CONSTRUCTION DICTIONARY

iUniverse books may be ordered through booksellers or by contacting:

iUniverse LLC
1663 Liberty Drive
Bloomington, IN 47403
www.iuniverse.com
1-800-Authors (1-800-288-4677)

ISBN: 978-1-4917-3081-2 (sc)
ISBN: 978-1-4917-3083-6 (hc)
ISBN: 978-1-4917-3082-9 (e)

Printed in the United States of America.

iUniverse rev. date: 04/17/2014

a acre, ampere, anode

A angstrom unit, argon

A.A.S.H.T.O. American Association of State, Highway and Transportation Officials

ABC aggregate base course

abs absolute

AC alternating current, air conditioning

ACD automatic closing device

A.C.I. American Concrete Institute

acoust acoustical

ACU air conditioning unit(s)

addl additional

addtns/add/addns addition, additions

adj adjoining

ADP apparatus dew point

advt advertisement

AFF above finished floor

agcy agency

agric agricultural

ah ampere-hour

AHP air horsepower

AHU air handling unit

air cond air conditioning

A.I.S.C. American Institute of Steel Construction

AISE American Iron & Steel Engineers

Al/alum aluminum

ALT altitude

ALTRN alteration

AMB ambient

amp ampere

amp hr ampere hour

amt amount

anhyd anhydrous

ANSI American National Standards Institute

apt apartment

ar area

arch architect, architectural

AS aftersight

A.S.A. American Standard Association

asb asbestos

A.S.C.E. American Society of Civil Engineers

ash/ashl ashlar

ASHRAE American Society of Heating, Refrigeration and Air Conditioning Engineers

ASTM American Society for Testing & Materials

asp/asph asphalt

at airtight

atm atmosphere, atmospheric

aux auxiliary

av/ave/avg average

av/ave avenue

AW actual weight

AWG American wire gauge

AWS American Welding Society

AZ azimuth

ABC Aggregate base course used in highway surfacing to furnish a compact, stable and even surface.

A.B.C. process A method of deodorizing and precipitating sludge by the addition of alum, charcoal, or some other material, and clay to the raw sewage.

ABS Material used under a concrete slab, made up of crushed rock. Used in order to get a solid base for concrete.

A.M.F. The abbreviation of a parting remark by a construction superintendent as he buttons up a project and leaves it for the last time.

Aaron's rod An ornamental figure representing a rod with a serpent twined about it. It is sometimes confused with the caduceus of Mercury. The difference is that the caduceus has two serpents twined in opposite directions, the Aaron's rod but one.

abaciscus (1) A small abacus. (2) A stone or tile in mosaic. *(see abaculus)*

abaculus A unit tile in a geometrical pattern surface.

abacus The upper part of the capital of a column, either square or curved.

abamurus A block of masonry, in buttress form, for the support of a structure.

abate (1) To cutaway, as in stonework, or to beat down, as in metalwork, so as to leave parts in relief. (2) A diminution or reduction by amount of degree of discharges, such as pollutants into receiving waters.

abatement In carpentry, the wasting of timber when shaping it to size, hence a decrease in its strength.

abvatjour In building, a device for admitting daylight and deflecting it downward when it enters a window, as a sloping soffit of a lintel or arch; also a movable slat or screen; a skylight.

abatsons A contrivance for the purpose of directing sound vibrations downward.

abattoir A building for the slaughter of cattle.

abatvent A contrivance to break the force of, or prevent the entrance of wind, as in a louver or chimney cowl.

abatvoix A reflector of sound.

abbey The group of buildings forming the dwelling place of a society of monks or nuns. A place of worship connected now or formerly with a monastic establishment. A dwelling now or formerly the residence of an abbot or abbess.

abbeystead The land on which an abbey stands.

abney level A hand level for taking readings up steep slopes and as a clinometer.

above-grade subfloors Floors above ground level. Normally an air space of at least 18″ between the ground and the subfloor, with proper cross ventilation in both directions, should be provided to help assure dryness.

abraded yarns Continuous filament yarns in which filaments have been cut or abraded at intervals and given additional twist to produce a certain degree of hairiness, so as to simulate the character of yarns spun from staple. Abraded yarns are usually plied or twisted with other yarns before using.

Abrams' law A rule stating that with given concrete materials and conditions of test the ration of the amount of water to the amount of the cement in the mixture determines the strength of the concrete provided the mixture is of a workable consistency. *(see water-cement ratio)*

abrasion (1) The process of wearing away by friction; the act of reducing material by grinding instead of cutting with tools. (2) Wear or scour by hydraulic traffic.

abrasion resistance Ability of a surface to resist being worn away by a rubbing or friction process.

abrasion-resistant refractory Hard-fired, dense, high-duty fire-clay bricks (alumina-silica, containing less than 50 percent alumina) which resist physical wear or abrasion.

abrasive A hard material used for wearing away or polishing a surface by friction; grinding material such as sandstone, emery, carborundum, etc.

abrasive paper Paper or cloth covered on one side with a grinding material glued to the surface, used for smoothing and polishing.

abrasive tools All implements used for wearing down materials by friction or rubbing; includes grindstones which are made of pure sandstone, whetstone, emery wheels, sandpaper, and emery cloth.

abreauvior In masonry, the mortar joint between stones in a wall or between two arch stones.

absolute (1) In the trades, a term often used to designate perfection or exactness. (2) Anything which is complete in its own character. (3) A chemical substance relatively free of impurities.

absolute maximum grade Steepest grade on paved highways 17%; steepest grade on urban streets 32%.

absolute pressure The sum of the atmospheric pressure and gauge pressure.

absolute specific gravity Ratio of the mass of a given volume of a solid or liquid, referred to a vacuum, at a stated temperature to the mass, referred to a vacuum, of an equal volume of gas-free distilled water at a stated temperature. *(see specific gravity)*

absolute volume Of ingredients of concrete or mortar, the displacement volume of an ingredient of concrete or mortar; in the case of solids, the volume of the particles themselves, including their permeable and impermeable voids but excluding space between particles; in the case of fluids, the cubic content which they occupy.

absolute zero The zero point on the absolute temperature scale, 459.69 degrees below the zero on the Fahrenheit scale, 273.16 degrees below the zero on the Celsius scale.

absorbed moisture Moisture that has entered a solid material by absorption and has physical properties not substantially different from ordinary water at the same temperature and pressure. *(see absorption)*

absorbent A material which, due to an affinity for certain substances, extracts one or more such substances from a liquid or gaseous medium with which it is in contact, and which changes physically or chemically, or both, during the process. Calcium chloride is an example of a solid absorbent, while solutions of lithium chloride, lithium bromide, and the ethylene glycols are examples of liquid adsorbents.

absorber (1) A device containing liquid for absorbing refrigerant vapor or other vapors. In an absorption system, that part of the low side used for absorbing refrigerant vapor. (2) A particular material or device which has been designed for the removal of a specific substance, like a pollutant, from a stream of water by either a chemical or mechanical means, or both.

absorber plate The part of the collector which ultimately takes solar energy into the system is designated an absorber or base plate. The plate transfers the heat to a working fluid whose internal energy is thereby increased.

absorbing well (well drain) A well to drain away water.

absorptance The soaking up of heat in a solar collector. Measured as a percentage of total radiation available.

absorption (1) The process by which a liquid is drawn into and tends to fill permeable pores in a porous solid body; also the increase in weight of a porous solid body resulting from the penetration of a liquid into its permeable pores. *(see absorbed moisture)* (2) When light strikes an object, some light is reflected and absorbed. The darker the object the more light it absorbs. (3) The property of a fiber, yarn or fabric which enables it to attract and hold gasses or liquids within its pores. (4) A process whereby a material extracts one or more substances present in an atmosphere or mixture of gases or liquids; accompanied by physical change, chemical change, or both, of the material.

absorption air conditioning Solar systems which include air conditioning may use the absorption method of "cooling with heat." Solar heated water is used, much like the flame in gas refrigerators or air conditioners to fuel the system which cools and dehumidifies the desired space.

absorption field A drainage system consisting of a series of pipes laid in trenches filled with sand, gravel or crushed stone, through which septic tank effluent may seep or leach into the surrounding ground.

absorption loss Water losses which occur during the first filling of a ditch or reservoir in wetting the soil.

absorption rate The amount of water absorbed by an item when it is partly immersed in water for one minute.

absorption refrigeration A cooling process system operated by hot water (solar heated) instead of mechanical compressor.

absorption spectroscopy Study of spectra obtained by the passage of radiant energy from a continuous source through a selectively absorbing medium. The basis of several chemical analysis techniques.

absorptive coating   (see coating)

absorptive power   The rate of emission or absorption of heat from an item compared with the rate from a similarly shaped black item under the same conditions.

absorptivity   The capacity of a material to absorb radiant energy. Absorbtance is the ratio of the radiant flux absorbed by a body to that incident to it.

abstract   (1) A land deed recording the continuous history of the plot from the date of the original deed. (2) General order sheet that indicates power supply for the elevator motor, signals and special features of an installation.

abstract of bids   A summary of unit prices furnished by the owner or his representative for a given job, for the purpose of selecting the contractor to be awarded the job on the basis of low bid.

abut   To meet or touch with an end, as one construction member meeting another; usually called butt; to be contiguous or adjoining.

abutment   The part of a bridge that supports the end of the span and prevents the bank from sliding under it; a foundation that carries gravity and also thrust loads; an anchorage for the cables of a suspension bridge; a point or place where the support joins the thing supported.

abutment piece   In framing a building, the lowest structural member which receives and distributes the thrust of an upright or strut; the soleplate of a partition to which studding is nailed; same as foot plate or sole piece.

abuttals   The boundings of a piece of land, street, river, etc.

abutting joint   A joint produced by the meeting of two pieces end on, with the grain of one piece forming an angle with the grain of the other piece.

abutting tenons   In carpentry, two tenons entering from opposite sides and abutting in the center of a mortise.

Abyssinian well   A perforated tube which is driven into the ground by hammering or ramming with a light pile hammer. Water is extracted from it by pumping.

acanthur (acanthine)   An architectural ornament patterned after the leaves of the acanthus, a plant native the Mediterranean regions. It is a distinguishing characteristic of the Corinthian and Composite capitals.

accelerated weathering   The exposure in testing of paints or other building materials to cycles of heat, frost, wetness and dryness that are more severe than naturally experienced.

acceleration   (1) Increase in velocity or in rate of change, especially the quickening of the natural progress of a process, such as hardening, setting, or strength development of concretes. (see accelerator) (2) The increasing of the speed of a moving vehicle by the application of surplus power from the engine. The rate of acceleration depends on the weight of the vehicle and the surplus rimpull that is available for accelerating.

accelerator   (1) An admixture which, when added to concrete, mortar, plaster or grout, increases the rate of hydration of a hydraulic cement, shortens the time of set, or increases the rate of hardening or strength development; a hardener or catalyst. (2) A pump for circulating water through a heating system.

accepted bid   The bid or proposal accepted by the owner or his representative as the basis of entering into an agreement for the proposed construction.

accepted engineering requirements (practices)   (OSHA) Those requirements or practices which are compatible with standards required by a registered architect, a registered professional engineer, or other duly licensed or recognized authority.

access   A passageway or means of approach to a room or building; a corridor between rooms; also a term used in building construction referring to points at which concealed equipment may be reached for inspection and repair.

access connection Any roadway facility by means of which vehicles can enter or leave an arterial highway; included are intersections at grade, private driveways and ramps, or separate lanes connecting with cross streets or frontage roads.

access door Any door which allows access to concealed equipment, or parts of a building not often used, such as a door to concealed plumbing parts.

access eye (cleanout) An opening in a drain closed by a plate which is often provided at pipe bends to enable the pipe to be rodded. It is also called a rodding eye.

access switch A key-operated corridor switch to run the elevator car at inspection speed for purposes of elevator maintenance.

accessable (1) In wiring methods, capable of being removed or exposed without damaging the building structure. (2) In equipment, admitting close approach, not guarded by locked doors, elevation, etc.

accessories Those items other than frames, braces, or post shores used to facilitate the construction of scaffold and shoring.

accessory An extra building product which supplements a basic solid sheeted building such as door, window, skylight, ventilator, etc.

accident In insurance terminology, a sudden, unexpected event identifiable as to time and place. *(see occurrence)*

accidental air *(see entrapped air)*

accidental error In surveying, a compensating error.

acclivity A slope or steepness of a line or plane inclined to the horizon, taken upward; in contradiction to declivity, which is taken downward.

accolade A decorative use of molding over a door or window, in which two ogee curves meet centrally at the top.

accordian doors Folding doors supported by carriers with rollers which run on a track; the doors fold up in a manner similar to the bellows of an accordian, hence the name.

accouple To join or couple; to bring together as ties or braces joined together in building construction.

accouplement (1) In carpentry, a tie or brace of timber. (2) In architecture, the placing of two columns or pilasters close together, as in pairs of columns forming a colonnade.

accumulator (1) A machine used to maintain constant hydraulic pressure in a power-operated system for jacking. An accumulator is essentially a set of two differential pistons with hydraulic pressure on the smaller one and compressed air on the other, together with a compressed air reservoir and switches which are operated by the moving piston to start and stop the hydraulic pump. (2) In refrigeration, also known as a surge drum or surge header. (3) A storage chamber for low-side liquid refrigerant also known as surge drum, surge header. Also, a pressure vessel whose volume is used in a refrigerant circuit to reduce pulsation.

acetone A highly flammable, organic solvent used for removing paint.

acetylene A colorless gaseous hydrocarbon made by action of water on calcium carbon and used chiefly in organic synthesis and as a fuel in welding and soldering.

acid Either an inorganic or organic compound (1) that reacts with metals to yield hydrogen; (2) that reacts with a base to form a salt; (3) that dissociates in water to yield hydrogen or hydronium ions; (4) that has a pH of less than 7.0; (5) that neutralizes bases or alkaline media. All acids contain hydrogen and turn litmus paper red. They are corrosive to human tissue and are to be handled with care.

acid & alkali-resistant grout A grout that resists the effects of prolonged contact with acids and alkalis.

acid etch A method of cleaning concrete by scrubbing it with acid, and then rinsing it with water.

acidity   The ability of the acidity of a sample of water to produce hydrogen ions, i.e., hydrated protons, upon treatment with sodium hydroxide, sodium carbonate, or other similar alkaline materials. This acidity may result from nitric, hydrochloric and sulfuric or other fully-ionized strong acids; carbonic, acetic, tannic, or other poorly-ionized weak acids; or such hydrolyzing metallic salts as chlorides or iron and aluminum, or the sulfates.

acid polishing   The polishing of any surface by acid treatment.

acid refractory   High-silica and alumina-silica refractories. Alumina-silica materials vary in refractoriness or resistance to high temperatures; the higher the alumina content, the greater the refractoriness.

acid steel   Steel made by a process in which the flux is silica, or where the furnace is silica lined.

acoustic absorptivity   *(see sound absorption coefficient)*

acoustical   Related to, pertaining to, or associated with sound, but not having its properties or characteristics.

acoustical board   Any type of special material, such as insulating boarding, used in the control of sound or to prevent the passage of sound from one room to another.

acoustical correction   Treating an auditorium, church, theater, concert hall, etc., to make the hearing conditions in the room as ideal as possible; the problem is especially present in such instances where large audiences assemble

acoustically satisfactory auditorium   Optimum acoustic conditions in an auditorium are obtained when an average sound rises to a suitable intensity in every part of the auditorium with no echoes or distortion of the original sound, and then decays quickly enough not to interfere with succeeding sounds. This ideal is seldom reached, but the human ear allows a rather wide variation from ideal without damaging the over-all effect.

acoustical materials   Sound-absorbing materials for covering walls and ceilings; a term applied to special plaster, tile, or any other material for wall coverings composed of mineral, wool or vegetable fibers; also, cork or metal used to control or deaden sound.

acoustic mill feed control   A system used for the control of mill feed rate based on changes in the noise level of the mill.

acoustical plaster & plastics   Sound absorbing finishing materials mill-formulated for application in areas where a reduction in sound reverberation or noise intensity is desired. These materials usually are applied to a minimum thickness of $\frac{1}{2}''$ and generally provide a noise reduction coefficient of at least .45 decibels.

acoustical reduction factor   The opposite of the acoustical transmission factor. *(see sound-reduction factor)*

acoustical tile   Any tile composed of materials having the property of absorbing sound waves, hence reducing the reflection of sound; any tile designed and constructed to absorb sound waves.

acoustical transmission factor   The ratio which sound energy is transmitted through and beyond the surface, partition, or device. The sound-reduction factor is its reciprocal.

acoustical clip   *(see floor clip)*

acoustic construction   A building method aimed at measurably reducing sound, e.g., discontinuous construction, etc.

acoustic mill feed control   A system used for the control of mill feed rate based on changes in the noise level of the mill.

acoustic plaster   Wall plaster with a high sound absorbency.

acoustic power   The sound energy emitted per second measured in watts.

acoustics   The branch of physics dealing with phenomena and laws of sound. The qualities of an enclosed space with respect to the transmission of sounds.

acoustic tile Tile-shaped blocks of sound-absorbent material used for ceilings or as wall facing.

acoustometer An apparatus for measuring acoustic values.

acre Unit for measuring land, equal to 43,560 square feet; 4,840 square yards; or 160 square rods.

acre foot A unit for measuring volume, equal to 43,560 cubic feet. Equal to an area of one acre one foot deep. Used sometimes in measuring coal or water volume.

acropolis The citadel of an ancient Greek city, usually a high plateau.

across (1) A term used in carpentry when cutting or sawing across a board at approximately a right angle to the length of the piece. (2) The application of gypsum board where long dimension is applied at right angles to the framing.

acroter A small pedestal placed on the apex or at the basal angle of a pediment to support a statue or other ornament.

acroterion (acroteria) A pedestal upon the ends or apex of a pediment to support a statue or other ornament; also the statue or ornament itself.

acrylic One of the resins in latex paints used to bond other ingredients.

acrylic fiber Acrylic fiber is made from a long chain of synthetic polymer composed of at least 85 per cent by weight of acrylonitrile, a liquid derivative of natural gas and air. The fiber appeared on the market in 1949, went into full-scale production in 1952 and made its first appearance on carpets in 1957.

acrylic plastic glaze A synthetic material which comes in sheets for use on windows in high breakage areas; results in a comparatively shatterproof window.

acrylic plastics Noncrystalline thermoplastics with optical clarity.

acrylic resin A synthetic material such as Lucite, which comes in flat, shaped or corrugated panels.

acrylic/wood The generic name for wood-plastic-composites utilizing woods impregnated with acrylic monomers and polymerized within the wood cells by gamma irradiation. In the case of acrylic/wood parquet, a built-in finish is developed.

Act Section 107 of the Contract Work Hours and Safety Standards Act, commonly know as the Construction Safety Act.

actinic glass Glass designed to filter out the actinic rays from daylight.

action level The exposure level (concentration of the material in air) at which certain OSHA regulations to protect employees take effect (CFR 1910.1001-1047). E.g., workplace air analysis, employee training, medical monitoring, and record keeping. Exposure at or above the action level is termed occupational exposure.

activated alumina A form of aluminum oxide which absorbs moisture readily and is used as a drying agent.

activated carbon A form of carbon made porous by special treatment by which it is capable of absorbing various odors, anesthetics and other vapors.

activated sludge Sludge settled out of sewage previously agitated in the presence of abundant atmospheric oxygen.

activated sludge process A sewage treatment method which entails the introduction of oxygen and support bacteria which feed on organic matter in the sewage. As the sewage settles, the bacteria mass falls out and forms a sludge. Part of this "activated" sludge is recycled to treat fresh sewage.

active earth pressure The horizontal push from the earth on a wall.

active layer The layer at the surface of the ground, which moves seasonally as the soil-volume changes, expanding when frozen and shrinking when it thaws and dries.

active solar energy system A system which utilizes outside energy to operate the system and to transfer the collected solar energy from the collector to storage and distribute it throughout the living unit. Active systems can provide space heating and cooling and domestic hot water.

active storage The volume of the reservoir that is available for use either for power generation, irrigation, flood control, or other purposes. Active storage excludes flood surcharge.

active system A system which incorporates an assembly of parts for the collection and storage of solar energy is termed active. Such a system may not require external energy to operate, or it could include forced air circulation. *(see passive system; thermosyphon)*

activity *(C.P.M.)* A task or item of work that must be performed in order to complete a project.

activity duration The amount of time estimated as required to accomplish an activity.

actual dimension The measured dimension of a concrete masonry unit.

actual site preparation and construction Any construction activity undertaken in reliance upon a foundation or building permit.

Acute Toxicity The adverse (acute) effects resulting from a single dose of or exposure to a substance.

adament plaster A quick-hardening gypsum plaster, sometimes combined with sand or sawdust, for floating coats.

Adam's arm *(slang)* A shovel.

adaptor An electrical fitting for taking power from an outlet in a way for which it was not designed.

addenda (addendum) Written or graphic instruments issued prior to the execution of the contract which modify or interpret the bidding documents, including drawings and specifications, by additions, deletions, clarifications or corrections. As such, addenda are intended to become part of the contract documents when the construction contract is executed.

addition (1) To cement, processing additions designed to aid the cement manufacturer in grinding or otherwise processing or handling his cement; functional additions added primarily to modify the end properties of the cement. (2) To a structure, a construction project physically connected to an existing structure, as distinct from alterations within an existing structure. (3) To contract sum, amount added to the contract sum by change order. *(see extra)*

addition polymerization Polymerization in which monomers are linked together without the splitting off of water or other simple molecules.

additional services (of the architect or engineer) Professional services which may, upon the owner's request or approval, be rendered by the architect or engineer in addition to the basic services identified in the owner-architect agreement.

additive (1) Any material added to a propellant to achieve a more even rate of combustion, or to improve quality of fuels and lubricants. (2) For cement, see addition.

additive alternate An alternate bid resulting in an addition to the same bidder's base bid. *(see alternate bid)*

additive constant In surveying stadia work, an amount added to the product of the intercept on the staff and the multiplying constant to give the true distance between telescope center and staff, often less than one foot.

add to set The slight overhang on the point of a saw-tooth to make the kerf slightly wider than the saw so that the saw can run easily.

adduct A substance formed by a simple addition reaction. Adducts formed from amines and epoxy resins are used to cure epoxy paint films.

adhesion (1) The soil quality of sticking to buckets, blades and other parts of excavators. (2) In painting, the attachment of a paint or varnish film to its ground. (3) The sticking together of structural parts by mechanical or chemical bonding using a cement or glue. (4) The bond between mortar or grout and masonry units or steel.

adhesive (sealant) (1) In roofing, material applied to composition shingle to seal or adhere the tab of the shingle to the preceding course or underlying shingle. (2) Any substance used to hold materials together by surface attachment. It is a general term and includes cements, mucilage, paste and glue. (3) A compound, glue or mastic used in the application of gypsum board products to framing or for laminating one or more layers of gypsum boards.

adhesive application A means of applying gypsum board utilizing adhesives and supplemental mechanical fasteners.

adhesive bond (1) A relationship between two materials in contact with each other causing them to stick or adhere together by means other than cohesion. (2) The adhering characteristics of adhesives as determined by a test method.

adhesive spreader A notched trowel or special tool to aid in the application of laminating adhesives.

adhesive wall clips Special clips or nails with large perforated bases for mastic application to most firm surfaces.

adiabatic A condition in which heat neither enters nor leaves a system.

adiabatic curing The maintenance of surrounding conditions during the setting and hardening of concrete so that heat is neither lost to nor gained from the surroundings of the concrete; during very cold weather the concrete must be heated and during very hot weather it must be kept cool.

adiabatic process A thermodynamic process during which no heat is added to, or taken from, a substance or system.

Adirondack sandstone (see Malone sandstone)

adit (aditus) (1) In ancient classical architecture, the entrance or approach to a building. (2) A nearly level tunnel to underground workings which is slightly sloped towards the entrance for drainage.

adjoining (adj) To be next to or to be in contact with.

adjustable attachments Angles, plates, and brackets with devices which allow for three plane adjustments to compensate for minor irregularities in the building structure; used to attach supports to building structure.

adjustable clamp Any type of clamping device that can be adjusted to suit the work being done.

adjusted base cost The base building cost per square foot of living area with ± adjustments for alternate components.

adjusting lever On a carpenter's plane, a lever for adjusting the bit so it will cut shavings of uniform thickness.

adjusting nut Any button or nut by means of which adjustments may be made on tools or other devices.

adjusting plane A carpenter's plane having attachments which provide for the adjustments of the bit so it will cut shavings to any thickness desired.

adjusting screw (1) A threaded screw on a surveying instrument to provide a final adjustment for focus, level, or position. (2) A leveling device or jack composed of a threaded screw and an adjusting handle used for the vertical adjustment of shoring and formwork.

admixture Material added to cement or the concrete mix to increase workability, strength, or imperviousness; to lower freezing point; to prevent scaling; or otherwise to affect the concrete. Accelerators, plasticizers, and air-entraining agents are admixtures.

adobe An aluminous earth from which unfired brick is made, especially in the western United States.

adobe construction A type of construction in which the exterior walls are built of blocks that are made of soil mixed with straw and hardened in the sun; this type of construction is employed chiefly in the warm, dry climate of the southwestern United States.

adsorbed water Water held on surfaces of a material by electrochemical forces and having physical properties substantially different from those of absorbed water or chemically combined water at the same temperature and pressure. (see absorption)

adsorbent A material which has the ability to cause molecules of gases, liquids or solids to adhere to its internal surfaces without changing the absorbent physically or chemically. Certain solid materials such as silica gel, activated carbon and activated alumina have this property.

adsorber A device designed and built for the adsorption of pollutants.

adsorption (1) Development at the surface of a liquid or solid of a higher concentration of substance than exists in the bulk of the medium, especially formation of one or more layers of molecules of gases, of dissolved substances, or of liquids at the surface of a solid, such as cement, cement paste, or aggregate, or of air-entraining agents at the air-water interfaces; also the process by which a substance is absorbed. *(see adsorbed water)* (2) The action, associated with surface adherence, of a material in extracting one or more substances present in an atmosphere or mixture of gases and liquids, unaccompanied by physical or chemical change. Commercial adsorbent materials have enormous internal surfaces.

advancing slope grouting A method of grouting by which the front of a mass of grout is caused to move horizontally through preplaced aggregate by use of suitable grout injection sequence.

advancing slope method A method of placing concrete, as in tunnel linings, in which the face of the fresh concrete is not vertical and moves forward as concrete is placed.

advection The transfer of heat by the horizontal mass motion of the atmosphere.

adversed grade(s) Grade or grades contrary to the general rise or fall between terminals.

advertisement (Advt) A public notice.

advertisement for bids Published public notice soliciting bids for a construction project. Most frequently used to conform to legal requirements pertaining to projects to be constructed under public authority, and usually published in newspapers of general circulation in those districts from which the public funds are derived.

adz (adze) A cutting tool resembling an ax; the thin arched blade is set at right angles to the handle and is used for rough-dressing timber.

adze-eye hammer A claw hammer with the eye extended giving a longer bearing on the handle than is the case in hammers not having an extended eye.

A.E.C. (Atomic Energy Commission) The United States Atomic Energy Commission, a civilian agency created by the Federal Government in 1946 to take over the Army's World War II Manhattan Project. Its purpose was to direct atomic research toward peaceful purposes in addition to those of national security. The Commission was disbanded in January, 1975. *(see ERDA)*

aeolian Wind-blown; usually settling to loess.

aerated concrete A light-weight material made from a specially prepared cement used for subfloors. Due to its cellular structure, this material is retardant to sound transmission. *(see cellular concrete)*

aeration (1) The bringing about of contact between air and water. This process is accomplished by spray, bubbling, agitation or other natural or mechanical means. (2) Exposing a substance, or area to air circulation.

aerator A mechanical device which is used to introduce a controlled flow of air into raw or waste water. It is the means by which aeration is accomplished.

aerial sewer An unburied sewer (generally sanitary type), supported on pedestals or bents to provide a suitable grade line.

aerial surveying Surveying done by photographing the area from an airplane. Base points, for easy identification, are usually pre-marked on the ground.

aerial tramway A line of towers carrying wire ropes to serve as tracks for carriers for building materials in mountainous areas.

aerobe An organism, particularly a bacterium, which uses oxygen to sustain life. Almost every natural body of water contains aerobes. These aerobes live on carbohydrates, fats, proteins and other waste material. The primary means of water self-purification is provided by the activity of aerobes.

aerobic environment One in which free or uncombined oxygen is found.

aerocrete Type of concrete used for insulation or fill which has low compressive strength (1,000 psi @ 28 days).

aerodynamic instability A flutter during strong wind so large as to endanger a structure; used to describe the failure of the Tacoma Narrows bridge.

aerograph A spray gun used in the application of paint. The paint passes from attached container to a small nozzle where it is blown by compressed air into a fine spray which can easily be directed onto the surface to be covered.

aerosol An assemblage of small particles, solid or liquid, suspended in air. The diameters of the particles may vary from 100 microns down to 0.01 micron or less, e.g., dust, fog, smoke.

affidavit of non-collusion A sworn statement, by bidders for the same work, that their proposal prices were arrived at independently without consultation between or among them.

affinity The tendency of two substances to chemically unite, such as the fiber and dyestuff in carpets.

A-frame (1) An open structure tapering from a wide base to a load-bearing top. (2) A building with gabled roof extending to the foundation. (3) A portable structural steel frame used to support a chain fall or hoisting sheave for moving and hoisting material or equipment. The side members of the frame support a horizontal cross beam and are usually shaped in the form of an A.

African mahogany A large tree remotely related to the mahogany family. The tree produces exceptionally fine figured timber of unusual lengths and widths.

after-cooler Any device which will cool compressed air after it is fully compressed.

after-tack A defect of paint which has been tack free and then becomes tacky.

afwillite A mineral with composition $3CaO \cdot 2SiO_2 \cdot 3H_2O$ occurring naturally in South Africa, Northern Ireland, and California, and artificially in some hydrated portland cement mixtures.

agency Relationship between agent and principal; organization acting as agent; administrative subdivision of an organization, particularly in government.

agent One authorized by another to act in his stead or behalf.

agglomeration (1) Gathering into a ball or mass. (2) To gather, through adhesion, suspended colloidal particles into large masses called flocs.

aggregate (1) An inert material used as a filler with cementitious material and water to produce plaster, concrete, etc. The term used in conjunction with plaster usually implies sand, vermiculite or perlite. (2) In the case of materials of construction, essentially inert materials which when bound together into a conglomerated mass by a matrix form concrete mastic, mortar or plaster; crushed rock or gravel screened to size for use in road surfaces, concrete or bituminous mixes; any of several hard materials such as sand gravel, stone, slag, cinders or other inert materials used for mixing with a cementing material to form concrete. Aggregate, in a surface course in the building of roads, is often called road metal.

Aggregate base course (ABC) A foundation course consisting of mineral aggregate. coarse That retained on the No. eight sieve.

coarse-graded One having a continuous grading in sizes of particles from coarse through fine with a predominance of coarse sizes.

fine That passing the No. eight sieve.

fine-graded One having a continuous grading in sizes of particles from coarse through fine with a predominance of fine sizes.

heavyweight Aggregate of high specific gravity such as barite, magnetite, limonite, ilemenite, iron or steel used to produce heavy concrete.

interlock The projection of aggregate particles or portions of aggregate particles from one side of a joint or crack in concrete into recesses in the other side of such joint or crack so as to effect load transfer in compression and shear, and maintain mutual alignment.

lightweight Aggregate of low bulk specific gravity such as expanded or cindered clay, slate, slag, fly ash, vermiculite or pumice or natural pumice and scoria used to produce lightweight concrete.

macadam A coarse aggregate of uniform size usually of crushed stone, slag or gravel.

open-graded One containing little or no mineral filler or in which the void spaces in the compacted aggregate are relatively large.

well-graded Aggregate that is graded from the maximum size down to filler with the object of obtaining an asphalt mix with controlled void content and high stability.

aggregate blending The process of intermixing two or more aggregates to produce a different set of properties; generally, but not exclusively, to improve grading.

aggregate/cement ratio The weight of the aggregate divided by the weight of the cement in concrete.

aging (1) In painting, the storage of varnishes after manufacture to improve gloss and reduce crawling, pinholing, and lining. (2) A process used by builders to make materials appear old or ancient by artificial means. (3) The effect on materials of exposure to an environment for an interval of time.

agitating speed The rate of rotation of the drum or blades of a truck mixer or other device when used for agitation of mixed concrete.

agitating truck (mixer; concrete truck) A vehicle carrying a drum in which freshly mixed concrete can be conveyed from the point of mixing to that of placing, the drum being rotated continuously so as to agitate the contents; designated agitating lorry in United Kingdom.

agitation (1) The process of providing gentle motion in mixed concrete just sufficient to prevent segregation or loss of plasticity. (2) The mixing and homogenization of slurries or finely ground powders by air or mechanical means.

agitator (1) A device for maintaining plasticity and preventing segregation of mixed concrete by agitation. *(see agitation)* (2) A device causing turbulent motion in a fluid confined in tank.

aglite Lightweight aggregate from expanded clay.

agonic line In surveying, a line on a map along which the magnetic declination is zero.

A-grade wood Best standard veneer, smooth and paintable. May be composed of more than one piece well jointed. Repairs that are neatly made are permitted.

agreement A meeting of minds; a legally enforceable promise or promises between two or among several persons; on a construction project, the document stating the essential terms of the construction contract which incorporates by reference the other contract documents; the document setting forth the terms of the contract between the designer and owner or between the owner and the contractor. *(see agreement form)*

agreement form A document setting forth in printed form the general provisions of a agreement, with spaces provided for insertion of specific data relating to a particular project.

aiguille In masonry, an instrument for boring holes in stone or other masonry material.

aile *(see aisle)*

aileron A wing wall to hide the aisle of a church.

air alternator A device which automatically switches the air from one side of the ice tank to the other.

air, ambient Generally speaking, the air surrounding an object.

air and gas *(slang)* Oxygen and acetylene as used for welding.

air atomization Process of using air to break the oil into small particles to prepare for combustion.

air base In aerial surveying, the distance between the stations of overlapping aerial photographs.

air blast Forced air circulation.

air blown Refers to the process of converting petroleum to asphalt for use in the manufacture of composition roofing and roofing products by the use of air.

air-blown mortar *(see shotcrete)*

air blow pipe Air jet used in shotcrete gunning to remove rebound or other loose material from the work area.

airborne transmission Sound traveling by air through a structure.

air brick (1) A hollow or perforated brick specially prepared for ventilating purposes. (2) A brick-sized box made of metal with grated sides which allows air to enter a building where ventilation is otherwise restricted.

air brush In painting, devices for spraying paint onto a surface by means of compressed air.

air bubble (blistering) (1) A bubble of trapped air or a lump of paste under wall covering. (2) Results when air is trapped under the installed floor covering. Most common causes of air bubbles are: irregular subfloor, failure to properly roll the floor after installation and preset adhesive.

air change The quantity of fresh air of the volume of a room being ventilated. Standard of ventilation is described by the number of air changes per hour.

air circulation The movement of air from the heating or the air conditioning unit throughout the home or building.

air cleaner A device used to remove airborne impurities.

air conditioner One or more factory made assemblies which include an evaporator or cooling coil and an electrically driven compressor and condenser combination, and may include a heating function.

air conditioner, room A factory-made encased assembly designed as a unit for mounting in a window, through a wall, or as a console. It is designed for free delivery of conditioned air to an enclosed space without ducts.

air conditioner, window Self-contained room conditioner arranged to be supported in or connected with a window opening, circulating outside air over the high side and room air over the low side.

air conditioning (1) The process of treating air so as to control simultaneously its temperature, humidity, cleanliness, and distribution to meet the requirements of the conditioned space. (2) The process of heating or cooling, cleaning, humidifying or de-humidifying, and circulating air throughout the various rooms of a house or public building.

air conditioning, comfort The process of treating air so as to control simultaneously its temperature, humidity, cleanliness and distribution to meet the comfort requirements of the occupants of the conditioned space.

air conditioning condenser A unit which is either air or water cooled, and the function of which is to condense hot, compressed refrigerant gases. In the water-cooled condensing units, a cooling tower is commonly used to cool the water within the condenser system.

air conditioning, industrial Air conditioning for other uses than comfort.

air conditioning, summer Comfort air conditioning carried out primarily when outside temperature and humidity are above those to be maintained in the conditioned space.

air-conditioning unit An assembly of equipment for the treatment of air so as to control simultaneously its temperature, humidity, cleanliness and distribution to meet the requirements of a conditioned space.

air-conditioning unit, cooling (heating)
A specific air treating combination consisting of means for ventilation, air circulation, air cleaning, and heat transfer, with control means for cooling (or heating).

air conditioning, winter   Heating, humidification, air distribution, and air cleaning, where outside temperatures are below the inside or room temperature.

air contaminants   Solid, liquid, or gaseous materials (or combinations thereof) which, by their presence, may produce undesirable effects on humans, animals, plants, surfaces, or materials.

air content   The volume of air voids in cement paste, mortar, or concrete, exclusive of pore space in aggregate particles, usually expressed as a percentage of total volume of the paste, mortar, or concrete.

air-cooled blast-furnace slag   The material resulting from solidification of molten blast-furnace slag under atmospheric conditions. Subsequent cooling may be accelerated by application of water to the solidified surface. *(see blast-furnace slag)*

air-cooled jacket   Jacket around a burner pipe, open at both ends, to allow cool outside air to be drawn along the outside of the burner tip by the fuel or air-fuel mixture as it leaves the tip.

air-cooled slag   The product of relatively slow-cooling molten blast-furnace slag, resulting in a solid mass of tough, durable material which is excavated, crushed and screened for commercial purposes, such as concrete and bituminous aggregate.

air cooler   A factory-encased assembly of elements whereby the temperature of air passing through the device is reduced.

air cooler, dry   Removes excess heat from the dehydrated air whenever it leaves the dehydrator at an elevated temperature.

air cooler, dry-type   A forced circulation air cooler wherein heat transfer is not implemented by a liquid spray during the operating period.

air cooler unit   Specific air treating combination consisting of means for air circulation and cooling.

aircore   A type of a transformer that utilizes air as the medium through which magnetizing flux links the primary and secondary coils.

air diffuser   A circular, square, or rectangular air distribution outlet, generally located in the ceiling and comprised of deflecting members discharging supply air in various directions and planes, and arranged to promote mixing of primary air with secondary room air.

air drain   A flue or passageway for conveying fresh air to foundation walls to keep them dry; to wood work to preserve it; or to a fireplace.

air-dried lumber   Any lumber which is seasoned by drying in the air instead of a kiln or oven.

air drill   *(see jackhammer)*

air dry   Dry to such a degree that no further moisture is given up on exposure to air.

air drying   The process of drying block or brick by exposing to ambient air without any special equipment.

air duct   A pipe for conducting air for ventilating the rooms of a house, or to a furnace; sometimes applied to lights of temporary construction as opposed to an air drain of masonry.

air entraining   The capability of a material or process to develop a system of minute bubbles of air in cement paste, mortar of concrete. *(see entrainment)*

air-entraining agent   An addition for hydraulic cement or an admixture for concrete or mortar which causes air to be incorporated in the form of minute bubbles in the concrete or mortar during mixing, usually to increase its workability and frost resistance.

air-entraining hydraulic cement   Hydraulic cement containing an air-entraining addition in such amount as to cause the product to entrain air in mortar within specified limits.

air entrainment   The occlusion of air in

the form of minute bubbles, generally smaller than one mm, during the mixing of concrete or mortar. (see air entraining)

air escape In plumbing, a contrivance for discharging excess air from a water pipe. It consists of a ball cock which opens the discharging air valve when sufficient air has collected and closes it in time to prevent loss of water.

airfield soil classification (ac system) A soil classification based on sieve analysis and consistency limits.

air flue A flue which is usually fitted with a special type of valve built into a chimney stack so as to withdraw vitiated air from a room.

air grating A perforated metal register, sometimes with moveable slats, across an air duct where it enters a room.

air gun A spray gun. (see gun)

air injection A system of fuel injection in which metered fuel charges are forced through an injection nozzle into the cylinder by means of compressed air.

air lance A devise used to test, in the field, the integrity of field seams in plastic sheeting. It consists of a wand or tube through which compressed air is blown.

air lateral Pipe which supplies the air to the ice cans contained in the freezing tank.

air lift (1) A pump for raising sewage or other liquid by injecting air into and near the bottom of an open discharge pipe submerged in a well of the liquid to be raised. (2) Equipment whereby slurry or dry powder is lifted through pipes by means of compressed air.

airlock (1) An airtight chamber, under water or land as in caisson or tunnel excavation, serving to graduate the air pressure between adjacent atmospheres. (2) Weather stripping. (3) In plumbing, a stoppage of flow in a pipe due to a bubble of air being trapped in it.

air main Pipe which carries air to the air laterals supplying ice cans contained in the freezing tank.

airman (slang) An ironworker who erects transmission towers.

air meter A device for measuring the air content of concrete and mortar.

air permeablilty test A procedure for measuring the fineness of powdered materials such as portland cement.

air pocket A space which accidentally occurs in concrete work.

air pollution Presence in the atmosphere of one or more air contaminants in combinations, in such quantities, and of such duration as to be potentially harmful to human, plant, or animal life, or to property, or which unreasonably interferes with comfortable enjoyment of life or property or conduct of business.

airport lighting The application of lights or floodlighting as air-navigation facilities at airports.

air receiver The air storage tank on a compressor.

air ring Perforated manifold in nozzle of wet-mix shotcrete equipment through which high pressure air is introduced into the material flow.

air separator An upright cylindrical-conical apparatus, with internal rotating blades, which separates various size fractions of ground materials pneumatically; fine particles are discharged as product; oversize is returned to the mill as tailings.

airshaft An unroofed area within the walls of a multistory building, not necessarily starting from the ground level. Windows open on it to provide natural ventilation.

air slaking In masonry, the process of exposing quicklime to the air; as a result it will gradually absorb moisture and break down into a powder.

airslide Enclosed conveyor in which finely ground materials are transported by gravity over a slightly inclined porous fabric. Air flowing through the fabric keeps the powdered material fluid.

air space A cavity or space in walls or between various structural members.

air, standard Dry air at a pressure of

760mm (29.92 in.) Hg at 21 C (69.8 F) temperature and with a specific volume of 0.833 m³/kg (13.33 ft³/lb).

air survey   A survey made by aerial photography.

air-swept mill   A mill (i.e., ball mill, tube mill, rod mill, compartment mill or roller mill) in which a flow of gas transports the finely ground product out of the mill or grinding chamber.

air tight (at)   Too tight for air or gas to pass thru.

airtightness   The ability of heating unit and ductwork to be airtight at the seams, joints and connections.

air-to-air heat-transmission coefficient *(see U-valve)*

air-to-air resistance   Resistance to the passage of heat provided by the wall of building.

air trap   A chemical added to ready mixed concrete to increase workability.

air tunnel   (1) A tunnel in muck, dug out under compressed air. (2) A refrigerated tunnel with rapid air circulation through which the product to be frozen is passed.

air valve   A device that releases air from a pipeline automatically without permitting loss of water.

air vessel   A small tank containing air in the pipe on the discharge side of a reciprocating pump. It is present to even out the pulsations of the pump.

air void   A space in cement paste, mortar, or concrete filled with air; an entrapped air void is characteristically one mm or more in a size and irregular in shape; an entrained air void is typically between 10 and 1000 microns in diameter and spherical.

air washer   A water spray system or device for cleaning, humidifying, or dehumidifying the air.

air-water jet   A high velocity jet of air and water mixed at the nozzle used in clean-up of horizontal construction joints in preparation for the next concrete placement.

air waves   Air borne vibrations caused by explosions.

airway   a space between roof insulation and roof boards for movement of air.

aisle   (1) The wings, inward side porticos of a church; the inward lateral corridors which enclose the choir, the presbytery and the body of the church along its sides. (2) A passage between rows of seats, as in a hall, theater, or school.

ajarcara   Brickwork in ornamental relief.

ajour   Carving pierced to transmit light.

ajutage   The nozzle of a fountain or jet d'eau.

Alabama marble   A fine-grained white variety, the chief attractiveness of which is due to its life and warmth of coloring; for the most part a cream white rather than the bluish white common to Italian white marbles.

Alabaster   A massive densely crystalline, softly textured form of practically pure gypsum.

Alaska yellow cedar   A wood of the Pacific Northwest, moderately light, low in strength, highly resistant to decay, easily worked.

albarium   A white lime used for stucco, produced by calcination of marble.

Alberene   Trade name for a dense and massive soapstone, blue-gray in color, quarried in Virginia.

albronze   Alloy of copper and aluminum.

alcove   A large recess in a room generally separated by an arch.

alder   A red wood of the Pacific Coast, with heartwood and sapwood, a pale, pinkish brown; used for interior work, sometimes in imitation of mahogany or walnut.

alectorium   In ancient Roman architecture, a room for dice players.

alette   (1) A minor wing of a building. (2) Side of a pier under the impost of an arch. (3) A door jamb.

Alfol   Trade name for an insulating material made of aluminum foil.

algae   (1) A low form of plant life. Algae have no true roots, stems or leaves. They often float in water, as scum. Certain chemicals are frequently found in streams nourishing algae. These are usually nitrates. Algae, like other plants, are able to produce foodstuffs by photosynthesis in sunlight or artificial radiation. This manufacturing process results in the release of oxygen. **(2)** Minute fresh water plant growths which form a scum on the surfaces of recirculated water apparatus, interfering with fluid flow and heat transfer.

algicide A substance or blend fatal to algae.

alidade A rule equipped with simple or telescopic sights used for determination of direction; a part of a surveying instrument consisting of a telescope and its attachments.

aliform Wing-like extensions as on a box culvert.

align To adjust or arrange in a line.

alignment The points for the correct lines for laying out a road, railway, wall, transmission line, canal, etc.; a ground plan showing a route, as opposed to a profile or section showing levels and elevations.

alignment wire *(see ground wire)*

alite A name used by Tornebohm (1897) to identify tricalcium silicate including small amounts of MgO,Al_2O_3,Fe_2O_3, and other oxides; a principal constituent of portland cement clinker. *(see belite, celite, felite)*

alkali Water soluble salts of alkali metals, principally sodium and potassium; specifically sodium and potassium occurring in constituents of concrete or mortar; usually expressed in chemical analysis as the oxides Na_2O and K_2O. *(see cement, low-alkali)*

alkali-aggregate reaction Chemical reaction in mortar or concrete between alkalis (sodium and potassium) from portland cement or other sources and certain constituents of some aggregates; under certain conditions, deleterious expansion of the concrete or mortar may result.

alkaline salts Occurs in concrete subfloors when water carries diluted alkaline salts to slab. Can cause floor fail-

ure by destroying the adhesive's bond; can work its way through sheet goods seams and tile joints.

alkalinity The ability of a water sample to neutralize added free or combined hydrogen ions. Powerful alkalis like sodium and potassium hydroxide and such weak alkalis as carbonates, bicarbonates; or hydrolyzable metallic salts of weak acids such as sodium cyanide may cause alkalinity.

alkali reactivity (of aggregate) Susceptibility of aggregate to alkali-aggregate reaction.

alkyd A common term for oil-base paints; cleanup and thinning are done with solvent.

alkyd paint Paint with a binder consisting of synthetic resin producing a quick drying, tough paint surface.

alkyd plastics Thermoset plastics that are fast-curing, dimensionally stable, have good heat and electrical insulation properties, low impact strength, and are self-extinguishing, with maximum use temperatures of 3000 to 4000 F; used for paints, lacquers and molded ignition parts.

alkyd resins In painting, a modified form of resin used principally for lacquer paints, varnishes and metal finishes.

alkyl aryl sulfonate Synthetic detergent from petroleum fractions.

allege A thinning of part of a wall, as in a spandrel under a windowsill.

alley An established passageway for vehicles and pedestrians affording a secondary means of access in the rear to properties abutting on a street or highway.

all heart Of heartwood throughout; free of sapwood.

alligatoring **(1)** Cracks in the surface layer of materials only, which widen from contraction caused by a sudden change in temperature, lack of binder, not sufficient drying time between coats, poor penetration or applying a hard film over a soft undercoat. **(2)** Extensive breaking of paint film resulting from the second coat being applied over a primer not thoroughly dried. Sometimes referred to as crocodiling.

alligator head *(slang)* A device that attaches to a Universal stick that has various uses in hot electrical work.

alligator wrench *(slang)* A pipe wrench.

allowable load The ultimate load divided by factor of safety.

allowable stress Maximum permissible stress used in design of members of a structure and based on a factor of safety against rupture or yielding of any type.

allowance Classification of the tightness or looseness of mating parts.

alloy A mixture of two or more metals usually made to combine their qualities.

alloy steel Steel compounded with other metals to improve its quality.

all-purpose compound A joint treatment compound that can be used as a bedding compound for tape, a finishing compound, and as a laminating adhesive or texturing product.

all-rowlock wall In masonry, a wall built with two courses of stretchers standing on edge, alternating with one course of headers standing on edge; sometimes called rat trap bond.

alluvial soil Soil, sand or gravel deposited by flowing water, especially during times of floods. Such soil is not stable enough to insure a firm foundation for heavy structures.

alluvium Sedimentary matter deposited by flowing water. Such matter as clay and silt.

aloring The parapet walls of a church.

alpha gypsum A term denoting a class of specially processed calcined gypsums having properties of low consistency and high strength. Alpha Gypsums can be produced having strengths in excess of 10,000 PSI.

alterations A construction project, or portion of a project, comprising revisions within or to prescribed elements of an existing structure, as distinct from additions to an existing structure; remodeling.

alternate bid Amount stated in the bid to be added to or deducted from the amount of the base bid if the corresponding change in project scope or alternate materials and/or methods of construction is accepted.

alternate lane construction A method of constructing concrete roads, runways, or other paved areas, in which alternate lanes are placed and allowed to harden before the remaining intermediate lanes are placed.

alternating current (A.C.) An electric current which reverses the direction of its flow at regular intervals, usually 60 cycles per second.

alternating device A device where-by sewage may be automatically delivered into different parallel treatment units in a cycle following a predetermined sequence.

alternator A machine which generates alternating current by rotation of its rotor, usually driven by a steam or water turbine.

altitude Angular distance from the horizon to the sun.

altitude level A level tube on the vertical circle of a theodolite; used to accurately measure vertical angles.

alum Chemical used in sewage treatment plants which reduces suspended solids and biochemical oxygen demand (B.O.D.)

alumina Aluminum oxide, Al_2O_3.

alumina ratio (Alumina Modulus) AR = Al_2O_3; the proportion of Fe_2O_3 alumina to iron oxide.

Alumina refractory Brick composed essentially of alumina and silica, with the alumina in proportions ranging between 40 and 70 percent.

aluminate concrete Concrete made with calcium-aluminate cement; used primarily where high-early-strength or refractory or corrosion-resistant concrete is required.

aluminous cement A calcium aluminate cement manufactured by melting or by sintering a mixture of limestone and bauxite. Has high early strength and refractory properties.

aluminum (Al) The most important element in light alloys. When used to carry load, it is alloyed to form stronger metals.

aluminum coated steel Steel coated with aluminum for corrosion protection.

aluminum foil Aluminum sheet which reflects both visible light and infrared rays. It is used as an insulator.

aluminum nails Nails that are lightweight, stainless, rustless, and sterilized.

aluminum oxide Alumina.

aluminum stearate Used in the manufacture of lacquers to produce a flat finish.

alure A passage or gallery, as on the top of a wall.

alveated Beehive-shaped.

ambient This term is usually applied to the air temperature surrounding a part of the system such as the collector. The monthly average ambient air temperature difference between the collector inlet and the air. The smaller the temperature difference between these two values, the more efficiently the collector will operate.

ambrain An insulating material made from fossils and silicates. It is strong, heat resistant and nonhygroscopic; used for molded insulation.

ambulatory A covered passage or sheltered walk generally located just within the main walls of a building, or between the columns and walls of a circular building.

American bond A method of bonding brick in a wall whereby every fifth, sixth, or seventh course consists of headers, the other courses being stretchers.

American Oriental Axminster, Wilton or tufted rugs with Oriental rug colors and pattern designs. Soft, pliable, without sizing.

American (Briggs) Standard A list of pipe sizes, thicknesses, etc. compiled by Robert Briggs in 1862 and subsequently adopted as a standard.

American Standard Institute Code The National safety code governing the installation of elevators.

American Table of Distances (Quantity Distance Tables) American Table of Distances for storage of explosives as approved by the Institute of the Makers of Explosives.

AMES Taping Tool Specially designed tool to mechanically apply taping compound and tape.

Amherst sandstone A light gray or light buff, or variegated stone, quarried in Lorain County, Ohio.

amino plastics Thermoset plastics which come in all colors, are scratch resistant, glossy surfaced and good as electrical insulation. They require careful molding; have low impact strength. The weather resistance is not good.

ammeter An electrical instrument used to measure the number of amperes flowing through a circuit.

ammonal A powdered nonnitroglycerine explosive consisting of TNT, ammonium nitrate, and powdered aluminum. It is used for heavy blasts in dry boreholes and tunnels. It absorbs moisture and does not keep well.

amorphous Without regard for definite form; uncrystallized; structureless.

amount (amt) A quantity or the whole value or effect.

ampacity Current carrying capacity expressed in amperes.

ampere The intensity of electric current produced by one volt acting through a resistance of one ohm; the practical unit which indicates the rate of flow of electricity through a circuit.

amphiprostyle With columned portico at front and rear but no columns at sides; applied to the Classic temple.

amphitheater Originally an arena encircled by tiers of seats; now usually semicircular.

amplification Amplification is the artificial strengthening of sound by mechanical and/or electrical means.

amplitude The maximum displacement from the mean position in connection with vibration.

amyl acetate (banana oil) A solvent

used in cellulose lacquers, bronzing fluids. and metallic paints. It has an unpleasant banana-like smell.

anaerobes Those microorganisms which only survive and multiply in environments which have no free oxygen. Their food supply can be the same as aerobes, but they use the combined oxygen in the nutrients rather than oxygen in the water, or air. Foul-smelling hydrocarbons and sulfur-containing gasses often result from anerobic bacterial action.

anerobic environment One which has no uncombined or dissolved oxygen.

analog signal The representative value of a physical variable by a continuous device or record. There is no sharp break from one value to another. This in contrast with a digital signal made up of direct numerical values.

anaglyph Sculpture or other ornament in relief more pronounced than bas-relief.

analysis The determination of the nature or proportion of one or more constituents of a substance, whether separated out or not.

analyzer Device in high side of absorption system for increasing the concentration of refrigerant in the vapor entering rectifier or condenser.

anchor (1) In prestressed concrete, to lock the stressed tendon in position so that it will retain its stressed condition; in precast concrete construction, to attach the precast units to the building frame; in slabs on grade or walls, to fasten to rock or adjacent structures to prevent movement of the slab or wall with respect to the foundation, adjacent structure or rock. (2) That bolt or fastening device which attaches to the anchorage. (3) An egg-shaped ornament alternating with a dart-like tongue used to enrich a molding.

anchorage In post-tensioning, a device used to anchor the tendon to the concrete member; in pretensioning, a device used to anchor the tendon during hardening of the concrete; in precast concrete construction, the devices for attaching precast units to the building

frame; in slab or wall construction, the device used to anchor the slab or wall to the foundation, rock, or adjacent structure. Sometimes called a dead man.

anchorage bond stress The bar forces divided by the product of the bar perimeter or perimeters and the embedment length.

anchorage deformation (slip) The loss of elongation or stress in the tendons of prestressed concrete due to the deformation of the anchorage or slippage of the tendons in the anchorage device when the prestressing force is transferred from the jack to the anchorage device.

anchorage device *(see anchorage)*

anchorage loss *(see anchorage deformation or slip)*

anchorage zone In post-tensioning, the region adjacent to the anchorage subjected to secondary stresses resulting from the distribution of the pre-stressing force; in pretensioning, the region in which the transfer bond stresses are developed.

anchor blocks Blocks of wood built into masonry walls, to which partitions and fixtures may be secured.

anchor bolt A bolt with the threaded portion projecting from a structure, generally used to hold the frame of a building secure against wind load or a machine against the forces of vibration; known also as hold-down bolt, foundation bolt, and sill bolt.

anchor bolt plan A plan view showing the size, location, and projection of all anchor bolts for the metal building systems components, the length and width of the foundation (which may vary from the nominal metal building size). Column reactions (magnitude and direction), and minimum base plate dimensions may also be included.

anchor gate A gate similar to a canal lock gate which is held in position at the top by the pintle of an anchor and collar or similar hinge.

anchor plates Small flat pieces often made of perforated metal, through the center of which various types of hangers may be inserted.

ancillary A subordinate, auxiliary building in a group composition; a dependency.

ancon A boss or projection left on a block of masonry to serve as a console or small bracket; a vertical corbel supporting a cornice. Ancons are also sometimes used to support busts or figures.

anemometer An instrument for measuring the velocity of a fluid.

anesthetizing location Any area in which it is intended to administer any flammable or nonflammable inhalation agents in the course of examination or treatment and includes operating rooms, delivery rooms, and other areas where anesthesia is used.

angle (1) The difference in direction of two lines which meet or tend to meet. Usually measured by degrees. (2) The angle at which the collectors are tilted to the sun depends upon both the application and the latitude. Tilting the collector surface from the horizontal to be more nearly at right angles to the sun's rays is the optimum angle. *(see orientation)*

angle beam (angle iron) A rolled-steel beam of L section, the wings usually at right angles.

angle board In carpentry, a board used as a guide, so as to plane lumber to a specific angle.

angle bond In masonry work, brick or metal ties used to bind the angles or corners of the walls together.

angle brace A bar put across an angle to stiffen it.

angle bracket A type of support which has two faces usually at right angles to each other. A web is sometimes added to increase the strength.

angle brick Any brick shaped to an oblique angle to fit a salient corner.

angle capital A capital at the corner where a range of columns turns.

angle cleat A small bracket of angle section fixed in a horizontal position to support a structural member.

angle closer In masonry, a portion of a whole brick which is used to close up the bond of brickwork at corners.

angle dividers A tool primarily designed for bisecting angles, but can also be used as a try square.

angledozer A bulldozer with the moldboard set at an angle so that it pushes earth both sideways and ahead.

angle float A finishing tool having a surface bent to form a right angle.

angle gauge A tool used to set off and test angles in work done by carpenters, bricklayers, and masons.

angle iron A section or strip of structural iron bent to form a right angle.

angle joint In carpentry, a joint between two pieces of timber at a corner, as distinguished from a lengthening joint.

angle of internal friction For very dry or submerged soils without cohesion, such as clean sands, the angle of internal friction is approximately the angle of repose.

angle of repose *(OSHA)* The greatest angle above the horizontal plane at which a material will lie without sliding.

angle rafter A hip rafter.

angle section A metal section shaped like an L; the leg lengths may be equal or unequal.

angle staff A wooden or pressed steel angle bead which is sometimes decorated.

angle tie (dragon tie) A horizontal timber which holds one end of the dragon beam and joins the wall plates together at a corner of the building; an angle brace.

angle tile (arris tile) A plain tile molded to a right angle for covering a hip or ridge in the corner of a building.

angle trowel In plastering, a margin trowel.

angle valve A shut-off valve in which the pipe openings are set at right angles to each other.

angling dozer A bulldozer with a blade

which can be pivoted on a vertical pin so as to cast its load to either side.

angstrom Unit of wavelength, equal to a hundred-millionth of one centimeter.

angular aggregate Aggregate, the particals of which possess well-defined edges formed at the intersection of roughly planar faces.

anhydride A compound derived from another compound (as an acid) by removing the elements of water.

anhydrite A mineral, anhydrous calcium sulfate ($CaSO_4$); gypsum from which the water of crystallization has been removed, usually by heating above 325°F (160°C); natural anhydrite is less reactive than that obtained by calcination of gypsum.

anhydrous Matter containing no water.

anhydrous calcium sulphate A stable form of gypsum from which practically all of the water of crystallization has been removed. Described by the term dead-burned gypsum.

anhydrous lime Unslaked lime which is made from almost pure limestone.

anion A negatively charged particle of molecular proportions. It is attracted to the anode when in solution. anneal To reduce the brittleness and increase the ductility of metal by heating to a certain temperature, then cooling slowly in air or oil.

annealed wire A soft pliable wire used extensively in the building trade for tie wires, especially for wiring concrete forms.

annex A supplementary building added to, or used in connection with, a previously existing structure.

annotation A note on a drawing providing an explanation or comment.

annual growth ring The growth layer put on a tree in a single growth year. Includes spring wood and summerwood.

annual ring The arrangement of the wood of a tree in concentric rings, or layers, due to the fact that it is formed gradually, one ring being added each year.

annular Ring-shaped.

annular bit A key-hole saw.

annular ring-nail A deformed shank nail with improved holding qualities specially designed for use with gypsum board.

annular vault A vault rising from two parallel walls; the vault of a corridor; same as barrel vault.

annulated columns Columns clustered together by rings or bands.

annulet A small square molding used to separate others. The fillet which separates the flutings of columns is sometimes known by this term.

annunciator An electromagnetic device to indicate which of several circuits has been activated.

annunciator, car An electrical device in the car which indicates visually the landings at which an elevator landing signal registering device has been actuated.

anode The opposite pole from the cathode in electrolysis.

anodic metallic coating Prevents corrosion of exposed areas of the base metal by galvanic protection. The coating becomes the anode and undergoes increased corrosion so that the base metal cathode is protected from further corrosion until all the nearby coating metal is gone.

anodize To give an aluminum oxide coating by electrolytic action.

anomaly Something that deviates more than would be expected from normal variations.

anta (antal) A name given to a pilaster when attached to a wall.

antechamber An apartment preceded by a vestibule and from which another room is approached; an entry.

antefixa In Classical architecture (gargoyles, in Gothic architecture), the ornaments of lions and other heads below the eaves of a temple, through channels in which, usually by the mouth, the water is carried from the eaves. Also, the upright ornaments above the eaves in ancient architecture, which hid the ends of the Harmi or joint tiles.

anterides In ancient architecture, the buttresses of a wall.

anteroom (antechamber) A room of secondary use, often serving as a waiting room or reception room to a space of greater importance.

ante-solarium A balcony which faces the sun.

anthemion Conventionalize, decorative designs based on the honeysuckle or palmette; common in Greek architecture.

anthracite A hard, natural coal which contains approximately 85-95 percent carbon and a low percentage of volatile matter.

anti-actinic glass Heat-absorbing glass.

anticipating control One which, by artificial means, is actuated sooner than it would be without such means, to produce a smaller differential of the controlled property.

anti-corrosive paints Paints that contain pigments to inhibit and delay corrosion of metal surfaces; metal priming coats.

anticum A porch of a front entrance, as distinguished from posticum, a porch of a rear entrance.

antidegradant A compounding material used to retard deterioration caused by oxidation, ozone, light and combinations of these. Note-antigegradant is a generic term for such additives as antioxidants, antiozonants and waxes.

antioxidant A substance which prevents or slows down oxidation of material exposed to air.

antimony oxide A brilliant white paint with a faint pink undertone that will not bleed.

anti-noise paint A rough surfaced paint with high noise absorption.

anti-sag bar (sag bar) A vertical tie rod from the ridge of a truss down to the horizontal tie beam. It may also be used to connect horizontal steel rails in wall framing or purlins in roofing, to reduce their deflection.

anti-siphon trap In plumbing, a trap in a drainage system designed to preserve a waterseal by preventing siphonage.

anti-static The ability of a carpet or an agent to disperse electrostatic charges and reduce the build-up of static electricity.

anvil block In a paving breaker, a movable piece of steel between the air piston stem and the steel.

apartment A residential unit of one or more rooms, providing complete living facilities for a family or an individual; usually called a flat in Britain.

aperature In building, an opening left in a wall for a door, window or for ventilating purposes.

apex Top or peak of a pyramidal or conical form.

apex stone A triangular stone at the top of a gable wall, often decorated with a carved trefoil.

apophyge The lowest part of the shaft of an Ionic or Corinthian column, or the highest member of its base if the column is considered as a whole. The apophyge is the inverted cavetto or concave sweep, on the upper edge of which the diminishing shaft rests.

apparent mass of object 8.0 grams per cubic centimeter is mass of material of density 8.0 grams per cubic centimeter that produces exactly the same balance reading as the object when the comparison is made in air with density of 1.2 grams per cubic centimeter at 20 degrees celsius. Used to determine actual weight of object.

apparent specific gravity (see specific gravity)

appendage In building, any structure appended or attached to the outer wall of a building but not necessary to its stability.

appentice A hood over an entrance, supported by attachment to the wall.

apples and pears (slang) Stairs or a staircase.

application for payment Contractor's written request for payment of amount due for completed portions of the work and, if the contract so provides, for materials delivered and suitably stored pending their incorporation into the work.

application rate The quantity (mass,

volume or thickness) of material applied per unit area.

applied molding The arrangement of molding to give the effect of paneling. Applied molding was commonly used in a type of architecture of the seventeenth century known as Jacobean architecture.

appraisal Evaluation or estimate, preferably by a qualified professional appraiser, of the market or other value, cost, utility or other attribute of land or other facility.

apprentice A person who works under a skilled craftsman for a number of years and is taught to be a tradesman or journeyman.

approach In an evaporative cooling device, the difference between the average temperature of the circulating water leaving the device, and the average wet-bulb temperature of the entering air.

approval, architect's (engineer's) Architect's or engineer's written or imprinted acknowledgment that materials, equipment or methods of construction are acceptable for use in the work, or that a contractor's request or claim is valid.

approval drawings Approval drawings may include framing drawings, elevations and sections through the building as furnished by the manufacturer for approval of the buyer. Approval by the buyer affirms that the manufacturer has correctly interpreted the overall contract requirements.

approved *(OSHA)* Sanctioned, endorsed, accredited, certified, or accepted as satisfactory by a duly constituted and nationally recognized authority or agency.

approved equal Material, equipment or method approved by the architect or engineer for use in the work as being acceptable as an equivalent in essential attributes to the material, equipment or method specified in the contract documents.

appurtence A structure that is attached to, or sufficiently near a main structure to be considered a part of it.

apron (1) The front gate of a scraper body; short ramp with a slight pitch. (2) A plain or molded piece of finish below the sill of a window put on to cover the rough edge of the plastering. (3) A floor or lining of concrete, timber, etc., to protect a surface from erosion, such as pavement below chutes or spillways. (4) The portion of an airport, usually paved,immediately adjacent to hangars and other buildings, used for parking, loading and unloading of aircraft. (5) *(OSHA)* The area along the waterfront edge of the pier or wharf.

apron feeder Short conveyor comprised of uniform overlapping pans attached to chains or joined by links to form an endless conveying medium over supported rollers reinforced to withstand pressure. It is used for controlled rate feeding of crushed materials. Also known as plate-belt feeder.

apron molding Molding on the lock rail of a door

apron piece In carpentry, a pitching piece.

apron wall That part of a panel wall between the window sill and the support of the panel wall.

apse The semicircular or polygonal termination to the chancel of a church. The term also applies to similar forms in other buildings.

apteral A temple without columns on the flanks or sides.

aquastat A device for regulating the temperature of the hot water supply.

aqueduct An artificial canal for the conveyance of water either above or below ground.

aqueous (aq.) Describes a water-based solution or suspension. Frequently describes a gaseous compound dissolved in water.

Aquia Creek stone A light gray and buff cretaceous sandstone quarried in Stafford County, Virginia.

arabesque A decorative pattern combining animal, plant, and occasionally, human forms, used in Roman and Renaissance design; also, a decorative pattern of interlaced lines or bands in geometrical forms, developed in Arabian design.

arbitration Method of settling claims or disputes between parties to a contract, rather than by litigation, under which an arbitrator or a panel or arbitrators, selected for his or their specialized knowledge in the field in question, hears the evidence and renders a decision.

arbor (1) A type or detached latticework or an archway of latticework. (2) A drive shaft.

arc (1) An arch; a division or foil or a trefoil, quatrefoil, cinquefoil, or multifoil arch; any part of the circumference of a circle. (2) To strike an arc is to light a welding torch.

arcade A range of arches supported either on columns or on piers and detached or attached to the wall; A passageway with an arched roof, frequently with shops on one or both sides.

arcature A small arcade, such as an arched balustrade.

arch A curved structural member used to span an opening or recesses; also built flat. Structurally, an arch is a piece, or assemblage of pieces, so arranged over an opening that the supported load is resolved into pressures on the side supports, and practically normal to their faces.

miter An arch which is really a lintel with opposed halves at an angle.

relieving A segmental arch, usually a blind arch, above a lintel, for the purpose of relieving the lintel of the weight above.

segmental A round arch whose intrados includes less than a semicircle.

stilted An arch in which the enter is above the impost line.

arch (In water treatment terminology) A condition found in the chemical feeding of dry chemical in which the dry material packs in an arch-shaped formation in or above the discharge throat of the feed hopper. This formation, which is also known as "bridging," prevents further flow of material to the feed hopper.

arch band The visible portion of a rib in vaulting.

arch bar A support for a flat arch. The support may be either a strip of iron or a flat bar.

arch brace A sloping arch-shaped strut in a wooden truss near its support; a curved timber in a frame.

arch brick Special wedge-shaped brick used in the building of an arch; also suitable for other similar work.

arch-buttress Sometimes called a flying buttress; an arch springing from a buttress or a pier.

arch corner bead A job-shaped length of corner bead used to define the curved portion of arched openings.

arch dam A dam held up by horizontal thrust from the sides of the valley (abutments). It must be built on rock, since yielding ground would cause the dam to fail. It can be of concrete, stone or brick, with concrete being the commonest. The arch is curved in a horizontal plane. Variations include arch centerline, angle arch, radius arch, crown cantilever, double curvature, fillet, etc.

arched construction Building with arches, i.e., carrying wall or floor loads on arches instead of on lintels or beams.

Archimedes screw A spiral feed screw, set at an incline, which turns and lifts water and other material from the submerged lower end, sometimes through a pipe; ancient water lifting device.

architect Designation reserved, usually by law, for a person or organization professionally qualified and duly licensed to perform architectural services, including analysis of project requirements, creation and development of the project design, preparation of drawings, specifications and bidding requirements, and general administration of the construction contract.

architect's scale A 3-sided rule with 15 scales on it so chosen that by placing the rule's edge on a reduced-scale drawing the scale of the drawing may be converted directly into the dimensions of the object.

architect-engineer An individual or firm offering professional services as both architect and engineer; term generally used in government contracts, particularly those with the federal government.

architect-in-training *(see intern architect)*

architectonic Having the constructive characteristic of architecture.

architectural area Sum of the areas of the several floors of the building including basements, mezzanine and intermediate floored tiers and penthouses of headroom height measured from the exterior faces of exterior walls or from center line of walls separating buildings.

architectural concrete Concrete which will be permanently exposed to view and which therefore requires special care in selection of the concrete materials, forming, placing and finishing to obtain the desired architectural appearance.

architectural drawing A drawing which shows the plan view and/or elevations of the finished building for the purpose of showing the general appearance of the building, indicating all accessory locations.

architectural terra cotta Hand-burned, glazed or unglazed clay building units, plain or ornamental, machine-extruded or hand-molded, and generally larger in size than brick and used as a facing.

architrave A chief beam; that part of an entablature which rests upon a column head and supports the frieze. A decorative molding framing a panel, doorway or window.

architrave block A block at the base of an architrave into which the skirting board fits.

architrave cornice An entablature consisting of an architrave and cornice, without the intervention of the frieze, sometimes introduced when inconvenient to give the entablature the usual height.

architrave (of a) door The finished work surrounding the aperture; the upper part of the lintel is called the traverse, and the sides the jambs.

architrave jamb A molding on the side of a window or door opening.

archivolt A collection of members forming the inner contour of an arch, or a band or frame adorned with moldings running over the faces or the arch-stones, and bearing upon the imposts.

arch rib A load-bearing main member of a ribbed arch; a deepening of an arch.

arch ring The load-bearing portion of an arch.

arch stone A wedge-shaped stone for use in an arch.

archway An opening or passageway spanned by an arch.

arclight An electric light source depending on a voltaic arc between the ends of two carbon rods.

arcograph An instrument for drawing arcs of a circle without striking them from a center as with a compass.

arc spetography Spectrographic identification of elements in a sample of material, heated to volatilization in an electric arc or spark.

arcuated construction Stone masonry in compression, using the arch and vault.

arc-welding Electric fusion welding process used for heavy and medium-heavy structural welding.

are A metric unit of area, 100 square meters; 100 ares equals one hectare.

area (1) Total inside surface of anything, measured in square units. The quantitative measure of a plane or surface; two-dimensional extent measured in square units. (2) An uncovered space surrounding foundation walls to give light to the basement. (3) An open space or court within a building.

area divider A raised, double wood member attached to a properly flashed wood base plate that is anchored to the roof deck. It is used to relieve thermal stresses in a roof system where no expansion joints have been provided.

area drain A drain set in the floor of a basement areaway, any depressed entry way, a loading platform, or a cemented driveway which cannot be drained otherwise.

area method (of estimating cost) Method of estimating probable total construction cost by multiplying the adjusted gross floor area by a predetermined cost per unit of area.

area separation wall Fire-rated partition, usually with 2- to 4-hour rating, designed to prevent spread of fire from an adjoining occupancy; also usually provides good sound attenuation. Extends from foundation to or through the roof.

area wall (1) The masonry wall surrounding or partly surrounding an area. Also the retaining wall around basement windows below grade. (2) A metal devise, shaped like a horseshoe 3' in height. Used for an access to a crawl space under a house. It is connected to the stem or foundation wall.

areaway Recessed area below grade around the foundation to allow light and ventilation into a basement window or door. Also called area.

arena The open space in the middle of the amphitheater or other place of public resort.

arenaceous Composed primarily of sand; sandy.

aerostyle The style of building in which the columns are distant from one another from four to five diameters. Strictly speaking, the term should be limited to intercolumniation of four diameters, which is only suited to the Tuscan order.

argillaceous Composed primarily of clay or shale; clayey.

argon (A) A chemical element, an inert gas found in the air and used in light bulbs, radio tubes, etc.

Arizona marble A stone varying to the extent of every color of the spectrum and in a wide scale of veinings. The principal productions are known as Apache Gold, Geronimo, and Navajo Black and Gold.

Arkansas marble A group name given to several colorful and decorative varieties quarried near Batesville and known as Ozark Famosa, Ozark Fleuri, Ozark Rouge, and St. Clair.

armature (1) Iron bars of framing to help support slender columns. (2) The rotating part of a motor, caused to move because of a magnetic field. Also the movable part of a relay which moves due to a magnetic field.

armor coat A type of asphalt paving involving the spreading of two or more thin layers of different sizes of aggregate sprayed with asphalt.

armored cable Rubber-insulated wires which are wrapped with a flexible steel covering; often called BX.

armored concrete Concrete which has been strengthened by reinforcing steel or steel plates.

armory A room or building serving as a depository for arms and armor; a building or establishment for the manufacture of arms, especially one maintained by the government; a building for the use of a body of militia, with storage for their arms and equipment.

Armstrong's Acoustical Slide Rule Designed by Don Graf of PENCIL POINTS magazine for use in quick figuring for both acoustical correction and noise quieting problems.

Armstrong scale A divided scale, arranged so that eight different relationships are obtained. Eight commonly used scales are arranged in pairs on each edge.

aromatic red cedar An aromatic wood available from Nova Scotia west to the Dakotas and from that line south to the Gulf of Mexico; used chiefly for plywood and for lining storage closets as a deterrent measure against moths.

array A group of collectors placed so as to best collect the sun's rays.

arrester In air pollution control, a wire screen secured to the top of an incinerator to confine sparks and other products of burning; also used on smoke stacks of equipment working in heavy timber.

arrest point A critical point.

arris The edge of an external angle; the ridge between adjoining flutes of a Doric column.

arris tile *(see angle tile)*

arrissing tool A tool similar to a float, but having a form suitable for rounding an edge of freshly placed concrete.

arrisways In building, a term used when referring to tile or slates laid diagonally.

arrow (1) In critical path method, a line drawn to represent each activity included in the network for a project, joining two events. (2) In surveying, a short rigid piece of wire used to mark temporary points on the ground.

arrow diagram *(C.P.M.)* An arrangement of arrows representing activities that describe a project. The head to tail relationship of the activity arrows indicate the sequence in which activities will be performed.

arterial highway A general term denoting a highway primarily for through traffic, usually on a continuous route.

article (1) A subdivision of a document. (2) In project specifications, the primary subdivision of the section, often further subdivided into paragraphs, subparagraphs and clauses.

articled clerk In Britain, an indentured apprentice.

articulated Jointed; bending in the middle; a type of steering mechanism.

articulation *(see percentage articulation)*

artificial harbor A harbor made by building one or more breakwaters around an area of water.

artificial horizon A container of mercury used to give a true horizontal direction by reflection when measuring altitudes with a sextant.

artificial stone A special kind of manufactured product resembling a natural stone. A common type is made from pulverized quarry refuse mixed with portland cement and water.

artisan (artificer) A skilled craftsman; an artist; one trained in a special mechanical art or trade; a handicraftsman

who manufactures articles of wood or other material.

asbestine Talc; an extender used in paint.

asbestos A fibrous mineral used in many ways as a fire barrier.

asbestos blanket In plumbing, a small asbestos blanket wrapped around the pipes being welded to keep the heat in.

asbestos board A fire-resistant sheet made from asbestos fiber and portland cement.

asbestos cement A fire-resisting, waterproofing material made by combining portland cement with asbestos fibers.

asbestos-diatomite Insulating, fire-resisting boards or building blocks made from asbestos fiber, diatomaceous earth and a binder.

asbestos felt A sheet of matted asbestos fibers used as a basis for saturated asbestos felt and asbestos asphalt coated roofing.

asbestos-free compound Joint treatment products that have no asbestos fiber.

asbestos plaster A nonflammable insulation for pipes, made of asbestos-diatomite.

asbestos protection Fibers of asbestos felt embedded in the galvanized coating of sheet steel to enable bituminous coatings to adhere more tenaciously and to provide greater corrosion resistance.

asbestos sheeting Sheets for roofing and wall covering made of asbestos cement.

asbestos shingles A type of shingle made for fire-proof purposes. The principal composition of these shingles is asbestos, which is non-combustible, non-conducting, and chemically resistant to fire.

asbestos wallboard Panels with a high proportion of asbestos, therefore higher fire resistance and better insulating value, than asbestos-cement sheet.

as-built drawings *(see record drawings)*

ash 1. Hardwoods of the eastern U.S.A., ranking high in weight, strength, resistance to shock and wear, and ability to hold a formed shape. 2. The incombustible material that remains after a substance has been burned.

ashlar (ashler) (1) Squared and dressed stones used for facing a masonry wall. (2) Short upright wood pieces extending from the attic floor to the rafters forming a dwarf wall.

ashlar brick A brick that has been rough-hackled on the face to resemble stone.

ashlar facing Facing of a faced or veneered wall composed of solid rectangular units usually larger in size than brick, having sawed, dressed, or squared beds, and mortar joints.

ashlar masonry Masonry composed of rectangular units usually larger in size than brick and properly bonded, having sawed, dressed, or square beds, and mortar joints.

ashpit *(see soot door)*

ash ring Internal buildup near the kiln discharge end promoted by the fallout of ash particles on the load or lining.

askarel A synthetic nonflammable insulating liquid which, when decomposed by the electric arc, evolves only nonflammable gaseous mixtures.

askew Crooked, distorted, out of position such as a warped or misapplied timber or stud.

aspect ratio In air distribution outlets, the ratio of the length of the core opening of a grille, face, or register to the width. In rectangular ducts, the ratio of the width to the depth.

asphalt A dark brown to black cementitious material; solid, semi-solid, or liquid in consistency; in which the predominating constituents are bitumens which occur in nature as such or which are obtained as residue in refining petroleum. Asphalt is a constituent in varying proportions of most crude petroleums. Asphalt, air blown - An asphalt produced by blowing air through molten asphalt at an elevated temperature to raise its softening point and modify other properties.

asphalt base course A foundation course consisting of mineral aggregate, bound together with asphaltic material.

asphalt binder course Intermediate course between base and asphalt courses, usually coarse graded aggregate asphaltic concrete but seldom containing mineral matter passing No. 200 sieve.

asphalt blocks Asphalt concrete molded under high pressure. The type of aggregate mixture composition, amount and type of asphalt, and the size and thickness of the blocks may be varied to suit usage requirements.

asphalt block pavements Pavements in which the surface course is constructed of asphalt blocks. These blocks are laid in regular courses as in the case of brick pavements.

asphalt, blown or oxidized Asphalt that is treated by blowing air through it at elevated temperature to give it characteristics desired for certain special uses such as roofing, pipe coating, undersealing portland cement concrete pavements, membrane envelopes, and hydraulic applications.

asphalt, cake *(slang)* Broken asphalt to be remolded in chunks.

asphalt, catalytically blown An air-blown asphalt produced by using a catalyst during the blowing process.

asphalt cement Asphalt that is refined to meet specifications for paving, industrial, and special purposes. Its penetration is usually between 40 and 300. The term is often abbreviated A.C.

asphalt color coat Asphalt surface treatment with cover of mineral aggregate selected to produce desired color.

asphalt concrete High quality, thoroughly controlled hot mixture of asphalt cement and well-graded, high quality aggregate, thoroughly compacted into a uniform dense mass typified by Asphalt Institute Type IV Mixes.

asphalt, cut back A term generally applied to liquid asphalts such as Rapid Curing, Medium Curing, Slow Curing, and Emulsified Asphalts. It simply indicates some additive has been mixed with heavy asphalt to liquify the material.

asphalt dip Protective coating and linings for steel culverts; pipes can be spun, dipped and invert paved with this material.

asphalt, emulsified This grade of liquid asphalt is an asphaltic cement mixed with water and a detergent which keeps the asphalt in a liquid condition. After this material is mixed with an aggregate and is exposed to the air, the water evaporates and leaves a stable dense mix.

asphalt emulsion slurry seal **(1)** A mixture of slow-setting emulsified asphalt, fine aggregate and mineral filler, with water added to produce slurry consistency. **(2)** A homogenous mixture of emulsified asphalt, a graded aggregate and water which is spread on a pavement surface. The cured slurry has an even appearance, fills all cracks, adheres firmly to the surface, and has skid resistant texture.

asphalt filler An asphalt product used to fill cracks and joints in pavements and structures.

asphalt fog seal A light application of liquid asphalt without mineral aggregate cover. Slow setting asphalt emulsion diluted with water is the preferred type.

asphalt from petroleum Almost all asphalt produced and used in the U.S. is refined from petroleum. Such asphalt is produced in a variety of types and grades ranging from hard brittle solids to almost water-thin liquids. Liquid asphaltic products are generally prepared by cutting back or blending asphalt cements with petroleum, by distillates or by emulsifying them with water.

asphalt intermediate course (binder course) A course between a base course and an asphalt surface course.

asphalt joint filler An asphaltic product used for filling cracks and joints in pavement and other structures.

asphalt joint fillers, preformed Premolded strips of asphalt mixed with fine mineral substances, fiberous materials, cork sawdust, etc.; manufactured in dimensions suitable for construction joints.

asphalt leveling course A course (asphalt aggregate mixture) of variable thickness used to eliminate irregularities in the contour of an existing surface prior to superimposed treatment or construction.

asphalt, liquid An asphaltic material having a soft or fluid consistency that is beyond the range of measurement by the normal penetration test, the limit of which is 300 maximum. Liquid asphalts include the following:

(a) *cutback asphalt* Asphalt cement which has been liquified by blending with petroleum solvents (also called diluents), as for the RC and MC liquid asphalts *(see b and c below).* Upon exposure to atmospheric conditions the diluents evaporate, leaving the asphalt cement to perform its function.

(b) *rapid-curing (RC) asphalt* Liquid asphalt composed of asphalt cement and a naphtha or gasoline-type diluent of high volatility.

(c) *medium-curing (MC) asphalt* Liquid asphalt composed of asphalt cement and a kerosene-type diluent of medium volatility.

(d) *slow curing (SC) asphalt* Liquid asphalt composed of asphalt cement and oils of low volatility.

(e) *road-oil* A heavy petroleum oil, usually one of the slow-curing (SC) grades of liquid asphalt.

(f) *asphalt emulsion* of asphalt cement and water which contains a small amount of an emulsifying agent, a heterogeneous system containing two normally immiscible phases (asphalt and water) in which the water forms the continuous phase of the emulsion and minute globules of asphalt form discontinuous phase. Emulsified asphalts may be of either the anionic, electro-negatively charged asphalt globules or cationic, electro-positively charged asphalt globules types, depending upon the emulsifying agent.

asphalt macadam   A type of pavement construction using a course, open-graded aggregate that is usually produced by crushing and screening stone, slag or gravel. Such aggregate is called macadam aggregate. Asphalt may be incorporated in macadam construction either by penetration or by mixing.

asphalt mastic   A mixture of asphalt and fine mineral material in such proportions that it may be poured hot or cold into place and compacted by troweling to a smooth surface.

asphalt mastic board dummy joint   For use as a longitudinal and/or traverse contraction joint of the plane of weakness type for all concrete structures and pavements. asphalt, milling A thin layer of old asphalt paving removed by special milling equipment so an area can be resurfaced without raising the grade.

asphalt, mineral filled   Asphalt containing finely divided mineral matter passing No. 200 sieve.

asphalt, natural (native)   Asphalt occurring in nature which has been derived from petroleum by natural processes of evaporation of volatile fractions leaving the asphalt fractions. The native asphalts of most importance are found in the Trinidad and Bermudez Lake deposits. Asphalt from these sources often is called Lake Asphalt.

asphalt overlay   One or more courses of asphalt construction on an existing pavement. The overlay generally includes a leveling course, to correct the contour of the old pavement, followed by uniform course or courses to provide needed thickness. When overlaying rigid-type pavements the overlay should be not less than 4

inches thick to minimize reflection or cracks and joints through the overlay. Greater thickness of overlay may be required depending upon conditions or old pavement and traffic to be served.

asphalt paint   A liquid asphaltic product sometimes containing small amounts of other materials such as lampblack, aluminum flakes and mineral pigments.

asphalt panels, premolded   Generally made with a core of asphalt, minerals, and fibers, covered on each side by a layer of asphalt-impregnated felt, coated on the outside with hot applied asphalt. The panels are made under pressure and heat to a width of three to four feet by ⅛ to one inch thick, and to any desired length.

asphalt pavement structure (flexible pavement structure)   Courses of asphalt-aggregate mixtures, plus any non-rigid courses between the asphalt construction and the foundation or subgrade. The term flexible sometimes used in connection with asphalt pavements denotes the ability of such a pavement structure to conform to settle- ment of the foundation.

asphalt pavements   Pavements consisting of a surface course of mineral aggregate coated and cemented together with asphalt cement on supporting courses such as asphalt bases; crushed stone, slag, or gravel; or on portland cement concrete, brick or block pavement.

asphalt paving machine (lay-down machine)   A machine which receives asphaltic concrete from dump trucks and spreads it to the specified thickness on the area being paved.

asphalt paving plant (hot plant)   A specially constructed plant designed to heat and mix crushed aggregate with heated asphalt to the specified consistency for application on any area to be paved with asphaltic concrete.

asphalt penetration   A measure of the hardness or consistency of asphalt expressed as the distance that a standard needle will penetrate a sample under known conditions of temperature, loading and time.

asphalt, petroleum Asphalt refined from crude petroleum.

asphalt planks Premolded mixtures of asphalt fiber and mineral filler, sometimes reinforced with steel or fiberglass mesh. They are usually made in three to eight-foot lengths and six to twelve inches wide. Asphalt planks may also contain mineral grits which maintain a sandpaper texture throughout their life.

asphalt, powdered Solid or hard asphalt crushed or ground to a fine state of subdivision.

asphalt prime coat An application of low viscosity liquid asphalt to an absorbent surface. It is used to prepare an untreated base for an asphalt surface. The prime penetrates into the base and plugs the voids, hardens the top and helps bind it to the overlying asphalt course. It also reduces the necessity of maintaining an untreated base course prior to placing the asphalt pavement.

asphalt primer A liquid asphalt of low viscosity which penetrates into a non-bituminous surface upon application.

asphalt, rock Porous rock such as sandstone or limestone that has become impregnated with natural asphalt through geologic processes. asphalt, rubberized Made of ground up tires, asphalt cement, crude petroleum and mineralized aggregate used as a surface course.

asphalt, sand A mixture of sand and asphalt cement or liquid asphalt prepared with or without mineral filler. Either mixed-in-place orplant-mix construction may be employed. Sand asphalt is used in construction of both base and surface courses.

asphalt seal coat A thin asphalt surface treatment used to waterproof and improve the texture of an asphalt wearing surface. Depending on the purpose, seal coats may or may not be covered with aggregate. The main types of seal coats are aggregate seals, fog seals, emulsion slurry seals and sand seals.

asphalt, semi-solid Asphalt which is intermediate in consistency between liquid asphalts and solid or hard asphalt, that is, normally has a penetration between 10 and 300.

asphalt, sheet A hot mix of asphalt cement with clean, angular, graded sand and mineral filler. Its use is ordinarily confined to surface course, usually laid on an intermediate or leveling course.

asphalt shingles composition roof shingles made from asphalt impregnated felt covered with mineral granules.

asphalt soil stabilization (soil treatment) Treatment of naturally occurring non-plastic or moderately plastic soil with liquid asphalt at normal temperatures. After mixing, aeration and compaction provide water resistant base and sub-base courses of improved load bearing qualities.

asphalt, solid or hard Asphalt having a normal penetration of less than 10.

asphalt, stone-filled sheet A sheet asphalt containing up to 25 percent coarse aggregate. asphalt surface course The top course of an asphalt pavement, sometimes called asphalt wearing course.

asphalt surface treatments Application of asphaltic materials to any type of road or pavement surface, with or without a cover of mineral aggregate, which produces an increase in thickness of less than one inch.

asphalt tack coat A very light application of liquid asphalt applied to an existing asphalt or portland cement concrete surface. Asphalt emulsion diluted with water is the preferred type. It is used to insure a bond between the surface being paved and the overlying course.

asphalt viscosity Means of controlling application temperatures of asphalt.

asphaltene A high molecular weight hydrocarbon fraction precipitated from asphalt by a designated paraffinic naphtha solvent at a specified temperature and solvent-asphalt ratio. Note-The asphaltene fraction should be identified by the temperature and solvent-asphalt ratio used.

aspiration Production of movement in a fluid by suction created by fluid velocity.

assembly rod An external bolt holding a machine together.

assignment of contract A document specifying payments due on a contract be paid to a person or an agency other than the contractor or subcontractor.

assimilative capacity The pollutant-absorbent capability of receiving waters.

assize In masonry, a cylinder-shaped block of stone which forms part of a column or of a layer of stone in a building.

associate (of an office or firm) A member of an engineer's or architect's staff who has a special employment agreement.

associate (or associated) architect (or engineer) An architect or engineer who has a temporary partnership, joint venture or employment agreement with another architect or engineer to collaborate in the performance of services for a specific project or series of projects. *(see joint venture)*

astragal (1) A small semicircular molding, either plain or ornamented. (2) A molding on the leading edge of hoistway doors. Usually a rubber molding extending the full height on center opening doors, and either metal or rubber running the full width of the upper panel on by-parting freight-type doors.

astylar Lacking a column or pilaster.

asympote A straight line which continually approaches a curve without touching it.

atactic A chain of molecules in which the position of the side methyl groups is more or less random.

athey wagon A large bottom-dump

type of hauling trailer usually pulled by a hauling unit. These units range in size from 15-ton capacity to 100-tons, or larger.

atlantes (atlases) Male figures corresponding to the more familiar female figures, caryatids; used as masonry supports.

atmospheric pressure Pressure of air enveloping the earth, averaged as 14.7 pounds per square inch at sea level, or 29.92 inches of mercury as measured by a standard barometer.

atmospheric steam curing Steam curing of concrete products or cement at atmospheric pressure, usually at maximum ambient temperature between 100-200°F (40-95C).

atom A particle of matter that cannot be divided by chemical means. An atom consists of a nucleus, which is composed of two kinds of primary particles called protons and neutrons, and electrons, which surround the nucleus. It is estimated that it would take 100 million atoms to cover the head of a pin.

atomic absorption spectroscopy Production, measurement, and interpretation of spectra arising from either emission or absorption of electromagnetic radiation by atoms.

atomic number Defined by the number of protons in the nucleus of a chemical element.

atomic weight The mass of an atom of an element, compared to the mass of carbon 12.

atomization Breaking up paint, lacquer or varnish into fine drops by compressed air before it is ejected from a spray gun.

atomize Reduce to fine spray.

atrium A large hallway or lobby with galleries at each floor level on three or more sides; often glass enclosed. An open court within a building.

attached columns Those which project three quarters of their diameter from the wall.

attachment plug (plug cap, cap) A device which when inserted into a receptacle, establishes connection between the conductors of the attached flexible cord and the conductors connected permanently to the receptacle.

attenuation The sound reduction process in which sound energy is absorbed or diminished in intensity as the result of energy conversion from sound to motion or heat.

attenuation factor The difference in noise level measured in decibels between a source room and an adjacent receiving room when it is assumed that all the sound entering the receiving room travels by way of the common ceiling of the two rooms.

Atterberg limits Arbitrary water contents (shrinkage limit, plastic limit, liquid limit) determined by standard tests, which define the boundaries between the different states of consistency of plastic soils.

Atterberg test A method for determining the plasticity of soils.

attic A garret; the room or space directly below the roof of a building.

attic base A base for columns commonly used by the Romans, the upper and lower torus with scotia and fillets between.

attic order A term used to denote the low pilasters employed in the decoration of an attic story.

attic ventilators In home building, openings in gables or roof; also, mechanical devices to force ventilation by the use of power-driven fans in the ventilators.

attorney in fact A person authorized to act for or in behalf of another person or organization, to the extent prescribed in a written instrument known as a power of attorney. (see power of attorney)

attrition (1) Wear and tear. (2) Grinding in which size reduction is accomplished by rubbing or friction.

audiograph An acoustic measuring instrument to determine the rate at which sound dies away in a room. This gives a measure of the sound absorption of a room.

auditorium A room or building designed to meet the needs and comfort of an audience.

auger A rotating drill having a screw thread that carries cuttings away from the face.

auger bit An auger without a handle to be used in a brace. Such a bit has square tapered shanks made to fit in the socket of a common brace. This combination tool is known as a brace and bit.

authorized person *(OSHA)* A person approved or assigned by the employer to perform a specific type of duty or duties or to be at a specific location or locations at the jobsite.

autoclave (1) A pressure vessel in which an environment of steam at high pressure may be produced; used in the curing of concrete products and in the testing of hydraulic cement for soundness. (2) An apparatus for carrying out certain finishing operations, such as heat-setting yarn under pressure in a super heated steam atmosphere.

autoclave curing Steam curing of concrete products, sandlime brick, asbestos cement products, hydrous calcium silicate insulation products, or cement in an autoclave at maximum ambient temperatures generally between 340° and 420°F (170° and 215°C).

autoclave cycle The time interval between the start of the temperature-rise period and the end of the blow-down period; also a schedule of the time and temperature-pressure conditions of periods which make up the cycle.

autoclaving (see autoclave curing)

autogenous grinding Grinding with few or no grinding media in relatively large-diameter, short mills where the cascading load produces the impact upon itself.

autogenous healing A natural process of closing and filling of cracks in concrete or mortar when the concrete or mortar is kept damp.

autogenous volume change Change in volume produced by continued hydration of cement exclusive of effects of external forces of change of water content or temperature.

automatic Self-acting; operating by its own mechanism which is actuated by some impersonal influence, i.e., change in pressure, temperature, or mechanical configuration.

automatic grouter A pressurized steel form, faced with foam rubber, which forces grout in and around stones or brick after it has been poured in from the top of stonework.

automatic welding A welding operation utilizing a machine to make a continuous, unbroken weld.

automation That system, process or apparatus operation that is controlled by electronic or mechanical means. These controlling devices complement or replace human observation, effort, decision and action.

autopatrol British word for motorgrader.

auxiliary A helper or standby engine or unit.

auxiliary heat The heat provided by a conventional heating system for periods of cloudiness or intense cold, when a solar heating system cannot provide enough heat.

auxiliary lane The portion of the roadway adjoining the traveled way for parking, speed-change or for other purposes supplementary to through traffic movement.

auxiliary loads All specified dynamic live loads other than the basic design loads which the building must safely withstand, such as cranes, material handling systems and impact loads.

auxiliary reinforcement In a prestressed member, any reinforcement in addition to that participating in the prestressing function.

available oxygen The quantity of atmospheric oxygen dissolved in a given amount of water.

availability factor Percentage of total possible operating time that a piece of equipment is available for service.

avalanche protector Guard plates that prevent loose material from sliding into contact with the wheels or tracks of a digging machine.

avenue A way of approach, a street, drive, etc.

average Usual; normal; The result of dividing the sum of two or more quantities by the number of quantities.

average bond stress The force in a bar divided by the product of its perimeter and its embedded length.

average dimension The average of the corresponding dimensions of units of a sample taken at random.

average frost penetration U.S. Weather Bureau designation of depth frost will penetrate soils ranging from 0″-60″.

average haul The average distance a grading material is moved from cut to fill.

avoirdupois weight A system of weights still in use in some countries for weighing commodities except for precious stones and metals. In this system 16 ounces equal one pound; 2,000 pounds equal one short ton; a long ton contains 2,240 pounds.

award The decision of an owner/ agent to accept the proposal of the lowest responsible bidder for the work, subject to the execution and approval of a satisfactory contract and bond to secure the performance therof, and to such other conditions as may be specified or otherwise required by law. Also the communication of acceptance.

awarding agency The owner, or owner's representative, for whom contract work is done.

awl A small sharp pointed instrument used by the carpenter for making holes for nails or screws.

awl haft The handle of an awl.

awning A roof-like shelter extending over a doorway, window, porch, etc., which provides protection from the sun or rain.

awning window A window in which the vent or vents pivot outward about the top edge giving an awning effect.

ax (axe) (1) A tool for cutting rough-dressing lumber. (2) A bricklayer's hammer.

axed work   Stone faced with the ax: showing ax marks.

axhammer   A type of cutting tool, or ax having two cutting edges, or one cutting edge and one hammer face used for dressing or spalling the rougher kinds of stone.

axial loading   Tension or compression applied longitudinally on columns.

axis   (1) The spindle or center of any rotative motion. (2) In a sphere, an imaginary line through the center. (3) The center line of a tunnel.

axis line (corridor line)   This is the point in the building from which the elevator is located; it is always shown on the layout drawings and is usually the center of a group of columns or the center of two hallways.

axis of symmetry   A line, imaginary or real, about which a geometrical figure or drawing is symmetrically developed, and in which the center of gravity is located.

axle   A pin or shaft on or with which a wheel or pair of wheels revolves.

axle-dead   A fixed shaft functioning as a hinge pin; a fixed shaft or beam on which a wheel revolves.

axle-live   A revolving horizontal shaft.

axle load   The portion of the gross weight of a vehicle transmitted to a structure or a roadway through wheels supporting a given axle.

axle pulley (sash pulley)   A wheel placed on each side at the top of the window to carry the sash cord.

axle steel   Steel from carbon-steel axles for railroad cars.

axle steel reinforcement   Plain or deformend reinforcing bars rolled from axle steel.

axonometric perspective   A way of showing a plan and partial elevation on the same drawing. The plan is turned 30°or 45° and vertical lines are drawn to show the partial elevations.

azeotrope   Azeotropic mixture: a mixture whose vapor and liquid phases have identical compositions at a given temperature.

azimuth   The azimuth of a line on the ground is the horizontal angle measured from the plane of the meridian to the vertical plane containing the line.

azimuthal projection   A map which from one central point all points are on their true bearings.

azimuth traverse   A continuous series of lines of sight related to one another by measured angles only.

azulejo   A Spanish glazed decorative tile in which blue is prominent.

B boron, brightness

Ba barium

bat batten

BB Ballbearing

bb baseboard

BBC Basic Building Code"(se BOCA)

b&cb beaded on the edge and center

bd/bds board, boards

bd ft. board foot

bdl bundle

bev sid beveled siding

Beth.B Bethlehem beam

BEV billion electron volts

BG below ground

BHN Brinell hardness number

BHP brake horsepower

bkt bracket

BI black iron

B/L Bill of lading

bldg building

blk block

BM bench mark, board measure

B/M bill of material

BMEP brake mean effective measure

B&O back-out punch

BOCA Building Officials and Code Administrators International, Inc

B.O.D. biochemical oxygen demand

BPG beveled plate glass

BR bedroom

brk/br brick

brl barrel

bsmt basement

BTB bituminous treated base

BTU British Thermal Unit

bur bureau

but buttress

b/bo Dry rodded bulk volume of coarse aggregate per unit volume of concrete; the ratio of the solid volume of coarse aggregate particles per unit volume of freshly mixed concrete to the solid volume of the coarse aggregate particles per unit volume of dry rodded coarse aggregate.

BCF Bulked continuous filament. Continuous man-made fiber made into yarn that has been texturized to increase bulk and covering power.

BG A tractor-drawn scraper box usually used to maintain the haul road by keeping it as smooth as possible for the scrapers, trucks or other hauling units.

BM (bench mark) An established elevation for comparing with other elevations.

B&O A back-out punch with a special snap, or head, that fits in a riveting gun to drive out a faulty rivet.

Btu British thermal unit; the amount of heat required to raise one pound of water one degree Fahrenheit at or near its greatest density.

BX A cableform of insulated wire, the outer covering of which is a helical binding of interlocking, flexible steel strips. Also called armored cable.

babbit A soft antifriction metal composed of tin, antimony and copper, in varying proportions.

back (1) The extrados of an arch. (2) In plastering, the surface of gypsum wallboard having a double thickness of paper on two long edges designed to be plastered. The opposite side is the face. (3) The top edge of a saw; the following edge of a sawtooth behind the face. (4) The upperface of a slate. (5) The side of a panel that is of a lower veneer quality; a panel whose outer plugs are of different veneer grades.

backacter (drag shovel) A mechanical shovel which digs towards the machine. It can dig to a depth of about 12 feet below the tracks, but does not make as clean-walled a trench as a trencher.

back arch A concealed arch carrying the backing or inner part of a wall where the exterior facing material is carried by a lintel.

backband Molding used on the side of a door or window casing for ornamentation or to increase the width of trim.

back blocking A short piece of gypsum board adhesively laminated behind the joints between each framing member to reinforce the joint.

back clip A specially designed clip attached to the back of gypsum board that fits into slots or other formations in the framing to hold the gypsum board in place. Often used in demountable partition designs.

back coating Asphalt coating applied to the back side of shingles or roll roofing.

back drop (drop manhole) A connection at a manhole where the branch drain enters by a vertical pipe.

back end That portion of project where pipe is lowered into the ditch and tested.

backer rod Open-cell polyurethane foam in various shapes and densities used for many years in the caulking and sealant trade. Used to fill joints prior to application of caulking or sealant.

backfill (1) Earth or other material used to replace material removed during construction, such as in culvert and pipe line trenches and behind bridge abutments; also refers to material placed between an old structure and a new lining. (2) Backing brickwork or bricknogging.

backfill concrete Non-structural concrete used to correct over-excavation, or fill excavated pockets in rock, or to prepare a surface to receive structural concrete.

backfill density Percent compaction for backfill required or expected.

backfire (1) A fire deliberately started to burn against and cut off a spreading fire. (2) An explosion in the intake or exhaust passages of an engine.

backflow The flow of water or other liquids, mixtures or substances into the distributing pipes of a potable supply of water from any source or sources other than its intended source.

backflow preventer (anti-siphon valve) A device or means to prevent backflow into the potable water system.

backform *(see top form)*

backfurrow The first cut of a plow from which the slice is laid on undisturbed soil.

back gutter (chimney gutter) A gutter placed between the upper side of a chimney and a sloping roof; usually lined with flexible metal.

back haul A line which pulls a drag scraper backward from the dump point to the digging.

back hearth That part of a fireplace floor between the side walls and behind the face.

backhoe An excavating machine whose bucket is attached to a hinged stick on the boom and is drawn towards the machine in operation.

backhousing *(see dust chamber)*

backing (1) Of a rafter or rib, the forming of an upper or outer surface that it may range with the edges of the ribs or rafters on either side. (2) Of a wall, the rough inner face of a wall; earth deposited behind a retaining wall, etc. (3) Of a window, that piece of wainscoting which is between the bottom of the sash frame and the floor. (4) In plastering, the rendering coat of plaster, called, on lath, the pricking up coat. (5) The bricks in a wall which are hidden by the facing bricks; coursed masonry built over an extrados. (6) Material that forms the back of the carpet, regardless of the type of construction. (7) Strips of wood nailed at the inside angles of walls and partitions to provide solid corners for nailing the wallboard.

primary back In a tufted carpet, the material to which surface yarns are attached. Made of jute, kraftcord, cotton, woven or non-woven synthetics.

secondary back Also called "double backing." Any material (jute, woven or non-woven synthetics, scrim, form or cushion) laminated to the primary back.

backing board (1) Material, often gypsum wallboard, fastened to wall studs before paneling; gives paneling rigidity, offers sound insulation, and provides fire resistance. (2) A base layer in ceilings for the adhesive application of acoustical tile. *(see water resistant gypsum backing board)*

backing hip rafter The beveling arris as at corners of hip rafters to tie up with adjacent roof surfaces.

backing material The material applied to the back side of shingles or roll roofing to prevent sticking in the bundles or rolls.

backing tier In masonry, the tier of rough brick work which backs up the face tier of an exterior wall for a residence or other well-built brick structure.

backing up Using a lower grade brick for backing than for the facing of a wall.

back iron The steel plate which reinforces the cutting iron of a carpenter's plane and breaks up the shavings.

back lintel A lintel supporting the wall backing; not seen on the face.

backnailing The practice of blind nailing(in addition to hot-mopping)all the plies of a substrate to prevent slippage. *(see blind nailing)*

back observation (back sight) In surveying, any sight taken towards the last station passed.

back of a window A piece of wainscoting between the bottom of the sash frame and the floor.

back-plastering (1) A term denoting plaster applied to one face of a lath system following application and subsequent hardening of plaster applied to the opposite face. Back-plastering is used primarily in construction of solid plaster partitions and certain exterior wall systems. (2) Mortar covering on the back of a brick veneer.

back primed When a coat of paint is applied to the back of woodwork and exterior siding to prevent moisture from getting into the wood and causing the grain to swell, it is said to be back primed.

back prop A raking strut to transfer the weight of the shoring of deep trenches to the ground, usually inserted under every second or third frame.

back putty Bed putty.

backsaw Any saw with its blade stiffened by an additional metal strip along the back. The backsaw is commonly used in cabinet work as a bench saw.

back sawing An Australian process of flat sawing timber enabling the heart to be boxed.

backscatter The number of neutrons reflected back as contrasted to passing through a substance.

back seams While all carpet seams are located on the back or underside of the carpet, those made when the carpet is turned over or face-down are called "back seams," while those made with the carpet face-up are called "face seams."

backset The horizontal distance from the front of a door lock to a centerline through the keyhole, or through the door knob.

back sight The British term for leveling. *(see back observation)*

back-siphonage The flowing back of used, contaminated or polluted water from a plumbing fixture or vessel into a water-supply pipe due to a negative pressure in the pipe.

backspill The material which periodically spills out of the feed end of the kiln caused by operating of mechanical problems.

back stay *(see brace)*

backup The inner, load bearing or structural portion of a masonry wall, usually finished with face brick, stone ashlar, stucco or other decorative or protective veneer.

back-up plate A rigid plate to support an end lap to provide uniform compression.

backup strips Pieces of wood nailed at the ceiling-sidewall corner to provide fastening for ends of plaster base or gypsum panels.

back vent A fresh air intake.

back water (backed) Water held back by some obstruction, natural or artificial.

back water gate A device for preventing the back flow of sewage or water.

bacteria Those microscopic components of the plant kingdom found extensively distributed on plants and animals and in soil and water. They comprise single cells groups, chains, rods or filaments. They neither possess pigment nor require light for their life processes. Non-living materials are used as food by most bacteria. They can be grown by culturing and promote decay of organic matter and soil fertility.

bacterial corrosion The destruction of a material by chemical processes brought about by the activity of certain bacteria which may produce substances such as hydrogen sulfide, ammonia and sulfuric acid.

badger (1) An implement used to clean out the excess mortar at the joints of a drain after it has been laid. (2) In cabinetwork, a large wooden rabbet plane.

badigeon (badijun) In building, a kind of cement or paste made by mixing suitable materials for filling holes or covering defects in stones or wood.

baffle A surface used for deflecting fluids, usually in the form of a plate or wall.

baffle-piers Obstructions set in the path of high velocity water, such as piers on the apron of an overflow dam, to dissipate energy and prevent scour; a groyne.

baffle, refrigerator A plate, wall, or partition which is designed to perform one or more of the following functions:

(a) prevent contact of food with refrigerated surfaces; (b) prevent dripping of condensate on food; (c) regulate and/or direct circulation of refrigerated air.

bag (of cement; sack) A quantity of portland cement: 94 pounds in the United States, 87.5 pounds in Canada, 112 pounds in United Kingdom, and 50 kg in most countries using the metric system; for other kinds of cement, a quantity indicated on the container. *(see barrel)*

bag dam In soil conservation, a dam made of bags partly filled with soil or concrete.

baghouse The building that houses the fabric filters used to collect dust emissions in cement manufacture.

bagnio (1) A bath or bathhouse. (2) A brothel. (3) In Turkey, a prison.

bag plug In testing plumbing, an inflatable drain plug used to block the lower end of a drain.

baguette A small molding of the astragal type, sometimes embellished by carving.

bahut (1) A medieval cupboard. (2) The rounded top course of a masonry wall.

bail A hinged loop used for lifting; a hoist yoke for bracket.

bailer (1) A hollow cylinder used for removing rock chips and water from churn drill holes. (2) A sand pump.

baked finish Paint or varnish requiring baking at temperatures above 150°F for the development of desired properties. British term is stoving.

bakelite One of the earliest plastics developed (Dr. Baekeland, 1916) for use in electrical fittings, door handles, pulls, etc.

balance bar In hydraulics, a large beam, usually wooden, projecting from a lock gate; by pushing this beam when the water level is the same on each side, the lock gate can be opened.

balance box A weight at the far side of a crane from the jib and load; used for counterbalance.

balance bridge A bascule bridge.

balanced cuts Cuts of tile at the

perimeter of an area which will not take full tiles. Also the same sized cuts on each side of a miter.

balanced earthworks An excavation method designed so the cuts equal the fills. Theoretically no earth is left over and no back cutting is needed to complete the last fill.

balanced load Load capacity at simultaneous crushing of concrete and yielding of tension steel.

balanced moment Moment capacity at simultaneous crushing of concrete and yielding of tension steel.

balanced reinforcement In working stress design, an amount and distribution of reinforcement in a flexural member such that the allowable tensile stress in the steel, and the allowable compressive stress in the concrete, are attained simultaneously when the member is loaded. In ultimate strength design, an amount and distribution of reinforcement that reaches its yield point when the concrete reaches ultimate strain in compression as the member is loaded to its capacity.

balance point An intersection between a mass-haul curve and the datum line indicating the point where all excavated material has been used in fill.

balata A rubber latex from South America used for making conveyor and power transmission belts.

balconet The combination of railing and opening as in a balcony, but without the latter's floor space.

balcony A projection from a face of a wall supported by columns or consoles, and usually surrounded by a balustrade.

baldachin A building in the form of a canopy, supported with columns, and serving as a crown or covering to an altar.

bales catch A kind of ball catch.

bale tack A lead tack.

balk (baulk) (1) Earth between excavations; a dumpling. (2) A large roughly squared timber, beam or rafter.

ballast (1) In railroad and highway use, broken stone, slag, sand, etc., used to keep railroad ties in place and to provide drainage. (2) Stone placed on any work mattress to sink it and make it conform to the river bed. (3) Heavy material carried by a moving unit to keep it held down or steady. (4) A current-regulating auxiliary device required to operate a fluorescent lamp.

ballast-tamper A portable machine actuated by compressed air or electricity or any other mechanical device for compacting ballast under the ties or a railroad.

ball-and-race mill Vertical grinding mill for dry raw materials, coal or clinker. The material is ground by steel balls (8-in. to 12-in. diameter) rotating horizontally in a race.

ball coating Reconsolidation of finely ground, dry material on the surface of the grinding media which inhibits further comminution.

ball cock An automatic arrangement in flushing tanks or other cisterns whereby a floating copper or plastic ball opens the cock when the cistern is empty and closes it as it floats up while the cistern fills.

ball-flower An ornament roughly spherical in shape, the front separation of three conventionalized petals revealing an inner ball; usually the ball-flower is one of a series set in a concave molding.

ballie pole A rough-hewn pole used in Iran for structural framework and scaffolding.

balling A name applied to the hydrometric scale used in measuring the strength or worts. This scale gives directly the amount of extract dissolved in the wort, as the weight percentage of sugar in water.

ball mill Horizontal, cylindrical, rotating mill containing steel or ceramic bals as grinding media.

balloon framing A system of framing wooden buildings in which the corner posts and studs are continuous in one piece from sill to roof plate, the intermediate joist being carried by girts spiked to, or let into, the studs, the pieces being secured only by nailing.

without the use of mortises and tenons or the like.

ball peen hammer A hammer having a peen which is hemispherical in shape; used especially by metal workers and stone masons.

ballroom A large room for social assemblies.

ball test A test to determine the consistency of freshly mixed concrete by measuring the depth of penetration of a cylindrical metal weight with a hemispherical bottom.

ball valve A valve controlled by a lever with ball float.

balsa Known also as corkwood; lightest in weight of all woods, weighing seven and one-half pounds per cubic foot when oven dry. The wood is pinkish white, soft and porous.

balteus (1) Literally, a belt; the band forming the junction of the volutes in an Ionic capital. (2) The wide step between tiers of seats in an ancient theater or amphitheater.

baluster (1) A short vase-shaped supporting column or member. (2) A support for a railing, especially one of the upright columns of a balustrade.

balustrade A railing or parapet consisting of a handrail on balusters, sometimes on a base member and sometimes interrupted by piers.

band (1) Small bars or wire encircling the main reinforcement in a member to form a peripheral tie. (2) A flat, horizontal member usually ornamental of relatively slight projection, marking a division in the wall plane. (3) Scots for bond.

band chain A surveyor's steel tape usually 100 feet or more in length, graduated in feet.

banded Having masonry of different colors or textures arranged in alternating courses.

banded column One with its drums alternately larger in diameter than the shaft proper, or more or less richly decorated; fairly common in the French Renaissance.

bandelet A small band encircling a column shaft.

bander A laborer who bolts the metal bands on corrugated metal pipe.

banderize To coat steel with a patented phosphate solution for protection against corrosion.

banderole A sculptured or painted band, ribbon-like, as for an inscription.

banderolle In surveying, a range pole.

bandings Inlays or strips to cover edges of veneer or ends of cores.

band iron Thin metal strap used as form tie, hanger, etc.

band saw A mechanical saw used for cutting intricate shapes or for converting timber. It consists of an endless steel belt with teeth at one edge, running on two pulleys.

band screen An endless band or belt of wire mesh, bars, plates or other screening medium which passes around upper and lower rollers or guides.

band shell A bandstand supplied with a sounding board of shell shape.

banger *(slang)* Refers to number of cylinders of internal combustion in engines (like two-banger, four-banger).

banister Corruption of baluster.

banjo *(slang)* A short-handled shovel.

banjo bar *(slang)* A big U-shaped bar or dolly that an ironworker holds hard against a rivet head while the riveter forms a head on the other end of the red-hot rivet.

banjo taper A mechanical device which dispenses tape and taping compound simultaneously

bank *(OSHA)* A mass of soil rising above a digging level. Specifically, a mass of soil rising above a digging or trucking level. Generally, any soil which is to be dug from its natural position.

banker In masonry, a type or work bench on which bricklayers and stonemasons work when shaping materials.

bank gravel A natural mixture of cobbles, gravel, sand and fines.

bank measure Volume of soil or rock

in its original place in the ground before excavation.

bank of elevators A group of two or more elevators in adjacent hoistways, designed to be installed and wired to operate as a unit. May also pertain to a group of elevators with entrances facing each other from opposite sides of common corridor.

bank of transformers A group of power transformers installed together.

bank protection Various methods used to reduce erosion of the banks of canals, rivers, freeway underpass slopes, etc. by use of gunite, rubble, turfing, etc.

bank run gravel Common term used to describe material six inch maximum to less than $\frac{1}{4}$ inch minimum size, which is excavated from a naturally occurring deposit, and containing some finer material.

banksman The British term for a crane-operator's helper. He signals to the driver when to raise, lower, swing the jib, etc. U.S. equivalent is the oiler.

bank storage Water absorbed by the banks of a stream and which is returned to the stream as the water level falls.

bank yards Yards of soil or rock measured in its original position before digging.

banquette (1) A sidewalk of about 18 inch width. (2) A berm. (3) A footbridge above road level.

baptistery (baptistry) That part of a church set apart for the rite of baptism; the pool for baptism by immersion.

bar (1) A metal member used to reinforce concrete. (2) A glazing bar. (3) A counter over which refreshments are served, or the room in which the counter is located.

barabara A sod house of Alaska.

barbed dowel pin A piece of barbed steel wire pointed at one end; used by carpenters for fastening mortise-and-tenon joints.

bar bender A tradesman who cuts and bends steel reinforcement; or a machine for bending reinforcement.

bar chair A device for supporting reinforcement bars during the placing of concrete in forms or molds.

bar clamp A device consisting of a long bar and two clamping jaws, used by woodworkers for clamping large work.

bar, deformed *(see deformed bar)*

bar ditch Highway ditch.

bargeboard A decorative board covering the face of a projecting gable rafter; often ornate. *(see verge board)*

barge couple One of two projecting rafters covered by bargeboards; also, two beams fitted together to strengthen a building.

barge course (verge course) Brick coping to a gable wall which slightly overhangs the wall; a course of bricks-on-edge laid across a wall as a coping; tiles next to the gable, which overhang it slightly.

barite A mineral, barium sulfate ($BaSO_4$), used in pure or impure form as concrete aggregate primarily for the construction of high-density radiation shielding concrete; designated barytes in Britain.

barium plaster A type of plaster containing barite aggregate with gypsum plaster or portland cement as a binder. It is used on the walls of X-ray rooms to reduce the amount of radiation passing through them.

bar joist A truss form of steel top and bottom members, of plates, channels, or T-sections, with heavy wire or rod web lacing; used for floor and roof supports.

bark pocket A patch of bark nearly, or entirely, enclosed in the wood.

bar lock A type of door interlock used with manually operated doors.

bar mat An assembly of steel reinforcement composed of two or more layers of bars placed at right angles to each other and secured together by welding or ties.

barminutor Bar screen and comminutor assembly at entrance to sewage treatment plant which breaks up or filters out large solids.

barn A building for housing cattle or

horses, for storage of hay or other crops. or for a combination of such purposes.

barn-door hanger A set of pulleys over a door and attached to it by steel strap carrying the weight of the door. The pulleys travel on a rail hung from the lintel. This arrangement is often used for garage and other heavy doors.

Barnes's formula for flow A more accurate formula than Crimp and Bruges. The velocity in feet per second equals $107m^{0.7}$ i where m is the hydraulic mean depth in feet and i the slope.

barney (*slang*) A small truck used to push tunnel mucking cars.

barometer An instrument showing atmospheric pressure.

barometric damper A smoke pipe damper for use in cutting down the natural draft.

Baroque A style developed during the late Renaissance in reaction from Classical forms; characterized by elaboration of scrolls, curves and carved ornament.

barrabkie An Eskimo hut.

barrack Structure resembling a shed or barn to provide temporary housing.

barrage A diversion dam; an artificial dam to increase depth of water or to divert it into a channel.

barranca Steep bank or bluff.

barrel (1) Weight measure for portland cement corresponding to 4 bags; in United States 376 pounds net; in Canada 350 pounds net; most other countries use a ton of (a) 2000 pounds (20 bags at 100 pounds), or (b) 1000 kg (20 bags at 50 kg); also wood or metal container formerly used for shipping cement. The United States converted in 1972 to the use of the short ton (2000 pounds) weight measure. (2) The water passage in a culvert.

barrel light A roof window or curved shape. actually made with curved glass and glazing bars.

barrel nipple A short length of pipe, outside threaded on each end. bare in the middle; a tubular.

barrel shell (*see barrel vault*)

barrel vault Semicircular vaulting unbroken by ribs or groins.

barrel-vault roof A thin concrete roof taking the form of a part of a cylinder.

barricade (*OSHA*) An obstruction to deter the passage of persons or vehicles. Any of several devices to detour or restrict passage.

barrier protection Protection from the environment by a physical, inert barrier. If broken, the underlying base metal is unprotected. Contrasts with anodic coatings which. if breached, continue to protect the underlying base metal.

barrier rail (K-rail) Continuous concrete barrier in the shape of an inverted V. used to maintain separation between high speed traffic lanes going in opposite directions.

barrow A wheelbarrow.

bar screen A screen composed of parallel bars or rods.

bar spacing The distance between parallel reinforcing bars, measured center to center of the bars perpendicular to their longitudinal axes.

bar support (bar chair) A rigid device used to support and/or hold reinforcing bars in proper position to prevent displacement before or during concreting.

bartisan (1) A turret for a flagstaff. (2) A turret projecting from a corner of a tower or of a parapet.

basalt An igneous rock of fine grain, high density and dark color.

bascule (1) A moving span that rotates in a vertical plane about an axis that may be either fixed or movable. (2) An apparatus in which one end is counterbalanced by the other, such as a bascule bridge

bascule bridge A bridge having a balancing section to form a draw-bridge.

base (1) A subfloor slab or working mat, either previously placed and hardened or freshly placed, on which floor topping is placed in a later operation; also the under-lying stratum on which a concrete slab, such as a pavement, is placed. (2) A foundation, or roadbed or paint; the bottom of anything or the chief ingredient of anything. (**3**) The center electrode of a junction transistor. It is similar in circuit operation to the electron tube grid.

base angle An angle secured to the perimeter of the foundation to support and close wall panels.

base bead Base screed.

base bid Amount of money stated in the bid as the sum for which the bidder offers to perform the work, not including that work for which alternate bids are also submitted.

base bid specifications The specifications listing or describing only those materials, equipment and methods of construction upon which the base bid must be predicated, exclusive of any alterante bids. *(see specifications, closed specifications)*

base block The squared block terminating a molded baseboard at an opening.

baseboard A horizontal decorative element used to cover the joint between a wall and floor.

base coat Any plaster or paint coat, or coats, applied prior to application of the finish coat.

base course (**1**) A layer of aggregate, treated soil, or soil-aggregate which rests upon the sub-base or natural foundation. The materials of the base course are usually held together with a binder, but with certain materials, good base courses may sometimes be made without the addition of an outside binder. The purpose of a base course is to furnish a compact, stable and even surface on which to lay a wearing course. (**2**) In masonry, the lowest course, or footing, of a wall or pier.

basehoe A moulding designed to be attached to existing base moulding to cover expansion space. Similar to quarter-round in profile.

base layer The first or interior layer of gypsum board applied in a multilayer system.

base line (**1**) The main traverse or surveyed line running through the site of proposed construction from which property lines, street lines, buildings, etc., are located and plotted on the plan. (**2**) The center line of location of a railway or highway, often called baseline of construction; a reference line for the construction of a bridge or other construction. (**3**) In aerial surveying, an air base.

basement A full story space below the first floor, usually part or all below grade.

basement wall A foundation wall enclosing useable area under a building.

base molding Molding used to trim the upper edge of interior baseboard.

base of a column That part which is between the shaft and pedestal; if there is no pedestal, between the shaft and the plinth.

base plate (**1**) A plate of metal or other approved material formerly placed under pavement joints and the adjacent slab ends to prevent the infiltration of soil and moisture from the sides or bottom of the joint opening; also a device used to distribute vertical loads as for building columns or machinery. (**2**) Part of a surveyors theodolite carrying the lower ends of three footscrews whose upper ends are attached to the tribrach. (**3**) A plate attached to the base of a column which rest on a foundation or other support, usually secured by anchor bolts.

base ply The base ply is the first ply when it is a separate ply and not part of a shingled system.

base screed A preformed metal screed with perforated or expanded flanges to provide a ground for plaster, and to separate areas of dissimilar materials.

base sheet The asphalt saturated and coated composition roofing used in the laying of a built-up roof; specifically the underlying sheets comprising the base or principal part of a roof.

base shoe Molding used next to the floor on interior baseboard. Sometimes called a carpet strip.

base trim Any molding used to decorate the base of a wall, pedestal, column, etc.

basic The theoretical or normal standard size from which all variations are made.

basic module A unit of dimension used to coordinate the size of components and of building elements.

basic refractory Kiln lining made from magnesite or chrome ore. These bricks exhibit greater refractoriness and better resistance to chemical attack by slags and metallic oxides than the alumina or silica types.

basic safety circuit A portion of the elevator control wiring that includes a number of mechanical swing contacts and relay contacts in series. Usually includes the final limits, emergency stop button, governor contacts and a safety operated switch. The cease of operation of any one of these contacts constitutes a possible hazardous operation of the elevator and therefore stops all elevator operations.

basic services The architect's basic services consisting of the following five phases: schematic design; design development; construction documents; bidding or negotiation; and construction contract administration.

basil *(see bezel)*

basilica A large early Christian or medieval church, usually having a cruciform-shaped floor plan; derived from early Roman structures used as public meeting halls and court rooms.

basin Implies circular with sloping sides; any basin-like hollow or depression; a receptacle for water. In plumbing installations, the lavatory.

basket A load-transfer assembly.

basket boom A boom whose foot is supported by a network, or basket, of guy cables; usually surrounded by a tower of framework.

basket crib An enclosure of interlocking timbers used as a shaft lining, as protection around a concrete pier in water, or as a floating temporary foundation.

basketweave A checkerboard pattern used in masonry, wood inlay and painting.

bas-relief Sculpture or carving with slight projection from the background.

bastard Anything not typical or uniform or true.

bastard cut Bastard file.

bastard file A fine or medium grained flat surfaced file used primarily to smooth metal surfaces.

bastard granite A laminated or foliated rock corresponding in composition to granite, though not a true granite formation, hence the name bastard granite; suitable for use in wall construction.

bastard masonry Facing stones of a rubble wall, dressed and built like ashlar; stones for ashlar work which are not completely quarry dressed.

bastard pointing In masonry, pointing with a projection from the face of the brickwork from the same mortar as the pointing.

bastard-sawn (1) A term for lumber that is flat-sawn, plain-sawn or slash-sawn. (2) Hardwood lumber in which the annual rings make angles of 30° to 60° with the surface of the piece.

bastion As in a fort, a projection extruding outward with two flanks.

bat (batt) (1) A piece of brick with one end whole and the other end broken off; any part of a brick. (2) A unit of flat-wrapped insulation. (3) A lead wedge.

batch Quantity of concrete or mortar mixed at one time.

batch box Container of known volume used to measure constituents of a batch of concrete or mortar in proper proportions.

batched water The mixing water added by a batcher to a concrete or mortar mixture before or during the initial stages of mixing.

batcher A device for measuring ingredients for a batch of concrete.

automatic A batcher equipped with gates or valves which, when actuated by a single starter switch, will open automatically at the start of the weighing operation of each material and close automatically when the designated weight of each material has been reached, interlocked in such a manner that: (a) the charging mechanism cannot be opened until the scale has returned to zero; (b) the charging mechanism cannot be opened if the discharge mechanism is open; (c) the discharge mechanism can- not be opened if the charging mechanism is open; (d) the discharge mechanism cannot be opened until the designated weight has been reached within the allowable tolerance; and (e) if different kinds of aggregates or different kinds of cements are weighed cumulatively in a single batcher, interlocked sequential controls are provided.

manual A batcher equipped with gates or valves which are operated manually, with or without supplementary power from pneumatic, hydraulic or electrical machinery, the accuracy of the weighing operation being dependent on the operator's observation of the scale.

semiautomatic A batcher equipped with gates or valves which are separately opened manually to allow the material to be weighed by which are closed automatically when the designated weight of each material has been reached.

batching The controlling of each material that goes into a load of concrete. Weighing or volumetrically measuring and introducing into the mixer the ingredients for a batch of concrete or mortar.

batch mixer A machine which mixes batches of concrete or mortar in contrast to a continuous mixer.

batch plant An operating installation of equipment including batchers and mixers as required for batching or for batching and mixing concrete materials; also called mixing plant when mixing equipment is included.

batement light A window with its sill slanting from the usual horizontal; the shape implies abatement of the light.

bath The tub for human bathing; or the room containing it and other plumbing fixtures, when it is usually called bathroom.

bathtub A tub for human bathing usually a fixed plumbing installation.

batt (bat) A unit of insulation designed to be installed between framing members.

batten Raised rib, in a metal roof, or a separate part or formed portion in a metal roofing panel.

batten (batten strip) A narrow strip of wood or metal used to cover vertical joints between boards or panels.

batten door A door made of sheathing, secured by strips of board, put crossways and nailed with clinched nails.

battening In carpentry work, common grounds put on a wall for use as a base for lathing.

batter (1) Inward slope from bottom to top of the face of a wall. (2) A pile driven at an angle to widen the area of support and to resist thrust. (3) A term used by bricklayers and carpenters to signify a wall, piece of timber, or other materials, which do not stand upright; the opposite of corbel.

batter boards Pairs of horizontal boards nailed to wood stakes adjoining an excavation, used as a guide to elevations and to outline the building.

batter brace In construction work, an inclined brace set at the end of a truss to give added strength and support.

batter level A clinometer to measure the slope of earth cuts and fills.

batter pile A pile driven in at an angle.

battery (1) A storage battery or dry cell. (2) In blasting, often a blasting machine.

battledeck floor A steel floor system for bridges and buildings, devised and developed by the A.I.S.C., consisting of steel plates and beams welded together so as to develop the whole, as a T-beam section with continuity in all directions.

battlement A parapet, the top of which is broken by slots or embrasures.

battleship *(slang)* A large steel bucket, for mucking out shafts or tunnels, that spills its load by being tripped with a cable and opening like a huge clamshell bucket.

baulk *(see balk)*

bauxite A reddish rock composed principally of hydrous aluminum oxides; the principal ore of aluminum, and a raw material for manufacture of calcium aluminate cement. Jamaica is a large exporter.

bay (1) The space between frame center lines or primary supporting members in the longitudinal direction of the building. (2) Any division or compartment of an arcade, roof, etc. (3) Bay window is any window projecting outward from the wall of a building, either square or polygonal in plan, and commencing from the ground.

bayonet gauge (rail gauge) A pair of gauges to be attached to the end of a piece of pipe. These gauges indicate the DBG (distance between guides) and whether or not the rails are square with one another.

bay window An alcove of a room projecting from an outside wall and having its own windows and foundation. Oriel window is a similar structure but supported on projecting corbels.

bazaar A group of retail shops.

bazooka A portable auger used for unloading bulk cement from trucks or freight cars; unloading range is from 0 feet to 15 feet; *(slang)* an Ames taping tool.

beach The face of a hydraulically filled earth dam.

beach pipe Hydraulic fill pipe that carries a slurry of earth and water to make an earth dam.

beacon A light used to indicate a geographical location, producing high-power beams directed slightly above the horizontal, and rotated to produce flashing lights to an observer.

bead (1) In glazing, a sealant or compound after application in a joint, however applied, such as caulking bead, glazing bead, etc. Also, a molding or stop used to hold glass or panels in position. (2) A circular molding. When several are joined, it is called reeding; when flush with the surface, it is called quirk-bead; and when raised, cock-bead. (3) A strip, usually of wood and with one edge molded, against which a sash slides or a door closes. (4) The excessive flow of paint or varnish causing an accumulation at a lower edge. (5) A strip of sheet metal usually formed with a projecting nosing and two perforated or expanded flanges. The nosing serves to establish plaster grounds while the flanges provide for attachment to the plaster base. Used at the perimeter of a plaster membrane as a stop or at projecting angles to define and reinforce the edge. Types are corner beads, base beads, casing beads, etc.

bead-and-reel A molding having a profile of approximately half a circle or more, in which bead forms, singly or in groups, alternate with disc forms.

bead butt (bead and butt) A thick door-panelling which is flush on one face with the frame and recessed on the other without moldings. The flush side is usually decorated with moldings so that the panel butts against the rails of the frame without a bead. These thick doors have high fire resistance.

bead butt and square Door panelling flush on one face and bead butt on the other.

bead molding One having a small half-round of half-spherical section, continuous or divided into beadlike forms.

bead plane A special type of plane used for cutting beads.

beak A drip mold.

beak-head molding One common in Norman architecture, using grotesque heads in a series, all heads terminating in a pointed chin or beak.

beak molding Bird's beak molding.

beam (1) A term generally applied to the principal horizontal members of a building so installed as to support the load of the structure. Beams may be made of wood, steel or other materials; also called girders. There are three types: simple, continuous and cantilever. (2) A structural member subjected primarily to flexure. (3) The graduated horizontal bar of a scale on which the balances ride. **(4)** A long thick piece of wood or metal; standard metal shapes are: I-beam, H-beam, WF beam and junior beam. **(5)** A structural member used to support a load applied across it. **(6)** Large, horizontal spools holding yarns ready to be fed into the loom or tufting machine.

beam and column A primary structural system consisting of a series of rafter beams supported by columns. Often used as the end frame of metal building.

beam-and-slab floor A reinforced concrete floor system in which the floor slab is supported by beams of reinforced concrete.

Beaman stadia arc A direct reading tachometer used in surveying.

beam bender A machine used to straighten or bend rolled-steel joists.

beam block (bond beam) A hollow concrete masonry unit which has short webs, or a channel in which horizontal reinforcement can be placed for embedment in grout or concrete.

beam bottom Soffit or bottom form for a beam.

beam ceiling A type of construction in which the beams of the ceiling, usually placed in a horizontal position, are exposed to view. The beams may be either true or false, but if properly constructed the appearance of the ceiling will be the same.

beam compass A drawing instrument used to draw large circles, similar to a compass except it is held in both hands.

beam filling Brick nogging or masonry between the floor or ceiling joists at their supports which stiffens the joists and provides a fire stop in the ceiling or floor.

beam form A retainer or mold so erected as to give the necessary shape, support and finish to a concrete beam.

beam hanger A wire, sheetmetal, strap or other hardware device that supports formwork from structural members; a stirrup strap.

beam haunch A poured concrete section that extends beyond a beam to support the sill.

beam pocket Opening left in a vertical member in which a beam is to rest; also an opening in the column of girder form where forms for an intersecting beam will be framed.

beam saddle Beam hanger.

beams & stringers Large pieces of lumber (nominal dimensions, 5" and thicker, width more than 2" greater than thickness, e.g. 5 by 8 inches and up) of rectangular cross section graded with respect to their strength in bending when loaded on the narrow face.

beam side Vertical side panels or parts of a beam form.

beam test Aa method of measuring the flexural strength (modules of rupture) of concrete by testing a standard unreinforced beam.

bean sheet *(slang)* A union card used to get food or lodging.

bearer *(OSHA)* A horizontal member of a scaffold upon which the platform rests and which may be supported by ledgers.

bearing **(1)** The portion of a beam truss, etc., that rests on the support. **(2)** The horizontal angle turned between a datum direction such as true north and a given line. **(3)** A wall which supports the floor and roofs in a building. **(4)** A part in which a shaft or pivot revolves.

anti-friction A bearing consisting of an inner and outer ring, separated by balls or rollers held in position by a cage.

needle An anti-friction bearing using very small diameter rollers between wide faces.

pilot A small bearing that keeps the end of a shaft in line.

solid A one-piece bushing.

throwout A bearing that permits a clutch throwout collar to slide along the clutch shaft without rotating with it.

bearing capacity The maximum unit pressure which a soil or other material will withstand without failure or without settlement to an amount detrimental to the integrity or the function of the structure.

bearing pile A pile which carries weight, as distinguished from a sheet pile which takes earth preasure or a raker which takes thrust. It may be a friction pile or an endbearing pile.

bearing plate A plate that provides support for a structural member.

bearing pressure (bearing stress) The load on a bearing surface divided by its area.

bearing stratum The stratum or bed chosen as the most suitable to carry the load being considered.

bearing wall A wall which supports any vertical load in a building as well as its own weight.

bear's den gray A granite of warm gray color, medium grain, quarried at Mason, New Hampshire.

bear-trap dam An obstruction built of hinged leaves that are raised and held up by the pressure of water admitted to the inside. The dam is lowered by draining the interior.

beat When two sounds have nearly the same frequency they alternately reinforce and cancel each other producing a pulsation known as a beat.

beater (1) A bridge man's maul. (2) *(slang)* Sledge hammer. (3) *(slang)* Single jack.

beating block A wooden block used to embed tiles in a flat plane. Method is called beating in.

Beaufort scale A scale of wind velocity ranging from 0 for calm to 12 for hurricane force (over 75 mph).

beaver-tail *(slang)* A main jack.

bed (1) In bricklaying and masonry, the horizontal surfaces on which the stones or bricks of walls lie in courses. (2) A base for machinery, (3) In glazing, the bead of compound applied between a light of glass or panel and the stationary stop or sight bar of the sash or frame. (4) To set firmly and permanently in place.

bed coat Commonly the first coat of joint compound over tape, bead, and fastener heads; occasionally used in reference to taping coat (embedment of tape).

bedding Ground or supports on which pipe is laid.

bedding plane A separation or weakness between two layers of rock, caused by changes during the building up of the rock-forming material.

bed dowel A dowel in the center of the bed or a stone.

bed joints Horizontal joints in brick or masonry; the radiating joints of an arch.

bed load The quantity of silt, sand and gravel or other debris rolled along the bed of a stream, often expressed as weight or volume per time.

bed molding A molding in an angle, as between the overhanging cornice, or eaves, of a building and the side walls; a flat area in a cornice.

bed of a slate The lower side.

bedplate A foundation plate used as a support for some structural part; a metal plate used as a bed, or rest, for a machine; a foundation frame forming the bottom of a furnace.

bed putty The glazier's putty placed under glass, on which the glass is bedded.

bedrock Solid rock which underlies any superficial formation; hence a firm foundation on which to erect a building especially a heavy structure.

bedroom A room designed primarily for sleeping.

beech A hard, stiff, strong hardwood with reddish brown heartwood and white sapwood; plentiful throughout eastern U.S.A.; low in resistance to decay; difficult to season because of shrinkage and tendency to warp.

beetle (mall) A heavy mallet for striking pegs, paving slabs and material which might be damaged by use of a sledge hammer.

beetle head *(slang)* A drop hammer.

bel A unit of sound intensity equal to 10 decibels.

Belanger's critical velocity *(see critical velocity)*

Belfast truss A wooden bowstring girder for spans of up to 50 feet built of relatively small timber. The truss is curved at the top, has a horizontal tie which is joined by sloping members to the curved top chord.

belfry A cupola, turret or framework to enclose a bell.

Belgian truss A fink truss.

belite A name used by Tornebohm (1897) to identify one form of the constituent of portland cement clinker now known when pure as decalcium silicate ($2CaO-SiO^2$) *(see alite, celite, felite)*

bell (1) An expanded part at one end of a pipe section into which the next pipe fits. (2) In Classical architecture, the bare vase form of the Corinthian capital, around which the acanthus leaves are grouped.

bell and hopper A charging device on top of a blast furnace.

bell and spigot In plumbing, pipe joints formed with sections of cast iron pipe with a wide opening (bell) at one end and a narrow end (spigot) at the other; fitted by caulking with oakum and lead.

bell arch A semicircular arch supported on quarter-round corbels.

bellboy *(slang)* A signalman who lets a hoist operator or a cableway operator know when to raise and lower, move away or come closer.

bell crank A level with two arms forming an angle at the fulcrum, or a triangular plate hinged at one corner.

bell curve The shape of a curve depicting the distribution of results of data in which the data follows a normal or Gaussian distribution.

belled excavation *(OSHA)* A part of a shaft or footing excavation, usually near the bottom and bell shaped; i.e., an enlargement of the cross section above.

bell heater Means of heating a small quantity of heavy oil in the oil tank.

bell hole Excavation around pipe that is big enough to work in.

bell joint Sewer or drain tile made with a bell-shape on one end. The plain end on the next section fits inside the bell.

bellmouth overflow Overflow from a reservoir, usually through a tunnel, via towers built from the bed to overflow level.

bell of a capital In Gothic work, immediately above the necking is a deep, hollow curve; this is called the bell of a capital. It is often enriched with foliages. It is also applied to the body of the Corinthian and Composite capitals.

bellows seal Metal bellows used in a shaft seal, or in place of a packing for valves. Also used in long pipe lines instead of gaskets to compensate for expansion of the line with temperature.

bell pier A pier, usually underwater, shaped like a bell and usually supported by both straight and batter piles.

belly board *(slang)* Usually a $1'' \times 10''$ board used to cover a seam in the siding of a building. Usually more than one story.

belly dump A material mover that empties from the bottom.

belly rod *(see camber rod)*

below-grade A floor which is located below the ground level, usually a concrete slab. Presence of moisture is automatically assumed; should be properly tested to determine the moisture level. Proper floor and installation procedure must be selected.

belt (1) A course of stones or brick projecting from a brick or stone wall, generally placed in a line with the sills of the window; sometimes called stone string. (2) A flexible endless band that passes around two or more pulleys, cylinders, etc., for conveying material or communicating motion.

belt conveyor Conveyor by which dry materials are transported on a continuous flat or slightly curved belt of rubber and / or fabric traveling over rollers.

belt course A horizontal course of masonry of a different size or color, usually projecting and generally in the line with window sills or heads or the point of bearing of joists.

belt driven Driver and driven, as motor and compressor, equipped with suitable sheaves or pulleys, and connected by one or more belts to operate at a speed ratio established by the relative diameters of the pulley.

belt highway An arterial highway for carrying traffic partially or entirely around an urban area or portion thereof. Also called circumferential highway.

belt mark A surface defect caused by the gypsum board machine forming belt during manufacture.

belt tightner A pulley unit installed on a conveyer belt system to loosen or tighten the belt by counterweight and positioning of pulley unit.

bench (1) A working level or step in a cut which is made in several layers. (2) A berm. *(see pretensioning bed)*

bench dog A wooden or metal peg placed in a hole near the end of a workbench to prevent a piece of work from slipping out of position or off the bench.

benched foundation (stepped foundation) A foundation placed on a sloping bearing stratum, cut in steps to prevent sliding when loaded.

bench flume A conduit on a bench, cut on sloping ground.

bench hook In cabinetwork, a piece of flat wood placed on the bench to protect the bench top from scarring. Often fitted with a small cleat at each end.

benching (1) Concrete cast in a manhole around a half-round drainage channel so that water flow falls gradually and no solids are left behind. (2) A berm above a ditch. (3) Quarring with benches about 10 feet deep or more.

bench knife In carpentry, a knife blade projecting from a bench surface and used, like a bench stop, for steadying a board being worked.

bench mark A point of known or assumed elevation used as a reference in determining and recording other elevations in topographical surveys.

bench plane Any plane used constantly and kept handy on the bench; a plane used on the bench as a jack plane, a truing plane or a smoothing plane.

bench sander A stationary wood sanding machine of three types: disc sanders or grinders, belt sanders, and reciprocating pad sanders. All grind with glass paper or glass cloth.

bench stop An adjustable metal device, usually notched, attached near one end of a workbench to hold a piece of work while it is being planed.

bench terrace A more or less level step between steep risers, graded into a hillside.

bench trimmer A trimming machine used in cabinetmaking.

bench work In cabinetwork, hand work rather than machine work.

bend (1) A short piece of curved pipe, as an elbow, used to connect two adjacent straight lengths of a conduit. (2) The intertwining of the ends of two ropes to make one continuous rope.

bender gain The distance saved by the arc of a 90° bend.

bending Bowing of a member that results when a load or loads are applied laterally between supports.

bending formula The formula for bending beams of any homogeneous material is: bending moment = stress × modulus of section.

bending machine Machine used ro bend joints of pipe in the field.

bending moment The bending effect at any section of a beam. It is equal to the sum of all moments to the right or left of the section, and represented by the symbol M.

bending moment diagram A graph giving the amount of bending moment at any given point along a beam for a particular loading.

bending schedule A list of reinforcement prepared by the designer or detailer of a reinforced concrete structure, showing the shapes and dimensions of every bar and the number of bars required.

bends (caisson disease) A cramping disease induced by too rapid decrease of air pressure after a stay in compressed atmosphere, as in a caisson.

bend test A test of the weld or of the steel in a flat bar by cold bending it through 180° to verify its ductility. If there is no cracking, the piece is considered ductile.

beneficial occupancy   Use of a project or portion thereof for the purpose intended.

beneficiation   Improvement of the chemical or physical properties of a raw material or intermediate product by the removal of undesirable components or impurities.

benefits, mandatory and customary   Personnel benefits, required by law such as social security, worker's compensation and disability insurance; and by custom, such as sick leave, holidays and vacation; and those which are optional with the respective firm such as life insurance, hospitalization programs, pension plans and similar benefits.

bent   (1) A group of two or more piles or posts which support a trestle deck or falsework. A transverse framework to carry lateral as well as vertical loads. (2) A piece of lumber curved by lamination or steaming. (3) Land unenclosed and covered only with grass or sedge, as opposed to wood, such as a wasteland.

bent bar   Longitudinal reinforcement bent to pass from one face to the other of a member, to use steel efficiently for resistance of moment and diagonal tension, or for anchorage of the bar.

bentonite   A clay composed principally of minerals of the montmorillonite group, characterized by high absorption and very large volume change with wetting or drying.

Berea sandstone   A fine-grain Ohio sandstone, quarried at Amherst, Ohio.

berliner   A type of terrazzo topping using small and large pieces of marble paving, usually with a standard terrazzo matrix between pieces.

berm   (1) An artificial ridge of earth, generally side slopes of a roadbed and commonly called the shoulder. The space between the toe of a slope and excavation made for intercepting ditches or borrow pits. Berms are built to hold water on land that is to be flood

irrigated. (2) In dam construction, a horizontal step or bench in the sloping profile of an embankment dam.

Bernoulli's assumption   Sections of a bent beam which were plane before bending are plane after bending.

berth   Docking place where a ship can tie up to load or unload.

berthing impact   Forces on piers and jetties during the berthing of vessels.

Bessemer process   A process for making steel by blowing air through molten pig iron contained in a suitable vessel, thus removing the impurities by oxidation.

bevel   (1) Any inclination of two surfaces other than 90°. (2) An instrument for taking angles.

beveled edge   The factory edge of gypsum board that has been angled to form a "vee" grooved joint when two pieces are placed together.

bevel of compound bead   In glazing, a bead of compound applied to provide a slanted top surface so that water will drain away from the glass or panel.

bevel siding   Finish siding for the exterior of houses or other structures. It is resawn from square surfaced boards to make two wedge shaped pieces.

bevel square   An adjustable tool, similar to a try square but with a blade that can be set at any angle.

bezantee and billet   A name given to an ornamental molding.

bezel (basil)   The bevel of the cutting edge of a chisel, plane or other cutting tool.

B-grade wood   A grade of solid surface veneer; circular repair plugs and tight knots are permitted.

b-horizon   In soil science, the lower part of the topsoil; the horizon between the a-horizon and c-horizon which contains metal oxides and other materials leached from the a-horizon above it.

bias   A steady DC voltage applied across a PN junction to establish the required junction operating conditions.

bib (bibcock)   A water tap which is fed by a horizontal supply pipe. A stopcock or faucet having a bent down nozzle.

Bible *(slang)* Book of specifications.

bicottura Method for producing tile by firing twice (first fire for body, second to fuse glazes onto body). Can be produced using three different clays - red or cottoforte, yellow or majolica and white clay. Usually have two glazes on the tile, the first a non-transparent on the body and a transparent glaze on the surface.

bid **(1)** The offer of the bidder submitted in the prescribed manner to furnish all labor, equipment and materials, and to perform the specified work within the time prescribed therein for the consideration of payment at the prices stated in the bid schedule. **(2)** To make a price on anything; a proposition, either verbal or written, for doing work and for supplying materials and/or equipment. **(3)** *(slang)* Wild guess carried out to three decimal places.

bid abstract (summary) Abstract of bids; a list of bidders and their bid prices on a given project, usually broken down by items in the project.

bid bond A form of bid security executed by the bidder as principal and by a surety; bid security; surety.

bid call A published notice that bids will be accepted at a designated time and place for specified construction work.

bid date The date established by the owner, architect or engineer for the receipt of bids; bid time.

bidder **(1)** An individual, firm or corporation submitting a proposal for work on a project. **(2)** One who submits a bid for a prime contract with the owner, as distinct from a sub-bidder who submits a bid to a prime bidder. Technically; a bidder is not a contractor on a specific project until a contract exists between him and the owner.

selected *(see selected bidder)*

invited *(see invited bidders)*

bidding documents The advertisement or invitation to bid, instruction to bidders, the bid form and the proposed contract documents including any addenda issued prior to receipt of bids.

bidding or negotiation phase The fourth phase of the architect's basic services, during which competitive bids or negotiated proposals are sought as the basis for awarding a contract.

bidding period The calendar period beginning at the time of issuance of bidding requirements and contract documents and ending at the prescribed bid time. *(see bid time)*

bidding requirements Those documents providing information and establishing procedures and conditions for the submission of bids. They consist of the notice to bidders or advertisement for bids, instructions to bidders, invitation to bid, and sample forms. *(see bidding documents)*

bid form A form furnished to a bidder to be filled out, signed and submitted as his bid.

bid guarantee The required security submitted with the bid to insure execution of the contract and the furnishing of the required bonds.

bid letting Bid opening.

bid opening The opening and tabulation of bids submitted by the prescribed bid time and in conformity with the prescribed procedures. *(see bid time)*

bid price The sum stated in the bid for which the bidder offers to perform the work.

bid security The deposit of cash, certified check, cashier's check, bank draft, money order or bid bond submitted with a bid and serving to guarantee to the owner that the bidder, if awarded the contract, will execute such contract in accordance with the bidding requirements and the contract documents.

bid shopper A term used to describe a buyer who generally plays one proposed supplier or subcontractor against another for the purpose of reducing his purchase price.

bid tabulation A summary sheet listing all bid prices for a project showing the base price together with exclusions or alternates as quoted by the bidders, and usually the estimate of the owner or his representative. A bid abstract.

bid time   The date and hour established by the owner, engineer or architect for the receipt of bids. *(see bid date)*

bifurcation gate   A structure that divides the flow between two conduits.

big bull   *(slang)* A foreman.

big inch   *(slang)* Usually refers to pipe 24 inches in diameter and larger.

big savage   *(slang)* A foreman.

bilateral tolerance   Tolerance specified in two directions from a basic size.

billet   (1) A piece of lumber with three sides sawn and the fourth left round. (2) A steel slab for distributing a load, such as a column, to a grillage or footing.

billet steel   Steel, either reduced directly from ingots or continuously cast, made from properly identified heats of open-hearth, basic oxygen, or electric furnace steel, or lots of acid bessemer steel and conforming to specified limits on chemical composition.

bill of materials   Quantity survey; a detailed listing of all items of material required for construction of a project.

bill of quantities   British term for bill of materials or progress estimate.

billywebb   A wood from Mexico, Central and northern South America, light brown and lustrous; used mainly for veneer.

bimetallic element   One formed of two metals having different coefficients of thermal expansion, used as a temperature control device.

binary   Two-state or two conditions; a counting system.

binder   (1) The fine soil (clay) fraction inherent in or added to sands and gravels for cohesion; soil fraction passing No. 40 sieve; also admixture for stabilizing. Binders include bituminous materials, portland cement, clay, ground limestone, ground shell, and other materials which tend to cement together the separate particles of road metal. Fines which hold gravel together when it is dry. (2) That part of a paint medium which holds the pigment in a coherent film and is not volatile. It may be oil, size or resin. (3) A small diameter rod (stirrup) used for holding together the main steel in a reinforced-concrete beam or column. (4) *(slang)* Term used for the IHC (International Harvester) truck because when running it sounds like a grain binder. (5) A chemical additive to gypsum board core formulation, frequently starch, to improve the bond between the surfacing papers and the core.

binding   A strip sewn over a carpet edge to protect against unraveling and/or to add to its appearance.

binding rafter   A purlin.

binding yarn   Synthetic or natural yarn running lengthwise of the woven fabric, used to "bind" the pile tufts firmly; often called "crimp warp" or "binder warp."

binder bars   Made of metal, vinyl or rubber and used to finish off raw edges, such as doorways or between two different types of floors.

bin-wall   A series of connected bins, generally filled with earth or gravel to serve as a retaining wall, abutment, pier or as protection against explosions or gunfire.

bioaeration   Modification of the activated sludge process in which the sewage and sludge are activated and aerated by mechanical means, such as paddle wheels or turbines.

biocide   That substance able to destroy living organisms.

biodegradable   The attribute of a substance which makes it subject to attack and subsequent deterioration to simpler ingredients by bacteria.

bioecology   The interrelationship of animals and plants with their common environment.

biofiltration   The recirculation of sewage from a trickling filter to a settling tank preceding the filter. This process is covered by the Jenks patent.

biological treatment   The treatment of water-borne pollutants by bacterial or enzyme activity.

biolytic tank   A continuous flow tank

with hopper bottom, with inlet arranged so as to agitate the sludge by the entry of sewage at the apex of the hopper shaped bottom. This agitation tank is sometimes followed by a settling tank in which the sludge is detained until removed.

biosphere That portion of the earth capable of sustaining living organisms.

biota Regional animal and plant life.

biotite Brown or dark green mica, a magnesium iron silicate.

bi-parting doors Doors used on freight elevator to give clear passage as wide as the width of the car. The doors part vertically in the center, with the top section counterbalanced by the bottom one.

bi-parting dumbwaiter doors Two door panels which meet at the center of the opening, one sliding downward and the other sliding upward when opening.

birch A wood of northeastern U.S.A., commercially distributed in two varieties, yellow birch and sweet birch; even-textured, hard, strong wood used for flooring, interior woodwork and veneer.

bird (*slang*) A round piece of foam with a steel rod through the middle with eyes on both ends for the string to be tied onto. With air pressure behind it the bird glides through the conduit.

birdbath (*slang*) A concavity in a pavement surface which holds water after a shower or rain.

bird block A wood block used to separate trusses on the top of an exterior wall. Usually half have holes with screen and half is solid.

bird house (*slang*) Attic ventilator.

bird peck A small hole or patch of distorted wood grain which results from birds pecking through the growing cells in the tree.

bird's-beak molding A drip mold found notably in the cap of the anta or pilaster of the Doric order.

bird screen Wire mesh used to prevent birds from entering the building through ventilators and louvers.

bird's-eye A group of grain patterns visible in many veneers, particularly in maple; a small localized area in wood where the fibers are indented and otherwise contorted.

bird's-eye view (bird's-eye perspective) (1) One of which the station point is above the object. (2) An oblique aerial photograph.

bird's-head molding A medieval molding using a conventionalized, pendant bird.

birdsmouth joint A British term for the cut into the end of a timber to fit it over a cross timber, especially the cut in a rafter to fit it over a wall plate.

Birmingham wire gauge (Stub's iron wire gauge) Wire and sheet steel thicknesses rated by numbers which increase; the smaller the number, the larger the wire.

biscuit A term applied to unglazed tile.

bisect To divide or cut a line, plane or solid into two equal parts.

bit A unit of computer information equivalent to the result of a choice between two alternatives.

bit The part of a drill which cuts.

carbide A bit having inserts of tungsten carbide.

chopping A bit that is worked by raising and dropping.

coring A bit that grinds the outside ring of a hole, leaving an inner core intact for sampling.

diamond A rotary bit having diamond set in its cutting surface.

drag A diamond or fishtail bit; a bit that cuts by rotation of fixed cutting edges or points.

fishtail A rotary bit having cutting edges or knives.

multi-use A bit that can be sharpened for new service when worn.

plug A diamond bit that grinds out the full width of the hole.

roller A bit that contains cutting elements that are rotated inside it as it turns.

soldering The working head of a soldering iron, usually made of copper.

throwaway A bit that is discarded when worn.

bit brace A curved device used for holding boring or drilling tools; a bit stock, with a curved handle, designed to give greater leverage than is afforded by a boring tool with a straight handle.

bitch A three-dimensional steel spike similar to the dog, only with spikes pointing in directions at right angles to each other.

bite In glazing, the amount of overlap of the stop on the panel or light.

bit extension A steel rod which is held on one end by a brace, the other grips a bit; made for drilling holes deeper than the length of the bit in use.

bit gauge (bit stop) A small metal piece attached to a bit to prevent the hole from being drilled too deeply.

bit stock A brace.

bitt Post or vertical timber on a ship's deck or dock to which cables, ropes etc., are made fast.

bitting A indentation or cut on that portion of a door lock key which sets the tumblers.

bitty Paint or varnish defect if small pieces of broken paint skin or other material sticks up above the surface.

bitumen Mixtures of hydrocarbons of natural or pyrogenous origin or combinations of both, frequently accompanied by their non-metallic derivative, which may be gaseous, liquid, semisolid or solid, and which are completely soluble in carbon disulfide. Strictly the portion of bituminous material completely soluble in carbon disulfide. Used loosely as a term for any bituminous material, tar or asphalt.

bitumen content The term used to describe the percent of binder material used in a bituminous mix. In most mixes the bitumen content will vary from three to six percent, depending upon the type of product being mixed.

bituminous Composed of or containing bitumen materials; as asphalt, macadam, tar macadam, tar cement or asphalt cement.

bituminous base course (black base) A foundation for surface and binder courses made of aggregates bound together with bituminous material.

bituminous binder course An intermediate course between a base course and a surface course.

bituminous coal Soft coal which contains about 50 to 80 percent carbon and about 15 to 40 percent volatile matter.

bituminous concrete The highest type of bituminous pavement in use today. It is composed of carefully graded coarse and fine aggregates, and bound together with asphaltic cement. Its graduation is carefully controlled to give a dense, high strength pavement capable of sustained heavy traffic loads.

bituminous emulsion (1) A suspension of minute globules of bituminous material in water or in an aqueous solution; (2) A suspension of minute globules of water or an aqueous solution in a liquid bituminous material (invert emulsion).

bituminous grout A mixture of bituminous material and fine sand that will flow into place without mechanical manipulation when heated.

bituminous leveling course Usually a plant mix of sand and asphalt used to true or crown an old pavement or a rough base before applying a surface.

bituminous macadam In some localities, a term used for coarse stone, gravel or slag fragments coated with bituminous material in a mixing plant or by mix-in-place methods.

bituminous mat A mat of bituminous cemented aggregate, from $\frac{3}{4}$ inch to $1\frac{1}{4}$ inch or more, resulting from repetitions of surface treatment and aggregate covering, using viscous bitumens.

bituminous material A combination of asphalt or tar, inert materials and impurities, distillates or emulsifiers.

bituminous mix-in-place A mixture of aggregates and liquid bituminous material mixed directly on the road or runway base by means of blade graders, road drags, harrows, rotary tillers, or a traveling plant machine. Two general types are the open and coarse graded type. This process is also known as road mix or mulch.

bituminous paint Paint with a high proportion of bitumen, usually dark in color; e.g., black Japan.

bituminous pavements Layers of aggregate over ¾ inch thick, coated and cemented together with bituminous material.

bituminous penetration macadam A pavement constructed by spreading and compacting coarse, uniform rock fragments bound together by aggregated interlock and surface applications of hot asphalt cement, emulsified asphalt or road tar which penetrate the layer of stone.

bituminous plant mix (black top) Aggregates and bituminous materials mixed in a mechanical mixing plant, the finished mix being hauled and laid on the road or runway.

bituminous plastics Plastics made with natural bitumens and used for door furniture and electrical fittings, etc.

bituminous prime coat A spray application of low viscosity asphalt on an untreated base prepatory to construction of the asphalt pavement. For tightly bonded bases in hot climates MC 70 or SC 70 is recommended. In cooler climates where curing may be slow, RC 70 is recommended. For open bases in hot climates MC 250 is recommended. In cooler climates where curing may be slow RC 250 is recommended.

bituminous seal coat (carpet coat) A thin bituminous application to a surface or wearing course to seal and waterproof small voids and/or to embed sand or chips to provide better traction.

bituminous stabilization The process of thoroughly mixing soils, gravel or sand with liquid bituminous materials by blade, harrows, rotary tillers or other methods. Similar to mix-in-place or road mix.

bituminous surface treatments Spray applications of bituminous materials to any type of road or pavement surface, with or without aggregate cover.

bituminous tack coat Very light bituminous application to a primed base, a binder course, a concrete base or any existing pavement, to insure thorough bond with a surface course.

black alum Waterworks alum. It includes a small degree of activated carbon.

black body A theoretical object that absorbs all the radiant energy falling on it and emits it in the form of thermal radiation.

black bolts Bolts covered with a black iron oxide called scale. Less uniform in shape than bright turned bolts.

black diamond Igneous rock of the gabbro or black granite class, with a fine and uniform grain; quarried at Escondido, California.

black ebony A hard, heavy wood from India, the heartwood of which becomes black; often streaked with brown or purple, and can be highly polished.

black Japan The best black varnish; bituminous paint.

black powder Gunpowder. A mixture of carbon, sodium or potassium nitrate, and sulphur. Sometimes used for blasting.

blacktop A broad term used in referring to asphalt pavement.

black vista A cross-grained, easily worked granite, classed among the blacks, quarried near San Diego, California.

blackwall hitch A loop of rope that runs back on itself around the shank of a lifting hook so that it will not slip when lifting.

blade (1) Usually a part of an excavator which digs and pushes dirt but does not carry it; a common term for motor patrol or motor grader. (2) In plastering, that part of the trowel which touches the plaster. (3) The cutting part of a tool, such as a saw blade, chisel blade, etc.

blading back Pushing soil in the windrow back to the position from which it came, usually with a grader.

Blaine apparatus Air-permeability apparatus for measuring the surface area of a finely ground cement, raw material or other product.

Blaine fineness The fineness of powdered materials such as cement and pozzolans, expressed as surface area usually in square centimeters per gram, determined by the Blaine apparatus. *(see specific surface)*

Blaine test A method for determining the fineness of cement or other fine material on the basis of the permeability to air of a sample prepared under specified conditions.

blank door (window) A door or window which has been walled up.

blanket (1) Soil or broken rock left or placed over a blast to confine or direct throw or fragments. (2) Insulating material with paper lining on each face. *(see blasting mat)* (3) In dam construction, an impervious layer placed on the reservoir floor. In the case of an embankment dam, the blanket may be connected to the impermeable element in the dam. (4) Mats used to cover pipe weld.

blanket insulation Fiberglass insulation in roll form, often installed between the metal roof panels and the supporting purlins.

blank flue A chamber built in and closed off at the top in order to conserve material and labor, and to balance weight if the space on one side of a fireplace is not needed for a flue.

blank wall A wall with no openings.

blast To loosen or move rock or dirt by means of explosives or an explosion.

blast area *(OSHA)* The area in which explosives loading and blasting operations are being conducted.

blaster (powder monkey) The person or persons authorized to use explosives for blasting purposes.

blast furnace slag The non-metallic product, consisting essentially of silicates and aluminosilicates of calcium and of other bases, which is developed in a molten condition simultaneously with iron in a blast furnace.

air cooled Material resulting from solidification of molten blast furnace slag under atmospheric conditions; subsequent cooling may be acceler-

ated by application of water to the solidified surface.

expanded The lightweight, cellular material obtained by controlled processing of molten blast furnace slag with water, or water and other agents, such as steam or compressed air, or both.

granulated The glassy, granular material formed when molten blast furnace slag is rapidly chilled, as by immersion in water.

blast heater A set of heat transfer coils or sections used to heat air which is drawn or forced through it by a fan.

blast hole A vertical drill hole, four or more inches in diameter, used for a charge of explosives.

blasting Removing rock from a quarry wall by means of explosives or blasting agents.

blasting agent Any material or mixture consisting of a fuel and oxidizer used for blasting, but not classified an explosive and in which none of the ingredients is classified as an explosive provided the mixed product cannot be detonated with a No.eight test blasting cap when confined. A common blasting agent presently in use is a mixture of ammonium nitrate (NH_4NO_3) and carbonaceous combustibles, such as fuel oil or coal, and may be either procured, premixed and packaged from explosives companies or mixed in the field.

blasting cap *(OSHA)* A metallic tube closed at one end, containing a charge of one or more detonating compounds, and designed for and capable of detonation from the sparks or flame from a safety fuse inserted and crimped into the open end.

blasting gelatin A jelly-like high explosive made by dissolving nitrocotton into nitroglycerin.

blasting machine A hand operated generator used to supply firing current to blasting circuits.

blasting mat A steel blanket composed of woven cable or interlocked rings. Used to confine debris loosened by a blast.

bleach An imperfection resulting from incomplete grinding of plate glass, caused by a low area in the plate which retains part of the original rough surface.

bleaching Restoring discolored or stained wood to its normal color or making it lighter by using oxalic acid or other bleaching agents.

bleed (1) To remove unwanted air or fluid from passages. (2) To undergo bleeding. *(see bleeding)*

bleeder Pipe attached, as to a condenser, to lead off liquid refrigerant, parallel to main flow.

bleeder tile Pipes placed through the foundation of a building to drain water from outside the basement retaining wall into drains within the building.

bleeding (1) In wood finishing, a term often applied to the use of mahogany and red dye stains. Unless some quick-setting material such as shellac, is used as a finish coat, the undercoat may partially dissolve and bleed through the top coat. (2) The discharge or freeing of water from freshly placed concrete. (3) Sap or resin seeping from green lumber. (4) Loss of color when wet due to improper dyeing or from the use of poor dyestuffs. Fabrics that bleed when wet will stain fabrics which come in contact with them.

bleeding capacity The ratio of volume of water released by bleeding to the volume of paste or mortar.

bleed-off Withdrawing a small amount of water from a system. This is done on a controlled, continuous basis usually to limit concentrations of dissolved solids, like those found in cooling systems. *(see blow-down)*

bleeding rate The rate at which water is released from a paste or mortar by bleeding.

blemish Any imperfection which mars the appearance of wood, concrete, paint or other finished surface.

blended cement A product consisting of a mixture of portland cement and other material such as granulated blast-furnace slag, pozzolan, hydrated lime, etc., combined either during the finish grinding of the cement at the mill or by the blending of the materials after grinding.

blender A soft, round paint brush with a blunted tip, used for blending colors and removing brush marks left by coarser brushes.

blight In a city or community, an existing area in which the property has deteriorated below acceptable standards.

blind arch A relieving arch concealed behind a wall facing.

blind bond Bond used to tie the front course to the wall in brickwork where it is not desirable that any headers should be seen in the face work.

blind floor A sub-floor or rough floor.

blind header A half-brick or header which is not seen on one face.

blind hinge A hinge which is concealed.

blinding (1) Compacting soil immediately over a tile drain to reduce its tendency to move into the tile. (2) The application of a layer of weak concrete or other suitable material to reduce surface voids, or to provide a clean dry working surface. (3) The filling or plugging of the openings in a screen or sieve by the material being separated.

blind mortise A mortise which does not pass through the lumber and which encloses a stub tenon.

blind nailing Driving nails in such a way that the holes are concealed; sometimes called secret nailing.

blind rivet A small headed pin with expandable shank for joining light gauge metal. Typically used to attach flashing, gutter, etc.

blinds (shutters) Light wood sections in the form of doors to close over windows to shut out light, give protection, or add temporary insulation. Commonly used now for ornamental purposes, in which case they are fastened rigidly to the building.

blind stop A rectangular molding, usually $\frac{3}{4}$ by $1\frac{3}{8}$ inches or more, used in the assembly of a window frame.

blister (1) A loose raised spot on the gypsum board face, usually due to an air space or void in the core. **(2)** A tape blister under the joint reinforcing tape, usually caused by insufficient compound beneath the tape.

blistering **(1)** The irregular raising of a thin layer at the surface of placed mortar or concrete during, or soon after, completion of the finishing operation. **(2)** A condition similar to the preceding in the case of pipe after spinning. **(3)** A condition usually characterized by a bulging of the finish plaster coat as it separates and draws away from the basecoat. The resulting protuberances are often termed "turtle backs." **(4)** Bubbles in a paint surface caused by vaporization of moisture or resin under the surface. Not to be confused with a bitty film. **(5)** Breaking boulders by firing a charge or high-velocity dynamite plastered on with a few shovels of mud. It makes a terrific air blast.

bloated Swollen as in certain lightweight aggregates, as a result of processing.

block **(1)** A concrete masonry unit, usually containing hollow cores. The most common sizes are 8″x8″x16″; 8″x10″x16″; 8″x12″x16″. **(2)** In carpentry, the solid wood members nailed between joists to stiffen the floor; also called bridging. **(3)** An area of land bounded by streets. **(4)** A small piece of lead or wood which supports the glass in glazing. **(5)** A pulley and its case.

bond beam A hollow unit with web portions depressed to form a continuous channel or channels.

corner A unit with a flat end for construction or the end or corner of a wall.

crown A sheave set suspended at the top of a derrick.

h-block A hollow unit with both ends open.

ribbed A unit with vertical ribs molded into the face.

sash A unit with an end slot for use in openings to receive jambs of doors or windows.

sling A frame containing two sheaves mounted on parallel axis so they will line up when pulled from opposite directions.

split A unit with one or more faces having a rough surface from being split during manufacture.

split rib A unit with vertical ribs which have a rough surface from being split during manufacture.

snatch A sheave in a case having a pull hook or ring.

traveling A frame for a sheave or set of sheaves that slides in a track.

block beam A flexural member composed of individual blocks which are joined together by prestressing.

block caving A method of mining material from the top down in thick successive layers of blocks. Each block is undercut over the greater part of its bottom area and the supporting pillars blasted out.

block holing *(OSHA)* The breaking of boulders by firing a charge of explosives that has been loaded in a drill hole.

blocking **(1)** In carpentry, the process of fastening together two pieces of board by gluing blocks of wood in the interior angle. **(2)** Short lengths of 2 by 4 installed horizontally between studs to provide a nailing base for paneling. **(3)** A method of bonding two adjoining or intersecting walls not built at the same time by means of offsets whose vertical dimensions are not less than eight inches. **(4)** The use of wood blocks as filler pieces between framing members. Serves to stabilize the framing.

blocking course In masonry, a course of stone placed on the top of a cornice crowning the wall.

blockout **(1)** A space within a concrete structure under construction in which fresh concrete is not to be placed; called core in the United Kingdom. **(2)** Openings in a wall provided by a general contractor for the insertion of fixture boxes.

block plan A small-scale plan showing the outlines of existing buildings.

block plane A tool used for working end grain. This type of plane is usually small in size. The cutting bevel is placed up instead of down, and has no cap iron. Designed to use in one hand when in operation.

block tin In plumbing, pure tin.

blockwork Masonry of precast concrete blocks, usually hollow. Usually less expensive than brickwork.

blockyard A plant where concrete blocks are manufactured, hardened and stored.

bloom (1) A surface film on glass resulting from attack by the atmosphere, or by deposition of smoke or other vapors. (2) A roughly prepared mass of iron or steel nearly square in section and comparatively short in proportion to its thickness. (3) A thin film, like the bloom on fruit, that forms on old glossy paint or varnish, veiling the color or reducing the gloss.

blossom *(slang)* A detonating cap used in blasting.

blow Eruption of sand and water inside a cofferdam causing flooding. *(see boil)*

blow (throw) In air distribution, the distance an air stream travels from an outlet to a position at which air motion along the axis reduces to a velocity of 50 fpm. For unit heaters, the distance an air stream travels from a heater without a perceptible rise due to temperature difference and loss of velocity.

blow count Amount of drops of known-weight hammer to drive a pile or other structure to refusal. blow-down Removing small amounts of water from a system using a controlled or scheduled intermittent basis to withdraw accumulated suspended solids and/or dissolved solids. The expressions blow-down and bleed-off are often used interchangeably.

blowdown period Time taken to reduce pressure in an autoclave from maximum to atmospheric.

blower (1) An electrically powered fan for forcing hot air into ducts, and for drawing cold air back to heating unit.

(2) *(slang)* Turbo used to blow bulk cement into bin.

blowhole A hole produced during the solidification of metal by evolved gas which, in failing to escape is held in little pockets.

blowing (popping, pitting) Small pits formed by the expulsion of plaster from the expanding surface behind it; may be caused by lime which slakes slowly, or the oxidation of coal in the lime.

blowing agent A compounding ingredient used to produce gas by chemical or thermal action, or both, in manufacture of hollow or cellular articles.

blown joint In plumbing, a joint in soft metal, such as lead, made by the use of a blowpipe.

blow off In sewage work, a pipe outlet for discharging sediment or water or for emptying a low sewer.

blow sand Wind borne, free moving dune sand.

blow up (1) Localized buckling or shattering of rigid pavement caused by excessive longitudinal pressure. (2) An enlarged section of a plan or map, showing more details than the larger view.

blub A British term for a plaster cast, formed by an air bubble; blistering.

blueprint A positive print with white lines on blue background, made on ferroprussiate paper from a translucent drawing as negative, and developed in water. Plans of a project are usually called blueprints even if copies are made using another process.

bluestone A bluish gray sandstone of fine texture used for paving, coping, stair treads, etc.

blue tops Grade stakes whose tops indicate finish grade level.

blushing A term describing a milky opalescence of lacquer, which is usually caused by moisture or a lack of compatibility of ingredients.

board A flat piece of wood having a nominal thickness of one inch or less and a width of four inches or more; for hardwood, the term is interchangeable with plank.

board and batten A type of siding composed of wide boards and narrow battens. The boards, generally 12 inches wide, are nailed to the sheathing so that there is ½ inch space between them. The battens, generally three inches wide, are nailed over the open spaces between the boards.

board butt joint Shotcrete construction joint formed by sloping gunned surface to a one inch board laid flat.

board foot A unit of measure represented by a board one foot long, one foot wide and one inch thick, or 144 cubic inches: (1″ × 12″ × 12″).

boarding Boards closely laid over rafters or studs to act as a surface for fastening insulation, cladding, tiles, slates, flexible metal sheet, etc.

board knife A hand tool holding a replaceable blade to sharply score or trim gypsum board products. Commonly referred to as a "Stanley" knife.

board lath (1) Wood lath used in plastering. (2) Gypsum plank.

board measure The common measure of lumber, of which the unit is the board foot.

board rule A measuring stick with a scale for computing board feet.

board saw A short hand saw with very coarse teeth for cutting gypsum board for door and window frame openings.

boar's nest *(slang)* A bunkhouse on a construction job.

boast To surface a stone with broad chisel, boasting chisel, and mallet.

boaster A mason's chisel for chopping and shaping brick or block.

boasting In masonry, the dressing of stone a with broad chisel and mallet.

boatswain's chair (bos'n's) *(OSHA)* A seat supported by slings attached to a suspended rope, designed to accommodate one workman in a sitting position.

bob A plumb bob.

bobbin cable hanger A type of insulated support for a traveling cable.

BOD (Biochemical Oxygen Demand)
The oxygen requirement of a water sample, or that amount of elemental oxygen necessary to react with oxidizable or biodegradable material dissolved or suspended in the sample. The amount is normally expressed as milligrams of oxygen per liter of sample. If a population of bacteria is the agency through which oxidation is effected, the needed oxygen is referred to as the biochemical oxygen demand (BOD). BOD tests generally span a five-day period.

bodied linseed oil Linseed oil that has been thickened in viscosity by suitable processing with heat or chemicals. Bodied oils are obtainable in a great range in viscosity from a little greater than that of raw oil to just short of a jellied condition.

bodied solvent adhesive An adhesive consisting of a solution of the membrane compound used in the seaming of membranes.

BOD load The pollutant makeup of a body of water. It is generally given in pounds of oxygen necessary to treat the pollutants. *(see Biochemical Oxygen Demand)*

body (1) The load-carrying part of a truck or scraper. (2) The stiffness of paint or the solidity of the dried film. (3) The descriptive texture of mortar; too much body is too stiff.

quarry A dump body with sloped sides.

rock A dump body with oak planking set inside a double steel floor.

bodying in A process used in painting which includes staining, filling and the first priming.

bog Wet, spongy ground sometimes filled with decayed vegetable matter.

bogie (tandem) A two axle driving unit in a truck; also called tandem drive unit or a tandem.

boil A run of wet material, usually quicksand, on the bottom of an excavated hole, under the sheeting of an excavation or under the cutting edge of a caisson; caused by greater water pressure on the outside than on the inside.

boiled linseed oil   Linseed oil in which enough lead, manganese, or cobalt salts have been incorporated to make the oil harden more rapidly when spread in thin coatings.

boiler   The heating unit of a hot water or steam heating system.

boiler heating surface   All of the surface of the heat-transfer apparatus in contact on one side with the water or wet steam being heated and on the other side with the gas or refractory being cooled, in which the fluid being heated forms part of the circulating system, this surface to be measured on the side receiving heat.

direct heating surface   is generally understood to be the boiler heating surface subject to direct radiation from the surface of the grate, or from the surfaces of oil or gas burners.

indirect heating surface   is the boiler heating surface within the flues.

boiler horsepower   The equivalent evaporation of 34.5 lb of water per hr from and at 212°F. This is equal to a heat output of 970.3 × 34.5 = 33,475 Btus.

boiling point   The temperature at which the vapor pressure of a liquid equals the absolute external pressure at the liquid-vapor interface.

boiler rating   A boiler's heating capacity expressed in British thermal units (Btu) per hour.

boiling water reactor   Water is boiled directly in the reactor core, thereby producing steam which is transported through pipes to the turbine generator set.

Boise sandstone   Trade name for an Idaho sandstone of medium grain, varying from light gray and buff to darker tones, often with brown and purple veinings.

bolection molding   Originally a panel molding which projected beyond the face of the rails and stiles; hence a molding of unusually large and broad convex projection.

bollard   (1) A stone guard against damage to a wall corner by encroaching traffic; also a free-standing stone post to obstruct or direct vehicular traffic. (2) A metal post anchored deeply into the masonry of a quay wall, used for mooring vessels.

bolster   (1) A wide chair used in concrete work to hold up and keep at proper intervals a series of reinforcing rods on a form. (2) A short horizontal timber resting on the top of a column for the support of beams or girders. (3) Padding around the edge of a limpet dam to make a watertight joint with the dock. (4) A bricklayer's chisel.

bolt   (1) The tongue of a lock, which prevents a door opening. (2) A cylindrical bar which is threaded at one end for a nut and forged with a square or hexagonal head at the other end. One of the oldest and commonest methods of fixing metal parts together. (3) Two or more rolls of wallpaper in a single package.

bolt sleeve   A tube surrounding a bolt in a concrete wall to prevent concrete from sticking to the bolt and acting as a spreader for the formwork.

bolt stretcher   *(slang)* What the new men are sent for.

bolt, veneer   A short log cut to length suitable for peeling in a lathe.

bona fide bid   Bid submitted in good faith, complete and in prescribed form which meets the conditions of the bidding requirements and is properly signed by someone legally authorized to sign such bid.

bond   (1) Adhesion and grip of concrete or mortar to reinforcement or to other surfaces against which it is placed, including friction due to shrinkage and longitudinal shear in the concrete engaged by the bar deformations; the adhesion of cement paste to aggregate; adherence between plaster coats or between plaster and a substrate produced by adhesive of cohesive properties of plaster or supplemental material. (2) In bricklaying and masonry, that connection between bricks or stones formed by lapping them upon one another in carrying up the work, so as to form an inseparable mass of building, by preventing the vertical joints falling over each other. In brickwork there are several kinds of bond. In common brick walls, in every sixth or seventh course the bricks are laid crossways to the wall, called headers. In face work, the back of the face brick is clipped so as to get in a diagonal course of headers behind. In Old English bond, every alternate course is a header course. In Flemish bond, a header and stretcher alternate in each course. **(3)** A short length of wire rope used to fix loads to a crane. **(4)** The state of adherence between plaster coats or between plaster and a plaster base produced by adhesive and/or cohesive properties of plaster or special supplementary materials. **(5)** The layer of adhesive in a plywood joint. **(6)** The degree of firmness with which the paper adheres to the gypsum board core. **(7)** *(see bid bond, labor and material payment bond, performance bond, surety bond.)*

bond agent (bonding agent) An independent agent, representing bonding or surety companies, who acts as the liaison between the contractor and the surety company.

bond area The area of interface between two elements across which adhesion develops or may develop, as between concrete and reinforcing steel.

bond beam A horizontal reinforced concrete or concrete masonry beam designed to strengthen a masonry wall and to reduce the probability of objectionable cracking.

bond breaker A material used to prevent adhesion of newly placed concrete and the substrate.

bond course The course consisting of units which overlap those below.

bonded member A prestressed concrete member in which the tendons are bonded to the concrete either directly or through grouting.

bonded post-tensioning Post tensioned construction in which the annular spaces around the tendons are grouted after stressing, thereby bonding the tendon to the concrete section.

bonded roof A roof which carries a written warranty with respect to weather-tightness for a stipulated number of years.

bonded rubber cushion Comes in two different forms: **(1)** as cushion prepared in strips prior to its application to the carpet back; **(2)** as cushion manufactured and cured in place in seamless widths. Rubber cushion is usually either sponge rubber or latex foam, and its quality is generally estimated by its density.

bonded tendon A prestressing tendon which is bonded to the concrete either directly or through grouting.

bonder (header) A masonry unit which ties two or more wythes or leaves of a wall together by overlapping.

bonderize To coat steel with an anticorrosive phosphate solution, usually in prep for the application of paint, enamel, or laquer. also a trademark.

bonding Any material used to join two surfaces and tie them together.

bonding agent **(1)** A substance applied to a suitable substrate to create a bond between it and a succeeding layer as between a subsurface and a terrazzo topping or a succeeding plaster application. **(2)** *(see bond agent.)*

bonding company A firm or corporation executing a surety bond, or bonds, payable to the owner, securing the performance of a contract either in whole or in part; or securing payment for labor and materials.

bonding compound (bitumen) In roofing with bitumen-felt, an oxidized bitumen melted and while hot, applied to fix layer of felt to the roof and to each other. Sealing compound is applied while cold.

bonding conductor A length of cable or wire which grounds cable sheaths or metal frames of electrical apparatus.

bonding jumper *(OSHA)* A conductor to assure the required electrical conductivity between metal parts required to be electrically connected.

bonding jumper, circuit The connection between portions of a conductor in a circuit to maintain required ampacity of the circuit.

bonding layer A layer of mortar, usually ¹/₈ to ¹/₂ inch (3 to 13 cm) thick spread on a moist and prepared, hardened concrete surface prior to placing fresh concrete.

bond length The length of grip of a reinforcing bar.

bond plaster A especially formulated gypsum plaster designed as first coat application over monolithic concrete.

bond prevention Procedures whereby specific tendons in pretensioned construction are prevented from becoming bonded to the concrete for a predetermined distance from the ends of flexural members; measures taken to prevent adhesion of concrete or mortar to surfaces against which it is placed.

bond strength Resistance to separation of mortar and concrete from reinforcing steel and other material with which it is in contact; a collective expression for all forces, such as adhesion, friction due to shrinkage, and longitudinal shear in the concrete engaged by the bar deformations, that resist separation.

bond stress (1) The shear stress at the surface of a reinforcing bar, which prevents relative movement between concrete. (2) The force of adhesion per unit area of contact between two bonded surfaces such as concrete and reinforcing steel or any other material such as foundation rock; sheer stress at the surface of a reinforcing bar, preventing relative movement between the bar and the surrounding concrete.

bond timbers Timber placed in a horizontal direction in the walls of a brick building in tiers, and to which the battens, laths, etc., are secured.

bonnet (1) In building, a wire netting used to cover the top of a ventilating pipe or a chimney. (2) In plumbing, a cover for guiding and enclosing the tail end of a valve spindle. (3) A roof over a bay window. (4) (slang) A steel head or shoe placed over the top of a pile for driving. (5) British term for the hood of a vehicle.

bonnet tile (hip tile) A roofing tile of approximately semi-cylindrical shape, used for covering the roofing along a hip.

bonus and penalty clause A provision in the construction contract for payment of a bonus to the contractor for completing the work prior to a stipulated date, and a charge against the contractor for failure to complete the work by such stipulated date.

bonus clause A provision in the construction contract for additional payment to the contractor as a reward for completing the work prior to a stipulated date.

boojee pump A grouting machine in Britain.

book tile A type clay tile used for roof and wall coverings.

boom In a revolving shovel, a beam hinged to the deck front, supported by cables; any heavy beam which is hinged at one end and carries a weight-lifting device at the other; a tree, beam or pole extending from a mast of a derrick to lift and guide anything being lifted.

lattice A long, light shovel boom fabricated of crisscrossed steel or aluminum angles or tubing.

live A shovel boom which can be lifted and lowered without interrupting the digging cycle.

boom crane A long, light boom, usually of lattice construction.

boomer (1) (load binder) A tool to boom down or cinch up a load, particularly referring to trucking loads. (2) (slang) A floater or itinerant tradesman, who moves from town to town following the boom of construction.

boom jack A boom whose function is to support sheaves that carry lines to a working boom.

boomplacer A specialized boom designed for the use of concrete placement.

booster An auxiliary device that increases force of pressure.

booster fan A small fan for installation in individual heat ducts.

booster heater An electric water heater

to raise the water temperature in one part of the system.

booster pump A pump that operates in the discharge line of another pump either to increase pressure, or to restore pressure lost by friction in the line or by lift.

boosters *(slang)* Boost-a-load ready-mix trucks.

boot (1) A projection from a beam or floor slab to carry facing brickwork. (2) The cold air return fitting that fits into the furnace casing.

boot truck A truck with an insulated tank equipped with heating and pumping devices and used to spray asphaltic products under pressure on the surface of a road, runway or other area to be paved; also called a distributor truck.

Bordeaux connection A thimble for a steel wire rope with a link fitted permanently into it; a convenient way to join wire rope to short-link crane chain.

border (1) An earth ridge built to hold irrigation water within prescribed limits in a field; also called berm. (2) A piece around the edge of anything. (3) A narrow decorative strip of paper, usually placed at the joining of the wall and ceiling.

border stone A curb stone.

bore (1) The internal diameter of a pipe. (2) A borehole, or to make a borehole. (3) In hydraulics, a wave advancing upstream with nearly vertical front during the flowing tide in an estuary.

bore and stroke *(slang)* The measure of a man's capabilities.

bored pile (cast-in-situ pile) A pile formed by pouring concrete into a hole formed in the ground, usually containing some light reinforcement.

borer holes Voids made by woodboring insects, such as grubs or worms.

boring (1) Rotary drilling; the process of making holes in wood or metal for the insertion of bolts or other fasteners used in building construction. (2) A drilling into the earth to bring up samples of the soil to be found at various depths, with the purpose of estimating the load-carrying capacity of the soil.

boring approach excavation the back hoe makes to put boring machine in place.

boron loaded concrete High-density concrete including a boron-containing admixture of aggregate, such as mineral colemanite, boron frits of boron metal alloys, to act as a neutron attenuator.

borrow In highway construction, materials used in the roadbed which are excavated from native materials in ground generally close to roadbed; the term borrow implies the excavation, hauling and spreading of the material from pits designated by the agency building the road.

borrowed light opening A glazed window unit in an interior partition.

borrow pit An excavation made for the purpose of obtaining earth for use in construction.

borts Commercial diamond chips on the face of a rock-boring bit.

boss (1) An ornamental projecting block. (2) The enlarged part of a shaft. (3) A cone for opening pipes. (4) A keystone to a dome, sometimes of glass.

bossage A stone in the rough left projecting from a wall to be sculptured later; coursed ashlar with a roughly dressed or projecting face.

bossing stick In plumbing, a shaper for applying a sheet lead lining to a tank, etc.

Boston Caisson A Gow caisson.

Boston hip roof A method of shingling used to cover the joint, or hip, of a hip roof. To insure a watertight job, a double row of shingles or slate is laid lengthwise along the hip.

Boston lap A method of finishing the ridge of a shingled roof with a shingle course having overlapping vertical joints.

Boston ridge A method of applying asphalt or wood shingles as a finish at the ridge or hips of a roof.

bottle-nose drip A rounded edge of a drip of a metal roof.

bottom dead center Lowest point

reached by a piston on its stroke toward the crankshaft.

bottom dump A type of trailer used to haul sand, gravel, dry earth and coal; best used when material is to be distributed in layers on a fill.

bottoming The last few inches of excavation usually removed by hand to insure that the bottom is smooth and to correct level.

boulder A rock which is too heavy to be lifted readily by hand.

bouldering Paving with cobblestones.

boulevard A wide street in cities which is usually landscaped.

Boulton process A process for pressure creosoting in which the timber is dried, put under vacuum and then put under pressure with creosote.

boundary light One of a series of lights used to indicate the limits of a landing area or a landing field.

boundary survey A mathematically closed diagram of the complete peripheral boundary of a site, reflecting dimensions, compass bearings and angles. It should bear a licensed land surveyor's signed certification, and may include a metes and bounds or other written description.

Bourdon pressure gauge An oval tube which tends to become circular as the pressure inside it increases.

boutell An obsolete term for a round molding, or torus. When it followed a curve, it was called a roving boutell.

bow (1) Any projecting part of a building in the form of an arc of a circle. (2) A warping of lumber at right angles to its face.

bow compass A drafting instrument for drawing small circles; its radius is adjusted by a setscrew working against a spring.

Bower-Barff process (blueing) A protective treatment for steel or cast-iron pipes and fittings.

bowk A kibble.

bowl The bucket or body of a carrying scraper, sometimes the moldboard or blade of a dozer.

bowl classifer Consists essentially of a shallow cylindrical tank in which agitation is maintained by rakes or plows and a means to convey coarse settled particles out of the classifying medium.

bowl mill vertical grinding mill in which materials are ground between centrally suspended rollers and a revolving annular ring.

bowled floor A floor sloping towards one end, as in a church or auditorium.

bow saw A special type of saw used for making curved cuts. The blade, which is thin and narrow, is held in tension by the leverage obtained through the twisting of a cord, or by means of rods and turnbuckle.

bow string truss A truss form in which both upper assembly and bottom chord are convex with their projections above the horizontal.

bow trowel A finishing trowel with a slight curve for "crowning" the final application for joint treatment.

bow window A window placed in the bow of a building.

box (1) A poured concrete culvert. (2) A transmission. (3) A dump body.

box beam A box girder.

box caisson A large open-topped reinforced concrete box built on shore, floated out, and sunk in the site selected for a foundation. Commonly used for bridge piers, since it allows construction to be done where dry.

box casing In cabinetwork, an inside lining.

box cornice A hollow cornice built from wood. The box shape is enclosed by shingles or a gutter above, a fascia in front, the plancier below, and the wall of the building behind it. The soffits of the rafters are hidden, unlike the open cornice.

box cutter A specially designed hand tool for shear-cutting electrical outlet holes in gypsum board.

box drain A small, usually rectangular, drain of concrete or brick.

boxed gutter A roof gutter sunk behind the eaves so as to be concealed.

box frame   A window frame containing boxes for holding the sash weights.

box girder   A hollow steel beam with a square or rectangular cross section.

boxing up   In carpentry, closing in, nailing sheathing to studs or otherwise encasing something.

box nail   A nail that has a flat head, is slightly lighter and has a smaller shank diameter than a common nail. Its predominate use is in rough framing.

box out   To form an opening or pocket in concrete by a box-like form.

box pile   A pile made from two sheet piles or channels or angle sections or joists.

box shear test   A standard method of measuring shear strength of soil; in a box split in two, pressure is applied at the same time as a shearing force.

box stair   An enclosed stair.

box the paint   After the paint has been thoroughly mixed by stirring or shaking, boxing consists of pouring it back and forth from one pail to another to insure consistency of a uniform nature.

box thread   The female side of A.P.I. tapered thread.

boxwood   A hardwood used for making handles, dressers, etc.

boxwood dresser   A wooden tool for straightening lead sheet and pipe.

boziga   Old term for a dwelling.

brace   (1) A tie that holds one scaffold member in a fixed position with respect to another member. (2) *(OSHA)* A strut or pusher, usually horizontal though sometimes inclined, of timber or steel, acting in compression to hold earth material or a structure against lateral movement.

brace frame   A type of framework for a building in which the corner posts are braced to sills and plates.

brace framing   The system of framing buildings by which all vertical structural elements of the bearing walls and partitions extend for one story only, corner posts excepted.

brace jaws   The parts of a bit brace which clamp around the tapered shank of a bit.

brace mold   Two ressaunts or ogees united together like a brace in printing, sometimes with a small bead between them.

brace rod   (1) Any rod that extends from the elevator platform framing to another part of the elevator carframe or sling for the purpose of supporting the platform or holding it securely in position. (2) Rods used in roof and walls to transfer loads, such as wind loads, and seismic and crane thrusts to the foundation. Also often used to plumb buildings but not designed to replace erection cables.

braces, trench   *(OSHA)* The horizontal members of the shoring system whose ends bear against the uprights or stringers.

bracing   Structural elements, which due to their ability to transmit direct stress, are provided to either prevent buckling of individual members subject to compression, to add rigidity to a structure as a whole, or to resist lateral loads. A member used to support, strengthen, or position another piece or portion of a framework.

bracket   (1) A projecting ornament for supporting something or decorating a structure. (2) A knee or knee brace connecting a post or batter brace to an overhead strut. (3) A structural support projecting from a wall or column on which to fasten another structural member. Examples are canopy brackets, lean to brackets and crane runway brackets.

bracket capital   A capital having bracket forms projecting as a continuing support of the lintel; found particularly in Hindu, Saracenic and early Spanish Renaissance, work.

bracket scaffold   An obsolete type of scaffold; a grappler is firmly driven into a brick joint and a steel framed bracket hooked over it.

bracketed stair   One in which the exposed ends of steps bear a decorative scroll-bracket form.

brad A slender wire nail with a small deep round head.

bradawl An awl with chisel edge used to make holes for brads or screws.

bragger A projecting shelf of masonry, built out from a wall in steps, to support something above.

brake (1) A machine for bending, flanging, folding and forming sheet metal. (2) A device for slowing, stopping, and holding an object. (3) A mechanical device used to prevent the elevator from moving.

disc A brake which utilizes friction between fixed and rotating discs and shoes.

friction A brake operated by friction between two surfaces rotating or sliding on each other.

self-energizing A brake that is applied partly by friction between its lining and the drum.

tooth (jaw breaker) A brake used to hold a shaft by means of a tooth or teeth with fixed sockets. Not used for slowing or stopping.

brake drum A rotating cylinder with a machined inner or outer surface upon which a brake band or shoe presses.

brake horsepower The horsepower output of an engine or mechanical device, measured at the flywheel or belt, usually by some form of mechanical brake.

branch In plumbing, an inlet or outlet from pipe.

branch circuits *(OSHA)* (1) That portion of a wiring system extending beyond the final overcurrent device protecting the circuit. A device not approved for branch circuit protection, such as thermal cutout or motor overload protective device, is not considered as the overcurrent device protecting the circuit. (2) Individual circuit off the main riser.

branch interval A length of soil or waste stack corresponding in general to a story height, but never less than eight feet, within which the horizontal branches from one floor or story of a building are connected to the stack.

branch vent Any vent pipe connecting from a branch of the drainage system to the vent stack.

brander In plastering, a fillet nailed at 12 to 15 inch centers to the joists soffit. Ceiling laths are nailed to the branders.

branding iron *(slang)* An indenting roller.

brandrith A rail or fence enclosing a well.

brashness A condition of wood characterized by low resistance to shock and by an abrupt failure across the grain without splintering.

brass (1) An alloy of copper and zinc, with decorative and wearing qualities. Movable parts of much hardware are of brass. (2) A generic term given inscription plates countersunk in the face of tombs and the like. (3) *(slang)* Finish plumbing hardware, drains, spouts, etc.

brattishing Battlement, parapet or cresting.

braze To solder with brass or other hard alloys.

brazed Joined by fusion using a spelter on the order of brass. This is considered equivalent to hard soldering.

break (1) A lapse in continuity. (2) In building, any projection from the general surface of a wall; an abrupt change in direction as in a wall. (3) To twist open or disconnect. (4) An overlap at a purlin between tiers of patent glazing. (5) A short rest period.

breaker A relatively poor conductor of heat used to join the liner and outer shell of an internally refrigerated container such as a refrigerator.

breaker plate heavy, wear-resistance liners for jaw crushers or roll crushers

breaker strip, refrigerator cabinet A cabinet breaker strip is a separate insulating element or integral insulating extension of the cabinet interior surfaces around the periphery of the cabinet door or drawer opening(s), which functions as a thermal barrier to minimize heat flow to the interior of the cabinet.

breakfast room A room designed for the serving of the morning meal.

break ground To start an excavation;

formal start of a construction project; groundbreaking.

breaking factor Tensile at break in force per unit of width ; units, SI:Newton per meter, customary:pound per inch.

breaking strength Property of a fabric which allows resistance to rupture from evenly applied tension. Expressed as pounds of force applied to one inch width in both the direction of the warp and the filling yarn.

breaking stress The crushing strength of brick, concrete or stone; the ultimate tensile strength.

break iron An iron fastened to the top of the bit of a plane. The purpose of the iron is to curl and break the shavings.

break joints (breaking) To arrange a course of masonry so that its vertical joints are not in line with those of the course just below; in plywood sheeting, the same principle.

break lines Lines used when the entire view of the object is not needed, or the object is so large that it could not be properly illustrated on the print.

breakwater (mole) A wall built into the sea to protect a harbor from waves. Two main types are rubble mound and blockwork.

break your pick *(slang)* To quit or be fired.

breast (1) A projecting portion of a wall, usually in connection with a chimney. (2) The moldboard of a plow or dozer. (3) A riser of a stair. (4) The wall under the sill of a window down to the floor level.

breast board A temporary barrier to prevent the digging face from caving or flowing into a tunnel.

breast drill A small tool used for drilling holes by hand in wood or metal. A handturned crank transmits power through bevel gears to the drill chuck.

breast of a window The masonry forming the back of the recess and the parapet under the window sill.

breast-summer *(see bressummer)*

breast timber A leaning brace from the floor of an excavation to a wall support.

breather plug A removable plug, cap, or other means of venting a space containing insulating material through vaportight sheathing to the interior of a refrigerated compartment.

breccia Stone in which angular pieces are imbedded in a matrix of the same or another composition. Many of the marbles are breccias.

bredigite A mineral, alpha prime dicalcium silicate ($2CaO–SiO^2$), occurring naturally at Scawt Hill, Northern Ireland; and at Isle or Muck, Scotland; also in slags and portland cement.

breeder reactor One which produces more fuel than it burns. It is designed so that the uranium 238 in the core absorbs neutrons which then transforms into plutonium, which is fissionable. There is not actually more fuel than you started with, It's a matter of turning the Uranium 238, which is not good fission material, into plutonium, which is easy to fission.

breeze Clinker; fine divided material from coke production.

breeze fixing brick A brick made of cement and breeze and built into a wall for nailing purposes.

breezeway A covered passage, open at each end, which passes through a house or between two structures increasing ventilation and adding an outdoor living effect. Also called a dogtrot.

bressummer A lintel, beam or iron tie intended to carry an external wall itself, supported by piers or posts.

Briar Hill sandstone An Ohio stone with decided variegations in the marking of its general buff color, blending from a golden buff to mottled and banded markings of deeper shades.

brick A structural unit of kiln-burned clay; its shape is generally that of a rectangular parallelepiped. The standard size of a brick is $8'' \times 3\frac{3}{4}'' \times 2\frac{1}{4}''$ or $2'' \times 4'' \times 8''$.

brick and brick Gauged brickwork.

brick ax A bricklayer's hammer.

brick cement A waterproofed masonry cement employed for every kind of brick, concrete brick, tile or stone masonry, and also in stucco work.

brick construction A type of building construction where the exterior walls are bearing walls built of brick or a combination of brick and tile masonry.

brick core Brickwork filled in between the top of a wood lintel and soffit of a relieving arch.

brick facing The same as brick veneer.

bricklayer A craftsman who builds and repairs brickwork.

bricklayers' square scaffold *(OSHA)* A scaffold composed of framed wood squares which support a platform; limited to light and medium duty.

brick mason A bricklayer.

brick masonry Masonry with units of baked clay of shale of uniform size small enough to be placed with one hand and laid in courses with mortar joints.

brick nogging Brickwork filled in between wood posts or studs.

brick-on-edge coping A coping of headers placed on edge.

brick roll A sheet of granule surfaced, asphalt saturated, and coated felt embossed to simulate a brick design.

brick seat Ledge on a wall or footing to support a course of masonry.

brick set A chisel used for cutting bricks.

brick veneer The outside facing of brickwork used to cover a wall built of other material; an outer covering of a four inch brick wall tied to a wood-frame wall.

brick whistle A weep hole; a hole in a mortar joint at the foot of a wall to let out and water that might get in the wall behind the brick.

brick work Masonry of brick, either structural or paving.

bridge (1) A structure built over a drainage channel, a depression or obstruction such as water, highway or railway, and having a roadway surface or track for carrying traffic or other moving loads. (2) In an electric blasting cap, the wire that is heated by electric current so as to ignite the charge; sometimes the shunt connection between the cap wires. (3) A straightedge used as a starting line for the laying of tile. The straightedge can be blocked up to support tile over an opening.

bridge board In carpentry, a cut stringer.

bridge cap The highest part of a bridge pier on which the bearings or rollers are seated.

bridge crane A load lifting system consisting of a hoist which moves laterally on a beam, girder or bridge which, in turn, moves longitudinally on a runway made of beams and rails. Loads can be moved to any point within a rectangle formed by the bridge span and runway length.

bridge deck The load-bearing floor of a bridge which carries and spreads the load to the main beams.

bridge pier A support for a bridge placed on bedrock.

bridge reamer A long thin reamer used to make a rivet hole bigger or to make two holes line up by making them both bigger.

bridge seat That part of the top of a bridge pier or abutment that receives directly the pedestals or shoes of the super structure.

bridge thrust The horizontal force on an arch bridge caused by its shape.

bridge trust A suitable truss for carrying bridge loads, e.g., a Warren Pratt truss.

bridging (1) Bracing floor joists by fixing lateral members between the joists; called strutting in Britain. (2) In painting, the covering over of a gap in a ground by the film. Bridging by paint or varnish weakens the film.

bridging floor A floor carried only on common joists.

bridging joist A common joist.

bridging piece A short bearer between or across the common joists; to carry a partition.

bridle cable An anchor cable that is at right angles to the line of pull.

bridle hitch A connection between a bridle cable and a cable or sheave block.

bridle iron A support by which the end of one beam is carried by another, usually at right angles to the first. Also called stirrup iron or stirrup.

bridle rod In railroad work, a rod that holds the tracks at the right spacing for spiking.

bright A term used to indicate that lumber is free from discoloration.

bright tin plate Sheet-steel coated with tin. Terne plate is a similar roofing material with a coating over the steel of 20 percent tin and 80 percent lead.

brightness The degree of apparent lightness of any surface emitting or reflecting light.

brilliance In paint, the clearness of a varnish or lacquer, and the absence of opalescence and other defects. The cleanness and brightness of color.

brine Any liquid cooled by the refrigerant and used for the transmission of heat without a change in its state, having no flash point or a flash point above 150°F as determined by American Society for Testing and Materials Method D93.

brine, electrolytic Any brine capable of causing chemical decomposition of one of two dissimilar metals by electrolysis.

Brinell test A method of determining the hardness of metal by the indentation of a standard steel ball of known hardness under a definite load.

briquette (briquet) A molded specimen of mortar with enlarged extremities and reduced center having a cross section of definite area; used for measurement of tensile strength.

brisance The shattering or crushing effect of an explosive.

brise-soleil Literally, sun-break; an architectural shield, fixed or movable, on the exterior of a building to block the entrance of unwanted sun rays.

British imperial gallon A fluid gallon equal to approximately 1.2 U.S. gallons; contains 277.42 cubic inches; there are 6.23 such gallons per cubic foot.

British thermal unit (Btu) A unit of measurement of the quantity of heat required to raise the temperature of one pound of water one degree Fahrenheit.

broach (1) To enlarge or ream a hole, usually in stone. (2) To dress a stone roughly. (3) A squinch. (4) One of the semi-pyramidal slopes at the corners of an octagonal spire springing from a square tower.

broaching (line drilling) An excavation method used when the rock left in place must not be shattered by explosive. A line of holes is drilled close together along the break line. The rock between them is knocked out with a chisel, called a broach, and the block is removed with wedges.

broach spire An eight-sided spire developed directly upon its tower walls, without interruption of setback or parapet.

broad base terrace In soil conservation, a long ridge of earth 10 to 30 inches high, and 15 to 30 feet wide with gently sloping sides, a rounded crown and broad shallow channel along the upper side, constructed to control erosion by diverting run-off along the coutour at low velocity instead of permitting it to rush down the slope.

broadcast To toss granular material, such as sand, over a horizontal surface so that a thin, uniform layer is obtained.

broad irrigation A method used for the disposal of sewage effluent by allowing it to flow over levelled land; pipe drains are not normally used. This process is not common in the U.S.A.

broad knife A wide flexible finishing knife for applying joint finishing compound.

brocade A carpet or rug in which a raised pattern or engraved effect is formed using heavy twisted yarn tufts on a ground of straight fibers. Colors of the two fibers are often the same.

broken joint tile A single-lap tile.

broken pediment One interrupted at the top by the return of its molding on themselves, leaving a space usually filled by a vase form or other ornament on a centered pedestal.

broken range Masonry construction in which the continuity of the courses are broken at intervals.

broken range ashlar Uncoursed rubble.

broken tape switch A switch to prevent further operation of the elevator in the event the selector tape breaks.

broken white (off white) A white paint which has been toned down, usually to a creamy tone.

bronze An alloy of copper and tin, frequently including other elements; widely used for sculpture castings and for the most durable metalwork.

bronzing Surface covering of a metallic powder carried in a liquid vehicle.

broom finish A rough surface texture obtained by stroking a broom over freshly placed concrete.

brooming (1) Brushing a floating coat of plaster with a broom. (2) The crushing and spreading of the top of a wooden pile without a driving band when it is driven into hard ground.

brothers A chain or rope sling; may mean either a two-leg or four-leg sling.

brown coat A coat of plaster which is applied with a fairly rough finish to receive the finish coat; in two-coat work the term refers to the base coat of plaster which is applied over the lath; the second coat in three-coat plaster application. Not actually a brown color.

brownline A drawing printed on brownish tinted paper, showing dark brown lines. Similar to a blueprint.

brownmillerite A ternary compound originally regarded as $4CaO-Al_2O_3$, $Fe_2O_3(C_2F)$ occurring in portland cement and high alumina cement; now used to refer to a series of solid solutions between $2CaO-Fe_2O_3(C2F)$ and $2CaO-Al_2O_3(C_2A)$.

brown out To complete application of basecoat plaster.

brown oxide A brown mineral pigment having an iron oxide content between 28 and 95 percent.

brown stone A sandstone of reddish brown color. Many so-called brownstone fronts, however, were of imitation masonry in stucco.

brush The device, usually of carbon or graphite composition, used to connect with the rotating or moving portion of a motor, generator or other electrical device, which carries electrical current to or from the nonmoving parts or connections.

brushability The ability of a liquid to be brushed on. Brushable paints are not gummy or ropy and join easily with paint applied earlier.

brush hand *(slang)* A painter whose sole ability lies in his skill in applying material.

brush lines Fine parallel surface lines in glass having the general appearance of brush marks in paint; also called end lines.

brush or spray coating A water proofing application of one or more coats of asphalt, pitch or a commercial waterproofing on the exterior of the foundation below the grade line with a brush, trowel, or by spraying; may be used where subgrade moisture problems are not severe.

brushed surface A sandy texture obtained by brushing the surface of freshly placed or slightly hardened concrete with a stiff brush for architectural effect or, in pavements, to increase skid resistance. *(see also broom finish)*

bubble (1) The air bubble in a level, or the level tube itself. (2) A large void in the core of gypsum board caused by the entrapment of air while the core is in a fluid state during the manufacturing process.

bubble tube In a level, the tube containing the bubble.

bubbling A defect of paint or varnish films containing very volatile solvents. It consists of bubbles of air or solvent vapors; these may disappear before the film dries.

bucker An ironworker who "bucks" up or backs up a hot rivet with his dolly bar so that the driver can form the head on it.

bucket A part of an excavator which digs, lifts and carries dirt.

slat An openwork bucket made of bars instead of plates used in digging sticky soil.

bucket elevator An endless chain with buckets attached; usually for moving excavated material.

bucket ladder excavator A trencher; a trench excavator.

bucket loader Usually a chain bucket loader, sometimes a tractor loader or shovel dozer.

bucket of kilowatts *(slang)* What the new men are sent for.

bucket sheave (padlock sheave) A pulley attached to a shovel bucket through which the hoist or drag cable is reeved.

Buckeye sandstone A siliceous sandstone of Ohio that is available in several varieties which are uniform in texture and possess unusual enduring qualities: B. Gray, B. Buff, B. Golden Vein, B. Mohogany, B. Spiderweb.

buckle (1) To curve from the normal line of face under strain. (2) A bubble or rupture which eventually cracks exposing the lath beneath.

buckling Failure by lateral or torsional instability of a structural member, occurring with stresses below the yield on ultimate values.

buckling load In structural work, the crippling load on a long column.

bucks (1) The metal frame that forms the entrance to the elevator hoistway. Doors are hung from the "header," or top inside of these elevator door frames. (2) Framing around an opening in a wall. A door buck encloses the opening in which a door is placed.

buckstay (1) An upright member, usually in cross-connected pairs, reinforcing a masonry furnace of flue. (2) Any similar brace member.

buckup An aid to erecting hollow metal frames made up of tow telescoping tubes with clamps at either end.

budget *(slang)* A pocket for carrying nails, used by roofers and bricklayers.

budget construction The sum established by the owner as available for construction of the project. The stipulated highest acceptable bid price or, in the case of a project involving multiple construction contracts, the stipulated aggregate total of the highest acceptable bid prices.

budget, project The sum established by the owner as available for the entire project, including the construction budget, land costs, equipment costs, financing costs, compensation for professional services, contingency allowance, and other similar established or estimated costs.

buffer (1) A pile of blasted rock left against or near a face to improve fragmentation and reduce scattering from the next blast. (2) A movable metal plate used in tunnels to limit scattering of blasted rock. (3) A device designed to stop a descending elevator car or counterweight beyond its normal limit of travel by storing or by absorbing and dissipating the kinetic energy of the car or counterweight. (4) A substance that reduces the change in hydrogen ion concentration (pH) that other wise would be produced by adding acids or bases to a solution.

oil buffer A buffer using oil as a medium which absorbs and dissipates the kinetic energy of the descending car or counterweight.

spring buffer A buffer utilizing a spring to cushion the impact force of the decending car or counterweight. (5) An intermediate storage area for storing computer data.

buffer solution A solution which contains two or more properties, which, when combined, resist marked changes in pH after moderate quantities of either strong acid or base have been added.

buffer switch A switch to prevent normal operation of the elevator car in the event the buffer fails to return.

buffing A router trimming of the shear cut end of gypsum board to smooth cut and adjust for length tolerance prior to the bundling tapes being applied.

bug A parallel connector used for splicing large wires. (Not to be confused with "rail bug.")

buggy A two-wheeled or motor-driven cart, usually rubber-tired, for transporting small quantities of concrete from hoppers or mixers to forms; sometimes called a concrete cart.

bug holes Small regular or irregular cavities, usually not exceeding 15 mm in diameter, resulting from entrapment of air bubbles in the surface of formed concrete during placing and compaction.

build Application of coats of paint for required film thickness.

build a high line *(slang)* To tell a tall tale.

builder's equipment In general, machinery used by builders. Also called builder's plant and machinery.

builder's level A level tube set in a straight edge; a dumpy level used on a building site, but not usually very sensitive.

builder's tape (tape measure) Steel measuring tape usually 50 or 100 feet in length, contained in a circular case. Builder's tape is sometimes made of fabricated materials.

building A structure enclosed within a roof and within exterior walls or fire walls designed for the housing, shelter, enclosure and support of individuals, animals or property of any kind.

building blocks Hollow or solid blocks of burnt clay, gypsum, concrete or other material; larger than bricks.

building brick A solid masonry unit made primarily for building purposes and not especially treated for texture or color; formerly called common brick.

building code The legal requirements set up by various governing agencies covering the minimum requirements for all types of construction. *(see codes)*

building drain That part of the lowest horizontal piping of a building drainage system which receives the discharge from soil, waste and other drainage pipes inside the walls of the building and conveys it to the building sewer outside the inner face of the building wall.

building-drainage system All piping provided for carrying waste water, sewage or other drainage from the building to the street sewer or place of disposal.

building envelope (1) The elements of a building which enclose conditioned spaces through which thermal energy may be transferred to or from the exterior. (2) The outer structure of the building.

building equipment Services, furniture and other plant equipment used in completed building.

building in (1) Fixing a wall tie, air brick, bracket or other building part by bedding it in mortar and laying bricks or stones over and around it. May be done while the wall is being built, or later, by leaving or breaking a hole. (2) Building equipment or similar components in during the course of construction.

building inspector A representative of a governmental authority employed to inspect construction for compliance with applicable codes, regulations and ordinances.

building line A line established by law or agreement, usually parallel to property line, beyond which a structure may not extend. This generally does not apply to uncovered entrance platforms, terraces and steps.

building main The water-supply pipe, including fittings and accessories, from the water main or other source of supply to the first branch of the water-distributing system.

building materials The materials used for building elements, e.g., sand, clay, cement, lumber.

building official The officer or other designated authority charged with the administration of a building code, or his duly authorized representative.

building paper Paper used as inter lining, as between sheathing and outside wall covering, or between rough and finish flooring.

building permit A permit issued by appropriate governmental authority allowing construction of a project in accordance with approved drawings and specifications.

building process The entire process which embraces every step from the conception to the total satisfaction of all building requirements.

building sewer That part of the horizontal piping of a building-drainage system extending from the building drain outside of the inner face of the building wall to the street sewer or other place of disposal and conveying the drainage of one building site.

building storm drain A building drain used for conveying rain water, surface water, ground water, subsurface water, condensate, cooling water or other similar discharge to a building storm sewer or combined building sewer extending to a point as specified outside the building wall.

building storm sewer The extension from the building storm drain to the public storm sewer, combined sewer or other point of disposal.

building subdrain That portion of a drainage system which cannot drain by gravity into the building sewer.

building trade Any one of the skilled and semi-skilled crafts used in the construction industry.

building trap A device, fitting or assembly of fitting installed in the building drain to prevent circulation of air between the drainage system of the building and the building sewer.

build-up Gunning of shotcrete in successive layers to form a thicker mass.

built-in *(see building in)*

built-in garage A garage which is part of a residence and has living quarters above; contrasted with attached garage which has no living quarters above.

built-up (1) Two or more layers of roofing material, covering the same roof area, which are cemented together, built-up, on the job; roll roofing produced especially for the use of built-up roofs. (2) A term indicating the assembly of pieces or layers to complete a product.

buke Simple houses enclosed by ditch and fence.

bulb angle A metal angle section which is enlarged to a bulb on one end.

bulb edge In sheet glass manufacture, the extreme lateral edge of the sheet as drawn.

bulb of pressure The mass of compressed material under a footing.

bulk cement Cement which is transported and delivered in bulk, usually in specially constructed vehicles instead of in bags.

bulk density The weight of a material, including solid particles and any contained water, per unit volume including voids. *(see specific gravity)*

bulker (1) A bulk cement hauler. (2) A specially constructed tank mounted on a truck with a side metering device for proportioning bulk cement into a windrow.

bulkhead (1) In building construction, the increase in the size of materials due to the absorption of moisture. (2) A partition in the forms blocking fresh concrete from a section of the forms or closing the end of a form at a construction joint. (3) A structure above the roof of any part of a building, sometimes defined as synonymous with penthouse. (4) A wall or partition erected to resist ground or water pressure.

bulkhead wall Retaining wall for a marginal warf.

bulking (1) Increase in the bulk volume of a quantity of sand in a moist condition over the volume of the same quantity dry or completely inundated. (2) Processing yarn, usually by mechanical means, to fluff it up and give more coverage with the same weight. Also known as texturizing and lofting.

bulking curve Graph of change in volume of a quantity of sand due to change in moisture content.

bulking facture Ration of the volume of moist sand to the volume of the sand when dry.

bulk loading Loading of unbagged cement in containers, specially designed trucks, railroad cars or ships.

bulk modulus Elastic constants.

bulk specific gravity *(see specific gravity)*

bulk spreader A machine for carrying cement or other material for soil stabilization, and spreading it on the prepared soil.

bull *(slang)* Roofing cement.

bull clam A bulldozer fitted with a curved bowl hinged to the top of the front of the blade.

bulldog clip A floor clip.

bulldog grip A U-bolt threaded at each end.

bulldozer (1) Tractor driven machine having a broad, blunt, horizontal blade for clearing land and road building. (2) A machine for bending reinforcing rods into U-shapes.

bulldozer hole A penetration through a floor or deck structure to allow access for insertion of a cellar nozzle which is a piece of equipment that allows a fireman to extinguish a fire in an inaccessible space.

bullet-proof glass A lamination of thin sheets cemented together under heat and pressure, usually three layers of glass and two of the colorless binding material. Shatterproof glass is similar but with fewer and thinner laminations.

bull float (1) A tool used to spread out and smooth the concrete. (2) A tool comprising a large, flat, rectangular piece of wood, aluminum, or magnesium usually eight inches (20 cm) wide and 42 to 60 inches (100 to 150 cm) long, and a handle 4 to 16 feet (1 to 5 m) in length used to smooth uniformed surfaces of freshly placed concrete.

bullfrog *(see barney)*

bull gear *(slang)* The largest or strongest toothed driving wheel.

Bullgrader Trade name for an International Harvester angling dozer.

bullhead A plumbing tee in steam and water fitting; the branch is longer than the run.

bull header In masonry, a brick having one rounded corner usually laid with the short face exposed to form the brick sill under and beyond a window frame; also used as a quoin or around doorways.

bull point A pointed, steel hand drill used with a striking hammer for breaking off small quantities of rock or masonry.

bullnose (1) Convex rounding of a member, such as the front edge of a stair tread. (2) A rounded-end tile or brick.

bullnose block A concrete masonry unit which has one or more rounded exterior corners.

bullnose brick A brick with a quadrant end, usually purposely made and used for quoins, sills, etc.

bull-nose plane A small plane which can be used in corners or other places difficult to reach. The mouth can be adjusted for coarse or fine work.

bull of the woods *(slang)* Shop or job superintendent.

bull pin A pin used in steelwork to line up holes so that a driftpin can be driven prior to riveting or bolting connections.

bull prick *(slang)* (1) A pointed steel hand drill used with a striking hammer for breaking off small quantities of rock or masonry. (2) A tapered steel shaft used to help align rivet holes.

bull's liver A water-bearing mixture of sand and red clay found in lower Manhattan Island and elsewhere. It quakes when stepped on and is subject to mass movement.

bull stick A capstan bar inserted in the base, or bull wheel, of a guy derrick to turn the derrick.

bull-stretcher A ro-lok brick laid with its longest dimension parallel to the face of the wall.

bull wheel A large driving wheel or sprocket.

bulwark The side of a ship above the upper deck.

bumboat A small boat equipped with a hoist and used for handling dredge lines and anchors.

bumper A device other than an oil or spring buffer, designed to stop a descending elevator car or counterweight beyond its normal limit of travel by absorbing the impact.

bumper (guard) A slotted or perforated plate that holds a check type air valve near its seat.

bumper up A laborer who helps the riveting crew by backing the holder up with a second hammer.

bundle A unit or stack of wood panels held together for shipment with metal bands. Stack size varies throughout the industry, with the average stack running about 30 to 33 inches high. A bundle 30 inches high for example, contains 120 sheets of ¼ inch panels, 80 sheets of ⅜ inch panels, or 60 sheets of ½ inch panels.

bundled bars A group of four parallel reinforcing bars in contact with each other and enclosed in stirrups or ties, used as a reinforcing element.

bung *(slang)* Impregnated sheathing applied to houses under siding (Celotex).

bungalow A one-story house with low sweeping lines and a wide veranda; sometimes the attic is finished as a second story. This type of dwelling was first developed in India. In the United States, the bungalow has become especially popular as a country or seaside residence.

bunker (1) A protective embankment mostly below ground and often built of reinforced concrete. (2) In crushing or screening, a device built of metal that protects and feeds the belt feeding the crusher or screening plants. (3) A storage container for ore and stone. (4) Space in refrigerator given to ice or cooling element.

buoyancy The power of a supporting floating body, including the tendency to float an empty pipe by exterior hydraulic pressure.

buoyant foundation A reinforced concrete raft foundation designed so that the total of its own weight and all loads is approximately equal to the weight of the displaced soil or water.

burden The distance from a drill hole to the face; or the volume of rock to be moved by the explosive in a drill hole.

burin A steel cutting tool with blade ground to a sharp point.

burl Wood taken from a knotty part of a tree; usually a veneer having a characteristic curly pattern.

burlap (1) A coarse fabric of jute, hemp, or, less commonly, flax, for use as a water-retaining covering in curing concrete surfaces. (2) A wallcovering—woven fibers fashioned into rolls and colored for decoration.

burling An inspection process following carpet construction to correct loose tufts, etc.; also the process of replacing missing tufts by hand.

burn (1) to cut metal off with an acetylene flame. (2) To pulverize with very heavy explosive charges.

burnability The ability of raw materials to react chemically on heating. Softer and more finely ground and intimately mixed raw materials of the proper chemical content combine into cement clinker more

burn cut A narrow section of rock pulverized by exploding heavy charges in parallel holes.

burner The part of a gas or oil heating unit where fuel is ignited and burned.

burner (or burner man) The operator who controls the burning process of a cement kiln.

burner floor The platform or floor at the lower end of the kiln on which are located controls, and where the burner regulates the operation.

burner glasses Special glasses for viewing the burning operation in a kiln. Blue or green glasses containing cobalt or iron stop the passage of infrared rays.

burner pipe The pipe through which the fuel (coal, oil, or gas), and usually part of the combustion air, is blown into the kiln.

Burnett's process The infusion of timber with chloride of zinc as a preservative.

burning off Removing old paint by heating with a torch and scraping it off while hot.

burning zone The zone near the discharge end of the kiln in which the dried and calcined raw materials are chemically converted to portland cement clinker at temperatures near 2800 deg. F (1450 deg. C).

burnishing tool A mold abrasive tool used to clean contact points.

burnt clay Clay burnt in a kiln to make tiles, bricks, earthenware pipes, etc.

burnt lime Quicklime, calcium oxide (CaO).

burr (1) A nut with a screw thread. (2) The rough projecting edge of a drilled hole in steel work. (3) The curly figure obtained by cutting through the enlarged trunk of certain trees, particularly walnut.

burred edges Most often caused by cutting seam with dull knife, leaving a jagged edge. Can be removed by aluminum foil and electric iron, scraping and sandpapering, rubbing with hammerhead or with scrap material.

burring reamer In plumbing, a tool turned in a brace to remove the burr left inside a pipe by the pipe cutter.

burse (bourse) A public edifice for the assembly of merchant traders; an exchange.

bush hammer A hammer having a serrated face, or rows of pyramidal points; used to obtain an exposed aggregate-finish for concrete.

bush-hammer finish A finish on concrete obtained by means of a bush-hammer.

bushing (1) A metal cylinder between a shaft and a support or a wheel that serves to reduce rotating friction and to protect the parts. (2) In electrical work an insulated tube which protects cables. (3) In plumbing, a screwed pipe

fitting which connects two others of different diameters.

bushing split A bushing made in two pieces, for ease of insertion and removal.

business agent In trade unions, the one who runs the affairs of the union. He represents the union in wage negotiations and disputes, and checks projects for compliance with union regulations and union contracts.

buster A machine for cutting off the heads of rivets; also the edged tool which does the cutting.

bus wire An expendable wire, used in parallel or series circuits, to which are connected the leg wires of electric blasting caps.

butane A paraffin hydrocarbon gas (C_4H_{10}) obtained from refining petroleum.

butt To join end to end; abut.

butterflies Color variations on a lime putty finish wall.

butterfly roof A roof constructed to appear as two sheds roofs connected at the lower edges.

butterfly valve A double cock valve.

buttering (1) In masonry, the process of spreading mortar on the edge of a brick before laying it. (2) In glazing, the application of putty or compound sealant to the flat surface of some member before placing the member in position, such as the buttering of a removable stop before fastening the stop in place.

buttering trowel A smaller trowel than a brick trowel.

buttery A store-room for provisions.

butt gauge In cabinetwork, a marking gauge.

butt hinge The common two-plate door hinge, with fixed or removable pivot pins.

butt joint A plain square joint between two members.

butt plate The end plate of a structural member usually used to rest against a like plate of another member in forming a connection. Sometimes called a split plate or bolted end plate.

button **(1)** A small bar of wood or metal, turning on a central screw pivot, to fasten doors. **(2)** *(slang)* A raised pavement marker. *(see pavement marker)*

button-bottom pile Steel pile with pentagonal point.

button-headed screw (half-round screw) A screw with hemispherical head.

buttonwood *(see sycamore, American)*

butt plate The end plate of a structural member, usually used to rest against a like plate of another member.

buttress A structure of any material built against a wall to strengthen it. A flying buttress is a detached buttress or pier of masonry at some distance from a wall and connected to it by an arch so as to discharge the thrust of another arch on the other side of the wall.

buttress dam Variations include multiple arch, flat slab, solid head, diamond head, etc. A dam consisting of a watertight upstream face supported at intervals on the downstream side by a series of buttresses.

buttress, flying A type of masonry structure in which a detached buttress or pier at a distance from a wall is connected to the wall by an arch, or portion of an arch.

buttress screw thread A screw thread designed to carry a heavy axial load in only one direction.

buttress shafts Slender columns at the angle of buttresses, chiefly used in the Early English period.

butt seam The joining of one panel to another without interlocking.

butt strap A steel plate to cover a butt joint; connects the two members by welding or riveting.

butt veneer Veneer having a strong curly figure caused by roots coming in at all angles to the trunk.

butt weld A butt joint made by welding.

butyl rubber A synthetic rubber based on isobutylene and a minor amount of isoprene. It is vulcanizable and features low permeability to gases and water vapor and good resistance to aging, chemicals and weathering.

butyl sterate A colorless oleaginous, practically odorless material $(C_{17}H_{35}COOC_4H_9)$ used as a dampproofer for concrete.

buzzer An electric signaling device resembling a small electric bell but with a buzzing sound instead of a ring.

buzz saw *(slang)* A circular saw.

byatt A horizontal timber to support decking and walkways in trench excavations.

bye channel A spillway leading water around a reservoir when it is already full.

bypass **(1)** In plumbing, pipes for directing the flow around instead of through a certain pipe. **(2)** A pipe or duct, usually controlled by a valve or damper, for conveying air or fluid around an element of a system.

byproduct nuclear material Secondary radioactive material derived from nuclear refining processes in the manufacture of nuclear fuels. This type of material is used in nuclear moisture meters.

byte A group of adjacent binary digits often shorter than a word that a computer can process.

byzant A circular disc in series upon a molding; common in Norman architecture.

c   candle, cathode, cycle, channel

C   carbon, centigrade

Ca   calcium

CAD   Computer aided design

CAD   Computer aided drafting

CADD   Computer aided design and drafting

CAE   Computer aided engineering

cal   calorie

CAM   Computer aided manufacturing

cap   capacity

CB   catch basin

CBR   California bearing ratio

cc   cubic centimeter

CCW   counterclockwise

ceil   ceiling

cem   cement

cem.fin.   cement finish

cem.m   cement mortar

cent   centigrade, central

cer   ceramic

CF   centrifugal force

cfm   cubic feet per minute

cfs   cubic feet per second

CG   center of gravity

cham   chamfer, chamfering

CI   cast iron, certificate of insurance

ckt/cct   circuit

cm   centimeter

CM   construction management

CMP   corrugated metal pipe

CMPA   corrugated metal pipe arch

coeff/coef   coefficient

col   column

com   common

comp   composition

conc   concrete

conc.bl./blk   concrete block

cond   conductivity

const   constant, construction

constr   construction

conv   convector

cop   coping

corb   corbelled

corn   cornice

corr   corrugated

CP/cp   candlepower

CPFF   cost plus fixed fee

CPM   cycles per minute

crib   cribbing

CRN   cost or reproduction/replacement new

CRP   controlled rate of penetration

CRT   cathode-ray tube

C-Section   A member formed from steel sheet in the shape of a block C, that may be used either singularly of back to back.

CS   cast stone

c/s   cycles per second

csmt   casement

ct   coat, coats

CTB   cement treated base

c to c   center to center

ctr   center

cu   cubic

cu.ft.   cubic feet

cu.in.   cubic inches

cu.yd.   cubic yard

cw   clockwise

C.W.pt.   cold water point

cwt   hundred weight

cyl   cylinder

cyp   cypress

C.M.U.   Concrete Masonry Unit. Type of building construction such as cinder block, concrete block, slump block, etc.

COP (Heating):   Coefficient of performance. The heat effect divided by the power input. Both must be in the same units. Watts or BTU. A COP of above 2.2 is recommended.

CPM Critical path method. A graphical method of showing the relationship of tasks on a project. The critical path is that sequence of tasks which determines the length of the project.

C.S. Commercial standard usually associated with petroleum products.

C/S ratio The molar or weight ratio, whichever is specified, of calcium oxide to silicon dioxide; usually of binder materials cured in an autoclave.

cabana In its Spanish origin, a hut, cabin or hovel; in recent use, a bathhouse.

cab guard On a rock or quarry dump truck, a heavy metal shield extending up from the front wall of the body and forward over the cab.

cabinet A piece of furniture fitted with shelves or drawers, sometimes both, and enclosed with doors, for holding small equipment; the doors for such cases are often made of glass, especially when the cases are used for display purposes.

cabinet finish A highly varnished or polished finish on hardwood, like that on good furniture.

cabinet latch A name applied to various kinds of catches, ranging from the type of catch used on refrigerator doors to the horizontal spring-and-bolt latch operated by turning a knob, as on kitchen cabinets.

cabinet maker A worker who makes fine furniture.

cabinet projection A way of showing solid objects on a drawing. The object is drawn in plan or elevation. Perpendicular faces are drawn at an angle of 45°.

cabinet scraper (scraper plane) A tool, made of a flat piece of steel, designed with an edge in such a shape that when the implement is drawn over a surface of wood any irregularities, plane marks or other uneven places will be removed, leaving the surface clean and smooth. The cabinet scraper

is used for final smoothing of surfaces before sandpapering.

cabinetwork (1) The work of one who makes fine furniture, or beautifully finished woodwork of any kind. (2) Generic term for interior woodwork that is the product of the joiner or woodworking plant.

cabin hook A hooked bar on a cupboard door or window frame which engages in a screw eye on the door to hold it shut or open; a type of fastener, consisting of a small hook and eye, used on the doors of cabinets.

cable (1) A bead set in the lower third of a flute. (see tendon) (2) The copper conductors through which an electric appliance receives its power. The conductors are separately insulated but laid together within a common insulating sheath. (3) Heavy wire rope or group of parallel wires for a member in tension; rope made of steel wire.

backhaul In a cable excavator, the line that pulls the bucket from the dumping point back to the digging.

drag In a dragline or hoe, the line that pulls the bucket toward the shovel.

inhaul (digging line) In a cable excavator, the line that pulls the bucket to dig and bring in the soil.

cable chain A chain designed to operate over a smooth sheave, as opposed to a roller chain which operates over a sprocket.

cable control unit A high speed tractor winch having one to three drums under separate control; used to operate dozers and towed equipment.

cable excavator A long range, cable-operated machine which works between a head mast and an anchor.

cable molding A ropelike molding, as found in Norman architecture.

cabling The flutes of columns are said to be cabled when they are partly occupied by solid convex masses or appear to be refilled with cylinders after they have been formed.

cadastral survey A survey made to determine the lengths and directions of boundary lines and the area of the tract bounded by these lines; or a survey made to establish the positions of boundary lines on the ground.

cadillac *(slang)* The mobile container used by roofers to carry their roof tar in.

cadmium plating A protective finish for steel articles such as wood screws.

cafeteria A self-service restaurant.

cage (1) A circular frame that limits the motion of balls or rollers in a bearing. (2) An elevator for temporary use during the construction of a building, usually incompletely enclosed. (3) A rigid assembly of reinforcement ready for placing in position.

cage screen A screen consisting of a cage, with sides of bars, rods or mesh, so arranged that it may be lowered into the sewage and raised for cleaning.

cairn A pile of stones used as a marker.

caisson (1) A wood, steel, concrete or reinforced concrete, air-and-water-tight chamber in which it is possible for men to work under air pressure greater than atmospheric pressure, to excavate material below water level. (2) Panel sunk below the surface in flat or vaulted ceilings. *(see coffer)*

caisson disease A disease which affects workers in compressed air who come too quickly out of the air lock. It is caused by bubbles of nitrogen forming in the blood. Also called the bends.

caisson foundation A foundation system in which holes are drilled in the earth to bearing strata and then filled with concrete.

caisson pile A cast-in-place pile made by driving a tube, excavating it and filling the cavity with concrete.

caking The settling or hardening of paint into a mass.

calathus The bell or core of the Corinthian capital.

calcareous Containing calcium carbonite or, less generally, containing the element calcium.

calcimine A cold-water paint of whiting, glue, coloring matter and water,

used chiefly as a wash for ceilings or other interior plasterings.

calcinator Machine for drying and preheating slurry through intimate contact with hot kiln exit gases, passing in counterflow through a vessel charged with heat-exchanging elements. Normally little if any calcination (liberation of CO_2) takes place.

calcine To alter composition or physical state by heating below the temperature of fusion; to heat ore or mineral at a high temperature to drive off carbon dioxide and water.

calcined gypsum Gypsum partially dehydrated by heat.

calcining zone That zone in the kiln where calcium carbonate is decomposed into CaO and CO_2 at temperatures ranging from 1380-1740 deg.F (750-950 deg. C).

calcite ($CaCO_3$) Crystalline calcium carbonate; the principal constituent of limestone, chalk and marble; usually a major raw material used in manufacture of portland cement.

calcium A sliver-white metallic element of the alkaline-earth group occurring only in combination with other elements.

calcium-aluminate cement The product obtained by pulverizing clinker consisting essentially of hydraulic calcium aluminates resulting from fusing or sintering a suitably proportioned mixture of aluminous and calcareous materials; called high-alumina cement in United Kingdom.

calcium carbonate Found in nature as calcite and used in making lime and portland cement.

calcium chloride ($CaCI_2$) An admixture used to accelerate the hardening of cement. For this reason it is added to concrete during frost to accelerate its rate of heating, and therefore its setting and hardening rates.

calcium hydroxide ($CaOH_2$) Slaked lime.

calcium oxide (CaO) Quicklime; when water is added, it becomes calcium hydroxide.

calcium-silicate brick A concrete product made principally from sand and lime which is hardened by autoclave curing.

calcium-silicate hydrate Any of the various reaction products of calcium silicate and water, often produced by autoclave curing.

calcium stearate Product of the reaction of lime and stearic acid used as an integral water repellant in concrete.

calcium sulphate (CaSO₄) The mineral anhydrite having the same composition as calcined gypsum.

calcium sulphate hemihydrate (CaSO₄¹/₂H2₀) Plaster of Paris or casting plaster. The basis of retarded hemihydrate plasters.

calender A machine which presses materials between rollers or plates in order to smooth and glaze or thin into sheets.

calender cut In roofing material, the cut or break in the dry felt caused by a fold in the sheet before passing through the calender.

calf's-tongue molding One having a series of pointed, tongue-like members in line in relief against a plane or curved surface; sometimes radiating from a common center.

caliber The bore or internal diameter of a hollow cylinder or pipe; the width of the mouth of a piece of ordnance; the diameter of any round body.

calibrate To check the graduations of an instrument or machine, and to graduate it correctly if necessary.

calibrated sand method Method of determining weight per cubic foot of soil in place.

calibration Process of dividing and numbering the scale of an instrument; also of correcting or determining the error of an existing scale, or of evaluating one quantity in terms of readings of another.

calibration tank Small slurry tank equipped with float or electronic probe, and electrically remote-controlled by kiln-operator, located between kiln feeder and feed pipe. In the automatic measuring cycle the time of filling the tank is recorded on a stop watch on the control panel. Tables for various water content provide actual kiln feed rate (solids) within 0.1% accuracy.

caliche Gravel, sand or desert debris cemented by porous calcium carbonate or other salts; found in southwestern United States.

caliduct A pipe for conveying hot air, hot water or steam for heating purposes.

California bearing ratio The ratio of the force per unit area required to penetrate a soil mass with a three square inch (19.4 sq cm) circular piston at the rate of 0.05 inch (1.27 mm)per minute to the force required for corresponding penetration of a standard crushed-rock base material; the ratio is usually determined at 0.1 inch (2.5 mm) penetration.

California bearing ratio method (CBR method) A design method using the CBR test.

California bearing ratio test (CBR test) A standard test to determine the CBR.

calk (caulk) (1) Fish-tailed steel bar built into masonry. (2) To fill a joint with mastic, usually with a pressure gun.

calking (caulking) The process of filling seams with mastic material to prevent leaking.

calking compound Mastic used to seal joints of wall openings against water.

calking tool Tool or device used for driving a calking compound into seams and crevices to make joints watertight and airtight.

call for bids A request for interested or invited qualified contractors to submit a proposal to perform work in question.

calliper (caliper) (1) An instrument for measuring diameter as of logs or trees. (2) A pair of metal legs pivoted together like a draftman's divider that is used to measure the bore of pipes or their outside diameter.

callout A note on a drawing with a leader to the feature.

calorie The amount of heat required to

raise the temperature of one gram of water through one degree centigrade.

calorifier A closed tank, in which water is heated, usually by a submerged coil of pipe containing steam or hotter water.

calorimeter An instrument for measuring heat exchange during a chemical reaction such as the quantities of heat liberated by the combustion of a fuel or hydration of a cement.

calyon In building, flint or pebble stone used in wall construction.

cam (1) A rotating or sliding piece, or projection on a wheel, used to impart exactly timed motion to light parts; used for lifting the valves of internal combustion engines. (2) A device for converting regular rotary motion into irregular rotary or reciprocating motion.

camarin A room in which privacy may be found. The sacristy or vestry of a church; the greenroom or actor's dressing-room of a theater; a closet.

camber (hog) (1) A slight, usually upward, curvature of a truss, beam or form to improve appearance or to compensate for anticipated deflection such as that produced as a normal consequence of the eccentricity from the center of gravity of the section of the prestressing tendons. (2) A curvature which is domed to allow water to run off a road, to hide the deflection of a girder, etc. (3) Rise or crown of the center of a bridge, or flowline thru a culvert, above a straight line through its ends.

camber arch An arch with concave intrados approaching the flat.

camber beam A beam that is cambered on its upper surface. An old term for a truss.

camber rod (belly rod) The tensioning rod below a trussed beam.

camber slip A shaped piece of wood, cambered on its upper surface, which is used in the centers of a flat brick arch to ensure that the arch soffit at the midspan is slightly cambered above the springing line.

cambium The layer of cells between the bark and the wood of a tree.

came (calm) A soft metal H-shaped division strip between adjacent pieces of glass in leaded or stained glass windows.

camel-hair mop A paint brush like a dabber.

camouflet A blasting hole which is made larger in size by chambering.

campanile A bell tower, especially one that is separated from a church building.

camp ceiling A ceiling in which the center is horizontal while a border slopes with the roof rafters; an attic ceiling with four sloping surfaces.

campo An Italian measure of land, roughly an acre.

camp sheathing (sheeting) A retaining wall used to hold river banks; it consists of two connected rows of piles with the space between being filled with earth. A light sheet pile wall.

can (1) A housing for a recessed fixture. (2) A colloquial expression for the bucket on a drag-line, shovel or loader; also, for the carry-all.

canal A channel built to carry water for navigation, irrigation, water for power or other purposes.

canaletta A hard, dense wood from tropical America having a tobacco or reddish brown color.

canalis The space, usually concave, between the fillets of the Ionic volute.

canal lift A wheel-drawn tank moving up or down an incline or vertically to pass barges through a lock with a large lift.

canal trimmer Heavy equipment used for final trimming of the bottom and sides of an earthen canal prior to placing of water tight membrane.

cancellation A system or arrangement of web members in a truss.

cancelli Bars or thin balusters in a screen or railing; originally the railing dividing the semicircular court of a pagan basilica, and perhaps the origin of chancel.

candle beam A beam so called because of its minor use to support candles for lighting an interior.

candlepower A measure of luminous intensity.

candy bucket *(slang)* A bucket used to raise dirt from a shaft.

candy wagon *(slang)* The term used by men on the job for the utility truck to haul miscellaneous items of material, supplies, and also to haul personnel from one part of the job to another. In some cases, it has all the lubricants, oil, grease, gear oil, etc., on it for servicing the equipment; some carry fuel, water and air also.

cane Open weaving of cane or rattan, used for seats and backs of chairs and for screens and grilles.

can of fade *(slang)* What the new men are sent for.

canopy (1) An ornamental rooflike covering supported by posts or suspended from a wall; a sheltering member, as over a niche, a doorway or a seat of honor; a gauze covering over a bed to keep off insects; a mosquito curtain. (2) A device, like an open cab, on a piece of equipment, to protect the operator from the weather. (3) That part of an elevator cab, located above and supported by the walls; it contains the ceiling and completely encloses the top of the cab.

cant To slope, tilt or bank; set at a slant from horizontal or vertical; also a molding formed of plain surfaces and angles rather than curves.

cant bay A three-sided bay window with splay sides.

cant beam A beam with edges chamfered or beveled.

cant brick A splay brick.

cant dog *(slang)* A cant hook for handling logs and timbers.

canted Splayed, bevelled or off square.

canted wall A wall joining another at an angle.

cant hook A stout wooden lever with an adjustable steel or iron hook near the lever end. The cant hook is used for rolling logs and telephone or telegraph poles.

cantilever (1) A projecting beam supported only at one end; a large bracket for supporting a balcony or cornice. (2) Two bracketlike arms projecting toward each other from opposite piers or banks to form the span of a bridge, making what is known as a cantilever bridge.

cantilever arm The part of a cantilever bridge overhanging from the support into the central span and carrying one end of the suspended span.

cantilever bridge A bridge made of two cantilevers whose projecting ends meet but do not support each other. Also a symmetrical threespan bridge with the two outer spans anchored at the shore and overhang into the central span. The suspended span, resting on the cantilever arms, occupies the remaining space of the central span.

cantilever crane A transport crane with one or both ends overhanging.

cantilever formwork Climbing formwork.

cantilever foundation A foundation for a column or stanchion used when there is not enough space for a true central brace.

cantilever wall (1) A reinforced concrete retaining wall stabilized by the weight of the retained material. (2) A sheet pile wall stabilized by its length of penetration below ground level on the free side.

cantilevered beam A projecting beam that is supported and restrained at one end only.

canting strip A projecting molding near the bottom of a wall to direct rain water away from the foundation wall.

canting table A saw bench with a working surface which can be tilted and thus rip at any angle required for bevel cutting.

cant strip (chamfer strip) Beveled strip placed in the angle between the roof and an abutting wall to avoid a sharp bend in the roofing material; the strip placed under the lowest row of tiles on a roof to give it the same slope as the rows above it.

cap (1) Detonator set off by electric current or a burning fuse. (2) Fitted or threaded piece to protect the top of a pile from damage while being driven. (3) Pipe plug with female threads. (4) Roof or top piece of a three-piece timber set used for tunnel support. (5) Top parts of columns, doors, windows and moldings. (6) Smooth, plane surface of suitable material bonded to the bearing surface of a test specimen to insure uniform distribution of load during strength testing. (7) The decorative uppermost part of a newel post.

capacitance The ability to hold or store electrical energy.

capacitor A device, the primary purpose of which is to introduce capacitance into an electric circuit.

capacity (1) The volume of concrete permitted to be mixed or carried in a particular mixer or agitator, usually limited by specifications to a maximum percentage of total gross volume; also the output of concrete, aggregate or other product per unit of time, as plant capacity or screen capacity. (2) The load-carrying limit of a structure.

capacity curve A graph showing the volume contained in a reservoir or tank at any given water level.

capacity, heat The amount of heat necessary to raise the temperature of a given mass one degree. Numerically, the mass multiplied by the specific heat.

capacity reducer In a compressor, a device such as a clearance pocket, movable cylinder head, or suction bypass, by which compressor capacity can be adjusted without otherwise changing the operating conditions.

cap and lining A plumbing connection.

cap cables Short cables or tendon introduced to prestress the zone of negative bending only.

capillarity (1) The movement of a liquid in the interstices of soil or other porous material due to surface tension. (see capillary flow) (2) The action by which the surface of a liquid, where it

is in contact with a solid, is raised or lowered.

capillary action The action in soil by which water rises in a channel in any direction above the horizontal plane of the supply of free water.

capillary attraction The tendency of water to move into fine spaces, as between soil particles, regardless of gravity.

capillary flow Flow of moisture through a capillary pore system, such as in concrete.

capillary groove (break) A space between two surfaces, large enough to prevent capillary movement of water into a building, as in a water checked casement.

capillary movement Movement of underground water in response to capillary attraction.

capillary potential The amount of work required to pull a unit mass of water from a unit mass of soil.

capillary pressure *(seepage force)* In ground being drained from outside an excavation, capillary pressures are those which help the excavated earth to stand. If the ground is being drained from inside the excavation, the capillary pressures will help the earth face to collapse. *(see wellpoint)*

capillary space In cement paste, any space not occupied by anhydrous cement or cement gel. Air bubbles, whether entrained or entrapped, are not considered to be part of the cement paste.

capillary tube A tube of small internal diameter used as a liquid refrigerant flow control or expansion device between high and low sides; also used to transmit pressure from the sensitive bulb of some temperature controls to the operating element.

capital The ornamental uppermost part of a column, pilaster or pier; best known are the Greek types, Corinthian, Doric and Ionic; and the Roman types, Tuscan and Composite.

capping (1) The uppermost part on top of a piece of work; a crowning or topping part. **(2)** Procedure and material used for self-coved tile and/or sheet goods installation. The cap strip, usually metal but also can be vinyl or rubber, has a flange into which the top edge of the coved floor covering fits.

capping brick In masonry, brick which are especially shaped for capping the exposed top of a wall.

capping piece A horizontal timber placed over the ends of two walings. It transfers the thrust of a strut to the walings.

capping plane A plane to round off the top of a handrail.

cap plate A plate located at the top of a column or end of a beam capping the exposed end of the member.

cap sheet The top or last sheet of composition roofing used in the laying of a built-up roof; the sheet or layer which is exposed to the weather.

cap, short delay (millisecond delay) A detonating cap that fires from 20 to 500 thousandths of a second after the firing current passes through it.

capstan A machine for moving or raising heavy weights by winding cable around a vertical spindle-mounted drum that is rotated manually or driven by steam or electric power.

capstone The crowning stone of a structure; differing from capital in that it is not a supporting member; a coping.

caravansary A huge, square building, or inn, in the eastern hemisphere, for the reception of travelers and lodging of caravans.

carbide Tungsten carbide, a very hard and abrasion-resistant compound used in drill bits and other tools.

carbide bit A steel bit which contains inserts of tungsten carbide.

carbolineum A name applied to an oily, dark-brown substance consisting of anthracene oil and zinc chloride, used as a preservative for wood or timber.

carbon **(1)** A non-metallic chemical element. Diamond and graphite are pure carbon. It is also found in coal. **(2)** As a

rule, refers to activated carbon. It is often employed for adsorption of taste and odor-generating organic contaminants dissolved in water. It is also used to remove dissolved organic content in waste water as a tertiary treatment step.

carbon-arc welding Electric arc welding with one electrode carbon rod, the other the piece being welded. Extra metal is supplied by a filler rod held in the arc; used for building up metal and filling in holes.

carbonation Reaction between carbon dioxide and calcium compounds, especially in cement paste, mortar or concrete, to produce calcium carbonate.

carbon black A finely divided amorphous carbon used to color concrete; produced by burning natural gas in a supply of air insufficient for complete combustion; characterized by a high oil absorption and a low specific gravity.

carbon dioxide ice Solid CO_2; dry ice.

carbonization Formation of carbonaceous deposits, which may be produced by decomposition of lubricating oil or other organic materials.

carbon monoxide Colorless, odorless, poisonous gas (CO). It is produced when carbon or carbonaceous fuels are burned with insufficient air.

carbon steel Usually a hardened steel not alloyed with other metals.

Carborundum A trade-mark for an abrasive made from a combination of carbon and silicon, and sometimes used instead of emery.

Carborundum cloth or paper An abrasive cloth or paper made by covering the material with powdered Carborundum held in place by some adhesive, such as glue.

carcass The loadbearing part of a structure without windows, doors, plaster or finishes; the frame of a house; the unfinished framework, or skeleton, of a building or ship.

carcassing **(1)** In building, the work involved in erecting or constructing the framework of a structure. **(2)** The layout and installation of gas pipe for a building.

car counterweight A set of weights roped directly to the elevator car, which on drum-type installations will equal the car in weight.

card A machine used in the processing of staple yarns. Its functions are to separate, align and deliver staple fibers in a sliver form. This process is achieved by passing the staple into a series of rolls which are covered with many projecting wire teeth.

car door or gate power closer A device or assembly of devices which closes a manually opened car door or gate by power other than by hand, gravity, springs or the movement of the car.

car enclosure The top and the walls of the car resting on and attached to the elevator car platform.

car frame (sling) The supporting frame to which the car platform, upper and lower sets of guide shoes, car safety and the hoisting ropes or hoisting-rope sheaves, or the plunger of a direct plunger elevator are attached.

car frame, overslung A car frame to which the hoisting-rope fastenings or hoisting-rope sheaves are attached to the crosshead or top member of the car frame.

car frame, underslung A car frame to which the hoisting-rope fastenings or hoisting-rope sheaves are attached at or below the car platform.

car frame, sub-post A car frame all of whose members are located below the car platform.

carol A space enclosed with partitions, screens or a railing.

carolithic column A column with a foliated shaft.

carpenter A worker who erects wood framework, fits joints, wood floors, stairs and window frames, asbestos sheeting and other wallboard, and builds other wooden structures.

carpenters bracket scaffold A scaffold consisting of wood or metal brackets supporting a platform.

carpenter's hammer A hammer with striking face on one end of head, a claw for withdrawing nails on the other.

carpentry work Work which is performed by a craftsman in cutting, framing and joining pieces of timber in construction.

Carpet fibers (*see individual listings under acrylic, modacrylic, nylon, polyester, polypropylene (olefin), and wool*)

car platform The structure which forms the floor of the car and which directly supports the load.

carport Shelter for the automobile in conjunction with a dwelling; usually roofed, but not fully enclosed, thus differentiated from the garage.

carreau A unit of glass or encaustic tile, usually square or diamond shaped.

carrelage An area of tile, terra cotta or bricks in pattern.

carriage The support for the steps of a wooden stairway; these supports may be either of wood or steel. An inclined timber placed between the two strings against the underside of wide stairs to support them in the middle.

carriageway (*see roadway*)

carrier A product added to a dyebath to promote the dyeing of hydrophobic man-made fibers and characterized by affinity for, and ability to swell, the fiber.

carryall A self-loading carrier for hauling earth and crushed rock.

carry back Joint of pipe out of sequence.

carrying capacity The current which a fuse or cable can carry without overloading.

carrying channel Main supporting member of a suspended ceiling system to which furring members or channels attach.

car tip A hoisting mechanism used to raise one side or one end of a specially designed railroad car or truck, or its body, to dump the contents.

cartographer One who prepares charts or maps.

cartoon A full-size drawing intended to

facilitate the making of a fresco, mosaic, stained glass or the like.

cartouche An ornament like an escutcheon; a shield or an oval or oblong panel with the central part plain, and usually slightly convex, to receive an inscription, armorial bearings, or an ornamental or significant piece of painting or sculpture.

cartridge A wrapped stick of dynamite or other explosive.

caryatides Human female figures used as piers, columns or supports. Caryatic is applied to the human figure generally, when used in the manner of caryatides.

casa (Spanish) A house.

cascading The rolling and falling motion of grinding balls in a mill, or of clinker in a kiln, as the equipment rotates. In mills, particularly, the movement of grinding media rolling down the surface of the load as the mill rotates.

case (1) The framework of the structure in building construction. (2) In masonry, the external facings of a building when these are of better material than the backing. (3) The surface of steel which has been hardened by case-hardening, leaving a relatively ductile core within the case.

cased Covered with other materials, generally of a better quality.

case harden (1) To harden the surface of iron through a process of carbonization. (2) A term used to describe wood which, during seasoning, dries more quickly on the outer skin than on the inner part, causing warping.

casein glues Glues made from milk.

casein paint Paint in which a casein solution takes the place of the drying oils of common paints. For outdoor use, lime and cement supply the hiding property; for inside work, lime, powdered chalk or kaolin. The paint is sold as a powder to be mixed with water for use.

casement A type of window having sash with hinges on the side allowing window to open vertically.

casement door (French door) A hinged door or pair of doors almost completely glass. *(see espagnolette)*

case mold Plaster shell used to hold various parts of a plaster mold in correct position.

cash allowance An amount established in the contract documents for inclusion in the contract sum to cover the cost of prescribed items not specified in detail, with provision that variations between such amount and the finally determined cost of the prescribed items will be reflected in change orders appropriately adjusting the contract sum.

cash flow statement A projection prepared at the onset of a project indicating the amount of money to be earned and spent monthly during the construction life of the contract.

casing (1) The framework around a window or door. (2) Outer jacket of a heating unit. (3) Formwork for concrete. (4) Steel pipe lining to oil or water wells or other boreholes. (5) A steel plate enclosure to a fan which widens out to a final volute.

casing bead A bead used at the edge of plaster or around openings to provide a stop.

casing spider A frame and wedge set that supports the top of a casing string while new sections are added.

casino A building for public social gatherings; a building or a room for games of chance.

cassoon A sunken panel in a ceiling or vault.

cast To form in a mold by pouring or pressing.

castable refractory A packaged, dry mixture of hydraulic cement, generally calcium-aluminate cement, and specially selected and proportioned refractory aggregates which, when mixed with water, will produce refractory concrete or mortar.

castellated Having turrets or battlements, like a fortified castle.

caster A wheel mounted in a swivel frame so that it is steered automatically by movements of its load.

casting Any substance as metal or plastic cast in a mold (i.e.: manhole covers, catch basin tops, etc.).

casting resin (cast resin) A synthetic resin of which shapes can be cast often a epoxide or phenol resin.

cast-in-place Mortar or concrete which is deposited in the place where it is required to harden as part of the structure, as opposed to precast concrete.

cast-in-place pile A concrete pile concreted either with or without a casing in its permanent location, as distinguished from a precast pile.

cast-in-situ (see cast-in-place)

cast iron A commercial variety of iron containing more than 1.7 percent carbon, poured molten into a mold so as to solidify in a desired shape.

castle Originally a fortified house; more recently, the residence of royalty.

cast steel Steel not forged or rolled after casting. All steel is cast during manufacture but most is subsequently worked so as to change its shape considerably. Crucible steel is cast steel.

cast stone Concrete or mortar cast into blocks or small slabs in special molds so as to resemble natural building stone.

Cat A trademarked designation for any machine made by the Caterpillar Tractor Company; widely used to indicate a crawler tractor or mounting of any make.

catalyst (curing agent; promotor) A substance that accelerates or causes a chemical reaction without itself being transformed by the reaction. (see accelerator)

catalytic oxidation A system of gaseous pollution control. Gases are reduced to easy-to-handle—and in some instances marketable—components by means of activating materials known as catalysts.

Cat and can Crawler tractor drawn scraper. Under certain conditions, these machines can operate where the rubber-tired scrapers cannot go.

cataracting The motion of grinding media in a ball mill described by a par-abolic free fall above the mass to a point of impingement on the active layer of media below.

catch A device for latching a light door or gate, or the like.

catch basin (1) A cistern or depression at the point where a gutter discharges into a sewer to catch any object which would not readily pass through the sewers; a reservoir to catch and retain surface drainage. (2) A trap to catch and hold fats, grease and oil from kitchen sinks to prevent them from passing into the sewer. Sometimes called a catch pit.

catch basin and manhole block Solid, curved and battered concrete masonry units used in construction of catch basins and manholes.

catch feeder Minor irrigation canal.

catchment area (basin) A water shed or drainage basin; also the area of such basin.

catch off The sideboom on lowering in whose functions is to assist the cradle tractor.

catch pit A pit in a drainage system at an accessible point, designed to catch grit and prevent it from blocking inaccessible parts of the drain.

catchpoint On a cross section view of a cut on engineering drawings, that surface point where the natural material will start to be cut away. On a cross section view of a fill, that surface point where the natural material will meet the fill material.

catenary The curve assumed by a cord fastened at both ends and subjected only to the additional force of gravity.

catenated Bearing a line, incised or embossed to suggest the form of a chain.

caterpillar gate A large metal gate for controlling the flow of water through a spillway. Usually carried on crawler tracks with steel rollers bearing on steeply sloped rails at each side of the opening.

cat eye (1) A seed or blister near the glass surface of sheet glass, usually with a leading or trailing (or both) tail often open. **(2)** A pin knot in lumber.

catface (holiday) **(1)** Blemish or rough depression in the finish plaster coat caused by variations in the base coat thickness. **(2)** Skip in the application of paint; flaw in the finish coat similar to a pock mark.

cat head A notched wedge placed between two formwork members meeting at an oblique angle; a spindle on a hoist; a capstan winch, non-winding, used with soft rope.

cathedral A large or impressive church; the principal church of a diocese, containing the bishop's throne.

cathedral ceiling **(1)** High ceiling formed by or suggesting an open timber roof. **(2)** A ceiling as in a living room, higher than that of other rooms in the house.

cathedral glass Sheet glass with a lightly hammered surface, used in ecclesiastical work and also in other locations where an obscure glass is wanted.

catherine wheel A circular window, or circular panel of a larger window, the muntins or cames of which are radii.

cathetus The vertical axis of the Ionic volute upon which is based the construction of the spiral.

cathode In electrolysis, the plate at which metal or hydrogen are released or at which chemical reduction occurs.

cathodic protection Preventing corrosion of a pipeline by using special cathodes and anodes to circumvent corrosive damage by electric current. Also a function of zinc coatings on iron and steel drainage products.

cation A particle the size of a molecule that carries a positive charge. Cations move toward the cathode in electrolysis. Magnesium, sodium, potassium, manganese and other metal ions, as well as ionized hydrogen (H+), are examples of cations.

cat ladder (duck board) A board with cleats nailed on it, laid over a roof slope to protect it and give access for workmen to the slope.

cat run A 2x4 to connect trusses on the top of the bottom cord.

cat's ass *(slang)* A kink in a cable.

cat's head molding A medieval molding using cat's head grotesques.

catskinner *(slang)* Operator of a crawler tractor.

cattle pass A culvert type passageway for livestock built under a highway.

catty *(slang)* A term used to describe an ironworker's ability to walk high steel with ease.

catwalk A walk, usually of wood or metal, that gives access to parts of large machines, usually elevated; a gangway around the upper outside walls of high buildings, giving access to the roof and eaves for painting, cleaning or other purposes.

caul A tool used in forming veneer to the shape of a curved surface; a sheet of aluminum in hot pressing, or plywood in cold pressing, to protect veneers from contact with the presses.

cauliculus A slender stem branching from beneath the abacus of a Corinthian column.

caulis One of the lower circlet of acanthus stems forming the middle portion of a Corinthian capital.

caulk To seal and make weather-tight joints, seams, or voids by filling with a waterproofing compound or material.

caulking (calking) Filling of cracks and crevices, chiefly along the intersection of wood or metal with masonry, using a non-hardening putty-like compound often applied from a pressure gun; the blocking of a seam or joint to make it air-tight, water-tight or steam-tight.

caulking compound A semidrying or slow-drying plastic material used to seal joints or fill crevices around windows, chimneys, and the like. It usually is applied with a caulking gun or with a putty knife.

caulking gun (pressure gun) An injecting tool for sealing joints with mastic.

causeway A raised or paved way across wet ground or water.

caustic To burn, eat away or destroy by chemical or corrosive action.

cave (caving) Collapse of an unstable bank.

cavetto Quarter round concave molding; a concave ornamental molding opposed in effect to the ovolo; the quarter of circle called the quarter round.

cavil ax (kevel; jedding ax) A small ax with a pointed peen and an ax blade for cutting stone.

cavitation When pumping at high speeds, certain parts of a pump may move faster that the water. The result is corrosion of metal parts due to the freeing of oxygen from the water.

cavitation damage Pitting of concrete caused by implosion; the collapse of vapor bubbles in flowing water which form in areas of low pressure and collapse as they enter areas of higher pressure.

cavity block Precast concrete blocks, hollowed so that when laid over each other they form a cavity wall.

cavity flashing A damp course crossing the gap of a cavity wall.

cavity wall (core wall) A wall built of masonry units or of plain concrete, or a combination of these materials, so arranged as to provide an air space within the wall, with or without insulating material, and in which the inner and outer wythes of the wall are tied together with metal ties.

C-clamp A device or tool used to clamp two surfaces together.

cedar A wood of moderate strength, with a fine and uniform texture; used for Venetian blinds, interior finish, shingles, posts and furniture. Varieties include red and white, with several subtypes.

Cedartex An embossed design applied to the granule surfaced roofing sheet.

ceil To apply an interior sheathing.

ceiling (1) Interior sheathing of an overhead surface. (2) A lumber pattern featuring a center and edge V and/or bead.

ceiling floor Joists or other supports for a ceiling.

ceiling joist A joist carrying the ceiling beneath it but not the floor over it.

ceiling outlet A round, square, rectangular, or linear air diffuser located in the ceiling which provides a horizontal distribution pattern of primary and secondary air over the occupied zone and induces low velocity secondary air motion through the occupied zone.

ceiling strap A wooden strip nailed to rafters or floor joists for suspending ceiling joists.

celature The art of surfacing metals by cutting or embossing.

celite A name used to identify the calcium alumino ferrite constituent of portland cement. *(see alite, belite and felite)*

cell One of the hollow spaces in building tile.

cella The inner enclosed room of an ancient temple.

cellar A story, or portion thereof, more than one-half below the average grade of the ground surrounding the building; not counted as a story in determining the height of the building.

cellular cofferdam A gravity retaining structure from the series of interconnected straight web steel sheet pile cells filled with soil, usually sand, or sand and gravel. The interconnection provides watertightness and self-stability against the lateral pressures of water and earth.

cellular concrete A lightweight product consisting of portland cement, cement-silica, cement-pozzolan, lime-pozzolan or lime-silica pastes, of pastes containing blends of these ingredients and having a homogeneous void or cell structure, attained with gas-forming chemicals or foaming agents. For cellular concretes containing binder ingredients other than, or in addition to, portland cement, autoclave curing is usually employed.

cellular construction A method of constructing concrete elements in which part of the interior concrete is replaced by voids.

cellulose (1) The most important ingre

dient of a tree, constituting 60 percent of the tree's wood and giving wood fibers their strength. **(2)** Re-cycled wood fiber (paper) chemically treated to retard flame spread and smoke development

cellulose enamel *(see lacquer)*

cellulose sheet A sheet of flooring made from cork dust, sawdust, wood flour, and pigments with gelatinized nitrocellulose on a backing of woven jute.

Celotex An asphalt impregnated composition building board made mostly of cane stalks. It is used as siding and as underlayment for roofing, with or without a finished surface. It also provides insulating properties and serves as a vapor barrier. Celotex is a brand name and is available in various widths plus an assortment of edges; shiplap, tongue and groove, square and V-joint.

Celsius A temperature scale on which the freezing point of water at sea level atmospheric pressure is indicated as 0° and its boiling point as 100°. Degrees Celsius (C) equals Fahrenheit (F) minus 32 multiplied by ⅝.

celure A canopy of its decoration.

cement **(1)** A substance made by burning a mixture of clay and limestone; in essence, a mixture of silicates and aluminates of calcium and used as an ingredient of mortar and concrete. This term is frequently used erroneously by the layman when he means concrete, as in the expression, "Our house has cement floors." **(2)** A substance which, by hardening between two surfaces to which it adheres, binds them together.

cement-aggregate ratio The ratio, by weight or volume, of cement to aggregate.

cement aluminous *(see calcium-aluminate cement)*

cementation A term applied to the setting of a plastic; also, the process of uniting and binding articles or materials together so they will adhere firmly by using an adhesive such as asphalt or portland cement.

cementation process The process of injecting cement grout under pressure into certain types of ground to solidify it. Cement-based waterproof coating compounds which seal the pores in basement walls or floors, providing protection against water pressure and dampness in the ground. These compounds usually come in a cement base, but some can be purchased in paste, powder or liquid forms, to be mixed with cement before application.

cement-base waterproof coating Compounds which seal the pores in basement walls or floors, providing protection against water pressure and dampness in the ground. These compounds usually come in a cement base, but some can be purchased in paste, powder or liquid forms, to be mixed with cement before application.

cement, bituminous A black solid, semisolid, or liquid substance at natural air temperatures and appreciably soluble only in carbon disulfide or some volatile liquid hydrocarbon, being composed of mixed indeterminate hydrocarbons mined from natural deposits, produced as a residue in the distillation of petroleum, or obtained by the destructive distillation of coal or wood.

cement body tile Tiles with a structure made from a mixture of sand and portland cement. The surface can be finished with portland cement, spheroids marble or other materials.

cement-coated nails Nails coated with cement which are used for fixing parquet floors and for nailing green timber because they have high holding power.

cement colors A special mineral pigment for coloring concrete used for floors.

cement content Quantity of cement contained in a unit volume of concrete or mortar, preferably expressed as weight.

cement cooler Equipment for cooling finished cement after grinding. May consist of water-jacketed screw conveyor with water-cooled impeller shaft and blades, or a vertical cylinder, with the outside cooled by running water and along the inner surface of which a thin layer of cement is moved.

cemented carbides Materials used for the tips of very-high-speed tools. Tungsten and molybdenum carbides are the main components, with some titanium, cobalt and tantalum.

cement, expansive (see expansive cement)

cement factor The number of bags or cubic feet of cement per cubic yard of concrete. (see cement content)

cement gel The colloidal material that makes up the major portion of the porous mass of which mature hydrated cement paste is composed.

cement grout (see grout)

cement gun A machine in which a mixture of cement and small aggregate is forced by compressed air through a hose to a nozzle, where water brought through a separate hose is added, and the combined materials are driven forcibly from the nozzle to the point of placement. (see shotcrete)

cement, high-early-strength Cement characterized by producing earlier strength in mortar or concrete than regular cement, referred to in United States as Type III.

cement hydration The process of combining cement with water.

cement, hydraulic A cement that is capable of setting and hardening under water due to interaction of water and the constituents of the cement.

cementitious Having the property of binding substances together.

cement joggle A method of preventing relative movement between concrete blocks by leaving an indentation for the height of each block opposite a corresponding notch in the next block. When the blocks are set, this cavity is poured full of mortar. (see joggle)

cement, Keene's The whitest finish plaster obtainable that produces a wall of extreme durability. Because of its density it excels for a wainscoting plaster for bathrooms and kitchens and is also used extensively for the finish coat in auditoriums, public buildings and other places where walls will be subjected to unusually hard wear or abuse.

cement kiln (see kiln, cement)

cement, low alkali A portland cement that contains a relatively small amount of sodium or potassium or both; in the United States a cement containing not more than 0.6 percent Na_2O equivalent, percent $Na_2O + (0.658 \times percent K2O)$.

cement, low-heat A cement in which there is only limited generation of heat during setting, achieved by modifying the chemical composition of normal portland cement, referred to in United States as Type IV.

cement, masonry Hydraulic cement produced for use in mortars for masonry construction where greater plasticity and water retention are desired than is obtainable by the use of portland cement alone; such cements always contain one or more of the following materials: portland cement, portland-pozzolan cement, natural cement, slag cement, hydraulic lime, and usually contain one or more of the following: hydrated lime, pulverized limestone, chalk, talc, pozzolan, clay or gypsum; many masonry cements also include air-entraining and water-repellent additions. (see masonry mortar)

cement-modified soil A soil material that has been treated with a relatively small amount of portland cement; less than is required to produce hardened soil-cement. Small quantities of cement reduce the soil's plasticity, decrease its water-holding and volume-change capacities and increase its bearing value and shearing strength.

cement mortar Mortar usually composed of four parts sand to one of cement, with a suitable amount of water; either lime of plasticizer may also be added. (see lime mortar)

cement, natural The product obtained by finely pulverizing calcined argillaceous limestone burned at a temperature no higher than in necessary to drive off carbon dioxide.

cement, oil-well Hydraulic cement

suitable for use under high pressure and temperature insealing water and gas pockets and setting casings during the drilling and repair of oil wells; often contains retarders to meet the requirements of use.

cement paint A paint consisting generally of white portland cement and water, pigments, hydrated lime, water repellents or hygroscopic salts.

cement paste A mixture of cement and water; may be either hardened or unhardened. *(see neat cement)*

cement plaster Plaster containing portland cement; gypsum plaster which is prepared to be used with the addition of sand as a base coat plaster; called neat of hardwall.

cement, portland The product obtained by pulverizing clinker consisting essentially of hydraulaic calcium silicates; usually containing calcium sulfates as an interground addition. The federal government and the American Sociecty of Testing Materials recognize five major types of portland cement; Type I—Standard portland cement is a general purpose cement for concrete construction. Type II—A modification of Type I is resistant to sulphate attack and decrease rate of heat evolution, sometimes used for massive structures. Type III—A high early strength of quick hardening cement. Type IV—Designed for a low heat of hydration, also used in massive structures. Type V—Designed for extreme sulphate resistance, is similar to Type II.

cement, portland blast-furnace slag Essentially an intimately interground mixture of portland cement clinker and granulated blast-furnace slag or an intimate and uniform blend of portland cement and fine granulated blast-furnace slag in which the amount of the slag constituents falls within specified limits.

cement, portland-pozzolan Essentially an intimately interground mixture of portland cement clinker and pozzolan or an intimate and uniform blend of portland cement and fine pozzolan in which the amount of the pozzolan constituent falls within specified limits.

cement rock Natural impure limestone which contains the ingredients for production of portland cement in approximately the required proportions.

cement screed A screed of cement mortar laid on a concrete slab floor.

cement, slag Finely divided materials consisting essentially of an intimate and uniform blend of granulated blast-furnace slag and hydrated lime in which the slag constituent makes up more than a specified minimum percentage.

cement slurry A liquid cement-water mix; for injection, or used as a wash on a wall.

cement, sulfate-resistant portland cement, low in tricalcium aluminate, to reduce susceptibility of concrete to attack by dissolved sulfates in water or soils, desiganted Type V in United States.

cement, suslfoluminate *(see expansive cement)*

cement, supersulfated A hydraulic cement made by intimately intergrinding a mixture of granulated blast-furnace slag, calcium sulfate, and a small amount of lime, cement or cement clinker; so named because the equivalent content of sulfate exceeds that for portland blast-frunace slag cement.

cement treated base A low grade concrete produced by the addition of cement to a base course on the area to be mixed.

cement, white portland cement which hydrates to a white paste; made from raw materials of low iron content the clinker for which is fired by a reducing flame.

center A fixed point about which the radius of a circle, or of an arc, revolves; the point about which any revolving body rotates or revolves; the middle, or center, or activity.

center bit A simple drill bit for use with the brace.

center cut *(see wedge cut)*

centering The highly specialized falsework used in the construction of arches, shells and space structures or any continuous structure where the entire falsework is lowered as a unit to avoid the introduction of injurious stress in any part of the structure; also the use of metal lath as a form for lightweight concrete in roof construction.

center line On plans, a broken line, usually indicated by a dot and dash, showing the center of an object and providing a convenient line from which to lay off measurements.

center matched Tongue-and-groove lumber with the tongue and groove at the center of the piece rather than offset as in standard matched.

center mixer A stationary concrete mixer from which the fresh concrete is transported to the work.

center of gravity (1) That point in a body about which all the weights of all the various parts balance. It is found experimentally by balancing on a knife edge. (2) The center of mass of a cut or fill.

center of mass (1) In a cut, of fill, a cross section line that divides its bulk into halves. (2) Center of gravity.

centerpiece A plaster rosette or larger decoration for the center of a ceiling.

centerpin (center pintle) In a revolving shovel, a fixed vertical shaft around which the shovel deck turns.

center punch A small hard-steel bar with a blunt point. The point is placed over the center of a hole to be drilled and the other end of the bar is struck with a hammer. The small dent thus ensures that the bit starts drilling in the correct place.

centers (centering) Temporary curved supports, usually wooden, for an arch or dome during casting or laying up.

center-to-center Measurements taken from the center of one joist to another, or from one rafter to another, or from one stud to another.

centigrade *(see celsius)*

centimeter (cm) A measure of length in the metric system equal to the one-hundredth part of a meter, or .3937 inch.

central air conditioner An air conditioner which provides service to an entire structure from a single, central, source.

central heating A system of heating a building, which depends upon one source, with distribution ducts or pipes.

centralizer A device that lines up a drill steel or string between the mast and the hole.

central-mixed concrete Concrete which is completely mixed in a stationary mixer from which it is transported to the delivery point.

central mixer A stationary concrete mixer from which the freshly mixed concrete is transported to the work.

centrifugal brake A mechanism on hoist drums which throws the brake shoes outward onto the fixed brake drum if the load begins to fall.

centrifugal compressor A non-reciprocating air compressor; usually made of several centrifugal blowers in series.

centrifugal force Outward force exerted by a body moving in a curved line. It is the force which tends to tip a car over in going around a curve. *(see centripetal force)*

centrifugal pump A pump with a rotating high-speed impeller. Water enters near the center of the impeller and is thrown outwards by the blades.

centrifuge Device for separating substances of different densities by centrifugal action.

centrifuge moisture equivalent The water content retained by a soil which has been first saturated with water and then subjected to a force equal to 1,000 times the force of gravity for one hour.

centripetal force The force exerted inward to keep a body moving in a curved line. The force which keeps a car from being thrown out of a curve about which it is moving is centripetal force.

centroid Center of mass.

ceramic bond The development of fired strength as a result of thermochemical reactions between materials exposed to temperatures approaching the fusion point of the mixture, such as that which may occur under these conditions, between calcium-aluminate cement and a refractory aggregate.

ceramic mosiac Flooring or wall tiles of glazed clay; often sold in sheets for easier installation.

ceramics Bricks, terra cotta, glazed tiles, stoneware pipes, clay blocks and other pottery items.

ceramic tile A thin, flat piece of fired clay, usually square and attached to walls, floors or counter tops with cement or other adhesives creating durable, decorative and dirt-resistant surfaces.

ceramic veneer A fired, glazed clay veneer for facing buildings; made in sheets, moldings, corners and varied shapes. There is also a spray-on wall finish with ceramic or vitreous surface qualities that is resistant to temperature, acid and alkali.

CERCLA An acronym for the Comprehensive Environmental Response, Compensation, and Liability Act, passed in 1980 and commonly known as Superfund. CERCLA gives the federal government the power to respond to releases, or threatened releases, of any hazardous substance into the environment as well as to a release of a pollutant or contaminant that may present an imminent and substantial danger to public health or welfare. CERCLA established a Hazardous Substance Trust Fund (Superfund), which is available to finance responses taken by the federal government.

certificate for payment A statement from the architect to the owner confirming the amount of money due contractor for work accomplished or materials and equipment suitably stored, or both.

certificate of occupancy Document issued by governmental authority certifying that all or a designated portion of a building complies with the provisions of applicable statutes and regulations, and permitting occupancy for its designated use.

cesspool A pit into which household sewage or other liquid waste is discharged and from which the liquid leaches into the surrounding soil or is otherwise removed.

cetane number An indication of diesel fuel ignition quality. The cetane number of a fuel is the percentage by volume of cetane in a mixture of cetane and alpaha-methyl-napthlalene which matches the unknown fuel in ignition quality. American diesel fuel usually varies from 30 to 60 cetane.

C-frame An angling dozer lift and push frame.

C-grade wood Minimum veneer permitted in exterior type. Repairs are permitted on knotholes to one inch splits and plugs.

chain (1) A tow line or drive belt made of interlocked links. (2) A surveyor's steel tape measure, equivalent to 100 feet.

chainage A surveying length measured by chain or steel tape.

chain binders Yarns running lengthwise in the back of a woven carpet, binding construction yarns together in a woven construction.

chainblock (chainhoist) A pulley hoist in which chain takes the place of rope.

chainfall Same as chain block.

chain bond In masonry, the bonding together of a stone wall by the use of a built-in chain or iron bar.

chain book A field book in which a surveyor records his measurements.

chain, breakaway A safety chain that holds a tractor and a towed unit together if the regular fastening opens or breaks.

chain-bucket dredger A bucket-ladder dredging machine.

chain-bucket loader A mobile loader that uses a series of small buckets on a roller chain to elevate spoil to the dumping point.

chain dogs *(see dog)*

chaines A term applied to quoins when the stones are square.

chain, leaf A chain designed for low speed heavy duty work.

chain, logging A chain composed of links of round bar pieces curved and welded to interlock, with a grab hook at one end and a round hook at the other.

chainman (axman) Junior member of a survey party who carries the chain.

chain of locks In hydraulics, a series of interconnected lock.

chain-pipe vise When fitting steam pipes, a portable vise which utilizes a heavy chain to fasten the pipe in the jaw.

chain reaction The process which sustains fission. For every one neutron that causes a reaction, there will be an average of two and a half neutrons that are freed by the splitting of the atomic nucleus, or five neutrons freed for every two atoms that are split. As they move in the material, two of them will cause other fissions, and the other three will be absorbed by graphite or whatever material surrounds the core.

chain, roller Generally, any sprocket-driven chain made up of links connected by hinge pins and sleeves. Specifically, a chain whose hinge sleeves are protected by an outer sleeve or roller that is free to turn.

chain saw A power saw with teeth linked together for constant cutting action; used for cross-cutting trees or logs; also used for cutting building stone.

chain, silent A roller-type chain in which the sprockets are engaged by projections on the link side bars.

chain sling A sling of iron or manganese steel.

chain, stud type A roller chain in which the inner, or block, links are connected solidly by non-rotating bushings.

chain survey A survey in which no angles, only lengths are measured. If by triangulation, the angles can be deduced.

chain system A system of chains suspended in the feed end of a kiln to promote heat transfer to the raw mix which can be wet or dry. Two types of

chain systems are: Curtain chains (attached only on one end to the kiln interior) or garland chains (attached at both ends to the kiln interior).

chain tongs A plumber's heavy pipe grip, which holds the pipe by a chain linked to a toothed bar.

chair A wire seat or support for reinforcing bars to maintain their designed location while concrete is poured around and over them. *(see bar support)*

chair rail A plain or molded strip on wood or plaster wall as a protection against chair backs.

chalet A wooden dwelling house of the type common in Switzerland.

chalk A soft limestone composed chiefly of the calcareous remains of marine organisms.

chalking Disintegration of coatings such as paint, manifested by the presence of a loose powder evolved from the paint at, or just beneath, the surface.

chalk line (1) A light cord that has been rubbed with chalk (usually blue) for marking. (2) The line left by a chalked string.

chamber A bedroom; a room of state; the private rooms of a judge, adjoining his courtroom.

chambering (springing; squibbing) The firing of successively larger charges of explosive until the bottom of the hole is sufficiently enlarged or chambered to take the final charge. The method is much used for heavy blasts in quarrying. *(see camouflet, jet drilling, torpedo)*

chamfer The beveled edge formed at the right-angle corner of a construction member.

chamfer stop The ending, usually decorative, of a chamfer where it approaches the end of its length and the beginning of an arris.

chamfer strip Triangular or curved insert placed in an inside form corner to produce a rounded or flat chamfer; also called fillet, cant strip, skew back.

chancery The group of rooms, or building, used for the business activities of an ambassador.

chandelier A branching light source hanging from ceiling of roof.

change of state Change from one phase, such as solid, liquid, or gas, to another.

change order A written order to the contractor signed by the owner and engineer or architect, issued after the execution of the contract, authorizing a change in the work or an adjustment in the contract sum or the contract time. A change order may be signed by the architect of engineer, provided they have written authority from the owner for such procedure and that a copy of such written authority is furnished to the contractor upon request. A change order may also be signed by the contractor if he agrees to the adjustment in the contract sum or the contract time. The contract sum and the contract time may be changed only by change order. *(see deduction)*

change point (turning point) **(1)** In survey leveling, a point at which two readings of the staff are taken, a foresight and a backsight. **(2)** Critical point.

changes in the work Changes ordered by the owner consisting of additions, deletions or other revisions within the general scope of the contract, the contract sum and the contract time being adjusted accordingly. All changes in the work, except those of a minor nature not involving an adjustment to the contract sum or the contract time, should be authorized by change order. *(see field order)*

channel **(1)** In glazing, a three-sided U-shaped opening in sash or frame to receive a light or panel, as with sash or frame units in which the light or panel is retained by a removable stop; this is contrasted to a rabbet, which is a two-sided L-shaped opening, as with face glazed window sash. **(2)** A rolled form of structural steel in varying sizes, each a straight web with equal right-angled flanges on both edges and on the same side of the web. **(3)** A natural or artificial water course. **(4)** Term sometimes used to describe the "L" and "T" shaped metal beams used in suspended ceiling installations.

channel beam A member having U-shaped cross section.

channel depth In glazing, the measurement from sight line to base of channel.

channel glazing In glazing, the sealing of the joints around lights or panels set in U-shaped channel employing removable stops.

channel-hotrolled A member formed while in a semi-molten state at the steel mill to a shape having standard dimensions and properties.

channel iron A rolled iron bar, with the sides turned upward forming a rim, making the channel iron appear like a channel-shaped trough.

channeled quoin An ashlar quoin with rebated upper edge.

channel pipe A semi-circular or three-quarter round open pipe used in drainage, particularly at manholes.

channel terrace A contour ridge built of soil moved from its uphill side which serves to divert surface water from a field.

channel tile The under-tile for Spanish or Italian tiling.

channel width In glazing, the measurement between stationary and removable stops in a U-shaped channel at its widest point.

chapel A small house of worship usually serving a residence or institution.

chapter house The meeting place, and sometimes the residence, of the clergy serving a cathedral or other collegiate church.

chaptrel In Gothic architecture, the capital of a pier or column which receives an arch.

charging Introducing, feeding or loading materials into a concrete or mortar mixer, furnace or other container or receptacle where they will be further treated or processed.

Charley Paddock *(slang)* A hacksaw.

Charpy test An impact test in which a notched test-piece supported at both ends is broken by a blow on the face immediately behind the notch.

charring The process of scorching or burning a surface for construction purposes.

chase A recess on the inside of a wall to accommodate plumbing, heating, or other pipes; usually a vertical groove.

chase hole An opening in the rough flooring, through which to pass materials, etc.

chase mortising Cutting a mortise in lumber which is in position. The bottom of the blind mortise is archshaped so that the tenon can be slipped into it sideways.

chasers *(slang)* Pipe cutting tools.

chase wedge In plumbing, a wooden wedge used in bossing lead.

chasing The decorative features produced by grooving or indenting metal.

chat The gangue material which is found intimately mixed with the lead-zinc ores of Missouri and Oklahoma. It is a by-product of metal mining.

chateau A country house of France; originally the French word for castle.

cheapener *(slang)* Paint extender.

check (1) A crack in wood caused by seasoning stresses; in veneer, fine checks may add character and value. (2) An ornamental design composed of inlaid squares. (3) A verification of a survey, a calculation, etc. (4) A structure which controls the water level in an irrigation canal or ditch.

check dam Short (usually 0'6" to 1'-0") berm used as erosion protection on steep banks.

checkdraft An opening and door in smokepipe.

checker (1) An engineer section leader who is usually fully qualified to check structural drawings. (2) A storemen or his helper who counts stores or supplies as they arrive on site and checks that they agree with the invoices.

checker work Masonry of squareface stones not breaking joints.

check-fillet An asphalt curb formed on a roof surface to help control rainwater.

checking (1) Development of shallow cracks at closely spaced but irregular intervals on the surface of mortar or concrete. (2) Very small cracks in flat glass, usually at the edge; though small at first, they can be intensified under strain. (3) Fissures that appear with age in many exterior paint coatings; at first superficial, but which may continue to penetrate entirely through the coating. (4) Blemishes in timber due to uneven seasoning. *(see "craze cracks")*

checkrails Meeting rails sufficiently thicker than a window to fill the opening between the top and bottom sash made by the parting stop in the frame. They are usually beveled.

check stop A molding for holding the bottom sash of a double-hung window in place in a window frame.

check throat A capillary groove under a door or window sill.

check valve Any device which will allow fluid or air to pass through it in only one direction; in plumbing, a valve preventing the back-flow of water or other liquid by automatically closing.

cheeks (cheek pieces) Any pair of upright facing members, as the cheeks of a window embrasure, or of a doorway, of a flight of steps.

cheesiness A paint film which is soft and incompletely dry; the opposite of a flexible, tough film. A film which is tough on the surface may be cheesy underneath.

Chelmsford Gray A light gray, medium-grain, muscovite-biotite granite from Massachusetts, used for heavy masonry and monument building.

chemical bond Bond produced by cohesion between separate laminae of similar crystalline materials. Based on formation and subsequent interlocking of crystals.

chemical gauging (chemi-hydrometry) Measuring the quantity of water flow by determining the dilution of a chemical solution introduced upstream at a known rate and concentration.

chemical precipitation The settlement of sewage, hastened by flocculation.

chemical resistance The degree to which a material resists stains and/or corrosive action of various household and industrial chemicals.

chemistry The chemical properties, composition, reactions and uses of substances.

cheneau An ornamental upper portion of a cornice or gutter.

cherry picker *(slang)* **(1)** A small derrick made up of an A-frame, winch line and hook, mounted on a truck; often used for setting pipe, lifting pipe, engines, or any relatively light load. **(2)** Any small crane or derrick that can work and lift in cramped spaces. **(3)** Hydraulic lift.

chert Non-crystalline silica which is found in limestones; an impure flint used for ballast; fine-grained, dense textured gray, white or black rock found in the southern United States.

chevron The meeting place of rafters at the ridge of a gable roof; a zigzag pattern used as an ornamentation of Romanesque architecture.

chevron drain (herringbone drain) Stone-filled trenches laid in a herringbone pattern to drain into drains laid out along the line of steepest slope.

Chicago boom A boom hinged to the steel framework of a building and used to raise materials into the structure.

Chicago cassion (Chicago well) A small cofferdam used in medium stiff clays lined with planks sunk to hard ground for pier foundations. The plank sheeting is held in place by steel rings wedged against the side.

chicken ladder *(slang)* A crawling board.

chicken wings A steel arm attached to a pole to put an insulator on to hold the wire.

chick sale *(slang)* A portable out-door toilet used on construction jobsites.

chief Draftsman, generally a designer, with high qualifications and much experience.

chill bar A thick copper bar placed under welding area to absorb the heat.

chiller An air conditioning unit consist-

ing of a compressor, condenser and evaporator tank. Chilled water is piped through a building and the cold is emitted into the air. The water returns to be rechilled and recirculated.

chilling Deterioration of paints or varnishes which have been stored at low temperature.

chimney A flue, approximately vertical, for conducting the smoke and gases of combustion from above a fire to the outside air.

chimney block Concrete masonry units designed for use in chimney construction, usually in conjunction with flue lining.

chimney breast The chimney wall which projects into a room and contains the fireplace and flues; a mantel.

chimney cowl A metal revolving ventilator over the chimney.

chimney effect The tendency of air or gas in a duct or other vertical passage to rise when heated due to its lower density compared with that of the surrounding air or gas. In buildings, the tendency toward displacement of internal heated air by unheated outside air due to the difference in density of outside and inside air.

chimney gutter A back gutter.

chimney lining Rectangular or round tiles placed within a chimney for protective purpose. The glazed surface of the tile provides resistance to the deteriorating effects of smoke and gas fumes.

chimney piece The ensemble of architectural and decorative treatment about and over the fireplace.

chimney pot A short extension of a flue in round section above the chimney wall.

chimney shaft Part of a chimney which stands free of other structures, usually limited to a large chimney containing one or two flues.

chimney stack A group of flues contained within a common covering.

chimney throat The narrow horizontal slot above a fireplace through which the gases of combustion pass.

Chinese fingers *(slang)* A split wrap-around cable grip, used to support wires.

Chinese white *(see zinc oxide)*

chink In a building, a crack or small fissure in a wall surface; to fill cracks or interstices as between logs or stones of a wall.

chip blasting Shallow blasting of ledge rock.

chipboard *(see particleboard)*

chip cracks Fine cracks, similar to check cracks except that bond is partially destroyed producing a series of concave fragments of the surface material. The condition is also termed "egg shelling," fire cracking, etc.

chippage The breaking off of particles on the stretcher or header surfaces of face brick, usually after they are burned.

chipped grain An area in which pieces of wood have been pulled or chipped away from the surface during machining; also called torn grain.

chipping (1) A process of cutting off small pieces of metal or wood with a cold chisel and a hammer. (2) Treatment of a hardened concrete surface by chiseling away a portion of the material. (3) Loosening of shallow rock by light blasting or air hammers.

chips Broken fragments of marble or other mineral aggregate screened to specified sizes. A common term for a sealing or top layer of roadway materials.

chisel A cutting tool with a wide variety of uses. The cutting edge on the end of the tool usually is transverse to the axis. The cutting principle of the chisel is the same as that of the wedge.

chisel edge A slanted factory edge on gypsum board.

chisel knife A narrow striping knife with a square edge used in painting.

chlorination Applying chlorine to water or wastewater. This is usually done to disinfect. Often, however, it is used to accomplish other biological or chemical results.

chlorine An element which usually exists as a greenish-yellow gas. It weighs about 2.5 times as much as air.

chock A block used under and against an object to prevent it from rolling or sliding.

choir loft Often above the rear of a sanctuary, designed for the seating of a body of trained singers.

choke The inductor used in a filter to help smooth out the DC voltage.

choker A short length of cable with eyes spliced into either end, usually wrapped around a load, threaded through itself and hooked to a crane hook.

choker hook (round hook) A hook that can slide along a chain.

chop The movable outer plate of the jaw of a carpenter's bench vise.

chord An essential member, approximately horizontal, of a truss; a straight line connecting two points on a curve.

chord modulus *(see modulus of elasticity)*

chorometry The science of measuring land.

chroma (saturation) A term used to designate the color strength as it extends from a gray of the same value to the greatest saturation of the color.

chromacity The characteristics of light specified by dominant wavelength and purity.

chromating (1) Priming with lead or zinc chromate to prevent rust forming under the paint. (2) A protective coating for magnesium alloys formed by dipping the article in hot solutions of alkaline dichromate or chromic and nitric acids.

chromium A grayish white metal, resistant to corrosion and widely used as a plating.

chronotherm A combination clock and thermostat that can be set to produce desired heat at given times during day or night.

chuck (1) A device used to secure a tool or piece of material in position; in a brace and bit, the chuck holds the auger bit in the brace. (2) The part of a drill that rotates the steel.

chuffy brick One swollen by inner steam or air while in the kiln.

chunk out *(slang)* To clear out access roads.

chunk sample method Method of determining weight per cubic foot of soil in place.

churn drill (spudding; well drill) A machine that drills holes by dropping and raising a bit and drill string hung by a cable.

churn molding A zigzag molding often used in early Norman architecture.

chute A sloping trough or tube for conducting concrete, cement, aggregate or other free flowing materials from a higher to a lower point.

cill The usual British spelling for sill.

cincture An encircling fillet, ring or girdle at the top and bottom of a column, serving to divide the shaft of the column from its capital and base.

cinder block Clinker block.

cinerator A furnace in a crematory. *(see incinerator)*

cinquefoil arch An arch of five arcs.

circle The perimeter of a circle; a line that bounds a circular plane surface; the distance around a circle or an ellipse; radius × 6.283185.

circle cutter An adjustable scribe for cutting circular patterns or openings for lighting fixtures and other devices.

circlehead window A small, decorative, half-oval window usually over a door.

circle of a motor grader The rotary table which supports the blade and regulates its angle.

circle reverse The mechanism that changes the angle of a grade blade.

circuit In electricity, the path taken by an electrical current in flowing through a conductor from one terminal of the source of supply to the other.

circuit breaker A device designed to open and close a circuit by manual means, and to open the circuit automatically on a predetermined overload of current, without injury to itself when properly applied within its rating.

circuit vent A branch vent that serves two or more traps and extends from in front of the last fixture connection of a horizontal branch to the vent stack.

circular plane A carpenter's compass plane.

circular saw A saw with teeth spaced around the edge of a circular plate, or disk, which is rotated at high speed upon a central axis, or spindle, used for cutting lumber or sawing logs.

circular stair A spiral stair.

circulating water Water contained in a closed loop circuit of a central heating system.

circumscribe The process of drawing a line to enclose certain portions of an object, figure, or plane; to encircle; to draw boundary lines; to enclose within certain limits.

cistern An artificial reservoir or tank, often underground, for the storing of rain water collected off a roof.

citadel A stronghold; originally one protecting a city.

civic center In a community, that part where the main public buildings are located.

civil engineer A trained engineer who designs harbors, roads, bridges, waterworks, and other heavy engineering projects.

cladding (1) British term for the surface material of a non-loadbearing wall; in the U.S.A., called siding. (2) Composite plate made of base with a plate of corrosion or heat-resistant metal on one or both sides.

clam *(slang)* A clamshell bucket.

clam gun *(slang)* Shovel.

clamp A device for holding portions of work together, either wood or metal; an appliance with opposing sides or parts that may be screwed together to hold objects or parts of objects together firmly. *(see tie; coupler)*

clamping screw A screw used in a clamp; a screw used to hold pieces of work together in a clamp.

clampman In pipeline work, a member of the gang that pulls the pneumatic clamp through a length of pipe to clamp into position a new length for welding.

clamshell A shovel bucket with two jaws which clamp together by their own weight when it is lifted by the closing line. A shovel equipped with a clamshell bucket handles loose material such as sand, gravel, crushed stone, coal, etc.

clapboard (bevel; lapsiding) A board that is thin on one edge and thicker on the other, to facilitate overlapping horizontally to form a weatherproof, exterior wall surface.

clarification drawing A graphic interpretation of the drawings or other contract documents issued by the architect or engineer as part of an addendum, modification, change order or field order.

clarifiers Mechanical devices used to remove, by gravity, suspended particles in liquid. They are employed in the treatment of drinking water and the purification of sewage.

Clarke beam A type of built-up beam, formed to two or more joists bolted together and reinforced with short diagonal pieces, placed solidly along the length of a beam on each side.

clasp nail A cut nail of square section with a head having two points which sink into the wood.

Classical Of, or based upon, the architecture of ancient Greece and Rome.

classified product A product labeled and listed by an approved laboratory having a factory follow-up and inspection service.

class of concrete An arbitrary characterization of concrete of various qualities or usages, usually by compressive strength.

class of refrigerating system. Formerly in extensive use, now becoming obsolete as a result of code change to classification rather than weight. Refers to total weight of refrigerant contained; Class A system is one containing 1000 lb or more of refrigerant; Class B system is one containing more than 100 lb but less than 1000 lb of refrigerant; Class C system is one con-

taining more than 20 lb but not more than 100 lb of refrigerant; Class D system is one containing more than 6 lb but not more than 20 lb of refrigerant; Class E system is one containing 6 lb or less.

claw (pinch bar; crow bar) A carpenter's bar with a split end for pulling nails.

claw hammer (carpenter's hammer) A hammer with one split, claw-shaped peen for drawing nails and one face for striking nails; much used for erecting and dismantling formwork.

claw hatchet A shingling or lathing hatchet.

clay Natural mineral material having plastic properties and composed of very fine particles; the clay mineral fraction of a soil is usually considered to be the portion consisting of particles finer than 2 microns (0.002 mm); clay minerals are essentially hydrous aluminum silicates or occasionally hydrous magnesium silicates. Used principally for brick, tile and earthenware.

hard Clay that must be excavated with pick and cannot be remolded with the fingers.

medium Clay that can be excavated with spade and remolded with difficulty.

soft Clay that can be excavated with shovel and easily remolded with the fingers.

clay content Percentage of clay by dry weight of a heterogeneous material, such as a soil or a natural concrete aggregate.

clay masonry unit A solid or hollow masonry unit with clay or shale as the principal binder, usually formed into a rectangular prism while plastic, and burned or fired in a kiln.

clay mortar mix A dried clay powder used for making masonry mortar for bricklaying.

clay slip A suspension of clay in water prepared for ease of handling and proportioning.

clean Free of foreign material; in reference to sand or gravel, lack of binder.

clean aggregate Sand or gravel which is free from clay or silt.

cleaning eye An access eye; an opening or cleanout.

cleanout (1) An opening in the forms for removal of refuse, to be closed before the concrete is placed. (2) A screw-plugged opening in drain piping. (3) An opening in a chimney or heating unit for cleaning, sometimes called an access eye, soot door, etc.

cleanup (1) Scraping, smoothing and sanding of finished carpentry work. (2) Treatment of horizontal construction joints to remove all surface material and contamination down to a condition of cleanness corresponding to that of a freshly broken surface of concrete. (3) Final detailing and cleaning of a construction project prior to final inspection by owners and agent.

clear (1) Term for milled wood, without knots. (2) Ratio of height web to thickness of web in steel beams.

clearance (1) Space to spare above actual need, as the height, greater than normal headroom, between a stair tread and the closed ceiling above it. (2) Space between a moving object and a stationary object. (3) Space in cylinder not occupied by piston at the end of compression stroke, or volume of gas remaining in cylinder at same point; measured in percentage of piston displacement.

clearance pocket In a compressor, a space of controlled volume to give the effect of greater or less cylinder clearance thereby changing compressor capacity.

clear cole A priming or sizing used in Great Britain; white ground lead mixed in water and glue.

clearing (clearing and grubbing) Removal of tree stumps, shrubs and roots before excavation of a site.

clearing hole (clearance hole) A hole drilled slightly larger than the bolt which passes through it.

clear span The distance, or clear and unobstructed opening, between two supports of a beam; always less than the effective span.

cleat (1) A strip of wood or metal fastened across a door or other object to give it additional strength; a strip of wood fastened to a surface to serve as a support for another board, such as a shelf; a small board used to connect formwork members or used as a brace in concreting. (2) A strip of insulator across a cable, holding it in position; a metal fastener for ductwork connections. (3) A ladder crosspiece.

cleavage membrane A membrane that provides a separation and slip sheet between the mortar setting bed and the backing or base surface.

cleavage plane Any uniform joint, crack or change of quality of formation along which rock will break easily when dug or blasted.

clerestory Part of roof extending above the main roof, usually with windows.

clerestry window A window or series of windows in a wall above the primary roof line, for additional lighting and ventilation of central part of building.

clerk of the works A British term for one who supervises the construction of a building and keeps a record of the materials used and sometimes, of workmen's time. The American term is project representative or supervisor.

clevis A connecting iron bent into the form of a horseshoe, stirrup or letter U; a line in a chain shaped like the letter U; an adjusting piece for bridge members of varying length; a shackle; a split end of a rod, drilled for insertion of a pin through the two sections or for connecting steel wires to a load.

client The person or firm employing an architect or engineer and to whom they are responsible.

cliff dwelling Prehistoric habitation of certain Indian tribes in southwestern U.S.A., and in northern Mexico; partly excavation, partly stone-walled on narrow shelves of the cliffs.

climatology In architecture, the science of planning and building in accord with regional climatic variations.

climbing form A form which is raised vertically for succeeding lifts of concrete in a given structure, usually supported on anchor bolts or rods embedded in the top of the previous lift. The form is moved only after an entire lift is placed and partially hardened; this should not be confused with a slip form which moves during placement of the concrete.

climbing lane (passing lane) Used in highway design, an extra uphill lane for faster traffic.

clinch The process of securing a driven nail by bending down the point; to fasten firmly by bending down the ends of protruding nails.

clink (1) A pointed steel bar about 12 inches long used for breaking up road surfaces where a concrete breaker is not available. (2) A seam between adjacent bays of flexible metal roofing.

clinker A partially fused product of a kiln which is ground to make cement; also other vitrified or burnt material.

clinker block (cinder block) An inexpensive and strong building block of clinker concrete.

clinker breaker A series of hammers or rollers installed at the discharge end of a clinker cooler to break lumps for more rapid cooling.

clinker brick A type of rustic brick in the manufacture of which metallic residues are used; clinker bricks are very hard.

clinometer A hand instrument for measuring grades by sighting.

clip A kind of metal fastener used in places where penetrating or adhesive fasteners reduce the efficiency of the construction; clips of various kinds hold members together by tension in opposing clips. Clips can be used where there is no overlapping of members and where it is desirable to have semi-independent members in construction to minimize stresses, as well as for other purposes.

clip joint A joint of abnormal thickness to bring the course up to the required height. Usually used in the layout course to make up for low elevations of footings.

clipped header A bat placed to look like a header for purposes of establishing a pattern. Also called false header.

clod buster *(slang)* A drag that follows a grading machine to break up lumps.

cloister A square court surrounded by an open arcade.

close-boarded Term describing a roof or wall that is covered with boards below the slates or tiles.

close-couple (couple-close) Describing a roof of common rafters joined at the wall plate level with a tie-beam.

close-cut hip (valley) In roofing, a hip or valley in which the slates, shingles, or tiles are cut to meet on the hip or valley line.

close fit A term applied to a type of machine thread used on structural parts where accuracy is essential.

closed-circuit grinding Grinding system in which the mill product is passed to a screen or separator so that fines may be removed from the circuit and oversize tailings or sands returned for further grinding.

closed-circuit grouting Injection of grout into a hole intersecting fissures or voids which are to be filled at such volume and pressure that grout input to the hole is greater than the grout take of the surrounding formation, excess grout being returned to the pumping plant for recirculation.

closed-circuit TV Cameras and monitors connected by wires without use of antennas.

closed container A container so sealed by means of a lid or other device that neither liquid nor vapor will escape from it at ordinary temperatures.

closed cornice A box cornice.

closed list of bidders *(see invited bidders)*

closed sandwich type panel A sandwich panel in which all edges of panel are closed except for weep holes and vents.

closed specifications Specifications stipulating the use of specific products or processes without provision for substitution. *(see base bid specifications)*

closed stack A plumbing system that has no vents. Not practical because of internal pressures caused by sudden and rapid discharges of water.

closed stair (box stair) A stair walled in on each side and closed by a door at one end.

closed system (1) A building system having interchangeability of its own subsystems and components only. (2) A heating or refrigerating piping system in which the circulating water or brine is completely enclosed, under pressure above atmospheric, and shut off from the atmosphere except for a vented expansion tank at the high point of the system.

closed valley In building construction, a valley in which the courses of shingles meet and completely cover the lining of tin or other material; a secret gutter.

close fit A term applied to a type of machine thread used on structural parts where accuracy is essential.

close-grained Wood with narrow and inconspicuous annual rings; sometimes used to designate wood having small and closely spaced pores, but in this sense the term "fine textured" is more often used. Wood with more than six rings per inch.

close nipple (parallel nipple) A short nipple with threads from one end to the other; for making short or close connections.

closer (closure) The last brick or part of brick built in to complete a course of masonry; a brick or portion of brick used to break bond at quoins and openings in brick walls.

   king closure A brick cut diagonally to have a two inch end and one full width end.

   queen closure A half-brick with a nominal two inch horizontal face dimension made by cutting a whole brick longitudinally.

close string (box string) A method of finishing the outer edge of stairs, by building up a sort of curb string on which the balusters set, and the treads and risers stop against it.

closet (1) A privy, a water closet. (2) A small room or a cupboard generally for storage of clothes or linens.

closet lining Thin tongue-and-groove boards used for lining clothes closets; usually such boards are of red cedar, the odor of which protects clothing against moths.

closing line (digging line) The cable which closes the jaws of a clamshell bucket.

closure The process of bringing two parts of a cofferdam together to divert a river from its channel.

closure strip A resilient strip, formed by the contour of ribbed panels used to close openings created by joining metal panels and flashing.

cloth, wire Screen composed of wire or rod woven and crimped into a square or rectangular pattern.

clouding In painting, loss of luster usually caused by a porous undercoat.

cloudy A painted surface not uniformly covered.

clout nail (felt nail) A short galvanized nail with a large round flat head; used for attaching roofing felt and plasterboard, etc.

cloverleaf System of on and off ramps for a highway that resembles a 4-leafed clover or one or more petals of a clover.

club hammer (mash hammer; lump hammer) A double-face hammer used by bricklayers and masons.

cluster In lighting, a fixture having two or more lamps on it.

clustered column A group of shafts, with their bases and capitals engaged as one support.

clutch A device which connects and disconnects two shafts which revolve in line with each other.

   automatic A clutch whose engagement is controlled by centrifugal force, vacuum or other power without attention by the operator.

brake A device to slow the jackshaft when a clutch is released, to permit more rapid gear shifting.

centrifugal A clutch that is kept in engagement only by centrifugal force, so that it automatically disconnects the power train when the engine idles.

denture A jaw clutch.

disc A coupling that can be engaged to transmit power through one or more discs squeezed between a back-plate and a movable pressure plate, and that can be disengaged by moving the plates apart.

fluid A fluid coupling other than a torque converter.

lockup A clutch that can be engaged to provide a non-slip mechanical drive through a fluid coupling.

jaw (positive; denture clutch) A toothed hub and a sliding toothed collar that can be engaged to transmit power between two shafts having the same axis of revolution.

overrunning (free wheeling unit) A coupling that transmits rotation in only one direction, and disconnects when the torque is reversed.

slip (safety clutch) A friction clutch that protects a mechanism by slipping under excessive load.

wet (oil clutch) A clutch that operates in an oil bath.

coach screw *(see lag bolt)*

coagulant A substance which, when added to waters above a certain pH, forms a bulky precipitate, or floc. Great amounts of suspended solids adhere to the floc because of its large surface area. This increases the weight of the floc and produces settling.

coal storage The storage area where stocks of coal are maintained.

coal tar bitumen A dark brown to black, semi-solid hydrocarbon formed as a residue from the partial evaporation or distillation of coal tar. It is used as the waterproofing agent in dead-level or low-slope built-up roofs. It differs from COAL TAR PITCH in having a lower front-end volatility. (For

specification properties, see ASTM Standard D 450, Type III.)

coal tar enamel A bituminous black coal liquid especially used to coat vessels before being buried in the ground.

coal tar felt *(see tarred felt)*

coal tar pitch A dark brown to black, semi-solid hydrocarbon formed as a residue from the partial evaporation or distillation of coal tar. It is used as the waterproofing agent in dead-level or low-slope built-up roofs. (For specification properties, see ASTM Standard D 450, Types I and II.)

coaming The raised frame, as around a hatchway in the deck to keep out water.

coarse aggregate Aggregate predominantly retained on the No. 4 (4.76 mm) sieve; or that portion of an aggregate retained on the No. 4 (4.76 mm) sieve. *(see aggregate)*

coarse grained (1) Wide ringed timber. (2) Soil in which the larger grain sizes, such as sand and gravel, predominate.

coarse stuff The material for the first and second coats of plaster, made either with hydrated lime or with lime putty.

coat A film or layer as of asphalt, paint or plaster applied in a single operation.

coated base sheet (or felt) A felt that has been impregnated and saturated with asphalt and then coated on both sides with harder, more viscous asphalt to increase its impermeability to moisture; a parting agent is incorporated to prevent the material from sticking in the roll.

coated macadam *(see tarmacadam)*

coating (1) Material applied to a surface by brushing, dipping, mopping, spraying, troweling, etc., so as to preserve, protect, decorate, seal or smooth the substrate. (2) The dark or blackened finish which is applied to the side of the collector plate exposed to the sun's rays is called a coating. Often called a wavelength or optically selective coating, its purpose is to maximize absorption of the sun's energy. The absorptivity and emissivity characteristics of coating affect collector performance.

coating asphalt The layer of asphalt applied to the surface of the roofing material during manufacture into which roofing granules or some other form of surfacing material is embedded; this coating and surfacing provides the weather-resistant surface.

coating in Applying a coat of paint.

cob A small mixture of unburned clay usually with straw as a binder; when used in building walls it is known as cob walls.

cobble In geology, a rock fragment between 2½ and 10 inches (64 and 256 mm) in diameter; as applied to coarse aggregate for concrete, the material in the nominal size range three to six inches (75 to 150 mm).

cob wall A wall built of clay blocks made of unburnt clay or calk mixed with straw; also a wall constructed of cobs, such as clay bats.

cobwebbing A painting term for the ejection from a spray gun of a series of cobweb-like threads. The same difficulty may occasionally occur in brushing.

cock A valve for controlling a pipeline of water, gas or other fluid. Plug cocks are usual for gas, fullway valves for water supplies with low pressure, and screw-down valves for a high pressure water supply.

cocking (1) In carpentry, a type of joining used to connect one beam to another across which it is bearing. (2) Tipping sideward or running off center neither horizontal or vertical.

cockle A "crease-like" wrinkle or small depression in gypsum board face paper usually running in the long or machine direction.

cockling A curliness or crimpiness appearing in the cut face pile of carpet as a result of a yarn or machine condition, but not necessarily a defect, depending on the style.

cockpit The part of a tractor or grader containing the operator's seat and controls.

cockscomb *(slang)* A mason's drag.

cocoa mat A fabric of wood fibers used to distribute water evenly over a smooth surface, such as over a roll on a road roller.

codes Regulation, ordinances or statutory requirements of a governmental unit relating to building construction and occupancy, adopted and administered for the protection of the public health, safety and welfare.

coefficient A factor that contributes to produce a result, as in mathematics or physics.

coefficient of accoustics That property of a material which reduces echoes in the room. It has little effect on passing of sound through a wall or floor, except insofar as it reduces sound within the room.

coefficient of compressibility The change in the voids ratio per unit increase of pressure expressed in square centimeters per gram.

coefficient of consolidation A value expressed in square centimeters per minute, in the consolidation of soils.

coefficient of contraction In hydraulics, the ratio of the smallest cross-sectional area of a jet discharged from an orifice under pressure to the area of the orifice.

coefficient of discharge The ratio of the observed discharge to the theoretical discharge of a liquid through an orifice or pipe.

coefficient of expansion A value denoting the rate at which a material expands with rising temperature.

coefficient of friction Ratio between the force causing a body to slide along a plane and the force normal to the plane.

coefficient of imperviousness Impermeability factor.

coefficient of internal friction The tangent of the angle Ø, the angle of internal friction.

coefficient of heat transmission A term applied to any one of a number of coefficients which may be used to calculate heat transmission by either conduction, convection, or radiation, through various materials and structures.

coefficient of linear thermal expansion Length change per unit of length per degree of temperature change.

coefficient of performance (COP) The ratio of the rate of useful heat output delivered by the complete heat pump unit (exclusive of supplementary heating) to the corresponding rate of energy input, expressed in consistent units and under designated operating conditions. British thermal units are converted to kilowatt hours at the rate of 3413 British thermal units per kilowatt hour.

coefficient of subgrade friction The coefficient of friction between a grade slab and its subgrade; used to estimate shrinkage reinforcing steel requirements by calculating stresses induce in the concrete by its shrinkage and the subgrade restraint.

coefficient of subgrade reaction An experimentally determined ratio between the vertical subgrade reaction and the deflection at a point on the surface of contact. *(see contact pressure)*

coefficient of thermal conductance (C) Amount of heat (in Btu) that passes thru a specific thickness of a material (either homogeneous or heterogeneous) per hr., per sq. ft., per °F. Measured as temperature difference between surfaces.

coefficient of thermal conductivity (k) Convenient factor represents the amount of heat (in Btu) that passes by conduction through a homogeneous material, per hr., per sq. ft., per in. thickness, per °F. Measured as temperature difference between the two surfaces of the material.

coefficient of traction The factor by which the total load on a driving tire or track should be multiplied in order to determine the maximum possible tractive force between the tire or track and the surface just before slipping will occur.

coefficient of uniformity The ratio between grain diameter larger than 60 percent by weight of the particles in a soil sample, to that diameter, the effective size, larger than 10 percent by weight of the particles. Non-uniform soils have a relatively flat grading curve; uniform soils a steep one.

coefficient of variation Standard deviation divided by the mean.

coefficient of velocity The ratio of the measured discharge velocity to the theoretical discharge velocity.

coefficient of volume change The modulus of volume change.

coffer (1) A recessed panel in a flat or vaulted ceiling. (2) A recessed ceiling source of artificial light; a troffer.

cofferdam (1) A watertight enclosure usually built of piles of clay, within which excavation is done for foundations; also a watertight enclosure fixed to the side of a ship for making repairs below the water line. A caisson. (2) In dam construction, a temporary structure enclosing all or part of the construction area so that construction can proceed in the dry. A diversion cofferdam diverts a river into a pipe, channel, or tunnel.

coffered ceilings Ceilings made up of sunken or recessed panels.

coffing hoist A small chain hoist used in steam fitting and steelwork.

cog (1) In carpentry, the solid middle portion which remains in a structural timber after two notches have been cut to form a cogged joint. (2) In roofing, a nib in the tiles.

cogeneration (1) The sequential production of useful shaft power and thermal energy from a primary energy source. (2) simultaneous generation of electrical energy and low grade heat from the same fuel.

cogged joint A joint having one member notched so as to form a cog and the other member notched to fit over the cog.

cohesion of soil The quality of some soil particles to be attracted to like particles, manifested in a tendency to stick together, as in clay.

coil A cooling or heating element made of pipe or tubing.

coil deck Insulated horizontal partition between refrigerated space and bunker.

coil heating Heating a concrete floor slab by water pipes or electric cables cast into it.

cold cathode An instant-starting variety of fluorescent lamps, using electrodes of cylindrical form; hot-cathode lamps use electrodes of coiled tungsten filaments.

cold chisel A name applied to a chisel made of tool steel of a strength and temper that will stand up under the hardest usage. A chisel suitable for cutting and shaping cold metal.

cold cut (cold cutter) A cold chisel mounted on a handle-like hammer; used with the application of a maul.

cold drawing (wire drawing) Making steel wire by drawing it through successively smaller round holes in steel dies which hardens the steel, raises its ultimate tensile strength and reduces its diameter.

cold face The surface of a refractory not exposed to the source of heat.

cold forming Process of using press brakes or rolling mills to shape steel into desired cross sections; done at room temperature.

cold joint A joint or discontinuity formed when a concrete surface hardens before the next batch is placed against it, characterized by poor bond unless necessary procedures are observed.

cold joint lines Visible lines on the surfaces of formed concrete indicating the presence of joints where one layer of concrete had hardened before subsequent concrete was placed. (see cold joint)

cold-laid plant mixture (cold mixes) Plant mixes spread and rolled at normal temperatures; cold mixes are made of emulsified asphalt, powdered asphalt, liquid asphalt cement, cutback asphalts or tars and either heated and dried or cold aggregates.

cold patch Aggregates and liquid bitumin mixed up by hand or plant and stockpiled for patching or maintenance.

cold process A roofing application wherin cold asphalt of a cutback type is used as adhesive between the three layers of roofing.

cold rolling Cold bending of steel plates to make very light structural section.

Cold Spring Agate A medium-to coarse-grain granite, reddish with broad, dark veining and a clouding of red, pearl gray and a bluish shade, quarried at Odessa, Minnesota.

Carnelian A porphyritic granite of medium grain and a general brownish red color, quarried at Milbank, South Dakota.

Diamond Pink A coarse-grain granite, pinkish with mixed pearl gray and reddish colorings, quarried at St. Cloud, Minnesota.

Pearl Pink A porphyritic granite of medium grain, quarried at Cold Spring, Minnesota.

Pearl White A light pink granite, classed as white of medium grain, quarried at Isle, Minnesota.

Rainbow A medium-to coarse-grain pink granite with black and gray wavings, quarried at Morton, Minnesota.

Red A medium-grain reddish granite with black and gray spottings, quarried at Odessa, Minnesota.

cold strength The compressive or flexural strength of refractory concrete determined prior to drying or firing.

cold-water paint A paint in which the binder or vehicle portion is composed of latex, casein, glue, and some similar material dissolved or dispersed in water.

cold working The shaping of metals at room temperature.

collapse Irregular shrinkage in wood above the fiber saturation point; caused by collapse of wood cells as free water is drawn out of the cell cavities without replacement with air or more water.

collapsible pans Telescopic centering.

collar (1) In carpentry, an encircling band resembling a collar; a molding extending around a leg of furniture. (2) The open end of a drill hole. (3) A sliding ring mounted on a shaft so that it does not revolve with it; used in clutches and transmissions. (4) Asphalt built up around a pipe passing up through an asphalt roof to insure a water-tight joint at the pipe. (5) An enlargement outside a pipe or a reduction inside its bore; often made to bear on another collar and ensure a tight joint between pipes.

collar beam A horizontal tie beam in a roof truss, connecting two opposite rafters at a level considerably above the wall plate.

collar joint The interior, longitudinal, vertical joint in a multi-unit masonry wall.

collaring Starting a drill hole; when the hole is deep enough to hold the bit from slipping out of it, it is collared.

collateral load All specified additional dead loads other than the metal building framing, such as sprinklers, mechanical and electrical systems and ceilings.

collecting system Each drain or sewer of a sewerage system between the house and the outfall line.

collection device Unit used to collect particulate or gaseous material of interest.

collection line A drain for plumbing.

collection system A term often associated with the transfer of sewage and wastewater from the point of generation to the point of treatment.

collective bargaining The negotiation for mutual agreement in the settlement of a labor contract between an employer or his representatives and a labor union or its representatives.

collective elevator An elevator that has the ability to "store" both hall and car calls, and to stop for them as they are reached.

collector A device for intercepting the sun's rays and directly converting them to a conveniently transportable form of energy such as heat or electricity.

collector box Transition piece between a gutter and downspout to facilitate water flow.

collector efficiency The ratio of the energy collected to the incident radiation on the collector is used to measure collector efficiency.

collector tilt The angle at which a solar heat collector is tilted to face the sun for better performance.

collimation error Error in surveying instruments from the line of sight not being horizontal or otherwise being out of line.

collimation line Line of sight of a surveying instrument; it passes through the intersection of the cross hairs in the reticule.

collimation method In levelling, also known as height of instrument method as opposed to the rise and fall method. During field work, the instrument height is always known by taking the first sight on a point of known level. The method is convenient to obtain levels of many points from one set-up.

colloid (1) A substance that, when apparently dissolved in water, diffuses very slowly or not at all through a membrane; composed of particles ranging from 105 to 107 cm in diameter. (2) A gluey, jelly-like substance like glue, starch, gelatin, flour, paste and gum, which sticks fast when the solvent evaporates.

colloidal grout A grout which has artificially induced cohesiveness or ability to retain the dispersed solid particles in suspension.

collusion A secret agreement or cooperation for a fraudulent or deceitful purpose. Non-collusion statements are often required when bidding on governmental contracts.

colluvial soil Soil or rock transported by gravity (i.e., cliff debris, avalanches, masses of rock waste).

cologne earth In painting, a lignite which yields a deep brown transparent earth color.

colonnade A series of columns at regular intervals, usually carrying an architrave.

colonnette A small column of secondary use, such as applied to the face of panel stiles.

color Color includes hue, value and saturation. Hues are red, yellow, green, blue, purple, etc. Value is the amount of light reflected. Saturation is the intensity of a hue compared with a neutral grey of similar value. The colors of the spectrum are the most intense.

color-coding (polarizing) Identification of wires, etc. by color.

colored cement Any of the cements when mixed with mineral pigments.

colored finishes Plaster finish coats containing integrally mixed color pigments or colored aggregates.

colorimetric value An indication of the amount of organic impurities present in fine aggregate.

coloring pigment In painting, a pigment or stainer which is added to paint when a final color is required, different from that of the base used; sometimes called stainer.

color systems Efforts to arrange the colors of the spectrum in orderly graphic relationship, such as the systems of Munsell and Ostwald.

colter (slang) A cutting wheel.

column A compression member, vertical or nearly vertical, the width of which does not exceed four times its thickness and the height of which exceeds four times its least lateral dimension.

  analogy An analogy between the equations for slope and deflection of a bent beam and those for load and moment in a short eccentrically loaded column. Particular cases of fixed-base portals and arches can be rapidly analyzed by this method.

  capital An enlargement of the end of a column designed and built to act as an integral unit with the column and flat slab and increase the shearing resistance.

  combination A column in which a

structural steel member, designed to carry part of the load, is encased in concrete of such quality and in such manner that the remaining load may be allowed thereon.

  composite A column in which a metal structural member is completely encased in concrete containing special and longitudinal reinforcement.

column clamp Any of various types of tying or fastening units used to hold column form sides together; a manufactured device surrounding a column form, to hold the pressure exerted by wet concrete. *(see yoke)*

column footings Concrete footings, reinforced with steel rods, used as supports for columns which in turn carry the load of I-beams which serve as supports for the superstructure of a building.

columination Arrangement of columns where their placing and relation to each other from a principal feature of a design.

column load A continuous charge of explosive in a blasthole, with no stemming between charges.

column, long A column whose load capacity must be reduced because of its slenderness.

column sections In building construction, steel beams and steel columns used extensively in large structures.

column, short A column whose load capacity need not be reduced because of its slenderness.

column side One of the vertical panel components of a column form.

column strip The portion of a flat slab over the columns and consisting of the two adjacent quarter panels on each side of the column center line.

Colusa sandstone A blue-gray stone of very even grain, quarried in Colusa County, California.

comalong (slang) A tool used to pull materials together to fit-up for welding; capable of six feet of hoist.

comb (1) In carpentry, the ridge of a roof. (2) In masonry, a tool used to give a finish to the face of stone. (3) In house painting, an instrument used for graining surfaces. (4) In plastering, a tool for scratching plaster to give a key for the following coat.

combed joint An angle joint formed by a series of tenons engaging in corresponding slots in carpentry. *(see dovetail)*

combination A term which refers to yarns or fabrics: (1) A combination yarn is composed of two or more yarns having the same or different fibers or twists, e.g., one yarn may have a high twist; the other, little or no twist; (2) A combination fabric is one which uses yarns as described above.

combination doors Doors with an inside removable section so that the same frame serves for both summer and winter protective devices. A screen is inserted in warm weather to make a screen door, and a glazed or a glazed-and-wood-paneled section in winter to make a storm door.

combination fixture A trade term designating an integral combination of one sink and one or two laundry trays in one fixture.

combination man A workman who has skills, or who holds union cards, in two different crafts or trades.

combination plane A universal plane.

combination pliers A pincerlike tool, with long, flat, roughened jaws adjustable for size of opening by means of a slip joint. The inner grip is notched for grasping and holding round objects; the outer grip is scored. The tool is also used for cutting or bending wire.

combination square A tool which combines in handy compact form the equivalent of several tools, including an inside try square, outside try square, mitre square, plumb, level, depth gauge, marking gauge, straight edge, bevel protractor, and center head in addition to square head.

combination tank A combination plumbing tank and cylinder.

combined aggregate grading Particle size distribution of a mixture of fine and coarse aggregate.

combined escutcheon plate Metal plate for a door with both a knob socket and a keyhole.

combined footing A structural unit or assembly of units supporting more than one column load.

combined sewer (combined system) A sewer designed to receive both storm water and sewage.

combined stresses Twisting or bending stresses combined with direct tension or compression stresses.

combined water The water, chemically held as water of crystallization, by the calcium sulphate dihydrate, or hemihydrate crystal.

combing In the shingle roof, a top course which projects somewhat above the ridge from the direction of prevailing winds.

comb roof A double-sloping or gable roof.

combustible liquids Any liquid having a flash point at or above 140°F (60°C) and below 200°F.

combustion Any chemical process that involves oxidation sufficient to produce light or heat.

combustion chamber The drum of firebox of a heating unit where combustion takes place.

come-along (1) A hoe-like tool with a blade about four inches high and 20 inches wide; curved from top to bottom, used for spreading concrete. (2) A colloquial name for a device (load binder) used to tighten chains holding loads in place on a truck bed.

comfort chart A chart showing effective temperatures with dry-bulb temperatures and humidities (and sometimes air motion) by which the effects of various air conditions on human comfort may be compared.

comfort cooling Refrigeration for comfort as opposed to refrigeration for storage or manufacture.

comfort zone (average) The range of effective temperatures over which the majority (50 percent or more) of adults feels comfortable; (extreme). The range of effective temperatures over which one or more adults feels comfortable.

comfort line (comfort zone) The distance from the floor that adults require a constant, comfortable temperature.

comfort station A building, or part of a building, providing toilet facilities for public use.

commercial matching Matching of colors within acceptable tolerances, or with a color variation that is barely detectable to the naked eye.

comminution Progressive reduction in size by crushing, grinding or pulverizing.

comminutor Device at entrance to sewage treatment plant used to reduce solids to minute particles.

commode step A riser curved in plan, usually at the foot of a stairway.

common A line, angle, surface, etc., which belongs equally to several objects.

common bond (running bond) Bond patten in which head joints are staggered or broken in adjacent courses. Sometimes known as American bond.

common duct A duct common to two or more services; a duct common to two or more elevator cars.

common dovetail A dovetail joint with both wooden members showing end grain.

common excavation Soil with boulders less than ½ cubic yard.

common ground A strip of wood solidly fixed to a wall or sub-frame as a base for plaster, cabinetry, sheeting, etc.

common joist Boards set on edge to span a gap between walls; floorboards are nailed directly to them.

common partition A wooden non-load-bearing framed partition consisting of a head and sill joined by vertical studs, strutted apart by short horizontal pieces.

common rafter The rafter that extends past the walls to form the eaves.

common room A central, heated gathering-room in a chapter house, monastery, dormitory or clubhouse.

commons A term describing the ordinary grades of knotty lumber.

common sewer A sewer in which all abutters have equal rights.

common wall The wall between two distinct sections of a building, one-story and two-story section of residence, or between house and attached garage; also known as party wall.

community center In urban planning, the chief location of provision for public, social and sometimes recreational facilities.

compact To reduce in bulk by tamping, rolling, soaking, etc.

compacted volume The volume of the earth after it has been placed in a fill, such as a dam or roadbed, and compacted.

compacted yards Measurement of soil or rock after it has been placed and compacted in a fill.

compacting factor The ratio obtained by dividing the observed weight of concrete which fills a container of standard size and shape when allowed to fall into it under standard conditions of test, by the weight of fully compacted concrete which fills the same container.

compaction (1) The process of inducing a closer packing of the solid particles in freshly mixed concrete or mortar during placement by the reduction of the volume of voids, usually by vibration, tamping or some combination of these actions; also applicable to similar manipulation of other cementitious mixtures, soils, aggregate, or the like. (2) The compression of any material into a smaller volume.

compactor Usually refers to sheepsfoot or mesh-type rollers either pulled by another tractor in gangs or self-propelled. In the case of a self-propelled compactor, the wheels themselves are made to compact; used to compact a fill area.

companion fabrics A fabric that has been printed in the same pattern as that on a wall covering.

companion papers A set of two papers usually designed or colored to coordinate decoration in one room or adjoining rooms. One paper may consist of a large, bold pattern, the other a stripe or other semi-plain effect, both with the same coloring.

comparator An instrument for comparing or measuring comparisons between similar or like things.

compartment A subdivision of enclosed space.

compass (1) In drawing, an instrument with two pointed legs connected by a pivot used to inscribe a circle or an arc. (2) An instrument carrying a magnetic needle which indicates the true north-south direction.

compass brick In masonry, a curved or tapering brick for use in curved work, such as in arches.

compass plane A cutting tool used for smoothing concave or convex surfaces; a plane with an adjustable sole.

compass roof A roof having its rafters bent to the shape of an arc; also, a timber roof in which each truss has its rafters, collar beams and braces combined into an arched form.

compass saw A small handsaw of a special type with a thin tapering blade designed for cutting a small circle or other small opening. Compass saws are often sold in sets called nests.

compass window A bay oriel window.

compatibility A term describing materials such as paints and plasters, which blend perfectly and look well. An incompatible paint mix will be cloudy, coagulating or precipitating pigment. An incompatible film may show pinholing, low adhesion, poor gloss, greasiness or crawling.

compensating diaphram A fitting to a telescope which alters the space between stadia hairs when a sloping sight is made. Thus the horizontal distance of the staff from the surveyor can be directly calculated from the staff intercept.

compensating drive In a four-wheel drive truck, a free wheeling unit in the front propeller shaft that allows the front wheels to go farther than the rear on curves.

compensating error (Accidental error) One of two kinds of error in measurement, the other being systematic.

compensating-rope sheave switch A device which automatically causes the electric power to be removed from the elevator driving-machine motor and brake when the compensating sheave approaches its upper or lower limit of travel.

compensation (1) Payment for services rendered or products or materials furnished or delivered. (2) Payment in satisfaction of claims for damages suffered. (3) The use of ropes or chains to counterbalance the shift in weight of the hoist ropes from the car side to the counterweight side of a hoisting machine, or visa versa, as an elevator car travels.

competent person *(OSHA)* One who is capable of identifying existing and predictable hazards in the surroundings or working conditions which are unsanitary, hazardous or dangerous to employees, and who has authorization to take prompt corrective measures to eliminate them.

completion bond A document given by the contractor to the owner and lending institution to guarantee the work will be completed, and funds will be provided for that purpose.

completion date The date established in the contract documents for substantial completion of the work. *(see date of substantial completion; time of completion)*

completion list *(see inspection list)*

compluvium (1) An opening in the roof above the atrium of an ancient Roman house for the admission of light and air. (2) An area in the center of such a house, so built to receive the waters from the roof; a cistern.

compo (1) Stucco. (2) Lead alloy used in gas pipes for making flexible connections to an appliance.

Compo board Trade name for a type of building board made from strips of wood glued together or from various products formed into board shape; widely used as sheathing, lath, insulation and interior wall surfacing.

compo mortar Composition, as for plastering or stucco-work; lime-cement mortar.

component An industrial product which is manufactured as an independent unit capable of being joined with other building elements to make a whole.

component method A method of building up cost of a residence with component and element costs; detailed method for use by persons experienced in building construction.

Composite The last of the five classical orders, a combination of Corinthian and Ionic devised by the Romans.

composite arch The pointed or lancet arch.

composite column A column in which a steel or cast-iron section is completely encased in concrete containing spiral and longitudinal reinforcement.

composite concrete flexural construction A precast concrete member in cast-in-place reinforced concrete so interconnected that the component elements act together as a flexural unit.

composite construction A type of construction made up of different materials, e.g., concrete and structural steel, or of members produced by different methods, e.g., cast-in-place concrete and precast concrete.

composite masonry Masonry in which at least one wythe has strength or compression characteristics different from the other wythe or wythes and the wythes are adequately bonded together to act as a single structural element.

composite pile A pile made up of different materials, usually concrete and wood or steel fastened together end to end, to form a single pile.

composite sample Sample obtained by blending two or more individual samples of a material.

composition board Panels manufactured by subjecting wood fibers, with

or without binding agents, to heat and pressure.

composition roofing A roofing consisting of asbestos felt saturated with asphalt and assembled with asphalt cement; also called prepared roofing and roll-roofing.

composition shingles Shingles made or formed from composition roofing material.

composition siding A manufactured wall covering often finished in an imitation brick pattern.

composition tile A hard tile surfacing unit made from a mixture of chemicals. The finished surface can be the mixture of chemicals or can be marble chips to create a terrazzo finish. The unit is made hard by the set of the chemicals and the product is not fired as in the manufacture of ceramic tile.

compound (1) Units put together to form a whole. (2) A term often applied to a base coat plaster to which sand is to be added on the job; in some localities the term refers to compound, joint sealing neat goods or to cement plaster. (3) An enclosure, by wall or fence, securing protection and privacy. (4) In electricity, a material used for insulating conductors. (5) A cluster of columns or arches.

compound, joint sealing An impervious material used to fill joints in pavements or structures.

compound plaster A regional term denoting neat calcined gypsum for use in basecoat plasters.

compound, sealing An impervious material applied as a coating or to fill joints or cracks in concrete or mortar. *(see joint sealant)*

compound shake Several types of shakes used in combination.

compound walling Walls constructed in two or more skins of different materials.

compound, waterproofing Material used to impart water repellency to a structure or a constructional unit.

comprehensive services Professional services performed by the architect or engineer in addition to the basic services, in such related areas as project analysis, programming, land use studies, feasibility investigations financing, construction management and special consulting services.

compressed-air disease   Caisson disease; bends.

compression (1) For steel wheel rollers, the compacting effect of the weight at the bottom of the roll, measured in pounds per lineal inch of roll width. (2) A force which tends to shorten a member; the opposite of a tension. (3) In a compression refrigeration system, a process by which the pressure of the refrigerant is increased.

compression efficiency   Ratio of work required to compress, adiabatically and reversibly, all the vapor delivered by a compressor (per stage) to the actual work delivered to the vapor by the piston or blades of the compressor.

compression flange   The widened portion of an I, T, or similar cross section beam which is shortened or compressed by bending under normal loads, such as the horizontal portion of the cross section of a simple span T-beam.

compression-ignition engine   A diesel engine as opposed to a spark ignition engine. Ignition of fuel occurs from high temperatures created by compression of the fuel and air.

compression ratio   The ratio of the volume of space above a piston at the bottom of its stroke to the volume above the piston at the top of its stroke.

compression reinforcement   Reinforcement designed to carry compressive stresses.

compression roll (drive roll)   The drive wheel of a steel-wheel roller.

compression set   Caused when wood strips or parquet slats expand so tightly that the cells along the edge of adjoining pieces of the floor are crushed. This causes them to lose their resiliency, creating cracks when the floor returns to its normal moisture content.

compression system   Refrigerating system in which the pressure imposing element is mechanically operated.

compression test   Test made on a test specimen of clay, mortar or concrete to determine the compressive strength; in the United States, unless otherwise specified, compression tests of mortars are made on two inch (5 cm) cubes and compression tests of concrete are made on cylinders six inches (15 cm) in diameter and 12 inches (30 cm) high.

compressive strength   The measured maximum resistance of a concrete or mortar specimen to axial loading; expressed as force per unit cross-sectional area; or the specified resistance used in design calculations; in United States expressed in pounds per square inch (psi) and designated fc.

compressor   A machine for compressing air or other gases, such as used in come cooling systems.

computer (Date processing system)   Aggregate of electronic equipment to which information may be fed(input) and processed through previously programmed instructions for arithmetical procedures, and which delivers the results of these calculations (outputs). Analog computers translate mathematical equations into physical (electric) quantities for solution of the problems, similar to a slide rule. In digital computers the mathematical quantities are represented by symbols or counters. Business computers produce solutions to problems of cost accounting, orders, shipments, billing, inventory, warehousing, payroll, and preventive maintenance. Process computers (production line control) receive input of process variables from sensing instruments and, based on mathematical models actuate control devices to produce or maintain intended temperature, load, pressure, draft, flow, speed, composition, fineness, etc.

concave   A curved recess hollowed out like the inner curve of a circle or sphere; the interior of a curved surface or line; a bowl-shaped depression.

concave bead   In glazing, a bead of

compound with a concave exposed surface.

concave joint A mortar joint, hollowed by pushing a bar along it while it is green. *(see jointing)*

concavex Grinding balls characterized by surface indentations which produce both concave and convex areas in the surface.

concealed gutter In building, a gutter which is constructed in such a manner that it cannot be seen.

concealed heating *(see panel heating)*

concealed nailing Secret nailing; toe nailing.

concentrated load The weight localized on, and carried by, a beam, girder or other supporting structural part.

concentration A number specifying the composition of a solution with respect to the constituent names, as lb of salt per gal of brine.

concentrating collectors A focusing or concentrating collector is a solar collector that contains mirrors, reflectors or refractors which concentrate the solar energy falling on the aperture onto an absorber plate of smaller surface area than the aperture. This type collector achieves high temperatures but can utilize only direct solar radiation.

concentric circles Circles having common centers.

concha (1) The half-dome of an apse. (2) The concave, ribless surface of a pendentive.

concordant tendons Tendons in statically indeterminate structures which are coincident with the pressure line produced by the tendons; such tendons do not produce secondary moments.

concrete A composite material which consists essentially of a binding medium within which are embedded particles or fragments of aggregate; in portland cement concrete, the binder is a mixture of portland cement and water. When set it attains hardness and strength not unlike stone.

aerated (see foamed concrete)

colloidal (see colloidal concrete)

dense Concrete containing a minimum of voids.

dry-packed (see dry-packed concrete)

fat A concrete containing a large proportion of mortar.

field Concrete delivered or mixed, placed and cured on the job site.

foamed Concrete made very light and cellular by the addition of a prepared form or by generation of gas within the unhardened mixture.

granolithic (see granolithic concrete)

green Concrete which has set but not appreciably hardened.

heavy (see heavy concrete)

high-density (see high-density concrete)

in-situ (cast-in-place) Concrete which is deposited in the place where it is required to harden as part of the structure, as opposed to precast concrete.

lean (see lean concrete)

lightweight (see lightweight concrete)

mass (see mass concrete)

monolithic (see monolithic concrete)

no-fines (see no-fines concrete)

normal-weight Concrete having a unit weight of approximately 150 pounds per cubic foot (2400 kg per cubic meter) made with aggregates of normal weight.

no-slump (see no-slump concrete)

plain Concrete without reinforcement, or reinforced only for shrinkage or temperature changes.

precast (see precast)

preplaced-aggregate Concrete produced by placing coarse aggregate in a form and later injecting a portland cement-sand grout, usually with admixtures, to fill the voids.

prestressed (see prestressed concrete)

ready-mixed (see ready-mixed concrete)

refractory (see refractory concrete)

reinforced (see reinforced concrete)

spun (see spun concrete)

structural lightweight Structural concrete made with lightweight aggregate; the unit weight usually is in the range of 90 to 115 pounds per cubic foot (1440 to 1850 kg per cubic meter).

transit-mixed   (see transit-mixed concrete)

translucent   A combination of glass and concrete used together in precast or prestressed panels.

vacuum   (see vacuum concrete)

vibrated   (see vibrated concrete)

concrete bent construction   A system of construction in which precast concrete bent framing units are the basic load-bearing members; a concrete bent consists of a vertical and horizontal load-bearing member which is cast in one piece and designed on the cantilever principle.

concrete block (cement block)   A hollow building block, usually 8″ × 8″ × 16″, formed of cast concrete.

concrete breaker   A compressed air tool specially designed and constructed to break up concrete; a jack hammer.

concrete brick   A solid concrete masonry unit made from water, portland cement and suitable aggregates with or without the inclusion of other materials, usually not larger than 4 × 4 × 12 inches.

concrete curing blanket   Insulated blanket for winter concrete curing.

concrete curing compounds   Compounds which provide a water-impervious film over the surface of the concrete.

concrete curing mats   Burlap mats laid on fresh concrete, the mats are wetted and retain moisture for better curing.

concrete finishing machine   A machine mounted on flanged wheel which rides on the forms or on specially set tracks, used to finish surfaces such as those of pavements; or a portable power driven machine for floating and finishing of floors and other slabs.

concrete masonry unit   A solid or hollow masonry unit made from water, portland cement, and suitable aggregates such as sand, gravel, crushed stone, bituminous or anthracite cinder, expanded clay or shale, pumice, volcanic scoria, aircooled or expanded blast furnace slag, with or without other materials and molded into various shapes. *(see block)*

architectural concrete masonry unit   A solid or hollow unit with special treatment to the exposed surfaces to provide a specified appearance in the wall. Also called a customized concrete masonry unit. Often given a name which reflects the treatment such as a split face concrete masonry unit or ribbed concrete masonry unit.

hollow concrete masonry unit   A concrete masonry unit whose net cross-sectional area in every plane parallel to the bearing surface is less than 75 percent of the gross cross-sectional area in the same plane.

solid concrete masonry unit   A concrete masonry unit whose net cross-sectional area in every plane parallel to the bearing surface is 75 percent or more of its cross-sectional area measured in the same plane.

structural   Concrete used to carry structural load or to form an integral part of a structure; concrete of a quality specified for structural use; concrete used solely for protective cover, fill, or insulation is not considered structural concrete.

concrete mixer   A metal drum of several cubic yards capacity which can be revolved to mix the ingredients of concrete; usually motor driven.

concrete nail   A hard square cut nail for fixing to brick or concrete.

concrete paint   A specially prepared thin paint, consisting of a mixture of cement and water, applied to the surface of a concrete wall to give it a uniform finish and to protect the joints against weathering by rain or snow.

concrete paver   A concrete mixer, usually mounted on crawler tracks, which mixes and places concrete pavement on the subgrade.

concrete pavement   A layer of concrete over such areas as roads, sidewalks, airfields, canals, playgrounds, and those used for storage or parking.

concrete pile   A precast reinforced or

prestressed concrete pile driven into the ground by a pile driver or otherwise placed. *(see cast-in-place pile)*

concrete pipe Pipe made of concrete, varying in capacity from 3 inches to several feet, porous for use as underground and storm drains; capable of withstanding considerable water pressure.

concrete pump An apparatus which forces concrete to the placing position through a pipeline or hose. *(see pumped concrete)*

concrete spreader A machine usually carried on side-forms or on rails parallel thereto, designed to spread concrete, from heaps already dumped in front of it, or to receive and spread concrete in a uniform layer.

concrete terrazzo Marble-aggregate concrete that is cast-in-place or precast and ground smooth for decorated surfacing purposes on floors and walls.

concrete vibrating machine A machine, commonly carried on side forms or on parallel rails, which compacts a layer of freshly mixed concrete by vibration.

concrete wall In building construction, any wall made of reinforced concrete such as a basement wall.

concussion Shock or sharp air waves caused by an explosion or heavy blow.

condemn (1) To sieze, by public authority and for public benefit, property of an individual, making due recompense. (2) To declare unfit for use.

condensate The liquid formed by condensation of a vapor. In steam heating, water condensed from steam; in air conditioning, water extracted from air, as by condensation on the cooling coil of a refrigeration machine.

condensation (1) The conversion of moisture in air to water, as on the warm-room side of a cold wall; the forming of water on a surface can usually be prevented by insulating the inner wall so that its surface is kept warmer. (2) Cure of a synthetic resin. (3) The process of changing a vapor into liquid by the extraction of heat. Condensation of steam or water vapor is effected in either steam condensers or dehumidifying coils and the resulting water is called condensate.

condensing refrigerating effect The condensing heat added to the refrigerant vapor in the refrigerant compressor unit.

condensation groove Part of the sheath of a lead-clothed glazing bar projecting under the glass to catch water and channel it to the condensation gutter at the foot of the pane.

condenser (1) An apparatus for storing, or intensifying, an electric charge. (2) An apparatus for reducing vapor to a liquid. (3) An apparatus for compressing air. (4) A heat exchanger in which the refrigerant, compressed to a suitable pressure, is condensed by rejection of heat to an appropriate external cooling medium.

conditioned space Space, within a building, which is provided with a positive heat supply or a positive method of cooling.

conditions of the bid Conditions set forth in the instructions to bidders, the notice to bidders or advertisement for bids, the invitation to bidders or other similar documents, prescribing the conditions under which bids are to be prepared, executed, submitted, received and accepted.

conditions of the contract Those portions of the contract documents which define, set forth or relate to: contract terminology; the rights and responsibilities of the contracting parties and of others involved in the work; requirements for safety and for compliance with laws and regulations; general procedures for the orderly prosecution and management of the work; payments to the contractor; and similar provisions of a general, non-technical nature. The conditions of the contract include general conditions and supplementary conditions.

conduction The transmission of heat by the passage of energy from particle to particle is called conduction.

conductive mortar A tile mortar to which specific electrical conductivity is imparted through the use of conductive additives.

conductive tile   Tile made from special body compositions or by methods that result in specific properties of electrical conductivity while retaining other normal physical properties of ceramic tile.

conductivity (K-value)   The ability of a material to carry an electrical charge from a point of high potential to a point of lower potential. The carrier of the charge in metals is the electron. In aqueous solutions ions are the carriers. Dissolved salts increase the conductivity of aqueous solutions. Therefore, the conductivity is a measure of the amount of ionized salts in the solution.

conductor   (1) A pipe to carry rain water to the ground or storm sewer; also called leader or downspout. (2) A substance with a high conductivity for heat, electricity or other energy; a wire or cable used for leading power from the supply to the consumer. (3) A lightning conductor.

conduit   (1) A natural or artificial channel for carrying fluids, as water pipes, canals and aqueducts. (2) A tube, or trough, for receiving and protecting electric wires. (3) A long narrow passage between two walls.

conduit box   An electrical distribution box.

conduit layout sheet   Engineering drawings describing the conduit, flex, fittings, etc., necessary for a particular installation.

cone bolt   A form of tie rod for wall forms with cones at each end inside the forms so that a bolt can act as a spreader as well as a tie.

cone crusher   Crusher which operates by use of two concentric cones, one of which gyrates.

cone of depression   The dried up area of soil around a single underground suction point.

cone penetrometer   Instrument used to determine the consistency of masonry mortar in the field for correlation with laboratory mixes.

confined concrete   Concrete containing closely-spaced special transverse reinforcement which is provided to restrain the concrete in directions perpendicular to the applied stresses.

conge   A British term for quarter round.

conglomerate   Rock composed of rounded fragments, varying in size from boulder to pebble in cement-like clay.

conical light   A skylight built up from glazing bars and flat panes of glass. It is shaped like a many-sided pyramid.

conical mill   A rod mill in which the conical head facilitates uniform entrance of feed, permitting maximum grinding efficiency at highest rates allowable.

conical roll (batten roll)   In preparation for flexible metal roofing, a roll joint formed over a triangular wood roll.

Connecticut brownstone   One of the first building stones to be widely used in America; fine grain, even texture, of a uniform, warm brown.

connection   in   parallel   System whereby flow is divided among two or more channels from a common starting point or header.

connecting rod   A device connecting the piston to a crank and used to change rotating motion into reciprocating motion, or vice versa, as from rotating crankshaft to reciprocating piston.

connecting wire   An insulated expendable wire used between electric blasting caps and the leading wires or between the bus wire and the leading wires.

connector   *(slang)* Iron work which connects red iron.

conoid   A cone-shaped geometrical figure or solid.

consent of surety   Written consent of the surety on a performance bond and/or labor and material payment bond to such contract changes as change orders or reductions in the contractor's retainage, or to final payment, or to waiving notification of contract changes. The term is also used with respect to an extension of time in a bid bond.

conservation of energy The principle which assumes that energy can be neither created nor destroyed.

conservatory A room which, in its abundance of glazed openings and provision for artificial heat, is suited to the growing of plant life.

consistency A term literally denoting the fluidity or viscosity of a plaster mortar or cementitious paste. The term is often used to denote the quantity of water required to bring a given quantity of dry cementitious material or mixture of cementitious material and aggregate to a given state of fluidity.

consistency factor A measure of grout fluidity roughly analogous to viscosity, which describes the ease with which grout may be pumped into pores or fissures; usually a laboratory measurement in which consistency is reported in degrees of rotation of a torque viscosimeter in a specimen of grout.

consistency index The ratio of the difference between the liquid limit and the natural water content to the difference between the liquid limit and the plastic limit.

consistency limits (Atterberg limits) The liquid limit, plastic limit, shrinkage limit, and sticky limit of a clay; all descriptive of the water content of clay in certain conditions.

consistometer An apparatus for measuring the consistency of cement pastes, mortars, grouts or concretes.

console In architecture, any bracket, or bracket-like support usually ornamented by a reverse scroll; an ornamental bracket-like support for a cornice or bust; any ornamental bracket-like architectural member used as a support.

consolidation Compaction of freshly placed concrete or mortar to minimum practical volume, usually by vibration, centrifugation, tamping, or some combination of these, to mold it within forms or molds and around embedded parts and reinforcement, and to eliminate voids other than entrained air. (*see compaction*)

consolidation settlement The settlement of loaded clay over a period of years; sometimes accelerated by vertical sand drains. The leaning Tower of Pisa is an example of unequal consolidation settlement.

consolidation test Method of determining coefficient of permeability of soils.

constant A quality or factor that does not vary.

constant head feeder A raw meal or slurry feeder equipped with supply tank and overflow to assure a constant fluid pressure at the feeder.

constant head permeameter Apparatus and method of determining the permeability of soils.

constant pressure control A type of elevator control where the elevator runs up only when the "UP" button is pressed, and vice versa, and stops when pressure is removed from the button.

constriction A narrowing of the free path of flow such as a dam in a kiln.

construct To put together parts in building.

construction (1) The process of assembling material and building a structure; that which is constructed of various elements. (2) A service industry whose primary responsibility is to convert plans and specification into a finished project.

brick A type of construction in which the exterior wall are bearing walls made of brick or a combination of brick and tile masonry.

brick-veneer A type of construction in which a wood frame construction has an exterior surface of brick applied.

composite Construction consisting of cast-in-place reinforced concrete and members made of some other material so interconnected that the component elements act together as a unit.

drywall A type of construction in which the interior wall finish is of a material other than plaster or material similar to it, applied without the use of mortar.

exterior protected A type of building construction in which the exterior walls, party walls and the fire walls are of incombustible materials, self-supporting, and the interior structure framing is wholly or partly of wood or similar materials.

fireproof A type of construction designed to withstand a complete burnout of the contents for which the structure was intended without the impairment of structural integrity.

frame A type of construction in which the structural parts are of wood or dependent upon a wood frame for support.

incombustible A type of building construction which has all structural elements of incombustible materials with fire-resistance ratings of one hour or less.

ordinary Usually refers to construction in which the exterior walls are of masonry or of reinforced concrete and in which the interior structural elements are wholly or partly of wood.

prefabricated A type of construction so designed as to involve a minimum of assembly at the site, usually comprising a series of large units or panels manufactured in a factory.

rammed earth A type of construction in which the exterior walls are bearing walls composed of a controlled combination of sand, clay, coarse aggregate and moisture compacted by pressure into forms.

reinforced concrete A type of construction in which the principal structural members, such as floors, columns and beams, are made of concrete poured around isolated steel bars or steel meshwork in such a manner that the two materials act together in resisting force.

skeleton A type of construction in which all external and internal loads and stresses are transmitted to the foundations by a rigidly connected framework of metal or reinforced concrete; the enclosing walls are supported by the frame at designated intervals, usually at each story.

steel frame A type of construction in which the structural parts are of steel or dependent on a steel frame for support.

unprotected metal A type of construction in which the structural parts are of metal unprotected by fireproofing.

construction cost The cost of all of the construction portions of a project, generally based upon the sum of the construction contract(s) and other direct construction costs. Construction cost does not include the compensation paid to the architect and engineer and consultants, the cost of the land, rights-of-way or other costs which are defined in the contract documents as being the responsibility of the owner.

construction documents Working drawings and specifications.

construction documents phase The third phase of the architect's basic services. in this phase the architect prepares from the approved design development documents, for approval by the owner, the working drawings and specifications and the necessary bidding information. In this phase the architect also assists the owner in the preparation of bidding forms, the conditions of the contract and the form of agreement between the owner and the contractor.

construction inspector *(see project representative)*

construction joint The surface where two successive placements of concrete meet; frequently with a keyway or reinforcement across the joint. *(see lift joint)*

construction loads The loads to which a permanent or temporary structure is subjected during construction.

construction management (CM) A project delivery system that differs from the traditional design-bid-build system by utilizing the services of a construction manager who becomes a member of the team of owner-architect-construction manager. The manager's role is to coordinate and communicate the entire project process utilizing his skill and knowledge of construction to clarify cost and time consequences of design decisions as well as their construction feasibility; and to manage the bidding, award and construction phases of the project. The project owner's objective in utilizing construction management is to minimize project time and cost while maintaining quality, function and aesthetics.

construction management contract An arrangement wherein responsibilities for coordination and accomplishment of project planning, design and construction are given to a single construction firm. Usually, a contractor serves as part of a building team consisting of himself, the owner and an architect/engineer.

construction phase — administration of the construction contract The fifth and final phase of the architect's services, which includes the architect's general administration of the construction contract(s). *(see contract administration)*

construction surveys Surveys executed to locate or lay out engineering works.

constructor An individual who, through education and experience, is capable of implementing significant facets of construction on a timely and economical basis with proficiency and integrity.

consultant An individual or organization engaged by the owner, the architect or the engineer, to render professional consulting services complementing or supplementing the architect's or engineer's services.

consulting engineer A person retained to give expert advice in regard to all engineering problems; an experienced engineer of high rating in his profession.

continuity The terminology given to a structural system denoting the transfer of loads and stresses from member to member, as if there were no connection. **(1)** The continuous effective contact of all parts of an electrical circuit to give it high conductance (low resistance). **(2)** The joining of floors to beams, of beams to other beams and columns so effectively that they bend together under load and so strengthen each other. This is easily done in concrete or welded steel, less so in other materials.

contract aerator A device consisting of a crate holding broken stone, coke, brushwood or other media which is placed in a single or two story sedimentation tank and through which the sewage is made to flow upward and return on the outside and become activated by the admission of compressed air below.

contract bed In sewage treatment, a bacteria bed.

contract breaker An electric switch actuated by overload.

contact ceiling A ceiling which is secured in direct contact with the construction above without use of furring.

contract pressure Pressure acting at and perpendicular to the contact area between footing and soil, produced by the weight of the footing and all forces acting on it.

contact print A print on light-sensitive paper, made by placing a drawing in opaque ink or pencil on transparent paper in contact with the light-sensitive paper and exposing them to light for a given period of time. *(see blueprint)*

contact splice A means of connecting reinforcing bars in which the bars are lapped and in direct contact. *(see lap splice)*

containment grouting *(see perimeter grouting)*

contaminant Unwanted matter in what otherwise would be a pure material.

contingency allowance A sum designated to cover unpredictable or unforseen items of work or changes subsequently required by the owner.

contingent agreement An agreement, generally between an owner and an architect or engineer, in which some portion of the architect's or engineer's compensation is contingent upon the owner's obtaining funds for the project, such as by successful referendum, sale of bonds or securing of other financing, or upon some other specially prescribed condition.

continuous beam A timber that rests on more than two supporting members of a structure.

continuous filament Continuous strand of synthetic fiber extruded in yarn form, without the need for spinning which all natural fibers require.

continuous filter A type of bacteria bed in sewage treatment.

continuous footing A combined footing of prismatic or truncated shape, supporting two or more columns in a row.

continuous grading A particle size distribution in which all intermediate size fractions are present, as opposed to gap-grading.

continuous header The top plate replaced by 2x6's turned on edge and running around the entire structure. This header is strong enough to act as lintel over all wall openings, eliminating some cutting and fitting of stud lengths and separate headers over openings; this is especially important because of the emphasis on one story, open planning houses.

continuously reinforced pavement A pavement without transverse joints,except tied construction joints placed between successive days concreting, with sufficient longitudinal reinforcement, adequately lapped to develop tensile continuity, so that transverse cracks will be held tightly closed.

continuous mixer A mixer into which the ingredients of the mixture are fed without stopping, and from which the mixed product is discharged in a continuous stream.

continuous slab A slab or beam which extends as a unit over three or more supports in a given direction.

continuous stave pipe A pipe of wooden staves held together by encircling bands; the assembly is made in the field.

continuous string An outer string continued around a stairwell, usually under a continuous handrail.

continuous vent A vertical vent that is a continuation of the drain to which it connects. *(see vent pipe)*

continuous waste Waste from two or more fixtures connected to a single trap.

continuous-waste-and-vent A vent that is a continuation of and in a straight line with the drain to which it connects. A continuous-waste-and-vent is further defined by the angle made by the drain and vent at the point of connection with the horizontal; for example, vertical continuous-waste-and-vent, 45° continuous-waste-and-vent, and flat continuous-waste-and-vent.

contour Outline of a figure or mass of land; the face of a molding or other outline of a solid.

contour line A level line crossing a slope. On a land map denoting elevations, a line connecting points with the same elevation.

contract The written agreement executed between an owner, a department or agency and the successful bidder, covering the performance of the work and the furnishing of labor and materials by which the contractor is bound to perform the work and furnish the labor and materials, and by which the owner, department or agency is obligated to compensate him therefor at the mutually established and accepted rate or price. *(see agreement)*

contract administration The duties and responsibilities of the architect and engineer during the construction phase.

contract bond The approved form of security, executed by a contractor or subcontractor and his surety or sureties, guaranteeing complete execution of the contract and all supplemental agreements pertaining thereto and for the payment of all legal debts pertaining to the construction of the project.

contract date *(see date of agreement)*

contract documents The owner-contractor agreement, the conditions of the contract (general, supplementary and other conditions), the drawings, the specifications, all addenda issued prior to execution of the contract, all modifications thereto, and any other items specifically stipulated as being included in the contract documents.

contracted weir A restricted structure across a stream or ditch for diverting or measuring the flow of water.

contracting officer The person designated as an official representative of the owner with specific authority to act in his behalf in connection with a project.

contraction joint A plane, usually vertical, separating concrete in a structure or pavement, at a designed location such as to interfere least with performance of the structure, but so as to prevent formation of objectionable shrinkage cracks elsewhere in the concrete.

contraction-joint grouting Injection of grout into contraction joints.

contraction of concrete (expansion) The sum of volume changes occurring as the result of all processes affecting the bulk volume of a mass of concrete. *(see shrinkage)*

contract item (pay item) An item of work specifically described and for which a price, either unit or lump sum, is provided. It includes the performance of all work and the furnishing of all labor, equipment and materials described in the text of a specification item included in the contract or described in any subdivision of the text of the supplemental specifications or special provisions of the contract.

contract limit A limit line or perimeter line established on the drawings or elsewhere in the contract documents defining the boundaries of the site available to the contractor for construction purposes.

contractor The individual, firm or corporation undertaking the execution of the work under the terms of the contract and acting directly or through its agents or employees; a person or company who agrees to furnish materials and labor to do work for a certain price.

contractor's affidavit A certified statement of the contractor, properly notarized, relating to payment of debts and claims, release of liens or similar matter requiring specific evidence for the protection of the owner. *(see non-collusion affidavit)*

contractor's option A provision of the contract documents under which the contractor may select certain specified materials, methods of systems at his own option, without change in the contract sum.

contract overrun (underrun) The difference between the original contract price, including adjustments by change order, and the final completed cost.

contract payment bond The security furnished by the contractor to guarantee the payment to all persons supplying labor and materials in the prosecution of the work in accordance with the terms of the contract.

contract performance bond The security furnished by the contractor to guarantee the completion of the work in accordance with the terms of the contract.

contract period The period from the specified date that the specified number of working days or calendar days, as the case may be, has elapsed; or from the specified date of commencing work to the specified date of completion, as specified in the contract.

contract sum The price stated in the owner-contractor agreement, which is the total amount payable by the owner to the contractor for the performance of the work under the contract documents. The contract sum can be adjusted only by change order.

contract time The period of time established in the contract documents within which the work must be completed; usually set out in working days or calendar days. The contract time can be adjusted by time extensions through change orders.

contractual liability Liability assumed by a party under a contract. An indemnification or hold harmless clause is an example of contractual liability.

contraflexure When stress is placed on

a rigid frame member, an S-curve bend results. The portion of the S-curve which is opposite to the direction of the inflected stress is contraflexure.

control (1) Any device for regulation of a system or component in normal operation, manual or automatic. If automatic, the implication is that it is responsive to changes of pressure, temperature or other property whose magnitude is to be regulated. (2) The system governing the starting, stopping, direction of motion, acceleration, speed and retardation of the moving member.

control, generator-field A system of control which is accomplished by the use of an individual generator for each elevator or dumbwaiter wherein the voltage applied to the driving-machine motor is adjusted by varying the strength and direction of the generator field.

control, multi-voltage A system of control which is accomplished by impressing successively on the armature of the driving-machine motor a number of substantially fixed voltages such as may be obtained from multi-commutator generators common to a group of elevators.

control, rheostatic A system of control which is accomplished by varying resistance and/or reactance in the armature and/or field circuit of the driving-machine motor.

control, single speed alternating current A control for a driving-machine induction motor which is arranged to run at a single speed.

control, two speed alternating current A control for a two-speed driving-machine induction motor which is arranged to run at two different synchronous speeds by connecting the motor windings so as to obtain different numbers of poles.

control factor The ratio of the minimum compressive strength to the average compressive strength.

control flume An open conduit or arti-ficial channel arranged for measuring the flow of water.

control joint Formed, sawed or tooled groove in a concrete structure to regulate the location and amount of cracking and separation resulting from the dimensional change of different parts of a structure so as to avoid the development of high stresses.

control joint block Concrete masonry units used to facilitate construction of vertical shear-type control joints.

control-joint grouting *(see contraction-joint grouting)*

controlled atmosphere storage (gas storage) Artificial addition of carbon dioxide to the atmosphere, particularly in large concentration, with no attempt to regulate the amount of oxygen.

controlled concrete Concrete for which working stresses are based on the ultimate strength; the mix is designed by preliminary trials and tests to give the ultimate strength desired.

controller A device which functions to automatically keep a process variable within a chosen range of values.

control rods Neutron absorbing material, usually boron or cadmium, which is inserted into the reactor core to control the number of fissions taking place. When the rods are inserted far enough, they absorb neutrons faster than they are formed and the chain reaction dies out.

control survey A survey made to establish the horizontal or vertical positions of arbitrary points.

control valve A regulating valve.

convection (1) The vertical transport of warm air from the earth's surface. Or, the transport of warm water upward through a body of cold water. (2) Heat travel by the movement of fluid currents is called convection. It is partly for this reason that transparent cover plates are placed over the absorber plate, to reduce the loss of heat by convection to moving air currents.

convector An electric hot water or steam heating room unit.

convector radiator Type of heating in

which steam or hot water runs through a pipe core, heating metal plates or fins attached to it at short intervals; air passed over these fins picks up heat and distributes it through vents in an enclosure to the area to be heated.

convent A building for the use of a group of nuns.

conventional design Design procedure using moments or stresses determined by widely accepted methods.

conventional engine (Otto cycle) The type of engine originally used in automobiles, trucks and tractors; of four cycle type, using a carburetor for mixing fuel and spark plugs for ignition.

conventional installation Method of installing ceramic tile with portland cement mortar.

conversion (1) A short conduit for uniting two others having different hydraulic elements. (2) A transition as in the reduction of lumber.

conversion burner A gas or oil burner designed for installation in a heating unit that was originally meant to use another fuel.

conversion factor A number enabling the units of one system to be readily transformed into corresponding units of another system.

converter (Bessemer converter) Furnace used in the Bessemer steelmaking process.

convertibility The adaptability of a heating unit to change from one fuel to another.

convex bead In glazing, a bead of compound with a convex exposed surface.

conveying hose (see delivery hose)

conveyor A device for moving materials; usually a continuous belt, an articulated system of buckets, a confined screw, or a pipe through which material is moved by air or water.

apron One or more endless chains carrying overlapping or interlocking plates that carry bulk material on their upper surface.

decline A conveyor that transports downhill.

feeder A short conveyor belt that supplies material to a long belt.

screw A revolving shaft fitted with auger-type flights that moves bulk materials through a trough or tube.

conveyor belt An endless belt of rubber-covered fabric that transports materials on its upper surface.

convolute To twist, coil, roll or wind materials together with one part upon another.

cookie (slang) 1. Concrete masonry unit. 2. Pertain to clay tile - the cover for the tile opening.

cookie cutter (slang) A steel caisson with a circular base; floated into position like a huge barge and sunk all the way to bedrock to make a base for a bridge pier.

cooler nail A nail with special size and head configuration for use in gypsum board applications.

cooling (heating) air-conditioning unit A specific air treating combination consisting of means for ventilation, air circulation, air cleaning, and heat transfer, with control means for cooling (or heating).

cooling coil An arrangement of pipe or tubing which transfers heat from air to a refrigerant or brine.

cooling element Heat transfer surface containing refrigerating fluid in location where refrigerating effect is desired.

cooling medium Any substance whose temperature is such that it is used, with or without a change of state, to lower the temperature of other bodies or substances.

cooling of air Reduction in air temperature due to the abstraction of heat as a result of contact with a medium held at a temperature lower than that of the air. Cooling may be accompanied by moisture addition (evaporation), by moisture extraction (dehumidification), or by no change whatever of moisture content.

cooling pond A large body of water that loses heat from its surface, largely by evaporation but also by convection and radiation.

cooling range In a water cooling device, the difference between the average temperature of the water entering the device, and the average temperature of the water leaving it.

cooling tower (1) A device usually placed outdoors for cooling the water used in an air conditioning condenser so that it may be re-used, thus conserving water. (2) A sizable structure through which heated water is circulated. This water is cooled by heat transfer and evaporation into a stream of air which is moved through the tower by mechanical draft or convective means.

cooling unit A refrigeration coil that can be installed in the ductwork of a forced air heating system for summer cooling.

cooling water Water used for condensation of refrigerant; condenser water.

cool white Flourescent lamp whiter than filament lamp; blends well with daylight.

cooperative apartment house One in which ownership of the individual apartments is held by different people, usually stockholders in a corporation that holds title to the property.

coordinates Measured distances from fixed straight lines which intersect at the origin. The purpose of coordinates is to locate a point. The system invented by Descartes, using Cartesian coordinates, is the most commonly used surveying system.

copal A resin from several tropical trees, used in varnishes.

cope (1) To dress or notch. (2) To cut a structural steel member so that another member may be fitted against it. (3) To join two molded strips at an angle by fitting one over the other, instead of mitering. (4) To cover a wall with stones, bricks or precast slabs which usually overhang as a protection to the wall from rain.

coped joint The seam, or juncture, between molded pieces in which a portion of one piece is cut away to receive the molded part of the other piece. *(see scribe)*

coping (1) The cap or top course of a wall, usually of stone, set to shed water. (2) Splitting stones by drilling and driving in wedges along the drill line.

coping block A solid concrete masonry unit for use as the top and finishing course in wall construction.

coping saw Narrow blade in a U frame to cut curved outlines.

coping stone A brick, stone or concrete weather protection for the top of a wall.

copper One of the metallic elements. A reddish, extremely ductile metal; used for wire, flashing, eave gutter, downspouts, etc.

copper bit A soldering iron used in plumbing work.

copper fittings Fittings for copper tubing, many of them not made of copper, but of brass or gunmetal. The two main types are compression and capillary joints. Capillary fittings, often of copper, must be completed by heat. Compression fittings are completed by tightening screw threads.

copper glazing Copper cames welded together. *(see electro-copper glazing)*

copper pipe Pipe used for plumbing service in buildings.

copper plating (1) A film of copper deposited by electrical, immersion, or other means on the surface of another material such as iron or steel; in refrigeration usually on compressor walls, pistons, discharge valves, and shaft or seal. (2) Copper electroplating providing a protective finish to steel nails, wood screws, wire, etc.

coppersmith's hammer Hammer with a long, bent ball peen, used for beating copper.

copper water tube Seamless copper tube of certain standard sizes, in straight lengths and coils, used with flared or soldered joints for the conveyance of gases and liquids.

copper welding Fusion welding copper materials.

coquina ½ to ⅝-inch sea shells bound

along present or former saltwater shorelines; used as calcareous raw material. The shells are firmly cemented together and are used as building material in Florida.

corbel (1) A piece of wood, stone or brick projecting from the face of a wall to form a support for a timber or other weight; a bracket-like support; a stepping out of courses in a wall to form a ledge; one of a series of brackets, often ornamental, projecting from the face of a wall. (2) A corbeling iron.

corbeling Courses of masonry set out beyond the face of a wall in order to form a self-supporting projection.

corbeling iron Metal supports built into brickwork to carry a wall plate instead of corbeling the brickwork out.

corbel out To build out one or more courses of brick or stone from the face of a wall, to form a support for timbers.

corbel table A range of corbels supporting a superstructure or upper moldings, commonly used beneath a spire or parapet or below the eaves line.

cordon A string course.

Cordova Pink A coarse-grain, deep pink granite, mottled with black; quarried in Llano County, Texas.

corduroy (1) A road made of logs laid at right angles to the center line of the road, on the ground or on other logs. (2) *(slang)* Used to describe a bumpy, badly rutted road.

core (1) The soil material enclosed within a tubular pile after driving; it may be replaced with concrete. (2) The mandrel used for driving casings for cast-in-place piles. (3) That portion of a reinforced concrete column inside the center line of the principal reinforcement. (4) A cylindrical sample of hardened concrete or rock obtained by means of a core drill. (5) The molded open space in a concrete masonry unit. (6) The impervious center of an earth-fill dam or other embankment. (7) In electricity, a conductor within a cable including its insulation. (8) A cut-off wall of clay, concrete or other material. (9) The brick core below a relieving arch. (10) In plastering, the base to a

cornice or other complicated work. It may be bracketing, hollow core, or a mass of reinforced coarse stuff, solid core. (11) In plywood, the innermost portion, also referred to as the center. (12) The inner material of a veneered door. (13) A combination of utilities, sometimes including elevators, for the central stem of a building.

core area The total plane area of the portion of a grille, face, or register, bounded by a line tangent to the outer edges of the outer openings through which air can pass.

coreboard A gypsum board product normally 1″ thick or less either laminated or homogenous. Usually manufactured in 24″ widths and lengths as per job requirements. May have either square, rounded or tongue and groove edges.

core box A large wooden box, divided by partitions into narrow strips. It holds the cores from a borehole in the order in which they were extracted.

core catcher a steel spring for keeping samples of sand from falling out of a soil sampler.

core cutter (core lifter) An attachment at the foot of the core barrel which grips the core and breaks it at the root when the core is withdrawn for examination; a soil sampler; a rotary drill for cutting a cylinder from a road for test purposes.

cored beam A beam whose cross section is partially hollow, or a beam from which cored samples of concrete have been taken.

cored hole A hole cast by leaving a core in a concrete, metal or plastic piece. The core is removed shortly after the material is poured, leaving a neat hole.

core drill A rotary drill equipped with a hollow bit and core lifter.

core pool The center of a hydraulically filled earth dam.

core separation A split in the gypsum core often accompanying an over calcined condition.

core test Compression test on a concrete sample cut from hardened concrete by means of a core drill.

core wall A wall of masonry, sheet piling or puddled clay built inside a dam or embankment to reduce percolation.

coring (1) The act of obtaining cores from concrete structures or rock foundations. (2) After parging a flue, the removal of loose parge with a bundle of rags called a cripple. The cripple is left in the flue during parging to catch droppings.

Corinthian One of the Greek orders, in which the column capitals show conventionalized acanthus leaves, the shaft being slender and sometimes fluted.

cork The bark of the cork oak, grown in Mediterranean countries and North America. Granulated cork is used as a loose-fill insulation.

corkboard (compressed cork; baked cork) Granulated cork which has been compressed and baked to form slabs for flooring or insulation; has a K-value of 0.29.

corkboard insulation Granules of pure cork bark compressed and baked into blocks. This material is also used for decorative and sound proofing purposes.

corking In carpentry, a method of connecting one beam to another across which it is bearing.

corkscrew stair A circular stair.

cork setting asphalt A type of asphalt used to glue, cement or adhere cork to some surface when used for insulation purposes.

cork tiles Tiles made from pressed cork and used as flooring.

corkwood Balsa wood; a very lightweight and fragile wood.

corner batt The term used to describe the three corner points from which a concrete form is started.

corner bead A strip of formed galvanized iron, sometimes combined with a strip of metal lath, placed on corners before plastering to reinforce them. Also, a strip of wood finish three-quarters-round or angular placed over a plastered corner for protection.

corner bit brace A specially designed bit brace for use in positions where it is difficult for a workman to operate the regular bit brace; a corner brace is useful for working close to perpendicular surfaces and in corners.

corner boards Used as trim for the external corners of a house or other frame structure against which the ends of the siding are finished.

corner braces Diagonal braces let into studs to reinforce corners of frame structures.

corner chisel A chisel used to cut out mortises. Its blade is L-shaped, with no handle, so that both ends can be used for cutting.

cornerite Strip of metal lath fitted into a corner to prevent cracking of the plaster.

corner posts (studs) The two or three studs spiked together to form a corner in a frame structure.

corner reinforcement Plaster reinforcement used at reentrant or internal angles to provide continuity between two intersecting plaster planes. Usually a strip of diamond mesh metal lath bent to form a right angle.

cornerstone A conspicuous stone in the base of a building on which is usually carved the date the building was erected.

corner tool An angular finishing knife to allow the simultaneous application of joint treatment to both sides of a 90 degree interior angle.

cornice Projection at the top of a wall; a term applied to construction under the eaves or where the roof and side walls meet; the top course, or courses of a wall when treated as a crowning member.

cornice return That portion of the cornice that returns on the gable end of a house.

cornice trim The exterior finish on a building where the sloping roof meets the vertical wall.

corona The brow of the cornice which projects over the bed moldings to throw off the water.

Corps of Engineers Branch of the Army which performs engineering tasks in peacetime and wartime.

corporation cock The valve of a public water or gas main between it and the system being served.

corporation stop Fitting inserted into main under pressure for gas or water service.

corral (1) a pile-supported enclosure in deep water, used to position a caisson as it is being sunk. (2) An enclosure for livestock.

corresponding values Simultaneous values of various properties of a fluid, such as pressure, volume, temperature, etc., for a given condition of fluid.

corridor A long passageway or hall connecting parts of a building.

corrosion disintegration or deterioration of metal, concrete or reinforcement by electrolysis or by chemical attack. *(see abrasion resistance; cavitation damage)*

corrosion inhibitor Chemicals such as sodium nitrite or chromate which protects metals from corrosive materials.

corrosive Having chemically destructive effect on metals (occasionally on other materials).

corrugated Formed into alternate ridges and valleys in parallel, giving greater rigidity to thin plates; usually galvanized steel, asbestos or aluminum for roofing or side walls.

corrugated glass Glass rolled to produce a corrugated contour; when wired it is used especially for skylights, roofs and sidewalks.

corrugated surface The uneven coating surface on roll roofing produced when the coating rollers revolve with the direction of the sheet travel.

corrugated toothed ring A connector made of corrugated metal.

corrugations Parallel grooves and ridges, as in corrugated sheet iron or steel, which is used for buildings and road culverts.

coslettizing *(see phosphating)*

cost breakdown *(see schedule of values)*

cost codes A number-coding system given to specific kinds of work for the purpose of facilitating cost control.

cost of work Costs incurred in the proper performance of the work required by the plans and specifications, and paid by the contractor.

cost per ton-hour The cost to make and distribute one ton of refrigeration per hour. It includes, but is not limited to; energy charges, demand charges, cost of water, cost of water treatment chemicals, equipment repairs, maintenance costs (materials and labor), cost of operating labor (& reg. and O.T.), overheat, amortization, and fixed charges.

cost-plus contract *(see cost plus fee agreement)*

cost plus fee agreement (cost plus) An agreement under which the contractor (in an owner-contractor agreement) or the architect and engineer (in an owner-architect-engineer agreement) is reimbursed for his direct and indirect costs and, in addition, is paid a fee for his services. The fee is usually stated as a stipulated sum or as a percentage of cost.

cotter Steel wedge driven into a cottered joint to tighten it.

cottered joint Joint between the king post of a truss and the tie-beam below it. The king post is held to the beam by a metal U-strap passing under the tie-beam. The strap holds the tie-beam tight to the king post by wedges and gibs through king post and strap.

cotton mats Cotton-filled quilts fabricated for use as a water-retaining covering in curing concrete surfaces.

cottonwood A light, weak wood which warps and splits easily and decays quickly in contact with the ground; used for boxes and crates and in veneer.

coulisse (cullis) A piece of lumber grooved to allow a sluice or similar frame to slide into it.

Coulomb A system for measuring electricity, named after French physicist Charles A. DeCoulomb. The amount conveyed by one ampere in one second; such as 1 Ampere equals 1 coulomb per second; the letter Q is used to symbolize this measurement.

coumarone resins (cumarone-indene resins) Synthetic resins used as the medium for painting metal, electrical insulating varnish, or for an alkali-resistant finish.

counter A built-in table for a business establishment, the customer's side of which is usually closed to the floor, the other side usually shelved; a fixed shelf or top member of a floor mounted cabinet for use as work space.

counter battens (1) Battens fixed across the back of boards to stiffen them, often held in place by screws to allow slight movement. (2) Battens parallel to the rafters and nailed over them on a boarded and felted roof. The tiling or slating battens are nailed over them.

counterbore A cylindrical enlargement of the end of a cylinder bore or of a bore hole.

counterbracing Diagonal bracing which transmits a strain in an opposite direction from the main bracing; in a truss or girder, bracing used to give additional support to the beam and to relieve it of transverse stress.

counter ceiling A false ceiling.

counter cramp (clamp) A batten, with small pieces of wood attached, against which several boards can be held with folding wedges while they are being glued at the edges.

counter-flashing Sheet metal strip in the form of an inverted L built into a wall to overlap the flashing and make the roof water-tight.

counter floor (sub-floor) The lower of two-layer floor boards, often laid diagonally to carry parquet or other finished flooring. It is also called a blind floor or rough floor.

counterflow In heat exchange between two fluids, opposite direction of flow, coldest portion of one meeting coldest portion of the other.

counterfort Vertical slabs used to stiffen walls, especially high retaining walls.

counter gauge A mortise gauge.

counter-lathing *(see brander)*

counter proposal A response to an original proposal; often used in negotiations between labor and management.

countershaft A shaft which receives power from a parallel mainshaft and transmits it to another part of the mainshaft or to working parts.

countersink (1) An added depression below a surface to receive the head of a nail, screw or bolt; also the tool used to make such a recess. (2) The sinkage of any small area beneath the plane of the surface.

counter unit The base unit of a cabinet having a working surface.

counterweight A dead or nonworking load attached to one end or side of a machine to balance weight carried on the opposite end. A working part attached or positioned partly for the purpose of improving machine balance.

counting interval The time period during which meter detector tubes are measuring nuclear backscatter. Since isotopic discharges (disintegrations) occur randomly, a mean average can be obtained after a suitable interval. Precision improves by 30 percent when the time segment is doubled. Normal counting intervals range to 30 seconds.

coupled columns Pairs of columns.

coupler (1) A device for connecting reinforcing bars or prestressing tendons end to end; also known as a clamp. (2) A device for locking together the component parts of a tubular metal scaffold. The material used for the couplers are of a structural type, such as a drop-forged steel, malleable iron or structural grade aluminum.

couple roof A pitched roof used for short spans with common rafters and no tie-beam.

coupling A mechanical device for joining parts together such as pipes.

coupling pin An insert device used to connect lifts or tiers, or formwork scaffolding vertically.

course (1) A horizontal layer of concrete, usually one of several making up a lift. *(see lift)* (2) In masonry, a horizontal range of units the length and thickness of the wall. (3) A horizontal row of shingles; one of numerous rows forming the covering of a roof area.

coursed ashlar Regular coursed rubble.

coursed masonry Coursed blockwork.

coursed squared rubble (random ashlar) Squared rubble built to occasional courses.

coursing joint (1) A bed joint. (2) The joint in an arch, concentric with and separating two string courses.

court (1) An uncovered area partly or wholly surrounded by buildings or walls. (2) A building or a room where justice is administered.

cove (1) A concave molding. (2) The curved junction between a ceiling and side wall; above a cornice if there is one.

cove base Made of vinyl, rubber and/or metal in a variety of heights and shapes for a wide range of sheet goods and tile installations. Installed with adhesives, or self-stick.

cove base (sanitary) A trim tile having a concave radius on one edge and a convex radius with a flat landing on the opposite edge. This base often is used as the only course of tile above the floor tile.

cove-bracketing The wooden skeleton mold or framing of a cove, applied chiefly to the bracketing of a cove ceiling.

cove ceiling A ceiling curving from the walls.

coved and flat ceiling A ceiling in which the section is the quadrant of a circle, rising from the walls and intersecting in a flat surface.

cove lighting That in which the light sources are concealed from below by a cove, cornice or horizontal recess and direct their light upon a reflecting ceiling.

cove molding A quarter round, or concave molding; a molding called the cavetto.

cove strip Used for flash cove installation, this is usually a ⅛" strip of muslin-backed wax. Installed at floor level so that floor covering can be curved up over it in forming the cove.

cover (1) In reinforced concrete, the least distance between the surface of the reinforcement and the outer surface of the concrete. (2) That part of a course of tiles, slate or shingles which is covered by the overlapping course. (3) A piece of land artificially raised to a required level such as an embankment and/or the material used to accomplish it; also called fill.

cover block *(see spacer)*

cover fillet (cover strip) A narrow strip used to cover joints in ceiling or wall board.

cover flap A panelled flap covering boxing shutters.

cover plate (1) The glass or optically suitable plastic which is placed over the solar absorber plate. Most flat plate collectors use two covers for space and water heating applications. (2) A plastic or metal plate used to cover a switch or plug electrical outlet.

coverage The surface area to be continuously covered by a specific quantity of a particular material.

coving (1) The projection of upper facades beyond the lower, as common in Elizabethan architecture. (2) Also referred to as flash coving or self coving. Usually sheet goods, although tile can also be coved. The floor covering is installed up the wall to the desired height and finished at the top with capping.

cowbell *(slang)* Cam locks used in securing 2" × 4" whaler tight to forms (accessory in plywood and whaler forming system).

cowl A hood-shaped top for a chimney or ventilating pipe made to turn or revolve or to turn like a vane so that the opening will always be away from the wind, thus assisting the draft.

cow tool *(slang)* A useless tool.

coyote holes *(slang)* Horizontal tunnels

in which explosives are packed for blasting a high rock face.

crab A short axle in a frame, with square ends that fit a hand crank, used for raising materials.

crab clamps *(slang)* A clamp used to hold 4/0 wire on the walls or in vaults for grounding inside the vault.

Crab Orchard stone A quartzite, easily lifted in layers, of variegated buffs and grays, quarried in Cumberland County, Tennessee.

crack A fracture in the monolithic surface of gypsum board.

crack-control reinforcement Reinforcement in concrete construction designed to prevent opening of cracks, and usually effective in limiting them to uniformly distributed small cracks.

cracked section A section designed or analyzed on the assumption that the concrete has no resistance to tensile stress.

cracking (1) In paint, the breakdown of the paint film with cracks through at least one coat. Some of the types of cracking are hair cracking, crocodiling, crawling, crazing. (2) In plaster, cracks caused by shrinkage, or when lath twist or are too thinly plastered, or when the structure settles differentially.

cracking load The load which causes tensile stress in a member to exceed the tensile strength of the concrete.

cradle (1) A footing structure shaped to fit the conduit it supports. (2) to incline suspending cables to the vertical. (3) A carriage or scaffold. (4) Sling equipped with rollers designed to lift pipe while travelling.

cradle tractor Side-boom used to carry pipe cradle.

cradling Timber work for sustaining the lath and plaster of vaulted ceilings.

craft Manual skill; a trade; an occupation; skill in the execution of manual work; special skill in a manual art or handiwork.

cramming In plumbing, plugging a pipe before making a repair.

cramming (clamp) (1) In masonry, a contrivance consisting of iron rods or

bars with the ends bent to a right angle; used to hold blocks of stone together. (2) In carpentry, a tool to squeeze together wood parts during gluing.

crampon (crampoon) Nippers.

crandall A multi-pointed hammer for dressing the face of a stone.

crane (1) A mobile machine used for lifting and moving loads without use of a bucket. (2) A bracket-like pivoted fireplace accessory.

crane, gantry *(see gantry)*

crane operator A skilled operator who controls the working of the crane from its cab.

crane post The upright mast of a jib crane; holds the upper end of the jib by a tie rod or ropes at its top end and at its lower end it is pivoted to the ground.

crane rail A track supporting and guiding the wheels of a bridge crane or trolley system.

crane runway beam The member that supports a crane rail and is supported by columns or rafters depending on the type of crane system. On underhung bridge cranes, a runway beam also acts as crane rails.

crane tower (king tower) The tower on a derrick which carries the mast and the crane machinery.

crank (1) A bar with a right-angle bend in it to give leverage in turning the obsolete starting handle of a car. (2) A carpenter's brace. (3) An internal combustion engine crankshaft.

crank brace A carpenter's brace for drilling holes.

cranked sheet A corrugated asbestos-cement sheet bent to fit into the junction of two roof slopes.

crankshaft The engine shaft that converts the reciprocating motion and force of pistons and connecting rods to rotary motion and torque.

cranky *(slang)* A term used to describe a cable that has been bent sharply and snarls up.

crapaudine Pivoted on a vertical axis.

crawl (creep) A fault in painted work when freshly applied paint tends to overlap rather than keep to a plane surface. A mild crawl is called ciss.

crawler track One of a pair of roller chain tracks used to support and propel a machine mounted on such tracks.

crawling board (chicken ladder) A plank with cleats spaced and secured at equal intervals, for use by a worker on roofs, not designed to carry any material.

crawl space In some cases where houses have no basements, the space between the first floor and the surface of the ground is made large enough for a man to crawl through for repairs and installation of utilities. Also called a crawlway.

craze cracks Fine, random fissures or cracks which may appear in a plaster surface caused by plaster shrinkage. Also termed check cracking, these cracks are generally associated with a lime finish coat that has not been properly gauged or troweled.

crazing The occurrence of numerous fine cracks which appear on the surface of concrete in a hexagonal or octagonal pattern similar to a crushed eggshell.

cream paper A highly sized and calendered paper used as the face paper in the manufacture of gypsum board.

creel A frame device which holds cones of yarn, which are fed through tubing into the needles of a tufting machine.

creep (1) The property of a substance which allows it in time to become permanently deformed when subject to a stress. Creep is greater at higher temperatures. (2) Very slow travel of a machine or a part. (3) Unwanted turning or motion of a shaft due to drag in a fluid coupling or other disconnected device.

creeper A traveling derrick used in bridge construction.

creeper lanes Reduced speed lanes of a highway for heavy trucks, usually on steep grades.

creeping (crawling) A result of too glossy an undercoat not permitting the oil and finish coat to make a bond; paint runs together in little bubbles.

cremorne bolt A locking device for a French or similar door, consisting of two long rods, the ends of which engage at sill and head; espagnolette.

crenelated Describing a parapet in which the top is alternately and uniformly depressed; battlemented.

crenelle (crenel) An embrasure which, alternating with the elevated portions of a wall, forms a battlement.

creosote Oil distilled from coal tar, used as a timber preservative.

creosoting A method of preserving lumber by impregnating it with creosote under pressure.

crescent A building or row of buildings the facades of which follow the line of an arc in plan.

crest (1) The crown of an overflow section of a dam. In the United States, the term crest of dam is often used when top of dam is intended. To avoid confusion, the terms crest of spillway and top of dam should be used for referring to the overflow section and dam proper, respectively. (2) A decorative ridge for a roof, usually as a continuous series of finals.

crib (grillage) (1) A layer of lumber or steel laid on the ground, or two layers laid across each other, to spread a heavy load. (2) The lining of a shaft.

cribbled Descriptive of a perforated or dotted background on wood or metal.

crib dam A barrier made of timber, forming bays or cells which are filled with stone or other suitable material.

cribwork Large wooden cells which are sunk full of concrete to make a bridge foundation.

crick A small screw jack used to jack up falsework or scaffolding.

cricket A small roof structure, either single or double sloped, that is normally used with a flat roof in such a fashion as to divert drainage toward a downspout or scupper.

crimp To bend metal sheets sharply, as in a lock joint of metal roofing; to corrugate.

Crimp and Bruges' formula A formula connecting rate of flow, hydraulic mean depth, and the slope of sewer. The units are in feet per second and feet. *(see Barnes's formula)*

Crimped wire   Wire which is deformed into a curve which approximates in sine curve as a means of increasing the capacity of the wire to bond to the concrete; also welded wire fabric crimped to provide an integral chair.

crimper   (1) A hand operated tool used to attach metal studs to runners by crimping. (2) An indenting roller.

crimping   Processing yarn, usually by heat or pressure, to fix a wavy texture and increase bulk.

cripple   (1) A structural member that is cut less than full length, such as a studding piece above a window or door; framing member used to support rafters. (2) A bend in a chimney.

crippling load (buckling load)   The load at which a long span begins to bend noticeably.

criteria   The owner's minimum requirements for the design and construction of a particular type of building, or structure.

critical   Of, relating to, or being a turning point or specially important juncture; relating to or being a state in which a measurement or point at which some quality, property or phenomenon suffers a definite change.

critical angle   The least angle of incidence at which total reflection takes place.

critical density   Zone separating the levels of backfill compaction that will or will not prevent deflection failure of a pipe.

critical density of sands   *(see critical voids ratio)*

critical height   The height to which vertical cuts in cohesive soil will stand without shoring.

critical mass   The quantity of fissionable material which is necessary to sustain a chain reaction. The number of neutrons generated by fission has to balance the number of neutrons lost, otherwise there would be no chain reaction.

critical path method (C.P.M.)   A planning, scheduling and control technique whereby a construction project is completely planned and scheduled and an arrow diagram drawn to show the interconnected individual tasks involved in constructing the project. It permits determination of the relative significance of each event, and establishes the optimum sequence and duration of operations. *(see PERT schedule)*

critical point   Of a substance, stated point at which liquid and vapor have identical properties; critical temperature, critical pressure and critical volume are the terms given to the temperature, pressure and volume at the critical point. Above the critical temperature or pressure there is no line of demarcation between liquid and gaseous phases.

critical speed (velocity)   (1) That speed in an engine at which the power impulses of the engine are synchronized with the natural vibrational frequency of the crankshaft, thus amplifying the vibration. (2) On a bridge it is the speed at which a vehicle produces the maximum impact.

critical velocity   The velocity above which fluid flow is turbulent.

critical voids ratio   Critical voids ratio is equal to the voids ratio corresponding to critical density. Critical density is the unit weight of a saturated granular material below which it will lose strength and above which it will gain strength when subjected to rapid deformation. The critical density of a given material is dependent on many factors, for example compaction and loading.

crizzle   An imperfection resulting in the formation of a multitude of very fine surface fractures of wrinkles in rolled glass.

crock   Clay tile sewer pipe.

crocking   Term used to describe excess color rubbing off as the result of improper dye penetration of fixation.

crocket   A projecting ornament common to Gothic architecture; the blunt terminal of conventionalized foliage, as frequently occurs along the edges of a spire.

crocodiling *(see alligatoring)*

crook Warping in wood or boards resulting in distortion of the material causing the edge to become either convex or concave lengthwise.

crop The end or ends of an ingot containing the pipe of other defects which are cut off and discarded; also termed crop ends or discard.

cross In plumbing, a fitted connection consisting of two short pipes meeting at right angles on a pipe run.

cross band To place the grain of the layers of veneer at right angles in order to minimize swelling and shrinking.

cross bond Bond in which the joints of the stretcher in the second course come in the middle of the stretcher in the first; course composed of headers and stretchers intervening.

cross brace Any crosspiece which diverts, transmits, or resists the weight or pressure of a load.

cross bracing A system of members which connect frames or panels of scaffolding laterally to make a tower or continuous structure.

cross-connection Any physical connection or arrangement between two otherwise separate piping systems, one which contains potable water and the other water of unknown or questionable safety, whereby water may flow from one system to the other, the direction of flow depending on the pressure differential between the two systems.

cross-cut In carpentry, to saw at right angles to the grain of wood.

cross-dyed Multi-colored effects produced in a fabric with fibers of different dye affinities.

crossed nicols Two nicol prisms placed so that their vibration planes of transmitted light are mutually at right angles. *(see nicol prism)*

crosses Fabricated fitting for steel pipes or culverts.

crossette (crosset) The side projection of an architrave at top, the double-mitered ear *(see ancon)*; a side lug at

the upper side of an arch stone, entering a corresponding space on the adjoining stone; joggle jointing.

cross furring Furring members attached to other structural components to support lath in suspended ceilings. Generally ¾" steel channels or pencil rods.

cross-garnet A T-shaped hinge, in a wide variety of decorative forms.

cross grain Fibers which do not run parallel to the length of the piece. Fibers which are spiral grain, diagonal grain or interlocked grain are contrary of straight grain and make the wood hard to work.

cross-grained float A wooden plastering float like the hand float but thicker, with the grain parallel to the short side; used for scouring.

cross hair A hair mounted horizontally in the reticule of the telescope so as to divide the field of view into halves.

cross hatch Lines drawn closely together, generally at an angle of 45°, to denote a sectional cut.

crosshead (1) A connection between a connecting rod and a piston rod which is guided so as to move in a straight line. (2) The steel frame that slides between guides in a sinking shaft. It is carried up and down by the bail of the kibble but is not attached to it, thus preventing the kibble from swaying during hoisting. (3) The top horizontal member of an elevator car sling.

crossing (1) A cross band for lumber. (2) Putting on a coat of paint with a brush by a series of strokes each at right angles to the previous series. (3) The intersection of naves and transepts in the cruciform plan.

cross joint The joint at the end of individual formboards between subpurlins.

cross joints *(see butt joints)*

crosslap A joint where two pieces of timber cross each other; formed by curring away half the thickness of each piece at the place of joining so that each piece will fit into the other.

crosslinking A general term referring to the formation of chemical bonds between polymeric chains to yield an insoluble, three dimensional polymeric structure. Crosslinking of rubbers is vulcanization, qv.

cross nogging Bridging common joists in a herringbone pattern.

crossover A plumbing pipe bent into a U-shape to pass another pipe.

cross peen A description of the hand hammer with a wedge shape opposite the face of the hammerhead. The wedge is horizontal when the handle is vertical.

cross poling In trench excavation, short horizontal poling boards to cover a gap between runners.

cross seam A procedure used to join two ends of the floor covering together.

cross section The section of a body perpendicular to a given axis of the body; a drawing showing such a section; a vertical section of the ground suitable for calculating earthwork quantities.

cross section paper Paper ruled in squares for convenience of drawing and measuring; graph paper.

cross-springer Transverse ribs of a vault.

cross system A system of segments or crosses of steel or refractory material in the upper end of a kiln and at right angles to the axis. Aids in heat transfer by increasing the surface area exposed.

cross-tee A light-gauge metal member resembling an upside-down T; used to support the abutting ends of formboards in insulating concrete roof construction.

cross tongue (loose tongue) A piece of plywood or strip of wood with diagonal grain, glued between two members to stiffen an angle joint.

cross-vaulting A common name given to groins and cylindrical vaults.

cross welt A seam between joining sheets of flexible-metal roofing, usually parallel to the gutter or ridge. *(see staggering)*

crotch veneer Veneer cut from the crotch of a tree, revealing unusual and irregular grain patterns.

crowd The process of forcing a bucket into digging, or the mechanism which does the forcing; used chiefly in reference to machines which dig by pushing away from themselves; crowd or face shovel.

crowding the line Laying units in such a way as to prevent the line or string from being clear of the face; building with a tendency to make the wall overhang.

crowfoot (1) In electricity, a small fitting fastened in an outlet box to which fixtures are fastened. (2) In stone, descriptive of the veining that contains dark, uncemented material.

crown (1) The buildup of joint compound over a joint to conceal the tape. The higher the crown the wider the compound must be feathered to make the joint less visible. (2) In plumbing, the highest part of an arch shape, particularly the inside of a drain or sewer. *(see invert)* (3) The elevation of a road surface at its center above its elevations at its edges to encourage drainage. (4) The curved roof of a tunnel. (5) In architecture, the uppermost member of the cornice. (6) Of an arch, the top of the opening. (7) Of a horizontal timber, the camber of a slightly warped length, always set at the top.

crown cover A protective cover placed over a circular saw.

crown glass Glass blown into large, circular discs, afterwards cut to the desired rectangular or other shape.

crowning A specific type of warping when a slat assumes the shape of an inverted "U" across the face. Often an illusory condition caused by premature sanding of a cupped floor.

crown molding a molding used above eye level; usually the corner molding under the roof overhang.

crown plate A bolster.

crown post A king post; short vertical posts near the middle of a hammerbeam roof.

crucible steel Cast steel.

cruciform Descriptive of the characteristic form of Gothic church plans; nave, apse, and transepts.

crumb boss *(slang)* Cook or other person in charge of a construction camp.

crumber A bulldozer blade that follows the wheel or ladder of a ditching machine to clean out loose material and shape the bottom.

crumbs Ragged chunks of gypsum on cut ends or cut outs.

crushed gravel The product resulting from the artificial crushing of gravel with substantially all fragments having at least one face resulting from fracture. *(see coarse aggregate)*

crushed stone The product resulting from the artificial crushing of rocks, boulders or large cobblestones, substantially all faces of which have resulted from the crushing operation. *(see coarse aggregate)*

crusher A machine which reduces rocks to smaller and more uniform sizes.

gyratory A crusher having a central conical member with an eccentric motion in a circular chamber tapering from a wide top opening.

hammermill A rock crusher or a shredder employing hammers or flails on a rapidly rotating axle.

jaw A fixed and a movable jaw widely spaced at the top and close at the bottom, with means to move one jaw toward and away from the other.

primary Usually a jaw-type crusher which reduces very large rocks to a size that can be processed by a secondary crusher.

roll A crusher having two large flat spring loaded steel rolls which revolve toward each other; the rock size required is determined by the spacing between the rolls.

secondary A machine which reduces rocks to smaller and more uniform sizes; usually a combination of jaw and roll crusher.

crusher-run aggregate Aggregate that has been broken in a mechanical crusher and has not been subjected to any subsequent screening process.

crushing strength Load at which material fails during compression, divided by cross-sectional area, properly called its crushing stress.

crushing test Any test in which material is made to fail.

crush plate An expendable strip of wood attached to the edge of a form or intersection of fitted forms to protect the form from damage during prying, pulling or other stripping operations; the term is also used to designate a wrecking strip.

cryohydrate A frozen mixture of water and a salt; a brine mixed in eutectic proportions to give the lowest freezing point.

crypt The vaulted basement of a building, usually a church or cathedral, often with its own chapels and sometimes tombs.

cryptoporticus A gallery or portico having side walls with openings or windows rather than columns.

crystal formation, zone of maximum Temperature range in freezing in which most of the freezing takes place (about 25° to 30° F for water).

crystalline fracture Term usually reserved for cleavage fracture.

crystallized finish The wrinkles formed in paints containing tung or similar oils; true crystallizing of certain lacquers.

C-scroll A C-shaped carved design used as ornamental work, especially on furniture.

"C" section A member formed from steel sheet in the shape of a block "C", that may be uesd either singly or back to back.

cub *(slang)* Apprentice carpenter.

cubage The architectural volume of a building; the sum of the products of (a) the areas and (b) the height from the underside of the lowest floor construction system to the average height of the surface of the finished roof above, for the various parts of the building.

cube A solid with six equal square sides.

cube root A given number which taken three times as a factor produces a number called its cube, as 3x3x3 equals 27, hence 3, the given number is the cube root of 27.

cube strength The load per unit area at which a standard cube fails when tested in a specified manner.

cubical aggregate Angular aggregate most of whose particles have length, breadth, and thickness approximately equal.

cubic content In building construction, the number of cubic feet contained within the walls of a room or combination of rooms and used as a basis for estimating cost of materials and construction; cubic content is also important when estimating cost of installing heating, lighting and ventilating systems.

cubicle A diminutive room.

cubic measure The measurement of volume in cubic units, as follows:

1,729 cubic inches = 1 cubic foot
27 cubic feet = 1 cubic yard
231 cubic inches = 1 gallon
128 cubic feet = 1 cord

cubit An obsolete unit of linear measure, usually considered about 18 inches.

cucumber tree *(see magnolia)*

cul-de-sac A minor street with entrance and exit at the same end.

cull Material rejected as below a stated grade, as brick or lumber.

cullet Broken glass, excess glass from a previous melt, or edges trimmed off when cutting glass to size.

culling Sorting masonry units for size, color or quality.

culvert (1) A drain pipe or masonry crossing, under a road or embankment, made of galvanized corrugated metal, aluminum or steel, or corrugated polyethylene tubing which can be full circle or arched in shape; also can be concrete; any structure not classified as a bridge, which provides a waterway or other opening under a road or highway. (2) In dam construction, a gallery or waterway constructed through any type of dam; normally dry but is used occasionally for discharging water, hence the terms scour culvert, drawoff culvert, and spillway culvert.

cumdom *(slang)* A sock shaped from small cables or nylon string, used to hold or pull wire through conduit, as pulling electric power cables through duct.

cumulative batching Measuring more than one ingredient of a batch in the same container by bringing the batcher scale into balance at successive total weights as each ingredient is accumulated in the container.

cumulose soils Organic accumulations (ie., peat muck, swamp soils, humus, bog soils).

cup (1) A warp common in glat-sawn timber and sometimes seen in floor boards when they bend up at the edges or in the middle becoming either channel-shaped or cambered across. (2) A hollow metal cone fitted into a countersunk hole in cabinetwork, to take the thrust of a countersunk screw.

cupboard A shallow closet with shelves.

cupronickel An alloy of copper and nickel, used in condenser tubes, some coins, etc.

cuphead The descriptive shape of the head of a rivet or bolt rounded like the inside of a shallow cup.

cup joint In plumbing, a blown joint.

cupola (1) A dome; a small structure built on top of a roof. (2) A vertical cylindrical furnace for melting cast iron to make iron castings.

cupped taper A condition where the outer edge of the taper is in the same plane as the surface causing a ridge to appear in the tapered edge.

curb (1) The stone or concrete edging of a sidewalk or paved street; the raised edge of a floor or well opening. (2) A timber upright sometimes used as a roll. (3) A cast-iron or reinforced segmented concrete ring forming an anchorage for mine shaft linings. *(see crib)* The British spelling is kerb.

curb form A retainer or mold used in conjunction with a curb tool to give the necessary shape and finish to a concrete curb.

curb roof (mansard roof) A roof formed of four contiguous planes, each two having an external inclination.

curb tool A tool used to give the desired finish and shape to the exposed surfaces of a concrete curb.

cure (1) To provide conditions conducive to completion of the hydration process. (2) Generally used in conjunction with portland cement plaster; to maintain a sufficient quantity of water in contact with portland cement plaster to insure complete hydration throughout the period required for this process to take place.

curie The official unit of radioactivity, defined as 3.70×10^{10} disintegrations per second. *(see Roentgen)*

curing (1) Maintenance of humidity and temperature of freshly placed concrete during some definite period following placing, casting or finishing to assure satisfactory hydration of the cementitious materials and proper hardening of the concrete. (2) The chemical change in timber which occurs when resins are heated, or when an accelerator is added to a cold-setting resin. (3) An agent used with concrete subfloors to reduce evaporation rate of water and achieve a harder and denser finished slab.

curing agent A catalyst; hardener.

curing blanket A build-up covering of sacks matting, hessian, straw, waterproof paper or other suitable material placed over freshly finished concrete.

curing compound A liquid that can be applied as a coating to the surface of newly placed concrete to retard the loss of water or, in the case of pigmented compounds, also to reflect heat so as to provide an opportunity for the concrete to develop its properties in a favorable temperature and moisture environment.

curing cycle *(see autoclaving cycle, and steam curing cycle)*

curing delay In steam curing of concrete products, the period between the completion of placement of concrete in molds and forms or forming of masonry units by machine and the application of steam.

curing kiln *(see steam box)*

curing membrane *(see membrane curing)*

curl A spiral or curved marking in wood grain; a feather-form mark in wood.

curling The distortion of an essentially linear or planar member into a curved shape such as the warping of a slab due to creep or to differences in temperature or moisture content in the zones adjacent to its opposite faces.

current The flow of electrically charged particles due to an electromotive force being applied to them.

current meter (rotary meter) (1) An instrument which measures current flow, particularly in wide rivers. It has a vane like a windmill which rotates to keep the instrument head on into the current. (2) An instrument which ascertains the velocity of water flow. This is done by determining the speed at which a vane or series of cups is rotated by the flowing stream.

cursor A pointer on a computer display.

curstable A course of stones bearing moldings, to produce a string course.

curtain step The bottom step in an open-string stair, extending in a half-round or volute following the volute of the handrail.

curtain In painting, a scallop effect resulting from paints sagging or running down the wall.

curtain chains Chains suspended in the feed end of the kiln in lengths approximately ⅓ of the kiln diameter and with only one end of each length attached.

curtain drain (intercepting drain) A drain that is placed between the water source and the area to be protected.

curtain grouting Injection of grout into a subsurface formation in such a way as to create a zone of grouted material transverse to the direction of anticipated water flow.

curtain wall (1) A non-bearing wall built between piers or metal columns. (2) A wall acting merely as a screen to hide something. (3) An enclosing wall around property.

curvature friction Friction resulting from bends or curves in the specified profile of post-tensioned tendons.

curve ranging Setting out points on a curve when surveying.

curves (French curves) (1) Bends. (2) Aids in drafting in the form of thin plastic or wood cut to the profiles of various irregular curves.

curve, vertical A change in gradient of the center line of a road or pipe.

curvilinear gable A gable in which the upper slopes have geometric curves.

curvometer A measuring instrument registering units of length by running a small wheel along curved or irregular lines.

cusec A unit flow of water equalling one cubic foot per second. *(see acre foot)*

cushion (1) In plumbing, air pocketed beyond and above a faucet or valve to alleviate water hammer. (2) A pad-stone. (3) A seating, usually of asbestos, plastic cord or lead, for glass running the full length of a patent glazing bar.

cushion-back carpet A carpet having a cushion or padding as an integral part of its backing.

cushion capaital A capital common to Romanesque and early Medieval architecture, and, in another form, to Norman work.

cushion-edged tile Tile on which the facial edges have a distinct curvature that results in a slightly recessed joint.

cushion head Term for a pile helmet.

cusp A terminal point marking the conjunction of arcs in Gothic tracery.

custom-tufted Carpets or rugs in which pile yarns are manually tufted with a hand machine through the back.

cut (1) An excavation, usually a trench; to lower an existing grade. (2) An artificial depression. (3) To stop an engine or throttle it to idling speed. (4) To penetrate with an edged instrument. (5) Descriptive of the size of the ridges on

a file; a fine cut is one with small ridges which provides a smooth finish.

gross The total amount of excavation in a road or road section without regard to fill requirements.

net The amount of excavation material to be removed from a road section after completing fills in that section.

cut-a-foot *(slang)* "Dummy" end of the tape where measurements start.

cut and cover A work method which involves excavation in the open, and placing of a temporary roof over it to carry traffic during further work.

cut and fill A process of building canals, roads or embankments by excavating part of the depth and using the excavated material for the adjacent fills, shoulders and embankments. In a balanced cut and fill operation the excavated material is precisely enough for the embankments with an allowance for fill.

cut-and-mitered hip (valley) A close-cut hip or valley roof.

cutback asphalt Asphalt cement which has been liquified by blending with petroleum solvents, also called diluents; upon exposure to atmospheric conditions, the diluents evaporate leaving the asphalt cement to perform its function.

cut boss *(slang)* The top skinner or the foreman of a crew of men operating heavy earthmoving equipment in a cut or excavating operation.

cut brick A brick cut to shape with an ax or bolster; much rougher in shape than a gauged brick.

cut end The end of the gypsum board with the exposed core.

cut-full lumber Lumber intentionally manufactured in larger than normal thickness and width usually to allow for shrinkage; a term sometimes confused with full-cut lumber.

cut-in A device operating an electric circuit which connects two circuits.

cut nail One cut out of an iron sheet, as contrasted with the wire nail; squared instead of round; commonly used for nailing into concrete.

cut out Damaged or improperly welded pipe that must be removed.

cut pile A fabric, the face of which is composed of cut ends of pile yarn.

cutoff (1) A wall or other structure intending to reduce or eliminate percolation through porous strata. (2) The angle from the vertical at which the reflector or shielding medium cuts off the view of the light source. (3) A short piece of lumber cut from the end of a measured piece; an excess, often used later as bridging, etc.

cutout (1) A means of breaking an electric circuit, usually because of overload. (2) The upper end of a patent glazing bar that is cut off to let the glazing be flashed.

cutout box In electricity, the box in which fuse-holder blocks, fuses and circuit breakers are located.

cut stone Building stone cut to size and shape, each piece fabricated to conform to drawings and to be installed in a designated location in the finished structure.

cutter A hand operated tool used to cut studs and metal runners on the job.

cutter (cutterhead) On a hydraulic dredge, a set of revolving blades at the end of the suction line.

cutting Excavating or lowering a grade.

cutting gauge A gauge similar in construction to regular marking gauges except that it has an adjustable blade for slitting thin stock, instead of the marking pin.

cutting in Painting a clean edge, usually a straight line at the edge of the area painted.

cutting iron The sharpened steel blade of a plane as distinguished from the back iron.

cutting list A list showing the sizes and types of lumber needed for a job.

cutting oil Material used when drilling or machining to hold down heat caused by action of tool against metal; can be combined with water and other materials for greater efficiency in certain operations.

cutting pliers A type of pliers which has a pair of nippers placed to one side for cutting wire, in addition to the flat jaws.

cutting screed Sharp etched tool used to trim shotcrete to finished outline. *(see rod)*

cutting torch An acetylene torch used to burn a piece of metal into two pieces.

cycle (1) A complete course of operation of working fluid back to a starting point, measured in thermodynamic terms (functions). (2) Used in general for any repeated process on any system. (3) (acoustic) One full repetition of a motion sequence during periodic vibration. Movement from zero to +1 back to zero to -1 back to zero. Frequency of vibration is expressed in cycles per second. *(see Hertz)*

cycle, digging complete set of operations a machine performs before repeating them.

cyclone Conical sheet steel vessel for separation of solids from fluids (air or water) by centrifugal action. A cylindrical or conical cone used to collect dust by centrifugal action that has a diameter ranging from 12 to 90 inches in groups of one, two, four or six unit combinations.

cyclopean concrete Mass concrete in which large stones, each of 100 pounds (50kg) or more, are placed and embedded in the concrete as it is deposited; the stones are called pudding stones or plums, and are preferably not less than 6 inches (15cm) apart and not closer than 8 inches (20 cm) to any exposed surface. *(see rubble concrete)*

cyclostyle The Greek term for a circle of columns and their entablature without an inner temple.

cylinder (1) Any geometrical solid bounded by a curved surface and two equal parallel planes. (2) In hydraulic systems, a hollow cylinder of metal, containing a piston, piston rod and end seals, and fitted with a port or ports to allow entrance and exit of fluid. (3)

Steel tubes, driven through bad ground to bedrock, excavated inside, filled with concrete and used as a pile foundation for skyscrapers and in underpinning. **(4)** A monolith of circular cross section.

cylinder caisson A drop shaft.

cylinder lock One in which a set of interior tumblers prevents a cylinder from turning until the right key releases them.

cylinder, slave A small cylinder whose piston is moved by a piston rod controlled by a larger cylinder.

cylinder strength *(see compressive strength)*

cylinder test A laboratory test for compressive stress of a field sample of concrete; usually six inches in diameter by 12 inches in length, although four by eight inches is now also used.

cylindrical slide A rotational slide.

cylpebs (Cylindrical pebbles) Cast or clipped cylindrical grinding media for tube mills, approximately ½ in. in diameter and 1 in. long.

cyma A molding in common use, similar in section to an italic f. Called cyma recta, when the concave part is uppermost; known as cyma reversa, if the convexity appears above and the concavity below.

cymatium In Classic architecture, the crowning molding of an entablature; in the form of a cyma it is known as the cymatium.

cymbia A fillet.

cymograph An instrument for recording the profiles of moldings.

cypress A wood found in the low swamplands in southeastern U.S.A. and in the Mississippi River valley. The heartwood is particularly resistant to decay, so that the wood is used for exterior woodwork and work in contact with the ground.

cyrtostyle A circular projecting portico.

d   degree, density, penny

D   diameter, dimensional

dbl   double

DBG   distance between guides

DC   direct current

deg   degree,degrees

dem   demurrage

depr   depreciation

desc   description

dev   deviation

DF   damage free, direction finder

dg   decigram, decigrams

DH   double hung (door, window)

dia/diam   diameter

diag   diagonal

diff   differential

dil   dilute

dk   deck, dock

dkg   decagram

dkl   decaliter

dl   decilter

dm   decimeter

D&M   dressed and matched (lumber)

D&MB   dressed and matched beaded

do   ditto

doz   dozen

DP   couble pitched, degree of polymerization

DR   dining room

drwl   drywall

DS   double strength (glass)

DTA   differential thermal analysis

dup   duplicate

dwt   deadweight ton, pennyweight

DX   distance

dynam   dynamics

dz   dozen

D & B   Dun & Bradstreet. A credit rating agency.

DBA   (1) Decibels of sound measured on an A-scale. (2) Doing business as; when using a company name other than the actual incorporated name.

D4S   A symbol used on lumber meaning dressed on four sides.

DUNS   Data Universal Numbering System. Used by governmental agencies. D & B number can be used when a company does not have a DUNS number.

dab   To dress the face of a stone by picking with a pointed tool.

dabber   A soft round-tipped brush for applying spirit varnish.

dabbing (daubing)   Dressing a stone face.

dado   (1) Decorative molding on lower interior wall. (2) The flat space between the base and crown molding on a Classical pedestal. (3) A rebate or groove in woodwork.

dado capping (dado molding)   The highest edge part of a framed dado.

dado joint   A recessed joint on the face of a board to receive the end of a perpendicular board.

dagger   (slang) Anything that stands in a diagonal position.

dagmar   A reflective or non-reflective barrier device used to guide vehicles into desired paths of travel along the roadway.

dago float   A slang term used to describe the use of a fresh mortar screed in lieu of float strips to rod floor mortar. This method is commonly used in floor work.

dago stick   Slang term used by tile setters when referring to a small piece of wood used to rod off mortar that has been applied to fill in the holes caused by the removal of the float strips.

dias   A raised platform at the end of a hall.

dallage   A floor or pavement of marble, tile or stone.

Dalton's Law of partial pressure   Each constituent of a mixture of gases behaves thermodynamically as if it alone occupied the space. The sum of the individual pressures of the constituents equals the total pressure of the mixture.

dam   (1) A wall to hold back water. (2) Pairs of cast-steel plates with interlocking fingers built into the road surface of a bridge over an expansion joint to allow traffic to pass over the joint.

damages   Sums which can generally only be recovered from the contractor if it can be proven that they are related to the loss caused by a delay. *(see liquidated damages)*

dammar   A natural gum resin, soluble in many organic solvents; pale yellow or colorless when used in varnish.

damp course   A course or layer of impervious material which prevents capillary entrance of moisture from the ground of a lower course. Often called damp check.

damper   (1) A device used for regulating the draft in the flue of a furnace. (2) A device for checking vibrations.

damping   A force which tends to reduce vibration in the same way that friction reduces ordinary motion. Dampproofing treatment of concrete or mortar to retard the passage or absorption of water, or water vapor, either by application of a suitable coating to exposed surfaces, or by use of a suitable admixture or treated cement.

Dampproofing   Treatment of concrete or mortar to retard the passage or absorption of water, or water vapor, either by application of a suitable coating to exposed surfaces, or by use of a suitable admixture or treated cement.

dancers   *(slang)* Stairs.

dap   To notch; a notch cut in one timber to receive another.

darby   A flat wooden or metal tool about 4″ wide and 42″ long with handles; used to smooth or float the brown coat; also used on finished coat to give a preliminary true and even surface.

darbying   Smoothing the surface of freshly placed concrete or plaster with a darby to level any raised spots and fill depressions.

Darcy's law   The velocity of percolation of water in saturated soil; this law states that velocity = coefficient of permeablilty × hydraulic gradient.

dart valve   A drain for a well bailer that opens automatically when rested on the ground.

dashboard running jean   *(slang)* A carpenter's bib overalls.

dash-bond coat   A thick slurry of portland cement, sand and water dashed on smooth monolithic concrete surfaces with a paddle or whiskbroom to provide a key for subsequent portland cement plaster coats.

data   Information used as basis for reasoning or calculation.

data base   Organized information stored in a computer for retrieval for multiple applications.

data logging   Scanning and recording (typeout or memory tapes), at regular intervals, of process or test date (temperatures, drafts, weights, speeds, analyses, etc.).

date of agreement   The date stated on the face of the agreement. If no date is stated, it could be the date on which the agreement is actually signed, if this is recorded, or it may be the date established by the award. Also, sometimes referred to as the contract date.

date of commencement of the work   The date established in a notice to proceed or, in the absence of such notice, the date of the agreement or such other date as may be established therein or by the parties thereto.

date of substantial completion   The date certified by the architect when the work or a designated portion thereof is sufficiently complete, in accordance with the contract documents, so the owner may occupy the work or designated portion thereof for the use for which it is intended.

datum   Any level surface taken as a surface of reference from which to measure elevations.

daubing (dabbing)   (1) Process of giving a rough stone finish to a wall by throwing a rough coating of plaster upon it. (2) A term applied to the dressing of a stone surface with a special hammer so as to cover the surface with small holes.

davit The structure on large firetube boilers from which the front and rear doors are suspended when opened.

daylight width The width of the actual opening which lets light through a window. *(see sight size)*

daywork A British term for a method of payment for construction, involving agreement between the owner and the contractor on the hours of work done by each man, and the materials used. Payment to the contractor consists of his expenses in labor and materials, plus an agreed percentage for overhead and profit. *(see cost-plus)*

D-cracking The progressive formation on a concrete surface of a series of fine cracks at rather close intervals often of random patterns, but in highway slabs paralleling edges, joints and cracks and usually curving across slab corners. Also termed D-cracks and D-line cracks.

dead The opposite of live wire describing a conductor which is disconnected from its power source.

deadbolt A locking bolt without a spring, that is, one not automatically actuated.

dead burned dolomite A refractory material generally produced in rotary kilns at high temperatures often with admixture of controlled amounts of other materials such as iron oxide for stabilization.

dead end (1) In the stressing of a tendon from one end only, the end opposite that to which stress is applied. (2) The part of a pipe between a blocked-off end and the first branch. When it contains air it is useful in preventing the noise of water hammer. (3) The point of termination and fastening of hoist ropes, or of any wire rope or cord.

dead end anchorage Anchorage at that end of a tendon which is opposite the jacking end.

deadening The use of insulating materials made for the purpose of preventing sounds passing through walls and floors. Also called pugging.

deadheading Traveling without load, as from the dumping area to the loading point.

dead knot A knot whose fibers are not inter-grown with surrounding wood and can be easily knocked out. It is a worse defect than a live knot.

deadlatch A springless lock, actuated from the outside by a key, on the inside by a knob or handle.

dead leg A hot water connection in which the water is stationary, not circulating, except when being drawn off. Since the water cools down between draw-offs the dead leg therefore wastes both water and heat.

dead level (1) Absolutely level or without slope. (2) A grade of asphalt to be used on roof areas that have extremely small or no pitch.

dead light A window in which the glass is fixed direct to the framing; a window or part of a window which does not open.

dead load An inert, inactive load such as in structures due to the weight of the members, the supported structure and permanent attachments; a constant weight or pressure, used in computing strength of beams, floors or roof surfaces. *(see static load)*

dead lock A lock worked only by key from both sides and having no door knobs.

deadman (1) An anchor for a guy line, usually a beam, block or other heavy item buried in the ground, to which a line is attached. (2) Stake.

dead shore One of two heavy up-right timbers which carries the weight of a wall below a needle.

deadwood (1) Timber from dead standing trees. (2) *(slang)* Unproductive labor.

dead zone That area immediately above and below the floor level in which leveling of the elevator is not effective.

deaerator   Service to remove gases from feed water system to boilers.

deal   British term for a commonly used pine; a general term used in many parts of the world for board and plank sizes of softwoods.

debris   Accumulated rubbish or waste matter resulting from remodeling or construction operations.

decant   To pour off a liquid without disturbing a sediment or precipitate.

decanting   A method used for decompressing under emergency circumstances. In this procedure, the person is brought to atmospheric pressure with a very high gas tension in the tissues and then immediately recompressed in a second and separate chamber or lock.

decastyle   A temple or portico of ten columns in front.

decay   Disintegration of wood or other substance through the action of fungi.

deceleration lanes   Highway lanes specifically designed for vehicles which are slowing to exit.

decenter   To lower or remove centering or shoring.

decibel   (1) A unit of loudness of sound derived from the vocabulary of communication engineering. It is the equivalent of the loss in power in one mile of standard cable at 860 cycles. (2) One-tenth of a bel or ten times the logarithm to the base ten of the ratio for any two sound intensities. ($10 \log_{10} I_{10}$). It is an increase of 26% in sound intensity. (3) A unit used to express the relation between two amounts of power. By definition the difference in decibels between two powers P_1 and P_2, P_2 being the larger, is: db difference = $10 \log_{10} P_2/P_1$.

decibel reduction   A reduction in the intensity level expressed in decibels.

deciduous   Pertaining to trees which shed their leaves annually; all hardwoods and a few softwoods.

decimal   A fractional part of a number, proceeding by tenths, each unit being ten times the unit next smaller.

decimal equivalent   The value of a fraction expressed as a decimal, as ¼ equals .25.

decision tree   A device for setting forth graphically the pattern of relationship between decisions and chance events.

deck   (1) The form upon which concrete for a slab is placed, also the floor or roof slab itself. (2) A main upper frame of a shovel containing engine clutches, drums, cab, etc. (3) An unsheltered floor of wood construction.

deck charge   A charge in a blasthold made up of cartridges separated from each other by stemming.

decking   (1) Sheathing material for a deck or slab form. (2) Separating charges of explosives by inert material which prevents passing of concussion and placing a primer in each charge; deck charge. (3) Any lumber generally two inches or thicker, laid as the roof or floor of a structure.

deck-on-hip   A flat roof capping a hip roof.

deck paint   An enamel with a high degree of resistance to mechanical wear, designed for use on such surfaces as porch floors.

deck screen   Two or more screens, usually of the vibrating type, placed one above the other.

declination   A bending downward. Angular distance north or south from the celestial equator measured along a great circle passing through the celestial poles.

declination of sun   The angle above or below the equatorial plane. It is plus if north of the plane, and minus if below. Celestial objects are located by declination.

decomposition   Process of chemical change; breaking up of structures; spoilage.

decompression   Process of reducing high air pressure gradually enough not to injure men who have been working in it. *(see decanting)*

decorated   A term applied to the Medieval architecture in England prevailing during the reigns of the first three

Edwards. it followed the Early English period.

decorative tile Tile with a ceramic design on the surface.

decoupling Separating elements to retard the transmission of structurally borne sound, thermal conductance or physical loads.

deduction (from contract sum) Amount deducted from the contract sum by change order.

deductive alternate An alternate bid resulting in a deduction from the same bidder's base bid. (see alternate bid)

Deed A legal document giving a right to property.

de-energized An electrical circuit not carrying any current.

deep-seal trap An anti-siphon trap with a deep seal, used in one-pipe plumbing systems.

deep-strength asphalt pavement An asphalt pavement structure in which the top six or more inches consist of compacted, high-quality, dense-graded, asphalt hot mix.

deep well pump A centrifugal pump used for raising water more than 25 feet.

Deer Isle A coarse, pinkish lavender-tinted, medium-gray granite of Maine.

defect Any characteristic or condition which tends to weaken or reduce the strength of the tool, object or structure of which it is a part.

defective work Work not complying with the contract requirements.

defibering The process whereby wood chips are reduced into fibers or fiber bundles.

deficiencies (see defective work)

deflagration To burn with sudden and startling combustion; describes explosion of black powder in contrast with more rapid detonation of dynamite.

deflected tendons Tendons which have a trajectory that is curved or bent with respect to the gravity axis of the concrete member.

deflection (1) A deviation, or turning aside, from a straight line. (2) Bending of a beam or any part of a structure under an applied load. (3) Change in shape or decrease in diameter of a conduit, produced without a fracture of the material.

deflection curve (see elastic curve)

deflection limitation Maximum allowable deflection is dictated by code or good practice. Often expressed as ratio of span (L) divided by criterion factor (120, 240, 360). For example, in a 10-ft. or 120″ high wall, allowable deflection under $^1/_{240}$ criterion equals $^{120}/_{240}$ or $^1/_2$″ maximum.

deflectometer An instrument for measuring the deflections of structures, usually of beams under load.

deflocculation The dispersion of flocs or agglomerated particles of fine materials. (cf. slurry thinners).

deformation A change in dimension or shape due to stress. (see time dependant deformation)

deformed bar A reinforcing bar with manufactured surface deformations which provide a locking anchorage with surrounding concrete.

deformed metal plate A metal plate with horizontal deformations or corrugations used in construction to form a vertical joint and provide a mechanical interlock between adjacent sections.

deformed reinforcement Metal bars, wire, or fabric with a manufactured pattern of surface ridges which provide a locking anchorage with surrounding concrete.

deformed tie bar Deformed bar used to hold two slab elements in close contact.

defrosting The process of removing unwanted ice or frost from a cooling surface.

defrosting, hot gas Use of high pressure or condenser gas in the evaporator or low side to effect removal of frost.

degree One 360th part of a circumference of a circle, or of a round angle.

degree day A unit, based upon temperature difference and time, used in estimating fuel consumption and specifying nominal heating load of a building in winter. For any one day, when the mean temperature is less than 65 F, there exist as many degree days as there are Farenheit degrees difference in temperature between the mean temperature for the day and 65 F.

degree electrical The 360th part of the angle subtended at the axis of the machine by two consecutive field poles of like polarity. One mechanical degree is thus equal to as many electrical degrees as there are pairs of poles in the machine.

degree of compaction The measure of density of a soil sample, estimated by a standard formula.

degree of curve The number of degrees at the center of a circle subtended by a cord of 100 feet at its rim; occasionally in highway surveying it is defined as the central angle subtended by an arc of 100 feet.

degree of density Measure of compaction.

dehumidification The condensation of water vapor from air by cooling below the dewpoint or removal of water vapor from air by chemical or physical methods. Dehumidify.

dehumidifier (1) An air cooler or washer used for lowering the moisture content of the air passing through it. (2) An adsorption or absorption device for removing moisture from air.

dehumidifier, surface An air-conditioning unit, designed primarily for cooling and dehumidifying air through the action of passing the air over wet cooling coils.

dehydration (1) The removal of water vapor from air by the use of absorbing or adsorbing materials. (2) The removal of water from stored goods.

delamination Separation of the plies through failure of the adhesive.

delay An electric blasting cap which explodes at a set interval after current is passed through it. *(see curing delay)*

deliquesce To dissolve gradually and become liquid by absorbing moisture from the air, as certain salts. The opposite of efflorescence.

delivery box A structure for the control and measurement of water delivered to a form unit.

delivery hose Hose through which shotcrete materials or pumped concrete pass; also known as material hose or conveying hose.

Delta T As used in solar work, the term designates the difference in temperature between outside ambient air and either inlet or outlet temperature of the fluid passing through the solar collector. As a rule, the higher the Delta T, the lower the collector efficiency. When comparing the performance of two collectors at a given Delta T, the one with the higher efficiency is the better performer. The term Delta T is commonly used to designate temperature differences between any two temperature readings.

delustered yarns Subduing or dulling the natural luster by chemical or physical means.

demarcation In masonry, a fixed line for making a boundary limit.

demi-metope The half of a metope, which is found at the retiring or projecting angles of a Doric frieze.

demising partition Partition between two rental areas in a shopping center, etc., unfinished on one side.

demising wall A separating between two different uses; basically the same as a party wall.

demolition The deliberate razing of a building.

demountable partition An assembly designed to be dismantled and reassembled with a minimal loss of components.

denier Unit of weight for the size of a single filament. The higher the denier, the heavier the yarn.

dense concrete *(see concrete, dense)*

density control Control of density of concrete in field construction to insure that specified values as determined by standard tests are obtained.

dense graded aggregate A mineral aggregate uniformly graded from the maximum size down to and including sufficient mineral dust to reduce the void space in the compacted aggregate to exceedingly small dimensions approximating the size of voids in the dust itself.

density (1) In urban planning, the number of people dwelling upon an acre of land or sometimes, upon a square mile. (2) The ratio of the mass of a specimen of a substance to the volume of the specimen. The mass of a unit volume of a substance. When weight can be used without confusion, as synonymous with mass, density is the weight per unit volume. (3) Closeness of pile yarn; amount of pile packed into a given area of carpet, usually measured in ounces per square yard.

dentil (1) A tooth-like projection on an apron or other surface to deflect or break the force of flowing water; a form of baffle. (2) One of a series of small rectangular close spaced blocks projecting like teeth; used as a decorative motif under a cornice.

departure The distance which a line extends in an east or west direction from the vertical.

dependency In architecture, a minor building flanking a major one in a single composition; usually dependencies are in symmetrical pairs.

deposit for bidding documents Monetary deposit required to obtain a set of construction documents and bidding requirements, customarily refunded to bona fide bidders on return of the documents in good condition within a specified time.

depot (1) A railroad station. (2) A storage or collection center. (3) In France, a building for military storage.

depressed arches (drop arches) Those of less pitch than the equilateral.

depressed sewer A sewer, often crossing beneath a valley or a watercourse, which runs full or under greater than atmospheric pressure because its profile is depressed below the hydraulic grade line.

depth gauge A measuring instrument used for testing the depth of holes or recessed portions of any structural work. It consists of a narrow rule which slides through a cross piece.

depth of a column The agate line or inch measurement of the length of a column from top to bottom.

derby float (see darby)

derrick Usually a non-mobile tower equipped with a hoist; may be used as a synonym for crane.

derricking To lift with a derrick or crane.

derrick tower gantry Strong steel staging of three towers, one crane tower for the mast and jib or the derrick, and two anchor towers for the legs and their kentledge. The towers are tied together at the top by the derrick legs.

desalination The conversion of brackish or sea water to fresh water. Dissolved salts are removed in this process. Various distillation processes are involved in the desalination. In one process, the salt water is heated to the evaporation point. "Fresh" water vapor results that can be condensed and recovered. Ion exchange, reverse osmosis and freezing are other methods of salt removal.

describe To draw graphically with a compass, as to describe an arc.

desiccant Any absorbent or adsorbent, liquid or solid, that will remove water or water vapor from a material. In a refrigeration circuit, the desiccant should be insoluble in the refrigerant. In a solar collector, a desiccant may be used to provide a dry atmosphere between the cover plates minimizing condensation. Silica gel is a common desiccant.

desiccate To dry thoroughly or to make dry by removing the moisture content, as the seasoning of timber by exposing it in an oven to a current of hot air.

desiccation Any process for evaporating water or removing water vapor from a material.

desiccator An apparatus in which a substance is dried.

design The plans, elevations, sections and whatever other drawings may be necessary for a building or other structure. The term plan has a restricted application to a technical portion of the design.

designated person Authorized person or agent.

design-build Construction arrangement in which the contractor provides the design work and building construction services.

design-construct contract A single contract to provide both design and construction services.

design development phase The second phase of the architect's basic services. In this phase the architect prepares from the approved schematic design studies, for approval by the owner, the design development documents consisting of drawings and other documents to fix and describe the size and character of the entire project as to structural, mechanical and electrical systems, materials and such other essentials as may be appropriate. The architect also submits to the owner a further statement of probable construction cost.

design heating load The total heat loss from a building under the most severe winter conditions likely to occur.

design life The length of time for which it is economically sound to require a structure to serve without major repairs.

design load The weight or other force for which a building, plant or part of a building or plant is designed. The worst possible combination of weight or force.

design professions Architects and engineers, for example. *(see environmental design professions)*

design strength The load-bearing capacity of a member computed on the basis of the allowable stresses assumed in design; the assumed values for the strength of the concrete and the yield stress of the steel on whose basis the theoretical ultimate strength of a section is computed.

design working pressure The maximum allowable working pressure for which a specific part of a system is designed.

detachable bit A threaded piece of metal screwed to the end of a rock-drill steel for a cutting point. The steel remains at the work site and only the bits need to be retipped or resharpened. The cutting edges are coated with hard facing.

detail A drawing, at a larger scale, of part of another drawing, indicating in detail the design, location, composition and correlation of the elements and materials shown.

detailer One who prepares small drawings for shop use; a draftsman who makes detailed drawings.

detector A device which generates electrical signals based upon the intensity of some phenomenon such as neutrons or light waves striking it.

detergent A chemical compound that acts to clean surfaces and to keep foreign matter in solution or suspension.

deterioration *(see disintegration)*

detonating cord A flexible cord containing a center core of high explosives which, when detonated, will have sufficient strength to detonate other cap-sensitive explosives with which it is in contact.

detonation Practically instantaneous decomposition or combustion of an unstable compound with tremendous increase in volume.

detonator Blasting caps, electric blasting caps, delay electric blasting caps and non-electric delay blasting caps.

detritus Loose material produced by the disintegration of rocks through geological agencies or processes simulating those of nature.

detritus chamber or pit *(see detritus tank)*

detritus slide (creep slide) The slow movement of detritus downhill. A common kind of landslide, generally not dangerous.

detritus tank (chamber) A detention chamber larger than a grit chamber usually with provision for removing the sediment without interrupting the flow of sewage; a settling tank of short detention period, designed primarily to remove heavy settleable solids.

detrusion The shearing of wood parallel to the grain. Connectors have been developed to prevent this kind of failure.

developed length The length of a pipe along the center line of the pipe and fittings.

developed surface A curved or angular surface graphically represented as flattened out upon a plane.

developement bond stress *(see anchorage bond stress)*

deviation (1) The difference between the value of one set and the average of the set; used in estimating the reliability and variability of a test. (2) Any departure of a borehole from the straight. (3) Any major departure from standard.

devil A firegrate used for heating asphalting tools or for softening a small patch of bituminous road.

devil's float A wooden float with two nails protruding from the toe; used to roughen the surface of the brown plaster coat.

dewar vessel A thermos-type container used for storing very low temperature (cryogenic) liquids.

dewatering Removing water by pumping, drainage or evaporation.

dew point The temperature at which air becomes oversaturated with moisture and the moisture condenses.

dextrin A starch gum obtained by boiling starch alone or with dilute acids; used for sizing and as an adhesive.

D-grade wood Used only in interior type wood for inner piles and backs, where specified.

diabase A granular igneous rock, dark gray to black, sometimes called dolerite.

diaglyph Sculpture sunk below the general surface.

diagonal A straight oblique line connecting two nonadjacent angles of a quadrilateral, polygon or polyhedron; a straight line which divides a rectangle into two equal triangles; the struts, ties

and braces of a lattice girder are its diagonals.

diagonal band A group of reinforcing bars covering a width approximately 0.4, the average span placed symmetrically with respect to the diagonal running from corner to corner of the panel of a flat slab.

diagonal bond (herringbone bond) In very thick brickwork, approximately one course in six is a header course with bricks placed at 45° to the face. A bond for facing bricks laid in a decorative herringbone pattern.

diagonal brace A sloping member which carries compression or tension forces, or both, generally used to stabilize a frame against wind or other forces.

diagonal crack An inclined crack, usually at about 45° to the center line beginning at the tension surface of a concrete member.

diagonal cracking Development of diagonal cracks.

diagonal eyepiece The eyepiece of a surveyor's prismatic telescope.

diagonal grain A defect in which the fibers of wood are at an angle to the length due to faulty conversion of straight grained timber.

diagonal slating Laying of asbestos-cement diamond slates with one diagonal horizontal. The corners are cut off and the head is nailed.

diagonal tension The principal tensile stress resulting from a combination of the vertical and horizontal stresses in a beam.

diagram A figure which gives the outline or general features of an object; a line drawing, as a chart or graph used for scientific purposes; a graphic representation of some feature of a structure.

diagrid floor A network of diagonally intersecting metal or concrete prestressed ribs spanning a rectangular space. It admits a large amount of light, is not heavy, and occupies a small depth.

diameter (1) The line in a circle passing through its center, or thickest part.

(2) The diameters of the lower and upper ends of the shaft of a column are called its inferior and superior diameters, respectively; the former is the greatest, the latter the least diameter of the shaft.

diameter, grain (grain size; particle size) The size of grain, usually in millimeters, as determined by sieve analysis or wet mechanical analysis; hence not a true grain size except for spherical grains.

diametral compression test *(see splitting tensile test)*

diamicton A manner of constructing walls with the exterior of masonry and the interior of rubble.

diamond One of the carbon minerals, a gem formed in volcanic necks. The hardest mineral, it is extremely useful as a cutting agent.

diamond drill A light rotary drill most often used for exploratory work and blast holes.

Diamond Gray A coarse-grain granite in gray with brown and black markings; quarried at Isle, Minnesota.

diamond interchange System of on and off ramps of a highway resembling a diamond shape.

diamond mesh A type of metal lath having a characteristic geometric pattern produced by the slitting and expanding of metal sheets.

diamond pyramid hardness test Testing of the hardness of a metal surface by pressing a diamond pyramid point into it and measuring the indentation. *(see Vickers hardness test)*

diamond saw A circular saw which cuts stone with diamonds set in its cutting face.

deamond washer A curved washer used over roof sheeting which fits its corrugations like the limpet washer.

diaper (1) A design formed by the repetition of one or more units usually combined on a geometric basis and producing an interlaced diagonal pattern. (2) A method of decorating a wall, panel, stained glass or any plain surface by covering it with a continuous design.

diaphragm (1) A flexible partition between two chambers. (2) A stiffening plate in a bridge between the main girders, or a stiffening web across a hollow building block. (3) A brass fitting in a surveying telescope carrying the reticule. (4) An instrument to measure the flow of water in pipes. (5) A metal collar at right angles to a drain pipe to retard seepage or the burrowing of rodents.

diaphragm action The resistance to racking generally offered by the covering system, fasteners, and secondary framing.

diaphragm pump A reciprocating pump without a ram or piston, but with a flexible partition moved back and forth by a rod. It can handle gritty water and even small stones with little wear.

diaphragm wall Generally an underground concrete retaining wall built in a mechanically excavated trench which has been filled with mud to support it during excavation. Reinforcement is dropped into the mud, and the concrete is lowered into the bottom of the trench by tremie. Like sheet-piling methods, it is used when ground-water has to be kept out of an excavation or when high earth pressure must be resisted.

diastyle A spacious intercolumniation, to which three diameters are assigned.

diatomaceous earth A friable earthy material composed of nearly pure hydrous amorphous silica (opal) and consisting essentially of the frustules of the microscopic plants called diatoms. Used for the fine filtration of water.

diatomite *(see diatomaceous earth)*

dicalcium silicate A compound having the composition $2CaO.SiO_2$, abbreviated C_2S, that occurs in portland cement clinker. *(see belite)*

dice The more or less cubical pattern of fracture of tempered glass; the edges of the dice being roughly equal to the thickness of the glass.

dictyotheton (1) A Greek term for masonry laid up in meshlike courses. (2) An open latticework.

die (1) A steel former or device for shaping, impressing, threading or cutting out something. (2) The cube or dado of a pedestal. (3) The enlarged square part at the upper and lower ends of a baluster which meets the rail or plinth.

dielectric (1) Non-conducting. (2) Name for a substance through or across which electric induction takes place.

dielectric constant A number which defines the relative efficiency of a dielectric material for passing lines of electric force compared to that of vacuum. Number will be greater than one.

diesel engine An internal-combustion engine which burns a relatively inexpensive oil about the consistency of light lubricating oil. The oil is pumped into the cylinder by a pump and is ignited by the high compression in the cylinder, without electrical spark.

diesel hammer *(see pile hammer)*

dieseling In a compressor, explosions of mixtures of air and lubricating oil in the compression chambers or other parts of the air system.

die square A squared piece of lumber generally 4×4 inches or larger.

difference in elevation Between two points, the vertical distance between two level surfaces containing the two points.

differential (1) Of a control, the difference between cut-in and cut-out temperatures or pressures. (2) A device that drives two axles and allows them to turn at different speeds to adjust to varying resistance.

non-spin (limited action) A differential that will turn both axles even if one offers no resistance.

two-speed A differential having a high-low gearshift between the drive shaft and the ring gear.

differential pulley block (chain block) Lifting tackle consisting of an endless chain fed over two wheels of slightly different diameters, but turning on the same shaft. The lifting power increases as the diameters become closer.

differential settlement (relative settlement) Uneven sinking of different parts of a building.

differential thermal analysis (DTA) Indication of thermal reaction by differential thermocouple recording of temperature changes in a sample under investigation compared with those of a thermally passive control sample that is heated uniformly and simultaneously.

diffraction The tendency of sound waves to flow readily around obstacles which are small in comparison with the wave length of the sound. (On perforated acoustical material, the sound waves are diffracted into the holes where absorption takes place.)

diffuse One of two components of solar energy arriving at the earth's plane, the other being direct.

diffuser (1) Inner shell and water passages of a centrifugal pump. (2) A porous plate or other device through which air is forced and enters the sewage in the form of minute bubbles.

diffuse reflection Light reflection from a surface, such as smooth, matte, white paper reflects light equally in all directions.

diffuse-reflection factor The ratio of light diffusely reflected from a surface, to that which falls upon it.

diffusion (1) The scattering of light rays so that the light is emitted or reflected from all directions. (2) The movement, often contrary to gravity, of the molecules of gases in all directions causing them to intermingle. (3) Preservation of wood by laying on a stiff paste or a concentrated solution and allowing it to penetrate slowly.

diffusivity, thermal *(see thermal diffusivity)*

digester An apparatus in which sewage sludges are processed under anaerobic conditions. These sludges are used to produce such gases as methane and carbon dioxide, water and an innocuous solid or semi-solid residue.

digestion In sewage, the biochemical decomposition of organic matter which results in the formation of simpler organic and mineral compounds.

digging line On a shovel, the cable which forces the bucket into the soil. Called crowd in a dipper shovel, drag in a pull shovel, and dragline and closing line in a clamshell.

digital Data expressed in numerical form as opposed to analog form.

diglyph Double-grooved, as triglyph is triple-grooved.

dike (dyke) Earth dam or embankment. (2) A thin rock formation that cuts across the structure of surrounding rock. (3) A large ditch.

diluent A liquid or solid substance mixed with the active constituents of a formulation to increase the bulk or lower the concentration: in painting, a thinner.

dilution Reducing a concentration of soluble material by adding pure water.

dimension A distance between two points, lines or planes.

dimensional stability In describing building materials, material is dimensionally stable if it has no moisture movement, little temperature movement, and does not shrink or expand for any other reason.

dimension line On plans, a line with arrowheads at either end to show the distance between two points.

dimension lumber Material pre-cut to specified standardized sizes.

dimension shingles Shingles cut to uniform rather than random widths.

dimension stone Rock quarried in blocks to predetermined sizes in such a manner as not to weaken or shatter it.

diminishing courses Courses of roofing shingles so laid that the gauge between them diminishes from eaves to ridge. The slate widths usually also diminish.

diminishing piece (diminishing pipe) In plumbing, a taper pipe.

diminution Tapering; the gradual reduction in size toward the end of an object or column.

dimple The impression formed in the surface of gypsum wall board when the nail is driven to the proper depth. Later filled and smoothed, if wall is to receive paint or paper finish surface.

dimpling gun A tool used to attach flange to rectangular duct work.

ding bats *(slang)* Leader guard; plastic wire protector for electrical wire inside the conduit to keep the wire from being cut by the edge of the conduit.

dinging In plastering, a rough, single-coat stucco on walls, consisting of cement and sand, sometimes marked to imitate masonry joints.

dinky *(slang)* A small crane with under 20 ton lifting capacity.

dinky skinner *(slang)* One who drives a dinky engine, a small locomotive used in tracklaying and tunneling.

diorite Granular, crystallized igneous stone composed of feldspar and hornblende.

dip The slope of layers of soil or rock, sometimes used to describe a fault.

dip needle (dip compass) A magnetic needle with a horizontal pivot. The needle is set in the magnetic meridian and the inclination to the horizontal of the needle is read. This angle is the dip of the earth's magnetic field at that point.

dipper A digging bucket rigidly attached to a stick or arm.

dipper stick A name for the standard revolving shovel, dipper shovel; and for the straight shaft which connects the bucket with the boom.

dipper trip A device that unlatches the door of a shovel bucket to dump the load.

direct One of two components of solar energy arriving at the earth's plane, the other being diffuse. Direct beams of the sun's rays reach the earth by passing through the atmosphere in a straight line without being diffused by striking clouds, air contaminants, etc.

direct-acting pump A simple compressed-air or steam-driven reciprocating pump having the power cylinder and water cylinder at opposite ends of the same piston rod, and having no important rotating parts.

direct band A group of reinforcing bars, covering a width approximately 0.4 of the distance between columns, placed symmetrically with respect to the center lines of the supporting columns of a flat slab.

direct current (D C) An electric current flowing over a conductor in one direction only, and substantially constant in value.

direct dumping Discharge of concrete directly into place from crane bucket or mixer. In open forms this permits good distribution of concrete without lateral flow.

direct expense All items of expense directly incurred by or attributable to a specific project, assignment or task.

direct heating Heating a room from a heat source located within it. *(see indirect heating)*

direction limits switch The switch that prevents an elevator from further travel in one direction only.

direction of irrigation Direction of flow of irrigation water; usually at right angles to the supply ditch or pipe.

direction selecting circuit That portion of a wiring diagram which determines the direction an elevator should travel to answer a call.

direct lighting A lighting system in which all or nearly all of the light is distributed downward. Fixtures that send somewhat more light upward, but are still the direct type are called semidirect.

direct nailing (face nailing) Nailing perpendicular to the initial surface of to the junction of the pieces joined.

direct personnel expense Salaries and wages of principals and employees engaged on a project, including mandatory and customary benefits.

direct-reading tachometer A tachometer from which the plan length and the difference in level between staff and instrument can be read without measuring the vertical angle.

direct stress A stress created entirely by compression or tension and involving no bending or shear.

dirtjob Any construction which requires the movement of soils, i.e. dams, highways, etc.

dirty money A British term for the premium pay to a construction worker for working in difficult or unusual conditions.

disappearing stair An attic ladder, usually hinged for raising and lowering.

disc sander A small sanding machine with a rotating disc used for sanding corners and other areas which the ordinary floor sander cannot reach. It can usually be fitted to a hand electric drill.

discharge (1) Flow from a culvert, sewer, channel, etc. (2) The output rate of a plant such as a pump.

discharge valve A control valve for reducing or increasing the flow in a pipe, as distinguished from a stop valve.

discharging arch Any architectural member, or strut, designed to resist pressure and to distribute the weight of a wall above an opening, such as over a door or window.

discoloration Departure of color from that which is normal or desired.

disconnecting trap In plumbing, an intercept trap.

discontinuous construction Sound insulation using minimum insulating materials by making breaks in the construction in walls, floors and ceiling.

disintegrated granite Granular soil derived from advanced weathering and disintegration of granite rock.

disintegration Deterioration into small fragments or particles from any cause.

diskette *(see floppy disk)*

dispatching device An elevator device, the principal function of which is to either operate a signal in the car to indicate when the car should leave a designated landing; or actuate its starting mechanism when the car is at a designated landing.

dispersant A material which deflocculates or disperses finely ground materials by satisfying the surface energy requirements of the particles; used as a slurry thinner or grinding aid.

dispersing agent An additive or admixture capable of increasing the fluidity of pastes, mortars or concrete by reduction of inter-particle attraction.

dispersion In painting, a suspension of very fine particles in a liquid medium. Most paints and some varnishes are dispersions.

displacement (1) The volume displaced by a piston or ram moving to the top or bottom of its stroke. (2) In hydraulics, the volume of water displaced by a floating vessel.

displacement pump Any ram-operated or piston-operated pump; generally used when referring to diaphragm pumps or air-lift pumps in which compressed air displaces the water.

distance The distance or difference in elevation between two sloping pipes is the distance between the intersection of their center lines with the center line of the pipe to which both are connected.

distemper A term applied to a composition used for painting walls; a paint in which the colors are tempered or mixed with any of various glutinous substances.

distemper brush A well-packed flat brush with long bristles. The older two-knot brush is wire bound with two knots attached to one stock.

distressed A surface which has been scraped, scratched or gouged to give it a time worn look.

distributed load In building, a load spread evenly over an entire surface, or along the length of a girder, expressed in pounds or tons per foot.

distribution (1) The movement of freshly mixed concrete toward the point of placement either by hand or motorized tools (2) The movement of collected heat to the living areas from collectors or storage.

distribution box In electricity, the main feed line of a circuit to which branch circuits are connected.

distribution line The main electrical

circuit, to which branch circuits are connected.

distribution panel In electricity, an insulated board from which connections are made between the main feed lines and branch lines.

distribution pipe In plumbing, a pipe carrying water from a storage tank.

distribution reservoir In hydraulics, a service reservoir.

distribution steel The subsidiary reinforcement in a reinforced-concrete slab which is placed at right angles to the main steel to hold it in place during concreting and to distribute the loads over a larger area.

distribution tile Clay agricultural drain tiles which distribute the overflow from a septic tank to the soil.

distributor Device for dividing flow of liquid fluid between parallel paths in an evaporator or in other types of heat transfer apparatus.

distributor, sewage A device used to apply sewage to the surface of a filter. There are two types, fixed and moveable. The fixed type may consist of perforated pipes or notched troughs, sloping boards or sprinkler notches. The moveable type may consist of rotating or reciprocating perforated pipes or troughs applying spray or a thin sheet of sewage.

distributor truck A truck with an insulated tank equipped with heating and pumping devices and used to spray heated asphaltic products under pressure on the surface of a road, runway or other area to be paved. Also called a boot truck.

distributed sample In soils a sample which has beed mixed, therefore not representative of its original characteristics.

distyle A portico of two columns. This is not generally applied to the mere porch with two columns, but to describe a portico with two columns in antis.

ditch (1) Generally a long narrow excavation for drainage, irrigation or burying underground pipe lines. (2) In rotary drilling, a trough carrying mud to a screen.

ditch check   Barrier placed in a ditch to decrease the slope of the flowline and thereby decrease the velocity of the water.

ditcher (trencher)   A mechanical trench excavator.

   ladder   A machine that digs trenches by means of buckets mounted on a pair of chains traveling on the exterior of a boom.

   wheel   A machine that digs trenches by rotation of a wheel fitted with toothed buckets.

ditching by explosives   A line of holes loaded with cartridges of dynamite fired simultaneously.

Ditch Witch   A brand name of a trenching machine.

ditriglyph   An intercolumination in the Doric order, of two triglyphs.

diurnal temperature gauge   The variation in outdoor temperature between day and night.

diver   An underwater worker supplied with air, usually by a pipeline from the surface, who lays foundations for bridge piers, repairs underwater walls, uses underwater cutting and welding tools and the cement gun; also may do underwater carpentry, steel plating, and shipwright's work.

divers paralysis   Caisson disease or bends.

diversion (diversion cut)   A channel excavated to make a stream or river bypass, either permanently or during construction.

diversion chamber   A chamber that contains a device for diverting all or part of the flow.

diversion dam   A barrier across a stream built to divert or turn all or some of the water.

diversion valve   A valve which permits flow to be directed into any one of two or more pipes.

divide   To separate into parts; to cut apart into two or more pieces; to separate as by a partition.

divided scale   Black iron oxide covering iron or steel which has been forged or otherwise hot worked. It should be removed before painting.

dividers   A drafting instrument like a compass but with both ends having sharp points.

divider strips   In terrazzo work, nonferrous metal or plastic strips of different thicknesses usually ⅛ or 1¼ inches deep used to form panels.

divining rod   A forked branch, usually of hazel, by which it is claimed that the location of underground water can be ascertained.

division (of the specification)   One of the basic organizational subdivisions used in the uniform system for construction specifications, data filing and cost accounting.

division box   A structure for dividing and diverting water into other channels. Also called diversion box.

division gate   A structure that divides the flow between two or more laterals.

division wall (fire wall)   A fire-resistant wall from the lowest floor to the roof.

D-line cracks   *(see D-cracking)*

doat   *(see dote)*

dobie   Precast concrete block used as a support for reinforcing bars.

dobying   *(see blistering)*

dock   An artificial basin or harbor for landing and anchoring of ships.

dock wall   A marginal wall on a wharf or pier.

document deposit   *(see deposit for bidding documents)*

dog   A heavy-duty latch. **(2)** A name for various mechanical devices, tools, etc. that usually grip something. **(3)** A strip of clay cut with a clay knife. **(4)** A grappling iron used to lift a pile driver's hammer. **(5)** A hand tool for rotating pipes. **(6)** *(slang)* To dog it means to deliberately slow down the work pace. **(7)** *(slang)* A device to tighten and hold form ties in concrete formwork.

dog anchor   An iron rod or bar with the

ends bent to a right angle; used for holding pieces of timber together.

dog bars Vertical intermediate members in the lower part of a gate.

dog ear A box-like external corner which if formed by folding a metal roofing sheet without cutting it. *(see gusset piece)*

dog house *(slang)* (1) Storage room. (2) A shanty in which workmen change to work clothes.

dogleg Permanent short bend or cinch in a wire rope caused by improper use; a kink.

dog-leg chisel A bent chisel for cleaning out grooves.

dog-leg stair A stair that makes a right-angle turn by means of a landing.

dog-off To tie off or hold to prevent from slipping.

dogtooth (1) In architecture, a toothlike ornament or a molding cut into projecting teeth. (2) A type of early architectural decoration in the form of a four-leafed flower, probably so named from its resemblance to a dogtoothed violet. (3) A string course where bricks are laid so that one corner projects.

dogtrot A covered passage joining two parts of a house, such as a covered porch between house and a wing; a breezeway.

dolly (1) A unit consisting of a draw tongue, an axle with wheels and a turnable platform to support a trailer gooseneck. (2) A small wheeled carriage designed to support heavy machines. (3) A block of wood or plastic placed on a pile head to take the blows of the hammer ram; an extension on the top of a pile to let the hammer reach it when the pile top is below the driving rig. (4) In steelwork, a steel bar with a shaped head held against a rivet being driven. The bucker holds the dolly, the driver holds the rivet gun.

doloment A name applied to a composition used in making floors without joints.

dolomite (1) A mineral having a specific crystal structure consisting of calcium carbonate and magnesium carbonate in equivalent chemical amounts of 54.27 and 45.73 respectively. (2) A rock containing dolomite as the principal constituent.

dolphin A cluster of piles driven in water for mooring purposes or for protection against floating objects.

dome (1) The square prefabricated pan form used in two-way, waffle, concrete joint floor construction. (2) An inverted cup on a building, as a cupola, especially on a large scale; the vaulted roof or a rotunda, so constructed as to exert equal, oblique thrust stresses in all directions. (3) A spherical shape of rock strata.

dome light A curved roof window.

domestic architecture That branch relating to private buildings.

donegan *(slang)* A portable toilet on a construction site.

doniker *(slang)* A large boulder; an outcropping of rock.

donkey A winch with two drums which are controlled separately by clutches and brakes.

donkey doctor *(slang)* A mechanic for power equipment.

donut (see doughnut) (1) A large washer of any shape to increase bearing area of bolts and ties. (2) A round concrete spacer with hole in the center to hold vertical bars to the desired distance from form.

dooly *(slang)* Dynamite.

door A hinged, pivoted or sliding member, permitting passage through a wall.

door area Total area of outside doors and facings. Used in computing heating and cooling of a house.

door arm A long piece of steel which extends down from the elevator door operating mechanism, parallel with the door panel, and transmits door open and close force through one or more connecting links.

door buck A doorframe of rough material to which the finished doorframe is attached.

door casing The architrave and other trim around a door opening.

door check An automatic door closer.

door cheeks The vertical members of a door frame.

door control circuit That portion of the wiring diagram that controls the operation of the elevator car and hoistway doors.

door dike A projection on the door which extends into the refrigerated compartment and which functions primarily as a barrier to minimize heat flow to the interior of the cabinet.

door frame The surrounding case into and out of which the door shuts and opens. It consists primarily of two upright pieces, called jambs and a head, generally fixed together by mortises and tenons, and wrought, rebated and beaded.

door furniture (hardware) Handles, escutcheons, finger plates, locks, bolts, latches, hinges, etc.

door guide An angle or channel guide used to stabilize or keep plumb a sliding or rolling door during its operation.

doorhead The upper frame of a door.

door jack A frame used by carpenters for holding a door while it is being planed and the edges fitted to the size of a door opening.

doorjamb The surrounding case into which a door closes and opens. It consists of two upright pieces, called jambs, and a head, fitted together and rabbeted.

door post A vertical member of a door frame.

door sill A horizontal piece at the base of the frame of an outside door. It is connected to the door posts and is designed to keep out rain.

doorstop A device used to hold a door open to any desired position; a device, usually attached near the bottom of a door, to hold it open and operated by the pressure of the foot. The doorstop may or may not be attached to the door. The strip against which a door closes on the inside face of a door frame is also known as a doorstop.

door switch In electrical work, a switch automatically operated by the opening or closing of a door.

doorway An opening for passage through a wall.

dooryard Fenced or walled space before a principal entrance.

dope (1) A viscous liquid put on pipe threads to make a tight joint. (2) Additives made to any type of mortar to accelerate or retard its set.

dope gang A crew of workers who apply bitumen coating and wrap pipes.

dope hot Liquid tar like substance for coating pipe.

dope machine Machine which applies bitumen coating and wraps pipe, operated by dope gang.

Doric frieze That part of the entablature between the cornice and the architrave in Doric architecture.

Doric order The oldest and simplest of the three Greek orders of architecture. It is distinguished by the absence of a base to the column.

dormer A minor gable in a pitched roof, usually bearing a window or windows on its front vertical face; also, the window.

dormer cheek The upright side of a dormer, gable or window.

dormer window A vertical window in a projection built out from a sloping roof.

dormitory A residential building in an institution; a common sleeping room.

Dorr thickener (clarifier) A device placed in a tank by which a system of scrapers, driven by a central shaft, revolves slowly pushing the deposited sludge to a central outlet from which it is removed by gravity or pumping.

Dortmund tank A vertical-flow sedimentation tank with hopper bottom. The sewage, introduced near the bottom, rises and overflows at the surface. Sludge is removed from the bottom.

dosing siphon An automatic siphon for discharging the contents of a dosing tank.

dosing tank A tank into which raw or partly treated sewage is introduced and held until the desired quantity has been accumulated, after which it is discharged automatically for treatment.

dosy timber Wood which has started to rot.

dot A small lump of plaster placed on a surface between grounds to assist the plasterer in obtaining the proper plaster thickness and aid in aligning the surface.

dote (doat) Early stage of decay indicated by dots or speckles; also called dosy, foxy, etc.

dotting on In British estimating, a dot added to the times column indicating that the quantity occurs more than once.

double In rotary drilling, two pieces of drill rod left fastened together during raising and lowering.

double-acting Describing the action of reciprocating pumps or compressed-air or steam engines. It means that both sides of the piston are working under pressure so that every stroke of an engine is a power stroke and every stroke of a pump delivers fluid.

double-acting butt A type of butt hinge which allows a door to swing in either direction; commonly used between a kitchen and dining room.

double bead Two parallel beads with a quirk separating them.

double block & bleed Two safety shut off valves with a vent valve between them.

double breasted A firm which operates both union and open shop, usually via two or more divisions of a parent company, or with separate firms in different states.

double-bridging In carpentry, two rows of herringbone strutting dividing the floor area of each span into three equal parts.

double cleat ladder One that is similar to a single cleat ladder, but is wider, with an additional center rail which will allow for two-way traffic for workmen ascending and descending.

double-clutching Disengaging and engaging the clutch twice during a single gear shift in order to synchronize gear speeds.

double connector In plumbing, a short piece of pipe with a long parallel thread fitted with a back nut and a socket enabling a gas supply to be interrupted in an emergency.

double corner block Concrete masonry units which have two flat or flush ends for use in pilasters, piers or corner construction.

double-cut (full-lapped) Always used with non-patterned flooring goods; can also be used on patterned goods with large-sized blocks with sufficient selvage. Double-cutting is done by lapping the edges of the material (¾″) and striking a chalk line ⅛″ from edge of top sheet, along entire length. A cut is then made on the chalkline completely through the top sheet and deep enough to leave a guide for the cutting of the bottom sheet.

double door (see folding door)

double-dovetail key (dovetail feather; hammerhead key) A wooden key like two dovetail pins joined at the narrow ends, driven into a butt joint between two timbers to hold them together.

double-drum hoist A hoisting engine with two drums which can be separately driven, connected or disconnected by a clutch.

double eaves course (doubleing coures) A double row or shingles laid at the foot of a roof slope or vertical section of shingling.

double end area volumes Method for determining volumes in earthwork computations.

double faced Architraves, skirting boards, etc. with moldings which face in two different directions.

double-face hammer A hammer having a striking surface at each end of the head.

double Flemish bond Brickwork showing Flemish bond on both faces of the wall.

double floor (double-framed floor) A floor with joists spanning between binders; a single floor consisting of a counter floor with a second, finished timber floor.

double glazing The use of two sheets of glass with rarefied-air space between, serving as insulation against passage of heat.

double-handed saw A long cross-cut saw pulled by a workman at each end.

double-headed nail (duplex-headed nail) A round nail on which two heads are formed, so that the nail can be driven to fix concrete formwork; the second head, higher than the first, enables the nail to be pulled easily.

double header A trimmer joist, near an opening or wall, made by nailing together two joists.

double house *(see duplex)*

double hung window A type of window containing two moveable sash sections which open vertically.

double jack *(slang)* A sledge hammer; usually six or eight pounds in weight.

double laths Laths twice the thickness of single laths.

double layer Two layers of gypsum board. Various thicknesses may be combined to improve the fire, sound or structural characteristics.

double lock In hydraulics, two parallel canal-lock chambers with a sluice between them.

double-lock welt A cross welt.

double nailing A method of applying gypsum board by using two nails spaced approximately 2 inches apart every 12 inches in the field along the framing member to insure firm contact with the framing.

double offset Two offsets installed in succession or series in the same line.

double partition A partition built with two rows of studding either for soundproofing or to form a cavity for a sliding door.

double-pitch roof A roof having two slopes; sometimes called a saddleback roof, a mansard roof or a pitched roof.

double-pitch skylight A skylight designed to slope in two directions.

double pole scaffold (independent pole) A scaffold supported from the base by a double row of uprights, independent of support from the walls, and constructed of uprights, ledgers, horizontal platform bearers and diagonal bracing.

double-pole switch A switch to connect or break two sides of an electric circuit.

double-quirk bead (return bead) A bead recessed in a surface or corner by a quirk at each side.

double rebated A wide door post or jamb lining which is rebated on both edges so that the door may be hung to open in or out.

double-return stairs A stair with one wide flight up to the landing and two flights from the landing to the next floor.

double-roll verge tile A single-lap tile with a roll on each edge so that the verges on both sides are alike.

double roof A roof in which the common rafters are carried on purlins which rest on a roof truss or other intermediate supports.

double-rope tramway An aerial tramway with two track cables and one continuous traction rope.

double-skin roof A roof consisting of an upper layer, the weathering, and a lower layer, the underlay, which is flat and forms the ceiling.

double skirting A skirting made higher than usual by a second, upper skirting board.

double sling A chain or rope two-leg sling.

double step In heavy lumber framing, such as the support of a rafter on a tie-beam, a W-shaped notch to reduce the possibility of horizontal shear in the tie-beam.

double strength glass Sheet glass $1/8$ inch thick. Single strength glass is $1/10$ inch thick.

double surface treatments Two successive applications of asphaltic material and mineral aggregate; treatments as armor coat, multiple lift, and inverted penetration are essentially double surface treatments.

double T-beam A member composed of two beams and a top slab projecting on both sides; also a flat slab panel with projecting stems.

double-tier partition A framed partition two floors high.

double time The method of payment used after normal time pay and time-and-a-half pay have been used; a premium pay for overtime which is twice the normal wage.

double-up A method of plaster placement characterized by application in successive operations with no setting or drying time allowed between coats. Also called: double-back, doubled-up, laid off, laid on, or two coat work.

double vault Formed by a duplicate wall; wine cellars are sometimes so formed.

double-wall cofferdam A cofferdam consisting of two rows of sheet piling. The space between may be filled with clay, or if stability is all that is required, other material. Used primarily when the height of a single wall would be too great for stability.

double-walled heat exchanger A heat exchanger which separates the collector fluid from the potable water by two surfaces; it is required if the collector fluid is nonpotable.

double window (1) A storm window. (2) Double glazing.

doubling course A double eaves course.

doubling piece In carpentry, a tilting fillet.

doughnut (donut) (1) A large washer of any shape to increase bearing area of bolts and ties. (2) A round concrete spacer with a hole in the center to hold bars the desired distance from the forms.

dovetail In carpentry, an interlocking joint; to join in interlocking fashion.

dovetail cutter A tool used for cutting the inner and outer dovetails for joints.

dovetail feather A double-dovetail key.

dovetail-halved joint. A joint which is halved by cuts narrowed at the heel, as in dovetail joint.

dovetailing A method of fastening boards or timbers together by fitting one piece into the other as with dovetail joints.

dovetail joint A dovetail.

dovetail margin A banding or edging which is dovetailed.

dovetail molding A molding in which interlocked triangles are used.

dovetail saw A small saw similar to a backsaw, with smaller teeth and a different-shaped handle.

dovetail sheeting Dovetailed lathing.

dowel (1) A pin of wood or metal used to hold or strengthen two pieces where they join; a pin or tenon fitting into a corresponding hole and serving to fasten two pieces of wood together. (2) A piece of wood driven into a wall so that other pieces may be fastened to it; also called plugging.

dowel bit A carpenter's drilling bit of half-cylindrical cross section, similar in shape to a pod auger.

dowel deflection Deflection caused by the transverse load imposed on a dowel.

doweling The method of fastening two pieces of timber together by the use of dowels; butt joints are sometimes secured by the use of glue and dowel pins.

dowel lubricant Lubricating material applied by bars in expansion joints to reduce bond with the concrete and promote unrestrained longitudinal movement.

dowel pin A short round wire nail pointed at both ends; a headless nail with one point and a barbed shank driven into a mortise-and-tenon joint to fasten it permanently; a wood dowel.

dowel plate A metal plate in which holes are drilled. It can be used for verifying the diameter of a dowel or for making a dowel by driving a peg through it to remove excess wood.

dowel screw A metal screw with coarse wood-screw threads at both ends, useful for joining two wooden parts.

dowel shear The force applied in the plane of the cross section of the dowel.

downcomer *(slang)* Tube in a water tube boiler designed for the downward flow of heated liquids.

downfeed distribution A water distribution system that uses gravity to develop pressure.

downlight Small, concentrated direct lighting unit recessed in ceiling.

downspout A pipe for carrying rain water from roof gutters to the ground or the storm sewer system.

downstream face The dry side of a dam.

downtime The time a machine is not working because of repairs or adjustments.

dowsing Non-scientific method of searching for water or ore deposits by holding a branch or a pendulum in the hand; witching.

dozer Abbreviation for bulldozer shovel dozer, angle dozer or calf dozer.

dozer shovel A tractor equipped with a front-mounted bucket that can be used for pushing, digging and truck loading.

dozy *(see dote)*

draft (1) Resistance to movement of a towed load. (2) The drawing power of a chimney and its smoke pipe for furnace. (3) A smooth strip, either curved or straight, worked on stone for leveling or squaring the stone.

draft chisel A chisel used to make a draft on the face of a stone by striking it with a mallet.

draft gauge Usually a manometer for measuring the static pressure of the gases passing through a flue.

drafted margin A smooth, uniform margin worked into the edges of the face of a stone.

draftsman (draughtsman) One who translates a design into drawings.

draftsman's scale A measuring scale used by draftsmen; usually triangular in shape but sometimes flat. One edge is graduated $1/16$, $1/8$, $1/4$, $1/2$ and so on, as on a standard scale. Other edges are divided into other fractional parts to facilitate reducing measurements.

draft stop (fire stop) Any obstruction placed in air passages to block the passing of flames or air currents upward or across a building.

draft tube The metal casing by which water exits a turbine; similar to the diffuser of a centrifugal pump.

drag (1) Pulling a bucket into the digging; or the mechanism by which the pulling is done or controlled. (2) A metal plate with serrated edges used to level plaster surfaces and to produce a key for the next coat of plaster. (3) Resistance to the brush by paint or varnish while it is being applied. (4) *(slang)* To quit work just to draw pay.

drag brake On a revolving shovel, the brake which stops and holds the drag or digging drum.

dragged work A rock surface which has been smoothed with a drag.

dragging off Process of straight-edging, or rodding, concrete to a specific grade.

dragline A power shovel attachment used to remove earth from a ditch, canal, or pit. A revolving shovel which carries a bucket attached only by cables and digs by pulling the bucket toward itself.

dragon beam A horizontal timber into which the end of the hip rafter is framed with the outer end and carried on the corner of the building where the wall plates meet, the inner end placed at the angle tie.

dragon's blood In painting, any of several substances, mostly red in color, obtained from a variety of trees, not soluble in water but soluble in alcohol and ether; used for coloring varnishes.

dragon tie In carpentry, an angle tie.

drag scraper A digging and transporting device consisting of a bottomless bucket working between a mast and an anchor. A towed bottomless scraper used for land leveling; called leveling drag scraper to distinguish it from cable type.

dragshovel (hoe; backhoe; pullshovel)

A shovel equipped with a jack boom, a live boom, a hinged stick and a rigidly attached bucket that digs by pulling toward itself.

drag up *(slang)* To quit the job.

drain A conduit or pipe, usually underground, for carrying off, by gravity, liquids other than sewage and industrial wastes, but including ground or subsoil water, surface water and storm water.

drainage The interception and removal of water from, on or under an area or roadway; the process of removing surplus ground or surface water artificially. A general term for gravity flow of liquids in conduits. It may include sewage.

drainage area (drainage basin) A catchment area.

drainage basin (1) An area from which runoff water, rain or snow collects to feed a stream. As an example, the drainage section of a trunk river consists of the basins of its tributaries. (2) Area where water is collected at the end of irrigation rows and from which water can be pumped for reuse.

drainage ditch An artificially constructed open depression constructed for the purpose of carrying off surface water.

drainage fill Base course of granular material placed between floor slab and sub-grade to impede capillary rise of moisture. Also, lightweight concrete placed on floors or roofs to promote drainage.

drainage head The furthest or highest spot in a drainage area.

drainage-piping All or any part of the drain pipes or a plumbing system.

drainage system A system, drainage-piping, which includes all the piping within public or private premises; it conveys sewage, rain water, or other liquid wastes to a legal point of disposal, but does not include the mains of a public sewer system or private or public sewage treatment or disposal plant.

drainage wells Vertical wells or boreholes usually downstream of impervi-ous cores, grout curtains, or cutoffs, designed to collect and control seepage through or under a dam so as to reduce uplift pressures under or within a dam. A line of such wells forms a drainage curtain.

drainback A type of liquid heating system which is designed to drain into a tank when the pump is off.

drainboard The surface adjacent to the rim of a kitchen sink, usually sloped or grooved to drain into the sink.

drain chute A special drain pipe, the upper half tapered at the point where a drain enters or leaves a manhole. It is shaped in such a way that removal of obstructions can be done easily.

drain cock A cock or faucet at the lowest point of a water system whereby the system can be drained, if desired.

draindown A type of liquid heating system which protects collectors from freezing by automatically draining when the pump is turned off.

drain, intercepting (curtain drain) A drain that intercepts and diverts ground water before it reaches the area to be protected.

drain pipes Underground pipes which remove sewage, waste water or rainwater.

drain tile Pipe of burned clay, concrete, etc., in short lengths, usually laid with open joints to collect and remove drainage water.

draped tendons *(see deflected tendons)*

draught (draft) (1) Old term for drawing. (2) The pressure difference at the foot of a chimney between the air inside and outside which draws air up from the fire into the chimney.

draught bead A deep bead.

draughtsman British spelling for draftsman.

draw A small valley or gully.

drawbar In a tractor, a fixed or hinged bar extending to the rear, used as a fastening for lines and towed machines or loads; in a grader, the connection between the circle and the front of the frame.

drawbar horsepower A tractor's flywheel horsepower minus friction and slippage losses in the drive mechanism and the tracks or tires.

drawbar pull The pull a tractor can exert on a load attached to the drawbar; depends on power, weight and traction.

draw bolt A barrel bolt or any other simple bolt pushed by hand.

drawbore In carpentry, to drill holes through a tenon and a mortised piece about ⅛ inch out of line so that a tapered pin driven through the hole will draw the pieces more closely together.

draw bridge A bridge made to draw up or let down, much used in fortified places. In navigable rivers, the arch over the deepest channel is made to draw or revolve in order to let the masts of ships pass through.

draw-door weir A weir with gates which can be vertically elevated.

drawdown (1) Difference between static water table and height of water table at a working well. (2) In dam construction, the resultant lowering of water surface level due to release of waste from the reservoir.

draw-file Pushing a file across a surface with its length at right angles to the direction of movement, to produce a smoother surface than the usual method of filing and remove less metal.

drawing board A rectangular, smooth-surface slab, usually less than an inch thick and usually of soft wood, on which is fastened paper, linen or other thin material on which a drawing is to be made.

drawings The portion of the contract documents showing in graphic or pictorial form the design, location and dimensions of the elements of a project; a graphic representation.

draw-in system In electrical work, a carefully planned wiring system placed in conduits or ducts whereby the cables can be pulled and replaced when required.

drawknife A curved, two handled knife used in digging clay or in woodworking.

draw pin A removable pin that attaches a load to a drawbar.

drawpoint A spot where gravity-fed ore from a higher level is loaded into hauling units.

draw tongue A bar hinged to a towed machine, fitted with some device for attaching it to a tractor.

draw works The power distribution and control machinery of a rotary drill.

drayage The shipment of materials from point of manufacture to point of use.

dredge To dig under water.

dredging well The opening in a dredging machine through which the ladder or cutter passes to the bottom of the water.

dress To plane and sandpaper lumber; to cut and shape stones.

dressed and matched (tongue and groove) Boards or planks machined in such a manner that there is a groove on one edge and a corresponding tongue on the other.

dresser coupling Used on plain-end pipe for flexible joints and expansion joints; consists of a bolted cast iron ring and gasket.

dressing Term applied to smoothing lumber or facing stone.

dressing compound Hot or cold bituminous liquid for dressing the exposed surface of roofing felt.

dress up To fasten together, in subassemblies, structural members of the ground before erection.

dried strength The compressive or flexural strength of refractory concrete determined after first drying in an oven at 220°F to 230°F (105 to 110C) for a specified time.

drier (1) A varnish-like liquid that is added to paints or varnishes to hasten their drying; driers are usually metallic compositions, available also in solid form. (2) A manufactured device containing a desiccant placed in the refrigerant circuit, its primary purpose being to collect and hold within the desiccant all water in the system in excess of the amount which can be tolerated in the circulating refrigerant.

drift (1) To enlarge a hole with a conical pin. (2) A small nearly horizontal tunnel. (3) The speed of movement of a body of water. (4) In aerial survey, the angle made by the fore-and-aft line of an airplane with its actual course. The difference between the two is caused by the wind. (5) In a water spray device, the entrained unevaporated water carried from the device by air movement through it.

drift barrier A structure built across a waterway to catch driftwood by wire ropes or chains.

drift bolts Bolts used to connect members by driving into a prebored hole of smaller diameter.

drifter (1) An air drill mounted on a column or crossbar and used for horizontal drilling from underground, or drilling blastholes. (2) An underground mine or tunnel laborer.

drift pin A tapered pin used during erection to align holes in steel members to be connected by bolting or riveting.

drift plug In plumbing, a wooden plug driven through a lead pipe to straighten out a kink.

drill To cut a cylindrical hole; the machine used for such cutting.

blast hole A machine capable of drilling holes four inches or more in diameter to a depth of 100 or more feet

churn spudding A drill that cuts its hole by raising and dropping a chisel bit.

core A drill that cuts around a cylinder of rock or soil and lifts it to the surface for inspection.

diamond A rotary drill that uses a diamond-studded bit.

percussion A drill that hammers and rotates a steel and bit; sometimes limited to a large blast hole drill of the percussion type.

quarry A blast hole drill.

well A churn drill mounted on a truck.

drill bow The bow portion of a bow drill.

drill carriage (jumbo) A movable stage which has several rock drills attached to it and is used in tunneling. it travels on the tunnel floor.

drill collar Thick-walled drill pipe used immediately above a rotary bit to provide extra weight.

drill doctor *(slang)* A mechanic or shop that sharpens and services drill bits, tools and steel.

drill feed (1) The mechanism to push a drilling tool into a hole. (2) The speed at which a drilling tool operates.

drilling core Exploratory drilling that includes cutting cylinders of rock or soil and bringing them to the surface for inspection.

drilling mud Drilling fluid.

drilling, sectional Curving a rotary drill hole to avoid obstacles or to reach side areas.

drilling, solid In diamond drilling, using a bit that grinds the whole face without preserving a core for sampling.

drill pipe The sections of a rotary drilling string connecting the kelly with the bit or collars.

drill steel Hollow steel connecting a percussion drill with the bit.

drill string In rotary drills, all revolving parts below the ground. In churn drills, the tools hanging from the drilling cable.

drip (1) A cutout in the underside of a projecting piece of wood, stone or concrete to prevent water from working its way back to the wall. (2) A condensation drain line in vapor heating systems or plumbing.

drip cap A molding placed on the exterior top side of a door or window to cause water to drip beyond the outside of the frame.

drip channel A throat of drip.

drip edge The edge of a roof which drips into a gutter or into the open; often stiffened with a bead.

drip mold A molding designed to prevent rain water from running down the face of a wall.

dripping eave An eave with no gutter.

drip-stone The label or hood molding which serves as a canopy for an opening, and to throw off the rain. It is also called weather molding.

drive (1) To dig or make a tunnel. (2) To hammer down piling. (3) The means of transmitting mechanical power. (4) An access to property.

drive clamp A collar fitted on a churn drill string to enable it to be used as a hammer to drive casing pipe.

driven cast-in-place pile A reinforced-concrete pile cast in a hole formed in the ground by driving a steel casing. The casing is then filled with concrete which is tamped in place. The casing is withdrawn as soon as the concrete is placed.

driven pile A piling of wood, steel or reinforced concrete forced into the ground by striking it with a pile hammer.

drive, positive A drive connection to two or more wheel or shafts that will turn them at approximately the same relative speed under any conditions.

driver One who forms the heads on hot rivets with a pneumatic rivet gun.

drive screw (screw nail) A type of screw which can be driven in with a hammer but is removed with a screw driver.

driveway A private access. In Britain, simply called a drive.

driving band A steel band placed around the head of a timber pile to prevent it from brooming or mushrooming.

driving cap (driving helmet) A steel cap placed over the upper end of steel pile to reduce damage done by driving.

driving clearance Minimum distance from any other feature to the center of a rivet (usually diameter of rivet plus ¼″).

driving home (1) In shop work, the placing of a part, a nail or screw in its final position by driving it with the

blows of a hammer or screw driver. (2) Used in describing pile driving.

drop (1) A structure for dropping the water in a conduit to lower level and dissipating its surplus energy. (2) The throw of a rock fault measured vertically.

drop apron (drip) In roofing, a metal strip fixed vertically at eaves, verges and gutters and held by a lining plate.

drop arch A form of the lancet arch in which the centers of the two halves are located within the span.

dropback A reduction in the softening point of bitumen that occurs when bitumen is heated in the absence of air. *(see softening point drift)*

drop ball (skull cracker) A heavy weight which is raised by a crane and dropped on large pieces of rock in the quarry for crushing, to eliminate the need for secondary blasting.

drop-bottom bucket A container for placing concrete arranged so that the bottom opens when it touches the surface on which the concrete is to be deposited or previously has been deposited.

drop ceiling (dropped ceiling) A false or lowered ceiling.

drop cloth A protective sheet (as of cloth or plastic) used by painter to cover floors or furniture.

dropchute A device used to confine or to direct the flow of a falling stream of concrete.

articulated A dropchute consisting of a vertical succession of tapered metal cylinders which are so designed that the lower end of each cylinder fits into the upper end of the one below.

flexible A dropchute consisting of a heavy rubberized canvas tube.

drop connection *(see drop manhole)*

drop elbow (tee) A small tee or elbow with ears for ease in screwing it in close to a wall.

drop escutcheon (drop key plate) A small metal plate pivoted to cover a keyhole when the key is not in the lock.

drop hammer A pile driving hammer

that is lifted by a cable and obtains striking power by falling freely.

drop-in beam A simple beam, usually supported by canteilver arms, with joints so arranged that it is installed by lowering into position.

drop inlet A type of catch basin top which is set lower than the surrounding pavement.

drop manhole A shaft in which sewage falls from a sewer to a lower level.

drop match When the design in a carpet or wall covering is dropped in the next combining width of carpet to maintain the pattern.

drop molding Panel molding below the framing surface.

drop of beam A term used in testing materials to indicate that a test piece has passed the yield point as shown by the sudden dropping of the weighing beam of the testing machine.

drop-out bin or box Dust housing (dust chamber) at feed end of rotary kiln, for collection of coarsest dust particles in kiln exhaust.

drop panel The structural portion of a flat slab which is thickened throughout an area surrounding the column, column capital or bracket.

drop panel form A retainer or mold so erected as to give the necessary shape, support and finish to a drop.

drop siding Exterior wall covering of horizontal boards rebated on the lower edge to overlap.

drop system In plumbing, a heating circuit in which the flow pipe rises immediately to its highest level and then feeds downward through branches which drop as nearly vertically as possible to a return main.

drop wire An electrical cable dropped from the nearest pole to connect a building with electrical service.

drove A mason's blunt chisel for facing stone.

drum (1) A circular wall which carries a dome. (2) A round stone block forming part of a stone column. (3) A rotating cylinder with side flanges used for winding in and releasing cable. (4) A truck-mounted concrete mixing cylinder.

drum dryer A welded steel cylinder with two riding rings supported on rollers. Includes counter-flow dryers and parallel-flow dryers, depending on the flow direction of materials and hot gases.

drum gate A spillway gate, shaped like a portion of a circle, which releases water through appropriate valves.

drummer (1) In Britain, the worker who makes the tea on a building site. (2) A smith's striker.

drum screen In sewage, a screen shaped like a cylinder turning on its center line.

drum, spudding In a churn drill, the winch that controls the drilling line.

drum-type machine A hoisting machine with a winding drum, on which the ropes or counterweight ropes wind during hoisting.

drunken saw A circular saw which is purposely set slightly off the perpendicular so that it makes a wide cut for cutting open mortises.

dry area A narrow roofed area between the basement wall and the retaining wall outside. It is designed to keep the basement wall dry.

dryback boiler Firetube boiler with a refractory lined back door. Door opens to allow maintenance and/or inspection.

dry batch weight The weight of the materials, excluding water, used to make a batch of concrete.

dry-bulb temperature The temperature of the air as recorded by the ordinary, as differentiated from the wet-bulb, thermometer.

dry-bulb thermometer An ordinary thermometer which indicates the dry bulb temperature. *(see hygrometer)*

dry construction Building without plaster or mortar as in methods using prefabricated building sections. The building is ready for occupancy very quickly but may be expensive.

dry density The weight of dry material in a soil sample after drying at 105C.

dry-density/moisture-content relationship The relationship between dry-density and moisture-content of soil for a specific amount of compaction. The relationship is often drawn on a graph so that optimum moisture content can be determined.

dry dock A docking enclosure, into which a vessel can be floated, and from which water can be pumped and excluded; generally used in repair and construction of boats.

dryer A mechanical drying machine used to take moisture out of veneer.

dryers Process equipment designed to remove moisture from cement raw materials - coal, slag, etc. - before grinding. Types include: drum dryers, rapid dryers, impact dryers, tandem drying-grinding; drying also in mechanical air separators and in autogenous grinding mills.

dry galvanizing The galvanizing process in which steel is first fluxed in hot ammonium chloride solution, then dried in hot air, and finally passed through a bath of molten zinc.

dry grinding A comminution process wherein the mill feed is partially or completely dry and the mill product is essentially dry.

drying-grinding A dry grinding process wherein moisture in the mill feed is removed during grinding by heat supplied from an outside source. Grinding and drying are carried out simultaneously in the mill circuit.

drying oil In painting, an oil possessing the property of taking up oxygen from the air and changing to a relatively hard, tough and elastic substance when exposed in a thin film to the air.

drying shrinkage Contraction caused by drying.

drying zone That zone near the feed end of the kiln, in which the moisture in the slurry evaporates, usually at temperatures between 400-1200 deg. F. (200-650C).

dry joint A joint between two structures or parts of a structure that allow for relative movement caused by shrinkage, expansion or settlement.

there is no actual connection between the adjacent parts.

dry-jointed Without mortar.

dry kiln An ovenlike chamber in which wood is seasoned artificially to hasten the process of drying.

dry masonry Block or brick laid without mortar.

dry measure A system of units of measuring any capacity:

    2 pints (pts.) = 1 quart (qt.)

    8 quarts (qts.) = 1 peck (pk.)

    4 pecks (pks.) = 1 bushel (bu.)

    105 quarts (qts.) = 1 barrel (bbl.)

dry mix A mixture containing little water in relation to its other components.

dry mixing Blending of the solid materials for mortar or concrete prior to adding the mixing water.

dry-mix shotcrete Pneumatically conveyed shotcrete in which most of the mixing water is added at the nozzle. *(see pneumatic fed)*

dry mortar In masonry, mortar which contains enough moisture to cause it to set properly, but is not wet enough to cause it to be sticky; also, mortar which still retains a granular consistency.

dry-out A condition occasionally occurring in gypsum plaster work which by excessive evaporation or suction has lost some or all of the water necessary for crystallization. Appears as a light colored, friable area.

dry-pack To fill with concrete by ramming in a damp concrete mixture usually by means of a piece of timber and a striking hammer; also the mixture so placed.

dry-packed concrete A concrete mixture sufficiently dry to be consolidated only by heavy ramming.

dry-press Making cast stone with a very dry mix so that the stone can be unmolded quickly.

dry-press brick A brick of good quality made from nearly dry clay, five percent to seven percent moisture, pressed into molds at pressures from 550 to 1150 psi.

dry process In the manufacture of cement, the process in which the raw materials are ground, conveyed, blended and stored in a dry condition.

dry-rodded volume The volume which would be occupied by an aggregate if it were compacted dry under the standardized conditions used in measuring unit weight of aggregate.

dry-rodded weight Weight per unit volume of an aggregate compacted dry by rodding under standardized conditions.

dry-rodding In measurements of the weight per unit volume of coarse aggregates, the process of compacting dry material in a calibrated container by rodding under standardized conditions.

dry-rot A rapid decay of timbers by which its substance is converted into a dry powder which issues from minute cavities resembling th borings of worms.

dry sand method Method of determining field density of soils.

dry-set mortar A water-retentive hydraulic cement mortar usable with or without sand. When this mortar is used, neither the tile nor walls have to be soaked during the installation process.

dry shake See monolithic surface treatment.

dry stone wall British term for drywall.

dry tamp process The placing of concrete or mortar by hammering or ramming a relatively dry mix into place.

dry tape The application of tape over gypsum board joints with adhesives other than conventional joint compound.

dry to handle In painting, the last stage in the drying of a paint film when it can be handled freely without damage.

dry topping (*see monolithic surface treatment*)

dry vent Any vent that does not carry water or water-borne wastes.

dry-volume measurement Measurement of the ingredients of grout, mortar or concrete by their bulk volume.

drywall A wall laid without the use of mortar; also, a wall constructed of material which is put in place without the use of plaster. Preformed sheets of such material. (*see plasterboard*)

dry wall A type of construction where the interior finish material used is something other than plaster, such a gypsum wallboard; also the common term for gypsum wallboard.

dry weather flow The sewer flow during 24 hours of dry weather, usually roughly equivalent to water consumption in 24 hours as opposed to usage plus storm runoff.

dry well (1) A deep hole, covered and usually lined or filled with rocks, that holds drainage water until it soaks into the ground. (2) The part of a pumphouse containing the machinery as opposed to the wet well which contains water.

dry wood Any lumber from which the sap has been removed by seasoning.

dual system In plumbing, the two-pipe system.

dual vent A dual vent, sometimes called a unit vent, is a group vent connecting at the junction of two fixture branches and serving as a back vent for both branches.

dubbing out In plastering, the rough formation of a cornice or other elaborate form before the finishing coat is run.

Duchemin's formula A formula for determining wind pressure normal to a roof sloping at 0 degrees to the horizontal when the wind pressure on a vertical surface is known.

duckbill A dowel bit.

duckbill nail A nail which is chisel pointed.

duckboard A cat ladder.

duct A passage for air or gas flow. (1) In post-tensioning, a hole made in a post-tensioned member to accommodate a tendon. (2) In a house, usually round or rectangular metal pipe for distributing warm air from the heating plant to rooms, or air from a conditioning device. (3) Underground encased conduit, or group of them, for electric wiring, telephone, or other utilities. **(4)** A square or rectangular shaped trough, with or without stamped knockouts for conduit fittings, that serves as a wireway.

ductility That property of metal which allows the metal to be permanently deformed before final rupture, as in drawing out into a wire.

ductube An inflated tube used to form cable ducts in concrete. It is left until the concrete is partly set, then deflated and withdrawn.

due care A legal term indicating the requirement for a professional to exercise reasonable care, skill, ability and judgement in the performance of his duties and services consistent with the level of such services provided by reputable professionals in the same geographical area and at the same period of time.

duff **(1)** Vegetable matte on the ground; twigs; leaves or dead logs. **(2)** *(slang)* Used for incentive, as in "get off your."

Duff Abrams' law See Abrams' law.

dumb barge A barge, used to carry dredged material which may be self-powered and self discharging.

dumbbell kiln A kiln in which the center section is of a lesser diameter than the ends.

dumbwaiter A small elevator for transporting material or other small objects between stories. Not used for passenger service.

dummy **(1)** *(CPM)* A pseudoactivity with duration of zero. A dummy is a dotted line arrow and used solely to indicate sequence. **(2)** In plumbing, a lump of metal fixed on the end of a long rod used as an internal mallet to straighten large pipes. **(3)** In masonry, a round lump of zinc or lead with a short handle used in working soft stone.

dummy joint A joint placed in sidewalks and patios, strictly for design.

dumpling In a large excavation, a mass of ground with excavation on two or more sides. It is left untouched until the end of the dig and is used as an abutment for timbering the sides of the dig

which eliminates the need for long heavy timbers.

dumpman (spotter) A laborer who directs dump trucks and spots the sites for dumping material.

dumpy level A commonly used surveying level in which the telescope with its level tube is attached rigidly to the vertical spindle.

Dunagan analysis A method of separating the ingredients of freshly mixed concrete or mortar to determine the proportions of the mixture.

dunnage **(1)** Waste lumber. **(2)** Temporary timber decking. **(3)** Strips of wood used in stowing cargo to provide air space between pieces or packages.

dunter A mason who prepares large faces of monument granite for polishing with a pneumatic surfacing machine; a pneumatic surfacing machine.

Dunville stone Very fine-grain, light buff sandstone, soft when first quarried, but hardening on exposure; susceptible to finest carving; much used in interior work.

duodecimal system The feet and inches system or other systems in which 12 small units make up a large unit.

duplex A house containing two separate dwelling units.

duplex apartment One having rooms on two floors, with private stairway between.

duplex cable *(see twin cable)*

duplex nail A double headed nail used in forming; designed for easy removal, as the top head is not flush with the wood.

duplex outlet Electrical wall outlet having two plug receptacles.

durability The ability of materials to resist weathering action, chemical attack, abrasion and other conditions of service.

Duralumin Trade name for an alloy of aluminum used in construction, largely in rolled sheets.

duramen The heartwood of an exogenous tree trunk.

duration (D)　*(CPM)* Estimated time to perform an activity.

Dur-O-Wal　Trade name for a horizontal reinforcement in masonry design.

dust　(1) An air suspension of particles of any solid material, usually with particle size less than 100 microns. (2) Organaic or inorganic particles formed by operations other than combustion process.

dust chamber　The chamber or housing at the feed end of a kiln where coarse dust is trapped or deposited through changes in gas velocity or direction.

dust collectors　Equipment used to entrap and control dust effluent from a process. Types used to control dust emissions in cement manufacture include: cyclone collectors, gravity settling chambers, fabric filters, gravel bed filters, and electrostatic precipitators.

dust free　In painting, a stage in drying of a finish after which dust will not stick to the finish.

dusting　The development of a powdered material at the surface of hardened concrete.

dusting brush　A round or flat brush used to remove dust before painting.

dust laying oil　Oil of sufficiently low viscosity to be applied without preheating; may be slow curing liquid asphaltic product or non-volatile petroleum distillate containing no asphalt.

dust palliative　Type of asphalt emulsion sprayed onto gravel roads to control dust and stop erosion.

dust-press　The principal processes used for forming ceramic tiles. The tiles are dried to a dust consistency before being pressed into shapes.

dusty butt　*(slang)* Laborer.

Dutch arch (French arch)　An arch, flat at top and bottom in which only the center bricks are wedge shaped.

Dutch barn　A steel-framed building with no walls and a curved roof.

Dutch bond　Similar to English bond except at the corners, where a three-quarter brick finishes the stretcher course and the closer is omitted in the header course. Also can mean English cross bond or Flemish bond.

Dutch door　A door consisting of separately hinged halves, so that the bottom may be left shut while the top is open. Usually used as a stable door.

Dutch lap　A type of shingle application wherein the shingles have both a side lap and a head lap.

Dutchman　(1) An odd piece inserted to fill an opening or to cover a defect in carpentry or other trades. (2) A simple gin-pole crane mounted on a base frame with wheel so that it can be moved by hand and anchored with guy cables. (3) Colloquial name for a narrow strip of carpet side, seamed to standard width broadloom to compensate for unusual offsets, sloping walls, etc., but never used as a substitute for good planning and proper stretching techniques.

Dutch mattress　In hydraulics, a mattress of reed and timber for protecting the river or sea bed from scour.

dwang　(1) In Scotland, strutting between floor joists. (2) A crowbar.

dwarf partition　Partition which ends short of the ceiling.

dwarf wall　The walls enclosing courts, above which are railings of iron. Walls between the topmost ceiling level and the finished roof level.

dwelling　A building designed or used as the living quarters for one or more families.

dye beck　A large vat into which rolls of carpet are submerged for piece dyeing.

dyeing　Impregnating fabric with dye.

　solution dyeing　Synthetic yarn which is spun from a colored solution; the filament is thus impregnated with the pigment.

　stock dyeing　Fibers are dyed before spinning.

　yarn (or skein) dyeing　Yarn dyed before being fabricated into carpet.

　piece dyeing　Carpet dyed "in a piece" after tufting but before other finishing processes such as latexing or foaming.

　cross dyeing　Method of dyeing fabrics with dyestuffs which have different affinities for different types of yarns.

space dyeing Process whereby different colors are "printed" along the length of yarn before it is manufactured into carpet.

continuous dyeing The process of dyeing carpet in a continuous production line, rather than piece-dyeing separate lots. Most often done on Kuster continuous dyeing equipment which flows on dyestuffs, as distinguished from submerging carpet in separate dye becks.

dye penetrant A penetrating dye used to locate defects in metals, welds, etc.

dyestuff The substance which adds color to textiles by absorption into the fiber.

dymaxion A word coined by R. Buckminster Fuiller and defined as mass-produced logic. The term is known widely in connection with his Dymaxion House, a design for a dwelling of hexagonal plan supported by a central mast and cables, surrounding a core of utilities.

dynamic Forces tending to produce motion.

dynamic analysis Analysis of stresses in framing as functions of displacement under transient loading.

dynamic balance A condition of rest created by equal strength of forces tending to move in opposite directions.

dynamic load A load which is variable, i.e., not static, such as a moving live load, earthquake or wind.

dynamic loading Loading from units, particularly machinery, which by virtue of their movement of vibration, impose stresses in excess of those imposed by their dead load.

dynamic modulus of elasticity The modulus of elasticity computed from the size, weight, shape and fundamental frequency of vibration of concrete test specimen or from pulse velocity.

dynamic penetration test (drop penetration test) Tests such as the Raymond standard test as distinguished from static penetration tests.

dynamic pile formula Formula for the safe load on a pile calculated from the energy of the hammer-blow and the penetration of the pile from each blow.

dynamic strength The resistance to loads applied suddenly.

dynamite A mixture of an explosive or explosives with relatively inert material.

dynamite, straight A dynamite in which nitroglycerin is the principal or only explosive.

dynamo A machine for transforming mechanical work into electric current.

dynamometer A device for applying and measuring power developed by an engine or motor.

Dywidag bar An abbreviation of "Dykerhoff & Widmann, AG. A very high tensile strength steel bar which has coarse threads and can be used with associated high strength nuts. Commonly used in post tensioning concrete.

e   erg

E   engineer

ea   each

E and OE   errors and omissions excepted

ecol   ecology

EE   Electrical engineer, errors excepted

EEO   Equal Opportunity Employer

eff   efficieny

EG   edge grain

ehf   extremely high frequency

EHP   effective horsepower, electric horsepower

elec   electrical, electricity

elev   elevator

EM   electromagnetic, end matched, engineer of mines

EMF   electromotive force

emu   electromagnetic unit

enam   enameled

enc/encl   enclosure

eng/engr   engine, engineer

EPA   Environmental Protection Agency

EPCRA   Emergency Planning and Community Right to Know Act (of 1986).

eq   equation

equip   equipment

equiv   equivalent

erec   erection

est   estimate

esu   electrostatic unit

Et   ethylEV   electron volt

evap   evaporate

ex   extra, example

exc   excavation, except

ext   extension, exterior, external

extg   extracting

exx   examples

E   1. The rating of elasticity or stiffness of a material. 2. Symbol for voltage, electrical pressure, electromotive force.

ear   In plumbing, a projection on a metal pipe by means of which the pipe may be nailed to a wall. *(see crossette)*
earliest event occurrence time *(C.P.M.)* The earliest point in time that all activities that precede (whose arrows enter) the event will be completed.

earliest finish (EF)   *(C.P.M.)* Earliest time an activity can be finished.

earliest start (ES)   *(C.P.M.)* Earliest time an activity can be started.

earliest start time   *(C.P.M.)* The first day upon which work on an activity can begin if every preceding activity is finished as early as possible.

early strength   Strength of concrete developed soon after placement; usually during the first 72 hours.

earth   (1) The softer materials of the outer surface of the earth. Its basic constituents are the products of rock disintegration, glaciation and erosion, consisting of boulders, cobbles, pebbles, sand, silt and clay. (2) British term for an electrical ground.

earth auger   A tool for boring holes in the earth, such as post holes. Used in underpinning for removing earth from an underpinning cylinder.

earth berm   A mound of dirt that abuts a building wall to stabilize interior temperature or to deflect the wind.

earth borer   A truck-mounted drill rig.

earth closet   A privy utilizing dry dust as and absorbent for the wastes.

earth dam (earthfill dam)   (1) A water barrier composed of earth, clay, sand, gravel or combinations of these. (2) An embankment dam in which more than 50 percent of the total volume is formed of compacted fine-grained material obtained from a borrow area.

earth drill   An auger.

earth electrode   *(British)* A metal plate, pipe or other conductor electrically connected to earth, preferably where the earth is always damp, to ensure a low electrical resistance. *(see earth)*

earthenware   Pottery from brick earth, distinguished from stoneware which is harder. Earthenware is generally considered too soft for use as drainage pipes.

earthing lead   The conductor which makes the final connection to an earth electrode.

earth-moving plant   Machinery such as scrapers, dozers, excavators, graders, loading shovels, scarifiers, etc.

earth pigments   The class of pigments which are produced by physical processing of materials mined directly from the earth. Frequently termed natural or mineral pigments of color.

earth pin   *(slang)* A steel, wood or other strong substance rod that is driven into the ground for use as an anchor for pulling, or anything that needs to be tied down.

earth plate   An earth electrode made of a large copper plate sunk in water or damp ground.

earth pressure   The push from retained earth which varies between two extremes, the minimum, or active earth force, which is the force from earth tending to overturn a free retaining wall, and the maximum, that is the passive earth force which is the resistance of an earth surface to deformation by other forces.

earth pressure at rest   The thrust from earth to a fixed retaining wall midway between the active and the passive earth forces.

earthwork   Includes all grubbing, drainage and roadway excavation, excavation for embankments, borrowing, machine grading, rock filling and preparing subgrades.

earthwork operations   The determination of the volumes of materials which must be excavated or embanked on an engineering project to bring the ground surface to a predetermined grade, and the setting of stakes to aid in carrying out the construction work according to the plans.

eased edges   Slightly rounded surfacing on pieces of lumber to remove sharp edges. Lumber four inches or less in thickness is frequently shipped with eased edges unless otherwise specified.

easement   (1) A vested or acquired right to use land other than as a tenant, for a specific purpose; such right being held by someone other than the owner who holds the title to the land. *(see right-of-way)* (2) In architecture, a curved member used to prevent abrupt changes in direction as in a baseboard or handrail. (3) In stairway construction, a triangular piece to match the inside string and the wall base where these join at the bottom of the stairs.

easement curve   A transition curve.

easing the wedges   Loosening the wedges that hold the shoring after completion of underpinning, or of arch centers after building an arch.

easting   An eastward deviation from the north-south axis of a survey.

eaves   That part of a roof which projects over the side wall; a margin or lower part of a roof hanging over the wall.

eaves course   The first course of tiles or shingles on a roof, including the course of tiles at the eaves on which the first course of single-lap tiles is bedded.

eaves fascia   A board on edge nailed along the eaves ends of the rafters. It may carry the eaves gutter and also act as a tilting fillet.

eaves flashing   A drop apron on an asphalt roof dressed into the eaves gutter.

eaves gutter (eaves trough)   A rainwater gutter built along the eaves.

eaves height   The vertical dimension from finished floor to the eave.

eaves plate   A wall plate reaching between posts or piers at the eaves. It carries the feet of the rafters when there is no wall to carry them.

eaves pole   A tilting fillet.

eaves trough (eaves gutter)   A gutter at

the eaves of a roof for carrying off rain-water.

eave strut A structural member at the eave to support roof panels and wall panels. It may also transmit wind forces from roof brace rods to wall brace rods.

ebony A fine-textured wood of Ceylon and India; heartwood is jet black or, rarely, streaked.

ebullator A device inserted in flooded evaporator tubes to prevent the evaporator from becoming oil bound or the refrigerant liquid from becoming quiescent at a pressure lower than its boiling point.

EC Electrical Conductor of Aluminum.

eccentric (1) Away from the center, whether on purpose or not. (2) A wheel or cam with an off-center axis of revolution.

eccentric load A load on a column applied at a point away from the column center causing bending; puts a bending moment on the column equal to the load multiplied by arm.

eccentric tendon A tendon which follows a trajectory not coincident with the gravity axis of the concrete member.

ecclesiastical architecture That of the church in general.

ECCS (Emergency Core Cooling System) (nuclear power) A system to flood the fueled portion of the reactor and remove the residual heat produced by radioactive decay.

echelle French term for scale, as of a drawing.

echinus An ornamental molding supporting the abacus of a capital in the Doric order of architecture; egg-and-dart molding.

echo A single reflection which can be heard as a distinct repetition of the original sound.

eclectic architecture That based on, or imitative of, styles selected by personal preference.

economic life The estimated period during which a property is expected to be useful and profitable; usually shorter than physical life; an estimate of future life.

economic obsolescence A loss in value caused by unfavorable economic influences occurring outside a structure; e.g., development of rubbish disposal area near a residence.

economizer Heat exchanger beyond the waste heat boilers in which further energy recovery is attained by using the heat from exhaust gases at temperatures of 400-600 deg. F to heat feed water for the boilers.

economy brick Brick made to fit the four-inch height module.

economy wall A four-inch thick brick wall plastered or stiffened at intervals with eight-inch piers to carry roof trusses, and projecting outwards at the sides of door and window openings.

eddy currents Circulating currents induced in conducting materials by varying magnetic fields; usually considered undesirable because they represent loss of energy and cause heating.

Eddy's theorem The bending moment in an arch at any point is equal to the product of the horizontal thrust and the vertical distance between the arch center line and the line of thrust.

edge The narrow face of a rectangular-shaped piece of lumber.

edge bar A bar used at the edge of a slab to keep it straight.

edge-bar reinforcement Tension steel sometimes used to strengthen otherwise inadequate edges in a slab, without resorting to edge thickening.

edge bonded tile Term sometimes used to designate a particular type of pre-grouted tile sheet having the front and back surfaces completely exposed.

edge form (1) A retainer used to limit the horizontal spread of fresh concrete on flat slabs. (2) A stiffening beam at the edge of a slab.

edge grain (vertical grain) Descriptive of lumber in which the annual rings form an angle of 45° or more with the surface.

edge joint A joint running in the direction of the grain between two veneers.

edge nailing Hidden or toenailing of floor boards, etc.

edger A tool used on the edges of concrete objects before hardening, to provide a rounded corner.

edge-raised A tapered, slightly rounded factory edge of gypsum board.

edge roll A decorative molding used in furniture making; the design is of Greek origin.

edgeset A unit set on its narrow side instead of on its flat side.

edge sheets Felt strips that are cut to widths narrower than the standard width of the full felt roll. They are used to start the felt-shingling pattern at a roof edge.

edge-shot board A board having a planed edge.

edge stripping Application of felt strips cut to narrower widths than the normal width of the full felt roll. They are used to cover joints.

edge toenailing A method of joining board surfaces by driving the nails at a slant so the heads of the nails will be concealed.

edge tools Tools with a cutting edge such as the hatchet, chisel, plane gouge, knife.

edge trimmer A plane with a perpendicularly recessed bottom for making square face on small timber.

edge venting The practice of providing regularly spaced protected openings along a roof perimeter to relieve moisture vapor pressure.

edging (1) The protective finishing operation of rounding off the edge of a slab to prevent chipping or damage. (2) Made of metal, vinyl or rubber, it protects the floor covering's edge at doorways and/or other areas where raw edges are exposed.

edging strip A band for the edge of a flush door.

edging trowel A rectangular concrete finishing trowel with one edge turned down so as to trim the edges off curbs, etc.

edifice A structure or building; usually the term is applied only to large structures which are distinguished as an architectural masterpiece.

Edison base The standard screw base used for ordinary lamps and Edison-base plug fuses.

EDR Equivalent direct radiation is the rate of heat transfer from a radiator or convector. It is equivalent to the square feet of surface area necessary to transfer heat at the same rate at which it is produced by a generator. A single boiler horsepower equals 140 ft_ EDR.

EER (Energy Efficiency Ratio) (Cooling) The refrigeration effect in Btu/Hr divided by the power input in watts. The higher the EER, the more efficient the unit. An EER of 8.0 or greater is recommended.

effective age The age of a building indicated by its condition and architectural appearance; may be less than actual age if building is modernized; more, if it is not in repair; an estimate of past life.

effective area (1) Area of a section assumed to be effective in resisting the applied stresses. (2) The net area of an outlet or inlet device through which air can pass; it is equal to the free area of the device times the coefficient of discharge.

effective area of concrete Area of a section assumed to be active in resisting the applied stresses; the area of a section which lies between the centroid of the tension reinforcement and the compression face of the flexural member.

effective area of reinforcement The area obtained by multiplying the right cross-sectional area of the metal reinforcement by the cosine of the angle between its direction and the direction for which its effectiveness is considered.

effective area of reinforcement in diagonal bands The area obtained by multiplying the normal cross-sectional area of the reinforcement by the cosine of the angle at which the band is inclined to the direction for which its effectiveness is considered.

effective depth Depth of a beam or slab

section measured from the compression face to the centroid of the tensile reinforcement.

effective flange width Width of slab adjoining a beam stem assumed to be effective as the flange element of a T-beam section.

effective height of a column In calculating slenderness ratio, a value × the actual column length. The value varies depending on whether the column is fully or partially restrained at both ends.

effective length of column The distance between inflection points in a column when it bends.

effective modulus of elasticity Combination of elastic and plastic effects in an over-all stress-strain relationship in the service structure.

effective opening The minimum cross-sectional area between the end of the supply-fitting outlet and the inlet to the controlling valve or faucet. The basis of measurement is the diameter of a circle of equal cross-sectional area.

effective prestress The stress remaining in concrete due to prestressing after all losses have occurred, excluding the effect of superimposed loads, but including effect of weight of member.

effective reinforcement Reinforcement of a section assumed to be active in resisting the applied stresses.

effective span The lesser of the two following distances: (1) The distance between centers of supports. (2) The clear distance between supports plus the effective depth of the beam or slab.

effective stress (effective pressure) In prestressed concrete, the stress remaining in the tendons after all losses of the prestressing load have occurred.

effective temperature An experimentally determined scale of temperature, independent of radiation.

effective thickness of a wall In the calculation of the slenderness ratio for plain brick or masonry walls, the actual thickness; for hollow walls, two-thirds the thickness of the two leaves added together.

effective value The value of AC as read on an AC voltmeter. The value of AC that gives the same amount of heat dissipation in a resistor as DC of the same value.

effective width of slab That part of the width of a slab taken into account when designing T- or L- beams.

effervesce A bubbling reaction caused when dilute hydrochloric acid contacts corbonatee minerals present in the soil.

efficiency (1) The efficiency of a lighting fixture is the ratio of the light it emits to the total light produced by the bare lamp. (2) For an engine or motor, it is the power output divided by the power input. Efficiency is always less than 100 percent. (3) The ratio of the output to the input.

efflorescence A deposit of soluble salts, usually white in color, appearing on the surface of concrete and masonry construction. Also called whiskering and saltpetering.

effluent Partially or completely treated wastewater or other liquid which flows out of a reservoir, basin, treatment plant, or industrial treatment plant, or part thereof.

egg-and-dart (egg-and-tongue; egg-and-anchor) A molding familiar in classical architecture, with the appearance of an engaged egg shape alternating with an engaged dart form.

egg crate A form of baffle diffuser used beneath fluorescent tubes for ceiling lighting.

egg-shaped sewer A sewer shaped like an egg with the small end down, chosen for its satisfactory flow when nearly empty.

eggshell (1) A painting finish. (2) A smooth, matte face to building stone.

eggshelling Chip-cracked plaster, either base or finish coat.

egress A path of exit.

ejector (1) A cleanout device, usually a sliding plate. (2) In plumbing, a power pump for raising water or sewage to a drain at a higher elevation. (3) A device which builds up a high fluid velocity in a restricted area to obtain a lower static pressure at that point so that fluid from another source may be drawn in.

ejector grill A ventilating grill with slots shaped to force the air out in different directions.

elastic A material is said to be elastic if it expands and contracts by foreseeable amounts when pulled or pushed by known forces, and resumes original shape when forces are released.

elastic constants Three constants: the modulus of elasticity; the shear modulus; and the bulk modulus, the change in stress per unit change in volume. A fourth, Poisson's ratio is sometimes included.

elastic curve (deflection curve) A curve showing the deflected shape of the neutral surface of a bent beam; an essential part of the bending theory.

elastic design A design concept utilizing the proportional behavior of materials when all stresses are limited to specified allowable values.

elasticity That property of a material by virtue of which it tends to recover its original size and shape after deformation or compaction.

elastic limit The limit of stress beyond which the strain is not wholly recoverable. In most materials, it is also the limit of proportionality.

elastic loss In pretensioned concrete, the reduction in prestressing load resulting from the elastic shortening of the member.

elastic moduli *(see elastic constants)*

elastic shortening In prestressed concrete, the shortening of a member which occurs immediately on the application of forces induced by prestressing.

elastomeric Any of various elastic substances resembling rubber.

elastomers Plastic, synthetic or natural rubber concrete additives to increase bond strength and give it other rubbery properties.

elbow A fitting, either round or rectangular, that makes a 90° turn. Round elbows are adjustable.

elbow lining The panel over a window jamb, from sill to floor.

electric-arc welding *(see arc welding)*

electric blasting cap *(OSHA)* A blasting cap designed for and capable of detonation by means of an electric current.

electric cable An insulated wire or flexible built-up conductor for transmitting a current.

electric charge A physical phenomena caused by an isolated imbalance between the number of protons and electrons in a substance.

electric delay blasting caps Caps designed to detonate at a predetermined period of time after energy is applied to the ignition system.

electric digger Electrically powered hand tool which penetrates the earth by strong vibratory action. There are various kinds for special uses, such as hole or trench digging.

electric eye A phototube used to detect the presence or absence of light.

electric field The force of attraction between opposite charges when they are brought close together but not touching.

electric heat Heat by means of electricity with coils in walls, ceiling, floors or baseboards.

electrician A person who installs or repairs electrical circuits, wiring, machines or plants.

electric precipitator Device for removing dust from the air by means of electric charges induced on the dust particles.

electric radiant heat A method of heating utilizing the energy of electric current. It has gained usage through the reduction in cost of electric current. Additional insulation is necessary in homes using electric heat since electric heat is pure energy and heat losses are expensive.

electric screwdriver A tool like an electric drill. It is used on mass-production work because of speed of operation and the exactness to which all screws are driven with the same force.

electric welding This may also mean arc welding or resistance welding.

electric duct Enclosed metal runway for electrical conductors or cables.

electrical insulation Nonconducting material wrapped around the current carrying electrical wires.

electricity Relating to the flow or presence of charged particles; a fundamental physical force or energy.

electro-copper glazing (copper glazing) Pieces of glass between flat copper cames are pressed tightly together, then placed in an electrolyte containing copper salts so that the copper strips are made the cathode and more copper is deposited on them. The glass is thus held tightly in place.

electrode A conductor leading electric current into an electrolytic cell, furnace, or welding implement. In welding, the meaning is specialized as follows: (a) in metal-arc welding the filler rod, bare or covered; (b) in carbon-arc welding, a carbon rod; (c) in atomic-hydrogen welding, a tungsten rod; (d) in resistance welding, a bar wheel or clamp which presses together the metal parts to be welded.

electrode boiler A boiler, generally larger than domestic size, which differs from the immersion heater in that the water is heated by alternating current passing through it.

electrolier A hanging electric light fixture.

electrolysis The conduction of electric current through electrolytes. Direct current causes metal to be deposited on the cathode and acid radicals or oxygen to be freed at the anode.

electrolyte A liquid or solid that conducts electricity by the flow of ions.

electrolytic Special type of capacitor which can be charged in only one direction.

electrolytic corrosion Corrosion by electrolysis.

electromagnet A soft iron bar with thick copper wire wound around it, through which a heavy direct magnetizing current passes.

electronic controls Any of the electrically operated controls used in the operation of heating or air conditioning.

electronic glue gun An instantaneous curing glue gun with its own electronic heat unit for synthetic thermosetting resin adhesives. The gun is lightweight and portable, eliminates nailing and filling of nailheads and hammer marks on many jobs.

electronics The science dealing with the development and application of devices and systems involving the flow of electrons in vacuum, gaseous media, and semi-conductors.

electro-osmosis A ground-water lowering process, used in silts to speed up natural drainage and to produce a flow of water away from an excavation. It is also used to reduce the voids in concrete and increase its strength (similar to the vacuum concrete process) and to dry walls which have a defective damp course.

electroplating Applying a surface deposit of one metal on another by electrolysis.

electrostatic flocking Specially treated fibers charged by electrostatic field. Charged fibers move vertically, at a high speed, and embed firmly in the adhesive. Process used for majority of flocked commercial carpets.

element (1) The outline of the design of a decorated window, on which the centers for the tracery are formed. (2) The term used to designate an individual construction item, stairs or picture window, or a basic part making up the construction component; e.g., each layer (element) of the exterior wall sandwich (component). (3) A substance which cannot be separated by any known mechanical or chemical means into substances different from itself.

electrostatic precipitator Collector for fine dust, whose operation is based on gas ionization in a strong electrical field. Dust-laden air is passed through a large chamber where the dust particles are ionized by contact with chains or rods connected to one pole of a high-voltage rectifier, and then attracted to and collected on the sides of ducts or collector plates connected to the other (grounded) pole. Collectors are rapped periodically to discharge dust.

elephant trunk   *(slang)* **(1)** An articulated tube or chute used in concrete placement, especially to place concrete under water. *(see dropchute and tremie)* **(2)** A steel flex tube with a bell on the input end that guides the wire into the conduit smoothly.

elevation   A two-dimensional graphic representation of the design, location and certain dimensions of the project, or parts thereof, seen in a vertical plane viewed from a given direction; distance above or below a prescribed datum or reference point; drawings representing the front, sides or rear face of a structure, or some element of the structure; usually made as though the observer were looking straight at it.

elevator   A hoisting and lowering mechanism equipped with a car or platform which moves in guides in a substantially vertical direction, and which serves two or more floors of a building or structure.

elevator, direct-plunger   A hydraulic elevator having a plunger or piston directly attached to the car frame or platform.

elevator, electric   A power elevator where the energy is applied by means of an electric driving-machine.

elevator, electro-hydraulic   A direct-plunger elevator where liquid is pumped under pressure directly into the cylinder by a pump driven by an electric motor.

elevator, freight   An elevator primarily used for carrying freight and on which only the operator and the persons necessary for unloading and loading the freight are permitted to ride.

elevator, gravity   An elevator utilizing gravity to move the car.

elevator, hand   An elevator utilizing manual energy to move the car.

elevator, hydraulic   A power elevator where the energy is applied, by means of a liquid under pressure, in a cylinder equipped with a plunger or piston.

elevator, passenger   An elevator used primarily to carry persons other than the operator and persons necessary for loading and unloading.

elevator, power   An elevator utilizing energy, other than gravitational or manual to move the car.

elevator, roped hydraulic   A hydraulic elevator having its piston connected to the car with wire ropes.

elevator, sidewalk   An elevator of the freight type for carrying material exclusive of automobiles and operating between a landing in a sidewalk or other area exterior to a building and floors below the sidewalk or grade level.

elevator landing   That portion of a floor, balcony, or platform used to receive and discharge passengers or freight.

ell (el)   **(1)** An extension or wing of a building at right angles to the main section. **(2)** A pipe shaped like a bent elbow or L.

ellipse   A curve that is longer than it is wide.

ellipsoid   A solid of which every plane section is an ellipse or a circle.

elliptical arch   An arch which is elliptical in form, described from three or more centers.

elliptical reinforced concrete pipe   Pipe which has inside width greater than inside height.

elliptical stair   A stair with a well which is shaped like an ellipse in plan.

elm   A dull brown hardwood which warps badly if not carefully seasoned; has a twisted grain, and is harder to split than oak. In other respects, it is slightly weaker.

elongated piece   One in which the ratio of the length to the width of its circumscribing rectangular prism is greater than a specified value. *(see flat piece)*

elongation   1) The fractional increase in length of a material stressed in tension.

2) The amount of stretch of a material in a given length before breaking.

elutraitor A classifier which works on the principle that large grains sink faster through liquid than small grains of the same material. Used in soil analysis.

elutriation A process of grading fine particles in a fluid such as water or air. Elutriation can be carried out by decantation or rising fluid currents. The infrasizer is an example of an air elutriator.

eluvium A deposit of material which disintegrates in place, such as gravel.

EMA (Electrical Moisture Absorption) A water tank test during which the sample cables are subjected to voltage while the water is maintained at rated temperature; the immersion time is long, in order to accelerate failure due to moisture in the insulation; simulates buried cable.

embankment A fill whose top is higher than the adjoining surface. When used near water, it is called a levee.

embankment dam Variations include homogenous earthfill, hydraulic fill, rockfill, zoned, rolled fill, etc. Any dam constructed of excavated natural materials or of industrial waste materials.

embankment wall A retaining wall placed at the foot of a bank to prevent it from sliding.

embattlement An indented parapet; battlement.

embedded reinforcement Reinforcing bars embedded in concrete.

embedment (1) The process of pressing a felt, aggregate, fabric mat, or panel uniformly and completely into hot bitumen adhesive to ensure intimate contact at all points; (2) The process of pressing granules into coating in the manufacture of factory prepared roofing, such as shingles.

embedment length The length of embedded reinforcement provided beyond a critical section.

embossed (1) Ornamental designs raised above a surface; figures in relief, as a head on a coin; decorative protu-

berances. (2) The process of raising the asphalt-coated and granule-covered surface of roofing to produce a design. The reproduction of a design on roofing. (3) Tile or sheet goods with a high-low surface. (4) In carpet, the type of pattern formed when heavy twisted tufts are used in a ground of straight yarns to create an engraved appearance. Both the straight and twisted yarns are often of the same color.

embossed hardboard A variety of hardboard that has a decorative pattern imprinted or pressed into its surface.

embrasure The opening in a battlement between the two raised solid portions or merlons, sometimes called a crenelle.

emergency lock An air lock designed to hold and permit the quick passage of an entire shift of employees.

emergency stop switch A device located in the elevator car which, when manually operated, causes the electric power to be removed from the driving-machine motor and brake of an electric elevator or from the electrically operated valves and/or pump motor of a hydraulic elevator.

emery An impure corundum stone of a blackish or bluish gray color used as an abrasive. The stone is crushed and graded.

cloth A cloth used for removing file marks and for polishing metallic surfaces. It is prepared by sprinkling powdered emery over a thin cloth coated with glue.

wheel A wheel composed mostly of emery and used for grinding or polishing purposes. It is revolved at high speed.

EMI Electromagnetic interference.

eminent domain The right to expropriate or condemn private property for public use.

emissarium A canal for the drainage of swamps, or a floodgate for the same.

emission Act of passing air contaminants into the atmosphere by a gas stream or other means.

emissivity The rate at which particles

of electricity or heat are radiated from an object.

emission spectroscopy A method of identification of elements in a sample by bombardment of electrons and ions in an arc or spark.

emittance The amount of heat radiated back from the solar collector. Measured as a percentage of energy absorbed by the collector.

Empire The design of the period of the first French Empire (18th century).

empirical formula (rule) A formula or rule based on the result of trial or experiment and not on theoretical calculations.

emplection A type of masonry in which both exterior faces are built of ashlar in alternate headers and stretchers and the core of the wall is filled with rubble.

empty-cell process Any process for impregnating wood with preservatives or chemicals in which air is imprisoned in the wood under the pressure of the entering preservative and then expands when the pressure is released, to drive out part of the injected preservative.

emulsified asphalt Emulsion of asphalt cement and water containing small amounts of emulsifying agent.

emulsifier A substance which modifies the surface tension of colloidal droplets, keeping them from coalescing, and keeping them suspended.

emulsion A relatively stable suspension of small but not colloidal particles of a substance in a liquid, the suspended particles being undissolved.

enamel A material which dries with a hard finish when applied as a paint; provides a smooth finish, either glossy or semiglossy.

enameled brick A glazed brick.

en axe French for on axis.

encase To enclose with a case or lining.

encased knot A knot whose rings of annual growth are not intergrown with those of the surrounding wood; a dead knot.

encastre The end fixing of a built-in beam.

encaustic Colored or painted and having the hues fixed or determined by the agency of heat, as encaustic tile.

encaustic decoration Decoration burnt onto bricks, tiles, glass or porcelain.

encaustic tile Tile with a surface or decoration in vitreous color.

enceinte wall An outer wall enclosing a group of buildings. Enceinte is the French word for pregnant.

enclosed knot A knot which does not appear on the surface of a board.

enclosed stair A closed stairway.

enclosure wall Nonload-bearing walls intended only to enclose space and not to support any other portion of structure.

end anchorage Mechanical device to transmit prestressing force to the concrete in a post-tensioned member. *(see anchorage)*

end area Method of computing earthwork volumes.

end bearing pile Pile acting like a column; the point has a solid bearing in rock or other dense material.

end block An enlarged end section of a member designed to reduce anchorage stresses to allowable values.

end check A surface check at the end of a piece of lumber.

end construction *(see contracted weir)*

end-grain Describing the face of a piece of timber exposed when the fibers are cut crosswise.

end frame A frame at the endwall of a building to support the roof load from one half the end bay.

end honeycomb A check on the end grain of a piece of lumber which does not extend to any lateral face of the piece.

end joint A butt joint.

end-lap joint A joint formed at a corner where two boards lap. The boards are cut away to half their thickness so that they fit into each other. They are halved to a distance equal to their width, and when fitted together the outer surfaces are flush.

endless saw A band saw.

end manhole   One at the upstream end of a sewer.

end matched   Lumber with tongues and grooves milled at the ends so that lengths may be joined without a nailing member, such as a stud or joist, under each joint.

endothermic   Pertaining to a reaction which occurs with the absorption of heat.

end product specifications   Provisions for compaction which allow results instead of specifications to be the determining factor in the selection of equipment.

end section   Flared metal attachment on the inlet and outlet of a culvert to prevent erosion of the roadbed, improve hydraulic efficiency, and improve appearance.

end span   A span which is a continuous beam or slab only at its interior support, often shorter or more heavily reinforced than interior spans. *(see exterior panel)*

end spider   Cover plate on the ends of pipe stop logs in dams.

end split   A lengthwise separation of the wood fibers at the end of a piece of lumber.

end thrust   The push from the end of a member, especially the thrust of a centrifugal pump towards the suction end, which must be resisted by a special bearing called a thrust bearing.

endurance limit   A limiting stress, below which metal will withstand an indefinitely large number of applications of such stress without fracturing.

energy audit   An accounting of the forms of energy used during a designated period, such as monthly.

Energy Conservation Design Manual   The Energy Conservation Manual for Nonresidential Buildings, developed pursuant to the Health and Safety Code Section 19878.4, to aid designers, builders and contractors of nonresidential buildings in meeting energy conservation standards.

energy efficiency ratio (EER)   The ratio of net cooling capacity in Btu/hr to total rate of electric input in watts under designated operating conditions.

energy gradient   Slope of a line joining the elevation of the energy head of stream.

energy head   The elevation of the hydraulic gradient at any section, plus the head.

enfilade   The alignment of doors on an axis extending through a series of rooms.

engage   To attach one element to a simpler and more extensive one so that the first element seems partly embedded, as an engaged column or baluster not free standing.

engaged column   One of less than circular section set flatwise against a vertical surface.

engine   (1) A machine driven by electrical, hydraulic, compressed air, internal-combustion, steam, or other power to do work such as traction, hoisting, pumping, sawing and ventilation. (2) On equipment, the prime mover; device for transforming fuel or heat energy into mechanical energy.

engineered 24" framing   A building system using structural wood panels over lumber framing spaced 24 inches on center in walls, floors and roof. The system's series of in-line frames — trusses, studs and joists — provide cost-effective materials utilization and simpler, faster construction. It is recognized by major model codes and the FHA.

engineering   The science through which the properties of matter and the sources of power are utilized for man's benefit.

engineering officer   A person designated, usually by a military component or a corporation, as having authoritative charge over certain specific engineering operations and duties.

engineer-in-training   Designation prescribed by statute for a person qualified for professional engineering registration in all respects except the required professional experience.

engineer's chain A survey chain of 100 one-foot links.

engineer's hammer (fitter's hammer) A hammer which has a striking face and a ball peen, cross peen or a straight peen.

engineer's level A telescope with a level tube attached.

engineer's transit A theodolite having a vertical graduated arc and a telescope bubble, as opposed to a plain transit which measure only horizontal angles, since it has no telescope bubble or vertical circle.

English basement A basement with half its height above grade level.

English bond A brick bond pattern in which alternate courses are composed entirely of stretchers or entirely of headers.

English cross bond Alternate courses of headers and of stretchers, with the stretcher course breaking joints with its neighboring stretcher courses. Also called St. Andrew's cross bond.

English garden-wall bond *(see American bond)*

English roofing tile A flat-top tile of clay with interlocking side joints.

engrailed Indented with curved lines or small concave scallops.

enneastyle In Classical architecture, having nine columns.

enrichment A process which treats natural uranium in such a way that a greater percentage of it is fissionable.

enrichments Cast ornament which cannot be made by a running mold.

enrockment *(see rip-rap)*

entablature A term in Classical architecture; the entire horizontal beam or component supported by columns or piers. Three major elements of the entablature are architrave, frieze and cornice.

entail (1) An early English term, derived from the French, for sculptured ornament or for any embellishment produced by carving or moldings. (2) To bequeath with restrictions.

entasis A slight convex curve in the vertical outlines of the shaft of a pilaster or of a column.

entasis of a column The swelling or outward curve of the shaft of a column to avoid the hollow appearance which would result if the column were made absolutely straight with no bulge.

entourage Environment; the grounds immediately surrounding a building.

entrained air Microscopic air bubbles intentionally incorporated in mortar or concrete during mixing.

entrainment The induced flow of room air by the primary air from an outlet, creating a mixed air path (commonly called secondary air motion).

entrance frame The door frame through which a passenge enters or leaves an elevator; consists of two side jambs and one head jamb.

entrance head The head required to cause flow into a conduit or other structure, including both entrance loss and velocity head.

entrance loss In hydraulics, the head lost in eddies and friction at the inlet to a conduit.

entrance switch An electric switch to which the wires entering a building are connected.

entrapped air Air in concrete which is not purposely entrained.

envelope An imaginary assembly of planes to represent the maximum volume of a building with regard to zoning and other volume restrictions.

environmental design professions The professions collectively responsible for the design of man's physical environment, including architecture, engineering, landscape architecture, urban planning and similar environment-related professions.

EPA (Environmental Protection Agency) The federal regulatory agency responsible for maintaining and improving the quality of our living environment - mainly air and water.

EPDM A synthetic elastomer based on ethylene, propylene, and a small amount of a non-conjugated diene to provide sites for vulcanization. EPDM features excellent heat, ozone and weathering resistance, and low temperature flexibility.

epi A topmost point, as a spire.

epichlorohydrin rubber This synthetic rubber includes two epichlorohydrin-based elastomers which are saturated, high molecular weight, aliphatic polyethers with chloro-methyl side chains. The two types include a homopolymer (CO) and a copolymer of epichloro-hydrin and ethylene oxide (ECO). These rubbers are vulcanized with a variety of reagents that react difunctionally with the chloromethyl group; including diamines, urea, thioureas, 2 mercaptoimidazoline, and ammonium salts.

epistle side The epistle side of a church, the right-hand side as one faces the altar. The left-hand side is sometimes called the gospel side.

epistomium The spout of a water pipe, or its valve.

epistlye (epistylium) In Classical architecture, the architrave, or lowest of the three divisions of an entablature.

epitaxial A very significant thin-film type of deposit for making certain devices in microcircuits involving a re-alignment of molecules.

epitithedes Greek term for the crown of upper moldings of an entablature.

epoxy (1) A common name applied to an exceptionally durable plastic-like paint. (2) A very strong glue; often comes in two parts which must be mixed before using.

epoxy grout A two-part adhesive system employing epoxy resin and epoxy hardener used for bonding ceramic tile to back up material.

epoxy plastics Thermoset plastics which have excellent adhesion properties, good resistance to chemicals, heat, weather, and a slow curing rate; used for adhesives, laminates, chemical exhaust ducts and printed circuit boards.

epoxy resins Chemical bonding systems used in the preparation of special coating or adhesives for concrete, or as binders in epoxy resin mortars and concretes.

equal angle An angle section having legs of equal length.

equalization of boundaries In surveying, a method of calculating areas which have irregular lines are replaced by straight lines which cut off on one side an amount equal to what they add on the other side. The area can then be calculated by adding the area of the triangles so formed.

equalizing bed A bed of ballast or concrete on which pipes are laid in the bottom of a trench. *(see bedding)*

equalizer (1) A culvert placed where there is no channel but where it is desirable to have standing water at equal elevations on both sides of a fill. (2) A piping arrangement to maintain a common liquid level or pressure between two or more chambers.

external In a thermostatic expansion valve, a tube connection from a selected control-point in the lowside circuit to the pressure sensing side of the control element. control-point pressure is transmitted to the actuating element (diaphragm or bellows) which provides a means for compensating for the pressure drop through accessories and the evaporator.

internal In a thermostatic expansion valve, an integral internal part of passage which provides exposure of the actuating element (diaphragm or bellows) to pressure leaving the valve.

equal loudness contours Contours on a chart are plotted for varying frequencies and intensity levels. Each point on each contour appears to the average normal ear to be just as loud as the sound represented by every other point on the same contour.

equilateral arch An arch whose span and radii of the two halves form an equilateral triangle.

equilibrium The state of a body which does not move. A body is in stable equilibrium when any slight movement increases its potential energy so that it tends to fall back to its original position when released. When moved slightly, a body in unstable equilibrium tends to move farther away from its original position.

equilibrium moisture content The moisture content of (a) soil in a given environment, at which no moisture movement occurs, and (b) in timber, when subjected to a constant condition of humidity and temperature.

equipment All machinery and equipment together with the necessary supplies for upkeep and maintenance; also tools and apparatus necessary for the proper construction and acceptable completion of the work.

equipotential Having the same voltage at all points.

equipotential lines Contours of equal water pressure in the soil mass around a water-retaining structure, such as an earth dam or river bank. *(see flow lines)*

equivalent circuit An arrangement of circuit elements that has characteristics over a range of interest electrically equivalent to those of a different circuit or device.

Equivalent Direct Radiation (EDR) A unit of heat delivery of 240 Btu per hr.

equivalent evaporation The amount of water a boiler would evaporated, in pounds per hour, if it received feed water at 212° F and vaporized it at the same temperature and corresponding atmospheric pressure.

equivalent rectangular stress distribution An assumption of uniform stress on compression side of neutral axis in a reinforced concrete section; used in Whitney method of ultimate strength design to approximate actual conditions at ultimate bending load.

equivalent temperature British term similar in meaning to effective temperature, except that it does not take into account humidity in the air and is therefore not used in heavy industry where perspiration is a factor.

equivalent thickness The solid thickness to which a hollow unit would be reduced if there were no voids and the same face dimensions. The percent solid volume times the actual width divided by 100.

Equiviscous Temperature (EVT) Range The optimum application temperature of asphalt. It is the temperature range at which a viscosity of 125 centistokes is attained, plus or minus 25F.

ERDA Energy Research and Development Administration. ERDA was created in January, 1975 to consolidate all of the energy research, development and demonstration functions that had been carried on by the U.S. Environmental Protection Agency, Department of the Interior, National Science Foundation, and Atomic Energy Commission.

erect (1) To build. (2) In geometry, to draw a line at right angles to a specified base.

erecting Raising and setting in an upright position, as the final putting together in perpendicular form the structural parts of a building.

erecting bill A bill of material for a structure so arranged as to facilitate the finding and placing of members during erection.

erecting shop A large open area where steel frames are joined after fabrication to make sure that they fit, before being shipped in separate pieces to the site.

erection The assembling of the members of a structure in the field and making the necessary permanent connections.

ergonomics The interactions between people and work, particularly the design of machines, chairs, tables, etc. to suit the body, and to permit work with minimum fatigue.

erisma A buttress of shoring to support a wall.

erosion Wear or scouring caused by the abrasive action or moving water or wind. Not to be confused with corrosion.

erratum (erratta) Correction of a printing, typographical or editorial error. Not to be confused with addendum.

escalator A system of treads, risers and handrails actuated by machinery on a concealed loop, forming a moving stairway.

escape A wasteway for discharging the entire stream flow.

escape stair British term for fire escape.

escoinson Old French term for the inner edge of a window jamb. In Scotland it is called a scuntion.

escutcheon Shield or decorative plate for door hardware, plumbing fixtures, etc.

escutcheon pin A decorative nail having a round head, used in fastening ornamental and/or protective metal plates to wood.

esker In geology, long narrow ridges of sand and gravel with steeply sloping sides and soft, winding outlines. Formed by glacial deposits.

espagnolette A kind of fastening for a French casement window, usually consisting of a long rod with hooks at the top and bottom of the sash, and turned by a handle.

esplanade A concourse of landscaped plateau with drives and walks.

esquisse Sketch from which project is developed with least possible deviation.

Essex board measure A method of rapid calculation for finding board feet; the Essex board measure table usually is found on the framing squares conveniently located for the carpenter's use.

establishment charges British term for overhead costs.

estimate (1) A forecast of construction cost, as opposed to a firm proposal. (2) A term sometimes used to denote a contractor's application or request for a progress payment. *(see application for payment)*

estimate of construction cost, detailed A forecast of construction cost prepared on the basis of a detailed analysis of materials and labor for all items of work, as contrasted with an estimate based on current area, volume or similar unit costs.

estimating A process of judging or calculating the amount of material required for a given piece of work, also the amount of labor and equipment necessary to do the work by multiplying the volume by costs per unit or measurement, and finally an approximate evaluation of the finished product.

etage *(French)* A story, or mere range of openings, of a building.

etched nails Chemically treated nails to improve their holding power in wood framing.

etching Lines cut into a metal surface, either by a cutting tool or by acid guided by wax or other covering; removal of the surface of concrete with acid to expose the aggregate.

ettringite A mineral high sulfate calcium sulfoaluminate occurring naturally or formed by sulfate attack on mortar and concrete; designated as cement bacillus in older literature.

E.U.I. (Energy Utilization Index) Btu's per gross conditioned square foot.

eutectic mixture (solution) A mixture which melts or freezes at constant temperature and with constant composition. Its melting point is usually the lowest possible for mixtures of the given substances.

eurythmy Harmonious relationship among all the parts of a building.

eustyle In Classical architecture, descriptive of intercolumniation of 2¼ diameters, center to center.

EVA Family of copolymers of ethylene and Vinyl Acetate used for adhesives and thermoplastic modifiers. They possess a wide range of melt indexes.

evaporable water Water in set cement paste present in capillaries or held by surface forces; measured as that removable by drying under specified conditions. *(see non-evaporable water)*

evaporation Change of state from liquid to vapor.

evaporative cooler An air conditioner which cools the air by the effect of water evaporation. Outdoor air is drawn through a moistened filter pad in a cabinet and the cooled air is then circulated throughout the house.

event *(C.P.M.)* The starting point in an arrow diagram for an activity. Also the completion of an activity. It requires no time. Indicated on the arrow diagram by a number enclosed in a circle.

evaporator That part of a refrigerating system in which refrigerant is vaporized to produce refrigeration.

excavate To dig earth below ground level.

excavation *(OSHA)* Any man-made cavity or depression in the earth's surface, including its sides, walls or faces; formed by earth removal and producing unsupported earth conditions by reasons of the excavation. If installed forms or similar structures reduce the depth-to-width relationship, an excavation may become a trench.

excavation, unclassified A bid item; excavation paid for at a fixed price per yard regardless of whether it is earth or rock.

excavator A power-driven digging machine, usually mounted on crawler tracks. The backhoe, dragline and face shovel are fittings which can be attached to give a different function to the excavator. It can also be used as a crane.

excess air A term used to describe the amount of air that is supplied over and above the amount theoretically required for complete combustion.

exciter (1) Lime, alkali and sulphates, when added to a crushed blast furnace slag, cause it to set when mixed with water. Portland cement acts as an exciter. (2) In electricity, a direct current generator which energizes the field magnets of an alternator or similar electric machine.

exercise en loge *(French)* Drawings prepared without assistance, criticism or the use of documents.

exfiltration Air flow outward through a wall, leak, membrane, etc.

exfoliation Disintegration occurring by peeling off in successive layers; swelling up and opening into leaves or plates like a partly opened book. Usually caused by weather.

exhaust fan A fan used to withdraw air under suction.

exhaust opening Any opening through which air is removed from a space which is being heated or cooled, or humidified or dehumidified, or ventilated.

exhaust shaft A ventilating duct to remove stale air from a room.

exothermic Pertaining to a reaction which occurs with the evolution of heat.

expanded blast-furnace slag The lightweight cellular material obtained by controlled processing of molten blast-furnace slag with water, or with water and other agents such as steam or compressed air or both. *(see blast-furnace slag)*

expanded clay *(see lightweight aggregate)*

expanded metal A metal network, often used as reinforcement in concrete construction, formed by suitable stamping or cutting sheet metal and stretching it to form open meshes, usually of diamond shape. *(see diamond mesh)*

expanded shale A lightweight aggregate made by expanding shale or clay to form strong, lightweight aggregate for concrete and concrete masonry units.

expanding bit (expansion bit) In carpentry, a drill bit with a cutter which can be adjusted to varying size. Expanding bits have no twist.

expanding cement *(see expansive cement)*

expanding plug A bag plug or screw plug used to relieve pressure.

expansion Enlargement of length or bulk by reason of temperature rise, or less commonly, through absorption of water.

expansion bend A loop in a pipe in which expansion or contraction can be taken up without damaging the pipe.

expansion bolt A bolt with a sleeve or bushing that, when set into a hole in masonry, expands and anchors itself firmly as the bolt is tightened to it.

expansion cork A cork product used to fill the expansion space in a hardwood floor installation.

expansion end The movable end of a structure, trestle, span, truss, etc.

expansion joint (1) A break or space in construction to allow for thermal expansion and contraction of the materials used in the structure. (2) A separation between adjoining parts of a concrete structure which is provided to allow small relative movements, such as those caused by temperature changes, to occur independently. **(3)** A device usually formed from sheet metal and having a "W" shaped cross section, used to provide controlled discontinuity at locations in a plaster membrane where high stresses may be encountered. Also known as a "relief joint" or "control joint."

expansion joint filler The primary purpose of an expansion joint filler is to prevent foreign material from entering the joint and rendering it ineffectual for the purpose intended. They are often made of rubber or felt material.

expansion sleeve A tubular metal covering for a dowel bar to allow its free longitudinal movement at a joint.

expansion strip Material used in discontinuous construction to fill the joint between a partition and a structural wall or column. Also used to separate a glass block wall from any structural material abutting it so as to prevent the glass cracking.

expansion tank In a hot-water heating system, an open tank in which the expansion of the hot water can take place.

expansive cement (general) A cement which, when mixed with water, forms a paste that, after setting, tends to increase in volume to a significantly greater degree than portland cement paste; used to compensate for volume decrease due to shrinkage or to induce tensile stress in reinforcement (post-tensioning).

concrete (mortar or grout) A concrete made with expansive cement.

type K An expansive cement containing anhydrous aluminosulfate burned simultaneously with a portland cement composition, or burned separately when it is to be interground with portland cement clinker or blended with portland cement, calcium sulfate and free lime.

type M A mixture of portland cement, calcium aluminate cement and calcium sulfate.

type S A portland cement containing a large computed C3A content and modified by an excess of calcium sulfate above usual optimum content.

expected total error Where different portions of a testing procedure have measurement errors, this refers to the accumulated effects of these individual errors.

expediter One who checks and hastens the arrival of building materials or equipment to meet a progress schedule. In Britain, the expediter is known as a progress chaser.

expletive In masonry, a stone which is used to fill a cavity.

exploit To excavate in such a manner as to utilize material in a particular vein or layer, and waste or avoid surrounding material.

explosion process Separation of fibers by the sudden release of high-pressure steam.

explosionproof apparatus Apparatus enclosed in a case that is capable of withstanding an explosion of a specified gas or vapor that may occur within it, and also capable of preventing the ignition of a specified gas or vapor surrounding the enclosure by sparks, flashes, or explosion of the gas or vapor within, and which operates at such an external temperature that a surrounding flammable atmosphere will not be ignited thereby.

explosives Any chemical compound, mixture or device, the primary or common purpose of which is to function by explosion; that is, with substantially instantaneous release of gas and heat, unless such compound, mixture or device is otherwise specifically classified.

class A (OSHA) Possessing detonating hazard, such as dynamite, nitroglycerin, picric acid, lead azide, fulminate of mercury, black powder, blasting caps and detonating primers.

class B Possessing flammable hazard, such as propellent explosives, including some smokeless propellents.

class C Includes certain types of manufactured articles which contain class A and class B explosives, or both, as components, but in restricted quantities.

high A material that detonates (explodes) almost instantaneously.

exposed *(OSHA)* **(1)** As applied to live parts, means that a live part can be inadvertently touched or approached nearer than a safe distance by a person. This term applies to parts not suitable guarded, isolated or insulated. **(2)** As applied to toxic contaminants, means contact by inhalation, ingestion, skin absorption or contact with any material or substance which may have immediate or latent harmful effects on health.

exposed-aggregate finish A decorative finish for concrete work achieved by removing, generally before the concrete has fully hardened, the outer skin of mortar and exposing the coarse aggregate.

exposed area That portion of roofing or a shingle which is not covered and bears the full effect of the sun, rain and weathering elements.

exposed concrete Concrete surfaces formed so as to yield an acceptable texture and finish for permanent exposure to view. *(see also architectural concrete)*

exposed masonry Masonry construction which has no type of surface finish other than paint applied to the wall face.

exposure **(1)** The transverse dimension of a roofing element not overlapped by an adjacent element in any roof system. The exposure of any ply in a membrane may be computed by dividing the felt width minus 2 inches by the number of shingled plies; thus, the exposure of a 36-inch-wide felt in a shingled, four-ply membrane should be 8 ½ inches; **(2)** the time during which a portion of a roofing element is exposed to the weather.

exposure limits The amount of radiation which humans can tolerate.

expressway A divided arterial highway for through traffic with full or partial control of access and generally with grade separations at intersections.

extended overhead Additional overhead costs incurred beyond those estimated when bidding because of completion delays and extended work schedule.

extended surface Heat transfer surface, one or both sides of which are increased in area by the addition of fins, discs, or other means.

extender A finely divided inert mineral added to provide economical bulk in paints, synthetic resins and adhesives, or other products.

extending ladder A telescopic ladder which can extend up to 50 feet.

extensibility The maximum tensile strain that hardened cement paste, mortar or concrete can sustain before cracking occurs.

extension The increase in length produced in the gage length of a test specimen during a creep test.

extension bolt (monkey-tail bolt) Usually a barrel bolt, with a handle longer than normal, that can be pushed into place or released without stooping or stretching.

extension device Any device, other than an adjustment screw, used to obtain vertical adjustment of shoring towers.

extensions Extended prices on bid sheets or estimates of cost.

extensometer An apparatus for measuring minute degrees of expansion or contraction in metal bars under the influence of temperature or stress.

exterior **(1)** The outer surface or part, as in building the exterior of the structure, or the exterior wall. **(2)** A term frequently applied to plywood, bonded with highly resistant adhesives, that is capable of withstanding prolonged exposure to severe service conditions without failure in the glue bond.

exterior glazed Glass set from the exterior of the building.

exterior panel In a flat slab, a panel having at least one edge which is noncontinuous. Sometimes called an end span.

exterior stop In glazing, the removable molding or bed that holds the light or panel in place when it is on the exterior.

exterior trim Wooden moldings for

cornices, barge boards and eaves gutters.

exterior wall Any outside wall or vertical enclosure of a building.

externally operable Capable of being operated without exposing the operator to contact with live parts.

external vibration External vibration employs a vibrating device attached at strategic positions on the forms and is particularly applicable to manufacture of precast items and for vibration of tunnel lining forms.

external wall A wall with one or more faces exposed to the weather or the earth.

extinguishing media The type of fire extinguisher or extinguishing method appropriate for use on a specific chemical. Some chemicals react violently in the presence of water, so other suggested methods, such as foam or CO_2, should be followed.

extra An item or work involving additional cost. *(see addition)*

extractables Components or substances removable from a solid or liquid mixture by means of an appropriate solvent.

extrados The outer or upper surface of an arch. *(see intrados)*

extrapolate To project tested values, assuming a continuity of an established pattern, to obtain values beyond the limit of the test results.

extra work Additional construction items which are not included in the original contract.

extreme compression fiber A fiber farthest removed from the neutral axis on the compression side of a member subjected to bending.

extruded Pushed out through a die. Bars of ice, metal rods, shapes and tubes are made by this method.

extruded section The most common light-alloy structural sections, formed by extrusion.

extruded tile A tile or trim unit that is formed when plastic clay mixtures are forced through a pug mill opening (die) of suitable configuration, resulting in a continuous ribbon of formed clay. A wire cutter or similar cut-off device is then used to cut the ribbon into appropriate lengths and widths of tile.

extruder A machine with a driven screw that forces ductile or semisoft solids through a die opening of appropriate shape to produce continuous film, strip, or tubing.

extrusion Forming rods, tubes or sections of a specified shape by pushing hot or cold metal or plastics through a shaped die.

exudation A liquid or viscous gel-like material discharged through a pore, crack, or opening in the surface of concrete.

eye (1) An opening at the top of a dome or cupola. (2) The center of the volute of an Ionic capital. (3) In hardware, the metal loop which engages a hook, such as the eye bolt.

eye bar A bar with an eye at either one end or each end.

eye bolt A bolt with a looped head or an opening in the head.

eyebrow A dormer, usually of small size, the roof line over the upright face of which is an arch curve dying into a reverse curve to meet the horizontal at either end. A gablet.

eye of a dome The opening at its summit.

eye of a volute The circle in its center.

eyelet Something used on printed circuit boards to make reliable connections from one side of the board to the other.

F   Fahrenheit, fluorine

f   fine, focal length, force, frequency

fac   facsimile

FBM   foot board measure

fdn/fdtn/tds   foundation foundations

fdry   foundry

Fe   ferrum (iron)

FE   fire escape

FEA   Federal Energy Administration

FFA   full freight allowance

FG   fine grain, flat grain

fill   filling

fl   floor, fluid

flash   flashing

fl oz   fluid ounce

fm   fathom

FM   frequency modulation

FM   factory mutual

FMV   fair market value

FOC   free of charge

fp   fireplace, freezing point

f.pfg.   fireproofing

fpm   feet per minute

fps   feet per second

fr   frame

frmg   framing, forming

frt   freight

frwy   freeway

FST   flat seam tin

ft   foot, feet

ftc   foot candle

ft lb   foot pound

ftg   footing

fth   fathom

fv   face velocity

fwd   forward

F.O.B.   Free on board; designates the location from which a shipping charge is made.

fabric   In building construction, a term often applied to the walls, floors, and roof of a building; also the framework of a structure. *(see wire-mesh reinforcement)*

fabric filters   Dust collectors of the bag type which can be tubes or envelopes fabricated from woven or felt cloth made from natural or synthetic fibers that can effectively handle particles in the submicron range. *(see bag-house)*

fabric reinforcement   A fabric, scrim, etc., used to add structural strength to a 2 or more ply polymeric sheet. Such sheeting is referred to as "supported".

fabricate   (1) Build, construct, manufacture. (2) Make by fitting together standardized parts.

fabrication   The manufacturing process performed in a plant to convert raw material into finished metal building components. The main operations are coldforming, cutting, punching, welding, cleaning, and painting.

fabricator   A maker or manufacturer.

facade (face)   The whole exterior side of a building that can be seen at one view; strictly speaking, the principal front.

face   (1 The more or less vertical surface of rock exposed by blasting or excavating. An edge of rock used as a starting point in figuring drilling and blasting. (2) The width of a crusher roll. (3) To overlay one material with another, as to face a brickwall with marble; the exposed side of a unit of masonry. (4) The wider surface of a piece of lumber; any piece of rectangular cross section that has two faces and two edges; the better side of a panel in any grade of plywood calling for a face and back. (5) The front cutting surface of a drill or of a sawtooth. (6) The surface of gypsum wallboard that can be painted without plaster. (7) The working surface of a tool, such as the part of the hammer that drives the nail in.

face-bedded stone Stone laid so that the natural bed is vertical. Only arch-stones are correctly laid like this.

face brick Brick made or selected for color, texture, or other characteristic, to be used on the exposed surface of a wall, probably to be backed up with cheaper brick or other material.

faced block Concrete masonry units having a special ceramic, glazed, plastic, polished or ground face or surface.

faced plywood Plywood faced with metal, plastics or any sheet other than wood.

faced wall A wall in which the masonry facing and the backing are of different materials and are so bonded as to act together under load.

face glazing On a rabbeted sash without stops, the triangular cross section bead of compound applied with a glazing knife after bedding, setting, and clipping the light in place.

face hammer A hammer with a striking face and a cutting peen.

face joint The portion of the cross joint which is seen on the wall face.

face layer The outer layer of gypsum board in multilayer applications.

face left The position of a theodolite when the verticle circle is left of the telescope when viewed from the eyepiece.

face mark In woodworking, a mark placed on the surface of a piece of wood to indicate that part as the face, according to which all other sides are dressed true.

face measurement The measurement of the area of a board. Not the same as board measure except on one-inch thick board.

face mix In masonry, a mixture of stone dust and cement sometimes used as a facing for concrete blocks in imitation of real stone.

face mold The pattern for marking the plank or board out of which ornamental hand-railings for stairs and other works are cut.

face-nail To nail through the face.

face piece A face waling.

face plate That part of a marking gauge pressed against the face of a board while it is being marked.

face putty The triangular fillet of glazier's putty on the exposed surface of glass.

face right The position of a theodolite when the verticle circle is right of the telescope as seen from the eyepiece.

faces (sides; walls) The vertical or inclined earth surfaces formed as a result of excavation work.

face seams Seams, either sewed or cemented, that are made without turning the entire carpet over or facedown. These are made during installation where it is not possible to make back seams.

face shell The side wall of a hollow concrete masonry unit.

face shell bedding Mortar applied on the face shells for the bed joint and to a depth equal to the face shell thickness for the head joint.

face shovel An attachment fitted to an excavator which digs away from itself into a bank with a toothed bucket attached to a rigid arm.

face side (work face) In carpentry, the surface which carries the face mark.

face string The string on a wood stairway away from a wall, as opposed to the wall string.

face veneer A veneer for decoration and not strength.

face waling A waling across the end of a trench held by the ends of the main walings which support the end of the trench in combination with the end strut.

facia (fascia) A flat board, band or face, used sometimes by itself but usually in combination with moldings; often located at the outer face of the cornice.

facial defect That portion of the tile's facial surface which is readily observed to be non-conforming and which detracts from the aesthetic appearance or serviceability of the installed tile.

facing (see face)

facing bond Any bond showing primarily stretchers.

factor of safety The ratio of the ultimate strength, or yield point, of a material to the working stress assumed in design, stress factor of safety; or the ratio of the ultimate load, moment, or shear, respectively, assumed in design; load factor of safety.

factory square 108 square feet (10 square meters) of roofing material.

fadding A painting, the lightening of a color by aging or weathering.

faggot A South African term for a special facing brick about two inches wide.

Fahrenheit A thermometric scale in which 32° denotes freezing and 212° the boiling point of water under normal pressure at sea level (14.696 psi).

faience Rough grade enameled clay products, not including the highest grades such as porcelain. They are fired twice, once without and once with the glaze.

faience mosaic A type of glazed floor mosaic.

faience tile Features characteristic variations in the face, edges and glaze which gives a hand-crafted, nonmechanical, decorative effect. Generally made by the plastic process with glazed or unglazed tile.

failure The breaking point, as that of a material tested for compressive strength to failure.

fair-faced brickwork A term for brick surface which is built neatly and smoothly.

fair-face concrete A concrete surface which, on completion of the forming process, requires no further (concrete) treatment other than curing. (see also architectural concrete)

fairlead A device which lines up cable so that it will wind smoothly onto a drum.

fall In water supply or drainage, the slope, usually given in inches per foot.

fallback A reduction in bitumen softening or overheating in a relatively closed container. (see also softening point drift)

fall-down lumber Lumber not up to a particular grade.

falling head permeameter Apparatus and method used to determine the permeability of soils.

falling mold the developed elevation of a handrail center line.

fall pipe A downpipe for a rain gutter.

false body The stiffness of a thixotropic paint which is always lessened when the paint is mixed.

false ceiling (drop ceiling) A ceiling built with a space between it and the floor above, to provide an area for cables, pipes and ductwork.

false header (see header)

false rafter A short extension added to a main rafter over a cornice, especially where there is a change in the roof line.

false set The rapid development of rigidity in a freshly mixed portland cement paste, mortar or concrete without the evolution of much heat, which rigidty can be dispelled and plasticity regained by further mixing without addition of water; premature stiffening, hesitation set, early stiffening, and rubber set are terms referring to the same phenomenon, but false set is the preferred designation.

false tongue (see slip tongue)

falsework The temporary structure erected to support work in the process of construction; composed of shoring or vertical posting formwork for beams and slabs, and lateral bracing.

fan (1) A power-driven blower. (2) A floor of scaffold boards projecting over a pedestrian area or street so that falling objects are deflected back toward the wall during building or demolition. (3) An air-moving device comprising a wheel or blade, and housing or orifice plate.

fan, attic An exhaust fan to discharge air near the top of a building while cooler air is forced (drawn) in at a lower level.

fan, centrifugal A fan rotor or wheel

within a scroll type housing and including driving mechanism supports for either belt drive or direct connection.

fan coil A unit consisting of a fan and a heat exchanger which transfers heat from liquid to air (or vice versa); usually located in a duct.

fan economizer Device which prevents the operation of the fan motor as a cold diffuser during the shutdown period after the coil has been defrosted.

fanlight An overdoor window, usually semi-eliptical or semi-circular in shape, with radial muntins or leads.

fan, propeller A propeller or disc type wheel within a mounting ring or plate and including driving mechanism supports for either belt drive or direct connection.

fan tracery The very complicated mode of roofing used in the Perpendicular style, in which the vault is covered by ribs and veins of tracery.

fan, tubeaxial A propeller of disc type wheel within a cylinder and including driving mechanism supports for either belt drive or direct connection.

fan, vaneaxial A disc type wheel within a cylinder, a set of air guide vanes located either before or after the wheel and including driving mechanism supports for either belt drive or direct connection.

fan vaulting A system of vaulting used in the Perpendicular period, in which a group of ribs springs from a slender shaft or from a corbel and then diverges. Occasionally, ribs also spring from a pendant at the center of the vaulting.

fang The shank of a tool, or the fishtailed end of a metal railing built into a wall.

farad The unit of electrical capacitance.

fascia (facia) (1) A flat member or band at the surface of a building or the edge beam of a bridge; exposed eave of a building. (2) A decorative trim or panel projecting from the face of a wall.

fascine A brushwood bundle firmly tied

into a cylindrical shape which is used as a protective facing on sea walls or river banks, or to float a road over waterlogged soil.

fastener A mechanical device for attaching gypsum board to wood or metal framing.

fastigium The apex of a pediment; a top roof ridge.

fastness The property of a dye to retain its color when the dyed textile is exposed to light, atmosphere gasses, shampooing, or other color destroying agents.

fast powder Dynamites or other explosives having a high speed detonation.

fast sheet A permanent, or non opening, window.

fast to light A painting term describing color which is unaffected by light.

fast track (fast tracking) A method of construction management which involves a continuous design-construct operation. Construction work starts before final plans and specifications are complete. For example, excavation may start before superstructure plans and details are finished.

fat Material accumulated on the trowel during the finishing operation often used to fill in small imperfections. Also a term used to describe working characteristics of a mortar containing a high proportion of cementitious material. Also used to describe working characteristics of highly plastic mortars.

fat board The bricklayer's mortar board used when pointing

fat concrete (see concrete, fat)

fat edge A ridge of wet paint which collects at the bottom edge of a painted area when too much has been put on, or because the paint flows too much.

fatigue The weakening of a material caused by repeated or alternating loads; a weakening of elasticity.

fatigue resistance The property of a material to withstand repeated or alternating stresses.

fatigue strength The greatest stress which can be sustained for a given number or stress cycles without failure.

fatigue test Testing under repeated reversals or fluctuations of stress to determine the endurance limit.

fat lime A quicklime made by burning a pure or nearly pure limestone, such as chalk; used especially for plastering and masonry work.

fat mix Term used to describe a rich mix containing more cement, lime or other binder than usual.

fat mortar A mortar that tends to be sticky and adheres to the trowel.

fattening A painting term for an increase in the viscosity of paint during storage which is not sufficient to make it unusable.

fattening up in plastering, increasing the plasticity of lime putty by storing lime in excess water for about 30 days after slaking.

faucet A terminal valved outlet in a pipe line bearing a liquid; the socket end of a pipe which is joined to a spigot.

faucet ear In plumbing, a projection from a pipe socket used for nailing the pipe to the wall.

faulting Differential vertical displacement of a slab or other member adjacent to a joint or crack.

favas A latin word meaning honeycomb; one piece in a paving of hexagonal units.

faying surface The face of a metal plate, block, end of a timber, etc., which joins another surface so closely as to leave no space between them.

feasibility study A detailed investigation and analysis conducted to determine the financial, economic, technical or other advisability of a proposed project.

feather (1) To blend the edge of new material smoothly into the old surface. (2) A cross tongue which joins matchboards. (3) The slip separating the sash weights in a sash window.

feather edge (1) A wood or metal tool having a beveled edge; used to straighten re-entrant angles in finish plaster coat; also edge of a concrete or mortar placement such as a patch or topping that is beveled at an acute angle. (2) Procedure to reduce the gauge of the tile or thickness of sheet goods by tapering the edge in order to achieve level installation across width and length of floor.

feather-edge brick A compass brick.

feather-edged board Tapered boards which are used as weather boarding or close-boarded fencing.

feather-edged coping A coping stone with one edge thicker than the other so that its upper surface slopes one way only.

feather-edge rule A rule used in plastering after a floating rule or for working angles.

feather joint In carpentry, a joint made between two boards with squared edges butted together, each board having a plowed groove into which a common tongue is fitted.

feature strip Special stripping made of rubber, vinyl or of the floor covering being installed; used to create borders and/or special effects in the finished floor.

feather tongue A cross tongue.

fee A term used to denote payment for professional ability, capability and availability of organization, excluding compensation for direct, indirect and/or reimbursable expenses, as an agreement based on a professional fee plus expenses. Sometimes used to denote compensation of any kind for services rendered. *(see compensation)*

fee curve A graduated curve used by engineers to determine fee percentages based on estimated construction costs.

feed (1) A mechanism which pushes a drill into its work. (2) The process of supplying material to a conveying or processing unit.

feed-back control Adjustments of feed, speed, and other process parameters, based on analyses of subsequent product samples.

feeder (1) A pushing device or short belt that supplies material to a crusher or conveyor. (2) A channel supplying a reservoir or canal with water. (3) A cable connecting power stations to sub-stations that has a high current-carrying capacity.

feeding (livering) A painting term for the thickening of paint or varnish in the container to a rubbery jelly so that it cannot be used.

feed pipe In plumbing, a main-line pipe which carries a supply directly to the point where it is to be used or to secondary lines; also, a pipe supplying feed, as water to a boiler.

feed pump A pump, often duplex, which provides a steam boiler with water.

feed travel The distance a drilling machine moves the steel shank in traveling from top to bottom of its feeding range.

feed wheel Material distributor or regulator in certain types of shotcrete equipment.

feel The painter's term for the working qualities of paint.

fee plus expense agreement *(see cost plus fee arrangement)*

feint A slightly bent edge of cappings or flashings to form a capillary break; used in flexible-metal roofing.

feldspar Any of a group of crystalline minerals composed primarily of aluminum silicates.

felite A name used by Tornebohm (1897) to identify one form of dicalcium silicate, $2CaO.SiO_2$, one of the crystalline components of portland cement clinker. *(see alite; belite; celite)*

felt (1) A sheet of matted organic fibers used as a basis in the manufacture of composition roofing. (2) Compacted fibers of various materials in flexible sheet form used for insulation.

felt-and-gravel roof A roof covered with bitumen felt and by gravel to lessen its U-value.

felting down A painting term for flatting a dry varnish or paint surface with a felt pad loaded with abrasive powder and lubricated with water.

felt mill ream The mass in pounds of 480 square feet of dry, unsaturated felt; also termed "point weight".

felt nail A clout nail.

felt paper A paper sheathing on walls and roofs which insulates against heat, cold and dampness.

female Any item having an end that slips over a like item.

female coupling A pipe with threads on the inside.

femerell A ventilating shaft through a roof.

fence (1) An enclosing framework for land bearing pickets, boards, rails or other means of barring passage. (2) Cast shop term describing a wall placed around the model before pouring material. (3) A guide for the lumber on a bench saw.

fender clusters Clusters of fender piles.

fender pile A wooden piling, usually upright and free-standing, driven into the ground beneath water to absorb some of the impact of docking vessels, thus protecting the berth.

fender wall A small wall which carries the hearth slab to a ground floor fireplace.

fenestral A window opening closed with cloth or translucent paper instead of glass; having an opening like a window.

fenestration The design and disposition or arrangement of windows or other openings in a building wall.

ferriferous Composed largely of iron-bearing materials.

ferroconcrete Concrete work reinforced by steel bars or steel mesh embedded in the material before it sets to provide increased strength. The common term is reinforced concrete.

ferrous Containing iron

ferrous oxide A black easily oxidizable powder FeO that is the monoxide of iron.

ferrule (1) A short unthreaded tube or bushing shrunk or soldered onto a tube or line. (2) The metal band around the handle of a chisel which prevents it from splitting.

festoon   A sculptured swag or garland in a catenary curve between two points.

fetch   In dam construction, the straight line distance between dam and the farthest reservoir shore. The fetch is one of the factors used in calculating wave heights in a reservoir.

fettle   (1) To remove the roughness from a metal casting and prove it is free of flaws by hanging it in chains and striking it with a hammer. (2) The finishing-off work in any trade.

FGR   Flue Gas Recirculation or the recirculation of flue gas with combustion air to reduce NOx emissions.

fiber   (1) Animal hair or sisal, manila or glass fibers of appropriate length added to plaster mortar to increase its cohesiveness. (2) Any substance, natural or synthetic, strong enough to be used in thread or yarn form for processing as a textile.

fiberboard   A prefabricated building board of wood or other plant fibers compressed and bonded into a sheet.

fiber conduit   Tubing of molded fiber for insulating purposes.

fibered   Term pertaining to basecoat plaster containing animal, vegetable or glass fiber. Note: not included in this defination is neat gypsum basecoat plaster containing wood fiber as an aggregate and designed for use either with or without addition of other aggregates which is termed "wood-fibered plaster.

Fiberglas   Trade name for products of glass fibers; of a wool-like consistency for insulation; longer fibers are used for weaving fabrics that are noncombustible.

Fiberlic   A special type of building board; a trade name for a particular building-board product.

fibrous concrete   A concrete containing a fibrous aggregate such as asbestos or sawdust, used for lightness or ease in nailing.

fibrous plaster   Prepared plaster slabs produced by coating canvas with a thin layer of gypsum plaster.

fictile   Describing clay, capable of being molded.

fiddle   *(slang)* (1) To mark ties placing rails. (2) Saw.

fiddle drill   *(slang)* A bow drill.

fiddler's gear   *(slang)* Lifting tackle for laying large blocks at any angle, often used for work under water.

fiducial line (fiducial point)   In surveying, a reference point or line.

field   A term used to designate a construction project site. (Masonry) The expanse or area of wall between openings, corners, etc. composed for the most part of stretcher units.

field bending   Bending or reinforcing bars on the job rather than in a fabricating shop.

field book   A surveyor's note book in which to record field measurements.

field concrete   *(see concrete, field)*

field-cured cylinders   Test cylinders cured as nearly as practicable in the same manner as the concrete in the structure to indicate when supporting forms may be removed, additional construction loads may be imposed, or the structure may be placed in service.

fielded panel   An elevated panel.

field engineer   Term used by certain governmental agencies to designate their representative at the project site. *(see project representative)*

field joints   Joints in kilns where the prefabricated sections are assembled on site by means of welding or butt-straps.

field moisture equivalent   The minimum water content at which a drop of water placed on a smoothed surface of soil will not immediately be absorbed by the soil but will spread over the surface and give it a shiny appearance.

field order   A written order effecting a minor change in the work not involving an adjustment to the contract sum or an extension of the contract time; issued by the architect or engineer to the contractor during the construction phase.

field representative   *(see project representative)*

field stone   Loose stone found in the soil.

field tile   An area of tile covering a wall or floor. Most often bordered by tile trim.

field work order   An order issued from the project site for services or materials to a subcontractor or a vendor.

fifth wheel   (1) The weight-bearing swivel connection between highway type tractors and semi-trailers. (2) *(slang)* An unnecessary machine or person working on a job.

figure   Decorative natural designs in wood which are prized in the furniture and cabinet making industries.

figure of merit   For a thermoelectric material used in a thermoelectric device whose operation is based on the Seebeck effect or the Peltier effect, the quotient of the square of the absolute Seebeck coefficient by the product of the electrical resistivity and the thermal conductivity.

figuring   (1) The process of adding dimensions to working drawings. (2) The process of estimating quantities and costs from working drawings and specifications.

filament   A single strand of any kind of fiber, natural or synthetic. In textile use, filaments of natural fiber must be spun into yarns, and synthetic filaments are extruded as yarns.

file   (1) A tool, with teeth, used principally for finishing wood or metal surfaces. Single-cut files have parallel lines of teeth running diagonally across the face of the file. The double-cut files have two sets of parallel lines crossing each other. Single-cut files have four graduations—rough, bastard, second cut, and smooth; double-cut files have an added finer cut known as dead smooth. (2) On computers, a collection of data.

filigree   Any one of a number of decorative patterns stamped out of a hardboard or plywood panel.

fill   (1) An earth or broken rock structure or embankment; soil or loose rock used to raise a grade; soil that has no value except bulk. (2) Procedure in subfloor

preparation to level low spots, depressions, holes and the like to a level surface. Usually a trowelled-on product.

net   In sidehill work, the yardage of fill required at any station, less the yards of material obtained from the cut at that station.

net corrected   Net fill after making allowance for shrinkage during compaction.

fill dam   *(see earth dam)*

filler   (1) Finely divided inert material such as pulverized limestone, silica or colloidal substances sometimes added to portland cement paint or other materials to reduce shrinkage, improve workability or act as an extender. (2) Material used to fill an opening in a form. (3) Fuller's earth or clay or similar material used in the mix of back coating agents, in carpeting. (4) A material for filling nail holes, checks, cracks or other blemishes in surface of wood before application of paint, varnish or other finishes.

filler block   Concrete masonry units for use in conjunction with concrete joists for concrete floor or roof construction.

filler coat   A term used by painters when referring to the first coating of paint, varnish or other similar materials; applied to woodwork to fill the pores of the wood and make a smooth surface for the finish coat; also, the paint used for the first coat.

filler plate   A steel plate or shim used for filling in space between compression members.

fillet   (1) A narrow flat architectural member which adds beauty and strength by avoiding sharp angles. (2) A brace, usually poured concrete, where the pier and decking meet; the fillet is usually part of the concrete form when forming stressed concrete piers. *(see chamfer strip)*

filletster   *(see fillister)*

fillet weld   A weld of approximately triangular cross-section at right angles between two pieces.

filling-in piece   A piece of lumber

which is shorter than its neighbors, such as a jack-rafter.

filling piece A piece of lumber placed on another to make a plane surface.

filling yarn Yarns, usually of cotton, jute or kraftcord, running across a woven fabric and used with the chain yarns to bind the pile tufts to the backing yarns.

fillister (1) A plane used for cutting grooves; also, a rabbet, or groove, as the groove on a window sash for holding the putty and glass. (2) In mechanical work, the rounded head of a cap screw slotted to receive a screw driver.

fill-type insulation A loose-fill insulation material which is poured in place from bags or is hand packed between framing members or in hollow blocks.

film A painting term for dried paint or varnish of one or several coats.

filter (1) Granular material placed around a subdrain pipe to facilitate drainage and at the same time strain or prevent the admission of silt or sediment. (2) A screen made from spun glass, oil-treated paper or synthetic materials. (3) A device to remove solid material from a fluid.

filter bed A fill of previous soil that provides a site for a septic field.

filter block A hollow, vitrified clay masonry unit, sometimes salt-glazed, designed for trickling filter floors in sewage disposal plants.

filter cake (mud cake) A deposit of mud of the walls of a drill hole.

filter material Granular material that has been graded to allow water to pass through it while retaining solid matter.

filter press A device for separating solid and liquid matter under pressure so that the solid residue is compressed into briquettes to facilitate removal.

filter zone *(see filter (1))*

filtrate The fluid which passes through a filter.

Filtros (sewage) The trade name applied to an artificial porous stone of carefully graded silicious sand made by molding, pressing, firing, annealing and grinding; used as a filtering

medium and for diffusing air in the activated sludge process.

fin (1) A narrow linear projection on a formed concrete surface, resulting from mortar flowing out between spaces in the formwork. (2) An extended surface to increase the heat transfer area, as metal sheets attached to tubes.

final acceptance The owner's acceptance of the project from the contractor upon certification by the architect or engineer that it is complete and in accordance with the contract requirements. Final acceptance is confirmed by the making of final payment unless otherwise stipulated at the time of making such payment.

final completion Term denoting that the work is complete and all contract requirements have been fulfilled by the contractor.

final drive A set of reduction gears close to or inside a drive wheel.

final inspection Final review of the project by the architect or engineer prior to his issuance of the final certificate for payment.

final payment Payment made by the owner to the contractor, upon issuance by the architect or engineer of the final certificate for payment, of the entire unpaid balance of the contract sum as adjusted by change orders. *(see final acceptance)*

final prestress *(see final stress)*

final set A degree of stiffening of a mixture of cement and water greater than initial set, generally stated as an empirical value indicating the time in hours and minutes required for a cement paste to stiffen sufficiently to resist, to an established degree, the penetration of a weighted test needle; also applicable to concrete and mortar mixtures with use of suitable test procedures. *(see initial set)*

final setting time The time required for a freshly mixed cement paste, mortar or concrete to achieve final set. *(see initial setting time)*

final setting basin A tank through which the effluent of a trickling filter or other oxidizing device passes for the purpose of removing the settleable solids before its discharge.

final stress In prestressed concrete, the stress which exists after substantially all losses have occurred.

fine adjustment screw The tangent screw on a surveyor's telescope.

fine aggregate (1) Aggregate passing the ⅜ inch (9.5 mm) sieve and almost entirely passing the No. 4 (4.76 mm) sieve and predominantly retained in the No. 200 (74 micron) sieve. (2) That portion of an aggregate passing the No. 4 (4.76 mm) sieve and predominantly retained on the No. 200 (74 micron) sieve. *(see aggregate)*

fine cold asphalt A wearing course of aggregates or bituminous material which is spread and compacted while cold or warm.

fine grained soil Soil in which the smaller grain sizes predominate, such as fine sand, silt and clay.

fine mineral surfacing A water-insoluble, inorganic material, more than 50 percent of which passes through the No. 35 sieve, that may be used on the surface of roofing material.

fineness 1. A measure of particle-size distribution. *(see particle-size distribution)* 2. The sizing of the particles of raw meal and/or cement generally measured by air permeability (Blaine test), turbidity (Wagner turbidimeter), or sieve analysis. fineness of cement affects the rate of hydration. The greater the fineness the faster the rate of hydration and the more accelerated the strength development.

finenes modulus An abstract number used to compare different particles or graduations of aggregate. The fineness modulus is computed by adding the cumulative percentages retained on the six standard screens (#4, #8, #16, #30, #50 and #100) and dividing the sum by 100.

fines (1) Commonly the binder of silt and clay passing a No. 4 sieve. (2) In hydraulic sluicing, the material that slowly settles to the bottom of a mass of water. (3) Finely crushed or pow-

dered material or fibers; especially those smaller than the average in a mix of various sizes.

fine solder A type of solder made of an alloy of tin and lead used in plumbing to make a blown joint. It has the lowest melting point of all solders.

fine stuff In plastering, the material for the finishing coat.

finger-joint Pieces of lumber machined on the ends and bonded together with glue. The joint is similar to slipping the fingers of two hands together.

finger plate A plate fastened near the doorknob to protect the door surface from finger marks.

fingers In plastering, a comb or drag made by nailing together several laths with pointed ends.

finial A terminal form at the top of spire, gable, gatepost, pinnacle or other point of relative height.

fining off A term used to describe the application of the finishing coat of plaster.

finish (1) The texture and smoothness of a surface after compacting and finishing operations have been performed. (2) Last and final coat of plaster. (3) The final coat of a paint system. (4) Exterior or interior millwork. (5) A term including the higher grades of lumber; sound, relatively free of blemishes.

ground A finish made on an object by grinding.

planed A finish produced by planing.

rough The finish which is left by the original forms, molds, etc.

finish carpentry A term used to describe the installation of doors, skirtings, architraves, etc. The British term is joinery.

finish coat (1) Final thin coat of shotcrete preparatory to hand finishing. (2) Exposed coat of plaster and stucco.

finished interior The interior of a dormer, attic, basement recreation room, or lower level of a split level house, which is completed with floor, wall and ceiling coverings (floor tile, drywall, paneling, etc.).

finished string The end string of a stair

fastened to the rough carriage. It is cut, mitered, dressed and often finished with a molding or bead.

finisher (trowel man) A skilled laborer who gives a smooth finish to cast-in-place or precast concrete units, sometimes patching blemishes with concrete of matching color. A specialist in architectural stone finishing smooths the surface with a stone and polishes it with an emery wheel or buffing wheel.

finish floor The top or wearing surface of a floor system; usually made of hardwood, like oak or maple, linoleum, terrazzo or tile.

finish grade The final grade required by specifications.

finish grinding The final grinding of clinker into cement, with calcium sulfate in the form of gypsum or anhydrite generally being added; the final grinding operation required for a finished concrete surface, e.g., bump cutting of pavement, fin removal from structural concrete, terrazzo floor grinding.

finish hardware Hardware that is seen and is therefore given a special finish.

finishing (finish work) (1) Leveling, smoothing, compacting and otherwise treating surfaces of fresh or recently placed concrete or mortar to produce desired appearance and service. *(see float and trowel)* (2) The final perfecting of the workmanship on a building, such as the adding of casings, baseboards and ornamental moldings.

finishing brushes Brushes used to apply water to a smooth lime finish coat during final troweling.

finishing machine A power-operated machine used to give the desired surface texture to a concrete slab.

finishing off Preparing the finished surface of cabinetwork or fine carpentry.

finishing tools Plaster's cement finisher's or composition floor layer's trowels or floats for shaping curved or other difficult surfaces.

finish plaster Final or white coat of plaster.

fink truss (Belgian truss, French truss) A type of roof truss commonly used for short spans because the shortness of its struts makes it economical and prevents waste.

fins Concrete that has oozed out of joints between form boards, and has hardened into finlike projections.

Fir, Douglas Also called Oregon Pine, although neither a fir nor a pine; found abundantly in the northwest U.S.A.; a wood of strength and density approximately equal to those of southern yellow pine; widely used for flooring, sheathing and timber.

fir, white A wood cut mainly in Idaho and California; both heartwood and sapwood are a reddish tinge of white; a wood of many architectural uses.

fireback A plate of cast or wrought iron, usually ornamented, placed vertically at the back of a fireplace just above hearth level to protect the masonry from excess heat.

fire, bisque The process of kiln-firing ceramic ware prior to glazing.

fire block Solid bridging built into floors or wooden walls which constitute a fire stop.

firebox The combustion chamber of any heating unit.

fire breaks Fire-protecting doors, closed stairs, concrete floors, division walls, etc., to reduce the risk of fire to a standard acceptable to insurance companies or the law.

fire brick Brick made to withstand high temperatures for lining chimneys, incinerators and similar structures.

fire clay Clay which is capable of being subjected to high temperature without fusing or deforming for making brick, firebrick and laying of firebrick.

fire cracks Cracks caused in a plastered surface by exposure to sun or other heat during drying. *(see cracking; crazing)*

fire cut The angular cut at the end of a joist, designed to rest on a brick wall.

fire, decorating The process of firing ceramic or metallic decorations on the surface of glazed ceramic tile.

fire division wall A wall which subdivides a building to help resist the spread of fire. Unlike a division wall it does not necessarily rise through more than one floor.

fire door A metal-sheathed door that will resist fire, often held from sliding shut by a fusible link.

fire endurance Measure of elapsed time during which an assembly continues to exhibit fire resistance under specified conditions of test and performance. As specified to elements of buildings, it shall be measured by the methods and to the criteria defined in ASTM Methods E119, Fire Tests of Building Construction and Materials ASTM Methods E 152, Fire Tests of Door Assemblies or ASTM Methods E163, Fire Tests of Window Assemblies.

fire, single The process of maturing an unfired ceramic body and its glaze in one firing operation.

fired strength The compressive or flexural strength of refractory concrete determined after first firing to a specified temperature for a specified time and subsequent cooling.

fired unit weight The unit weight of refractory concrete after having been exposed to a specified firing temperature for a specified time and subsequent cooling.

fire escape A fixed or movable supplementary means of egress from a building.

fire-extinguishing equipment Fire hydrants, sprinklers, emulsifiers, fire extinguishers, etc.

fire hydrant An outdoor water-supply outlet with wrench-actuated valve and a connection for fire hose.

firing A step during the manufacture of ceramic using kiln or furnace to develop desired properties through controlled heat treatment.

fire lintel A horizontal flap member attached to the upper door panel to close the space between that panel and the hoistway wall when doors are closed. It is required to seal the hoistway in case of fire.

fire partition A wall designed to pre-

vent or restrict the spread of fire or to provide an area of refuge in case of fire. *(see fire division wall)*

fireplace An opening on a hearth, served by a chimney flue, where an open fire may be laid.

fireplace unit A metal form whose front rim is usually covered by the fireplace facing; the form often includes a special heating chamber, in addition to firebox, throat damper, downdraft shelf and smoke chamber.

fire point The lowest temperature at which the vapor from asphalt will ignite and remain burning; also called burning point or flash point.

fire-polish To make glass smooth or glossy by the action of fire.

fireproof Protected against fire; relatively noncombustible.

fireproof construction A building constructed of fire-resistive material for the purpose of protecting the contents of the structure against loss by fire.

fireproof encasement The structural steel members are encased in concrete, to protect them against deterioration caused by overheating.

fireproofing The use of noncombustible materials to protect structural components of a building so it can withstand a complete burnout of contents without losing structural integrity.

fireproof wood Chemically treated wood, fire resistive, used where noncombustible materials are required.

fire rated doors Doors designed to resist standard fire tests and labeled for identification.

fire resistance The ability of a material or assembly to withstand fire or give protection from it; the ability to confine a fire or to continue to perform a given structural function, or both.

fire-resistance rating The measured time in hours or fractions thereof that the material or construction will withstand fire exposure as determined by fire tests conducted in conformity to recognized standards.

fire-resisting finishes Paints based on silicones, polyvinyl chloride, chlorinated waxes, urea formaldehyde resins, casein, borax, and other noncombustible substances which reduce the rate of spread of fire on a combustible material.

fire-resisting floor (wall) A floor or wall which has a fire rating appropriate to the occupancy and fire load of the building. Any openings in this floor or wall must be protected from fire passing through them.

fire-resistive In the absence of a specific ruling by the authority having jurisdiction, applies to materials for construction not combustible in the temperatures of ordinary fires and that will withstand such fires without serious impairment of the usefulness for at least one hour.

fire-resitve construction A method of construction which prevents or retards the passage of hot gases or flames as defined by the fire-resistance rating.

fire-retardant chemical A chemical or preparation of chemicals used to reduce flammability or to retard spread of flame.

fire retardant rating A standard test rating of fire-resistive and protective characteristics of a building material or assembly.

fire stop A solid, tight closure of a concealed space placed to prevent the spread of fire and smoke through such a space.

fire taping The taping of gypsum board joints without subsequent finishing coats. A treatment method used in attic, plenum or mechanical areas where esthetics are not important.

fire tower A stairway enclosed with fire-resistant construction, usually entered from the various floors of a building through fire doors.

firetube boiler A boiler with combustion gases inside the tubes.

fire wall A wall, starting at the foundation and extending continuously through all stories to and above the roof, to restrict the spread of fire. *(see fire division wall)*

fire welding Forge welding.

fir fixed Unplaned lumber held in place by nailing only.

fir framed Unplaned lumber fixed by preparing the joints as in roof trusses.

firing (1) Exposure to heat of bricks or other clay products, in a kiln. (2) The charging of fuel into a furnace, generally steam.

firing line The third, last, and principal welding team that works on a welded pipeline joint.

firmer chisel A carpenter's chisel, stronger than a paring chisel, but not as strong as a socket chisel.

firmer gouge A chisel with a blade curved like that of a gouge.

firmer tools In woodworking, the tools commonly used on the workbench, such as the ordinary chisels and gouges.

firm heart stain A brownish or reddish discoloration, and in the lumber grades where specified, does not affect the use of the piece to any greater extent than the other characteristics of the grade.

firring *(see furring)*

first floor In U.S. buildings with a basement or cellar, the first floor is the first one above ground level. In Britain the floor which is above the floor at ground level is called the first floor.

first moment *(see static moment)*

fish bellied *(slang)* A term applied to a structural member such as a beam, girder or joist which bends downward, bulging out like a fish's belly.

fish mouth Crescent shaped wrinkle in roofing felt.

fish tape Snake.

fish eyes *(slang)* (1) Small blemishes occasionally found in lime finish coats. Approximately ¼" in diameter, they are caused by lumpy lime. (2) Opening in the surface of concrete, usually caused by gravel.

fish glue A type of glue made from parts of certain fish, usually the bladder-like portions of hake.

fishing (1) The operation of recovering an object left or dropped in a drill hole.

(2) Bolting fishplates to rails or other members.

fish-joint A splice where the pieces are joined butt end to end, and are connected by pieces of wood or iron placed on each side and firmly bolted to the timbers, or pieces joined.

fish ladder A channel with small lifts along which fish can travel up or down past a weir or dam.

fishmouth (1) A half-cylindrical or half-conical opening formed by an edge wrinkle; (2) In shingles, a half-conical opening formed at a cut edge.

fishplate A plate or plank fastened to the sides of two beams or rails placed end to end, to effect a splice; flitch-plate.

fish rods (slang) A fiberglass rod used to protect wire (neutral or dead wire) from hot wire. Principally used on down-guys to break ground between phases on the down-guy.

fishtail A wedge-shaped piece of wood used as part of the support form between tapered pans in concrete joist construction.

fishtail bolt An anchor bolt, with a split tail, cast into masonry or concrete.

fishway (see fish ladder)

fissile (fissility) Capable of being split, as for slate tiles.

fission A process whereby the nucleus of an atom is split in two nearly equal parts which results in the release of energy.

fitch A long-handeled small paint brush, bound with tin, to reach nearly inaccessible areas.

fitment In milwork and furniture making, any portion of a wall, room, or built-in furniture which is fitted into place, including chimney pieces, wall paneling, cabinets and cupboards.

fitting That part of the tile or sheet goods installation where the floor covering is fitted to walls, doorways, around projections, etc. Methods most often used are pattern-scribed, or hand-fitted.

fitting, poured A wire rope attachment fastened by separating the wires, ex-

panding them in a conical socket and filling it with molten zinc.

fittings, pipe Bends, couplings, crosses, elbows, tee, unions, etc., which are connectors and fittings for screwed pipes. for gas pipe, the fittings are usually of malleable cast iron.

fitting, wedge socket A wire rope attachment in which the rope lies in a too-small groove between a wedge and a housing so that pull on the rope tightens the wedge.

fit-up A term describing formwork which is framed so that it can be struck without destroying it. It is suitable for repeated use.

fixed base A column base that is designed to resist rotation as well as horizontal or vertical movement.

fixed beam A beam having a fixed end.

fixed capacitors These use materials such as paper, mica or glass and are built to certain capacities that cannot be changed.

fixed end The anchored end; an end of a girder or strut so firmly connected as to prevent all motion in the vicinity of the end.

fixed fee A specific amount set forth in a contract to be paid for all necessary services and materials.

fixed joint A connection between two members in such a manner as to cause them to act as a single continuous member, provides for transmission of forces from one member to the other without any movement in the connection itself.

fixed light (1) A window which does not open; a dead light. (2) A flush lighting fixture.

fixed limit of construction cost The maximum allowable cost of the construction work as established in the agreement between the owner and the engineer or architect. (see budget, construction)

fixed resistor Any resistor with a preset ohmic value that cannot be changed.

fixing Glass panes are fixed when they are fastened to ceilings or walls for such purposes as flush lighting fittings.

For other uses, the word glazing is used.

fixing bracket A fitting on a glazing bar for fastening it to a structural member.

fixing fillet A piece of wood, the thickness of a mortar joint, which is inserted into a joint as a fixing for carpentry.

fixing moment (fixed-end moment) The bending moment at the support of a beam required to fix it in such a way that it has a fixed end and cannot move.

fixing strip A device for fixing board or sheet covering to partitions or for attaching cladding to a wall frame or sub-frame.

fixture An article of equipment in a building, usually the part that is added last, making a system operative, as lighting fixtures, plumbing fixtures.

branch The supply pipe between the fixture and the water-distributing pipe.

drain The drain from the trap of a fixture to the junction of the drain with any other drain pipe.

unit A factor so chosen that the load-producing values of the different plumbing fixtures can be expressed approximately as multiples of that factor.

fixtures Display and storage units.

fixture-unit flow rate The total discharge flow in gallons per minute of a single fixture divided by 7.5, which provides the flow rate of that particular plumbing fixture as a unit of flow.

flagging Flagstone paving or other flat stones, for walkways, etc.

flagman A laborer who controls vehicular traffic by means of brightly colored flags and/or signs.

flagstone (flagging; flags) Flat stones from one to four inches thick, used for rustic walks, steps, floors, and the like.

flail A hammer hinged to an axle so that it can be used to break or crush material.

flaking A fault in painting; the peeling off of the coating.

flambeau A torch or torchlike lighting fixture.

flame cleaning A technique used for removing mill scale and water from weathered structural steelwork with a very hot flame. The surface is then immediately painted.

flame gun A large blow torch using kerosene for fuel.

flame photometer An instrument used to determine elements, especially sodium and potassium in portland cement, by the color intensity of their unique flame spectra resulting from introducing a solution of a compound of the element into a flame. Also known as flame spectrophotometer.

flame safeguard A control that sequences the burner through several stages of operation to provide proper air purge, ignition, normal operation, and shutdown for safe operation.

flame spread classification A standard test rating of fire-resistive and protective characteristics of a building material.

flammable *(OSHA)* Capable of being easily ignited, burning intensely, or having a rapid rate of flame spread.

flammable liquids *(OSHA)* Any liquid having a flash point below 140°F and having a vapor pressure not exceeding 40 pounds per square inch (absolute) at 100°F.

flammability A material's ability to burn.

flange (1) A ridge that prevents a sliding motion. (2) A projecting rim or rib for strength or for attachments.

flange brace A bracing member used to provide lateral support to the flange of a beam, girder, or column.

flane In architecture, the side of an arch.

flanking paths Paths by which sound travels around an element that is intended to impede it.

flanking window A window set beside an outside door which is often used to light a hallway.

flanks The intrados of an arch, near the springings.

flank wall A side wall of a building.

flanning The interior splay of a window jamb.

flap trap *(slang)* A sewage term for an antiflood valve.

flap valve A check valve with a hinged disc opening when the flow is normal and closing by gravity or by the flow when the flow tends to reverse.

flare The funnel-like widening of a tubular form.

flare fitting A type of soft-tube connector which involves the flaring of the tube to provide a mechanical seal.

flared column head A circular column widening to a cone shape just below the floor slab; sometimes used in mushroom construction.

flaring inlet A funnel-shaped entrance to facilitate flow into a pipe or conduit.

flash (1) To make a joint weather-tight, usually with sheet copper but also with composition flashing, such as the joint between a chimney and a roof, or the joint between wall and windowhead. (2) A variation in the color of paint due to wall suction.

flash chamber Separating tank placed between the expansion valve and evaporator in a refrigeration system to separate and bypass any flash gas formed in the expansion valve.

flashboard A plank or slab, generally held horizontally by end girders or by other supports, on the crest of a dam, check structure, or in a spillway to control the water level; a stop plank.

flash coat A light coat of shotcrete used to cover minor blemishes on a concrete surface.

flash drying A method used to rapid dry paint or varnish by exposing it to radiant heat for a short time.

flash gas The gas resulting from the instantaneous evaporation of refrigerant in a pressure-reducing device to cool the refrigerant to the evaporation temperature obtaining at the reduced pressure.

flashing (1) Sheet metal, copper, lead or tin used to cover open joints of exterior construction such as roof-valley joints or roof-parapet joints to make them waterproof. (2) Burning bricks with alternately too much or too little air to give them various colors. (3) In painting, the formation of patches in a finish which are glossier than the remainder, especially at joints or laps.

flashing board A board to which the flashings are fastened.

flashing cement A trowelable mixture of cutback bitumen and mineral stabilizers, including asbestos or other inorganic fibers.

flash point *(OSHA)* Flash point of liquid is the temperature at which it gives off vapor sufficient to form an ignitable mixture with the air near the surface of the liquid or within the vessel used as determined by appropriate test procedure and apparatus as specified. (1) The flash point of liquids having a viscosity less than 45 Saybolt Universal Second(s) at 100°F (37.8C) and a flash point below 175°F (79.4C) shall be determined in accordance with the Standard Method of Test for Flash Point by the Tag Closed Tester. (2) The flash point of liquids having a viscosity of 45 Saybolt Universal Second(s) or more at 175°F (79.4C) or higher shall be determined in accordance with the Standard Method of Test for Flash Point by the Pensky Martens Closed Tester.

flash set The rapid development of rigidity in a mixed portland cement paste, mortar or concrete, usually with the evolution of considerable heat. This rigidity cannot be dispelled nor can the plasticity be regained by further mixing without addition of water; also referred to as quick set or grab set.

flat (1) A bar of thin rectangular iron or steel. (2) A finish paint without a gloss. (3) British term for an apartment on one floor level.

flat arch An arch whose intrados is a horizontal line. Also called French arch and Dutch arch, especially when of bricks that are not wedge-shaped; sometimes known as a jack arch.

flat asphalt A roofing asphalt that has a softening point of approximately 170F (77C) and that conforms to the requirements of ASTM Standard D 312, Type II.

flat carving A type of carving where the design is left flat and only the background is cut away.

flat coat In painting, a coat of filler.

flat cost The cost of only labor and material.

flat-drawn sheet glass Ordinary window glass.

flat grain (F.G.) Lumber sawn approximately parallel to the annual growth rings so that all or some of the rings form an angle of less than 45 degrees with the surface of the piece.

flat jack A hydraulic jack consisting of light gauge metal bent and welded to a flat shape which expands under internal pressure.

flat joint A mortar joint with surface flush to the brickwork.

flat molding A thin, flat molding used only for finishing work.

flat paint An interior paint that contains a high proportion of pigment and dries to a flat or lusterless finish.

flat piece One in which the ratio of the width to thickness of its circumscribing rectangular prism is greater than a specified value. *(see elongated piece)*

flat plate A flat slab without column capitals or drop panels. *(see flat slab)*

flat plate collector **(1)** One which is capable of collecting both direct and diffuse components of solar radiation. This is an obvious advantage over focusing collectors, which collect only direct radiation. **(2)** A panel of metal or other suitable material that converts sunlight into heat. Usually a flat black color, the collector transfers its heat to circulating water or air.

flat pointing Pointing of brickwork so as to make flat joints.

flat roof A roof having only sufficient slope for drainage.

flat sawing Sawing logs with parallel cuts, a conversion method that wastes less timber than others.

flat skylight Any skylight which has only enough pitch to carry off rain water or water from melting snow.

flat slab A concrete slab reinforced in two or more directions, generally without beams or girders to transfer the loads to supporting members.

flat slab buttress dam A flat slab deck dam.

flat slab construction Reinforced concrete floor construction of uniform thickness which eliminates the drops of beams and girders.

flat spots In painting, spots which lack gloss on a finished surface indicating porous undercoat or improper surfacing.

flatting **(1)** In veneering, a process of flattening out buckled veneers. **(2)** A finish given to painting which leaves no gloss.

flatting agent A material added to paints, varnishes and other coating materials to reduce the gloss of the dried film.

flatting down (rubbing) A painting term describing the sanding of the painted surface with powdered pumice and felt, cuttle fish, glass paper or other abrasives.

flatting varnish A varnish which contains a great deal of hard resin and is suitable for an undercoating varnish. It can be flatted down to make a smooth surface for the finish.

flat wall brush A brush similar to a distemper brush, only narrower.

flaunching A cement mortar fillet around the top of a chimney stack to throw off the rain.

fleam A term used in woodworking to indicate the angle of bevel of the edge of a saw tooth with respect to the plane of the blade.

fleece Term used to describe mats of felts of usually non woven fibers.

fleet angle The maximum angle between a rope and a line perpendicular to the drum on which it winds.

Flemish bond Pattern of bonding in brickwork consisting of alternate headers and stretchers in the same course.

Flemish diagonal bond Alternating

headers and stretchers in a course, followed by a course of stretchers.

Flemish double-stretcher bond A header alternating with two stretchers.

flex Flexible metal conduit; also called Greenfield.

flex-duct A flexible rounded duct, made of spiral wire covered with plastic, etc., for use in transfer of air in heating, cooling and ventilating systems; made in various diameters.

flexibility factor Relative elastic deflection of a conduit.

flexible drop chute A drop chute consisting of a heavy, rubberized canvas tube.

flexible metal conduit Electrical conduit of spirally wound steel strip.

flexible metal roofing Roof coverings or flashings of flat flexible metal sheet. These roof coverings need a smooth roof underneath.

flexible pavement Highway or airstrip construction with a waterproof wearing surface of bituminous material which is assumed to have no tensile strength. The load is transferred to the foundation soil by the base course; considerably cheaper than concrete pavements.

flexibility The degree to which the floor covering will bend without cracking or breaking; will vary with temperature.

fleximer A flooring without joints which is also flexible.

flexlock Type of gasketed joint used in tongue & groove pipes.

flex plug and socket A plug-in connector.

flexural bond In prestressed concrete, the stress between the concrete and the tendon which results from the application of external load.

flexural moment *(see positive moment)*

flexural rigidity A measure of stiffness of a member, indicated by the product of modulus of elasticity and moment of inertia divided by the length of the member.

flexural strength A property of a solid that indicates its ability to withstand bending. *(see modulus of rupture)*

flier (1) Any single one of a flight of stairs whose treads are parallel to each other; a stair tread that is of uniform width throughout its length. (2) In carpentry, a flying shore.

flight (1) The screw thread, helix, of an auger. (2) A run of steps or stairs from one landing to another.

flint wall One built in the English custom, its outer shell of flints with their faces rough.

flitch The portion of a log sawed on two or more sides for remanufacture into lumber; one of the planks of a beam constructed by fastening two or more planks together.

flitch beam A built-up beam formed by a metal plate sandwiched between two wooden members and bolted together for additional strength.

flitch plate A thin strip of steel or other strong material inserted between two planks to strengthen them.

float (1) In reference to a dozer blade, to rest by its own weight or to be held from digging by upward pressure of a load of dirt against its moldboard. (2) A tool, usually non-metallic, used in finishing operations to impart a relatively even, but not smooth, texture to an unformed concrete surface; not a darby. (3) In hydraulics, a small floating object whose direction and speed of travel are taken to measure the speed of the water carrying it. (4) A body floating on water, which opens a valve in a water tank when the water level falls. (5) In plumbing, a metal drain pipe hung just below floor level taking waste from the floor above.

float coat In cement work, a term frequently applied to the mortarsetting bed which is put on with a float; also a term applied to a coat of finishing cement; sometimes called float finish which is put on with a float.

float-cut file A single-cut file.

floated coat in plastering, the second of three coats of plaster; the coat applied over the scratch coat; also called brown coat, although not brown in color.

floater (1) A tool used for finishing

mortar screeds. (**2**) *(slang)* An itinerant tradesman.

float finish A finish coat texture which is rougher than a trowel finish. The roughness is derived primarily from aggregate particles contained in the plaster mortar.

floating The process of spreading plaster, stucco or cement on the surface of walls to an equal thickness by the use of a board called a float. The operation of finishing a fresh concrete or mortar surface by use of a float.

floating angle A method of applying gypsum board designed to allow structural movement at interior corners.

floating crane A crane carried on a large pontoon.

floating edge A factory edge applied in such a manner that the edge does not lie directly over a framing member and is unsupported.

floating foundation In building construction, a special type of foundation made to carry the weight of a superstructure which is to be erected on swampy land or on unstable soil.

floating harbor A breakwater of pontoons attached end to end.

floating joint A condition where the butt joint does not lie directly over a framing member. Floating joints should be backblocked.

floating pipeline A pipeline carried on pontoons and used for removing the material dredged by a suction dredger which pumps fluid sand or silt into the pipeline. The dredged material is usually deposited on land to make a hydraulic-fill dam, etc.

floating rule (rod) In plastering, a long wooden rule with which a float coat is levelled to a plane surface between screeds.

float, ship scaffold *(OSHA)* A scaffold hung from overhead supports by means of ropes and consisting of a substantial platform having diagonal bracing underneath, resting upon and securely fastened to two parallel plank bearers at right angles to the span.

floatstone A porous opal stone or an iron block used for rubbing gauged bricks.

float switch A switch operated by a float for starting or stopping the pump motor when the water level rises or falls. It is also used for automatically opening or closing spillway gates and is thus a ball cock on a large scale.

float valve In plumbing, a valve actuated by a floating ball on a lever, as in a flush tank; a ball cock.

floc Gluelike masses created in fluids by adding coagulating properties by accretion or biochemical means.

flocculation (coagulation) The intentional grouping of colloids in a suspension in water or other liquids in order to increase the settlement rate of the solids in sewage. In paints this grouping increases the viscosity.

flocculent gypsum *(see gypsum insulation)*

flocking (**1**) In painting, blowing soft, fluffy fibers from cotton, silk or other textiles onto a sticky surface to form a textile-appearing surface. (**2**) Short, chopped fiber or flock is adhered, usually by electrostatic processes, to a base fabric, resulting in a short-pile material with a velvety texture in carpeting.

flogging An obsolete term for smoothing a wood floor with hand tools.

flood coat The top layer of bitumen into which the aggregate is embedded on an aggregate-surfaced built-up roof.

flood level In reference to a plumbing fixture, the level at which water begins to overflow the top or rim of the fixture.

floodlighting The bathing of an exterior in light by night, using carefully positioned and unobtrusive lights with reflectors.

flood plain An area adjoining a body of water or natural stream that has been or may be covered by flood water.

floor The lower horizontal surface of a room or building; the horizontal structure dividing a building into stories; also, less frequently, an outdoor paving.

floor arch (jack arch)   A structural vault form supported by longitudinal beams.

floor beam   A transverse beam or girder placed at the panel points of a span to support the stringers that carry the floor.

floor brick   Smooth, dense brick, highly resistant to abrasion and moisture used as finished floor surfaces.

floor chisel   An all-steel chisel used especially for removing floorboards.

floor clip   Strips of steel sheeting pushed into and anchored in the surface of a concrete floor slab or screed after levelling. When the concrete has hardened, the edges of the strip are pulled up and bent. They are then nailed to floor battens to which the finished wooden floor is fixed. Also called a bulldog clip or a sleeper clip.

floor cramp   A cramp for forcing floorboards together before nailing them down.

floor drain   A plumbing fixture used to drain water from floors into the plumbing system. Such drains are usually located in the laundry and near the furnace and are fitted with a deep seal trap.

floor framing   The common joists, together with strutting and supports.

floor furring   Furring strips of wood laid over a sub-floor construction when electrical conduits and piping are to be laid on top of the floor or sub-floor.

floor grille   Same as floor register, only for cold air return.

floor hole   *(OSHA)* An opening measuring less than 12 inches but more than one inch in its least dimension in any floor, roof or platform through which materials but not persons may fall, such as a belt hold, pipe opening, or slot opening.

flooring tiles   Concrete or clay tiles set in cement mortar, bituminous or other adhesive. For a more sound-absorbent, heat-insulating, decorative or comfortable walking surface, linoleum, glass, cork, rubber, asphalt or plastic tiles are used.

floor joist   A common joist.

floor line   A mark made on a wall, stanchion, etc., to show finished floor level.

floor lining   A layer of paper, felt or similar material laid between the subfloor and the finish floor; a term sometimes erroneously applied to the blind or sub-floor.

floor opening   *(OSHA)*   An opening measuring 12 inches or more in its least dimension in any floor, roof or platform, through which persons may fall.

floor plan   An architectural drawing showing the length and breadth of a building and the location of the rooms which the building contains. Each floor has a separate plan.

floor plug   An electrical outlet in the floor.

floor register   A grille, or floor covering, that fits over a floor register box.

floor sander   A large sanding machine used for finish sanding wood floors.

floor slab   A reinforced concrete floor, especially that between reinforced concrete or steel beams.

floor strutting   Herring bone, solid strutting, or other strutting between floor joists.

floppy disk   A circular magnetic disk in a holder either plastic or cardboard used for storing computer information.

flotation   (1) Separation of minerals by floating the lighter ones in a fluid. (2) The weight-supporting ability of a tire, crawler track or platform on soft ground.

floury soil   A fine-grained soil which looks like clay when wet but is actually a powder when dry. It is a silt or rock flour, not a clay.

flow   (1) Time dependent irrecoverable deformation. *(see rheology)* (2) A measure of the consistency of freshly mixed concrete, mortar or cement paste in terms of the increase in diameter of a molded truncated cone specimen after jiggling a specified number of times. (3) A property of paints and varnishes which insures spreading into a smooth film and will not show brush marks or orange peeling.

flow cone   A device for measurement or

grout consistency in which a predetermined volume of grout is permitted to escape through a precisely sized orifice; the time of efflux, flow factor, is used as the indication of consistency. The mold used to prepare a specimen for the flow test.

flow gradient A drainageway slope determined by the elevation and distance of the inlet and outlet and by required volume and velocity.

flow index Slope of the flow curve.

flowing-through chamber The upper compartment of a two-story sedimentation plant.

flow line Contour line representing the normal elevation of the water in a reservoir; the path traced by a particle in a moving body or water.

flow meter An instrument, such as a Venturi meter, for measuring the quantity of fluid such as water, air or gas which flows in a unit of time.

flow net Pictorial description of water's path through a dam.

flow promoter Substance added to coating to enhance brushability, flow and leveling.

flow reisistance A measure of the ability of a material to impede the flow of air through it.

specific flow resistance The resistance of one cubic centimeter of material. It is measured in rayls per centimeter.

flow table A jigging device used in making flow tests for consistency of cement paste, mortar or concrete. *(see flow (2))*

flue (1) An enclosed passageway such as a pipe or chimney, for carrying off smoke, gases or air. (2) Any duct, breeching, stack, or other passageway for air, gases, or airborne materials to be conducted to the atmosphere. Within limitations, these terms are used somewhat interchangeably.

flue blast protection Asbestos plates bolted on underside of a bridge over a railroad.

flue gas The gaseous by-products of combustion.

flue lining A smooth hollow tile unit used for the inner lining of masonry chimneys.

fluffing Appearance on carpet surface of loose fiber fragments left during manufacture; not a defect, but a characteristic which disappears after carpet use and vacuuming.

fluid (1) Gas, vapor, or liquid. (2) Solar heat transfer fluid is a liquid, such as water or anti-freeze, which is circulated through the collector and then sent to the point of use.

fluid-applied elastomer An elastomeric material, which is fluid at ambient temperature, that dries or cures after application to form a continuous membrane.

fluid clutch A hydraulic coupling which does not increase torque.

fluid drive A power transmitting device between two shafts that transmits torque by means of fluid in motion.

fluidifier An admixture employed in grout to decrease the flow factor without changing water content.

flume An open conduit of wood, concrete, metal, etc., on a prepared grade, trestle or bridge.

fluorescent lamp A light source in which light is produced by a fluorescent powder, phosphor, coated on the inner surface of a glass tube. A mercury vapor arc between electrodes sealed into each end of the tube generates ultra-violet radiation which is changed by the phosphor into visible light.

fluorocarbons Substituted ethylene polymers. Featuring outstanding formability, heat resistance, color retention, and resistance to solvents and chalking.

fluosilicate A salt, usually of magnesium or zinc, used on concrete as a surface-hardening agent.

flush (1) The continued surface of two contiguous masses on the same plane. (2) To send a quantity of water down a pipe or channel to clean, it or fill and empty it.

flush bead In cabinetwork, a bead placed level with the surrounding surface by forming a quirk on each side of it.

flush bolt A fastening bolt which is flush with the surface.

flush door A door any size, not paneled, having two flat surfaces; flush doors are frequently of various types of hollow core construction.

flush joint (1) In masonry, when the joint mortar is pressed by the trowel flush with the surface. (2) Aligning two joined members so that the surfaces form a continuous plane.

flushing manhole A manhole provided with a gate so that sewage and water may be accumulated and then discharged rapidly for flushing a sewer.

flushometer valve A device which discharges a predetermined quantity of water to a fixture for flushing purposes and is actuated by direct water pressure.

flush panel A panel that is flush with the framing.

flush seal An application to a road surface of approximately 0.15 gallons per square yard of asphaltic material, such as RC-70, without a cover aggregate.

flush tank A chamber in which water or sewage is accumulated and discharged at intervals for flushing a sewer; the reservoir from which a toilet is flushed with water.

flush valve *(see float valve)*

flush water *(see wash water)*

flute (1) A concave channel. (2) Columns whose shafts are channeled are said to be fluted, and the flutes are collectively called flutings.

flutter A multiple echo set up between parallel reflecting surfaces.

flux (flux oil) (1) A thick relatively nonvolatile fraction of petroleum which may be used to soften asphalt to a desired consistency; often used as base stock for manufacture of roofing asphalts. (2) A substance which makes the impurities in the ore and fuel, such as silica and alumina, more easily fusible and provides a fusible slag in which these and other impurities may be carried off. The flux used in the blast

furnace is usually limestone. (3) In soldering and welding, fusible substances like borax which coat the joint and prevent oxidation.

fly (flies) The space in a theater, above and behind the proscenium arch, in which scenery is hung.

fly ash (1) The finely divided residue resulting from the combustion of ground or powdered coal which is transported from the firebox through the boiler by flue gases. (2) Noncombustible, inorganic residue remaining after combustion of inorganic materials and subsequently entrained in a gas stream (includes ash, cinders, and sand).

flyer A flier; a rectangular stair tread or a flying shore.

flying bond In bricklaying, a bond formed by inserting a header course at intervals of from four to seven courses of stretchers.

flying buttress A type of masonry structure in which a detached buttress or pier at a distance from a wall is connected to the wall by an arch or portion of an arch.

flying scaffold A scaffold hung from an outrigger beam.

flying shore (flier) A horizontal strut between two walls above ground level.

fly rafter A barge board which is decorated.

flywheel effect The damping of interior temperature fluctuations by massive construction. *(see diurnal)*

foam concrete Concrete made very light and cellular by the addition of a prepared foam or by generation of gas within the unhardened mix.

foamglas Cellular glass, closed cell, exceptionally strong and very stable. Will not burn.

foaming The formation of a foam or froth of an oil-refrigerant mixture due to rapid boiling out of the refrigerant dissolved in the oil when the pressure is suddenly reduced. This occurs when the compressor starts operating and, if large quantities of refrigerant were dissolved, large quantities of oil may boil out and be carried through the refrigerant lines.

foaming agent A chemical which, when foamed by a generator and measured into cement mix, controls the cellular density of the resulting aerated material.

focusing of sound *(see sound foci)*

fog Suspended liquid droplets generated by condensation from the gaseous to the liquid state, or by breaking up a liquid into a dispersed state, such as by splashing, foaming, and atomizing.

fog curing Storage in a moist room in which the desired high humidity is achieved by the atomization of fresh water. *(see moist room)*

fog seal A very thin bituminous application (0.1 gallon per square yard) of material to a road surface, without cover aggregate.

foil (1) A rounded leaflike architectural ornamentation used especially for window decoration, sometimes consisting of three divisions or four, known respectively as trefoil and quatrefoil. (2) A description of metals such as copper, zinc, aluminum or lead which is thinner than sheet or strip.

foil back A gypsum board with a reflective aluminum foil composite laminated to the back surface.

foil wallpaper A very thin flexible metallic sheet—either aluminum or simulated metal—laminated to a paper or fabric back.

folded plate (1) A framing assembly composed of sloping slabs in a hipped or gabled arrangement. (2) Prismatic shell with open polygonal section.

folding doors The assembly of two or more hinged leaves which, when straightened in a line, can close the opening.

folding rule A fourfold or zigzag rule.

folding stair An attic ladder, hinged so it can be raised and lowered.

folding wedges Wedges used in pairs to tighten up or slack off dead shores, flying shores, raking shores, and falsework and centers of all sorts.

follow block That part of a pile driver that rests on top of the piling to be driven.

follower A piston that maintains a light pressure against a variable amount of fluid in a container.

foot (1) In tamping rollers, one of a number of projections from the base of a cylindrical drum. (2) Linear unit of measure; 12 inches. (3) The base of a structure or object.

foot block An architrave block.

foot bolt A vertically set tower bolt.

footcandle (ft-c) A quantitive unit for measuring illumination. It is approximately the illumination produced by a plumber's candle at a distance of one foot.

footing (1) A foundation for a column; spreading courses under a foundation wall. (2) An enlargement at the bottom of a wall to distribute the weight of the superstructure over a greater area to prevent settling. That portion of the foundation of a structure which spreads and transmits load directly to the piles, or to the soil or supporting grillage. (3) Ground in relation to its load bearing and friction qualities.

footing beam In roofing, the tie beam for the roof.

footing forms Forms made of wood for shaping and holding concrete for footings of columns which support beams and girders.

footing materials Footings usually are made of concrete reinforced with steel rods; however, other materials such as stone blocks are sometimes used.

footlambert (apparent footcandle) Unit of brightness; that emitted or reflected from any surface emitting or reflecting one lumen per square foot.

footlight One of a series of lights along the front edge of a stage, lighting the stage but sheltered from the audience.

footpace A resting space in the form of a platform set lengthwise in a straight flight of stairs. Sometimes loosely used as synonym for halfpace.

foot pins The hinge which attaches the boom to a revolving shovel.

foot plate A horizontal board laid over

and crossing the wall plate, joining the foot of the rafter to the foot of an ashler piece; sole plate.

foot-pound Unit of energy equal to the force in pounds multiplied by the distance in feet through which it acts. When a one pound force is exerted through a one foot distance, one foot-pound of energy is done.

footprints (pipe tongs; combination pliers) *(slang)* A pipefitter's adjustable wrench with serrated jaws.

foots Settlings of linseed oil.

foot screws In surveying, three screws which connect the tribrach of the theodolite or level to the plate which is screwed onto the tripod head; used for levelling the instrument.

footstall The pedestal of a column.

footstone (springer; kneeler) A stone built into the lower end of a gable to support its coping.

foot valve A check valve in the inlet end of a pump suction hose.

force In structural work, that which tends to accelerate a body or to change its movement; e.g., the weight of a body is a force which tends to move it downwards.

compression force A force acting on a body, tending to compress the body. (Pushing action).

shear force A force acting on a body which tends to slide one portion of the body against the other side of the body. (Sliding action).

tension force A force acting on a body tending to elongate the body. (Pulling action).

torsion force A force acting on a body which tends to twist the body. (Twisting action).

Force account (1) Term used when work is ordered to be done without prior agreement as to lump sum or unit price cost thereof and is to be billed for at cost of labor, materials and equipment, insurance, taxes, etc., plus an agreed percentage for overhead and profit. (2) Describes work done with a governmental agency's own forces, rather than letting the work out for bid.

force cup British term for the rubber cupped plunger used to unplug drains by means of force and suction.

forced air Hot or cold air blown from a heating or air-conditioning unit by means of a fan or blower.

forced air furnace Any heating unit with a fan or blower attached.

forced circulation air cooler A cooler which includes a fan or a blower for positive air circulation.

forced draft burner A burner that supplies combustion air with a fan and does not rely on chimney effect for draft.

forced drying Drying of paint at a temperature not exceeding 150°F.

forced fit The fitting of a structural member in place by means of force with the result that the parts become joined as a unit.

force pump A pump to deliver fluids to a level considerably higher than the cylinder, as distinguished from a spout-delivery pump.

ford A place where a road crosses a live stream but where there is no bridge or culvert.

forebay A reservoir or pond at the head of a penstock or pipe line; the water immediately upstream of any structure.

foreman The overseer of a specific trade or construction project who is in charge of a group of workers, and usually is responsible to a superintendent or manager.

fore observation Any observation made by surveying towards the next station in the forward direction of a survey.

fore plane A bench plane intermediate between the jointer plane, which is larger, and the jack plane, which is smaller.

forepole A plank driven ahead of a tunnel face to support the roof or wall during excavation.

forge (1) To work wrought iron into shape by first softening by heat and then hammering into required form. (2) The apparatus of a furnace in which the iron is heated before being worked.

forge welding Joining pieces of steel by hammering; a form of pressure welding. The oldest method of joining metal.

forging A metal product shaped by hammering while softened by heat.

fork A two-pronged rod or yoke used to slide shifting collars along their shafts.

forked tenon In cabinetwork, a joint formed by a tenon cut in a long rail and inserted into an open mortise.

fork head A wheel-guiding frame with a swivel connection to the machine or vehicle that rests on it; a caster frame.

fork-lift truck A power-driven truck with steel forks projecting in front which can lift, travel with and stack heavy loads at a height. The loads are often lifted on a pallet.

form (formwork) A temporary structure or mold for the support of concrete while it is setting and gaining sufficient strength to be self supporting.

form anchor Device used to secure formwork to previously placed concrete of adequate strength; the device is normally embedded in the concrete during placement.

format (for construction specifications) Standardized arrangement for the project manual including bidding information, contract forms, conditions of the contract, and specifications subdivided into divisions.

foremeret The arch rib lying next to the wall in groined vaulting shorter than the others.

form hanger Device used to support formwork from a structural framework; the dead load of forms, weight of concrete, and construction and impact loads must be supported.

Formica The trade name for a hard, durable plastic sheeting used for table, sink and counter tops or for wall covering; resistant to heat and chemicals.

forming tool A term frequently applied to any device which will facilitate a mechanical operation; a tool especially designed for a particular type or work with its cutting edge shaped like the form to be produced on the work.

form insulation Insulation material applied to outside of forms between studs and over the top in sufficient thickness and air tightness to conserve heat of hydration and maintain concrete at required temperatures in cold weather.

form lining Selected materials used to line the concreting face of formwork in order to impart a smooth or patterned finish to the concrete surface, to absorb moisture from the concrete, or to apply a set-retarding chemical to the formed surface.

form oil A special blend of oils applied to interior surfaces of formwork to promote a clean break from concrete when forms are removed.

form scabbing Removal of the surface of concrete because of adhesion to the form.

form spreader *(see spreader)*

form tie (snap tie) A tensile unit adapted to prevent concrete forms from spreading due to the fluid pressure of freshly placed, unhardened concrete.

formwork (falsework) *(OSHA)* The total system of support for freshly placed concrete, including the mold or sheathing which contacts the concrete as well as all supporting members, hardware, and necessary bracing; called shuttering in the United Kingdom.

formy *(see pattee)*

Forstner bit A carpenter's bit with a sharp ring at its outside edge, for sinking blind holes.

foss A moat; a barrier of water.

foul air duct A suction line in a tunnel ventilation system; a flue.

foul water Sewage.

found (1) To make a foundation. (2) To make a metal casting.

foundation The entire masonry substructure below the first floor or frame of a building, including the footing upon which the building rests; the soil or rock upon which a building or other structure rests.

foundation bolt *(see anchor bolt)*

foundation failure Failure of a building foundation in several ways, usually by differential settlement or by shear failure of the soil.

foundation wall A wall below the floor nearest grade serving as a support for a wall, pier, column or other structural part of the building.

foundry A place where metal casting is done.

fourble In rotary drilling, a unit of four drill pipes left coupled together.

four-by-four (4×4) (1) A vehicle with four wheels or two sets of wheels, all engine driven. (2) A piece of lumber approximately four inches by four inches in dimension.

four-centered arch An arch approximating elliptical form in which the entrados is a combination of four arcs of circles in two symmetrically disposed pairs.

four-leg sling A chain or rope sling with four hooks hung from one link or thimble.

four-part line A single rope or cable reeved around pulleys so that four strands connect the fixed and the movable units.

four-way reinforcement *(see reinforcement, four-way)*

four-way switch A switch used in wiring when a light is to be turned on or off at more than two places. For three places, two three-way and one four-way switches are used; for four places, two three-way and two four-way switches are used; an additional four-way switch is used for each additional place of control.

fox bolt A bolt with a split end holding a wedge, when the bolt is driven, it expands and can be concreted tight in place.

foxtail The wedge for a fox bolt.

foxtail wedging A method of mortising in which the end of the tenon is notched beyond the mortise and is split and a wedge inserted, which, being forcibly driven in, enlarges the tenon and makes the joint firm and immovable; secret wedging.

foyer A subordinate space between an entrance and the main interior to which

it leads in a theater, hotel, apartment or house.

fraction Any part as distinct from the whole; any part of a unit.

fractional-horsepower motor An electric motor with a rating of less than one horsepower; may be a universal motor.

fractional sampling Mechanical sampling by equipment which divides or decimates a sample without segregation and processes the sample with less time and labor than coning and quartering.

fracture *(see crack)*

fractured faces Freshly broken surface of aggregate normally produced in crushing.

frake *(see limba)*

frame (panel) (1) The principal prefabricated, welded structural unit in a scaffolding tower; also beam and column skeleton of a building. (2) In carpentry, the timber work supporting the various structural parts such as windows, doors, etc.; and the entire lumber work supporting the floors, walls, roofs and partitions.

frame construction Building of houses, apartments, etc. with wood framing members.

framed opening Frame work (headers and jambs) and flashing which surround an opening in the wall or roof of a building. Usually for field installed accessories such as overhead doors or powered roof exhausters.

framed partition A partition built of timber.

frame high In masonry, the level at which the lintel or arch of an opening is to be laid; also, the height of the top of window or door frames.

frames Racks at back of the Wilton loom holding spools from which yarns are fed into the loom, each frame holding separate colors.

framework The frame of a building; the various supporting parts of a building fitted together into a skeleton form.

framing (1) The primary and secondary members (columns, rafters, girts, purlins, brace rods, etc.) which go together to make up the skeleton of a structure to which the covering can be applied. (2) Wood or metal members, such as studs, joists and headers.

balloon A system of framing a building in which all vertical structural elements of the bearing walls and partitions consist of single pieces extending from the top of the sole-plate to the roofplate and to which all floor joists are fastened.

platform A system of framing a building in which floor joists of each story rest on the top plates of the story below or on the foundation sill for the first story, and the bearing walls and partitions rest on the subfloor of each story.

framing drawings Plans and erection instructions which identify all individual parts in sufficient detail to permit the proper erection and installation of all parts of the metal building system furnished by the seller; also known as erection drawings.

framing member The stud, plate, joist or furring component to which the exterior and interior surfacing materials are attached. Normally composed of wood or metal.

Francis turbine A low-to medium-head water turbine used on many large hydroelectric projects. The water enters it radially inwards and leaves it downwards. The turbine shaft is often vertical.

Franki pile Trade name for a driven cast-in-place pile which has the advantage of a bulbous toe, clubfoot. Its main disadvantage is the large amount of space needed for the pile frame, limiting its erection to large open sites.

frazil ice (slush ice) Granular or spiky ice formed in rapids or other agitated water during long cold spells.

free area The total area across the face of a pipe or duct.

free board The crest of a dam, etc., left to allow for wave action.

free end The end of a beam which is unsupported, as that end of a cantilever which is not fixed; the hinge of a beam.

free delivery-type unit A device which takes in air and discharges it directly to the space to be treated without external elements which impose air resistance.

free face In rock blasting, an exposed surface. Usually each round has one free face; holes with more than one free face need much less explosive.

free fall Descent of freshly mixed concrete into forms without dropchutes or other means of confinement; the distance through which such descent occurs; also uncontrolled fall of aggregate.

free-falling velocity *(see velocity, terminal)*

free float *(C.P.M.)* The amount of extra time available for an activity if every activity in the project starts as early as it is possible. It is thus the amount of float that can be allocated to an activity without interfering with subsequent work.

free flow Flow over a weir or dam which is so high that it is not affected by the level of the tailwater.

free form Most often refers to installation of two different colors or patterns together in a curved-type shape or design.

free haul The distance every cubic yard is entitled to be moved without an additional charge for haul.

free lime Calcium oxide (CaO) as in clinker and cement which has not combined with SiO_2, Al_2O_3 or Fe_2O_3 during the burning process, usually because of underburning, insufficient grinding of the raw mix or the presence of traces of inhibitors.

free moisture Moisture not retained or absorbed by aggregate. *(see surface moisture)*

free retaining wall A retaining wall tilting slightly at its base so that the movement of the top is in the neighborhood of half on one percent of the wall height. By this method the earth force in granular material is reduced to the fully active earth pressure.

free-standing Independent of an adjacent wall or other background, as a free-standing column.

freestone Stone which can be used for molding, tracery and other work required to be executed with the chisel. The oolitic and sandstone are those generally included by this term.

free water *(see surface moisture)*

freeway An expressway with full control of access.

freezeline The depth at which the soil freezes, depending on the various climates. Footings should be below freezeline to guard against failure due to expansion and contraction.

freeze-thaw Single cycle going from complete freeze to complete thaw. Generally used to test soil-cement and concrete mixtures.

freeze-up Failure of a refrigerating unit to operate normally due to formation of ice at the expansion device. A valve may freeze shut or open, causing improper refrigeration in either case. On a coil, frost formation to the extent that air flow stops or is severely restricted.

freezing time Time for any complete freezing process to take place.

freight elevator Term for an elevator used for hoisting furniture and other heavy loads in a building, but not for carrying passengers.

French arch *(see Dutch arch)*

French chalk A finely ground talc.

French creek granite A fine-grain, hard, dark-colored granite of Pennsylvania; when polished the surface is almost black, the hammered faces light.

French curve A drafting aid in template form, enabling the draftsman to draw various curves or arcs by guiding his pencil or drawing pen along an edge.

French door *(see French window)*

French drain (rubble; stone drain) A covered ditch containing a layer of fitted or loose stone or other pervious material.

Frenchman *(slang)* A knife with the end bent and used with a jointing rule for trimming mortar joints.

French polish A finish for wood obtained by repeated rubbing with shellac or a varnish gum dissolved in an abundance of alcohol.

French roof A mansard roof.

French roofing tile A flat, corrugated tile with interlocking flush side joints.

French stuc A plaster work which imitates stone.

French truss A fink truss.

French varnish A varnish made with shellac and methylated spirit.

French window A doorway equipped with two glazed doors hinged at the jambs.

Freon A trademark applied to a group of refrigerants; used extensively in air-conditioning systems because of its non-toxic and non-flammable properties.

frequency The speed of light divided by the wave length (for electromagnetic radiation).

frequency scale The audible frequency scale extends from approximately 20 cycles per second to 20,000 cycles per second. In acoustical work the range from 100 to 7000 cycles per second is most important. The absorption of acoustical materials is measured at octave intervals between 125 and 4000 cycles per second.

fresco A term applied to the process of painting on wet plaster; some times incorrectly used in reference to dry painting on plastered walls or ceiling.

fresh-air inlet (1) In plumbing, a connection made to a house drain above the drain trap leading to the outside atmosphere for the purpose of admitting fresh air into the drainage system to dispel the foul gases. (2) An opening for the introduction of fresh air into a ventilating system.

fresno A long-handled concrete finishing tool.

fresno scraper A non-automotive scraper pulled by four horses or mules, consisting of a long span open in front and above, with a heaped capacity of about ⅓ cubic yard; an ancestor of the bowl scraper.

fret Ornament, usually in band form, which originated in Greece; a geometrically meandering strap pattern.

fret saw A saw used for cutting around sharp curves consisting of a thin, narrow, replaceable blade held in a frame.

fretting The breaking away of aggregate from the paved surface of a road. Also called ravelling.

fretwork Any ornamental openwork or work in relief in masonry.

friable particles Particles which crumble easily between fingers.

friction Resistance to motion when one body is sliding or tending to slide over another. May be divided into sliding or rolling friction. Friction at rest is greater than when in motion; therefore, it requires a greater force to start a body in motion than to keep it going.

frictional soil Clean silt or sand or gravel, or a soil whose shearing strength is mainly decided by the friction between particles.

friction head In hydraulics, the energy lost by friction in a pipe; sometimes considered to include losses at bends and elsewhere.

friction latch (friction catch) A spring-actuated device, mortised in the edge, for holding a small door closed.

friction loss The stress loss in a tendon resulting from friction during stressing between the tendon and duct or other device.

friction pile A bearing pile with supporting capacity produced by friction with the soil in contact with the pile.

frieze (1) A decorative horizontal band at or near the top of a wall; in Classical architecture the middle portion of an entablature. (2) A tightly twisted yarn that gives a rough, nubby appearance to carpet pile.

frieze block Piece of lumber between rafters on the eaves to close off the attic.

frieze panel The uppermost panel in a door having more than four panels.

frig bob saw A long handsaw used in Britain for cutting Bath stone at the quarry.

fringe water A term for temporarily or permanently held water just above the water table.

frog A depression, such as a groove or recess, in one or both of the larger sides of a brick or building block providing a key for the mortar at the joints.

front (1) The working attachment of a shovel, dragline hoe, or dipper stick. (2) The more important face of a building, or that containing its main entrance.

frontage street or road A local street or road auxiliary located on the side of an arterial highway for service to an abutting property and adjacent areas, and for control of access.

front end loader A tractor loader with a bucket which operates entirely at the front end of the tractor.

front end loading The practice of overpricing items of work done at the beginning of a job and underpricing those at the end so that the contractor or subcontractor can receive disproportionately larger payments at the beginning of the contract.

frontispiece In architectural drawing, a composition of several related elements resulting from an exercise in undergraduate design and rendering.

front lintel A lintel supporting the wall seen over an opening.

fronton A pediment, particularly the pediment form used over door or window.

front putty Face putty.

frost Frozen soil.

frost back The flooding of liquid from an evaporator into the suction line accompanied by frost formation of suction line in most cases.

frost boils Soil approaching a liquid condition from melting ice lenses erupting in surface failures.

frosted finish A surface treatment for glass, consisting of an acid etching on one or both surfaces, that improves distribution of transmitted light and reduces glare.

frost heave Lifting of soil caused by accumulation of ice lenses.

frosting A painting term describing the translucent, finely wrinkled finish formed during drying; a characteristic of tung and other oils which have not been properly heat-treated.

frost line The greatest depth to which ground may be expected to freeze.

frost proof tile Product manufactured for use where freezing and thawing conditions occur.

frowy *(slang)* A description of lumber that is brittle or soft.

fudge *(slang)* To depart from correct drawing for the sake of appearance.

fuel adjustment As the price of fuel for generation over and above what is included in the rate changes, this increase or decrease is passed on to the customer. This adjustment is in ¢/Kwh.

fuel heater May be stream or electric. Means of raising the oil temperature to lower the viscosity of numbers 5 & 6 oil (number 4 oil in very cold climates).

fuel oil A liquid fuel derived from petroleum or coal that requires little further refinement and is commonly used to fuel boilers.

No. 1 distillate oil, vaporizing burners

No. 2 distillate oil, general use

No. 4 blended oil, no preheating required

No. 5 blended residual oil, preheating between 120-220 degrees F required

No. 6 blended residual, preheating between 180-260 degrees F required

No. 6 low sulfur residual oil, less preheating required than with No. 6 blended residual

fuel-to-steam efficiency Fuel-to-steam efficiency can be calculated using either of two methods as prescribed by the ASME Power Test Code, PTC 4.1 The first method is input-output. The second method is heat balance. This method considers stack tempera.

fugitive Of colors, those prone to early fading.

fulcrum A pivot for a lever.

full-cell process Any process for impregnating wood with preservatives or chemicals in which a vacuum is drawn to remove air from the wood before admitting the preservative.

full coat A painting term for as thick a coat of paint or varnish as can be properly applied.

full-cut lumber Lumber that in thickness and width measures fully up to specified sizes; a term sometimes confused with cut-full lumber, the latter meaning lumber intentionally manufactured in larger than nominal thickness and width.

full-depth asphalt pavement An asphalt pavement structure in which asphalt mixtures are used for all courses above the subgrade or improved subgrade.

Fuller's curve An empirical curve for gradation of aggregates; also known as the Fuller-Thompson Ideal Grading Curve; the curve is designed by fitting either a parabola or an ellipse to a tangent at the point where the aggregate fraction is one-tenth of the maximum size fraction.

fuller's earth A fine earth resembling clay but lacking plasticity. Much the same chemically as clay but with a decidedly higher percentage of water. It possesses the property of decolorizing oils and fats by retaining the color matter. it is sometimes used as a filtering agent.

fuller's faucet In plumbing, a faucet in which a rubber ball is forced into the opening to stop the flow of water.

full gloss A painting term for the highest possible grade of gloss.

full length lumber Cut so the ends can be squared to exact length.

full-tide cofferdam A cofferdam built high enough to keep out water at all tides.

full trailer A towed vehicle whose weight rests entirely on its own wheels or crawlers.

fully fixed In structural work, describing a member in a frame which has a fixed end.

fume To treat finish woodwork with the

fumes of ammonia to secure certain colors.

fumes (1) Solid particles commonly formed by the condensation of vapors from normally solid materials such as molten metals. Fumes may also be formed by sublimation, distillation, calcination, or chemical reaction wherever such processes create airborne particles predominantly below one micron in size. Such solid particles sometimes serve as condensation nuclei for water vapor to form smog. (2) Smoke from an explosion, or an invisible vapor.

excellent Fumes that contain a minimum of toxic and irritating chemicals.

poor Toxic or irritating chemicals produced by an explosion.

fumigation Disinfecting with gas for the destruction of germs, animal or insect life.

functionalism The principle of establishing form and structure on the basis of the most economical statisfaction of physical needs.

functional obsolescence A loss in value occurring within a structure, caused by changes in design, overcapacity or inadequacy; e.g., high ceilings, old-style fixtures or cabinets, poor floor plan in residences.

fundamental The lowest frequency in a group of harmonically related frequencies.

fungicide A chemical that is poisonous to fungi.

funny papers *(slang)* Blue prints.

furan resin A furan resin, composition used as a chemical-resistant setting adhesive or chemical-resistant grout.

furnace (1) The fire-containing apparatus for central heating by warm air. (2) That part of a boiler or warm air heating plant in which combustion takes place. Also a complete heating unit for transferring heat from fuel being burned to the air supplied to a heating system.

furnished by others Materials or apparatus to be installed by the contractor but to be supplied by the owner, a different contractor, or others.

furniture Equipment for inhabited interiors and outlying spaces; e.g., chairs, tables, beds, desks, cabinets and the like.

furr down Drop ceiling in kitchen, baths or halls; used to conceal ducts.

furred In plumbing, a description of pipes and boilers which have become encrusted with hard lime or other salts deposited from the water heated in them.

furred ceiling A ceiling having spacer elements, (usually furring channels, round rods, or wood strips) interposed between it and the supporting structure above.

furring The strips of wood or metal applied to a wall or other surface to make it level, to form an air space, or to provide fastening surface for a finish covering.

furring channels Term generally applied to ¾″ cold or hot rolled steel channels used in plaster base construction.

furrowing The practice of striking a 'V' shaped trough in a bed of mortar.

fusarole A member, the section of which is a semicircle, carved into beadlike forms, as under the echinus of certain columns in the Doric and Ionic orders.

fuse (1) A replaceable fusible link in the wiring for an electric circuit to break the circuit by melding in the event of overload. (2) For blasting, a thin core of black powder surrounded by wrappings; when lit at one end it will burn to the other end at a fixed rate of speed.

fuse block In electricity, an insulated block designed to hold fuses.

fuse box A term sometimes applied to a distribution fuse board when it is enclosed in a box.

fuse cutout An insulated block with fittings for holding fuses.

fuse, detonating A stringlike core of PETN, a high explosive, contained within a waterproof reinforced sheath. Primacord is the best known.

fuse lighters Special devices for the purpose of igniting safety fuses.

fuse link A length of fuse wire for refilling fuses; the necessary or fusible part of a cartridge fuse.

fuse plug A fuse mounted in a screw plug which is screwed into the fuse block like a lamp in a socket.

fusestat In electricity, a special type of plug fuse with a time lag and an adapter that makes it impossible to bridge the fuse with a coin; also called S fuse.

fuse strip A length of ribbon fuse as distinguished from a wire fuse.

fuse switch A switch containing a fuse.

fusetron In electricity, a special type of fuse with a time lag that will carry the current or motors without opening the circuit.

fuse wire A wire made of an alloy which melts at a comparatively low temperature.

fusible link A link that is broken by the melting of a short length of low-melting-point metal in an electric circuit, thus releasing a fire door, sprinkler valve or the like.

fusible plug A device having a prede-termined melting temperature member for the relief of pressure.

fusion The combination of the nuclei of atoms. Fusion is what is going on in the sun where hydrogen atoms are continuously converted to helium atoms. Energy from fusion may well become the best source of energy for man to use, but the technical problems inherent in the control of fusion are enormous.

fusion welding That type of welding where material is joined by fusion, with or without depositing at the same time filler metal in a molten or molten-and-vapor state.

fuzzing Hairy effect on fabric surface caused by wild fibers or slack yarn twist; or by fibers slipping out of yarn or contour in either service or wet cleaning. Carpet of continuous filament yarn is fuzzed by filaments snagging and breaking. It is corrected by shearing in manufacturing or by the professional cleaner.

fuzzy grain Roughening of the surface of the wood, resulting from absorption of moisture sufficient to expand the wood cells at the immediate surface. The result is a fuzzy feel when touched.

g   gauge, gram, gravity

ga   gauge

gal   gallon

galv   galvanized

gar   garage

GCF   greatest common factor

Gl   galvinized iron

gl   glass, glazing

GMV   gram-molecluar volume

Goth   Gothic

gov/govt   government

gpd   gallons per day

gpm   gallons per minute

gr   grade, grains, gravity, gross

gr.fl.   ground floor

gr.fl.ar.   ground floor area

gr. wt.   gross weight

GT   gross ton

gtd   guaranteed

g.u.p.   grading under pavement

gabbro   Generic name for igneous granular stone composed chiefly of pyroxene, augite or diallage, and plagioclase.

gabions   As used in modern engineering practice, compartmented rectangular containers made of galvanized steel hexagonal wire mesh and filled with stone.

gable   The end of a building as distinguished from the front or rear side; the triangular end of an exterior wall above the eaves; the end of a ridged roof which at its extremity is not returned on itself but is cut off in a vertical plane which above the eaves is triangular in shape due to the slope of the roof

gableboard   A board placed along the sloping edge of a gable roof covering the timbers that project over the gables; a barge board.

gable coping   Coping for a gable wall, projecting above the roof.

gabled towers   Those finished with gables instead of parapets. Many German Romanesque towers are gabled.

gable end   An end wall having a gable.

gable molding   The molding used as a finish for the gable end of a roof.

gable post   A short post at the apex of a gable into which barge boards are placed.

gable roof   A ridged roof which terminates either at one end or both ends in a gable.

gable shoulder   Projection formed by the gable springer at the base of a gable coping.

gable springer   A stone overhang at the foot of a gable coping below the lowest kneeler. Also called a foot stone or skew block.

gablet   A miniature gabled top, as over a buttress; a small gable-like decoration.

gable wall   A wall topped by a gable.

gable window   A term sometimes applied to the large window under a gable, but more properly to the windows in the gable itself.

gaboon   An African mahogany.

gad   A chisel or pointed iron or steel bar for loosening rock.

gaffer   *(slang)* A foreman, pusher or ganger. In general, anyone in charge of work.

gage   *(see gauge)*

gage glass   Device for showing a liquid level.

gag process   The process of bending structural shapes in a gag press.

gain   (1) The notch or mortise where a piece of wood is cut out to receive the end of another piece of wood. (2) A beveled shoulder on the end of a mortised brace, for the purpose of giving additional resistance to the shoulder. (3) A notch or mortise cut to receive a hinge or other hardware.

galbestos   Type of siding used in the building of manufactured housing.

galite   Type of expanded shale used as an aggregate in lighweight concrete.

gallery   (1) The space provided by inserting an intermediate floor over part of an enclosed space, this floor projecting from one or more of the enclosing walls and being terminated by a balustrade or parapet; a roofed passageway above grade projecting from an exterior wall; a connecting room in a formal interior; a museum or a room thereof. (2) In mining, a roadway or tunnel for collecting water in rock or in a concrete dam.

gallery apartment house   An apartment house where access to the units is obtained from an open corridor.

gallet   A chip of rock; a spall.

galleting   In rubble work, a term applied to the process of filling in the coarse masonry joints of fresh mortar with small stone or flint chips or gallets; same as garreting.

gallon   A standard liquid measure; the British Imperial gallon contains 10 pounds of water; one American gallon contains 8.33 pounds of water.

gallon per minute (gpm)   A unit measure of flow. Equals a flow rate of one gallon in one minute.

gallows bracket   A bracket of triangle framing which projects from a wall.

galvanic cell   A cell in which chemical change is the source of electrical energy. It usually consists of two dissimilar conductors in contact with each other and an electrolyte.

galvanic corrosion   Accelerated corrosive action brought about by two different metals touching each other while wet with any solution capable of conducting an electric current. This sets up a galvanic voltage which tends to accelerate corrosion in one of the metals and protect the other.

galvanize   To dip iron or steel into molten zinc, hot-dip galvanizing, or to electroplate with zinc. This process prevents rusting. Not all zinc coatings are galvanized.

galvanized iron   Steel or steel sheet coated with zinc; usually not iron.

galvanized pipe   Zinc coated pipe for water flow. Gas pipe is black.

galvanized sheet steel   Sheet steel on whose surface are developed an adherent, protective coating of zinc and zinc compounds by immersing them in a bath of molten zinc.

galvanized steel   Steel coated with zinc for corrosion resistance.

gambrel roof   A type of roof which has its slope broken by an obtuse angle, so that the lower slope is steeper than the upper slope; A roof with two pitches. Also referred to as a mansard, half-hipped or curb roof.

gamma protein   Protein derived from soya bean meal; used as an extender for casein in water base paints.

gandy dancer   (slang) A section man in railroad work who does earth-moving and tracklaying by sections.

gandy stick   (slang) A tamping bar used in railroad work.

gang   (1) A combination of several tools, machines, etc., operated by a single force or so contrived as to be made to act as one. (2) A company or crew of men. (3) Entry to a Swedish dwelling. (4) Connecting hall between rooms of the Dutch dwelling.

gang-boarding   A cat ladder.

ganged forms   Prefabricated panels joined to make a much larger unit, up to 30 × 50 feet (9 × 15 m) for convenience in erecting, stripping and reusing; usually braced with walers, strongbacks or special lifting hardware.

ganager   The worker in charge of a gang of laborers. He may be a working ganger who works with one gang or a traveling, or walking, ganger who supervises several gangs.

gang mold   A mold for simultaneous casting of several similar concrete units.

gang saw   A reciprocating mechanical saw, e.g., a frame saw.

gang-sawn   Adjective descriptive of a moderately smooth granular surface of building stone that results from the gang sawing alone.

gangue Valueless minerals in an ore, often quartz or calcite.

gangway In building, a temporary footway made of planks and used as a passageway by workmen on a construction job.

ganister A material made of ground quartz and fire clay used for fire-proofing purposes, especially around the hearths of furnaces and for furnace linings. It is a highly refractory siliceous sedimentary rock.

ganosis The dulling of polished surface on marble.

gantry (1) An overhead structure that supports machines or operating parts. (2) An upward extension of a shovel revolving frame that holds the boom line sheaves.

gap-filling glue A glue for joining surfaces which cannot be fitted closely or pressed tightly enough for a close-contact glue.

gap-graded aggregate Aggregate having a particle-size distribution characterized by gap grading.

gap-grading A particle-sized distribution in which particles of certain intermediate sizes are wholly or substantially absent.

garchey sink A domestic sink installed in some British kitchens. All ordinary household rubbish can be emptied through it and no waste bins are needed except for tins, bottles and newspaper.

garden apartment A multiple dwelling of two or three stories in height, usually in a suburban residential community, with a minimum of landscaping on the site.

garden bond A type of masonry construction usually consisting of three stretchers in each course followed by a header; this bond may have from two to five stretchers between headers.

garden city One in which the single family detached house and open spaces are predominant.

garderobe A room for keeping articles of clothing, a wardrobe; also a small private room as a bedroom or a privy.

gargoyle A grotesque sculptural projection from a roof scupper, to drop rain water clear of the walls; characteristic of Gothic church architecture.

garland Sculptured ornament, usually in relief, in the form of a swag or festoon of flowers and fruits.

garnet A gallet, used in galleting.

garnet hinge A cross garnet hinge.

garneting (garreting) *(see galleting)*

garnet paper An abrasive paper used for polishing and finishing surfaces of woodwork. The paper is prepared by covering one side with glue and a reddish abrasive material. Originally the abrasive material used was finely powdered garnet stone.

garret (1) Unfinished space under a pitched roof. (2) A room in a dwelling immediately under the roof. If the garret has a ceiling, the space above it is sometimes called the cockloft or cotloft; same as attic.

garreting In masonry, a term applied to the process of pressing small splinters of stone into the joints of coarse masonry; also called galleting.

garth An enclosed yard in connection with a building.

gas Usually a highly superheated vapor which, within acceptable limits of accuracy, satisfies the perfect gas laws.

gas carbonizing Carbonizing steel by heating it in a current of gas containing carbon.

gas cock A manual shut-off valve.

gas concrete Lightweight concrete produced by developing voids with hydrogen gas bubbles generated within the unhardened mix, usually from the action of cement alkalies on aluminum powder used as an admixture. *(see foam concrete)*

gas constant The coefficient R in the perfect gas equation $pv = RT$.

gas-cooled reactor A reactor in which helium takes the place of water in the primary loop. Pressurized helium is raised to a high temperature in the reactor and then flows to a steam generator.

gas engine   An internal-combustion engine which uses as fuel a form of gas.

gases   Formless, dimensionless fluids that occupy any confined space where the molecules tend to separate from each other. Gases are changed to the liquid or solid state by increased pressures at controlled temperatures or by decreased temperatures at controlled pressures. Materials in the gaseous state at standard conditions are considered to be gases.

gasket   Washer-type device of plastic, rubber or other pliable material used in faucets or other screwed joints to make a water or air tight seal. Hemp fibers wound around the threads of a screwed joint in a water pipe before it is tightened. When wet, the hemp expands.

gaskin   In jointing stoneware pipes with cement mortar, a ring of rope put into the socket before any mortar is inserted.

gas main   The community supply line of gas for heating, illuminating and cooking.

gas meter   A measuring and recording device for gas used from the main by an individual building.

gas storage   Artificial addition of carbon dioxide to the atmosphere, particularly in large concentration, with no attempt to regulate the amount of oxygen.

gas vent   In sewage, an opening which allows gases, liberated in an Imhoff tank sludge-digestion chamber, to reach the atmosphere without passing up through the sewage in the settling chamber.

gate   (1) A barrier, hinged or hung, usually of open structure. (2) In dam construction, a device in which a leaf or member is moved across the waterway from an external position to control or stop the flow.

gate hook (gudgeon)   A metal bar which is driven by its point into a wooden post or built into a masonry or brick gate pier. It has an exposed, upright pin on which the hinge of the gate is dropped to hang the gate.

gatehouse   A house or small building near an important entrance gateway.

gatepost (gate pier)   A post to which a gate is hinged or against which it latches.

gate tower   Entrance to a walled city.

gate valve   A valve consisting of a brass gate; the gate is lifted and lowered by means of a screw stem which is operated by a cast iron wheel handle; a valve for piping utilizing the guillotine gate action.

gather   To bring flues together in a stack.

gauge (gage)   (1) The proportions of different materials in a mortar or plaster mix; to add lime putty to cement mortar; to slow the setting of plaster by adding a substance such as glue; to hasten the setting of plaster by the addition of plaster of Paris. (2) To rub brick for contrast in color and texture to adjacent brickwork. (3) The exposed depth of a tile; the distance between the bottom edge of one row of tiles and the bottom edge of the next row above or below. (4) A boundry strip used in asphalting to show the correct thickness of asphalt; screed. (5) The thickness measure of sheet metal and glass; or of wire, the diameter. (6) The spacing of tracks or wheels. (7) A tool used by carpenters and other woodworkers to make a line parallel to the edge of a board.

gauge board   (1) A board for carrying plaster and tools. It is usually placed on a stand. (2) In carpentry, a pitch board.

gauge box   A batch box.

gauged brick   Brick which have been ground or otherwise produced to accurate dimensions.

gauge glass   Device for showing a liquid level.

gauge/pitch   The number of ends of surface yarn counting across the width of carpet. In woven carpet, pitch is the number of ends of yarn in 27 inches of width, e.g., 216 divided by 27 = 8 ends per inch. In tufted carpet, gauge also means the number of ends of surface yarn per inch counting across the carpet e.g., ⅛ gauge = ends per inch.

gauge stick A piece of material cut to a specific dimension; used for measuring repetitive dimensions.

gauged arch An arch built from gauged bricks, i.e., soft bricks sawn to shape or rubbed smooth on a stone or another brick. They are laid with very fine joints, often of lime mortar without cement or sand (pure lime putty).

gauged mortar In plastering, any mortar mixed with plaster of Paris to make it set more quickly; also called gauged stuff.

gauged stuff Lime putty, generally used for the finishing coat of interior cornices, ceilings and moldings, to which plaster of Paris has been added to counteract shrinkage and hasten the set.

gauging A cementitious material (usually calcined gypsum, Keene's cement, or portland cement) added to lime putty to provide and control set. Also the act of adding gauging material.

gauge pot A container for pouring liquid grout.

gauge pressure (p.s.i.g.) Pressure measured by a gauge and indicating the pressure exceeding atmospheric.

gauge rod A storey rod.

gauge size The width of a drill bit along the cutting edge.

gauging board A device for mixing mortar, plaster, etc.

gauging plaster Gypsum plaster or plaster of Paris.

gaul A hollow in a finishing coat caused by bad troweling.

Gaussian curve The cgs (centimeter-gram-second) unit of magnetic induction equal to the magnetic flux density that will induce an electromotive force of one-hundred millionth of a volt in each linear centimeter of a wire moving laterally with a speed of one centimeter per second at right angles to a magnetic flux.

gazebo (1) A belvedere. (2) A spherical mirror on a pedestal, used as a garden ornament.

G-clamp A G-shaped screw clamp often used when gluing wood.

gear A toothed wheel, cone or bar.

bevel A gear made of teeth cut in the surface of a truncated cone.

bull A gear or sprocket that is much larger than the others in the same power train.

cluster Two or more gears of different sizes made in one solid piece.

helical A gear with straight or curved teeth cut at an angle of less than 90° to the direction of rotation.

herringbone A gear with V-teeth.

idler A gear, meshed with two other gears, that does not transmit power to its shaft; used to reverse direction of rotation in a transmission.

pinion A drive gear that is smaller than the gear it turns.

planetary set A gear set consisting of an inner sun, gear, an outer ring with internal teeth and two or more small planet, gears meshed with both the sun and the ring.

sprocket A gear that meshes with roller or silent chain.

rack A toothed bar.

gear jammer *(slang)* Truck driver.

geison In Classical architecture, the total projection of the entablature beyond the plane of the wall or face of column shafts, or that of the tympanum of a pediment.

gel Matter in a colloidal state that does not dissolve, but remains suspended in a solvent from which it fails to precipitate without the intervention of heat or of an electrolyte. *(see cement gel)*

gelatin A product of the packing house which can be cast into a semi-rigid mold. Because of its flexibility, it is particularly adaptable to molds containing undercuts, etc.

gleatin, blasting A high explosive made by dissolving nitrocotton in nitroglycerin; it is the strongest and highest velocity commercial explosive.

gelating molding A method for making

jelly molds for complicated undercut fibrous plaster castings.

gelling   Conversion of liquid to a jelly-like consistency.

general conditions   That part of the contract documents which sets forth many of the rights, responsibilities and relationships of the parties involved or of the contract.

general contract   Under the single contract system, the contract between the owner and the contractor for construction of the entire work. Under the separate contract system, that contract between the owner and a contractor for construction or architectural and structural work.

general contractor   The prime or main contractor.

general drawing   A drawing showing elevation plan and cross section of the structure; also the borings for substructure and the main dimention, etc.

general estimate method   A quick method of estimating cost of a residence on the basis of its area and general construction. Only simple arithmetic and one page of cost data is needed.

general foreman   The contractor's representative on a site, in charge of all labor under the agent. He coordinates the work of trades foremen, whether employed by the general contractor or by a subcontractor. He has usually graduated from a trade and been a trade foreman. Often called superintendent on large projects.

general lighting   Lighting designed to uniformly illuminate an entire area.

generator   (1) An electromechanical machine that converts mechanical energy into electrical energy. It generates electrical power either as an alternating current, an alternator; or as a direct current, a dynamo. (2) Basic part of an absorption system; a still provided with means of heating used to drive refrigerant out of solution.

Genessee Valley bluestone   A dark gray stone of New York State used for trim, flagging and steps.

gentese   Cusps in the arch of a doorway, such as are found in early English architecture.

geodesy   Geodetic surveying.

geodetic construction   Stressed-skin construction.

geodetic surveying   Surveying areas of the earth which are so large that the curvature must be allowed for in calculations. All distances and horizontal angles are projected onto the surface of the spheroid which represents mean sea level on the earth.

geodimeter   A surveying instrument which uses the length of a modulated wave or pulse of light as the unit of measurement to obtain the slope distance between the transmitting device and a reflecting mirror.

geological map   A map which shows outcrops of all strata or igneous rocks, or only the outcrops of the solid with the overlaying drift removed.

geometrical stair   A winding stair which returns on itself with winders built around a well. The balustrade follows the curve without newel posts at the turns. It is also known as a spiral stair and often there are no landings between floors.

Georgia buggy   *(slang)* A wheelbarrow with heavy rubber wheels to carry concrete to its destination at a site.

Georgia marble   A group name for sparkling, crystalline varieties with white or light gray grounds.

Georgian glass   Thick glass with a square mesh wire embedded in it.

geotechnical processes   Processes which change the properties of soils; for instance compaction, electro-osmosis, freezing, ground-water lowering, injection, or vibroflotation.

German siding   A type of weatherboarding with the upper part of the exposed face finished with a concave curve and the lower portion of the back face rebated.

German silver   An alloy of nickel, copper and zinc.

gesso   A plaster surface composed of

gypsum plaster, whiting and glue, used as a base for decorative painting.

ghanat *(see quanat)*

ghosting A coating of paint with a skimpy appearance.

giant (monitor) In hydraulicking, a large, high-pressure nozzle mounted in a swivel on a skid frame.

gib A piece of metal in the shape of an elongated channel, used as a clamp.

gig stick A radius rod.

Gillmore needle A device used in determining time of setting of hydraulic cement.

gilsonite A from of natural asphalt, hard and brittle, occurring in rock crevices or veins from which it is mined, like coal.

gimlet A small tool with a handle at right angles to the point, used for drilling holes smaller than ¼ inch diameter. It was used by the ancient Greeks.

gin Any vertical pole or frame used to raise things. Originally spelled gyn.

gin block A single pulley for fiber rope, carried in a steel frame with a hook at the top from which it can be hung.

gingerbread work A gaudy type of ornamentation in architecture, especially in the trim of a house.

ginnywink *(slang)* An A-frame derrick with a fixed rear leg.

gin pole A mast or vertical pole guyed to the ground by cables; used in connection with blocks and tackle for raising weight.

girandole A wall bracket with branching arms for holding candles or electric lights, usually with a circular convex mirror against the wall.

girder Any heavy, strong or principal flexural member, usually horizontal, on which the weight of a floor is carried; a main supporting beam, either timber or steel; used for supporting a superstructure; used to support concentrated loads at isolated points along its length.

girder bridge A bridge supported by girders or large beams.

girder casing (1) Material which cov-

ers and protects from fire the part of a steel girder that is below ceiling level. (2) Formwork.

girt (1) A horizontal member between columns or bents, acting as a stiffener. (2) Old term for heavy timber used in the location of the present day plate, supporting rafter ends. (3) A beam of an outside wall to receive the ends of floor joists; it also supports the summer when the summer does not rest on a post. (4) The same as girth; the circumference of round timber. *(see ledger)*

girth The circumference of any circular object; the distance around a column.

girt strip A board attached to studding to carry floor joists; a ledger board.

give-and-take lines The straight lines used for equalization of boundaries in the calculation of land area.

glacial till A mixture of material which may include sand, gravel, silt and clay; deposited by glacial action.

gland (1) In plumbing, a compressible copper or brass ring which is slipped over the copper tube and under the screwed fitting. When the fitting is tightened, the soft metal of the gland is compressed, thus closing the gap between the tube and the fitting. (2) In electrical work, the seal used at the end of a cable to prevent water from entering. A similar gland is used at water taps and stop valves to prevent leakage outward.

gland bolt A bolt used for tightening or slackening an unthreaded gland.

gland joint A joint on hot water or soil pipes which allows temperature movement.

glare Brightness in the field of view which causes either visual disability or a sensation of discomfort.

glass An inorganic product of fusion which has cooled to a rigid condition without crystallizing; it is typically hard and brittle; it may be colorless or colored, and transparent to opaque.

quartz Pure quartz transmitting the ultraviolet rays of daylight which are beneficial to health.

obscure Sheet glass that has been

made translucent instead of transparent. It is sand-blasted or molded to make the surfaces irregular.

shatter-proof *(see bullet-proof glass)*

stained A combination of pigmented glass and that which is painted and fired, arranged in a design of leading.

structural Cast glass in squares or rectangles, one inch to two inches thick, sometimes laid up between concrete ribs, frequently as tile. Larger units are made in hollow or vacuum blocks. The wide use of the porduct is in colored and polished sheets for interior wall surfacing.

wire Glass in which wire mesh is embedded to prevent shattering.

glass blocks Hollow translucent blocks of glass obscured by patterns molded on one or both faces. When used as partitions, they give a pleasant diffused light, but they have low heat insulation value and low fire resistance. In pavement lights, solid glass is used.

glass-concrete construction **(1)** Concrete pavement lights, or floor or roof slabs with glass lenses cast in. **(2)** Walls with loadbearing concrete mullions between which glass blocks are built.

glass cutter A tool for cutting glass using either a diamond or a hard, sharp metal wheel.

glass fiber felt A felt sheet in which glass fibers are bonded into the felt sheet with resin. Glass fiber felts are suitable for impregnation and coating. They are used in the manufacture and coating of bituminous waterproofing materials, roof membranes, and shingles.

glassed surface *(see polished plate)*

glass mat A glass fiber mat sheet with random textile fibers used in production of roofing.

glass mosaic tile Made of glass usually in sizes not over 2″ square and ¼″ thick, mounted on sheets of paper. Sheets are usually 12″×12″.

glasspaper Abrasive paper made from glass, flint, garnet, corundum or similar powders glued to cloth or paper. Sandpaper and emery cloth are common types.

glass size The glazing size.

glass stop A device at the lower end of a patent glazing bar to stop panes from sliding down. A glazing bead.

glass tile Transparent or translucent units to admit light through a roofing surface. *(see glass blocks)*

glass transition The reversible change in an amorphous polymer or in amorphous regions of a partially crystalline polymer from (or to) a viscous or rubbery condition to (or from) a hard and relatively brittle one.

glass wool (glass silk) Flexible fibers, formed from molten glass, used as insulation for heat and sound. It is highly fire resistant and can be obtained in rolls covered with waterproof papers, resin-bonded, bitumen-bonded or loose.

glauber's salts A term for sodium sulfate decahydrate, which melts at 90°F, a component of eutectic salts.

glaze **(1)** The process of installing glass panes in window and door frames and applying putty to hold the glass in position. **(2)** A glass-like protection fired onto bricks and tile. **(3)** In painting, the process of applying a nearly transparent coat to enhance the color below. **(4)** A ceramic coating matured to the glassy state on a formed ceramic product. Also refers to the material or mixture from which the coating is made.

bright glaze A high glass coating with or without color.

clear glaze Transparent with or without color.

crystalline glaze Contains microscopic crystals.

fritted glaze Uses all or part of prefused fluxing constituents.

mat glaze A low gloss glaze with or without color.

opaque glaze A non-transparent coating with or without color.

raw glaze Compounded primarily of raw constituents and contains no prefused materials.

semimat glaze A medium gloss finish with or without color.

speckled glaze Features granules of oxides or ceramic stains of contrasting colors.

glaze coat (1) The top layer of asphalt in a smooth-surfaced built-up roof assembly; (2) A thin protective coating of bitumen applied to the lower plies or top ply of a built-up roof membrane when application of additional felts or the flood coat and aggregate surfacing are delayed.

glazed brick Building brick prepared by fusing on the surface a glazing material; brick having a glassy surface.

glazed doors Doors which have been fitted with glass usually having a pattern or lattice of woodwork between the panes.

glazed structural unit A solid or hollow unit with a surface of applied smooth glossy nature, e.g. a tile with a fired glaze finish.

glazed tile A type of masonry tile which has a glassy or glossy surface; generally for interior use.

glazed ware (glazed stoneware) Pipes and drain fittings, made of stoneware, glazed by vapor from salt thrown into the kiln during firing.

glazement In building, a facing material which gives a glazed waterproof surface; used for concrete or brickwork construction.

glazier One who installs glass panes.

glazier's chisel A glazier's putty knife shaped like a chisel.

glazier's points Small headless nails used to hold glass in place while putty is being applied. They are often triangular pieces of flat metal.

glazier's putty (painter's putty) A plastic material used for bedding glass in lights and for making a weatherproof fillet of putty outside the glass holding it to the frame.

glazing (1) The securing of glass in prepared openings in windows, door panels, screens, partitions, etc. (2) The filling up of interstices in the surface of a grindstone or emery wheel with minute abraded particles detached in grinding.

glazing bar (sash bar; astragal) A wood or metal bar which holds the panes of glass in a window. The term glazing bar is often reserved for roof lights or patent glazing.

glazing bead (glass stop) A small wood strip, mitered and nailed or screwed around a rebate, to hold the glass instead of putty.

glazing size (glass size) The size of a piece of glass cut for glazing.

glazing sprig (glazier's point; brad) A small beadless nail in the face putty around a pane of glass. It holds the glass in place while the face putty is being applied.

glitch *(slang)* (1) A seemingly insolvable design problem. (2) Contractor's headache.

globe valve One in which a circular disc shuts off the flow of a liquid, moving in a plane parallel to the connected piping. It has a bulbous appearance and higher resistance than a gate valve.

glory hole *(slang)* (1) A vertical pit, material from which is fed by gravity to hauling units in a shaft under the pit bottom. (2) A small excavation mined to determine ore quality but found to be unproductive.

gloss In paint or enamel, that which contains a relatively low proportion of pigment and dries to a sheen or luster. Of painted surfaces, a highly polished finish, such as that given by certain enamels, without after-polish.

glossing up An undesirable gloss which develops on a matte surface when it is handled.

glossy The shininess or lack of shininess of a paint finish. Paint finishes described as "glossy" have the highest luster; those described as "flat" have little luster; "semi-gloss" has a medium luster.

glue To attach materials together by means of glue; a cementing substance.

casein Made from casein and borax.

flake Made from animal substances.

marine Waterproof glue made with a

shellac or rubber base and oil solvent.

waterproof Made from synthetic resins.

glue block An angle block.

glue gun A hand tool for the application of bulk or cartridge-type adhesives.

glue line The line visible on the edge of a plywood panel indicating the layer of glue.

Glu-lam Trade name for glued and laminated wood structural timbers, such as arches or trusses.

glyph In architecture, an ornamental channel, or groove; a short vertical groove.

glyptic Carved or incised.

gneiss Crystalline rock with a tendency to cleave in slabs.

gob bucket *(slang)* Bucket used on a crane for transferring concrete to forms.

gob hopper *(slang)* Surge bin.

go-devil *(slang)* A ball of rolled-up burlap, paper or specially fabricated device put into the pump end of a pipeline and forced through the pipe by water pressure to clean the pipeline.

gofer *(slang)* (1) Runner. (2) Lowest qualified person on jobsite.

going on stairways, the horizontal distance between two consecutive nosings is the going of a tread. The sum of the tread goings is the going of the flight.

going rod A rod for setting out the going of a flight of stairs.

gold bronze Copper or copper alloy powder for bronzing.

gold leaf A sheet gold of extra fineness used for gilding exterior or interior surfaces.

gold size An oleo-resinous varnish which dries quickly to the tacky state but then hardens slowly; used for fixing gold leaf to a surface. Also an oleo-resinous varnish with a high proportion of driers which hardens quickly and is used for making filler.

goliath crane A heavy portable frame used for shop erection of heavy steel and for other heavy lifting jobs. Is usually of about 50 tons capacity, with a crane crab.

goober A bubble formed of concrete escaping from concrete form.

goods lift British term for freight elevator.

goop *(slang)* Lubrication used for tight pipe fittings.

gooseneck (1) A plumbing fitting so shaped; a prefabricated fitting for connecting a corporation stop to the service line. (2) An arched connection between a tractor and a trailer. (3) The curved or bent section of the handrail on a stair. (4) In steel work, a dolly shaped like the neck of a goose.

gorge A throat; the necking of a column or pilaster.

Gothic In architecture, a particular type and style of classic ornamentation.

Gothic arch A type of arch usually high and narrow, coming to a point at the center at the top, especially one with a joint instead of a keystone at the apex.

gouge A cutting chisel which has a concave-convex cross section, or cutting surface, arc edge.

gouge bit A drill bit with a rounded end.

gouge slip (slipstone) An oilstone slip.

gouge work Incised woodwork for which the gouge is the principal tool, as in trim and mantels of the so-called Dutch Colonial architecture of New Jersey and Pennsylvania.

government anchor In steelwork, a V-shaped anchor, usually made of half-inch round bars to secure the steel beam to masonry.

gow caisson (Boston caisson; caisson pile) Small shafts sunk through soft clay or silt to prevent excessive loss of ground.

grab set *(see flash set)*

gradability Maximum slope up which a crawler or wheel-type prime mover can move at a uniform speed; stated in percentage or degree.

gradation The particle size distribution of aggregate as determined by separation with standard screens. Sieve analysis, screen analysis, and mechanical analysis are terms used synonymously in referring to gradation of aggregate. Gradation of aggregate is expressed in terms of the individual percentages retained on U.S. standard screens designated by the numbers 4-8-16-30-50 and 100.

grab sample A sampling of water or wastewater used for laboratory diagnosis. It is collected with a bottle or jar.

grade (1) The slope of a road, channel or natural ground. (2) The finished surface of a canal bed, road bed, top of embankment or bottom of excavation. (3) Any surface prepared for the support of a conduit, paving, ties, rails, etc. (4) In lumber, any of the quality classes into which lumber is segregated for marketing. (5) The ground level around a building. (6) In plumbing, grade is usually expressed as the fall in inches per foot length of pipe. (7) Refers to the subfloor: above-grade, on-grade or below grade *(see specific categories)*.

grade Designation for durability of a brick.

grade mw (moderate weather) Brick intended for use where exposed to temperatures below freezing but not likely to be permeated with water.

grade nw (negligible weather) Brick intended for use as a backup or interior masonry.

grade sw (severe weather) Brick intended for use where a high degree of resistance to frost action is desired and the exposure is such that the brick may be frozen when permeated with water.

grade beam A horizontal loadbearing foundation member, end-supported like a standard beam, not ground-supported like the foundation wall, which forms a foundation for the walls of a superstructure.

grade block Concrete masonry unit for use in top course of foundation wall where the masonry wall above is of a smaller or greater thickness.

graded aggregate One having a continuous grading in sizes of particles from coarse to fine.

graded standard sand Ottawa sand accurately graded between the U.S. Standard No. 30 (590 micron) and No. 100 (149 micron) sieves for use in the testing of cements. *(see Ottawa sand; standard sand)*

grader (1) A machine with a centrally located blade that can be angled to cast to either side, with independent hoist control on each side. (2) Employees who hand trim the ditch, where necessary, after the ditch has been dug.

grade stake A stake indicating the amount of cut or fill required to bring the ground to a specified level.

grade-stiff *(slang)* A grade foreman.

grade strip Usually a thin strip of wood tacked inside forms at the line to which the top of the concrete lift is to come, either at a construction joint or the top of the structure.

gradetto A fillet molding; an annulet.

gradient Change of elevation, velocity, pressure or other characteristics per unit length; slope along a specific route as of a road surface, channel or pipe. The term grade is more commonly used.

gradienter A micrometer fitted to the vertical circle of a level allowing the telescope to be moved through a known small angle. In this way, the telescope can be used as a tachometer without stadia hairs, and as a grading instrument.

grading (1) Modification of the ground surface by cuts, fills or both. (2) Filling in around a building with rubble and earth so the ground will slope downward from the foundation at an angle sufficient to carry off rainwater. (3) The percentage by weight of different grain sizes in a sample of soil or aggregate, expressed on a grading curve. (4) Modification of the proportions of the different grain sizes in an aggregate for concrete, or in a soil for an earth dam or other structure, so as to produce the most stable material. *(see particle-size distribution)*

grading curve A graphical representation of the proportion of different particle sizes in a material obtained by plotting the cumulative or separate percentages of the material passing through sieves in which the aperature sizes form a given series.

grading instrument In surveying, a level with a telescope which can be raised or lowered to lay out a required gradient.

gradiograph A leveling rule for checking drain slopes.

gradiometer *(see grading instrument)*

gradual load The gradual application of a load to the supporting members of a structure, so as to provide the most favorable conditions possible for receiving the stress and strain which these members will be required to carry when the building is completed.

graduate To mark with degrees of measurement, at the division marks of a scale; the regular dividing of parts into steps or grades.

graduated acting Term applied to a control instrument or device which functions to give throttling control, that is, operates between full on and full off position.

graduated courses Diminishing courses of bricks, block, etc.

graduation The process of separating a unit of measure into equal parts; also, one of the division marks or one of the equal divisions of a scale.

graffito A plaster surface decorated by scoring a pattern on it while soft thus exposing a lower coat of a different color, often black or dark red.

grain (1) Composition and texture of stones. (2) An outmoded practice of imitating the grain of woods with paint. (3) The general direction, size and arrangement of the fibers and other elements in wood.

edge (vertical) Edge-grain lumber which has been sawn parallel to the pith of the log and approximately at right angles to the growth rings; e.g., the rings form an angle of 45° or more with the surface of the piece.

flat Flat-grain lumber has been sawn

parallel to the pith of the log and approximately tangent to the growth rings; e.g., the rings form an angle of less than 45° with the surface of the piece.

quartersawn Another term for edge grain.

grainer A painter who paints wood or stone to imitate wood grain, knot marks, marble veins, etc.

grain size curve A graph of the analysis of a soil showing the percentage size variations by weight.

granite A crystalling igneous rock composed chiefly of feldspar and some quartz and mica; used extensively in construction work and for monuments. It is extremely hard and will take a high polish.

granitic finish A face mix, resembling granite, on precast concrete.

granny bar *(slang)* A big crow bar.

granny rag *(slang)* A rag that the ragman uses in pipeline work to touch up with asphaltic compound, or dope, spots that the dope machine may have missed.

granolith A concrete used for paving, the coarse aggregate being pulverized granite.

granolithic concrete Concrete suitable for use as a wearing surface finish to floors; made with specially selected aggregate of suitable hardness, surface texture and particle shape.

granolithic finish A surface layer of granolithic concrete which may be laid on a base of either fresh or hardened concrete.

grantee A person to whom property or property rights are granted by deed or other documents, e.g., the buyer.

grantor A person who transfers property or property rights by deed or other documents, e.g., the seller.

granular Technical term referring to the uniform size of grains or crystals in rock.

granular material A sandy type of soil whose particles are coarser than cohesive material and which do not stick to each other.

granulated blast-furnace slag The nonmetallic product consisting essentially of silicates and aluminosilicates of calcium which is developed simultaneously with iron in a blast furnace and is granulated by quenching the molten material in water or in water, steam and air. *(see blast furnace)*

granulated cork *(see cork: corkboard)*

granule Natural colored or artificially colored particles of silicious material used on composition roofing.

grapple A clamshell-type bucket having three or more jaws.

grappler The wedge-shaped spike for the top end of a bracket scaffold; when driven into a brick joint, an eye is left exposed by which to attach the scaffolding.

grasshopper *(slang)* Any small crane.

grate A screen consisting of parallel bars, two sets being transverse to each other in the same plane.

graticulate To superimpose a system of squares in line upon a design or drawing, with the purpose of enlargement to a like system or larger squares.

grating A framework or grate-like arrangement of bars either parallel or crossed; used to cover an opening; or set as a strainer across a flow of liquid.

grasscloth A wallcovering made from the arrowroot bark and laminated to a paper for backing.

gravel (1) Granular material predominantly retained on the No. 4 (4.76 mm) sieve and resulting from natural disintegration and abrasion of rock or processing of weakly bound conglomerate. *(see coarse aggregate)*

gravel fill Crushed rock, pebbles or gravel deposited in a layer of any desired thickness at the bottom of an excavation; the purpose is to insure adequate drainage of water.

gravel, pit run (bank run) Natural gravel deposits; may contain some sand, clay or silt.

gravel pump A centrifugal pump used for moving gravel loosened hydraulically.

gravel roof A roof made waterproof with roofing felt, sealed or bonded, and covered with a layer of gravel to improve its insulation value and protect it from the sun.

gravel stop A strip of metal with a vertical lip used to retain the gravel around the edge of a built-up roof.

gravitational water Water above the standing-water level.

gravity The force that tends to pull bodies towards the center of mass; e.g., to give bodies weight. *(see specific gravity)*

gravity-arch dam A dam which obtains its resistance to the water thrust from arch action and from its own weight.

gravity circulation of hot water In plumbing, a circuit which works only by virtue of the difference in densities between hot and cold water, not by a pump.

gravity correction A tape correction to a band standardized at one place and used at another place of different gravity.

gravity dam A dam depending solely on its weight to resist the water load.

gravity fault *(see normal fault)*

gravity furnace A furnace for basement installation. Pipes or ducts are sloped upward allowing the warm air, which is lighter than cold air, to rise.

gravity main A pipeline in which water flows from the impounding reservoir to the service reservoir.

gravity mills Horizontal grinding mills which include ball mills, tube mills and compound mills in which the material being ground flows through the mill by gravity.

gravity retaining wall A retaining wall which, like a gravity dam, is prevented from overturning by depending on its own weight, not the weight of any soil which it carries. It must be designed to take no tension; the line of thrust must pass through the middle third of the wall.

gravity scheme A water-supply scheme in which almost all flow into or out of the impounding reservoir is by gravity and not by pumping.

gravity settling chambers Usually used to pre-clean high dust-laden gases. Dust is removed by reducing the velocity of the gas or air stream, and/or by changing stream direction.

gravity water A term for gravitational water; a water supply from a gravity scheme.

Gray Canyon A fine-grain Ohio sandstone of light blue gray, even in texture and resistant to fire.

gray paper The unsized, uncalendered paper used on the back side of regular gypsum board products and as the face and back paper on backing board products.

grease Thick oil. A solid or semi-solid mixture of oil with soap or other fillers.

grease monkey *(slang)* Service man who lubricates and refuels the equipment; sometimes applied to the mechanic who repairs the equipment.

grease trap A device by means of which the grease content of sewage is cooled and congealed so that it may be skimmed from the surface.

greasiness A greasy surface on paint caused by lack of compatibility.

Greathead shield A protective shield for workmen tunneling in soft ground; first used successfully in London by Greathead in 1879, and still used for driving circular tunnels.

Greco-Roman An architecture of the beam and column, the lintel being used pure and unmixed by the Greeks, but forced into union with the arch by the Romans.

green (1) Freshly applied, not hard; refers to concrete, plaster and sometimes to paint. (2) A description of unseasoned timber. *(see green wood)*

greenbelt A boundary, or division, of a community consisting mainly of a belt of trees or other plantings.

green board A gypsum board having a tinted face paper usually tinted green (or blue) to distinguish special board types. This term has also been used to describe gypsum board that is damp.

green brick A clay brick, before burning, during drying.

Green County sandstone A light gray Pennsylvania stone, massive bedded, of even grain, soft and easily worked when freshly quarried.

greencutting *(slang)* To prepare freshly placed concrete for successive lifts before the final set by using air or water jetting to the concrete surface.

greenhouse effect The process of converting the sun's rays to heat in the collector. A green house is warm inside although the outside air may be cool.

green room A waiting room for the cast in a theater.

greenfield Flexible metal conduit.

green wood A term used by woodworkers when referring to timbers which still contain the moisture, or sap, of the tree from which the wood was cut. Lumber is said to be seasoned when the sap has been removed by natural processes of drying or by artificial drying in a kiln.

grees Early English term for steps or a staircase.

griege goods (Pronounced "gray" goods.) Term designating carpet just off the tufting machine and in an undyed or unfinished state.

greystone lime Lime burnt from chalk and containing enough silica and alumina to make it somewhat hydraulic.

grid (1) A set of surveyor's closely spaced reference lines laid out at right angles with elevations taken at line intersections. (2) In structural work, the plan layout for any given building. (3) A mat of crossed reinforcing bars for incorporation in a concrete footing.

grid bearing The angle between a line in a grid, generally a north-south line, and a required direction.

grid foundation A combined footing formed by intersecting continuous footings, loaded at the intersection points and covering less than 75 percent of the total area within the outer limits of the assembly.

gridiron A term used to describe the rectangular plotting of city streets.

grid line A line in a reference pattern. *(see planning grid)*

grid plan A plan in which grid lines coincide with the most important walls and other building components. Buildings are often designed to fit a grid plan.

grid roller A compaction roller with wheels forming an open grid pattern.

grids, testing of Testing done by nitrogen under 250 psi pressure over a period of 12 hours.

grief *(slang)* Harsh criticism from a boss.

grief stem (kelly) A square or fluted pipe which is turned by a drill rotary table while it is free to move up and down in the table.

griffe An ornamental form, some-what like a claw, extending from the torus of a column base and lying on the four corners of the plinth.

grillage Horizontal members, usually of steel, for spreading the load of a structure over its footing or underpinning.

grillage foundation In building, a foundation formed of a framework of sleepers and crossbeams of timbers or steel beams superimposed on a layer of concrete.

grille (grill) (1) A grating of open-work barrier, usually of metal but sometimes of wood, used to cover an opening, or as a protection over the glass of a window or door. A grille may be plain but often it is of ornamental or decorative character. (2) A grating or screen through which air passes into, rather than from, a ventilating duct. The grille has no damper and connects to a return air duct. (3) A louvered or perforated covering for an air passage opening which can be located in the sidewall, ceiling or floor.

grin A term used to indicate that condition where the backing of the carpet shows between the row of pile tufts; e.g., some carpet may show the backing when layed over the nosing of a step.

grind To reduce any substance to powder by friction or crushing. To wear down or sharpen a tool by use of an abrasive, such as a whetstone, emery wheel or grindstone. To reduce in size by the removal of particles of material by contact with a rotating abrasive wheel.

grindability The response of a material to grinding effort. One grindability index is expressed in grams per mill revolution of ground material, passing the 200 mesh sieve. Other grindability indexes include: hardgrove, bond, etc.

grinder Any device used to sharpen tools, or remove particles of material by any process of grinding.

grinding aids Materials used to expedite the process of grinding by eliminating ball coating or by dispersing the finely ground product, or both.

grinding media Hard, free-moving charge in a ball or tube mill between which particles of raw material, coal, or clinker are reduced in size by attrition or impact. Usually of steel, and spherical in shape with graded sizes, the maximum in a ball mill being about 3 to 4 times the maximum feed size.

grinding medium A hard, free-moving charge in ball or tube mill to reduce the particle size of introduced materials by attrition or impact.

grinding mills Machines used for reducing coarse particles to fine particles by application of impact and attrition. Includes: ball mills, tube mills, compound mills, ring ball mills, ring roll mills, and impact mills.

grinding slip An oilstone slip.

grindstone A flat, rotating stone wheel used to sharpen tools or wear down materials by abrading or grinding. Grindstones are natural sandstone.

grinning through *(slang)* The showing through plaster of lathing beneath, or the showing of a lower coat of paint through a top coat.

grip length (bond length) The length of straight rebar, stated in bar diameters, needed to anchor the bar in concrete.

grisaille (1) Surface painting in several

tones of gray, suggesting bas-relief. **(2)** Uncolored and non-transparent glass elements in leaded windows, sometimes with occasional color.

grit   The heavy mineral matter contained in sewage such as sand, gravel, cinders, etc.; particles of sand or gravel.

grit blasting   Sand blasting with grit.

grit chamber (catcher)   A chamber usually placed at the upper end of a depressed sewer, or at other points of protection on combined or stormwater sewers, of such shape and dimension as to reduce the velocity of flow and permit the settling of grit.

gritcrete   Type of concrete used as fill.

grizzley (grizzlie)   A simple, stationary screen or series of equally spaced parallel bars set at an angle to remove oversize particles in processing aggregate or other material; a gate or closure on a chute.

grog   Burned pulverized refractory materials such as broken pottery on firebrick, utilized in the preparation of pottery bodies; a potsherd; shard.

groin   **(1)** The ridge formed by the meeting of two vaulting sections. **(2)** Structure built from shore into water for protection against erosion. Used in river training as construction works to establish normal channel width; to direct the axis of flow; to promote scour and sediment deposition where required; and to trap bedload to build up new banks.

groin arch   A rib form accenting the intersection of two vaulted surfaces and dividing the vault into bays or travees.

groin centering   In groining without ribs, the whole surface is supported by centering during the erection of the vaulting. In ribbed work, the stone ribs only are supported by timber ribs during the progress of the work.

groined   A term applied to the curved intersection of two vaults meeting each other at any angle.

groined ceiling   In architecture, an arched ceiling consisting of two intersecting curved planes.

groined vaulting   The intersecting, or crossing, of two stone, brick, wood or plaster vaults, so that they form a projecting solid angle which grows more obtuse at the top; a system of covering a building or passageway with intersecting stone vaults.

groin point   The name given to the arris or line of intersection of one vault with another where there are no ribs.

groin rib   The rib which conceals the groin point, or joints, where the spandrels intersect.

groins, Welsh (underpitch)   A system of vaulting where the main longitudinal vault of any groining is higher than the cross or transverse vaults which run from the windows.

grommet   **(1)** An eyelet, washer, soaked in compound and fitted between the nut and socket to make a tight joint. There are many types of grommets. **(2)** A metal eyelet used principally in awnings or along the edges of sails.

groove   A rectangular or round-bottomed channel lengthwise of a piece or running with the grain, usually small, used in woodworking and building for different purposes; sometimes practical but often merely decorative.

groove joint   A construction joint created by forming a groove in the surface of a pavement, floor slab or wall to control random cracking.

grooved couplings   Clamped type gasketed couplings used for pipe connections. The pipe is grooved rather than threaded, to receive the connection.

groover   A tool used for form grooves or weakened plane joints in a concrete slab before hardening to control crack location or provide pattern.

gross area   **(1)** The total enclosed floor area of a building measured from the outside surface of the exterior walls. **(2)** In roofing, the whole or entire area. **(3)** In shingles, the entire area of material including cutout waste needed to produce one shingle.

gross cross-sectional area   The total area of a section perpendicular to the direction of the load, including areas within cells and within reentrant spaces in the masonry unless these spaces are to be occupied by portions of adjacent masonry.

gross error In surveying, a mistake easily detected because it is large in proportion to the value being measured. This mistake would be detected by making three measurements. Two measurements would show the one measurement was incorrect and could be rejected.

gross measure The board measure contents of lumber calculated for measurements of named sizes.

gross vehicle load The weight of a vehicle plus the weight of any load.

gross volume (of concrete mixers) In the case of a revolving-drum mixer, the total interior volume of the revolving portion of the mixer drum; in the case of an open-top mixer, the total volume of the trough or pan calculated on the basis that no vertical dimension of the container exceeds twice the radius of the circular section below the axis of the central shaft.

grotesque A decorative detail, usually sculptural, expressing an extravagantly whimsical idea.

ground (1) A conducting connection, whether intentional or accidental, between an electrical circuit or equipment and earth, or to some conducting body which serves in place of the earth. (2) Synonym for grade, as at ground level. (3) A strip, usually of wood, to which the thickness of plastering or cement is worked. (4) Any surface which is or will be painted; the first of several coats of paint. (5) An electrical reference point; the earth.

ground apples *(slang)* Rocks.

ground area The area computed from the exterior dimensions of the ground floor.

ground beam A reinforced-concrete beam at or near ground level acting as a foundation for the walls or floors of the superstructure. It may reach between foundation piers or piles or may be a strip foundation itself.

ground brush A round or oval paint brush, used for painting large areas, grounds.

ground casing In carpentry, a blind casing.

ground color The background color against which the top colors create the pattern or figure in the design.

ground control In aerial photography, marking points on the ground so that they can be recognized in the photograph. Some surveying work must be done to verify or measure the positions and altitudes of these points.

ground cover *(see soil cover)*

grounded Connected to earth or to some conducting body which serves in place of the earth.

ground floor The floor of a building which is approximately level with the ground. Sometimes called first floor.

ground glass Double strength glass that has one side ground to a nonglare finish, thus transforming the clear glass to an obscure glass.

grounding A connection, either intentional or accidental, between an electrical circuit or equipment and the earth or to some connection body which serves in place of the earth.

ground joint (1) A closely fitted joint in masonry, usually without mortar. (2) A closely fitted joint between metal surfaces in piping or valves.

ground joist Joist that is blocked up from the ground.

ground line In building construction, the ground level or natural grade line from which measurements for excavating are taken.

ground plate In carpentry, the lowest horizontal timber of a building frame; also called a sole plate.

ground pressure The weight of a machine divided by the area in square inches of the ground directly supporting it.

ground rent The rent paid for the use of ground by the owner of a building upon it.

grounds A piece of wood or metal attached to the plaster base so that its exposed surface acts as a gauge to determine the thickness of paste to be applied. Also used by the carpenter as a nailing base or spacer for attachment of trim. A term denoting plaster thickness.

groundsill (grundsill; gunsel) The bottom horizontal frame member in buildings of wood frame construction; now called just sill.

ground storey In Britain, the space between ground floor and first floor in a building.

ground water Water in the soil below the standing-water level.

ground-water drain A drain which carries away ground water.

ground-water lowering Lowering the level of the ground water to keep an excavation dry or to make the sides of the excavation stand up. Ground-water lowering in this sense is always accomplished from outside the excavation, often by well points and pumping.

ground water table Upper surface of the zone of saturation in permeable rock or soil.

ground waves Vibrations of soil or rock.

ground wire Small-gauge high strength wire used to establish line and grade, as in shotcrete work; also called alignment wire or screed wire.

groundwork Battens as a base for slating or tiling for either siding or roofing.

grouped columns Three, four or more columns put together on the same pedestal. When two are placed together, they are said to be coupled.

group vent A branch vent that performs its function for two or more traps.

grouser (1) A ridge or cleat across a track shoe which improves its grip on the ground. (2) *(slang)* A workman who complains or grouses.

grout A mixture of cementitious materials and aggregates to which sufficient water has been added to produce pouring consistency without segregation of the constituents.

grout box A cone-shaped metal box, set into concrete with an anchor plate at the narrow end of the cone through which an anchor bolt passes.

grout curtain A row of holes drilled downwards below the cut-off wall under a dam and also upstream and downstream. The holes are drilled vertically and are filled with grout, drilled out and filled at a higher pressure until the engineer is satisfied that the cracks in the rocks are all filled or that the rock can take no higher pressure without breaking up.

grouted-aggregate concrete Concrete which is formed by injecting grout into previously placed coarse aggregate. *(see concrete; pre-placed-aggregate)*

grouted macadam A road built with coarse aggregate with the voids filled by pouring in a bituminous of cement grout.

grouted masonry Masonry composed of hollow units in which designated cells are solidly filled with grout, or masonry of two or more wythes in which the cavities between wythes are solidly filled with grout.

grouted scarf joint Mortar filled joint used in tongue and groove jointed pipes.

grouting The process of injecting cement grout into foundations and decayed walls for reinforcing and strengthening them, and into dams and mass fills for the purpose of stabilization; often referred to as pressure grouting. Grouting by hand is the operation in which grout material is placed as a filler between ceramic, quarry, mosaic tile and under structural columns and machine bases.

grout lift An increment of grout height within the total pour; a pour may consist of one or more lifts.

groutnick *(see joggle)*

grout pour The total height of masonry to be filled with grout prior to the erection of additional masonry. A pour consists of one or more lifts.

grout prism Compressive strength grout specimen which has been molded in a mold fabricated out of block or brick.

grout slope The natural slope of fluid grout injected into preplaced aggregate concrete.

growth rings Increments of growth which appear as figures in the floor. Seen in a cross-section of a log as rings around the center of the log. When only one growth ring is formed during a year, it is called annual ring. Viewing the end of a parquet slat, they appear in bands or layers.

groyne (jetty; groin) A spur dike. It may be built of facines, stone or piling. *(see wing dam)*

grub (grubbing) To clear land, to remove trees, stumps, roots, shrubs and the like.

grub axle A tool with an adze-like blade at one end for pulling up roots and with a regular axe blade at the other end.

grub saw A hand saw for cutting stone.

grummet A grommet.

grunt *(slang)* Term used to describe a common laborer. An apprentice lineman.

grunter *(slang)* An electrician's assistant. *(see grunt)*

guarantee Legally enforceable assurance of the duration of satisfactory performance or quality of a product or work.

guaranteed maximum cost Amount established in an agreement between owner and contractor as the maximum cost of performing specified work on the basis or cost of labor and materials plus overhead expense and profit.

guaranty bond (1) Bid bond. (2) Labor and material payment bond. (3) Performance bond. (4) Surety bond. *(see bonds)*

guard A protective railing or enclosure around moving parts of machinery, or around an excavation or materials.

guard bead *(see inside stop; stop bead)*

guard board A board placed on edge at the outside of a gantry crane to prevent objects from falling.

guard lock A lock separating a dock from tidal water.

guardrail A rail secured to uprights and erected along the exposed sides and ends of platforms or as a barrier between or beside, lanes of a highway.

Guastavino A method of constructing the inner shell of a dome with two or more layers of rectangular tiles; named for the inventor.

gudgeon (1) A reinforced bushing or a thrust absorbing block. (2) The stationary leaf of a hinge. (3) A metal dowel for locking neighboring stones together. (4) A gate hook.

guide coat A very thin coat of paint applied over a surface before it is rubbed down. Used as a guide for showing high places.

guide pile In excavation supported by sheet piles, a heavy vertical square timber which is driven close to them and carries the full earth pressure from the walings.

guilloche An ornamental motif in band from consisting of intertwined strips of curved form.

guillotine A trimming machine.

guinea A survey marker driven to grade and blue topped with paint for finishing operation.

guinea chaser A member of the crew who uncovers the blue topped stakes and signals the blade operator as to cut or fill required.

gula Synonym for ogee.

gullet (1) The length of a saw-tooth from point to base; also the gap between teeth. (2) A narrow trench dug wide enough to take a track for the carriers which are removing the material. The trench is widened, as necessary, to the full width.

gulley sucker A heavy truck with a large tank and a pump for taking silt out of a road gulleys and forcing it into the tank. used in Britain.

gumbo Soil of finely divided clays of varying capillarity. Dark-colored, very sticky, highly plastic and soapy in appearance and ground in central and southern United States. In the East, it's mud; in the Midwest, it's clay.

gummy The heavy drag on a brush from a sticky paint or gummy paint. May be caused by cold weather, excessive evaporation of the solvent, etc.

gum vein Accumulation of resin in a streak; occurs in some hardwoods.

gun (1) Shotcrete material delivery equipment, usually consisting of double chambers under pressure; equipment with a single pressure chamber is used to some extent. (2) Pressure cylinder used to propel freshly mixed concrete pneumatically. (3) *(slang)* Transit (shoots grades).

gun finish Undisturbed final layer of shotcrete as applied from a nozzle, without hand finishing.

Gunite Trade name for a construction material composed of cement, sand, crushed slag and water mixed together and forced through a cement gun by pneumatic pressure; used to stabilize slopes; the method of applying dry-mix shotcrete through a hose using compressed air.

gunman Workman on shotcreting crew who operates delivery equipment.

gunning Act of applying shotcrete; ejection of material from a nozzle and impingement on surface to be gunned.

gunning pattern Conical outline of material discharge stream in shotcrete operation.

Gunter's Chain A measure used by surveyors, equivalent to 66 feet.

gun-type oil burner An oil burner which shoots a mixture of oil and air into the combustion chamber where it is ignited.

gusset A brace or angle bracket used to stiffen a corner or angular piece of work.

gusset plate Bracing steel plate to which pairs of angles are riveted, forming a joint or bracket.

gut burglar *(slang)* Construction camp cook.

gut hammer *(slang)* A musical triangle or triangular piece of steel used to call crews to meals in a camp.

gut line A large diameter steel cable that is the load line on a cableway.

gutta (guttae) In architecture, one of a series of droplike ornaments, or cone-shaped pendants, used in the decoration of the Doric entablature.

gutter (1) A shallow channel or conduit of metal or wood set below and along the eaves of a house to catch and carry off rainwater. An eave trough. (2) A ditch along the edge of a road.

gutter plate In carpentry, a wall plate below a lead gutter; side of a valley gutter, lined with flexible metal, to carry the feet of the rafters.

gutter tool A tool used to give the desired shape and finish to concrete gutters.

guy A line that steadies a high piece or structure by pulling against an off-center load.

guy derrick A standard steel-erecting derrick, with a guyed mast and a hinged boom at its base, both able to swivel on the base.

guyed-mast *(see derrick)*

guy rope A galvanized rope consisting of six strands of seven wires each, covering a hemp core; used to hold a structure in a desired position.

gymmer *(see jimmer)*

gyneceum The women's section of a Greek dwelling.

gypo *(slang)* Under-financed, struggling small company.

gypsite An earthy deposit found at or near the surface of the ground, consisting of finely crystalline gypsum mixed with loam, clay, sand, and humus. Gypsum content generally ranges from 60% to more than 90%.

gypsum A naturally occurring mineral consisting of calcium sulphate combined with two molecules of water, in crystalline form, having the approximate chemical formula $CaSo_4 2H_2O$.

gypsum block A lightweight masonry unit made from gypsum plaster, water, and fiber cast in metal molds.

gypsum board lath A plaster base made in sheet form composed of a core of fibered gypsum faced on both sides with paper; gypsum board lath is highly fire and heat resistant and comes in two common types, plain and perforated.

gypsum plaster Ground calcined gypsum combined with various additives to control set. Also used to denote applied gypsum plaster mixtures.

gypsum plasterboard A common building material made with a core of gypsum or anhydrite plaster, usually enclosed between two sheets of heavy paper. Primarily used for sheeting interior walls.

gypsum sheathing A gypsum board, usually tongue and grooved, covered with a weather-proofed paper for use as exterior sheathing.

gypsum trowel finish Various proprietary ready-mixed finish coat materials consisting essentially of calcined gypsum.

gypsum-vermiculite plaster *(see vermiculite-gypsum plaster)*

gypsum wallboard A prefabricated sheet used in drywall construction as a substitute for plaster; made of gypsum covered with paper which can be painted, textured or wall papered. *(see gypsum plasterboard)*

gypsy spool (cat head) *(slang)* A capstan winch.

gyratory crusher A crusher for rock or clinker in which a steel center cone rotates eccentrically to crush the material against the outside cylindrical or conical steel wall.

H   Hydrogen

h   harbor, hard, height, hours, house, hundred

HA   Hour angle

HB   H-beam

HD   heavy duty

hdwr   hardware

He   helium

HE   high explosive

hem   hemlock

hex   hexagon

hf   half, high-frequency

H.F.   hot finished

hg   hectogram

hgt   height

HI   height of instrument

hip   hipped (foof)

hl   hectoliter

hm   hectometer

HM   hollow metal

hor/horiz   horizontal

hp   horsepower

HP   half pay, high pressure

hr   hour

ht   height

HT   high-tension

htg   heating

HV   high voltage

hvy   heavy

HW   high water

HWM   high-water mark

hwy   highway

hyd   hydraulics, hydrostatics

hydraul   hydraulics

hyp/hypoth   hypothesis, hypothetical

H section   A steel member with an H cross section.

hachure   Cross hatching on a drawing.

hacienda   South American term for a productive estate in the country.

hack   An unworkmanlike manner of cutting work; rough cutting of any kind.

hacking   (1) In stone masonry, the introduction of two courses in place of one; usually done because of a lack of the larger stones. (2) The roughening of a surface by striking with a tool. (3) The procedure of stacking brick in a kiln or on a kiln car; laying units with the bottom edge set in from the plane surface of the wall.

hacking knife   A knife used to remove old putty from a window before reglazing it.

hack saw   A narrow, light-framed saw used for cutting metal; a fine-toothed, narrow-bladed saw stretched in a firm frame. It may be operated either by hand or by electric power.

haft   The handle of any thrusting or cutting tool, such as a dagger, knife, sword or awl.

hagioscope   An oblique slit in an interior wall of a medieval church, to afford a view of the altar. *(see squint)*

haha   A drop in grade level to serve as a barrier to grazing stock, preventing their approach to lawns about the house.

hair cracks   Cracks which are just visible to the naked eye.

hair hook   A plasterer's tool similar to a hoe but with two bent tines instead of a hoe blade for mixing hair into coarse stuff.

hairline cracking   (hair checking) Small cracks of random pattern in an exposed concrete surface.

hairpin   The wedge used to tighten some types of ties; a hairpin-shaped anchor set in place while concrete is unhardened; a light hairpin shaped reinforcing bar used for shear reinforcement in beams, tie reinforcement in columns or prefabricated column shear heads.

hair pounder *(slang)* A horse teamster.

half-and-half solder An alloy of equal parts of tin and lead.

half-back bench saw A cutting tool in which a stiffening bar extends over only a portion of the blade length, combining the action of both the handsaw and the backsaw.

half bat (snap header) A half-brick, cut in two across the length.

half-brick wall A wall the thickness of a brick, built entirely of stretchers.

half bubble off *(slang)* One who acts to be a bit crazy. Not having a full tool box.

half-hatchet A carpenter's hatchet with a notch for drawing nails, like a plasterer's lath hammer.

half height block Concrete masonry units which have a height of four inches.

half-joist A joist cut in two along the web to form a T-section; used in welded steelwork.

half-landing A platform between the two floors of a building joined by stairs.

half-lap joint A jointing of two pieces by cutting away half the thickness of each piece so that the pieces fit together with the surfaces flush.

half-lattice girder A Warren girder.

half-pace (halpace) (1) A landing interrupting a stair where a turn of 180° is made. (2) A raised section of flooring, as in some bay windows.

half-principal A rafter which does not reach the ridge.

half-rip saw A rip saw with teeth closer than the usual rip saw.

half-round A molding of semicircular section.

half-round file A tool which is flat on one side and curved on the other; however, the convexity never equals a semicircle.

half-space landing A landing whose length is the width of both flights and the well.

half-span roof A lean-to roof.

half story (1) An attic in a pitched roof structure having a finished ceiling and floor and some side wall. (2) A mezzanine.

half-tide cofferdam A cofferdam which is not built high enough to exclude water at high tide; it therefore needs de-watering after every full tide.

half-timbered A style of architecture characteristic of the Elizabethan period; timber framing members of walls are exposed; spaces between are filled with masonry or plaster. May be simulated in current construction.

half track *(slang)* A heavy truck with high speed crawler track drive in the rear and driving wheels in the front.

halide torch A flame tester generally using alcohol and burning with a blue flame; when the sampling tube draws in halocarbon refrigerant vapor, color of flame changes to bright green.

hall (1) A building of importance for public use. (2) The main livingroom of a large house in England. (3) A corridor. (4) An entry.

Hallinger shield A Hungarian shield, used successfully in tunneling in very soft ground. It uses a mechanical excavator and no timbering is needed to protect the workers.

Hallowell granite A light gray of fine texture, of Maine, used for monumental work, building and bridges.

hallway (1) A corridor. (2) An entry.

halon One of a variety of fire-suppressant gases used in room where conventional fire extinguishers would damage expensive equipment.

Halon System Trade name for the system which used halon gas for fire protection; used for water sensitive equipment.

halpace (half-pace) A raised floor, as in a bay window or before a fireplace; also a dais or even a stair landing.

halve (halving) To splice or cross two lengths of wood or other material by halving the thickness of each for a lap joint.

halved joint A joint made by halving two pieces of lumber.

hammer A hand tool consisting of a solid head of metal, wood or stone set crosswise on a handle; used for breaking, beating or driving.

air A machine hammer driven by compressed air, as an air riveting hammer.

axe A hammer like the lath hammer.

bust A hammer, used in riveting work, having a rivet buster on one end and a hammer on the other end.

Cleveland One of the numerous makes of air riveting hammers.

flogging A very large hammer used with a flogging chisel for chipping iron castings.

holding-up A heavy engineer's hammer on a long handle, used in times past for bucking up rivets.

jack A heavy vibrating hammer for breaking pavement or rock.

lath (see lath hammer)

peen A hammer having a peen on one or both faces.

pile The part of a pile driver or steam hammer that strikes the blow.

pneumatic A hammer operated by compressed air.

power A hammer used for forging work.

rivet A pneumatic or hand hammer for driving rivets; also, an engineer's light hammer for testing the tightness of rivets after driving.

hammer beam A beam at the foot of a rafter.

hammer brace The member bracing a hammer beam against the pendant post.

hammer crusher Used for size reduction of hard to medium hard limestone and marl. There are two types: single shaft and double shaft crushers which work with the impact effect of hammers.

hammer drill The compressed-air rock drill which has taken the place of the piston drill.

hammer finish A finish like hammered metal produced by applying color enamels containing metal powder.

hammer fracture A tear in the gypsum board face and core caused by improperly hitting or overdriving the nail.

hammerhead *(slang)* A big crane shaped like a T; its crossbar rotates freely.

hammer-headed chisel A mason's chisel with a flat conical steel head which is struck by a hammer and not by a mallet.

hammer-head key A joint of wood or stone, in which a squared dumbbell key is cut in across the face of the joint.

hammer loss A test to determine the impact resistance of gypsum board.

hammerman One of a team working on a pile hammer who controls the hoist or the steam jet which operates the hammer. Other members of the team are the ladderman and topman.

hammer mill An impact rock crusher or shredder employing hammers or flails on a rapidly rotating axle.

hammer post A post with its base on the hammer beam. It corresponds to an ashler piece resting on a footplate.

Hamm tip Flared shotcrete nozzle having a larger diameter at mid-point than either inlet or outlet; also designated premixing tip.

hance **(1)** A small arch joining a straight line to its jamb; a haunch. **(2)** In lighting, a horizontal member mounted across the top of a window to conceal light sources.

hand brace A carpenter's brace.

hand drill (brace and bit) A hand-operated tool used for drilling holes.

hand file A tool used in finishing flat surfaces.

hand fitting Installation in which instead of guidelines or scribe marks, the contour of the baseboard trim or other irregularities is used as the guide for the knife (i.e., fitting floor covering to the perimeter of the room).

hand hole Small access opening used in cleaning and repairing vessels. Typically 3×4 to 4×6.

hand float (1) A wood tool for laying on the finishing coat of plaster. (2) A hand tool for finishing concrete.

handle In a dipper shovel or hoe, the arm that connects the bucket with the boom.

hand level A sighting level that does not have a tripod base of telescope.

handling tight Couplings screwed onto a pipe sufficiently tight so that they cannot be removed except by use of a wrench.

handrail A bar or pipe supported on brackets from a wall or partition, as on a stairway or ramp, to furnish persons with a handhold.

handrail screw (1) A dowel screw. (2) A bolt, used for installing handrails.

handrail scroll A spiral ending to a handrail.

handrail wreath The curved section of a stair rail. *(see wreath)*

handsaw Any ordinary wood saw operated with one hand; that is, a one-handed saw, either a ripsaw or a cross cut saw; never a power-operated saw.

hand screw A clamp with two parallel jaws and two screws used by woodworkers; the action is provided by means of the screws, one operating through each jaw.

hand sprayer (hand distributor) A hand-directed spray for spreading road asphalts, in which the pressure is developed by a hand or power-operated pump.

hand tight Couplings tightened by hand with such effort as an average man can continuously exert.

hand tools Any tools which are operated and guided by hand.

handy billy *(slang)* Block and tackle.

hang To install a door or window in a building.

hanger (1) A device used for suspending one object from another such as the hardware attached to a building frame to support forms; a stirrup strap, also called a beam hanger. (2) A tradesman who applies gypsum board products.

hanger bearing A shaft which is supported by a hanger.

hanger bench A low scaffold board that allows the hanging crew to easily reach the ceiling area.

hanger bolt A bolt used for attaching hangers to woodwork; it consists of a lag screw at one end with a machine bolt at the other end.

hanging buttress A buttress not rising from the ground, but supported on a corbel; applied chiefly as a decoration and used only in the Decorated and Perpendicular styles.

hanging gutter A metal eaves gutter fastened to rafter ends or to a fascia.

hanging leaders A steel frame hung from a pivot at the top of a crane or excavator jib, used to guide a driven pile on its downward path. Unlike false leaders, the steam hammer or drop hammer is carried by the crane rope. Hanging leaders do not rest on the ground but are anchored back to the crane by a strut at the foot of the jib.

hangings (tapestry) Originally invented to hide the coarseness of the walls of a chamber. Different materials were employed for this purpose, some of them exceedingly costly and beautifully worked in figures, gold and silk.

hanging stile On a door or window, the vertical part to which the hinges are fixed.

hard asphalt Solid asphalt with normal penetration of less than 10.

hardboard Wood fibers joined together under pressure to form a sheet of material.

hard-burnt (1) Burnt clay brick, tile etc., which has been burnt at high temperature, giving the material high compressive strength, durability and low absorption. (2) Plasters such as Keene's cement are called hard-burnt.

hard compact soil All earth materials not classified as running or unstable.

hard disk Rigid metal magnetic disk mounted in a disk drive for storing large amounts of data.

hard dry A stage in the drying of a paint film when it is nearly free from tackiness and is dried throughout its depth so that another coat can be safely applied.

hard edge A special core formulation used along the paperbound edges to improve resistance of gypsum board.

hardenability In welding, a loss of ductility between the weld and parent metal. This defect causes cracking and may bring about failure of the weld. It usually increases with the carbon content of the steel and is the opposite of weldability.

hardener (1) A chemical, including certain fluosilicates or sodium silicate, applied to concrete floors to reduce wear and dusting. (2) In a two-component adhesive or coating, the chemical component which causes the resin component to cure.

hard facing Welding a hard surface onto steel or other metal of tungsten carbide to form an abrasion-resistant cutting edge on a drilling tool, excavator bucket, etc.

hard finish In building, a smooth finishing coat of hard fine plaster applied to the surface of rough plastering.

hard hat A protective helmet worn by construction workers, miners, etc.

hard-head (slang) A lag screw used in pole bands and x-braces for cross arms.

hard-metal sheathed cable An electrical cable covered with hard metal, such as copper but not lead, over the cable insulation.

hardness test A means of determining the resistance to penetration, occasionally employed to obtain a quick approximation of tensile strength. There are several methods, such as Brinell, Rockwell, and Vickers, which have been standardized to give a hardness scale of several hundred numbers.

hardpan A compact, cemented mass of clay with sand, gravel or boulders, or any two or all of them, usually of glacial origin. The term is rather loosely used but always implies a very dense material, difficult to excavate without picks or the equivalent.

hard solder Any solder which melts at red heat or hotter.

hard standing Any hard surface suitable for parking heavy vehicles such as automobiles, airplanes or construction equipment.

hard stopping In painting, a stiff paste made with water and powder, applied by putty knife to fill holes in a surface. It sets hard quickly as it contains plaster of Paris.

Hardwall Term used for gypsum basecoat plaster. In some cases it refers to sanded or neat plaster.

hardware Metal fittings permanently incorporated in a building as adjuncts to doors, windows, drawers, etc. (see finish hardware)

hardwood Wood of the broadleaved trees, i.e., oak maple, ash and walnut, as contrasted with softwoods of the needle-leaved trees such as pine, spruce, hemlock, etc.

hardwood plywood Usually carries no commercial standard mark due to its specialty classification.

Hardy cross A method of moment distribution in continuous beams named after its inventor; a sign convention. (see positive movement)

harmonics (see overtones)

harmus Greek term for a tile covering the joint between two common tiles.

harped tendons (see deflected tendons)

harsh mixture A concrete mixture which lacks desired workability and consistency due to a deficiency of mortar or aggregate fines.

hasp The arm with a slot which, fitting over a staple, permits the use of a padlock.

hass The inside curvature of a bent pipe.

hatch (hatchway) An opening in floor or roof, with removable cover, for the passage of packing cases, furniture, etc.

hatchet A multi-purpose hand tool with a special head configuration (convex) to properly dimple the nail. The hatchet (axe) blade may be used to cleave and adjust framing and wallboard edges to fit or as a jacking wedge.

hatchet iron A soldering iron shaped like a hatchet; used in plumbing.

hatching Parallel lines drawn closely together for the purpose of shading or to indicate a section of an object shown in a drawing. The lines are generally drawn at an angle of 45° with the horizontal.

haulageway A main tunnel connecting underground excavation areas with an exit.

haulaway An excavation method which involves hauling the spoil away from the site.

haul distance (average haul) The distance measured along the center line or most direct practical route between the center of the mass of excavation and the center of mass of the fill as finally placed; the distance material is moved.

free The distance every cubic yard is entitled to be moved without an additional charge for hauling.

over The distance, in excess of that given at the stated haul distance, to haul excavated material.

station yards The number of cubic yards multiplied by the number of 100-foot stations through which it is removed.

haul road A primitive, temporary road built along the route of a job to provide means for moving equipment and men; the road usually between the cut and the fill or between the source of crushed material and the roadsite.

haunch (1) In pipe, the sides of the lower third of the circumference. (2) A bracket built on a wall or column used to support a load outside the wall or column; also that portion of a girder or arch which is thickened near the supports. (3) The outermost strip of a road. *(see flank)*

haunching (1) The increased depth of beam or slab near the supports, to increase its strength. (2) Concrete support to the sides of a drain or sewer pipe above the bedding. (3) Work done in strengthening or improving the outer strip of a roadway.

hawk A tool used by plasterers to hold and carry plaster mortar; generally a flat piece of wood or metal approximately 10 to 12 inches (25 to 30 cm) square, with a wooden handle centered and fixed to the underside.

haydite (serlite) An expanded clay used as aggregate for lightweight concrete.

hazard A hazard is considered to include casualty, fire and shock, when applicable.

hazardous substance A substance which, by reason of being explosive, flammable, poisonous, corrosive, oxidizing, irritating, or otherwise harmful, is likely to cause death or injury.

Hazen-Williams formula Formula used in water distribution for velocity of flow in pipes.

H-Beam Steel beam with wider flanges than an I-beam.

head (1) The top of anything, e.g., the top of a window is a window head. (2) Difference in elevation between two points in a body of fluid, as a measure of the pressure of the fluid. *(see bonnet)* (3) A stone that has one end dressed to match the face because the end will be exposed at a corner or reveal.

headache ball *(slang)* Round iron ball which swings from cable to boom; a demolition tool.

headache rack *(slang)* Pipe structure, like a frame mounted over the operator of a Cat, used as protection for operator. Also called ROPS, for roll-over protection system.

head bay The part of a canal lock upstream from the lock gates.

head block A block bolted to the end of a lumber tie to take the thrust of a rafter. It may also be keyed into the tie.

head button The head of a bar, bolt or rivet having the shape of a button.

head casing The part of the architrave outside and over a door. It may be topped by a drip cap or other weathering.

head, chord The enlarged head of a

chord bar through which the pin passes.

head, dynamic or total   In flowing fluid, the sum of the static and velocity heads at the point of measurement.

header   (1) In masonry, a brick or building stone laid across the thickness of a wall with one end toward face of wall. (2) In carpentry, a wood beam set at right angles to joists to provide a seat or support; a wood lintel. (3) In waterworks, any conduit or pipe which distributes fluid to or extracts it from other conduits or pipe. (4) *(slang)* An axman who trims the head of a wooden pile.

header block   Concrete masonry units which have a portion of one side of the height removed to facilitate bonding with adjacent masonry such as brick facing.

header board   The board used to contain the concrete at the end of a pour.

header bond   Bond showing only headers on the face, each header divided evenly on the header under it.

header joist   In carpentry, the large beam or timber into which the common joists are fitted when framing around openings for stairs, chimneys or any opening in a floor or roof; placed so as to fit between two long beams and support the ends of short timbers.

head, eye-bar   The enlarged end of the eye-bar through which the pin passes.

head gate   The upstream gate of a lock conduit or irrigation system.

heading   In a tunnel, a digging face and its work area.

heading bond   A wall brick-length in thickness, with all headers on both faces.

heading courses   Courses of a wall in which the stone or brick are all headers.

heading joint   A cross joint; in carpentry, the line on which two boards butt.

head joint   The vertical mortar joint between ends of masonry units; sometimes called the cross joint. The line on which two boards butt.

headlap   That portion of a shingle which is covered by the succeeding shingle and is not exposed to weathering.

head mast   In cable excavator, the tower that carries the working lines.

head molding   A molding over an opening.

head pressure   This term designates the capacity of a liquid circulator and is another way of expressing pressure drop. The maximum "head" of a pump is actually the maximum pressure drop against which the pump can induce a flow of liquid. The rating of a circulator is usually expressed in feet of water.

head race   A channel leading water to a water wheel from a forebay; a free-flow tunnel or open channel that conveys water to the upper end of a penstock.

head room   (1) The vertical space in a doorway. (2) The clear space in height between a stair tread and the ceiling or stairs above. (3) The distance between the top of a finished floor and the lowest part of the floor above.

head, static   The static pressure of fluid expressed in terms of the height of a column of the fluid, or of some manometric fluid, which it would support.

headstone   A principal stone in masonry, as a cornerstone or keystone.

head, velocity   In a flowing fluid, the height of the fluid or of some manometric fluid equivalent to its velocity pressure.

headwall   A wall of any material at the end of a culvert or drain to serve one or more of the following purposes: protect fill from scour or underminings; increase hydraulic efficiency; divert direction of flow, or serve as a retaining wall.

headway   On a stairway, the unobstructed distance from a landing or the face of a step to the ceiling above.

head, welded   Heads first worked into desired shape and then welded onto bars.

heap   Material carried above the sides or above the top of a loaded carrier.

hearth   The floor of a fireplace; also the portion of the floor immediately in front of the fireplace, usually made of brick, tile or stone.

hearthstone Originally the single large stone used for the hearth; now used figuratively for the fireside.

hearting The filling in of a wall faced on one or both sides with quality or finish material.

heartwood The wood extending from the pith to the sapwood, the cells of which no longer participate in the life process of the tree.

heat A form of energy which is an internal motion of molecules, imparting a change in temperature or the performance of work. The unit measurement of heat is the British thermal unit, Btu, the amount of heat required to raise one pound of water one degree Fahrenheit.

heat balance A method of accounting for all the heat units supplied, transferred, utilized in, and lost from a kiln.

heat capacity The amount of heat necessary to raise the temperature of a given mass one degree. Numerically, the mass multiplied by the specific heat.

heat conductor A material capable of readily conducting heat. The opposite of an insulator or insulation.

heater (1) A general term, most often used to refer to stoves and individual heating units. (2) *(slang)* In steel work, a man who heats the rivets over a small forge; when they are hot, he throws them to the sticker.

heat exchanger A device specifically designed to transfer heat between two physically separated fluids.

heat exchanger, double-pipe One in which two pipes are arranged concentrically one within the other, and in which one fluid flows through the inner pipe and the other through the annulus between them.

heat, humid Ratio of increase of enthalpy per pound of dry air with its associated moisture to rise of temperature under conditions of constant pressure and constant specific humidity.

heat of hydration The heat given off by cement paste during the chemical combination of cement with water. An exothermic process.

heating element The part of an electric heater or stove which consists of a wire or metal unit heated by an electric current.

heating load The rate of heat flow required to maintain indoor comfort; measured in Btu per hour.

heating rate The rate expressed in degrees per hour at which the temperature of the kiln or autoclave is raised to the desired maximum temperature.

heating season The period of time that is necessary to operate heating equipment for indoor comfort.

heating system Any device or system for heating a building.

heating system, high pressure steam A steam heating system employing steam at pressures above 15 psig.

heating system, high pressure water A heating system in which water having supply temperatures above 350 F is used as a medium to convey heat from a central boiler, through a piping system, to suitable heat distributing means.

heating system, hot water A heating system in which water having supply temperatures less than 250 F is used as a medium to convey heat from a central boiler, through a piping system, to suitable heat distributing means.

heating system, low pressure steam A steam heating system employing steam at pressures between 0 and 15 psig.

heating system, low temperature water *(see heating system, hot water)*

heating system, medium-temperature water A heating system in which water having supply temperatures between 250 F and 350 F is used as a medium to convey heat from a central boiler, through a piping system, to suitable heat distributing means.

heating system, panel A heating system in which heat is transmitted by both radiation and convection from panel surfaces to both air and surrounding surfaces.

heating system, perimeter warm air

A warm air heating system of the combination panel and convection type. Warm air ducts embedded in the concrete slab of a basementless house, around the perimeter, receive heated air from a furnace and deliver it to the heated space through registers placed in or near the floor. Air is returned to the furnace from registers near the ceiling.

heating system, radiant A heating system in which only the heat radiated from panels is effective in providing the heating requirements. The term radiant heating is frequently used to include both panel and radiant heating.

heating system, split A system in which the heating is accomplished by means of radiators or convectors supplemented by mechanical circulation or air (heated or unheated) from a central point. Ventilation may be provided by the same system.

heating system, steam A heating system in which heat is transferred from the boiler or other source of heat to the heating units by means of steam at, above, or below atmospheric pressure.

heating system, vacuum A two pipe steam heating system equipped with the necessary accessory apparatus which will permit operating the system below atmospheric pressure.

heating system, vapor A steam heating system which operates under pressures at or near atmospheric and which returns the condensate to the boiler or receiver by gravity.

heating system, warm air A warm air heating plant consisting of a heating unit (fuel-burning furnace) enclosed in a casing, from which the heated air is distributed to various rooms of the building through ducts.

heating unit, electric A structure containing one or more heating elements, electrical terminals or leads, electric insulation, and a frame or casing, all assembled together in one unit.

heat insulation The ability of a material to impede heat flow which is inversely proportional to the air-to-air heat transmission coefficient of the material.

heat interchanger A device to transfer heat from the liquid refrigerant to the suction gas; also known as heat exchanger.

heat latent Change of enthalpy during a change of state, usually expressed in Btu per lb. With pure substances, latent heat is absorbed or rejected at constant pressure.

heat, latent, or condensation or evaporation(specific) Thermodynamically the difference in the specific enthalpies of a pure condensable fluid between its dry saturated vapor state and its saturated (not subcooled) liquid state at the same pressure.

heat loss (1) Total amount of heat lost through openings around doors, windows, etc., and through exposed walls and floors. (2) Term used to describe loss of heat which solar collector has absorbed from the sun's rays. The losses occur through conduction, convection, and radiation.

heat, mechanical equivalent of An energy conversion ratio of 778.177 ft lb = 1 Btu.

heat method Procedure for determining moisture content of soils.

heat of fusion Latent heat involved in changing between the solid and the liquid states.

heat of hydration Heat evolved by chemical reactions with water, such as that evolved during the setting and hardening of portland cement; the difference between the heat of solution of dry cement and that of partially hydrated cement. (see heat of solution)

heat of reaction Heat per unit mass or per mol of one of the reagents or products of reaction in a chemical reaction; exothermal if given off, endothermal if absorbed.

heat of solution Heat evolved by the solution of a material in a solvent.

heat of the liquid Enthalpy of a mass of liquid above as arbitrary zero.

heat vaporization Latent heat involved

in the change between liquid and vapor states.

heat pump A refrigerating system employed to transfer heat into a space or substance. The condenser provides the heat while the evaporator is arranged to pick up heat from air, water, etc. By shifting the flow of air or other fluid a heat pump system may also be used to cool the space.

heat pump, cooling and heating A refrigerating system designed so that the heat extracted at a low temperature and the heat rejected at a higher temperature may be utilized alternately or simultaneously for cooling and heating functions respectively.

heat pump, heating A refrigerating system designed primarily to utilize the heat rejection from the system for a desired heating function.

heat quantity (Btu) Common unit of measure of quantity of heat is the British thermal unit (Btu). One Btu is the amount of heat required to raise one pound of water from 63° to 64°F. (1 Btu=1055.06 J). This is about the amount of heat given off by one wooden match. A pound of coal can produce 13,000 Btu.

heat rejection effect, subcooling The total refrigerant heat rejection effect less the condensing heat rejection effect.

heat rejection effect, total refrigerant Total useful capacity of a refrigerant condenser for removing heat from the refrigerant circulated through it.

heat-resistant concrete Any concrete which will not disintegrate when exposed to constant or cyclic heating at any temperature below which a ceramic bond is formed.

heat-resistant paint Paint or enamel which can be used on radiators or similar equipment; often containing silicone resins.

heat seaming The process of joining two or more thermoplastic films or sheets by heating areas in contact with each other to the temperature at which fusion occurs. The process is usually aided.

heat, sensible Heat which is associated with a change in temperature; in contrast to a heat interchange in which a change of state (latent heat) occurs.

heat-set Stabilization of yarns to insure no change in size or shape; the process of heat-setting in an autoclave, using super-heated steam under pressure.

heat sink A medium (water, earth, or air) capable of accepting heat.

heat, specific The ratio of the quantity of heat required to raise the temperature of a given mass of any substance one degree to the quantity required to raise the temperature of an equal mass of a standard substance (usually water at 59 F) one degree.

heat tinting Heating a specimen, with a suitable surface finish, in air for the purpose of developing a desired color.

heat transfer Heat always flows toward a substance of lower temperature until the temperatures of the two substances equalize. It travels by one or more of three methods: conduction, convection or radiation.

heat transmission Any time-rate of heat flow; usually refers to conduction, convection and radiation combined.

heat transmission coefficient Any one of a number of coefficients used in the calculation of heat transmission by conduction, convection, and radiation, through various materials and structures. *(see thermal conductance, thermal conductivity, thermal resistance, thermal resistivity, thermal transmittance, etc.)*

heat treatment An operation of combination of operations involving the heating and cooling of a metal or any alloy in the solid state for the purpose of obtaining certain desirable conditions or properties. Heating and cooling for the sole purpose of mechanical working are excluded from the meaning of the definition.

heat value Heat value of a solid fuel is expressed in Btu's per pound of fuel on as-received, dry, or moisture-and-ash free basis. Heat values for gases, in Btu's per 1000 cu ft., and for liquid fuels, in Btu's per gallon, are usually computed by adding together the heat contributed by the constituent gases or hydrocarbons.

heave (1) In rock, the horizontal displacement between the ends of a faulted seam, or other bed, measured at right angles to the direction of the fault. (2) The rising of the floor of a deep excavation in soft silt or clay.

heavy-bodied paint A viscous paint, or a paint which makes a strong film.

heavy concrete *(see high density concrete)*

heavy duty scaffold A scaffold designed and constructed to carry a working load not to exceed 75 pounds per square foot.

heavy duty tile Tile suitable for areas where heavy pedestrian traffic is prevalent. Can be specified to meet higher test values as determined by job requirements.

heavy-edge reinforcement Wire fabric reinforcement, for highway pavement slabs, having one to four edge wires heavier than the other longitudinal wires.

heavy joist In woodworking, a timber measuring between four and six inches in thickness and eight inches or over in width.

heavy-media separation A method in which a liquid or suspension of given specific gravity is used to separate particles into a portion lighter than (those that float), and a portion heavier than (those that sink), the medium.

heavy soil A soil which is largely clay; damper than sand and therefore heavier.

heavy timber A building code designation for a particular type of construction with good fire endurance. Heavy timber is widely recognized as comparable to one-hour construction. A panel roof deck of 1⅛ inch tongue-and-grooved plywood with exterior glue over 4 inch wide supports meets the heavy timber requirements and provided the same fire performance as nominal 3 inch tongue-and-groove.

heavy wall ⅞ inch and over

heavy water Water which possesses an isotope of hydrogen. It has an atomic weight of 2 rather than 1.008. It is known as deuterium oxide.

heavyweight (volumetric components) Room-size, or smaller, volumes of concrete, steel sandwich, wood or fiber-reinforced plastic, which can be grouped horizontally and/or stacked vertically, if bearing, and dry connected to form single family or multifamily attached or detached housing. Other types of systems employ discontinuous room units to provide for mechanical chases, sound insulation and structural fireproofing.

heavyweight aggregate *(see aggregate, heavyweight)*

heavyweight concrete *(see high density concrete)*

heel (1) A floor brace or socket for wall-bracing timbers. (2) The trailing edge of an angled blade. (3) The water side of the base of a dam or retaining wall. *(see toe)*

heel bead In glazing, a compound applied at the base of the channel after setting a light or panel, and before the removable stop is installed. Its purpose is to prevent leakage past the stop.

heel dolly bar A type of dolly used in steelwork.

heeler *(slang)* One who gives tracklaying directions to a crew.

heeling in Temporary planting of trees and shrubs, often at an angle in a trench, for easy removal.

heel of rafter The seat cut in a rafter that rests on the wall plate.

height Overall distance from top to bottom; the dimension measured at right angles to the direction of the thickness and length of a concrete masonry unit.

height money In Britain, the term for additional pay for working more than 30 or 40 feet above the ground or above a building. In the United States, this is called high pay or high time.

height or cover Distance from crown of a culvert or conduit to the finished road surface or the base of rail.

height of instrument A term used in leveling, meaning the vertical height of the line or collimation, line of sight, of a level; or the horizontal axis of a theodolite above a given datum plane; or a datum that has been assumed to suit the work in hand.

held water British term for free water or vadose water.

helical Spiral.

helical chain Each chain length in a CHAIN SYSTEM is advanced along the kiln shell longitudinally as well as circumferentially. The total system is in the form of a spiral along the shell.

helical conveyor (screw; worm conveyor) A conveyor which consists primarily of a horizontal shaft with helical paddles or ribbons, rotating on its center line within a tube; an Archimedes screw.

helical hinge A hinge for a swing door hung from its frame.

helical reinforcement Steel rod reinforcement bent into a spiral curve, sometimes used for reinforcing columns.

helical stair Correct, but not the usual, name for a spiral staircase.

helicline A spiral ramp.

heliograph An instrument used that reflects sunlight in flashes so as to make a distant surveying station visible.

heliostat A mirror which reflects the sun's rays into a collector.

helmet (see bonnet)

helm roof A steeply pitched roof in which four faces rest diagonally between gables and converge at the top.

helve The handle of a tool, such as a hammer, hatchet or ax.

hematite An important ore of iron, Fe_2O_3; red when powdered.

hemiglyph The half-channel which forms a chamfer on each vertical edge of a triglyph.

hemihydrate A hydrate containing one-half molecule of water to one molecule of compound; the most commonly known hemihydrate is the partially dehydrated gypsum, plaster of Paris.

hemihydrate plaster Plaster made by

heating gypsum, which loses part of the water and becomes the hemihydrate. It is commonly called plaster of Paris.

hemitriglyph A half-triglyph.

hemlock, Eastern A wood from the Lake states and eastern U.S. mountain country; used chiefly for framing, sheathing, roofing and subflooring; more brittle and liable to splinter than spruce.

hemp wallcovering A wallcovering made from the fibers of the hemp plant and laminated to a paper backing.

Hercules piles Steel pipe piles filled with high strength concrete.

Herculite Trade name for a specially tempered, thick plate glass, usually used for doors without framing.

herringbone bond In masonry, the arrangement of bricks in a course in a zigzag fashion, with the end or one brick laid at right angles against the side of a second brick.

herringbone drain A chevron drain.

hertz A unit of frequency equal to one cycle per second.

hesitation set (see false set)

hessian (see burlap)

hewn Of wood, roughly dressed by ax or adze; of stone, cut to form by mallet and chisel.

hexaprostyle In Classical architecture, having a main front of six columns, and no columns at sides.

H-hinge A hinge in the shape of an H.

hickey bar (slang) A bar for bending slab reinforcement to shape.

hick joint In masonry, a mortar joint finished flush with the surface of the wall.

hickory A strong timber with high shock resistance and bending strength.

hiding power (opacity) The ability of paint to obscure color beneath it.

high air (slang) Air pressure used to supply power to pneumatic tools and devices.

high alumina cement (see calcium-aluminate cement)

high-bond bar (see deformed bar)

high calcium lime A type of lime containing principally calcium oxide or hydroxide and not more than 5% magnesium oxide or hydroxide.

high capacity unit An air distribution unit consisting of a factory made assembly of dual duct modulating dampers and integral volume control station together with a temperature mixing station to supply air volumes greater than 2000 cfm from an external source. These units are designed for furred-in application and distribution ducts to provide sound attenuation and air delivery to the occupied room.

high-carbon steel Carbon steel containing over .5 percent carbon and up to 1.5 percent carbon. Low-carbon steel has 0.04 percent to 0.25 percent carbon and medium-carbon steel has 0.25 to 0.5 percent carbon.

high chair *(slang)* A chair-shaped device used to hold reinforcing steel off of the framework.

high density concrete Concrete of exceptionally high unit weight, usually obtained by use of heavyweight aggregates; used especially for radiation shielding.

high-density foam Rubber product applied as a liquid foam, then cured, to form an integral part of the carpet back. Weights vary from 38 oz. to 45 oz. per square yard.

high-discharge mixer *(see inclined-axis mixer)*

high-early-strength concrete Concrete which, through the use of high-early-strength cement or admixtures, is capable of attaining specified strength at an earlier age than normal concrete. It is frequently used when the temperature is below freezing.

high explosive An explosive containing at least one chemical compound which, when fired, decomposes at high speed, a process called detonation. Low explosives combine at least two materials giving a heaving slow explosion.

highlighting To emphasize surface texture by making some portions paler than the primary color.

high lime rock Limestone which contains approximately 75 percent or more of calcium carbonate.

high line A high tension electric line; electric power supplied by a utility.

high-low A multi-level pile, sometimes combining cut and looped surface yarns.

high magnesium lime Lime containing over five percent magnesium oxide or hydroxide.

high pressure steam curing *(see autoclave curing)*

high pressure unit An air distribution unit consisting of a factory-made assembly with either a dual duct modulating damper (or a single duct pressure reducing damper), an integral volume controller together with temperature mixing and sound attenuation stations, which supply air volumes up to approximately 2000 cfm and static pressures greater than 0.40 in water from an external source. Units may be designed for a furred-in application in a plenum for exposed installation in the space with or without an enclosure.

high rise (1) A popular term for multi-storied buildings, usually over six stories. (2) *(slang)* A barricade eight feet to ten feet, used for traffic control at each end of the construction zone. It has three flagged arms usually set at 10:00, 12:00 and 2:00 o'clock.

high side (high pressure side) (1) Parts of a refrigerating system subjected to condenser pressure or higher. (2) *(slang)* The "outside" of a bend in a pipe, conduit or cylinder.

high speed neutron High velocity neutrons such as would emanate directly from atomic nuclei such as the radioactive isotopes used in roof moisture meters. *(see Thermalization)*.

high spiker *(slang)* One who drives spikes that other workmen missed.

high-strength friction-grip bolts Fixings for steelwork. *(see high tension bolts)*

high strength steel Steel with a high yield point; in the case of reinforcing bars, generally greater than 60,000 psf. *(see reinforcement, high tensile)*

high temperature steam curing *(see atmospheric-pressure steam curing; autoclave curing)*

high tension bolts High strength steel bolts tightened with calibrated wrenches to high tension; used as a substitute for conventional rivets in steel frame structure.

high time (high pay) *(see height money)*

high wall A face which is being excavated as distinguished from spoil piles; undisturbed soil or rock bordering a cut.

highway (street; road) A general term denoting a public way for purposes of vehicular travel, including the entire area within the right-of-way.

hillbilly bar *(slang)* Short hook bar.

hinge A connection which allows swinging motion in one plane.

hinge joint Any joint which permits action with no appreciable separation of the adjacent members.

hip The external angle formed by the meeting of two sloping sides of a roof which have their wall plates running in different directions. The place at which the top chord meets the batter brace or inclined end post.

inner The intersection of the inner inclined end post with the top chord in the arm of a swing span.

outer The hip at the outer end of one of the arms of a swing span.

hip and ridge shingle A piece of composition roofing cut to an individual nominal size of approximately nine inches by twelve inches; used on the hips and ridges of roofs.

hip heeler *(slang)* The man who works next to the heeler.

hip jack rafter Short rafter extending from the plate to the hip ridge.

hip jacks Jacks running from plate to hip, usually meeting at the hip in pairs.

hip-knob The finial on the hip of a roof or between the barge boards of a gable.

hipped end The triangular sloping end of a hipped roof.

hip rafters Rafters which form the hip of a roof as distinguished from the common rafter.

hip roll The half-cylindrical surface, usually of metal, for finishing the hip of a roof.

hip roof A roof which rises by inclined planes from all four sides of a building; the line where two adjacent sloping sides of a roof meet is called the hip.

hip tiles Tiles covering those roofing tiles which meet at a hip. Hip tiles do not generally overlap each other.

histogram A chart showing a distribution of data, e.g. the number of occurrences of a value plotted versus the value itself. Sometimes called a bar chart.

hitch (1) A horizontal shelf along the side of a rock tunnel that supports roof timbers. (2) A connection between two machines. (3) A loose knot used in a rope when hoisting material.

hoarding (boarding) An enclosure of rough boards around building sites for the protection of the public and the contractor.

hockle *(slang)* A kink in a rope or cable.

hod A portable trough for carrying mortar, bricks, etc., fixed crosswise on top of a pole and carried on the shoulder.

hod carrier A laborer, usually one who transports concrete or mortar from the delivery truck to the work area.

hoddability A term descriptive of the ease with which a plaster mortar may be handled with a hod or hawk. Dependent upon flow characteristics and angle of repose of the mortar.

hoe (backhoe; pullshovel) A shovel that digs by pulling a boom-and-stick mounted bucket toward itself.

hog To hog the bond is a term used by bricklayers to denote that there is a closer in the middle of a course; in some bonds, it means that there is not the proper sequence of stretchers and headers along the course.

hog barge *(slang)* A waterborne dredge.

hog box *(slang)* A concrete box in which dirt and water are mixed before they are pumped out to a hydraulic fill.

hogging moment *(see negative moment)*

hoist A machine for lifting weights or loads of various kinds; to elevate by means of block and tackle or by machinery of any kind.

air A hoisting device, usually consisting of a cylinder and piston rod, operated by compressed air.

assembling A hoist for lifting and assembling the component parts of trusses, spans, etc., in the shop or yard of a bridge plant.

cable A hoist in which cables winding about a drum or drums are used to lift a load.

chain A hoist in which chains are used for lifting loads.

electrical A hoist operated by an electric motor.

hydraulic A hoist operated by hydraulic power.

pneumatic An air hoist.

steam A hoist operated by steam.

hoistway access switch A switch, located at a landing, the function of which is to permit operation of the car with the hoistway door at this landing and the car door or gate open, in order to permit access to the top of the car or to the pit.

hoistway, elevator or dumbwaiter A shaftway for the travel of one or more elevators or dumbwaiters. It includes the pit and terminates at the underside of the overhead machinery space floor or grating, or at the underside of the roof where the hoistway does not penetrate the roof.

blind hoistway The portion of a hoistway which passes floors or other landings at which no normal landing entrances are provided.

multiple hoistway A hoistway for more than one elevator or dumbwaiter.

single hoistway A hoistway for a single elevator or dumbwaiter.

hoistway enclosure The fixed structure, consisting of vertical walls or partitions, which isolates the hoistway from all other parts of the building or from an adjacent hoistway and in which the hoistway doors and door assemblies are installed.

holdback An automatic safety device that prevents a conveyor belt from running backward.

holder-up A dolly bar for bucking up rivets; also called bucker-up.

hold harmless *(see indemnification; contractual liability)*

holding-down bolt An anchor bolt.

holding line The hoist cable for a clamshell bucket.

holding period *(see presteaming period)*

holding point The value selected as a basis for controlling raw material proportions, usually depending on chemical analysis and calculation of raw mix moduli.

hold-over In an evaporator, the ability to stay cold after heat removal from the evaporator stops. A material used to store heat in latent or sensible form.

holiday A skip in the application of material or paint.

hollow-backed flooring Floorboards hollowed out on the underside to improve ventilation and bedding of the boards on the joists.

hollow block A concrete masonry unit whose net cross-sectional area in any plane parallel to the bearing surface is less than 75 percent of its gross cross-sectional area measured in the same plane.

hollow chamfer A concave chamfer.

hollow-core door A flush door in which plywood or hardwood for both faces is glued to a skeleton framework. It is lighter and less expensive than a solid door.

hollow dam A barrier, usually of reinforced concrete, consisting essentially of slabs supported by transverse buttresses; the load is taken by the slabs and transferred to the foundations through the buttresses.

hollow partition A partition built of hollow blocks, a partition built in two sections with a gap between for sound insulation, thermal insulation or to accommodate a sliding door.

hollow tile Tile made in a variety of forms and sizes; used extensively as a building material for both exterior walls and partitions.

hollow unit masonry Masonry consisting, wholly or in part, of hollow masonry units laid contiguously in mortar.

hollow wall A wall of masonry so arranged as to provide an air space within the wall between the inner and outer parts of the wall.

hollow-web girder A box girder.

hollow-wood construction Plywood using decorative or structural construction glued on both faces as in hollow-core doors.

homogeneity (nick and break test) A test consisting of nicking a piece of metal transversely and breaking it for the purpose of disclosing, by ocular examination of the surface fracture, such internal defects as piping or other unsoundness.

homogenizer A bin or tank in which fluids or powders are thoroughly mixed and blended by compressed air, paddles or rakes.

honcho *(slang)* The boss.

honeycomb (1) A cell-like structure. (2) Concrete that is poorly mixed and not adequately puddled, having voids or open spaces. *(see honeycombing)*

honeycomb core A structure of air cells resembling a honeycomb, often made of paper, which is placed between plywood panels; this type of wall construction provides lighter prefabricated walls with excellent insulating properties.

honeycombing (1) A common fault in concrete; voids caused by incomplete filling of the form. (2) Separation of fibers in lumber due to drying stresses.

honeycomb wall A half-brick wall constructed of stretchers with gaps between; they are held only by bed joints at their ends, above and below.

honey wagon A tank truck used to clean portable toilets.

honing (1) The process of giving stone a very smooth finish by rubbing; it is usually found only in interior work. (2) Sharpening a tool's cutting edge.

hood (1) A casing on the end of a suction line that causes it to pick up material from the bottom only. (2) A curved baffle that prevents scattering and separation of material discharged by a conveyor belt. (3) A canopy to throw water off a window, door or other opening. (4) Overhead cover of a chimney or a kitchen range; an inverted funnel leading into a ventilating flue. *(see bonnet)*

hood mold A drop molding over a door or window.

hook (1) Extension of the cutting edge past the sole of the plate. (2) A bend in the end of a reinforcing bar. (3) *(slang)* A crane. (4) A curved or bent implement for catching, holding or pulling.

bolt A bolt bent in a U-shape at the unthreaded end.

cable A round hook with a wide beveled face.

grab A chain hook that will slide over any one link but will not slide along the chain.

hand A tool for twisting iron or steel bars.

pintle A towing bracket having a fixed lower part, and a hinged upper one, which when locked together makes a round opening that can hold a tow ring.

round-slip A hook that has smooth inner surfaces and will slide along a chain.

safety lock-on A round hook with a hinged piece across the opening that allows a line to enter it readily, but requires special manipulation to remove it.

sister A pair of hooks on the same axis facing each other and fitting closely together when in use.

swivel A hook with a swivel connection to its base or eye.

hooked bar A reinforcing bar with the end bent into a hook to provide anchorage.

Hooke's law A law stating that the deformation of an elastic body is proportional to the force applied, or that the intensity of stress is proportional to the rate of strain. *(see proportional limit; modulus of elasticity)*

hook knife A special curved knife commonly called a Linoleum Knife.

hook tender *(slang)* A straw boss or foreman.

hopper A storage bin or a funnel that is loaded from the top and discharges through a door or chute in the bottom.

hopper head A rain-water head.

hoppit A kibble.

horizon In perspective drawing, the intersection of the picture plane by a plane at right angles passing through the station point.

horizon glass A glass in a sextant which is half silvered and half clear.

horizon line An imaginary line parallel to the ground line, used in perspective work.

horizon of soil One of the layers in a cross section of soil.

horizontal Parallel to the line where the earth meets the sky

horizontal angle An angle measured in a horizontal plane between two vertical planes.

horizontal application The application of gypsum board with the long dimension at right angles to the framing members. Also referred to as a perpendicular.

horizontal-axis mixer A concrete mixer of the revolving drum type in which the drum rotates about a horizontal axis.

horizontal brace *(see ledger)*

horizontal branch A branch drain extending laterally from a soil or waste stack or building drain, with or without vertical sections or branches, which receives the discharge from one or more fixture drains and conducts it to the soil or waste stack or to the building drain.

horizontal circle (of a theodolite or transit) The circular, graduated plate under the telescope, for accurately measuring horizontal angles.

horizontal curve A curve in plan.

horizontal distance The distance between the points projected onto a horizontal plane.

horizontal flow tank A tank or basin, with or without baffles, in which the direction of flow is generally horizontal.

horizontal line At any point, any line which is perpendicular to the vertical at the point.

horizontal plane The plane which is perpendicular to the vertical line at a given point.

horizontal shaft mixer A mixer having a stationary cylindrical mixing compartment, with the axis of the cylinder horizontal, and one or more rotating horizontal shafts to which mixing blades or paddles are attached.

horizontal shoring Adjustable span members, either beam or truss type, used to support forms over relatively long spans thereby reducing the number of vertical supports.

hornblende A mineral containing iron, silicate of magnesium, calcium and aluminum, black or greenish-black in color.

Horn Book An old out-dated book that contained general information of surveying and field engineering.

horse **(1)** *(slang)* A sawhorse or other simple framing used as a temporary support. **(2)** The string carrying the treads and risers of a stair. **(3)** A short board housed to receive the wood backing to the shaped metal templet which forms a plaster molding to the required profile. **(4)** A wood finial which is to be covered with lead.

horsed mold A wooden stock housed into a horse and fixed by wooden stays. The horsed mold is pushed along the angle between ceiling and wall by one plasterer. A second plasterer feeds the plaster onto the molding.

horse dolly A heavy dolly used in steel-work.

horsehead (1) A light framework or headframe used over a pit for supporting a pulley block for use in hoisting and lowering men and materials. (2) A temporary support for forepoles used in tunneling soft ground.

horsepower Unit of the rate of work, 33,000 pounds lifted one foot in one minute; applied to a boiler, the rating indicates the amount and pressure of steam that will drive an engine to perform at that rate; applied to an electric motor, one horsepower requires 745.941 watts.

drawbar Horsepower available to move a tractor and its load after deducting losses in the power train

indicated The horsepower developed in the cylinders determined by use of an indicator gauge; does not include engine friction losses.

rated Theoretical horsepower of an engine based on dimensions and speed; power of an engine according to a particular standard.

shaft Actual horsepower produced by the engine after deducting the drag of accessories.

horsepower hours The horsepower developed multiplied by the number of hours it is developed.

horse scaffold A scaffold for light or medium duty, composed of horses supporting a work platform.

horseshoe arch An arch continuing beyond a semicircle.

horsing up In plastering, building up a horsed mold for running a cornice, etc.

hosecock *(see sillcock)*

hose coupling A joint or connection from a hose to a steel pipe or another hose.

hospital door A flush door.

hot *(slang)* A "live" or energized wire or electrical component.

hot-air heater A system of heating by driving warm air into a room through vents in the walls or floor.

hot bend Short radius bend prepared at pipe mill.

hot cathode The variety of fluorescent lamps using coiled tungsten filaments; there are both instantstarting and preheating types.

hot cement Cement which is at a high temperature, usually due to inadequate or insufficient cooling after manufacture.

hot-dip galvanizing Dipping metal parts in molten zinc or tin to give a protective coating.

hot-drawn A term used to signify the product of drawing when the operation is performed on material that is hot, usually red hot, e.g. hot-drawn seamless tubes.

hot face The surface of a refractory section exposed to the source of heat.

hot gas line A line used to convey discharge gas from the compressor.

hot-finished (HF) tubing The product of piercing, rolling and other operations, carried on while the metal is hot, to prevent workhardening.

hot-laid mixtures Plant mixes which must be spread and compacted while in a heated condition; the highest types of asphalt pavements are constructed with hot laid mixtures known as asphaltic concrete, sheet asphalt and stone-filled sheet asphalt according to grading of mineral aggregate.

hot line Pipeline in service.

hot line stakes Stakes marking hot line (in service).

hot load test A test for determining the resistance to deformation of shear of a refractory material when subjected to a specified compressive load at a specified temperature for a specified time.

hot melt A blend of polymer and filling applied in a heated state to a carpet back, to lock in surface yarns and for lamination.

hot mill To heat metal, and then shape it.

hot mix (black top) Plant mixes of the highest type made of hot, dried aggregates and heated asphalt or road tar spread and rolled while still heated.

hot mud *(slang)* Concrete that has been in a mixer for longer than an hour and not placed.

hot pass Second weldings pass around pipe.

hot plant *(see asphalt paving plant)*

hot rolled shapes Steel sections (angles, channels, I-beams, etc.) which are formed by rolling mills while the steel is in a semi-molten state.

hot rolling The method of making rolled-steel sections in a rolling mill by passing hot steel bars through pairs of massive steel rolls.

hot shot A condition of brittleness in iron or steel due to the presence of sulfur.

hot spot An exterior area of the kiln shell, usually in the burning zone, which becomes heated to a temperature sufficient to cause the shell to be red hot or to glow. Usually caused by the loss of coating or lining.

hot spraying Spraying lacquers and paints which have been heated to reduce their viscosity instead of adding thinners. Used to form a thicker coat.

hot stuff (slang) The roofer's term for hot bitumen.

hot wall Plastered wall unusually heavy in free lime which burns out paint film.

hot-water heating A system of heating, utilizing hot water circulated through pipes, coils and radiators.

hot wires The power-carrying wires, usually black or red, as distinguished from the neutral wires, usually white.

hot wrench *(slang)* Using a cutting torch to disassemble or loosen lug bolts.

house A general term designating any building used as a residence.

house drain In plumbing, the main, lower, horizontal pipe or pipes which connect with the sewer.

housed stair A complete stair that is built between two walls.

housed string A stair string with horizontal and vertical grooves cut on the inside to receive the ends of the risers and treads. Wedges covered with glue are often used to hold the risers and treads in place in the grooves.

house sewer (sewage) A pipe conveying the sewage from a single building to a common sewer; loosely used for domestic sewage

housing (1) Dwelling units in quantity. (2) A sinking in one member to engage a projection from another. (3) A heavy cased enclosure for rotating parts.

Howe truss A type of truss used both in roofs and in construction of bridges; a form of truss especially adapted to wood and steel construction.

Hoyer effect In prestressed concrete, frictional forces which result from the tendency of the tendons to regain the diameter which they had before they were stressed.

Hoyer method *(see pretensioning)*

HSWA The acronym for the Hazardous and Solid Waste Amendments of 1984 (Public Law 98-616), which significantly expanded both the scope and the coverage of RCRA.

hub The strengthened inner part or mounting of a wheel, gear or sewer pipe.

Hudee rim Metal frame used to secure sink in countertop.

hue Refers to a color family; a basic color as it appears in the spectrum. A dark red and a light pink are the same hue.

hue, lightness Refers to the tonal quality of a color from light to dark.

humidification (1) The process of adding moisture to heated air by means of evaporation. (2) The process of adding moisture to finished boards.

humidified bond The ability of the surfacing paper to resist delamination from the core under extremely high humidity conditions.

humidifier A mechanical device which controls the amount of water vapor to be added to the atmosphere or any material.

humidify To add water vapor to the atmosphere; to add water vapor or moisture to any material.

humidifying effect The latent heat of

vaporization of water at the average evaporating temperature times the weight of water evaporated per unit of time.

humidistat A regulatory device, actuated by changes in humidity, used for the automatic control of relative humidity.

humidity Water vapor within a given space.

humidity of air (absolute humidity) The weight of moisture present in air, as contrasted with relative humidity which is a percentage or ratio.

humidity, percentage The ratio of the weight of water vapor associated with a pound of dry air to the weight of water vapor associated with a pound of dry air saturated at the same temperature.

humidity ratio *(see humidity, specific)*

humidity, relative The ratio of the mol fraction of water vapor present in the air, to the mol fraction of water vapor present in saturated air at the same temperature and barometric pressure; approximately, it equals the ratio of the partial pressure or density of the water vapor in the air, to the saturation pressure or density, respectively, of water vapor at the same temperature.

humidity, specific Weight of water vapor steam associated with one pound weight of dry air; also called humidity ratio.

humper *(slang)* Formerly and usually a Swedish section man; an earthmover in 19th century railroad work who used only a shovel and a wheelbarrow and contracted to move a section of earth.

humus Decayed organic matter; a dark fluffy swamp soil composed chiefly of decayed vegetation; also called peat.

humus tank A tank for collecting humus sludge. *(see final settling basin)*

hundredweight A British unit of weight, 112 pounds; 20 hundredweight make one long ton, or 2,240 pounds, the ton used in Britain.

hungry (starved) Descriptive of a surface which is too absorptive for the amount or kind of paint put on it, making a paint film that is thin and patchy.

hunting tooth A sprocket and roller chain combination in which one has an odd number so that no tooth will contact the same pin twice in succession.

hurricane anchor Metal fastener nailed to rafter and top plate to provide a wind and seismic tie for trusses.

HVAC System A system that provides either collectively or individually the processes of comfort heating, ventilating, and/or cooling within or associated with a building.

Hveen Stabilometer A device for determining the strength of compacted asphalt concrete mixtures, also used to determine strength of compacted soils.

hydrant A connection to water main used for discharge of water.

hydrate To combine with water or elements of water. A term used to denote hydrated lime.

hydrated lime The dry, relatively stable material produced by treating quicklime with just enough water to satisfy its chemical affinity for water under the conditions of its hydration.

hydration Formation of a compound by the combining of water with some other substance; in concrete, the chemical reaction between cement and water.

hydraulic (1) Relating to the flow of fluids, particularly water. (2) Descriptive of limes or mortars which set and harden under water.

hydraulic actuator Used in duct work for opening and closing dampers.

hydraulic cement A type of cement which hardens under water.

hydraulic dredge A floating pump that sucks up a mixture of water and soil and usually discharges it on land through pipes.

hydraulic ejector (elephant trunk) A pipe for removing sand, mud or small gravel from the working chamber of a pneumatic caisson; the pipe also used for pumping stiff silt which will not flow through a pump.

hydraulic excavation Excavation by giants shooting a jet of water at high velocity against an earth or gravel bank. The flowing water carries the mud and soil to flumes and from there to the embankment or treatment plant as required.

hydraulic fill Fill moved and placed by running water.

hydraulic fill dam A dam composed of earth, sand, gravel, etc. sluiced into place; generally the fines are washed toward the center for greater imperviousness.

hydraulic friction (loss of head) The flow resistance caused by roughness or obstructions in a pipe or channel.

hydraulic gradient The slope of the surface of open or underground water. *(see Darcy's law)*

hydraulic hydrated lime The hydrated dry cementitious product obtained by calcining a limestone containing silica and alumina to a temperature short of incipient fusion so as to form sufficient free calcium oxide to permit hydration and at the same time leaving sufficient unhydrated calcium silicates to give the dry powder its hydraulic properties.

hydraulic jack A lifting device operated by a lever from the outside, and put into action by means of a small force pump, through the use of a liquid, such as water or oil.

hydraulicking *(slang). (see hydraulic excavation)*

hydraulic lime A lime having the property of hardening under water.

hydraulic limestone A limestone which contains some silica and alumina, yielding a quicklime that sets or hardens under water.

hydraulic mortar In masonry, a mortar which will harden under water; used for foundation or any masonry construction under water.

hydraulic pile driving A method of driving sheet piles by hydraulic force.

hydraulic radius The cross-sectional area of a stream of water divided by the length of that part of its periphery in contact with its containing conduit. The ratio of area to wetted perimeter.

hydraulics That branch of science or engineering which deals with water or other fluid in motion.

hydraulic sluicing The process of moving materials by water; colloquially.

hydraulic test In plumbing, the water test for drains. Also a test for pipes, boilers, etc. which are filled with water to design pressure or slightly above it.

hydrocarbons Any member of a family of organic compounds which contains only hydrogen and carbon atoms in a variety of alignments.

hydrodynamics The branch of hydraulics which deals with flow over weirs, through openings and pipes and channels.

hydroelectric power station A power station which generates electricity by the energy of falling water, causing turbines to turn and drive generators.

hydrogen ion Acidity of alkalinity of water or soil.

hydrograph A graph showing the stage, flow, velocity or other property of water with respect to time.

hydrographic survey The determination of the configuration of the bottom of a body of water.

hydrology That science concerned with the properties, occurrences, distribution and circulation of water.

hydrolysis The splitting up of compounds by reaction with water; e.g., reaction of dichlorodifluoromethane or methyl chloride with water, in which case acid materials are formed.

hydrolytic tank In general, any sewage tank in which hydrolysis occurs; specifically applied to a special form of vertical-flow tank.

hydrometer A device, usually a float in a glass tube, for measuring the specific gravity of fluids.

hydronics The science of heating and cooling with liquids.

hydrostatic press (hydraulic press) A large ram whose surface is acted on by fluid in contact with a small ram. The small ram is moved back and forth to increase the liquid pressure producing a large force on the large ram.

hydrostatic pressure (1) The pressure at any point in a liquid at rest; equal to the depth of the liquid multiplied by its density. (2) Takes place with on-grade or below-grade concrete slabs when either excessive water is present or there is a high water table. Pressure forces water through the slab, which can cause a flooring job to fail.

hygrometer An instrument for measuring the degree of moisture suspended in the air.

hygrometric expansion All materials, particularly those of organic origin, expand and contract in relation to their moisture content which varies with environment. The Hygrometric Coefficient of Expansion is expressed in "Inches Per Inch Per Percent Of Relative Humidity.

hygroscopic Any material having a tendency to absorb water from the atmosphere.

hygroscopic moisture Moisture contained in the air-dried soil which evaporates if the soil is dried at 105 C.

hygrostat Automatic control responsive to humidity.

hyperbolic paraboloid A concrete umbrella used for beauty only.

hyphen The connecting link between a main building and an outlying wing, such as is found in the South Atlantic states and in the Georgian mansions of the eighteenth century.

hypogeal Construction under the surface of the earth or in the sides of a hill or mountain.

hypoid A pinion-and-ring gear set transmitting rotation through a right angle by means of teeth having structure intermediate between a bevel and a worm set.

hysteresis Loop formed in the stress-strain curve when a specimen is strained beyond its elastic limit in alternating cycles of tension and compression.

I   inclination, intensity, moment of inertia

IB   I-beam

IC   ironclad

ICBO   International Conference of Building Officials.

ID   improvement district, inside dimension, inside diameter

ihp   indicated horsepower

imp/imperf   imperfect

impr/impts   improvements

in   inch

inc   incorporated, increase

ind   industrial, index, independent

ins   inches, insurance

insol   insoluble

insp   inspector

inst   instant, installation

instr   instrument

insul   insulation

int   interior, interest

IP   intial point, intermediate pressure

ipm   inches per minute

ips   inches per second

IR   infrared

irreg   irregular

I   *(C.P.M.)* A symbol that describes the event at the tail of an activity arrow.

I-J   *(C.P.M.)* Any arrow in an arrow diagram.

IRA   Initial Rate of Absorption (suction). The weight of water that will be absorbed by 30 square inches of brick in one minute.

I-beam (H-beam)   A beam of rolled steel, having in cross section the shape of an I with somewhat exaggerated top and bottom horizontal strokes.

ice apron (ice breaker)   A ramp, upstream of a bridge pier, which slopes up from below water level. Ice carried downstream is lifted and broken by this device.

ice bank   A thermal accumulator in which, during off-peak periods of refrigeration demand, ice is formed, and in which, during peak periods of refrigeration demand, compressor capacity is supplemented by melting ice.

ichnography   That branch of knowledge dealing with graphic representation; therefore, a horizontal section of a building or other object, showing its true dimensions according to a geometric scale; a ground plan.

icos   Method of making an underground diaphragm wall.

idealite   A type of lightweight aggregate used in structural concrete.

identification index   A set of numbers used in the marking of sheathing grades of plywood. The numbers are related to the species of panel face and back veneers and panel thickness in a manner to describe the bending properties of a panel.

idiot stick   *(slang)* Shovel; slide rule.

idler   A wheel or gear which changes the direction or rotation of shafts; or the direction of movement of a chain or belt.

igneous   Rock-solidified molten material. One of the three basic rock formations including sedimentary and metamorphic.

igneous intrusion   Molten rock forced out of the center of the earth to form thick masses or thin flat deposits covered by other rocks. They crystallize slowly and therefore have crystals large enough to be seen by the naked eye, unlike volcanic, extruded rocks which have very few visible crystals.

ignition loss   *(see loss on ignition)*

ignition powder   A mixture, usually of powdered aluminum and oxidizing material, which starts the reaction in thermit welding.

ignition temperature The lowest temperature at which a combustible material will catch on fire in air and will continue to burn independently of the source of heat when heated.

illumination The amount of light brought to bear upon a surface.

ilmenite A mineral, iron titanate, which in pure or impure form is commonly used as aggregate in high density concrete.

imbow To arch over.

imbrex In Classical architecture, a half-round roofing tile which fits over the under-tile, or tegula.

imbricated Overlapping and breaking joints, as tiles, slate or shingles on a roof, and as in some ornaments. A description of any surface which looks like a tiled roof.

Imhoff tank A deep two-storied tank, invented by Karl Imhoff, consisting of an upper or continuous sedimentation chamber and a lower or sludge digestion chamber. Sewage ferments to form methane and the sludge is drawn off and dried after settling.

immersion heater An electric resistance heater which is submerged in a water tank.

impact The act of striking; the forcible momentary contact of a moving body with another, either moving or at rest. The stress in a structure caused by the force of a vibratory dropping of moving load. This is generally a percentage of the live load.

impact-allowance load A percentage allowance for impact applied to the equivalent uniform live load.

impact crusher An apparatus for coarse size reduction which occurs in three stages: impact of the impeller bars; impact against the breaker plate; and impact of material against material.

impact dryer An impact crusher that contains a drying arrangement.

impact factor A factor between one and two by which the weight of a moving load is multiplied to give its full effect on a bridge or floor. The factor for the same load is larger for a short span than for a long span.

impact flow meter A device that senses the passage of fine or granular dry material and whose output is in weight per unit of time. The force of falling material on an impact sensor is translated into an electric signal.

impact indentation The degree to which the floor covering recovers from indentation created by dropped objects or foot traffic.

impact insulation class Values which rate the capacity of floor assemblies to control impact noise such as footfalls. FHA requirements (and some local building codes) specify minimum acceptable ratings.

impact load An assumed dynamic load resulting from the motion of machinery, elevators, craneways, vehicles, and other similar moving forces.

impact noise rating Minimum noise level standards for multiple housing. Test measures the noise that results from dropped objects, foot traffic and the like.

impact resistance The ability of a layer of asphalt to resist cracking or breaking when the material on which it is applied receives a hard blow or knock.

impact spanner *(see impact wrench)*

impact test A test in which one or more blows are suddenly applied to a specimen. The results are usually expressed in terms of energy absorbed or number of blows, of given intensity, required to break the specimen.

impact transmission Sound transferred through a wall or floor into another area.

impact wrench A compressed-air wrench which tightens high-strength friction-grip bolts and stalls when it reaches the correct torque for the nut being tightened. These impact wrenches must be re-calibrated every shift and for every change of bolt diameter.

impedance The ratio of voltage to current in an alternating current circuit.

impeller A rotary pump member using

centrifugal force to discharge a fluid into outlet passages

impending slough The consistency obtained with shotcrete containing the maximum amount of water that can be used without flow or sag after placement.

imperfect frame A frame having fewer members than are needed to make it stable.

Imperial Mahogany A medium grain granite, pinkish with black and gray spottings; quarried near Minneapolis, Minnesota.

impervious Resistant to movement of water. Generally a description of waterproof soils, such as clays, through which water percolates at about ¹/₁₀₀₀ of the speed with which it passes through gravel.

impervious core (impervious zone) In dam construction, a zone of material of low permeability in an enbankment dam; hence the terms central core, inclined core, puddle clay core, and rolled clay core.

imperviousness, coefficient of The amount of rain which runs off a surface in relation to that which falls on it; a factor from which run-off can be calculated. *(see Lloyd Davies formula)*

impervious zone *(see impervious core)*

impinge To strike directly upon (as a flame may impinge on the load in a kiln).

impluvium *(see compluvium)*

impost The uppermost member of a column, pillar, pier or wall upon which the end of an arch rests.

impounding reservoir A large reservoir for storing fluids.

impoundment A pond, lake, tank or basin used to store, regulate and control water. It may be a natural creation or developed in whole or part by construction or engineering.

Impreg Trade name for wood veneers impregnated with resin, dried, stacked and cured under low pressure.

impregnation (1) The impregnation of timbers with preservatives under pressure or with alternating vacuum and pressure. (2) Allowing a water proofing liquid to pass through a soil to reduce leakage. An example of base exchange.

impressed current Current of electricity introduced for cathodic protection.

improved Venturi flume The Parshall measuring flume.

improvement district A specific district formed by property owners for the purpose of improvements, water, sewer, storm drains, paving and appurtenances, etc. The district, as sole beneficiary of the improvement, pays for them in cash or by bonds.

improvement district bonds Interest bearing bonds used to pay for improvements to a district and retired over a period of years as determined by the improvement district board.

improvement line A building line or the line of an improved road.

impulse turbine A steam or water turbine in which driving energy is provided by the speed of the fluid rather than by its change in pressure.

inband A header stone visible in a reveal.

inbark Bark embedded in the wood; ingrown bark.

incandescent light A light source consisting of a glass bulb containing a filament that may be kept incandescent by the transmission of an electric current. *(see electric filament lamp)*

inceptor A device designed and installed so as to separate and retain deleterious, hazardous or undesirable matter from normal wastes and permit normal sewage or liquid wastes to discharge into the disposal terminal by gravity.

incertum Wall masonry of rough stones without horizontal course lines.

inch Unit of linear measure; the twelfth part of a foot.

inch and a half *(slang)* Time-and-one-half payment for work performed.

inch of water A unit of pressure equal to the pressure exerted by a column of liquid water 1 in. high at a temperature of 4 C or 39.2 F.

inch-pounds A unit of energy. Force in

pounds multiplied by the distance in inches through which it acts.

incident radiation Energy arriving at the surface of the solar collector, including both direct and diffuse components.

incinerator A furnace for consuming waste by fire; a furnace for cremation; a cinerator.

incise To cut in; to carve; to engrave.

inclinator An armchair elevator used on stairs. Installed in the home of comedian Groucho Marx, who also invented the word.

incline (1) A sloping way. (2) A length of track laid at a uniform slope.

inclined-axis mixer A truck with a revolving drum which rotates around an axis inclined to the bed of the truck chasis.

inclined cableway A monocable cableway in which the track cable has a slope along its full length, usually one to four; steep enough to allow the carrier to descend by its own weight.

inclined gauge Sloping staff graduated to read vertical heights, or depths, above a certain datum.

inclined grate cooler An enclosed, inclined system of moving grates. Clinker dropped on the high end moves progressively to the lower discharge end while cool air is forced through the grates and load from below.

inclined plane (1) A surface inclined to the plane of the horizon; the angle which it makes with the horizontal line is known as the angle of inclination. (2) A slope used to change the direction and speedpower ratio of a force.

incombustible construction A type of building construction which has all structural elements of incombustible materials with fire-resistance ratings of one hour or less.

incombustible material Material which will not ignite or actively support combustion in a surrounding temperature of 1200° F during an exposure of five minutes; will not melt when the temperature of the material is maintained at 900° F for a period of at least five minutes.

increaser Pipe increasing in diameter in the direction of flow.

incrustation (1) Materials deposited in water pipes or conduits. (2) A layer of corrosive material which collects on a stone wall surface.

indemnification A contractual obligation by which one person or organization agrees to secure another against loss or damage from specified liabilities.

implied An indemnification which is implied by law rather than arising out of a contract.

indent A gap left in a course of brickwork or stone between toothers to bond with future work.

indented Toothed together.

indented bars Steel reinforcement for concrete which has indentations increasing the mechanical bond between the steel and the concrete.

indented bolt An anchor bolt which is a plain bar with forged indentations to increase its grip in concrete or grout.

indented joint A joint in which wooden fishplates and main timbers are cut with mating notches; also sometimes wedged. The fishplates are bolted to the main timbers.

indented wire Wire having machine-made surface indentations intended to improve bond; depending on type or wire, may be used for either concrete reinforcement or pretensioning tendons.

indenting *(see toothing)*

indenting roller (branding iron; crimper) A roller with a patterned surface which is impressed into hot asphalt when pushed over it making a non-slip surface.

indenture (1) A formal agreement between the issuer of a bond and the bondholders. (2) A deed of mutual covenants. (3) In England and early America, a legal agreement between an apprentice and his employer or master. Apprentices enrolled in formal apprenticeship programs are still referred to as indentured apprentices.

index of liquidity (liquidity index)

$$\frac{(\text{water content of sample}) \\ \text{minus} \\ (\text{water content at plastic limit})}{\text{index of plasticity}}$$

This figure is the reverse of the consistency index and gives a value of 100 percent for a clay at the liquid limit and 0 for a clay at the plastic limit.

index of plasticity (plasticity index) The difference between water contents of a clay at the liquid and at the plastic limits. It shows the range of water contents for which the clay is plastic.

index properties Those features which distinguish one soil from another. There are two types: the soil grain properties, size, shape and chemical constitution; and the soil aggregate properties, dry density, moisture content and consistency limits.

Indiana limestone Oolitic limestone produced by a group of quarries in the state of Indiana.

indicated horsepower The horsepower developed in the cylinders; determined by use of an indicator gauge. Does not include engine friction losses.

indicating bolt A door bolt sometimes installed on a bathroom or toilet door to show whether it is vacant or in use.

indicator An apparatus which shows, by the position of a pointer or level of a liquid, the temperature, speed, level, or other parameter of equipment or process.

indicator valve One which indicates by a sign an open or shut position.

indirect expense Overhead expense; expense indirectly incurred and not chargeable to a specific project or task.

indirect heating Heating of rooms by a distant source of heat, the heat being brought to the room by steam, water or hot air; central heating.

indirect lighting A system of artificial lighting in which light from the sources is directed at ceiling or wall to be reflected for general illumination.

indirect solar A type of passive solar heating system in which the storage is interposed between the collecting and the distributing surfaces (e.g., Trombe wall, water wall, or roof pond).

indirect waste pipe A pipe that does not connect directly with the drainage system but conveys liquid waste by discharges into plumbing fixtures or receptacles which are directly connected to the drainage system.

indoor/outdoor Type of carpet, regardless of construction, which is made entirely of components (surface yarns, backing, adhesives, or laminating materials) which have been especially designed or treated to withstand moisture, extremes of temperature, ultraviolet rays and other types of exposure.

induced draft The negative pressure created by a suction fan.

induction The entrainment of room air by the jet action of a primary air stream discharging from an air outlet.

industrial diamond Black diamond or bort.

industrialized building system The total integration of all subsystems and components into an overall process fully utilizing industrialized production, transportation and assembly techniques. This integration is achieved through the exploration of the underlying organizational principles rather than the external forms of industrialization, mechanization and programming to structure the entire building process.

industrial wastes Liquid wastes resulting from the processes employed in industrial establishments; they are free of fecal matter.

inelastic behavior Deformation that does not disappear on removal of the force that produced it. (see elasticity)

inelastic scattering Scattering of particles as a result of collisions in which part of the kinetic energy is lost as heat or radiation. (See thermalizing)

inert Having inactive chemical properties.

inertia The property of matter by which it will remain at rest, or in uniform motion in a straight line, unless acted upon by an external force.

inert pigment A pigment which, unlike

a drier. does not react chemically in a paint; a paint extender.

infiltrated air Outside or ambient air leaking into the pyroprocessing system, generally at the back seal ring, dust valves, etc.

infiltration The uncontrolled inward air leakage through cracks and interstices in any building element and around windows and doors of a building, caused by the pressure effect of wind and/or the effect of differences in the indoor and outdoor air density.

infirmary A room or building in which patients are received for, or given, treatment.

inflammable (see flammable)

inflecture point The point where reversal of curvature occurs; point of contraflexure.

influence line A graph for examining the effects of different loads on beams. The curve extends the full span, or half span, of the beam. Its ordinates show, for any point on the beam, either the shears or the bending moments caused by unit load at any given position.

inflexion Contraflexure.

influent Raw or partly treated water which flows into a reservoir, basin, sewage treatment plant or industrial complex, usually, it refers to any material entering a process or facility.

infra-red detector A sensor that can detect an infra-red spectrum of light.

infra-red drying (see stoving)

infra-red light Light which is given off by objects which contain heat.

infra-red photography Photography on special film which is more sensitive to heat radiation, infra-red rays, than to light.

infra-red spectroscopy The use of a spectrophotometer for determination of infra-red absorption spectra (2.5 to 18-micron wave lengths) of materials; used for detection, determination and identification especially of organic materials.

infrared spectrum Those wave lengths of the electromagnetic spectrum which are by convention called infrared, gen-

erally considered to be of wave lengths from just beyond the visible (.77 microns) to about 3000 microns, (longer wavelengths).

ingle A fireplace.

inglenook A fireplace recess or corner, usually provided with built-in seats.

ingot A large mass of metal cast in a mold.

ingot iron An open-hearth iron very low in carbon, manganese and other impurities.

ingress Entrance.

inhaul The line or mechanism by which a cable excavator bucket is pulled toward the dump point.

inhibiting pigment Zinc chromate, red lead, aluminum, graphite powders, etc., added to paints, particularly priming coats; used to prevent corrosion of a metal surface.

inhibitor Materials such as arsenic or antimony compounds which delay a chemical action in pickling acids, or small proportions of antioxidants which stabilize the paint in a tank in which objects are painted by dipping.

initial drying shrinkage The difference between the length of specimen, molded and cured under stated conditions, and its length when first dried to constant length; expressed as a percentage of the moist length.

initial prestress The prestressing stress, or force, applied to the concrete at the time of stressing.

initial set A degree of stiffening of a mixture of cement and water less than final set; generally stated as an empirical value indicating the time in hours and minutes required for cement paste to stiffen sufficiently to resist, to an established degree, the penetration of a weighted test needle; also applicable to concrete or mortar with use of suitable test procedures. (see final set)

initial setting time The time required for a freshly mixed cement paste, mortar or concrete to achieve initial set. (see final setting time)

initial stresses The stresses occurring

in prestressed concrete members before any losses occur.

initial tangent modulus *(see modulus of elasticity)*

injector In a diesel engine, the unit that sprays fuel into the combustion chamber.

inked *(slang)* To fire a person.

inkwell *(slang)* The base plate of a guy derrick.

inlaid parquet Parquet flooring fixed in blocks about two feet square to a wood backing and then attached to floor boards.

inlaid work (inlay) A decorative design laid in the body of a surface by setting in small pieces of material different from the material used in the ground work.

inlet A surface connection to a closed drain; a structure at the diversion end of a conduit; the upstream end of any structure through which matter may flow.

inlet well A well or opening at the surface of the ground to receive surface water which is then conducted to a sewer.

inner casing A metal partition between the heating unit and the outer casing or jacket.

inner plies All layers of a plywood panel except face and back.

inorganic Being or composed of matter other than hydrocarbons and their derivatives, or matter that is not of plant or animal origin.

input system A method of ventilating by drawing air into an electric fan from the roof to the rooms through ducts. A simple air cleaner is usually included, together with an automatically controlled air heater.

insert (patch; shim) An inlay of veneer which fills a knot hole or other hole in plywood.

insets Installing a design into the overall floor covering. Methods include: drawing design directly on the floor and then cutting it out; making a template; using pre-cut designs; drawing design on heavy paper backed with carbon paper and then tracing to transfer design for cutting out; mill-produced pieces to be fitted; etc.

inside-angle tool A float for shaping internal angles.

inside calipers In shopwork, a type of calipers having the points at the ends of the legs turned outward instead of inward so the tool can be used for gauging the inside diameters.

inside glazing External glazing placed from within the frame.

inside lining The inner member of a cased frame; also called the inside casing or box casing.

inside stop In building, a strip of wood, usually with a bead or molding on one edge, used for holding window sash in place.

inside trim (casing trim) The architrave within a door or window.

in-situ The natural undisturbed soil in place. *(see cast-in-place)*

in-situ concrete piles Concrete bored piles poured in place in holes bored or driven in the ground, as opposed to precast piles which are fixed into the ground by driving, jacking or jetting.

in-situ soil tests Tests made on soil in a borehole, tunnel or trial pit.

insolation (1) Exposure to direct sunlight; penetration of sunlight; extent to which sunlight enters an interior space. (2) The radiant energy from the sun received by a surface such as the solar collector.

insoluble residue The portion of a cement or aggregate that is not soluble in dilute hydrochloric acid of stated concentration.

inspection Examination of work completed or in progress to determine its compliance with contract requirements.

inspection chamber (manhole) A shaft down to a sewer or duct, arranged so that a man can enter it from the surface.

inspection fitting (inspection eye) An access eye.

inspection junction A special length of drain pipe with a branch, consisting of a short pipe leading up to ground level, through which the flow can be inspected.

inspection list (punch list) A list of items of work to be completed or corrected by the contractor.

inspector An authorized representative assigned to make a detailed inspection of any or all portions of the work or materials therefor. *(see building inspector; owner's inspector; resident engineer)*

install To place in position for use.

instructions to bidders Instructions contained in the bidding requirements for preparing and submitting bids for a construction project. *(see notice to bidders)*

instrument A surveying tool which requires more than ordinary skill to be used effectively, e.g., a theodolite, transit, dumpy level, sextant or planimeter.

instrumental shaft plumbing Looking into a shaft with a theodolite to obtain the bearing of a point at the foot of a shaft from a set-up at the top; or the set-up may be at the bottom and the point at the top.

instrument board A panel of recording instruments, switches, and the like, usually the electric-control center of a building; the term is also used in referring to an engine room, laboratory, theater and other operational centers.

insufflation Practice of adding dust to the kiln by blowing it into the burning zone.

insulate To protect a room or building from sound, heat or loss of heat, usually by the use of discontinuous construction to break up the sound paths, combined with insulating materials. Any part of a building separated from other parts of the structure, to prevent the transfer of heat or sound, is said to be insulated.

insulated metal roofing Insulated panels faced with light gauge flexible metal.

insulating board (fiberboard) A building board made of compressed plant fibers such as wood, cane or corn stalks; usually formed by a felting process, dried and pressed to specified thickness of ½ inch to ⅔ inch.

insulating concrete Concrete having low thermal conductivity; used as thermal insulation.

insulating fiber board lath Insulating fiber board made with special edges as a base for plaster.

insulating plasterboard (foil back) Plasterboard backed with brightly polished aluminum foil.

insulating refractory A refractory with a large percentage of open pore space having a low rate of heat transmission. This type of refractory may be in the form of bricks or refractory concrete. Used to conserve heat in kilns, ducts, preheater vessels, etc.

insulating strip An expansion strip.

insulation (1) Any material used in building construction for the reduction of fire hazard or for protection from heat or cold. Insulation also prevents transfer of electricity. (2) Material used to reduce the passage or leakage of heat. The back and sides of a solar collector are insulated to prevent loss of absorbed heat.

fill Granulated, shredded, or powdered material, prepared from vegetable, animal, or mineral origin. It can come in bulk or batt form.

sound Acoustical treatment of fan housings, supply ducts and other parts of system and equipment for isolation of vibration, or to reduce transmission of noise.

thermal A material having a relatively high resistance to heat flow, and used principally to retard the flow of heat.

insulator Glass or ceramic devices used to carry electric wires.

insurance The action or process of insuring; the business of insuring persons or property; coverage by contract whereby one party undertakes to indemnify or guarantee another against loss by a specified contingency or peril.

bodily injury Physical injury, sickness or disease sustained by a person. *(see personal injury)*

builder's risk A specialized form of property insurance to cover work in the course of construction.

care, custody and control The term used to describe a standard exclusion in liability insurance; does not apply to damage to property in the care or custody of the insured, or to damage to property over which the insured is for any purpose exercising physical control.

certificate of A memorandum issued by an authorized representative of an insurance company, stating the type, amounts and effective dates of insurance in force for a designated insurance.

completed operations Liability insurance coverage for injuries to persons or damage to property occurring after an operation is completed but attributed to that operation. An operation is completed (a) when all operations under the contract have been completed or abandoned; or (b) when all operations at one project site are completed; or (c) when the portion of the work out of which the injury or damage arises has been put to its intended use by the person or organization for whom that portion of the work was done. Completed operations insurance does not apply to damage to the completed work itself.

contractor's liability Insurance purchased and maintained by the contractor to protect him from specified claims which may arise out of or result from his operations under the contract, whether such operations be by himself or by any subcontractor or by anyone directly or indirectly employed by any of them, or by anyone for whose acts any of them may be liable.

employer's liability Insurance protection for the employer against claims by employees for damages which arise out of injuries or diseases sustained in the course of their work and which are based on common law negligence rather than on liability under workmen's compensation acts.

errors and omissions *(see professional liability insurance)*

extended coverage *(see property insurance; steam boiler and machinery insurance)*

fire and extended coverage *(see property insurance)*

liability Insurance which protects the insured against liability on account of injury to the person or property of another. *(see completed operations insurance; contractor's liability insurance; employer's liability insurance; owner's liability insurance; professional liability insurance; property damage insurance; public liability insurance; special hazards insurance)*

loss of use Insurance protecting against financial loss during the time required to repair or replace property damaged or destroyed by an insured peril.

owner's liability Insurance to protect the owner against claims arising from his ownership of property and which may be extended to cover claims which may arise from operations of others under the construction contract.

personal injury Injury or damage to the character or reputation of a person, as well as bodily injury. Personal injury insurance usually covers such situations as false arrest, malicious prosecution, willful detention or imprisonment, libel, slander, defamation of character, wrongful eviction, invasion of privacy or wrongful entry. *(see bodily injury)*

professional liability Insurance designed to insure an architect or engineer against claims for damages resulting from alleged professional negligence.

property Insurance on the work at the site against loss or damage caused by perils of fire, lighting, extended coverage (wind, hail explosion except steam boiler explosion, riot, civil commotion, aircraft, land vehicles and smoke), vandalism and malicious mischief and additional perils as otherwise provided or requested. *(see special hazards insurance)*

property damage Part of general liability insurance covering injury to or destruction of tangible property, including loss of use resulting therefrom, but usually not including property which is in the care, custody and control of the insured. *(see care, custody and control)*

public liability Insurance covering liability of the insured for negligent acts resulting in bodily injury, disease or death of others than employees of the insured, and /or property damage.

special hazards Additional perils insurance to be included in property insurance, as provided in contract documents or requested by the contractor or at the option of the owner, such as sprinkler leakage, collapse, water damage, all physical loss, or insurance on materials and supplies at other locations and/or in transit to the site. *(see property insurance)*

steam boiler and machinery Special insurance covering steam boilers, other pressure vessels and related equipment and machinery. This insurance covers damage or injury to property, resulting from explosion of steam boilers, which is not covered by extended coverage perils.

workman's compensation Insurance covering liability of an employer to his employees for compensation and other benefits required by workmen's compensation laws with respect to injury, sickness, disease or death arising from their employment.

intaglio Surface decoration by slightly depressed plane of line or pattern.

intake Any structure in a reservoir, dam, or river through which water can be drawn into an aqueduct.

intake belt course In building, a belt course with the molded face cut so that it serves as an intake between the varying thicknesses of two walls.

intake heading Headworks.

intarsia (tarsia) Surface decoration of wood by the use of inlay in contrasting colors; similar to parquetry.

intergral curb Curbing formed together with the roadway.

integrally-stiffened plating Extruded aluminum sheet shaped like an upside down L; used for decking.

integral waterproofing A British term for the waterproofing of concrete by including an admixture with the mixing water or cement.

integrating meter A device which records the total quantity of fluid or electricity which has passed it, usually simply called a meter.

intelligibility *(see percentage articulation)*

intensity The amount of energy per unit area of a wave front. It is one of the factors which determines loudness.

intensity of stress Stress.

interaction, soil-steel The division of load carrying between pipe and backfill and the relationship of one to the other.

intercept The length of a staff seen between the two stadia hairs of a telescope.

intercepting drain A ditch or trench filled with a previous filter material around a subdrainage pipe. A curtain drain.

intercepting sewer A sewer which receives the dry-weather flow from a number of transverse sewers or outlets, with or without a determined quantity of storm water, if from a combined system.

interceptor A device designed and installed so as to separate and retain deleterious, hazardous or undesirable matter from normal wastes which discharge into the disposal terminal by gravity.

intercolumniation The distance from column to column; the clear space between columns.

intercom A commonly used term for

the intercommunicating telephone system not using a central switchboard.

interconnection Physical connection or arrangement of pipes between two otherwise separate building water-supply systems whereby water may flow from one system to the other, the direction of flow depending upon the pressure differential between the two systems. Where such connection occurs between the sources of two such systems and the first branch from either, whether inside or outside the building, the term cross-connection applies and is generally used.

intercooler A radiator or tank in which air is cooled while moving from low pressure cylinders or a two-stage compressor.

interdome The space between the inner and outer shells of a dome.

interface (1) A common boundary between two parts of a system. (2) In fluid dynamics, a surface separating two fluids across which there is a discontinuity of some fluid property, such as density or velocity or of some derivative of these properties, in a direction normal to the interface.

interface strength *(see bond)*

interference Conflict between waves of light or of sound.

interference body bolt A bolt having high bearing strength and shear strength which are claimed to be better than those of rivets. They have V-shaped corrugations on the threaded part of the shank which are deformed during driving, fully gripping the shank against the walls of the hole.

interference settlement The sinking of a foundation due to loads on foundations near it and the natural extension of their settlement beyond their own boundaries.

intergranular pressure Effective pressure.

intergrown knot One partially or completely intergrown on one or two faces with the growth rings of the surrounding wood; a live knot.

interheater A reheater.

interim certificate The British term for partial payment for construction work which is not the final certificate.

interim financing Funds supplied, usually by a bank, to be utilized by the project owner until long-term financing can be arranged.

interior finish A term applied to the total effect produced by the inside finishing of a building, including not only the materials used but also the manner in which the trim and decorative features have been handled.

interior glazed Glass set from the interior of the building.

interior hung scaffold A scaffold suspended from the ceiling or roof structure.

interior plywood A term frequently applied to plywood bonded with adhesives that maintain adequate bond under conditions usually existing in the interior of buildings. The glue used is usually not waterproof.

interior span A continuous beam or slab with supports that are continuous with neighboring spans.

interior stop In glazing, the removable molding or bead that holds the light or panel in place when it is on the interior, as contrasted to an exterior stop for exterior glazing.

interlace The intermixing of more than one complete field of scan lines. Instead of scanning each line sequentially from the top to the bottom, some lines are left as spaces and are filled in on the display by a subsequent field.

interlaced arches Arches where one passes over two openings; they consequently cut or intersect each other.

interlock In piling, a combination of grooves and projections at the side of the units of steel sheet pile for holding one pile to the adjacent piles.

interlocking joint A joint in ashlar in which a projection on one stone beds in a groove on the next one.

intermediate bend Any bend between the end bends.

intermediate girder Any girder between two outside girders.

intermediate rafter A common rafter.

intermediate shaft A shaft which is driven by one shaft and drives another.

intermediate sight In levelling, a staff reading which is neither a back sight nor a fore sight.

internal combustion engine A gasoline, natural gas or diesel powered engine in which the burning of a gas or vapor provides the energy which turns the wheels. Generally the burning takes place in a cylinder in which a piston is driven down by the increased gas pressure formed by burning. The latest types are jet engines, turbo-jets and rotary engines which do not have pistons or cylinders.

internal dormer A vertical door or window in a sloping roof within the general line of the roof.

internal force Stress.

internal friction This soil particle's resistance to sliding within the soil mass. For sand, the internal friction is dependent on the gradation, density and shape of the grain and is relatively independent of the moisture content. For a clay, internal friction will vary with the moisture content. *(see angle of internal friction)*

internal glazing Glazing inside walls. *(see interior glazed)*

internal honeycomb An internal check, not visible on the surface of lumber.

internal pressure Pressure inside a building which is a function of wind velocity and number and location of openings.

internal thread A thread on the inside or a part, such as the threads inside a pipe end; designed to accept threads on the outside of connector or another pipe. Also called inside thread.

internal vibration In concrete, the use of a vibrating element which can be inserted into the concrete at selected locations and is more generally applicable to in-place construction.

intern architect One pursuing a program of training-in-practice under the guidance of a practicing architect, with the objective of qualifying for registration as an architect.

interpile sheeting (sheathing) Horizontal sheeting, usually of wood, installed between underpinning piles and supported by the piles.

interpit sheeting (sheathing) The same as interpile sheeting but between concrete underpinning pits.

interpolate To estimate untested values which fall between tested values.

interrupted arch A pediment in the form of an arch with the central portion cut away.

interruptions Secondary cutters in auger drills.

intersection (1) The set of elements common to two sets, especially the set of points common to two geometric configurations. (2) A place or area where two or more things intersect, for example, two or more streets. (3) The crossing of a cruciform plan.

intersection angle A deflection angle.

interstice A small or narrow space between things or parts; crevice; crack.

interstice bin An interior bin formed by the exterior walls of three or more silos or bins; also called STAR BIN.

interstitial Of, forming, or occurring in interstices. Situated between the components of a structure.

interstitium (intersticium) The crossing in a building of cruciform plan.

intertie An intermediate horizontal member in a framed partition, to strengthen it at a door head or elsewhere between floor levels.

in the clear A term to describe the measurement of an unobstructed space as between the floor and beam soffit rather than between the floor and ceiling.

intrados (soffit) The under surface or interior curve of an arch or vault.

inverse square law Applies to a process where the intensity of radiation decreases as the square of the distance—that is if one went twice the distance, the intensity would be ¼.

invert The lowest visible surface; the

floor of a drain, sewer, tunnel, culvert or channel.

invert block A voussoir-shaped hollow tile built into the invert of a masonry sewer.

inverted arch In masonry, an arch where the keystone is located at the lowest point of the arch; used to distribute weight over a foundation.

inverted asphalt emulsion An emulsified asphalt in which the continuous phase is asphalt, usually a liquid asphalt, and the discontinuous phase is minute globules of water in relatively small quantities. This type of emulsion may also be either anionic or cationic.

inverted crown The fall, or pitch, from sides to center as in a driveway or road.

inverted display The transposition of the grey scale (i.e. black for white) in a CRT display.

inverted penetration A type of surface course on which the bituminous materials are first spread and then covered with stone chips, slag or gravel. The term surface treatment is often applied to this type of highway construction.

invert elevation The lower inside point of a pipe or sewer, at a given location and in reference to a bench mark.

invitation to bid A portion of the bidding requirements soliciting bids for a construction project.

invited bidders The bidders selected by the designer and the owner as the only ones from whom bids will be received.

involute A curve that could be described by the unwinding of a string from a cylinder.

ion That part of an electrolyte which moves to an electrode in electrolysis. Cations move to the cathode; anions move to the anode.

Ionic order A style of architecture developed by the Ionians. It is distinguished especially by the scroll which is the most important decorative feature of the capital which surmounts the columns.

ionizing radiation Radiant energy emitted by way of radioactive materials or X-ray devices.

Iowa lip curb Type of curb usually used on rural roads which is simply a triangular notch about three inches in depth and nine inches plus or minus from notch to shoulder.

Irish confetti *(slang)* Bricks.

Irish fan *(slang)* A shovel.

Irish mail *(slang)* A tunnel car with benches that is used to bring men out at the end of their shift.

iron **(1)** *(slang)* The contractor's heavy equipment. **(2)** A common but important and abundant metal. The pure metal has a white, lustrous appearance, does not harden appreciably on quenching and is strongly attracted by a magnet. It cannot be made magnetic except when containing carbon, or while an electric current is passed around it.

cast A blast-furnace product high in compressive strength. Its chief use is in parts that are readily and thus cheaply formed by casting, with occasional machining.

malleable Cast iron that has been put through an annealing process that gives it some ductility and some resistance to shock through bending or twisting. It cannot be forged or rolled.

wrought Pig iron that is puddled and rolled, never cast or melted; it is less dense and homogeneous, usually containing less than 0.23 percent carbon and from one percent to two percent slag. After puddling it is squeezed, hammered and rolled into muck bars. These bars when piled together, heated and rolled into plates, rounds, squares, etc., are known as merchant bars.

iron cement A mixture of iron turnings, sal ammoniac and sulfur used to join cast iron pipes and mend cracks in cast iron pipes.

iron driver *(see driver)*

iron expansion shield A type of shield used with an anchor bolt for securing wood structural parts to a masonry wall.

iron free glass A glass which minimizes internal absorption of heat, thus reducing the amount received by the solar absorber plate.

ironmongery Cast iron or wrought iron; hardware.

iron oxide A substance used in pigments both manufactured and natural; for example, Venetian red. Magnetite or a mixture of oxides make black or purple pigments. The umbers, siennas and ochres are oxides or hydrated oxides of a yellow to chestnut or dark brown color and were among the earliest pigments known and used by man.

iron pan *(slang)* Hardpan. A cemented or compacted and often clayey layer in soil that is impenetrable by roots.

iron sand, fine chilled A type of sand that is shot fed with water into a cut during the sawing of hard stone.

ironwork A term applied to the use of iron for ornamental purposes. Elaborately designed ornamentation in ironwork was used for hinges, door knockers and escutcheons in the architecture of the Middle Ages and is again in vogue.

irradiated hardwood A process wherein a hardwood floor is bonded at the molecular level with acrylic through the use of gamma radiation.

irregular coursed rubble Rubble walls built to courses of various depth.

irrigating head The flow for irrigation of a particular tract of land; the flow of water distributed at a single irrigation or in a single form lateral.

irrigation (1) Distribution of water to land for farming usually involving the digging of canals and building dams. (2) The disposal of sewage by spreading it over the land. *(see broad irrigation)*

isacoustic Equal in acoustic correction.

I-section A beam cross section consisting of top and bottom flanges connected by a vertical web.

isochromatic lines In photo-elastic stress analysis, colored streaks which

are lines of equal difference of principal stress.

isoclinic lines In photo-elasticity, or other studies of stress concentration, dark lines which join all points at which the principal stresses are parallel to the planes of polarization.

isocyanate plastic Thermoset plastics having good heat and electrical insulation properties but poor wear resistance. They are self-extinguishing and have maximum use temperatures of 140°F to 300°F; can be poured as a liquid and then expanded.

isodomun Masonry having courses of uniform thickness, the blocks being of equal length and the vertical joints being over the middle of the blocks of the course below.

isolated solar gain A type of passive solar heating system in which heat is collected in one area to be used in another (e.g., greenhouse or attic collector).

isolating membrane An underlay.

isolation An acoustical term used to describe sound privacy by reducing direct sound paths.

isolation joint A joint placed to separate concrete into individual structural elements or from adjacent surfaces.

isolator (link) A part of a circuit which can be removed to break the circuit when no current is flowing.

isometric A form of orthogonal perspective in which all three of the main dimensions are at the same inclination to the plane of project; it has no perspective.

isometric drawing A form of three-dimensional projection in which all of the principal planes are drawn parallel to corresponding established axes and at true dimensions. Horizontals are usually drawn at 30° from the normal horizontal axes; verticals remain parallel to the normal vertical axes.

isotherm Contours or lines depicting equal apparent temperatures on the display screen. On imaging scanners, these areas are electrically highlighted on the display as bright white.

isotherm thermogram   A picture of a thermal image showing areas of equal apparent temperature.

isothermal compression   Compression of air at constant temperature; a condition which is approached by using intercoolers between stages.

isothermal units   A unit of thermal measurement common to a particular IR system. It must be converted to temperature by correcting for instrument settings, detector output, emissitives, and ambient conditions.

isotropy   The behavior of a medium having the same properties in all directions, e.g., metal. Wood is not isotropic since it is much stronger along the grain than across the grain.

Italian tiling   (pan and roll tiles) Single-lap tiles which form a roof covering with two different kinds of tile; the curved over-tile and the flat trayshaped under-tile.

item   A term used to describe particular kinds of work to be performed or materials to be supplied under the contract plans and specifications.

ivory paper   *(see cream paper)*

ivorywood   White to pale yellow-brown from South America, sometimes with a slight greenish tinge; hard, heavy, tough and strong but not durable. It is used for cabinet and lathe work.

Izod test   A type of impact test in which a specimen is struck by swinging pendulum and the energy absorbed in the fracture is measured.

J jack
jct junction
jour journeyman
JP jet propulsion

jsts joists
jt/jnt joint
junc junction

J *(C.P.M.)* A symbol that describes the event at the head of an activity arrow.

J-bolt A bolt shaped like a letter J, used to grasp a structural member from the back side.

jacal A mud-plastered pole or wicker construction found in Mexico and among the Indians of southwestern U.S.A.

jack A portable mechanical device of varying design used to apply force to prestressing tendons, adjust elevation of forms or form supports, and raise weights small distances. The smallest jacks are operated by a screw and called screw jacks; larger jacks work by a hydraulic ram.

jack arch One having horizontal or nearly horizontal upper and lower surfaces; may also be called a flat or straight arch. The term is also used for any temporary arch roughly built and is sometimes called a French arch or Welsh arch. Much used before reinforced concrete was developed.

jack beam A beam used to support another beam or truss and to eliminate a column support.

jack boom A boom which supports sheaves between the hoist drum and the main bit; can usually be operated by one man.

jacked pile A pile forced into the ground by jacking against the building above it.

jacket (1) A covering of insulation, usually applied to exposed heating pipes. (2) Also used for cooling pipes and not necessarily exposed. Also used in concealed areas to prevent condensation.

jacketing Surrounding by a confined bath or stream of fluid for temperature control or heat absorption.

jack hammer (1) A device driven percussively by compressed air. (2) A pneumatically operated percussive rock drilling tool.

jacking conduit A method of providing an opening for drainage or other purposes underground, by cutting an opening ahead of the pipe and forcing the pipe into the opening by means of horizontal jacks.

jacking device The device used to stress the tendons for prestressed concrete; also, a device for raising a vertical slipform.

jacking dice Blocks, usually of five inch steel pipe filled with concrete, used for temporary fillers during jacking operations.

jacking force Temporary force exerted by the device which introduces tension into prestressing tendons.

jacking plate A steel plate placed on top of a pile during the jacking to transmit the load of the jack to the pile.

jacking stress The maximum stress occurring in a prestressed tendon during stressing.

jackknife (1) A tractor and trailer assuming such an angle to each other that the tractor cannot move forward. (2) The accidental raising, by the load, of a boom on a derrick.

jack lagging Timber bearing members used in building forms for odd shapes, especially arches.

jackleg (1) An outrigger post. (2) *(slang)* A worker who doesn't know what he's doing.

jack plane A bench plane, appropriately named for a beast of burden often called upon to do the hardest and roughest kind of work. The jack plane, likewise, is called upon to do the hardest and roughest work on a piece of timber as it first comes from the saw. This plane is the one used to true up the edges and rapidly prepare the rough surface of a board for the finer work of the smoothing planes.

jack rafter A short rafter of which there are three kinds: those between the plate and a hip rafter; those between the hip and valley rafters; and those between the valley rafters and the ridge board. Jack rafters are used especially in hip roofs.

jack rib A curved jack rafter used in a small dome roof.

jackscrew A mechanical device operated by a screw, used in lifting weights and for leveling work.

jack shaft A short drive shaft, usually connecting a clutch and transmission.

jack shore A telescoping, or otherwise adjustable, single post metal shore.

jack truss A truss used to support another truss or beam and to eliminate a column support.

Jacob's ladder A marine ladder of rope or chain with wooden or metal rungs.

jag A bundle of scrap steel used like a wrecking ball.

jagger A toothed chisel used for dressing a stone.

jalousies Window blinds or shutters with fixed or movable slats sloping upward from the outside to admit light and air, serving to exclude rain, water and sunlight; somewhat like a venetian blind.

jamb In building, the exposed lining of an opening, such as the vertical side posts used in the framing of a doorway or window. The jambs of a window outside the frame are called reveals.

jamb lining A board facing covering a jamb.

jamb posts (jamb stone) A post or stone forming a door jamb.

jamb-shafts Small shafts to doors and windows with caps and bases; when in the inside arris of the jamb of a window they are sometimes called esconsons.

jam riviter A riveting hammer with an air-operated telescopic casing for holding the hammer to the work.

Japan A resin varnish used chiefly as a drier in paints.

Japanning Painting with a black Japan which is stoved.

jars A tool in the churn drill string which contains slack to allow hammering upward to free a stuck bit.

jaspé Irregular stripes of two or more huse, shades or values of the same color used to produce a particular effect on the pile yarn of plain or evenly designed fabrics. Various jaspé effects can be produced by varying the twist of the yarn.

jaw In a clutch, one of a pair of toothed rings, the teeth of which face each other. One ring slides along its shaft to engage or disengage from the other.

jawab A building duplicating or matching another architecturally.

jaw crusher A fixed and a movable jaw widely spaced at the top and close at the bottom, with means to move one jaw toward and away from the other; used in crushing rock to specified sizes. Roughly the same duty as gyratory crushers.

jeep trailer A two-axle trailer which fits between truck and semi-trailer to increase load-carrying capacity.

Jeffcott tachometer A direct-reading tachometer.

jemmy A pinch bar about 15 inches long.

jenny British term for gin block.

Jenny Linde A type of window.

jerkinhead A roof form in which the top of a gable is cut off by a secondary slope forming a hip; the opposite of a gambrel roof.

jerry builder *(slang)* One who produces flimsy construction due to poor materials and workmanship.

jesting beam   A beam introduced into a structure for ornamental purposes only.

Jesus pin   *(slang)* A tiny hairpin shaped lockpin. So called because of the expletive used when it is dropped.

jet   **(1)** A pipe end or nozzle from which water, or water and compressed air, is emitted under pressure; the water emitted from the nozzle; to use such a jet to loosen the ground to facilitate the driving of a pile, or to loosen and suspend the material in an underpinning pile so that it can be removed by pumping. **(2)** A sprue or gate for the introduction of molten metal in the casting process.

jet drilling   A method of drilling rock with fuel which is injected with oxygen through a water-cooled pipe and burned within the hole.

jetting   **(1)** Drilling with high pressure water or air jets. **(2)** A method of sinking piles when a pile hammer is not practical due to locality. **(3)** Jet engines retired from flying service used in the USSR to propel excavated material by a sort of airborn hydraulic fill and to excavate in the same manner as giants; claimed to be highly economical.

jetty   **(1)** A portion of a building projecting beyond the parts below, whether corbeled or supported on brackets. **(2)** A dike built of piles, rock or other material, extending into a stream or into the sea at the mouths of rivers to induce scouring or bank building or for protection. **(3)** A deck on pilings at water's edge used for landing purposes.

jewel   A boss of glass in a leaded window.

jib   **(1)** The lifting arm of a crane or derrick. At the outer end the hoisting rope passes over a pulley. **(2)** The arm carrying the cutting chain of a power-operated chain saw. **(3)** The steel armature that holds a drifter on a jumbo drilling rig.

jib boom   An extension piece hinged to the upper end of a crane boom.

jib crane   **(1)** A crane with a jib, as compared to overhead traveling cranes or transporter cranes which usually have none. **(2)** A cantilevered boom or horizontal beam with hoist and trolley. This lifting machine may pick up loads in all or part of a circle around the column to which it is attached.

jib door   A door whose face is flush with the wall and decorated to be seen as little as possible.

jig   A clamp or guide used in shaping pieces of wood or metal to facilitate the assembly of duplicate pieces of construction.

jig saw   In woodworking, a type of saw with a thin, narrow blade to which an up-and-down motion is imparted either by foot power or by mechanical means. It is used for cutting sharper curves than those cut by a band saw.

jim   *(slang)* To spoil or to render unfit for use.

jimmer   A hinge of which the two leaves are inseparable; usually further described, as for example, cock's head jimmer.

jimmy   *(slang)* Refers to either GMC motor or truck.

jinnie wheel   A British term for gin block.

jitterbug   *(slang)* **(1)** A grate tamper for concrete. *(see tamper)* **(2)** A hand tool used to cause sand and cement grout to come to the surface of wet concrete when placing a slab.

job (jobsite)   **(1)** Terms commonly used to indicate the location of a construction project. **(2)** The whole of a work of construction, or some individual part of it; a piece of work. *(see project; work)*

job-average basis   A technique for determining the average dimensions or quantities of materials, by analysis of roof test cuts. The technique requires a minimum of three test cuts per roof area, plus one cut for each additional 10,000 square feet of roof area. Job-average basis is computed by dividing the sum of all measurements taken by the number of measurements taken. The result would describe the job-average for the quantity or dimension.

jobber (builder's handyman)   One semi-skilled to do any sort of building repairs such as bricklaying, plastering, painting, plumbing, carpentry, etc.

job captain Member of the designer's staff normally responsible, on a given project, for the preparation of drawings and their coordination with other documents.

job made Made on the building site.

jobsite *(see site; job)*

job superintendent *(see superintendent)*

Joe McGee *(slang)* An unpopular ironworker.

jog An offset; a change of direction in a surface.

joggle A projection or shoulder to receive the thrust of a brace; also, a key to projecting pin set in between two joining surfaces for the purpose of reinforcing the joint; or, a joint between two bodies so constructed by means of jobs or notches as to prevent their sliding past each other.

joggle piece A post shouldered like the foot of a king post to provide an abutment for a strut.

joggle post King post.

joggy *(slang)* A saw.

johnny ball *(slang)* A porcelain insulator.

Johnson bar *(slang)* A long pry bar.

joiner A craftsman in woodworking who constructs joints; usually a term applied to the workmen in shops who construct doors, windows and other fitted parts of a house or ship; a carpenter.

joiner's gauge A marking gauge.

joiner's hammer A hammer with a head with a striking face and a nail-pulling end.

joiner's laborer (carpenter's mate) A helper to a carpenter or joiner, who is known as a gluer-up if he prepares glue and joints.

joinery *(British)* The more intricate branches of carpentry; cabinetry or other fine woodwork.

joining Sometimes termed a jointing, denotes the juncture of two separate plaster applications usually within a single surface plane.

joint (1) The space between and the meeting of two or more building elements; the connection point. (2) In masonry, the space between units; to break joints, in masonry, to avoid continuous joints between units in successive courses. (3) In carpentry, the place where two or more surfaces meet; also, to form, or unite, two pieces into a joint; to provide with a joint by preparing the edges of two pieces so they will fit together properly when joined. (4) A gap or space between rocks. *(see rift)* (5) In steel sheet piling, a clutch.

joint bolt A handrail bolt.

joint box A cast-iron box built up around a joint formed between the end of one electrical cable and the beginning of the next. The wire armoring or lead sheathing is gripped by bolted clamps outside the box. The box may be filled with insulating compound after the joint is made.

joint, brazed (high temperature) A gas-tight joint obtained by the joining of metal parts with alloys which melt at temperatures higher than 1500 F but less than the melting temperature of the joined parts.

joint, brazed (low temperature) A gas-tight joint obtained by the joining of metal parts with metallic mixtures or alloys which melt at temperatures below 1500 F but above 1000 F.

jointer A metal tool about six inches (15 cm) long and from two to four and one-half inches (5 to 11 cm) wide and having shallow, medium or deep bits, cutting edges, ranging form $\frac{1}{8}$ inch to $\frac{3}{4}$ inch (5 to 20 mm) or deeper used to cut a joint partly through fresh concrete.

jointer plane A large bench plane used chiefly for long work and for final truing up of wood edges or surfaces for joining two pieces of wood; an iron or wood plane suitable for all kinds of plane work, and especially adaptable for truing large surfaces required in furniture making.

jointer saw A saw for cutting stone.

joint fastener A corrugated fastener.

joint filler (sealant) (1) A powder, often called spackle, that is usually mixed with water and used for joint treatment in gypsum-wallboard finish to provide a smooth surface. Also comes ready to use, in a clay-like consistency. *(see mud)* (2) Compressible strip material (bitumen, felt, cork, etc.) used as a spacer between precast concrete units, permitting them to expand or contract without developing serious compressive stress in the concrete. (3) Compressible material used to fill a joint to prevent the infiltration of debris and to provide support for sealants.

jointing Working the surface of mortar joints to give a finished face while green rather than raking them out and refilling them.

jointing compound A material like paste, paint or iron cement used to make a tight joint between steel or iron pipes.

jointing material A sheet material from which gaskets or washers can be cut to shape for insertion in the joints of flanged pipes, pumps, etc., to make them watertight; often rubber for cold water, and asbestos for steam.

jointing rule A long straight edge used with the jointer by bricklayers.

jointless flooring (composition flooring) Flooring, often epoxy based, which can be laid or poured without joints. In spite of the name, many jointless floors, particularly those containing cement, are best laid with joints about eight feet apart to allow for shrinkage.

joint, mechanical A gas-tight joint obtained by the joining of metal parts through a positive holding mechanical construction (such as flanged joint, screwed joint, flared joint).

joint reinforcement Steel wire, bar or prefabricated reinforcement which is placed in or on mortar bed joints.

joint rule A steel rule used by plasterers in forming the mitres at the junctions of cornice moldings. One end is formed at an angle of 45°.

joint sealant Material used to exclude water and solid foreign materials from joints.

joint, soldered A gas-tight joint obtained by the joining of metal parts

with metallic mixtures or alloys which melt at temperatures below 1000 F.

joint tape Paper or paper-faced cotton tape which is placed over the joints between wallboards.

joint venture A collaborative undertaking by two or more persons or organizations for a specific project or projects, having the legal characteristics of a partnership.

joint, welded A gas-tight joint obtained by the joining of metal parts in the plastic or molten state.

joist (1) A heavy piece of horizontal timber to which the boards of a floor, or the lath of a ceiling, are nailed. Joists are laid edgewise to form the floor support. They rest on the wall or on girders. (2) A horizontal structural member supporting deck from sheathing; usually rests on stringers or ledgers.

joist anchor A wall anchor.

joist and plank Pieces of lumber with nominal dimensions of two to four inches in thickness by four inches and wider, of rectangular cross section and graded with respect to their strength in bending when loaded either on the narrow face as a joist or on the wide face as a plank.

joist hanger A steel or iron stirrup used to support and align the ends of joists which are to be flush with the girder.

Jonesboro A pinkish gray biotite granite of Maine, with a medium coarse grain.

Joosten process Injection of two separate solutions, calcium chloride after sodium silicate, through pipes driven or jetted into the soil. The two solutions meet in the ground react to form a gel, strengthen the soil and make it watertight.

joule The unit of energy in the meter-kilogram-second system of units equal to the work done by a force of magnitude of one newton; the point at which the force applied is displaced one meter in the direction of force.

Joule's equivalent Mechanical equivalent of heat.

Joule-Thomson effect The ratio of

temperature change to pressure change (*dT/dp*) of an actual gas in a process of throttling or expansion without doing work or interchanging heat.

journal That part of a rotating shaft or axle which turns in a load-supporting bearing.

journeyman A skilled worker, competent in his trade, who has usually served as an apprentice to learn his skill.

joy stick *(slang)* Truck driver's term for the gear shift.

jubilee wagon *(British)* A tipping wagon.

judas An inspection panel in an entrance door.

juicer *(slang)* An electrician.

jumbo (1) A number of drills, or drillers, mounted on a mobile carriage for drilling tunnels in rock. (2) Traveling support for forms, commonly used in tunnel work.

jumbo brick A brick of larger than usual size either intentionally or by mistake.

jumper (1) In snecked or squared rubble, a stretcher which covers more than one cross joint. (2) A temporary electrical connection made of a round circuit. (3) A mushroom-shaped part of a domestic water tap, whether for sink, basin or bath; the washer fits on the lower face of the mushroom disc. The stalk of the mushroom points upwards into the screw-down part of the tap. When the tap opens, the force of the water lifts the jumper into the guide, raising the washer with it. (4) *(slang)* A short length of wire used to temporarily short out electrical terminals or circuits.

jumping jack *(slang)* A hand tamper with the motor in the head.

jumping shoe A big bracket in which

the foot of the boom in a guy derrick is placed when the ironworkers are jumping the derrick to the next tier of steel.

jumping up *(slang)* Upsetting.

jump join A forge weld made by upsetting the ends of two bars prior to welding them.

jumpover *(see return offset)*

junction A drain pipe with a socket to take a branch.

junction box A box which covers the joints between the ends of conductors in house wiring. It also joins up ends of the metal sheaths.

junction chamber A converging section of a sewer used to facilitate the flow from one or more sewers into a main sewer.

junction manhole A manhole at the junction of two or more sewers.

junction point A point of a curve where the circular part joins the non-circular part of either a straight or transition curve.

junior beam Light weight structural steel sections rolled to a full I-beam shape.

Jurgenson formula Formula used to determine shear strength of moist soils based on unit pressure and depth of stratum.

jurisdictional dispute Disagreement between two or more labor unions over which union shall do certain work.

jut in building, a term applied to any part of a structure which projects outward, as a jut window.

jute Derived from fibrous plant native to India and the Far East. It is shredded and spun into yarn, which may be used as the backing yarn for woven carpets, or woven into a backing fabric for tufted carpets.

K Kalium

k kilo, knot

Ka cathode

kc kilocycle

kcal kilocalorie

kc/s kilocycles per second

KD kiln dried

KDN knocked down

kg keg, kilogram

KIT kitchen

kl kiloliter

KLF kips per lineal foot

km kilometer

kmps kilometers per second

kn knot

Kr krypton

kv kilovolt

kvar kilovar

kw kilowatt

kwhr/kwh kilowatt hour

k Coefficient of permeability (in soils) units ft/min, in/hr, in/day, etc.

kva Kilovolt-ampere. Approximately ⁷/₁₀ of a kilowatt.

Kalamein door A fireproof door with a metal covering.

Kaolin A rock, generally white, consisting primarily of clay minerals of the Kaolinite group, composed principally of hydrous aluminum silicate, of low iron content, used as raw material in the manufacture of white cement.

Kaolinite A common clay mineral having the general formula $Al2 (Si_2O_5) (OH_4)$; the primary constituent of Kaolin.

kaplan turbine A propeller type water turbine having blades of a pitch that can be automatically varied with the load to increase efficiency.

keblah (kibleh) The point in a mosque designating the direction in which Mecca lies.

keckle To cover something or protect it by winding it with wire, rope or cable.

keel arch The inflected or ogee arch.

keel molding A molding having a section resembling the keel of a ship, two ogee curves meeting in an arris.

Keene's cement A cementitious material used principally in finish coats as gauging for lime putty. Capable of producing a very hard, smooth surface. Keene's Cement consists of gypsum, calcined to a point where all but 0.1% to 1% of the water of crystallization has been removed, and compounded with an accelerator. Also termed anhydrous calcined gypsum.

keep That part of a medieval castle, often circular, used as its chief defense.

keeper The receiving member of a lock bolt or latch.

keeping the gauge Maintaining the spacing of the brick or masonry courses; often four per foot height for a standard brick of 2¾ inch depth.

keeping the perpends Laying bricks, stones, slates or tiles accurately so that the cross joints, perpends, or the visible edges of slates and tiles in alternate courses are in the same vertical line.

Kellem's Grip A wrap-around cable grip, used to support wires.

kellstone In architecture, a stucco with crushed finish.

kelly A square or fluted pipe which is turned by a drill rotary table while it is free to move up and down in the table, with its earth auger attached on the end.

kelly ball An apparatus used for indicating the consistency of fresh concrete, consisting of a cylinder six inches (15 cm) in diameter with a hemispherically shaped bottom and handle weighing 30 pounds (14 kg) and a stirrup to guide the handle and serve as a reference for measuring depth of penetration. *(see ball test)*

kelly ball test *(see ball test; kelly ball)*

kelly crowd A mechanism to keep the kelly bearing down into the ground.

kentledge (cantledge) Loading to give stability to a crane, provide a reaction over a jack, push down a plate in the plate bearing test, or to test a bearing pile or a caisson. Scrap metal, large stones, tanks filled with water, or any other convenient material may be used.

Kentucky bluestone A light bluish-gray sandstone, hard and durable.

keratin A retardant for plaster of Paris, obtained from horns, hoofs, nails, and scales of animals.

kerb British equivalent of curb.

kerb form (kerb tool) *(see curb form; curb tool)*

kerf (kerfing) The process of cutting grooves or kerfs across a board or beam to make it flexible for bending. Kerfs are cut down to about two-thirds of the thickness of the piece to be bent. An example is found in the bullnose of a stair which frequently is bent by the process of kerfing; also a cut or notch in a member such as a rustication strip to avoid damage from swelling of the wood and permit easier removal; also used in stone.

kerfed beam A beam cut with several saw-cuts that allows it to be bent.

kern A section core, as for a test sample.

kern area The area located within the kern distance from the centroid of a footing as seen in plan.

kern distance The ratio of the section modulus of the cross section about the axis perpendicular to the kern distance, divided by the area of the cross section.

kerosene value (kerosene number) The amount of kerosene absorbed or taken in by a piece of felt; used as a measure of the ability of the felt to absorb saturant asphalt.

Kessener brush A metal brush, cylindrical in shape, which is used to promote circulation and provide oxygen in the activated sludge process, or in aerated ponds.

Kesternich test Simulates acid rain conditions by subjecting samples to a sulfur dioxide atmosphere at 140 degrees F.

kettle The tank or container in which asphalt is stored for use on the roofing machine; also an open vessel for melting glue or holding paint.

kevel A strong piece of wood used to secure a rope's end.

key **(1)** The removable operating member of a lock. **(2)** A wedge cross-reinforcing a miter joint or locking a tenon. **(3)** A wedge-shaped floor board. **(4)** A roughened surface that receives glued veneer. **(5)** The plaster or mortar extruded behind lath which, when hard, serves to hold the plaster in place. **(6)** A sinkage in tile or terra cotta to engage mortar.

key block Keystone.

key course A course of stones used in place of a keystone at the crown of a wide arch.

key drop An escutcheon cover.

keyed **(1)** Fastened or fixed in position in a notch or other recess, as forms become keyed into the concrete they support. **(2)** A dowel which is grooved to allow air and excess glue to be forced out.

keyed beam A beam with a lap joint into which joggles have been cut in each member. Keys are driven into these holes to increase the bending strength of the joint.

keyed joint Concave pointing of a mortar joint.

keyed mortise and tenon In carpentry, a tusk tenon.

keyhole saw A small cutting tool with a tapered blade used for cutting keyholes, fretwork and other similar work.

keyhole slot A slot enlarged at one end to allow entrance of a chain or bolt that can then be held by the narrow end.

keying A process used for strengthening miter joints.

keying-in Bonding a brick or block wall to another already built.

key plan A small plan showing the position of the units in a layout.

key plate Escutcheon.

keystone The uppermost and last set stone of an arch, which completes it and locks its members together. It is usually wedge-shaped.

key switch An electric switch operated by a removable key rather than by a button or tumbler.

key valve A valve operated by a removable key rather than by a fixed handle.

keyway (1) A recess or groove in one lift or placement of concrete which is filled with concrete of the next lift giving shear strength to the joint; also called a key. (2) A square-edged lengthwise slot in a shaft or hub.

kibble A bucket used to raise dirt, rock, water, men and tools from a shaft.

kick (1) The raised fillet on a brickmaster's mold or pallet which forms the frog in the brick. (2) The difference in pitch between patent glazing and the surrounding roof.

kick lift A jacking wedge used to elevate or shift gypsum board into proper nailing position on the wall during the application procedure.

kick-out A lower downspout section used to direct water away from a wall.

kicker (1) A wood block or board attached to a formwork member in a building frame or formwork to make the structure more stable. (2) In formwork it acts as a haunch. (3) Cleat. (4) (slang) Admixture.

kicking piece A short timber nailed to a waling to absorb the thrust of a raking shore.

kick off Starting point of pipeline.

kickouts Accidental release or failure of a shore or brace.

kick plate (kicking plate) A metal plate, or strip, placed along the lower edge of a door, to prevent the marring of the finish by shoe marks.

kick strip (see kicker)

kidding Faggoting.

kill (1) Cut off electrical current from a circuit. (2) Stop an engine. (3) To cover the knots in wood to prevent resin from bleeding through later coats of paint.

killesse A gutter, groove or channel.

kiln A furnace or oven for drying, charring, hardening, baking, calcining, sintering or burning various materials; a chamber used for drying lumber. (see steam-curing room)

kiln bedding The degree of filling by the load in a rotary kiln, normally 3 to 10 percent of the free cross section.

kiln, cement A kiln in which the ground and proportioned raw mix is dried, calcined and burned into clinker at a temperature of 2600° to 3000°F (1420 to 1650C); can be of the rotary, shaft, fluid bed or traveling grate type; fuel may be coal, oil or gas.

kiln department The department of a cement plant which includes the kilns with all auxiliaries (feeders, drives, coolers, dust collectors, burner's platform, fans, dampers, and fuel injection device).

kiln-dried Said of lumber which has been freed of excess moisture by heating in a kiln instead of open air.

kiln gun Special industrial gun used for shooting down clinker rings or for breaking up large clinker balls in rotary kilns.

kiln hood Refractory-lined steel plate housing around discharge end of rotary kiln, furnished with openings for fuel pipe, radiation pyrometers, television cameras, observation openings, and cleanout and access doors.

kiln inclination The lengthwise slope in a vertical plane of a rotary kiln from feed end to discharge end; stated in inches per foot (e.g. ½ in. per ft), or in percent (such as 4 percent).

kiln insulation Low heat transmission material, placed between kiln shell and refractory lining to minimize heat loss.

kiln lining A layer of refractory, brick or concrete, placed inside a rotary kiln to protect the steel shell against heat and abrasion.

kiln paint Heat-resistant paint sometimes applied to outside of rotary kilns for protection, and to reduce heat loss.

kiln pier Concrete or steel support for rotary kiln, one pier located under each set of supporting rollers for the kiln tires.

kiln quadrant Cross-plates installed in the feed end of a rotary kiln to divide the load into several streams for increased heat transfer.

kiln run Brick or structural clay tile from one kiln which have not been sorted or graded for size, burning or color variation.

kiln seal Adjustable plates or rings installed around feed end or discharge end of rotary kiln for prevention of infiltration of air.

kiln shell The cylindrical outer mantle of a rotary kiln made of steel plate. Shipped in sections and riveted or welded together during erection. Rarely equipped with stiffener rings to maintain cylindrical shape.

kiln speed Speed of rotation of rotary kiln stated in revolutions per hour (rph), less frequently in revolutions per minute.

kilo A prefix meaning 1000 times; for example, a kilogram is 1000 grams. Kilo is also an abbreviation for kilogram.

kiloampere One thousand amperes.

kilovolt One thousand volts.

kilowatt (kw) An electrical unit of work or power; equal to one thousand watts, 1.34 horsepower, and 1.18 kilovoltampere (kva). The kilowatt-hour is usually the unit by which electrical energy is sold.

kinematic viscosity Describes the flow properties of liquids. Units of kinematic viscosity are called strokes. The greater the number of strokes, the thicker the liquid.

kinetic energy The energy of a moving body due to its weight and motion, equal to $Wv/2g$ foot-pound where W is the weight in pounds, v its speed in feet per second, and g is 32.2 feet per second, each second.

kinetic head *(see velocity head)*

king bolt A vertical tie rod replacing the king post of a truss.

king closer A portion of a brick greater than a half-length, to complete a dimensional course.

king pile In a wide, strutted sheet-pile excavation, a long pile driven at the strut spacing in the center of the trench before it is dug. King piles have the length of the main timbers from side to side since the main timbers from each side bear on the king piles. A guide pile.

kingpin (king pin) A vertical swivel or hinge pin usually supported at both top and bottom.

king post In a roof truss, the central upright piece against which the rafters abut and which supports the tie beam.

king tower *(see crane tower)*

Kingwood stone Trade name for a hard West Virginia quartzite, medium to coarse in grain and varying from antique yellow and light buff to a rather purplish buff; ground mass is white quartz, and color is caused by innumerable brown spots of completely oxidized iron; used for heavy masonry.

kiosk A small structure, generally polygonal or circular in construction, with open sides, and surmounted by a dome-shaped or tent-shaped roof carried on pillars; used as a bandstand, summer house, etc.

kip (1) A kilopound, 1000 pounds (454 kg), which constitutes a convenient unit of force for use in structural calculations. (2) *(slang)* A bunkhouse on a construction job.

kiss marks Marks where bricks have touched in the kiln.

kite A sheet of Kraft paper applied to the sheet of coated roofing in production as a means of measuring the weight of surfacing granules applied to the roofing.

kite winder The central of three winders turning a right angle so called because in plan it looks like a kite.

klaw notch *(slang)* To notch wood for adjoining lumber, wiring, etc. with the claw end of a hammer.

Knapen system Patented method of drying out damp walls by drilling holes into them from outside at about the internal floor level. The holes do not pass completely through the wall and are left open so as to drain outwards and be kept ventilated.

knapping hammer A hammer for shaping stones.

knee (1) A convex length of handrail; the reverse of a ramp, which is concave. (2) A timber following its natural bent, usually employed as a brace; in formwork, etc., it acts as a haunch. (3) A sharp right-angle bend in a pipe.

knee board A tool used to kneel on, while finishing concrete.

knee brace Brace between horizontal and vertical members in a building frame or formwork to make the structure more stable; in formwork it acts as a haunch.

kneeler (1) In masonry, a stone cut to provide a change in direction as in the curve of an arch, or a stone built into the lower end of a gable to support its coping. (2) Pitching laid to protect a bank from erosion divided into panels to localize damage. The boundaries of the panels are reinforced-concrete beams sunk deep into the bank.

knife The dirt-cutting edge of a digging machine.

knifing Procedure in which a knife is used to gradually cut the floor covering to fit the room.

knitting A method of fabricating a carpet in one operation, as in weaving. Surface and backing yarns are looped together with a stitching yarn on machines with three sets of needles.

knob A projecting handle, usually round or oval, operating a latch. *(see knot)*

knob-and-tube wiring An early system of electrical wiring, without conduits, in which the insulated wires were supported on porcelain knobs and through porcelain tubes in traversing timbers.

knobbing (**knobbling; skiffling**) Rough dressing in the quarry by removing protruding humps from stone.

knock-outs Stamped sections of ducts on electrical boxes which can be knocked out so fittings or wires can be installed in the duct or box.

knocked down Construction material, as for a house, which is complete in its various parts, delivered to a job unassembled but cut and ready for assembling.

knocker (1) A hinged striker on a door, usually of metal. (2) A detonating cap used in blasting.

knockings Stone chips that are smaller than spalls.

knocking up Restoring stiffened lime mortar to a plastic condition by working without the easier process of adding more water.

knock over Method of fastening one duct into another duct.

knot (knob) (1) A cluster of leaves or flowers, as a terminal of a label or the boss at the intersection of vaulting ribs. (2) Variation in grain of wood surface where interrupted by a branch of the tree. (3) The intertwining of the end of a rope or cable.

knot brush A thick brush with its bristles or fibers bunched in round or oval shapes; often used for distempering.

knot cluster A group of two or more knots such that the wood fibers are deflected around the entire grouping.

knothole Void produced when a knot drops out of veneer.

knotting Shellac dissolved in methylated spirit, used as a local sealer over knots in new wood so that it can be painted without danger of the knots bleeding sap through the paint. Other quick-drying compositions are also used.

knotty score A ragged cut edge.

knuckle That part of a hinge consisting of holes through which the pin passes.

knuckle buster *(slang)* A wrench.

knuckle joint The curb joint in a mansard roof.

knuckle soldered joint A right-angled joint made between two lead pipes.

Ko-Cal Asphalt windrow elevator.

Kraftcord A tightly twisted yarn made

from plant fiber, used as a backing yarn for carpeting.

Kraft paper A type of strong brown paper used extensively for wrapping purposes, and as a building paper.

K-rail (barrier rail) Concrete barrier in the shape of an inverted V used as a barricade along high speed traffic lanes.

Kuster dyeing Piece-dyeing technique that allows uniform and continuous dyeing in great quantities. Named after Kuster dye machine.

Kutter formula Used to determine quantity of flow of drainage in open channels.

K-value The thermal conductivity of a material. *(see U-value)*

Kyan's process In woodworking, a method of preserving wood by infusing the timber with bichloride of mercury; to kyanize.

l   length, liter, lumen

L   lambert, large

lam   laminated

L&CM   lime and cement mortar

L&L   latch and lock

L&O   load and oil (paint)

L&P   lath and plaster

lat   latitude, lattice

lav   lavatory

lb/lbs   pound, pounds

lbr   lumber, load backrest

LCL   less-than-carload lot

LCM   least common multiple

ld   loadldg   loading, landing

LE   leading edge

LECA   light expanded clay aggregate

lf   lightface, low frequency, lineal foot

lg   large, long

LG   liquid gas

lgt   light

lin   linear, lineal

lino   linoleum

LL&B   latch, lock and bolt

LM   lime mortar

LP/LPG   liquid petroleum, liquid petroleum gas

LR   living room

LS   lump sum

LT   long ton

ltd   limited

ltg   lighting

ltr   lighter

lts   lights

lub   lubricant

lvd   louvered

LW   low water

LWM   low-water mark

L.A. Abrasion   Test for aggregate to determine the resistance to abrasion using a Los Angeles Testing Machine.

label   (1) A molding or dripstone over a door or window, especially one which extends horizontally across the top of the opening and vertically downward for a certain distance at the edges, also called label mold or hood mold. (2) Any written, printed or graphic material displayed on or affixed to containers of hazardous chemicals. A label should contain identity of the hazardous chemical; appropriate hazard warnings; and name and address of the chemical manufacturer, importer, or other responsible party.

label stop   An ornamental terminal of a drip mold; a knot or knob.

labor and material payment bond   A contractor's bond in which a surety guarantees to the owner that the contractor will pay for labor and materials used in the performance of the con-

tract. The claimants under the bond are defined as those having direct contracts with the contractor or any subcontractor.

laboratory   The testing laboratory of the owner/agency or any other testing laboratory which may be designated by the engineer.

labor constant   The amount of labor required to perform a specific unit of work.

laborer   A workman qualified for only unskilled or semi-skilled work.

lac   a resinous exudation of an East Indian insect, used as a base of shellacs, varnishes and lacquers.

laced column   A column built using lacing from several members.

laced fall   A line reeved through multi-sheaved pairs of blocks or pulleys to get a big mechanical advantage.

laced valley   A valley formed without a valley gutter. A wide board is fixed in the valley, on which tiles of 1½ times the normal width are placed. The two slopes intersect sharply and do not blend into each other as in the swept valley.

lacing (1) small boards or laths that prevent dirt from entering an excavation through spaces between sheeting or lagging planks; horizontal brace between shoring members. (2) A course of brick in a wall of rubble; a bonding course between brick courses of an arch. (3) The distribution steel of a reinforced concrete slab.

lacing course A course of bricks, stones or tiles laid together to strengthen a wall. Also a course of upright bricks or deep stones which cuts through two or more arch rings and bonds them together.

lacquer A glossy finish which dries rapidly by evaporation. Modern Lacquers are distinguished from varnish and enamel by being based on cellulose compounds.

lacuna (1) A depression in a finished surface, such as for inlay. (2) A sunken panel in a soffit or ceiling.

lacunaria Panels or coffers in a ceiling, in the soffit of a cornice, etc.

ladder (1) a structure for climbing up or down that consists of two long sidepieces joined at intervals by crosspieces. (2) The digging boom assembly in a hydraulic dredger or chain and bucket ditcher.

ladder ditcher A machine that digs ditches by means of buckets on a chain that travels around a boom.

ladder jack scaffold (1) A light duty scaffold supported by brackets attached. (2) Light scaffold used for painting and other similar work.

ladderman A man who works the ropes which pass over the head of a pile frame; works with a topman and hammerman to form a team.

ladder scraper Similar to a regular scraper with exception of a conveyor loading device to load the bowl. Usually these machines are smaller and do not require push Cats for loading purposes. They are also referred to as paddle wheels.

ladkin (latterkin) A wooden tool used for opening the cames of leaded windows.

lag (1) Delay in one action following another. (2) To install lagging or increase the diameter of a drum. (3) To wrap hot pipes or tanks to reduce heat losses.

lag bolt A large pointed screw which is driven into wood by turning the square head with a spanner. Part of the hole must be drilled for it.

lagging (1) designates heavier sheathing used in underground work to withstand earth pressure, etc. In a tunnel, planking placed against the dirt or rock walls and ceiling outside the ribs. (2) The surface or contact area of a drum or flat pulley, especially a detachable surface or one of special composition. (3) Boards fastened to the back of a shovel for blast protection. (4) Temporary support for the masonry of an arch or vault.

lagging, split Drum lagging made in two pieces to allow changing it without dismantling the drum.

lag screw A heavy wood screw with a square head. Since there is no slot in the head, the screw must be tightened down with a wrench; *(British)* a coach screw.

laitance (1) A layer of weak and nondurable material containing cement and fines from aggregates, brought by bleeding water to the top of overwet concrete, the amount of which is generally increased by overworking or overmanipulating concrete at the surface, by improper finishing or by job traffic. This condition also exists in over-trowelled mortar. (2) The soft water-laden concrete on the top three or four inches of an underwater pour of concrete.

lake asphalt Native asphalt occurring as surface deposits in natural depressions of the earth's crust.

lake dwelling Primitive dwelling of those who built upon piles over the water.

lake sand Sand consisting predominantly of fine, rounded particles.

Lally column Trade name for a cylindrically-shaped steel member, sometimes filled with concrete; used as a support for girders or other beams.

lambert Unit of brightness; the average brightness of any surface emitting or reflecting one lumen per square centimeter.

lamb's tongue A molding combining a small ovolo and a fillet, as in wood muntins; the fillet was originally a long pointed section.

Lamella roof A large-span vault built of wooden, concrete or metal members joined by bolts or other means, connected in a diamond pattern. Patented by a German engineer in 1925.

laminar flame Rotary kiln flame, all parts of which flow essentially parallel and in the same direction. Mixing occurs by molecular diffusion only. Generally long and low temperature.

laminar flow In laminar flow, particles of a substance move in parallel layers without the layers mixing with each other.

laminar velocity The speed in a particular channel for a certain liquid, below which streamline flow always occurs and above which the flow may be streamline or turbulent.

laminate (1) Impregnation of many layers of paper, textile or veneer with a synthetic resin and compression of them at high temperature to make a sheet of durable, strong material. (2) To build up from sheets glued together, generally with resin glues, such as the construction of plywood.

laminated Any type of construction built up out of thin parallel sheets or plates, which are fastened together with glue, cement or other similar adhesive. This method eliminates cross-grain wood and provides strength, especially on thin curved members.

laminated arches Arched rafters formed by nailing or gluing thin strips of wood together.

laminated fiber wallboard Fiber board made in thin layers cemented together. It is used for panelling walls, ceilings, etc. and is made with a surface which is smooth or pebbled, painted or prepared for painting.

laminated insulation Several layers of insulation, sometimes of different materials, bonded together in the most effective order.

laminated joint A combed joint.

laminated lead sheet A weather-resistant covering for walls, consisting of thin layers of lead glued to other material.

laminated plastic Sheets of paper or textile, soaked with a synthetic resin, sandwiched between layers of the resin to make a stiff board with glossy-surfaced covering; e.g. Formica.

laminated wood Wood built up of plies or laminations that have been joined either with glue or with mechanical fasteners. Usually, the plies are too thick to be classified as veneer and the grain of all plies is parallel.

laminating compound A cementitious material (usually regular joint compound) used to adhere two or more layers of gypsum board together.

laminator A distributor, fabricator of faced fiberglass blanket insulation products for metal buildings.

lammie A brick swelled out of shape in the kiln.

lamphole A British term for a small shaft built over the center of a sewer so that a lamp can be lowered into it. A man at a manhole can look along the sewer boards towards the light and see whether there is any obstruction in the flow or damage to the sewer.

lanai The Hawaiian veranda or terrace.

lancet The sharply pointed Gothic arch or window. It is commonly formed by a radius equal to the span of the opening and struck from both sides on the springing line; the springing line may be far above the impost line.

land A backfurrow.

landing A platform in a flight of stairs between two stories; the terminating or the changing of the direction of a stairway.

landing, elevator That portion of a floor, balcony, or platform used to receive and discharge passengers or freight.

landing, bottom terminal The lowest landing served by the elevator which is equipped with a hoistway door and hoistway door locking device which permits egress from the hoistway side.

landing, top terminal The highest landing served by the elevator which is equipped with a hoistway door and hoistway-door locking device which permits egress from the hoistway side.

landing, moving walk The stationary area at the entrance to or exit from a moving walk or moving walk system.

landing newel A post at the landing point of a stair supporting the handrail.

landing tread A term used when referring to the front end of a stair landing. The method of construction usually provides the front edge with a thickness and finish of a stair tread while the back has the same thickness as the flooring of the landing.

landing zone A zone extending from a point eighteen inches below a landing to a point eighteen inches above the landing.

land leveler A towed scraper with a bottomless bucket centrally mounted in a long frame; used chiefly in agricultural and highway grading.

land plaster A term used to describe coarsely ground natural gypsum used agriculturally as a soil conditioner.

land reclamation Gaining land from the sea or from a marsh by dumping of dredged mud or other material on an enclosure and then pumping water out of the enclosed area.

landscape architecture The design, planning or management of the land, arrangement of natural and manmade elements thereon through application of cultural and scientific knowledge with concern for resource conservation to the end that the resultant environment serves a useful and enjoyable purpose.

landslide A sliding down of soil on a slope because of an increase of load due to rain, new building, etc.; or a removal of support at the base due to cutting away of earth.

land survey A survey made to determine the lengths and directions of boundary lines and the area of the tract bounded by these lines; or a survey made to establish the positions of the boundary lines on the ground. *(see boundary survey; survey)*

land surveyor (topographical surveyor) A person who measures land and buildings for mapping. Most engineers, structural, civil or mechanical, can act as surveyors since designing requires a knowledge of surveying.

land tie A tie-rod holding sheet pile or retaining wall to a buried deadman or stay pile.

land tile Porous clay pipe with open, butt, joints. This pipe is laid end to end with a small opening between pieces to allow easy water seepage.

land use In urban planning, a division of available land into categories such as residential, industrial, commercial, recreational, public, etc.

lang lay (Lang's lay) A wire rope with strands twisted in the same direction as the wires. This type of rope can only be used for hoisting a guided load because it spins and loses its twist when hoisting a free bucket. It wears less than a rope of ordinary lay.

Langley A unit of measurement of solar radiation. This is the manner in which most meteorological stations report solar radiation received on a horizontal surface at ground level. One Langley, named for American astronomer S. P. Langley, equals one calorie of radiation energy per square centimeter per minute. This is equivalent to 220 Btus per sq. ft. per hour.

lantern (1) A superstructure on a roof, a dome, or a tower, glazed at the sides and sometimes without its own floor. (2) In a centrifugal pump, a hollow casing on the engine side of the pump body.

lap (1) The length by which one bar or sheet of fabric reinforcement overlaps another. It is equal to the grip length. **(2)** To overlap one surface with another, as in shingling, and the actual length of such overlap. **(3)** To place a coat of paint or varnish beside another and over its edge so as to make an invisible joint. **(4)** In paving, the same principle as paint.

lap cement An asphaltic material used to cement or stick the seams of two sheet of roofing. *(see sealing compound)*

lap joint The overlapping of two pieces of wood or metal. In wood working, such a uniting of two pieces of board is produced by cutting away one-half the thickness of each piece. When joined, the two pieces fit into each other so that the outer faces are flush. The two pieces may be welded, bolted or riveted together. Halvings is a development of the lap joint.

lapped Overlapped and fitted together.

lapped tenons Two tenons which enter a mortise from opposite ends and lap within it.

lapping The overlapping of reinforcing steel bars, welded wire fabric or expanded metal so that there may be continuity of tensile stress in the reinforcing when the concrete member is subjected to flexural or tensile loading.

lap siding Clapboard. *(see siding, beveled)*

lap splice A connection of reinforcing steel made by lapping the ends of the bars.

lap weld To weld overlapping edges.

larch, European (1) A tree found throughout northern Europe; in England it is an important softwood. **(2)** A native of Montana, Idaho, Washington, Oregon and southeastern Canada; the wood splits easily, is heavy, strong and stiff; it is frequently logged with Douglas fir and sold as Larch fir.

Larder British equivalent of pantry; originally, a room in which meat was hung.

large calorie A kilogram calorie, equivalent to 3.97 Btu.

large knot In woodworking, a sound knot measuring more than 1½ inches in diameter. *(see sound knot)*

large-panel construction A pre-fab building method, first used in the USSR, consisting of reinforced concrete panels one or two stories high; sometimes made of lightweight insulating concrete.

larmier The corona, or, by extension, any drip member.

Larnite A mineral; beta dicalcium silicate (Ca2SiO4); occurs naturally at Scawt Hill, Northern Ireland, and artificially in slags and as a major constituent of portland cement.

larry *(slang)* **(1)** A mortar hoe. **(2)** A small truck used to push tunnel mucking cars. **(3)** Fluid mortar. *(see hair hook)*

larrying (larrying up) *(slang)* Using fluid mortar so that the bricks are slid into position and not laid; mortar is then poured in to fill the vertical joints.

lashing (whip; bond) A short length of fiber or steel rope for tying scaffold timbers.

latch A catch for a door, usually a pivoted arm, the outer end of which engages a slot. When the door is closed, it engages by a spring with a key being turned.

latent heat The change in heat content that occurs with a change in phase and without change in temperature; the heat stored in the material during melting or vaporization. Latent heat is recovered by freezing a liquid or by condensing a gas.

lateral A small irrigation canal.

lateral movement Horizontal movement of a structure, earth, sheeting or bracing.

lateral pressure The horizontal component of the force due to a wedge of earth and surcharge, if any, moving or tending to move downward along its natural cleavage plane.

lateral reinforcement *(see reinforcement, lateral)*

lateral sewer A sewer which discharges into a branch or other sewer and has no other common sewer tributary to it.

lateral shift　*(see heave)*

lateral support　The means whereby walls are braced either vertically or horizontally by columns, pilasters or crosswalls or by floor or roof constructions.

latest event occurrence time　*(C.P.M.)* The deadline by which time an event must be completed if the project is not to be delayed.

latest finish date　*(C.P.M.)* The latest point in time by which all work must be done on an activity if the project is not to be delayed.

latest start date　*(C.P.M.)* The latest possible point in time by which an activity must be started if the project is not to be delayed.

latex　A milky, rubbery fluid found in several seed plants, today mostly synthetic, used to seal the back of carpets and for lamination. May be used on tufted or woven carpets.

latex emulsions　Dispersions in water of rubber or one of many synthetic resins; the best known is polyvinyl acetate (PVA).

latex paints　Water-base paints, sometimes called 'vinyl' or 'acrylic' paints; cleanup and thinning are done with soap and water.

Latex - portland cement grout　Combines portland cement grout with a special latex additive to make a less rigid, less permeable grout than regular portland cement.

Latex - portland cement mortar　A mixture of portland cement, sand and special latex additives used for bonding tile to back-up material. It is less rigid than portland cement mortar.

lath　In building, a term applied to a strip of wood or metal usually about 1½ inches in width, ⅜ inches in thickness and four to eight feet in length. Used as a foundation for plastering, slating and tiling.

lath and plaster membrane　A thin slab of lath and plaster including any integral supporting and stiffening members. A term describing lath and plaster as a unit of structure.

lathe　A mechanical device used in the process of producing circular work, for wood or metal turning.

lathe work　In either woodworking or in metal work, the lathe work includes practically all branches of production by turning or boring which commonly is done in the lathe.

lath hammer (claw hatchet; shingling hatchet)　A plaster's hammer for nailing lath. It has an ax edge and a hammer face with the ax side being notched near the handle to form a claw for pulling.

lathing　(1) In architecture, the nailing of lath in position; also a term used for the material itself. (2) Any base for plaster.

lathing hammer　A lath hammer.

lath, plaster, and set　Two-coat work; a floating coat and a finishing coat often used on backings such as plasterboard or insulating board.

lath, plaster, float, and set　Three-coat work.

latitude　Of a line, the distance which the line extends in a north or south direction of a reference line which runs east and west.

latrine　A privy, such as those used in military camps and temporary dwellings.

latrobe　A stove heater set against a chimney breast and heating its surroundings by direct radiation, heating one or more rooms above by warm air.

latten　An early English alloy, resembling brass.

lattekin　A ladkin.

lattice　(1) Any work of wood or metal made by crossing laths, rods or bars, and forming a net-work (2) A reticulated window, made of laths or slips or iron, separated by glass windows and only used where air rather than light is to be admitted, as in cellars and dairies.

lattice truss　A truss in which the upper and lower members are joined by lattice-like struts.

lattice window　A window in which

small panes of glass are bedded in metal frames.

latticework Any work in wood or metal made of lattice or a collection of lattices.

lavatory A built-in washbasin; also a washroom or the room containing the toilet.

lay A term used in connection with a wire rope to denote the direction of rotation of twist, or helix, of either the wires in the strand or the strands in the rope.

lang A wire rope construction in which the wires are twisted in the same direction as the strands are twisted in the rope.

regular A wire rope construction in which the direction of twist of the wires is opposite to that of the strands in the rope.

lay bar A horizontal glazing bar.

laydown machine A piece of equipment used to spread and give initial compaction to asphaltic concrete; it may be towed or self-propelled.

laydown plus 2 *(slang)* Six feet plus two inches.

layed down The first floating of concrete.

layer 1. *(see course)* 2. A layer is a single veneer ply or two or more plies laminated with parallel grain direction. Two or more plies laminated with grain direction parallel is a "parallel laminated layer".

layer board (lear board) A board on which to place the lowest sheet of box gutter.

layered map A contour map which has areas designating the different contours shown in different colors.

lay-in Describes tile or panels which are installed into metal channels in suspended ceiling systems.

laying-and-finishing machine *(British)* A self-propelled laydown machine which receives road material, spreads it and compacts it into a finished road surfacing which may later be rolled.

laying line (laying guide) Lines printed on saturated felt and certain roll

roofing to provide a visible means of measure of the amount of lapping in laying a built-up roof.

laying trowel (laying-on trowel) A brick trowel or a rectangular steel trowel with which plaster is laid onto a surface.

lay light A window fixed horizontally in a ceiling.

layout (1) The plan or design of the project to be constructed; a schematic. (2) A scaled mechanical drawing showing dimensioned plan views and elevations of an elevator hoistway and machine room. It indicates space conditions, dimensions, sizes, and location of the components of the installation.

layout stick A long strip of wood marked at the appropriate joint intervals for the tile to be used. it is used to check the length, width, or height of the tilework. A common name for this item is 'idiot stick.'

lay panel A door or other panel with its length horizontal.

layshaft A fixed shaft supporting revolving drums.

lazaretto A ward or building for the quarantine of diseased person.

lazy flame Kiln flame characterized by slow undulating movements, approximately following the velocity of the flow of surrounding air. Long and low temperature.

lazy jack A system of levers pivoted together to give a mechanical advantage.

L-beam A beam whose section has the form of an inverted L, usually occurring in the edge of a floor, of which a part forms the top flange of the beam.

L-column The portion of a precast concrete frame, composed of the column, the haunch and part of the girder.

L/D ratio Length of rotary kiln or ball mill divided by internal diameter; Varies between 15 and 40 for rotary kilns.

leach To remove salts from soil, or minerals from an ore by passing water through it.

leaching Removing soluble constituents, such as salts and alkalis, from the soil. Removal is accomplished by the dissolving action of water percolating through the earth.

leaching cesspool A cesspool built so as to permit waste liquids to percolate through its wall into the surrounding soil.

lead (1) /'led/ A metallic element, soft and heavy, with many uses in building. Used by the early Romans and Saxons but now too expensive for common use. (2) /'lēd/ An electrical conductor. Short lengths of insulated wires which conduct electric current to and from a device or appliance. (3) /'lēd/ In masonry, a part of a wall built as a guide for the laying of the balance of the wall. (4) /'lēd/ Lead corner, a section of brickwork plumbed exactly and built up ahead of the rest by steps in the courses called raking back. (5) /'lēd/ In a pile driver, the usually vertical hanging beam that guides the hammer and the pile. (6) /'lēd/ The distance a screw thread advances axially in one complete turn.

lead and oil /'led/ Popular name for white lead, carbonate of lead, as a pigment in linseed oil, forming a paint widely used before the present improved techniques of paint making.

lead burning /'led/ Welding lead without solder. It requires a more direct flame than soldering.

lead-capped nail /'led/ A nail with a lead washer forming the underside of the head. When driven into roof sheeting, it makes a watertight joint.

lead cesspool /'lēd/ A hopper at the low end of a parapet gutter to collect rainwater before it enters a down pipe.

lead dot /lēd/ (see dots)

lead driers /'led/ Lead compounds which quicken the hardening of drying oils in paint.

leaded light (lead glass; lead glazing) /'led-ed/ A window in which small diamond-shaped panes of glass are held in lead cames.

leaded zinc oxides /'led-ed/ White pigments which are mixtures of zinc oxide and basic lead sulphate. These pigments are made from sulphide ores of lead and zinc, burnt without separating them.

leader /'lēd-er/ (1) A pipe draining water from the roof to a storm sewer or other means of disposal. (2) The person on a survey crew who holds the leading end of a chain or tape, and who is aligned by the follower.

leader head /'lēd-er/ A rainwater head.

lead-free paint /'led/ Paint with no lead compounds; used in food packing, etc.

lead glazing /'led/ (see leaded light)

lead joint /'led/ A joint in large cast iron pipes, made by pouring molten lead into the gap or caulking it with lead wool.

lead-light glazier /'led/ A worker who sets out and solders lead or copper cames, cuts glass, glazes the light, and fixes it. If he specializes in stained glass he may be known as a fret glazier or decorative glass worker. If he is also fixing, he is called a stained-glass fitter and fixer.

lead line (sounding line) /'l-ed/ A strong cord knotted at fathom intervals and used for taking soundings in hydrography. It is weighted with a hand lead.

lead nail /'led/ A small copper alloy nail for fixing lead sheet to a roof.

lead paint /'led/ Paint containing lead pigment, particularly white lead. All lead pigments are poisonous since they are soluble in the stomach juices and can be absorbed by the body.

lead plug /'led/ (1) A small cylinder of lead driven into a joint or hole in a wall as a tight fixing for a screw. (2) A lead skin placed into a groove cut into neighboring stones in a course, to hold them together.

lead sheath /'led/ (1) A lead tube covering a power or communication cable. (2) An enclosure of the core of a glazing bar which has lead wings and condensation grooves.

lead soaker /'lēd/ (see soaker)

lead spitter /'lēd/ A short outlet from a hopper or gutter to a down pipe.

lead wedge (bat) /'led/ A tapered piece

of lead scrap used for fixing a flashing to a raglet.

lead wing /'led/ A projecting lead fin forming part of the lead sheath of a lead-clothed glazing bar in patent glazing. It is dressed down onto the glass to hold it and to prevent water entering at the edge of the glass.

lead wires /'lēd/ In blasting, the heavy wires that connect the firing current source or switch with the connecting or cap wire.

lead wool /'led/ Lead cut up into thin strands and used for caulking iron pipes when it is impossible to pour molten lead into the joint.

leaf (1) One of a pair of doors or windows, or one of the tiles at the tile ridge. (2) One solid half of a cavity wall. *(see withe)*

leafwork In furniture making, designs of small cluster of leaves carved on the legs and splats of chairs and other details of furniture. Used extensively by cabinetmakers during the last quarter of the 18th century.

leakage current Current that crosses a PN junction when reverse bias is applied.

leak detector Device used to detect refrigerant leaks in a refrigerating system.

leaks (sound) Small openings for electrical boxes and plumbing, cracks around doors, loose-fitting trim and closures all create leaks that allow sound to pass through, reducing the effectiveness of a sound wall, floor or ceiling system.

lean concrete Concrete of low cement content.

leaning edge The factory edge formed out of a square with the surface in gypsum board.

lean lime An impure lime that slakes slowly and does not yield much putty; a hydraulic lime.

lean mixture A term denoting any plaster mortar containing a relatively high ratio of aggregate to cementitious material. The term 'harsh' is often used to describe the working properties of a mortar mix that is too lean.

lean mortar Mortar which is difficult to spread due to a deficiency of cementitious material; the opposite of fat.

lean-to A small building with a single pitch roof whose rafters pitch or lean against another building or a wall. Can also be used to describe lean-to roof.

lear board A layer board.

lease A contract securing the tenure of real property for a specified time.

least count The smallest measurement made using a vernier.

Lebanon cedar A wood from Europe, Asia and Africa; yellowish brown when first cut but darkening with exposure to a rich lustrous brown with darker ring markings; used for exterior construction work and fencing.

Le Chatelier test A standard test for the soundness of cement; used in England and Europe.

ledge Any shelf-like projection from a wall.

ledge batten The top or bottom batten securing the vertical boards of a batten door.

ledge drain Type of drainage system installed in upstream face of a concrete dam constructed on ledge.

ledge water stop Notch formed in ledge near upstream face of concrete dam to intercept water passing through the dam.

ledged and braced door A batten door which is diagonally braced between the ledges; an unframed door of medieval type, still used for many purposes.

ledgement A string course or horizontal molding.

ledger (stringer) (1) Horizontal formwork member, especially one attached to a beam side, that supports the joists; also may be called girt, sill, purlin or stringer. (2) A slab of stone used horizontally to cover a tomb. (3) A horizontal scaffold member which extends from post to post and which supports the putlogs or bearers forming a tie between the posts.

ledger board (1) The top covering

board of a fence. **(2)** A board let into the face of studding to support on its upper edge the floor joists; a ribbon. **(3)** Horizontal member of a scaffold.

ledger strip   A strip of lumber nailed along the bottom of the side of a girder on which joists rest.

leech   A limpet dam.

left lay   When the strands of a wire rope are twisted in a counterclockwise arrangement.

leg   **(1)** A side post in tunnel timbering. **(2)** A wire or connector in one side of an electric circuit.

Leighton Buzzard sand   *(British)* A closely graded, clean white sand, quarried for building purposes, and used as a standard for testing cements.

Leipzig market halls   Circular buildings of 248 foot span with concrete dome roofs; the first large shells were built according to membrane theory. They are remarkably light, having a weight per square foot of floor area about one-tenth that of St. Peter's, Rome, which has a span of 131 feet.

lelite   Type of lightweight aggregate used in concrete construction.

length   The longer or longest dimension of an object; a measured distance or dimension; a piece constituting or usable as part of a whole or of a connected series. For example, the dimension measured between the ends of a concrete masonry unit.

length of engagement   The length of contact between two mating parts, measured axially.

lengthening joints   Joints which increase the length of timbers, as opposed to angle joints. Some are scarfed, lapped, halved, fished and indented joints. They are seldom used now.

leno fabric   An open fabric in which two warp yarns wrap around each fill yarn in order to prevent the warp or fill yarns from sliding over each other.

Lepol Kiln (trade name)   Combination of a relatively short rotary kiln and a preheater embodying a traveling grate, conveying a layer of nodulized raw meal towards the kiln, while hot exit gases are drawn through the layer. Provides high fuel economy.

lesbian rule   A thin strip of lead which is used to record temporarily the profile of moldings.

lessee   One to whom a lease is granted.

lessor   One who grants a lease.

let in braces   In wood house framing, the diagonal braces notched into studs.

letter agreement (letter of agreement)   A letter stating the terms of an agreement between addressor and addressee, usually prepared to be signed by the addressee to indicate his acceptance of those terms as legally binding.

letter of intent   A letter signifying an intention to enter into a formal agreement, usually setting forth the general terms of such agreement.

letting, bid   *(see bid opening)*

letting down   Reducing the hardness and brittleness of steel by tempering it.

levee   A dike or embankment for the protection of lands from inundation, or for the purpose of confining stream flow. It may or may not have an impervious core.

level   **(1)** To make level or to cause to conform to a specified grade. **(2)** Any instrument that can be used to indicate a horizontal line or plane. **(3)** The elevation of a point in Britain; and in the USA, grade. **(4)** A drainage canal in England.

level book   A surveyor's field book with special vertical rulings for recording readings taken with a dumpy level.

level control   Means of sensing and maintaining water level in the boiler.

leveling   **(1)** The operation in surveying performed to determine and establish elevations of points, to determine differences in elevation between points, and to control grades in construction surveys. **(2)** In painting, the flow or pulling over of the liquid being applied.

leveling device, elevator car   Any mechanism which will, either automatically or under the control of the operator, move the car within the leveling zone toward the landing only, and automatically stop it at the landing. Where controlled by the operator by means of up-and-down continuous-pressure switches in the car, this device is known as an 'inching device.' Where used with a hydraulic elevator to correct automatically a change in car level caused by leakage in the hydraulic system, this device is known as an 'anticreep device.'

leveling device, one-way automatic A device which corrects the car level only in case of under-run of the car, but will not maintain the level during loading and unloading.

leveling device, two-way automatic maintaining A device which corrects the car level on both under-run and over-run, and maintains the level during loading and unloading.

leveling device, two-way automatic non-maintaining A device which corrects the car level on both under-run and over-run, but will not maintain the level during loading and unloading.

leveling zone The limited distance above or below an elevator landing within which the leveling device is permitted to cause movement of the car toward the landing.

leveling instrument A leveling device consisting of a spirit level attached to a sighting tube and the whole mounted on a tripod; used for leveling a surface to a horizontal plane. When the bubble in the level is in the center, the line of sight is horizontal.

leveling plate A steel plate used on top of a foundation or other support on which a structural column can rest.

leveling rod (staff) A telescoping rod marked in feet and fractions of feet and fitted with a movable target or sighting disc. The most commonly used types are the target rod read only by the rodman, and the self-reading rod which is read directly by the person who does the leveling.

leveling rule A straight edge used with a spirit level for bringing dots and screeds to a uniform surface.

leveling screw A foot screw.

level loop Carpet construction with face yarns tufted or woven into loops of same pile height.

level man The surveyor who has charge of the leveling instrument.

level recorder A pressure or float operated instrument which continuously records the water level in a channel.

level surface A continuous surface which is at all points perpendicular to the direction of gravity.

level trier (bubble trier) An instrument which measures the slope corresponding to a noted number of graduations through which the bubble has moved.

level tube (bubble; bubble tube) A transparent tube filled with liquid. The upper surface is graduated and convex, and the bubble tends to remain near the summit at all times. It is an indispensable part of all levels and of the theodolite.

lever A bar that pivots so that force applied at one part can do work at another, usually with a change in the force-distance ratio.

first class A bar having a fulcrum or pivot point, between the points where force is applied and where it is exerted.

second class A lever whose force is exerted between the fulcrum and the point where it is applied.

third class A lever to which force is applied between the fulcrum and the work point.

lever arm In a structural member, the distance from the center of the tensile reinforcement to the center of action of the compression.

lever boards Adjustable louvers.

lever cap A metal piece above the back iron of a metal plane holding the back and cutting irons in place by cam action.

lever lock A lock in which the key must move several levers in order to shoot the bolt.

levy facing A watertight facing on the water face of a dam. The facing is built onto a row of small arches in a horizontal plane forming vertical openings the full height of the dam. The arches are drained at the foot. Any leaks which occur through the facing cannot produce dangerous hydrostatic pressures within the dam, since the water within the levy facing is never at a pressure higher than atmospheric.

lewis (lewis anchor) A device for lifting blocks of stone; there are various forms but all depend on dovetail-shaped keys fitting into mortices cut in the stones to receive them.

lewis bolt An anchor bolt with a ragged tapering tail inserted in masonry and held in place by a lead casing.

lewis holes Sinkages in stones on surfaces that will be hidden in building, for engaging lewis anchors in hoisting and placing the stones.

lewising tool A chisel for cutting lewis holes.

L-head The top of a shore formed with a braced horizontal member projecting on one side forming an inverted L-shaped assembly.

licensed architect *(see architect)*

licensed contractor A person or organization certified by governmental authority, where required by law, to engage in construction contracting.

licensed engineer *(see professional engineer)*

lien, mechanic's or material A charge put against a project for satisfaction of unpaid debts on work performed or materials supplied.

lien release A document designating that materials and services furnished to a project have been paid for.

lien waiver An instrument by which a person or organization who has or may have a right of mechanic's lien or materials lien against the property of another relinquishes such right. *(see mechanic's lien; release of lien)*

lierne French term for a subordinate rib in vaulting.

lierne vaulting Vaulting in which lierne ribs are freely employed.

life-cycle costing The LCC concept is where lifetime ownership costs, rather than just first costs, are the basis of comparison for the purchase of goods. (To advance the use of solar systems one of the factors which lenders will need to become cognizant of is the LCC concept as the payoff time for solar versus conventional heating systems is much longer.)

lift (1) A step or bench in a multiple layer excavation. (2) The concrete placed between two consecutive horizontal construction joints; usually containing several layers, or courses. (3) An elevator; a sidewalk lift is an elevator rising through iron doors in a sidewalk. (4) A metal aid in lifting a sash or door. (5) The distance through which a vessel rises or falls in passing through a lock. (6) A power-operated hoist for raising or lowering vessels from one reach to the next without using a lock.

lifter A wide chisel like pointer for taking stone out of the rough. *(see devil)*

lifter hole A shot hole drilled near the floor of a tunnel and fired after the cut holes and relief holes.

lift gate (1) A lock gate which opens by rising vertically. (2) A hydraulically powered tailgate on a truck which acts like an elevating dock or platform. (trucking term)

lifting (raising) The softening of a dry film of paint or varnish when another coat is applied over it, causing a wrinkling of the first coat.

lifting block A set of pulleys to enable heavy weights to be lifted, such as a differential pulley block.

lifting magnet An electromagnet hanging from a crane hook used for lifting iron or steel. It lifts only magnetic material thus separating it from non-magnetic materials or non-ferrous metals.

lifting pin A lewis.

lifting shutters *(British)* Shutters balanced by cords and weights like a sash which drop behind the window back when not in use.

lifting tackle The entire lifting apparatus, including blocks, hooks, ropes, chains, slings, eyebolts, pulleys or hoists used for raising or lowering heavy weights. Power-operated devices are called cranes or derricks.

lift joint Surface at which two successive lifts meet.

lift latch A thumb latch.

lift pump A suction pump.

lifts (tiers) The number of frames of scaffolding erected one above each other in a vertical direction. (see lift)

lift shaft (lift well) *(British)* Elevator shaft.

lift slab A method of concrete construction in which floor and roof slabs are cast on or at ground level and hoisted into position by jacking; also a slab which is a component of such construction. First used in U.S.A. in 1948.

light (lite) (1) The term used in the glass industry for a piece of glass or a section of a window sash for a single pane of glass. (2) The amount of illumination, generally daylight, captured in a room or an interior. Borrowed light is that which is received through or over a partition from an outside lighted space. (3) A light fixture.

light alloys Alloys of aluminum, used in building; alloys of magnesium, which have only recently been developed, are even lighter.

light duty scaffold A scaffold designed and constructed to carry a working load not to exceed 25 pounds per square foot.

light emitting diode (LED) A PN diode designed to emit light when forward current flows.

light-gauge copper tube Very thin copper pipes. Since these pipes are too thin to have a screw thread cut on them, they are joined by fittings. Close tolerances insure the close fit needed for capillary joints.

lightning shake Failure of wood, by compression, seen as a cross break.

light plant A usually portable generator used to supply power to small equipment.

light rail way *(British)* A narrow gauge railway.

light reflectance values The percentage of total light reflected back to the eye from the floor. Color of the floor covering surface is the influencing factor. Measured with a reflectometer, using standard light source.

light sap stain A slight difference in color which will not materially impair the appearance of a piece of lumber given a natural finish.

lightweight aggregate Aggregate such as vermiculite and perlite used instead of sand in plaster, and in concrete for roofs of large span. Pumice, foamed slag or clinker aggregates can also be used to make lightweight concrete.

lightweight block Used where load reduction is important. Uses a special aggregate made by processing and burning shale into vesiculated pieces ranging in size from coarse dust to crushed stone.

lightweight concrete Concrete of substantially lower unit weight than that made from gravel or crushed stone.

lightweight units (mobile-home types) Totally self-contained housing units which can retain their mobility, or be permanently installed and grouped or stacked with the addition of a demountable frame. In most cases mobile homes are completely preassembled and finished, and require only site utility connections for occupancy.

light well An open area within a building or in a subsurface space around a basement window, which provides light and air.

lignified wood A special plywood pressure-impregnated with lignin.

lignin The second important item in the makeup of wood, after cellulose, consisting of resins which cement the wood fibers together.

lime Specifically, calcium oxide (CaO); also, loosely, a general term for the various chemical and physical forms of quicklime, hydrated lime and hydraulic hydrated lime.

lime concrete A mixture of gravel, sand and lime which has a hard set. It was used in Roman times and later until portland cement was made.

lime mortar Lime and sand which is

mixed with water as a bricklaying mortar and sometimes with cement. If the quantity of cement is equal to the quantity of lime, the mortar can be considered to be cement mortar because cement is more powerful and quicker acting than lime.

lime plaster   A term generally referring to basecoat plaster, consisting essentially of lime and an aggregate.

lime powder   The powder obtained by air slaking lime.

lime putty   A plastering material resulting from slaking quicklime or soaking and mixed hydrated lime with a sufficient quantity of water to form a thick paste.

lime ratio   Ratio of lime to silica plus alumina and iron. Used in design or control of raw mix.

lime rock   A natural material, essentially calcium carbonate with varying percentages of silica; hardens upon exposure to elements. Some varieties provide excellent road material.

lime saturation factor   The ratio of the theoretical effective lime content to the maximum possible lime content of a given clinker.

limestone   Natural rock of sedimentary origin composed principally of calcium carbonate or calcium and magnesium carbonates in either its original chemical, fragmental or recrystallized form. *(see oolite)*

limewash (whitewash)   A milk formed with quicklime by soaking in excess water.

limit control   A furnace thermostat that prevents overheating of the heating unit.

limit design   A method of proportioning reinforced concrete members based on calculation of their ultimate strength. *(see ultimate strength design method; plastic design)*

limit of liquidity (of plasticity)   *(see liquid limit; plastic limit)*

limit switch   (1) A safety device on an electrically-driven lift, engine or hoist. Limit switches begin operating at the end of the trip to prevent the cage over-

winding or underwinding. (2) A mechanically or magnetically operated device wired into an elevator circuit to restrict travel of a moving object, such as an elevator, elevator door, etc.

limits   The extreme permissible dimensions of a part.

limnology   A specialized form of ecology directed at the study of biological productivity and characteristics of inland water, lakes in particular.

limonite   An iron ore composed of a mixture of hydrated ferric oxides; occasionally used in high density concrete because of its high density and water content which contribute to its effectiveness in radiation shielding.

limpet asbestos   A sprayed asbestos.

limpet dam (leech)   A small open caisson shaped to fit into a dock wall. It is lowered by a crane into the water, placed in contact with the wall section to be repaired, and pumped out. The water pressure forces it even closer to the wall and holds it in place. Access is through the top.

limpet washer   A conical washer placed under the nut of a hook bolt to hold down a corrugated sheet. A diamond washer has the same function.

line   (1) A cable, rope, chain or other flexible device for transmitting pull. (2) To line pieces up in order to couple them together. (3) A cord used for setting out building work especially by foundation workers and bricklayers.

lineal expansion   The increase in one dimension, expressed as a percentage of that dimension at the shrinkage limit, of a soil mass when the water content is increased from the shrinkage limit to any given water content.

lineal foot   Pertaining to a line one foot in length as distinguished from a square foot or a cubic foot.

lineal shrinkage   The decrease in one dimension, expressed as a percentage of that dimension originally; of a soil mass when the water content is reduced from the original percentage to the shrinkage limit.

line and pin   A chalk line attached to

iron pins driven into brick courses at each end of a wall in process of erection, acting as a guide to the true alignment of the intermediate courses.

linear (1) Resembling a line, or thread; narrow and elongated. (2) Involving measurement in one direction; pertaining to length.

linear measure A system of measurement in length; also called long measure:

12 inches = 1 foot
3 feet = 1 yard
16½ feet = 1 rod
320 rods = 1 mile
5280 feet = 1 mile

linear perspective Graphic representation in two kinds, in both of which it is assumed that the line of sight is perpendicular to the plane of projection; centrolinear, or stationpoint, perspective (conic projection) in which the spectator is assumed to be at a local fixed distance from the object; orthogonal perspective (cylindrical projection) in which the spectator is assumed to be at an infinite distance from the object.

linear prestressing Prestressing as applied to linear members, such as beams, columns, etc.

linear transformation The method of altering the trajectory of the prestressing tendon in any statically indeterminate prestressed structure by changing the location of the tendon at one or more interior supports without altering its position at the end supports and without changing the basic shape of the trajectory between any supports; linear transformation does not change the location of trajectory of the pressure line.

line drawing A drawing of lines, dots, and solid masses, as distinguished from the tonal variations of a wash drawing. A line drawing is capable of reproduction for printing by the line process of photoengraving.

line drilling (1) The drilling of a series of holes in rock along the line to which it is to be excavated; the holes are usually drilled about four inches apart, center to center, after which the rock is blasted off with light shots or broken off with plugs and feathers. (2) In a churn drill, the cable that supports and manipulates the tools.

line drop (1) In electricity, the loss in voltage in the conductors of a circuit due to their resistance. (2) Commonly refers to the line between the power station and the consumer.

line level In building construction, a type of level used when laying foundations, tile pipe, determining grades, or for other similar work.

line manhole A manhole in the line of a sewer at a point where no other sewers connect; it may be at a point where the sewer changes direction either in line, slope or grade.

line of electric flux Invisible conceptual lines connecting opposite electrical charges in a dielectric medium.

line of flight The angle of ascent of a stair.

line of least resistance In blasting, the shortest distance between the center of the explosive charge and the nearest free face. It is usually slightly shorter than the burden.

line of thrust The locus of the points through which the force in an arch or retaining wall passes. (see Eddy's theorem)

line oiler An oil reservoir and metering device placed in a compressed air line to lubricate air tools.

line pin A metal pin used to attach the line used for alignment of masonry units.

line pins The metal pins inserted in the mortar joint at the ends of a wall, used for holding a bricklayer's line.

line printer plot A method by which computer generated moisture maps are made.

liner (1) In painting, a lining tool. (2) In plumbing, a sleeve piece. (3) In timbering, a board cut to the length available between members of a frame and nailed to lock them in place. (see stretcher) (4) The enclosure forming the interior of the general refrigerated compartment and/ or some freezer compartment(s). The complete liner comprises the compartment liner in the cabinet, the exposed breaker strip surfaces and the door liner(s).

liner panel A panel applied as an interior finish.

liner plate Formed steel unit used to line or reinforce a tunnel or other opening.

line resistance method A current limiting method for starting A.C. motors.

lines per fame The number of times that the electron beam sweeps across the face of the cathode ray tube in a TV-like display.

line spinning A line wrapped around a threaded pipe, so that a pull will rotate the pipe to fasten or unfasten it from another.

line strainer An accessory wire mesh strainer placed in the oil line to catch foreign matter before it enters the power unit.

lining (1) Any sheet, plate or layer of material attached directly to the inside of the forms to improve or alter the surface texture and quality of the finished concrete. (2) The interior refractory lining of a heating unit. (3) A layer of clay, concrete, brick, stone or wood on the bed of a canal to reduce scour, friction and leakage. (4) A concreted, gunited or bricked surface to a tunnel or shaft. (5) Covering for the interior, as casing for the exterior surface of a building; also, linings of a door for windows, shutters and similar work. (6) An insulating fiber board, wood or corkboard, fixed to a framed partition under the surface covering to improve the sound insulation, absorption or the thermal insulation of a partition. (7) Continuous or discontinuous parallel troughs or ridges in the direction which a paint or varnish has drained or been brushed. Silking is very fine-grained lining.

lining felt Produced in widths of 36″, it is made of dry felt, semi-saturated felt and fully-saturated felt. It absorbs the normal movement of wood subfloors and helps eliminate shifting of resilient floors, adds to quietness and resiliency.

makes floors easier to remove for replacement.

lining paper (1) Paper pasted onto plaster as a wallpaper base. (2) An inexpensive paper stock recommended for use under foils and other fine quality coverings. Lining paper absorbs excess moisture.

lining plate In flexible-metal roofing, a metal strip nailed to the eaves or verge and attached to the roofing sheet.

lining tool (liner) A small flat tool with a slanting edge used for painting lines.

link dormer A large dormer, sometimes with side windows. It may join one part of the roof to another or incorporate a roof projection such as a chimney.

linked switch Two or more switches joined by bars so that they open or close simultaneously or in sequence.

link fuse A fuse not protected by a cover plate.

linoleum A finish floor covering made of linseed oil, ground cork, etc., oxidized upon a fabric base.

linseed oil One of the most commonly used paint oils, processed from flaxseed.

lintel (1) A piece of wood, stone or steel placed horizontally across the top of door and window openings to support the walls immediately above the openings. (2) In steel work, the horizontal steel member spanning an opening to support the load above.

lintel block U or W shaped concrete masonry units for use in construction of horizontal bond beams or lintels.

Linville truss *(see Pratt truss)*

lip (1) The cutting edge of a bucket; applied chiefly to edges including tooth sockets. (2) The banding on a flush door.

lip block (lip piece; lipping) A piece of wood nailed over a strut in trench timbering. It overhangs the waling so that if the sides of the trench cave, the strut will not drop on the men below.

lip joint In terra cotta, a joint similar to a carpenter's rebate.

lip mold A molding of the perpendicular period like a hanging lip.

lipped The process of laying units with the lower face projecting over the one below.

lipping *(see lip block)*

lip union In plumbing, a union with a ring-like inner projection which keeps the gasket from being forced into the pipe thereby blocking it.

liquefaction Change of state to liquid, generally used instead of condensation in case of substances ordinarily gaseous.

liquefied petroleum gasses LPG and LP gas mean and include any material which is composed predominantly of any of the following hydrocarbons, or mixtures of them, such as propane, propylene, butane (normal butane or iso-butane), and butylenes.

liquid asphalts Products so soft that their consistency cannot be measured by the normal penetration test, such as road oils or asphaltic cutbacks.

liquidated damages An amount of money established in a construction contract, usually as a fixed sum per day, as the measure of damages suffered by the owner due to failure to complete the work within a stated time. *(see bonus and penalty clause; bonus clause*

liquid driers A painting term for soluble driers.

liquid indicator A device, frequently combined with a strainer, located in the liquid line of a refrigerating system and having a sight port by which liquid flow may be observed for presence of bubbles.

liquidity index *(see index of liquidity)*

liquid limit Water content, expressed as a percentage of the dry weight of the soil at which the soil passes from the plastic to the liquid state under standard test conditions; the minimum moisture content which will cause soil to flow if jarred slightly. *(see Atterberg limits)*

liquid line The tube or pipe carrying the refrigerant liquid from the condenser or receiver of a refrigerating system to a pressure-reducing device.

liquid-membrane curing compound A sealant.

liquid refrigerant receiver A vessel in refrigerating system designed to insure the availability of adequate liquid refrigerant for proper functioning of the system and to store the liquid refrigerant when the system is pumped down.

liquids Substances having free flow and movement of molecules among themselves, but without the tendency to separate from each other. Substances in the liquid state at standard conditions are considered to be liquids.

liquid/solid cyclone Relatively small conical cyclone classifier operating in closed circuit with wet grinding mill, for classifying slurry into coarse and fine fractions by centrifugal action.

liquid, volatile One which evaporates readily at atmospheric pressure and room temperatures.

liquid-volume measurement Measurement of grout on the basis of the total volume of solid and liquid constituents.

liquid waste The discharge from any fixture, appliance or appurtenance, in connection with a plumbing system which does not receive fecal matter.

liquor A solution used in absorption refrigeration.

liquor, strong Solvent with relatively high concentration of solute.

liquor, weak Solvent with relatively low concentration of solute.

list (listel) A small square molding to crown a larger one; also termed a fillet.

listing mark An independent laboratory mark or manifest indicating the material bearing this mark may be used in tests certified by the lab.

liter weight test Method of determining the density in grams per 1000 cc of clinker of uniform, screened size. Indicates degree of burning and, by correlation, the free lime.

litharge (lead monoxide) (PbO) A drier and pigment ranging in color from pale yellow to brown.

Lithonia granite A blue-gray, fine-grain granite of Georgia.

lithopone Zinc sulphate and sulphate of baryta used as a white paint pigment.

lithosphere That rocky portion of the earth comprised mainly of solid material, i.e., rocks, clay, earth, gravel, sand, etc.

little inch *(slang)* Usually refers to pipe 24 inches in diameter and smaller.

little joiners *(slang)* Small pieces of wood which are used to conceal or fill holes in wood.

little red wagon *(slang)* A portable toilet.

live edge An edge of paint which although painted for some time, can still be blended with newly applied paint without the lap showing.

live knot A knot whose fibers are intergrown with the wood. It is allowable in structural timber within certain size limits.

live load The non-permanent load to which a structure is subjected in addition to its own weight. It includes the weight of persons occupying the building and free standing material, but does not include wind loads, earthquake loads or dead loads.

livering Feeding in painting.

live wire A conductor with the electrical power turned on and therefore dangerous to touch.

living area The area computed using exterior dimensions of the entire living area of a residence; e.g., both floors of a two-story residence, excluding attic, basement, breezeway or porch.

Lloyd Davies formula A method used in Britain for calculating the run-off, from which the sizes of sewers are calculated; runoff water in cubic feet = 60.5 × area drained in acres × rainfall in inches per hour × impermeability factor.

IN$_2$ Liquid nitrogen - the reference temperature material used by many IR imaging systems. Boiling point - 196°C or .324°F.

load (1) In electricity, the work required to be done by a machine; also,
the current flowing through a circuit. (2) To place explosives in a hole. (3) To transfer material to a hauling unit or hopper. (4) 50 cubic feet of timber.

dead Total downward pressure of all fixed elements of the structure.

live Downward pressure that might be added to the structure temporarily.

load-bearing wall Any wall which bears its own weight as well as other weight and the force of wind; same as a supporting wall. Partitions and panel walls are usually not load bearing.

load binder A lever that pulls two grab hooks together and holds them by locking over center.

load current Total current across a power source.

load deck Charges of dynamite spaced well apart in a borehole and fired by separate primers or by detonating cord.

loaded filter The filter at the foot of an earth dam, which stabilizes the toe of the dam by its weight and permeability since water cannot exist in it under pressure.

loader One of a variety of types of equipment loading material onto or into something.

belt, elevating grader A machine whose forward motion cuts soil with a plowshare or disc and pushes it to a conveyor belt that elevates it to a dumping point.

bucket A machine having a digging and gathering rotor, and a set of chain mounted buckets to elevate the materials to a dumping point.

front end A tractor loader that both digs and dumps in front.

paddle A belt loader equipped with chain driven paddles that move loose material to the belt.

reversed A front end loader mounted on a wheel tractor having the driving wheels in front and steering at the rear.

swing A tractor loader that digs in front and can swing the bucket to dump to the side of the tractor.

tower A front end loader whose

bucket is lifted along tracks on a more or less vertical tower.

tractor A tractor equipped with a digging bucket that can dump into hauling equipment.

load factor (1) The ratio of the collapse load to the working load on a structure or section. (2) Average load carried by an engine, machine or plant expressed as a percentage of its maximum capacity. (3) The percentage of the total connected fixture unit flow rate which is likely to occur at any point in the drainage system. It varies with the type of occupancy, the total flow unit above this point being considered, and with the probability factor of simultaneous use.

load-indicating bolt A high-strength friction-grip bolt, which gives a reliable easily inspected indication that the specified minimum tension has been achieved. The head of the bolt has small projections on its underside, which compress as the bolt is tightened. The gap indicates the amount of bolt tension, and can be measured simply by feeler gauges pushed under the bolt head.

load indicator washer A washer for high strength bolts in which pre-tension load can be measured as a function or amount of compression on raised portions or the washer.

loading boom An overhanging structure from which material is loaded into trucks.

loading hopper A hopper in which concrete or other free flowing material is placed for loading by gravity into buggies or other conveyances for transport to the forms or to other place of processing, use or storage.

loading pipe Before bending a pipe, it is filled with a bending spring, molten lead, low melting-point alloy, pitch, resin or compressed sand. Such loading prevents the pipe from distorting during bending.

loading pump A hand pump for filling bulk materials into application tools.

loading shovel A mechanical shovel on pneumatic tires, originally designed for lifting and loading rubbish, sand, coal, etc. It can be used for digging or dozing and as a crane. It can also be used as a fork-lift for stacking bricks or raising them up to scaffolding. It is a very light and fast-moving excavator but unsuitable for traveling on bad ground because of its rubber tires.

load rating The weight or load required to compress the spring by an amount equal to its stroke.

loads Anything that causes a force to be exerted on a structural member. Examples of different types are:

a. *Dead Load*

b. *Impact Load*

c. *Roof Live Load*

d. *Seismic Load*

e. *Wind Load*

f. *Crane Load*

g. *Collateral Load*

h. *Auxiliary Load*

load-transfer assembly Most commonly, the unit, basket or plate, designed to support or link dowel bars during concreting operations so as to hold them in place in the desired alignment.

load, usage The sum of the air change, product and miscellaneous loads on a refrigerator; the sum of the loads exclusive of the wall heat gains.

loam In some localities, a friable mixture of sand, clay and silt; in other localities an organic topsoil suitable for cultivation and plant growth.

lobby An anteroom; a large vestibule; the main-floor circulation center of a hotel.

local attraction Deviation of the compass needle from the magnetic north. It may be due to iron or steel in the ground or metal on the compass-holder's person.

lock (1) In a compressed air system, a chamber that can be opened to pressure air at one end, and to atmospheric air at the other. (2) A mechanical means of fastening a door, drawer or the like. (3) A chamber in a canal or river with gates on each side though which barges or ships can pass up or downstream.

lock block A wood block in a door into which the lock can be fastened.

Locke level A hand level.

lock gate A gate which separates the water in a channel from that in the lock chamber. Sometimes a lock gate divides a chamber into two compartments.

locking device A device used to secure a cross brace in scaffolding to the frame or panel.

locking stile The vertical section of a door to which the lock is fastened.

lock nut A second nut screwed onto a bolt after the nut which carries the load, to prevent it unscrewing.

lock rail The rail of a door into which the lock is set.

lock seam (lock joint) In sheet metal, the joining of two surfaces in the same plane in which the edges to be united are folded back for a suitable distance, the folds interlocked, and the joint then pressed tight. Also used for the longitudinal seam in a pipe.

lock sill The part of the floor of a lock chamber against which the gates rest when shut.

lockspit A narrow V-shaped cut in the ground to mark the line of a dig.

lockup *(slang)* A building or room for temporary imprisonment.

locust, black A tree of North America, the hard, heavy wood of which is particularly resistant to decay underground.

lodge A hut; a cabin; a meeting place of certain fraternal organizations; a gate lodge, or porter's lodge, a small building attending the entrance to the grounds of a large residence or an institution.

loess Windblown, pale-colored silt and clay, very porous and cavitated; it is characterized by thick beds and vertical cleavage; cut slopes usually stand vertically.

loft Originally the unfinished story just under the roof of a commercial building or warehouse; now, any undivided floor of a commercial building, the subdivision and equipment of which is left to the tenant; the unfinished space under the rafters of a large building, as a barn, church or schoolhouse.

lofting *see bulking)*

loft ladder (disappearing stair) A folding ladder which is fixed at the top to a trap door into a loft or attic space and is invisible from below when the trap door is closed. The trap door is hinged to open down and is counterbalanced to carry the ladder by weights.

logarithm The exponent indicating the power to which a base number (10 in the decimal system) must be raised to produce a given number.

logarithmic spiral A spiral which intersects all of its radiants at the same angle.

log chute (logway) A passage through or beside a dam for logs and driftwood.

loggia In architecture, a roofed arcade, or gallery, usually within the body of the building at the height of the second story, or higher, with one side open to the air making an open air room.

logging tongs Tongs with end hooks that dig in when the tongs are pulled.

long break lines Thin lines drawn with a straight edge and free hand 'zigzags' to indicate the structure or object has been broken to permit convenient presentation of them on the drawing sheet.

long column *(see column, long)*

long dolly A follower.

long dummy *(slang)* A tool for straightening out kinks in lead pipe.

long float A float requiring two men to handle it.

longitudinal Pertaining to length.

longitudinal bar *(see longitudinal reinforcement)*

longitudinal bead test (slow bend test) A test for weldability. A steel plate, on which a welding bead is dropped, and then bent double. If the plate or weld metal is not weldable, it will crack.

longitudinal bond Occasional courses of bricks laid as stretchers to form a bond in thick walls.

longitudinal joint In building construction, a joint which fastens two pieces of timber together in the direction of their length, a joint parallel to the long dimension of a structure or pavement.

longitudinal profile A vertical section through the center line of a road or similar structure to show the original and final grade.

longitudinal reinforcement Reinforcement essentially parallel to the long axis of a concrete member or pavement.

longitudinal section In shopwork and drawing, a lengthwise cut of any portion of a structure; also, pertaining to a measurement along the axis of a body.

long oil A high ratio of oil to resin in a varnish.

long-oil alkyd An alkyd resin containing more than 60 percent oil as a modifying agent.

long-oil varnish An oleo-resinous varnish, other than an alkyd, containing not less than 2½ parts of oil to one part of resin.

long screw In plumbing, a connector.

long term financing Funds provided by a lending institution for construction purposes, and repaid over an extended period of time by the owner.

long ton 2,240 pounds.

lookout (1) A cantilevered beam or a bracket for support of overhanging construction. (2) A place from which observations are made, as from a watchtower.

lookout ledger Usually a 1 × 4 band around a building at the top of the wall, to which the lookouts are attached.

lookouts Short wooden framing members attached to a ledger board at the top of the wall and to the rafter tails for attachment of the plancier.

loop Normally any section of pipeline between valves.

loop chain Length of chain, suspended at both ends, inside upper fourth of rotary kiln to increase heat transfer from hot gases to load.

loop circuit A continuous circuit connecting the motor and generator armatures.

looped pile Pile surface in which looped yarns are left uncut. In woven carpets, sometimes referred to as 'round wire.'

looper That part of a roofing machine which forms and allows the sheet of roofing to land in loops to facilitate cooling. On the wet end of the machine, it allows the saturant to soak into the sheet. The looper is also used as a means to provide continuous operation of the finishing end of the roofing machine.

loophole A slotlike aperature in a wall, originally used for small-arms action in defense; a crenelle.

looping in A method of reducing the number of T-joints in wiring conduits by keeping one cable permanently connected to the socket, the other passing through the switch. More wire is needed, but the cable is cut at fewer points, therefore making fewer joints.

loop vent The same as a circuit vent except that it loops back and connects with a waste stack vent instead of the vent stack.

loose end The point in the pipeline where one section ends and another begins.

loose-fill insulation Insulating materials such as granulated cork, loose asbestos, expanded clay, foamed slag, gypsum insulation, mineral wool or vermiculite placed between rafters, studs, or in the cavity formed in hollow block walls, to increase the insulating value of a dry air space.

loose fit A fit allowing considerable freedom; used when accuracy is not essential.

loose-joint butt Hinges which can be taken apart by lifting one leaf from the other. A door so hinged that it can be easily unhung without unscrewing its hinges.

loose knot In woodworking, a term applied to a knot which is not held in position firmly by the surrounding wood fibers. Such a knot is a severe blemish in a piece of lumber making the board unfit for first-class work.

loose-lay Floors installed without use of adhesive, generally rotovinyl products. Around perimeter, floor covering is put beneath quarter round. Adhesive is used at seams, by adhering to heavy wrapping paper or shade cloth and not to floor.

loose-measure volume Volume of the earth after it has been removed from its natural position and deposited in trucks, scrapers or spoil piles. Usually expressed in cubic yards.

loose-pin butt A butt hinge with a removable hinge pin which enables the door to be unhung by removing the pins from the hinges.

loose rock Rock that can be moved without blasting, e.g., ripped or dug out with power equipment.

loose tongue In carpentry, a cross tongue.

loose yards Measurement of soil or rock after it has been loosened by digging or blasting.

Los Angeles Abrasion Test Test for abrasion resistance of concrete aggregates.

loss of head Hydraulic friction.

loss of prestress The reduction of the prestressing force which results from the combined effects of creep in the steel, and creep and shrinkage of the concrete; does not normally include friction losses but may include the effect of elastic deformation of the concrete.

loss on ignition The percentage loss in weight of a sample ignited to constant weight at a specified temperature, usually 900-1000°C.

lost ground Material which runs into an excavation under or through the sheeting, or as a boil in the bottom; material outside the sheeting which moves downward because of the run or boil, voids left behind the sheeting when it was placed, or movement of the sheeting.

lost head The friction loss in a pipe or channel. A loss in potential energy.

lost-head nail A round wire nail having a very small head.

lot A measured portion of land, usually a building site.

lot line A building term referring to the line which bounds a plot of ground described as a lot in the title of a property.

loudness level The loudness level of any sound is defined as the intensity level of a sound of 1,000 cycles frequency which sounds equally loud.

loud spots Places in a room where sound focuses and increases the intensity level.

louver (1) Horizontal openings in or between pieces of horizontal sheeting for the purpose of filling any voids which may occur behind the sheeting. (2) An opening for ventilating closed attics or other used spaces. (3) A lantern or turret on a roof for ventilating or lighting purposes, commonly used in medieval buildings.

louver boards In architecture, a series of overlapping sloping boards or slats in an opening so arranged as to admit air but keep out rain or snow.

louvre damper Damper, for control of kiln draft, consisting of a set of horizontal rectangular plates which, like a venetian blind, can be adjusted to various angles through a gear mechanism. Installed in the duct between kiln and draft fan.

louvered awning blinds Adjustable louvers on slanted outside blinds to control the amount of shade or sunlight entering windows.

low air Air supplied to pressurize working chambers and locks.

low-alkali cement (see cement, low-alkali)

low bed (low boy) A machinery trailer with a low deck.

low bid Bid stating the lowest bid price, including selected alternates, and complying with all bidding requirements.

low carbonate stone Limestone for cement raw material containing less than 75 percent calcium carbonate.

low carbon sheet steel Steel containing carbon up to about 2% and only residual quantities of other elements, except those added for dioxidation, with silicon usually limited to 0.60% and manganese to about 1.65%. Also termed "plain carbon steel," "ordinary steel," and "straight carbon steel."

low-consistency plaster A neat gypsum base coat plaster that has been specially processed during manufacture so that less mixing water is required to produce workability than in standard gypsum basecoat plaster.

lower plate The limb of a theodolite.

lowest responsible bidder Bidder who submits the lowest bonafide bid and is considered by the owner and the architect to be fully responsible and qualified to perform the work for which the bid is submitted.

lowest responsive bid The lowest bid which is responsive to and complies with the bidding requirements.

low frequency An electric current which has a small number of cycles per second.

low-heat cement (see cement, low-heat)

low pressure side That part of a refrigerating system operating at approximately the evaporator pressure.

low-pressure steam curing (see atmospheric-pressure steam curing)

low slump Very stiff concrete.

low speed neutron A high-speed neutron that has been slowed down after repeated collisions with a hydrogen atom. (see thermalizing)

lozenge molding An ornamental molding used in Norman architecture, characterized by diamond shaped ornaments resembling a lozenge.

L-shore A shore with an L-head.

lubricant Material such as grease and oil used to decrease friction between moving parts.

lucarne A small window in a dormer or spire; if in a spire it is often capped by a gablet and finial.

Lucite Trade name for a plastic material available in transparent sheets and other forms.

lucullite A black, fine-textured marble, named for Lucullus, a consul of ancient Rome.

luffing Derricking.

lug (1) A small projecting member of a larger body used to engage an adjoining unit or to serve as an aid in handling. (2) The part of a sill for window or door opening that extends horizontally beyond the opening into the masonry. (3) A connector for fastening the end of a wire to a terminal.

lug down To slow down by increasing load beyond capacity.

lumber Any material, such as boards, planks or beams cut from timber to a size and form suitable for marketing.

    board Yard lumber less than two inches thick and two or more inches wide.

    dimension Yard lumber from two inches to but not including five inches thick, and two or more inches wide. Includes joists, rafters, studding, plank and small timbers.

    dressed size The dimensions of lumber after shrinking from the green dimension and after planing, usually ⅜ inch less than the nominal or rough size. For example, a 2×4 stud usually measures 1⅝ by 3⅝ inches.

    matched Lumber that is edge-dressed and shaped to make a close tongue-and-groove joint at the edges or ends when laid edge to edge or end to end.

    shiplap Lumber that is edge-dressed to make a close rabbeted or lapped joint.

    timber Yard lumber five or more inches in least dimension. Includes beams, stringers, posts, caps, sills, girders and purlins.

lumber mucker (slang) A laborer who carries the lumber from storage to work, etc.

lumen A quantitative unit for measuring light output.

lumen-hour Unit of lighting; lighting at a rate of one lumen for one hour.

lumiline A tubular incandescent light source which has a filament extending the length of the tube and is connected at each end to a disc base.

luminaire (1) A complete lighting unit; ceiling fixture, wall bracket, portable lamp or built-in or applied units. (2) In highway lighting, a complete lighting device consisting of a light source, plus a globe, reflector, refractor, housing and such support as is integral with the housing. The light standard, bracket or pole, is not considered a part of the luminaire.

luminosity Quality of flame which produces light and heat through radiation.

lump hammer A club hammer.

lump lime Quicklime as it comes from the kiln.

lump sum agreement *(see stipulated sum agreement)*

lump sum bid A bid of a set amount to cover all labor, equipment, materials, overhead and profit necessary for construction of a variety of unspecified items of work.

lump sum contract A contract which provides that the owner will pay the contractor a specified sum of money for the completion of a project.

lunette The French term for a small round or arched-top window in a vaulted or coved ceiling or roof.

Lu-Re-Co A system of panel and truss construction emphasizing flexibility and economy.

luster fabric Any cut pile fabric woven with surface yarns spun from special types of staple and chemically washed, like handwoven Oriental fabric, to give a bright sheen or luster.

luthern A window above the cornice of a Classical building, rising vertically in line with the outside wall; types are square, arched, bull's eye, semicircular, etc.

lyceum A building for an institution of learning.

lying panel In carpentry, a lay panel.

lyophilization The process of dehydrating a frozen substance under conditions of sublimation; e.g. vacuum-freeze drying.

lytag A lightweight aggregate made of fly ash.

m   meter, mile, minute, month

M   metal, per thousand, moment

ma   milliampere

MA   mechanical advantage

mach   machine, machinist

mag   magazine, magneto

man. page   manual page

manuf   manufacture

mas   masonry

mat   material

max   maximum

mb   millibar

me   marbled edges

Me   methyl

ME   mechanical engineer

meas   measure

mech   mechanic, mechanical

med   medium

meg   megohm

mep   mean effective pressure

meq   milliequivalent

mer   meridian

met   metullurgy

MEV   million electron volts

mezz   mezzanine

mfg   manufactured

mg   milligram

Mg   magnesium

MG   motor generator

mgmt   management

mh   millihenry

MHW   mean high water

mi   mile

mid   middle

mil. stnd.   Military Standard

min   minimum, minor, minute

misc   miscellaneous

mixt   mixture

mks   meter-kilogram-second

ml   milliliter

mL   millilambert

MLW   mean low water

mm   millimeter

MMF   magnetomotive force

mmfd   micromicrofarad

Mn   manganese

MN   magnetic north

Mo   molybdenum

mod/modif   modification

mol   molecule

mol. wt.   molecular weight

mp   melting point

mpg   miles per gallon

mph   miles per hour

mphps   miles per hour per second

mpl   maple

mps   meters per second

mr   milliroentgen

MR   mill run

msec   millisecond

MSF   per 1000 sq. ft.

msl   mean sea level

MT   metric ton

mtg/mtge   mortgage

mull   mullion

mult   multiplier

mun/munic   municipal

mv   millivolt

MV   mean variation

mw   milliwatt

mxd   mixed

myg   myriagram

myl   myrialiter

mym   myriameter

MA (mechanical advantage) Increase in force obtained at the expense of speed or distance.

M.E. (M. Eng.) Abbreviation of the degree Master of Engineering.

Mfbm 1,000 feet board measure of lumber.

macadam A commonly used method of paving with crushed stone, named for John L. Macadam (1756-1836), a Scottish engineer. The road may be water-bound, cement-bound or coated with asphalt or tar.

macadam aggregate A uniformly coarse-size aggregate usually of crushed stone, slag or gravel. When compacted, voids are relatively large.

macadam spreader A machine similar to the laydown machine.

MacArthur piles Type of piles formed by steel casing filled with concrete and then withdrawn.

machine burn A darkening of the wood due to overheating by the machine knives or rolls when pieces are stopped in a machine.

machined (1) A smooth surface finish on metal. (2) Shaped by cutting or grinding.

machine, driving The power unit which applies the energy necessary to raise and lower an elevator or dumbwaiter car or to drive an escalator, a private residence inclined lift or a moving walk.

machine rating In electricity, the amount of load, or power, a machine can deliver without overheating.

machine stress-rated (MSR lumber) Lumber that has been evaluated by mechanical stress rating equipment; each piece is nondestructively tested and marked to indicate the modullus of elasticity. MSR lumber is also required to meet certain visual requirements.

machine tools A group of specially designed tools to mechanically apply joint treatment products.

macromolecule A large molecule in which there is a large number of one or several relatively simple structural units, each consisting of several atoms bonded together.

macroscopic *(see megascopic)*

made ground (land) In construction, a portion of land or ground, formed by filling in natural or artificial pits with rubbish or other material. Land brought to a higher level by earth fill, sometimes brought out of water.

magazine (1) In architecture, a warehouse or storehouse for merchandise. (2) Any building or structure, other than an explosives manufacturing building, used for the storage of explosives.

magister In medieval times, a master craftsman.

magnesia Magnesium oxide. Can appear in clinker as free MgO (periclase); in cement compounds as a solid solution.

magnesite A material usually combining calcined magnesium oxide and magnesium chloride, applied in plastic state for flooring, integral bases and wainscots on wood with metal lath, or in concrete.

magnesium A silver-white metal, used in alloys of light weight.

magnetic bearing The horizontal angle from magnetic north to a given survey line.

magnetic domains The magnetic molecules in a material such as iron, each having its own magnetic field.

magnetic driver A tool used to hold short concrete nails while they are being driven.

magnetic effect Results when a current produces a magnetic field.

magnetic field A region in space surrounding a magnet or a conductor through which current is flowing.

magnetic flow meter Line instrument for measuring liquid flow such as slurry. Sometimes used to govern regulating valve on discharge of kiln feed slurry pump.

magnetic flux The sum of all the magnetic tubes of force from a magnetic source.

magnetic hammer A special designed hammer magnetically sensitized to hold a metal fastener during application.

magnetic induction When conductors are caused to cut a magnetic field or when a magnetic field moves across conductors.

magnetic particle Nondestructive test method for ferrous material. Specimen is magnetized, iron oxide particles introduced, discontinuities gather particles to disclose defects.

magnetic repulsion A condition or state that exists when like magnetic poles repel each other.

magnetite A mineral, ferric oxide (Fe_3O_4); the principal constituent of magnetic black iron ore; specific gravity about 5.2 and Mohs hardness about 6; used as an aggregate in high density concrete.

magneto (magneto generator) A small electric generator in which the magnetic field is carried in a permanent magnet.

magnolia A Southern evergreen; also called cucumber tree.

magusalem *(slang)* Plastic roof cement.

mahogany The reddish-brown wood of a tropical American tree.

Maihak strain gauge A type of acoustic strain gauge made in Germany.

main (1) In electricity, the circuit from which all other smaller circuits are taken. (2) A major supply pipe for liquids or gases.

main bar *(see main reinforcement)*

main beam In floor construction, one of the principal beams which transmits loads directly to the columns, not onto another beam.

main contractor (prime contractor) The contractor who is responsible for the work on a site, including the work of the subcontractors.

main couple In building construction, the principal truss in a timber roof.

main rafter A roof member extending at right angles from the plate to the ridge.

main reinforcement Steel reinforcement designed to resist stresses resulting from design loads and moments, as opposed to reinforcement intended to resist secondary stresses.

main runners The heaviest integral supporting members in a suspended ceiling. Main runners are supported by hangers attached to the building structure and in turn support furring channels or rods to which lath is fastened.

main sewer A sewer which receives one or more branch sewers as tributaries.

main squeeze *(slang)* A foreman.

maintenance bond A document given by the contractor to the owner, guaranteeing to rectify defects in workmanship or materials for a specified time following completion of the project. A one-year bond is normally included in the performance bond.

maintenance period The period of time after completion of a contract during which a contractor is required to make good at his own expense any work which needs repair. Also called warranty time.

main vent *(see vent stack)*

maisonette (duplex apartment) A self-contained apartment on two levels and having its own internal stairs.

major arch Arch with spans greater than 6 ft. and uniform loads greater than 1000 lb. per ft. Typically semicircular arch, Gothic arch or parabolic arch. Has rise to span ratio greater than 0.15.

make good To repair or correct a defect.

makeup water Water supplied to replenish, as water replacing that lost by evaporation.

male nipple Pipe with threads on the outside.

mall (1) A shaded walk or an area in a retail section or shopping center for pedestrians. (2) A heavy wooden mallet. *(see maul)*

malleability The property of metal enabling it to be hammered or bent without breaking.

malleable iron *(see iron)*

mallet A small maul, or hammer, usually made of wood; used for driving another tool, such as a chisel.

Malone, Potsdam (Adirondack sandstone) A dense, strong, very hard quartzite of New York State composed wholly of quartz grains with siliceous cementing material and varying in color from a rather light pink to a reddish brown.

maltha A very viscous or stiff asphalt petroleum which hardens rapidly when exposed; used in ancient times as a mortar or stucco.

mandatory and customary benefits *(see benefits, mandatory and customary)*

mandrel (1) The cylindrical arbor or spindle on which a roll of felt or roofing is wound in the process of manufacture. (2) A piece of wood which is pushed through a pipe to enlarge it or remove distortions. *(see arbor)*

manganese A metal which is added to nearly all steels.

manganese steel *(see steel)*

manhole (1) A shaft or chamber from the surface of the ground to a sewer, large enough to enable a man to have access for the purpose of inspection and cleaning. (2) An access hole, with cover, for a boiler or a tank.

manhole cover A cast-iron plate fitting into a metal frame embedded in a concrete slab over a manhole.

manhole head The cast-iron fixture covering a manhole. It is made up of two parts: a frame, which rests on the masonry of the shaft and a removable cover. Frames are either fixed or adjustable in height.

man hour The amount of work done by one man in one hour.

manifest The shipping document-EPA Form 8700-22, used to identify the quantity, composition, origin, routing, and destination of hazardous waste during its transportation from the point of generation to the point of treatment, storage, or disposal.

manifold A chamber or tube having a number of inlets and one outlet, or one inlet and several outlets.

manipulative joint A compression joint in which the ends of the copper tubes are enlarged slightly. One advantage is that a gasket is not usually needed; the soft copper of the belled-out tube acts as a packing.

man lock A chamber through which men, not materials, pass from one air pressure environment into another. It is used as an access to a shaft, tunnel or caisson.

Manning formula Method of determining amount of flow in pipes or channels.

manometer (1) Tube containing a liquid, the surface of which moves proportionally to changes of pressures; a U-tube; a tube-type differential-pressure indicator; a pressure gauge. (2) An instrument for measuring pressure; essentially a U-tube partially filled with a liquid.

mansard roof A roof with two slopes or pitches on each of the four sides, the lower slopes steeper than the upper. Convenient for adding another story to the building. *(see curb roof)*

mansion A dwelling of large and pretentious size.

mantel (mantelpiece) The shelf and facing embellishment of a fireplace opening.

mantel tree A beam across the opening of a fireplace.

mantle The outer wall and casing of a blast furnace above the hearth.

mantlerock Unconsolidated material that overlies the earth's solid bedrock.

manual Capable of being operated by personal intervention.

manually propelled mobile scaffold A portable rolling scaffold supported by castors.

manufactured sand *(see sand)*

manufacturer's bond A security company's guarantee that it will stand behind a manufacturer's liability to finance membrane repairs occasioned by ordinary wear within a period generally limited to 5, 10, 15, or 20 years.

map cracking *(see crazing)*

maple, hard (sugar) A wood occurring from Newfoundland and Quebec to southern Manitoba and south to Georgia and Oklahoma; of dense texture, strong and durable; used for flooring particularly and for cabinetwork.

Marb-l-cote A paint in powder form;

when mixed with water and applied to a surface it will set within 24 hours and has the appearance of marble.

marble Calcium carbonate with other components which give it color, pattern and texture suitable for a desirable building stone.

marble tile Marble cut into tiles 12"×12" or less, usually ⅛" to ¾" thick. Available in various finishes, including polished, honed and split faced.

marbling The process of painting a wood surface so that it will resemble marble. Also called marblizing.

marchioness In building, a size of roofing slate measuring 22x12 inches.

marezzo An imitation marble formed with Keene's cement to which colors have been added. It is cast on smooth glass or marble beds.

margin *(see verge)*

marginal wharf A wharf parallel to the shore.

margin draft *(see drafted margin)*

margin light A narrow pane of glass at the edge of the window sash.

margin temple A pitch board with an edge strip the same width as the margin.

marine borers Any of several types of small marine animals which attack wood piers and bridge abutments.

marine glue In woodworking, an adhesive substance composed of crude rubber, pitch and shellac; the proportions are: one part rubber, two parts shellac and three parts pitch. It was used before the synthetic resins were developed.

marked face The face side of timber.

marker (1) A distinguishing threadline woven in the back toward the right hand edge to enable the workroom or the installer to assemble breadths of carpet causing the pile to lay in the same direction. (2) A pattern marking point of a distinguishing color woven into the back close to each edge to enable the workroom or the installer to assemble breadths of carpet and match

the pattern when working on the underside.

marking paint The material used to mark the laying lines on saturated felt and roofing.

markouts Paint markings on streets showing approximate locations of buried utilities and underground structures.

marl Calcareous clay, usually containing from 35 to 65 percent calcium carbonate ($CaCO_3$), found in the bottoms of shallow lakes, swamps or extinct fresh water basins.

marquee (marquise) A hood or canopy projecting over an entrance to provide protection from the weather.

marquetry Mosaic of varicolored woods, sometimes interspersed with other materials such as mother-of-pearl.

Maryland Verde Antique A serpentine that ranks high as a beautiful green marble. It is a mottled light and dark grass-green with interlocking veins of lighter green.

mash hammer Term used in Scotland for a club or sledge hammer. This hammer is used on non-headed chisels.

mashrebeeyah A latticed window.

masking During painting, the protection of the edges of a painted surface by masking them with tape or paper stuck on, or by holding a firm paper or metal mask over them.

masking tape *(see masking)*

mason A workman skilled in constructing masonry or finishing concrete surfaces.

Masonite A brand name for a hardboard product having a variety of uses such as roofing, siding, paneling, and doorskins.

masonry Construction composed of shaped or molded units, usually small enough to be handled by one man and composed of stone, ceramic brick or tile, concrete, glass, adobe or the like; sometimes used to designate cast-in-place concrete.

masonry bonded hollow wall A hollow wall built of masonry units in which the inner and outer withes of the walls are bonded together with masonry units.

masonry cement   Hydraulic cement produced for use in mortars for masonry construction where greater plasticity is desired than is obtainable by the use of portland cement alone.

masonry fill   Insulating material used to fill the cores or open spaces in masonry construction for insulation purposes.

masonry filler unit   Masonry unit used to fill in between joists or beams to provide a platform for a cast-in-place concrete slab.

masonry mortar   Mortar used in masonry structures. *(see cement, masonry; mortar)*

masonry panel wall   Exterior non-load-bearing wall whose outer surface may form the exterior building face or may be used in back of a panel curtain wall to provide fire rating as required by local code. In the latter case, it is sometimes called back-up.

masonry reinforcing   Lateral steel reinforcing rods or mesh used between courses in masonry construction.

masonry unit   A construction unit in masonry. *(see block)*

mason's adjustable multiple point suspension scaffold   A scaffold having a continuous platform supported by bearers suspended by wire rope from overhead supports, so arranged and operated as to permit the raising or lowering of the platform to desired working positions.

mason's joint   A mortar joint which consists of a projecting triangle of mortar.

mason's miter (mason's stop)   An angle joint formed by shaping the corner out of the solid stone which is not a miter but usually a butt joint away from the corner.

mason's putty   A lime putty mixed with portland cement and stone dust used for jointing ashlar.

mass   A measure of the quantity of matter in a body determined by comparing the resultant changes in velocities when the body impinges upon a standard body.

mass center   The center of gravity.

mass concrete   Any large volume of concrete cast-in-place, generally as a monolithic structure, intended to resist applied loads by virtue of its mass. It is distinct from other types of concrete because its dimensions are of such magnitude as to require that measures be taken to cope with the generation of heat and attendant volume changes.

mass curing   Adiabatic curing in sealed containers.

mass diagram   A plotting of cumulative cuts and fills used for engineering computation of highway jobs; also used in hydraulics and other fields.

mass haul curve   The curve showing the amount of excavation in a cut which is available for fill.

mass profile   A road profile showing cut and fill in cubic yards.

mass shooting   Simultaneous exploding of charges in all of a large number of holes, as contrasted with firing in sequence with delay caps.

mast   A tower or vertical beam carrying one or more load lines at its top.

master gear   Annular gear ring around rotary kiln or ball or tube mill to which the rotation is transmitted from a master pinion.

master key   A key made to operate two or more locks requiring different keys.

master pinion   Gear wheel on end of driving shaft of motor or speed-reducer, transmitting rotation to a master gear of a kiln or mill.

master plan   A plan, usually of a community or city, made to guide or restrict future development.

master switch   An electric switch controlling the operation of two or more subordinate circuits.

mastic   A term applied to thick adhesive consisting of a mixture of bituminous preparations, such as asphalt and some foreign matter, usually fine sand. Also, a quick setting waterproofing form of cement or caulking compound that retains a measure of elasticity. It may be applied with a putty knife or a pressure gun; organic tile adhesive.

mat (1) A heavy, flexible fabric of woven wire rope or chain used to confine blasts. (2) A wooden platform used in sets to support machinery on soft ground. (3) Blanket of brush lumber or poles interwoven or otherwise lashed together and weighted with rock or concrete blocks or otherwise held in place, placed to cover an area subject to scour. (4) A grid of reinforcement for foundation concrete.

matched boards Boards tongued and grooved on opposite edges to achieve a close finished joint.

match marks Indicate the pattern repeat point for ease of matching sheet goods; shown on selvage.

matching The placing of sheets of veneer to obtain a particular pattern.

match—set or drop In a set-match carpet pattern, the figure matches straight across on each side of the carpet width; in a drop match, the figure matches midway of the design; in a quarter-drop match, the figure matches one-quarter of the length of the repeat on the opposite side.

material Any substance specified for use in the construction of the project and its appurtenances.

material hose (see delivery hose)

material safety data sheet (MSDS) Written statement of the hazardous nature of a material that describes the hazards, proper protective work clothing, and emergency procedures.

materials lock A chamber through which materials and equipment pass from one air pressure environment into another.

material supplier (see supplier)

mat foundation A continuous footing supporting an array of columns in several rows in each direction, having a slab-like shape with or without depressions or openings, covering an area at least 75 percent of the total area within the outer limits of the assembly. (see raft foundations)

mathematical model Arithmetical

equations relating the variables of a process in rigid terms. Used in computer simulation of industrial processes.

matrix On as-is mortar, the cement paste in which the fine aggregate particles are embedded; in the case of concrete, the mortar in which the coarse aggregate particles are embedded. Used for cementing material in mortar, concrete and terrazzo.

mat sinkage A depression in a floor near an entrance so that a doormat placed there will be approximately at floor level.

matte finish A term applied to surfaces free from gloss or polish.

matte surface A dull non-glossy surface. Light reflected from matte surface is diffused.

mattress A ground level concrete slab used as a base for transformers or other plants, or for other similar purposes.

maturing (1) Fattening up mortar. (2) Aging of varnish to improve its properties. (3) The aging of various materials, i.e., of wood, concrete, etc.

maul (mall) A heavy wooden mallet.

maximum demand In electricity, the greatest simultaneous power demand from consumers.

maximum dry density The dry density obtained by a specified amount of compaction of soil at the optimum moisture content.

maximum rated load The total of all loads including the working load, the weight of the scaffold and such other loads as may be reasonably anticipated.

maximum size of aggregate The largest size aggregate particles present in sufficient quantity to affect the physical properties of concrete; generally designated by the sieve size on which the maximum amount permitted to be retained is five or ten percent by weight.

maximum temperature period A time interval over which the maximum temperature is held constant in an autoclave or steam-curing room.

MBDA Metal Building Dealers Associated *(see SBA)*.

MBMA Metal Building Manufacturers Association.

McDermott sandstone An even-bedded sandstone with a medium fine grain, in buff and blue colors; easy to work with and carve.

McKinlay entry borer A type of entry borer.

McMath formula Used in drainage computations; it determines quantity of runoff.

mean Intermediate as to position occupied; between extremes, equal distance from given limits; average.

mean depth In hydraulics, the cross-section area of a stream divided by its surface width.

measurement Estimating from drawings the amount of work to be done; measuring, on the site, the work done and to be paid for.

measurement and payment A system of paying for work completed by measuring the work in place and applying a previously agreed unit cost to the measured amount to determine the total payment.

measuring chain *(see engineer's chain; Gunter's chain)*

measuring water In hydraulics, a rectangular, trapezoidal or triangular notch in a thin vertical plate. From the depth of water in the notch the amount of flow can be easily determined.

mechanic A person skilled in some branch of handicraft or manual art; one trained in the repair and maintenance of mechanical equipment.

mechanical advantage The ratio of the load raised by a machine to the applied force. The mechanical advantage divided by the velocity ratio gives the efficiency of the machine.

mechanical analysis The process of determining particle-size distribution of an aggregate. *(see sieve analysis; particle-size distribution)*

mechanical anchorage Any mechanical device capable of developing the strength of the reinforcement without damage to the concrete.

mechanical application Application of plaster mortar by mechanical means: generally pumping and spraying. Distinguished from hand application with a trowel.

mechanical atomization Means of breaking the oil down into very, very small particles to allow optimum combustion. Typical range 100 to 300 psi.

mechanical bond The physical keying of one plaster coat to another or to the plaster base by plaster keys to metal lath, or by interlock between adjacent plaster coats by scratching or cross raking; also between concrete and reinforcing bars. The bond attributed to keying or interlocking action other than adhesion. Distinguished from chemical bond, which implies formation of interlocking crystals or fusion.

mechanical drawing Plans showing the plumbing, heating and related equipment layout for the building.

mechanical efficiency The ratio of the useful horsepower available at the flywheel, or power takeoff, to the horsepower developed in the engine cylinders; expressed in percent.

mechanical engineer A person trained in mechanical engineering.

mechanical engineering The design and construction of engines and machines of every sort. It overlaps electrical engineering but does not include the design of electrical circuits.

mechanical equivalent of heat (Joule's equivalent) The amount of mechanical energy which can be transformed into one unit of heat. It is equivalent to 778 foot-pounds per Btu.

mechanical key *(see mechanical bond)*

mechanical loading *(see excavator)*

mechanically rated lumber Stress grade stamped on lumber that is mechanically and automatically stamped with an assigned E and corresponding F rating.

mechanical saw The best known mechanical saws for lumber are the circular saw, band saw and jig saw.

mechanical trowel A power machine used to smooth and compact plaster finish coats. Capable of producing an extremely smooth, dense surface. Consisting of revolving metal or rubber blades. Also termed 'power trowel.'

mechanical units Plumbing and electrical components and heating or air conditioning units, which may be assembled on-site in the traditional manner, or subassemblies which may be fabricated off-site and connected together on-site. Subassembly may range from plumbing trees to completely preassembled bathrooms, kitchens and similar components.

mechanic's level A level.

mechanic's lien A lien on real property, created by statute in many areas, in favor of persons supplying labor or materials for a building or structure for the value of labor or materials supplied by them. In some jurisdictions, a mechanic's lien also exists for the value of professional services. Clear title to the property cannot be obtained until the claim for the labor, materials or professional services is settled.

median The portion of a divided highway separating traffic traveling in opposite directions.

median barrier A double-faced guardrail or other divider in the median of two adjacent highways.

median lane A speed change lane within the median to accommodate left-turning vehicles.

medical lock A special chamber in which employees are treated for decompression illness. It may also be used in pre-employment physical examinations to determine the adaptability of the prospective employee to changes in pressure.

medium In paint or enamel, the liquid part which becomes the binder after it has hardened.

medium-carbon steel (see high-carbon steel)

medium curing asphalt Liquid asphalt composed of asphalt cement and a kerosene-type diluent of medium volatility.

medium curing cutback An asphalt cement cutback with kerosene.

medium duty scaffold A scaffold designed and constructed to carry a working load not to exceed 50 pounds per square foot.

medium fit Used for a running fit under 600 rpm and with a journal pressure less than 600 psi.

medium force fit A fit requiring considerable pressure to assemble and generally resulting in a permanent assembly.

meeting rail A strip of wood or metal which forms the horizontal bar separating the upper and lower sash of a window. (see check rail)

meeting stile The stile of a door on which the lock is set; in a double door, the stiles which meet when the doors are closed.

megalith A large hewn or unhewn stone such as is found in cyclopean masonry. The Stonehenge in England is a well known example.

megalith masonry Masonry of very large stones so exactly hewn that a knife blade cannot be inserted in the joints.

megascopic Visible to the unaided eye.

melilite A group of minerals ranging from the calcium magnesium silicate, ackermanite, to the calcium aluminate silicate, gehlenite, that occur as crystals in blast-furnace slag. (see merwinite)

melt The molten portion of the raw material mass during the burning of cement clinker; firing of lightweight aggregates or expanding of blast-furnace slags.

melting Change of state from solid to liquid.

melting point For a given pressure, the temperature at which the solid and liquid phases of a substance are in equilibrium.

member (1) A part of a molding. (2) A component part. (3) A structural member; can be a wall, column, beam or tie, or a combination of these. The various structural parts of a building or the parts of one unit of a building.

membrane 1. In dam construction, a sheet or thin zone or facing made of a flexible impervious material such as asphaltic concrete, plastic concrete, steel, wood, copper, plastic, etc. A cut-off wall, or core wall, if thin and flexible, is sometimes referred to as a diaphragm wall or diaphragm. 2. A flexible or semi-flexible roof covering or waterproofing layer, whose primary function is the exclusion of water.

membrane curing A process that involves either liquid sealing compound, e.g., bituminous and paraffinic emulsions, coal tar cut-backs, pigmented and non-pigmented resin suspensions or suspensions of wax and drying oil; or nonliquid protective coating, e.g., sheet plastics or waterproof paper. Both types function as films to restrict evaporation of rising water from the fresh concrete surfaces.

membrane fireproofing A lath and plaster membrane having among its functions that of providing a barrier to fire and intense heat.

membrane theory A theory of design for thin shells, based on the premise that a shell cannot resist bending because it deflects; the only stresses that exist in any section, therefore, are shear stress and direct compression or tension.

membrane waterproofing System of waterproofing masonry walls with layers of felt, canvas or burlap and pitch.

memory Stored data on a computer.

mensuration The process of calculation of lengths, areas and volumes.

menu A list of commands on a computer.

mer The repeating of structural unit of any high polymer.

merchant bars (see iron, wrought)

mercury vapor light An electric light source of tubular form dependent on mercury.

merlon That part of a parapet which lies between two embrasures.

merwinite One of the principal crystalline phases found in blast-furnace slags.

mesh (1) In building construction, any material consisting of a network formed by the crossing of wires or strings. (2) In wire screen, the number of openings per lineal inch. (see welded wire fabric)

mesh reinforcement (see welded-wire fabric reinforcement)

metabolism Chemical changes in living cells by which energy is provided for vital processes.

metal (1) Any of various opaque, fusible, ductile and typically lustrous substances; one that is a chemical element as distinguished from an alloy. (2) Glass in its molten state. (3) Broken stone used in road building.

metal-arc welding Electric-arc welding with a metal electrode, usually using low-voltage direct current.

metal building fiber glass insulation A grade of fiberglass insulation blanket specifically manufactured for lamination to a vapor retarder.

metal cramp A bent bar for placing stones in the same course. (see cramp)

metal deck A sheet metal roofing for flat roofs.

metal defects In glass, the opposite of surface defects; applying to those defects in the body of the glass that are independent of the forming process.

metal flashing (see flashing); metal flashing is frequently used as through-wall flashing, cap flashing, counter-flashing or gravel stops)

metal gutters A type of attached gutter prefabricated of sheet metal.

metal lath A term denoting a metallic plaster base manufactured from sheet metal by slotting and subsequent expansion or by punching and forming. Types are diamond mesh, rib lath and sheet lath. Distinguished from wire lath, or wire fabric lath which is a welded or woven wire mesh.

metallic fiber A manufactured fiber composed of metal, plastic-coated metal, metal-coated plastic or a core completely covered by metal. The most important characteristic of metallic fiber in carpet is to reduce build-up of static electricity.

metallurgical cement A supersul-
phated cement.

metal sash block Concrete masonry
unit which has an end slot for use in
openings where metal sash is used.

metal trim Architraves, skirtings, picture rails and angle beads of sheet
metal placed before plastering and incorporated in the plaster surface.

metal valley A valley gutter lined with
metal, e.g., copper, lead, zinc or aluminum.

metal wall ties Strip of corrugated
metal used to tie a brick veneer wall to
framework.

metamorphic rock Pre-existing rock
altered to such an extent as to be
classed separately. One of the three
basic rock formations including igneous and sedimentary.

meter (1) Unit of linear measure in the
metric system now used in many countries equivalent to 39.37 inches, or to
1,000 millimeters or to 100 centimeters; 1,000 meters are equal to one kilometer; metre, in some areas. (2) An apparatus for measuring the flow of
liquid, gas or electrical current.

metering pin A valve plunger that controls the rate of flow of a liquid or a
gas.

metes and bounds The boundaries,
property lines or limits of a parcel of
land, defined by distances and compass
directions.

metric systems A weights and measure
system based on the meter and its decimal divisions. A cubic centimeter (1
cc) of water weighs one gram. A liter of
water (1,000 cc) weighs one kilogram.
A pressure of one kilogram per square
centimeter is equivalent to a column of
10 meters of water. Because of its very
simple relationships the metric system
is remarkably convenient for engineering calculations and is now being commonly used in most countries. *(see
complete metric tables in table section
of book)*

Mexican paver tile Used mainly on
floors, the handmade tiles vary in color,
texture and appearance. The terracotta-
like tile in hexagon, octagon, elongated

hexagon, fleur de lis, squares up to 12"
and other shapes. Coated with various
types of sealers to provide a wearing
surface.

mezzanine A story of lesser height and
area midway between the floor and
ceiling of a high story; an entresol.

mica A silicate mineral used as either a
surfacing or backing material on composition roofing.

Micarta A trade name for a plastic material made of resin soaked layers of
paper or cloth fused together under
heat and pressure. Used in sheet form
for table tops and similar durable and
decorative needs, and in many other
forms for insulation, gears, etc.

mica schist Mica mixed with quartz,
hornblende or feldspar. A dry ground
mineral used on a roofing machine of a
specified screen grading.

micro climate Local climate conditions
peculiar to a given area.

microclimatology In architecture, the
science of planning a building in accord with climatic characteristics of the
individual building site. This was a fa-
vorite practice of Frank Lloyd Wright
and is carried on by his protegeés.

micrometer gauge (micrometer) A
length-measuring instrument which
measures up to one-thousandth of an
inch. It consists of a G-shaped frame,
one leg of which is a round bar accurately threaded with 100 divisions per
inch. A nut on it is marked outside with
lines which represent 0.001 inch.

micron A unit of length; one-thousandth of a millimeter or one-millionth
of a meter.

microscopic analysis Qualitative and
quantitative identification of minerals
(including cement phases) and distribution of phases in polished, etched
samples by reflected or transmitted
light.

middle strip In flat slab framing, the
slab portion which occupies the middle
half of the span between columns. *(see
column strip)*

mid-feather (1) A parting slip. (2) The
central withe of a chimney.

mid-ordinate An ordinate which occurs midway between extremes.

midpoint (midrange) The average value of two extreme observations.

midrail A rail approximately midway between the guardrail and platform, secured to the uprights erected along the exposed sides and ends of platforms.

midspan A point midway between the supports of a beam.

mihrab (mehrab) A niche, or other feature of a Mohammedan mosque, indicating the direction in which Mecca lies.

mil One-thousandth part of an inch or .001 inch.

mild steel Steel containing from 0.2 percent to 0.5 percent carbon, having more nearly than ordinary steel the properties of wrought iron.

Milford pink granite A pink granite of a medium to coarse grain, mottled with black mica spottings, quarried in Massachusetts; it is used for monumental and general building work.

miliary pillar On Roman highways, a stone indicating a distance of 1,000 paces.

milkiness A whitish or translucent defect in a varnish film.

milk of lime Lime slaked in water.

mill (1) A building containing machinery but originally a building in which grain is ground. (2) A machine for grinding or crushing, such as a ball mill, hammer mill or pug mill.

mill construction A type of fire-resistant construction; masonry walls, heavy timber framing and planked or laminated wood floors much thicker than ordinary joist construction.

milled Having a serrated surface useful in circular metal forms that are to be turned by hand.

milled lead Lead rolled from slabs into sheets.

miller The operator who controls the grinding operation of one or several mills by regulating feed rate, circulating load, water, additions or additives, etc.

mill charge Grinding media (balls, cylpebs, concavex, slugs or flint pebbles) with which a grinding mill is partially filled.

mill file A coarse-grained file used primarily to remove excess material on metal surfaces.

mill liners Heavy cast or rolled alloy steel plates mounted inside grinding mills to (1) protect mill shell against abrasion and impact from load and charge, (2) improve grinding action, and (3) sometimes classify grinding media.

mill scale Iron-containing waste material obtained from steel rolling mills and often used as a component of the cement raw mix.

millimeter (mm) One thousandth of a meter.

millimeter of mercury A unit of pressure equal to the pressure exerted by a column of mercury 1 mm high at a temperature of 0°C.

millimicron One millionth of a millimeter.

millisecond delay (short period delay) A type of delay cap with a definite but extremely short interval between passing of current and explosion.

mill-mixed Term referring to plaster materials that have been formulated and dry-mixed by the manufacturer requiring only the addition and mixture of water at the job.

millrun mortar A mortar made in a pug mill or other types of mixers.

mill scale The black iron oxide layer formed during the hot rolling of metals, such as that formed on hot-rolled reinforcing bars. Because of this scale, untreated bars are called black bars.

Millstone A buff, blue and pink granite of Connecticut.

millwork Generally all building materials made of finished wood and manufactured in millwork plants and planing mills are included under the term millwork, such as doors, window and door frames, sash, blinds, porch work, mantels, panel work, stairways and special wood work; does not include flooring.

ceiling or siding. Often referred to as prefabricated.

millwright A mechanic specializing in installation of heavy machinery in permanent plants.

minaret Specifically, a tower of a mosque from which the muezzin calls to prayer; an alkorane; more loosely, a slender tower, usually among others.

minch house A place of shelter and rest, usually a small inn.

mineral aggregate A blend of sand, gravel and crushed rock used in asphaltic concrete.

mineralogical analysis Application of DTA, XRD, or microscopy, or other methods for identification and characterization of cement phases or constituents or raw materials.

mineral dust The portion of the fine aggregate passing the No. 200 sieve.

mineral fiber felt A felt with mineral wool as its principal component.

mineral filled asphalt Asphalt containing an appreciable percentage of finely divided mineral matter, passing the 200 sieve.

mineral filler A finely divided mineral product at least 65 percent of which will pass a No. 200 sieve. Pulverized limestone is the most commonly manufactured filler, although other stone dust, hydrated lime, portland cement and certain natural deposits of finely divided mineral matter are also used.

mineral granules Opaque, natural, or synthetically colored aggregate commonly used to surface cap sheets, granule-surfaced sheets, and roofing shingles.

mineralizer A material added to the raw mix that aids in the production of calcium silicates in the clinkering process.

mineral stabilizer A fine, water-insoluble inorganic material, used in a mixture with solid or semi-solid bituminous materials.

mineral streak A general term used to describe discoloring in hardwoods. The discoloring ranges from greenish brown to black and has a high mineral content; also called mineral stain.

mineral surface Siliceous rock granules used to cover asphalt-coated composition roofing.

mineral wool A fibrous material made from mineral slag and used for insulation. Common types are rock wool, glass wool, slag wool and others.

miner's dip needle A meter with a needle which indicates the presence of magnetic material in the ground.

miner's inch A unit used in western United States for measuring the rate of flow of water. Originally it was the flow through a one inch square hole.

minimum detectable temperature difference A quantification of the smallest temperature difference which may be discerned between one point and another on an object using an infrared sensor.

mining Usually removal of soil or rock having value because of its chemical composition.

Minnesota Black An igneous rock of the gabbro or black granite class, of medium grain, quarried at Ely, Minnesota.

Minnesota Mankato A fine- to coarse-grained, compact, semi-crystalline limestone, ranging from buff to cream, yellow and gray. There are also pink and pink-buff varieties.

minor arch Arch with maximum span of 6 ft. and loads not exceeding 1000 lb. per ft. Typically jack arch, segmented arch, or multicentered arch. Has rise to span ratio less than or equal to 0.15.

minor change (in the work) A change of minor nature in the work not involving an adjustment in the contract sum or contract time, which may be effected by field order or other written order issued by the architect or engineer.

minor diameter The smallest diameter of a screw thread.

minor structure (1) In engineering construction, any structure not classed as a bridge or a culvert; includes catch basins, inlets, manholes, retaining walls, steps, fences and other miscellaneous items. (2) In building construction, an out-building or other small structure not attached to the major structure.

minus sight In surveying, a term recommended by the ASCE instead of foresight.

minute (part) (1) One-thirtieth of Palladio's module of the Classic orders. Vignola divided the module into 12 parts in the Tuscan and Doric orders, 18 parts in the Ionic, Corinthian, and Composite orders. (2) In measurement of angles, 1/60th of a degree. (3) Minute of arc is a measurement to find the proportion of a column. *(see module)*

mirror glazing quality In plate glass, a quality used where a very high standard of glazing is required, and imperfections are discoverable only upon close inspection.

miscible The extent to which liquids or gases can be mixed or blended.

miser A large hand auger for test holing loose soil.

misfire An explosive charge which fails to detonate.

mission roofing tile (Spanish tile) A clay tile 14 inches to 18 inches long, curved to the arc of a circle, slightly tapered lengthwise, laid alternately with the convex side up, flanked by units with the concave side up.

Missouri marble A crystalline limestone generally gray with a light bluish tint and consisting of irregular grains of calcite and shells bound in a mass of calcite.

Missouri Red granite A granite of medium to coarse grain and with a rich red color.

mist coat In painting, a very thin sprayed coat, usually of cellulose lacquer.

mists Suspensions of finely-divided liquid droplets in a gas or gaseous stream.

miter The joining of two pieces at an angle that bisects the angle of junction.

miter arch French name for a pediment form used in early Greek, Celtic and Norman work.

miter box A device used by a carpenter for guiding a back saw at the proper angle for cutting a miter joint in wood.

miter brad A corrugated fastener for connecting mitered corners.

miter cut In carpentry, a cut made at an angle for joining two pieces of board cut so that they will form an angle.

miter dovetail (secret dovetail) A dovetail joint in which the pins cannot be seen and only the miter joint shows.

mitering The joining to two pieces of board at an evenly divided angle; joining two boards by using a miter joint.

miter knee A miter joint between the horizontal part of a handrail and a steeply falling part, curved like a bent knee.

miter plane A tool used for any type of utility work where a joint is made without overlapping of the boards, as in butt or miter joints.

miter-saw cut (miter-sawing board; miter box) A device used to guide a saw at a desired angle.

miter square A square similar to the try square, but with one edge of the handle having a 45° angle so it can be used for laying out miter joints.

miter templet A small frame made to guide a chisel when mitering small moldings.

mix A colloquial term designating a particular type of concrete mixture, e.g., six sack mix, lean mix, paving mix, etc.; the preferable term is mixture.

mix design *(see proportioning)*

mixed face In tunneling, digging in dirt and rock in the same heading at the same time.

mixed glue A synthetic resin glue with the hardener mixed with it in the pot.

mixed granules Various colors of granules recovered from the roofing machine when blends are run.

mixed-in-place Mixing on the roadway of mineral aggregate and liquid asphaltic road materials by graders or special road-mixing equipment.

mixed media A wood based floor that

incorporates other materials, such as stone, slate ceramic, marble or metal.

mixer   Machines employed for blending the constituents of concrete, grout, mortar or other mixture.

batch   (*see batch mixer*)

colloidal   A mixer designed to produce colloidal grout.

tilting   A horizontal-axis mixer, the drum of which can be tilted; the materials are fed in when the discharge opening of the drum is raised and the mixture is discharged by tilting the drum.

mixer efficiency   The adequacy of a mixer in rendering a homogeneous product within a stated period; homogeneity is determinable by testing for relative differences in physical properties of samples extracted from different portions of a freshly mixed batch.

mixer pan   A mixer comprising a horizontal pan or drum in which mixing is accomplished by means of the rotating pan, or fixed or rotating paddles, or both; rotation is around a vertical axis.

mixer truck   Colloquialism for the mobile unit, truck, on which is mounted a metal drum of several cubic yards capacity which is revolved to mix the ingredients of concrete while the truck is moving or stationary. (*see transit mix concrete*)

mixing   The mechanical combination of ground raw material components (such as limestone, shale or clay). Equipment used includes tanks or basins with mechanical or air agitation, circulation by pumping, or fluidization of dry meal with compressed air.

mixing cycle   The time taken for a complete cycle in a batch mixer, e.g., the time elapsing between successive repetitions of the same operation, such as successive discharges.

mixing plants   Mechanical means of storing, drying, heating and mixing aggregates and bitumen; may be permanent, temporary, traveling or improvised. (*see batch plant*)

mixing speed   Rotation rate of a mixer drum or of the paddles in an open top.

pan or trough mixer, when mixing a batch; expressed in revolutions per minute (rpm), or in peripheral feet per minute of a point on the circumference at maximum diameter.

mixing time   The period during which the constituents of a batch of concrete are mixed by a mixer; for a stationary mixer, time is given in minutes from the completion of mixer charging until the beginning of discharge; for a truck mixer, time is given in total minutes at a specified mixing speed or expressed in terms of total revolutions at a specified mixing speed.

mixing varnish   A varnish which can be mixed into oil base paint to give additional gloss.

mixing water   The water in freshly mixed sand-cement grout, mortar or concrete, exclusive of any previously absorbed by the aggregate, e.g., water considered in the computation of the net water-cement ratio. (*see batched water; surface moisture*)

mixture   The assembled, blended, commingled ingredients of mortar, concrete or the like; or the proportions for their assembly.

mnemonic   A device to aid the memory; often used in engineering formula, the symbols being chosen so that they are easily remembered; e.g., an engineering mnemonic is the bending formula MfEI yR remembered as Mifyer.

mobile crane   A crane powered by gasoline or diesel fuel and traveling either on crawler tracks or rubber tires. When lifting, these cranes are usually stabilized by outriggers.

mobile hoist   A platform hoist which can be towed. It can lift 1,000 pounds to a height which varies with the hoist from 20 to 80 feet.

mobile home   A portable structure built on a chassis or a frame and designed to be moved to a site and used, with or without a permanent foundation, as a dwelling unit when connected to utilities.

modacrylic fiber   This is a modified acrylic, composed of 35 to 85 per cent by weight of acrylonitrile—a liquid derivative. While used alone in bath or scatter rugs, in carpeting it's usually blended with an acrylic, with the exception of 100 per cent modacrylic. fabrics using a recently introduced solution-dyed fiber.

model analysis (1) Building of models to scale, subsequent testing by loading them up to design loads and measuring their deflections. (2) For hydraulic models, measuring the heads and flows of water and the interpretation of the results.

model codes Codes established to provide uniformity in regulations pertaining to building construction. Examples:
UBC - Uniform Building Code
BOCA - *(see BOCA)*
NBC - National Building Code
SBC - Standard Building Code

model method A method of estimating cost of a residence on the basis of area, perimeter and general construction.

modem A device that sends and receives data over telephone lines.

moderate heat of hydration and sulfate-resistant cement Cement (Type II) generating heat more slowly during hydration in concrete than Types I, III and V, although faster than Type IV; also makes concrete more resistant to attack by sulfate-containing water than Types I and III.

moderator Material that is used to slow down neutrons, making it easier for them to hit the nuclei of Uranium 235.

modification (to the contract documents) A written amendment to the contract signed by both parties; a change order; a written or graphic interpretation issued by the architect or engineer; a written order for a minor change in the work issued by the architect or engineer. *(see change order; field order)*

modified loose-lay Similar to procedure for loose-lay, except that adhesive is used for cementing seams to floor and at doorways. *(see loose-lay)*

modillion An ornamental bracket under the cornice of an entablature, usually in a series.

modular coordination A dimensional system affording more efficient assembly of buildings from standard building products by correlating the dimensions of a structure and the unit sizes of the materials going into it, through reference to a four inch cubical module. Efficient use eliminates extra work hours and waste of materials.

modular dimension A dimension based on a given module; usually four inches in the case of concrete masonry.

modular masonry unit One whose nominal dimensions are based on the four inch module.

modular ratio The ratio of modulus of elasticity of steel, E, to that of concrete, EC; usually denoted by the symbol n.

modular system The planning of buildings and building components to fit into a planning grid relating to a module.

modulating Of a control, tending to adjust by increments and decrements; also one modified by variation of a second condition.

module A repetitive dimensional or functional unit used in planning, recording or constructing buildings or other structures; a distinct component forming part of an ordered system.

modulus Unit of measure used in describing the strength of materials.

modulus of deformation A concept of modulus of elasticity expressed as a function of two time variables: strain in loaded concrete as a function of the age at which the load is initially applied and the length of time the load is sustained.

modulus of elasticity The ratio of normal stress to corresponding strain for tensile or compressive stresses below the proportional limit of the material; referred to as elastic modulus, Young's modulus, and Young's modulus of elasticity, denoted by the symbol E. *(see modulus of rigidity)* (Note: Few materials conform to Hooke's law throughout the entire range of stress-strain relations; deviations from it are caused by inelastic behavior. If the deviations are significant, the slope of the tangent to the stress-strain curve at any given stress, the slope of the secant drawn from the origin of any specified point on the stress-strain curve, or the slope of the chord connecting any two specified points on the stress-strain curve, may be considered as the modulus; in such cases the modulus is designated, respectively, as the initial tangent modulus, the tangent modulus, the secant modulus, or the chord modulus, and the stress stated. The modulus is expressed as force per unit of area, e.g., psi or kg per square mm.)

modulus of incompressibility The ratio of pressure in soil mass to the volume change caused by this pressure.

modulus of resilience (see resilience)

modulus of rigidity The ratio of unit shearing stress to the corresponding unit shearing strain; referred to as shear modulus and modulus of elasticity in shear, denoted by the symbol G. (see modulus of elasticity)

modulus of rupture A measure of the ultimate load-carrying capacity of a beam and sometimes referred to as rupture modulus or rupture strength. It is calculated for apparent tensile stress in the extreme fiber of a transverse test specimen under the load which produces rupture. (see flexural strength)

modulus of subgrade reaction (see coefficient of subgrade reaction)

moellon The inner filling of a masonry wall, e.g., spalls, broken stones and grout.

Moh's circle of stress Graphical representation which enables the stresses in a cross-section to be easily determined if the principal stresses are known. Commonly used for determining stresses in two directions; with slight further complication, it can also be used for determining three-dimensional stresses.

Moh's scale A standard gauge of hardness for minerals.

moil (see gad)

moist room A room in which the atmosphere is maintained at a selected temperature and a relative humidity of at least 98 percent, for the purpose of curing and storing cementitious test specimens.

moisture barrier Vapor barrier or damp-proof course.

moisture conduction Migration by wicking as contrasted to vapor movement.

moisture content Weight of water contained in wood, expressed as a percentage of the weight of the wood when oven dry; the weight of water in a soil mass divided by the weight of the solids and multiplied by 100.

moisture contour map A map with lines connecting continuous levels of moisture. When drawn by computer the wettest areas are often indicated by darkest symbols and the dryest areas left blank.

moisture movement The process by which moisture moves through a porous medium; the effects of such movement on the dimensions of a material such as concrete, mortar, cement paste or rock. (see drying shrinkage)

moisture tests Prior to installing resilient floors over a concrete subfloor, the subfloor should be tested for dampness. Mill specs should be checked to be sure the floor is proper for the installation. Test methods are:

chemical A ring of caulking compound or putty, 6" in diameter and ½" high, is securely bonded on the concrete at each corner of the room and at the center. A small hole is drilled in the concrete inside each ring and granulated anhydrous calcium chloride is placed on a watch or clock crystal, covered with a piece of glass and pressed down on the putty. If there is dampness in the slab, moisture will appear on the cover glass in 48 to 72 hours and the calcium chloride will be all or partially dissolved.

electrical Works on principle of resistance to electricity passing through the moisture in the slab. To detect deep-seated moisture, holes must be drilled halfway through the slab with pins inserted in the holes.

humidity test A relative humidity

meter is placed on the surface of the concrete next to interior walls and pillars. The meter is covered with an 18" square polyethylene sheet, sealed at the edges with tape or cement. On a slab 4" thick, test should run 24 hours; up to 72 hours on a thicker slab. If the meter reading stays at 80% slab is too wet.

mat test 24" squares of goods to be installed are placed at several points on the subfloor and installed with adhesive to be used. Seal all edges (tape) firmly to the subfloor and let remain from 24 to 48 hours. Remove patches. If beads of water are found on the subfloor, moisture is present. Test can also be performed using a water soluble adhesive. If adhesive fails to dry after 48 hours, or if it is partly or completely dissolved, there is an abnormal amount of moisture in the slab.

primer test Spread primer in several locations on the floor, including the corners. Scrape primer with a putty knife. If the primer peels off of the floor, moisture is rising to the surface of the concrete too rapidly.

mol A weight of a substance numerically equal to its molecular weight. If the weight is in pounds the unit is a *pound mol*, in grams the unit is a *gram mol*.

mold (1) A device containing a cavity into which neat cement, mortar or concrete test specimens are cast. (2) A form used in the fabrication of precast mortar or concrete units. Those used by plasterers are called running and casting. Running molds are used for cornice, rails, ribs, molding or anything run in place. Casting molds are used for additional ornamentation that cannot be run in place.

mold oil A mineral oil that is applied to the interior surface of a clean mold, before casting concrete or mortar therein, to facilitate removal of the mold after the concrete or mortar has hardened. (*See also form oil, bond breaker, and release agent.*)

moldboard Curved surface of a plow, dozer, grader blade or other dirt mover.

molded insulation A form of insulation material which can be placed in a mold and pressed into shape.

molded rubber back Carpet, on which liquid rubber is coated on the back, then rolled out with an embossed roller.

molding Material, usually patterned strips, used to provide ornamental variation of outline or contour, such as cornices, bases, window and doorjambs and heads.

mole (1) A huge self-propelled tunneling machine that augers and chews its way through soft rock to make a tunnel. (2) A sea wall, dam or quay.

mole ball An egg-shaped device pulled behind the tooth of a subsoil plow to open drainage or cable passages.

mole run A meandering ridge in a roof membrane not associated with insulation or deck joints.

molecular sieve An adsorbent composed of porous alumino-silicates with pores of uniform molecular dimensions which will selectively adsorb molecules of the substance to be gathered.

mole drain A drainage ditch cut by drawing a mole ball through it.

moler brick Brick made from diatomite.

molly (1) A loose or broken strand in a wire cable. (2) A type of threaded holder inserted into plaster and concrete to receive a bolt for hanging shutters, draperies, etc.

moment 1. The tendency of a force to cause rotation about a point or axis. 2. (*see positive moment; negative moment*)

momentary switch A switch that is operated only when pressure is applied. As soon as the pressure is released, the switch returns to its normal state.

moment, bending The moment which produces bending in a beam or other structure. It is measured by the algebraic sum of the products of all the forces multiplied by their respective lever arms.

moment connection A rigid connection between two members which transfers the moment from one side of the connection to the other side and maintains under application of load the same angle between the connected members that exist prior to the loading. Also, a connection that maintains continuity.

moment distribution A method of structural analysis for continuous beams and rigid frames whereby successive converging corrections are made to an assumed set of moments until the desired precision is obtained; also known as the Hardy Cross method.

moment of inertia Function of some property of a body or figure such as weight, mass, volume, area, length or position, equal to the summation of the products of the elementary portions by the squares of their distances from a given axis.

momentum The product of mass times velocity.

Monel metal Trade name for an alloy of nickel and copper having high resistance to corrosion.

monial (1) A division piece between the sash in a frame; a mullion. (2) An upright in any framing.

monitor (1) A raised structure on a roof having windows or louvers for ventilating or lighting the building, as a factory or warehouse. (2) In hydraulics, a high pressure nozzle mounted in a swivel on a skid frame. *(see giant)*

monk bond Flemish bond modified to show on the face two stretchers and a header repeating in each course.

monkey *(slang)* A pile-driving hammer.

monkey blood *(slang)* Liquid compound sprayed on concrete surfaces to prevent the rapid evaporation of water in the concrete mix, and to aid in the curing.

monkey milk *(slang)* A mix used in cement mortar for patching concrete.

monkey pole *(slang)* Similar to a Dutchman, but braced more firmly with two A-frames.

monkey slide *(slang)* A slanting cable-way or elevator, particularly to a canyon bottom.

monkey tail *(slang)* A scroll at the underside end of a handrail.

monkey tail bolt *(slang)* Extension bolt.

monochrome image (grey image) A thermal image with a blending of grey tones from dark to light but without the presence of isotherms.

monocottura Method of producing tile by a single firing in which body and glazes are fired once in kilns at temperature over 2000 degrees. Can have two different bodies red or white. Can be frost proof.

monofilament A filament large and strong enough to be used directly as a yarn for making textiles through any established process.

monoform base sheet A type of composition sheet roofing manufactured especially for use in the monoform system of roofing. The surfacing material is slate.

monolith A body of plain or reinforced concrete cast or erected as a single integral mass or structure.

monolithic A structure cast entirely in solid concrete.

monolithic concrete Concrete cast with no joints other than construction joints.

monolithic construction A method of pouring concrete grade beam and floor slab together to form the building foundation without forming and pouring each separately.

monolithic surface treatment A dry mixture, usually one part cement to two parts sand, which is sprinkled evenly on an unformed surface after water has largely disappeared following the strikeoff, and then worked in by floating; also called dry shake.

monolithic terrazzo The application of a ⅞ inch terrazzo topping directly to a specially prepared concrete substrata, eliminating an underbed.

monolithic topping On flatwork: a higher quality, more serviceable topping course placed promptly after the

344 monolithic unit (boxes)

base course has lost all slump and bleeding water.

monolithic unit (boxes) Units that are generally factory produced and pre-assembled volumetric elements with a high degree of finish and a minimum amount of required site erection time.

monomer A simple molecule which is capable of combining with a number of like or unlike molecules to form a polymer.

monorail A single rail support for a material handling system. Normally a standard hot rolled I-beam.

monostyle Of a single column, as a shaft monument.

montant Any vertical member of a framework, as a stile.

montmorillonoid (montmorillonite) A group of clay minerals, including montmorillonite, characterized by a sheet-like internal molecular structure; consisting of extremely finely-divided hydrous aluminum or magnesium silicates that swell on wetting, shrink on drying, and are subject to ion exchange.

monument (1) A structure whose chief purpose is commemorative. (2) A boundary stone, set by land surveyors, locating a property line or corner.

moonbeam An upward curving beam, at the base of a pile-driving rig, used to set the leads that hold the pile at an angle to the vertical for driving batter piles.

Moorish (Moresque) In the architectural or decorative manner of the Moors; Saracenic.

mop-and-flop An application procedure in which roofing elements (insulation boards, felt plies, cap sheets, etc.) are initially placed upside down adjacent to their ultimate locations, are coated with adhesive, and are then turned over and applied to the substrate.

mopboard (baseboard) A skirting board, usually with moldings, extending along an interior wall or partition primarily as a protection against de-

facement of the wall surface at floor level.

mopping An application of hot bitumen applied to the substrate or to the felts of a built-up roof membrane with a mop or mechanical applicator.

Solid Mopping a continuous mopping of a surface, leaving no unmopped areas.

Spot Mopping a mopping pattern in which hot bitumen is applied in roughly circular areas, leaving a grid of unmopped, perpendicular bands on the roof.

Sprinkle Mopping a random mopping pattern wherein heated bitumen beads are strewn onto the substrate with a brush or mop.

Strip Mopping a mopping pattern in which hot bitumen is applied in parallel bands.

mopstick A rounded handrail with a small flat surface underneath.

moresque Single strands of different colors of yarn twisted, or plied, together to form one multicolored yarn.

mortar (1) A material used in a plastic state, which can be troweled and becomes hard in place. The term is used without regard to the composition of the material or its specific use. (2) A mixture of cement paste and sand; when used in masonry construction, the mixture may contain masonry cement, or ordinary hydraulic cement with lime, and possibly other mixtures, to afford greater plasticity and durability than are attainable with ordinary hydraulic-cement paste. *(see cement, masonry; masonry mortar)*

type M High strength mortar for reinforced brick masonry and for plain masonry below grade and in contact with the earth, such as foundations, retaining walls, walks, sewers, manholes and catch basins. It is also used where very high compressive strength is important.

type N Medium strength mortar for general use in exposed masonry above grades and recommended specifically for parapet walls, chimneys and exterior masonry walls subjected to severe exposures.

type O Medium low strength mortar for non-load-bearing interior masonry walls, and for load-bearing walls of solid masonry units in which compressive stresses do not exceed 100 psi and where exposures are not severe.

type S Medium high strength mortar used where very high compressive strengths are not required, but where bond and lateral strength are important considerations.

mortar aggregate (mortar sand) Aggregate consisting of natural or manufactured sand.

mortar board A board about three feet square laid on the scaffold to receive the mortar ready for the use of a bricklayer.

mortar box The box in which the ingredients for mortar are mixed.

mortar cube A compressive strength sample of mortar made in 2″×2″×2″ cube mold.

mortar mixer A machine which mixes mortar by means of paddles in a rotating drum. These machines are usually power-driven and sometimes a large one is mounted on the back of a truck. The truck-mounted machine mixes the mortar as it travels to the job.

mortar sand *(see mortar aggregate)*

mortgage A pledging of property by the debtor, mortgagor, to the creditor, mortgagee, as security for a money debt to be paid in a specified time.

mortise (1) A cut-out receptacle in one member to receive the tenon of another to which it is to be joined. (2) A cut-out receptacle or depression to receive a lock mechanism, a hinge leaf or the like.

mortise and tenon joint A joint usually between members at right angles to each other, such as a door rail tenoned into its stile.

mortise chisel A tool used in woodworking for cutting mortises; a heavy-bodied chisel with a narrow face.

mortise gauge A carpenter's tool consisting of a head and bar containing two scratch pins which may be adjusted, for scribing parallel lines to cut mortises to whatever width may be desired.

mortise lock A lock designed to be let into a mortise extending edgewise into the stile of a door or the like, and occasionally even deeper into the rail.

mortising machine A carpenter's tool used for cutting mortises in wood, either by using a chisel or a circular cutting bit.

mosaic (1) In building, a design formed of inlaid work using small irregular-shaped fragments of marble, glazed pottery or glass, or using small colored tiles. (2) In aerial survey, a map made by fitting together many vertical photographs that have been enlarged to the same scale.

mosaic tile Formed by either dust-pressed or plastic method usually ⅛″ to ⅜″ thick with a facial area of less than six square inches. Made of porcelain or natural clay composition, in plain or with an abrasive mixture throughout.

motive power Term used to express the source from which a device such as a diaphragm valve, relay, or motor obtains its power (electric or fluid).

motor, air An air operated device which is used primarily for opening or closing dampers.

motor, capacitor A single-phase induction motor with a main winding arranged for direct connection to a source of power and an auxiliary winding connected in series with a capacitor.

motor patrol Same as blade or grader. In Britain, an auto patrol.

mottler A thick brush used for graining and marbling.

mottling Uniform, rounded marks; a defect of sprayed coats.

moulding *(see molding)*

mound breakwater A rock mound breakwater.

mount A fitted piece used to strengthen a structural member designed to add a decorative feature.

mounted tile Tile assembled into units or sheets either back mounted or face mounted, and bonded by suitable material to facilitate handling. Back mounted has perforated paper, fiber mesh, resin or other suitable material permanently attached to the back and/or edges so that a portion of the back of each tile is exposed to the bond coat. Face mounted has paper applied to the face of the tile, usually by water soluble adhesive so it is easily removed prior to grouting of the joints.

Mt. Airy granite Trade name for a medium-grain, even-textured, light gray to nearly white biotite granite quarried at Mt. Airy, North Carolina.

Mt. Waldo A light to medium gray granite of Maine.

mouse A short piece of curved lead attached to a string and slipped over a sash pulley. The other end of the string is tied to the sash cord, then pulled over the pulley by the string as the mouse is drawn through the pocket.

moused A method of winding with wire for the purpose of securing an object.

mouse hole *(slang)* A rotary drill substructure; a socket that holds a single piece of drill pipe ready to be added to the string.

mousing *(slang)* The lashing around the open jaw of a lifting hook on a crane, used to close it off so that the load won't slip.

movable bridge A bridge which can be moved to allow a ship to pass through. Drawbridges are more common.

movable dam A barrier that may be opened in whole or in part. The movable part may consist of gates, stop logs, needles, wickets or any other device whereby the area for flow, through or over the dam, may be controlled.

moving forms Large prefabricated units of formwork incorporating supports, and designed to be moved horizontally on rollers or similar devices with a minimum amount of dismantling between successive uses.

moving load A live load which moves; e.g., pedestrians, automobiles, etc.

moving walk A type of passenger-carrying device on which passengers stand or walk, and in which the passenger-carrying surface remains parallel to its direction of motion and is uninterrupted.

moving walk, belt type A moving walk with a power-driven continuous belt treadway.

moving walk, belt pallet type A moving walk with a series of connected and power-driven pallets to which a continuous belt treadway is fastened.

moving walk, pallet type A moving walk with a series of connected and power-driven pallets which together constitute the treadway.

moving walk, edge supported belt type A moving walk with the treadway supported near its edges by a succession of rollers.

moving walk, roller bed type A moving walk with the treadway supported throughout its width by a succession of rollers.

moving walk, slider-bed type A moving walk with the treadway sliding upon a supporting surface.

moving walk system A series of moving walks in end to end or side by side relationship with no landings between treadways.

MSDS The acronym for material safety data sheets—standard information sheets that are provided by chemical manufacturers with their chemicals, identifying any hazards associated with the product and outlining ways to respond to accidental spills.

muck Excavated material or material to be excavated; mud rich in humus or decayed vegetation.

muckers Laborers who muck out tunnels and excavations.

mucking tools Earth auger; small orange-peel bucket, jet, etc.; used for excavating underpinning cylinders too small to be entered and dug out by men.

muck shifting Muck or mud moving.

mud (1) Generally any soil containing enough water to make it soft. (2) In rotary drilling, a mixture of water with fine drill cuttings and added material which is pumped through the drill string to clean the hole and cool the bit. **(3)** *(slang)* Concrete or mortar. **(4)** *(slang)* Drywall taping compound.

mudcapping (1) Blasting boulders or other rock by means of explosive laid on the surface and covered with mud. *(see blistering)* **(2)** Sometimes known as bulldozing, adobe blasting or dobying. So called because the explosives are not confined in a drill hole.

mud cracking Surface cracking resembling a dried mud flat.

mud flush *(slang)* A drilling fluid.

mud jacking Boring a hole through a concrete slab which has sunk and connecting it to a mud jack by flexible pipe. The mud jack is a truck on which there is a slurry mixer for a pump which forces the mix under the slab and elevates it.

mud ring *(slang)* Receptacle cover for use on plastered surfaces.

mud scrapper *(slang)* Brick layer.

mudsill A plank, frame or small footing on the ground used as base for a shore or post in form work or to support framed construction.

mudslab A two to six inch layer of concrete below a structural concrete floor, or footing over soft, wet soil.

mud slinger *(slang)* Special concrete mixer that discharges concrete forward rather than from the rear.

mud wall A wall made of tamped mud, sometimes stuccoed.

mud wave The front face of a mud slide.

muffle A layer of mortar covering a horsed mold to the thickness of the finishing coat; used for roughing out the core of a molding. Before the finishing coat is run, the muffle is chipped off the mold.

muistanden Literally, mouse teeth; the introduction into the brickwork, at edge of a gable, of brick set at right angles to the slope. In Virginia the practice is called tumbling.

mulch saturant A petroleum asphalt used only as a saturant for mulch as differentiated from felt or roofing saturant.

mule A template used to shape the profile of a curb and gutter.

mullen A test of the ability of a sheet of material to resist puncture.

mullet A piece of grooved wood which is moved along the edge of a panel to check it for thickness.

mullion The thin vertical bars which divide lights in a window or panels in a door.

multi-cord A cable with two or more wires.

multielement prestressing Prestressing accomplished by stressing an assembly of several individual structural elements as a means of producing one integrated structural member.

multifilament Yarns made of many filaments plied or spun together. The finer the filaments spun together, the softer and more luxurious the yarn and textiles made from it.

multi-gable building Buildings consisting of more than one gable across the width of the building.

multiple lines A single line reeved around two or more sheaves so as to increase pull at the expense of speed.

multiple of direct personnel expense A method of compensation for professional services based on the direct expense of professional and technical personnel including cost of salaries and mandatory and customary benefits, multiplied by an agreed factor.

multiple surface treatments Commonly two or three successive applications of asphaltic material and mineral aggregate. Treatments designated armor coat, multiple lift and inverted penetration are essentially multiple surface treatments.

multiplier The factor by which an architect's direct personnel expense is multiplied to determine compensation for his professional services or designated portions thereof.

multi-span building A building consisting of more than one span across the width of the building. Multiple gable buildings and single gable buildings with interior posts are examples.

multi-stage stressing Prestressing performed in stages as the construction progresses.

multi-unit wall A wall composed of two or more wythes of masonry.

multi-use bit A detachable drill bit that can be sharpened and reshaped when worn.

municipal engineering The design and maintenance of public service such as roads, sewers, water supply, airfields, etc.

munnion (muntin) A mullion.

muntil *(see mullion)*

muntin Surface applied dividers on windows.

mushroom construction Reinforced concrete slabs carried by columns which may be flared at the top but which are not joined by beams. The slabs may be thickened around the columns.

music wire Steel wire used in aligning. *(see plumb lines)*

mustard *(slang)* Concrete.

mustard mixer *(slang)* A concrete mixer.

Mylar (trademark) Tough and translucent polyester drafting film.

myrtle burl Also called California laurel or baytree; a wood of the West Coast, hard, strong, golden brown and yellowish green in color, sometimes with dark purple blotches; used for veneer.

n noon, number

N nitrogen, normal, north

Na sodium

nav navigable

NBC National Building Code

NBFU National Board of Fire Underwriters

NC nitrocellulose, no charge

Ni nickel

NIC not in contract

NM nautical mile, not marked

no north, number

NOP not otherwise provided for

norm normal

N.Pl. nickel-plated

NPSH Net Positive Suction Head

nr near, number

N.R.C. Nuclear Regulatory Commission.

NS not specified

ntp normal temperature and pressure

nt.wt./n.wt. net weight

num numeral

nail A slender piece of metal pointed at one end for driving into wood, and flat or rounded at the other end for striking with a hammer; used as a wood fastener by carpenters and other construction workers. The sizes of nails are indicated by the term penny, abbreviated d, which originally indicated the price per hundred, but now refers to the length. Although the sizes of nails may vary as much as ⅛ to ¼ inch from that indicated, the approximate lengths sold are:

  4 penny nail — 1¼ inches
  6 penny nail — 2 inches
  8 penny nail — 2½ inches
  10 penny nail — 3 inches
  20 penny nail — 4 inches
  60 penny nail — 6 inches

nailable Material into which nails can be driven and which will hold nails.

nailable concrete Concrete usually made with a suitable lightweight aggregate, with or without the addition of sawdust, into which nails can be driven.

nailer A strip of wood or other fitting attached to or set in concrete, or attached to steel to facilitate making nailed connections.

nail float A devil float with a nail projecting from it.

nailing blocks Wood members set in masonry to anchor other members to the masonry with nails or screws.

nailing ground A common ground.

nail pop An abnormal flaw, where the fastener has moved outward relative to the board, usually because of improper wallboard application or lumber shrinkage.

nail puller Any small pinch bar suitable for prying purposes, with a V-shaped, or forked, end which can be slipped under the head of a nail for prying it loose from the wood; also, a mechanical device provided with two jaws, one of which serves as a leverage heel for gripping a nail and prying it loose from a board.

nail punch (nail set) A tool usually made from a solid bar of high-grade tool steel measuring about four inches in length, used to set the heads of nails below the surface of wood. One end of the tool is drawn to a taper and the head is shaped so there is slight possibility of the device slipping off the head of a nail.

nail spotter A small box-type applicator for covering dimpled nail heads with joint compound. *(see ames tools)*

naked flooring The timbers of a floor before the boards are laid.

naked wall In plastering, a term applied to a wall which is lathed and ready for the plastering; an unplastered, lathed wall.

naphtha A thinner distilled from organic material at temperatures from 160°C to 270°C, particularly from petroleum consisting mainly of paraffins and olefines. It is used in painting with caution due to its strong smell.

nappe A sheet of water which flows over the crest of a weir or dam.

narrow back *(slang)* Inside wireman; electrician.

narrow London A long narrow trowel used in bricklaying.

narrow-ringed timber Wood which has grown slowly and has narrowed, less conspicuous annual rings. It is therefore stronger than wood which has grown quickly.

narthex The entrance vestibule of a church; sometimes the near end of the nave behind a screen.

natatorium A building or room sheltering a swimming pool.

National Coil Coaters Association Association composed of North American coil coasters charged with the promotion of the use of coated coils.

nattes A basket-weave surface decoration.

natural asphalt (native asphalt) Asphalt occurring in nature which has been derived from petroleum by natural processes of evaporation of volatile fractions leaving the asphalt fractions; the native asphalts of most importance are found in the Trinidad and Bermudez Lake deposits; asphalt from these sources often is called lake asphalt. Natural asphalt usually must be refined and softened prior to use.

natural beds In stratified rocks, the surface of a stone as it lies in the quarry. If not laid in walls in their natural bed, the layers may separate.

natural cement A cement made from natural earth requiring little preparation; similar to hydraulic lime. *(see cement, natural)*

natural clay tile A ceramic mosaic or paver tile made by dust-pressed or plastic method. Made from clays that produce a dense body with a distinctive slightly textured appearance.

natural convection air cooler An air cooler depending upon natural convection for air circulation.

natural draft A means of creating air flow through the combustion chamber by a chimney effect.

natural finish A transparent finish, usually a drying oil, sealer or varnish, applied on wood for the purpose of protection against soiling or weathering. Such a finish may not seriously alter the original color of the wood or obscure its grain pattern.

natural frequency conveyor Horizontal or slightly inclined conveyor for dry materials, consisting of a pan or trough suspended from springs, the conveying action being caused by lengthwise reciprocal movements of the trough. The number of these movements per minute (free oscillations) depends on the weight and design of the pan and frame, length, weight and rigidity of the springs, and weight of material.

natural frequency of a foundation The frequency of free vibration of a soil foundation system. Frequency should be appreciably different from that of any machines carried by the foundation, to avoid resonance.

natural gas Gas which flows from the ground and which can be used as a fuel. It usually contains methane and other paraffins and olefines.

natural harbor A harbor made by the shape of the coastline.

natural rock asphalt Rock such as sandstone or limestone which contains asphalt or bitumen in the voids.

natural seasoning The drying of timber by stacking it so that it is exposed to the air but sheltered from sun and rain. The process usually takes years and is therefore costly. This method is older than kiln seasoning and is sometimes preferred.

natural stone Stone which has been quarried and cut as opposed to cut stone.

nave That portion of a church interior on the main axis, and not including the transepts, for occupation by lay worshippers.

Navier's hypothesis An assumption used by engineers in the design of beams. The stress or strain at any point, due to bending, is assumed to be proportional to the distance from the neutral axis. This hypothesis is fairly accurate and, together with Bernoulli's assumption and Hooke's law, greatly simplifies beam calculations. Galileo made the first recorded attempt at formulating this hypothesis early in the 17th century.

navvy (*slang*) A power shovel with excavator attachments.

navvy pick (*slang*) A heavy double-pointed pick, or a pick with a point at one end and a chisel at the other.

neat Used without addition of other materials, as neat cement or neat plaster.

neat cement In masonry, a pure cement uncut by a sand admixture.

neat cement grout A fluid mixture of hydraulic cement and water with or without admixture; also the hardened equivalent of such mixture.

neat cement paste A mixture of hydraulic cement and water, both before and after setting and hardening.

neat line A line defining the proposed or specified limits of an excavation or structure. Any material removed beyond the neat line is overbreak.

neat plaster A term applied to plaster made without sand.

neat size The dimensions of a piece of lumber after cutting and planing.

neat work (**1**) (*slang*) Brickwork above the footing that is visible. (**2**) A pure cement uncut by a sand admixture. (*see neat cement*)

nebule A form of ornament characteristic of Norman architecture, the lower edge of which is undulating.

neck In architecture, that part of a column immediately below the capital and directly above the astragal at the head of the shaft.

necking (**1**) In architecture, any narrow molding encircling a column near the head, between the top of the shaft and the projecting part of the capital. (**2**) The contraction that occurs when a ductile metal fails in tension. It is seen in broken tensile test pieces and is an example of plastic deformation.

needle (needle beam) A horizontal beam or group of beams for carrying the load of a column, wall or other part of a structure, usually while it is being underpinned; an underpinning beam supporting radially arranged beams all around it to support the walls of a tunnel; in flying or raking shores, a short horizontal piece which passes through the vertical wall piece and the wall. It holds the wall piece in place and forms an abutment for the sloping shores.

needle bath A shower bath in which water jets strike the user horizontally.

needle beam scaffold A light duty scaffold consisting of needle beams supporting a platform.

needle instrument A surveying instrument controlled by a compass needle.

needle punched A mechanical entanglement of dry laid (usually cross-lapped, carded staple fiber) webs where barbed needles achieve, in multiple punches, mechanical bonding.

needle scaffold Scaffolding hung on needles driven into the wall.

needle valve A cone-shaped valve ending in a sharp point. It is used to regulate flow into large turbines.

needle weir A fixed frame weir carrying heavy vertical timbers, (needles), in contact. The timbers can be withdrawn as needed to lower the water level.

needling Inserting a needle into a wall.

negative moment A condition of flexure in which top fibers of a horizontally placed member, or external fibers of a vertically placed exterior member, are subjected to tensile stresses. Also called hogging moment.

negative reinforcement Steel reinforcement for negative moment.

negotiation phase (*see bidding*)

Neo-Classic Any revival of Classical architectural forms.

Neo-Gothic A revival of Gothic forms, such as occurred both in England and the United States in the nineteenth century.

Neo-Greek A revival of Greek forms; Neo-Greque in France, where a revival developed in the first half of the nineteenth century.

neon lights Elements of illumination depending upon electrical discharge in tubes of neon gas.

Neoprene Trade name for an oil-resistant synthetic rubber, like PVC, with other excellent properties of non-flammability and light resistance. Neoprene rubber bridge bearing pad used on prestressed concrete or steel construction, providing a smooth and uniform transfer of load from the beam to the substructure.

nervure A side or secondary rib of a groined vault.

nest of saws A set of detachable saw blades intended for use in the same handle. Such a collection of thin, narrow-bladed saws usually consists of one or more compass saws and a keyhole saw designed primarily for cutting out small holes.

net cross-sectional area The gross cross-sectional area of a section minus the area of cores or cellular spaces. The cross-sectional area of grooves in scored units is not deducted from the gross cross-sectional area to obtain the net cross-sectional area.

net cut In sidehill work, the cut required, less the fill required, at a particular station or part of a road.

net fill The fill required, less the cut, at a particular station or part of a road.

net line (neat line) The limit within which no material may be left in an excavation; it refers to the sides, not to the bottom or sub-grade, of an excavation.

net mixing water (see mixing water)

net seam A neat flooring seam which results from the angle at which the knife blade is held. If the blade is held at a true 90 degrees to the floor, a net seam results. Tilting the blade away from the edge will result in an open seam; toward the edge produces too tight of a seam.

net ton (see short ton)

network (C.P.M.) A synonym for arrow diagram drawn to represent the relations of the activities and events of a construction project.

neutral axis A line where the longitudinal stress is zero in the plane of a structural member which is subject to bending.

neutralizing Preparation of concrete, cement mortar or plaster surfaces for painting, so that the lime in such surfaces does not attack the paint.

neutral pressure (neutral stress) The hydrostatic pressure in the pore water of the soil.

neutral refractory Refractory which is neither definitely acid nor definitely basic. The most nearly neutral of all common refractory materials is chrome ore.

neutral sealants Acidic acid-free and aimine-free sealants.

neutron Fundamental particle of matter having a mass of 1.009 but no electric charge. It is a constituent of the nucleus of all elements except hydrogen.

neutron absorption The process by which a neutron is "captured" by an atom of the target material, thereby transferring its nucleus to the next higher isotope of the target.

neutron activation analysis Determination of trace components in a sample of detecting and interpreting beta or gamma radiation induced by irradiating the sample with thermal velocity or high energy neutrons.

neutron sources Neutrons may be produced by reactors, accelerators, or certain radioactive isotopes. In most portable gauging applications neutrons are produced by isotopes. They are the reaction between alpha particles and beryllium, with radium 226 or americium 241 being the source of alpha particles.

newel (newel post) An upright post supporting the handrail at the top and bottom of a stairway, or at the turn on a landing; also, the main post about which a circular staircase winds; a stone column carrying the inner ends of the treads of a spiral stone staircase.

newel cap A top or cap for the newel post. *(see newel)*

newel drop A downward decorative projection on a newel post through a soffit.

newel joint A joint between the newel and the handrail.

new energy Electrical or chemical energy converted to thermal or mechanical energy expressly for the purpose of comfort heating or cooling.

newton SI unit of measure for force (N).

New York rod A leveling rod marked with narrow lines, ruler-fashion.

N grade wood A special order, natural finish, veneer. Heartwood, free of open defect, should be selected.

nib (cog) (1) A lug pointing downward at the upper end of a tile and hooking over the tiling batten. (2) The part of the top edge of a vertical sheet of asphalt which fits into a chase in the wall, which it protects. (3) A small solid particle which projects above a varnished surface. A varnish with nibs is called bitty.

nib grade (nib rule) A 2x⅞ inch straight edge nailed on the floating coat of a ceiling on which a cornice mold is to be run. It holds the upper end of the horsed mold in position just as the running rule holds the lower edge.

niche A recess sunk in a wall, generally for the reception of a statue. Niches sometimes terminate by a simple label, but more commonly by a canopy, and with a bracket or corbel for the figure, in which case they are often called tabernacles.

nickel A mineral used widely, as is chromium, for electroplating upon other metals, e.g., in plumbing fixtures.

nickel steel *(see steel)*

nicker A mason's broad chisel for grooving a stone before splitting. *(see center bit)*

nicol prism A system of two optically clear crystals of calcite, Iceland spar, used in producing a plane-polarized light.

nidged (nigged) ashlar Stone, particularly granite, roughly dressed with a pick or pointed hammer. The hardest granite can be dressed only in this manner.

night latch A spring lock, knob-operated inside, key-operated outside.

night vent (ventlight; vent sash; ventilator) A small opening pane with horizontal hinges, at the top of a casement window.

ni-hard (trade name) Grinding media and mill liners made of special alloy steel containing nickel.

Nineteen-inch selvage A prepared roofing sheet with a 17-inch granule-surfaced exposure and a nongranule-surfaced 19-inch selvage edge. This material is sometimes referred to as SIS or as Wide-Selvage Ashalt Roll Roofing Material Surfaced with Mineral Granules.

ninety-pound A prepared roll roofing with a granule surfaced exposure that has a mass of approximately 4400 g/m^3 (90 lb/108 ft^3).

nip The seizing of stone between the jaws or rolls of a crusher.

nip, angle of In a roll crusher, the angle between tangents to the roll surfaces at the widest point at which they will grip a stone.

nipper Power tongs that grab a pile-driving hammer to raise it.

nipple (thimble) (1) A short piece of pipe, male-threaded for connecting two lengths of pipe or hose. (2) A small valve at the high points of a hot-water system through which air can be released to prevent air locks. (3) A small brass tube screwed into a machine part; grease is injected through it by use of grease gun.

nipple, close A nipple so short that its two sets of threads meet in the middle.

Nissen hut A semicylindrical structure

of corrugated steel, adapted to military use, taking its name from the designer, a British engineer.

nitramon   An insensitive, safe explosive which can be detonated only by a detonating fuse. With a good detonating fuse, it is one of the safest known explosives.

nitriding (nitrogen hardening)   Case-hardening of steel by holding it at about 500°C for 2½ days in ammonia gas to introduce nitrogen into the surface of the metal. No subsequent heat treatment is needed and this process distorts the steel less than carburizing or cyanide hardening.

nitrile rubber   A family of copolymers of butadiene and acrylonitrile that can be vulcanized into tough oil resistant compounds. Blends with PVC are used where ozone and weathering are important requirements in addition to its inherrent oil and fuel resistance.

nitrocellulose (cellulose nitrate; guncotton)   An important constituent of most modern lacquers used for lacquering metal, wood or textiles. It is also used for making plastic wood and some glues. Another use is as a solid explosive, used with nitroglycerin in gelatin explosives.

nitroglycerin   A powerful liquid explosive that is dangerously unstable unless combined with other materials.

nitrous fumes   Reddish fumes of NO_2 and N_2O_3 produced when nitroglycerine explosives burn instead of detonating. They are very poisonous.

NO   Notation used to represent two toxic gaseous nitrogen oxides, nitric oxide (NO) and nitrogen dioxide (NO), emitted during combustion of fuels in air, etc.

noble metal   A metal with marked resistance to chemical reaction, particularly to oxidation and to solution by inorganic acids.

nocturnal cooling   A method of cooling through radiation of heat from warm surfaces to a clear night sky.

nocturnal radiation   Exchange of infrared radiation between the solar collector and the atmosphere. This takes place in daylight as well, but is much more noticeable at night.

node   A point in a framed structure, particularly a truss, where two or more members meet.

nodules   (1) Moist, ball-shaped agglomerations of raw materials containing about 10-12 percent water, up to 1 in. in diameter; used as feed to semidry process rotary kilns, shaft kilns, or Lepol grates. (2) Lumps of nearly dried slurry sliding out of chain section and passing down through wet-process rotary kiln. Depending on a number of operational factors and physical characteristics of the raw materials, these nodules contain between 5 and 12 percent residual moisture. The physical strength of the nodules has a considerable influence on kiln capacity, heat economy and dust loss.

nodulizer   Machine for producing nodules for semi-dry process kilns or Lepol grates. May be: (1) an inclined rotating drum, (2) a rotating disc, up to 30 ft. diameter with a rim, inclined about 30 degrees from horizontal, (3) a pug mill or (4) an extruder.

no-fines concrete   A concrete mixture containing little or no fine aggregate.

nog   A fixing or bracing brick.

nogging (nogging piece; nog)   (1) Horizontal short timbers which stiffen the studs of a framed partition. (2) Filling of brick, clay or other solid material, between the closely spaced studding of a frame wall. *(see bricknogging)*

noise   Any undesired sound which usually contains many frequency components over a wide range.

noise absorption   The noise level within a room reduced before it is built by discontinuous construction, or after it is built by noise absorption; that is, by surrounding it or filling it with absorbent, nonechoing material.

noise energy   The accumulative effect when continuous noise in a room bounces off walls, floors and ceilings.

noise insulation   The prevention of sound transmission of walls, floors and ceilings.

noise quieting The elimination by absorption of as much sound energy as possible.

noise reduction A reduction or loss in sound transmission from one space to another space, through one or more parallel paths of: ceiling-furred plenum-ceiling, through partitions, along ventilation ducts, or door-corridor-door.

noise reduction coefficient The average sound absorption coefficient of a material, to the nearest .05 at the four frequencies of 250, 500, 1000 and 2000 cycles.

nominal term indicating that the full measurement is not used; usually slightly less than the full net measurement, as with 2"x4" studs which have an actual size when dry of $1\frac{1}{2}"x3\frac{1}{2}"$.

nominal dimension (1) The actual masonry dimension plus an amount equal to the thickness of a mortar joint, but not more than $\frac{1}{2}$ inch. (2) The size you ask for when buying lumber; actual size is less, because of surfacing and shrinkage. For example, a nominal 2x4 is actually about $1\frac{1}{2}x3\frac{1}{2}$.

nominal mix The proportions of the constituents of a proposed concrete mixture.

nominal size (1) The dimension of timber after sawing but before planing or otherwise working on it. It is usually about $\frac{1}{8}$ to $\frac{1}{8}$ inch larger than the final size after planing. (2) A term used to express the sizes of pipe fittings, $\frac{1}{2}$ inch, 1 inch, $1\frac{1}{2}$ inch, although the dimensions by which they are called are not exact.

nomogram (alignment chart) A diagram used for eliminating or shortening calculations. The simplest form consists of three straight lines graduated for the variables in a relationship. By joining any two of them with a ruler, the third can be read off. One line showing the velocity of flow in a pipe can be related to a second showing the internal diameter and to a third showing either the quantity flowing or the friction loss. Nomograms are much simpler to read than graphs showing the same amount of information, since they have no confusing background of squared lines. They give no indication of variation, and this may be a slight disadvantage.

non-agitating unit A truck-mounted container for transporting central mixed concrete, not equipped to provide agitation, slow mixing, during delivery.

non-air-entrained concrete Concrete in which neither an air-entraining admixture nor air-entraining cement has been used.

non-asphaltic road oil Non-hardening petroleum distillate used as dust laying oil.

non-bearing partition or wall A wall which merely separates space into rooms, but does not carry overhead partitions or floor joists. Carries only its own weight, as opposed to a load-bearing wall.

non-cohesive soil A frictional soil such as sand, gravel, etc.

non-collusion affidavit Notarized statement by a bidder that he has prepared his bid without collusion of any kind.

non-combustible A term preferred to the old word incombustible, meaning that which does not burn.

nonconcordant tendons In statically indeterminate structures, tendons that are not coincident with the pressure line caused by the tendons. *(see cap cables)*

non-conductor Any material that does not readily conduct electrical current; used as insulation.

non-conforming work Work that does not fulfill the requirements of the contract documents.

nondepletable energy source Energy source which cannot be exhausted by use, such as wind and solar energy.

non-destructive testing (NDT) Methods which can evaluate the strength or composition of material without damaging the object under test.

non-drying In glazing, descriptive of a compound that does not form a surface skin after application.

non-electric delay blasting cap A blasting cap with an integral delay element and capable of being detonated by a detonation impulse or signal from miniaturized detonating cord.

non-evaporative water The water that is chemically combined during cement hydration; not removable by specified drying. *(see evaporative water)*

non-ferrous Containing no iron; said of metal such as brass or copper.

non-flammable A term used to mean material which will not burn with a flame.

non-hydraulic lime A high calcium lime.

non-ionizing radiation An amplification of light through ultraviolet and infrared rays by means of instruments such as the laser. Non-ionizing radiation includes microwave frequencies beginning at approximately 100 megahertz (108) and extending to 100 gigahertz (1011) and the infrared and ultraviolet and visible light frequencies as may be utilized in microwave, maser and laser equipment.

non-manipulative joint A compression joint requiring no work on the pipe other than cutting the ends square.

non-metallic minerals Minerals containing no metal, i.e.: abrasives, asbestos, asphalt, building stone, clay, lime, coal, petroleum, gems, fossil gums, natural gas, pigments.

non-pressure drainage A condition in which a static pressure cannot be imposed safely on the building drain. This condition is sometimes referred to as gravity flow and implies that the sloping pipes are not completely filled.

non-pressure treatments for timber Application of a wood preservative by brush, spray, dipping, steeping, etc.

non-prestressed reinforcement Ordinary or high tensile strength reinforcing steel, as used in prestressed concrete construction, and subjected neither to prestressing nor post-tensioning.

non-return valve A check valve.

non-simultaneous prestressing The post-tensioning of tendons individually rather than simultaneously.

non-slip floor (non-skid floor) A concrete floor surface roughened by treatment with iron filings, carborundum powder or indented while it is wet.

non-staining mortar A mortar with a low free-alkali content to avoid efflorescence or staining of adjacent masonry units by migration of soluble materials.

non-tilting mixer A drum-shaped concrete mixer with two openings, rotating about a horizontal axis. The mixed concrete is extracted by inserting a chute which catches the concrete as it drops from the side baffles.

non-union *(see open shop)*

non-vitreous When water absorption exceeds 7% in ceramic tile, it is considered non-vitreous.

non-woven A carpet fabric made up of a web of fibers held together by a chemical or fibrous bonding agent.

nook A recess in, or extension beyond, a room, without separation from the main body unless by a slight change of level.

norm The meter CPM reading of hydrogen found in a BUR in its dryest area (lowest reading). *(see background count)*

normal Load applied perpendicularly to a beam or other structural member.

normal condition When working under compressed air, a situation in which exposure to compressed air is limited to a single continuous working period followed by a single decompression in any given 24 hour period; the total time of exposure to compressed air during the single continuous working period is not interrupted by exposure to normal atmospheric pressure, and a second exposure to compressed air does not occur until at least 12 consecutive hours of exposure to normal atmospheric pressure has elapsed.

normal consistency The degrees of wetness exhibited by a freshly mixed concrete, mortar or neat cement grout when the workability of the mixture is considered acceptable for the purpose at hand.

normal curve *(see Gaussian curve)*

normal distribution Also known as Gaussian distribution. The distribution of results of random events which follow specific probability rules, e.g. flipping of coins.

normal fault (gravity fault) A rock fracture which has been caused by pulling the rocks apart. Therefore, the two intersections of a faulted seam are seen to be separated at a width equal to the heave. The contrary of a reversed fault.

normal haul The cost of a haul which is included in the cost of excavation so that no separate charge is made for it.

normalizing Heating of steel or other metal to above the range of critical points, followed by cooling by air. This softens the metal and makes it less brittle.

normal-weight concrete *(see concrete, normal-weight)*

Norman architecture The development of Romanesque in Normandy and England for a century after the Conquest.

Norman brick A brick measuring 2⅔×4×12 inches, including mortar joints. Three courses of this size lay up eight inches in height.

north-light roof (saw-tooth roof) A sloping roof having one steep slope and one gentle slope. In the northern hemisphere, the steep slope is usually glazed and faces north. It is often built facing south in the southern hemisphere.

North River bluestone A New York stone used for trim, curbing and paving.

Norwood blender That part of the roofing machine which distributes granules to the roofing sheet surface in a predetermined amount and position.

Norwood hopper The hopper part of the Norwood blender.

nose (1) Any blunt overhang; a nosing. (2) That portion of a tread projecting beyond the face of the riser immediately below.

nose castings Heat resistant metal segments for holding kiln lining at discharge end.

nosing (1) A half round, over-hanging edge to a stair tread, flat roof, window sill, etc., in concrete, stone or timber; the projecting part of a buttress. (2) The lateral load from a locomotive wheel in either direction, usually taken in bridge design as 10 tons at rail level perpendicular.

nosing line An angular line touching the edges of the nosings on a stair. The margin of a close string is measured from this line.

no-slump concrete Concrete with a slump of one inch (25 mm) or less.

notch (gain) A groove cut in a timber to receive another timber. *(see dap)*

notched bar test An impact test.

notch effect The locally increased stress at a point in a member which changes in section at a sharp angle. Close to a right angle notch the stress can be three times as high as the average across the reduced section. Notches are therefore avoided in highly stressed members. *(see impact test)*

notcher A machine in a steel fabricating shop which strips the flanges from the ends of rolled joists.

notching (1) Joining two pieces of lumber by cutting a piece of one or both. (2) Excavating by cutting a series of horizontal steps; fabricating.

notch plate A small weir used in laboratory models of hydraulic structures.

notice of award Written notice to the contractor that his proposal has been accepted.

notice to bidders A notice contained in the bidding requirements informing prospective bidders of the opportunity to submit bids on a project and setting forth the procedures for doing so.

notice to proceed Written communication issued by the owner to the contractor authorizing him to proceed with the work and establishing the date of commencement of the work. This also applies to a notice from the prime contractor to a sub-contractor to proceed, although such notices are often oral.

novelty siding (German siding) A term formerly used as descriptive of siding with a lower edge intended to be decorative.

nozzle (nozzle tip) **(1)** An outlet at the end of piping, open as for a fountain jet, or valved as in a hose nozzle. **(2)** Attachment at end of shotcrete material hose from which material is jetted at high velocity; attachment at end of hose used in machine-applied portland cement plaster.

nozzle liner Replaceable rubber insert in nozzle tip to prevent wear of metal nozzle.

nozzleman Workman on shotcrete gunite, or other similar crew who manipulates the nozzle, controls consistency and makes final disposition of the material.

nozzle tip *(see nozzle)*

nozzle velocity Velocity of material at exit from nozzle, usually stated in feet, or centimeters per second.

N-truss A Pratt truss.

nuclear magnetic resonance Qualitative and quantitative determination of elements in a sample of observation of the resonance characteristics of atomic nuclei in an applied magnetic field.

nuclear reactor A system consisting of fuel containing fissionable material (usually uranium pellets bound together in steel jacketed tubes), a moderator (often water is used) to carry away excess heat and slow down neutrons, a coolant to carry away heat (sometimes the same water used as a moderator), and control rods all of which are contained in a core where controlled chain reactions take place.

nuclear slurry density gauge Electronic instrument, located on raw mill discharge stream, to control moisture content in slurry by regulating water addition, feed, or in slurry storage basins by regulating "trim" water.

nulling In Jacobean architecture, a type of decorative detail carved on friezes and moldings, quadrant shaped in section.

nut A square or multi-sided block of metal, tapped with a through thread, for engaging the end of a screw bolt.

nylon fiber A thermoplastic polyamide resin derived from coal tar base, air and water. The fiber was first discovered by DuPont chemists in 1938.

o ohm

O oxygen

o/a on account

O.B.M. ordinance bench mark

obs obsolete

oct octagon

od outside diameter; outside dimension; ordinance datum

O/H overhead

O.J.T. on-the-job-training

opp opposite

opt optional

OR owner's risk

ord order, ordinance

oz ounce

o.c. On centers, an abbreviation frequently used in dimensioning working drawings, designating dimensions from the center of one member to the center of the next.

O.G. *(see ogee)*

O O (pronounced "oh-oh") Digging stick originally made of hard woods and later made of iron. Approximately 5 feet in length with one end tapered down and resembling a flat spade shape used for digging. The other end has a rounded flat surface used for tamping or pounding. The bar may also be used for prying and/or as a lever. This tool was used by the native Hawaiians as documented by the missionaries, and is still in use today.

oak Hard, heavy, strong woods used for heavy framing and prized for furniture, interior trim and flooring. There are two principal groups, white and red.

oakum A loose fiber from hemp or untwisted rope, used for caulking joints and seams.

oak varnish An oil varnish with a high proportion of oil to resin; normally used indoors. Elastic oak varnish can be used out of doors.

obelisk A four-sided shaft of stone, usually monolithic, tapering as it rises and terminating in a pyramid at the apex; usually commemorative.

objective probability distributions Probability distributions determined by statistical procedures.

oblique butt joint A butt joint at an angle other than 90° to the length of the piece.

oblique grain Diagonal grain.

oblique offset A distance from a survey line measured at an angle to it which is not a right angle.

oblique photograph An air photograph taken with the camera axis inclined away from the vertical. A high oblique is one which shows the horizon; a low oblique does not include the horizon.

oblique projection A pictorial view of an object showing its elevation, plan or section to scale with parallel lines projected from the corners to indicate the other side.

observation hole Opening in hood at front end of rotary kiln through which the burning, flame, consistency of clinker load, filling, position of cacined raw mix and burning zone can be observed.

observation of the work A function of the architect in the construction phase, during his periodic visits to the site, to familiarize himself generally with the progress and quality of the work and to determine in general if the work is proceeding in accordance with the contract documents.

observatory (1) An upper room or lantern. (2) A building, usually with glazed and rotating dome, for astronomical observations.

obsidian A natural, hard, dark-colored, volcanic glass of relatively low water content. *(see perlite)*

obsolescence The deterioration of a building, not so much physically as in failing to meet progressive change in needs and usage.

obstruction light A red light which indicates the presence of a fixed object that is dangerous to aircraft in motion.

occupancy permit *(see certificate of occupancy)*

occurrence An accident or a continuous exposure to conditions which result in injury or damage, provided the injury or damage is neither expected nor intended.

ocher (ochre) Used in painting; clays colored with oxides of iron in various proportions and ranging in color from pale yellow to brownish red.

Ocrate process Trade name for the treatment of concrete with gaseous SiF_4 to transform any free CaO into CaF_2.

octagon A polygon having eight equal angles and consequently eight equal sides.

octahedral Having eight equal surfaces.

octangular Having eight angles.

octastyle In Classical architecture, having eight columns across the main facade.

octave The interval between two sounds having a basic frequency ratio of two. The formula is 2n times the frequency, where n is the desired octave interval. The octave band frequency given in sound test results is usually the band center frequency, thus the 1000 Hz octave band encompasses frequencies from 707 Hz to 1414 Hz (n=−½). The 1000 Hz one-third-octave band encompasses frequencies from 891 Hz to 1122 Hz (n=−⅙).

oculus The circular opening occasionally formed at the top of a dome.

odd-pitch roof A roof on which the rise not an even fraction of the run.

odeum In architecture, a small gallery, or hall, used for musical or dramatic performances; in ancient Greece, a small roofed theater.

odometer An instrument for measuring the distance traveled by a vehicle.

odor threshold The lowest concentration of a materials vapor (or a gas) in air that can be detected by smell. Frequently expressed as a percentage of a panel of test individuals.

oeil-de-boeuf A bull's-eye window, circular or oval.

offer To bid, as a price or wages; a proposal to be accepted or rejected.

offhand Done without preparation.

official Authorized.

officiate To act as an officer in some business transaction.

offset (1) A displacement or abrupt change in line or the distance between two parallel lines. (2) In surveying, a horizontal distance measured at right angles to a survey line to locate a point off the line. (3) A term used in building when referring to a set-off, such as a sunken panel in a wall, or a recess of any kind; a horizontal ledge on a wall formed by the diminishing of the thickness of the wall at that point. (4) An offset in a line of piping is a combination of elbows or bends which brings one section of the pipe out of line with, but into a line parallel with, another section.

offset bend Any bend in a reinforcing bar that displaces the center line of a section of the bar to a position parallel to the original bar, in which the displacement is relatively small; commonly applied to column verticals.

offset digging In a ladder ditcher, digging with the boom not centered in the machine.

offset scale A scale for plotting details on a map which have been fixed by measured offsets in the field.

offset screwdriver A screwdriver which turns screws at right angles to its length; generally used in confined spaces.

offshoot Water table.

ogee (1) The name applied to a molding, partly a hollow and partly a round, and derived, possibly, from its resemblance to an O placed over a G. (2) An

S shaped curve, as in moldings or spill-ways.

ogee arch *(see inverted arch)*

ogee joint A type of spigot and socket joint in pipes.

ogive **(1)** A diagonal rib of simple vaulting intersection. **(2)** French term for pointed arch.

Oglesby blue granite A fine grain biotite granite of Georgia, with an azure blue color, taking a high polish.

Ohio cofferdam A double-wall cofferdam built from two lines of vertical timbers, held apart with tie-rods across the gap, anchored to horizontal walings on the outside of each wall. Built on land or near shore, floated into the river and sunk where desired by filling it with materials.

ohm Unit of electrical resistance; pressure (volts) divided by current (amperes) equals ohms.

ohmmeter An instrument for measuring electrical resistance in ohms.

oil **(1)** Any fluid lubricant. **(2)** Any liquid petroleum derivative that is less volatile than gasoline.

oil-base paints Paints with resins and other ingredients made of various oils; cleanup and thinning are done with solvent.

oil-bound distemper Distemper which contains a drying oil in the medium; commonly called oil-bound water paint.

oil cake *(slang)* Asphaltic concrete pavement.

oil-canning *(slang)* A term used to describe metal siding that is wrinkled; waves or crimping in metal sheet roofing.

oiler One who oils or lubricates machinery or equipment.

oil fired furnace Any furnace that is designed to burn oil or any furnace that has been converted to oil.

oil gloss paint Interior paint made with boiled oil and raw linseed oil.

oil immersed An object setting in a container of oil with the oil covering the whole object.

oil length The ratio of oil to resin in a varnish. *(see long oil; short oil)*

oillette A small loophole, usually circular, as contrasted with a crenelle.

oil paint A paint that contains drying oil or oil varnish as the basic vehicle.

oil separator A device for separating oil and oil vapor from the refrigerant, usually installed in the compressor discharge line.

oilslip A term used by woodworkers when referring to a small unmounted oilstone held in the hand while they sharpen the cutting edges of gouges. An oilstone slip or whetstone.

oil stain A thin oil paint, with very little pigment, used for staining wood.

oil still A device to separate oil from refrigerant by a distillation process.

oilstone A fine-grained whetstone (hone) whose rubbing surface is moistened with oil, when used for sharpening the cutting edges of tools.

oil well cement Cement used for sealing oil wells. Must be slow setting under conditions of high temperatures and pressures.

old gold A dull, metallic yellow color resembling tarnished gold.

old man *(slang)* **(1)** A tool used to increase leverage when drilling holes in steel or iron; usually a homemade tool. **(2)** A drilling post that gives firm positioning for a power drill used to drill holes in steel in the field.

old maude *(slang)* A large pipe wrench.

old woman's tooth *(slang)* The original form of the plane now called a plow. It consists of a chisel held by a wedge in a block of wood.

olefin plastics Plastics based on polymers made by the polymerization of olefins or copolymerization of olefins with other monomers, the olefins being at least 50 mass %.

oleo-resin A pine gum obtained by distilling dead wood or by bleeding the living tree.

oleo-resinous varnish A varnish containing vegetable drying oil and natural or synthetic hardening resin.

Oliensis test A method of determining whether or not two types of bituminous materials are compatible.

olive butt (see olive hinge)

olive hinge A hinge which, in the bearing between the two leaves, resembles a horizontally split olive.

on center The distance from the center of one structural member to the center of another; term used for spacing studs, joists and rafters.

on line Measuring or analyzing material, or conditions directly on process stream.

one-on-two (one-to-two) A slope in which the elevation rises one foot in two horizontal feet.

one-part line A single strand of rope or cable.

one-pipe system (1) In drainage systems, two vertical pipes, with waste and soil water flowing down the same pipe, and all the branches connected to the same anti-siphon pipe. (2) A heating circuit in which all the flow and return connections to the radiators come from the same pipe. The radiator at the far end is therefore much cooler than the radiator which is nearest the heat source.

one-way slab Concrete slab with reinforcing steel rods providing a bearing on two opposite sides only.

one-way system The arrangement of steel reinforcement within a slab that presumably bends in only one direction.

on-grade The entire concrete slab is directly on the ground.

on the ground (slang) Supervisory personnel.

oolite A rock consisting of small round grains, usually of calcium carbonate, cemented together.

oolitic limestone A variety of rock formation composed of rounded concretions, usually carbonate of lime, resembling the roe of fish, cemented together.

opacity The hiding property of paint; the opposite of transparency.

opal A mineral composed of amorphous hydrous silica ($SiO_2 \cdot nH2_O$).

opalescent A dark greenish gray gabbro granite with black and brown spottings, of coarse grain; quarried at Cold Spring, Minnesota.

opaline chert Chert composed entirely or mainly of opal.

opaqueness (see opacity)

open bidding Bidding procedure in which bids are accepted from all interested and qualified bidders.

open caisson A caisson (cylinder, monolith, or drop shaft) open both at bottom and top.

open circuit grinding Grinding arrangement whereby material passes through a mill and is ground to the desired fineness in one pass, without classification and regrinding. Alorso called one pass grinding.

open-circuit grouting A grouting system with no provision for recirculation of grout to the pump.

open cornice In wood construction, an eaves overhang in which the rafter soffits and usually the slates or roof sheathing can be seen.

open-cut A method of excavation in which the working area is kept open to the sky; used to distinguish from cut-and-cover and underground work.

open defect Any irregularity such as checks, splits, open joints, cracks, knot holes, or loose knots that interrupts the smooth continuity of the veneer.

open-end block Concrete masonry unit which has an end web removed to facilitate placing of the unit around vertical pipes or reinforcement.

open floor A floor in which the joists on the underside are exposed.

open-frame girder Vierendeel girder.

open-graded aggregate One containing little or no mineral filler, or in which the void spaces in the compacted aggregate are relatively large.

open grain Wide ringed or coarse textured timber.

open-hearth process (Siemens Maran process) The process by which 80 percent of British steel is made. Pig iron, scrap steel or iron, and lime are charged into a large, gas-heated shallow furnace. The process can be controlled more closely than the Bessemer process, being much slower.

opening leaf A leaf of a folding door which opens, as distinguished from a standing leaf.

opening light A light which opens, as opposed to a dead light.

opening of bids (see bid opening)

open-newel stair A geometrical stair; that is, one without newels.

open planning Planning of skyscrapers without air shafts. It may also mean the designing of a house with few, if any, fixed partitions.

open-planning millwork Millwork stock which includes special profiles for use in large window areas and open modular planning construction, where framing members are often used as finish members.

open production Mold sizes and incorporations modified to specification per project of about 300 dwelling units or more. A typical example would be a concrete panel incorporating any desired finish; the panels are usually either room-size or in manageable strips; semi-heavy, cast on-site or at a remote factory.

open roof A roof in which the beams can be seen from below, since it has no ceiling.

open sandwich-type panel Sandwich panel with top and bottom edges closed.

open sheeting Vertical poling boards that do not touch each other; held up by struts and walings.

open shop (merit shop; non-union) A firm whose employees are not covered by collective bargaining agreements.

open slating Slates or tiles laid with a gap between those in the same course.

open space In urban planning, that portion of a community site given over to roads, parks, and other land not containing the buildings.

open system A building system, designed to have interchangeability of its subsystems, components, or building elements with like subsystems, components, or elements of other systems.

open-top mixer A mixer consisting essentially of a trough within which mixing paddles revolve about the horizontal axis or a pan within which mixing blades revolve about the vertical axis.

open traverse A traverse in which the last line is not joined to the beginning point of the traverse.

open valley A roof valley where the shingles of the intersecting slopes leave open a space covered by metal flashing.

open web joist Steel joists built up out of light steel shapes with an open latticed web. A bar joist or trussed joist.

open-well stair A stair with a large stair well.

openwork Any type of construction which shows openings through the substance of which the surface is formed, especially ornamental designs of wood, metal, stone or other materials.

operating device The elevator car switch, push button, lever or other manual device used to actuate the control.

operating engineer A workman who operates heavy construction equipment and machines.

optical coatings Very thin coatings applied to glass or other transparent materials to increase the transmission (reduce the reflection) of sunlight. Coatings are also used to reflect back to the heat exchanger infrared radiation emitted from it.

optical losses Losses resulting from reflecting solar radiation from the surface of the cover plate.

optimum Best; highest quality.

optimum moisture content The percent of moisture of which the greatest density of that particular soil can be obtained through compaction. Especially important in road construction.

optimum time of reverberation The reverberation time for any given room which will give the best acoustical conditions for the intended use of the room.

option *(see contractor's option)*

orange peel (1) A type of self-opening and closing bucket in the shape of a half-orange peel cut into segments, used on a cable to excavate earth from an underpinning cylinder or elsewhere. (2) A description of poorly applied paint resulting in a pocked effect; pinholing. (3) A texture design applied to walls in drywalling.

orb (1) A boss at the intersection of vaulting ribs, perhaps originally to conceal the miters. (2) A blank window or panel.

order A type of column and its entablature considered as a unit of style in architecture, such as those used by the ancient Greeks: Doric, Ionic, and Corinthian, each distinguished by its particular style of entablature.

orders of architecture Classical architecture includes five orders; three used by the ancient Greeks, Doric, Ionic, and Corinthian; and two added by the Romans, Tuscan and Composite.

ordinance An authoritative decree or direction; a law set forth by governmental authority, specifically a municipal regulation.

ordinary lay A description of the lay of a wire rope in which each strand twists in the opposite direction from the wires of which it is made. Because of this type of manufacture, it is much less likely to untwist than a lang lay rope and can be used to hoist a bucket without guides.

ordinary portland cement A widely used hydraulic cement made by heating a slurry of clay and limestone in a kiln.

ordonnance French term for the proper arrangement and composition of any architectural work leaning upon traditional law.

ore Rock or earth, which is mined or worked, containing quantities of a mineral or minerals of commercial value.

or equal *(see approved equal)*

organic coating Coatings that are generally inert or inhibited. May be temporary (e.g., slushing oils) or permanent (paints, varnishes, enamels, etc.).

organic compound Originally a chemical compound produced by a life process. Now generally understood to include all compounds containing carbon.

organic content Usually synonymous with volatile solids in an ashing test; e.g. a discrepancy between volatile solids and organic content can be caused by small traces of some inorganic materials such as calcium carbonate that lose weight at temperatures used in determining volatile solids.

organic silt Mineral particles ranging in size from 0.05 to 0.074 mm containing appreciable quantities of organic materials.

oriel A projecting window with its walls corbeled or supported by brackets.

orient (1) To locate a building by points of the compass. (2) To locate a church so the altar end is toward the east.

Oriental granite A medium-grain pink granite with black and gray wavings, quarried at Morton, Minnesota.

Oriental rugs Handwoven rugs made in the Middle East and Orient.

orientation Collector panel position with relation to the points of the compass. Angle refers to the tilt of the collector to the sun; orientation refers to the compass direction in which the collector points.

oriented-core barrel A surveying instrument which takes and marks a core to show its orientation, and at the same time records the bearing and slope of the test hole.

orifice A small opening at the end of a vent pipe or any similar mouth-like aperture.

orifice meter A plate with a hole in it, placed across a pipeline or flowing liquid. The pressure difference between the two sides of the plate is metered to indicate the amount of the flow through the pipe.

orifice plate A metal plate erected across a pipeline. The pipeline carries gas or liquid which flows through a round hole or opening called an orifice, which has been machined into the plate. The orifice will promote a drop in pressure which is in proportion to the square of the rate-of-flow through the piping.

origin A point of intersection between two axis of a graph, the zero point of a graph where both y and x equal 0.

orlo (orle) (1) A fillet at the top or bottom of the shaft of a column. (2) The plane surface between adjacent flutes of a column or between channels of a triglyph; also called shank, femor, regela and meros.

ormolu Goldleaf-coated bronze.

ornament Detail that is incised, molded, painted or otherwise added to a building, usually against a foil of plain surface, with the purpose of embellishment.

ornamentation In masonry, a design formed by the laying of stone, brick or tile so as to produce a decorative effect.

orsat Manually operated, portable apparatus for analyzing kiln waste gases in which carbon dioxide, oxygen and carbon monoxide are successively removed from a given volume of gas by passing through chemical solutions.

orthogonal perspective A special type of orthogonal projection in which the rays are assumed to be not only parallel to each other but also perpendicular to the plane of projection.

orthogonal projection The graphic representation of a body upon a plane surface by drawing parallel lines to the surface from points on the body; sometimes termed orthographic.

orthographic projection A means of describing the exact shape of any object. The drawing is made up of a set of separate views of the same object. These are taken by the observer from different positions and arranged relative to each other in a definite way. Each view shows the shape of the object from a particular direction; a combination of two or more views will completely describe the object.

orthostyle In architecture, the placing of a series of columns in a straight row.

orthotropic A description of the physical properties of materials which, like wood, have distinct differences in two or more directions at right angles to each other. Also called orthogonally anisotropic.

oscillation Independent movement through a limited range, usually on a hinge.

oscillating conveyor Conveyor in which the pan or trough is suspended by a number of pendulums and is moved backward and forward with a relatively long oscillation. Actuated by mechanical means.

osmosis The diffusion of a liquid through a skin, permeable in only one direction, into the more concentrated solution. It is similar to the movement of water in soil during electro-osmosis.

Ottawa sand Naturally rounded grains of nearly pure quartz; produced by processing silica sand obtained by hydraulic mining of massive orthoquartzite situated in open-pit deposits near Ottawa, Illinois; used in mortar test specimens incident to testing hydraulic cement. *(see standard sand; graded standard sand)*

outage (1) The gallonage which has been removed from a tank car or distributor, or the gallonage which the tank lacks of being full to rated capacity. (2) A failure or interruption in use or functioning. (3) A period of interruption of electric current.

outband A stretcher stone which is visible in a reveal.

outbuilding A minor structure separated from a prime building.

outcrop An exposure of a stratum or body of ore at the earth's surface. A buried outcrop is one which would be seen if the recent loose deposits over the bedrock were stripped off.

outer separation The portion of an arterial highway between the traveled ways of a roadway for through traffic and a frontage street or road.

outfall In hydraulics, the discharge end of drains and sewers. It may be controlled by a gate or valve to prevent backup.

outfall sewer A sewer which receives the sewage from the collecting system and conducts it to a point of final discharge or to a disposal plant.

outhouse A detached privy.

outlet (1) A distribution source of electrical current, such as for a lighting fixture, or a socket into which can be plugged the wiring for portable lamps and the like. (2) A discharge point in piping. (3) A vent, in particular an opening in a parapet wall, through which rain water is discharged.

outlet pipe A pipe which conveys the effluent from a treatment plant to its final point of disposal.

outline specifications A set of material and workmanship requirements or design standards that establish the minimum technical performance of building systems.

out-of-plumb A term used when referring to a structural member which is not in alignment. Commonly not truly vertical or leaning away from the vertical.

out-of-sequence services Services performed in other than the normal or natural order of succession.

out of true In shopworking and the building trades, a term used when there is a twist or any other irregularity in the alignment of a form; a varying from exactness in a structural part.

output Capacity; duty; performance; net produced by a system.

outrigger (1) A projecting beam used in connection with overhanging roofs; (2) a projecting beam or foot used to give stability to a crane by widening its base.

outrigger scaffold A scaffold supported by outriggers or thrustouts projecting beyond the wall or face of the building or structure, the inboard ends

of which are secured inside of such building or structure.

outside air Air taken from outdoors and not previously circulated through the air conditioning system.

outside casing The boards forming the outside of a cased frame.

outside glazing Installing glass panes from outside the frame.

outside gouge In woodworking, a type of gouge where the bevel is ground on the convex, or outside, face.

Outsulation Registered Trademark name for exterior insulation panel system composed of Dryvit Insulation Board and expanded polystyrene cellular material. Various textured finishes are available. Also erroneously used as generic term to describe placing insulation on exterior surface of walls; elimination of thermal bridges; and the exterior wall structure itself.

out-to-out In measurements, a term meaning the dimensions are overall.

out of wind Description of wood or masonry surfaces which are plane, at right angles to the neighboring surfaces, and therefore not winding.

ovals Marble chips which have been tumbled until smooth oval shapes have resulted.

oval-wire brad A wire nail formed from oval wire. Not to be confused with brads.

oven dry The condition resulting from having been dried to essentially constant weight, in an oven the temperature of which has been previously fixed, usually between 221°F and 230°F (105 and 110°C); also the process of producing this condition.

overall An adjective describing measurements made from outside to outside.

overall coefficient of heat transfer (thermal transmittance) The time rate of heat flow through a body per unit area, under steady conditions, for a unit temperature difference between the fluids on the two sides of the body.

overbend The bend in a joint that fits on a hill.

overbreak Moving or loosening of rock as a result of a blast beyond the intended line of cut.

overburden The soil mantle found directly over a deposit of rock, sand or gravel either stripped off or broken down for mixing as a binder.

overburned Cement clinker is considered "overburned" if it has been exposed to too high a temperature. This results in mineralogical changes which can lead to lower strength potential and harder grinding.

overdesign To require adherence to structural design requirements higher than service demands, as a means of compensating for statistical variation or for anticipated deficiencies or both.

overdoor Architecturally treated space over a doorway.

overfall That part of a dam or weir over which the water pours; the overpouring water. *(see nappe)*

overflow stand A stand pipe in which water rises and overflows at hydraulic grade lines.

overgrainer A brush used for graining and marbling finishes.

overhand work In masonry, work performed on the outside of a wall from a scaffold constructed on the inside of the wall.

overhang The projecting area of a roof or upper story beyond the wall of the lower part; projecting parts of a face or bank.

overhaul (1) In many highway contracts, a movement of dirt far enough that payment, in addition to excavation pay, is made for its haulage. (2) The condition in a haulage engine when the load runs toward the engine faster than the rope, thus tangling the rope on the drum.

overhead That portion of the contractor's cost which cannot properly and accurately be allocated to a specific operation on any project. *(see indirect expense)*

overhead door A counterbalanced door that opens by following side tracks to a horizontal position above and behind the opening; used in garages, warehouses, etc. It may be in one or more leaves.

overhead shovel A tractor loader which digs at one end, swings the bucket overhead and dumps at the other end.

overhead structure All of the structural members, platforms, etc., supporting the elevator machinery, sheaves and equipment at the top of the hoistway.

overhead traveling crane A lifting machine generally power-operated at least in its hoisting operation. It is carried on a horizontal girder reaching between rails above window level at each side of a workshop and consists of a hoisting crab which can travel from end to end of the girder. The whole area between the rails can thus be traversed by the crab. *(see gantry; traveller)*

overland flow Water from precipitation and runoff which does not penetrate soil.

overlay A layer of concrete or mortar, seldom thinner than 1 in. (25 mm), placed on and usually bonded onto the worn or cracked surface of a concrete slab to either restore or improve the function of the previous surface.

overlay technique A method of producing composition roofing whereby a layer of asphalt is spread over another layer of asphalt previously applied.

overlimed A raw-mix is "overlimed" if it contains more CaO than required for the chemical combination with silica, alumina and iron oxide.

overload (1) In structures, a weight greater than the structure is designed to carry. (2) In electrical or mechanical engineering, a load greater than the plant is designed for.

overload trip Protective equipment on a motor starter or circuit breaker to ensure that the power is cut when the current exceeds a certain limit; usually operated by a solenoid.

overmantel Architecturally treated space above a fireplace mantel.

overrun (contract; quantity)   *(see contract overrun; quantity overrun)*

overrun brake (overriding brake)   A braked fitted to a towed vehicle such as a concrete mixer or trailer. It operates as soon as the towing truck slows down and the towed vehicle tends to push into it. Movement of the towed vehicle towards the towing vehicle applies the overrrun brake, making safe high-speed towing possible.

oversailing course   A brick or stone string course.

oversanded   Containing more sand than would be necessary to produce adequate workability and a satisfactory condition for finishing.

over-scribe   Technique of using a divider or compass to trace the contour of an irregular or off-square vertical surface (wall, pillar, offset, radiator leg, etc.) directly to the flooring or wall covering material.

oversite concrete   A layer of about six inches of concrete under the ground floor of a house, whether the floor is of wood or other flooring material.

oversize (underflow)   In classifying mineral, aggregate, etc., the larger of two sizes; the smaller size is the undersize or overflow.

overstretching   Stressing of tendons to a value higher than designed for the initial stress to (a) overcome frictional losses; (b) temporarily overstress the steel to reduce steel creep that occurs after anchorage; and (c) counteract loss of prestressing force that is caused by subsequent prestressing of other tendons.

overthrow   Ornamental ironwork spanning a pair of gate-posts.

overtime   Payment for time worked over the normal number of hours; paid for at a premium, e.g., time-and-one-half or double the normal hourly rate.

overtones   All of the frequencies emitted from a sound source at one time with the exception of the fundamental. Overtones are heard as a group and form the quality of the sound.

overtopping   Water flowing over the top of a dam or embankment.

overturning   Result of any combination of forces tending to overcome stable equilibrium.

overvibration   Excessive use of vibrators during placement of freshly mixed concrete causing segregation and excessive bleeding.

overwinding   A rope or cable wound and attached so that it stretches from the top of a drum to the load.

ovolo   A convex molding, forming or approximating in section a quarter of a circle; a quarter-round molding.

ovum   The egg, as in egg-and-dart molding.

owner   The architect's or engineer's client; the owner of a project such as a government agency; the person, firm or corporation with which a contract has been made for the payment of the work performed under that contract.

owner-architect agreement   Contract between architect and client for professional services.

owner-contractor agreement   Contract between owner and contractor for a construction project.

owner's inspector   A person employed by the owner to inspect construction in the owner's behalf.

owner's liability insurance   Insurance that protects an owner against claims arising from work performed by a contractor on behalf of the owner.

ox eye   A round or oval window, frequently in a dormer; an oeil-de-boeuf.

oxidation   (1) In asphalt refining, the addition of oxygen to the hot liquid bituminous material by blowing air through the melted material. (2) On a roof, the hardening of the asphalt coating caused by the action of the sun and air.

oxidized asphalt (blown asphalt)   Asphalt that is treated by blowing air through it at an elevated temperature to give it characteristics desired for certain special uses such as roofing, pipe coating, undersealing portland cement concrete pavement, membrane envelopes and hydraulic applications.

oxidizing flame Kiln flame to which more primary and secondary air is supplied than required for complete combustion.

oxy-acetyline flame A flame obtained by combining compressed oxygen and acetylene from separate steel cylinders; used for cutting metals, brazing or welding copper. For structural steel, arc welding methods are used.

oylet A small hole or perforation; an eyelet.

oystering In furniture making, a term applied to using a veneer obtained from the roots and boughs of certain trees.

ozone Triatomic oxygen, O_3, sometimes used in air conditioning or cold storage as an odor eliminator; can be toxic in certain concentrations.

p   part, per, pint, pipe, pitch, pole, post, port, power

P   phosphorus, pressure

PA   particular average, power amplifier, purchasing agent

pan   panel

par   parapet

part   partition

pat   patent

Pb   lead

pc/pct   percent

PCE   pyrometric cone equivalent

pcs   pieces

pd   paid, pressure drop

Pd   palladium

PD   per diem, potential difference

PE   professional engineer, probable error

pecky cyp   pecky cypress

PEP   Public Employment Program

per   perimeter, by the, period

PERT   Project Evaluation and Review Technique

PF   power factor

PFA   pulverized fuel ash

P&G   post and girder

ph   phase

Ph   phenyl

pil   pilaster

piv   pivoted

pk   park, peak, plank

pk.fr.   plank frame

pkwy   parkway

pl   place, plate

PL   private line

P/L   plastic laminate

platf   platform

plmb/plb   plumbing

pmf   probable maximum flood

pmh   production man-hour

pmp   probable maximum precipitation

P.M.S.   Pneumatic Mechanical Stress

pos   positive

pot   potential

ppd   prepaid

ppm   part per million

ppt/pptn   precipitate, precipitation

PR   payroll

PRA   Public Roads Administration

preb   prebend

prec   preceding

prelim   preliminary

prin   principal

prod   production

proj   project, projection

prop   property

pro   provisional

prs   pairs

PRV   Pressure Reducing Valve

ps   pieces

psf   pounds per square foot

psi   pounds per square inch

pt   paint, pint, payment, port, point

P.T.   pipe thread

ptfe   polytetrafluorethylene

PU   pickup

PUD   pickup and delivery

pur   purlins

PVC   polyvinyl chloride

PWA   Public Works Administration

pwr   power

pwt   pennyweight

PETN   Pentaerythrite tetranitrate; a material used in detonating fuse; primacord.

pH   Measurement of hydrogen ion concentrations. A measurement of acidity and alkalinity pH 7 is neutral, smaller readings are increasingly acid.

PVA Polyvinyl acetate. *(see latex emulsion)*

pace A dais; a staircase landing. *(see half-pace, quarter-pace, footpace)*

pache Color coding of plans or drawings for the estimator's use in bidding and quantity take-off.

pack (packing) A plate inserted between two others to fill a gap and fit them closely together.

packaged concrete (mortar; grout) Mixtures of dry ingredients in packages, requiring only the addition of water to produce concrete, mortar or grout.

package dealer A person or organization assuming responsibility under a single contract for the design and construction of a project to meet the specific requirements of another.

packaged terminal air conditioner A room air conditioner consisting of a factory selected combination of heating and cooling components, assemblies or sections, intended to serve an individual room or zone.

packer A device inserted into a hole in which grout is to be injected which acts to prevent return of the grout around the injection pipe; usually an expandable device actuated mechanically, hydraulically or pneumatically.

packer-head process A method of casting concrete pipe in a vertical position in which concrete of low water content is compacted with a revolving compaction tool.

packing (1) Small stones used to fill gaps in rubble walls. (2) Stuffing of oakum or the like to prevent leaking at a valve stem. (3) A cushion of sand between the helmet and the head of a driven pile.

packing machine Semi-automatic or automatic machine for filling paper bags with a fixed weight of cement.

pack set *(see sticky cement)*

pad (1) (shoe or plate) Ground contact part of a crawler type truck. (2) (template) A stone or precast concrete block placed under the end of a girder to spread the load in a loadbearing wall. (3) A tool pad.

padding Fine dirt used to protect the pipe from rock.

paddle mixer (twin pug) A mixer with two horizontal shafts rotating in opposite directions. *(see Pug mill)*

paddle wheel scraper *(see ladder scraper)*

paddock A fenced enclosure adjoining, or near, a stable.

pad foundation The isolated foundation of a separate column.

padlock A self-contained lock having a pivoted bow or ring which is closed to lock.

pad saw A small compass saw with a detachable handle, which also serves as a socket, or holder, for the narrow tapering blade when not in use.

padstone A concrete or stone pad in a wall; a stone template. *(see pad)*

pagoda In Far Eastern architecture, a tower-like or pyramidal structure; usually part of a temple.

pai-loo In China, a decorated gateway.

paint A mixture of pigment in a liquid vehicle which, spread thinly on a surface, dries to form an opaque solid film.

paint base Zinc, white lead, or any similar material.

paint drier A compound of lead and manganese.

painter One knowledgeable in the trade of painting.

painter's putty Like glazier's putty; used as a filler.

paint harling Throwing paint-coated stone chips onto a tacky paint film to make a rough textured surface.

paint remover A liquid solvent which softens a paint or varnish film, so that it can be scraped or brushed off.

paint system A succession of coats designed to protect a surface and give a decorative finish. The first coat is a sealer on wood or plaster, or a priming coat on corrodible metal. The next is usually an undercoat with good hiding power, followed by a high gloss coat and sometimes by a varnish.

paling (pale) One of the upright members of a picket fence, fastened to top and bottom rails between posts.

palisade A fence of poles driven into the ground.

Palladian (Palladian motive) A generic term for the form characterized by a round-arched opening flanked by narrower, square-top openings beyond slender mullions. In the manner of Andrea Palladio, an Italian architect of 1518–1580.

palladiana *(see berliner)*

pallet (1) A tray used for stacking material, usually brick or block, and lifting with a fork-lift. (2) A fixing fillet.

pallet brick (1) A brick which is rebated at one edge to receive a fixing fillet. (2) A brick made with a groove to hold a pallet.

pallet, moving walk One of a series of rigid platforms which together form an articulated treadway or the support for a continuous treadway.

palm An ancient Hebrew and Chaldean unit of linear measure; four digits = one palm; three palms = one span; two spans = one cubit. 1 cubit is 1 foot-9.888 inches.

palmate Having lobes or leaves in fan shape, as the Greek anthemion.

Palmer granite A pinkish biotite granite of medium texture, from Maine.

palmette The conventionalized palm-leaf ornament, widely used in Classical architecture; the anthemion.

pan (1) A prefabricated form unit used in concrete joist floor construction. (2) A container that receives particles passing the finest sieve during mechanical analysis of granular materials. (3) A bottom-dump scraper pulled by a tractor in earthmoving.

panache That portion of a groined vault between two ribs.

pan-and-roll roofing tile A roofing tile in two shapes, one of flat rectangular section, the other a half-round section, for covering the joints of the flat sections. *(see Italian tiling)*

pane (1) A sheet of glass for a comparatively small opening in a window sash or door. The term is rarely applied to large sheets of plate glass, as in a display window. Same as light. (2) In ancient times, a side or face of a building. (3) The peen of a hammer.

panel (1) A section of form sheathing, constructed from boards, plywood, metal sheets, etc., that can be erected or stripped as a unit. (2) A concrete member, usually precast, rectangular in shape, and relatively thin with respect to other dimensions.

paneling Decorative wood panels joined in a continuous surface.

panel box A box in which electric switches and fuses for branch circuits are located.

panel clip Independent clip used to attach roof panels to substructure.

panel creep The tendency of the transverse dimension of a roof panel to gain in modularity due to spring out or storage distortion.

panel curtain wall Exterior non-load-bearing wall made of panels; (a) attached directly to building structure with adjustable attachments; or (b) mounted on supports, subframe, which in turn are attached to building structure by adjustable attachments. Exterior surface of panels form face of building; interior surface may or may not form interior finish.

panel, drop *(see drop panel)*

panel-for-panel curtain wall Single element of any size or shape made of one material or assembly of materials, one side of which forms exterior building face and which protects the building from weather.

panel grids Prefabricated panels of radiant heating coils.

panel heating A method of home heating by means of electrical or hot water coils installed in ceilings, walls, floors or baseboards.

panel mold A mold in which plaster panels are cast.

panel pin A very slender wire nail with

a small head. It is nearly invisible when driven below the surface.

panel point In structural work, a node on a truss chord, especially one where a vertical meets the chord.

panel saw A carpenter's handsaw with fine teeth, making it especially suitable for cutting thin wood.

panel strip A strip used for design purposes extending across the length or width of a flat slab.

panel wall Exterior non-load-bearing wall whose outer surface may or may not form exterior facing of building and whose interior surface may or may not form the interior finish. It may rest on the building structure or may be hung from the structure.

pan feeder (1) Rugged, slow moving conveyor consisting of over-lapping heavy, cast steel or manganese steel pans, used for evenly feeding large-sized lumps of rock to a primary crusher. (2) Short, vibrating, trough-type feeder for dry materials.

pan handle A heavy concrete beam between footings, used to balance column loads that cannot be centered on their own footings.

pan head The head of a rivet or screw shaped like a cut-off cone.

panic bolt A door latch operated from the inside by pressure against a horizontal bar running practically across the full width of the door.

panier A corbel form breaking the angle between a pilaster and the beam it supports.

pan mixer *(see open-top mixer)*

panopticon A building planned on a radial scheme, so that a single attendant at the center can observe the converging corridors.

pan steps Prefabricated step forms.

pantheon Generic term for a temple dedicated to all the gods.

pantile A curved roofing tile, somewhat like a prone letter S.

pantograph A drafting instrument for copying at a different scale.

pants Steel plates bolted to a piledriving hammer to make a driving shoe for steel sheetpiling.

paoh-tah In China, a temple, especially the tower-like forms of the Buddhists; always of an uneven number of stories.

pap The vertical outlet from an eaves gutter.

paper, building A general term for papers, felts and similar sheet materials used in buildings without reference to their properties or uses.

paper form A heavy paper mold used for casting concrete columns, box beams, grid floors, etc.

paperhanger A worker who hangs wallpaper and related materials, as well as preparing surfaces for it by stopping cracks, and sizing.

paper latcher One who fits rolls of glass fiber and Kraft paper onto a pipeline wrapping machine.

paper rollers Curlings of paper torn from the surface of gypsum board. Usually occurs as a result of prolonged exposure to high humidity and sliding one board across the surface of another.

paper, sheathing A building material, generally paper or felt, used in wall and roof construction as a protection against the passage of air and sometimes moisture.

papier-maché A composition of paper pulp and glue size, easily molded before it hardens.

parabola (1) A shape made by cutting a cone parallel to one edge. (2) The curve of the bending-moment diagram for a uniformly distributed load on a simply supported beam.

parabolic reflector A reflector shaped to control the light in a narrow beam.

parachute *(slang)* A rubber or plastic balloon with a steel end for string to be tied onto; that with air pressure behind it, the parachute glides through the conduit.

parallel An arrangement of electric blasting caps in which the firing current passes through all of them at the same time.

parallel application The long dimension of gypsum board applied in the same direction as the framing members. *(Also referred to as vertical application)*

parallel, connection in System whereby flow is divided among two or more channels, from a common starting point or header.

parallel flow In heat exchange between two fluids, hottest portion of one meeting coldest portion of the other.

parallel gutter A box gutter.

parallelogram A four-sided plane figure whose opposite sides are parallel, hence equal.

parallel series Two or more series of electric blasting caps arranged in parallel.

parallel thread A screw thread with uniform diameter; used on mechanical connections such as bolts.

parallel-wire unit A post-tensioning tendon composed of a number of wires or strands which are approximately parallel.

parapet (1) In architecture, a protective railing or low wall along the edge of a roof, balcony or terrace. (2) A low wall along the top of a dam. (3) The wall on top of an abutment extending from the bridge floor and designed to hold the backfill.

parapet gutter In building construction, a gutter placed behind a parapet wall.

parapet wall (1) That portion of any wall which extends above the roof line. (2) A wall which serves as a guard at the edge of a balcony or roof. (3) A solid wall built along the top of a dam for ornament, for the safety of vehicles and pedestrians, or to prevent overtopping.

paretta Roughcast embellished with surface pebbles.

parge To coat with plaster, particularly foundation walls and rough masonry.

parge coat A thin coat of cement plaster applied to masonry wall for refinement of the surface or for dampproofing.

pargeting (1) The process of plastering the inside of a flue or the back of face brickwork or stone. (2) Ornamental plaster or plaster work; sometimes referred to as parging or back mortaring.

parging A thin coat of plastering applied to rough stone or brick walls for smoothing purposes.

Parian cement A gypsum plaster similar to Keene's cement.

paring A term used by wood turners when referring to a method of wood turning which is different than the scraping method commonly employed by patternmakers.

paring chisel A type of long chisel employed by patternmakers for slicing, or paring, cuts in wood to make a smooth surface which is difficult to obtain when cutting directly across the grain.

paring gouge A woodworker's bench tool with its cutting edge beveled on the inside, or concave face, of the blade.

parking device, elevator An electrical or mechanical device, the function of which is to permit the opening from the landing side of the hoistway door at any landing when the car is within the landing zone of that landing. The device may also be used to close the door.

parking lot Ground space devoted to the temporary occupation of vehicles, usually close to a building.

parks Ornamental landscaped areas.

parkway An arterial highway for non-commercial traffic with full or partial control of access and usually located within a park or a ribbon of park-like developments.

parliament hinge H hinge.

parquet floor A hardwood floor laid in small rectangular or square patterns, not in long strips, to form various designs.

parquet floor square Basically a 'tile' composed of individual slats held in place by a mechanical fastening. A square may or may not possess tongues & grooves to interlock.

parquet floor units A unit consists of four (sometimes three) or more squares or 'tiles' fastened together.

parquetry The inlaid patterns of a parquet floor.

parquet strip A floor consisting of tongued and grooved hardwood boards which are secret nailed and glued to a wooden subfloor.

parell A chimney breast.

Parshall measuring flume An improved Venturi flume used in hydraulics for measuring the flow in open channels.

part (minute) A subdivision of the Classic module. *(see module)*

parti The general scheme of a design, particularly in plan.

partial occupancy Occupancy by the owner of a portion of a project prior to final completion.

partial payment *(see progress payment)*

partial prestressing Prestressing to a stress level such that, under design loads, tensile stresses exist in the precompressed tensile zone of the prestressed member.

partial release Release into a prestressed concrete member of a portion of the total prestress initially held wholly in the prestressed reinforcement.

partially fixed End support of a beam or column which cannot develop full fixing moment to the beam or column.

partially reinforced concrete masonry Concrete masonry in which reinforcement is provided to carry the principal tensile stresses but which does not conform to the requirements for reinforced masonry.

particleboard A composition board consisting of distinct particles of wood bonded together with a synthetic resin or other added binder. Also called chipboard.

particle shape The shape of a particle. *(see cubical aggregate; elongated piece; flat piece)*

particle-size analysis Proportion by weight of different particle sizes in soil or sand as determined by mechanical analysis.

particle-size distribution The distribution of particles of granular material among various sizes; usually expressed in terms of cumulative percentages larger or smaller than each of a series of diameters, sieve opening, or the percentages between certain ranges of diameters.

particulate matter Material or substance emitted into, or present in, the atmosphere in a finely-divided form of the solid or liquid state (or combination thereof), normally at standard conditions. This does not include chemically or physically uncombined water vapor.

parting bead (parting strip) A vertical guide strip on a double-hung window frame separating the sashes.

parting slip A long narrow vertical strip of wood which hangs from the pulley level to the bottom of the cased frame of a sash window and prevents the sash weights from colliding when the window is being opened or closed.

parting stop (strip) A small wood piece used in the side and head jambs of double-hung windows to separate upper and lower sash.

parting tool A narrow-bladed turning tool used by woodworkers for cutting recesses, grooves or channels.

partition (1) A dividing wall between rooms or areas, generally non-bearing. (2) Slotted cast steel or alloy steel grate separating two chambers in a compartment mill.

partition block Light-loadbearing hollow masonry unit, made as thin as two inches, usually scored for plastering both sides.

partition plate The horizontal member which serves as a cap for the partition studs, and also supports the joists, rafters and studding.

partition system An assembly of materials designed to perform a special function as a wall.

parts of line Separate strands of the same rope or cable used to connect two sets of sheaves.

part-swing shovel A shovel in which the upper works can rotate through only a part of a circle.

party wall A wall erected on a line between adjoining property owners and used in common. This can be an interior or exterior wall.

Pascal's law A law of hydrostatics developed in 1646 stating that in a perfect fluid the pressure exerted on it anywhere is transmitted undiminished in all directions.

pass (1) A working trip or passage of an excavating, grading or compaction machine. (2) Layer of shotcrete placed in one movement over the field of operation.

passage (passageway) A corridor or other horizontal means of intercommunication between elements of an interior.

passing lane A highway design to provide an extra lane for faster traffic.

passive earth pressure (passive resistance) The resistance to deformation usually due to active earth pressure.

passive solar energy systems & concepts Passive solar heating applications generally involve energy collection through south-facing glazed areas; energy storage in the building mass or in special storage elements; energy distribution by natural means such as convection, conduction or radiation with only minimal use of low power fans or pumps; and a method controlling both high and low temperatures and energy flows. Passive cooling applications usually include methods of shading collector areas from exposure to the summer sun and provisions to induce ventilation to reduce internal temperatures and humidity.

passkey *(see master key)*

paste Wheat paste used in connection with asbestos paper and tape when sealing the pipe, duct and furnace connections of a heating system.

paste content (of concrete) Proportional volume of cement paste in concrete, mortar, or the like, expressed as volume percent of the entire mixture. *(see also neat cement paste)*

pasteurization Heat treatment, usually at 131–158°F, for killing bacteria as in milk without greatly changing its chemical composition.

pasting *(see blistering)*

pat A neat cement paste specimen about three inches (76 mm) in diameter and ½ inch (13 mm) in thickness at the center and tapering to a thin edge on a flat glass plate for indicating setting time.

patand In early English carpentry, a sill or bottom member of a frame.

patch (shim) An insert in plywood or veneer.

patent glazing Any method of dry puttyless glazing.

patent plaster A hard plaster which is based on gypsum with an admixture; similar to Keene's cement.

patent plate *(see plate glass)*

patent stone *(see cast stone)*

patina Color and texture added to a surface by time weathering and various allies, particularly the green coating on copper or its alloys.

patio A courtyard or open paved area; may be partially or entirely surrounded by a residence.

patio block The solid concrete masonry units for use in walks, terraces, patios, etc.

pattée Small at the center and widening toward the ends.

pattern bond The pattern formed by the masonry units and the mortar joints on the face of a wall. The pattern may result from the type of structural bond used or may be purely a decorative one in no way related to the structural bonding.

pattern cracking Fine openings or cracks on concrete surfaces in the form of a pattern; resulting from a decrease in volume of the material near the surface or increase in volume of the material below the surface, or both.

pattern-maker's saw A small handsaw with a thin blade designed especially for accuracy in cutting patterns or for cabinetmaking.

pattern match Procedure for ensuring that when installed, sheet goods patterns fall correctly. Requires proper layout to lay the material in a straight line and to have patterns match properly. *(see repeat)*

pattern repeat The vertical distance between a point of a pattern and the next point where the pattern is identical.

pattern scribing An accurate and convenient procedure for fitting sheet goods (particularly in a small room). Consists of two operations: (a) scribing the contour of vertical surfaces to lining felt or heavy wrapping paper; and (b) transferring the pattern by rescribing the lines on the felt onto the floor covering being installed.

pavement, concrete A layer of concrete over such areas as roads, sidewalks, airfields, canals, playgrounds and those used for storage or parking. Also sometimes used to describe these areas when coated with asphalt.

pavement, invert Lower segment of corrugated metal pipe provided with a smooth bituminous material that completely fills the corrugations; intended to give resistance to scour and erosion and to improve flow.

pavement light Transparent or translucent element in paving to light a space beneath; vault light.

pavement marker A reflective or non-reflective barrier device used to guide vehicles into desired paths of travel along the roadway. This barrier device should not project more than 1 to 3 inches above the pavement surface.

pavement structure All courses of selected material placed on the foundation or subgrade soil other than any layers or courses constructed in grading operations.

paver An obsolete term for quarry tile. *(see concrete paver; slip-form paver)*

pavers Unglazed porcelain or natural clay tile formed by the dust-pressed method and similar to ceramic mosaics in composition and physical properties but relatively thicker with 6 in.^{2} or more of facial area. (ASTM C 242).

pavilion Originally a temporary or movable shelter, sometimes merely a tent; a small outbuilding; a wing or section of an institutional building, such as a hospital; a building for temporary use, as in an exposition.

pavilion roof (polygonal roof; pyramid roof) A sloped roof with equal hipped areas all around it.

paving Generally a layer of concrete, asphalt or coated macadam. Used on streets, sidewalks, parking areas and for airport hard-surfacing.

paving breaker An air hammer which does not rotate its steel.

paving brick Vitrified brick especially suitable for use in pavements where resistance to abrasion is important.

paving train An assemblage of equipment designed to place and finish a pavement.

pavior British term for stone mason.

pavonazzo Descriptive of brilliantly veined marbles.

pawl A tooth or set of teeth designed to lock against a ratchet.

payback The payback or payoff time of a solar system is viewed in terms of how many years are required to pay back the extra cost of the solar equipment with fuel savings.

pay formation A layer or deposit of soil or rock whose value is sufficient to justify excavation.

pay item Any item of work designated on the contract; or an item of work both parties agree will be paid for, if and when it should arise during the work on the project.

payment bond, labor & material Bond to insure payment of labor and materials costs. Frequently written as one bond with performance bond.

Payne's process A method of fireproofing wood by first treating it with an injection of sulphate of iron, then later infusing the wood with a solution of sulphate of lime or soda.

pea gravel Screened gravel, most of the particles of which will pass a ⅜ inch (10 mm) sieve and be retained on a No. 4 (5 mm) sieve.

pea gravel grout Grout to which pea gravel is added.

peak The uppermost point of a gable.

peaked roof A roof rising either to a point or a ridge.

peak load The maximum instantaneous demand for electrical power which determines the generating capacity required by a public utility.

peak sign A sign attached to the peak of the building at the endwall showing the building manufacturer.

peak-to-peak values The total value between the positive and negative peaks of an AC sine wave.

peak values The maximum values of voltage or current as measured from the zero value.

pearlite (see perlite)

pearl molding One simulating a string of beads.

peat (humus) A soft light swamp soil consisting mostly of decayed vegetation.

pea trap A trap under sinks and lavatories which prevents gas from backing into the house; somewhat describes the shape of the trap.

pebble dash A term used for finishing the exterior walls of a structure by dashing pebbles against the plaster or cement.

pebbles smaller pieces of material which have broken away from the bedrock; ⅛ to ¼ inch minimum size.

pecan A tree native to the U.S.A. with heartwood reddish brown in color, with darker brown stripes, and sapwood varying from pale red to white; can be stained and finished to resemble walnut.

peckerhead (slang) Electrical connection point on an electric motor.

pecking (see picking)

pecky Timber which shows signs of decay.

pecky cypress Cypress having disintegrated spots, caused by a fungus attack in the standing tree, which add interest to its texture and color.

pedestal An upright compression member whose height does not exceed three times its average least lateral dimension, such as a short pier or plinth used as the base for a column.

pedestal pile A cast-in-place concrete pile constructed so that concrete is forced out into a widened bulb or pedestal shape at the foot of the pipe which forms the pile.

pediment A low triangular ornamented crowning in front of a building and over doors and windows. Pediments are sometimes made in the form of a segment; the space enclosed within the triangle is called the tympanum. Also, the gable ends of Classic buildings, where the horizontal cornice is carried across the front forming a triangle with the end of the roof.

pediment arch (see miter arch)

peeler One of a set of blades that pick up and channel water moved outward by the impeller of a centrifugal pump.

peeling (1) A process in which thin flakes of mortar are broken away from a concrete surface; caused by deterioration or by adherence of surface mortar to forms as they are removed. (2) Rotary cutting of wood veneers.

peen The blunt, wedge-shaped or ball-shaped end of a hammer head, opposite to the striking face.

peen hammer A hammer with no flat striking face but with two cutting peens.

pee pot (slang) Hard hat.

peg (1) A small piece of wood used in place of nails for holding parts together. (2) A short pointed wooden stick driven into the ground used in surveying to mark a line or level. (3) A metal pin which secures glass to a metal window frame.

peggies British term for small random shingles usually sold by weight.

pellet powder Black powder made up into hollow cartridges.

Peltier effect The evolution or absorption of heat which occurs when an electric current is passed across the junction between two different metals.

penal sum The amount named in a contract or bond as the penalty to be paid by a signatory thereto in the event he fails to perform his contractual obligations.

penalty and bonus clause *(see bonus and penalty clause)*

penciling Painting the mortar joints of brickwork with a white paint to set off the contrast between the brickwork and the joints.

pencil rod Plain metal rod of about ¼ inch (6 mm) diameter.

pendant switch A small pushbutton switch hanging from the ceiling of a room by a drop cord; used to control the flow of electric current to a ceiling light.

pendent A name given to an elongated boss, either molded or foliated, such as hang down from the intersection of groins, especially in fan tracery, or at the end of hammer beams. Sometimes long corbels, under the wall pieces.

pendentive A name given to an arch which cuts off the corners of a square building internally, so that the superstructure may become an octagon or a dome.

pendentive bracketing (cove bracketing) Springing from the rectangular walls upward to the ceiling, and forming the horizontal part of the ceiling into a circle or ellipse.

pendent posts A name given to those timbers which hang down the side of a wall from the plate in hammer beam trusses, and which receive the hammer braces.

penetration (1) A test by means of weighted needle to determine the hardness of asphalt. (2) Of sheet piling, the cut-off depth. (3) The depth below ground level of a monolith or caisson.

penetration construction General method described for asphalt macadam, but also applying to similar use of emulsified asphalt and cut back asphalt with denser graded mineral aggregate in which void spaces are much smaller than for asphalt macadam.

penetration needle *(see Proctor plasticity needle)*

penetration probe A device for obtaining a measure of the resistance of concrete to penetration; customarily determined by the distance that a steel pin is driven into the concrete from a special gun by a precisely measured explosive charge.

penetration resistance The resistance, usually expressed in pounds per square inch (psi) (kg per sq mm) of mortar or cement paste to penetration by a plunger or needle under standardized conditions.

penetration tests Tests of in-place soil which give a more accurate indication of its load-bearing capacity than tests conducted in the laboratory.

penetrometer (wash-point) A cone-shaped instrument which is jetted into the ground to the required level and then forced in at a measured pressure; a static penetration test.

penitentiary (1) A prison. (2) *(obsolete)* A small building in which the penitent of a monastic order confined himself. That part of a church to which penitents were admitted during services.

penning gate A British term for the rectangular sluice gate which opens by lifting upwards.

Pennsylvania bluestone Also called Wyoming Valley stone; a fine-grain, compact, hard sandstone of gray-red, gray-green, or blue-gray; used for trim, paving, etc.

penny As applied to nails it originally indicated the price per hundred. The term now serves as a measure of nail length and is abbreviated by the letter d. In general, the larger the number, the larger the nail.

pennydog *(slang)* A straw boss or foreman.

penstock In dam construction, a pipeline or pressure shaft leading from the headrace or reservoir to the turbines; a sluice or floodgate controlling the discharge of water.

pentastyle In Classical architecture, having five columns across the main facade.

penthouse (1) A building on the roof of a structure to house equipment or residents. (2) A projecting hood over a door, window or wall to protect it from rain; sometimes spelled pentice.

pent roof A roof with a slope on one side only.

percentage agreement An agreement for professional services in which the compensation is based upon a percentage of the construction cost.

percentage articulation A measure of the number of discernible speech sounds correctly identified by a group of listeners with average hearing in any given room.

percentage fee Compensation based upon a percentage of construction cost. *(see fee)*

percentage of reinforcement The ratio of cross-sectional area of reinforcing steel to the effective cross-sectional area of a member, expressed as a percentage.

percent elongation In tensile testing, the increase in the gauge length, measured after fracture of the specimen within the gauge length. Usually expressed as a percentage of the original gauge length.

percent fines Amount, expressed as a percentage, of material in aggregate finer than a given sieve, usually the No. 200 (74-micron) sieve; also the amount of fine aggregate in a concrete mixture expressed as a percent by absolute volume of the amount of aggregate.

percent possible sunshine The amount of radiation available compared to the amount which would be present if there were no cloud cover; usually measured on a monthly basis.

perch A measure used in measuring stone work; 24¾ cubic feet or 16¾ cubic feet according to locality and custom.

perched water table Underground water lying over dry soil and sealed from it by an impervious layer.

perclose An enclosing barrier, such as a railing, protecting an area or an object.

percolating filter In sewage, a type of bacteria bed.

percolation The movement of gas or water through the void spaces of the earth. *(see Darcy's law)*

percolation test A test to determine the rate of sewage dispersal into the ground.

percussion tools Tools which operate by striking rapid blows. Most are driven by compressed air or electricity.

percussive-rotary drilling Rotary drilling combined with a percussion or vibratory motion on the bit.

perfa-tape Perforated paper joint tape approximately two inches wide; used to cover the joints in gypsum wallboard.

perfect frame A frame which is stable under loading from any direction but would become unstable if one of its members were removed or if one of its fixed ends became hinged.

perforated Pierced with holes.

perforated brick A brick with vertical perforations through the frog. Much used in Europe, particularly in Germany. *(see V-brick)*

perforated gypsum plasterboard A gypsum plasterboard which has uniformly spaced circular holes giving it a high sound absorption.

performance bond A bond of the contractor in which a surety guarantees to the owner that the work will be performed in accordance with the contract documents. Except where prohibited by statute, the performance bond is frequently combined with the labor and material payment bond. *(see surety bond)*

performance factor Ratio of the useful output capacity of a system to the input required to obtain it. Units of capacity and input need not be consistent.

performance factor, refrigerating system The ratio of the useful refrigerating effect of the system to the power input.

performance specification States how a building element must perform.

pergeting *(see pargeting)*

pergola An open, structural framework over an outdoor area usually covered with climbing shrubs or vines to form an arbor.

peribolus (peribolos) The wall bounding an enclosure, or the enclosure itself; more particularly around a temple.

periclase A crystalline mineral, magnesia, MgO, the equivalent of which may be present in portland cement clinker, portland cement, and other materials such as open hearth slags and certain basic refractories.

peridrome The space between the peristyle and the walls of a temple.

perimeter The total length of the periphery of a given area, i.e., equals the distance around the outside of a building.

perimeter grouting Injection of grout, usually at relatively low pressure, around the periphery of an area which is subsequently to be grouted at greater pressure; intended to confine subsequent grout injection within the perimeter.

perimeter heating A method of warm air heating, whereby the hot air registers are installed near outside walls beneath windows.

perimeter installation Procedure with approved sheet goods in which the floor is installed by using special adhesive system around the outer edges and at seams instead of spreading entire floor.

perimeter relief Construction detail which allows for building movement. Gasketing materials which relieve stresses at the intersections of wall and ceiling surfaces.

period The duration of time necessary for one cycle to complete itself.

period at maximum temperature (see maximum-temperature period)

peripheral discharge Design of ball or tube mill whereby the ground product is discharged through openings in the mill-shell.

peripheral instrumentation Sensing instruments integrated with, and feeding input information on process to, a computer.

periphery The entire outside edge of an object.

peripteral Having a row of columns around the cella of a temple.

perisphere A spherical form such as was used in connection with the trylon at the New York World's Fair in 1939.

peristyle The outer colonade surrounding a temple or other structure, or a court.

perk hole A six foot hole dug in the ground to test soil conditions for the septic system.

perk test (slang) (see percolation)

perling (see purlin)

perlite A volcanic glass having a perlitic structure, usually having a higher water content than obsidian; when expanded by heating, used as an insulating material and as a lightweight aggregate in concretes, mortars and plasters. (see vermiculite)

perlite plaster Gypsum plaster containing only perlite aggregate and no sand. A good insulator, and easy to work because it is lightweight.

perlitic structure A structure produced in a homogeneous material by contraction during cooling, and consisting of a system of irregular convolute and spheroidal cracks; generally confined to natural glass.

perm The unit of permeance. A perm is equal to 1 grain per (sq ft) (hr) (inch of mercury vapor pressure difference).

permafrost Permanently frozen ground such as is found in Siberia, Alaska and northern Canada.

permanent blasting wire A permanently mounted insulated wire used between the electric power source and the electric blasting cap circuit.

permanent form Any form that remains in place after the concrete has developed its design strength. The form may or may not become an integral part of the structure.

permanent magnet When the magnetic domains in a metal can be arranged in the same manner and kept in this alignment, the metal becomes a permanent magnet.

permanent set   Inelastic elongation or shortening.

permeability   Water vapor permeability is a property of a substance which permits passage of water vapor, and is equal to the permeance of a 1 inch thickness of the substance. When permeability varies with psychometric conditions, the spot or specific permeability defines the property at a specific condition. Permeability is measured in perm-inches.

permeability to water, coefficient of   The rate of discharge of water under laminar flow conditions through a unit cross-sectional area of a porous medium under a unit hydraulic gradient and standard temperature conditions, usually 20°C.

permeameter   An instrument for measuring the coefficient of permeability of a soil sample. Constant head permeameter is used for permeable materials like gravel or sand; the falling head permeameter is used for impermeable materials like clay or silt.

permeance   The water vapor permeance of a sheet of any thickness (or assembly between parallel surfaces) is the ratio of water vapor flow to the vapor pressure difference between the surfaces. Permeance is measured in perms.

permissible   Low-flame explosive used in gassy and dusty coal mines.

permit, building   (see building permit)

permit, occupancy   (see certificate of occupancy)

permit, zoning   (see zoning permit)

perpends (perpender)   (1) A header extending through a wall so that one end appears on each side of it; bondstone. (2) The so-called vertical sloping joints between adjacent shingles; the vertical joints in brick and block construction.

perpeyn wall   A projecting pier, buttress or pilaster, used to sustain additional weight upon or against the wall.

perron   An arrangement of exterior entrance steps, usually impressively elaborated.

perspective   (see linear perspective)

perspective drawing   Drawing of an object in a three dimensional form on a plane surface. An object drawn as it would appear to the eye.

PERT   In the pure sense, a probabilistic, event-oriented control technique. An acronym for Project Evaluation and Review Technique. In recent times, the term PERT has been used as a synonym for critical path method.

PERT schedule   A charting of the activities and events anticipated in a work process. (see critial path method)

pervibration   A British term used for the internal vibration of concrete.

pervious   Giving passage or entrance; permeable; sand is easily pervious to water.

petcock   A small drain cock or drain valve on a pipe line, boiler, radiator or the like, for draining or testing.

Petrograd standard (Petersburg standard)   The unit of lumber measurement (165 cubic feet) commonly used in Britain.

petrography   The branch of petrology dealing with description and systematic classification of rocks aside from their geologic relations, mainly by laboratory methods, largely chemical and microscopical; also, loosely, petrology or lithology.

petrol engine   A British term for an internal-combustion engine which runs on gasoline.

petroleum asphalt   Two types of asphalt are refined directly from petroleum: asphalts with asphalt base and asphalts with paraffin base. Asphaltic base asphalts are most desirable for bituminous road construction because they are more stable and adhesive in character; asphalts for paving construction are generally divided into six groups: rapid-curing (RC), medium-curing (MC), slow-curing (SC), emulsified, powdered, and asphalt cements (AC).

petroleum pitch   A dark brown to black, predominantly aromatic, solid cementitious material obtained by the processing of petroleum, petroleum fractions, or petroleum residuals.

petrology The science of rocks, dealing with their origin, structure, composition, etc., from all aspects and in all relations. *(see petrography)*

pew A benchlike seat for a church interior.

pewter An alloy of four parts tin and one part lead.

pextite resin A resinous substance usually in powder form added to soils used in embankments to increase stabilization.

pH Used in expressing acidity or alkalinity of substances.

phantom lines Similar to cutting plane lines only thinner. They are used to indicate repeated forms, details, or features. Also used to show alternate positions of moving parts or to show the position of nearby related parts.

phase (1) In thermodynamics one of the states of matter, as solid, liquid, gaseous. (2) Electrical, an alternating current whose alternations have a definite time relation to the rotational position of the alternator. In a polyphase machine, the phases are separated by 360 electrical degrees divided by the number of phases.

phased application The installation of a roof system or waterproofing system during two or more separate time intervals.

phase-change material A material used to store heat by melting. Heat is later released for use as the material solidifies.

phenolic resin A class of synthetic, oil-soluble resins, or plastics, produced as condensation products of phenol, substituted phenols and formaldehyde, or some similar aldehyde that may be used in paints for concrete.

Philadelphia rod A leveling rod in which the hundredths of feet or eighths of inches are marked by alternate bars of color the width of the measurement.

Philla-fencing 2½", 4½" wide × 6' or 8' length boards. (Material primarily utilized on porch ceilings, usually tongue and groove. Also utilized in other areas of construction.

Phillips recessed-head screw A recessed head screw with an X-shaped indentation rather than a slot; a special Phillips screwdriver must be used.

phon (1) The unit of loudness of sound as received by the average human ear. (2) The loudness level of a sound is measured in phons and is numerically equal to the intensity level in decibels of an equally loud sound at 1000 cycles.

phosphating Protecting a metal surface by application of hot phosphoric acid. Like pickling, it is a pretreatment and inhibiting coat rather than a finished surface and should be followed by surfacing with oil, wax, paint or lacquer.

phosphor-bronze An alloy metal in which copper, tin and a very little phosphorus are fused; it can be extremely ductile, tough or very hard.

phosphorous pentoxide A drier material; it becomes gummy on reacting with moisture and hence is not used as a drying agent in refrigerating systems.

photodiode A PN diode designed so the device can switch and regulate current in proportion to the intensity of the light striking the PN junction.

photo-elasticity Examining by model analysis the distribution of stresses in unusual shapes while under load. Polarized light is passed through a transparent model and shows isochromatic and isoclinic lines. This gives the directions of the axis of principal stress at any point and the magnitude of the difference of principal stresses.

photoelectric eye (photoelectric-cell-operated relay) A device depending on the interruption of a fixed beam of light to act as a trigger to door-opening mechanisms, counting machines, sorting machines, and many other such operations.

photogrammetry The science of measurement by means of photographs; used in aerial surveying.

photometer *(see flame photometer)*

photons Particles of energy that compose a light ray.

photovoltaic cell A device without any

moving parts that converts light directly into electricity by the excitement of electrons.

phreatic water An obsolete term for ground water.

pi (π) A number, approximately 3.1416 or 3¹/₇, which, when multiplied by the diameter of a circle, will give the circumference.

piano wire Steel wire used in aligning. *(see plumb lines)*

pick (1) A digging hand tool with two long sharp points used for breaking loose rock or digging stiff clay or gravel. *(see navvy pick)* (2) The number of weft yarns shuttled across the warp yarns, and indicating closeness of weave lengthwise.

pick and dip A method of bricklaying by which the bricklayer simultaneously picks up a brick with one hand and enough mortar to lay it with on the trowel in his other hand.

picket (1) One of the upright wooden members supported by upper and lower rails between posts in a type of fence; a paling. (2) *(slang)* To go on strike; the employees who carry picket signs in protest of some action of the employer.

picking (wasting; stugging) Surfacing a rubble stone with a steel point struck at right angles to their surface so as to make many small, closely spaced pits.

pickling of metal Dipping steelwork in hot sulphuric acid, then hot water, then hot phosphoric acid to remove scale in prepartion for galvanizing or painting. The steel is dried and painted while still warm.

picks A term used to describe the physical action when a coil becomes energized.

picks per inch The number of filling insertions required to make one inch of fabric.

pick up sags Too heavy a coating of paint that has been applied and starts to sag or run down the surface; the painter brushes up through the sagging paint to level it off.

picture-frame form A steel frame with a plywood sheet fitted to it; used as a reusable formwork panel in concrete.

picture plane An imaginary plane between the eye and the object drawn; used in perspective drawing.

picture window A large window, often a fixed sheet of plate or insulating glass, usually located because of the outside view.

pie card *(slang)* A union card used to get food or lodging.

piece mark A number given to each separate part of the building for erection identification. Also called mark number and part number.

piend An arris.

pier (1) One of the solid supports on which the arches of a bridge rest. (2) Any solid support of masonry. (3) The solid part of a wall between windows, doors, etc. (4) A wharf projecting from the shore.

pier cap (pier template) The top part of a bridge pier which distributes the concentrated loads from the bridge uniformly over the pier.

piercing *(see probing)*

pier-glass A mirror hanging between windows.

pier template *(see pier cap)*

piezometer An instrument for measuring pressure head, usually consisting of a small pipe tapped into the side of a conduit and flush with the inside, connected with a pressure gauge, mercury, water column or other device for indicating pressure head.

pig (1) An air manifold having a number of pipes which distribute compressed air coming through a single large line. (2) A lead or iron block cast at the smelting furnace for remelting at the foundry. The word ingot is used to describe other metals. (3) *(slang)* (mandrel) A device to clean conduit, roots out the garbage.

pigeon-holed wall A honeycomb wall.

piggy-back In staple application of tile to gypsum wallboard, a second staple is driven directly on top of the first. The staple spreads to form a firm bond between the tile and the gypsum board.

pig iron High carbon iron made by reduction of iron ore in the blast furnace.

pigment A coloring matter, usually in the form of an insoluble fine powder.

pigmented yarns A colored yarn spun from a solution to which a pigment has been added.

pig spout A sheet metal flashing designed to direct the flow of water out through the face of the gutter rather than through a downspout.

pigtail (1) A Y-shaped electrical connector. (2) A lamp socket with two wires attached used for lighting and testing purposes.

pilaster A right-angled columnar projection with capital and base from a pier or wall; a square engaged pillar.

pilaster block Concrete masonry units designed for use in construction of plain or reinforced concrete masonry pilasters and columns.

pilaster face The form for the front surface of a pilaster parallel to the wall.

pilaster side The form for the side surface of a pilaster perpendicular to the wall.

pile (1) A long slender timber, concrete, or steel structural element, driven, jetted, or otherwise embedded on end in the ground for the purpose of supporting a load or compacting the soil. (2) The upright ends of yarn, whether cut or looped, that form the wearing surface of carpets or rugs.

pile, bearing A member driven or jetted into the ground and deriving its support from the underlying strata and/or by the friction of the ground on its surface.

pile bent Two or more piles driven in a row transverse to the long dimension of the structure and fastened together by capping and sometimes bracing.

pile bridge A bridge carried on piles.

pile cap A structural member placed on, and usually fastened to, the top of a pile or a group of piles and used to transmit loads into the pile or group of piles, and in the case of a group, to connect them into a bent; also known as a rider cap or girder. A masonry, timber

or concrete footing resting on a group of piles; a metal cap or helmet temporarily fitted over the head of a precast pile to protect it during driving. Some form of shock-absorbing material is often incorporated.

pile core (mandrel) A steel rod or stiff pipe inserted, by driving, into a hollow cylinder pile when the pile is sunk. The force of the pile hammer is spent on the pile core which makes contact with the pile shoe. The cylinder is therefore not damaged by driving.

pile crush Bending of carpet pile by constant walking or the pressure of furniture.

pile density Number of tufts both across (needles per inch or gauge for tufted carpet) and lengthwise (stitches per inch) of the carpet.

piled foundation A foundation carried on piles to earth considerably beneath the surface.

pile driver A machine for driving piles; usually a high vertical framework with appliances attached for raising a heavy mass of iron which, after being lifted to the top of the framework, is allowed to fall, by the force of gravity or mechanical methods, on the head of the pile thus driving it into the ground. *(see pile hammer)*

pile extractor (pile drawer) Any piledriver which strikes a pile upwards and loosens the grip of the pile on the ground. The actual withdrawal of the pile is done by the crane from which the pile extractor hangs.

pile foot The lower extremity of a pile.

pile frame A pile-driver; appreciably taller than the longest pile to be used.

pile group Several piles placed close together to take a heavier load than a single pile could carry. A pile group is generally capped by a reinforced-concrete pile cap.

pile hammer Generally a drop hammer or a steam hammer. A steam hammer may be fully automatic, e.g., the steam admission is automatically controlled by valves, or semi-automatic. Fully automatic hammers are double-acting and are used for driving steel sheet piling. Semi-automatic hammers are single-acting and have a steam admission controlled by hand line. They are used for driving timber or concrete piles.

pile head The top of a pile.

pile height The height of pile measured from the surface of the back to the top of the pile, not including the thickness of the back.

pile helmet A cap which covers and protects the head of a precast-concrete pile during driving and holds the packing in place between it and the pile head.

pile hoop A driving band.

pile-placing methods Driving piles by means such as drop or steam hammer, jetting, jacking, boring, washing out, blowing out, coring, drilling or vibration.

pile ring A driving band.

pile setting Brushing done to carpet after shampooing to restore the damp pile to its original height. A pile lifting machine or a pile brush is used.

pile shoe A hard metal point on the foot of a wood or concrete driven pile to help it penetrate the soil.

pile yarn The yarn used to form the loops or tufts of a pile fabric.

piling (1) The behavior of very quick drying paint which becomes so sticky during application by brush that the resulting film is thick and uneven. (2) *(see pile)*

pilla A masonry support for roof timbers that is superimposed on a column.

pillar (1) A columnar support but not a Classical column. (2) In underground excavation, a mass of ore or rock left to support the overlying ground.

pillar tap In plumbing, a water tap used on washbasins and baths, equipped with a long vertical screw thread at the bottom, passing through the basin or bath, and connecting to the supply pipe.

pilling A condition in certain fibers in which strands of the fiber separate and become knotted with other strands, causing a rough, spotty appearance. Pilled tufts should never be pulled from

carpet, but may be cut off with sharp scissors at the pile surface.

pillow A supporting member of cushion shape, usually at the top of a column.

pillow block A metal-cased rubber block that allows limited motion of a support or thrust.

pill test *(see tablet test)*

pilot circuit In electrical work, a control circuit similar to that used in remote control or for conductors.

pilot hole In carpentry, a guiding hole, usually of smaller diameter than the main hole is to be.

piloti A heavy column, usually of reinforced concrete, supporting a structure above an open ground-level space.

pilot light (1) A small flame, used in gas-heating devices, which burns constantly. (2) A small electric light of very low wattage indicating a closed circuit.

pilot nail A temporary nail, driven to hold lumber in place while the main nails are being driven.

pilot valve In a compressor, an automatic valve which regulates air pressure.

pimp *(slang)* (1) Man who cleans wells. (2) Welder's helper.

pin (1) A cylindrical piece of wood, iron or steel, used to hold two or more pieces together by passing through a hole in each of them, as in a mortise and tenon joint, or a pin joint of a truss. (2) The only pin in an integrated crawler track that will open the track when driven out.

pincers A jointed tool, with two handles and a pair of jaws used for gripping and holding an object.

pinchbar A type of crowbar, or lever, on one end of which a pointed projection serves as a kind of fulcrum; used especially for rolling heavy wheels. *(see wrecking bar)*

pin connection In structural analysis, a member connection to a foundation; another member or structure is designed in such a way that free rotation is assumed.

pine Any of a genus of coniferous evergreen trees having slender elongated needles and including valuable timber trees as well as many ornamentals.

eastern white The first lumber used by early settlers in America; soft, fine-textured, easily worked; heartwood endures under exposure; now largely knotty second growth and replaced by western white pine under the names of California and Idaho pine.

ponderosa A tree of the Rocky Mountain and Pacific coast regions, with wood moderately light, rather uniform in texture, easy to work; used widely for millwork of doors, frames and sash.

red A member of the yellow pine group, growing in Canada and the Lake states; more contrast in texture, heavier, stronger and somewhat more resinous that the eastern white pine with which it is sold in the lower grades.

southern yellow Woods of the southeastern states, consisting chiefly of loblolly, slash, longleaf and shortleaf; the lumber is relatively strong and dense. The wood characteristics of the species overlap according to age and growth conditions.

sugar Grown in California, southern Oregon and Mexico. Large trees yield wide thick sizes of lumber for millwork.

pine oil A strong solvent used in paints made from the oleo-resin of pine trees or synthetically. It is an anti-skinning agent and is used to give good flow properties to the paint.

pin hinge A loose-pin butt hinge.

pinhole (1) A small hole appearing in a cast when the water-stucco ratio has not been accurately measured. Excess water causes pinholes. (2) A very small dark-stained worm hole in wood.

pin joint A structural hinge.

pin knot A term used by woodworkers when referring to a blemish in boards, consisting of a small knot of ½ inch or less in diameter. Also called a cat eye.

pinnacle A terminal ornament or pro-

tecting cap, usually tapered upward to a point or knob and used as a high point of a roof, a buttress or the like.

pinnings In Scotland, stones of different color or texture set in a rubble wall to give a checkered effect.

pin, taper A straight-sided pin that is smaller at one end that at the other.

pintle A vertical pin fastened at the bottom that serves as a center of rotation.

pintle hook A towing device consisting of a fixed lower jaw, a hinged and lockable upper jaw, and a socket between them to hold a tow ring.

pin, track A hinge pin connecting two sections or shoes of a crawler track.

pioneering The first working over of rough or overgrown areas. Usually done with a bulldozer.

pioneer road A primitive, temporary road built along the route of a job to provide means for moving equipment and men.

pipe A tubular conduit for liquid or gas.

pipe branches Special forms of vitrified tile and cast iron pipe for making connections to a sewer; called tee, Y, tee-Y, double Y and V from their shapes.

pipe buffer A worker on a welding crew who butts ends of pipe section with buffing machine prior to finish welding.

pipe column Column made of steel pipe; often filled with concrete.

pipe, copper or brass Seamless tube conforming to the particular dimensions commercially known as Standard Pipe Sizes.

pipe coupling In plumbing, a short collar consisting of a threaded sleeve to connect two pipes.

pipe cutter A tool for cutting pipes.

pipe diaper A piece of burlap or other fabric shaped like a diaper; two metal bands are sewn in the outside edge, wrapped around pipe joints and filled with hot tar or concrete as a sealer.

pipe drill A drill which cuts round holes in brickwork.

pipe duct A duct for piping.

pipe enamel   An asphaltic material used to coat gas pipe which is placed underground.

pipe fitter   A trained worker who installs pipes for water, steam, gas, oil or chemicals.

pipe fittings   In plumbing, a term used in reference to ells, tees and various branch connectors used in connecting pipes.

pipe gang   Where pipe is welded together on side of ditch.

pipe hook (J-hook)   A spiked fastener, driven into a wall joint or stud, with a curved end for holding a pipe.

pipe-jointing clip   In plumbing, an asbestos and metal ring which envelopes a pipe joint to be filled with molten lead.

pipe layer   A skilled worker who joints, in the trench, pipes of glazed clay, concrete, iron, steel or asbestos cement and lays them to correct levels.

pipeless furnace   A basement furnace with a large, single register.

pipe pile   A steel cylinder, usually between 10 and 24 inches (25 cm and 60 cm) in diameter, generally driven with open ends to firm bearing and then excavated and filled with concrete. This pile may consist of several sections from five to 40 feet (1.5 m to 8 m) long, joined by cast-steel sleeves or otherwise. Sometimes it is used with its lower end closed by a conical steel shoe.

pipe-pushing   A method of placing underground pipelines by assembly at the foot of an access shaft and pushing them through the ground, instead of assembling them in place.

pipe saddle   *(see saddle)*

pipe sleeve   *(see expansion sleeve)*

pipe stopper   A screw plug for drains.

pipe stretcher   *(slang)* What the new men are sent for.

pipe tongs (foot prints)   A plumbing wrench; a Stillson.

pipe wrench (Stillson wrench)   A heavy wrench with adjustable serrated jaws for gripping, screwing or unscrewing metal pipe.

piping   The installation of equipment to enclose and carry wires from termination to termination point.

pise (pise de terre)   A rammed-earth wall building.

piss coat   *(slang)* A term used by painters to indicate a thin coat of paint poorly applied.

piston   A sliding piece moved by or against fluid pressure that usually consists of a short cylinder fitting within a cylindrical vessel along which it moves back and forth.

piston displacement   The amount of air displaced by moving all pistons of an engine or compressor from the bottom to the top of their stroke.

piston, free running   A piston not connected with a rod, that does its work by hammer-like blows.

piston, slave   A small piston having a fixed connection with a larger one.

piston speed   Total feet of travel of a piston in one minute.

piston stroke   Length of travel (twice its crank radius).

pit   (1) Any mine, quarry or excavation area worked by the open cut method to obtain material of value. In underpinning, a pit is usually sheeted horizontally and seldom goes below water lines and practically never more than a few feet below water. (2) In a theater, the area between the lower range of boxes or seats and the stage.

pit boards (well curbing)   Horizontal sheeting for retaining the earth about the pit.

pitch   (1) Any of various dark-colored bituminous or resinous substances consisting of fusible, viscous to solid, materials, especially coal tar. (2) The slope of a surface or tooth relative to its direction of movement; in a roller or silent chain, the space between pins, measured center to center (3) The degree of inclination, as of a roof plane or a flight of stairs. (4) The auditory sensation which enables one to locate a sound on a scale from low to high. The higher the frequency the higher the pitch. (5) The distance from any point on a screw thread to a corresponding point on the next thread, measured parallel to the axis.

pitch arms (pitch braces) Rods, usually adjustable, which determine the digging angle of a blade or bucket.

pitch board In building, a thin piece of board, cut in the shape of a right-angled triangle, used as a guide in forming work. When making cuts for stairs, the pitch board serves as a pattern for marking cuts; the shortest side is the height of the riser cut and the longer side is the width of the tread.

pitch pan A metal sleeve surrounding a pipe protruding through a roof; filled with pitch to prevent leaks.

pitch pocket A metal flange around the base of any roof-penetrating member (or component) which is filled with pitch or flashing cement to provide a seal.

pitched roof The most common type of roof, usually with two slopes more than 20° to the horizontal, meeting at a central ridge.

pitcher A pitching tool. *(see pitch-faced stone)*

pitcher tee (pitcher cross) In plumbing, a tee or cross with a gently curved turn instead of the sharp elbow of ordinary tees and crosses.

pitch-faced stone Stone which has been worked at the quarry with the pitching tool. It can be rubble or ashlar but is always rough stone.

pitching (1) Lifting a runner or pile and placing it in position for driving. (2) Large stones placed on edge and rolled or wedged by small stones called spalls to make a road foundation or revetment to protect an earth slope. *(see rip rap)*

pitching ferrules One or two short lengths of pipe cast into a reinforced-concrete pile and used for lifting it.

pitching-piece A horizontal timber, with one of its ends wedged into the wall at the top of a flight of stairs, to support the upper end of the rough strings.

pitch mastic A mixture of aggregate and coal-tar pitch, fluid when hot,

spread as a topping for jointless floors. Not to be confused with mastic.

pitch of a roof The proportion obtained by dividing the height by the span; thus, it may be $\frac{1}{2}$, $\frac{1}{3}$ or $\frac{1}{4}$. When the length of the rafters is equal to the breadth of the building it is called Gothic.

pitch pocket An opening extending parallel to the annual rings of growth of a tree; usually contains, or has contained, either solid or liquid pitch.

pit, dig-down (sunken pit) A pit that is below the surrounding area on all sides.

pit, elevator That portion of a hoistway extending from the threshold level of the lowest landing door to the floor at the bottom of the hoistway.

pith The small, soft core at the original center of a tree around which wood formation takes place.

pith knot In lumber, a minor defect; a knot whose only blemish is a pith hole smaller than $\frac{1}{4}$ inch.

pitman arm An arm having a limited movement around a pivot.

Pitot tube A device for observing the velocity head of flowing water. It has an orifice held to point upstream in flowing water and connected with a tube by which the rise of water in the tube above the water surface may be observed. It may be constructed with an upstream and downstream orifice and two water columns; the difference of water levels is an index of the velosity head.

pit-run gravel Gravel direct from a pit.

pit sawing The method used for ripping lumber before mechanical saws were used. One man stood in a pit and another man stood at the top, each pulling at the same saw.

pitting (pinholing) Development of relatively small cavities in a surface, due to phenomena such as corrosion or cavitation or, in concrete, localized disintegration. Also describes the appearance caused by changes in atmospheric conditions during drying, by mixing different varnishes or rubbing a dirty varnish. *(see popout)*

pivot A non-rotating axle or hinge pin.

pivot bridge A swinging bridge.

pivoted casement A casement window which has its upper and lower edges pivoted.

pivot shaft A tractor dead axle, or any fixed shaft which acts as a hinge pin.

pivot tube A hollow hinge pin.

placage A thin application of material and architectural detail to an otherwise bare wall.

place (1) An open piece of ground surrounded by buildings, generally decorated with a statue, column or other ornament. (2) A building or space devoted to a special purpose. A court or short street. To put in a particular position or condition.

placeability *(see workability)*

placement The process of placing and consolidating concrete; a quantity of concrete placed and finished during a continuous operation; also inappropriately referred to as pouring.

place brick Underburned, soft brick used only for walls that are to be plastered.

placing (1) The deposition and compaction of freshly mixed mortar or concrete in the place where it is to harden. (2) The process of applying plastic terrazzo mix to the prepared surface.

placing drawings Detail sheets. Usually provided by the reinforcing steel manufacturers to aid in the installation of rebar.

placing plant A British term for the total equipment for placing wet concrete in position.

plain In roofing, rolls of roofing shipped without nails or cement; shingles that are not embossed with a Cedartex design.

plain ashlars Smoothed surfaced stones.

plain bar A reinforcing bar without surface deformations, or one having deformations that do not conform to the applicable requirements.

plain concrete Concrete without reinforcement; or concrete that does not conform to the definition of reinforced concrete; also loosely used for concrete lacking whatever the concrete with which a comparison is being made possesses, as non-air-entrained concrete.

plain masonry Masonry without reinforcement, or reinforced only for shrinkage or temperature changes.

plain sawing Cutting wood so the saw cuts are parallel to the squared side of a log.

plain tile The common, flat roofing tile of concrete or burnt clay, which actually has a slight spherical camber, convex, above.

plan A horizontal geometrical section of the walls of a building; indications, on a horizontal plane, of the relative positions of the walls and partitions, with the various openings, such as windows and doors, recesses and projections, chimneys and chimney-breasts, columns, pilasters, etc. This term is often incorrectly used in the sense of design.

plancier That part of a cornice directly under the corona, e.g., the soffit, or underside of the corona.

plancier piece (soffit board) A horizontal board forming the wooden or plaster soffit of an overhanging eave.

plancon A roughly octagonal hardwood timber with minimum dimension of 10 inches.

plane (1) In woodworking, a flat surface where any line joining two points will lie entirely in the surface. (2) A carpenter's tool used for smoothing boards or other wood surfaces.

plane iron The cutting iron of a plane.

plane of rapture In the wedge theory, the plane along which retained earth is expected to fail when a wall is being designed to retain it.

plane of saturation A technical term for water table.

plane of weakness The plane along which a body under stress will tend to fracture; may exist by design, by accident, or because of the nature of the structure and its loading.

planer (1) A planing tool for surfacing metal, stone or timber. (2) A large machine used to smooth a preheated road surface.

planer bite A groove cut in the surface of the face or edge of a slat, deeper than intended by the planer knives.

plane stock The body of a plane which holds the cutting iron and the back iron.

plane surveying That branch of surveying wherein all distances and horizontal angles are assumed to be projected onto one horizontal plane.

plane tabling Mapping with a plane table and alidade. A quick way of mapping small areas.

planetary cooler A cooler consisting of a number of cylinders built around and parallel to the shell at the discharge end of a rotary kiln; the hot clinker leaves the kiln through these cylinders in counterflow with cooling air which then enters kiln as secondary combustion air.

planimeter A device that measures an area on a map when run around its perimeter.

planimetry The location of artificial features of a given locality in topographic surveying.

planing machine *(see plane; planer)*

planing mill A place equipped with woodworking machinery for smoothing rough wood surfaces, cutting, fitting and matching boards with tongued-and-grooved joints; a woodworking mill.

planing mill products Floorboards, ceiling boards and weather-boarding, as distinguished from millwork.

planish (1) To make smooth with a plane or by light hammering. (2) To polish.

plank A length of wood having rectangular section not under 1½ inches or over 3½ inches in thickness and not under six inches wide.

plank truss Any truss work con-

structed of heavy timber such as planking in a roof truss or in a bridge truss.

planning grid A reference grid pattern used for the presentation of plans and elevations of buildings.

planometric projection A pictorial view showing the object plan with oblique parallel lines from the corners to show the front, side and thickness.

plans The official approved plans, profiles, typical cross sections, working drawings and supplemental drawings, or exact reproductions thereof, which show the location, character, dimensions and details of the work to be performed.

planted Fastened on or tongued in, as a molding separately wrought and then applied.

plant mix The mixing of mineral aggregates and asphalt cement or liquid asphalt in a central, or traveling, mechanical mixer after which the finished mix is laid on the road. Proportioning of aggregate constituents and asphalt is closely controlled and the mineral aggregate is usually dried and heated before mixing.

plan view The top view of an architect's drawing.

plaque An applied or inset decoration, usually of round or oval shape.

plaster From Greek, emplastron, to daub on; Latin, emplastrum; French, platre; old English, plaister. (1) A cementitious material or combination of cementitious materials and aggregate that, when mixed with a suitable amount of water, forms a plastic mass or paste which applied to a surface, adheres to it and subsequently sets or hardens, preserving in a rigid state the form or texture imposed during the period of elasticity. The term 'plaster' is used with regard to the specific composition of the material and does not explicitly denote either interior or exterior use. The term 'stucco,' however, is generally used to describe plaster applied on the exterior. (2) The term 'plaster' is used regionally to denote specifically neat calcined gypsum, lime-sand mixtures, etc. **(3)** To plaster (v). The act of applying plaster.

plaster base   A working ground for plaster. It may be wood, metal lathing, gypsum lath, insulating board, masonry or brickwork.

plaster bead   A built-in edging, usually of metal, to strengthen a plaster angle.

plasterboard   A composition sheet in various thicknesses used as a base for a thin finish coat of plaster.

plasterboard nail   A galvanized nail used for installing plasterboard.

plaster dab   A small pat of gypsum plaster stuck on brickwork or lathing used as a fixing for wall tiles, marble facing, or joinery.

plasterer   A tradesman who applies plaster, stucco, lathing and related work.

plasterer's float   *(see float)*

plasterer's lath hammer   A lath hammer.

plasterer's putty   Lime putty.

plaster grounds   Strips of wood nailed to walls to serve as guides for the plasterer.

plaster lath   Thin, narrow strips of wood nailed to ceiling joists, studding or rafters as a groundwork for receiving plastering.

plaster of paris   **(1)** Calcined Gypsum (calcium sulphate hemihydrate) without addition of material to control set. Principal use is in casting and industrial applications. **(2)** Gypsum from which three-quarters of the chemically bound water has been driven off by heating; when wetted it recombines with water and hardens quickly. *(see also hemihydrate)*

plaster set   *(see false set)*

plaster work   The finished product of the plasterer.

plastic   Possessing plasticity, or possessing adequate plasticity. A condition of freshly mixed cement paste, mortar or concrete that is readily remoldable and workable, is cohesive and has an ample content of cement and fines but is not overwet.

plastic centroid   Centroid of the resistance to load computed for the assumptions that the concrete is stressed uniformly to 0.85 its design strength and the steel is stressed uniformly to its specified yield point.

plastic clay (bond fire)   A fire clay of sufficient natural plasticity to bond nonplastic material; a fire clay used as a plasticizing agent in mortar.

plastic concrete   Easily molded concrete that will change its form slowly only if the mold is removed.

plastic consistency   Condition in which cement paste, mortar or concrete will sustain deformation continuously in any direction without rupture.

plastic cracking   Cracking that occurs in the surface of fresh concrete soon after it is placed and while it is still plastic.

plastic deformation   Deformation that does not disappear when the force causing the deformation is removed.

plastic design   *(see ultimate-strength design)*

plastic emulsion   *(see latex emulsion)*

plastic flow   *(see creep; plastic deformation)*

plastic foam   An expanded plastic material used for insulation purposes.

plastic fracture   Metal broken in tension by a drawing out called necking. The necking produces a more gradual failure than the abrupt cleavage fracture.

plastic glues   Synthetic resin glues used on wood; epoxy resins for gluing light metals and other substances.

plastic index   The numerical difference between the soil's liquid limit and its plastic limit. Also called plasticity index.

plasticine   A modeling clay that retains its plasticity without the addition of moisture.

plasticity   That property of plaster mortar that permits continuous and permanent deformation in any direction. A plastic material is distinct from a fluid material in that it requires a measurable force (yield value) to start flow. The property exists in varying degrees in different materials and in plaster mortar is sometimes regarded as an index of working characteristics.

plasticity index The range in water content through which a soil remains plastic; numerical difference between the liquid limit and the plastic limit. *(see Atterberg limits)*

plasticizer A material that increases plasticity of a cement paste, mortar or concrete mixture.

plastic limit The water content at which a soil will just begin to crumble when rolled into a thread approximately ⅛ inch (3 mm) in diameter. *(see Atterberg limits)*

plastic loss *(see creep)*

plastic mortar A mortar of plastic consistency.

plastic paint (texture paint) Paint which can be manipulated after application to provide a textured finish.

plastic roof or wall panels Panels used to admit light. They are normally of the same configuration as the metal roof or wall panels, and installed in the same plane.

plastic shrinkage cracks *(see hairline cracking)*

plastic soil A soil that can be rolled into ⅛ inch (3 mm) diameter threads without crumbling; a soft rubbery soil.

plastic welding Welding in the plastic state, such as forge welding; usually also pressure welding.

plastic wood A quick drying paste of nitrocellulose, plasticizers, wood flour, resins and other materials dispersed in solvent. Used for repairing wood, filling holes, etc.; surface can be painted in about one hour.

plastic yield Plastic deformation.

plastisols Mixtures of resins and plasticizers which can be cast or converted to continuous films by the application of heat.

plat A plan of land divisions, streets, etc., showing ownership and boundaries with their descriptions.

plat band A flat band or string course with a projection less than its breadth.

plate (1) In formwork for concrete, a flat, horizontal member at the top or bottom, or both, of studs or posts; a mudsill if on the ground. (2) In structural design, a member, the depth of which is substantially smaller than its length and width. *(see flat plate; load-transfer assembly)* (3) A flat-rolled iron or steel product. (4) A horizontal structural member placed on a wall or supported on posts, studs or corbels to carry the trusses of a roof or to carry the rafters directly.

plate bearing test An obsolete method of estimating the bearing capacity of a soil by digging a hole down to the proposed foundation level, placing a stiff steel plate on the foundation, and loading it until it fails by sinking rapidly.

plate cut In carpentry, a foot cut.

plate girder Built up girder resembling an I beam with a web of steel plate and flanges of angle iron.

plate glass Glass from the same molten mixture as is used for window glass; it is flowed on an iron plate, rolled to proper thickness, annealed and polished. Used for large expanses; thicker than used for window plates.

plate, pressure A flywheel-driven plate that can be slid along a clutch shaft to squeeze a lined plate against the flywheel.

plate screws In surveying, foot screws.

plate tracery Tracery formed by piercing a single large stone.

plate vibrator A self-propelled mechanical vibrator with a flat base, used to compact fill.

platform (1) A wood mat used in sets to support machinery on soft ground; also called a pontoon. (2) An operator's station on a large machine, particularly on rollers. (3) A raised section of flooring, as a dais or simple stage. (4) A working space for persons, elevated above the surrounding floor or ground, such as a balcony or platform for the operation of machinery and equipment.

platform framing System of wood frame house construction using wood studs one story high finished with a platform consisting of the underflooring for the next story.

platform gantry A gantry for a portal crane or other similar purposes.

platform hoist A power-driven hoist which lifts a platform carrying a load of 200 to 5500 pounds up to 200 feet in height.

plat line A boundary line on plat or plan of property.

play Clearance for movable parts.

plenum (1) Chamber or space forming a part of an air conditioning system. (2) Use of compressed air to hold soil from slumping into an excavation. (3) An air compartment connected to one or more inlets or outlets.

plenum chamber (1) A container into which air is forced for slower distribution through ducts. (2) An air compartment connected to one or more distributing ducts.

plenum system Provision for ventilation of an interior in which fresh or conditioned air is forced into a plenum chamber, from which it finds its way through ducts to the various rooms; used in factories or large buildings.

Plexiglass Trade name for a plastic material, usually in sheets; uses are similar to glass, e.g., windows, shower doors, light panels, etc.

plied yarns Two or more strands, ends or plies either twisted or otherwise cohesively entwined, intermingled or entangled into a heavier yarn.

pliers A gripping tool, pivoted like a pair of scissors, with blades for cutting thin wire built into the jaws.

plies Plural of ply; a sheet of veneer, bitumen felt, etc.

plinth The base block, usually of stone, of a column, pedestal or other isolated object; the base block at the juncture of baseboard and trim around an opening.

plinth block A small block slightly thicker and wider than the casing for interior trim of a door; placed at the bottom of the door trim against which the base or mop board is butted.

plinth course The top course of a brick plinth.

plot A definitely limited piece of land, as where a building stands or is to be built.

plot plan A scale drawing indicating the location of the construction in relation to the site.

plotter A computer device that produces images on paper or acetate by electrostatic, thermal or mechanical means.

plotting The laying out, in drawing, of a group plan or the governing points of a curve or graph.

plotting instrument (plotting machine) A large drawing machine used in aerial surveying, equipped with a mechanically-operated plotting arm, pencil and viewing window in which vertical photographs or projections can be viewed together with their ground-control points.

plough (plow) To cut a groove.

plowed and tongued joint A feather joint.

plow steel The steel from which wire is drawn for making steel ropes.

plug (1) A stopper for a plumbing fixture drain opening. (2) A male-threaded casting for closing the end of a pipe line. (3) A teminating fixture for the wires of portable electric lamps or appliances by which connection is made with an outlet socket. (4) A small pointed wooden peg pushed into a hole in a wall where a nail, screw or other fastening is to be driven. (5) A stoppage in the discharge line of a dredge, or in an underground drain. (6) *(slang)* 4" × 8" × 12" concrete masonry unit.

plug and feathers A set of two half-round pieces of hard steel and a gradual taper wedge used for splitting drilled boulders.

plug-center bit A bit used to widen holes. The center part is a plug inserted in the hole already drilled.

plug cock A simple valve, in which the fluid passes through a hole in a tapered plug. It is closed by turning the plug around 90°.

plug-driving gun *(see stud gun)*

plugging Drilling a hole in a masonry

surface to be filled with a plug of wood fiber or metal such as a fixing for a nail, drive screw, wood screw, etc.

plugging chisel (star drill) A short steel hand bar struck with a hammer to make holes in brick, concrete or masonry. *(see pipe drill)*

plug, magnetic A drain or inspection plug magnetized for the purpose of attracting and holding iron or steel particles in lubricant.

plug tenon In carpentry, a short tenon projecting from the head or foot of a post to stabilize it.

plum A large random-shaped stone dropped into freshly placed mass concrete to economize on the volume of the concrete. *(see cyclopean concrete)*

plumb True according to a plumb line; perpendicular; vertical; to true up vertically as a wall by use of a plumb line.

plumb and level (level) A well-finished hardwood or metal case containing a glass tube with the bubble set lengthwise for testing accuracy of horizontal planes and lines. It also contains a second glass tube with the bubble set crosswise for testing accuracy of vertical lines and perpendicular walls.

plumb bob A pointed weight hung from a string; used for vertical alignment. *(see plumb line; plummet)*

plumb cut In carpentry, the vertical cut at the foot of a rafter where it fits over the wall plate; also the vertical cut at the top ridge.

plumber A person skilled in the plumbing trade.

plumber's dope A soft sealing compound for pipe threads.

plumber's mate A laborer who helps the plumber by carrying tools and bringing materials; may help to make joints, etc.; may be an apprentice.

plumber's solder (coarse solder) An alloy of lead and tin used for joining lead pipes; its melting point is well below that of lead.

plumbing (1) The work or business of installing in buildings the pipes, fixtures and other apparatus for bringing in the water supply and removing liquid and water-borne wastes. The term is also used to denote the installed fixtures and piping of a building. (2) The transferring of a point at one level to a point vertically below or above it, usually with a plumb bob or plumb rule.

plumbing fixtures Receptacles which receive and discharge water, liquid or water-borne wastes into a drainage system with which they are connected.

plumbing system The water-supply distributing pipes; the fixtures and fixture traps; the soil, waste, and vent pipes; the building drain and building sewer; and the storm-drainage pipes; with their devices, appurtenances, and connections all within or adjacent to the building.

plumb line A string, braided to avoid spinning, on which a weight is hung to stretch it in a vertical direction. *(see plumb bob)*

plumb rule A narrow board having a plumb line and bob on one end, or more commonly, having a bubble in a tube. It is used for establishing vertical lines and horizontal lines.

plumb scratch An additional scratch coat that has been applied to obtain a uniform setting bed on a plumb vertical plane.

plume (1) Dark, as yet unignited, part of a flame, closest to the nozzle of the burner pipe. Its length depends on the temperature and velocity of the primary combustion air and the fineness and volatile content of coal. (2) Opaque or apparently opaque effluent emitted from a stack.

plummet A plumb bob.

plunge A small swimming pool.

plunger A hand operated suction device for cleaning out or unstopping drains. *(see ram)*

plunger pump Water, oil, or slurry pump consisting of reciprocating piston(s) in cylinder(s).

plush A single-level, cut-pile surface.

plus sieve The portion of a powder sample retained on a standard sieve of specified number.

plus sight The term for levelling recommended by ASCE. In Britain, called a back sight.

plutonium A man-made element which results from the capture of uranium 238 of an extra neutron. It is a highly fissionable as well as highly radioactive material.

ply (1) Thickness; fold; anything composed of distinct layers or thicknesses, as plywood used in building construction; also used to denote thickness of roofing paper and lumber. (2) The number of strands of yarn twisted together to form a single yarn, as in '2-ply' or '3-ply.'

plying cement Any bituminous material used for adhering layers of felts, fabrics, or mats to structural surfaces and to each other.

plymetal Plywood faced on one or both sides with sheet metal of galvanized steel, aluminum or other metals.

plypon The arched space over a window or door.

plywood A fabricated wood product constructed of three or more layers of veneer joined with glue, usually laid with grain of adjoining plies at right angles.

pneumatic Powered or inflated by compressed air.

pneumatically-applied mortar Mortar projected onto a surface by an air jet; sometimes called shotcrete.

pneumatic caisson A caisson in which the working chamber for the worker is kept full of compressed air at a pressure nearly equal to the water pressure.

pneumatic conveyor A tube through which cement is transported by an air blast.

pneumatic drill (rock drill) A drill operated by compressed air.

pneumatic ejector A means of raising sewage or other liquid by alternately admitting it through a check valve into the bottom of a pot and then ejecting it through another check valve into the discharge pipe by admitting compressed air to the pot above the liquid.

pneumatic feed Shotcrete delivery equipment in which material is conveyed by a pressurized air stream.

pneumatic mortar Mortar thrown on, as gunite. The mortar is built up in layers by successive passes of the gun. It cannot be used with heavily reinforced concrete, but is particularly suitable for prestressed concrete.

pneumatic pick A light, 20 to 30 pound, concrete breaker.

pneumatic riveter A very noisy percussive compressed air tool fitted with a rivet snap. It closes the rivet and, with about ten blows per second, it forms the head.

pneumatic roller A roller, either towed or self-propelled, having an unequal number of smooth wide tread tires. The greater number of tires are in the back and are arranged in such a manner that they half-track the front tires. This roller is used for finished compaction work.

pneumatic tool A tool worked by compressed air, usually a hand tool.

pneumatic water supply A water-supply system used in houses in isolated areas. The cistern is in the basement and consists of a closed tank from which water is forced into the pipes by compressed air.

Pocahontas coal Smithing coal used in a forge to heat up rivets.

pocket An opening in a wall into which a beam is to be inserted.

pocket chisel A chisel, for cutting the pocket in the pulley stile or a window frame, which has a wide, thin blade honed on both sides.

pock marking A painting term describing orange peeling or other depressions formed in the drying of a paint or varnish.

pod auger An obsolete type of wood drill with the upper part shaped like a bean pod to contain the chippings.

podger (construction spanner) A single-end, open-jaw spanner with a pointed handle. The pointed end is used for aligning two or more drilled steel plates which are to be bolted. The point is inserted through the holes and moved about until they are brought into line.

podium (1) A flat topped mass of masonry on which a Classical temple was built. (2) An elevated station point for the conductor of an orchestra; a speaker's stand.

podzol A relatively acid surface soil found in temperate climates from which considerable soluble material, iron and aluminum oxides, has been leached into underlying soils.

pogo stick *(slang)* (1) An air tamper run by compressed air. (2) A spring loaded devise on a semi-truck that secures connection hoist, air, and electric lines off the frames of truck and trailer.

point (1) The sharp end of a tooth of a saw. The number of teeth per inch of a saw is one less than the number of points per inch. (2) In electrical work, a lampholder, socket, outlet or other terminal from which power can be taken. A power point is one designed for circuits more powerful than lighting circuits. (3) Any outlet of a gas system, connected or ready for connection, in plumbing. (4) In a well, the pipe having a fine mesh screen and a drive point at the bottom. Used for pumping out ground water.

point-bearing pile An end-bearing pile.

point count Method for determination of the volumetric composition of a solid by observation of the frequency with which areas of each component coincide with a regular system of points in one or more planes intersecting a sample of the solid.

point, critical Of a substance, state point at which liquid and vapor have identical properties; critical temperature, critical pressure, and critical volume are the terms given to the temperature, pressure and volume at the critical point. Above the critical temperature or pressure there is no line of demarcation between liquid and gaseous phases.

pointed architecture An occasional term for Gothic.

point gauge In hydraulics, a sharp point fixed to an attachment which slides down a graduated rod for measuring water level. The point is lowered until it barely touches the water surface.

pointing In masonry, finishing of joints in a brick or stone wall.

pointing trowel The pointing trowel or pointer is probably the most essential tool in the trade. It comes in sizes ranging from 4″ to 7″ in length, but the 6″ trowel is the most popular. The tilesetter uses this trowel in every phase of the work, especially for straightening tiles on walls and floors, marking floated surfaces, filling small depressions on float coats, buttering tiles and trim work, and placing mortar in areas that are too small for the flat trowel. The butt of the handle is used for tapping in tiles that are not on a true plane with the rest of the tilework. The trowel's flat working surface must be protected. The tilesetter should not use it to pry or chop hardened materials such as concrete or plaster.

pointing trowel A small hand instrument used by stone masons or bricklayers for pointing up joints, or for removing old mortar from the face of a wall.

point load A concentrated load.

point of contraflexure The point on a structural member subjected to flexure at which the direction of curvature changes and at which the bending moment is zero; also called point of inflection.

point of inflection The point, on the length of a structural member subjected to flexure, at which the direction of curvature changes and at which the bending moment is zero; called also point of contraflexure. Location of an abrupt bend in a plotted focus of points in a graph.

points Thin, flat, triangular or diamond shaped pieces of steel used to hold glass in wood sash; inserted by driving them into the wood close to the glass. They are then usually covered with a putty bead.

point, triple State point at which three

phases of given substance (e.g., solid, liquid and gas) exist in equilibrium.

poisson distribution The distribution of results of random events which follow its specific probability rules, e.g. time rate of radioactive disintegration.

Poisson's ratio The ratio of transverse, lateral, strain to the corresponding axial, longitudinal, strain resulting from uniformly distributed axial stress below the proportional limit of the material; the value will average about 0.2 for concrete and 0.25 for most metals.

polariscope A device for examining the degree of stress in a sample of glass.

polarized light Light in which the vibrations are in one plane only. A Nicol prism filters out all light except that vibrating in one plane, and polarizes the light in a petrographic microscope.

polarizer One of the Nicol prisms used in a polariscope.

polarizing microscope A microscope equipped with elements permitting observations and determinations to be made using polarized light. *(see Nicol prism)*

polder In Holland, the low-lying land reclaimed from the sea by enclosure with dikes.

pole (1) Either extremity of an axis of a sphere. (2) A terminal of an electric supply; an electrode. (3) A varying unit of length; usually 16½ feet. (4) A point of guidance or attraction. (5) A stake.

pole plate In carpentry, the horizontal beam resting on, and perpendicular to, principal rafters of a wooden roof truss; supports the feet of the common rafters and the inner edge of the box gutter.

poling back Excavating behind preplaced shoring.

poling boards (shoring) Vertical boards which support the sides of a trench or pit.

polish (final grind) The final operation in which fine abrasives are used to hone a surface to its desired smoothness and appearance.

polished plate Plate glass.

polishing Wall paints where shiny spots or surfaces have resulted from washing, wiping or vigorous scrubbing.

polishing varnish (rubbing varnish) A short-oil varnish used for fine finishing; generally so hard and dry that it can be polished by abrasive and mineral oil without dissolving the resin.

poll The striking face of a hammer.

polychromatic finish A paint finish of many colors; a finish with a metallic lustre and an iridescent effect produced by lacquers or enamels containing metal flake powders as well as transparent coloring matter.

polychromy Decoration in colors.

polyester A fiber introduced in the 50's; entered the carpet industry about 1969. Has a feel and appearance similar to wool. Technically, it is a complex ester formed by polymerization. It is made either as staple or continuous filament.

polyester resin The synthetic resin in a fiberglass reinforced resin.

polyethylene A thermoplastic high-molecular-weight organic compound used in formulating protective coatings or, in sheet form, as a protective cover for concrete surfaces during the curing period, or to provide a temporary enclosure for construction operations.

polygonal roof *(see pavilion roof)*

polygonal rubble Rubble walls faced with stones of many sides and projections.

polyisobutylene The polymerization product of isobutylene. It varies in consistency from a viscous liquid to a rubber like solid with corresponding variation in molecular weight from 1,000 to 400,000.

polymer (1) The product of polymerization; more commonly a rubber or resin consisting of large molecules formed by polymerization. (2) In synthetics, the basic chemical unit from which fibers are made. It is made of large complex molecules formed by uniting simple molecules (monomers).

polymeric liner Plastic or rubber sheeting used to line disposal sites, pits, ponds, lagoons, canals, etc.

polymerization The reaction in which

two or more molecules of the same substance combine to form a compound containing the same elements, and in the same proportions, but of high molecular weight, from which the original substance can be regenerated, in some cases only with extreme difficulty.

polypropylene (olefin) A long-chain synthetic polymer composed of at least 95% by weight of propylene and may be modified with several per cents of another olefin, except amorphous (non-crystalline) polyolefins qualifying as rubber. The fiber is used for conventional carpet as well as indoor/outdoor carpets. Polypropylene is also being used in the manufacture of man-made backings. The fiber is produced in continuous filament, fibrillated and staple form; solution dyed and piece-dyed.

polystrene Expanded polystrene beads (also called bead board); lightweight. Polystrene insulation, expanded polystrene beads, may be poured into cavities where other types of insulation cannot reach. When pressed together during manufacture, it is known as styrofoam.

polystyle In Classical architecture, many-columned.

polystyrene resin Synthetic resins varying in color from white to yellow, formed by the polymerization of styrene on heating with or without catalysts; may be used in paints for concrete, for making sculptured molds or as insulation.

polysulfide coating A protective coating system prepared by polymerizing a chlorinated alkyl polyether with an inorganic polysulfide; exhibits outstanding resistance to ozone, sunlight, oxidation and weathering.

polytropic change Any set of changes in a gas represented by the equation, $pV2$=constant.

polyurethane (1) Reaction product of an isocyanate with any of a wide variety of other compounds containing an active hydrogen group; used to formulate tough, abrasion-resistant coatings; highly insulating. (2) A resin. Also the common name applied to the clear plastic coating material made from this resin.

polyvinyl acetate Colorless, permanently thermoplastic resin; usually supplied as an emulsion or water-dispersible powder characterized by flexibility, stability towards light, transparency to ultraviolet rays, high dielectric strength, toughness and hardness. The higher the degree of polymerization, the higher the softening temperature; may be used in paints for concrete.

polyvinyl chloride A synthetic resin prepared by the polymerization of vinyl chloride; used in the manufacture of nonmetallic waterstops for concrete.

pommel (pomel) (1) A knob terminating a conical or domical roof. (2) A punner with an iron foot for ramming earth.

pond (1) A small lake. (2) In dredge work, an area where discharge water is held long enough to allow fine soil particles to settle. (3) The stretch of water between two canal locks.

ponding (1) Curing method for flat surfaces whereby a small earth dam or other water-retaining material is placed around the perimeter of the surface and the enclosed area is flooded with water. (2) The gathering of water at low or irregular areas on a roof.

pontoon (1) A float supporting part of a structure, such as a bridge. (2) A wood platform used to support machinery on soft ground.

pontoon bridge A temporary or permanent bridge which floats on pontoons moored to the river bed; built in this fashion when the foundation material is poor.

pookee *(slang)* Any sticky sealant.

pool A water receptacle used for swimming or as a plunge or other bath, designed to accommodate more than one bather at a time.

poor lime (CaO) Lime containing a high proportion of material which is insoluble in acids and is therefore not pure lime.

pop-corn concrete No-fines concrete containing insufficient cement paste to fill voids among the coarse aggregate so that the particles are bound only at points of contact. *(see no-fines concrete)*

poplar, yellow (tulip poplar) A wood found southeast of the Mississippi River, soft, fine-textured, light; often called whitewood; used for doors, sash, general interior woodwork and veneer.

popout The breaking away of small portions of a concrete surface due to internal pressure which leaves a shallow, typically conical, depression.

poppet valve A valve shaped like a mushroom resting on a circular seat and opened by raising the stem.

popping Blowing of plaster.

poppy head In architecture, an ornament often elaborately carved at the top of the ends of benches or pews.

pop rivet *(see blind rivet)*

porcelain A glazed or unglazed vitreous ceramic whiteware used for technical purposes. This term designates such products as electrical, chemical, mechanical, structural, and thermal wares when they are vitreous.

porcelain tile A ceramic mosaic or paver tile, generally made by the dust-pressed method of a composition that produces a dense, impervious, fine grained tile with smooth and sharply formed face.

porch A roofed structure providing shelter at the entrance of a building; an open or enclosed room on the outside of a building.

pores (1) Wood cells of comparatively large diameter that have open ends and are set one above the other to form continuous tubes. The openings of the vessels on the surface of a piece of wood are referred to as pores. (2) Small cavities in soils, especially granular soils like sand.

porete Type of preformed floor slab.

pore-water pressure The pressure of water in a saturated soil.

porosity The ratio, expressed as a percentage, of the interangular space in a given soil mass to the total volume of the soil mass; must be clearly differentiated from void ratio.

porous wood Hardwoods.

portable belt conveyor A movable belt conveyor with a belt driven by a motor. The belt is usually troughed and provided with short steel angle cleats to prevent material slipping back down steep slopes.

portable crane A crane which is not self-propelled but which can be moved about on wheels. It has a power-driven hoist and sometimes power slewing and derricking.

portable electric tool A hand-held tool, driven by an electric motor or vibrating armature in the body. Electric drills, saws, nailers and sanders are common.

portable tank A closed container having a liquid capacity more than 60 U.S. gallons, and not intended for fixed installation.

portal (1) A door, gate or entrance, especially one of imposing appearance. (2) A nearly level opening into a tunnel. (3) An elevated open structure to carry a crane; a base.

portal crane (gantry crane) A jib crane carried on a four-legged portal. The portal is built to run on rails.

portal frame A rigid frame structure so designed that it offers rigidity and stability in its plane. It is used to resist longitudinal loads where X-rods are not permitted.

portcullis A lifting gate, with sharp spikes at the bottom, used at the entrance to a stronghold.

porte-cochere A shelter for vehicles outside an entrance doorway.

portico An open space before the door or other entrance to any building, fronted with columns.

portland blast-furnace cement (portland blast-furnace slag cement) Cement made by grinding not more than 65 percent granulated blast furnace slag with at least 35 percent portland cement.

portland cement The product obtained by pulverizing clinker consisting essentially of hydraulic calcium silicates to which no additions have been made subsequent to calcination other than water or untreated calcium sulfate, or both, except that additions not to exceed 1.0 percent of other material may be interground with the clinker, at the option of the manufacturer, provided such materials in the amounts indicated have been shown not to be harmful.

portland cement concrete *(see concrete)*

portland cement paint A specially prepared paint made by mixing cement and water; used on concrete walls as a finish and to protect the joints against water.

portlandite A mineral; calcium hydroxide, $Ca(OH)_2$; occurs naturally in Ireland; a common product of the hydration of portland cement.

portland-pozzolan cement Cement made by blending not more than 50 percent pozzolan, a material consisting of siliceous or siliceous and aluminous material, with at least 50 percent portland cement.

portland stone A limestone found in the Isle of portland, England. The name source for portland cement.

posada In countries of Spanish influence, an inn.

position head In hydraulics, the top level of a fluid.

position indicator A device that indicates the position of the elevator car in the hoistway. It is called a hall position indicator when placed at a landing or a car position indicator when placed in the car.

positive displacement Wet-mix shotcrete delivery equipment in which the material is pushed through the material hose in a solid mass by a piston or auger.

positive drainage The drainage condition in which consideration has been made for all loading deflections of the deck, and additional roof slope has been provided to ensure complete drainage of the roof area within 24 hours of rainfall.

positive moment In simple structures, flexural moment such as occurs in a simply supported beam under gravity loading; in complex and indeterminate structures, flexural moment of a sense determined by the particular sign convention, Hardy Cross or slope deflection, being used. *(see negative moment)*

positive reinforcement Reinforcement for positive moment.

post A vertical structure member carrying stresses in compression; used where strength in bending is not a requisite, and as a brace, shore, prop or jack.

post (end post) A secondary column at the end of a building to support the girts and in a beam-and-column end-wall frame, to additionally support the rafter.

post and girt Wood framed buildings consisting of load bearing wood posts, widely spaced, connected with horizontal members called girts.

post-and-lintel Description of trabeated construction; that is, upright supports bearing horizontal beams or lintels.

post-completion services Additional services rendered after issuance of the final certificate for payment, such as consultation regarding maintenance, processes, systems, etc.

postern A door of secondary importance, often beside a large gate.

postflare The straight or curved enlargement of a post towards its top to serve as a capital or bracket for the better support of the weight above.

post-hole auger A rotating tool held by one or two men, which bores down to about 20 feet in unsupported holes and deeper in cased holes.

postiche Applied inappropriate ornament.

post office A building or office for the mail service.

posts and timbers Square timbers 5x5 inches or larger, stress-graded for use as struts.

postscenium In ancient theaters, the back of the stage where the machinery was kept and where the actors dressed. The term is still used, although it is not common usage.

post purge In boilers, a ten to fifteen second period following the run period with only the fan running to remove any unwanted products of combustion.

post shore (pole shore) Individual vertical member used to support loads.

adjustable timber single-post Individual timber used with a fabricated clamp to obtain adjustment and not normally manufactured as a complete unit.

fabricated single-post (a) Type I: Single all-metal post, with a fine-adjustment screw or device in combination with pin-and-hole adjustment or clamp. (b) Type II: Single or double wooden post members adjustable by a metal clamp or screw and usually manufactured as a complete unit.

timber single-post Timber used as a structural member for shoring support.

post-tensioning A method of prestressing reinforced concrete in which tendons are tensioned after the concrete has hardened. Also called post-stressing.

pot A hollow tile.

potable water Water which is satisfactory for drinking, culinary and domestic purposes and meets the basic sanitary requirements.

potato dirt *(slang)* A loose soil such as the kind that would be good for growing potatoes.

potato masher A commercial kitchen device adopted by the drywall trade for convenient manual mixing of joint compounds. A compound mixer.

potential energy Possible energy due to position, such as an elevated head of water or the elastic energy of a coiled spring.

potentiometer An instrument for comparing small electromotive forces, or for measuring small electromotive forces by comparison with a known electromotive force. Its principal advantage is that, during the measure-

ment, no current flows through the source of electromotive force.

pot fireman Worker on dope gang who regulates temperature of the dope kettle.

pot floor A hollow-tile floor.

pot hole (1) A small steep-sided hole usually with underground drainage. (2) *(slang)* A hole in a roadway surface caused by traffic and weathering; a chuckhole.

pot life Storage time interval after mixing during which liquid material is usable with no difficulty.

potman A skilled laborer who prepares and heats solid asphalt for application.

Potsdam sandstone *(see Malone sandstone)*

pot shelf Framing method used to build a plant shelf in a wall. Usually 4'×5' from the ceiling.

potty seat *(slang)* A plastic cover for underground wires, until they are connected to a residence.

poulticing *(see blistering)*

pounce A process used in painting to transfer the elements of a drawing by rubbing powder through holes pricked through the lines of a paper pattern.

pound A common unit of weight equal to 454 grams (0.454 kilogram); 2,240 pounds are equivalent to one long ton; 2,000 pounds are equivalent to one short ton. Abbreviation lb.

pound calorie (centigrade heat unit) The amount of heat required to raise one pound of water 1 degree C.

pounder Wooden mallet used on mallet head chisels.

pound-foot The effect of one pound of force at a distance of one foot; a unit of bending moment.

pour The total height of masonry to be filled with grout prior to the erection of additional masonry. A pour consists of one or more lifts.

poured fitting A connecting device which is fastened to the end of a cable or wire rope by inserting the cable end in a funnel shaped socket, separating the wires and filling the socket with molten zinc.

pour point The temperature at which a liquid ceases or begins to flow or at which it congeals.

powder Black powder or gunpowder; general term for explosives including dynamite, but excluding caps.

powder, black A mixture consisting mostly of carbon, sodium or potassium nitrate, and sulphur; used as an explosive.

powdered asphalt Hard asphalt crushed or ground to a fine state of subdivision; must be softened by combining with flux oil.

powdering A gradual crumbling of varnish into dust, usually resulting from use of an improper varnish for the purpose intended, such as interior varnish used on the exterior.

powderman Usually a member of crew whose job it is to set dynamite charges and oversee blasting procedures.

powder monkey *(slang)* The man in charge of handling, placing and detonating explosives on a job; the assistant to a blaster or shooter who handles the explosives.

powder room Originally an anteroom in which to powder wigs; later, a retiring room for ladies.

powder spreader A bulk spreader.

power (1) Mechanical power provided by portable internal combustion engines or by stationary plants such as electric power plants or air compressors. (2) The rate of performing work. Common units are horsepower, Btu per hour, and watts.

power arm The part of a lever between the fulcrum and the point where force is applied to the lever.

power burner In boilers a burner that supplies combustion air to the flame through means of a motor and fan.

power consumption Power used multiplied by time, measured in kwhr, kphr, etc. (Power is the rate of work; power consumption is work.)

power control unit One or more winches mounted on a tractor and used to manipulate parts of bulldozers, scrapers or other machines.

power-divider A non-spin differential.

power earth auger A drilling rig mounted on a truck.

power float *(see rotary float)*

power of attorney An instrument authorizing another to act as one's agent. *(see attorney in fact)*

power panel In electrical work, a cutout box used for power circuits rather than lighting circuits.

power rammer A hand-operated compacting machine which is raised by its own internal combustion engine and rams the earth by dropping on it.

power shovel A general term for any excavator.

power take-off A place in a transmission or engine to which a shaft can be attached so as to drive an outside mechanism.

power train All moving parts connecting an engine with the point or points where work is accomplished.

power wrench An impact spanner.

poyntel A pavement of small lozenge-shaped tiles, or square tiles laid diagonally.

pozzolan A siliceous, or siliceous and aluminous, material, which in itself possesses little or no cementitious value but will, in finely divided form and in the presence of moisture, chemically react with calcium hydroxide at ordinary temperatures to form compounds possessing cementitious properties.

pozzolanic Of or pertaining to a pozzolan.

pozzolanic reaction *(see pozzolan)*

Pratt truss A special type of construction used in both roof and bridge building in which the vertical members are in compression and the diagonals are in tension.

preacher *(slang)* The term used to designate a U-shaped piece of wood used by masons to hold their line in place on a wall.

preacher collar *(slang)* Leader guard. Plastic wire protector for electrical wire inside the conduit to keep the wire from being cut by the edge of the conduit.

preamble A term used in Britain for the introduction to each trade in a bill of quantities.

preboring (1) In carpentry, drilling a hole to avoid splitting a board when nailing, or when the nail must have a high withdrawal load. (2) In piling, boring holes for timber piles through ground hard enough to damage the piles if they were driven.

precalciner kiln system A rotary kiln system which includes an external furnace in which cement raw meal is heated to calcination temperature. The system generally includes a multistage cyclonic preheater.

precast A concrete member that is cast and cured in other than its final position, such as precast concrete slabs, precast reinforced lintels, beams, columns, piles, parts of walls and floors, etc.

precast dam A dam constructed mainly of large precast concrete blocks or sections.

precast pile A reinforced concrete pile manufactured in a casting plant or at the site but not in its final position.

precast stone Cast stone.

precher U-shape of wood used to scribe base or moulding in a bastard corner.

precipitation (1) Process by which water in liquid or solid state, e.g., rain, sleet, snow, is discharged out of the atmosphere upon a land or water surface. (2) The settlement of sewage which is usually helped by flocculation.

precision Of a measurement, the fineness with which it has been read. For example, a precise tape measurement may be taken but may be inaccurate because of non-allowance for tape corrections; therefore, precision is different from accuracy.

precompressed zone The area of a flexural member which is compressed by the prestressing tendons.

precooler Cooler for the removal of sensible heat before shipping, storing,

or processing. Device for cooling a fluid before it enters some piece of apparatus.

precured period *(see presteaming period)*

predella The broad step at the base of an altar.

preen To trim.

prefabricate To pre-make the standardized parts of a house, bridge, etc. Erection of prefabricated structures requires merely the assembling of the various sections on the jobsite.

prefabricated Descriptive of units that have been manufactured before arrival at the building site.

prefabricated masonry Masonry fabricated in a location other than its final, inservice location. Also known as preassembled, panelized and prelaid masonry.

prefabricated tie A wall tie consisting of a wire in each leaf of a cavity wall joined by similar wires at right angles, and welded to them at intervals like a fabric reinforcement.

prefecture A building housing the offices of a governor or administrative official.

prefinished A completely finished product requiring installation only.

prefiring Raising the temperature of refractory concrete under controlled conditions prior to placing it in service.

preform In wire rope, to shape the wires so that they will lie in place.

preformed asphalt joint fillers Premolded strips of asphalt cement and cork, sawdust, fiber, mineral matter, etc. for insertion in construction joints of pavements and structures.

preformed foam Foam produced in a foam generator prior to introduction of the foam into a mixer with other ingredients to produce cellular concrete.

preformed rope Wire rope manufactured from wires and strands that have been formed to fit the pattern of twist in the rope.

pregrouted tile A surface unit consisting of an assembly of ceramic tile bonded together at their edges by a material, generally elastomeric, which seals the joints completely. Such material (grout) may fill the joint completely, or partially and may cover all, a portion or none of the back surfaces of the tiles in the sheets. The perimeter of these factory pregrouted sheets may include the entire, or part of the joint between the sheets or none at all. The term edge-bonded tile is sometimes used to designate a particular type of pregrouted tile sheets having the front and back surfaces completely exposed.

preheating In air conditioning, to heat the air in advance of other processes.

prehomogenization Pre-blending of cement raw material to reduce chemical fluctuation prior to raw milling.

preliminary drawings Drawings prepared during the early stages of the design of a project. *(see schematic design phase; design development phase)*

preliminary estimate *(see statement of probable construction cost)*

preliminator Short, large diameter ball mill or first-stage grinding of raw materials or clinker in a multi-stage grinding system.

premature stiffening *(see false set; flash set)*

premises A building and its grounds.

pre-mixed plaster (premix) (1) Bagged plaster which usually contains perlite or vermiculite. The low density of the aggregates makes them easy to apply or mix. Only water has to be added to them, making them convenient for small batches. **(2)** Premixed cement and sand in bags.

pre-painted coil Coil steel which receives a paint coating prior to the forming operation.

prepacked concrete *(see preplaced-aggregate concrete)*

preplaced-aggregate concrete Concrete produced by placing clean, graded coarse aggregate in a form and later injecting a cement-sand grout, usually with admixtures, to fill the voids.

pre-post-tensioning A method of fabricating prestressed concrete in which

some of the tendons are pre-tensioned and a portion of the tendons are post-tensioned.

prepurge In boilers, blowing air through the combustion chamber before ignition to remove any unwanted gases.

prequalification of prospective bidders The process of investigating the qualifications of prospective bidders on the basis of their competence, integrity and responsibility relative to the contemplated project.

presbyterium (presbytery) In a church, the space in the chancel set aside for the clergy.

pre-selective An arrangement by which a gear lever can be moved, but the resulting speed shift will not take place until the clutch or the throttle is manipulated.

present value In Life Cycle Cost analysis, the procedure of relating expenses at some future time to present time to permit comparison of alternatives in equivalent terms.

preservative Any substance that, for a reasonable length of time, will prevent the action of wood-destroying fungi, bores of various kinds, and similar destructive life when the wood has been properly coated or impregnated with it. **(2)** Metal coating, phosphating, painting and tarring, etc.; used as preservatives for steel and cast iron.

preshrunk Concrete which has been mixed for a short period in a stationary mixer before being transferred to a transit mixer. Grout, mortar or concrete that has been mixed one to three hours before placing to reduce shrinkage during hardening.

presidio An outpost or fort of Spanish America.

press (1) In the manufacture of plywood, an arrangement of steel plates between which sheets of veneer are glued to form plywood under pressure. Hot pressing is generally worked by hydraulic pressure. Screw presses are used only for cold gluing. **(2)** For steel fabrication, presses are utilized for punching holes, shearing, notching, joggling, etc.

press brake   A machine used in cold-forming metal sheet or strip into desired shapes.

pressed brick   Brick molded to a compact smooth face by mechanical pressure, as differentiated from brick made by the lighter pressure of filling a mold with the clay.

pressed edge   Edge of a footing along which the greatest soil pressure occurs under conditions of overturning.

pressed glass   Pavement lights, bricks, etc., made of glass pressed to shape.

pressure   A force acting on a unit area. Usually shown as pounds per square inch (psi).

pressure, absolute   Pressure referred to that of a perfect vacuum. It is the sum of gage pressure and atmospheric pressure.

pressure, atmospheric   The pressure due to the weight of the atmosphere. It is the pressure indicated by a barometer. Standard Atmospheric Pressure or Standard Atmosphere is the pressure of 76 cm of mercury having a density of 13.5951 grams per cu cm, under standard gravity of 980.665 cm per (sec) (sec). It is equivalent to 14.696 psi or 29.921 in. of mercury at 32°F.

pressure, back (suction)   Operating pressure measured in the suction line at the compressor inlet.

pressure, balance   Pressure in a system or container equal to that which exists outside.

pressure change of an expansion valve   The change in outlet pressure of a constant pressure expansion valve required to open the valve a predetermined amount.

pressure creosoting   An effective way of preserving timbers by creosoting, under pressure, in tanks. *(see Boulton process)*

pressure, critical   Vapor pressure corresponding to the critical state of the substance at which the liquid and vapor have identical properties.

pressure, discharge   An operating pressure in a refrigerating system measured in the discharge line at the compressor outlet.

pressure drainage   A condition in which a static pressure may be imposed safely on the entrances of sloping building drains through soil and waste stacks connected to them.

pressure drop   (1) This term expresses the fact that power is consumed in moving liquids through the piping, collectors and other parts of the solar system. Or, expressed in another way, pressure drop is the amount of pressure lost between any two points in a system. Pressure drop is caused by the friction created between the inner walls of the conveyor and the moving liquid. Pressure drop is a major factor in the design of forced circulation systems. The friction or pressure drop in the system is directly related to the size of piping used and the design of other liquid carrying components. *(see head pressure)* (2) Static pressure loss in fluid pressure, as from one end of duct to the other, due to friction, etc.

pressure equalizing   Allowing high and low side pressures to equalize or nearly equalize during idle periods as by use of an unloading valve or a vapor lock liquid control; or nearly equalizing inlet and discharge pressures on the compressors. In either case, to reduce starting torque load.

pressure, gage   Pressure above atmospheric.

pressure gauge   A instrument for measuring fluid pressure. *(see Bourdon pressure gauge)*

pressure gun (caulking gun)   A tool similar to a grease gun which is used to apply joint sealing material or mastic such as putty, etc., to a joint.

pressure head   In hydraulics, the head of water in a pipeline due to the pressure in it.

pressure, hydrostatic   The normal force per unit area that would be exerted by a moving fluid on an infinitesimally small body immersed in it if the body were carried along with the fluid.

pressure imposing element   Any device or portion of the equipment used for the purpose of increasing the pressure upon the refrigerant.

pressure-limiting device A pressure-responsive mechanism designed to stop automatically the operation of the pressure imposing element at a predetermined pressure.

pressure line Locus of force points within a structure resulting from combined prestressing force and externally applied load.

pressure, operating The pressure occurring at a reference point in a refrigerating system when the system is in operation.

pressure, partial Portion of total gas pressure of a mixture attributable to one component.

pressure plate In a clutch, a plate driven by the flywheel or rotating housing, which can be slid toward the flywheel to engage the lined disc or discs between them.

pressure regulator, evaporator (back-pressure valve) An automatic valve located between the evaporator outlet and compressor inlet that is responsive to its own inlet pressure or to the evaporator or refrigerator temperature and functions to throttle the vapor flow when necessary to prevent the evaporator pressure from falling below a selected value.

pressure-relief device A valve or rupture member designed to relieve excessive pressure automatically.

pressure, saturation The saturation pressure for a pure substance for any given temperature is that pressure at which vapor and liquid, or vapor and solid, can coexist in stable equilibrium.

pressure, static The normal force per unit area that would be exerted by a moving fluid on a small body immersed in it if the body were carried along with the fluid. Practically, it is the normal force per unit area at a small hole in a wall of the duct through which the fluid flows (piezometer) or on the surface of a stationary tube at a point where the disturbances, created by inserting the tube, cancel. It is sup-

posed that the thermodynamic properties of a moving fluid depend on static pressure in exactly the same manner as those of the same fluid at rest depend upon its uniform hydrostatic pressure.

pressure, suction (back) Operating pressure measured in the suction line at a compressor inlet.

pressure tank (1) A tank in which timber is impregnated with creosote, zinc chloride or other preservatives. (2) A closed tank for heating tar or bitumen and spraying it through jets onto a road.

pressure, total In the theory of the flow of fluids, the sum of the static pressure and the velocity pressure at the point of measurement. Also called dynamic pressure.

pressure-type air cooler A cooler for use with one or more external elements which impose air resistance.

pressure, vapor The pressure exerted by a vapor. If a vapor is kept in confinement over its liquid so that the vapor can accumulate above the liquid, the temperature being held constant, the vapor pressure approaches a fixed limit called the maximum, or saturated, vapor pressure, dependent only on the temperature and the liquid. The term vapor pressure is sometimes used as synonymous with saturated vapor pressure.

pressure, velocity In moving fluid, the pressure capable of causing an equivalent velocity, if applied to move the same fluid through an orifice such that all pressure energy expended is converted into kinetic energy.

pressure vessel Any refrigerant-containing receptacle of a refrigerating system, other than evaporators (each separate section of which does not exceed ½ cu ft of refrigerant-containing volume), expansion coils, compressors, controls, headers, pipe, and pipe fittings.

pressure welding Welding done by pressing the joint parts together while the weld metal is plastic. Many methods of electrical resistance welding use this process.

presteaming period In the manufacture of concrete products, the time between molding of a concrete product and start of the temperature-rise period.

prestressed A process of preparing concrete slabs and beams for extra strength by pouring the mix over tightly-drawn special steel wire rope or rods which are later released to provide strong dense concrete.

prestressed concrete Concrete in which internal stresses of such magnitude and distribution are introduced so that the tensile stresses resulting from the service loads are counteracted to a desired degree; in reinforced concrete the prestress is commonly introduced by tensioning the tendons.

prestressing Applying forces to a structure to deform it so that it will withstand its working loads more effectively or with less total deflection. Concrete beams are prestressed deflecting upwards slightly by an amount equal to their total downward deflection under design load. The struts or braces in deep excavations are sometimes prestressed to prevent settlement of the surface and damage to neighboring structures.

pretensioning (Hoyer method) A method of prestressing reinforced concrete in which the reinforcement is tensioned before the concrete has hardened.

pretensioning bed (bench) The casting bed on which pretensioned members are manufactured and which resists the pretensioning force prior to release.

pretest The process of testing with hydraulic jacks the bearing capacity of a pile, footing, brace, shore or other unit of a structure, and of permanently wedging up its load by the patented pretest method. The distinctive feature of the pretest process is that the full test pressure is maintained while the wedging is being done, thus holding in compression the pile, footing or shore, and the earth on which it bears, or in the case of a horizontal brace, the brace itself and the members against which it pushes.

pretrimmed Rolls of wallpaper from which selvage has been trimmed at the factory.

preventive maintenance System of planned maintenance based on foreknowledge of necessity of repairs and past history of performance, to forestall undue deterioration of equipment, buildings, roads, fences, etc., and prevent breakdown and interruption of production.

pricking up Scoring and roughing the first coat of plaster placed over lathing.

pricking-up coat The first coat of plaster placed on metal or wood laths.

prick post (1) A queen post. (2) Any intermediate post in a framed unit.

Primacord (PETN) High explosive fuse whose case is in a waterproof covering with high tensile strength; the core is a detonating fuse of pentaerythrite tetranitrate.

primary air That part of the combustion air in a rotary kiln which is blown in with the fuel.

primary backing Material on which carpet is tufted and to which the visible secondary backing is affixed. Usually jute or polypropylene.

primary blasting The blasting operation by which the original rock formation is dislodged from its natural location.

primary blower Centrifugal blower delivering primary air to kiln. In case of direct coal firing, it also draws air through the unit pulverizer.

primary branch In a building drain, the single sloping drain from the base of a soil or waste stack to its junction with the main building drain or with another branch.

primary crusher A heavy crusher suitable for the first stage in a process of size reduction of rock.

primary drilling Drilling of holes in rock formation for explosive charges for primary blasting.

primary excavation Digging in undisturbed soil, as distinguished from rehandling stockpiles.

primary flow-and-return pipes In plumbing, the pipes in which water circulates in a water-heating system; the flow pipe is that by which water leaves the boiler or heater returning to it by the return pipe.

primary framing The main load carrying members of a structural system, generally the columns and rafters or other main support members.

primary gluing The gluing in the manufacture of plywood and other veneering work, as distinguished from assembly gluing.

primary members The main load carrying members of a structural system, including the columns, end wall posts, rafters, or other main support members.

primary nuclear vessel Interior container in a nuclear reactor designed for sustained loads and for working conditions.

primary surfacing hopper That part of the roofing machine where the surfacing granules are applied following the application of the primary coating.

prime (1) To provide means to start a process, as to supply sufficient water to a pump to enable it to start pumping. (2) In blasting, to place the detonator in a cartridge or charge of explosive.

prime coat (1) Initial application of low viscosity liquid asphaltic material to absorbent surface preparatory to superimposed construction. (2) The first coat in a series of applications of paint. *(see primer)*

prime contract Contract between owner and contractor for construction of a project or portion thereof.

prime contractor Any contractor on a project having a contract directly with the owner; the principal contractor on a project.

prime in the spots In painting, to apply a primary coat to those spots that have been scraped, wire-brushed, shellacked, have had the old paint burned off, or which consist of newly patched plaster.

prime mover (1) A tractor or other vehicle used to pull other machines. (2) Device used to provide means for withdrawing gas from stack or duct into sample train.

prime professional Any person or firm having a contract directly with the owner for professional services.

primer (1) A cartridge or container of explosives into which a detonator or detonating cord is inserted or attached. (2) The first coat of paint in a paint job that consists of two or more coats; also the paint used for the first coat. (3) A bituminous adhesive coating used to stick roofing felt onto roof sheeting. (4) In soil stabilization, a bituminous covering over soil after compaction for the purpose of waterproofing.

primer paint The initial coat of paint applied in the shop to the structural framing of a building for protection against the elements during shipping and erection.

priming (1) The first, or prime coat. (2) In glazing, the sealing of a porous surface so that the compound will not stain, lose elasticity, shrink, etc., because of loss of oil or vehicle. (3) The filling of a pump or siphon with fluid before it begins to flow. (4) In hydraulics, the first filling of a canal or reservoir with water occurring annually or only once in the lifetime of a reservoir.

princess posts Any subsidiary vertical timbers between the queen posts and the wall used to stiffen a queen-post truss.

principal (1) In professional practice, any person highly responsible for the activities of a professional practice. (2) A principal rafter. (3) A roof truss. (4) An officer or owner of a construction business.

principal point A point on an aerial photograph where the optical axis of the camera intersects the film.

principal post A door post in a framed partition.

principal rafters The main rafters in the roof truss which carry the purlins and on which the common rafters are laid.

principle of Archimedes Buoyancy; when a body is immersed in fluid it loses weight by an amount equal to the weight of the fluid it displaces. The principle applies to floating or submerged bodies as well as those which do neither.

printing The process of producing a pattern with dyestuffs on carpets and rugs. May be done by several methods, such as screen printing (e.g., on Zimmer equipment, which may be flat bed or rotary screen printing), or on roller equipment operating on the relief-printing principle (e.g., Stalwart equipment).

prism Masonry of proper size to be tested in the appropriate testing machine.

prismatic beam A beam having both flanges parallel to its longitudinal axis.

prismatic compass A pocket compass by which accurate bearings as close as 1° of arc can be read by looking through the prism at the compass card while sighting.

prism glass Glass designed to change the direction of light rays by refraction.

prismoidal formula A formula to obtain the volume of earth from the length of the excavation using the two end areas and the area at midpoint.

prism square In surveying, an optical square containing a prism.

private residence A separate dwelling or a separate apartment in a multiple dwelling which is occupied only by the members of a single family unit.

private residence elevator A power passenger electric elevator, installed in a private residence, and which has a rated load not in excess of seven hundred (700) pounds, a rated speed not in excess of forty (40) feet per minute, a net inside platform area not in excess of twelve (12) square feet, and a rise not in excess of fifty (50) feet.

private residence inclined lift A power passenger lift, installed on a stairway in a private residence, for raising and lowering persons from one floor to another.

privy A small building to shelter the primitive and unsanitary prototype of the water closet; an outhouse.

probable maximum flood The flood that may be expected from the most severe combination of critical meteorologic and hydrologic conditions that are possible in the region.

probable maximum precipitation The maximum amount and duration of precipitation that can be expected to occur on a drainage basin.

probabilistic design Method of design of structures using the principles of statistics (probability) as a basis for evaluation of structural safety.

probing (piercing) Pushing or driving a pointed metal rod into the ground for determining the position of bedrock.

processed shakes Sawn shingles surface-textured on one face to look like split shingles.

Proctor A method developed by R. R. Proctor for determining the density-moisture relationship in soils. It is almost universally used to determine the maximum density of any soil in order that specifications may be prepared properly for field construction requirements.

Proctor, modified A moisture-density test of more rigid specifications than Proctor. The basic difference is the use of heavier weight being dropped from a greater distance in laboratory determinations. It is used principally by the U.S. Corps of Engineers and a few state highway departments.

Proctor plasticity needle (penetration needle) An instrument for measuring the resistance of a soil to penetration at a standard rate of ½ inch per second. Needles of various sizes are used and a spring balance shows the force needed to push the needle in. (see *California bearing ratio*)

professional advisor An architect engaged by the owner to direct an authorized design competition for the selection of an architect.

professional engineer Designation reserved, usually by law, for a person or organization professionally qualified and duly licensed to perform such engineering services as structural, mechanical, electrical, sanitary, civil, etc.

professional fee *(see cost plus fee agreement)*

professional practice The practice of one of the environmental design professions in which services are rendered within the framework of recognized professional ethics and standards and applicable legal requirements.

profile (1) A charted line indicating grades and distances and usually depth of cut and height of fill for excavation and grading work; commonly taken along the centerline; a side view, as distinct from a plan or overhead view. (2) A British term for batterboard. (3) In plastering, a template for shaping a mold.

profile grade The trace of a vertical plane intersecting the top surface of the proposed wearing surface, usually along the longitudinal centerline of the roadbed; means either elevation of gradient or such trace according to the context.

profile paper Graph paper on which profiles of ground levels are drawn.

profilograph (1) An instrument borne on wheels for recording automatically the profile of the land over which it travels. (2) An instrument for measuring smoothness of a surface (as of a metal casting, or a highway or road) by amplification of the minute variations from the plane or arc of smoothness.

program (1) A list of requirements, conditions and other governing data in an architectural competition or architectural problem. (2) A plan of operation with time and financing elements, divisions of responsibilities, and the like, for a building project. (3) Detailed instructions which will be followed by a computer.

progress chart A chart showing the various operations in the construction of a building, such as site clearing, excavation, foundations, steelwork, pouring ground floor, pouring first floor, pouring roof, outer walls, partitions, plastering, painting and so on. Each operation is shown with proposed starting and finishing dates. It can be seen at what point each trade should be at a particular time. *(see critical path method)*

progress chaser A British term for expediter.

progress payment Payment for work completed by measuring the work in place and applying a previously agreed unit cost to the measured amount to determine the total payment.

progress schedule A diagram, graph or other pictorial or written schedule showing proposed and actual times of starting and completion of the various elements of the work. *(see critical path method; PERT schedule)*

project (1) The total construction designed by the architect or engineer of which the work performed under the contract documents may be the whole or a part. (2) *(C.P.M.)* Two or more activities or tasks that, when performed, lead to a common goal. A project has a single starting point and a single ending point.

project cost Total cost of the project including professional compensation, land costs, furnishings and equipment, financing and other charges, as well as the construction cost.

projected pipe A pipe laid on the surface before building a fill that buries it.

projecting belt course A masonry term used when referring to an elaboration of a plain band course or cut-stone work projecting beyond the face of a wall for several inches.

projecting scaffold A working platform, such as a bracket scaffold, built out from an upper story and which does not reach to the ground.

projection (1) The representation of a body on a plane. (2) The extension of a member beyond another.

projection welding An electrical resistance welding process similar to resistance spot welding, except that projections are formed at the places to be welded before they are put in contact between electrodes.

project manager The individual assigned to carry out and be responsible for construction of all or specified portions of a project; also a representative of the owner supervising such work.

project manual   The manual prepared by the architect for a project, including the bidding requirements, conditions of the contract and the technical specifications.

project representative   The architect's or engineer's representative at the project site who assists in the administration of the construction contract. When authorized by the owner, a fulltime project representative may be employed.

project site   *(see site)*

promoter   *(see catalyst)*

prompt   A message from a computer asking for a response.

proof load   The load, in pounds, at which the links of a chain start yielding under the load.

proof rolling   A process accomplished by the application of heavy, rubber-tired rollers, usually as a supplement to initial compaction by conventional means, in order to locate unstable areas and to achieve additional compaction.

proof stress   Stress applied to materials sufficient to produce a specified permanent strain; a specific stress to which some types of tendons are subjected in the manufacturing process as a means of reducing the deformation of anchorage, reducing the creep of steel or insuring that the tendon is sufficiently strong.

prop   *(see post; shore)*

propagation   Spread of an explosion through separated charges by concussion waves in water or mud.

propeller shaft   Usually a main drive shaft fitted with universal joints.

propel shaft   In a revolving shovel, a shaft which transmits engine power to the walking mechanism.

property line   A recorded boundary of a plot.

property survey   A survey made to determine the lengths and directions of boundary lines and the area of the tract bounded by these lines; or a survey

made to establish the positions of boundary lines on the ground.

proper vent   Polystyrene trough shaped piece which attaches to the interior roof sheathing to allow air to circulate from the soffit vent to the attic space.

proportional dividers   An instrument consisting of two double-pointed bars joined by a movable pivot; lengths picked up by the points of one end are enlarged or reduced by the opposite pair of points in a proportion established by the movable pivot.

proportional limit (Hooke's law)   The greatest stress which a material is capable of developing without any deviation from proportionality of stress to strain.

proportioning   Selection of proportions of ingredients for mortar, concrete or plaster, to make the most economical use of available materials to produce mortar, concrete or plaster of the required properties.

proportioning feeder   Equipment for feeding components of raw material or clinker and gypsum to mills in predetermined amounts, and automatically maintaining the set proportions.

proposal   The offer of the bidder, submitted on the prescribed proposal form, to perform the work and to furnish the labor and materials at the prices quoted by the bidder. *(see bid)*

proposal form   *(see bid form)*

proposal request (architect's; engineer's)   A written request from the architect or engineer, to the contractor, to submit a proposal for alterations to the work.

proscenium   In a theater, the front area of the stage still visible to the audience when the curtain is lowered; also the curtain and the anchor framework that holds it.

prospecting, seismic   Underground exploration conducted by measuring vibrations caused by explosions set off in drill holes.

prostyle   In Classical architecture, having columns only across the front of a temple.

protected corner Corner of a slab with adequate provision for load transfer, such that at least 20 percent of the load from one slab corner to the corner of an adjacent slab is transferred by mechanical means or aggregate interlock.

protected opening In an internal, fire-resisting floor or wall, an opening which can be closed by a door or shutter of an appropriate fire rating.

protective equipment (1) Safety equipment such as hard hats, safety goggles, ear plugs, safety shoes, etc. **(2)** Electrical switches and circuits such as relays, breakers, overload trips, etc., which protect a machine or its operator from faults or overloads.

protective strip The strip of material applied to shingles during the process of manufacturing which prevents the factory-applied sealant from sticking in the package.

prothyride *(see ancon)*

protractor A drafting instrument for laying out angles.

proving ring A device for calibrating load indicators of testing machines, consisting of a calibrated elastic ring and a mechanism or device for indicating the magnitude of deformation under load.

provisional sum A British term for a sum put aside in the bill of quantities by the consultant to provide payment for work not foreseen.

pry bar A nail puller. *(see pinch bar)*

pseudodipteral A description of Classical dipteral temples in which the innerline of columns is omitted but where the space they would have occupied is retained.

pseudoheader A snap header; a false header.

pseudoperipteral A description of Classical temples having columns across the front and on the sides to the depth of the portico; the sides and rear of the cella have columns engaged upon their walls.

pseudoprostyle A description of Classical temples in which the front portico columns are located closer to the cella

than the space of the regular intercolumniation.

psychrometer A kind of hygrometer which has a dry and a wet bulb. It is used to measure the tension of the aqueous vapor in the air and to determine the relative humidity. The wet bulb reads lower than the dry bulb for it is wrapped in a moist cloth and is affected by the evaporation of the moisture surrounding it. The variation between the wet and dry bulb readings is in proportion to the ambient relative humidity. When used in association with certain tables, it will give the measure of the relative humidity.

psychometric chart A graphical representation of the thermodynamic properties of moist air.

psychrometry The branch of physics relating to the measurement or determination of atmospheric conditions, particularly regarding the moisture mixed with the air.

pteron In Classical architecture, that which forms a side or flank.

public building Any building which the public has the right to enter.

public housing Dwelling units provided by a municipality, or other government agency, upon a specified basis of tenant selection, with or without subsidy.

puckering A condition in a carpet seam, due to poor layout or unequal stretch, etc., wherein the carpet on one side of the seam is longer or shorter than that on the other side, causing the long side to wrinkle or develop a 'pleated' effect.

pudding stone *(see conglomerate)*

puddle To settle loose dirt by turning on water, so as to render it firm and solid; vibrate and/or work concrete to eliminate honeycomb, and to produce a denser mass.

puddle stick A stock or rod used to consolidate grout by hand.

puddling (1) Process of inducing compaction in mortar or concrete by use of a tamping rod. *(see rod, tamping)* **(2)** Undesirable placement of shotcrete wherein air pressure is decreased and water content is increased.

pueblo   A communal dwelling of the Indians of the southwest U.S.A., entered by ladders.

pueblo sandstone   A fine-grain, soft gray, white and gray veined stone quarried along Turkey Creek, Colorado.

puff blowing   Blowing chips out of a hole by means of exhaust air from the drill.

puffing   Uneven combustion in rotary kiln resulting from incorrect balance between amount of fuel, combustion air and kiln draft.

puff pipe   An anti-siphon pipe.

pugging   A coarse kind of mortar laid between floor joists to prevent passage of sound; also fire-retarding. *(see deadening)*

pug mill   The part of a hot plant which mixes asphaltic concrete.

pull   (1) To loosen the rock around the bottom of a hole by blasting. Usually used with a negative to describe a blast which did not shatter rock to the desired depth. (2) A handle for opening a door, drawer, etc.

pull box   In electrical work, a box placed in a length of conduit, through which the cables can be pulled.

pulley   A wheel that carries a cable or belt on part of its surface.

pulley stile   In architecture, the upright pieces at the sides of a double-hung window frame on which the pulleys for the sash weights are fastened.

pulling   (1) A painting term for drag. (2) Installing and connecting wires necessary for a job.

pulling up (picking up)   In painting, the softening of an underlying dry coat of paint or varnish when another coat is put on.

pull-lift   A chain or rope pulling device which is light enough to be carried by a man.

pull shovel (dragshovel; hoe)   A shovel with a hinge-and-stick mounted bucket that digs while being pulled inward.

pulp   A term used in some areas to de-note wood fiber added as an aggregate to neat calcined gypsum.

pulpit   A raised platform, as in a church, where the clergyman stands while preaching.

pulpwood   Wood to be used in making paper.

pulverizing mixer   A mixer with revolving tines used in soil stabilization for pulverizing the earth over which it passes and mixing it with a stabilizer previously spread on the surface.

pulvinated   Convex in face, as a molding or certain types of frieze.

pumice   A highly porous and vesicular lava usually of relatively high silica content composed largely of glass drawn into approximately parallel or loosely entwined fibers, which themselves contain sealed vesicles.

pumicite   Naturally occurring finely divided pumice.

pump   A machine operated by hand or by a prime mover to raise or impel liquids through a pipe.

centrifugal   A pump that moves water by centrifugal force developed by rapid rotation of an impeller.

diaphragm   A pump that moves water by reciprocating motion of a diaphragm in a chamber having inlet and outlet check valves.

jetting   A water pump that develops very high discharge pressure.

mud-slush   The circulating pump that supplies fluid to a rotary drill.

wellpoint   A centrifugal pump that can handle considerable quantities of air, and is used for removing underground water to dry up an excavation.

pumpability   The ease with which a slurry can be pumped. Depends partly upon the viscosity (inversely) of the slurry, which in turn depends on water content, fineness, particle size gradation, and degree of dispersion.

pump down   (refrigeration system) The operation by which the refrigerant in a charged system is pumped into the liquid receiver.

pumped concrete   Concrete which is

transported through hose or pipe by means of a pump.

pumped storage reservoir A reservoir filled entirely or mainly with water pumped from outside its natural drainage area.

pumphandle footing Common name for a type of cantilever footing.

pump handle *(see pan handle)*

pumping (1) Of pavements, the ejection of water, or water and solid materials such as clay or silt along transverse or longitudinal joints and cracks, and along pavement edges; caused by downward slab movement activated by the passage of loads over the pavement after the accumulation of free water on or in the base course, subgrade or subbase. (2) *(slang)* In scraper operation, raising and lowering the bowl rapidly to force a larger load into it.

punch A steel driving tool used principally for removing material of the same shape as the punch.

punched work Ashlar with rough, diagonal strokes across the face worked with a punch.

puncheon (1) A short upright member in framing; a stud. (2) A log adzed to show one plane surface.

punching shear (1) Shear stress calculated by dividing the load on a column by the product of its perimeter and the thickness of the base or cap, or by the product of the perimeter taken at ½ the slab thickness away from the column and the thickness of the base or cap. (2) Failure of a base when a heavily loaded column punches a hole through it.

punch list A list, made near the completion of work, indicating items to be furnished or work to be performed by the contractor or subcontractor in order to complete the work as specified in the contract documents. *(see inspection list)*

punch out (pipe hole) A close fitting hole in the gypsum board to allow penetration of plumbing lines.

puncture resistance Extent to which a material is able to withstand the action of a sharp object without perforation.

punkah A ceiling fan common in India and other warm climates.

punner A hand operated wood or metal block at the end of a handle, raised and dropped to compact earth; a steel bar plunged up and down in wet concrete to compact it.

punning A form of light ramming.

PUP Unusually short joint of pipe.

purchase Leverage.

purchase order A written authorization for the purchase of materials or services.

purchase requisition A written request to the purchasing department to issue a purchase order for materials or services.

purger Device for removing noncondensable gas from refrigerant condensers or for removing low concentration liquor from absorption system evaporators.

purging The act of blowing out gas from a refrigerant-containing vessel, usually for the purpose of removing noncondensables.

purlin (1) A horizontal member resting usually on trusses and supporting the roof rafters. *(see ledger)* (2) A horizontal structural member attached to vertical supports, side beams or walls used for a rest or attachment for rafters, joists, trusses, etc. *(see ledger, stringer, girt)*

pushbutton A button-operated electric switch; the pushing of the button against its spring momentarily closes the circuit.

push cat A crawler tractor with a push pad or push block either included in the dozer blade, or mounted separately, for pushing a scraper for loading.

pusher (1) A tractor that pushes a scraper to help it pick up a load of material. (2) *(slang)* An assistant foreman, usually in ironworking.

push penny A round piece of metal made to fit over the end of electrical conduit to protect it from foreign objects until wire can be pulled through it.

push plate A metal plate on a door at

the level of the hand, to protect the door from damage and provide easier cleaning.

push shovel A face shovel.

putlog (1) Horizontal pieces for supporting the floor of a scaffold, one end being inserted into putlog holes left for that purpose in the masonry. (2) A scaffold member upon which the platform rests.

putlog hole A small recess in masonry for the support of scaffolding.

putty A stiff, doughlike material consisting of pigment and vehicle, used for setting window panes and filling imperfections in wood or metal surfaces.

putty coat Final smooth coat of plaster.

putty knife A glazier's knife for use in applying putty when glazing.

putty, plastering Lump lime slacked with water to the consistency of cream, and then left to harden by evaporation till it becomes like soft putty. It is then mixed with plaster of Paris, or sand, for the finishing coat.

puzzolana A grayish earth used for building under water.

pycnometer The simplest type of specific-gravity bottle. It is weighed empty, then full of soil, then full of soil and water. If the density of the soil particles is known, the three weighings will enable the moisture content of the soil to be calculated.

pycnostyle Having intercolumniation of 1½ diameters.

pylon A truncated pyramidal form characteristic of Egyptian monumental architecture, where it was used largely in gateways.

Pyofoil Type of sheetrock.

pyramid A huge masonry form, originally marking the grave of an Egyptian

pharoah; square in base with triangular sides meeting at a point.

pyramidal light A roof light in which the glazing slopes to a point from a base shaped like a polygon.

pyramid cut A method of blasting several rings of holes. The holes of the central ring are shaped like a pyramid, with toes close together.

pyramidon The small flat pyramid terminating the top of an obelisk.

pyramid roof A pavilion roof.

pyranometer An instrument for measuring sunlight intensity. It usually measures total (direct plus diffuse) insolation over a broad wavelength range.

pyrgeometer An instrument that measures unidirectional (infrared) radiation.

pyrheliometer An instrument that measures the intensity of the direct beam radiation (direct insolation) from the sun. The diffuse component is not measured.

pyrometer An instrument for measuring high temperatures.

pyrometric cone A small, slender, three-sided oblique pyramid made of ceramic or refractory material for use in determining the time-temperature effect of heating and in obtaining the pyrometric cone equivalent (PCE) of refractory material.

pyrometric cone equivalent (PCE) The number of that cone whose tip would touch the supporting plaque simultaneously with that of a cone of the refractory material being investigated when tested in accordance with a specified procedure such as ASTM C24.

pyroprocessing Manufacturing a product by using very high temperatures.

q   quart
qda   quantity discount agreement
qf   quick firing
qr   quarter, quarter-round

qs   quarter-sawn
qt.   quart
quad   quadrant
quar   quarterly

Q block   Concrete masonry units made to special specifications as to quality.

quad   An enclosed court; a quadrangle.

quadra   (1) A square architectural frame, as for a bas-relief sculpture. (2) A fillet above and below the scotia in the base of an Ionic column. (3) The plinth block of a podium.

quadrangle   An open court or space in the form of a parallelogram, usually rectangular in shape, partially or entirely surrounded by buildings, as on a college campus; also, the buildings surrounding the court.

quadrant   (1) An instrument usually consisting of a graduated arc of 90° with an index or vernier; used primarily for measuring altitudes; sometimes a plumb line is attached to the quadrant for determining the vertical or horizontal direction. A curved scale for measuring angles. (2) A quarter of the circumference of a circle; an arc of 90°. (3) A curved guide for a lever. (4) A curved metal casement stay. (see quarter-round)

quadrantal bearing (reduced bearing)   A bearing of less than 90° measuring from east, west, north or south.

quadrant dividers   A pair of dividers; one limb slides on an arc fitted to the other limb and may be temporarily clamped together by a screw.

quadratic equation   An equation which contains the square of an unknown quantity but no higher power.

quadrel   A square tile or similar unit.

quadrifores   In ancient architecture, folding doors, their height divided in two parts.

quadrilateral   A polygon having four sides and four angles of any shape. Its area is equal to the product of the diagonals times half the sine of the angle between them.

quadripartite   Having four divisions, usually describing groined vaulting.

quad-track   Two connected crawler tractors usually controlled by one operator.

quaggy timber   Wood with many shakes in the center.

qualified   One who, by possession of a recognized degree, certificate, or professional standing, or who by extensive knowledge, training and experience, has successfully demonstrated his ability to solve or resolve problems relating to the subject matter, the work or the project.

qualitative test   Applied to determine the occurrence, the type and the distribution of a material's characteristics. A test which identifies the identity or the presence of a subject but does not identify how much.

quality assurance   A system of procedures for selecting the levels of quality required for a project or portion thereof to perform the functions intended, and assuring that these levels are obtained.

quality control   A system of procedures and standards by which a constructor, product manufacturer, materials processor, or the like, monitors the properties of the finished work.

quality of sound   (see overtones)

quality of wet vapor   Fraction by weight of vapor in mixture of liquid and vapor.

quanat (ghanat)   The ancient Persian

system of distributing water underground by gravity.

quantitative test A test which identifies numerically the amount of characteristics of a substance in addition to identifying the substance itself.

quantity Term used to indicate the amount of work to be performed under a variety of items and measurements, e.g., lineal feet, cubic yard, square yard, per each, etc.

quantity distance tables *(see American table of distances)*

quantity overrun/underrun The difference between the original estimated contract quantities and the quantities in the completed work.

quantity survey (takeoff) Detailed analysis and listing of all items of material and equipment necessary to construct a project.

quantity surveyor One who draws up quantities of labor and material upon which contractor's bids are based.

quantized grey scale A display scale for an infrared scanner which assigns discrete grey tones to particular temperature increments on the screen display.

quantum theory Albert Einstein's theory that light rays are composed of bundles of energy called photons which give up their energy when they strike an object.

quarrel A small square or diamond-shaped member, as a pane of glass, especially when set diagonally; same as quarry.

quarry (1) A diamond-shaped pane of glass; same as quarrel; also a small square stone or tile. (2) A rock pit. (3) An open cut mine in rock chosen for physical rather than chemical characteristics. (4) The location of an operation removing a natural deposit of stone.

quarry bench A cut-back in the quarry face used as an operating level.

quarry-face Ashlar as it comes from the quarry, squared off for the joints only, with split face. Distinct from rock-face, in that the latter may be

weather-worn, while quarry-face should be fresh split. The terms are often used indiscriminately.

quarryman (quarrier; rock getter; rock hand; rock man; stone breaker; getter or hewer) A man working at the face of a quarry, drilling and breaking rock.

quarry sap The moisture in freshly cut quarry stone. When dried out, the stone is harder to work.

quarry-stone bond In masonry, a term applied to the arrangement of stones in rubblework.

quarry tile In masonry, a name given to machine-made, unglazed tile; also called promenade tile.

quarter (1) Medieval term for a stud. (2) A square panel. (3) The flank of a road.

quarter bend A bend, as of a pipe, through an arc of 90°. Other bends are proportional to this, a one-eighth bend being 45°.

quartered (quarter-sawn) Descriptive of lumber that is sawn from the log approximately radially.

quartered log A log cut into four quarters.

quartered partition (quarter partition) A partition built from quarterings.

quarterfoil *(see quatrefoil)*

quarter-girth rule Method of computing volume of timber in a round log. It is approximately equal in cross sectional area to a square of side equal to the quarter girth of the log at the middle of its length.

quartering (1) A method of obtaining a representative sample by quartering a larger sample and discarding opposite-quarters successively until the desired size of sample is obtained. (2) Small timber used as studs in a framed partition. (3) Quarter-sawing.

quarter octagonal A square shaft with corners cut back.

quarter-pace A landing interrupting a stair where a turn of 90° is made.

quarter-peg (stake) A peg set at the quarter width of a road; in conjunction with center pegs, it defines the road surface.

quarter-round Small molding presenting the profile of a quarter circle.

quarter-sawed grain Another term for edge-grain lumber, used generally in hardwoods.

quarter-sawing The sawing of logs lengthwise into quarters, with the saw cuts parallel with the medullary rays, then cutting the quarters into boards.

quarter-sawn timber Timber cut by quarter-sawing.

quarter-space landing A small landing which is the same width and length of a tread. Compare half-space landing.

quartz (SiO) A crystalline silica. The major part of sand, gravel or sandstone; the transparent part of granite; the most common mineral.

quartzite A strong sandstone cemented by quartz and about 98 percent silica.

quatrefoil In architecture, a single decorative feature consisting of an ornamental unit in the form of a four-leaved flower or a four lobed figure in variations.

queen bolt A long bolt of steel or iron serving in a roof truss in place of a queen rod.

queen closure (closer) A half brick, or smaller section, made by cutting a whole brick to size; also, a half brick used in a course of brick masonry to prevent vertical joints falling above one another.

queen post One of the two vertical tie posts in a roof truss or any similar framed truss.

queen truss A truss framed with queen posts; that is, two vertical tie posts, distinguished from the king truss, which has only one tie post.

quench hardening A treatment for copper-aluminum alloy products consisting of heating above the betatizing temperature followed by quenching to produce a hard martensitic structure.

quenching Cooling rapidly by air or water.

quetta bond A bond like rat-trap bond in which gaps are formed in the middle

of the wall. The bricks are laid on bed, not on edge; the cavities in the middle are filled with grout as the wall rises and contain vertical steel.

quick clays Clays that undergo a drastic reduction in strength upon disturbance.

quick-hardening lime Hydraulic lime.

quick-leveling head A ball-and-socket fitting under a level instead of three leveling screws.

quicklime An unstable material generally produced by burning limestone, the major part of which is calcium oxide or calcium oxide in natural association with a lesser amount of magnesium oxide. Before it can be used in construction, quicklime must be slaked in water and aged for at least 2 weeks.

quicksand Fine sand or silt that is prevented from settling firmly together by upward movement of ground water; any wet inorganic soil so unsubstantial that it will not support a load.

quick set *(see flash set; false set)*

quick sweep In architecture, a term applied to circular work which has a relatively small radius.

quiescent Without agitation, particularly in regard to storage of slurry.

quill shaft A light drive shaft inside a heavier one, and turning independently of it.

quilt *(see blanket)*

quilted figure (blister figure) An elaborate figure of apparent knolls in birch, maple or other woods, caused by uneven annual rings.

quilting Insulation material between two sheets of paper.

quincunx A grouping of five objects so that one is at each corner of a square and one in the center.

Quincy granite A granite from Quincy, Massachusetts; from medium gray or bluish gray to a very dark bluish gray, all with blue or blue-black spots; its texture is from medium to coarse with an even grain, and takes a high polish due to the absence of mica.

quinquefoil (cinquefoil) A five-lobed

figure in variations typified by the trefoil and quatrefoil.

quirk   A small groove or channel separating a bead or other molding from the adjoining members; an acute angle between moldings or beads.

quirk bead   A bead molding separated from the surface on one side by a channel or groove. A double quirk bead refers to a molding with a channel on each side of the beads.

quirk molding   An architectural term usually applied to a molding which has a small groove, although sometimes the term is also used in reference to a molding with both a convex and a concave curve separated by a flat portion.

quirk router   A shaping tool for cutting quirks.

quoin header   A corner header in the face wall which also serves as a stretcher for the side wall.

quoin post   A heel post.

quoins   Large squared stones such as buttresses, set at the angles of a building; in stone masonry, the quoins are often made of stones much larger than those in the remainder of the wall; the external corner of a building.

Quonset hut   A semicylindrical shelter of insulated corrugated steel designed chiefly for military use, it takes its name from the place of manufacture in Rhode Island.

quotation (quote)   The price, generally confidential, submitted prior to bid openings, for which a subcontractor or supplier agrees to furnish work or materials in accordance with the contract plans and specifications.

r rain, range, rare, red, river, roentgen, run, thermal resistance

Ra radium

rab rabbeted

raft rafter

RCP reinforced concrete pipe

rd road, rod, round

recap recapitulation

recd received

recip reciprocal

rec. room recreation room

rect rectangle, rectified

red reduce, reduction

ref reference, refining

refrig refrigeration

reg registered

rein/reinf reinforced

remod remodel

rent rental

rep repair

repl replace, replacement

reqd required

ret retain, retainage

rev revenue, reverse, revised,revolution

rf roof

RF radio frequency

RFP request for proposal

Rh rhodium

RH relative humidity

RI refractive index

rib. gl. ribbed glass

riv river

RJ road junction

rm ream, room

r.mold. raised mold

rms root means square

rnd round

ROP record of production

ROPS roll-over protection system

rot rotating, rotation

rpm revolutions per minute

RRGCP reinforced rubber gasket concrete pipe

RRS railroad siding

RSJ rolled steel joist

rt right

Rub/rub Ruberoid (roofing), rubble

r.w. redwood, roadway, right-of-way

rwy/ry railway

rab In plastering, a stick or beater used for mixing hair with mortar.

rabbet (1) In woodworking, a term used in referring to a groove cut in the surface, or along the edge of a board, to receive another board similarly cut. (2) In glazing, a two-sided L-shaped recess in sash or frame to receive lights or panels.

rabbeted lock In building, a lock which is fitted into a recess cut in the edge of a door.

rabbet joint A joint consisting of a rabbet into which another piece fits, or one in which both pieces are rabbeted to fit together.

rabbet plane (rebate plane) A woodworking plane with a cutting iron and a mouth extending to the edge of the sole, for cutting rabbets.

rabbit *(slang)* Copper or aluminum scrap wire.

race (1) In hydraulics, a channel to or from a water wheel; headrace or tailrace. (2) The inner and outer ring of a ball or roller bearing; ball race.

raceway Any channel for loosely holding wires or cables in interior work which is designed expressly and used solely for this purpose. Raceways may be of metal, wood or insulating material, and the term includes wood and metal moldings consisting of a backing and capping, and also metal ducts into which wires are to be pulled.

rack A trash rack, usually installed in a waterway; a metal grid that is used to properly space and align floor tiles.

racked In carpentry, a term applied to a temporary timbering, braced so as to stiffen it against deformation.

racking (1) Stepping back successive courses of masonry. (2) Lateral stresses exerted on an assembly.

rack saw In carpentry, a saw having wide teeth.

RAD Unit of absorbed dose of ionizing radiation equal to an energy of 100 ergs per gram of irradiated material. *(see REM)*

radar In aerial survey, a system used to fix the position and altitude of an aircraft at the moment of exposure of a vertical photograph greatly reducing the need for closely spaced ground control points.

radial Lines converging at a single center.

radial bar A device made by attaching a point and pencil to a wooden bar which is then used for striking large curves.

radial brick A compass brick.

radial gate (Tainter gate) A dam gate with curved water face and horizontal pivot axis which is also the center of curvature of the water face.

radial highway An arterial highway leading to or from an urban center.

radial step A winder; a spiral stair.

radian An arc of a circle equal in length to the radius, or the angle at the center measured by the arc.

radiant heating (1) A method of heating, usually consisting of coils or pipes placed in the floor, wall or ceiling. (2) In painting, drying a finish with radiation from a hot surface.

radiation (1) A surveying technique of plotting the surrounding points on a plane table set up by radiating lines drawn with the alidade, and marking of the distance of the point to scale on each line. (2) The process of emitting radiant energy in the form of waves or particles. (3) The direct transfer of energy from a hotter to a colder body.

radiation pyrometer An instrument which measures temperature in the burning zone by focusing the thermal radiation emitted, causing the generation of electrical signals displayed on a recording instrument.

radiation, thermal The transmission of heat through space by wave motion; the passage of heat from one object to another without warming the space between.

radiator A heating unit exposed to view within the room or space to be heated. A radiator transfers heat by radiation to objects within visible range, and by conduction to the surrounding air which in turn is circulated by natural convection; a so-called radiator is also a convector, but the term radiator has been established by long usage.

radiator, hot water (steam) (1) The room heating unit of a hot water or steam heating system. (2) A gilled container, usually for water, often part of a central-heating system. Being at a low temperature it loses less heat by radiation than by convection, and in theory it should therefore be called a convector.

radioactivity Spontaneous nuclear disintegration with emission of corpuscular or electromagnetic radiation, or both.

radio-frequency heating A method used to rapidly heat thick plywood assemblies or gluing by connecting electrodes to a high frequency power source and placing them in the assembly.

radius Horizontal distance from the center of rotation of a crane to its hoisting hook.

radius- and safe-lock indicator A pendulum which hangs loose on a crane jib over a board on which the crane radius for any angle and the safe load for this radius are painted.

radius diffusion The horizontal axial distance an air stream travels after leaving an air outlet before the maximum stream velocity is reduced to a specified terminal level.

radius of gyration (1) A value used in

calculating the slenderness ratio of a strut. If A is the cross-sectional area and I the moment of inertia of the strut the radius of gyration equals I/A, usually known as k. (2) The distance from the reference at which all of the area can be considered concentrated that still produces the same moment of inertia. Numerically equal to the square root of the moment of inertia, divided by the area.

radius shoe A plasterer's tool on which a piece of zinc plate is screwed to one side of a radius rod over its center-point and drilled so that the center pin or nail can pass through the radius rod.

radius test A bending test for felt to determine its ability to resist checking or cracking when bent over a rod of a specified radius.

rafter One of a series of structural members of a roof designed to support roof loads. The rafters of a flat roof are sometimes called roof joists.

   hip A rafter that forms the intersection of an external roof angle.

   jack A rafter that spans the distance from a wallplate to a hip or from a valley to a ridge.

   valley A rafter that forms the intersection of an internal roof angle.

rafter filling The method of placing brick between rafters at wall plate level.

rafter tail That part of a rafter which extends beyond the wall plate—the overhang.

raft foundation A continuous slab of concrete, usually reinforced, laid over soft ground or where heavy loads must be supported to form a foundation. *(see mat foundation)*

rag bolt A Lewis bolt.

rag felt In building construction, a type of heavy paper composed of rags impregnated with asphalt; used in the manufacture of waterproofing membranes for making asphalt shingles and other types of composition roofing, such as asphalt roofing.

ragging off The procedure of spreading damp cheese cloth and pulling it over the tile surface during the tile grouting process in order to clean the tile.

raggle In masonry, a manufactured building unit provided with a groove into which a metal flashing is fitted; also a term applied to a groove made in stone to receive adjoining material; a groove in a joint or a special unit to receive roofing or flashing.

raglet A groove cut in a wall into which the edge of a flashing is turned.

ragman *(slang)* One who uses the granny rag to touch up parts of a pipeline that the dope machine may have missed with its asphaltic compound, who works in front of the wrapping machine.

rag work In masonry, a term applied to any kind of rubble work made of small thin stones.

rail (1) A piece of railroad track. (2) The chain or inner surface of a crawler track. (3) A horizontal bar of timber, wood or metal extending from one post or support to another as a guard or barrier in a fence, balustrade, staircase, etc. Also, the cross or horizontal members of the framework of a sash, door, blind or any paneled assembly. (4) A light structure serving as a guard at the outer edge of a ship's deck. (5) A steel T-rail, 16′ long with a milled surface and four holes on each end. One end of the rail is grooved and one end is tongued. The face, or running surface, is planed. (6) A horizontal bar of wood used to separate drawers and doors on the face of a cabinet.

rail bolt In stair building, a bolt which is threaded for a nut on both ends; used for fastening stair rails; a stair bolt; also called handrail bolt.

rail file A Vixen file, sometimes called a body file, with coarse, curved teeth. It is used to file rail joints smooth.

railing (1) An open fence or guard made of rails and posts. (2) In cabinetwork, a banding.

rail steel reinforcement Reinforcing bars hot-rolled from standard T-section rails.

raindrop figure A lumber term describing a mottled figure which may alternate with ribbon grain.

rain gauge   An instrument which collects falling rain and indicates the amount of rainfall. It usually consists of a funnel from which the rain drips into a cylinder graduated in inches.

rain rippers   A particular cut and style of lumber used to divert rain to the scuppers.

rainwash   The movement of rock and surface soil down a slope because of heavy rain.

rainwater head   A tank at the top of a downpipe acting as a funnel to receive rainwater from a roof gutter; also called cistern head.

rainwater hopper   A hopper-shaped rainwater head which can also be used in the middle of a long downpipe.

raise   A shaft being dug upward from a tunnel.

raised grain   A condition when dense summer wood is raised above the springwood on the surface of a slat but not torn loose. Usually caused by absorption of moisture.

raising   In painting and lacquer work, a wrinkled or blistered condition on a finished surface.

raising hammer   A hammer having a rounded face used in lifting or raising sheet metal.

raising plate (pole; wall plate)   In building construction, a horizontal timber resting on part of a structure and supporting a superstructure.

rake   A board or molding placed along the sloping sides of a frame gable to cover the ends of the siding.

   angle   Angle fastened to purlins at rake for attachment of endwall panels.

rake   (1) A tool used to remove mortar a given depth from the face of a wall. (2) To treat mortar joints with a tool to remove a given depth of mortar.

rake angle   Angle fastened to purlins at rake for attachment of endwall panels.

rake, blade   A dozer blade or attachment made of spaced tines.

rake bond   In masonry, a method of laying the courses of brick in an angular or zigzag fashion.

rake, brush   A rake blade having a high top and light construction.

rake, classifier   Machine for separating coarse and fine particles of granular material temporarily suspended in water; the coarse particles settle to the bottom of a vessel and are scraped up an incline by a set of blades, the fine particles remain in suspension to be carried over the edge of the classifier.

raked joint   Joint formed in brickwork by raking out some of the mortar an even distance from the face of the wall.

rake molding   Gable molding attached on the incline of the gable. The molding must be a different profile to match the similar molding along the remaining horizontal portions of the roof.

raker   (1) A sloping brace for a shore head. (2) Moldings whose arrises are inclined to the horizon.

rake, rock   A heavy duty rake blade.

rake trim   A flashing designed to close the opening between the roof and endwall panels.

raking bond   A diagonal bond.

raking cornice (raking coping)   A cornice or coping placed on a slope such as over a gable.

raking course   In masonry, a course of bricks laid diagonally between the face courses of an especially thick wall for the purpose of adding strength to the wall.

raking flashing   A cover flashing used, for example, between a stone chimney and a sloping roof. It is parallel to the roof slope and is let into a sloping raglet. A stepped flashing is not practical with stone since the joints are too far apart.

raking out   Cleaning mortar out of joints before pointing.

raking pile   A pile which is not placed vertically.

raking riser   A step riser which is not vertical and overhangs the tread below; used to provide more foothold, especially when the rise of the stair is steep.

raking shore   A long balk or several of

them erected as a temporary support to a wall or a building.

ram (1) To drive into place or to compact, as to compact relatively dry concrete with a piece of timber and a striking hammer. (2) The moving weight in a pile driving hammer. (3) A hydraulic cylinder and piston device.

one way (single acting) A hydraulic cylinder in which fluid is supplied to one end so that the piston can be moved only one way by power.

two way (double acting) A hydraulic cylinder in which fluid can be supplied to either end so the piston can be moved by power in two directions.

rambler A popular name in some localities for a dwelling of one story and rambling plan.

rammed earth A system of wall building with earth tamped into forms, practiced in south west and south central U.S., and also in the south of France where it is called pise.

rammer (1) In building construction, a term applied to an instrument which is used for driving anything by force, as stones or piles or for compacting earth. (2) In concrete work, a kind of stomper used to pack concrete by removing the air bubbles.

ramp (1) An inclined walk or driveway. (2) The concave bend of a handrail where a sharp change in level is required, as at the post of a stair landing. (3) A short length of drainpipe laid more steeply than the usual gradient. (4) A connecting roadway between two intersecting highways at a highway separation.

rampant arch An arch with one abutment higher than the other.

ram plug The cylinder used for anchoring bolts, wires, etc. in pavements and roofs.

ram-press Uses two metal dies to form the green tile. This process produces an uneven tile or one that has the appearance of being hand made.

ram pump A single action reciprocating pump having no piston but a ram.

The ram is of constant diameter and does not fit tightly in the cylinder.

rance (rans) A timber or piece of lumber placed in an oblique position against a wall or building to serve as a temporary support; same as shore.

ranch house originally the main dwelling on a stock farm; designating a style of dwelling of which the preceding was the prototype.

random Without uniformity of dimension or design; e.g., masonry wall with stones placed irregularly, not in a straight course.

random ashlar Stone cut to modular heights and set in discontinuous courses.

random courses Courses of varying depths.

random masonry That in which the course heights vary in size.

random process One which is based on probability and not on exact repeatability.

random rubble Masonry wall built of unsquared or rudely squared stones irregular in size and shape.

random-sheared Textured pattern created by shearing some of the top or higher loops and leaving others looped.

random shingles Shingles of different widths banded together.

random widths The term used in describing flooring and wall boards or shingles of varying widths.

random work Any type of work done in irregular order such as a wall built up of odd-sized stones.

range (cooling range) In a water cooling device, the difference between the average temperature of the water entering the device, and the average temperature of the water leaving it.

range masonry A regular coursed rubble.

range pole (banderolle; range rod) A tall straight staff held upright by a surveyor's chainman when setting out points in a straight line. It is usually marked in alternate red and white bands.

ranger (1) A horizontal bracing member used in form construction, also called a whaler or waler. (2) The difference between the highest and lowest value. (3) Alignment of points by eye with range poles or with a telescope.

range work Masonry construction in which courses of differing thicknesses are continued across the entire face.

ranging line A string stretched taut between batterboards to mark the alignment of a wall or other line.

rapid-curing asphalt Liquid asphalt composed of asphalt cement and a naphtha or gasoline-type diluent of high volatility.

rapid dryer A drum dryer that is equipped with paddles.

rasp A coarse file or a file-like tool which has coarse projections; used to reduce material by a grinding motion.

ratchet A set of teeth, vertical on one side and sloped on the other, which will hold a pawl moving in one direction, but will allow it to move in another.

bit brace A carpenter's tool consisting of a bit brace with a ratchet attachment which permits operation of the tool in close quarters.

drill A hand drill which is rotated by a ratchet wheel moved by a pawl and lever.

wheel A wheel with angular teeth on the edge, into which a pawl drops or catches, to prevent a reversal of motion.

rated load The load which the elevator, dumbwaiter, escalator or private residence inclined lift is designed and installed to lift at the rated speed.

rated speed The speed at which the elevator, dumbwaiter, escalator, or inclined lift is designed to operate under the following conditions:

elevator or dumbwaiter The speed in the up direction with rated load in the car.

escalator or private residence inclined lift The rate of travel of the steps or carriage, measured along the angle of inclination, with rated load on the steps or carriage. In the case of a reversible escalator the rated speed shall be the rate of travel of the steps in the up direction, measured along the angle of inclination, with rated load on the steps.

rate of decay The rate of decay of a reverberant sound is the slope of the decay curve when plotted with time and intensity.

rat hole In a rotary drill substructure, a socket that supports the kelly and swivel when they are not in use.

rathskeller (rat cellar) A room, originally a cellar, in which beer and other refreshments are served.

ratio The relationship between two similar magnitudes in respect to the number of times the first contains the second, either integrally or fractionally.

rational formula Used in drainage computations to determine amount of runoff within a watershed.

ratio of reduction The relationship between the maximum size of the stone which will enter a crusher, and the size of its product.

rat joint runner Asbestos rope used to hold joint material, poured lead, etc.

rat-tail file A round file tapering to small diameter at the opposite end from the handle.

rat-trap bond *(see all-rowlock wall)*

rat wall A deepened edge around a floating concrete slab.

ravelling The breaking away of aggregate from the paved surface of a road. Also called fretting.

raw department General designation of equipment, buildings and operations pertaining to preparation of kiln feed. Often subdivided into crushing, raw grinding, and blending departments.

raw linseed oil The crude product obtained from flaxseed usually without much subsequent treatment.

rawlplug A fastener or holding device used in wood, glass, masonry, plaster, tile, brick, concrete, metal or other materials. These devices are made of longitudinal strands of tough jute fiber compressed into a tubular form.

raw materials Naturally occurring

rocks or materials, or water products, suitable for cement manufacture. Includes limestone, chalk, marl, clay, shale, silica, sand, iron ore, bauxite, dolomite, etc.

raw material storage Exposed or covered stockpiles, bins or silos for crushed but as yet unground raw materials.

raw meal Finely ground mixture of raw materials as used for kiln feed in dry-process plants.

raw mix Blend of raw materials, ground to desired fineness, correctly proportioned, and blended ready for burning, such as that used in the manufacture of cement clinker.

raw water In ice making, any water used for ice making except distilled water.

ray Tissue formed in a living tree that radiates from the pith toward the perimeter of a tree across the growth rings. Rays are very distinct in the oak species.

ray flect A part of a ray appearing very distinctly on the face of a quartersawn slat.

rayl A material is said to have one rayl resistance when pressure differential of one dyne per square centimeter produces a flow velocity of one centimeter per second.

Raymond granite A biotitemuscovite, light gray, with biotite mica in excess of the muscovite, and an occasional crystal of black hornblende; this is a medium-fine-grain granite of California.

Raymond piles Type of tapered piles; a shell with inserted mandril driven to resistance; the core is withdrawn and the casing filled with concrete.

rayonnant Descriptive of a type of French Gothic tracery which emphasized radial lines.

raze To ruin or level by destroying everything above the ground.

RCRA The acronym for the Resource Conservation and Recovery Act of 1976. What we commonly refer to as RCRA is an amendment of the first piece of legislation related to federal solid waste, called the solid Waste Disposal Act of 1965. RCRA was amended in 1980 and 1984.

reach A comparatively short length of a stream or channel.

reactance Opposition offered to the flow of alternating current by induction or capacitance of a component or circuit.

reaction The upward resistance of a support, such as a wall or column, against the downward pressure of the load, such as a beam.

reaction turbine A turbine in which the jets or nozzles are on the moving wheel, as distinguished from an impulse turbine which has fixed jets.

reactive aggregate Aggregate containing substances capable of reacting chemically with the products of solution or hydration of the portland cement in concrete or mortar under ordinary conditions of exposure, resulting is some cases in harmful expansion, cracking or straining.

reactive silica material Several types of materials which react at high temperatures with portland cement or lime during autoclaving; includes pulverized silica, natural pozzolan and fly ash.

readily accessible Capable of being reached quickly for operation, renewal, or inspection, without requiring those to whom ready access is requisite to climb over or remove obstacles or to resort to the use of portable access equipment.

ready-mixed A term denoting a plaster which is mixed at the mill with mineral aggregate and other ingredients which control time of set. Generally used in conjunction with gypsum plasters. Also termed mill-mixed, pre-mixed.

ready-mixed concrete Concrete manufactured for delivery to a purchaser in a plastic and unhardened state. (see central-mixed concrete; shrink-mixed concrete; transit mixed concrete)

real estate Land and what is built upon it.

realignment   An alteration to the line of a highway which may affect the slope, vertical alignment, but more often alters its layout in plan or horizontal alignment.

ream   To enlarge or smooth a borehole or a hole in metal with a reamer.

reamer   A cutting device that enlarges or straightens a hole.

reamer shell   A cutter just above a diamond bit, used to assure a full-size hole.

rearing   Rising of the front of a tractor when pulling a heavy load.

reasonable care and skill   *(see due care)*

rebar   *(slang)* Term used for reinforcing steel; a deformed steel put in concrete to improve its tension quality.

rebate (rabbet)   A groove or recess cut into the edge of a board to receive the edge of another piece.

rebound   Sand and cement or wet shotcrete which bounces away from a surface against which shotcrete is being projected.

rebound hammer   An apparatus that provides a rapid indication of the mechanical properties of concrete based on the distance of rebound of a spring-driven missile.

receiver   (1) The air tank or reservoir on a compressor or a sump. (2) The portion of the electric eye system containing the phototube.

receptacle   A fixture interrupting an electrical supply circuit into which a plug connection may be made for an extension or branch circuit.

receptor   The shallow sink of a shower.

recess   A depth of some inches in the thickness of a wall, as a niche, etc.

recessed head screw (Phillips)   A screw with a cross-shaped recess into the head which a cross-shaped screwdriver blade fits; a screw designed to fit flush into the surface, instead of projecting up from the surface.

reciprocal   levelling   A   surveying method of eliminating instrumental error in levelling between two points by taking levels from two set-ups, one near each point.

reciprocating   Having a straight back-and-forth or up-and-down motion.

reciprocating drill   A drill consisting of a threaded shaft which carries a drill chuck at its lower end and a sleeve which fits this thread and which is pushed down the shaft rotating it.

reciprocating engine   A steam or internal-combustion engine with cylinder and piston. Not to be confused with a turbine or jet engine.

reciprocating pump (compressor)   A pump or compressor operated by pistons or rams.

reclaiming   (1) Digging from stockpiles, or reprocessing previously rejected material. (2) Using unclean water for road construction.

reconstructed stone   A cast stone.

recool   The application of cooling as a secondary process to either preconditioned primary air or recirculated room air.

record drawings   Construction drawings revised to show significant changes made during the construction process; usually based on marked-up prints, drawings and other data furnished by the contractor or the architect.

recorder   Instrument which makes a chart or graph (circular or strip) of the on-going history of process parameters such as temperature, draft, fuel consumption, exit gas analysis, fuel-air-ratio, etc.

recording gauge (recorder)   A hydraulic gauge which automatically records the level of the water in a stream or tank and the velocity and pressure in a pipe. It works by a float or by a submerged air tank with a rubber diaphragm which moves inward as the water levels rises, causing a pressure increase in the air.

recover   The addition of a new membrane over a major portion of a roof surface. This may or may not involve removal of the old membrane and may or may not include installation of additional insulation.

recovered   energy   Energy   utilized

which would otherwise be wasted from an energy utilization system.

recovery peg A surveying marker placed as a known relationship in level, direction and distance to another marker to enable one to be accurately replaced.

rectangular duct Any four-sided air duct, square or otherwise.

rectifier (1) In refrigeration: externally cooled heat exchanger in high side of absorption system for condensing absorbent and separating it from refrigerant before passing to condenser. (2) In electricity: a device for converting alternating current to direct current.

rectilinear A synonym for the perpendicular period in English Medieval architecture.

recuperator Equipment which reclaims heat that otherwise would have been lost. Most clinker coolers are also recuperators, returning some of the clinker sensible heat to the kiln.

redan A buttress of V-shape projecting from the lower side of a wall crossing a slope.

red eye *(slang)* Numerous orange pits located around the edges of a large sheet of polished plate glass.

red head A device to attach the mudsill to the foundation wall or stem.

red iron *(slang)* Structural steel.

red lead Textroxide of lead; widely used as a pigment in linseed oil for painting metal as protection against rust.

red mud Waste product from the manufacture of alumina (aluminum oxide); being high in FE_2O_3 it is often used as a raw material for cement.

red top Subgrade stake.

reduced level In surveying, an elevation calculated from stipulated datum.

reducer (1) In plumbing, any one of the various pipe connections, such as a reducing sleeve, reducing ell or reducing tee; so constructed as to permit joining pipe of different sizes. (2) A paint thinner. (3) A trim used to reduce the radius of a bullnose or a cove to another radius or to a square.

reducer, pressure, liquid refrigerant A device or devices, in a refrigerating system, in which the pressure of the fluid is reduced from that of condensed liquid to that of the evaporator.

reducing flame Kiln flame to which insufficient combustion air is supplied. At the high temperature in the kiln this condition may tend to convert some iron in the clinker to a reduced state giving the cement a light, tannish color.

reducing strip A metal or wood strip used to adjust elevation between carpet and vinyl tile.

reduction The extraction of mineral from its ores.

reduction factor A structural factor for a given slenderness ratio so that the permissible stress on a long column is reduced below that permitted on a short column in order to prevent buckling.

reduction gear, double Two sets of gears in series to both reduce speed and increase power.

reduction gear, single A gear set that causes one shaft to turn another at reduced speed.

reduction in area A contraction in the area of a tensile test piece.

reduction of levels The surveying calculation of the differences in level between various points using the staff readings in a field book.

redundant frame A structural frame which has more members or more stability than is required for it to be a perfect frame. Therefore it is necessary to remove a member or members, or some fixity, to make it perfect.

redwood A tree of California, the lightweight, reddish wood of which is decay resistant and is used in building for both exterior and interior work, and for structural timber.

reeding A molding, or a surface made up of closely spaced parallel, half-round, convex profiles.

reel A revolving rack used for storage of hose and cable; in a churn drill, the winches are usually called reels.

bull-spudding The churn drill winch that lifts and lowers the drill string.

calf-casing   The churn drill winch used for handling casing and for odd jobs.

dead   A storage reel

live   A reel that supplies air, water or electricity to the inner end of the hose or wire wound on it.

sand   In a churn drill, the high speed winch that lifts the bailing cylinder.

re-entrant corner   An inside corner of a surface, producing stress concentrations in the roofing or waterproofing membrane.

reeved fall   *(see laced fall)*

reeving   (1) Running lifting or load lines or cables through pulley blocks. **(2)** Threading or placement of a working line.

re-expansion line   Curve on indicator diagram, representing the pressure-total volume relationship of clearance fluid during the initial portion of the return stroke of the piston, prior to the opening of the suction valve.

refectory   A dining-room in the house of a religious order.

reference level   A reading or image associated with normal or dry condition.

reference lines   The lines of intersection of the image planes in an orthographic projection (sometimes call folding lines).

reference mark   In surveying, a distant point used for taking bearings and measurements to other points.

reference peg   A recovery peg in surveying.

reference temperature   A temperature of known value used as a basis to determine other temperatures.

reflectance (reflection factor)   The ratio of the light reflected by a surface to the light falling upon it.

reflected plan   A graphic horizontal section, shown looking up instead of down as in the normal plan.

reflected sound   Sound that has struck a surface and 'bounced off.' Sound reflects at the same angle as light reflects in a mirror; the angle of incidence equals the angle of reflection. Large curved surfaces tend to focus (concave) or diffuse (convex) the sound when reflected. However, when the radius of the reflecting surface is less than the wavelength of the sound, this does not hold true. Thus, a rough textured surface has little effect on diffusion of sound.

reflection coefficient   The fraction of sound returned into a room after a sound wave strikes a surface in the room.

reflective insulation   Sheet material with one or both surfaces of comparatively low heat emissivity. When used in building construction, reflective side faces air spaces, and reduces the radiation across the air space.

reflectivity (reflectance)   The ratio of light reflected from a surface to the light falling on the surface. The reflectivity plus the absorptivity equals one, since the incident sunlight is either reflected or absorbed.

reflector   (1) A polished surface to reflect light in a desired direction. **(2)** A baffle to reflect heated air.

reflector lamp   Spot or flood lamp with bulb coated with reflecting surface; for indoor use only.

reflux valve   A check valve for piping.

refractive index   The ratio of the velocity of light in the first of two media to its velocity in the second as it passes from one into the other. The first medium is usually a vacuum.

refractories   Materials, usually non-metallic, used to withstand high temperatures.

refractoriness   In refractories, the property of being resistant to softening or deformation at high temperatures.

refractory   (1) Resistant to high temperatures. **(2)** A heat-resisting unit for furnace lining and the like. **(3)** Inorganic, nonmetallic, ceramic materials which retain physical shape and chemical identity in the presence of high temperatures.

refractory aggregate   Materials having refractory properties which, when bound together into a conglomerate mass by a matrix, form a refractory body.

refractory concrete (mortar) Concrete or mortar having refractory properties and suitable for use at high temperature such as boilers and furnaces; usually made with calcium-aluminate cement and refractory aggregate.

refractory insulating concrete Refractory concrete having low thermal conductivity.

refrigerant The fluid used for heat transfer in a refrigerating system, which absorbs heat at a low temperature and a low pressure of the fluid and rejects heat at a higher temperature and a higher pressure of the fluid, usually involving changes of state of the fluid.

refrigerant charge The designated amount of refrigerant required for proper functioning of a closed refrigerating system.

refrigerant, flammable Any refrigerant which will burn when mixed with air, such as ethyl chloride, methyl chloride, and the hydrocarbons.

refrigerant, secondary Any volatile or nonvolatile substance in an indirect refrigerating system that absorbs heat from a substance or space to be refrigerated and rejects this heat to the evaporator of the refrigerating system.

refrigerating compressor performance factor The ratio of its capacity to its power input as follows: (a) compressor only: tons per bhp at shaft of the power source; (b) compressor and motor: Btu per watt-hr or ton per kw.

refrigerating effect, condensing The condensing heat rejection effect less the heat added to the refrigerant vapor in the refrigerant compressor unit.

refrigerating effect, net water (brine) cooler The product of the weight rate of water or brine flow and the difference in enthalpy of the entering and leaving water or brine expressed in heat units per unit of time. It is expressed also by the total refrigeration effect less the heat leakage losses.

refrigerating effect, subcooling The additional refrigeration effect made

available by subcooling the refrigerant liquid in the condenser.

refrigerating effect, total water (brine) cooler The product of the weight rate of refrigerant flow and the difference in enthalpy of the entering and leaving refrigerant fluid, expressed in heat units per unit of time.

refrigerating engineering Technique of design, manufacture, application, and operation of refrigerating machinery and its primary equipment. Refrigeration (except as exact measure in heat units) refers here to a more general science, more concerned with the use of coldness for commercial and other useful purposes.

refrigerating medium Any substance whose temperature is such that it is used, with or without a change of state, to lower the temperature of other bodies or substances below the ambient temperature.

refrigerating plant A complete refrigerating system and all accessories, controls and other apparatus required for its utilization, and its enclosing structure.

refrigerating system performance factor The ratio of the useful refrigerating effect of the system to the power input.

refrigeration (cooling), direct method of A system in which the evaporator is in direct contact with the material or space refrigerated or as located in air circulating passages communicating with such spaces.

refrigeration (cooling), indirect method of A system in which a liquid, such as brine or water, cooled by the refrigerant, is circulated to the material or space refrigerated or is used to cool air so circulated.

refrigeration pipe line Service to group of buildings with a refrigerant supply from a central refrigerating plant.

refrigerator, walk-in A refrigerated cooler or freezer with large entry doors suitable for foot traffic.

refusal The depth beyond which a pile

cannot be driven due to geological structure.

regain of moisture   The amount absorbed by any material in percent of weight of that material.

regelation   Refreezing of water that has resulted from the melting of ice under pressure; does not require refrigeration.

regenerative heating (or cooling)   Process of utilizing heat which must be rejected or absorbed in one part of the cycle, to perform a useful function in another part of the cycle, by heat transfer.

regime (regimen)   Description of a stream or canal whose flow rate is such that it neither picks up nor deposits material from its bed.

register   (1) The end of a duct for incoming or escaping air; usually covered with grillwork. (2) A combination grille and damper assembly covering an air opening.

register box   Metal pan at floor, wall or ceiling where the duct line enters a room.

registered architect   (see architect)

registered land   Land covered by a special type deed.

registration   The process of determining and certifying competency to practice under state laws.

reglet (raglet)   A groove in a wall or other surface adjoining a roof surface for use in the attachment of counterflashing.

reglette   A surveyor's short scale, usually divided into hundredths and tenths of a foot. It is used for accurate measurements of length with a steel band marked in feet only.

regula   In the Doric order of architecture, the flat block from which the small cone-shaped pendants drop.

regulated set cements   Cements containing calcium fluoraluminate, a very reactive aluminate phase. These cements have a controlled setting time ranging from one to sixty minutes and have a corresponding rapid early strength development.

reheater (interheater)   An accessory to

steam or compressed-air engines which reduces consumption of air or steam. It superheats the steam or reheats the air between expansion stages increasing pressure and reducing the likelihood of freezing.

reignier work   Ornamental wood inlay in colors, in the manner of boulle work.

reimbursable expenses   Amounts expended for or on account of the project which, in accordance with the terms of the appropriate agreement, are to be reimbursed by the owner.

reinforce   To strengthen by the addition of new material, or extra material; for the reinforcement of concrete, iron or steel rods are embedded to give additional strength.

reinforced concrete   Concrete containing reinforcement and designed on the assumption that the two materials act together in resisting forces.

reinforced masonry   Unit masonry in which reinforcement is embedded in such a manner that the two materials act together in resisting forces.

reinforced membrane   A roofing or waterproofing membrane reinforced with felts, mats, fabrics, or chopped fibers.

reinforcement (bars, wires)   Metal bars, wires or other slender members which are embedded in concrete in such a manner that the metal and the concrete act together in resisting forces.

cold-drawn wire   Steel wire made from rods that have been hot rolled from billets, cold-drawn through a die; such as for concrete reinforcement of small diameter, in gauges not less than 0.080 inches (2 mm) nor greater than 0.625 inches (16 mm).

cold-worked steel   Steel bars or wires which have been rolled, twisted or drawn at normal ambient temperatures.

distribution-bar   Small diameter bars, usually at right angles to the main reinforcement, intended to spread a concentrated load on a slab and to prevent cracking.

dowel-bar Short bars, extending approximately equally into two abutting pieces of concrete to increase the strength of the joint.

expanded metal fabric A form of reinforcement made by slitting a rolled steel sheet and then stretching it to form a diamond-shaped mesh. *(see expanded metal)*

four-way A system of reinforcement in flat slab construction comprising bands of bars parallel to two adjacent edges and also to both diagonals of a rectangular slab.

helical Steel reinforcement forming a helix.

high tensile Concrete reinforcing bars have a minimum yield strength above a specified value, such as 60,000 or 75,000 psi (413.68 or 517.11 mega newtons per square meter).

hoop Binders in the form of rings, other than helical, around the main reinforcement in columns and piles.

lateral Usually applied to transverse hoops, links or helical reinforcement in columns.

mesh An arrangement of bars or wire, normally in two directions at right angles, tied or welded at the intersections, or interwoven. *(see reinforcement, expanded metal fabric)*

secondary Reinforcement other than main reinforcement.

spiral *(see spiral reinforcement)*

transverse **(1)** Links or helical reinforcement for columns. **(2)** Reinforcement at right angles to the main reinforcement.

twin-twisted bar Two bars of the same nominal diameter twisted together.

two-way Reinforcement arranged in bands of bars at right angles to each other.

welded Reinforcement joined together by welding.

reinforcement displacement Movement of reinforcing steel from its specified position in the forms.

reinforcement ratio Ratio of the effective area of the reinforcement to the effective area of the concrete at any section of a structural member. *(see percentage of reinforcement)*

reisner work Surfacing of inlaid colored woods; a 17th century German practice.

rejointing Pointing.

related trades The different or allied building trades whose work is necessary for the completion of a project.

relating device A device that determines the ratio of door travel.

relative compaction The dry density of soil divided by the maximum dry density of soil as determined by standard compaction test; generally expressed as a percentage. *(see degree of compaction)*

relative density A measure of the density of sand which gives a better impression of its compaction than the voids ratio. Laboratory measurements are made of the sand in its loosest possible dry state and its densest possible state.

relative humidity The ratio of the quantity of water vapor actually present to amount present in a saturated atmosphere at a given temperature; expressed as a percentage.

relative measurement Measurements between two objects or substances without regard to the absolute value of either.

relative moisture Moisture level in CPM or pounds per cubic foot compared to other levels.

relative physical intensity scale Instrument similar to a calibrated thermometer, showing the relationship between decibels and physical intensity.

relative saturation = Volume of water in sample × 100 Maximum volume of water sample could hold.

relative settlement Differential structural settlement.

relaxation Decrease in stress in steel as a result of creep within the steel under prolonged strain; decrease in stress of the steel, such as results from shrinkage and creep of the concrete in a pre-stressed concrete unit.

relay (1) A valve or switch that amplifies or restores original strength to an air, hydraulic or electrical impulse. (2) An electrically operated device that controls the making or breaking of electrical contacts in a circuit.

release agent Material used to prevent bonding of concrete to a surface.

release of lien Instrument executed by one supplying labor, materials or professional services on a project which releases his mechanic's lien against the project property. *(see mechanic's lien)*

releasing carrier The clamping device attached to the carframe, generally to the crosshead, which prevents the accidental application of the safeties due to a momentary unbalance of inertia between the governor rope system and the car.

releve (1) A measured drawing of old work. (2) A restoration.

relief holes Holes drilled closely along a line, which serve to weaken the rock so that it will break along that line.

relief pressure valve A pressure-sensitive device which protects the pumping unit from excessive pressure.

relief valve A valve which will allow air or fluid to escape if its pressure becomes higher than the valve setting.

relief vent A branch from the vent stack, connected to a horizontal branch between the first fixture branch and the soil or waste stack, whose primary function is to provide for circulation of air between the vent stack and the soil or waste stack.

relief well A borehole drilled at the toe of an earthen dam to relieve high pressures created by the weight of the dam.

relieving arch An arch built over and clear of a weak support, to carry the main load.

relieving platform Decking at the land side of a retaining wall to transmit heavy loads vertically down to the wall and prevent them from becoming a surcharge on the wall. The platform is usually carried partly on the wall and partly on bearing piles or raking piles.

reluctance The opposition a material offers to magnetic lines of force.

REM Roentgen Equivalent Man—adjusts radiation measured in RAD to account for the differing effect on man.

remedial roofing The repair of selected, isolated portions of the roof system to return the roof to uniform condition. This normally involves the removal of wet materials along with correction of the original cause of the problem.

remixing Working (mixing) concrete less than approximately 1½ hours old that has stiffened or dried out slightly when left standing. Useable if it can be completely compacted in the forms. Adding water to make a mixture more workable (retempering) should never be permitted.

remodeling *(see alterations)*

remoldability The readiness with which freshly mixed concrete responds to a remolding effort such as jigging or vibration causing it to reshape its mass around reinforcement and to conform to the shape of the form. *(see flow)*

remolding index The ratio of the modulus of the elasticity, or deformation, of a soil in the undisturbed state to the modulus of elasticity, or deformation, of the soil in the remolded state.

remolding test A test to measure remoldability.

Renaissance In architecture, a style of structural ornamentation which follows the Medieval, originating in Italy in the 15th century.

render (1) To add the finishing stage of a drawing, usually in washes. (2) To make a presentation drawing.

render and set Two-coat plaster on plasterboard walls; rendering covered by a finishing coat.

render, float, and set Application of three-coat plaster.

rendering (1) The application, by means of a trowel or float, of a coat of mortar. (2) A perspective or elevation drawing of a project or portion thereof with an artistic delineation of materials, shades and shadows.

rendering coat A first coat of plaster on a wall. A first coat on lathing is called a pricking-up coat.

rent laths Plastering laths which have been split instead of sawn.

repeat (1) The distance from a point in a pattern figure to the same point where it occurs again, measuring lengthwise of the fabric. (2) Indicates the distance between identical design elements in sheet goods. The most widely used is an 18″ repeat, with range from 3″ to 54″. Common are 9″, 12″, 13½″, 27″ and 54″ repeats. (9″ and 12″ repeats are usually found in small block or tile designs.)

replacement value The estimated cost to replace the building in kind, based on current replacement costs.

replum The panel of a framed door.

reposting The construction operation in which the original shoring or posting is removed and replaced in such a manner as to avoid damage to the partially cured concrete. *(see reshoring)*

repousse With a pattern or design in relief, as embossed metalwork.

representative sample A select sample which can be chosen only by planned action to insure that a fair proprortion is drawn from the various parts of the whole. Sampling within the parts may be at random.

requisitions Written requests for something authorized, but not made available automatically. Usually made on requisition forms and used to order parts or materials.

reradiation This is the phenomena of small amounts of solar energy being absorbed by the cover plates and sent back to the colder sky temperature. In addition, a portion of the heat collected on the absorber is also returned to the outside by infrared radiation.

reroofing The practice of applying new roofing materials over existing roofing materials.

research class Highest possible quality of sampling with little regard to costs,

e.g., sampling on research project, or on very important or expensive foundation structures.

reservoir (1) A tank or basin primarily for storage or collection of a liquid. (2) An artificial lake.

resetting Setting of forms separately for each successive lift of a wall to avoid offsets at construction joints.

reshoring Temporary vertical support for forms or completed structures, placed after the original shoring support has been removed.

residence A dwelling; apartment; home.

residence time The average length of time a particle spends in a process or in contact with a catalyst.

resident architect An architect at a job site who supervises the work and protects the owner's interests during construction under the direction of the consulting architect.

resident engineer (inspector) A person representing the owner's interests at the project site during the construction phase; term frequently used on projects in which a governmental agency is involved. *(see owner's inspector)*

residual magnetism The magnetic lines of force remaining in the relay core after the coil circuit is opened electrically.

residium The residue from the distillation of petroleum.

residual errors Minor surveying errors which cannot be eliminated from a measurement despite careful work.

residual soil *(see eluvium)*

residual tack A fault of paint finishes which do not harden, caused by vegetable oils. The tackiness may last indefinitely in damp air.

resilience (1) The work done per unit volume of a material in producing strain. (2) The ability of a carpet fabric or padding to spring back to its original shape or thickness after being crushed or walked upon. (3) Measure of floor covering's return to its original shape and gauge after foot traffic, dropped objects, or in-place objects.

resilient channel   A metal furring member designed to absorb sound or noise impact which strikes the surfacing membrane.

resin   A natural or synthetic, solid or semi-solid organic material of indefinite and often high molecular weight having a tendency to flow under stress; usually has a softening or melting range and usually fractures conchoidally.

resin bonded   Lumber glued with a synthetic resin, therefore somewhat moisture-resistant.

resin-emulsion paint   Paint, the vehicle or liquid part of which consists of resin or varnish dispersed in fine droplets in water.

resistance (resistance losses)   In hydraulics, the resistance of a pipe or channel to flow. It is usually expressed in feet-head of water and can be obtained from various flow formulas.

resistance butt-welding   Welding by butting the two parts together.

resistance, thermal   The reciprocal of thermal conductance.

resistance welding   The welding of two pieces held tightly in contact by electrodes through which a heavy alternating current momentarily flows causing them to fuse together.

resist-printing   A dye-resist agent is printed on tufted carpet prior to piece dyeing.

resistivity, thermal   The reciprocal of thermal conductivity.

resistor, electric   A material used to produce heat by passing an electric current through it.

resolving power   The number of picture elements (pixels) per line on an infrared scanner.

resonance   (1) Condition reached when frequency of applied dynamic load coincides with natural frequency of load support. (2) That condition which occurs in an alternating current circuit when the inductive reactance in the circuit is just equal to, and hence neutralizes, the capacitive reactance.

resorcinol formaldehyde resin   A type of synthetic resin.

respond   In Medieval architecture, a half pillar or pier attached to a wall to support an arch.

responsible bidder   *(see lowest responsible bidder)*

resteel   *(slang)* Rebar.

restoration   Rebuilding to approach as nearly as possible the original form.

restraint (of concrete)   Restriction of free movement of fresh or hardened concrete following completion of placing in formwork or molds or within an otherwise confined space; restraint can be internal or external and may act in one or more directions.

restretch   A term applied to the remedial steps necessary for the correction of improperly laid carpet resulting from application of wrong stretching techniques, carpet defects or undetermined causes.

restricted list of bidders   *(see invited bidders)*

retainage (retention)   A sum withheld from progress payments to the contractor in accordance with the terms of the owner-contractor agreement. Paid after a given time upon completion of a project.

retained percentage   *(see retainage)*

retained wall   A wall built to keep a bank of earth from sliding or water from flooding.

retardation   Reduction in the rate of hardening or setting, e.g., an increase in the time required to reach initial and final set or to develop early strength of fresh concrete, mortar or grout. *(see retarder)*

retarded hemihydrate plaster   *(see hemihydrate plaster)*

retarder   An admixture used to delay the setting action of plaster. Generally used only with gypsum plasters or finish coat plaster contained calcined gypsum gauging.

retard switch   A switch used to regulate the speed at which the car strikes the buffer.

retempering   The addition of water and

remixing of concrete or mortar which has started to stiffen; a practice usually frowned upon, as it may change the strength of the finished product.

retention *(see retainage)*

reticulated work That in which the courses are arranged in a form like the meshes of a net. The stones or bricks are square and placed in a diamond shape.

reticule A set of fine spider webs which intersect and are held by the diaphragm at the optical focus of a telescope. The intersection of the central lines defines the sight line of the telescope.

retification Turning AC voltage into DC voltage.

retiring cam A retractable cam used to actuate landing interlocks. It is mounted to an elevator car and is in a retracted position when the car is in motion, then contacts and unlocks the landing interlocks by moving against the lock roller arm.

retract The mechanism by which a dipper shovel bucket is pulled back out of the digging.

retreading Repairing roads whose surface is breaking up or which are misshapen. The surface is first scarified and the road is then reshaped, rolled and surfaced.

retrochoir The chapels and other parts behind and about the high altar.

retrofit A modification of equipment to incorporate changes not available at time of original installation.

return (1) The right-angled change of direction of a molding or group of moldings, terminating the run. (2) A corresponding termination of a projecting member of any kind, including a wall. (3) A return pipe. (4) The end railings of a fire-escape balcony. (5) A surface turned back from the face of the principal surface.

return air Air returned from conditioned or refrigerated space.

return air duct Ducts through which the cold air or return air passes on its way back to the heating unit.

return corner block (L) Concrete masonry unit designed for use in corner construction for 6-inch, 10inch and 12-inch walls.

return, dry A return pipe in a steam heating system which carries both water of condensation and air. The dry return is above the level of the water line in the boiler in a gravity system. *(see return, wet)*

return end An end of a molding shaped to fit the profile of the molding.

return head One that appears both on the face and edge of a work.

return jamb That portion of a door frame behind which a sliding door passes during opening and closing. Sometimes called a slide jamb.

return mains Pipes or conduits which return a heating or cooling medium from the heat transfer unit to the source of heat or refrigeration.

return nosing In the building of stairs, the mitered, overhanging end of a tread outside the balusters.

return offset (jumpover) A double offset installed so as to return the pipe to its original line.

return pipe The pipe by which the water returns to the heater or boiler in a water heating system.

return sheave A pulley at a distance from a haulage drum. A tail rope from the drum passes around it and enables the haulage engine to pull away from itself.

return wall A short length of wall perpendicular to an end of a longer wall.

return, wet That part of a return main of a steam heating system which is filled with water of condensation. The wet return usually is below the level of the water line in the boiler, although not necessarily so. *(see return, dry)*

reveal The side of an opening in a wall for a window or door.

reveal lining The finish covering a reveal.

reverberation The prolongation of sound waves in a room.

reverberation period The period of time, in seconds, required for sound of a certain frequency to decrease, after the source is silenced. The time depends mainly on the volume and the absorption of the room; the higher the absorption, the lower the reverberation period.

reverberation time The time required for any average sound to reduce in intensity to a value one-millionth of its original intensity, or to reduce sixty decibels, after the sound source has stopped.

reverse In plastering, a templet cut to the reverse shape of a molding and placed on it to check its accuracy.

reverse bend A line bent over a drum or a sheave, and then over another sheave in the opposite direction.

reverse curve An S-shaped curve.

reversing clutch A forward-and-reverse transmission which is shifted by a pair of friction clutches.

reverse phase relay A device normally mounted on the elevator control panel that prevents power from being applied to an elevator motor if the building power supplied to the elevator control has reversed phases, or has an open phase.

revet To face with masonry, as an embankment.

revetment (1) A wall sloped back sharply from its base. (2) A masonry or steel facing for a bank. (3) Material such as rock, concrete blocks or mattresses placed on the bottom or banks of a river to prevent or minimize erosion.

revibration One or more applications of vibration to concrete after completion of placing and initial compaction but preceding initial setting of the concrete.

revolution The motion or the apparent motion of a body in orbit.

revolution counter An instrument for indicating the total number of revolutions of a piece of rotating machinery, such as mill, kiln, etc.

revolving-blade mixer (paddle) (see open-top mixer)

revolving door A widely used type of door for entrance to public buildings,

having four leaves pivoted at their inside stiles and enclosed in a circular vestibule.

revolving screen A trash track turned mechanically or by the force of the water passing through it.

revolving shovel A digging machine in which the upper works can revolve independently of the supporting unit.

rexangle A composition shingle cut to a parallelogram design and laid up on a roof with both a side and a headlap.

rextite A composition shingle cut to a modified parallelogram design and laid up on a roof with both a side and a headlap.

Reynolds' critical velocity (see critical speed velocity)

Reynolds' number A non-dimensional coefficient used as a measure of the dynamic scale of an air flow.

rheology The science dealing with flow of materials. Applies to pumping of raw material slurry and placing of concrete, mortar, grout, and oil well cement slurries.

rheostat (1) A device that regulates flow of electricity by varying the amount of resistance on the circuit. (2) A type of variable resistor used to adjust current flow to a load.

rhomboid A parallelogram whose angles are oblique and only the opposite sides are equal.

rib (1) One of a number of parallel structural members backing sheeting; the portion of a T-beam which projects below the slab; in deformed reinforcing bars, the deformations or the longitudinal parting ridge. (2) A ridge projecting above grade in the floor of a blasted area. (3) A transverse or diagonal structural member of arched vaulting, usually emphasized; the vaulted ceiling is sprung between the ribs.

ribbed panel A panel composed of a thin slab reinforced by a system of ribs in one or two directions, usually orthogonal.

ribbed slab (see ribbed panel)

ribbon (1) A horizontal board let into the face of studding, to support the floor joists on its upper edge in balloon-frame construction; a ledger board. (2) A narrow strip of wood or other material.

ribbon courses Alternate courses of tiles, laid to shorter or longer gauge, alternately showing long and short exposed depths.

ribbon development Extension of urban growth along radial highways.

ribbon grain (ribbon stripe; stripe figure) Alternating light and dark strips in quarter timber.

ribbon loading Method of batching concrete in which the solid ingredients, and sometimes also the water, enter the mixer simultaneously.

ribbon saw A narrow band saw.

ribbon screw Screw conveyor with continuous helical blade.

rib holes Holes in tunnelling or shaft sinking drilled at the sides of the tunnel or shaft, and fired last after the relief holes; trimmers in Britain.

ribs Parallel structural members backing sheathing.

rich concrete Concrete of high cement content.

rich mixture A concrete mixture containing a high proportion of cement.

Richter scale A scale for measurement of earth tremors, developed by Charles Richter at the California Insititute of Technology. The scale ranges from 0 to 8.9, with the higher numbers indicating severity of the tremor or earthquake. (see Rossi-Forel scale)

rider cap (see pile cap)

ride the brush (slang) Bear down on the brush to the extent that the paint is applied with the sides of the bristles instead of the flag ends; shortens the life of the brush.

ridge The top horizontal edge or peak of a roof.

ridge board The board placed on edge at the ridge of the roof to support the upper ends of the rafters.

ridge capping The covering of wood or metal which tops the ridge of a roof.

ridge cut The cut at the top of a hip rafter.

ridge pole Highest horizontal member of roof receiving upper ends of rafters; a horizontal member against which opposite rafters are butted where they meet the peak.

ridge roll The half-cylindrical surface, usually metal, for finishing a roof ridge.

ridge terrace A ridge built along a contour line of a slope to pond rainwater above it.

ridge tiles Tiles used to cap the ridge of a roof.

ridging An upward, tenting displacement of a membrane, frequently over an insulation joint.

RIEI The Roofing Industry Educational Institute.

riffler A rasp bent for reaching concave surfaces; a fillet rasp.

rifle bar A cylinder with curved splines.

rifle nut A splined nut that slides back and forth on a rifle bar.

rifling Forming a spiral thread on the wall of a drill hole which makes it difficult to pull out the bit.

rift (riven) Descriptive of wood split or sawn with the grain.

rig (1) (slang) A general term denoting any machine; more specifically, the front or attachment of a revolving shovel. (2) To furnish with special gear or equipment; tackle, equipment or machinery fitted for a special purpose.

rigger (1) A long-bristled brush with a flat end for painting lines or bands of different thicknesses. (2) A workman who is used to load, unload and move heavy items of equipment or materials. May prepare loads for lifting by crane.

right angle An angle formed by two lines which are perpendicular to each other; that is, the lines represent two radii that intercept a quarter of a circle, hence, is a 90° angle.

right bank That bank of a stream which is on the right when one looks downstream.

right hand rule When the fingers of the right hand are wrapped around a coil of wire with the fingers pointing in the direction of conventional current flow, the thumb will point to the north pole.

right lay Strands of a wire rope that rotate or are twisted around the core in a clockwise manner are said to have a right lay.

right line The shortest distance between two points; that is, a straight line.

right of way The land secured and reserved to the public for highway purposes, sidewalks, utilities, etc.

rigid Rigid metal conduit.

rigid arch An arch without hinges; completely fixed throughout.

rigid frame (1) A frame depending on moment in joints for stability. (2) A term used in structural analysis to describe a rafter-to-column connection which is assumed to have sufficient rigidity to hold virtually unchanged the original angles between intersecting members.

rigidity Resistance to twisting or shearing.

rigid pavement Pavement that will provide high bending resistance and distribute loads to foundations over comparatively large areas, e.g., portland cement concrete pavement, and bituminous, brick, or stone-block pavement supported on portland cement concrete base.

rime A rung of a ladder.

rim lock A lock designed to be affixed to the surface of the door, as differentiated from the mortise lock, which is set into the edge of the door.

rimpull The tractive force between the rubber tires of driving wheels and the respective surface, expressed in pounds.

ring compression The principal stress in a confined circular ring subjected to extreme pressure.

ring course The course closest to the extrados in an arch which is several courses deep.

Ringelmann chart A set of charts which are numbered 0 to 5. They emulate different smoke densities denoted in percentages of black. These charts are utilized to assess the opacity of smoke emanating from stacks and other sources. Emission standards are occasionally based on Ringlemann numbers.

ring road (concentric rings; circumferential street; circular highway) In urban planning, units of a plan that complement radial thoroughfares and incidental gridirons.

ring shake A separation of the wood between annual growth rings of a tree.

rip To saw lumber parallel to the grain; also called flat cutting.

riparian rights Rights of a land owner to water on or bordering his property, including right to prevent diversion or misuse of upstream water.

rippen To take a stone out of the rough.

ripper (1) A towed machine equipped with teeth for loosening hard soil and soft rock. (2) A rip saw. (3) A plastering or slating tool.

rippers A stud cut diagonally lengthwise and placed on top of roof joists on a flat roof to give the roof a slight pitch.

ripple amplitude The amount of voltage variation in the output waveform of the DC power supply.

ripple finish An intentional and uniformly wrinkled painting finish usually obtained by stoving.

ripples An uneven appearance in the surface of a floor covering, such as is caused by stripwood subfloor irregularities, failure to properly roll floor covering at time of installation, etc.

riprap A layer of large uncoursed stones, broken rock, or precast blocks placed in random fashion on the upstream slope of an embankment dam, or a reservoir shore, or on the sides of a channel as a protection against wave and ice action. Very large riprap sometimes is referred to as armoring.

ripsaw A saw having coarse, chisel-shaped teeth used in cutting wood in the direction of the grain.

rise (1) The vertical distance from the

top of a tread to the top of the next higher tread. (2) The height of an arch from springing to crown. (3) The vertical height from the supports to the ridge of a roof. (4) The vertical distance from the crown of a road to its lowest point.

rise and fall A method used in survey work to reduce staff readings by working out the rise or fall from each point to one following it. The readings are entered in a level book in special columns parallel to those for the staff readings.

rise-and-fall table A circular-saw bench, which can be raised or lowered relatively to the saw.

rise and run A term used by carpenters to indicate the degree of incline, as in a sloped roof.

riser (1) The vertical board under the tread in stairs. (2) A water supply pipe which extends vertically one full story or more to convey water to branches or fixtures. (3) The vertical raceway in a hoistway. (4) Tube in a water tube boiler designed for the upward flow of heated liquids.

riser duct Vertical conduit in a kiln preheater installation which carries hot gases and pulverized raw meal in a vertical direction, generally to a cyclone separator.

rising and lateral conductors Electric cables in a branch circuit.

rising main An electrical supply cable, main gas or water supply pipe which passes up one or more floors of a building.

rive To split with the grain of lumber, as riven cypress shingles.

riven laths Split laths, used in plastering, that are stronger and less likely to split than sawn laths.

rivet (riveting) A round bar of steel, driven while red-hot into a hole through two pieces of steel which are to be joined. The head is held in position by a holder-up with a dolly while another worker strikes the end with a hand hammer, thus forming a head on it. The high-strength friction-grip bolt is much more convenient and quicker, making riveting obsolete for site work.

rivet catcher A laborer who catches, in a bucket, the hot rivet thrown by the rivet heater and passes it to the holder-up.

riveter The worker who forms the head on a hot rivet.

riveting hammer A pneumatic riveting device.

riveting machine A pneumatic or hydraulic riveting device.

rivet snap A punch with a recess in its head, shaped like the rivet head it forms.

riving knife A steel blade projecting up from a sawbench protecting the back edge of the circular saw blade. Its thickness assures that the wood will not bind the saw.

roach coach *(slang)* Lunch wagon.

road An open way of travel for vehicles improved in varying degrees from simple grading to complete asphalt or concrete surfacing.

road forms Wood or steel forms set on edge to form the side of a road slab. They are set with their upper surface at the correct levels for the road, to guide the screeding operation.

road heater A traveling machine which heats a road surface by blowing a flame or hot air on it.

road metal Broken stone, gravel, slag or similar material used in road surface, base construction or maintenance; hard pavement.

road-mix *(see mixed-in-place)*

road-oil A heavy petroleum oil, usually one of the slow-curing (SC) grades of liquid asphalt.

roadside The portion of the right-of-way not occupied by surface courses, curbs, paved gutters or paved median areas. Where no surface courses are provided, the roadside includes only such width or area of the roadbed as may be indicated on the plans.

roadside development The landscape development of the highway including landscape development of adjacent lands publicly owned or controlled.

roadster Low priced model of a scraper or truck.

road surface The travelled surface; also called the topping, wearing course or carpet.

road tar A bituminous material obtained in making coke from bituminous coal or by cracking petroleum oil vapors; classified as liquid or cold road tar.

roadway That portion of the highway included between the outside lines of gutters or side ditches, including the appertaining structures and all slopes, ditches, channels necessary for proper drainage protection and use. That part of right-of-way required for construction.

rob (1) To remove part of an installation for use elsewhere. (2) To take out supporting pillars or walls of pay rock in a mine.

rock (1) The hard, firm and stable parts of earth's crust; any material which requires blasting before it can be dug. (2) *(slang)* Sheetrock or gypsum board; to install sheetrock. (3) *(slang)* To create labor unrest at the job site.

rock asphalt A porous rock which has become naturally filled with asphalt or maltha. Rock asphalt is rarely used.

rock asphalt pavements Pavements constructed of rock asphalt, natural or processed, and treated with asphalt or flux as may be required for construction.

rockbolt Commonly used bolts of various sizes. Normally installed into a coredrilled hole and grouted into place. Also rock hangers.

rock drill A pneumatic or electric drill for making holes in rock for broaching, blasting or other purposes.

rocker End dump rock wagon; a unit built specifically to haul rocks from blast area.

rocker arm (1) A lever resting on a curved base so that the position of its fulcrum moves as its angle changes. (2) A bell crank with the fulcrum at the bottom.

rocker bearing A bridge, or truss support, free to rotate but not to move horizontally, unless also carried on rollers.

rocker shovel A mechanical, high speed shovel used in tunnelling.

rocket tester A rocket used in testing for leaks in pipes; it gives off a dense smoke when it is directed into a pipe during tests. The pipe is plugged at both ends and subjected to a slight internal pressure of water.

rock-faced Descriptive of stone laid as masonry with faces as received from the quarry.

rock-fill dam A dam composed of loose rock usually dumped in place; often with the up-stream part constructed of hand placed or derrick placed rock and faced with rolled earth or with an impervious surface of concrete, timber or steel.

rock flour Rock crushed to a silt.

rocking Pushing a resistant object repeatedly, and backing or rolling back between pushes to allow it to reach or cross its orginal position.

rocking frame An oscillating frame on which molds are set during concrete placement. The vibration helps compact the concrete.

rock job *(slang)* Any construction where material exists that will require blasting before it can be dug by available equipment.

rocklath A plaster base made of gypsum composition.

Rocklin granite A light-colored granite of California, somewhat similar to Raymond granite.

rock pile *(slang)* A skyscraper.

rock pocket A porous, mortar-deficient portion of hardened concrete consisting primarily of coarse aggregate and open voids, caused by leakage of mortar from its form, separation during placement , or insufficient consolidation. *(see honeycomb)*

rock rake A dozer-type attachment for a tractor with a series of bars and teeth for clearing rocks or trees.

rock slinger A laborer who removes oversize rock from the belt feeding a crusher; or, who walks in front of a motor grader throwing oversize rock out of the path of the grader.

Rockville A coarse-grained granite with feldspar; color is pinkish grey, and it consists of pale pink feldspar, quartz, and black mica; quarried at St. Cloud, Minnesota.

Rockwell hardness test A metal hardness test in which the depth of penetration of a conical diamond point or a steel ball is measured.

Rockwood oolitic limestone A light gray or buff even-textured variety quarried near Rockwood, Franklin County, Alabama.

rock wool (mineral wool) A loose fibrous material, made from certain kinds of rock and molten slag; used for insulating purposes in walls, roofs, floors, etc.

rococo A type of Renaissance ornament combining in profusion rocklike forms, scrolls, and crimped shells, often without organic coherence but presenting a lavish display of decoration; excess in decoration.

rod (1) Sharp-edged cutting screed used to trim shotcrete to conform to forms or ground wires. *(see screed)* (2) In surveying, a staff. (3) A pole-like piece of lumber used by carpenters as a measuring device, for instance, determining the exact height of risers in stairs.

rodability The susceptibility of fresh concrete or mortar to compaction by means of a tamping rod.

rod buster *(slang)* One who installs concrete reinforcement. An ironworker.

rodding (1) In concrete work, the act of compacting freshly poured concrete in its form by freeing the mass of air pockets with repeated stabs of a rod; such compacting is now more efficiently done with a vibrator. (2) In plumbing, cleaning out drains with drain rods. (3) In plastering, the leveling done with a floating rule.

rodding eye Opening for cleanout purposes; an access.

rod man *(see staff man)*

rod mill Cylindrical mill (as a tube mill) in which the grinding media consist of steel rods extending the full length of the mill. The cascading and grinding action is generally similar to the action of balls in a ball mill. Used extensively for coarse grinding in ore mining industries and occasionally in cement manufacture.

rod sounding A quick method of checking soil and rock conditions by driving a metal rod into the ground.

rod stock Round steel rod.

rod, tamping A round, straight steel rod having one end rounded to a hemispherical tip.

roentgen Unit of quantity or dose for X-rays, gamma rays, etc. that will produce as a result of ionization one electrostatic unit of electricity in one cc of dry air.

roll (1) A wheel of a roller. (2) A piece of wood over which roofing sheets are lapped and folded. (3) To compact with a roller.

roll-and-fillet molding A molding of convex face with a square fillet projecting from the middle of the profile; found in Medieval architecture.

roll, compression The drive wheel of a roller.

rollcrete A no-slump concrete that can be hauled in dump trucks, spread with a bulldozer or grader, and compacted with a vibratory roller.

roll crusher Crusher consisting of one or two rolls, sometimes equipped with manganese steel teeth. Pieces of rock are crushed between the rotating rolls or between one roll and a stationary breaker plate.

roll goods A general term applied to rubber and plastic sheeting whether fabric reinforced or not. It is usually furnished in rolls.

roll roofing Coated felts, either smooth or mineral surfaced.

rolled-steel joist An I-beam made from one piece of steel passed through a hot-rolling mill.

rolled-strip roofing Roll roofing.

roller (1) A heavy vehicle, usually self-propelled but sometimes towed, for compacting road sufaces or earth fill. The two types are very different. Road rollers, such as rubber tired rollers, are never towed. Earth rollers, such as grid rollers, sheepsfoot rollers or vibrating rollers, often are towed. **(2)** Small hand-operated devices for smoothing flooring, wall covering, etc.

rollerbug A tool used to consolidate or compact concrete.

roller gate A hollow cylindrical crest gate with spur gears at each end meshing with an inclined rack anchored to a recess in the end pier or wall. It is raised or lowered by being rolled on the rack. It may close at a greater depth than its diameter by means of shields or aprons attached to the cylinder; used in dam spillways.

roller, guide The front or steering wheel of a roller.

roller, hook In a revolving shovel, a roller attached by a bracket to the revolving section, and contacting the lower face of a circular track on the travel unit.

roller mill An air-swept grinding mill in which two to four grinding rollers, with shafts carried on hinged arms, ride a horizontal grinding table to pulverize raw material or clinker.

roller, support In a crawler machine, a roller that supports the slack upper part of the track.

roller, swing In a revolving shovel, one of several tapered wheels that roll on a circular turntable and support the upper works.

roller, track In a crawler machine, the small wheels that rest on the track and carry most of the weight of the machine.

rolling **(1)** (see roller) **(2)** The use of heavy metal or stone rollers on terrazzo topping to extract excess matrix. **(3)** procedure for removing trapped air and properly setting the floor covering into the adhesive (linoleum roller). Also procedure for use on seams (seam roller).

rolling doors Doors that are supported on wheels which run on a track.

rolling lift bridge A bridge, the lifting part of which has at its shore end a section resting on a flat, or rolling, surface.

rolling load The moving load.

rolling resistance Resistance which is encountered by a vehicle in moving over a road or surface. It is expressed in pounds of tractive pull required to move each gross ton over a level surface.

rolling tail gate Roller on back of float for winch line to run over freely.

rolling-up curtain weir A frame weir in which the frame remains upright and the barrier planks are drawn up to open the weir.

roll marks A series of fine parallel scratches or tears on the surface of rolled glass in the direction of the draw; caused by a difference in velocity between rolls and the sheet of glass.

roll molding A cylindrical form occurring chiefly in Early English and Decorated periods of Gothic. With a slight edge at one part, it is called a scroll or edge molding.

roll-over protection system A device mounted over the open cockpit of vehicles and heavy equipment to protect the operator from injury.

roll roofing A roofing material made of compressed fibers saturated with asphalt; supplied in rolls.

roll square 108 sq. ft. of roofing.

rollway The overflow section of a dam; spillway to carry overflow.

rolock (see rowlock)

Roman arch The round arch.

Roman bricks Bricks measuring 2×4×12 to 16 inches, including the mortar joints.

Roman cement (Parker's cement) The forerunner of portland cement.

Roman mosaic (tessellated pavement) A terrazzo uniformly laid with pieces of marble placed by hand.

Roman tile A clay tile used in Britain for roofing.

rondelle A small disc of glass used in leaded windows.

rood A crucifix as used in the chancel of a Christian church.

rood beam A beam or bottom chord of a truss near the front of a chancel on which the rood is carried.

rood loft A gallery over the rood screen.

rood screen A screen in the chancel, supporting the rood.

rood spire A spire built over the intersection of nave and transepts.

rood tower A name of the central tower, or that area over the intersection of the nave and chancel with the transepts.

roof The outside top covering of a structure.

roof boards (sheathing) Boards laid touching each other, sometimes with tongue and groove joints, nailed to the common rafters as a base for asphalt, flexible-metal roofing or roofing felt under slates or tiles.

roof covering The exposed exterior roof skin consisting of panels or sheets, attachments and joint sealants.

roof curb An accessory used to mount and level units (such as air conditioning and exhaust fans) on the sloped portion of the building roof.

roof decking Lightweight panels made of different roofing materials, such as plywood, aluminum, steel or timber; usually covered with roofing felt or flexible-metal sheet.

roof dormer A small window projecting from a roof slope.

roof drain A drain installed to receive water collecting on the surface of the roof and discharge it into the leader.

roofer The trade name for the workman who applies roofing materials.

roof guard A device to check snow from sliding off a pitched roof.

roofing The material put on a roof to make it water-tight.

roofing bracket (bearer bracket) A bracket used in slope roof construction, having provisions for fastening to the roof or supported by ropes fastened over the ridge and secured to some suitable object.

roofing felt Waterproof sheets of matted fibers laid either under tiles, in built-up roofing, or as an underlay or for other purposes.

roofing paper A building paper, usually of asphalt base.

roofing saturant The saturating asphalt used in manufacturing roll roofing and shingles, as differentiated from saturating asphalt for saturated felt.

roofing square (1) A steel square used in carpentry work. (2) A method of selling certain types of roofing material, e.g., by the square. (see sales square)

roofing tiles Concrete, burnt-clay or asbestos-cement tiles for covering roofs. Tiles are of three general types: (a) plain tiles, (b) shingle-lap tiles, (c) Italian tiling or Spanish tiling.

roof insulation Lightweight concrete used primarily as insulating material over structural roof systems.

roof jack A sleeve with flashing, having a flat sheet, either lead or galvanized metal, used to flash vent pipes or having a rain guard on top used for ventilating purposes.

roof ladder A cat ladder.

roof light A skylight.

roof light sheet An asbestos-cement roofing sheet with an opening in the middle for glazing or a corrugated sheet of transparent plastic material which may be used as glazing for an opening light.

roof overhang A roof extension beyond the endwall/sidewall of a building.

roof pitch (see roof slope)

roof seamer Machine which crimps panels together.

roof sheathing The boards or sheet material fastened to the roof rafters on which the shingle or other roof covering is laid.

roof slope The angle that a roof surface makes with the horizontal. Usually expressed in units of vertical rise to 12 units of horizontal run.

roof span The shortest distance between two opposite common rafter seats.

roof system A system of interacting roof components (NOT including the roof deck) designed to weatherproof and, normally, to insulate a building's top surface.

roof terminal The open roof end of a ventilation pipe.

roof tree An old term for the ridge of a roof; by extension, the dwelling.

roof truss The structural support for a roof consisting of braced timbers or structural iron fastened together for strengthening and stiffening this portion of a building.

room An interior space enclosed by walls. It is usually given a specific name, e.g., dining room, bedroom, family room, etc.

room air conditioner A factory encased air conditioner designed as a unit for mounting in a window or through a wall, or as a console. It is designed for delivery of conditioned air to an enclosed space without ducts. Room air conditioner includes packaged terminal air conditioners.

room dry bulb The dry bulb temperature of the conditioned room or space.

room, quick freezer Room kept at very low temperature for the purpose of freezing foodstuffs rapidly.

room thermostat A thermometer-like instrument for regulating the temperature within the room or house.

root (1) In carpentry, the part of a tenon which widens out at the shoulders. (2) The part of the dam that merges into the ground where the dam joins a slope. (3) The bottom surface joining the sides of two adjacent threads.

rooter A heavy duty ripper.

root hook A very heavy hook designed to catch and tear out big roots when it is dragged along the ground.

rope Strands of fiber or wire twisted or braided together. Wire rope is used for most hoisting or haulage purposes. Fiber rope is used for lesser purposes.

rope construction The arrangement of twisting based upon a number of wires in each strand and the number of strands twisted together to form the rope.

rope diameter The greatest diameter across the outer edges of the strands. Fiber ropes are usually measured by circumference.

rope equalizer, suspension A device installed on an elevator car or counterweight to equalize automatically the tensions in the hoisting wire ropes.

rope-fastening device, auxiliary A device attached to the car or counterweight or to the overhead dead-end rope-hitch support which will function automatically to support the car or counterweight in case the regular wire-rope fastening fails at the point of connection to the car or counterweight or at the overhead dead-end hitch.

rope grade The material, such as iron or steel, of which the wires are made.

rope lay The direction in which the wires or strands are twisted. *(see lay)*

rope molding A molding simulating the twisted strands of cordage.

ropey Descriptive of paint material which remains as applied and does not flow out; dries with slight ridges.

rose (1) A guard plate or escutcheon between a doorknob and the door, with perforation for the shank. (2) An ornamental centerpiece in a ceiling.

rose bit A countersink wood bit.

rose nail A wrought nail.

Rosendale cement A light hydraulic cement first made about 1837 in Rosendale, Ulster County, New York.

rose window A circular window, particularly in church architecture, the tracery of which loosely suggests a rose; if the radial lines are strongly emphasized it is sometimes called a wheel window or catherine wheel.

Rosie O'Moore *(slang)* A door.

rosin sized sheathing A sheet of wood fiber paper of a nominal, four to six pounds per 100 square feet weight, used in the building industry; generally colored pink on one side and sized with wood rosin.

Rossi-Forel scale   A scale for the measurement of intensities of earthquakes, evolved by Rossi and Forel. It grades earthquakes from 1 (very slight) to 10 (catastrophic). *(see Richter scale)*

rostrum   A raised dais or pulpit for the use of a public speaker.

rot   Decay of lumber.

ro-tap   A mechanical shaker used to screen materials for analysis of grading on different screen meshes.

rotary   (1) A rotary machine. (2) A road junction formed around a central circle about which traffic moves in one direction only. Also called a traffic circle.

rotary cooler   A large rotating cylinder supported by riding rings and rollers, partially or completely lined with refractory which passes hot clinker discharge from rotary kiln countercurrent to a flow of ambient air.

rotary cut   Veneer obtained by rotating a log against a cutting knife in such a way that a continuous sheet of veneer is unrolled spirally from the log.

rotary driller (tiller)   A machine that loosens and mixes soil and vegetation by means of a high speed rotor equipped with tines.

rotary engine   Any of various engines, as a turbine, in which power is applied to vanes or similar parts made to move in a circular path; a radial engine in which the cylinders revolve around a stationary crankshaft.

rotary excavator   A machine used for excavating circular tunnels. *(see Hallinger shield)*

rotary float (power float)   A motor-driven revolving disc that smooths, flattens and compacts the surface of concrete floors or floor toppings.

rotary kiln   Cylindrical rotating kiln, inclined approximately ½ in. per foot toward its discharge end; for burning cement raw meal into clinker. Lined with refractory bricks and often equipped with internal heat-exchangers, it is divided into the following process zones: drying zone (for wet process), preheating zone, calcining zone, burning zone, and cooling zone.

When the rotary kiln is used in conjunction with a preheater, and/or precalciner, the first three kiln zones are virtually eliminated.

rotary oil burner   An oil-burning heating unit that operates by centrifugal motion.

rotary pump   A pump of geared wheels which drive the water or oil between the gear teeth, like a rotary blower. Delivers large volumes of water at a low pressure.

rotary switch   A switch that utilizes sequential switching action of the contacts. One or more decks may be operated with a single control.

rotary table   The part of a rotary drill which turns the kelly and drill string.

rotary tiller   *(see rotary driller)*

rotary valve   A mechanism consisting of a series of blades or pockets revolving about a central axis and enclosed in a gas-tight housing. Regulates the flow of pulverized material while blocking the flow of air or gas through the valve.

rotary veneer   A veneer made using rotary cutting.

rotating magnetic field   Magnetic lines of force traveling around the pole pieces in the stator of an AC motor, creating a rotating effect.

rotation firing   Crushing a small piece of rock with a first explosion, and timing the other holes to throw their burdens toward the space made by that and other preceding explosions; row shooting.

rotation recorder   An instrument to measure the very slight rotation of a bridge support during loading.

rotor   (1) Any unit that does its work in a machine by spinning and does not drive other parts mechanically. (2) The rotating part of an AC motor.

rotunda   A building which is round both within and without; a circular room under a dome in large buildings.

rough arch   A relieving arch.

rough bracket   An under-stair bracket.

rough carriage   An under-stair carriage.

roughcast A kind of external plastering in which small sharp stones are mixed and which, when wet, is forcibly thrown or cast from a trowel against the wall to which it forms a rough coating of pleasant appearance.

rough coat The rendering coat of plaster on a wall.

rough floor Rough floor boards on which the finished floor is laid. In quality work a layer of building paper separates the two floors.

rough grind The initial operation in which coarse abrasives are used to cut the projecting chips in hardened terrazzo down to a level surface.

rough hardware All the concealed fasteners in a building such as nails, bolts and hangers as distinguished from the finish hardware.

roughing in (1) Installation of all concealed plumbing pipes; includes all plumbing work done before setting of fixtures or finishing but does not include the fixtures. (2) In electrical and other work, essentially the same process; not finished work.

roughness coefficient A factor in the Kutter Manning and other flow formulas representing the effect of channel, or conduit roughness upon energy losses in the water flow.

rough opening Any unfinished opening in the framing of a building.

rough plate Heavy plate glass sheets.

rough sawn Lumber that has not been smoothed; a rough sawn finish.

rough work Brickwork, which will eventually be covered by plaster, wallboard, facing bricks, cabinetry, etc.

round (1) Sculpture in full three-dimensional form, as opposed to sculpture in relief or in the round. (2) The rung of a ladder. (3) A carpenter's plane that cuts a groove. (4) In tunneling, a set of holes drilled for charging and firing together when blasting; a blast including a succession of delay shots.

round arch An arch of semicircular form; also called Roman arch.

rounded step A bullnose step.

roundel (1) A small circular window or panel; an oel-de-boeuf. (2) A bead molding. (3) A semicircular bastion.

round-headed buttress dam A concrete dam built of parallel buttresses thickened at the water end until they touch. The appearance is like the multiple-arch dam. The spillway may be a curved slab which passes over, joins and strengthens the down-stream ends of the buttresses.

rounding A deflector; usually poured concrete at the base of bridge pier to deflect debris in flood times; sometimes a metal cap which is installed at base of pier. In each case, a deflector is used to prevent wear and damage by debris to piers.

round timber Felled trees before being made into lumber.

round-topped roll A joint formed over a wood roll with vertical sides and rounded top used in flexible-metal roofing.

round turn and two half hitches (slang) A knot commonly used by ironworkers for rope bracing.

rout A term in woodworking for cutting or gouging out material with a tool called a router, which is a special type of smoothing plane.

router A woodworking tool used for smoothing the face of depressed surfaces, such as the bottom of grooves or any other depressions parallel with the surface of a plane of work.

routine class sample A fairly good quality of sample but with some attention paid to keeping both the equipment fairly simple and the time of operation reasonably short in order to avoid excessive costs, e.g., sampling by specialist soil mechanics organizations for fairly important foundation excavations.

routing The cutting away of any unnecessary parts that would interfere with the usefulness or mar the appearance of a piece of millwork.

roving A fiberglass reinforcing material (put on with spray application) for roofing.

row house A house of a row joined to its

neighbors by party walls and covered by the same roof; some townhouses are so constructed.

rowlock or rolok   A masonry unit laid on its face edge so that the normal end is visible in the wall face; sometimes called bullheaders.

rowlock arch   An arch of brick used chiefly as a relieving arch and formed of concentric courses of headers.

rowlock-back wall   A brick wall with face laid on bed and backed with bricks laid on edge.

rowlock cavity wall (rat-trap bond)   Cavity wall of brick in which all brick in both withes are laid on edge.

rows (wires)   Rows of tufts counting lengthwise in one inch of carpet. In Axminster carpets, these are called rows; in Wilton and velvet, wires.

row shooting   In a large blast, setting off the row of holes nearest the face first and other rows behind it in succession. *(see rotation firing)*

rubbed brick   Brick selected for color and rubbed to a smooth surface on one or two vertical faces, as for window and door jambs and heads; gauged brick.

rubbed finish   A finish obtained by using an abrasive to remove surface irregularities from concrete. *(see sack rub)*

rubbed joint   A strong joint between two narrow boards glued to make one wide board. Both boards are planed smooth with a jointer, coated with glue and rubbed together tightly until no more glue and air can be expelled. No clamping is needed.

rubber   (1) A rubbed brick. (2) British term for concrete or masonry finisher. (3) A cushioned carpet back which may be applied in various forms, such as contoured, compressed or slab. Also, as a separate rug or carpet cushion.

rubber-emulsion paint   Paint, the vehicle of which consists of rubber or synthetic rubber dispersed in fine droplets in water.

rubber guts   *(slang)* An insulation protector used to put over energized wire.

rubber set   *(see false set)*

rubber tired rollers   Pneumatic-tired rollers.

rubbing   A finishing of concrete surface: the form boards are removed and the surface rubbed down at once with a carborundum brick and plain water or a paste of water and cement.

rubbing iron   *(slang)* Saw.

rubbing varnish   In painting, a flatting varnish.

rubbish pully   A gin block.

rubble   Rough, broken stone used in uncoursed work of walls or for other fillings; rough broken stone direct from the quarry.

rubble ashlar   An ashlar-faced wall filled with rubble.

rubble concrete   (1) Concrete similar to cyclopean concrete except that small stones, such as one man can handle, are used. *(see cyclopean concrete)* (2) Concrete made with rubble from demolished structures.

rubble drain   *(see French drain)*

rubble masonry   Masonry walls built of unsquared or rudely squared stones, irregular in size and shape; also, uncut stone used for rough work, such as for backing of unfinished masonry walls.

rubble-mound breakwater (mound breakwater)   One of two main types of breakwater. It is built of extremely large stones dumped on top of each other at slopes which are nearly flat between tide marks and about 1½-horizontal to 1-vertical at depths greater than 15 feet below low water. Underwater rubble is sometimes stabilized by grouting it with fluid bitumen and sand.

rubblework   Masonry built of rubble or roughly dressed stones laid in irregular courses.

rub brick   A silicon-carbide brick used to smooth and remove irregularities from hardened concrete surfaces.

Ruberoid roofing   Brand name of a covering for roofs and exterior side walls.

rubrication   The coloring, especially in red, of a background by use of enamel or other paints.

rub-test   A test devised to determine

how firmly granules are embedded in the surface coating on roofing.

rudenture Decorative feature similar to cable but frequently used on a shaft without the flutings; frequently used to fill up the flutings of columns, the convexity of which contrasts with the concavity of the flutings and serves to strengthen the edges. They are generally only used in columns which rise from the ground and do not reach above one-third the height of the shaft.

ruderation In paving with mortar and pebbles, ground well tamped or rolled to make it firm, with a stratum of pebbles laid upon a cement screed, to be pressed into it afterward.

rule (1) A straight edge of any length or construction, for measuring, for drawing straight lines or for laying out on the site. (2) In plastering, a straight edge for working plaster to a plane surface or for other purposes. They are of several types: floating rules, joint rules, levelling rules, running rules.

rule joint In woodworking, a pivoted joint where two flat strips are joined end to end so that each strip will turn or fold only in one direction. An example is the ordinary two-foot folding rule used by carpenters and other woodworkers.

rule of thumb A statement or formula that is not exactly correct but is accurate enough for use in rough figuring.

ruling pen A draftsman's instrument with which ink lines are drawn.

rumble Sections of roadway with uneven paint line or button marker to produce an audible warning to motorists.

Rumford fireplace A type invented by Count Rumford to throw more heat into the room and less up the chimney.

run (1) In plumbing, that part of a pipe or fitting which continues in the same straight line as the direction of flow in the pipe to which it is connected. (2) In building, a gangway especially for the passage of wheelbarrows conveying materials. (3) In roofs, the horizontal distance between the face of a wall and ridge of the roof. (4) Referring to stairways, the net width of a step; also the

horizontal distance covered by a flight of stairs. (5) To pass plaster or lime putty through a sieve. (6) In paint, a narrow ridge which has flowed down from a small bulb or teardrop at the lower edge of the painted area. (7) A term used in reference to a steady run of jobs following one another in rapid succession. (8) Subdivision of a test, corresponding to one-date observation at a single point in a sample location.

runby, bottom elevator car The distance between the car buffer striker plate and the striking surface of the car buffer when the car floor is level with the bottom terminal landing.

runby, bottom elevator counterweight The distance between the counterweight buffer striker plate and the striking surface of the counterweight buffer when the car floor is level with the top terminal landing.

runby, top direct-plunger hydraulic elevator The distance the elevator car can run above its top terminal landing before the plunger strikes its mechanical stop.

rung (round) The horizontal bar or step of a ladder.

run levels To survey an area or strip to determine elevations.

run line A painting term for the straight line painted by using a lining tool and straight edge, or by stencilling.

runner (1) The lengthwise horizontal bracing or bearing members or both. (2) The guide in front of a plow. (3) The rotating part of a turbine on a water wheel. (4) A channel used to anchor metal studs at the floor and ceiling.

runners Vertical sheet timber piles driven in by hand ahead of the digging at the edge of an excavation.

running (1) Operating, particularly a drill but used with reference to many types of equipment. (2) A plastering process of slaking lime and pouring the milk of lime formed through a sieve into a pit for maturing. (3) Forming a molding, such as a cornice, in place with a horsed mold.

running bond Brick bond consisting entirely of stretchers.

running ground Either water-bearing sand or very dry sand that will not stand up without sheeting.

running-off Applying the finish plaster coat to a molding.

running screed A narrow band of plaster used in place of a running rule when running a molding.

running shoes In plastering, metal pieces on a horsed mold where it touches the nib guide and running rule to enable the mold to slide easily and prevent wearing.

run number In wallpaper each printing is designated with a different run number shown on the bolt package. The run number and pattern number is used to reorder, to insure perfect color match.

runoff That part of precipitation carried off from the area upon which it falls; also the rate of surface discharge. Precipitation reaching a storm drain or sewer.

run-off coefficient The impermeability factor.

run period In boilers, point at which the timing stops and the burner is released to modulation.

run relay circuit That portion of the wiring diagram containing the hoist motor direction relays.

runway (1) Decking over areas of concrete placement, usually of movable panels and supports, on which buggies of concrete travel to points of placement. (2) A passageway for persons, elevated above the surrounding floor or ground level, such as a footwalk along shafting or a walkway between buildings.

rupture member A safety device which will automatically rupture at a predetermined pressure.

rusticated A texture of cut stone with the edges chamfered to emphasize recessed joints.

rustication (rustic work) A groove in a concrete or masonry surface. Masonry in which the principal face of each stone is rough, reticulated or vermiculated, with a margin tooled smooth along rectangular edges; or the principal face may be smooth and surrounded by a bevel margin returning to the face of the wall.

rustication strip A strip of wood or other material attached to a form surface to produce a groove or rustication in the concrete.

rustic finish (washed finish) A type of terrazzo topping in which the matrix is recessed by washing prior to setting so as to expose the chips without destroying the bond between chip and matrix; a retarder is sometimes applied to the surface to facilitate this operation. *(see exposed-aggregate finish)*

rustic joint A joint sunk in from the surface of the stone.

rustic siding Drop siding.

rustic woodwork Structures, wall panels or screens made of unpeeled logs and saplings.

rustic work (rock work) A mode of building in imitation of nature. The term is applied to courses of stone work whose face is jagged or picked so as to present a rough surface.

chamfered Work in which the face of the stones is smooth, and parallel to the face of the wall, and the angles beveled to an angle of 135° with the face so that two stones coming together on the wall will form beveling at an internal right angle.

frosted Margins of stones reduced to a plane parallel to the plane of the wall, with the intermediate area having an irregular surface.

vermiculated Rock having intermediate parts worked so as to have the appearance of having been eaten by worms.

rust joint In piping, a tight connection effected by induced rusting of the pipe ends; iron filings and sal ammoniac are used; obsolete usage.

rust pocket An access eye at the foot of a ventilating pipe where rust collects and from which it can be removed.

'R' Value The resistance to heat flow. The higher the 'R' Value, the more effective the insulation.

S   South, southern, subject, sulphur

SA   supply air

SAE   Society of Automotive Engineers

S&G   studs and girts

S&H   staple and hasp

sanit   sanitation

sat   saturate, saturation

sch   school

scp   spherical candlepower

SD   sea-damaged, standard deviation

S/D   shop drawings

SDA   specific dynamic action

Se   selenium

sec   second

sed   sediment

sel   select, selected

sep   separate

sf   surface foot, safety factor

S4S   surfaced four sides

sh   shingles

shf   superhigh frequency

shp   shaft horsepower

sht   sheet, sheath

Si   silicon

SIC   Standard Industrial Classification

sid   siding

sk   sack

sky   skylights

slid   sliding

s.mld.   stuck mold

so   south

SO   seller's option

soln   solution

sp   specific, specimen, spirit, single pitch (roof)

SP   self-propelled, single pole

sp. gr.   specific gravity

sp. ht.   specific heat

spl   spline

spr   spruce

SPT   Standard Penetration Test

sp. vol.   specific volume

sq   square

sq. e.   square edge

sq. ft.   square foot

sq. in.   square inch

sq. yd.   square yard

SR   sedimentation rate

ss   single strength (glass)

SS   stainless steel

sst   standing seam tin (roof)

st   stairs, stone, street

std   standard

STP   standard temperature and pressure

str   stringers

st. sash   steel sash

sty   story

sty. hgt.   story height

sub. fl.   subfloor

subpar   subparagraph

subsec   subsection

sup   supplementary, supplement

supp   supplement

supt   superintendent

supvr   supervisor

sur   surface

surv   survey, surveying, surveyor

svc   service

sw   switch

SW   seawater, southwest

SWG   standard wire gauge

sy jet   syphon jet (water closet)

syst   system

SAE The nominal inside diameter by which pipe is designated.

SCR brick A brick which lays up three courses to eight inches and measures, including joints, 2x6x12 inches. It can be used to make a six-inch thick wall.

sabin A unit of equivalent sound absorption equal to the equivalent absorption of one square foot of a surface of unit absorptivity (e.g., of one square foot of surface which absorbs all incident sound energy).

sack A quantity of cement; 94 pounds representing one cubic foot in the United States and 87.5 pounds in Canada. (see bag)

sack joint Joint that has been wiped or rubbed with a rag or object such as a rubber heel, a method of exterior finishing a flush cut joint.

sack rub A finish for formed concrete surfaces designed to produce even texture and fill all pits and air holes; after dampening the surface, mortar is rubbed over surface; before it dries, a mixture of dry cement and sand is rubbed over it with a wad of burlap or a sponge-rubber float to remove surplus mortar and fill voids.

sacrificial anodes Anodes used for cathodic protection.

sacrificial protection A property furnished in coatings of zinc, cadmium, aluminum, etc., to protect an iron surface, even though the coating may not cover the entire surface. The zinc, cadmium or aluminum is dissolved first by the water, like an anode in cathodic protection.

saddle (1) Fitting put on pipe usually with straps for holding corporation stop. (2) A threshold. (3) Short horizontal member set on top of a post to spread the load of a girder over it. (4) A tent shape built between a chimney and roof ridge to support flashing. (5) Bends in conduit needed to go over a surface obstruction such as another piece of pipe.

saddle bar An iron bar to which the cames of leaded glass are fastened for reinforcement.

saddle bead A glazing bead for attaching the glass to the sides of curved glazing bars.

saddle block In a dipper shovel, the boom swivel block through which the stick slides when crowded or retracted.

saddle joint (water joint) A saddle-shaped joint between stones in a cornice so as to throw water away from the joint.

saddle roof A gabled pitched roof.

saddle stone The apex stone in a gable.

safe (1) A strongbox. (2) A shallow pan with waste pipe, to gather and lead away an overflow.

safe carrying capacity A term used with reference to construction of any piece or part so it will carry the weight, or load, it is designed to support without breaking down.

safe-deposit vault A strong room, usually in a basement, to provide secure storage.

safe-edge A mechanical door protective and automatic door reopening device, used with electric power door operators. It is arranged so that in the event the elevator car door either approaches or meets an obstruction when closing, the safe-edge shall automatically stop and reopen. It is vertically mounted to extend from the bottom to the top of a door panel and projects forward of the leading edge of the panel.

safe leg load The load which can safely be directly imposed on the frame leg of a scaffold. (see allowable load)

safety Mechanical device attached to the elevator car or counterweight to stop and hold the car or counterweight when the elevator travels beyond a certain predetermined speed.

safety arch A relieving arch.

safety bulkhead A closure at the bottom of the cylinder located above the cylinder head and provided with an orifice for controlling the loss of fluid in the event of cylinder head failure.

safety can An approved closed container, of not more than five gallons capacity, having a flash-arresting screen, spring-closing lid and spout cover and so designed that it will safely relieve internal pressure when subjected to fire exposure.

safety, car or counterweight   A mechanical device attached to the car frame or to an auxiliary frame, or to the counterweight frame, to stop and hold the car or counterweight in case of predetermined overspeed or free fall, or if the hoisting ropes slacken.

safety circuit   *(see basic safety circuit)*

safety clutch   A clutch that slips instead of transmitting loads beyond the capacity of the machine.

safety edge   *(see safe-edge)*

safety factor   The ratio of the ultimate breaking strength of a member or piece of material or equipment to the actual working stress or safe load when in use.

safety fuse   A flexible cord containing an internal burning medium by which fire is conveyed at a continuous and uniform rate for the purpose of firing blasting caps.

safety glass   A laminate consisting of two or more sheets of flat glass, usually plate or sheet, with an intermediate layer of transparent plastic bonded together by a heat and pressure treatment.

safety head   In a compressor, a cylinder head held in place by a spring of such strength that it will not be compressed during normal operation, but will be moved by solid or liquid matter or abnormal gas pressure between it and the piston, thereby protecting the compressor.

safety lintel   A load-carrying lintel, used to protect another more decorative lintel.

safety-operated switch   A mechanically operated switch that removes power from the elevator motor when the safety mechanism is actuated.

safety plank   The bottom member of the elevator carframe, which contains the car guide shoes and required safety equipment.

safety plank switch   *(see safety-operated switch)*

safety rail   *(see check rail)*

safety releasing carrier   A clamping device usually attached to the elevator car crosshead. It prevents the accidental application of the safeties due to a momentary unbalance of inertia between the governor rope system and the car.

safety screen   An air and water tight diaphragm placed across the upper part of a compressed air tunnel between the face and bulkhead in order to prevent flooding the crown of the tunnel between the safety screen and the bulkhead, thus providing a safe means of refuge and exit from a flooding or flooded tunnel.

safety shoe   *(see safe-edge)*

safety valve   A mechanical valve designed to open automatically at a given pressure; used for water, steam, air, etc.

safing   A non-combustible product used at the perimeter of floor and around other penetrations as a fire barrier.

safing off   Installation of the fire safety insulation around floor perimeters between floor slab and spandrel panels and in 'poke-thru' openings in walls and floors. Insulation helps retain integrity of fire resistance ratings.

sag   To sink, droop or settle below a level line.

sag bar   A bar to prevent sagging.

sagging   (1) Subsidence of material from the gunned surface of a sloping or vertical concrete structural member or from the gunned surface of an overhead horizontal shotcrete structural member. *(see sloughing)* (2) In painting, the same as curtaining.

sagitta   Obsolete term for the keystone of an arch.

sag rod   A tension member used to limit the deflection of a girt or purlin in the direction of the weak axis.

sailer   A masonry unit laid on end with the normal bed surface showing on the wall surface.

sailing course   (oversailing course) A string course.

salamander   A small steel fire basket used to keep newly poured concrete above freezing so that it can set; also used as an aid in drying plastered walls.

sal ammoniac Solid ammonia used for cleaning and tinning soldering irons.

sales square The amount of material sold as a unit to cover 100 square feet of roof surface.

salient A projecting mass.

salinometer Hydrometer calibrated in salt concentration.

sally A re-entrant angle cut in a timber. *(see birdsmouth joint)*

salmon brick One of the more lightly burned upper bricks of a kiln.

salon A reception room; an exhibition room.

saloon (1) The public room of a passenger vessel. (2) A place for the sale and consumption of liquors.

salt and pepper blend Two or more different colored granules combined in a mix prior to application to a sheet of composition roofing or shingles.

salt glaze A gloss finish obtained by thermochemical reaction between silicates of clay and vapors of salt or chemicals.

saltpetering *(see efflorescence)*

sampler (mechanical sampler; sample splitter) (1) A device for reducing a crushed sample to a representative sample which can be handled in the laboratory. It may also be a device for taking samples at intervals from a stream of material. (2) An instrument for examining the deepest water in hydrographic surveying.

samples (1) Physical examples furnished by the contractor for the architect's or engineer's review and approval, which illustrate materials, equipment or workmanship, and which establish standards by which the work will be judged. (2) A small amount of rock or other material to by analyzed for its content.

sampling train Series of devices into which a stack gas of known volume is withdrawn to facilitate sample collection and analysis.

sanatorium A building for convalescent invalids; also spelled sanitarium.

sanctuary That part of a church where the principal altar is situated.

sand (a) Granular material passing the 3/8 inch (9.52 mm) sieve and almost entirely passing the No. 4 (4.76 mm) sieve and predominantly retained on the No. 200 (74 micron) sieve, and resulting from natural disintegration and abrasion of rock or processing of completely friable sandstone. (b) That portion of an aggregate passing the No. 4 (4.76 mm) sieve and predominantly retained on the No. 200 (74 micron) sieve, and resulting from natural disintegration and abrasion of rock or processing of completely friable sandstone. Note: The definitions are alternatives to be applied under differing circumstances. Definition (a) is applied to an entire aggregate either in a natural condition or after processing. Definition (b) is applied to a portion of an aggregate. Requirements for properties and grading should be stated in specifications. Fine aggregate produced by crushing rock, gravel, or slag is commonly known as manufactured sand. *(see fine aggregate; critical voids ratio)*

sand asphalt A mixture of local sand passing a ⅜ inch or ⅛ inch sieve and asphalt cement or liquid asphalt without special control of sand grading; either hot plant mix or cold mix-in-place or plant mix; used for low cost base and surfaces.

sand blast A system of cutting or abrading a surface such as concrete by a stream of sand ejected from a nozzle at high speed by compressed air; often used for cleanup of horizontal construction joints or for architectural exposure of aggregate.

sand box (sand jack) A tight box filled with clean, dry sand on which rests a tight-fitting timber plunger that supports the bottom of posts used in centering; removal of a plug from a hole near the bottom of the box permits the sand to run out when it is necessary to lower the centering.

sand catcher (sand-grain meter) A hydrographic instrument through which water flows and sand is trapped.

The instrument is brought up to the surface and sand quantity measured.

sand clay   A natural material found in many states which has the natural properties for a fine base or sub-base. The term sand clay is used because it is basically a well graded sand with about 10 percent clay, or just enough to make the material bind tightly when compacted.

sand-course aggregate ratio   Ratio of fine to coarse aggregate in a batch of concrete, by weight or volume.

sand down   To remove the gloss of an old finish and smooth it prior to refinishing.

sand-dry surface   Painting term for a surface on which sand will not stick.

sanded bitumen felt (mineral surface felt   A bitumen roofing felt which is saturated with bitumen and embedded with sand-like granules.

sand equivalent   A measure of the amount of clay contamination in fine aggregate.

sand filter   A domestic water cleansing filter through which water flows downwards. It consists of layers of coarse stone, coarse gravel, sand becoming finer toward the top, where it is a layer of clean quartz grains of nearly uniform size. Water is allowed to flow slowly through; the upper layers become clogged with bacteria but are replaced periodically. Also a filter working on the same principle as above but with a coarser sand for purifying sewage effluent.

sand finish   A final coat of plastering, usually of lime and sand, floated smooth.

sand grout   Generally, any portland cement grout in which fine aggregate is incorporated into the mixture. Also termed sanded grout.

sandhog   *(slang)* A laborer who works under compressed air, as in a caisson.

sanding   **(1)** Sandpapering wood to a smooth surface. **(2)** To apply sand to a surface, such as sand on an oiled road surface.

sanding machine (sander)   An electrically or mechanically powered machine used for smoothing wooden surfaces with sandpaper or other abrasives. Sanders may either be portable or bench sanders.

sanding pole   A sandpaper holder affixed to the end of a handle with a swivel to aid in the sanding process.

sanding sealer   A hard first coat of paint which seals or fills but does not hide the grain of wood. The surface can still be sanded after sanding sealer is applied. *(see filler; sealer)*

sand interceptor (sand trap)   A watertight receptacle designed and constructed to intercept and prevent the passage of sand or other solids into the drainage system to which it is directly or indirectly connected.

sand island   A temporary pier of sand in a river made by driving sheet piles in an enclosure and filling it with sand; it eliminates strong currents so that a caisson or pipe pile can be dropped accurately through the sand island to the river bed.

sand jack   *(see sand box)*

sand-lime brick   *(see calcium-silicate brick)*

sandpaper   Abrasive paper of various textures used by hand or on sanding machines.

sand piles   A way of deep compaction of soil by dropping a heavy weight such as a pile-drive ram into it. The ram makes a hole into which sand is poured. The ram then drives the sand deeper and the process is repeated as required. If done with a damp concrete, the process makes a driven cast-in-place pile. *(see vibroflot)*

sand pump (bailer; shell pump; sludger)   A long tube, open at the top and fitted with a check valve at the bottom. It is lowered into a borehole to extract mud and cuttings.

sand pump dredger   A suction dredger.

sand seal   An application, approximately 0.25 gallons per square yard of material, often a rapid curing cutback, covered by approximately 10 to 20 pounds per square yard of sand cover; very effective for airport runways.

sandstone A sedimentary rock consisting usually of quartz cemented with silica, iron oxide, or calcium carbonate.

sand streak Streak in the surface of formed concrete caused by bleeding.

sand trap A device, often a simple enlargement, in a conduit for arresting the sand, silt, etc., carried by the water and generally including means of ejecting them from the conduit.

sandwich (structural sandwich) A strongly bonded union of two thin, strong, hard outer skins with a core of relatively lightweight material possessing insulating properties; the sheet used in walls, partitions and roofs.

sandwich beam Flitched beam.

sandwich construction Composite construction of light alloys, plastics, plasterboard, etc., generally of a hard outer sheet glued to an inner core of foam plastics or paper honeycomb. Extremely strong, in relation to weight, particularly if deliberately arched or otherwise shaped.

sandwich panel A non-composite panel assembly used as covering; consists of an insulating core material with inner and outer skins.

sanitarium *(see sanatorium)*

sanitary engineering The science of guarding health through proper water supply, sewerage, and the like in the individual building and in a far broader field in public utilities, municipal, county and state works.

sanitary sewage Domestic sewage with storm water excluded by design; sewage originating in the sanitary conveniences of a dwelling, business, building, factory or institution; the water supply of a community after it has been used and discharged into a sewer.

sanitary sewer A sewer carrying only waste matter, not surface water.

santorin earth A volcanic tuff used as a pozzolan.

sap (1) In woody plants, the watery circulating fluid which is necessary to

their growth. (2) The moisture in freshly quarried stone.

saponify To turn to soap, as oil in contact with an alkali or alkaline refrigerant. Chemically, to cause an ester to react with an inorganic base, the products being an alcohol and an acid (either free or in the form of salt). By extension, to hydrolyse compounds other than esters.

sap streaks Streaks showing through a finished wood surface which contains sapwood. Such streaks must be toned out in order to secure a uniform finish.

sap wood The portion of a tree just beneath the bark, consisting of the newest growth.

SARA Superfund Amendments and Reauthorization Act (SARA) of 1986.

sarcophagus A stone tomb of coffin size or larger.

sash The framework which holds the glass in a window or door.

sash and frame A cased frame and a sash window.

sash balance A device, usually operated with a spring, designed to counterbalance window sash. Use of sash balances eliminates the need for sash weights, pulleys and sash cord.

sash bar A muntin; strips which separate the panes of glass in a window sash.

sash chain In a double-hung window sash, the chain which carries the weights; used especially on heavy sash; same as sash cord.

sash chisel A pocket chisel.

sash cord A small rope attaching one side of a window sash to its counterweight. *(see sash chain)*

sash door Any door which has the upper portion glazed.

sash pin A heavy-gauge barbed headless nail or pin used to fasten the mortise-and-tenon joints of window sash and doors.

sash pulley In a window frame, the small pulley over which the sash cord or chain runs.

sash run *(see pulley stile)*

sash weight A counterweight for a window sash.

sash window (vertical sash) A window in which the window panes slide up and down in a cased frame, balanced by sash cords passing over a sash pulley.

satellite In urban planning, an outlying community unit of secondary importance, dependent upon the larger city.

saturant The asphaltic material used to impregnate, or saturate, the felt used in roofing materials.

saturated Thoroughly soaked. When used in connection with composition roofing, it means the soaking of the felt base with asphalt.

saturated air Air containing the greatest possible amount of water vapor at a given temperature; a relative humidity of 100 percent.

saturated felt A felt which is impregnated with tar or asphalt.

saturated surface dry Condition of an aggregate particle or other porous solid when the permeable voids are filled with water and no water is on the exposed surfaces.

saturation (1) The percentage of hue in a color. Factors in color are hue, saturation and brightness. (2) The condition for coexistence in stable equilibrium of a vapor and liquid or a vapor and solid phase of the same substance. Example: Steam over the water from which it is being generated. (3) In a transistor or electron tube, a condition in which the output current has reached the maximum value it can attain.

saturation coefficient *(see C/B ratio)*

saturation, degree of The ratio of the weight of water vapor associated with a pound of dry air to the weight of water vapor associated with a pound of dry air saturated at the same temperature.

saturation line The existing water table.

saturation ratio *(see saturation, degree of)*

saucer dome A glass or plastic dome molded in a single piece like an overturned saucer; used as a roof light.

saw A steel blade for cutting wood, stone or metal. Major power-driven saws for wood are circular, band or jig saws. Hacksaws are used for metal cutting. For hard stone, frame-saws like large hacksaws, or circular saws with diamond cutting edges are used. *(see handsaw)*

saw arbor The spindle, or shaft, on which a circular saw is mounted.

saw bench A table or framework for carrying a circular saw.

saw cut A cut in hardened concrete utilizing diamond or silicone-carbide blades or discs.

sawdust concrete Concrete in which the aggregate consists mainly of wood sawdust.

sawdust pump *(slang)* A brace and bit used for drilling holes in wood.

sawed joint A joint cut in hardened concrete, generally not to the full depth of the member, by means of special equipment utilizing diamond or silicon-carbide blades or discs.

saw gullet The throat at the bottom of the teeth of a circular saw.

saw gumming Shaping the teeth of a circular saw. Usually a grinding process.

saw horse A four-legged bench made primarily for use while hand sawing. The legs are usually an inverted V with the top a 2x4 or 2x6 inch piece of lumber.

saw set An instrument used for giving set to saw teeth.

saw-toothed skylight In architecture, a term applied to a skylight roof with its profile shaped like the teeth of a saw.

saw-toothed roof a roof composed of a series of single-pitch roofs whose shorter or vertical side has windows for light and air.

sawyer One whose occupation is that of sawing wood or other material; sometimes used in a restricted sense meaning one who operates one of several saws.

saxony finish Dense cut-pile, usually made of plied and heat set yarns, so each tuft end has distinguished appearance.

saybolt A type of laboratory equipment used to measure the viscosity of petroleum materials at controlled temperature through a known size of aperture such as asphalt tip, Furol tip or universal tip.

scab (1) A small piece of wood fastened to two formwork members to secure a butt joint. (2) *(slang)* One who works for less than union wages, on non-union terms; or a worker who accepts employment or replaces a union worker during a strike.

scabbing (1) Loss of patches of surfacing from a road. (2) Replacing a union worker during a strike; working non-union.

scabble To dress off the rougher projections of stones for rubble masonry with a stone, axe or scabbling hammer.

scaffold Any temporary elevated platform and its supporting structure used for supporting workmen or materials, or both.

scaffold height The height of the wall which requires another raising of the scaffold to continue the building of the wall.

scagliola An imitation marble made by the plasterer. Composed of a combination of Keene's cement, glue, isinglass and coloring material. It takes a high durable polish.

scale (1) A measuring strip as an aid in proportional drafting. (2) In architecture, harmonious relationship of parts to one another and to the human figure.

scale drawing A drawing made to a size other than the actual size of the object represented; a drawing provided by the architect or engineer wherein all construction details are produced in miniature to scale, e.g., one inch equals one foot.

scaler Worker who cleans rock slope faces and removes loose rock from slope surfaces.

scaling (1) Peeling away of surface of concrete. (2) Prying loose pieces of rock off a face or roof to avoid danger of their falling unexpectedly. (3) Measuring dimensions from a proportional drawing by comparison with a scale.

scallops The up-and-down uneven effect along the edge of carpet caused by indentations where tacks are driven.

scalper A screen for removing oversize particles.

scalping The removal of particles larger than a specified size by screening.

scalping screen A vibrating grizzly.

scalp rock Rock which has passed over a screen and was rejected; sometimes called waste rock.

scanning line frequency The number of lines scanned by an infrared scanner per second. The number of lines in a TV picture divided by the number of times per second that the picture is repeated.

scantle A strip of wood or metal with two nails projecting from it to mark the position of, and line up, a hole measured from the back of slate.

scantling The dimensions of a piece of timber in breadth and thickness; also, studding for a partition when under five inches square; roughsawn timbers.

scared strap *(slang)* A rigger's or ironworker's safety belt.

scarf To cut the ends of reinforcing steel in preparation for mechanical splicing.

scarf (scarf joint) A lapped joint for timber, in variations.

scarfing The joining and bolting of two pieces of timber so they appear as one.

scarifier An accessory on a grader, roller or other machine used chiefly for shallow loosening of road surfaces.

scarify To make scratches or small cuts in; to break up and loosen the surface of; to cut or soften the wall of. *(see score)*

scavenge (1) To clean out thoroughly. (2) To pick up surplus fluid and return it to a circulating system.

schedule A listing of parts or details.

schedule of dilapidations *(see punch list)*

schedule of values A statement furnished by the contractor to the architect or engineer reflecting the portions of the contract sum allotted for the various parts of the work and used as the basis for reviewing the contractor's applications for progress payments.

scheduler The person authorized to schedule work or the flow of material pertaining to a project.

schematic A drawing or presentation showing principles of construction or operation without accurate mechanical representation.

schematic design phase The first phase of the architect's basic services. In this phase, the architect consults with the owner to ascertain the requirements of the project and prepares schematic design studies consisting of drawings and other documents illustrating the scale and relationship of the project components for approval by the owner. A statement of probable construction cost is also submitted at this time.

scheme The chief elements of a composition and their interrelationship; usually the preliminary stage of a design; a parti.

scheme arch (skene arch) A segmental arch.

schist Roughly, a rock or building stone that splits.

Schmidt hammer A device for the nondestructive testing of hardened concrete; based on the principle that the rebound of a steel hammer, after impact against the concrete, is proportional to the compressive strength of the concrete.

Schoklitsch formula Used to find amount of water lost to seepage through a dam.

scissors truss A form of truss which serves without a bottom horizontal chord.

scleroscope hardness test Estimating the hardness of metal by measuring the rebound of a standard diamond-tipped hammer.

scobey chart Graphical representation of Kutter's formula for determining flow in open channels.

sconce (1) A detached defensive work; (2) A protective cover or screen; (3) A bracket candlestick or group of candlesticks; (4) An electric light fixture patterned after bracket candlestick.

sconcheon That portion of the side of an aperture extending from the back of the reveal to the inner face of the wall.

scoop feeder Slurry feeder for rotary kiln, consisting of a casing in which the slurry is maintained at a constant level, and a slow-moving wheel with two hollow scoops discharging through the hollow shaft. Also, dust scoop feeder which places kiln return dust into the mid section of the kiln by means of scoops and ports arranged around the kiln circumference.

score To scarify a surface to make a better bond for the plaster or cement which is to follow.

scoria Lava with numerous cavities; particles of volcanic origin usually found in the western United States; used for base course and seal coating in highway construction, cinder block production and landscaping.

scoring (1) Partial cutting of concrete flat work for the control of shrinkage cracking. Also used to describe the roughening of a slab to develop mechanical bond. (2) Marking with a sharp tool.

Scotch bond *(see American bond)*

Scotch bracketing In plastering, lath cut to length and attached at a slope from wall to ceiling as a base for a hollow plaster cornice; a form of cradling.

scotia A concave molding with profile similar to a section of a parabola.

scour (1) Removal of sand or earth from the bottom or banks of a river by the erosive action of flowing water. (2) Erosion of a concrete surface, exposing the aggregate. (3) To give plaster a smooth hard surface by working with a cross-grained float.

scouring sluice An opening in a dam controlled by a gate through which the accumulated silt, sand and gravel may be ejected.

scour protection Protection of submerged earth or other material by sheet piling, revetments, rip rap, brushwood mattress or a combination of methods.

SCR (silicon controlled rectifier) A semiconductor device that conducts in the forward direction only under controlled conditions.

scraper (carrying scraper; pan) A digging, hauling and grading machine having a cutting edge, a carrying bowl, a movable front wall or apron and a dumping or ejecting mechanism.

  drag A digging bucket, operated on a cable between a mast and an anchor, that is not lifted off the ground during a normal cycle; a two wheel tractor-towed scraper equipped with a bottomless bucket.

  rear dump A two wheel scraper that dumps in the rear.

  self-powered A scraper built into a single unit with a tractor.

  two axle A full trailer-type carrying scraper.

scraper excavator An excavator with multiple buckets.

scratch awl A tool, used for marking on metal or wood, made from a sharp-pointed piece of steel.

scratch coat The first coat of plaster or stucco applied to a surface in three-coat work; usually cross raked or scratched to form a mechanical key with the brown, or second, coat.

scratch course A course separated from the binder course; placed on the base to overcome deficiencies or to adjust grade or superelevation.

scratch double-up *(see double-up)*

scratcher Tool used to detect rock defects in a core hole.

scratch tool A small plastering tool for completing embellishments.

scratch work Graffito; sgraffito.

screed (1) On a laydown machine, a flat plate on the rear of the equipment which is pulled over asphaltic concrete to smooth it and give it initial compaction. (2) (a) Firmly established grade strips or side forms for unformed concrete which will guide the strike off

in producing the desired plane or shape. (b) To strike off concrete lying above the desired plane or shape. (c) A tool for striking off the concrete surface, preferably called a strikeoff. (3) A layer of mortar laid to finish a floor surface or as a bed for floor tiles. (4) A device or material run across the base surface of a wall or ceiling to serve as thickness and alignment guides for the plasterer in subsequent applications. Plaster screeds are generally about 4 wide and of full basecoat thickness.

screed rail A heavy rule used for forming concrete or mortar surfaces to the desired level or shape.

screed wire *(see ground wire)*

screen (1) A thin partition, often with openwork; insect screen; wiremesh protection for door and window openings. (2) A metallic plate or sheet, woven wire cloth, or other similar device, with regularly spaced apertures of uniform size, mounted in a suitable frame or holder for use in separating material according to size; in mechanical analysis an apparatus with square openings is a sieve.

  deck Two or more screens placed one above the other for successive processing of the same run of material.

  scalping A coarse primary screen or grizzly.

  shaking A screen that is moved with a back and forth or rotating motion to move material along it and through it.

  vibrating A screen that is vibrated to move material along and through it.

screen analysis *(see sieve analysis)*

screened material Material which has passed over or through a screen.

screenings Rejects from screening, either undersize or oversize.

screw (set screw) A metal rod enlarged at one end into a head, with a screw thread cut or forged on the full length of the shank. On a bolt, the thread does not run the full length.

screw anchor A bushing of fiber, plastic or lead which, pushed into a hole in a plaster or masonry wall, expands to lock tightly when a screw is driven into it; a molly.

screw auger Any auger used for carpentry, soil mechanics or other purposes.

screw chunk A device for holding work in a wood-turning lathe, with a projecting screw as live center.

screw clamp A woodworker's clamp consisting of two parallel jaws and two screws; the clamping action is obtained by means of the screws, one operating through each jaw.

screw conveyor (1) Conveyor for dry material or slurry consisting of a steel or concrete casing enclosing a continuous helical strip projecting from a rotating shaft. (2) *(see helical conveyor)*

screwdriver A tool used for driving in or removing screws by turning them; made of a well-tempered steel bar or rod, flattened or shaped at one end to fit into the slots in screw heads. The steel bar is fitted into a handle of wood, plastic, etc., often reinforced to prevent splitting.

screw eye A screw with a head shaped into a completely closed ring, forming a loop or eye.

screw feeder Short screw conveyor arranged for feeding dry pulverulent material.

screw gun A hand held device resembling an electrical drill designed or adapted to mechanically drive and set screws.

screw jacks Jacks operated by screw action; used with base plates or casters where floors or formwork are uneven, or where a fine adjustment in height is required.

screw nail A screw designed to be driven by hammering.

screw-on bead (stop) In glazing, a stop, molding or bead fastened by machine screws as compared with those that snap into position without additional fastening.

screw plug (disk plug) An expanding rubber ring used to block the end of a length of drain when the two steel plates on each side of it are screwed together in a drain test.

screws *(slang)* Caisson disease or bends.

screw stair A spiral staircase built around a slender pole.

screw threads The helical ridge of a screw.

scribe (1) To cut the edge of a member in an irregular line so as to fit it snugly against another, as around moldings or against masonry. (2) Procedure for scoring the floor covering to facilitate and achieve accuracy when cutting for fitting.

scribe awl An awl used for marking on wood or metal.

scriber A carpentry tool, consisting of a compass of pressed steel with a pencil in one leg or end and a metal point in the other; used to draw a line to make the irregularities of a surface in fitting cabinets or other trim members to the wall or floor.

scribing Duplicating a wall's uneven contour on the surface of a panel; using an inexpensive 'scribe' or a drawing compass.

scrim Coarse canvas, cotton or metal mesh, used for covering the joints between board, sheet or slab coverings before they are plastered; also used as a reinforcement for fibrous plaster. *(see joint tape)*

scrim back A double back made of light, coarse fabric, cemented to a jute or kraftcord back in tufted construction.

scroll A volute; a band, usually in relief, to contain an inscription; a band of flowing ornament.

scrollwork In architecture, any decorative feature suggestive of an unfolding parchment roll. An example is the capital of the Greek Ionic order.

scrubber Type of dust collector in which dust-laden gases are cleaned by passing through fine sprays or high turbulence regions of water.

scrub board A skirting or base board.

sculptured A multi-level texture pattern.

scupper (1) Outlets for overflow of water in outside or court walls to drain the floor of water from automatic sprinklers or fire hose in case of fire. (2) An opening in a wall or parapet that allows the water to drain from a roof. (3) A device placed in such an opening to prevent clogging of the drain.

scuppers A steel catch basin located on the low point of the bridge slab which is designed to drain water off the slab.

scutch A bricklayer's tool with a cutting edge on each side, used for dressing, cutting and trimming masonry units. It resembles a small pick and is sometimes called a scotch.

scutcheon (see escutcheon)

scuttle A framed opening in a wall, ceiling or roof, fitted with a lid or cover.

seal (1) To permanently close off the bottom of a cylinder, caisson or other excavation by pouring in grout or concrete so that water or earth cannot flow in. (2) To apply an inner wall surface, as of plaster or matched boards. (3) The water head in a plumbing trap. (4) In manhole covers, the airtight joint between the cover and the frame. (5) An impression device, used in the execution of a formal legal document such as a deed or contract. The statute of limitations applicable to a contract under seal is ordinarily longer than to a contract not under seal. (6) An embossing device or stamp used by a design professional on drawings and specifications as evidence of his registration in the state where the work is to be performed. (7) Metal bellows used in a shaft seal, or in place of a packing for valves. Also used in long pipelines instead of gaskets to compensate for expansion of the line with temperature. (8) A rubbing seal or stuffing box used to prevent fluid leakage between the shaft and bearing of a compressor or other fluidmoving device.

sealant (sealing compound) (1) A fluid placed over a joint surface or the outside of a joint filler to exclude water. (2) A coating of plastic, such as epoxy resin or polyurethane, painted on form linings or formwork to allow for reuse of forms. (3) A treatment for a set concrete floor, strengthening the concrete surface or binding the aggregate and insuring that it does not dust. (4) An elastomeric material that is used to fill and seal the expansion joint. This material prevents the passage of moisture and allows horizontal and laterial movement at the expansion joint.

seal coat Bituminous coating applied to surface of pavement to water-proof and preserve surface and to provide resistance to traffic abrasion; seldom over ½ inch thick.

sealed bearing Conventional bearings with seals on both sides of the bearing. The seals help to retain the grease within the bearing so that the bearing can be used for long periods without being regreased.

sealed bid An offer, submitted sealed for opening at a designated time and place, to furnish all the necessary services and materials, and to perform the work set forth by the contract documents.

sealed hydraulic system A leakproof hydraulic system with the oil at rest.

sealer (sealing coat) Liquids, some transparent, used like size as priming coats to close the pores of wood, plaster and other building materials; a liquid laid over bitumen, creosote, etc., to prevent it from bleeding through other paints. The sealer must be insoluble in the paint applied over it, and must not dissolve the material under it.

sea-level correction An engineering process of deduction from the measured length of a base line above sea level to bring it to its value at sea level.

sealing compound (see joint sealant; membrane curing)

sealing washer A metal-backed rubber washer assembled on a screw to prevent water from migrating through the screw hole.

seam (1) A layer of rock, coal or ore. (2) A joint, as a sheet metal joint.

seam sealing Procedure for welding seams of vinyl sheet goods, using special applicator and sealant. Properly applied, welds the wearlayers for appearance, elimination of soiled seams and elimination of moisture penetration.

seam strength Strength of a seam of material measured either in shear or peel modes.

seam welding Resistance welding of seams and joints.

seasonal efficiency The ratio of the solar energy collected and used to the solar energy striking the collector; measured over an entire heating season.

seasoning (1) Drying timber to a specified moisture content by natural or kiln seasoning. (2) The hardening and drying of stone.

seat angle A small steel angle riveted to one member to support the end of a beam or girder.

seat cut The cut at the building line on the hip rafter.

seating A surface carrying a heavy load.

seat of settlement The soil thickness below a loaded foundation within which 75 percent of the settlement occurs.

seawall A retaining structure that is subjected to earth pressure on one side and wave thrust on the other.

secant modulus *(see modulus of elasticity)*

secondary air That part of the combustion air in a rotary kiln which is not blown in with the fuel. Usually derived from heated clinker cooler quench air.

secondary backing Backing material laminated to underside of carpet for additional dimensional stability and body. Usually latex foam, jute, polypropylene or vinyl.

secondary beam Any beam carried by other beams, not by columns or walls.

secondary blasting A reduction, by the use of explosives, of oversize material to the dimension required for handling; including mudcapping and blockholing.

secondary branch Any branch of the building drain other than a primary branch.

secondary combustion Burning which takes place in the kiln beyond the actual burning zone. May be caused by too coarsely ground coal or inadequate mixing of fuel and combustion air.

secondary crusher A crusher used for the second stage in a process of size reduction. *(see primary crusher)*

secondary drilling Drilling of holes for explosive charges in pieces of rock which have been blasted loose during primary shooting in quarries, but which are still too large for feeding to primary crushers.

secondary level The enclosed space just below the machine room in certain elevator installations. The deflector and secondary sheaves, when used, are located here. Sometimes, other machine room equipment is located here when sufficient space is not available in the machine room.

secondary members Members which carry loads to the primary members. In a metal building system, this term includes purlins, girts, struts, diagonal bracing, wind bents, flange, and knee braces, headers, jambs, sag members, and other miscellaneous framing.

secondary moment In statically indeterminate structures, the additional moments caused by deformation of the structure due to the applied forces.

secondary nuclear vessel Exterior container or safety container in a nuclear reactor subjected to design load only once in its lifetime.

secondary sheave A steel sheave used to enable double wrapping of hoisting ropes to increase the traction. It may also be used to deflect the ropes if necessary.

secondary winding Winding of a transformer normally connected to the load circuit.

second-foot In hydraulics, a unit of flow; one cusec.

second moment of area A technically correct term for moment of inertia of a section.

seconds (1) Any second-quality material but particularly clayware such as bricks and drain pipes. (2) Division of minutes of an angle (60 seconds = 1 minute, 60 minutes = 1 degree).

secret dovetailing A dovetail joint on a miter where the wood on the exposed face is undisturbed.

secret fixing Attaching joinery by means which cannot be seen at the surface; methods include secret screwing and secret nailing.

secret gutter (closed valley) A nearly hidden valley gutter. It has the disadvantage of being easily clogged by leaves and debris.

secret nailing Used on flooring or matched sheathing where the nails are driven through the tongue but not the face; blind nailing.

secret screwing A method used in carpentry for making a wide board when only two narrow ones are available or for joints. Screws do not show on the finish face.

sectilia Paving with hexagonal units.

section (1) An area equal to 640 acres or one square mile. (2) A part of a work area or strip. (3) Metal rolling mill reference to flanged products. (4) A drawing of an object cut lengthwise to show the interior makeup. (5) A subdivision of a division of the specifications which should cover the work of no more than one trade.

sectional insulation *(see molded insulation)*

sectional modulus The moment of inertia of the area of a section of a member divided by the distance from the center of gravity to the outermost fiber.

sectional overhead doors Doors constructed in horizontally hinged sections. They are equipped with springs, tracks, counter balances, and other hardware which roll the sections into an overhead position, clear of the opening.

sectional properties End area per unit of width, moment of inertia, section modulus and radius of gyration.

section lines Thin, evenly spaced slant lines which are placed on the cut surfaces in section views.

section modulus A physical property of a structural member. It is used in design and basically describes the bending strength of a member.

sector gate A roller type of gate in which the roller is a sector of a circle instead of a complete cylinder. *(see roller gate)*

sectroid The warped surface between groins in vaulting.

sediment Any material which settles in a liquid; the material which is carried and deposited by a river; often called silt.

sedimentation The sinking of soil or mineral grains to the bottom of the water which contains them. Larger particles settle much faster than smaller particles.

seed To sprinkle aggregate on the surface of weak concrete, to produce an exposed aggregate.

seedy (sandy) A condition caused by the dirty heel of a brush resulting in small specks or grains in the paint film.

seepage The percolation of water through the soil; infiltration. Seepage from a canal or reservoir represents a loss that is conveniently expressed as a depth over the surface or wet perimeter in a given time. Seepage into a body is referred to as influent seepage; that away from a body as effluent seepage.

seepage collar A projecting collar usually of concrete built around the outside of a pipe, tunnel, or conduit, under an embankment dam, to lengthen the seepage path along the outer surface of the conduit.

seepage force *(see capillary pressure)*

segment (1) A section of a number of suspension arrangements which, when combined, make a complete circle of the kiln for certain loop chain systems. (2) A lifter or feed-end construction.

segmental arch A type of masonry construction where the curve of an arch through an arc, or segment, or circle is always less than a semicircle.

segmental member A structural member made up of individual elements prestressed together to act as a monolithic unit under service loads.

segmental sluice gate   In hydraulics, a radial gate.

segregation   The tendency, as concrete is caused to flow laterally, for coarse aggregate and drier material to remain behind and for mortar and wetter material to flow ahead; also occurs in a vertical direction when wet concrete is overvibrated or dropped vertically into the forms, the mortar and wetter material rising to the top; also called stratification *(see bleeding)*

seismic design   *(see lateral force)*

seismic load   Seismic load is the assumed lateral load acting in any horizontal direction on the structural system due to the action of earthquakes.

seismograph   An instrument at ground surface to record the electrical effects transmitted to it by a seismometer, thus showing the times and amplitudes of earth shocks.

seismometer   A seismograph measuring the actual movements of the ground.

seize   To bind wire rope with soft wire to prevent it from ravelling when cut.

selected bidder   The bidder selected by the owner for discussions relative to the possible award of the construction contract.

selected list of bidders   *(see invited bidders)*

selective coatings   Have high solar radiation absorptance low emissivity or infrared emittance. Silicon polyester, electroplated black chromium or nickel and vapor deposited tungsten are examples of selective coating materials.

selective collective control   A type of automatic elevator operation which has the ability to store calls and stop for them only in the direction for which they were intended.

selective digging   Separating two or more types of soil while digging them.

selective surface   A special coating applied to solar flat plate collectors. The selective surface absorbs most of the incoming solar energy.

select material   Non-plastic material

hauled and placed on the roadway to provide a foundation for aggregate base course and final surfacing. The type and thickness of select material on a roadway is dictated by the native material used in the fills.

selector   Device mounted in elevator machine room which is synchronized with the travel of the elevator to pass electrical information regarding stopping, etc. to the elevator controller.

selects   The higher grades of lumber, sound, relatively free of blemishes.

selenitic lime (cement)   Lime or cement with 5 percent to 10 percent plaster of Paris added. *(see gauged stuff)*

selenium rectifier   Type of rectifier used on elevator equipment.

self-centering formwork   *(see telescopic centering)*

self-contained air-conditioning (cooling) unit   An air-conditioning unit having the means for ventilation, air circulation, air cleaning and air cooling, and the controls thereof, in the same cabinet with the condensing unit. Self-contained air-conditioning units are classified according to the method of rejecting condenser heat (water cooled, air cooled, and evaporatively cooled), method of introducing ventilation air (no ventilation, ventilation by drawing air from outside, ventilation by a combination of the two methods), and method of discharging air to the room (free delivery or pressure type).

self-desiccation   The removal of free water by chemical reaction so as to leave insufficient water to cover the solid surfaces and to cause a decrease in the relative humidity of the system; applied to an effect occurring in sealed concretes, mortars and pastes.

self-drilling screw   A fastener which combines the functions of drilling and tapping. It is used for attaching panels to purlins and girts.

self-faced stone   Flagstones and similar stones which split cleanly and need no further dressing.

self-furring   Metal lath or welded wire fabric formed in the manufacturing process to include means by which the material is held away from the supporting surface, thus creating a space for keying of the insulating concrete, plaster or stucco.

self-furring nail Nail with a flat head and a washer or a spacer on the shank; for fastening reinforcing wire mesh and spacing it from the nailing member.

self-reading staff A leveling staff graduated so that the user can read the elevation at which his line of sight cuts the staff while looking through the telescope of the level. *(see Sopwith staff; target rod)*

self-spacing tile Tile with lugs, spacers or protuberances on the sides which automatically space the tile for grout joints.

self-stressing concrete (mortar; grout) Expansive-cement concrete, mortar or grout in which expansion, if restrained, induces persistent compressive stresses in the finished product.

self-supporting scaffold A load bearing scaffold. *(see scaffold)*

self-supporting wall A non-load-bearing wall.

self tapping screw A fastener which taps its own threads in a predrilled hole. It is for attaching panels to purlins and girts and for connecting trim and flashing.

self-tone A pattern of two or more shades of the same color. When two shades are used in a design, it is called two-tone.

selsyn generator Special electric device which is used to send electric power to a selsyn motor so that the motor moves in synchronism with the movements of the generator.

selsyn motor Special electric motor which is driven in synchronism to the movements of a selsyn generator.

selvage (1) The edge of the sheet of roll roofing left free of granules and most of the coating asphalt; covered by lapping of the next sheet of roofing. (2) The edges of wallpaper or fabric covering that are trimmed off before paper is hung. They protect the paper, and carry instructions. (3) The edge of a carpet so

finished that it will not ravel or require binding or hemming. (4) A strip down the edge of sheet goods, marked with codes for matching and pattern repeat data. Also selvages provide overlap for cutting seams.

semiarch A half-arch, such as in an abutment or a flying buttress.

semiautomatic batcher *(see batcher)*

semichord One-half the length of any chord of an arc.

semicircle A segment of a circle which is bound by the diameter and one-half of the circumference.

semicircular arch In architecture, a type of masonry construction where the curve of an arch, the intrados, forms a half circle.

semiconductor A material that is neither a good conductor or a good insulator. Also a solid state device.

semidetached Descriptive of a pair of houses with a party wall between.

semidome A half dome, as one over a semicircular niche or apse.

semiflexible joint A connection in which the reinforcement is arranged to permit some rotation of the joint.

semigloss paint (enamel) A paint or enamel made with a slight insufficiency of non-volatile vehicle so that its coating, when dry, has some luster but is not very glossy.

semigrouser A crawler track shoe with one or more low cleats.

semihoused stair A complete stair that has a wall on one side only.

semihoused stringer A piece of lineal material cut out and fastened to the face of a solid stringer. The ends of the risers and treads are concealed in the finished stair.

semitrailer (semi) A towed vehicle whose front rests on the towing unit.

sensible heat ratio, air cooler The ratio of sensible cooling effect to total cooling effect of an air cooler.

sensible horizon The horizon which is visible.

sensitiveness The responsiveness of an instrument to slight adjustments in the quantity being measured, e.g., the sensitiveness of a level bubble is expressed in seconds of arc per millimeter of bubble movement.

sensitive switch A small switch consisting of closely spaced contacts that are snapped together or apart by a spring mechanism. The spring action causes the contacts to operate with the same force regardless of the external pressure applied to the switch.

sensitivity A measure of a system's minimum detectable limit under given condition.

sensitivity slope The change in the response of an instrument to a change in the property being measured. For example, the change in the speed of count rate of a detector tube to a change in moisture expressed as counts per minute, per pound, per cubic foot. The value at which the calculation is made should be specified.

separate contract One of several prime contracts on a construction project.

separate system A sewage drainage in which rainwater and sewage are carried in separate sewers.

separation The tendency, as concrete is caused to pass from the ends of chutes, conveyor belts or similar arrangements, for coarse aggregate to separate from the concrete and accumulate at one side; the tendency, as processed aggregate leaves the ends of conveyor belts, chutes or similar devices with confining sides, for the larger aggregate to separate from the mass and accumulate at one side; or the tendency for the solids to separate from the water by gravitational settlement. *(see bleeding; segregation)*

separator Sections of steel pipe forming spacers between I beams bolted together serving as a structural unit.

separator fines The finer of two fractions into which raw material or cement has been divided in an air-separator (classifier). Generally, the finished product of a closed circuit milling system.

separator tailings The coarser of two fractions into which raw material or cement has been divided in an air separator (classifier). Returned to mill for further grinding or conveyed to another mill for fine grinding.

sepia A copy of a drawing printed on a plasticized paper, which is used as an intermediate medium for printing blueprints, etc.

septic tank A settling tank intended to retain the sludge in immediate contact with the sewage flowing through the tank for a sufficient period to secure a satisfactory decomposition of organic solids by bacterial action.

septic system A system whereby liquids and solids are transferred to a holding tank. Liquids are pumped to a leach field; solids are disposed of by transporting same to a sewage disposal site.

sepulcher A tomb of masonry or one cut out of the rock.

sequence-stressing loss In post-tensioning, the elastic loss in a stressed tendon resulting from the shortening of the member when additional tendons are stressed.

serging Also known as over-sewing, this is a method of finishing the edge of carpet. It is customary to serge the side and bind the end.

series An arrangement of electric blasting caps in which all the firing current passes through each of them in a single circuit.

series circuit An electrical circuit in which the various components are connected end to end and across a power source. In a series circuit, current flow is the same in all parts of the circuit.

series field The field coils connected in series with the armature.

series motor An electric motor that has the armature circuit in series with the field windings.

serpentine (1) Curving alternately to right and left. (2) A building stone, hydrous magnesium silicate, generally dull green in color and often mottled; the presence of iron may add red or brown. In its fibrous form, it resembles asbestos. In polished slab form, it is used as one would use marble.

serpentine coil In a circulator pump, the numerous paths of flow in each grid which lowers the fluid friction, reducing the pump size necessary as well as the cost of pumping.

serrated An edge cut so as to form a line of teeth.

serration A formation resembling the toothed edge of a saw.

service dead load The calculated dead weight supported by a member.

service ell In plumbing, an elbow having an outside thread on one end with the other end enlarged to form a screwed socket.

service entrance switch The main panel or fuse cabinet through which electricity is brought into the building and then distributed to various branch circuits.

service live load The live load specified by the general building code, or the actual load applied in service.

service pipe A gas or water pipe between the main pipe and the building or service receiving the supply.

service riser A vertically mounted steel pipe whose function is to enclose utility electrical wiring to a house or building. It is used to support wiring and protect access to the same.

service road (access road) A small road parallel to the main road. It is used primarily by local traffic so as to avoid obstructing through traffic.

services British term for the supply and distribution pipes for water, steam and gas; also power cables, telephone cables, transformers, drains, elevator equipment, etc. Called utilities in U.S.A.

service stair A secondary stairway for service.

service systems The heating, ventilating, air conditioning, service water heating, electrical distribution, and illuminating systems provided in a building.

service water heating Heating of water for domestic or commercial purposes other than comfort heating.

set (1) The condition reached by a cement paste, mortar or concrete when it has lost plasticity to an arbitrary degree, usually measured in terms of resistance to penetration or deformation; initial set refers to first stiffening; final set refers to attainment of significant rigidity. (2) In hydraulics, the direction of the flow of water. (3) A bend in a piece of metal. (4) The penetration for each blow of the drop hammer of a piling being driven. (5) A carpenter's nail punch. (6) To apply a finishing coat of plaster. (7) Paint or varnish that has stopped flowing is said to have set. (8) The proper angle of the teeth of a saw. (9) A wide beveled chisel used for cutting masonry units; a change in mortar from plastic to a hard state.

setback The recession of an upper part of a facade due to smaller area of upper floors; the setback is usually an answer to certain zoning restrictions.

setback line A line established by law, deed restriction or custom, fixing the minimum distance from the right of way or property line of the exterior face of buildings, walls and any other construction form; a street, road or highway right-of-way line.

set-in-tractor Sideboom used to set pipe into clamps for welding.

set match (1) Geometric sheet goods with the pattern design matching straight across the sheet from edge to edge. (2) In a set match carpet pattern, the figure matches straight across on each side of the narrow carpet width; in a drop match, the figure matches midway of the design; in a quarter-drop match, the figure matches one-quarter of the length of the repeat on the opposite side.

set-off A horizontal line shown on the plans, where a wall is reduced in thickness.

set/reset relay A type of relay manufactured with a hardened steel core that will hold itself in residually until the magnetic field is neutralized electrically.

sett   A follower used in pile driving.

set, timbering   A tunnel support consisting of a roof beam or arch, and two posts.

setting   (1) The placement of lights or panels in sash or frames. (2) The action of a compound as it becomes firmer after application. (3) The laying of stones, lintels, bricks, etc., in a wall. (4) The sheeting or poling boards held in place by a set of timber frames supporting an excavation.

setting bed   (1) The mortar bed in which masonry units are laid in a floor or a wall. (2) The final coat of mortar on a wall or ceiling.

setting coat   The plaster finish coat.

setting out   Putting stakes in the ground to mark out an excavation, marking floors to locate walls or otherwise laying out the work.

setting shrinkage   A reduction in volume of concrete prior to the final set of cement; caused by settling of the solids and by the decrease in volume due to the chemical combination of water with cement.

setting time   *(see initial setting time; final setting time)*

setting-up   (1) The change in materials such as concrete or paint as it changes from a fluid state to firm, hard, or fixed. (2) The gelling of paint during storage. (3) To erect. (4) To begin to move onto a new jobsite.

settlement   (1) Downward movement of a structure, part of a structure or of underpinning. (2) Sinking of the solid particles in fresh concrete or mortar after placement and before initial set.

settling   The lowering in elevation of sections of pavement or structure due to their weight, the loads imposed on them, or shrinkage or displacement of the supporting earth.

settling basin   An enlargement in a conduit to permit the settlement of debris carried in suspension, usually provided with means of ejecting the material so collected.

settling velocity   *(see velocity, terminal)*

set up   (1) Concrete that has dried so that it is firm is said to have set up. (2) The stationing of a surveying instrument such as a theodolite. (3) In plumbing, to bend up the edge of a lead sheet. (4) To caulk a joint with lead by driving it in with a blunt chisel.

severy   A bay of a vault.

sewage   Waste matter mainly in liquid form carried from places of habitation by the drainage lines of a plumbing or sewer system.

sewage disposal   The use of subsoil bacterial action, filtering and the like to purify sewage.

sewage gas   Gas collection in tanks where sewage sludge is digested.

sewage treatment plant   Structures and appurtenances which receive the discharge of a sanitary drainage system, designed to bring about a reduction in the organic and bacterial content of the waste so as to render it less offensive or dangerous; on a small scale, includes septic tanks and cesspools.

sewer   A pipe or conduit, generally closed but normally not flowing full, for carrying sewage and other waste liquids.

sewerage   A sewer system; the removal and disposal of sewage and surface water by sewers.

sewer brick   Low absorption, abrasive-resistant brick intended for use in drainage structures.

sewer hog   *(slang)* A ditchdigger.

sewer rat   *(slang)* Person who cleans an activated sewer; a term used to describe people working in the construction of pipelines.

sewer tile   Glazed waterproof clay pipe with bell joints.

sewer trap   A device in a sewer system which prevents sewer gas from entering a branch pipe leading to a building.

sewing pole   Any piece of wood or other material, more or less rounded, over which carpet may be laid in order to facilitate sewing and other related operations. Most carpet installers prefer a wooden pole, about 4 inches in diameter, that has been slightly flattened on one side.

sexpartite Descriptive of the six-part groined vault.

sextant A hand instrument for measuring either horizontal or vertical angles.

sgraffito A decorative and artistic medium generally consisting of two layers of differently colored plaster. While still soft, the uppermost layer is scratched away, exposing the base or ground layer. Countless variations on the process are possible by modulation of pigments and combination with fresco techniques. Sgraffito in Italian means 'scratched.'

shack A rudely constructed shelter of small size.

shackle A connecting device for lines and draw bars which consists of a U shaped section pierced for a cross bolt or a pin; a lifting ring on a crane hook.

shade A fabric screen to obstruct the light passing through a window, usually hung from a spring-actuated roller.

shaded pole The pole of an AC motor produced by cutting away a section of a field pole and inserting one turn of a conductor, giving the effect of one pole becoming two poles.

shading An apparent change of color in carpet pile caused as light is reflected in different ways when pile fibers are bent; not a defect, but a characteristic especially of cut pile fabrics, including upholstery and clothing.

shading coefficient The ratio of the solar heating gain through a glazing system corrected for external and internal shading to the solar gain through an unshaded single light of double strength sheet glass under the same set of conditions.

shading coil A continuous loop of copper or other electrical conductive material inserted in frame of an AC relay to retard the magnetic flux change in one portion of the frame to keep the relay from chattering.

shadow Indication on a drawing of sunlight intercepted; the conventionalized sun location is assumed at an angle of 45° above the horizon and 45° in left front of the plane of the picture.

shadowal block (shadow) Concrete masonry unit with beveled face shell recesses which provide a special architectural appearance in wall construction.

shadowing When preceding coats show through a finish, it is said to be shadowing; also called show through.

shadow point A sheet of composition roofing material which is cut down the middle, lengthwise, in a definite pattern; when laid on a roof this pattern simulates a shingle design.

shaft (1) That portion of a Classical column between base and capital. (2) A chimney stack. (3) An elevator well. (4) A pit or well sunk from the ground surface into a tunnel for the purpose of furnishing ventilation or access to the tunnel. (5) A cylindrical rod that rotates on its center line and transmits power by its rotation.

cam (camshaft) A shaft carrying cams which open and close valves.

crank (crankshaft) The main shaft of a piston-type engine that converts reciprocating motion into rotation.

counter (countershaft) A shaft that allows one end of a main shaft to drive the other through reduction gears.

idler (idler shaft) A shaft that carries a gear that reverses direction of rotation in a transmission.

input (input shaft) The shaft that delivers engine power to a transmission or clutch.

jack (jackshaft) A short driveshaft, usually connecting a clutch and a transmission.

lay (lay shaft) A fixed shaft supporting rotating drums or gears.

main (mainshaft) The transmission shaft forming a continuation of the input shaft.

output A shaft that transmits power from a transmission or clutch.

reversing A shaft whose direction of rotation can be reversed by use of clutches or brakes.

shaft kiln Vertical cylindrical stationary kiln for burning cement clinker. Pelletized raw meal is fed at the top, and finished clinker withdrawn continuously from the bottom through rotating grates and air-locks. Has smaller capacity but somewhat better fuel economy than straight rotary kilns.

shaft seal A rubbing seal or stuffing box used to prevent fluid leakage between the shaft and bearing of a compressor or other fluid moving device.

shaft wall Fire-resistant wall that isolates the elevator and/or stairwell core in high-rise construction. This wall (also ducts and vents) must withstand the fluctuating (positive and negative) air-pressure loads created by elevators.

shag A deep-pile texture with long, cut surface yarns. Currently defined as having a pile height greater than ⅞ inch, with density not exceeding 1800.

shake A split in timber; a hand-split shingle widely used in the western states of the U.S.A.

shaker An obsolete term for the worker who held a rock drill while a steel driver drove it with his sledgehammer.

shaking screen A suspended screen which is moved with a back-and-forth or rotary motion with a throw of several inches or more.

shale A laminated and fissile sedimentary rock, the constituent particles of which are principally in clay and silt sizes.

shale pit A dumping place for coarse material screened out of rotary drill mud.

shale shaker A screen in the mud circulating system of a rotary drill.

shall Mandatory.

shallow manhole An inspection chamber of the same size from top to bottom.

shallow well A shaft sunk to pump surface water.

shank (1) The plain space between channels of a triglyph. (2) The connecting bar between a ripper or scarifier tooth and the frame. (3) The part of drill steel that fits into the drill; the metal rod on many tools between the head and the handle.

shanty A shack; a crude wooden shelter; the office of a contractor on a construction job.

shape A term used in shopworking when referring to planing of metal on a shaper.

shaped work Curved carpentry work.

shapes Metal rolling mill reference to flanged products.

shark fin In roofing an upward-curled felt side lap or end lap.

sharp coat A coat of white lead in oil, well thinned. When put on fresh plaster, it is called sharp color.

sharp-crested weir A measuring weir with its crest at the upstream edge or corner of a relatively thin plate; generally of metal.

sharp paint A fast drying flat paint, usually strongly pigmented, used for priming or sealing.

sharp sand Coarse sand of which the particles are of angular shape.

shave hook A plumber's tool used to scrape lead pipes before soldering, or by painters for scraping off burnt paint.

shear The strain upon, or the failure of, a structural member at a point where the lines of force and resistance are perpendicular to the member.

shear constellation In composite construction, a set of interrupted keys cut into wood; used to provide shear strength at the junction between dissimilar materials.

shear diaphragms Membrane-like members which are capable of resisting deformation when loaded by in-plane shear forces.

shearhead Assembled unit in the top of the columns of flat slab or flat plate construction to transmit loads from slab to column.

sheariness An oily opalescence of a painted surface which should have a high gloss and has failed because of greasy surface, lack of compatibility in the paint, or other defect.

shearing The process in manufacture in

which carpet is drawn under revolving cutting blades, in order to produce a smooth face on the fabric.

shearing stress An action or stress resulting from applied forces which cause or tend to cause two contiguous parts of a body to slide toward each other in a direction parallel to their plane of contact.

shearlegs (shears) Two poles lashed together at the top with a pulley hung from the apex; used for lifting heavy loads. *(see derrick)*

shear modulus The modulus of rigidity. It is equal to the shear stress divided by the shear strain. *(see Poisson's ratio)*

shear plate A round steel plate used primarily for connecting wood to non-wood in heavy timber construction.

shear reinforcement Reinforcement designed to resist shear or diagonal tension stresses; dowels are not considered to be shear reinforcement.

shear slide A landslide in which a mass of earth slides as a mass away from the material below it.

shear strain The angular displacement of a member due to a force across it; shear force.

shear strength The stress at which material fails in shear. It is the same in all directions for steel, different in different directions for wood.

shear stress The shear force per unit of cross-sectional area, expressed in pounds per square inch, (psi).

shear tests *(see box shear test; triaxial compression test; vane test)*

shear wall A wall which in its own plane carries shear resulting from wind, blast or earthquake forces.

sheath An enclosure in which post-tensioned tendons are encased to prevent bonding during concrete placement.

sheathing (sheeting) (1) The first layer of exterior wall covering nailed to the studding; roof boards are also referred to as sheathing. (2) Horizontal or vertical members of wood or steel placed in contact with earth, usually on a vertical plane, for the purpose of retaining an earth bank in position. Also called lagging.

sheathing paper Tough, water-resistant paper applied over studding or over sheathing, to be itself covered by shingles, siding or other outside facing.

sheave Grooved pulley-wheel for changing the direction of a rope's pull.

sheave beams Steel beams forming the overhead supports for an elevator.

sheave block A pulley and a case provided with means to anchor it.

sheave, padlock The bucket sheave on a dipper or hoe shovel; a sheave set connecting inner and outer boom lines.

sheave, traveling A sheave block that slides in a track.

she bolt A type of form tie and spreader bolt in which the end fastenings are threaded into the end of the bolt, thus eliminating cones found on the ends of many ties and reducing the size of holes left in the concrete surface.

shed A lightly built subordinate shelter, usually one story high, not always fully enclosed, and sometimes a lean-to.

sheen The gloss seen at a glancing angle on an otherwise flat paint finish.

sheen-type A carpet having a high luster, usually produced by a chemical washing.

sheepsfoot A tamping roller, with numerous projections, called feet, expanded at their outer tips, used in compacting the earth.

sheet A thin piece of material, as glass, veneer, plywood or rolled metal.

sheet asphalt A pavement surface composed of graded sand passing a 10-mesh sieve.

sheet erosion Lowering of land by nearly uniform removal of particles from its entire surface by flowing water.

sheet glass Ordinary window glass.

sheet groove (reglet) A notch or block out formed along the outside edge of the foundation to provide support for the wall panels and serve as a closure along their bottom edge.

sheeting (sheeters) A line of planks,

often tongued and grooved on the sides, driven endwise into the ground to protect subgrade operations. *(see sheathing)*

sheeting driver   An air hammer attachment that fits on plank ends so that they can be driven without splintering.

sheeting jacks   Push-type turnbuckles, used to set ditch bracing.

sheet lath   A type of metal lath formed by punching geometrical perforations in steel sheets. Made from heavier gauge steel than expanded laths, they consequently have greater stiffness.

sheet metal   Thin metal, usually galvanized iron, used in the manufacturing of pipe, ductwork and fittings.

sheet-metal work   Working steel or flexible metal done by a plumber or sheet-metal worker.

sheet pile   A pile, or sheeting, that may form one of a continuous interlocking line, or a row of timber, concrete or steel piles, driven in close contact to provide a tight wall to resist the lateral pressure of water, adjacent earth or other materials.

sheetrock   *(slang)* Drywall.

sheetrock screwdriver   An electric screwdriver with a special head.

Shelby tube   Thin walled steel sampler used to obtain samples of cohesive soils.

shelf   (1) A ledge or setback. (2) A horizontal board or slab of other material to serve as a resting place for small objects, as a bookshelf, a mantelshelf, a linen shelf.

shelf angle   An angle section riveted or welded to an I beam or channel section to support the formwork or the hollow tiles of a concrete slab.

shelf life   Maximum interval during which a material may be stored and remain in a usable condition.

shelf retaining wall   A reinforced-concrete retaining wall, with a relieving platform built into the upper part.

shell   The outer portion of a hollow masonry unit when laid.

shellac   A type of varnish consisting of lac carried in alcohol as a solvent.

shell and tube   Pertaining to heat exchangers in which a nest of tubes or pipes, or a coil of tube or pipe, is contained in a shell or container. The pipe (or pipes) carries a fluid through it while the shell is also provided with an inlet and outlet for a fluid flow.

shell construction   Construction using thin curved slabs.

shelling   Crazing of plaster.

Shell-perm process   Injection of bitumen emulsion into permeable soil to reduce the flow of water into an excavation. This closes the pores but does not strengthen the ground.

shell pump   A sand pump for pumping out boreholes.

shell-type apparatus   A refrigerant-containing pressure vessel.

shelter   Generic term for buildings serving as habitations for humans.

shelving   Shelves; material prepared for the building of shelves.

Sherardizing   A process to coat the surface of iron or steel with a condensation of volatile zinc dust for protection against corrosion. Named for inventor, Sherard Cowper-Coles.

shield   A steel hood to protect men driving a tunnel through soft ground.

shielded-arc welding   Arc welding with the weld metal protected by a shield of argon, helium or other inert gas added from the covered electrode or produced by other means.

shift   (1) The horizontal movement of a faulted seam. (2) The radial displacement from the circular shape needed to make a spiral curve from a circular curve. (3) A work period.

   day   The first shift, usually from 8:00 a.m. to 4:00 p.m. when more than one shift is to be worked.

   graveyard   A work shift, usually from midnight to 8:00 a.m.; the third shift.

   swing   Work shift, usually from 4:00 p.m. to midnight; occasionally refers to midnight to 8:00 a.m. shift; the second shift.

shim   (1) A relatively thin piece of steel used as a filler between two surfaces, such as a footing that has been forced down by pre-testing and the billet that formerly rested on it. (2) An insert in veneer. (3) A thin piece of wood used to align or level a wooden member; a shim shingle. (4) In glazing, small blocks of composition, lead, neoprene, etc., placed under the bottom rabbet or channel after setting glass, thus distorting the sealant.

shin The replaceable edge of a moldboard.

shiner A spot glossier than the rest of the area and sometimes caused by spot-sealing patched areas before applying finish; also the lapping of some paints not having proper wet edge; a brick laid inside out with the kiln marks showing.

shingle (1) Roof or wall covering of asphalt, asbestos, wood, tile, slate or other material cut into stock lengths, widths and thickness. (2) A wedge-shaped piece of wood or other material used in overlapping courses to cover a roof or an outside wall surface.

shingle roll A roll of roofing which is scored or cut down the center of the roll to give the appearance of a shingle-type edge when applied on a roof.

shingle siding Various kinds of shingles, some especially designed, that can be used as the exterior side-wall covering for a structure.

shingle tile A flat clay tile, used chiefly for roofing and laid like shingles.

shingling (1) The procedure of laying parallel felts so that one longitudinal edge of each felt overlaps and the other longitudinal edge underlaps, an adjacent felt. *(see ply)* Normally, felts are shingled on a slope so that the water flows over rather than against each lap; (2) The application of shingles to a sloped roof.

shingling hatchet (claw hatchet) A hatchet like a lath hammer, with a notch in the blade for pulling nails.

shiplap A type of lumber having a portion of the width cut away on both edges, but on opposite sides, so as to make a flush joint with similar pieces.

shipper *(slang)* A misshapen brick.

shipper shaft The cogged shaft on a power shovel's dipper stick; the shaft rides a cogged wheel that retracts or crowds the dipper stick.

shipping list A list that enumerates by part number or description each piece of material or assembly to be shipped. Also called talley sheet and bill of materials.

shive (1) A splinter in roofing felt. (2) A piece of wood which has not been sufficiently defibrated.

shlinkett *(slang)* Large chunk embedded in wall which should not be there (term used by painters).

shock hazard Considered to exist at an accessible part in a circuit between the part and the ground, or other accessible parts if the potential is more than 42.4 volts peak and the current through a 1,500-ohm load is more than 5 milliamperes.

shock load Impact of material such as aggregate or concrete as it is released or dumped during placement.

shoddy work Careless, unworkmanlike results.

shoe (1) A ground plate forming a link of a track, or bolted to a track link. (2) A support for a bulldozer blade or other digging edge to prevent cutting down; a cleanup device following the buckets of a ditching machine. (3) A short length at the base of a downpipe to direct the flow away from a wall. (4) An iron or steel socket enclosing the end of a rafter or other load-bearing timber. (5) In glazing, a fitting which holds the lower end of a glazing bar to a roof member such as a purlin and acts as a stop for the glass. (6) A pile shoe. (7) *(slang)* A tire. *(see bonnet)*

shoe mold The small molding covering the joint between the flooring and the baseboard on the inside of a room.

shoe tile A box towed behind a ditching machine in which tile can be laid on the ditch bottom.

shoo-fly A temporary electrical line to carry power while repairing an existing line or when installing new power lines.

S-hooks and locks Metal fastening devices for ductwork connections.

shoot (1) Blast. (2) To true the edge of a board with a plane.

shooter One who sets off a dynamite blast to shoot rock.

shoot the base *(slang)* To spray asphalt primer to rock paving base.

shooting (1) Placing of shotcrete. *(see gunning)* (2) Dynamiting. (3) Carpet tufts. *(see sprouting)*

shooting board A board framed to hold steady another board while its edge is being planed.

shop A building or lesser space for a retail sales business; a space set aside for making repairs or small manufacturing.

shop drawings Incidental drawings furnished by suppliers and manufacturers of various materials and equipment. They must conform to the original drawings, but are not part of the plans as such. Drawings, diagrams, illustrations, schedules, performance charts, brochures and other data prepared by the contractor or subcontractor, manufacturer, supplier or distributor, which illustrate how specific portions of the work shall be fabricated or installed.

shopping center That portion of a city, town or neighborhood on which retail stores are grouped.

shop primed (shop coated) A prefabricated article that has been primed at the factory.

shopwork Any type of work performed in a shop, as opposed to site work.

shore A temporary support for formwork and fresh concrete or for recently built structures which have not developed full design strength; also called prop, tom, post, strut.

shore d hardness The reading of a material's hardness on a durometer similar to the Shore A durometer, the scale of which is 0-100, used on rigid and semi-rigid materials such as polystyrene. Consists of a pinpoint depression into the material.

shore head Wood or metal horizontal member placed on and fastened to a vertical shoring member. *(see raker)*

shore protection Prevention of scour by breakwaters, groynes and other types of revetment.

shoring Props or posts of timber or other material in compression used for the temporary support of excavations, formwork or unsafe structures; the process of erecting shores.

shoring, horizontal Metal or wood load-carrying beam or fabricated trussed section used to carry a shoring load from one bearing point, column, frame, post or wall to another; may be adjustable.

shoring layout A drawing prepared prior to erection showing arrangement of equipment for shoring.

short In paint, a condition usually due to the absence of easy brushing liquids and therefore does not give uniform appearance.

short-break lines Heavy freehand lines which indicate short breaks in the structure of objects. *(see break lines)*

short circuit (short) A connection, by reason of low resistance or accident, by which a designed electrical circuit is nullified or broken.

short column *(see column, short)*

short length A term used by woodworkers when referring to lumber which measures less than eight feet in length.

short oil Low ratio of oil to resin in varnish. *(see long oil)*

short staker *(slang)* One who works only long enough to get money for a few weeks of leisure.

short ton 2,000 pounds.

short-working plaster Plaster which is difficult to mix, and from which the sand separates when the mix is worked on the board. It is caused by deterioration of plaster which has been stored in a damp place.

shot The number of weft yarns in relation to each row of pile tufts crosswise on the loom. A 2-shot fabric is one having two weft yarns for each row of pile tufts; a 3-shot fabric has three weft yarns for each row of tufts.

shot blasting Cleaning a steel surface

by projecting steel shot onto it with centrifugal steel impellers or compressed-air blast. A preparation for painting or metal coating.

shotcrete Mortar or concrete conveyed through a hose and projected at high velocity onto a surface; also known as air-blown mortar; pneumatically applied sprayed mortar or gunned concrete.

shot firing *(see blast)*

shotgun Hot stick used for grounds while doing electrical hot work, installing or removing ground wires.

shot pin A device for fastening items by the utilization of a patented device which uses a powdered charge to imbed the item in the concrete and/or steel.

shot rock Blasted rock.

shot-sawn A finish given building stone by using chilled-steel shot in the sawing process.

shot tower *(slang)* A toilet on a construction job.

should Recommended.

shoulder (1) The portion of a roadway between the edge of the metal wearing course and the top of the foreslope of a ditch or embankment. (2) The side of a horizontal pipe at the level of the centerline. (3) An unintentional offset in a formed concrete surface, usually caused by bulging or movement of formwork. (4) The surface of a tenon which abuts the wood beside the mortise.

shoulder bolt A fastener used to attach wall and roof paneling to the structural frame. It consists of a large diameter shank and a small diameter stud. The shank provides support for the panel rib.

shouldered architrave An architrave around a door which widens at the top.

shoulder nipple A plumbing nipple with a space of about ¼ inch between threads at the middle.

shoved joint Mortar joint produced by laying brick in a thick bed of mortar and forming a vertical joint of mortar

by pushing the brick against the brick already laid in the same course.

shovel A digging and loading machine or tool.

dipper (dipper stick) A revolving shovel that has a push-type bucket rigidly fastened to a stick that slides on a pivot in the boom.

dozer (dozer shovel) A tractor equipped with a front-mounted bucket that can be used for pushing, digging and truck loading.

hoe (dragshovel; pullshovel; ditching shovel; backhoe) A revolving shovel having a pull-type bucket rigidly attached to a stick hinged on the end of a live boom.

hydraulic A revolving shovel in which drums and cables are replaced by hydraulic rams and/or motors.

part swing A revolving shovel that cannot swing through a full circle.

revolving A digging machine that has the machinery deck and attachment on a vertical pivot, so that it can swing independently of its base.

shower (shower bath) The floor receptacle and plumbing provided for bathing by overhead spray.

show rafter An architectural term applied to a short rafter which may be seen below the cornice; often an ornamental rafter. Also called exposed beam.

show room A room for the display of merchandise.

shrine A building, or a particular part of one, that is held sacred.

shrinkage Volume decrease caused by drying and chemical changes; a function of time but not of temperature or of stress due to external load; loss of bulk of soil when compacted in a fill; usually is computed on the basis of bank measure. *(see contraction; expansion)*

compensating A characteristic of grout, mortar or concrete made using an expansive cement in which volume increase, if restrained, induces compressive stresses which are intended to approximately offset the tendency of drying shrinkage to induce tensile stresses. *(see expansive cement)*

shrinkage crack   Crack due to restraint of shrinkage.

shrinkage cracking   Cracking of a structure or member due to failure in tension caused by external or internal restraints as reduction in moisture content develops, or as carbonation occurs, or both.

shrinkage limit   The maximum water content at which a reduction in water content will not cause a decrease in volume of the soil mass. *(see Atterberg limits)*

shrinkage loss   The loss of stress in the prestressing steel resulting from the shrinkage of the concrete.

shrinkage ratio   The ratio between a given volume change, expressed as a percentage of the dry volume, and the corresponding change in water content above the shrinkage limit; expressed as a percentage of the weight of the oven-dried soil.

shrinkage reinforcement   Reinforcement designed to resist shrinkage stresses in concrete.

shrinkage test   The maximum water content at which a reduction in water content will not cause a decrease in volume of the soil mass.

shrink-mixed concrete   Ready-mixed concrete mixed partially in a stationary mixer and then mixed in a truck mixer. *(see preshrunk)*

shrouded screw conveyor   Screw conveyor with a close fitting casing.

shunt   (1) A connection between the two wires of a blasting cap which prevents building up of opposed electric potential in them. (2) A resistive element placed across the terminals of an ammeter to bypass a portion of the current.

shunt circuits   Another name for a parallel circuit connection.

shutter   An extra closure for a window or door, usually of wood, paneled, and one of a pair hinged at the outside jambs.

shutter bar   A pivoted bar for fastening shutters in position over a window.

shutter hinge   An H hinge.

shuttering   (1) British term used to indicate formwork in general or more particularly form panels in direct contact with the concrete. (2) Closures for shop windows and similar large areas, of metal or wood.

shuttle   A back and forth motion of a machine which continues to face in one direction.

SI   The international symbol for the metric unit used by the United States (Le Systeme International d'Unites).

siamese connection   A wye connection installed close to the ground on the exterior side wall of a building, providing two inlet connections for fire hoses to the standpipes and fire-protection sprinkler system of a building.

side bend   A joint bent to cause horizontal deflection.

sidecasting   Piling soil alongside the excavation from which it was taken.

side ditch   The open side drain adjacent to the roadbed designed to carry water running to it from the roadway and adjacent side slopes.

side-entrance manhole   A deep manhole in which the access shaft is built to the side of the inspection chamber. A passageway leads to the inspection chamber or the inspection chamber may be enlarged to merge with the shaft.

side flights   Double-return stairs.

side gutter   A small gutter on a roof slope at the intersection of a chimney or dormer or other surface vertical to the main roof.

sidehill   A slope that crosses the line of work.

sidehill cut   A long excavation in a slope that has a bank on one side and is near original grade on the other.

side hook   A bench hook.

side lap   The amount of lap by which single-lap tiles cover each other at the side; the amount by which the vertical joint in one course is covered by the slate, tile or shingle above.

side lap fastner A fastener used to connect panels together at the side lap.

side light (1) A source of artificial illumination located on an interior wall or partition. (2) One of a pair of narrow windows flanking a door.

side outlet Any fitting having an outlet or opening in the side.

side posts Princess posts.

side rail *(see check rail)*

sides (walls; faces) The vertical or inclined earth surfaces formed as a result of excavation work.

side seams Seams running the length of the carpet. Also called length seams.

side telescope An auxiliary telescope.

side vent A vent connecting to the drain pipe through a 45° Y fitting.

sidewalk Walkway for pedestrians, flanking a street.

sidewalls (wingwalls) Walls, of concrete or masonry, at end of a culvert.

sideways A slight sideways movement of a frame in its own plane; caused by wind or other horizontal forces such as uneven loading.

siding Exterior wall covering of horizontal boards nailed to a wood frame.

bevel (lap siding) The finish siding on the exterior of a house or other structure. It is usually manufactured by resawing dry square-surfaced boards diagonally to produce two wedge-shaped pieces. These pieces commonly run from 7/16 inch thick on the thin edge to 1/2 to 3/4 inch thick on the other edge, depending on the width of the siding.

drop Drop siding has tongue-and-groove joints, is heavier, and has more structural strength; it is frequently used on buildings that require no sheathing, such as garages and barns. Usually 3/4 inch thick and six inches wide, machined into various patterns.

sieve (screen) In testing, as defined by the American Society for Testing Materials, screens have round openings and sieves have square openings. *(see screen)*

sieve analysis A method of classifying aggregates according to proportional content of particles of various sizes. Classification is done with standard sieves. *(see graduation)*

sieve correction Correction of a sieve analysis to adjust for deviation of sieve performance from that of standard calibrated sieves.

sieve number A number used to designate the size of a sieve, usually the approximate number of sieve cross wires per linear inch.

sight distance Minimum distance required for passing vehicles to see each other on a highway.

sight glass Glass tube used to indicate the liquid level in pipes, tanks, bearings and similar equipment.

sight rule In surveying, an alidade.

sight size The width and height of the opening which admits light through a window. *(see daylight width)*

signal device, elevator car flash One providing a signal light in the car, which is illuminated when the car approaches the landings at which a landing signal registering device has been actuated.

signal registering device, elevator landing A button or other device, located at the elevator landing, which when actuated by a waiting passenger, causes a stop signal to be registered in the car.

signals Moving signs, provided by workers, such as flagmen, or by devices, such as flashing lights, to warn of possible or existing hazards.

signal system, elevator separate One consisting of buttons or other devices located at the landings, which when actuated by a waiting passenger illuminate a flash signal or operate an annunciator in the car indicating floors at which stops are to be made.

signal transfer device, elevator automatic A device by means of which a signal registered in a car is automatically transferred to the next car following, in case the first car passes a floor for which a signal has been registered without making a stop.

signal transfer switch, elevator A

manually operated switch, located in the car, by means of which the operator can transfer a signal to the next car approaching in the same direction, when he desires to pass a floor at which a signal has been registered in the car.

signs Warnings of hazard, temporarily or permanently affixed or placed, at locations where hazards exist.

silent pile drivers Vibrating pile drivers and hydraulic pile drivers.

silex lining Protective lining for tube mills made of a hard siliceous rock. Used when iron-contamination must be avoided, as in the manufacture of white cement.

silica Silicon dioxide (SiO_2).

silica acid ratio Ratio of silica to alumina. SiO_2/Al_2O_3.

silica flour A siliceous binder component which reacts with lime under autoclave curing conditions; prepared by grinding quartz to the fineness of portland cement.

silica gel A substance used in dehumidifying because of its ready absorption of moisture, and the readiness with which it gives up this moisture when heated.

silica rock Hard rock, high in silica(SiO_2), usually containing quartz. Used as a raw material.

silicate Salt of a silicic acid.

siliconized polyesters Polyesers modified by the addition of silicon, an inorganic substance. Possess superior exterior durability, non-chalking properties and goss retention features.

silicosis A lung disease caused chiefly by inhaling rock dust from air drills.

silking *(see lining)*

sill **(1)** The horizontal member supported by a foundation wall or piers, and which in turn bears the upright members of a frame. **(2)** A horizontal closure at the bottom of a door or window frame. **(3)** The horizontal overflow line of a dam spillway or other weir structure. *(see lock sill)* **(4)** A submerged structure across a river to control the water level upstream. **(5)** The crest of a spillway.

sill anchor (plate anchor) A bolt anchored in the concrete or masonry foundation of a framed house. The bolt passes through a hole drilled in the plate to hold the frame down against the wind pressure.

sill bead A deep bead.

sill block A solid concrete masonry unit used for sills of openings.

sillcock (hosecock) A faucet or hose connection, usually on the exterior of a building about sill height.

sill plate Horizontal member laid directly on a foundation on which the framework of a building is erected.

sill sealer 1″×6″ insulation. Insulation used to create a seal between the foundation wall and the mudsill.

silo **(1)** A stationary or portable tower-like building to hold cement. **(2)** A storage place for grain or silage.

silo block Solid curved or plane concrete masonry units for use in construction of concrete silos.

silo set A disadvantageous property of cement manifested after period of hot storage in silos (or other), in which cement lacks flowability. Generally attributed to the development of syngenite in the cement.

silt A granular material resulting from the disintegration of rock, with grains largely passing a No. 200 (47 micron) sieve; alternatively, such particles in the range from 2 to 50 microns diameter.

silt box A loose iron box at the bottom of a gulley for collecting loose sand. It is pulled and emptied occasionally.

silt displacement A method of using a shield for tunnel driving in nearly fluid silts. As the shield is driven forward, the silt is forced into the tunnel through two rectangular openings, like toothpaste from a tube. It is then loaded and removed from the tunnel.

silt ejector A hydraulic ejector.

silt grade Silt sized material.

silting Filling with soil or mud deposited by water.

silt trap A settling hole or basin that

prevents water-borne soil from entering a pond or drainage system.

silverlock bond   Rat-trap bond.

sima   The rain gutter of a Classical building.

simple beam   A beam without restraint or continuity at its supports.

simple bending   Bending a beam which is supported freely and has no fixed end.

simple curve   The arc of a circle joining two straights with no transition curve.

simple framework   A perfect frame.

simple span   A term used in structural analysis to describe a support condition for a beam, girt, purlin, etc., which offers no resistance to rotation at the supports.

simplex piles   Steel pipe with steel point driven to resistance, casing filled with concrete and withdrawn leaving steel point at bottom.

single-acting pumps (engines)   Reciprocating pumps or compressed air or steam engines in which only one side of the piston works; every second stroke is a power stroke. All internal combustion engines are single acting.

single cleat ladder   One which consists of a pair of side rails, usually parallel, but with flared side rails permissible, connected together with cleats that are joined to the side rails at regular intervals.

single coating technique   A method of producing composition roofing wherein the surface coating is applied in only one layer.

single contract   Contract for construction of a project under which a single prime contractor is responsible for all of the work.

single corner block   Concrete masonry unit which has one flat end for use in construction of the end or corner of a wall.

single-cut file   A file with cuts in only one direction; used for filing soft materials.

single family house   A dwelling designed for occupancy by one family.

single Flemish bond   Brickwork laid in Flemish bond, seen on one face only. *(see double Flemish bond)*

single floor   A wood floor in which the joists span from wall to wall.

single footing   A footing which carries a single column.

single jack   *(slang)* A small, usually four-pound, sledge hammer.

single-lap tiles   Curved roofing tiles which overlap only the tiles in the course immediately below them.

single-lock welt   In plumbing, a cross welt.

single-pass soil stabilizer   A machine with several rapidly rotating wheels or paddles in contact with the soil. These rotors pulverize the soil to a measured depth, mix it with a liquid binder, and mix the soil with cement or other binder which has been spread ahead of the machine.

single-pitch roof   A lean-to roof; it slopes in only one direction.

single-point adjustable suspension scaffold   A manually or power-operated unit designed for light duty use, supported by a single wire rope from an overhead support so arranged and operated as to permit the raising or lowering of the platform to desired working positions.

single-pole scaffold   Platforms resting on putlogs or cross beams, the outside ends of which are supported on ledgers secured to a single row of posts or uprights, and the inner ends of which are supported on or in a wall.

single-pole switch   An electric device for making or breaking one side of an electric current.

single Roman tile   *(see Roman tile)*

single roof   A roof carried by common rafters instead of roof trusses, purlins or pincipals.

single-sized aggregate   Aggregate in which a major portion of the particles are of sizes lying between narrow limits.

single sling   A sling with a ring at one end and a hook at the other end.

single slope   A sloping roof with one

surface. The slope is from one wall to the opposite wall of a rectangular building.

single span A building or structural member without intermediate support.

single-stage compressor A machine to compress air to its full pressure in one cylinder.

single-stage curing Autoclave curing process in which precast concrete products remain on metal pallets until stacked for delivery or yard storage.

sink A washbasin for kitchen, pantry or janitor's closet, provided with plumbing.

sinkage A recess or set-back panel of slight depth, usually occurring in wall, ceiling or floor.

sink bib (bib nozzle) The type of tap for a kitchen sink.

sinking (1) A recess cut into the surface of wood, e.g., where butt hinges are attached. *(see mat sinkage)* (2) Loss of gloss of a finish coat of paint due to absorption of its medium by the undercoat.

sinking pump (submersible pump) A pump built for keeping a shaft dry during sinking or otherwise designed to operate in a well or shaft.

sintered carbides A term for cemented carbides *(see sintering)*

sintered clay Expanded clay aggregate. *(see lightweight aggregate)*

sinter grate A slowly traveling horizontal grate on which combustion and clinkering of nodules take place. The nodules, made from cement raw meal, clinker dust, fuel and water, burn on top of a protective layer of under-burned clinker.

sintering (1) Formation of cemented carbides by mixing carbides and metal powders of different melting points with cobalt, thus cementing the hard cutting agents together. (2) Heating a material until it begins to melt, so as to strengthen it while maintaining its porosity; part of the manufacturing of lightweight aggregates.

sinuous flow Turbulent flow.

siphon A closed conduit, a part of which rises above the hydraulic grade line. It utilizes atmospheric pressure to effect or control the flow of water through it.

inverted A conduit or culvert with a U- or V-shaped line to permit it to pass under an intersecting roadway, stream or other obstruction.

siphon break A small groove to arrest the capillary action of two adjacent surfaces.

siphon spillway A spillway which is built as a siphon over the crest of the dam. The water must rise to the crest of the siphon before the siphon primes itself and begins to flow, but the siphon will go on flowing until the water falls below its inlet, which is below the crest.

siphon trap *(see S-trap)*

S-iron The visible end of a tie rod used to hold masonry walls together or to secure interior framing to a masonry wall; the end is often S-shaped.

sister block *(slang)* Two sheaves or pulleys arranged in tandem.

site Geographical location of the project, usually defined by legal boundary lines; where a building is located or is to be erected.

site exploration (site investigation) The examination of the surface and subsoil at a site to obtain the information needed for design.

six-by-six (6×6) *(slang)* A truck having drive to the front wheels and to tandem rear wheels.

six wheeler A truck with two rear axles.

size (1) Measurement in extent. (2) A liquid coating composition, usually transparent, for sealing a porous surface preparatory to application of finishing coats.

size analysis Grading curve.

sized slates Slates of standardized uniform width, not random slates.

size of pipe and tubing Unless otherwise stated, the nominal size by which the pipe or tubing is commercially designated. Actual dimensions of the different kinds of pipe and tubing are usually given in the applicable specifications.

size stick A scantle used by a slater.

sizing (pre-sizing) **(1)** Spreading diluted glue or size on a surface before gluing it. Size penetrates more than glue, and reduces the absorption of glue by the wood. **(2)** Sizing is the estimating of the demand to be placed upon the solar and supplemental heating systems by the heat requirement of the application. The principal components involved in solar system sizing are the collectors, storage capacity and quantity of supplemental heat needed. Detailed calculations are necessary to design an optimum system for each application.

skeleton An accurate network of survey lines obtained by triangulation.

skeleton construction A type of building in which all external and internal loads and stresses are transmitted to the foundation by rigidly connected frameworks of metal or reinforced concrete.

skeleton core The internal hidden frame of a hollow-core door.

skeleton steps Treads, often metal, with no risers.

skene arch Scheme arch.

sketch A preliminary presentation drawing in the field of design, plan, elevation or perspective.

skew (skew angle) **(1)** The acute angle formed by the intersection of a line normal to the centerline of the roadway with a line parallel to the face of the abutments, or in the case of culverts, with the centerline of the culverts. **(2)** A bevel-faced member, particularly a stone at the eaves end of a gable.

skew back Sloping surface against which the end of an arch rests, such as a concrete thrust block supporting thrust of an arch bridge. *(see chamfer strip)*

skewback or skew block A brick or stone cut to make an inclined surface for receiving thrust or pressure as of an arch; a coping stone or gable.

skewback saw A curved-back handsaw made to lessen its weight without sacrificing stiffness.

skew bridge A bridge which spans a gap obliquely; it is therefore longer than a direct span.

skew chisel A woodworking tool with a straight cutting edge, sharpened at an angle, used in wood turning.

skew corbel Gable springer.

skewed On a horizontal angle, or in an oblique course or direction.

skew flashing A flashing between a gable coping and the roof below it.

skew nailing In carpentry, a term referring to the driving of nails on a slant or obliquely. *(see toenailing)*

skid Timbers used to support pipe.

skim coat (skimming coat) In plastering, the finishing coat consisting of fine stuff to which fine white sand may be added.

skimming **(1)** Diverting surface water by shallow overflow to avoid diverting sand, silt or other debris carried as bottom load. **(2)** Removing irregularities of the surface of the soil.

skin friction The resistance of ground surrounding a pile or caisson to its movement; usually proportional to the area of pile or caisson in contact with the ground; increases with penetration depth.

skinner (Cat skinner) *(slang)* An equipment operator.

skinning **(1)** The formation of a skin on the paint or varnish surface while in the can; caused by oxidation of the drying oil. **(2)** Removing covering or insulation, as from wire.

skin patch A thin patch on a bituminous pavement to fill a depression. Patching over existing asphalt pavement.

skintled brickwork Irregularly formed brickwork arranged with variations in projections on the exterior-face wall; usually formed of bricks of irregular shape.

skin type panel Panel made of one material.

skip A non-digging bucket or tray that hoists material.

skip loader Equipment, either rubber tired or track, with a bucket on the front for picking up material, carrying it for short distances or loading it onto other equipment.

skippy Said of paint that causes the brush to skip on the surface leaving some spots uncoated and others too thickly coated; caused by lack of sufficient vehicle to permit easy, uniform application or by liquids that pull.

skips (1) Areas of lumber which the surfacing machine missed. (2) Areas left unpainted by mistake. *(see holiday)*

skip trowel A method of texturing resulting in a rough 'Spanish Stucco' effect.

skirt (1) In architecture, the border or molded piece under a window stool commonly called apron; also a baseboard; a finished board which covers the plastering where it meets the floor of a room. (2) A vertical strip placed on the side of a conveyor belt to prevent spillage.

skirtboard (skirt; skirting) A baseboard or finishing board at junction of interior wall and floor.

skirting block An architrave block.

skirts *(see pants)*

skive To dig in thin layers, as with a two-handed clay knife that is drawn along a surface of clay.

skive edge The outside edges of the paper joint tape that have been sanded to improve adhesion and reduce waviness.

skullcracker *(slang)* A steel ball swung from a crane boom to demolish buildings and for breaking boulders; wrecking ball or headache ball.

sky factor The daylight factor.

skylight An opening in a roof or ceiling for admitting daylight; also, the window fitted into such an opening.

skyscraper A very tall building, usually of skeleton construction.

slab (1) A flat, usually horizontal or nearly so, molded layer of plain or reinforced concrete usually of uniform thickness, but sometimes of variable thickness; the flat section of floor or roof either on the ground or supported by beams, columns or other framework. *(see flat slab)* (2) The outside lengthwise cut of a log. (3) A thick plate of material, as a slab of stone, glass, etc.

slab bar bolster A device for supporting rebar during the placing of concrete in forms or molds.

slab floor A reinforced concrete floor; a floor covered with slabs of marble, slate, limestone, granite, cast stone, terrazzo, etc.

slab form *(see form)*

slab on grade A non-suspended, ground-supported concrete slab, often reinforced, of one of the following types: (a) edge supported-slab rests atop the perimeter foundation wall (b) floating-slab terminates at the inside face of the perimeter foundation wall and is said to float independent of the foundation wall (c) monolithic-slab and foundation wall formed into one integral mass of concrete, also called slab-thickened edge.

slab spacer Bar support and spacer for slab reinforcement.

slab strip *(see middle strip)*

slab, structural A suspended, self-supporting, reinforced concrete floor or roof slab.

slack Fine coal screenings.

slack adjuster In air brakes, the connection between the brake chamber and the brake cam.

slackline (slackline cableway) A cable excavator having a track cable which is loosened to lower the bucket and tightened to raise it.

slack-rope switch A device which automatically causes the electric power to be removed from the elevator driving-machine motor and brake when the hoisting ropes of a winding-drum machine become slack.

slag Refuse from steel-making; usually makes good paving material; can be crushed into most any gradation; most are quite porous.

slag cement An artificial cement made by first chilling slag from blast furnaces in water, then mixing and grinding the granulated slag with lime; a process which produces a cement with hydraulic properties.

slag concrete Concrete in which blast furnace slag is used as an aggregate; used in almost every type of construction and valued because of its fire-resistant properties as well as for its insulating qualities against cold and sound.

slag plaster A plaster made of granulated slag; valuable as an acoustic plaster because of its superior absorbent properties.

slag strip In roofing, a strip of wood nailed to the edges of a graveled roof to give the edge a finish and to prevent the gravel from rolling off the roof.

slag wool A material made by blowing steam through fluid slag. The final product is similar to asbestos in appearance and is used for insulating purposes.

slake As applied to lime, to add water, starting a chemical action resulting in lime putty.

slaking Adding water to quick lime to prepare lime putty.

slam *(slang)* To go on strike.

slamming stile In carpentry, a term used when referring to the upright strip, at the side of a door opening, against which the door slams, or against which it abuts when closed; also, the strip into which the bolt on the door slips when the lock is turned.

slanting construction A type of construction in which blast and/or bomb resistant features are incorporated into a new structure without appreciable extra cost or reduction in efficiency.

slap dash *(slang)* Rough cast; hastily and not well done.

slash grain The exposed grain of flat-sawn timber.

slat A thin strip, usually of wood or metal, as used in a louver or blind, or for a trellis or other similar open work.

slat bucket A digging bucket of basket construction used in handling sticky, chunky mud.

slate A fine-grained metamorphic rock possessing a well-developed fissility; used for roofing, paving, etc.

slate boarding Close boarding over a roof under slates or tiles.

slate clad A composition roofing surfaced with slate granules

slate cramp A slate piece cut to a shape which, in plan, is shaped like an hourglass and has dovetailed ends.

slate hanging (weather slating) Wall slating.

slate powder A very fine impalpable powder of slate, used as a paint extender. It is fairly opaque but is too dark for use in light colored paint.

slate ridge (slate roll) A ridge made of a circular rod of slate with a V-cut beneath it. The roll is bedded on each side in a heavy slate called a wing.

slath *(slang)* Scraps of wood or metal slats.

slather A stream of watery concrete that oozes out of form.

slave unit A machine which is controlled by or through another unit of the same type.

sledge (sledgehammer) A heavy hammer with a long handle; usually wielded with both hands and used for driving posts or other large stakes; doublejack. *(see singlejack)*

sleeper A heavy beam or piece of timber laid on, or near, the ground for receiving floor joists and to support the superstructure; also strips of wood laid over a rough concrete floor to which the finished wood floor is nailed.

sleeper clips (sleeper plates; sleepers) Sheet metal strips used to anchor wood flooring to concrete; a floor clip.

sleeper wall Honeycomb wall.

sleepiness A reduction of the gloss as a paint film dries; a defect sometimes similar to seediness.

sleeve A coupling for underpinning cylinders; essentially a close fitting internal band with a shoulder on its outside that bears against the top and bottom of the cylinders joined.

sleeve piece (thimble)   In plumbing, a short thin-walled brass or copper tube used in soldering a lead or copper pipe to one of some other metal.

slender beam   A beam which, if overloaded, would tend to fail by buckling in the compression flange. For concrete, it applies to beams longer than 20 times their width. The compressive stress in such a beam must be reduced in proportion to its slenderness ratio.

slenderness ratio   The ratio of effective length or height of a wall or pier to effective thickness; used as a means of assessing the stability of a masonry wall or concrete panel or column.

slewing   Rotation of a crane jib so the load moves horizontally through an arc. Slewing and derricking may be simultaneous.

sliced blockwork   Breakwater blockwork built in sloping, nearly vertical courses so that the placing of the submerged blocks is much easier than in coursed blockwork. Each block must rest on two others and slides naturally into position.

slicing   The production of veneer by driving half log or flitch down against a pressure bar and knife while being held against a metal bedplate. The shearing action produces very smooth surfaces.

slicker   A tool often used by the plasterer in place of the darby. It is made of a thin board bevelled on both sides, about 4 feet long and 6″ to 8″ wide, held by the thicker edge.

slick hole   *(slang)* A blasthole loaded full with explosives.

slick iron   *(slang)* Term referring to structural iron.

slick line   End section of a pipeline used in placing concrete by pump which is immersed in the placed concrete and moved as the work progresses.

slick sheets   Thin steel plates spread on a tunnel floor before a blast to make mucking with power equipment easier.

slide   An instrument for performing certain mathematical calculations; widely used by building engineers, architects, shopmen and others who wish to make such calculations quickly and accurately

slide coupling   A slip joint.

slide damper   Winch-operated, large, rectangular steel and firebrick slide, which may be raised or lowered inside a duct to increase or throttle gas flow.

slide door   A single or double leaf door which opens horizontally by means of overhead trolleys.

slide rail   A steel or cast iron mounting for a belt-driven machine enabling it to be moved as the belt stretches to tighten the belt.

slide rule   (1) A flat board, usually beneath the counter shelf of a dresser, desk, bookcase, or the like, that may be partly withdrawn to serve as a support. (2) A sliding closure for an opening, as between kitchen or pantry and dining room. (3) A slip or movement of a bank of earth.

slide shoe bearing   Special type bearing for ball mill, consisting of steel shoe on which a tire attached to the mill slides, and mechanism for maintaining protective oil film.

sliding form   *(see slipform)*

sliding gate   An obsolete type of crest gate which has high frictional resistance to opening and can only be used in small sizes. A roller gate has been developed to replace it in most cases.

sliding panel weir   A frame weir with wooden panels sliding between grooved uprights.

slime spot   A weak spot in dry felt caused by slime and foam in the forming process on the felt machine.

slime line lamp   An instant start, single-pin, hot-cathode fluorescent lamp.

sling   A lifting hold consisting of two or more strands of chain or cable.

sling block   A frame in which two sheaves are mounted so as to receive lines from opposite direction.

slip   (1) A fixing fillet. (2) A parting slip. (3) A paint which is so easily applied it seems to be lubricated is said to have slip. **(4)** Fluid grout made from gypsum cement or plaster.

slip factor The coefficient of friction between high-strength friction-grip bolts and the steel members which are gripped.

slip feather A tongue in a joint such as a feather joint.

slipform **(1)** A form which is pulled or raised as concrete is placed; may move in a generally horizontal direction to lay concrete evenly for highway paving or on slopes and inverts of canals, tunnels and siphons; or vertically to form walls, bins or silos of uniform cross section from bottom to top. **(2)** A narrow section of formwork that can easily be removed, and is designed to be struck first, thus making it easy to strike the remaining larger panels. It may also be termed a wrecking piece or strip. **(3)** A temporary loose vertical piece in a wall mold used to separate the expensive face mix from the less expensive backing mix during casting, and designed to be withdrawn as soon as the mold is full.

slipform paver A machine which lays concrete roads, pulling the road forms with it. The concrete must be stiff or the edges will collapse as the forms slide off them.

slip joint In masonry, especially in brick work, a type of joint made by cutting a channel or groove in the old wall to receive the brick of the new wall.

slip mortise An open or chase mortise.

slippage The relative lateral movement of adjacent components of a built-up roof membrane. It occurs mainly in roof membranes on a slope, sometimes exposing the lower plies to the weather.

slipper guide A plasterer's running rule.

slip-resistant tile Tile having greater slip-resistant characteristics due to an abrasive admixture, abrasive articles in the surface or grooves or patterns in the surface.

slip sill A stone sill for window or door which does not project into the wall beyond the jambs.

slip stick *(slang)* A slide rule.

slip surface The surface of a failure in an earth bank.

slip tongue (false tongue) A tongue in a feather joint.

slip under the brush A term for coating materials that are easy to apply.

slobber-belt *(slang)* The side belts attached to a belt conveyor for catching overflow material. *(see skirt)*

slop *(see sludge)*

slope **(1)** The angle with the horizontal at which a particular earth material will stand indefinitely without movement. **(2)** The inclination of a surface expressed as one unit of rise or fall to so many horizontal units. **(3)** Inclination from the horizontal expressed in percent; also termed gradient or grade.

slope cat Equipment with a blade attached on one side at an angle for actually cutting a given slope angle in a cut.

slope correction In surveying, a deduction from a measured sloping length to bring it to the corresponding horizontal length.

sloped footing A footing having sloping top or sides.

slope gauge A staff gauge placed on an incline and graduated to indicate vertical heights.

slope, moving walk The angle which the treadway makes with the horizontal.

slope staking Marking the ground surface with stakes to indicate where cut or fill is needed.

slop sink A low, deep sink for service or janitor use.

slot mortise An open mortise.

slough **(1)** */slew/* Secondary river channel or branch through which the current is usually sluggish. **(2)** */sluff/* Of an earth slope, to break off or slide.

sloughing */sluffing/* Subsidence of material from a vertical surface of newly gunned shotcrete generally due to the use of an excessive amount of mixing water. *(see sagging)*

slow bend test *(see longitudinal bead test)*

slow-burning construction In building, a term often applied to construction in which treated material is used in order to make the structure as fire resistant as possible; a term also sometimes applied to heavy timber construction.

slow-curing asphalt (SC) Liquid asphalt composed of asphalt cement and oils of low volatility.

slow-curing liquid asphaltic materials Asphaltic residual oil from petroleum or blend of such oil with distillates which do not volatize readily.

slow-down switch A limit switch, located at the terminal landing to slow down an elevator.

slow powder Black powder, often called gunpowder. Also, some of the slow acting dynamites.

sloyd knife A type of woodworker's knife used in the sloyd system of manual training. A special feature of this system, which orginated in Sweden, is the used of wood carving as a means of acquiring skill in the use of woodworking tools.

sludge The waste material produced in the wet grinding process and consisting of finely ground terrazzo and water.

sludger (1) A centrifugal pump for sludge of any sort; a sand pump. (2) A tool for cleaning materials out of a hole drilled in rock before inserting the explosive.

sludge samples Samples of mud from a rotary drill or sand from a churn drill, used to obtain information about the formation being drilled.

slug Disc-shaped punchings of steel plates, or cylindrical cuttings of steel rods, used as inexpensive grinding media in tube mills.

slugger *(slang)* A tooth on a roll-type rock crusher.

slugging Pulsating and intermittent flow of shotcrete material due to improper use of delivery equipment and materials.

sluice (1) To cause water to flow at high velocities for wastage, for purposes of excavation, ejecting debris, etc. (2) A steep narrow waterway.

sluicing Moving earth, sand, gravel, etc., by flowing water; hydraulic sluicing; colloquially, hydraulicking.

slucing box *(see hog box)*

slum A section of a city or town in which many of the habitations have deteriorated to such an extent that they menace the health and security of the whole community.

slump A measure of consistency of freshly mixed concrete, mortar or stucco equal to the subsidence measured to the nearest ¼ inch (6 mm) of the molded truncated cone immediately after removal of the slump cone.

slump block Concrete masonry units, produced so they slump or sag before they harden, for use in masonry wall construction.

slump bottom *(slang)* Corrugated metal pipe arch.

slump cone A mold in the form of a truncated cone with a base diameter of eight inches (20.32 cm), top diameter four inches (10.16 cm), and height twelve inches (30.48 cm), used to fabricate a specimen of freshly mixed concrete for the slump test; a cone six inches (15.24 cm) high is used for tests of freshly mixed mortar and stucco.

slump test The procedure for measuring slump. *(see slump cone)*

slurry A thin, watery mixture of neat cement or cement and sand.

slurry agitator Mechanism, incorporating the constant or intermittent use of compressed air, to prevent sedimentation or segregation in slurry basins or tanks (cf). In tall cylindrical slurry tanks air is used exclusively; mechanical agitators or combinations (stationary or traveling) are used in cylindrical, oval or rectangular basins.

slurry basin Large concrete or steel container for raw material slurry, equipped with slurry agitators (cf). blending basins receive slurries from different slurry basins or tanks; mixing basins are used for homogenization of slurry; correcting basins receive slurries of pre-determined chemical composition in correct proportions to produce final raw mix; kiln basins serve as storage for one or several day's supply of finished slurry.

slurry coat A brushed application of slurry generally applied to back of adhered veneer units and to backing.

slurry seal machine A truck-mounted unit which is capable of metering, delivering, mixing and spreading the ingredients used in making an asphalt emulsion slurry seal. *(see asphalt emulsion slurry seal)*

slurry dryer Equipment for utilization of hot kiln exit gases for partial or total drying of slurry before it is fed to the kiln. Frequently designed as a drum charged with chains or specially designed heat-exchange elements.

slurry feeder Equipment for feeding slurry to kilns or mills at controlled rates.

slurry filter Continuously operating drum or disc-type filter for removing part of the water from slurry by application of vacuum. Special types of filter cloth are used to resist weat and rot. Depending on fineness and plasticity of the slurry, the water content may be reduced 15-20 percentage points.

slurry tanks Serve same purpose as slurry basins (cf); basins are generally larger in diameter than in height and made of concrete; tanks are generally smaller and taller and often made of steel plate.

slurry thinners A number of organic or inorganic chemicals or wast products which , when added in small amounts, make it possible to produce slurry with less than normal water without loss of fluidity. The use os such slurry sometimes results in reduced fuel consumption, more kiln and raw mill production, and larger slurry basin capacity.

slurry trench A narrow excavation whose sides are supported by a slurry made of mud, clay, or cement and mud filling the excavation. In dam construction, sometimes used to describe the cutoff itself.

slushed joints Head joints, filled after units are laid by throwing mortar in with edge of the trowel.

slusher A mobile drag scraper with a metal slide to elevate the bucket to dump point.

slush grouting Distribution of a portland-cement slurry, with or without fine aggregate as required, over a rock or concrete surface which is subsequently to be covered with concrete, usually by brooming it into place to fill surface voids and fissures.

slush ice *(see frazil ice)*

slushing Hydraulic filling.

slush mould A mould into which wet clay is poured to form tiles.

slush pump The mud pump for a rotary drill.

slype A passageway, such as from transept to chapter house or from cloister to deanery.

small tool (spoon) A small curved steel plastering tool for mitering, molding or scratching an indentation in a molding; used for finishing moldings by hand and made in several shapes.

smart aleck *(slang)* A limit switch that cuts off power if a machine part is moved beyond its safe range.

smithing The forging of steel or iron while hot.

smith's hammer A medium-weight hammer, shaped like a sledge, only with a cross peen.

smith welding Welding by forging.

smoke An air suspension (aerosol) of particles, usually but not necessarily solid, often originating in a solid nucleus, formed from combustion or sublimation. Also defined as carbon or soot particles less than 0.1 micron in size which result from the incomplete combustion of carbonaceous materials such as coal, oil, tar, and tobacco.

smoke chamber That part of the flue directly above the fireplace.

smokeless arch An inverted baffle placed in an up-draft furnace toward the rear to aid in mixing the gases of combustion, and thereby to reduce the smoke produced.

smoke pipe Pipe from heating unit to chimney that carries products of combustion.

smoker *(slang)* A diesel truck.

smoke radiator The part of a heating unit that connects onto the drum or combustion chamber. This part holds or retains the smoke and other products of combustion and obtains additional heat from them.

smoke test Test to determine the tightness of a pipe system, by filling it with smoke and tracing the odor.

smooth A description of the fine cut of a file.

smooth ashlar A squared smooth-faced stone.

smoother A planer with a blade from ½ inch to 1¼ inch wide.

smoother bar A drag that breaks up lumps behind a leveling machine.

smoothing iron A heated iron tool for smoothing asphalt and sealing the joints.

smooth roofing An asphalt-coated composition roll roofing with either mica or mica schist embedded in it.

smooth-surfaced roof A built-up roof membrane surfaced with a layer of hot-mopped asphalt, cold-applied asphalt-clay emulsion, cold-applied asphalt cutback, or sometimes with an un-mopped inorganic felt.

smudge (soil) (1) A mix of lamp black and size applied over a lead surface to prevent solder from adhering to it. (2) Waste paint used for formwork or the insides of iron gutters, but not for finish painting. (3) Sewage.

snafu Situation normal, all fouled up.

snag boat A boat equipped with a hoist and grapple for clearing obstacles from the path of a dredge.

snake (1) *(slang)* A coil of wire, designed to travel through bends and around corners when pulling wires through conduit. (2) A flexible metal cable made to travel through pipes, as when necessary to clear an obstruction, etc.

snake hole A hole driven into a toe for blasting, with or without vertical holes.

snakehole shot A charge placed in a hole under a boulder to break it out of the ground.

snakeholing Drilling under a rock or face in order to blast it.

snaking Towing a load with a long cable.

snap The head of a rivet gun that shapes the rivet head.

snap header (blind header) A half-brick, not actually a header.

snaphead rivet A rivet with a rounded head.

snappy flame Short, brisk, high temperature flame, resulting from a high percentage of primary air, fine grinding or atomization of the fuel, and effective mixing of fuel and air.

snap tie A wire wall-form tie, the conical end of which can be twisted or snapped off after the forms have been removed.

snatch block A pulley in a case which can be easily fastened to lines or objects by means of a hook, ring or shackle.

sneak circuit An unwanted feature of a designed circuit.

sneck In rubblework masonry, a small stone used to fill in between larger stones.

snibill A true hinge, having a pintle.

snips *(see tin snips)*

snivvey *(slang)* A guy wire or a sling.

snow density The moisture content of snow, expressed as a ratio of the snow depth after and before melting.

snow guard A device, usually in the form of projecting wires or the like, on a roof slope, to prevent or at least hinder snow slides.

snow load The live load for which a flat roof may be designed in temperate or cold climates.

snowman Formation of sticky clinker following discharge from rotary kiln.

snow plow A machine for removing snow from a road. A blade snow plow is towed by a tractor or truck; a rotary snow plow has a rotating blade or is a self-contained unit with blade in front.

snub To take two or three turns of rope around a shaft to ease a load down.

snub gable A gable roof that is snubbed or truncated at the top; done for architectural purposes.

snug fit Descriptive of the most precise and closest fit that can be assembled by hand.

SO₂ A toxic colorless gas (sulfur dioxide). Produced from burning sulfur-containing fuels and/or processing sulfur-containing raw materials.

soaker (1) A small piece of flexible metal cut to interlock with slates or tiles to make a watertight joint at a hip or valley or at an abutment between roof and wall. (2) A type of head used in underground sprinkler systems for watering areas planted with flowers or shrubs; also called a bubbler.

soaking (1) Saturating with water. (2) Prolonged exposure of clinker to heat. Kilns may be designed (or operated) to produce a soaking heat (to drive off alkalies).

soaking period In high-pressure steam curing, the time during which the live steam supply to the kiln or autoclave is shut off and the concrete products are left to soak in the residual heat or moisture; in low-pressure steam curing, the period after the concrete product has reached maximum temperature and during which the steam is shut off and the products are allowed to soak in the residual heat and moisture of the curing kiln.

soap (1) A masonry unit of normal face dimensions having a nominal two-inch thickness or half the normal width of material. (2) Lubricant used when pulling conductors (wires) through conduit.

sock (slang) A woven-cable sling.

socket (1) In plumbing, that portion of a pipe which, for a short distance, is enlarged to receive the end of another pipe of the same diameter. The joint thus made is secured by caulking. A coupling. (see bell; hub) (2) The cavity into which the pivot of a pivoted sash fits. (3) The mortise in a dovetail joint.

socket chisel A woodworker's tool with sharp cutting edges on each side. Usually the upper end of the shank terminates in a socket into which the handle is driven.

socket inlet (plug) An electrical fixture attached to the flex of an appliance for connecting it to the electrical supply through a socket outlet or an adaptor.

socket outlet (wall socket; receptacle) (1) An electrical fixture containing two or three holes into which the metal prongs of an adaptor or socket inlet are inserted. (2) That part of a plug-in connector for gas which is attached to the wall.

socle An architectural term applied to a projecting member at the base of a supporting wall or pier or at the bottom of a pedestal or column.

sod Grassy surface soil held together by the matted roots of grass and weeds.

sodium-vapor lamp A light source used chiefly in street lighting, utilizing electric discharge in the vapor; the yellow color of the light approaches the point of maximum luminosity in the spectrum.

soffit (1) The underside of any subordinate member of a building, such as the under surface of an arch, cornice or stairway. (2) The uppermost part of the inside of a sewer, drain or culvert; also called crown. (3) Any undersurface except a ceiling.

soffit block Concrete masonry unit for use in concrete floor or roof construction where a uniform ceiling texture is desired.

soffit board (planceer piece) A horizontal board attached to the underside of the rafters, forming a soffit under an overhanging eave.

soffit spacer A piece of metal used to hold the beam bottom a predetermined distance from the structural steel.

soft-burned Clay products which have been fired at low temperature ranges, producing relatively high absorptions and low compressive strengths.

softening point The temperature at which asphalt softens as determined by the special ASTM apparatus; sometimes erroneously called melting point.

soft ground   Earth as contrasted to hard ground or rock; usually, with depth, soft ground is water-bearing and semifluid.

soft-mud brick   Brick produced by molding relatively wet clay (20 to 30 percent moisture), often a hand process. When insides of molds are sanded to prevent sticking of clay, the product is sandstruck brick. When molds are wetted to prevent sticking, the product is waterstruck brick.

soft particle   An aggregate particle possessing less than an established degree of hardness or strength as determined by a specific testing procedure.

soft solder   Fine solder or plumber's solder which melts below red heat, unlike hard solder.

softwood   Lumber made from the trees of the conifer type known as the needle-bearing trees. The term has no reference to the actual hardness of the wood.

softwood sizes   *(see deal)*

soil   (1) Generic term for fine earth material produced by the decomposition of various rocks, mixed organic matter and decomposed vegetable matter above bedrock. (2) In plumbing, sewage as opposed to dirty water. *(see smidge)*

soil analysis   *(see mechanical analysis)*

soil borings   A boring made on the site in the general location of the proposed building to determine soil type, depth of the various types of soils, and water table level.

soil branch   A sewer branch leading to a soil pipe.

soil-cement   A mixture of pulverized soil and measured amounts of portland cement and water, compacted to high density. As the cement hydrates, the mixture becomes a hard, durable paving material.

soil cover (ground cover)   (1) A light roll roofing used on the ground of crawl spaces to minimize moisture permeation of the area. (2) A type of bank protection employed on inverted highways using fast growing shrubs and other plants to deter erosion of the slopes. It is less expensive and has greater aesthetic value than other types of protection.

soil drain   A drain for carrying sewage to the sewer.

soil, heavy   A fine grained solid, made up largely of clay or silt.

soil mechanics   The study of the composition of soils, their classifications, strength, water flow through them, and active and passive earth pressures in relation to them.

soil mortar   Soil fraction in mixtures passing a No. 10 sieve.

soil pipe (soil stack)   The drainage main, chiefly vertical, into which branch lines drain plumbing fixtures.

soil pressure   *(see contact pressure)*

soil profile   A section showing the vertical succession of soil on a site.

soil retardant   Agent applied to carpet pile yarns to resist soiling.

soil sample   Any soil specimen.

soil sampler (sampling spoon)   A tube driven into the ground to obtain an undisturbed sample. Used primarily for clays, since the technique of getting undisturbed samples of clean sand is much more complicated.

soil stabilization (soil solidification)   Any method of strengthening soil to reduce shrinkage and insure against movement.

soil stack   A general term for the vertical main of a system of soil, waste or vent piping.

soil survey   *(see subsurface investigation)*

soil test   A test to ascertain whether soil is suitable for leaching and to determine the size of the tile field.

solar access or solar rights   The ability to receive direct sunlight which has passed over land located to the south; the protection of solar access is a legal issue.

solar cell   *(see photovoltaic cell)*

solar collector   Device (normally constructed of glass, plastic and/or metal, with insulation) which receives radiation from the sun and transfers heat to a fluid or air.

solar constant   The average amount of solar radiation reaching the earth's atmosphere per minute. This is just under 2 langleys, 2 gram calories per square centimeter.

solar dryer   One simple form consists of two posts and a length of rope for drying clothes. Often called clothes line. Other similar devices used for drying crops, air, etc.

solar energy   The heat energy derived from the sun's rays is commonly referred to as solar energy. Solar energy arrives at the earth's plane in two components—diffuse and direct.

solar flat plate collector   Solar collector in fixed flat shape, distinguished from curved, concentrating collector.

solar flux   This is the incident radiation/unit time on a given collector surface and represents the available energy for heating purposes. This is a quantity, commonly measured in langleys or Btu per ft2, which must be established for rating the collector.

solar fraction   The percentage of a building's seasonal heating requirements provided by a solar system.

solar freeze protection   Antifreeze solution or drain down method which prevents the collectors from freezing.

solar furnace   A solar concentrator used to produce very high temperatures; also a trade name for a modular air heating system, usually ground mounted, with rock storage.

solar gain   The part of a building's heating load, or an additional cooling load, which is provided by solar radiation striking the building or passing into the building through windows.

solar heat   Heat trapped from the sun's rays.

solar heat exchanger   Relatively large surface area (normally coils or rock) which transfers the heat directly or from storage to the space to be heated. The area is large for flat plate collectors

because the temperatures are relatively low when compared to a boiler, furnace or electric coil.

solar heat gain   The increase in temperature resulting from the collision of solar energy with a surface through which the waves cannot penetrate, e.g., drapes, blinds, furniture, rugs, etc.

solarimeter   A simple solar radiation measuring instrument using solar cells.

solar insolation   (1) Total radiation available to the earth, or a collector. Comprised of:
(a) Direct Solar Radiation
(b) Difuse Solar Radiation
(c) Reflected Solar Radiation
(2) The amount of energy available from the sun per unit area of collector surface.

solarium   A living space enclosed by glazing; a greenhouse.

solar noon   Solar noon is when the sun is directly overhead and, on a clear day, solar insolation is maximum. The sun's rays pass direct through the atmosphere and on to the receiver with a minimum length of passage through the air.

solar orientation   The designing of a building with the large glass areas facing the south, to take advantage of winter sun.

solar pump   A device using solar energy to run a steam engine or electric motor to pump water.

solar radiation   The direct transfer of energy from the sun to some body of matter. This energy travels in straight lines through empty space or through suitably 'transparent' media, e.g., glass.

solar reflecting surface (spar finish)   Special finish to a flat roof consisting of materials such as white rock, chips, etc., to reduce the heating of the roof in sunlight.

solar still   Equipment for desalting water by using sun's heat.

solar storage   Medium (normally fluid and/or rocks) which holds solar energy to help carry the system through nights or cloudy days.

solar system   A solar system is an assembly of components which includes collectors, heat exchangers, transport system, storage, and controls and supplemental heat source. The purpose of the system is to collect and utilize solar energy through the movement of a fluid.

solar thermal electric power   The indirect conversion of solar energy into electricity by solar collectors, a heat engine, and electrical generators.

solar tracking collector   Collector which moves, orienting itself towards the sun.

solder   (1) Any alloy used to join metals except those which consist mainly of the pure parent metal. Plumber's solders and fine solders are lead-tin allows. Brazing or hard solders are copper-zinc alloys and sometimes silver alloys. (2) To make a tight junction of metallic sheets, piping, and the like, by the application of a molten alloy.

soldering iron (copper bit; soldering bolt)   A small bit, often copper, attached to thin steel rod with a wooden or other insulating handle. The copper bit may be heated electrically or by other means.

soldier   (1) In masonry, that side or face of a brick which shows on the face of the wall in a vertical position. (2) An upright column for holding timbers against the walls of an excavation for bracing. (3) Vertical wales used for strengthening or alignment. (4) Stretcher set on end with face showing on the wall surface.

soldier arch   A flat arch made of uncut bricks placed on end.

soldier beam   A rolled steel section driven into the ground to carry the force of a horizontal sheeting earth bank.

soldier course   A course of units set on end with the face showing on the wall surface; oblong tile laid with the long side vertical and all joints in alignment.

sole   (1) In carpentry, a term applied to a horizontal foot piece on the bottom of a wall to which the studs are nailed. (2) The smooth under-surface of a plane, from which the cutting iron projects.

solenoid valve   A valve opened by electromagnetic action and closed by gravity.

soleplate   (1) The horizontal member of a frame wall resting on the rough floor, to which the studs are nailed. (2) A sill.

Solétanche   A method of making an underground diaphragm wall.

solid block   A concrete masonry unit whose net cross-sectional area in every plane parallel to the bearing surface is 75 percent or more of its gross cross-sectional area measured in the same plane.

solid bossing   Bossing lead to shape instead of soldering it.

solid bridging (block bridging; strutting)   Bridging of floor joints by short lengths of joist cut to fit tightly between, and at right angles to, the joists at midspan.

solid door   (1) A flush door with a solid, not a skeleton, core. (see *hollow-core door*) (2) A fire-resisting door built with three thicknesses of tongued and grooved boarding, the inner one horizontal, the outer ones vertical. Sometimes such a door is plated with sheet metal.

solid loading   Filling a drill hole with all the explosive which can be crammed into it, except for stemming space at the top.

solid map   A geological map showing no drift but only the solid formation called bedrock.

solid masonry unit   Any block with a cross-sectional area in every plane parallel to the bed of 75 percent or more of the bed area. A hollow masonry unit has solid of less than 75 percent of the bed area.

solid molding (stuck molding)   A molding cut directly into the board.

solid panel   A solid slab, usually of constant thickness.

solid partition   A partition which has no cavity. It may be of brick, block or plastered on both sides.

solid plasterwork   Solid core plaster which is formed in place.

solid rock   Rock that can only be moved or processed after being blasted.

solids   (1) That part of paint, varnish or lacquer that does not evaporate but stays and dries on the surface to form the film. (2) Substances rigid and definite in form, without free movement between molecules and without tendency for molecules to separate from each other. Substances in the solid state at standard conditions are considered to be solids.

solid stop   A stop rebated into a solid frame.

solid strutting   Solid bridging.

solid top block   Concrete masonry unit which has a solid top for use as a bearing surface or in a top course of a wall.

solid unit masonry   Masonry consisting wholly of solid masonry units laid contiguously in mortar.

solid volume   *(see absolute volume)*

solid web   A web of a beam consisting of a plate or other rolled section. A box girder is usually considered to be a solid web girder.

solubility   The quantity of dissolved substance (solute) which is contained in a unit quantity of saturated solution at a given temperature and pressure.

solute   A component (originally solid, liquid, or gas) of a solution, usually present in lesser amount than the solvent.

solution   A liquid of at least two substances, one of which is a solvent in which the other or others are dissolved. solution, eutectic   A mixture which melts or freezes normally at constant temperature and with constant composition. Its melting point is usually the lowest possible for mixtures of the given substances.

solvent   (1) A liquid component of a solution usually present in greater amount than the solute. (2) A liquid in which another substance may be dissolved.

Somes Sound granite   A biotite granite of Maine; coarse, inclined to medium grain in a light grayish buff.

sommer   *(see summer beam)*

sones   Pertaining to sound.

sonic modulus   *(see dynamic modulus of elasticity)*

sonic pile driver   A vibrating pile driver.

Sonotube   A circular preformed casing made of laminated paper used for forming cylindrical piers or stems.

soot   Dark, organic particles formed by incomplete combustion of organic fuels.

soot door (ashpit door; cleanout door)   A door at the base of a chimney through which soot can be removed.

Sopwith staff   A telescopic self-reading leveling staff divided into three sections set one above the other when the staff is fully extended.

sorbent   A material which extracts one or more substances present in an atmosphere or mixture of gases or liquids with which it is in contact, due to an affinity for such substances.

Sorel's cement   *(see magnesite flooring)*

sotto portico   A covered public way beneath the overhanging upper story and behind the columns of a facade.

sound   A wave motion in the air.

sound absorbing units   One sound absorbing unit is equivalent to one square foot of a perfectly absorbing surface (e.g., open window).

sound absorption coefficient   The fraction of the instant energy absorbed (not reflected) by a material when a sound wave strikes it.

sound board   The covering of a pulpit to deflect the sound into a church.

sound boarding   Horizontal boards fitted between joists and resting on them to increase the sound insulation of the floor.

sound foci   When sound is reflected in such a way as to be concentrated in high intensity in a region of limited extent, these regions are known as sound foci.

sounding   (1) Determining the depth of a river or ocean by an echosounder or sounding line. (2) Driving a steel rod into the soil to determine the depth of bedrock. *(see penetration tests)*

sounding line   A surveying lead line.

sounding well   A vertical conduit in the mass of coarse aggregate for preplaced aggregate concrete, provided with continuous or closely spaced openings to permit entrance of grout; the grout level is determined by means of a float on a measured line.

sound intensity   Amount of sound power per unit area.

sound isolation   The method of preventing vibration and noise produced by machinery or equipment.

sound knot   A solid, tight undecayed knot at least as hard as the wood around it. *(see unsound knot)*

sound leaks   Cracks under doors, openings in a wall, pipe or wiring holes, etc., which allow sound to escape through a structure from one room to another.

sound lock   A small acoustically treated entrance vestibule usually used in broadcasting studios.

soundness   The freedom of a solid from cracks, flaws, fissures or variations from an accepted standard; in the case of a cement, freedom from excessive volume change after setting; in the case of aggregate, the ability to withstand the aggressive action to which concrete containing it might be exposed, particularly that due to weather.

sound pressure level (SPL)   Expressed in decibels, the SPL is 20 times the logarithm to the base 10 of the ratio of the pressure of sound to a reference pressure of 20 micropascals. *(see decibel)*

soundproofing   Insulation in the form of sound-deadening material in walls, ceilings or floors.

sound-reduction factor (acoustical reduction factor)   A value expressed in decibels, giving a measure of the reduction in intensity of the sound of any given frequency which passes through a wall.

sound transmission   *(see transmission loss)*

sound transmission class (STC)   A rat-

ing for evaluating the effectiveness of a construction in isolating airborne sound transmission. Higher numbers indicate more effectiveness.

sound wave   A pressure disturbance in air proceeding at a finite velocity (approximately 1120 ft./sec.).

source   Any point or place from which materials are emitted which are (or which may become) air contaminants.

southing   In surveying, a distance measured southwards from an east-west axis. *(see latitude)*

sowdel   *(see saddle bar)*

soya glue   A glue made from soya bean meal after the oil has been extracted.

space   (1) In a screen, the actual dimension of the clear opening between adjacent parallel wires or bars. (2) Of a saw, the length from one point of a tooth to the next.

spaced loading   Loading so that cartridges or groups of cartridges are separated by open spacers which do not prevent the concussion from one charge from reaching the next.

space frame   A three-dimensional frame stable against wind loads without further bracing.

space heating   Heating the space in a building by either direct or indirect heating.

space lattice   A space frame built of lattice girders.

spacer   (1) A worker in a pipe gang who sees that proper spacing is kept between pipe sections to permit strong weld. (2) A device which maintains reinforcement in proper position, or wall forms at a given distance apart before and during concreting. *(see spreader)* (3) Small block of composition wood, neoprene, etc., placed during installation on each side of lights or panels to center them in the channel and maintain uniform width of sealant beads; prevents excessive sealant distortion after settling.

space sheating   The framing method of using 1x4 or 1x6 boards on top of the trusses spaced 4″ to 6″ apart, for tile roofs. This method is used instead of using plywood.

spacing (1) The distance between drill holes along a line parallel to the face. (2) Distance between center lines of beams, columns, roof trusses, purlins, etc. *(see pitch)*

spackling (spackle; sparkling) A putty-like material for the filling of cracks and holes in plaster, sometimes in wood, to prepare the smooth surface for further finishing.

spad A surveyor's nail.

spading Consolidation of mortar or concrete by repeated insertions and withdrawal of a flat, spadelike tool.

spall A chip or small piece of stone broken from a large block; a small fragment removed from the face of a masonry unit by a blow or by action of the elements.

spall drain *(see French drain)*

spalling The cracking or flaking of particles from a surface.

span The clear horizontal distance between structural supports, as those of a bridge, or between columns of a structure.

spandrel (1) The surface at the side of a half-arch between a vertical line at the bottom of the archivolt and a horizontal line through its top. (2) In skeleton-frame buildings, the panel of wall between adjacent structural columns and between the window-sill and the window head next below it.

spandrel beam A beam which lies in the same vertical plane as the exterior wall.

spandrel wall That part of a curtain wall above the top of a window or door in one story and below the sill of a window or door in the story above.

Spanish roofing tile (mission tile) A rounded-top, interlocking side-joint tile.

span roof A pitched roof.

spar (1) Old term for timber. (2) A common rafter.

sparge pipe A perforated pipe used for flushing a urinal.

spark arrester A screen over the top of a chimney or the smoke stack of equipment.

sparked tape Drywall or joint tape with minute perforations that do not permit joint cement to squeeze through.

sparklers Particles of glowing pulverized coal that fall from the plume or flame through the kiln atmosphere onto the clinker bed. Usually caused by improper grinding of coal.

sparkling *(see spackling)*

sparky *(slang)* An electrician.

spar piece (span piece) A collar beam.

sparrow peck (1) Texture given to plaster by pitting with a stiff brush. (2) Texture given to stone by picking.

spatterdash A rich mixture of portland cement and coarse sand which is thrown onto a background by a trowel, scoop or other appliance, so as to form a thin, coarse-textured, continuous coating; as a preliminary treatment before rendering, it assists bond of the undercoat to the background, improves resistance to rain penetration, and evens out the suction of variable backgrounds. *(see parge, dash-bond coat)*

spave Peck wood used in natural stone and concrete.

spec *(slang)* Specification.

special conditions A section of the conditions of the contract, other than general conditions and supplementary conditions, which may be prepared for a particular project. Specific clauses setting forth conditions or requirements peculiar to the project under consideration, and covering work or materials involved in the proposal and estimate, but not satisfactorily covered by the general conditions. *(see conditions of the contract)*

special decompression chamber A chamber to provide greater comfort for employees when the total decompression time exceeds 75 minutes.

special detail drawings Larger-scaled and sometimes full-size detailed drawings of specific areas made to insure the builder full information.

special provisions *(see special conditions)*

special purpose tile A tile, either glazed or unglazed, made to meet or to have specific physical design or appearance characteristics such as size, thickness, shape, color, or decoration; keys or lugs on backs or sides; special resistance to staining, frost, alkalies, acids, thermal shock, physical impact, high coefficient of friction, or electrical properties.

special steep asphalt A roofing asphalt that has a softening point of 190°F or 88° Celsius and conforms to the requirement ASTM stand 312 Type 3.

specific adhesion Chemical bond between glued or cemented substances as opposed to mechanical bond.

specification A description, for contract purposes, of the materials and workmanship required in a structure, as also shown by the related working drawings. The written material containing the standard provisions and special provisions, as may be necessary, pertaining to the quantities and qualities of materials to be furnished under the contract.

specific gravity The ratio of the mass of a unit volume of a material at a stated temperature to the mass of the same volume of a gas-free distilled water at a stated temperature.

apparent The ratio of the mass in air of a unit volume of a material at a stated temperature to the mass in air at equal density of an equal volume of gas-free distilled water at a stated temperature. If the material is a solid, the volume is that of the impermeable portion.

bulk The ratio of the mass in air of a unit volume of a permeable material, including both permeable and impermeable voids normal to the material, at a stated temperature to the mass in air of equal density of an equal volume of gas-free distilled water at a stated temperature.

bulk (saturated-surface-dry) Same as bullk specific gravity except that the mass includes the water in the permeable voids. *(see absolute specific gravity)*

specific heat The amount of heat required to raise the temperature of one pound of substance one degree compared to the amount of heat required to raise the temperature of the same mass of water one degree.

specific production Kiln production per unit of volume or surface.

specific retention The ratio of the volume, or weight of water which a soil will retain against the force of gravity, after having once been saturated to its own volume or weight.

specific surface The surface area of particles contained in a unit weight or absolute unit volume of a material. *(see Blaine Fineness)*

specific yield Of soil, the ratio of the volume or weight of water which it will yield to the force of gravity after having once been saturated to its own volume or weight.

specified dimensions Dimensions specified for the manufacture or construction of masonry, masonry units, joints, or any other component of a structure.

spectral absorptance The quantity characterizing the ability of a substance to retain radiation which is incident upon it. It is equal to the ratio of the amount of radiation absorbed by a substance to that which would be absorbed by a black body for a given wave length.

spectral range A region of the electromagnetic spectrum defined by a continuity of wave lengths between two defined wave length limits.

spectral reflectance The quantity characterizing the surface of a substance equal to the ratio of the amount of incident radiation which is reflected to that which would be reflected by a black body for a given wave length.

spectrophotometer Instrument for measuring intensity of radiant energy of desired frequencies absorbed by atoms of molecules; substances are analyzed by converting the absorbed energy to electrical signals, proportional to the intensity of radiation. *(see infrared spectroscopy; flame photometer)*

speculative builder   One who develops and constructs building projects for subsequent sale or lease.

specus   Water channel for an aqueduct.

speed of sound   1,120 ft. per second or 763 miles per hour is the speed of sound in air.

speed reducer   Gear box used between engine and load to cut down rpm.

spelter   Ingot form of zinc.

speroni   Wall buttresses; anterides.

sphere   Any round body of space bounded by one surface. every part of which is equidistant from a point within called the center; also, any round solid with every point on its surface equidistant from the center.

spider   (1) Structural steel rotating framework supporting harrows in washmill or air pipes in slurry agitators. (2) *(see yoke)*

spider plate   *(slang)* The top plate of a guy-derrick mast to which all the guy cables are fastened.

spier   *(slang)* A fixed screen serving as a partition.

spigot   In plumbing. the plain end of a pipe which enters the enlarged end of the next pipe to form a joint between the two lengths; the plug or peg used to close the vent of a pipe; a term sometimes applied to a faucet or cock.

spike   A heavy type of nail used in fastening large timbers.

spike knot   In woodworking, a knot sawed lengthwise.

spikers   The laborer who drives in the spikes on a railroad; a railroad laborer; a gandydancer.

spile (forepole)   A plank driven ahead of a tunnel face for roof support. A wood pile.

spiling   Forepoling.

spillway   A structure over or through which flood flows are discharged. If the flow is controlled by gates, it is considered a controlled spillway; if the elevation of the spillway crest is the only

control, it is considered an uncontrolled spillway.

fuse plug spillway   A form of auxiliary or emergency spillway comprising a low embankment or a natural saddle designed to be overtopped and eroded away during a very rare and exceptionally large flood.

ogee spillway (ogee section)   An overflow in which the cross-section of the crest, downstream slope, and bucket forms an S or ogee curve.

primary spillway (principal spillway)   The principal or first-used spillway during flood flows.

shaft spillway (morning glory spillway)   A vertical or inclined shaft into which flood water spills and then is conducted through, under, or around a dam by means of a conduit or tunnel.

side channel spillway   A spillway in which the crest is roughly parallel to the channel immediately downstream of the spillway.

siphon spillway   A spillway with one or more siphons built at crest level.

spindle   (1) A small axle, as the spindle of a vane on which doorknobs are fixed. (2) A short turned part, as that on a baluster.

spinning   (1) Chemical Spinning) The process of producing manmade fibers, including the extrusion of the spinning liquid through a spinneret into a coagulating medium and the winding of the filaments onto bobbins or in cake form. (2) (Mechanical Spinning) Twisting together and drawing out short fibers into continuous strands of yarn.

spinning line   A chain or rope used as a wrench in attaching and detaching drill pipe sections.

spira   A group of moldings on the base of a column or pilaster.

spiral   Suspension pattern for chain system in rotary kiln in which the ends of each chain loop are separated a certain distance longitudinally in the kiln and at the same time a certain number of degrees in a circle transverse to the kiln axis.

spiral cleaner A device for removing dirt from a conveyor belt.

spiraling (1) Rifling. (2) A drill hole twisting into a spiral around its intended center line.

spirally reinforced column A column in which the vertical bars are enveloped by spiral reinforcement; e.g., closely spaced continuous hooping.

spiral reinforcement Coiled wire or bar held to a definite pitch or spacing.

spiral staircase A flight of stairs winding around a central vertical support or open space.

spire A tapering tower or roof; any elongated structural mass shaped like a cone or pyramid; also, the topmost feature of a steeple.

spiriting off The final operation in French polishing, in which the last trace of oil is removed by a rag dampened with methylated spirit rubbed, quickly and often, over the surface.

spirit level A glass tube containing fluid and an air bubble.

spirit stain Dye dissolved in alcohol, usually with shellac or other resin as a binder; used for darkening a wood surface.

spirit varnish Varnish made by dissolving a gum or resin in alcohol or other spirit.

spit The depth of one hand-shovel blade.

spit out A glaze defect of the pinhole type developed in the decorating kiln, due to evolution of minute gas bubbles from body or glaze.

spitzer Oversize particle in ground material.

splash block A solid concrete masonry unit which is laid with its top close to the ground surface to receive roof drainage and carry it away from the building.

splashboard (1) Board placed on edge against a wall beside a scaffold to help keep the wall clean. (2) A weather molding placed at the foot of an outside door.

splash lap That part of the overlap of flexible-metal drip or roll which ex-

tends over the flat surface of the next sheet.

splash plate Refractory or high alloy steel shelf located in a preheater riser duct below the raw meal entry pipe. It is used to disperse raw meal into the flowing gases in the riser duct.

splat A covering strip over joints in wallboards. *(see joint tape)*

splay A slanted surface or beveled edge; an oblique surface, bevel or chamber, as of the sides of a doorway or window; splay corner.

splay angle Two surfaces forming an angle over 90°.

splay brick (slope brick; cant brick) A special brick beveled at about 45° at one end, a splay header, or 45° along one edge, a splay stretcher.

splayed ground Ground with beveled or rebated edge to provide a key for the plaster when the ground also acts as a screed.

splayed heading joint Joint between the ends of floorboards cut at 45° so that one overlaps the other.

splayed skirting Skirting with top edge beveled, instead of molded.

splice (1) The joining together of two similar materials by weaving, welding, bolting, nailing or gluing; e.g., in piling, cable, bridge forms, etc. (2) The repaired break in a sheet of roofing or felt.

splice bar (splice piece) *(see fishplate)*

spline (1) A flexible strip with provision for holding it in desired curves, used as a drafting aid. (2) A thin strip forming a key between two boards or planks and locking their edges together; usually the spline is of rectangular section, but sometimes of X-section. (3) A wood strip screwed or nailed to a window frame for glazing. (4) A feather.

split (1) A masonry unit half the height of a full unit. (2) A separation in roofing material resulting from movement of the substrate. *(see crack)*

split batch charging Method of charging a mixer in which the solid ingredients do not all enter the mixer together;

cement, and sometimes different sizes of aggregate, may be added separately.

split block Concrete masonry units with one or more faces having a fractured surface appearance for use in masonry wall construction.

split cable grip A woven wire basket device used for gripping wires, traveling cables, etc. Also called 'Chinese fingers.'

split course A course of bricks cut lengthwise to reduce depth to less than an ordinary course.

split face A rough face formed by guillotining cast or natural stone units.

split level house A residence having living areas on two or more levels.

split loading Method of batching concrete in which the soil ingredients do not all enter the mixer together. *(see split batch charging)*

split pipe Pipe cut lengthwise; a channel.

split shakes Wooden shingles which have been split instead of sawn.

split spoon sampler Used in soils exploration, a type of drill core.

split sprocket A two-piece sprocket that can be assembled on a shaft without removing the shaft bearings.

split system A heating system utilizing two simple systems, such as radiators and also indirect warm air.

split tail *(slang)* A claw hammer.

splitter A wide chisel used for splitting stone.

splitting A condition occurring with flat wall paints when applied over a sealer coat that has not thoroughly hardened; a later stage of alligatoring.

splitting tensile strength Tensile strength of concrete determined by a splitting tensile test.

splitting tensile test (diametral compression test) A test for tensile strength in which a cylindrical specimen is loaded to failure in diametral compression.

splocket A sprocket.

splush Semi-dense cut-pile carpet, about half-way in appearance between shag and plush, whose tufts lie less irregularly than shag but not as regularly as plush.

spoil Dirt or rock which has been removed or separated from its original location or solid form.

spool (1) The moveable part of a slide-type hydraulic valve. (2) To wind in a winch cable. (3) A distance piece between timbers, usually cast iron.

spoon A special length of pipe split in half lengthwise and driven deep into the earth to take samples of underlying strata.

spoon bit A dowel bit.

spot To direct trucks to the exact loading or dumping place.

spot board (gauge board) A plasterer's board on which he works up the plaster before he applies it.

spot grounds Pieces of wood attached to the plaster base at various intervals for gauging plaster thickness.

spot level The elevation of a given point in surveying.

spot log A marker or log placed to show a truck driver the spot where he should stop to be loaded.

spot mopping Bitumin applied in roughly circular areas, generally about 460 mm (18 in.) in diameter, leaving a grid of unmopped, perpendicular areas.

spotter (1) In truck use, the man who directs the driver into loading or dumping position. (2) In a pile driver, the horizontal connection between the machinery deck and the lead or pile guide.

spotting (1) Directing trucks for loading or dumping. (2) In soil stabilization, laying bags of stabilizer in position on the ground. (3) A defect of a painted surface with spots of different color or gloss from the rest. (4) Adhesive material applied in plastic form that attaches thin veneer units to the backing.

spot wobbling A method of display on an IR scanner which broadens the lines of the display thereby filling the spaces between the lines on the screen. Sometimes used to improve the apparent resolution of the picture.

spout-delivery pump   A pump, like a diaphragm pump, to deliver water no higher than itself. *(see force pump)*

spray application   The use of mechanical equipment to apply ceiling or wall texture materials.

spray bar   A pipe with jets to spray binder onto a road surface from a pressure tank.

spray drying   A method of evaporating the liquid from a solution by spraying it into a heated gas.

sprayed asbestos (limpet asbestos)   Asbestos blown onto a surface by a spray gun.

sprayed concrete   *(see gunite)*

sprayed mortar   *(see shotcrete)*

spray gun (air brush; spraying pistol; paint spray)   A compressed air tool for ejecting a fine mist of paint, powder, metal coating or cement mortar.

spray lance   The pipe of a hand sprayer carrying the jets.

spray painting (spraying)   Putting paint, lacquer or other substance on with a spray unit.

spray texture   A mechanically applied material used to produce various decorative finishes. May contain aggregates for different effects.

spread   *(slang)*   The mobile power equipment under the direction of a spread superintendent.

spreader   (1) A temporary board placed in a horizontal position, halfway up the window or door frame, to prevent the masonry from crowding inward. (2) A piece of wood or metal used to hold the sides of a form apart until the concrete is poured.

spreader beam (yoke)   A beam hanging from a crane hook, with ropes or chains hanging from different points along it, used for lifting a long reinforced-concrete pile, a large glass sheet, or any other long fragile object to prevent its breakage during lifting.

spreader box   A machine that is designed to spread material on a roadway or area to be paved.

ABC   A tow-type spreader that lays down ABC to the specified thickness.

asphalt   *(see laydown machine)*

cement   A tow-type spreader that spreads the specified amount of cement on the flat surface to be mixed for a cement treated base course.

chip   A self-propelled or tow-type machine designed to spread finely graded aggregate.

spreader hopper   That part of a roofing machine which spreads the granule surfacing or backing mineral on the hot coated sheet.

spread footing   A generally rectangular prism of concrete larger in lateral dimensions than the column or wall it supports, to distribute the load of a column or wall to the subgrade.

spreading   The process of laying mortar on masonry units with a trowel to make a bed in which to lay subsequent units.

spreading rate   In painting, the square yards of surface covered by one gallon of mixed paint. This term is preferred to covering power.

spread recorder   An instrument used in bridge testing to measure the outward spread of an abutment during loading.

spread superintendent   Ranks with general superintendent in ordinary construction operations; has charge of all operations.

sprig   A small wire headless nail such as a glazing sprig.

sprig bit   A bradawl.

spring   (1) Of an arch, the initial rise from the impost. (2) In lumber, a variety of warp which consists of the bending of a board in a plane parallel to its face. (3) An elastic body or device that recovers its original shape when released after being distorted.

spring buffer   A heavy wire spring, mounted in an elevator pit. It cushions or stops a car or counterweight that descends beyond the normal limit of travel.

springer   The stone or unit from which an arch springs; the lowest stone of a gable is sometimes called a springer.

spring gear   Master spur gear for rotary

kiln fastened to shell by spring plates tangential to kiln.

spring, helper On a truck rear axle, an upper spring that carries no weight until the regular spring changes shape under load.

spring hinge A joint, with a spring built into it, used for self-closing doors.

springing The creation of a pocket in the bottom of a drill hole by the use of a moderate quantity of explosives in order that larger quantities of explosives my be inserted therein.

springing line (spring line) The imaginary horizontal line at which an arch or vault begins to curve; for minor arches, the line where the skewback cuts the soffit; for major, parabolic arches, the line where the arch intersects the skewback.

spring loaded Held in contact or engagement by springs.

spring washer A steel ring washer cut through and bent to a slow helical curve to prevent a nut from unscrewing; may be used in place of a lock nut.

sprinkle The distribution of additional chips on a terrazzo topping prior to rolling.

sprinkler system (1) In building, an arrangement of overhead pipes equipped with sprinkler heads or nozzles. In case of fire, these nozzles automatically release sprays of water for extinguishing the fire. (2) An outdoor underground lawn watering system.

sprocket A gear that meshes with a chain or a crawler track; a cocking piece.

sprocketed eaves Eaves tilting outward by use of sprockets.

sprouting Protrusion of individual tuft or yarn ends above the surface pile level of carpet.

spruce An important wood with a number of species, including eastern spruce, Engelmann spruce and Sitka spruce, of which the Sitka is in wide use; a strong, light, shock-resisting wood used for interior and exterior finish, siding and general construction.

sprue A projecting inlet in a mold through which metal is poured for casting.

sprung molding In carpentry, a term applied to a curved molding.

spud (1) A dowel in the foot of a door post attaching it to the floor. (2) A steel shaft driven by a pile driver through clay or old fill to open up a hole for the pile. Also raising and dropping a pile when little progress can be made with the driving hammer. (3) A nail used by surveyors for hanging a plumb bob as a mark for a survey station. (4) (anchoring spud A steel post under a dredger lowered by a toothed rack or by ropes until it is fixed in the bottom; serves as an anchorage for the dredger.

spudding drill (churn drill) A drill that makes holes by lifting and dropping a chisel bit.

spud keeper The framework on the back of a dredge that holds spuds or legs dropped down to anchor the dredge barge when dredging.

spudshovel Used by roofers to remove roofing material.

spud well On a dredge, a pair of guide collars for a spud.

spud wrench A long tapering steel handle with a wrench on one end; used by ironworkers to line up holes to make steel connections.

spunbonded A generic name for nonwoven fabrics formed directly from polymer chips, spun into continuous filaments which are laid down and bonded continuously, without an intermediate step.

spunlaced A Hydroentangled nonwoven fabric whereby a dry laid staple fabric is mechanically bonded by water jet which entangles the individual fibers.

spun concrete Concrete compacted by centrifugal action, e.g., in the manufacture of pipes.

spunware Circular forms of thin metal produced by spinning.

spun yarn A yarn consisting of fibers of regular or irregular staple length usually bound together by twist.

spur (1) A rock ridge projecting from a

side wall after blasting. (2) A sharp-pointed carpenter's tool used for cutting veneer. (3) An electrical single cable socket outlet connection from a ring main.

spurdike (wing dam) Used in river training as contraction works to establish normal channel width; to direct the axis of flow; to promote scour and sediment deposition where required; and to trap bed load to build up new banks.

spur valley A short branch valley.

square (1) A plane figure having four equal sides and four interior right angles. (2) An area of flooring, roofing, etc., which is 10 feet square. (3) An open rectangular space in a community; a park. (4) An instrument, sometimes combined with a measure, for determining right angles. (5) Descriptive of lines or planes at right angles to each other.

squared log (1) A baulk. (2) A half-timer, baulk sawn lengthwise, at least 5×10 inches in cross section.

square joint A butt joint.

square-mile foot A volume of water one foot deep over one square mile. *(see acre foot)*

square roof A roof which has rafters rising at 45° and meeting at a right angle at the ridge.

square shoot A formed wooden down-pipe.

square staff A rectangular wood fillet fixed as an angle bead, for plastering.

squaring (working up) Calculating areas, a process which follows taking off from the drawings or measuring up the work.

squeeze Of a molding, to press wet plaster over it to take a cast from which a template can be cut.

squeeze riveter A large single-stroke air cylinder which closes rivets by action of a toggle mechanism.

squib A detonation consisting of a firing device and a chemical that will burn with a flash which will ignite black powder.

squinch A small arch built across an interior corner of a room for carrying the weight of a superimposed mass, such as the spire of a tower.

squint An oblique opening in the interior wall of a medieval church to afford a view of the high altar for persons in the aisles; a hagioscope.

squint brick In masonry, a brick which has been shaped or molded to a special desired form; a purpose-made brick.

squint quoin A projecting building corner, not at a right angle.

squirrel-cage motor An alternating-current motor used for many purposes. The rotor consists of a number of parallel bars on the perimeter, joined to end rings. There need be no electrical connection between the rotor and the outside of the motor.

squirrel-tail pipe jointer A pipe-jointing clip.

stab (stabbing) (1) In adding to a drill string, the action of lining up and catching the threads of the loose piece. (2) In masonry, a term used when referring to the process of making a brick surface rough in order to provide a key for plasterwork.

stability A structure's resistance to sliding, overturning or collapsing.

stabilization The process of giving natural soils enough abrasive resistance and shear strength to accommodate traffic or loads.

stabilizer A substance which makes a solution or suspension more stable, usually by keeping particles from precipitating.

stable door (Dutch door) A door cut through horizontally at about half its height, with each half hung separately.

stack (1) A vertical range of bookshelves. (2) A chimney, particularly a large or tall one. (3) A vertical range of piping with branches, for heating or plumbing. (4) A rainwater downpipe.

stack bond (stacked bond) Bond pattern in which the head joints form a continuous vertical line.

stack effect The rising of heated air over a dark surface by natural convection to create a draft; used to provide summer ventilation in some passive homes.

stack effluent Outflow discharge from a stack carrying gaseous and particulate process wastes to the atmosphere. Usually passed through filters or precipitators.

stacker A large mobile elevating belt used for stockpiling material.

stack gas Aggregate of gaseous, liquid, and solid materials emitted from a source.

stackhead A wall or baseboard register box.

stack height The height of a gravity convector between the bottom of the heating unit and top of the outlet opening.

stack vent The extension at a soil or waste stack above the highest horizontal drain connected to the stack.

stacking tile A method of installation whereby glazed tiles are placed on the wall so that they are in direct contact with the adjacent tiles. The width of the joints is not maintained by the use of string or other means. The tiles may be set with either straight or broken joints.

stadhuis In the Netherlands, a town house or city hall.

stadia In surveying, a term used to denote the procedures for obtaining horizontal distances and differences in elevation by indirect methods which are based on the optical geometry of the instruments employed.

stadia rod A leveling staff with graduations for stadia work.

stadium A circular, oval or round-ended sports amphitheater.

staff (1) A short-lived exterior wall covering resembling stucco, used chiefly for exposition buildings and the like. (2) A rod of light metal or wood, with graduations painted on it; used in leveling or stadia work. (3) Plaster casts of ornamental details made in molds and reinforced with fiber. Usually wired or nailed into place.

staff bead (1) In plastering, an angle bead; a vertical member protecting or decorating the salient angle of a wall, particularly when it engages plaster, stucco or staff. (2) The outside molding member of an exterior architrave, fitting snugly against the adjoining wall.

staff gauge In hydraulics, a graduated scale on a rod, metal plate, or on the masonry of a pier for reading the level of the water.

staff man A worker who carries the leveling staff for a surveyor in leveling or stadia work.

stage (1) Elevation of the surface of a river; depends on such factors as amount of rainfall and runoff. (2) A platform raised above the floor level at the front of a theater, lecture hall, classroom or other large room.

stage grouting Sequential grouting of a hole in separate steps or stages in lieu of grouting the entire length at once.

stagger To arrange in parallel rows but with objects in one row opposite a space in the next.

staggered courses Courses of shingles laid with butts not in a horizontal line.

staggered-stud partition A partition made of two rows of studs separated from each other, each surfaced by its own covering. The rows of studs fit into the gap in the opposite row and may be separated by an insulating blanket. This discontinuous construction is used for reducing sound transmission between rooms.

staggering An arrangement of joints spread to distribute their weakness, or of supports which are spread to give uniform strength.

staging Temporary platform working space in and around a building under construction or repair; scaffolding.

stagnation A high temperature condition obtained in a solar collector when the sun is shining and no fluid is flowing through the collector; temperature range from 250 degrees F to 400 degrees F, depending on collector design. Any condition under which a collector is losing as much heat as it gains.

stain Color in a dissolving vehicle; when spread on an absorptive surface, it penetrates and gives its color to the wood or other material.

stained glass Glass given a desired color in its pot-metal state; or such glass disposed in decorative or pictorial compositions with the use of lead cames, metal frames and stiffeners.

stainless steel A hard, tough steel which retains polish; an alloy of steel which contains a high percentage of chromium, sometimes with the addition of nickel and copper. Has excellent resistance to corrosion.

stain, shingle A form of oil paint, very thin in consistency, intended for coloring wood with rough surfaces, such as shingles, without forming a coating of significant thickness or gloss.

stair A step, alone or in a series, facilitating walking from one level to another.

stair carriage A stringer for steps on stairs.

staircase A series of steps or a flight of stairs, sometimes with landings, handrails, newels, etc.

stairhead Top of a stair.

stair landing A platform between flights of stairs.

stair platform An extended step or landing breaking a continuous run of stairs.

stair railing A vertical barrier erected along exposed sides of a stairway to prevent falls of persons.

stair rise The distance from the floor to the top of a landing, or to the floor above.

stair run The horizontal distance between the first riser and the face of the platform, or stair opening above.

stairs (stairways) A series of steps leading from one level of floor to another, or leading to platforms, pits, boiler rooms, crossovers, or around machinery tanks and other equipment that are used more or less continuously or routinely by employees or only occasionally by specific individuals. A series of steps and landing having three or more rises constitutes stairs or stairway.

stair treads The upper horizontal boards of a flight of steps; the portion actually stepped upon.

stair well A compartment extending vertically through a building in which stairs are placed.

stake (staking out) (1) A short piece of lumber or metal pointed at one end for driving into the ground. (2) To mark, with stakes driven into the ground, the location of a proposed structure or work site.

side A stake on the line of the outer edge of the proposed pavement; any stake not on the centerline.

slope A stake marking the line where a cut of fill meets the original grade.

stake hound *(slang) (see short staker)*

stake notes A written record by the engineer or surveyor of the actual field location of the survey stakes.

stalk (1) The vertical portion of a reinforced-concrete retaining wall. (2) The central part of a tee-section.

stamba An isolated pillar serving as a memorial.

stanchion (1) A vertical post, two of which flank the animal's head, used to confine a cow in a stable. (2) An upright bar between mullions of a window.

standard In surveying, a U-shaped metal casting fixed on the upper plate of a theodolite, carrying the telescope trunnions.

standard brick In masonry, common brick size is $2\frac{1}{4} \times 3\frac{3}{4} \times 8$ inches; permissible variables are plus or minus $\frac{1}{16}$ inch in depth, $\frac{1}{8}$ inch in width, and $\frac{1}{4}$ inch in length.

standard conditions Used as reference point for compressible fluids for calculating and reporting results. Unless otherwise specified, 60 degrees F (15.6°C) and 1.0 atmosphere (total pressure) at dry-gas conditions. Standard atmospheric pressure at sea level is 29.92 inches of mercury (760.0 millimeters of mercury); barometric conditions other than these are to be corrected to standard pressure at sea level.

standard curing Exposure of test specimens to specified conditions of moisture or humidity and of temperature.

standard details Design drawing details which are common to many jobs, and have been made into permanent drawings.

standard dimension The manufacturer's designated dimension.

standard hexagonal A roofing shingle or strip with the edge cut to form a hexagonal pattern when applied on a roof surface.

standard hook A hook at the end of a reinforcing bar made in accordance with a standard.

standard matched Tongue and groove lumber with the tongue and groove offset rather than centered as in center matched lumber.

standard penetration test Made in boreholes by means of the standard two-inch outside diameter split-spoon sampler; sometimes known as the Raymond Sampler.

standard pile *(see guide pile)*

standard pressure In plumbing, a term applied to fittings and valves which are suitable for a working pressure of 125 pounds per square inch (psi).

standard provisions Contract and construction provisions which are common to many jobs and are used unless the project requires special provisions. Ordinarily used in conjunction with the special provisions.

standard railing A vertical barrier erected along exposed edges of a floor opening, wall opening, ramp, platform or runway to prevent falls of persons.

standard rating A standard rating is a rating based on tests performed at Standard Rating Conditions.

standard sand Ottawa sand accurately graded to pass a U.S. Standard No. 20 (841 micron) sieve and to be retained on a U.S. Standard No. 30 (595 micron) sieve, for use in the testing of cements. *(see Ottawa sand; graded standard sand)*

standards of professional practice Statements of ethical principles promulgated by professional societies to guide their members in the conduct of professional practice.

standing derrick *(see derrick)*

standing ladder A ladder with rectangular stiles, as distinguished from a builder's ladder. An extending ladder is built of two or more standing ladders.

standing pier A bridge pier with spans on each side, as opposed to an abutment pier.

standing pilot Pilot light that is on all the time.

standing seam A flexible-metal roofing seam, generally running from ridge to eaves.

standing waste A vertical overflow pipe inserted in the customary bottom outlet of a bowl or tank.

standing water level The level at which ground water finally stands in a hole or pit left open for some time.

standing water test Evaluations in which test panels are submerged in aqueous solutions and alternately dried in air.

standpipe (1) A tall vertical pipe for holding a liquid such as water; used to secure a uniform pressure in a city water supply system. (2) A pipe or tank connected to a closed conduit and extending to or above the hydraulic grade line.

stand up time Time an unsupported excavation can be maintained in a tunnel or drill pier. Used to test soil stability.

stank (1) A small timbered cofferdam watertight with clay. (2) To make watertight; to seal.

Stanley compensating diaphragm A compensating diaphragm used in surveying, designed specifically for stadia work. Others include Beaman stadia arc and Jeffcott direct-reading tachometer.

staple (1) A double-pointed U-shaped piece of metal. Used to attach mesh wire, electric cable, and for other purposes when nails will not suffice. (2) Fiber in the natural, unprocessed state, usually in short lengths, which must be spun or twisted into yarn, as opposed to continuous filament.

star drill A tool with a star-shaped point used for drilling in stone or masonry.

starling A piling, usually timber, driven into the river bed of a bridge pier to form an enclosure.

star molding A common molding in Norman architecture.

starter (motor starter) **(1)** Protective equipment, automatic or hand operated, which insures that a motor does not receive too high a current when starting up. **(2)** In drilling, a short steel used to start a drill hole.

starter frame *(see kicker)*

starter strip A strip of composition roofing applied to the lower edge of a roof surface before the first row of shingles is laid.

starting newel A post at the bottom of a staircase for supporting the balustrade.

starting platform A movable platform used to support a seaming machine as it begins to roll-seal a metal seam.

starting step The first step at the bottom of a flight of stairs.

stat Contraction of thermostat.

statement of probable construction cost Cost forecasts prepared by the architect or engineer during the schematic design, design development and construction documents phases of basic services, for the guidance of the owner.

statically-determinate frame (perfect frame) A frame in which the reactions and bending moments can be determined by the laws of statics.

statically-indeterminate frame (redundant frame) A frame in which the reactions and bending moments cannot be calculated from the law of statics because the frame has more members or more fixity than a perfect frame.

static balance A condition of rest created by inertia sufficient to oppose outside forces.

static cone penetration test A test where the cone is thrust down by hydraulic cylinder for a penetration of three inches into the soil. The results are correlated directly with bearing capacity and settlement of shallow foundation and piles.

static head The difference in water level between two points, such as between the reservoir and the tailwater of a water turbine.

static load The weight of a single stationary body or the combined weights of all of the stationary bodies in a structure such as the load of a stationary vehicle on a roadway; or, during construction, the weight of forms, stringers, joists, reinforcing bars and the actual concrete to be placed. *(see dead load)*

static load indentation Indentations in the floor covering caused by heavy objects (furniture, appliances, etc.) that remain in place for long periods of time.

static moment The static moment of a section about an axis YY, also called its first moment of area about the axis. It is the sum of the products obtained by multiplying each element of area (a) by its distance (x) from YY. It can be explained as: first moment + the sum of (x times a) or $E(xa)$.

statics A branch of mechanics; the basis of structural engineering. The study of forces and bodies at rest.

static Young's modulus of elasticity The value of Young's modulus of elasticity obtained by arbitrary criteria from measured stress-strain relationships derived from other than dynamic loading. *(see modulus of elasticity)*

station Any one of a series of stakes or points indicating distance from a point of beginning or reference.

 minus Stakes or points on the negative side of the zero point from which a job was originally laid out.

stationary hopper A container used to receive and temporarily store freshly mixed concrete.

station-point perspective (centro-linear projection) A form of linear perspective in which the point of sight is assumed to be fixed and the line of sight is perpendicular to the plane of projection.

station roof (umbrella roof) A roof cantilevered to one or both sides and carried on a single row of stanchions.

station yards of haul The number of cubic yards multiplied by the number of 100-foot stations through which it is moved.

statistical stability & drift Changes in the characteristics of the random process governing results of a test procedure.

statistics (1) The study of population measurements and variations from the mean. (2) Used in estimating the strength or mineral content of a batch of concrete or ore from a few samples.

stator In a torque converter, a set of fixed vanes to change the direction of flow of fluid entering the pump or the next stage turbine.

statumen A lime and sand mortar used in ancient Rome in paving.

statute of limitations A statute specifying the period of time within which legal action must be brought for alleged damage or injury. The lengths of the periods vary from state to state and depend upon the type of legal action. Ordinarily the period commences with the discovery of the act resulting in the alleged damage or injury, although in construction industry cases a number of jurisdictions define the period as commencing with completion of the work or services performed in connection with it.

statutory bond A bond, the form or content of which is prescribed by statute.

staunching piece (staunching bead) In concrete dams, a vertical gap left between successive bays of concrete. The gap is not concreted until most shrinkage in adjoining bays has occurred.

staunching rod A rubber rod in contact with a crest gate compressed between the gate and the structure to form a watertight joint.

stave A ladder rung.

staves Vertical sheathing in a circular column form.

stay A prop; a guy wire.

stay bar (1) A horizontal bar to strengthen a mullion or leaded light; a casement stay. (2) A temporary brace which holds the two opposite walls of a building in place and prevents them from spreading apart.

stay pile A pile driven or cast in place as an anchor for a land tie holding a sheet pile wall, etc.

stay tacking Temporary tacking of the carpet to hold the stretch.

steady flow In hydraulics, the stream line flow.

steady point A pointed steel bar which can be locked in a clamp, and is used to brace a drill frame against the ground.

steady state intensity The intensity level in a room when a sound source continues long enough for sound waves from the source to fill the room.

steam Water in the vapor phase.

steam atomization Process of using steam to break the oil into small particles to prepare for combustion.

steam blown (steam refined) Processing of residuum or petroleum flux by use of steam.

steam boiler *(see boiler)*

steam box Enclosure for steam curing concrete products.

steam cleaning Cleaning with steam, usually under pressure.

steam curing Curing of concrete or mortar in water vapor at atmospheric or high pressures and at temperatures between about 100° and 420° F (30° and 215° C). *(see atmospheric-pressure steam curing; autoclave curing; single-stage curing; two-stage curing)*

steam-curing cycle The time interval between the start of the temperature-rise period and the end of the soaking period or the cooling-off period; also a schedule of the time and temperature of periods which make up the cycle.

steam-curing room A chamber for steam curing of concrete products at atmospheric pressure.

steam engine A piston-driven engine operated by the force of steam on the piston; a reciprocating engine.

steam fitter   A worker skilled in piping for steam or hot water heating.

steam hammer   *(see pile hammer)*

steam kiln   *(see steam-curing room)*

steam pipe   A pipe for carrying steam.

steam shovel   A power shovel operated by steam.

steam trap   A device for allowing the passage of condensate, or air and condensate, and preventing the passage of steam.

steatite   Soapstone in slab form used for hearths, fireplace facings, laundry tubs, etc.

steel   Iron compounded with other metals to increase strength, wearing or rust resistance or to obtain other desired qualities.

air hammer   The hollow or solid steel bar which connects the hammer with the cutting tool.

chromium   An alloy of steel possessing extreme hardness; it can be machined when annealed; used chiefly for bearing plates.

drill   Steel with the end threaded to take a detachable bit.

steel casement   A window casement made of steel; may be fixed directly to the wall or to a subframe.

steel centralizer   On a wagon drill, a guide to hold the steel in proper alignment.

steel changes   The difference in length between successive steels used in drilling one hole.

steel drawings   Drawings proved by the architect, which show the arrangement and sizes of steel used in the construction of a building.

steel erector   A skilled worker, one of two who climbs onto a steel frame to fix each end of a steel beam as it is lowered by a crane.

steel-frame   Describing a building in which the support is achieved by a closely knit structure of steel.

steel-grit blasting   A type of shot blasting.

steel lathing   An expanded metal or steel wire mesh used as metal lathing in plastering.

steel puller   A hinged clamp on the bottom of a hand drill.

steel ring   A ring of pressed steel, used for lining a tunnel or other circular section. Shaft rings are usually of cast iron and known as tubbing.

steel sheet   Cold-formed sheet or strip steel shaped as a structural member for the purpose of carrying the live and dead loads in lightweight concrete roof construction.

steel sheet piling   Interlocking rolled-steel sections of sheet piling driven vertically into the ground, before excavation is begun, along the edge of a guide waling.

steel square   An instrument having at least one right angle and two or more straight edges; used for testing and laying out work for trueness. A term frequently applied to the large framing square used by carpenters.

steel trowel   A flat steel tool for smoothing and creating a dense finish on concrete surfaces.

steel wool   A mass of fine steel threads matted together and used principally for polishing and cleaning surfaces of wood or metal.

steelworker (iron worker)   A worker skilled in structural steel or reinforcing for concrete.

steening   Brickwork without mortar, as in a leaching cesspool.

steep asphalt   A roofing asphalt that has a softening point of approximately 220° F or 104° Celsius, that conforms to the requirements of ASTM Standard D312 Type 4.

steeple   A tower and spire, usually on a church.

steeplejack   A worker who repairs and /or builds steeples or other tall brick or masonry structures.

steering brake   A brake which slows or stops one side of a tractor.

steering clutch   A clutch which can disconnect power from one side of a tractor.

Steiner Tunnel Test   *(see tunnel test)*

stele An upright slab of stone bearing an inscription and occasionally bas-relief sculpture.

stellite A cobalt, chromium and tungsten alloy with a little carbon, manganese, silicon and iron. Much harder than steel; applied by welding to the wearing parts of drilling tools.

stem bars Bars used in the wall section of a cantilevered retaining wall or in the webs of a box; when a cantilevered retaining wall and its footing are considered as an integral unit, the wall is often referred to as the stem of the unit.

stemming A suitable inert incombustible material or device used to confine or separate explosives in a drill hole, or to cover explosives in mudcapping.

stem wall The part of a wall that extends from the top of a foundation footing up to the floor. Generally constructed of concrete or masonry.

step One unit of tread and riser, alone or in a series, in a flight of stairs.

step bracket A bracket form, carved or sawn, for ornamenting the end of a step in an open-string stair.

step down transformer A transformer which has a higher voltage at the primary winding terminals than at the secondary winding terminals.

step joint Joint between a rafter and tie-beam; the tie-beam is notched with a birdsmouth to receive the end of the rafter.

step ladder A ladder built with rectangular stiles and treads designed to be horizontal in use. Usually built in the form of an inverted V, with locking devices to hold it steady.

stepped Gabled roof; one whose rake is stepped rather than straight or curved.

stepped flashing Flashing, against a wall or chimney, where the masonry joint entered must necessarily change at intervals to keep at a safe distance above the sloped roof surface.

stepped footing A step-like support consisting of prisms of concrete of progressively diminishing lateral dimensions superimposed on each other to distribute the load of a column or wall to the subgrade.

stepped skirting Asphalt skirting placed at a sloped intersection with a roof.

step up transformer A transformer which has a higher voltage at the secondary winding terminals than at the primary winding terminals.

stereobate A substructure of a building without columns in Classical architecture.

stereometric map A graphic map showing valleys and elevations which can be easily visualized by looking at the map.

stereoscopic (three-dimensional vision) Ordinary vision in which depth and distance is seen and can be estimated. A plotting instrument enables vertical photographs to be seen stereoscopically.

stereotomy The art of properly sizing and placing cut stones in a masonry structure.

Stevenson's formula A formula to determine the height of waves developed by gales traveling over the water for a distance of F nautical miles or the fetch. It applies only to unobstructed deep water, since even submerged sandbanks cause waves to break.

stick (1) A waxed-paper cartridge of explosives, usually 1¼x8 inches. (2) A long piece of wood, as a stick of lumber. (3) In a dipper shovel or pull shovel, a rigid bar hinged to the boom and fastened to the bucket.

sticker (1) A small separator laid between sheets of freshly cut plywood in the direction in which warping is most likely to occur. (2) *(slang)* One who catches a hot rivet, thrown by a heater, and sticks it in the rivet hole with tongs.

sticking The cutting of a molding in a woodworking mill.

sticking board In carpentry, a framed board in which small pieces are held steady while being molded or stuck with a plane.

sticky cement Finished cement which

develops low or zero flowability during or after storage in silos, or after transportation in bulk containers, hopper-bottom cars, etc.; may be caused by (a) interlocking of particles, (b) mechanical compaction, or (c) electrostatic attraction between particles. *(see warehouse set)*

stiffback *(see strongback)*

stiffened suspension bridge Suspension bridge with stiffening girders.

stiffener (web stiffener) A small structural member added to a slender beam or column to prevent buckling.

stiffener lip A short extension of material at an angle to the flange of cold formed structural members, which adds strength to the member.

stiffener ring Steel ring, commonly of a rectangular cross section, welded to outside of kiln shell to help minimize elliptical deformation.

stiffening girder A girder built into a suspension bridge to distribute the load uniformly among the suspenders and reduce the local deflections under concentrated loads.

stiff frame A redundant frame.

stiff-mud brick Brick produced by extruding a stiff but plastic clay (12 to 15 percent moisture) through a die to form a column which is cut by wires into individual brick units.

stiffness Resistance to deformation.

stiffness factor A measure of stiffness, indicated by the ratio of moment of inertia of the cross section to the length of the member.

stile (1) Steps flanking a fence or wall to aid in passing over it. (2) A vertical framing member of a paneled door or paneling.

S-tile A roofing tile of which the cross section resembles a prone letter S.

stile end A junction between the patent glazing and the roof, including the flashing at the junction.

still Enclosed tank equipped with a method of heating and perforated pipes for introduction of air and/or steam; used for changing the characteristics of

bituminous residuum into material for use as roofing material.

stillicidium Dripping eaves of a Doric building.

stilling pool An enlarged deepening of the river at the foot of a dam spillway to lower the flow speed and reduce scour.

stilling well A pipe, chamber or compartment with closed sides and bottom except for a comparatively small inlet or inlets communicating with a main body of water; its purpose is to dampen waves or surges while permitting the water level within the well to rise and fall with the major fluctuations of the main body.

Stillson wrench A pipe wrench.

stilted arch (stilted vault) An arch or vault having some length of vertical intrados above the impost.

stilts Adjustable extensions worn on the shoes to reach higher than normal areas.

stinger *(slang)* A welding rod; welding rod holder or clamp.

stipple To dab a coat of paint with a stippler brush to remove regular brush marks immediately after a coat is put on; to break up the color coat with spots of a different color, or to break up its texture with a bristle or rubber stippler.

stippler A paint brush with many tufts of soft bristles set in a flat stock with the bristle tufts all ending in the same plane; used to even up the coat of paint, remove brush marks and leave the wet surface with a uniform, slightly granulated finish. A rubber stippler is used for breaking up texture.

stippling In surface painting, the use of the brush point, a sponge, or the like, to secure a texture unlike that given by brush strokes or spraying.

stipulated sum agreement Contract in which a specific amount is set forth as the total payment for performance of the contract. *(see lump sum contract)*

stirrup A reinforcing device to resist shear and diagonal tension stresses in a beam; typically a steel bar bent into a

U-shape and installed perpendicular to or at an angle to the longitudinal reinforcement and properly anchored.

stirrup strap (hanger; bridle iron) A steel strap, used in carpentry, built into brickwork or fixed to a post or beam for holding a horizontal member up to it.

stitch The number of lengthwise yarn tufts in one inch of tufted carpet.

stitch screw A fastener used to connect panels together at the side lap.

stoa In ancient Greek architecture, a portico or cloister.

stob *(slang)* A short grade stake.

stob-jobber *(slang)* A worker who drives the surveyor's stakes.

stock (1) Commonly used and commercially available patterns and sizes, as stock window sash, stock doors, etc. (2) Converted lumber, also called stuff. (3) The body or handle of a tool. (4) A tool which holds a die for cutting an external thread.

stockade A space surrounded by logs driven into the ground as a palisade.

stock brush A brush used to wet a wall before plastering, to prevent it absorbing too much water from the plaster.

stockhouse set *(see sticky cement)*

stock lumber Wood sawn to standard sizes.

stockpile Material dug and piled for future use.

stoker A mechanical device for feeding coal or other fuel into a fire chamber.

stoker timer A stoker control for allowing a stoker to run periodically, regardless of the thermostat. It prevents the fire from going out.

Stokes's law (Stokes's formula) The settling velocity of spherical particles in liquid; utilized for determining the diameters of those parts of a soil sample which cannot conveniently be sieved, being smaller than a 200 mesh sieve.

stone (1) Any natural rock deposit or formation of igneous, sedimentary and/or metamorphic origin, either in original or altered form. (2) A car-

borundum or other natural or artificial hone for putting a cutting edge on tools. (3) Individual blocks, masses, or fragments of rock taken from their original formation and considered for commercial use.

stone drain A rubble drain.

Stonehenge Megalithic remains on Salisbury Plain, England.

stone lime Any lime except that made from chalk.

stone mason A building craftsman skilled in constructing stone masonry, including preparation of the stone as necessary on the construction site.

Stone Mountain granite A medium-grain granite quarried in Georgia; widely used, of uniform light gray.

stone sand *(see sand; fine aggregate)*

stone seal (armor coat) An application of heavy bituminous material, approximately 0.3 gallon per square yard, such as a rapid curing cutback covered with 18 to 40 pounds of crushed rock, slag or gravel chips per square yard. Repeated applications form an armor coat or inverted penetration.

stone setters' adjustable multiple-point suspension scaffold A swinging type scaffold having a platform supported by hangers suspended at four points so as to permit the raising or lowering of the platform to the desired working position by the use of hoisting machines.

stone tongs Nippers.

stoneware Baked ceramic material from which channels, drains and other drainage fittings are made; it is nearly always salt glazed. *(see earthenware)*

Stonington Pink/Gray granite *(see Deer Isle)*

Stony Creek granite A warm reddish granite of Connecticut, varying from medium to coarse grain, with bold veinings.

stool (1) The flat, narrow shelf forming the top member of the interior trim at the bottom of a window. (2) A bathroom plumbing fixture; commode.

stoop A broad platform step at the entrance to a house.

stoothing Common grounds for carpentry, lathing, etc.

stop In building, any device which will limit motion beyond a certain point, as a doorstop in a building, usually attached near the bottom of a door and operated by pressure from the foot.

stop bead A strip on a door frame or window frame against which the door closes or the sash slides.

stop chamfer A chamfer which gradually merges into a sharp arris.

stopcock A valve in plumbing work to close a main or branch line of pipe.

stope An underground excavation that is made in a series of steps or benches.

stoper A heavy pneumatic hammer, sometimes a drifter, which delivers up to 200 blows per minute, with much greater force than an ordinary air hammer.

stop glazing Either the stationary lip at the back of a rabbet, or the removable molding at the front of the rabbet; either or both of these serve to hold a light or panel in the sash or frame with the help of spacers.

stop log A log, plank, cut timber or steel or concrete slab or beam, fitting into end guides between walls or piers to close an opening to the passage of water.

stop molding A molding which ends at the stop and does not continue to the end of the member.

stop mortise A blind mortise.

stopper (stopping) A filler used in painting and glazing for filling in holes or cracks. *(see spackle)*

stopping knife a glazier's putty knife, also used by painters for putting spackle into holes or cracks. Similar to a chisel knife, with one rounded edge and one splayed edge, meeting at a point.

stop valve A valve for turning on or off a supply of fluid.

stop work order An order issued by the owner's representative to stop project work for a variety of reasons, e.g., failure to perform according to contract

specifications, unsatisfied liens, labor disputes, inclement weather, etc.

storage Solar storage is storing heat collected during the day in excess of immediate requirements for use overnight or on cloudy days. Unless infinite storage is provided, a system cannot be fully utilized at all times except during periods of high demand. Storage capacity for space heating should match system requirements with regard to carrying peak load. Storage of heat may be accomplished by tanks in liquid base systems or rock piles in air systems.

storage hopper *(see stationary hopper)*

storeroom A room for miscellaneous storage.

storm cellar (cyclone cellar) An underground space for protection against violent windstorms.

storm door An additional outside door in the door frame, for better insulation against weather.

storm drain A drain used for conveying rain water, subsurface water, condensate, cooling water or other similar discharges, but not sewage.

storm overflow A weir, orifice or other device for permitting the discharge from a combined sewer of flow in excess of that which the sewer is designed to carry.

storm overflow sewer A sewer used to carry the excess of storm flow from a main or intercepting sewer to an independent outlet.

storm pavement A gently sloped bank of a breakwater.

stormproof window A casement window with additional protection against rain; for example, hood moldings and throatings, and lips in the joints.

storm sash (storm window) An extra window usually placed on the outside of an existing window as additional protection against cold weather.

storm sewer A sewer designed to carry away storm water or surface water not sewage; usually terminates in a river, dry run, lake or natural drainage basin.

storm sheet Roofing sheet curved

down at one edge to protect an eave against rain.

stormwater Runoff after heavy rain.

stormwater tanks Tanks in which the solid material in runoff settles before the water passes into a stream.

story (storey) That part of a building between any floor and the floor or roof next above.

story pole A long pole used instead of a leveling rod; a rod with grade markings on it, and used with the builder's level.

story rod A rod or pole cut to the proposed clear height between finished floor and ceiling.

stove bolt A bolt threaded from tip to bolt head.

stoving (baking) Drying of paint surfaces by heat.

straddle pole As sloping scaffolding pole laid along a roof line in a straddle scaffold from an upright to meet another straddle pole at the ridge of the roof.

straight arch Flat arch.

straight courses Shingles laid with butts in line.

straightedge A rigid, straight piece of wood or metal used to strikeoff or screed a concrete surface to proper grade. (*see rod; screed; strikeoff*)

straightedged/single-lapped Procedure for cutting flooring seams when there is not enough selvage on large block designs, or if small-scale designs or inerliner patterns are used. Edge of one piece is squared by cutting it along a straightedge. This is then lapped over the edge of the adjoining seam, and with knife held against the squared edge, the under piece is scored. Scored piece is then trimmed along the length of the seam.

straight flight A stair consisting of fliers and no winders.

straight-grain (comb-grain) Descriptive of lumber, particularly flooring, when the grain is clearly seen as continuous parallel lines.

straight joint (1) In carpentry, a butt joint. (2) In brickwork, the joint which is above another joint; a mistake if the bond is structural.

straight-joint tiles Single-lap tiles made so that edges in successive courses run in a line from eaves to ridge.

straight-line theory An assumption in reinforced-concrete analysis according to which the strains and stresses in a member under flexure are assumed to vary in proportion to the distance from the neutral axis.

straight line wiring diagram A wiring diagram that shows the circuits as they are wired, not as they are physically located.

straight-peen hammer A hammer which has a blunt wedge parallel to the shaft of the hammer and a striking face on the opposite end.

straights (*slang*) Flex or tubing connectors of 180°; used for connections which continue the flex or tubing in a straight line.

straight tee In plumbing, a tee which has all openings of the same size.

straight tongue One edge of a board made thinner by rebates so that the tongue can fit into a matching groove.

strain Deformation of a material expressed as the ratio of linear unit deformation to the distance within which that deformation occurs.

strain aging Increase in strength and hardness with aging; seen in steel and iron and in light alloys.

strain energy (1) Energy stored in an elastic body under load. (2) Method of structural analysis based on the amount of work or energy stored in a loaded frame. (*see resilience*)

strainer (1) A globe of wire mesh inserted in a gutter at the top of a downspout to prevent clogging with leaves and debris. (2) A pierced plate at the top of a sink outlet. (3) A device for withholding foreign matter from a flowing liquid or gas.

strain gauge A sensitive instrument to measure small deflections in machines or structures from which the strains can be calculated.

strain wire The steel center supporting wire in a traveling cable.

strain hardening Hardening from cold working.

straining beam Any horizontal strut, especially that between the heads of queen posts in a queen-post truss.

straining piece (strutting piece) A horizontal member attached to the middle of the central, horizontal flying shore as an abutment from which the shorter, sloping struts at each end obtain their thrust.

straining sill A timber on and attached to the tie-beam of a queen-post truss between the queen posts, or between the queen and princess posts, to keep them stabilized.

strake A metal lug or cleat placed on a pneumatic-tired wheel to improve its grip.

strand A prestressing tendon composed of a number of wires most of which are twisted around a center wire or core.

strand grip A device used to anchor strands.

stranded caisson A box caisson.

Stran-steel Cold-rolled steel sections, sport welded together in pairs to provide a nailing slot between them.

strap An iron plate for connecting two or more timbers, to which it is screwed by bolts. It generally passes around one of the timbers.

S-trap (siphon trap) The common trap in plumbing; an S-bend in the drain pipe beneath a fixture to provide a water seal against sewer gases.

strap hinge One in which one leaf is a flat decorative strap and leaves are attached to wall face of jamb and face of door rather than to the eges.

strapped elbow In plumbing, a drop elbow.

strapping Common grounds used as a base for lath and plaster.

strapwork A form of ornamentation employing interlaced raised bands.

stratification The separation of overwet or overvibrated concrete into horizontal layers with increasingly lighter material toward the top; water, laitance, mortar and coarse aggregate will tend to occupy successively lower positions in that order. A layered structure in concrete resulting from placing of successive batches that differ in appearance.

strawberry A small bubble or blister in the flood coating of a gravel-surfaced roof membrane.

straw boss *(slang)* An assistant foreman.

streamline Path of a particle of water which is flowing without turbulence; structure causing such flow, as a fin.

streamlined specifications Specifications containing adequate technical information for the construction of the work but written in an abbreviated manner.

streamline flow In hydraulics, fluid flow in which the movement is continuous and constant. Head loss due to friction is only proportional to the first power of the velocity. The upper limit of speed of streamline flow is Reynold's critical velocity.

street A strip of land used for a public highway in an inhabited area.

street ell A pipe elbow with male threads on one end and female on the other.

strength (1) Strength of material measured by the greatest safeworking stress. This is equal to the yield point, ultimate strength or proof stress divided by an appropriate factor of safety. *(see modulus of elasticity)* (2) The strength of a structural part is the ability to resist loads which rest on it. (3) In an explosive, the energy content in relation to its weight.

compressive (see compressive strength)

creep The stress that causes a given creep in a given time and at a specified temperature.

fatigue (see fatigue strength)

shear The maximum shearing stress which a material is capable of developing based on the original area of cross section.

tensile (see tensile strength)

ultimate   (see ultimate strength)

yield   (see yield strength)

stress   The intensity of the force developed per unit area within a body in resisting the forces acting on it; considered at a point within a plane passing through the body, stress may be divided into two components: normal stress acting perpendicular to the plane and shearing stress tangent to the plane.

stress analysis   Determination of the stresses in the various parts of a loaded structure.

stress circle   Mohr's circle.

stress concentration   A condition in which a stress distribution has high localized stressed; usually induced by an abrupt change in the shape of a member.

stress corrosion   Corrosion of a metal accelerated by stress.

stress diagram   A graphic chart showing direction and amount of each stress in a structural unit.

stressing end   In prestressed concrete, the end of the tendon from which the load is applied when tendons are stressed from one end only.

stress-number curve (S-N curve)   A curve obtained in fatigue testing; it shows the range of stress in a material plotted against the number of cycles to failure.

stress relaxation   Stress loss resulting from strain developed when a constant length is maintained under stress.

stress relieving   Heated steel which is slowly cooled to relieve internal stress.

stress-strain curve   A curve showing the test results on a metal test piece in which the strains are plotted against stresses.

stretch   (1) The width of the area on which a painter will normally apply paint across a ceiling or down a side wall. (2) A surface of single-tier patent glazing expressed in square feet.

stretcher   A masonry unit laid with its length horizontal and parallel with the face of a wall or other masonry member.

stretcher block   Concrete masonry unit which has a flat or concave end and is usually laid with its length parallel to the face of the wall.

stretcher face   The long face of a brick or block seen after it is laid.

stria   (1) The ridge separating adjacent flutes in a column shaft; an arris. (2) Striped. A striped effect obtained by loosely twisting two strands of one shade of yarn with one strand of a lighter or darker shade. The single yarn appears like irregular stripes.

striations   A series of narrow grooves cut lengthwise on the face of a softwood veneer panel for decorative effect.

striding level   A level tube used for cross-leveling a theodolite telescope; it is fitted at each end with a telescoping leg projectng downwards from the tube.

striges   The channels of a fluted column.

strigil ornament   In Roman architecture, a fascia bearing a series of vertical reedlike flutings.

strike   (1) To remove formwork. (2) A long thin piece of wood, metal or other material. (3) In masonry, to cut off with a trowel stroke the excess mortar at the face of a joint. (4) A work stoppage by a body of workers to enforce compliance with demands made on an employer.

strike fault   A rock fault whose strike line is roughly parallel to the strata which it cuts.

strikeoff   To remove concrete in excess of that which is required to fill the form evenly or bring the surface to grade; performed with a straight-edged piece of wood or metal by means of a forward sawing movement or by a power operated tool appropriate for this purpose. *(see screed)*

striking   The releasing or lowering of centering or other temporary support.

striking off   The smoothing off of excess compound at the sight line when applying a compound around lights or panels.

striking off lines   Lines drawn on wall or ceiling for setting plaster.

striking plate (striker plate)   The member of a lock set or latch set that is fastened to the jamb to engage the lock bolt or latch and at the same time to prevent damage by the latter to the wooden edge of the jamb.

strikethrough   A term used in the manufacture of fabric reinforced polymeric sheeting to indicate that two layers of polymer have made bonding contact through the scrim.

striking wedges   Folding wedges.

string   A term applied to one of the inclined sides of a stair supporting the treads and risers.

string board   A board placed next to the well hole in wooden stairs, terminating the ends of the steps. The string piece is the piece of board put under the treads and risers for a support and forming the support of the stair.

string course   A plain or molded horizontal continuous band on an exterior wall.

stringer (wales)   (1) A horizontal structural member supporting joists and resting on vertical supports. (2) The sloping outside strut or decorative end face of a stair.

stringers   *(slang)* Workers on a pipeline crew who distribute lengths of pipe.

stringing   Unloading pipe in approximate location it will be used.

stringing mortar   The procedure of spreading enough mortar on the bed joint to lay several masonry units.

string level   A spirit level equipped with prongs so that it can be hung from a string.

string line   String used as a guide when setting forms.

string loading   Filling a drill hole with cartridges smaller in diameter than the hole, without slitting or tamping them.

string of tools   In a churn drill, the tools suspended on the drilling cable.

strip   (1) A narrow or relatively long piece of roofing, e.g., a strip shingle. (2) Remove overburden or thin layers of pay material. (3) Complete removal of an old finish with paint removers. (4) To remove formwork or a mold. (5) A length of wallpaper cut to fit the height of the wall. In scenics, a single section of the design.

strip board   Obsolete term for blockboard, in which the core blocks are not glued together.

strip flooring   Solid boards designed to be installed in parallel rows, produced in these thicknesses: $\frac{5}{16}''$, $\frac{3}{8}''$, $\frac{1}{2}''$, $\frac{3}{4}''$, $3\frac{1}{2}''$; and these widths: $1\frac{1}{2}''$, $2''$ and $2\frac{1}{4}''$. Designed for nail-down installation over wood subfloors.

strip footing   A combined continuous footing of prismatic or truncated shape supporting two columns in a row. *(see continuous footing)*

strip foundation   A continuous foundation of which the length considerably exceeds the breadth.

stripite   *(see strip lath)*

strip lath   A narrow strip of diamond mesh metal lath sometimes applied as reinforcement over joints between sheets of gypsum lath, at the juncture of two different base materials, at corners of openings, etc.

strippable films   Added protection sometimes applied to continuous strip in coil coating process. Applied after prime and top coats to resist damage prior to and during erection.

strippable paper   A type of wall-paper that can be removed without tearing and without the use of water or steam.

stripper   A liquid compound formulated to remove coatings by chemical or solvent action, or both.

stripping   (1) The removal of forms from poured concrete after it has set. (2) Clearing a building site of the top soil level containing undesirable material. (3) Loss of binder or aggregate from a road surface.

stripping shovel   A shovel with a long boom and stick that enables it to reach farther and pile higher.

strix   A channel in a fluted column.

stroke   Of a piston, length of travel (twice its crank radius).

strongback   A frame attached to the

back of a form to stiffen or reinforce it; additional vertical wales placed outside horizontal wales for added strength or to improve alignment; also called stiff-back.

stroper A hand-size air drill mounted on a column or other support.

struck capacity The capacity of a container, calculated as if it were full of water, so that all material above the edges is imagined to be struck off with a straight edge. The rated capacity is the struck capacity.

struck joint In masonry, where the excess mortar exuding between units is removed by a flush stroke of the trowel.

structural Descriptive of that aspect of a structure or building which, in addition to its own weight, carries the weight and forces placed by all other parts of the structure.

structural analysis Early structural design to determine what forces are carried by all the parts of a structure and what proportions the forces bear to the loads placed on it.

structural bond The method by which individual masonry units are interlocked or tied together to cause the entire assembly to act as a single structural unit.

structural clay tile A term applied to various sizes and kinds of hollow and practically solid building units molded from surface clay, shale, fire clay or a mixture of these materials.

structural defects Cracks or laminations in the body of the tile which detract from the aesthetic appearances and/or the structural soundness of the tile installation.

structural design The proportioning of members to carry loads in a structure in the most economical way. A structural design is carried out in two parts, the first a rough estimate of the loads or structural analysis; the second half consists of proportioning the members according to the calculations of the first half, together with the adjustment of the original calculations to any final altered size of parts.

structural drawing Plans showing the structural components of the building; usually developed by the architect.

structural excavation The excavation and removal of all materials necessary for the construction of structures, pipelines and pipe culverts, including foundations and substructures, in accordance with the details shown on the plans and the specifications.

structural glass Rectangular tiles or panels of glass, used for wall facing.

structural lightweight concrete *(see concrete, structural lightweight)*

structural lumber Any lumber which is two inches or more in thickness and four inches or more in width intended for use in buildings where working stresses are required. The grading of structural lumber is based on the strength of the piece and the use for which the entire piece is intended.

structural steel members Load carrying members. May be hot rolled sections, cold formed shapes, or built-up shapes.

structural steelwork Rolled-steel joints of built-up members fabricated by riveting, welding or bolting.

structural systems (frames) Frames generally constitute parts of a structure such as beams and columns, fabricated offsite but assembled onsite. Into these are fitted infill units, walls, partitions, floors, ceilings and roofs. These latter elements are also sometimes fabricated offsite and assembled to the structural elements onsite.

structural terra cotta (hollow tile) Unit shapes for partitions, wall backing, floor arches, roof slabs, etc.

structure (1) An edifice, especially one of large size or imposing appearance; any kind of building. (2) Any construction composed of parts arranged and fitted together in some way such as a bridge or dam. (3) The loadbearing part of a building.

structure-borne sound Sound energy imparted directly to and transmitted by solid materials, such as building structures.

strut   A supporting piece; an inside brace resisting pressure along its length. *(see shore)*

strut tenon   A term applied to a piece of wood or iron, or some other member of a structure, designed to resist pressure or weight in the direction of its length; used on a diagonal piece, usually on heavy timbers, as a timber extended obliquely from a rafter to a king post. *(see king post)*

strutting   (1) In structural work, using struts as temporary supports. (2) In carpentry, solid bridging or herringbone strutting.

stubbies   *(slang)* Screwdrivers made with very short blades and handles for use in hard-to-get-at places.

stub length   A short end of pipe; not of any specific length.

Stub's iron wire gauge   *(see Birmingham wire gauge)*

stub tenon   A tenon inserted into a blind mortise which, if wedged, must be done by secret wedging.

stub wall   A low wall, placed monolithically with concrete floor and other members to provide for control and attachment to wall forms.

stucco   (1) A term denoting plaster used on exposed exterior locations. The term stucco is used without regard to specific composition of the material. Also termed 'exterior plaster.' (2) A term used within the manufacturing segment of the plaster industry to denote gypsum that has been partially or fully calcined but not yet processed into finished plaster. Also used to denote gypsum formulations for certain special industrial uses.

stuck molding   In carpentry, a molding cut out of a solid piece by a plane or sticker machine; the opposite of a planted molding.

stud   (1) Vertical member of appropriate size and spacing to support sheathing of concrete forms. (2) A series of slender wood members used to support elements in walls and partitions. (3) A bolt having one end firmly anchored.

stud brush   An appliance used to clean and smooth wall studs when spray-on insulation has been applied prior to drywall installation.

stud finder   A tool used to find the studding on a solid wall.

stud gun   An explosive-operated gun which shoots hard male- or female-threaded steel studs into concrete, brickwork or steel. The penetrating end of the stud is pointed, and a safety device prevents the gun from firing except when pressed against a wall.

studio   The workroom of an artist, usually with high ceiling and north light.

stud kicker   *(slang)* An inspector.

stud partition   In carpentry, a partition built of studs; a framed partition.

stud shear   A hand tool for cutting metal studs.

stud shooting   Driving threaded studs with a stud gun.

stud welding   Fixing a metal stud onto a steel frame by resistance welding after the frame is built. The welding is rapid, with the stud being held in place with a special type of gun during welding.

study   Preliminary sketch or drawing to facilitate the development of a design.

stuffing box   A space around a shaft filled with soft packing to prevent fluids or gases from leaking along it.

Stuko-Bak   A felt or paper used in back of exterior plaster or stucco.

stumper   A narrow heavy dozer attachment used in pushing out stumps.

stunt end (form stop; stop end)   Vertical shuttering across a wall, slab or trench to form a construction joint to end the day's concrete pour.

style   (1) Characteristic form, as of a specific period in history. (2) Distinctive or characteristic expression in any art.

stylobate   The main base of a building under the Classical columns.

stylus   An input device used with a computer.

styrofoam   Expanded polystrene (plastic) extruded into board form; closed cell. Highly resistant to moisture.

styrofoam insulation Expanded polystrene extruded into board form.

sub (1) Popular contraction for subcontractor. (2) A threaded thread protector used with drill pipe; a joint protector.

subbase (1) A layer in a pavement system between the subgrade and the base course or between the subgrade and a concrete pavement. The course in the asphalt pavement structure immediately below the base course is called the subbase course. If the subgrade soil is of adequate quality it may serve as the subbase. (2) The bottom front strip or molding of a baseboard. (3) The lowest part of a structural base, which consists of two or more horizontal members, as the base of a column.

sub-basement A story immediately below a basement, or one of several stories below a basement.

sub-bidder One who tenders, to a bidder on a prime contract, a proposal to provide materials and/or labor.

sub-cellar A cellar beneath a cellar.

sub-circuit In electricity, a branch circuit.

subcontract An agreement between the prime contractor and another contractor or a supplier for the satisfactory performance of services or delivery of material as indicated on the plans and specifications, all as evidenced by the contract documents.

subcontractor A secondary contractor who performs some part of the prime contractor's obligation under the contract.

subcontractor bonds A document given to the prime contractor by the subcontractor, guaranteeing performance of his contract and payment of all labor and materials bills in connection with that contract.

subdivision A parcel of land divided into blocks, lots or plots for immediate or future use or sale, or for building developments.

subdrain A drain built beneath a sewer to intercept ground water and prevent it from entering the sewer, especially during construction.

subfloor (1) A floor laid on top of the floor joists, to which the finished floor is fastened. (2) A frame, often of pressed steel, built into a wall as a fixing for a window or door.

subgrade The uppermost material placed in embankments or unmoved from cuts in the normal grading of the roadbed. It is the foundation for the asphalt pavement structure. The subgrade soil sometimes is called basement soil or foundation soil.

subgrade improved Any course or courses of select or improved material between the foundation soil and the subbase is usually referred to as the improved subgrade. The improved subgrade can be made up of two or more courses of different quality materials.

subgrade reaction (*see contract pressure*)

sublet To enter into contract for the performance of work one has himself contracted to perform; subcontract.

submerged orifice An opening which, in use, is drowned by having the tail water higher than all parts of the opening.

submerged weir A weir which, in use, has the tail water level equal to or higher than the weir crest.

submersible pump A centrifugal pump, driven by compressed air or electricity, which can be wholly submerged in water.

submittal Documentation or correspondence submitted to others for consideration, decision and or approval.

subparagraph In the contract documents, the first subdivision of a paragraph.

sub-purlin A light structural section used as a secondary structural member; in lightweight concrete roof construction, used to support the formboards over which the lightweight concrete is placed.

subrail In building, a closed string stair; a molded member called a subrail or shoe is placed on the top edge of the stair string to receive and carry the lower end of the balusters.

subrogation The substitution of one person for another with respect to legal rights such as a right of recovery. Subrogation occurs when a third person, such as an insurance company, has paid a debt of another or claim against another and succeeds to all legal rights which the debtor or person against whom the claim was asserted may have against other persons.

sub saver (sub) A protector for the thread protector on the kelly of a rotary drill.

subsidence (settlement) A sinking of the ground surface.

subsidized housing Housing for low-income groups, the construction costs or rental charges of which are at least partly borne by government or other authority.

sub-sill (sill drip molding) An additional sill fitted to the outside of the window sill after manufacture. Its purpose is to increase the distance from the wall at which the rain is thrown off.

subsistence Extra money paid to employees to compensate them for living costs away from home.

subsoil The materials lying below the surface soil, generally devoid of humus or organic matter. Also the ground below foundation level called the subgrade or foundation.

subsoil drain A drain installed for collecting subsurface or seepage water and conveying it to a place of disposal.

subsoil plow (pan breaker) A one-tooth ripper.

substantial completion (see date of substantial completion)

sub-station A building or room containing electrical equipment, usually with transformers to reduce the high voltage of incoming power to a voltage at which the consumer can use it.

substitution A material or process offered in lieu of and as being equivalent to a specified material or process.

substrate British term for painting ground; the underlying support for the ceramic tile installation.

substructure The lower portion of a structure forming the foundation which supports the superstructure of a building.

sub-subcontractor A person or organization who has a direct or indirect contract with a subcontractor to perform a portion of the work at the site.

subsurface float In hydraulics, an underwater float tied to a surface float so as to more easily read its movement.

subsurface investigation The soil boring and sampling program, together with the associated laboratory tests, necessary to establish subsurface profiles and the relative strengths, compressibility and other characteristics of the various strata encountered within the depths likely to have an influence on the design of the project.

subsystem A complete, physically integrated, dimensionally coordinated, series of parts which function as a unit.

subtense bar A surveyor's bar used in the subtense method of tachometry. The bar is held at the distant point and its distance calculated from the known length and the angle which it subtends at the observer.

suburb An outlying section of, or near, a city; predominantly for residential use.

subway Underground public transportation line.

successful bidder (see selected bidder)

suck The shape of the bottom of a cutting edge or tooth which tends to pull it into the ground as it is moving.

suction (1) The pull of a pump. (2) Absorption possessed by a plastered surface. (3) Atmospheric pressure pushing against a partial vacuum. (4) Adhesion of a mass of mud to the underside of an object being lifted out of it. (5) The adhesion of a brick to set mortar or of wet plaster to a wall. (6) A partial vacuum resulting from wind loads on a building which cause a load in the outward direction.

suction-cutter dredger A suction dredger, used in hydraulics, with a rotating clay cutter at the end of the suction pipe.

suction head (static suction life) The height to which a pump can lift water on its suction side, measured from the free water level in the sump.

suction valve A check valve on a suction pipe near the entry to the sump.

sudden drawdown A rapid drop in water level which produces a critical condition in the design of a dam, quay wall or any earth slope.

suitable That which fits, and has the qualities or qualifications to meet a given purpose, occasion, condition, function or circumstance.

suite A group of rooms and their connections to be used as a unit.

sulfate attack Harmful or deleterious chemical or physical reaction, or both, between sulfates in soil or ground water and concrete or mortar, primarily the cement-paste matrix.

sulfate resistance Ability of concrete or mortar to withstand sulfate attack.

sulfate-resistant cement *(see cement, sulfate-resistant)*

sullage Mud deposited by flowing water; silt.

sulphate of lime Gypsum, anhydrite or a calcium hemihydrate, used in plaster.

sulphur cement Equal parts of sulphur and pitch heated together.

summary of reinforcement A cutting list for reinforcing bars.

summer (summer beam) A heavy horizontal timber or girder serving as a support for some superstructure; a lintel. *(see bressummer)*

summit canal A canal crossing a summit, therefore requiring pumping of the water.

sump A tank or pit which receives sewage or liquid waste, located below the normal grade of the gravity system which must be emptied by mechanical means.

sump pump A small capacity pump for occasionally emptying a sump.

sundeck A deck or flat roof for sun bathing.

sun gears A planetary gear set consisting of a central gear, an internal-tooth ring gear, and two or more planet gears meshed with both of them.

sunk draft Margin of a building stone set below the rest of the face.

sunk face An ashlar face cut below the margins of the stone.

sunk gutter A secret gutter placed below the roof surface.

sunk panels Panels recessed below the surrounding surface.

sun parlor (sun room) A room with many windows.

sunspace A living space enclosed by glazing; a solarium or greenhouse.

sun-tempering A method that involves a significant daytime solar gain and an effective distribution system, but generally lacks a storage system.

sun tracking Following the sun with a solar collector to make it more effective.

super *(slang)* Superintendent.

superblock A reconstruction on the gridiron plan combining a number of blocks by eliminating the dividing streets.

supercapital A block of stone above the capital of a column, as in Byzantine architecture.

supercharger A blower that increases the intake pressure of an engine.

supercilium The molded lintel of a doorway; the fillet crowning the cymatium.

supercolumniation The use of one Classic order above another.

super-duty refractory Highly refractory, fire-clay brick for kiln lining. Has low porosity, high resistance to fluxing and thermal spalling, and strength and constancy of volume at high temperatures.

superelevation Exaggerated tilt of roadway on a curve to counteract centrifugal force on vehicles.

superficial measure Face measure of lumber.

superfund *(see CERCLA)*

superimposed load The live load imposed on a structure.

superintendent Contractor's representative at the site who is responsible for continuous field supervision, coordination, completion of the work and, unless another person is designated, for the prevention of accidents.

superload A structural live load or superimposed load.

supermarket A large retail food store of the serve-yourself type.

superposition A principle which simplifies structural calculations, and which can be used for solving the forces in redundant frames. Stresses in a member due to one system of loading can be added to the stresses in it due to another system of loading. The redundant frame is split first into two or more perfect frames having some members in common. The forces in the perfect frames are determined by statics and those which occur in the same member are added algebraically.

super-steep asphalt A roofing asphalt conforming to the requirements of Specification D 312, Type IV.

superstructure (1) That part of a building or other structure which is carried upon any main supporting level, as a foundation wall. (2) That part of a bridge above the bridge seats, above the spring line of the arches or above the bottom of the caps.

super-sulfated cement *(see cement, super-sulfated)*

supervision Direction of the work by contractor's personnel. Supervision is neither a duty nor a responsibility of the architect or engineer as part of his basic professional services.

supplemental conditions *(see supplementary conditions)*

supplementary conditions A part of the contract documents which supplements and may also modify provisions of the general conditions. *(see conditions of the contract)*

supplement of an angle An angle which is equal to the difference between the given angle and 180°. If the given angle is 165° its supplement is 15°

supplier A person or organization who supplies materials or equipment for the work, including that fabricated to a special design, but who does not perform labor at the site. *(see vendor)*

supply bond A document given by the manufacturer or supply distributor to the owner guaranteeing that materials contracted for will be delivered as specified in the contract.

supply mains (1) The primary piping system bringing water or gas, etc., into a facility. (2) The pipes through which the heating or cooling medium of a system flows from the source of heat or refrigeration to the runouts and risers leading to the heating or cooling units.

support That which upholds.

support moment Hogging moment.

suppressed weir A measuring weir notch whose sides are flush with the channel thus eliminating or suppressing end contractions of the overflowing water. A weir may be suppressed on one end, two ends, bottom, or any combination of them.

surbase (1) A dado capping. (2) A molding which crowns a baseboard.

surcharge Any elevated load which is level with the top of a retaining wall. Surcharges may be temporary live loads such as equipment or permanent dead loads such as earth sloping up from the top of the wall or a building above the top of the wall.

surcharged wall A retaining wall carrying a surcharge, such as an embankment.

surety A firm or corporation executing a surety bond, or bonds, payable to the owner, securing the performance of the contract, either in whole or in part; or securing payments for labor and materials. *(see bonding company)*

surety bond A legal instrument under which one party agrees to answer to another party for the debt, default or failure to perform of a third party.

surface To make plane and smooth.

surface active Having the ability to modify surface energy and to facilitate wetting, penetrating, emulsifying, dispersing, solubilizing, foaming, frothing, etc., of other substances.

surface area *(see specific surface)*

surface building characteristics Rating of interior and surface finish material providing indices for flame spread and smoke developed, based on testing conducted according to ASTM Standard F84.

surface burning characteristic Rating of interior and surface finish material providing indices for flame spread and smoke developed, based on testing conducted according to ASTM Standard E84.

surface conductance A unit of heat flow for heat exchange between a material and the air around it. Ventilation over a surface will decrease the thickness of the air film and reduce the thermal effect (increase the heat flow).

surface course Top course of asphalt pavement.

surface cure Curing or vulcanization which occurs in a thin layer on the surface of a manufactured polymeric sheet or other items.

surface depression A mark or indentation on gypsum board surface.

surface dressing A wearing surface on a roadway, consisting of a layer of chips or gravel on a thin layer of fresh tar or bitumen.

surface drying A material that dries faster on the surface than in the body of the film.

surface error Error introduced into a measurement due to irregularities or other characteristics of the surface.

surface finish A finish material which penetrates the pores of the wood, providing a finish that is in the wood rather than on the surface.

surface float A float on the water surface.

surface measure Face measure of timber, etc.

surface mineral Granules of rock used as a protective covering of the asphalt surface on composition roofing.

surface moisture Free water retained on surfaces of aggregate particles and considered to be part of the mixing water in concrete, as distinguished from absorbed moisture.

surface of pyramid or cone Circumference of base × ¹/₂ of the slant height plus area of base.

surface passivation The changing of the chemically active surface of a metal to a much less reactive state.

surface planer A steel bed-plate with the upper half in two parallel levels. Between the two halves the adzing cutter block rotates with its blades projecting above one half and level with the other half.

surface texture Degree of roughness or irregularity of the exterior surfaces of aggregate particles or hardened concrete.

surface vibrator A vibrator used for consolidating concrete by application to the top surface of a mass of freshly mixed concrete; four principal types exist: vibrating screeds, pan vibrators, plate or grid vibratory tampers, and vibratory roller screeds.

surface voids Cavities visible on the surface of a solid.

surface water *(see surface moisture)*

surface-water drain A pipe in the ground to handle rainwater.

surfaced timber (dressed timber) Timber planed on at least one surface.

surfacing The upper layers of a road or street.

surfacing of lumber In woodworking, symbols used to indicate how lumber has been surfaced, as S1E, surfaced on one edge; S1S, surfaced on one side; S2S, surfaced on two sides, etc.

surge (1) The horizontal force applied to a high level on a building, often by a crane accelerating or braking. (2) A sudden increase of pressure in a pipeline caused by a valve closing.

surge bin (1) A compartment for temporary storage which will allow converting a variable rate of supply into a steady flow of the same average amount. (2) Bin or tank, not used for storage, but inserted in process to absorb and equalize fluctuations in flow of material.

surge drum   Accumulator; a storage chamber for low-side liquid refrigerant.

surge header   A pressure vessel whose volume is used in a refrigerant circuit to reduce pulsation.

surge pipe   An open-topped stand pipe for releasing surge pressure. The water simply spills over the top.

surge tank   An open tank connected to the top of a surge pipe to avoid water loss during pressure surges.

surround   An enframement.

survey   (1) Boundary an/or topographic mapping of a site. (2) Measuring an existing building. (3) Analyzing a building for use of space. (4) Determining owner's requirements for a project. (5) Investigating and reporting of required data for a project.

surveying   To find and record elevations, locations and directions by means of instruments; the unit of measurement is the surveyor's chain, with 80 chains equal to one mile.

surveyor   One skilled in land measurement.

susceptibility   When not otherwise qualified, the degree of change in viscosity with temperature.

suspended ceiling   Usually refers to a false or drop ceiling; metal runners are attached by wire hangers, and panels of ceiling material, Celotex, etc., are placed on the runners.

suspended floor   A floor which is supported at the ends, but not in the middle.

suspended scaffold   A projecting or cradle scaffold.

suspended shuttering   Floor formwork which is carried on the supports of the floor and not propped up from below.

suspended span   The short, middle, freely-supported span of a cantilever bridge.

suspender   A vertical hanger of a suspension bridge.

suspension   Small solid particles distributed through a liquid; an emulsion in which one liquid carries the other liquid suspended within it in small separate drops.

suspension bridge   A road bridge hung from steel cables, carried by towers at each bank. The cables are anchored into rock or a large mass of masonry behind the towers. The weight of the road is carried by vertical rods or suspenders which are spaced at uniform intervals between road and cables at the sides.

suspension cable   The wire rope carrying a suspension bridge; any cable used to hold a load under stress.

suspension-cable anchor   The mass of masonry or a fixing deep into rock on the land side of a suspension bridge tower, to hold the ends of the suspension cables.

suspension preheater   A system of cyclones and riser ducts in which dry process kiln feed is preheated in contact with kiln exit gases.

sustained modulus of elasticity   Term including elastic and inelastic effects in one expression to aid in visualizing net effects of stress-strain up to any given time; computed by dividing the unit sustained stress by the sum of elastic and plastic deformation at that time. *(see modulus of elasticity)*

swage   A smith's tool used for shaping hot or cold metal, particularly rivet heads and saws. Swages are made in pairs, one male and one female; one acts as the hammer and the other as the anvil.

swage-setting   A method of setting circular saws to be used for ripping.

swale   A low, flat depression to drain off storm water.

swamper   *(slang)* A helper, particularly on a truck; also used as a name for the workman who performs janitorial and other cleanup work around a construction camp or field office. The assistant driver to a skinner.

swan neck   (1) An S-bend, particularly between a downpipe and eaves gutter under an overhanging eaves. (2) The joint ramp and knee in a handrail.

sway Sideways frame movement.

swaybrace A diagonal brace used to resist wind or other lateral forces. *(see X-brace)*

sweat To unite two closely fitting pieces by enlarging the outer one by heat; particularly descriptive of the process of joining copper tubing.

sweat board *(slang)* A hand concrete mixer.

sweat finish (swirl finish) A non-skid texture given to a concrete surface during final troweling by keeping the trowel flat and using a rotary motion.

sweating (condensation) (1) Separation of liquids in a paint resulting in one of them appearing at the surface of the film. (2) A gloss which may develop in a dry paint or varnish after sanding. (3) Beads of water that collect on the outside of cold pipes.

sweat joint In plumbing, a capillary joint.

sweat out A defective condition occasionally occurring in gypsum plaster. Characterized by a soft, damp area remaining after the surrounding area has set hard. Often caused by insufficient ventilation which inhibits normal drying.

Swedish break Slide or movement of clay or earth embankment with characteristic cylindrical or spherical fracture surface.

sweep tee In plumbing, a tee for screwed copper pipe; the branch is not precisely perpendicular to the run, as in a normal tee, but curves gently away from it.

swell (growth) Increase of bulk in soil or rock when it is dug or blasted.

swelling Volume increase caused by wetting or chemical changes, or both; a function of time but not of stress due to external load.

Swenson Buff Antique A muscovite-biotite granite of light to medium grayish buff color and fine to medium grain; quarried at Concord, New Hampshire.

Swenson Pink A biotite granite of light pink color, medium to coarse grain,

with occasional waves of closely segregated black and pink stripes; quarried at North Berwick, Maine.

swept valley A roof valley formed of slates, shingles or tiles cut or made to a taper to eliminate the need for a flexible-metal valley. A tile-and-a-half tile is cut to shape so that its tail is narrower than its head.

swift A reel or turntable on which prestressing tendons are placed to facilitate handling and placing.

swimming pool An artificial pool for recreational swimming.

swing (1) In revolving shovels, to rotate the shovel on its base. (2) In churn drills, to operate a string of tools.

swing angle The distance in degrees which a shovel must swing between digging and dumping points.

swing bridge (pivot bridge; turn bridge) A bridge pivoted at the center to swing open horizontally to allow a ship or barge to pass by.

swinger A pointed bar used for moving runners in trench shoring.

swing-jib crane A crane with one horizontal boom with a counterweight. It pivots through 360° and can travel on a track or be stationary.

swing saw A woodworker's tool consisting of a circular saw mounted on a hinged frame suspended from above. When needed, the saw is pulled to the work which remains stationary.

swirl finish *(see sweat finish)*

Swiss hammer *(see rebound hammer)*

switch A device for breaking the flow of electric current.

three-way A type used in pairs to control the same electric light from different points.

switchback A hairpin turn.

switchboard A panel to which electrical lines are brought for the purpose of connecting or disconnecting circuits.

switchgear Plant, including switches or circuit breakers, for protecting or controlling a power circuit.

swivel head In a diamond drill, the

mechanism that rotates the kelly and drill string.

swoles A low, flat depression to drain off storm water.

sycamore, American A tree of southern Ontario and the eastern U.S.A., south to Florida and Texas, the hard, reddish-brown wood of which develops, in veneer, small flakes more numerous than in quartered oak; also called buttonwood or American plane tree.

syenite Rock of the nature of granite but containing little or no quartz.

sylvester (donkey; prop drawer) A tool used for withdrawing timbers or steel posts. It consists of a hard-steel rack into which a lever engages to pull a chain attached to the timber or steel post to be drawn. Also used to apply tension to conveyor belts and for moving heavy machinery.

symbol An abbreviation standing for the name of something which is indicated by some mark, character, letter, figure or a combination of any such characters.

symbolism Representation, through an object or a form, of an idea, a person or a place to be remembered.

symmetrical Having identical forms or masses on either side of an axial line.

synagogue A meeting place for Jewish worship.

synchromesh A silent-shift transmission in which the hub speeds are synchronized before engagement by contact with cones of synthetic material.

synchronous motor A.C. motor, whose speed is directly proportional to the number of cycles of the current.

synergy (1) The combined action of 2 or more substances or agencies to achieve an effect greater than that of which each is individually capable. (2) An important by-product of membership in The Construction Specifications Institute.

synthetic paint A vague term sometimes meaning paints containing synthetic resin.

synthetic resin Urea-, melamine- or phenol-formaldehyde glues and casting resins and other synthetic resins which are immune from attack by molds and bacteria and are highly water resistant.

synthetic-resin-bonded paper sheet *(see laminated plastics)*

synthetic-resin cement A synthetic resin used as glue; synthetic resin without an accelerator.

systematic errors (cumulative errors) Surveying errors which are either always positive or always negative, as distinguished from compensating errors.

systems Combining prefabricated assemblies, components and parts into single integrated units utilizing industrialized production, assembly and methods; also called system building.

systyle A form of intercolumniation in Classic architecture in which the columns are two diameters apart, center to center.

t   temperature, time, ton

T   township, true

Ta   tantalum

t.b.   turnbuckle

TC   terra-cotta

Te   tellurium

TE   table of equipment, trailing edge

tech   technical

T.E.M.   Total Energy Management

temp   temperature, temporary

t.f.   tar felt

t.g.&d.   tongued, grooved and dressed

TH   true heading

therm   thermometer

thou   thousand

thp   thrust horsepower

Ti   titanium

TIMA   Thermal Insulation Manufacturer's Association.

tlr   trailer

TM   technical manual

tn   ton, town, train

TN   true north

tnpk/tpk   turnpike

t.o.   take off (estimate)

tonn   tonnage

topog/topo   topography

tp   title page, township, tar paper

tps   townships

tr   tread

trans   transom

transp   transportation

trf   tuned radio frequency

trib   tributary

trib.ar.   tributary area

ts   tensile strength

TSCA   Toxic Substances Control Act.

TSDF   The acronym for treatment, storage, or disposal facility.

TU   trade union, transmission unit

TV   terminal velocity

twp   township

T&M   Time and materials. Work agreed to between the owner and the contractor with payment based on the contractor's actual cost for labor, equipment and materials plus an add-on factor to cover the overhead and profit.

TNT   Trinitrotoluene, a powerful explosive.

T.U. (takeup)   A mechanism for adjusting belt or chain tension.

tab   That part of a composition strip that is exposed to the weather.

tabby   A mixture of stone or shell with mortar; a type of concrete made of lime, gravel, etc.

table   The flat part of a plumbing tee from which the stalk rises.

tablet test   Standard testing method for carpet flammability, using an ignition tablet (or methenamine 'pill') under controlled conditions. Better known in the trade as the 'Pill Test.'

tac tractor   Tractor fitted with welding machines used on firing line.

tachometer   (1) A device for indicating speed of rotation. (2) An instrument to indicate accurately the feet per minute and gallons per square yard covered by a bituminous distributor. In Britain, a tacheometer.

tack   A sharp, short nail with a large head as used in laying linoleum, carpeting, etc.

tack coat   Initial application of asphaltic material to existing surface to insure thorough bond between superimposed construction and old surface.

tackle   A construction of blocks and ropes, chains or cables used for hoisting purposes in heavy construction.

tack rag   Cheese cloth or other cotton fabric dampened with a slow-drying varnish used to remove dust from a surface after rubbing down and before putting on the next coat.

tack rivet A rivet which does not carry load and is put in for convenience or to comply with regulations.

tack welds Approximately one half inch long weld beads.

tacky Very sticky or gummy; adhesive.

taenia The fillet separating the Doric frieze from the architrave.

taft joint (finger-wiped joint) A joint between lead pipe and brass liner made by wiping in plumber's solder instead of pouring in fine solder as in a blown joint.

tag (1) Copper strip folded in several thicknesses and used as a wedge for holding copper sheet into a masonry joint. (2) *(OSHA)* Temporary sign, usually attached to a piece of equipment or part of a structure, to warn of existing or immediate hazards.

tagline (1) A line from a crane boom to a clamshell bucket that holds the bucket from spinning out of position. (2) A safety line used by a workman working in a high or otherwise unsafe location.

tail (1) The rear of a shovel deck. (2) The anchor end of a cable excavator. (3) The built-in end of a stone step.

tail anchor The anchor for a track cable, or the turn point for a backhaul line, a cable excavator.

tail bay (1) The end span of a wood fiber or roof. (2) Part of a canal downstream of the tail gate.

tail beams Joists or framing members that are supported by headers or trimmers at one or both ends.

tailblock The boom foot and idler sprocket assembly on a ladder ditcher.

tail bolts Bolts for securing the ends of asbestos-cement roof sheets.

tailgate (tailboard) The hinged rear wall of a dump truck body; the hinged or sliding rear wall of a scraper bowl.

tail heater Used to control the temperature of heavy oil for optimum combustion.

tailing In building construction, any

projecting part of stone or brick inserted in a wall.

tailing in Fixing the cantilevered member at a wall by laying stones or bricks to weigh it down.

tailing iron A steel section built into a wall to hold down the end of a cantilevered member which is below it.

tailings Second-grade or waste material separated from gravel during screening.

tail joist A relatively shorter joist that joins against a header or trimmer in floor framing; any building joist with one end fitted against a header joist.

tail piece A subordinate joist, rafter, or the like, supported on a wall or sill at one end and headed into another timber at the other end.

tail ring An annular dam located at the extreme feed end of a rotary kiln constructed from refractory brick, refractory casting, or high alloy coastings. Designed to retain raw meal or slurry feed in the kiln.

tail rope A hoisting rope which passes around a return sheave, as opposed to a direct rope.

tail swing The clearance required by the rear of a revolving shovel.

tail trimmer A trimmer next to the wall, into which the ends of joists are fastened.

tail water The water immediately downstream from a structure. Water lost from an irrigation system through headgates, spillways, etc., after being channelled into it.

Tainter gate Pivoted gate for regulating the flow of water; the face is usually an arc with the center of curvature at a pivot. Named for its inventor, Burnham Tainter.

tak dyeing Process of dyeing over a continuous dyed fabric by controlled sprinkle technique.

take off A list of materials, by quantities, from information contained in drawings and plans.

take-up In shopworking, any equipment or device provided to tighten or take up slack, or to remove looseness in parts due to wear or other causes; also called a clinger nut.

takspan Swedish pine roof shingles made like sliced veneer, approximately ⅛ inch thick.

Talbot process The protective coating of sand and bitumen inside cast iron pipes.

talc A mineral with a greasy or soapy feel, very soft, having the composition $Mg_3Si_4O_{10}(OH)_2$. (*see cement, masonry*)

tall boy A hood about five feet high, made of thick steel plate, galvanized and fixed over a chimney to prevent down drafts.

tally A brass label attached to a survey chain at every tenth link, thus marking 10 foot intervals with one notch cut in it for every 10 feet from the end of the chain.

tally slates Slates sold by number, not by weight.

talon Literally, heel; a molding, frequently enriched, with a profile in variation of the cyma reversa.

talus Sloping mass of fragments below a cliff.

talus wall The holding wall for an earth slope.

tambour (1) Literally, a drum. (2) The wall of a circular temple surrounded by columns. (3) The vertical-sided drum supporting a cupola.

tamp (1) To ram and concentrate, as in tamping freshly placed concrete in the form. (2) To compact earth.

tamper A hand-operated device for compacting concrete by the impact from the dropped device in preparation for strikeoff and finishing; contact surface often consists of open-mesh screen or a grid of bars to force coarse aggregate below the surface to prevent interference with floating or troweling.

tamping The operation of compacting freshly placed concrete by repeated blows. Compacting earth to achieve a desired density.

tamping rod (*see rod, tamping*)

tamping roller One or more steel drums fitted with projecting feet and towed by means of a box frame.

tandem (1) A pair in which one part follows the other, as in a tandem roller; a truck or other vehicle with two attached units, as a cab for pulling and a trailer to carry the load. (2) A double-axle drive unit for a truck or grader.

tandem drive A three-axle vehicle having two driving axles.

tandem drying-grinding A combination of a hammer mill and an air swept ball mill, utilizing hot gases in both to effect drying of the feed material.

tandem roller Rollers of about the same diameter behind each other on the same track.

tangent A straight line or a curve that touches another curve at only one point but does not cut or cross it.

tangent distance In setting out a road or railway curve, the distance from an intersection point to a tangent point.

tangential shrinkage Parallel to the growth rings as the shrinkage of timber.

tangent modulus (*see modulus of elasticity*)

tangent point The point at which a curve changes its curvature or becomes straight, in lining out roads or railways.

tangent screw (*see fine adjustment screw*)

tanking A waterproof skin, usually asphalt laid beneath a basement floor and up the basement walls. Also known as damp course.

tank, oil The metal storage tank for liquid fuel; sometimes buried underground.

tank sprayer Pressure tank on wheels.

tap (1) A threaded plug made of hard steel used for cutting internal threads. (2) To connect a public service supply line with a branch to serve a particular building. (3) A faucet.

tape A retractable ruler; any flexible narrow strip of linen, cotton, or steel marked off with measuring lines similar to the scale on a carpenter's rule. Usually the tape is contained in a circular case into which it can easily be rewound after using.

tape, asbestos Paper-like, non-combustible material used with paste in sealing up connections of ductwork and furnace connections.

tape corrections Corrections applied as a matter of course to all lengths measured by steel or invariable tape.

tape creaser A hand-held device to aid in folding joint tape for use in inside corners.

tapeless splicer or tapeless jointer A machine for gluing edges of sheets of veneer together without using joint tape.

tapered edge strip A tapered insulation strip used to (1) elevate the roof at the perimeter and at curbs that extend through the roof; (2) provide a gradual transition from one layer of insulation to another.

tapered-flange beam The inner surface of a rolled steel joist with its flanges tapered.

tapered member A built-up plate member consisting of flanges welded to a variable depth web.

tapered parapet gutter A flexible metal box gutter behind a parapet, narrower towards the lower end because of the roof slope.

tapered washer A bevelled washer.

taper file A fine-toothed triangular file for sharpening saws.

taper thread A standard screw thread used on pipes and fittings to insure a tight joint.

taping strips Roofing felt in strips laid over the joints between precast slabs in a roof before it is bonded and sealed.

tapping tile An inspection technique whereby a coin, key, or other small metallic object is tapped against an installed tile to determine by sound whether the tile is completely bonded to its backing. Tilesetters often tap the tile with a pointing trowel to determine that a good bond has been achieved.

tar A dark viscid oil, dry-distilled from resinous woods, coal, peat, and shale; used in roofing and as a road surface binder. Substances obtained by condensation of distillates resulting from destructive distillation of organic matter; tar products of consequence in road industry are gas-works coal tar, coke-oven coal tar and water gas tar.

tar boils Bubbles of moisture vapor encased in a thin film of bitumen, also known as blueberry, blackberry, etc.

tar cements Heavier grades (RT-10, RT-11, RT-12) prepared for direct use in construction and maintenance of bituminous pavements.

tar concrete A bituminous concrete made with tar.

tare (1) An allowance made for the weight of a container. (2) At an asphalt plant, the weight of the asphalt bucket including any residue and adhering bitumen.

target A usually red and white disc mounted on a leveling rod; used for certain types of readings in survey work.

target rod A leveling rod.

tar-gravel roofing Roof covering of felt mopped with hot tar or pitch and covered with gravel or sand.

tarmacadam A road material consisting of aggregate coated with tar or a tar-bitumen mixture. It has very little fines and a high proportion of voids.

tarpaulin (tarp) A waterproofed canvas or plastic covering for use in protecting unfinished work or stored materials against weather.

tarred felt A felt that has been saturated with refined coal tar.

task-oriented lighting Lighting designed specifically to illuminate one or more task locations, and generally confined to those locations.

taut Anything tightly drawn until it is tense and tight, with all sag eliminated, as a rope, wire or cord pulled taut.

T-beam A beam composed of a stem and a flange in the form of a T.

T-bevel A woodworker's tool used for testing the accuracy of work cut at an angle, such as a beveled edge.

teak An East Indian tree, the wood of which is dark, heavy and durable; used chiefly for fine flooring, decking, greenhouses, furniture and interior finish.

tear strength The maximum force required to tear a specified specimen, the force acting substantially parallel to the major axis of the test specimen. Measured in both initiated and uninitiated modes. Obtained value is dependent on specimen geometry, rate of extension, and type of fabric reinforcement. Values are reported in stress, e.g. pounds, or stress per unit of thickness, e.g. pounds per inch.

technical Any particular art or practical science, such as the mechanical or industrial trades, in which words or phrases are used in a special sense pertaining to one particular trade or profession.

technical assistant In Britain, the estimator's assistant. He is also described as a worker-up or as a taker-off according to the work he is doing.

tee A T-shaped pipe fitting that has two threaded openings in line, and a third at right angles to them.

tee-beam (tee iron; tee section) Part of a reinforced-concrete floor in which the beam projects below the slab.

tee iron A reinforcing device stamped from sheet metal, then drilled and countersunk; used for strengthening light wooden construction such as window screens.

tegula An undertile.

telecontrolled power station A remote-controlled hydroelectric power station which is not manned but wholly controlled by radio.

telescope To slide one piece inside another.

telescoped A condition in a roll of roofing, felt or other material where the layers have slid over one another giving the appearance of a telescope; also produces a roll with an over-all length greater than the actual width of the sheet in the roll.

telescopic centering Pans or self formwork for floors made of pressed-steel sections which fit into each other telescopically. The end sections are laid on the wall or beam which carries the floor.

telltale Any device designed to indicate movement of formwork, or of a pile under load.

tellurometer An electric measuring device used in surveying; it measures the transit time of microwaves traveling from a transmitter to a receiver and back to the transmitter.

telpher (telfer) An electrically driven hoist hanging from a wheeled cab rolling on a single overhead rail, occasionally from a rope; hung from roof girders indoors and over dams during their construction by means of an overhead gantry.

temo *(slang)* Teamster; a truck driver.

temper (1) To mix and blend lime, sand and water, or cement, sand and water to make mortar. To thin with water either of the above mixtures to make them workable; a practice usually forbidden in specifications. (2) The state of hardness of metal. (3) To toughen non-ferrous metal by beating and rolling.

tempera Pigment in water or in a vehicle soluble in water; distemper.

temperature The thermal state of matter with reference to its tendency to communicate heat to matter in contact with it. If no heat flows upon contact, there is no difference in temperature.

temperature cracking Cracking due to tensile failure, caused by temperature drop in members subjected to external restraints or temperature differential in members subjected to internal restraints.

temperature gradient The change in temperature per unit length, as in creating a vapor barrier.

temperature reinforcement Reinforcement designed to carry stresses resulting from temperature changes; also the minimum reinforcement for areas of members which are not subjected to primary stresses or necessary temperature stresses.

temperature rise The increase of temperature caused by absorption of heat or internal generation of heat, as by hydration of cement in concrete.

temperature reinforcing Light-weight deformed steel rods or wire mesh placed in concrete to resist possible cracks from thermal expansion or contraction.

temperature rise period The time interval during which the temperature of a concrete product rises at a controlled rate to the desired maximum in autoclave or atmospheric-pressure steam curing.

temperature steel Reinforcement steel which is inserted in a slab or other concrete member to prevent cracks due to shrinkage or temperature change.

temperature stress Stress in a structure or a member due to changes or differentials in temperature in the structure or member.

tempered (1) Descriptive of thoroughly mixed mortar or cement. (2) Descriptive of case-hardened metals, particularly steel.

tempered glass Glass that has been rapidly cooled from near the softening point, under rigorous control, to increase its mechanical and thermal endurance.

tempering air Cold air mixed with hot gases to reduce their temperature for protection of draft fan, dust collector, etc.

template (templet) (1) A pattern or mold used as a guide to the position or form of an installation or a piece being made. (2) A short piece placed in a wall under a beam to distribute the pressure; also, a beam spanning a doorway, or the like, and supporting joists. (3) Thin plate or board frame used as a guide in positioning or spacing form parts, reinforcement, anchors, etc. (4) The frame built at the top of the elevator hoistway to locate the lines for checking size, plumbness and squareness of hoistway, and to properly locate the lines for the rails. Lines are dropped from a template at the top to a target at the bottom.

temporary stress A stress which may be produced in a precast concrete member or component of a precast

concrete member during fabrication or erection, or in cast-in-place concrete structures due to construction or test loadings.

tender The bid of a contractor as used to tender, or offer; a bid.

tendering The British term for invitational or negotiated bid.

tendon A steel element such as a wire, cable, bar, rod or strand used to impart prestress to concrete when the element is tensioned.

tendon profile The path or trajectory of the prestressing tendon.

tenement A building containing low-rent apartments; an apartment in such a building.

tenia *(see taenia)*

Tennessee marble A group name for a great variety of marbles of excellent quality. Ground tones vary from light warm gray and shades of pink and brownish pink to dark chocolate.

tenon A projection on the shoulder of a wood member, to fit snugly into a socket or mortise in another wood member, forming a joint.

tenon saw In woodworking, any small backsaw used on the bench for cutting tenons. Also known as mitre saw.

tenpenny A size of nails, perhaps so-called because nails of this size once sold in England for tenpence a hundred.

tensile The ability to stand, stretch or pull without rupture or break.

tensile strength Maximum stress which a material is capable of resisting under axial tensile loading, based on the cross-sectional area of the specimen before loading. Also the measure of a material's ability to withstand stretching.

tensile stress Stress resulting from tension.

tensile test A test in which a standard piece of metal, mortar, concrete or wood is pulled in a testing machine until it breaks.

tension Stress in a structural member caused by forces tending to draw it apart longitudinally, as in a tie rod.

tension reinforcement Reinforcement designed to carry tensile stresses such as those in the bottom of a simple beam.

tension sleeve A screw shackle.

ten wheeler *(slang)* Tandem truck with ten wheels, commonly called a bogie; tandem dump truck.

teredo protection Coating on timber piles to protect against infiltration by the marine borers called teredos.

terminal (terminus) **(1)** An end feature, as the tip of a building, or a figure terminating a vista or an axis. **(2)** One end of an electrical conductor. **(3)** A station at the end of a railway.

terminal expenses Expenses incurred in connection with the termination of a contract.

terminal motion switch A switch used to stop the elevator car from running by the terminal floors under power if normal circuits fail.

terminal rail A section of door guide rail used for guiding the lower half of the elevator door at the bottom terminal landing and the upper half of the door at the top terminal landing.

terminal slow-down switch A mechanical switch that triggers an electrical contact to decelerate the elevator car.

terminal stopping device A device to slow down and stop an elevator or dumbwaiter car automatically at or near a terminal landing independently of the functioning of the operating device.

terminal velocity (free-falling velocity; settling velocity) The maximum velocity which a body can attain when freely falling in a fluid. For spherical particles, this can be found by using Stokes's law.

termite shield A sheet of metal serving as a barrier to termites between a foundation wall and the woodwork above.

terne (terne plate) Sheet steel coated with an alloy of 80 percent lead and 20 percent tin; used chiefly for roofing.

terpene Any of numerous hydrocarbons $(C_5H_8)n$ found especially in es-

sential oils, resins and balsams. Used especially as solvents and in organic synthesis.

terrace An elevated level surface of earth supported on one or more faces by a masonry wall, or by a sloping bank covered with turf. A long low embankment or ridge of earth constructed across a slope to control runoff and minimize soil erosion.

terra-cotta Cast and fired clay units, usually larger and more intricately modeled than brick. A composition of baked clay and sand.

terrain Ground surface.

terras A blemish in a marble block, removed and replaced by a composition filling.

terrazzo A type of Venetian marble mosaic in which portland cement is used as a matrix; a modern floor finish used also for bases, borders, wainscoting, as well as on stair treads, partitions and other wall surfaces.

terrazzo concrete *(see concrete, terrazzo)*

terrazzo flooring A term used in building trades for a type of flooring made of small fragments of colored stone or marble embedded irregularly in concrete; the surface is given a high polish.

terrazzo tile A terrazzo surface, on a portland cement and sand body, made by a mixture of marble chips and portland cement and usually ground smooth.

tertiary air Hot air taken from the clinker cooler to support combustion in a precalcining furnace.

tertiary treatment A phase of wastewater treatment utilizing such methods as carbon absorption, reverse osmosis, ion exchange and demineralization. This stage of treatment is beyond the 85-95% BOD removal of the secondary stage.

tessara, tessarare A small chip of glass or marble used in mosaic formations.

tesselatted Formed of cubes of stone, marble, glass or other suitable material arranged in a checkered pattern as in mosaic floors and pavements.

test (1) To find the bearing capacity of a pile, pier or footing, usually by means of hydraulic jacks. Such tests are usually not made up to the full bearing power of the pile or footing but to some predetermined limit. (2) To measure the quality of a material by trial.

test cut A sample of the roof membrane, usually 4 inches × 40 inches in size, that is cut from a roof membrane to :

*Determine the weight of the average interply bitumen poundages

*Diagnose the condition of the existing membrane(e.g.,to detect leaks or blister). National Roofing Contractors Association recommends that the test cut procedure NOT be used as a means of determining the quality of a roof system.

tester A canopy, as over a bed or a tomb.

testing machine A device for applying test conditions and accurately measuring results.

test piling A foundation piling installed on the proposed construction site. Structural engineers then make load test on the piling to determine how many and what size piling are needed for the project.

test pit An excavation to determine the nature of the material encountered or to disclose subsurface conditions.

tetracalcium aluminoferrite A compound in the calcium aluminoferrite series, having the composition $4CaO \cdot Al_2O_3 \cdot Fe_2O_3$, abbreviated C4AF, which is usually assumed to be the aluminoferrite present when compound calculations are made from the results of chemical analysis of portland cement. (see *brown-millerite*)

tetrastyle The type of classical building having four columns across the front.

tewel An opening for ventilation.

Texas Pink granite Of light pink, medium grain; quarried at Marble Falls, Texas.

Texas screed Motorized vibrating self-propelled screed for the placement of concrete slabs, bridge decks, etc.

texture Surface conformation or quality, independent of color.

texture brick Brick with a rough finish.

textured finish A rough wall finish formed by sand or stone chippings mixed with a paint or by working the paint into patterns. A rough finish to plaster, obtained by spraying or rough troweling the plaster on.

texture paint Paint which can be manipulated after its application to give it a textured finish.

texturing The process of producing a special texture on unhardened or hardened concrete.

thalweg The lowest point, in a drainage way, between the two banks.

thatch A roof covering of rushes, straw or the like fastened together to shed water.

T-head In precast framing, a segment of girder crossing the top of an interior column; also the top of a shore formed with a braced horizontal member projecting on two sides forming a T-shaped assembly.

theodolite An instrument for the measurement of angles in surveying.

theory An opinion, or ideal view, in an attempt to analyze a set of facts in their relation to one another.

therm (1) The heat unit on which the sale of natural gas is based. (2) A quantity of heat equivalent to 100,000 Btu.

thermal block A spacer of low thermal conductance material.

thermal conductance (C) The rate of heat flow, in BTUs per hour, through a square foot of material or a combination of materials whose surfaces have a temperature differential of 1 degree F.

thermal conductivity (k) The rate of heat flow, in BTUs per hour, through a square foot of material exactly one inch thick whose surfaces have a temperature differential of 1 degree. F.

thermal conductor A substance capable of transmitting heat.

thermal diffusivity Thermal conductivity divided by the product of specific heat and unit weight; an index of the facility with which a material undergoes temperature change.

thermal efficiency In a cement kiln system, the theoretical amount of heat required to clinker a given raw mix compared to the actual heat input of the process.

thermal expansion All materials expand and contract to some extent with changes in temperature. The Thermal Coefficient of Linear Expansion is expressed in 'Inches Per Inch Per Degree Fahrenheit.'

thermal fracture A compression crack caused by expansion of peripheral building components.

thermal image A visual representation of temperature distribution over a surface area. An image on a TV-like display presenting the response to infrared light waves.

thermal insulation A material applied to reduce the flow of heat.

thermal lag In an indirect gain system, the time delay for heat to move from the outer collecting surface to the inner radiating surface.

thermal level control The position in the temperature range where the thermal range is located.

thermal mass The heat capacity of a building material (brick, concrete, adobe, or water containers).

thermal overload A type of overload relay operated by bimetallic strips, surrounded by heaters that carry the motor current. Excessive heat causes the strips to bend, releasing a latch that holds the control contacts closed.

thermal profile The temperature of gas or solid material in a rotary kiln as related to the distance along the axis of the kiln.

thermal radiation The transmission of heat through space by wave motion; the passage of heat from one object to another without warming the space between.

thermal range control The amount of temperature difference between black and white in a thermal image.

thermal resistance (r-value) The tendency of a material to retard the flow of heat; the reciprocal of the coefficient of heat transmission.

thermal shock The subjection of a material or body, such as partially hardened concrete, to a rapid change in temperature which may be expected to have a potentially deleterious effect.

thermal transmittance (U) The rate of heat flow per square foot under steady conditions from the air on the warm side of a barrier to the air on the cold side, for $1°F.$ of temperature difference between the two. $(BTU/Ft^2\text{-}hr\text{-}1°F.)$

thermal unit Any unit chosen for the calculation of quantities of heat; that is, a unit of measurement used as a standard of comparison of other quantities of heat, such as Btu, British thermal unit.

thermalization of fast neutrons The process of reducing the energy of a neutron to a level where it is in equilibrium with its environment. Generally, thermal neutrons have energy levels in the 0.01 to 0.3 electron volts range. Thermalization occurs when the energy of fast neutrons is partially absorbed by moderators of hydrogen atom collisions.

thermel *(slang)* Term for any instrument which includes a thermocouple.

thermistor A resistor whose value can change when heat is applied; also known as thermal resistors or temperature sensitive resistors.

thermocouple A pair of dissimilar metals so joined as to produce a thermoelectric effect when heated. The magnitude of the thermo-electric effect shows the temperature to which the metals have been heated.

thermodynamics The science of heat energy and it transformations to and from other forms of energy.

thermogram A visible light record of the display of an infrared camera system via a Polaroid print, 35mm film, or video tape.

thermography   Process of converting heat emitting from any object into a visible picture.

thermometer   An instrument for determining the temperature.

Thermopane   Trade name for an insulating double-glazing pane for window or door.

thermopile   A group of thermocouples acting jointly to produce electric energy and used with galvanometer to measure temperature.

thermoplastic   Becoming soft when heated and hard when cooled.

thermoplastic elastomers   Polymers capable of remelt, but exhibiting elastomeric properties; related to elasticized polyolefins. They have a limited upper temperature service range.

thermoplastic putty   A soft glazier's putty which moves with the glass it touches.

thermoplastic resin   A material with a linear macromolecular structure that will repeatedly soften when heated and harden when cooled.

thermoset-n   A material that will undergo or has undergone a chemical reaction by the action of heat, catalysts, ultraviolet light, etc., leading to a relatively infusible state.

thermosetting   Becoming rigid by chemical reaction and not remeltable.

thermostat   An automatic device for regulating the temperature of a room by opening or closing the damper of a heating furnace. An electric switch actuated by changes in temperature.

thermosyphon   Natural circulation in which water circulates automatically between a flat plate collector and storage tank. The warm water rises as it transfers heat, cools, descends and continues to circulate through the system.

thickbutt   A strip shingle of the square-butted type in which the exposed area, or butt section, is thicker than the covered or unexposed area.

thickener   Large basin for slurry which has been ground with excess water. Suspended particles gravitate to bottom (underflow), whereas surplus water runs over rim.

thickness   (1) The dimension at right angles to the face of the wall, floor or other assembly in which concrete masonry units are used. (2) In sheet goods, the total nominal thickness of the floor covering, backing through wear surface.

thimble   In building, a term applied to a metal lining for a chimney or furnace pipe. *(see nipple)*

T-hinge   A type of joint with an abutting piece set at right angles to a strap, thus forming a T-shaped hinge, used mainly on outside work, such as barn doors and gates.

thinners (solvents)   Volatile liquids used to regulate the consistency of paint and other finishes; also for cleanup when using oil-base paints.

thin-set   A term used to describe the bonding of tile with suitable materials applied approximately $\frac{1}{8}''$ thick. *(see Dry-Set mortar)*

thin shell   A very thin poured slab roof, usually about two and one-half inches thick.

thin-shell precast   Precast concrete characterized by thin slabs and web sections. *(see shell construction)*

thin surfacing   A bituminous carpet.

thin wall   An electrical metal tubing.

thixotropy   The property of a material that enables it to stiffen in a short period on standing, but to acquire a lower viscosity on mechanical agitation, the process being reversible; a material having this property is termed thixotropic or shear thinning. *(see rheology)*

thole   A votive niche or recess.

tholobate   The circular substructure of a dome.

tholos   A circular building, or part of one.

threaded anchorage   An anchorage device which is provided with threads to facilitate attaching the jacking device and to effect the anchorage.

thread count   The number of threads per inch in each direction with the warp mentioned first and the fill second, e.g. a thread count of 20x10 means 20 threads per inch in the warp and 10 threads per inch in the fill direction.

threading Laying welded railroad rail with a machine that threads the long lengths of rail from the side of the embankment up onto the ties.

three-coat work (lath, plaster, float and set) The best quality plastering, in which the first coat fills the rough places, and the second forms a smooth surface for the third.

three-core block Concrete masonry unit which has three cores.

three-foot rule A three-foot-long fourfold rule, commonly used by building trades.

three part line A single strand of rope or cable doubled back around two sheaves so that three parts of it pull a load together.

three-ply Anything composed of three distinct layers or thicknesses, as plywood used in building construction or in furniture making, in which the material used consists of three separate plies or layers.

three-quarter bat A brick cut straight across to reduce its length by one quarter.

three-quarter header A header of length equal to three quarters of the wall thickness.

three-way switch A switch used in wiring when a light, or lights, is to be turned on or off from two places. A three-way switch must be used at each place.

threshold (1) A doorsill. The tread member of an entrance. (2) A saddle. (3) Raised member at the floor within the door jamb. Its purpose is to provide a divider between dissimilar flooring materials, or serve as a thermal, sound or water barrier.

thrible Three sections of drill pipe handled as a unit.

thriebeam A steel plate, usually galvanized, with three raised areas, or corrugations, running lengthwise to form a beam section. It is used as railing for bridges.

throat (1) Of a fireplace, the narrowed passage at a plane between fire chamber and smoke chamber or enlarged base of the flue. (2) The least thickness of a weld. (3) The opening from which shavings come out of a plane. (4) A channel or groove made on the underside of a string-course, coping etc., to prevent water from running inward toward the walls.

throating The undercutting of a projecting molding to form a drip.

through and through Sawing a log by parallel cuts, usually known as flatsawing.

through cut An excavation between parallel banks that begins and ends at original grade.

through lintel A lintel which measures the full thickness of the wall.

through shake A separation of wood between annual growth rings, extending between two faces of timber, similar to a windshake.

through stone A bond stone seen on both faces of the wall.

through-wall flashing A water-resistant membrane or material assembly extending totally through a wall and its cavities, positioned to direct any water within the wall to the exterior.

throw (1) The longest straight distance moved in the stroke or circle of a reciprocating or rotary part. (2) Scattering of blast fragments.

throwing power The ability of a plating solution to produce an approach to uniform metal distribution on an irregularly shaped cathode. It is measured by the percentage improvement of the metal distribution ratio over the primary current ratio.

throwout bearing A bearing sliding on a clutch jackshaft that carries the engage-and-disengage mechanism.

thrust (1) A force tending to push outward, as the thrust of a dome at its base, or that of a rafter on a plate. (2) The force that attempts to close an elevator door.

thrust arm A cable-controlled bar that can slide by power in two directions.

thrust borer Equipment for drilling an underground hole, as beneath an embankment, so as to insert pipes or cables.

thrust washer A washer that holds a rotating part from sideward movement in its bearings.

thumb latch (thum latch) A door fastener opened by thumb pressure on a lever.

thumb plane In woodworking, a term sometimes applied to a small plane not more than four or five inches in length, with a bit about one inch in width.

thumbscrew A screw with its head so constructed that it can be turned easily with the thumb and finger; also known as wing nut.

thumbtack A tack with a relatively large flat head and a sharp steel point for pressing with the thumb into a board; used especially by draftsmen for fastening down drawing paper.

thurm In cabinetmaking, working with saw and chisel across the grain so as to produce patterns, especially in upright work, like those produced by turning.

tie (1) A timber, rod, chain, etc., binding two bodies together which have a tendency to separate or diverge from each other. The tie-beam connects the bottom of a pair of principal rafters, and prevents them from breaking out of the wall. (2) Closed loop of reinforcing bars encircling the longitudinal steel in columns; also a tensile unit which holds concrete formwork secure against lateral pressure of unhardened concrete. (3) In architecture, anything used to hold two parts together, as a post, rod or beam. (4) In surveying, two or more scaled distances from known points to define a desired point.

tieback A rod fastened to a deadman, a rigid foundation, or a rock or soil anchor to prevent lateral movement of formwork, sheet pile walls, retaining walls, bulkheads, etc.

tie bar A deformed bar embedded in concrete construction at a joint and designed to hold abutting edges together,

but not designed for direct load transfer as a dowel.

tie beam (collar beam) A horizontal member in a roof structure tying together opposed rafters; any beam which ties together or prevents the spreading apart of the lower ends of the rafters of a roof.

tied column A column laterally reinforced with ties.

tie-down A mechanical device used to hold a machine bedplate in position and to prevent it from being lifted by the load on the hoist ropes.

tie iron A wall tie.

tier (1) A layer of brickwork half a brick thick. (2) One of a series of successively higher rows, as a tier of seats in an amphitheater.

tie rod In building, a steel rod used to hold structural parts together; a rod used to tie a truss in position and hold it there.

tie wire In form building, a wire used to hold the forms together so they will not spread apart when concrete is poured into the forms; also used in tying metal lath to columns and supports and for reinforcing for stucco.

tige A column shaft.

tight Soil or rock formations lacking veins of weakness; blasts or blast holes around which rock cannot break away freely.

tight fit A fit which requires light pressure for assembly and results in virtually permanent assemblies.

tight knot A knot held firmly in the wood around it, as found in high grade lumber.

tight sheathing Diagonal matchboards nailed to studs or rafters.

tight side The side of a sheet of sliced veneer which was not in contact with the blade while being cut.

tigna Tie beam of a timber roof.

tile (1) A unit of baked clay in various forms, for roofing or for wall or floor covering. Flat pieces of burned clay, either plain or ornamented, glazed or unglazed, used for floors, wainscoting and about fireplaces, etc. Structural tiles are units of baked clay, usually hollow, for self-supporting walls or partitions. Furring tiles are rough-faced hollow units for use in backing up masonry walls. Small square pieces of marble are also called tile. **(2)** A baked clay drain pipe.

bonnet A roofing tile of approximately semicylindrical shape, used for covering the roofing along a hip.

English roofing A flat, corrugated tile, with interlocking, flush side joints.

facing Tile for use in exposed masonry construction.

hip (*see bonnet tile*)

land Short pieces of porous pipe with butt, open, joints, used for underground drainage.

load-bearing Tile for use in masonry construction carrying superimposed loads.

mission roofing A clay tile 14 inches to 18 inches long, curved to the arc of a circle, slightly tapered lengthwise, laid alternately with the convex and concave side up.

non-load-bearing Tile for use in masonry construction and carrying no superimposed loads.

pan-and-roll roofing A roofing tile in two shapes, one of flat rectangular section, the other a half-round section, for covering the joints.

pantile A curved roofing tile, somewhat like a prone letter S.

screen Tile for use in screen walls.

sewer Glazed clay pipe with bell joints.

Spanish roofing A rounded-top, interlocking side-joint tile.

S-tile A roofing tile of which the cross section resembles a prone letter S.

tile-on A method, with certain flooring goods, that permits the installation of tile directly over existing floors without use of board underlayment, etc.

tilth Soil condition in relation to lump or particle size.

tilting concrete mixer (*see mixer, tilting*)

tilting dozer A bulldozer whose blade can be pivoted on a horizontal center pin to cut low on either side.

tilting gate A crest gate for dam spillways, designed so that water pressure opens it at a certain level and automatically closes it when the water level has dropped to normal.

tilting level A level with a bubble fitted on the telescope so that the axis of rotation does not need to be vertical; however, the telescope must be leveled at each site.

tilting mixer A small concrete or mortar mixer which discharges its contents by tilting the rotating drum.

tilt-up A method of concrete construction in which members are cast horizontally at a location adjacent to their eventual position, and tilted into place after removal of molds.

tilt-up compounds A slab separation medium for tilt-up slabs.

timber Structural lumber usually five inches or more in the least dimension. In dimension joists and timbers, the strength, stiffness and uniformity of size are of primary importance; appearance is secondary. Knots, checks, splits are permitted in the various grades in accordance with their effect upon the strength of the piece.

timber framing A load-carrying frame of timber, used in frame construction.

timbering Wood bracing in a tunnel or excavation.

timberman Workman who cuts and fixes timber shores, struts, walings. He also puts up timber frames, gantries, for temporary support of roads or railways, or for underpinning.

timber stresses Stresses for stress-grade lumber conforming to recognized values.

time (as the essence of the construction contract) Time limits or periods stated in the contract. A provision in a construction contract that time is of the essence of the contract signifies that the parties consider that punctual performance within the time limits or periods in the contract is a vital part of the performance and that failure to perform on time is a breach for which the injured party is entitled to damages in the amount of loss sustained.

time-and-a-half A 50 percent additional payment for time worked after normal working hours or at other designated periods.

time-dependent deformation Combined effects of autogenous volume change, contraction, creep, expansion, shrinkage and swelling occurring during an appreciable period of time; not synonymous with inelastic behavior or volume change.

time, drying The period of time during which an adhesive on an adherend or an assembly is allowed to dry with or without the application of heat of pressure, or both.

timekeeper A person who calculates wages for hours worked, usually at the jobsite.

time lag fuse A fuse that absorbs large amounts of surge currents, momentarily.

timely completion Completion of the work or designated portion thereof on or before the date required.

time of completion Date established in the contract, by name or by number of days, for substantial completion of the work.

time of haul In production of ready-mixed concrete, the period from first contact between mixing water and cement until completion of discharge of the freshly mixed concrete.

time of set Time required for addition of water for cement paste, mortar or concrete to attain a certain arbitrary degree of hardness.

timesing column A column on the British estimator's sheet for showing how many times the same quantity must be repeated.

tin A white lustrous metal, used chiefly for coating sheet steel, as in tin roofing.

tinbender (tinman) *(slang)* Sheet metal worker.

tine (1) A prong of a rake or harrow. (2) An excavating tooth in the mouth of a dragline, excavator bucket or scraper loader.

tingle (cleat; tab) (1) A lead, copper or zinc strip about 1½ inches wide, for fixing panes of glass in patent glazing, or fixing slates which replace broken slates. (2) A support at the middle of a long brick line.

tin horn *(slang)* Corrugated metal pipe.

tinker's dam In plumbing, a small dam made to enclose a spot which is to be flooded with solder.

tin-knocker *(slang)* Sheet metal worker.

tinman's solder Fine solder.

tinning Coating copper, steel or other metal with a tin alloy film to reduce corrosion.

tin pants *(slang)* Waterproof clothing.

tinplate Bright sheet-steel coated with a thin film of tin on both sides by dipping it in molten tin, commonly used in tin roofing. *(see terne)*

tin roofing Roofing with tinplate. Not recommended for wet climates due to its corrosive nature.

tin saw A masonry saw for cutting bricks.

tinsmith In Britain, a sheet metal worker.

tin snips *(slang)* A cutting tool, such as ordinary hand shears, used by sheet metal workers.

tint A color made by mixing white pigment with a small amount of colored pigment.

tinting Final color adjustment of paint.

tin whistle *(slang)* Corrugated metal culvert.

tip The thin end of a shingle which is laid at the upper end.

tip grade The toe line of piles.

tipping valve A mechanism which allows powdered material to flow vertically downward but blocks the passage of air or gas. Generally consists of one or a multiple of flaps in a housing which are actuated by weight of the pulverized material or by external means.

tipping wagon (jubilee wagon) A small wagon on narrow-gauge track, pivoted for side or end dumping.

tip-shearing Texture pattern of carpet, created in the same way as random-shearing, but generally less definite than random-sheared.

tip velocity The speed at which the fuel and primary air leave the burner pipe tip.

tire Hollow or solid cast steel riding ring for kiln or mill.

titan crane A crane of at least 50 tons capacity which can command a considerable distance outside the portal legs.

Title III The Emergency Planning and Community Right to Know Act of 1986, a stand-alone act that is contained in the Superfund Amendments and Reauthorization Act (SARA) of 1986. The Act has four major regulatory compliance sections: **(1)** emergency planning requirements, **(2)** emergency notification requirements, **(3)** chemical inventory reporting requirements, and **(4)** toxic chemical release reporting requirements.

title Legal documents indicating right of ownership.

title sheet The first sheet of a set of blueprints usually including a plot of the project, the name and location of the project, the name of the designer (architect or engineer), index, etc.

titration An analytical method using a standard solution for the determination of the amount of some substance in another solution. As an example, in cement manufacture, determination of the calcium-carbonate content of raw materials or raw mix, dissolved in hydrochloric acid, by measuring the smallest amount of alkali which will neutralize the solution, as indicated by a color change.

toat The handle commonly found on bench planes.

tobermorite A mineral found primarily in Northern Ireland, having the approximate formula $Ca_4 (Si_6O_{18}H_2)\cdot Ca\cdot$

$4H_2O$ identified approximately with the artificial product tobermorite (G) of Brunauer, a hydrated calcium silicate having CaO/SiO_2 ratio in the range 1.39 to 1.75 and forming minute layered crystals that constitute the principal cementing medium in portland cement concrete; a mineral with five mols of lime to six mols of silica, usually occurring in plate-like crystals, which is easily synthesized at steam pressures of about 100 psig and higher; the binder in several properly autoclaved products.

tobermorite gel The binder of concrete cured moist or in atmospheric-pressure steam, a lime-rich gel-like solid containing 1.5 to 2.0 mols of lime per mol of silica.

toe **(1)** The projection of the bottom of a face beyond the top. **(2)** The end of blasting hole where explosive is placed. **(3)** The base of a retaining wall away from retained material.

toe board *(OSHA)* A vertical barrier at floor level erected along exposed edges of a floor opening, wall opening, platform, runway or ramp to prevent falls of materials.

toe guard **(1)** A guard used to protect a passenger from catching his foot under a hoistway or elevator car sill projection. **(2)** A sheet steel plate fastened to the hoistway edge of a landing sill or to the edge of an elevator car platform beneath and in line with the entrance. The purpose of the toe guard is to reduce the shearing action of the edge of the sill or threshold, if it should interfere with any component projecting beyond the sill or threshold line.

toeing In carpentry, the driving of nails or brads obliquely; also, to clinch nails so driven.

toe joint In carpentry, the joint between a horizontal member and another at a vertical angle, as a rafter on plate.

toe level The depth to which piles are driven.

toenail The driving of a nail, spike or brad on a slant in a piece of lumber to attach another piece of lumber.

toe of dam The junction of the downstream face of a dam with the ground surface. Also referred to as downstream toe.

toggle bolt A corrogated device enabling a fixture to be fastened to a thin board.

tolerance Acceptable variation from a standard size.

tom *(see shore)*

ton A unit of weight. The short ton, 2,000 pounds; the long ton, 2,240 pounds.

ton (of refrigeration) A useful refrigerating effect equal to 12,000 Btu per hour; 200 Btu per minute.

tone on tone A carpet pattern made by using two or more shades of the same hue.

tongs A pair of curved arms pivoted to each other, scissor fashion, so that a pull on a ring or chain connecting the short ends will cause the long ends to close to grip an object between them.

tong tester Clamp-on ammeter used to measure alternating current in amperes.

tongue A projecting rib cut along the edge of a piece of timber so it can be fitted into a groove cut in another piece.

tongue and groove Sheeting, usually wood, in which one edge of the sheet is cut with a projecting tongue that fits into a corresponding groove or recess in the edge of the next sheet.

tonnage A charge per ton on cargo or freight on a canal, at a port, etc.; weight in tons.

tonk strips Slotted metal strips inserted into cabinets or book cases to carry clips which hold adjustable shelves.

ton slates Large, irregular pieces of slate sold by weight.

tool In construction, a saw, shovel, hammer, trowel, etc., called hand tools.

tooling Compressing and shaping the face of a mortar joint with a special tool other than a trowel.

tool of knowledge *(slang)* T-square.

tooth (1) A characteristic of good wall primer; a slight roughness for permitting better distribution of finish coat.

(2) A projection such as occurs on a gear, a saw, etc.

tooth base The inner part of a two-piece tooth on a digging bucket; occasionally, the socket in which a tooth fits.

toothing In masonry construction, the allowing of alternate courses of brick to project toothlike to provide for a good bond with any adjoining brickwork which may follow.

tooth ornament A pyramidal form having no antecedents in Classical architecture, based probably on the Norman nailhead and widely used in English thirteenth-century work and also on the Continent.

top beam *(see collar beam)*

top coat Follows prime coat application in coil coating process.

top colors Colors of the yarn used to form the carpet design, as distinguished from ground color.

top course tiles The course of tiles at the ridge, sized to maintain gauge of those below.

top cut The cut to level at the top of a rafter.

top form Form required on the upper or outer surface of a sloping slab or thin shell.

top-hung window A casement window hinged from the top.

top lighting Overhead lighting either by natural or artificial means.

topman One who holds a sheet pile in position as a crane lowers it slowly so that it interlocks with previously placed sheet piles.

top of car inspection station Controls on the top of the elevator car used by an elevator mechanic to operate the car at inspection speed.

topographical surveyor *(see land surveyor)*

topographic map A map indicating surface elevation and slope. Usually referred to as a topo.

topographic survey A survey conducted to determine the configuration of the ground.

topography The physically detailed description of a piece of land.

topped out The last piece; the uppermost section put in place; the top floor of a multi-story structure.

topping (1) A specially prepared substance in heavy paste form used to cover the perfa-tape and fill in the joint in gypsum wallboard. (2) A commercial mixture used to top concrete floor surfaces, to provide durability, safety & beauty. (3) An operation in putting a cutting edge on a handsaw.

top shadow line A line of dark colored granules applied to a thickbutt shingle in such a position that the shadow line will be accentuated.

topsoil The topmost layer of soil; soil containing humus which is capable of supporting a good plant growth.

top steam Steam introduced into the top, or gas and air area, above the bituminous residuum charge of a blowing still.

torchere An ornamental support for a flambeau or other source of light.

torpedo A tube containing the explosive which is used after chambering a hole which cannot be cooled enough to safely insert unprotected explosive.

torpedo sand A natural well-graded, plastering sand obtained from pits along the Fox River, west of Chicago, Illinois.

torque The twisting force exerted by or on a shaft without reference to the speed of the shaft. Turning or twisting power; the force causing rotation.

torque converter A hydraulic coupling which utilizes slippage to multiply torque.

torque rod A bar having the function of resisting or absorbing twisting strains.

torque viscosimeter A viscosimeter used for measuring consistency of slurries in which rotation of a device suspended in a rotating cup is the measure of viscosity.

torque wrench A wrench containing an adjustable mechanism for measuring and controlling the amount of torque or

turning force to be exerted-often used in tightening nuts or bolts.

torsade A ropelike molding.

torsion The force tending to right a twisted rod, cable or other long slender member.

torso An architectural term applied to a column with a twisted shaft.

torus In architecture, a type of molding with a convex portion which is nearly semicircular in form; used extensively as a base molding.

torus roll A horizontal roll covered with metal used where two slopes of a mansard roof join together.

total float *(C.P.M.)* The difference between the amount of time available to accomplish an activity and the time necessary. The difference between an activity's late start and its early start. The amount of extra time available to an activity assuming that all activities preceding have started as early as they can, and that all activities following will start as late as they can.

total rise of a roof The vertical distance between the plate line and the roof ridge.

total run The level distance which a rafter spans.

total systems (panels) Usually large concrete slabs or otherwise panelized units not made in the form of a box, but often large enough to constitute entire walls, partitions and floors, or substantial parts of floors and roofs, which form boxes when put together. They are fabricated in a shop and assembled at the site.

total weight Weight per square yard of total carpet pile, yarn, primary and secondary backings and coatings.

toughness The property of matter which resists fracture by impact or shock.

tough way *(slang)* The direction in rock along which the rock is tough to break.

tower A tall structure, usually square or round in plan, rising to a greater height than its surroundings.

tower gantry *(see derrick tower gantry)*

township The 36 square miles located between range and township lines.

tow tractor Tractor used to tow or winch equipment.

toxic Poisonous.

T-plate A T-shaped metal plate commonly used as a splice; also used for stiffening a joint where the end of one beam abuts against the side of another.

T-post A post built up of studs and blocking to form the intersection of the framing of perpendicular walls.

trabs A wall plate.

trace To make sketches, drawings or designs on tracing paper or on tracing linen for reproduction, as for blueprinting.

tracery An architectural term applied to any delicate ornamental work consisting of interlacing lines such as the decorative designs carved on panels or screens. Also, the intersecting of ribs and bars, as in rose windows, and the upper part of Gothic windows. Any decorative design suggestive of network.

tracing A drawing on translucent paper or linen.

track One of a pair of roller chains used to support and propel a machine; a metal way for wheeled components; one or more lines of ways, with fastenings, ties, etc., for a craneway, monorail or slide door.

track frame (truck frame) In a crawler mounting, a side frame to which the track roller and idler are attached.

tracking (1) Lines of wear in road surfaces. (2) Moving the solar collector to follow the sun and increase collector efficiency.

track roller In a crawler machine, the small wheels which are under the track frame and which rest on the track.

traction The total amount of driving push of a vehicle on a given surface; the friction developed between a powered surface and one in contact with it. As applied to elevators, traction refers to the friction developed between the hoist ropes and drive sheave.

traction steel Wire ropes used mainly for hoist ropes. They are a form of mild steel with an excellent combination of toughness, strength, ductility, and fatigue resistance.

tractive efficiency A measure of the proportion of the weight resting on tracks or drive wheels which can be converted into vehicle movement.

tractive effort (1) Force exerted by the weight and velocity of water which tends to cause erosion. (2) The driving force exerted against the ground surface by a track or wheel.

tractive resistance Identifies frictional resistance to motion per ton hauled.

tractor A motor vehicle on tracks or wheels used for towing or operating vehicles or equipment; equipment to pull or push loads.

tractor loader A tractor carrying a bucket which can dig and elevate to dump at truck height.

tractor-pulled scraper A scraper towed by a tractor used for loading, hauling and discharging material.

tractor shovel A loading shovel mounted on either crawler tracks or road wheels. It is tipped by reversing away from the material and moving towards the discharge point. It is suitable for confined spaces.

tractor driver *(slang)* Sideboom operator.

trade (craft) (1) Occupation requiring manual skill. (2) Members of a trade organized into a collective body.

trade union A combination of tradesmen organized for the purpose of promoting their common interest in regard to wages, fringe benefits, hours of work and other working conditions.

traditional architecture Contemporary architecture that holds closely to forms established in an earlier period.

traffic cone A cone-shaped device of pliable material used to define construction areas and route traffic.

trailer A towed carrier which rests on its own wheels both front and rear.

trailer, semi (semitrailer) A towed carrier that rests on the tractor in front and on its own wheels in the rear.

trailing cable A set of conductors providing power for crane, dragline, loader or similar machine.

train *(slang)* Cement or asphalt train; tractor and set of double carriers that haul bulk cement or asphalt products.

training wall In Britain, a retaining wall built to contain a river.

trajectory of prestressing force The path along which the prestress is effective in a structure or member; it is coincident with the center of gravity of the tendons for simple flexural members and statically indeterminate members which are prestressed with concordant tendons, but is not coincident with the center of gravity of the tendons of a statically indeterminate structure which is prestressed with non-concordant tendons.

trammel An instrument used for drawing arcs or radii too great for the capacity of the ordinary compass; a beam compass, with adjustable points attached to the end of a bar of wood or metal, used by draftsmen and shopworkers for describing unusually large circles or arcs.

tramp iron Scrap metal entering a crusher.

tramway *(see aerial tramway)*

transept Either of the lateral arms in a church of cruciform plan.

transfer The act of transferring the stress in prestressing tendons from the jacks or pretensioning bed to the concrete member.

transfer bond In pretensioning, the bond stress resulting from the transfer of stress from the tendon to the concrete.

transfer case In an all-wheel drive vehicle, a transmission or gear set that provides drive to the front shaft.

transfer length *(see transmission length)*

transfer medium The substance that carries heat from the solar collector to storage or from storage to the living areas.

transfer point Turning point.

transfer strength The concrete strength required before stress is transferred from the stressing mechanism to the concrete.

transformed section A hypothetical section of one material arranged so as to have the same elastic properties as a section of two materials.

transformer A device for converting one voltage of current to another voltage. The ease with which power can be transformed is the main reason for the use of alternating current over direct current when power is consumed far from the generator.

transit An instrument commonly used by surveyors consisting of four principal parts: (a) a telescope for sighting, (b) a spirit level, (c) a vernier or graduated arc for measuring vertical or horizontal angles, and (d) a tripod with leveling screws for adjusting the instrument.

transite (1) A fireproofing material used in walls, roofs and for lining ovens; composed of asbestos and portland cement molded under high pressure and sold under the trade name of Transite. (2) Cement-asbestos pipe. (3) A surveying instrument.

transition (1) The slow change from one distinct style to another distinct style following it. (2) A duct fitting that changes the size or shape of the duct or pipeline.

transition belt (feeder conveyor) A short belt carrying material from a loading point to a main conveyor belt.

transition curve (easement curve) Generally a spiral, the curve which eases the change between a straight and a circular curve.

transition spiral A transition spiral is a curve that provides a gradual curve between a straight line and a curve. Used in designing highways and railroads.

transit-mixed concrete Concrete, the mixing of which is wholly or principally accomplished in a mixer truck.

translucent Permitting the passage of light but not vision.

translucent concrete *(see concrete, translucent)*

transmission **(1)** In thermodynamics, a general term for heat travel; properly, heat transferred per unit of time. The amount of heat transmitted into a building or from it through the various components of the building envelope, including exterior walls, windows, doors; roof; floor, etc. **(2)** A gear set that permits change in speed-power ratio and/or direction of rotation.

clutch shifted A constant-mesh transmission in which power is directed through gear trains by engagement of friction clutches.

compound A gear set in which power can be transmitted through two sets of reduction gears in succession.

reduction type A transmission whose output shaft, usually the countershaft, always turns more slowly than the input shaft.

reversing A transmission that has only a forward and a reverse shift.

transmission length The distance at the end of a pretensioned tendon necessary for the bond stress to develop the maximum tendon stress; sometimes called transfer length.

transmission loss (TL) Essentially the amount, in decibels, by which sound power is attenuated by passing from one side of a structure to the other. TL is independent of the rooms on each side of the structure and theoretically independent of the area and edge conditions of the structure.

transom **(1)** An opening over a door or window, usually for ventilation, containing a glazed or solid sash, usually hinged or pivoted. **(2)** A panel or panels used to close a hoistway enclosure opening above a hoistway entrance.

transom bar A crossbar of wood or stone which divides an opening horizontally into two parts.

transport system The means through which the heat transfer fluid is moved to all parts of a solar system. Depending upon system design, the fluid may be propelled through ducts by fans or through piping by circulator or thermosiphon action.

transtra Horizontal roof timbers.

transverse joint A joint parallel to the intermediate dimension of a structure.

transverse prestress Prestress that is applied at right angles to the principal axis of a member.

transverse reinforcement Reinforcement at right angles to the principal axis of a member.

transverse strength *(see flexural strength; modulus of rupture)*

trap A device to prevent sewer air from backing up and escaping through a plumbing fixture. When made of cast iron or vitrified tile, it may be of various forms defined as running trap, P-trap, S-trap, etc.

trap door A covering for an opening in a floor, ceiling or roof; usually such a door is level, or practically so, with the surface of the opening which it covers.

trape notch A quadrilateral opening having only two sides parallel, used in a trapezoidal weir.

trapezoidal weir A contracted measuring weir with a trape notch.

trap rock A sized or graded, uncolored, natural rock used as an underlay between two layers of asphalt.

trap seal The vertical distance between the crown weir and the dip of the trap.

trash Waste matter resulting from a building operation.

trash rack A grid or screen across a stream designed to catch floating debris.

trass **(1)** A natural pozzolan of volcanic origin found in Germany. **(2)** Earth used in the making of hydraulic cement.

travel (rise) Distance in feet and inches that an elevator travels from its lowest landing to its highest landing.

traveler An inverted U-shaped structure usually mounted on tracks which permits it to move from one location to another to facilitate the construction of an arch, bridge or building.

traveling cable A cable made up of

electric conductors, which provides electrical connection between an elevator or dumbwaiter car and fixed outlet in the hoistway.

traveling forms Formwork for casting walls or the linings of tunnels or culverts, built on a carriage on rollers or wheels which allows the forms to be moved without dismantling them.

traveling nut Nut which travels along a screw when the screw is turned.

traveling screen (1) A diaphragm, usually of canvas in a frame moved by water in the direction of flow, for purposes of measuring directly the mean velocity; only useful in regular channels where the frame is shaped to the channel cross section and nearly fills it. (2) A revolving trash screen.

travel time Wages paid to workmen under certain union contracts and under certain job conditions for the time spent in traveling from their place of residence to and from the job.

traverse (1) To plane in a direction across the grain of the wood, as to traverse a floor by planing across the boards. (2) A series of connected lines of known length related to one another by known angles. (3) A gallery or loft of communication in a church or other building.

traverse closure The line which will exactly close the traverse.

tread (1) The ground contact surface on a tire or track shoe. (2) A high-friction lagging on a belt pulley. (3) The horizontal surface of a step; width measurement of a step.

treadle A foot pedal hinged to the floor at one end.

treadmill The source of power on building sites in the Middle Ages.

tread width The horizontal distance from front to back of tread, including nosing when used.

tree (slang) A group of wires or cables tied together to form a tree-like cluster.

tree-cutter (stumper; treedozer) A tractor or bulldozer equipped with a horizontal blade to clear trees.

tree nail (1) A wooden pin used in se-

curing together the ends of wooden framing. (2) A gutta.

trefoil In architecture, an ornamental three-lobed unit resembling in form the foliage of an herb whose leaf is divided into three distinct parts, such as the common varieties of clover.

treillage A latticework erected for supporting vines, as in a vine arbor; a trellis.

trellis An ornamental structure of latticework over which vines are trained, such as a summerhouse, usually made of narrow strips of wood which cross each other at regular intervals.

tremie A pipe through which concrete may be deposited under water, having at its upper end a hopper for filling and a bail by means of which the assembly can be handled by a derrick. (see elephant trunk)

tremie concrete Concrete placed by means of a tremie.

tremie seal Concrete placed under water by means of a tremie in a cofferdam or caisson so that it can be dewatered after the concrete hardens.

trench An excavation made for the purpose of installing or removing pipes, drains, catch basins, etc. and which is later refilled; a ditch; an excavation for a foundation wall.

trench excavator (ditcher; trenching machine) A self-propelled machine, specialized for digging trenches, using either a bucket-ladder excavator or a chain of buckets on a wheel.

trench jack Screw or hydraulic-type jacks used as cross bracing in a trench shoring system.

trench shield A shoring system composed of steel plates and bracing, welded or bolted together, which supports the walls of a trench from the ground level to the trench bottom and which can be moved along as work progresses.

trencher A trench excavator.

trenching machine (see trench excavator)

tresaunce A passageway.

trestle (1) A bridge, usually of timber

or steel, that has a number of closely spaced supports between the abutments. (2) A movable frame or support for anything; when made of a crosspiece with four legs it is called a carpenter's horse.

trestle table   A large drawing board supported by trestles.

trial batch   A batch of concrete prepared to establish or check proportions of the constituents.

triangular notch (triangular weir; vee notch)   A measuring weir of V-shape used for measuring small discharges.

triangular scale   A draftsman's three-faced measuring device having six graduated edges. On one edge is shown a scale of full-size measurements, while on the other edges are shown various reductions in scale.

triangular truss   A popular type of truss used for short spans, especially for roof supports.

triangular weir   A contracted measuring weir notch with sides that form an angle with its apex downward; a V-notch weir.

triangulation   The method of surveying called triangulation is based on the trigonometric proposition that, if one side and the three angles of a triangle are known, the remaining sides can be computed.

triaxial compression test   A test in which a specimen is subjected to a confining hydrostatic pressure and then loaded axially to failure.

triaxial test   A test in which a specimen is subjected simultaneously to lateral and axial loads.

tribble tie system   A system of modified truss-type Dur-o-wall hairpin ties and short pieces of rebar used to tie stone veneer facing to masonry block back-up in cavity walls.

tribrach   An adaptor for mounting an instrument on a surveyor's tripod which is, or is not, specifically designed for that instrument as the case may be.

tributary area   The area which con-

tributes to a specific structural component.

tricalcium aluminate (CA)   Chemical compound in portland cement that liberates a large amount of heat during the first few days of hardening. It also adds to early strength development. Cements low in C3A are resistant to sulfates found in soils and water.

tricalcium silicate   A compound having the composition $3CaO \cdot CiO_2$, abbreviated C_3S, an impure form of which (alite) is a main constituent of portland cement. *(see alite)*

trickle drain   A pond overflow pipe set vertically with its open top level with the water surface.

trickling water collector   A solar collector pioneered by Dr. Harry Thomason of Washington, D.C. Water pumped to the top of a roof trickles down the valleys of black corrugated collectors and is heated.

trig   The bricks laid in the middle of a wall between the two main leads to overcome the sag in the line and also to keep the center plumb; the metal clip used to hold the masons line; a short piece of line looped around the main line and fastened to the top edge of a brick that has been previously laid in proper position.

triglyphs   A structural member in a Doric frieze consisting typically of a rectangular block with two vertical grooves, or glyphs, and two chamfers, or half grooves, at the sides, which together count as a third glyph.

trig station   The base survey station used for large scale triangulation.

trilith   A megalithic gateway of two upright stones and a lintel.

trim   (1) In carpentry, a term applied to the visible finishing work of the interior of a building, including any ornamental parts of either wood or metal used for covering joints between jambs and plaster around windows and doors. The term may include also the locks, knobs and hinges on doors. (2) The light gauge metal used in the finish of a building, especially around openings and at intersections of surfaces. Often called flashing.

trim holes (relief holes) Unloaded drill holes closely spaced along a line to limit the breakage of a blast.

trimmer (1) One who sets a pace for working. (2) The longer floor framing member around a rectangular opening into which a header is joined. (3) A short beam engaging the ends of several other beams or joists, usually to support a floor around an opening or at a chimney breast.

trimmer arch An arch built in front of a fireplace, in the thickness of the floor, between two trimmers. The bottom of the arch starts from the chimney and the top presses against the header.

trimming (1) Framing strength at the opening through a floor, roof or wall, whether of timber or other material. (2) The final clean-up of an earthwork surface.

trimming joist A timber, or beam, which supports a header.

trinitrotoluene An explosive used in blasting; commonly known as TNT.

triode tube Three element vacuum tube.

trip A release catch.

trip coil A solenoid-operated device used for opening a circuit breaker.

triple course Three rows of shingles laid together at eaves for finish line.

triple grips Sheet metal anchor brackets, perforated with holes for nails, designed to tie framing members together.

triple seal-tab (tri-tab hexagonal) A strip shingle having three tabs, each of which is one-half of a modified hexagonal design.

tripod A three-legged support for a surveying instrument.

tripper A double pulley that turns a short section of a conveyor belt upside down in order to dump its load into a side chute.

tripping time The period of time required before excessive motor current forces an overload relay to open its control contact and remove power from the motor.

troffer A troughlike enclosure for light sources.

trombe wall Masonry, typically 8 to 16 inches thick, blackened and exposed to the sun behind glazing; a passive solar heating system in which a masonry wall collects, stores and distributes heat.

trommel Rotary screen.

trough gutter In sheet metal, a box gutter.

troughing (1) Making repeated dozer pushes in one track so that ridges of spilled material hold dirt in front of the blade. (2) Rolled steel sections shaped like a U welded in bridge decks with the U alternating in up or down positions.

trough mixer (see open-top mixer)

trowel A tool used by the plasterer to apply, spread, shape and smooth the various plastering mortars. The size of the trowel varies according to the mechanic's preference with regard to the tool's feel and balance. Common sizes are 10½" × 4½" and 11½" × 4¾". There are three parts of a trowel: These are called the blade, the mounting, and the handle. The following trowels are commonly used—margin trowel, angle trowel, joint trowel, panel trowel, and texture trowel.

troweled face Plaster or mortar surface with a trowel finish.

troweled stucco After ruling off and scoring stucco, a laying trowel is used for final surfacing.

trowel finish A term denoting the smooth finish coat surface produced by troweling.

troweling (1) Smoothing and compacting the unformed surface of fresh concrete by strokes of a trowel. (2) Spreading of adhesives or underlayment.

troweling machine A motor driven device which operates orbiting steel trowels on radial arms from a vertical shaft.

trowel man   Concrete or masonry finisher.

truck, bottom dump   (dump wagon) A trailer or semi-trailer that dumps bulk material by opening doors in the floor of the body.

truck frame   (see track frame)

truck-mixed concrete   (see transit-mixed concrete)

truck mixer (transit mixer)   A concrete mixer mounted on a truck, mixing the concrete while traveling from the batching plant to the site.

truck, platform (rack body truck)   A truck having a flat open body.

truck, rear dump (end dump)   A truck or semitrailer that has a box body that can be raised at the front so the load will slide out the rear.

true bearing   A horizontal angle between any survey line and true north.

true meridian   The geographic north to south plane.

true section   Drawing cross-section using the same vertical and horizontal scales.

true-to-scale print   A contact print or tracing on opaque paper or cloth.

truncated   Having the apex replaced by a plane section, especially one parallel to the base.

trunk   (1) That part of a pilaster corresponding to the shaft of a column. (2) Large sheet metal or iron pipe for ventilation.

trunk line   The main duct line from which individual lines branch.

trunnion (walking beam; walking bar)   An oscillating bar which allows changes in angle between a unit fastened to is center and another attached to both ends; a heavy horizontal hinge.

trunnion axis   On the theodolite telescope, the horizontal axis of rotation.

truss   Beams or other supports connected to support a roof, bridge, etc.; an assemblage of timbers, fastened together so as to mutually support each other and to prevent sagging or distortion of any kind; used as one of the principal supports of a roof.

trussed   Braced by an assembly of members into a rigid unit.

trussed arch   A steel arch built of rolled-steel sections; generally used in heavy bridge building.

trussed beam   An architectural term applied to a beam stiffened by a truss rod.

trussed partition   A framed partition, made of timber, strongly framed like a truss to carry weight in addition to its own. Rarely used now due to cheaper methods of construction.

trussed purlin   A purlin reinforced by use of a camber rod beneath it.

trussed rafter roof   (1) Collar-beam roof (2) Scissors truss.

trussed roof   A roof resting on trusses.

try square   A tool used for laying out right angles and for testing work for squareness.

T-shore   A shore with a T-head.

T-square   A tool used by draftsmen. It consists of a ruler, usually from two to three inches in width and from one to five feet in length, with a crosspiece attached to one end of the ruler or blade. The crosspiece, or head, is at least twice as thick as the blade.

T stat   Thermostat.

tub   The base of a walking dragline.

tubbing   Metal lining for tunnels or shafts formed from segments of a circle fitted and bolted together.

tube   A hollow product, metal or plastic, of round cross section, having a continuous periphery.

tube and coupler scaffold   An assembly consisting of tubing which serves as posts, bearers, braces, ties and runners, a base supporting the posts, and special couplers which serve to connect the uprights and to join the various members.

tube float   The machine used to level and finish the surface of concrete pavement.

tube mill   Cylindrical rotating mill, charged with grinding media; the length is several times the diameter.

tub mixer   (see open top mixer)

tubing *(see tube)*

tubular A pipe fitting, often copper, formed from pipe.

tubular saw A key hole saw.

tubular scaffolder In Britain, a workman who erects metal scaffolding joined with clips, fish plates, nuts and bolts. When erecting suspended scaffolds, he may be called a rigger.

tubular scaffolding Scaffolding of steel or light alloy tube measuring two inches outside diameter.

tubular welded frame scaffold A sectional panel or frame metal scaffold substantially built up of prefabricated welded sections which consists of posts and horizontal bearers with intermediate members.

tuck The horizontal line of a mortar joint filled with lime putty for a decorative white line.

tuck in Felt roofing cut and fit to cover the flashing next to a chase in the wall.

tuck pointing The filling in with fresh mortar of cut-out or defective mortar joints in old masonry.

tuft bind Force required to pull a tuft from a cut-pile carpet or to pull free one leg of a loop from a looped pile carpet.

tufting Surface, or pile, yarns are inserted into a pre-constructed backing.

tufts The cut or uncut loops forming the face of a tufted or woven carpet.

tumbler The parts of a lock which hold the locking bar in place until the key is turned.

tumbler switch A lever-operated switch.

tumbling in (tumbling courses) Courses of brickwork sloping to meet horizontal courses as at a gable wall.

tung oil (wood oil; China wood oil) An excellent water-resisting oil obtained from the seeds of aleurite trees grown in China and Japan.

tungsten carbide A hard material brazed onto cutting edges as bits and boring tools.

tungsten-filament lamp An incandescent electric light source using a filament of tungsten wire with a high melting point and a low evaporation rate in a bulb filled with a mixture of argon and nitrogen.

tunnel An underground passageway.

tunnel forms with accelerated curing Precision-made volumetric steel forms with integral heating equipment placed next to one another on a slab, and floors and walls cast in one single operation, in one-or-two-room widths. After casting, the heating accelerates the curing of the concrete and the formwork is easily removed to a new position for immediate reuse.

tunneling speed The time projection and record of advancement in tunneling procedures.

tunnel lining The covering placed over the rock and materials in the tunnel to prevent it falling in and to reduce the friction of the air passing through it.

tunnel test Standard testing method measuring flame spread, fuel contribution and smoke density of carpeting materials, under controlled conditions, with accepted minimum and maximum numerical rating from 10 to 75. This test is also known as the Steiner Tunnel Test.

tup A drop hammer.

tupper British for bricklayer's helper or apprentice.

turbidimeter A device for measuring the particle-size distribution of a finely divided material by taking successive measurements of the turbidity of a suspension in a fluid.

turbidimeter fineness The fineness of a material such as portland cement, usually expressed as total surface area in square centimeters per gram, as determined with a turbidimeter. *(see Wagner fineness)*

turbine A rotary engine driven by pressure of liquid or gas against its vanes, often used for driving an electric generator.

turbine mixer *(see open-top mixer)*

turbo-drill A oil well drilling machine designed to facilitate drilling at depths below two miles.

turbulent flame A flame in which the directions and velocities of the fuel and gases supporting combustion cause agitation and more complete mixing and rapid combustion.

turbulent flow Flow is said to be turbulent when its path lines are irregular curve which continually coss each other and form a complicated network which in the aggregate represents the forward motion of the entire stream.

turette A small turret.

turf Sod.

turkey tails Architectural design on the peak of gable roof.

turn angles To measure the angles between directions with a surveying instrument.

turnbuckle A type of coupling between the ends of two rods, used primarily for adjusting or regulating the tension in the rods which it connects. It consists of a loop or sleeve with a screw thread on one end and a swivel at the other, or with an internal screw thread at each end.

turn button A latch used on a cupboard door consisting of a pivoting metal or wood piece, held to the frame by a screw.

turned work Woodwork cut on a lathe.

turner A lathe operator who turns wood or metal in a machine.

turnkey contract Building arrangement in which a contractor is totally responsible for all design, financing, and construction until the building is delivered to the owner as a completed project.

turning The operation of making an object in a lathe.

turning gouge In woodworking, a tool used for roughing down wood-work in a lathe. The widths of gouges vary from ¼ to 1½ inches.

turning point (transfer point) A point whose elevation is taken from two or more instrument positions to determine their height in relation to each other.

turn-of-the-nut-method A method for pre-tensioning high strength bolts. The nut is turned from the snug tight position, corresponding to a few blows of an impact wrench or the full effort of a man using an ordinary spud wrench.

turnscrew British for screwdriver.

turnstile A rotating barrier through which one way passage is effected, sometimes with a counting or entrance-fee mechanism; primarily used in subways, supermarkets and museums.

turntable (1) A base that supports a part and allows it to rotate or swing. (2) In a shovel, the upper part of the travel unit.

turpentine A volatile oil used as a thinner in paints and as a solvent in varnishes. Chemically, it is a mixture of terpenes.

turpentine substitute Alcohol.

turret A small tower, usually corbeled, at the corner of a building and extending above it.

turret step A triangular step with rounded ends laid on top of each other from which a spiral stair is built.

turtle back (slang) (1) A term often used synonymously with blistering. (2) A term used regionally to denote a small localized area of craze-cracking.

Tuscan Pertaining to one of the five Classic orders of architecture, distinguished especially by the plain column and the absence of decorative detail.

tusks (tusses) Bricks, blocks or rocks projecting from the face of a structure.

tuyers The perforated casting fitted to the stoker retort. Air blasts pass through these from stoker fan.

tv compatible An infrared camera system whose frame rate and line frequency is compatible with closed-circuit TV systems.

twicher A trowel for edging the margins in finish plastering.

twin cable (duplex cable) Two conductors, both insulated, in a common insulating covering.

twining stem molding A molding in which a conventionalized tendril winds about a stem.

twin pug A mill with two horizontal shafts turning in opposite directions; also known as a pugmill.

twin-twisted reinforcement *(see reinforcement, twin-twisted bar)*

twist (1) The direction and shape yarn has been given to produce a particular texture effect. (2) A spiral warp in lumber.

twist bit In woodwork, a tool used for boring holes in wood for screws. A tool similar to the twist drill used for drilling holes in metal, except that the cutting edge of the twist bit is ground at a greater angle.

twist carpet Surface texture created with tightly twisted yarns, resulting in a nubby or pebbly effect.

twist drill A drilling tool having helical grooves extending from the point to the smooth portion of the shank. This type of drill is made of round stock with a shank that may be either straight or tapering and is used for drilling holes in metal.

twisted column (wreathed column) Carved or molded to give the appearance of having a twisted shaft or intertwined twin shafts.

twist gimlet A gimlet which has a helical groove by which the wood cuttings are removed.

two-blocked (1) A situation which occurs when the operator of a piece of equipment, such as a crane or cable-operated unit, reels up the cable too far, so that the top sheave block (pully wheel) and the bottom sheave block are run together. With no cable room to work with, it then becomes impossible to go either forward or back, resulting in a two-blocked condition. Anti-two-blocking devices are available to help avoid the situation. (2) *(slang)* Any situation out of which there is no apparent way out.

two-bolt lock A lock operated by a key, combined with a latch operated by a knob.

two-coat work Plastering, paint or asphalt generally applied in two layers, first coat and finish coat.

two-core block Concrete masonry unit which has two cores or cells.

two-handed saw A large saw with handles at each end, worked by two men for felling trees or cross cutting logs.

two-hinged arch (two-pinned arch) An arch-shaped or rectangular rigid frame hinged at both supports.

two-leg sling Two chains or ropes made into a sling hanging from one link with a hook attached at one end.

two-man rip rap Rocks of a size that two men could lift and place for facing a slope; usually used on waterways.

two-part line A single strand, rope or cable doubled back around a sheave so that two parts of it pull a load together.

two-pinned arch A two-hinged arch.

two-point suspension scaffold (swinging scaffold) A scaffold, the platform of which is supported by hangers or stirrups at two points, suspended from overhead supports so as to permit the raising or lowering of the platform to the desired working position by tackle or hoisting machines.

two-stage curing A process in which concrete products are cured in low-pressure steam, stacked and then autoclaved.

two tone When right of way dozer cuts a side hill on two elevations (bench) to keep from moving more material.

two-way footing A single footing using reinforcement steel.

two-way reinforced footing A footing having reinforcement in two directions, generally perpendicular to each other.

two-way system A system of reinforcement; bars, rods or wires placed at right angles to each other in a slab and intended to resist stresses due to bending of the slab in two directions.

T-wrench A tool for tightening a nut on a bolt. The T-wrench consists of a handle, or lever, with a T-shaped socket which fits over and completely encircles a nut or bolthead. It may have a ratchet or an extension to permit working in places not easily accessible.

tympanum The space enclosed by the

three molded sides of a pediment, or by the lines of a semicircular overdoor panel or the like.

Tyler standard Sieve sizes given in mesh per inch.

type The canopy sounding board over a pulpit.

tyrolea A porous plaster applied to provide a rainproof surface; plaster usually applied by hand operated machine.

u   unit

U   Uranium

UBC   Uniform Building Code

UDC   universal decimal classification

uhf   ultrahigh frequency

ult   ultimate

unins.   uninsurable

uns   unsymmetrical

up   upper

ur   urinal

UV   ultraviolet

U-bolt   An iron bar bent into a U-shaped bolt with screw threads and nuts on each end.

'U' factor   Coefficient of heat transfer. 'U' is equal to 1 divided by (hence, the reciprocal of) the total of the resistances of the various materials, air spaces and surface air films in an assembly. *(see thermal resistance)*

uffer   A copperground wire which is layed into the footer and run up to the electrical panel box.

U-gauge (water gauge)   A glass U-shaped tube half filled with water, one end being connected by a flexible rubber tubing to a system of drains or gas pipes being tested. It shows whether they are gas tight.

UL   Underwriters Laboratories, Inc., founded by NBFU and now operated in affiliation with AIA. UL is a nonprofit laboratory, operated for the purpose of testing devices, systems and materials as to their relation to life, fire and casualty hazard in the interest of public safety.

ultimate bearing pressure   The pressure at which a foundation sinks without increase of the load. In plate bearing tests, the ultimate bearing pressure is that pressure over all the plate at which the settlement amounts to one-fifth of the thickness of the plate.

ultimate compressive strength   The stress at which a material crushes; and the usual way of defining the strength of stone, brick and concrete.

ultimate design resisting moment   The moment at which a section reaches its

ultimate usable strength; most commonly the moment at which the tensile reinforcement reaches its specified yield strength.

ultimate elongation   The elongation of a stretch specimen at the time of break. Usually reported as percent of the original length. Also called elongation at break.

ultimate load   The maximum load which may be placed on a structure before its failure due to buckling of column members or failure of some component; also the load at which a unit or structure fails.

ultimate shear stress   The stress at a section which is loaded to its maximum in shear.

ultimate strength   The maximum resistance to load that a member or structure is capable of developing before failure occurs; or, with reference to cross sections of members, the largest moment, axial force or shear, a structural concrete cross section will support.

ultimate strength design   A method of proportioning structures or members for failure at a specified multiple of working loads, and assuming non-linear distribution of flexural stresses.

ultimate tensile strength (stress)   *(see ultimate strength)*

umbrella roof   *(see station roof)*

unbalanced bid   A contractor's bid proposal that does not reflect the true cost plus overhead and profit for each item bid. The most common practice is to front end load a bid proposal in order to obtain working capital to finance the project, e.g., putting extra money in items that will be performed early in the project.

unbalanced heating system A system that delivers unequal distribution of heat to various rooms.

unbonded member Post-tensioned, prestressed concrete element in which tensioning force is applied against end anchorages only, tendons being free to move within the element.

unbonded post-tensioning Post-tensioning in which the tendons are not grouted after stressing.

unbonded tendon A tendon which is not bonded to the concrete section.

unbraced length of column Distance between adequate lateral supports.

unbuffed end An untrimmed, serrated factory cut end on gypsum board.

unbuttoning Demolition, especially of steel framework by breaking off the rivet heads.

uncoursed rubble A description of random or snecked-rubble walls which may also be coursed. (*see broken range ashlar*)

underbed The base mortar, usually horizontal, into which strips are embedded and on which terrazzo topping is applied.

undercoat A coating applied prior to the finishing or top coats of a paint job. It may be the first of two or the second of three coats. In some usage of the word, it may be synonymous with priming coat.

undercroft A vaulted underground chamber.

undercuring Insufficient hardening of substances such as concrete, glue or paint caused by a low temperature or too short a setting-up period.

undercut (1) The action or result of cutting away from the underside of anything. (2) Cut or molded so as to present an overhanging part such as a drip mold.

undercut tenon A tenon with its shoulder cut at a slight angle to insure that it bears on the mortised piece.

underdrain Type of drain constructed with perforated pipe laid in a wedge of stone to intercept ground water.

under eaves course Course of eaves tiles in the eaves course.

underflow (1) In hydraulics, the water movement in the soil under ice or under a structure. (2) The oversize material of a classifier.

underground Beneath the surface of the ground, e.g., drainage systems, electric conduit, telephone cables, etc.

underlayment (1) A layer of sheathing that protects from moisture and prevents wind-driven rain from entering structures. In the case of asphalt shingles, it prevents contact between the shingles and the resinous areas in wood sheathing which, because of chemical incompatibility, may be damaging to the shingles. (2) Installed to cover subfloor irregularities and to absorb the movement of wood subfloors. A variety of underlayments are used to smooth and level irregularities: hardboard, particleboard, plywood, mastic with latex binders, mastic with asphalt binders, mastic with polyvinyl-acetate, etc.

underlay mineral Any type of sand or granules which are applied to a sheet of roofing and then covered by a layer of asphalt.

underpass A road, walkway, railroad, etc. crossing another at a lower level.

underpin (underpinning) To provide new permanent support beneath a wall or a column, without removing the superstructure, in order to increase the load capacity of a pre-existing building. The support for a structure by bracing, props, etc., sometimes temporary.

underpitch groin A joint of two cylindrical vaults of different height.

underreaming The widening of the base of a bored pile or of a foundation pier, e.g., the Gow caisson, to increase its area or to give the piling an anchorage against lifting by wind or heaving in permafrost regions.

underridge tiles (undertiles) Special undersize tiles laid in the top course of a roof below the ridge tiles.

undersanded With respect to concrete,

containing an insufficient proportion of fine aggregate to produce optimum properties in the fresh mixture, especially workability and finishing characteristics.

underscribe Procedure used for sheet goods seaming; fitting tightly to walls; for fitting tile; for fitting stair treads. etc. The edge of the top piece is inserted in the underscriber, with the guide pressed against the square edge of the bottom piece, allowing scoring of the top piece by drawing the underscriber along the edge of the bottom sheet.

undertone (tint) The color obtained when pigment is reduced with a large amount of white pigment. The color seen when colored paint is spread on glass and looked at with light passing through it.

Underwriter's Laboratories Label (UL) A label which shows the material is regularly tested by, and complies with the minimum standards of, the Underwriter's Laboratories specification for safety and quality. It is usually seen on electrical items.

undisturbed sample A soil sample of cohesive soil from a test hole which has been changed so little that it can safely be used for laboratory measurements of strength.

undressed lumber Lumber which has not been planed smooth.

unframed door A batten, or ledged and braced door.

ungauged lime plaster Plaster made with only lime, sand and water.

unglazed tile A hard, dense tile of uniform composition throughout, deriving color and texture from the materials of which the body is made.

Unified Soil Classification System of identifying soils by particle size developed by the U. S. Army Corps, of Engineers.

Unified thread A standardized uniform screw thread size.

uniformity coefficient *(see coefficient of uniformity)*

uniform sand A sand with most particles of uniform size. It is not a graded sand.

uniform system Coordination of specification sections, filing of technical data and product literature, and construction cost accounting organized into divisions based on an interrelationship of place, trade and function for material.

unilateral tolerance A tolerance specified in one direction only because the permissible variation can only lie in one direction.

UN/NA Number The hazardous material identification number assigned by DOT to chemicals, wastes, and other hazardous material. Under DOT regulation, UN/NA numbers for all hazardous material in a shipment must be listed on the shipping papers accompanying the shipments. For hazardous wastes, UN/NA numbers must be recorded on the Uniform Hazardous Waste Manifest accompanying all hazardous waste shipments under item 11 of the manifest, as part of the DOT description of the waste.

union (1) In the trades, a confederation of individuals who have joined together for a common purpose. Building trades unions comprise a large part of the unionized workforce in the construction industry, e.g., Carpenters Union, Painters Union, etc. (2) In plumbing, a joint in which an outer-threaded sleeve draws inner-threaded pipe ends into close contact.

union bend (union cock) In plumbing, a bend, cock, etc., with a union at one end.

unit (1) British thermal unit (Btu); the amount of heat required to raise the temperature of one pound of water, at its maximum density, through one degree Fahrenheit. (2) In electricity, the energy used when one kilowatt flows for one hour, e.g., one kilowatt hour (kwh).

unit cooler A direct-cooling, factory-made, encased assembly including a cooling element, fan motor (usually) and directional outlet.

unit heater A direct-heating, factory-made, encased assembly including a heating element, fan and motor, and directional outlet.

uni-thick (1) A term meaning uniform thickness. (2) A tri-tab, square butt or strip shingle which is uniform in composition in both the tab and headlap portion.

unit masonry A built-up construction or combination of masonry units set in mortar or grout.

unit of bond The shortest length of a brick course which repeats itself.

unit price contract A contract which provides the owner pay the contractor a specified amount of money for each unit of work completed in the performance of a contract. Usually this is used in situations where precise quantities cannot be predetermined.

unit prices Amounts stated in the contract as prices per unit of measurement for materials or services as described in the contract documents.

unit pulverizer Coal mill for service to one individual kiln, drying and grinding in one operation and operating as direct firing.

unit water content The quantity of water per unit volume of freshly mixed concrete, often expressed as pounds or gallons per cubic yard; the quantity of water on which the water-cement ratio is based, not including water absorbed by the aggregate.

unit weight The weight per unit volume of material or its density.

universal joint A connection between two shafts that allows them to turn or swivel at an angle.

universal motor A motor of usually less than one horsepower that can work on either alternating or direct current.

universal plane (combination plane) A hand operated metal plane with several cutting blades of different shapes to cut moldings, tongues or grooves, beads, rebates, etc.

unloader A device on or in a compressor for equalizing the high and low side pressures for a brief period during starting, in order to decrease the starting load on the motor; also a device for controlling compressor capacity by rendering one or more cylinders ineffective.

unprotected corner Corner of a slab with no adequate provision for load transfer, so that the corner must carry over 80 percent of the load. *(see protected corner)*

unreinforced concrete *(see plain concrete)*

unsound (1) In plastering, a description of slaked limes, plasters, cements and other mortars containing particles which may expand. (2) Not firmly made, placed, or fixed. (3) Subject to deterioration or disintegration during service exposure.

unsound knot A knot in lumber which is not as solid as the wood surrounding it, or which is loose or unconnected by fibers to the surrounding wood.

unstable The description of a structure which is apt to fail as a whole, usually by sliding or overturning. *(see unstable soil)*

unstable frame A frame containing too few members or of too little stability to be a perfect frame.

unstable soil Earth material, other than running, that because of its nature or the influence of related conditions, cannot be depended upon to remain in place without extra support, such as would be furnished by a system of shoring.

unsupporting sheeting A polymer sheeting one or more plies thick without a reinforcing fabric layer or scrim.

untrimmed floor A floor laid only on common joists.

upfeed distribution A water system that requires pumps to develop pressure.

upholster To equip with cushions under a fabric such as an upholstered seat.

uplift (1) In hydraulics, an upward force on the earth due to water leaking through a dam or any other point where water is under high pressure. (2) An upward force on a structure due to water, frost heave or wind force on the windward side of a structure. (**3**) Wind load on a building which causes a load in the upward direction. *(see suction)*

upper transit A term used in surveying to describe the upper culmination of the sun or a star.

upright Generally a term applied to a piece of timber which stands upright or in a vertical position such as the vertical pieces at the sides of a doorway, window frame or shoring.

upset (**1**) To thicken and shorten as by hammering a heated bar of iron on the end; to enlarge an end of a bar by shortening it. (**2**) A tear across the fiber of wood caused by shock, often during the felling of a tree.

upset price *(see guaranteed maximum cost)*

upshot burner In boilers, a gas fired unit with a row of burners on the firing chamber floor shooting upward.

upstand (upturn) That portion of a felt, metal flashing or roof covering which turns up beside a wall without being tucked into it and which is usually covered with stepped flashing.

upstand beam A beam set in a concrete floor rising out of the floor like a wall instead of projecting below it in the usual way.

up-start valve A bypass valve.

upthrust A device on the hanger assembly that limits the vertical motion of the elevator door panel.

upturn *(see upstand)*

uranium An element composed of the largest atoms known to exist naturally. There are several different kinds of uranium. U235 is easily fissionable. U238, which is much more abundant than U235, is much more difficult to fission.

urethane Plastic foam of rigid polyurethane, closed cell; most efficient (requiring less thickness). Made in board form or spray.

urethane insulation Plastic foam of rigid polyurethane; made into board form or sprayed on.

urinal A plumbing fixture for use in urinating.

usable life (**1**) The pot life of glue. (**2**) The useful life of a product, usually estimated before the fact.

U.S. gallon One U.S. gallon contains 8.336 pounds of distilled water at 62°F, equals 0.8327 British imperial gallons; 3.17 kilograms.

U-tie A wall tie made of heavy wire bent into a U-shape.

utility (public utility) A continuing service available to all citizens of a community, such as water, electricity, gas, sewage disposal, etc.

utility box Enclosure for compressed air and waterlines.

utility knife *(see board knife)*

utility room The space in a dwelling where the heating plant and other utilities are grouped; a room in a dwelling in which laundry equipment, water heater and the like are grouped.

U-value (thermal transmittance; air-to-air heat transmission coefficient) A figure, determined by experimentation, for a certain wall, floor or roof in a certain situation telling how many Btu per hour will pass through one square foot of the wall when the air temperature on one side is one-degree Fahrenheit higher than the air temperature on the other. In an exposed situation the same wall would have a higher U-value than one in a sheltered situation.

V   volt, valve

VAC   vacuum

val   value, valuation

van   vanity

var   variation, varnished, variable

VAR   visual-aural range, volt-ampere reactive

VD   vapor density

V.E.   Value Engineering

vel   velocity

ven   veneer

vent   ventilator

vert   vertical

VF   video frequency, visual field

vhf   very high frequency

vic   vicinity

VIF   verify in field

vil   village

vis   visibility, visual

vit. ch.   vitrious china

v.j.   V-joint

vlf   very low frequency

VLR   very long range

vol   volume

vou   voussoirs

VT   vacuum tube, variable time

VU   volume unit

V & C V   An abbreviation for the term meaning V-grooved and center V-grooved, that is, the board is V-grooved along the edge and also center V-grooved on the surface.

V-brick   A perforated brick with vertical cavities formed in it which make it equal in dryness and warmth to the cavity wall. It is easier to build than a cavity wall.

V-cut   *(see wedge cut)*

vacuum breaker   *(see back-flow preventer)*

vacuum-cleaning plant   A plant permanently installed in a building consisting of an exhaust fan and filter, usually in the basement, connected to all floors through a network of pipes.

vacuum concrete   Concrete from which water is extracted by a vacuum process before hardening occurs. The concrete reaches its normal 28-day strength in 10 days and has a 25 percent higher crushing strength.

vacuum heating   A steam-heating system for buildings in which a vacuum pump is connected to the return main. It removes moisture and air from the radiators and returns the water to the boiler feed tank.

vacuum lifting   Raising by crane hook and sling the concrete slabs cast on the ground through a suction attachment on the sling. The attachment works like a vacuum mat.

vacuum man   A skilled laborer who operates a vacuum plate in the lifting of precast concrete units from a mold while green to place them in their curing bed or oven.

vacuum mat   A stiff flat metal screen covered by a filtering fabric, the back of which can be kept under a partial vacuum by a pump connected to it through a hose. It is used in making vacuum concrete.

vacuum method   *(see ground-water lowering)*

vacuum method of testing sands   A triaxial testing of sand by maintaining a partial vacuum in the tube containing the sample. The outside of the tube is under atmospheric pressure and the resultant pressure on the tube is equal to the difference between the two pressures.

vacuum pump (air pump)   A pump which extracts air or steam from a space in order to maintain it at a pressure below the atmospheric pressure.

The pressure is usually measured in inches of mercury below atmospheric. These pumps are needed for all the vacuum processes and for the condensers of steam turbines.

vacuum saturation A process for increasing the amount of filling of the pores in a porous material, such as lightweight aggregate, with a fluid, such as water, by subjecting the porous material to reduced pressure in the presence of the fluid.

vacuum system A steam-heating two-pipe system with a thermostatic trap on the return end of each radiator and a vacuum pump on the return main, keeping the interior of the system at less than atmospheric pressure.

vadose water Water intermediate between soil water and fringe water; suspended water which may include all water in the soil from the water table to the ground surface. The British term is held water.

vagina The upper part of the shaft of a terminus, from which a bust or figure seems to rise.

valley In architecture, the term applied to a depressed angle formed by the meeting at the bottom of two inclined sides of a roof, as a gutter; also, the space, when viewed from above, between vault ridges. The opposite of a hip.

valley board A board fixed on and parallel to the valley rafter.

valley gutter (1) A channel used to carry off water from the 'V' of multi-gabled roofs. A gutter lined with metal in a valley, e.g., a secret gutter or a box gutter. (2) A type of street gutter which may be precast or cast in place.

valley jack A jack rafter which fits onto a valley board or a valley rafter.

valley rafter The diagonal rafter at the intersection of two intersecting sloping roofs.

valley shingle A shingle laid next to the valley, cut in a way that the grain is parallel to the valley.

valley tile A specially large concave tile

shaped for forming a valley without flexible metal.

value-cost contract (British) A cost reimbursement contract in which the contractor receives a larger fee when his final costs are lower than when the final costs are high.

value engineering A branch of engineering whose objective is to effect economy in the cost of constructing a project. Evaluating any object's function and bettering the object in terms of dollars and functional objectives.

valve A device to open or close a pipe, duct, or other passage, or to regulate a flow.

valve bag A paper bag for cement or other material, either glued or sewn, made of four or five plies of Kraft paper and completely closed except for a self-sealing paper valve through which the contents are introduced.

valve seat The stationary portion of the valve which, when in contact with the movable portion, stops flow completely.

vamure The walk on top of a wall behind the parapet; the allure.

vanadium The hardest known metal. It is used for making very strong alloy steels with manganese or chromium.

vane A blade or banner form pivoted on a tower, steeple or other high point to indicate the direction of the wind.

vane ratio In air distributing devices the ratio of depth of vane to shortest opening width between two adjacent grille bars.

vane shear test apparatus A device developed to measure the shear strength of very soft and sensitive clays. In Scandinavian countries the vane test is also regarded as a reliable means of determining the shear strength of stiff fissured clays.

vane test A four-bladed vane is inserted into soil at the foot of a borehole where it is rotated by a rod at the surface with a measured force until the soil shears. A measurement of the in-place shear strength of a soil is obtained which has been found to give consistent results to

100 foot depth except in stiff fissured clays.

vanishing point   A point to which lines in a parallel system converge in perspective drawing.

vapor   Gaseous phase of a substance normally in the liquid or solid state.

vapor barrier   Material used to retard the flow of vapor or moisture into walls and thus prevent condensation within them. There are two types of vapor barriers, the membrane that comes in rolls and is applied as a unit in the wall or ceiling construction, and the paint type, which is applied with a brush. The vapor barrier must be a part of the warm side of the wall.

vapor density   The weight of a vapor or gas compared to the weight of an equal volume of air; an expression of the density of the vapor or gas calculated as the ratio of the molecular weight of the gas to the average molecular weight of air, 29. MW of gas/29 = Vapor Density. Materials lighter than air have vapor densities of less than 1.0. Materials heavier than air have vapor densities greater than 1.0. All vapors and gases will mix with air, but the lighter materials will tend to rise and dissipate (unless confined). Heavier vapors and gases are likely to concentrate in low places (along or under floors; in sumps, sewers, manholes, trenches and ditches) creating fire, explosion, or health hazards.

vapor heating (vacuum vapor)   A system in which steam rises through piping and radiators in which the air pressure is less than atmospheric.

vapor migration   The movement of water vapor from a region of high vapor pressure to a region of lower vapor pressure.

vapor pressure   The pressure, measured in pounds per square inch (absolute), exerted by a volatile liquid as determined by the Standard Method of Test for Vapor Pressure of Petroleum Products (Reid Method) (ASTM D-323-58).

vapor retarder   Material used to retard the flow of water vapor into walls and

other spaces where this moisture may condense at a lower temperature.

vapor seal   A moisture-resistant material (plastic film, impregnated paper or aluminum foil) used in laminated roof decking manufacture to prevent moisture from passing through the finished material. *(see vapor barrier)*

variable resistor   A device used to increase or decrease resistance easily such as a potentiometer or rheostat.

variance   The square of the standard deviation; the average of the squares of the deviations of all the observations.

variation order   *(British)* A written order from the owner usually represented by the architect or engineer which authorizes an increase of the work above the amount shown in the contract. *(see change order)*

Varitone Mahogany   A medium-grain granite, reddish with black and gray spottings, quarried at Ortonville, Minnesota.

varnish   A thickened preparation of drying oil, or drying oil and resin, suitable for spreading on surfaces to form continuous, transparent coatings; or for mixing with pigments to make enamels.

varved   Banded; a varved clay is one formed by seasonal depositions extending over many years so that the seasons are indicated by the horizontal bands.

vault   An arched structure of masonry usually forming a ceiling or roof. Also, an arched passageway underground, or any room or space covered by arches. A room of massive construction for protection of valuables.

vault-light   The overhead, daylight-transmitting panel of an underground room; usually of rondelles set in a cement and steel frame in the sidewalk; a pavement light.

Vebe apparatus   A device for the measurement of the consistency of freshly mixed concrete; the measure of consistency is the time of vibration, in seconds, required to transform the concrete sample from a truncated cone, remaining after removal of the slump cone, into the right cylinder; the time is assumed directly proportional to the energy used in compacting the sample.

vee beam sheeting Asbestos-cement sheeting in which corrugations are formed by three flat surfaces instead of curves.

vee gutter A valley gutter.

vee notch *(see triangular notch)*

vee roof The shape made by two lean-to roofs which meet at a valley.

vee tool A wedge.

vehicle The liquid portion of a finishing material; it is made up of the binder, non-volatile, and volatile thinners, but no pigment.

vein A layer, seam or narrow irregular body of material different from the surrounding formations.

Veined Ebony Igneous rock of the gabbro or black granite class, of medium grain with pronounced darker veins, quarried at Mellen, Wisconsin.

vellum Treated, smooth white rag parchment drafting paper.

velocity A vector quantity that includes both magnitude, speed and direction relative to a given frame of reference. Commonly used as a synonym for the speed of any tangible or intangible thing.

velocity head (kinetic head) The energy per unit weight of water due to its velocity. It is also the vertical distance the fluid must fall freely under gravity to reach its velocity.

velocity in pipes Normal allowable velocities in pipes for different fluids measured in feet per second.

velocity of approach The average velocity in the channel of a measuring weir at the point where the depth over the weir is measured.

velocity of retreat The average velocity downstream from the measuring weir.

velocity ratio The distance through which the force applied to a machine moves, divided by the distance moved by the load.

velocity, terminal The maximum ve-

locity which a body can attain when freely falling in fluid. This can be found by using Stoke's law. It is also called free-falling or settling velocity.

velvet finish Surface of dense cut pile carpet usually produced on a tufting machine or velvet loom.

vendor A person or organization who furnishes materials or equipment not fabricated to a special design.

veneer (1) A thin layer of selected wood for glueing to a support. (2) A covering layer of material for a wall, as brick or marble veneer. A masonry facing which is attached to the backup but not so bonded as to act with it under the load.

veneer (adhered) Veneer in which the facing units are attached by adhesion to a backing.

veneer (ceramic) A type of architectural terra cotta characterized by larger face dimensions and thinner sections than ordinary terra cotta. The sections range from $1\frac{1}{4}''$ in thickness to $2\frac{1}{2}''$ in thickness.

veneer base A special design gypsum board product used as a base for thin coat veneer plaster finish.

veneered construction A method of construction in which thin layers of marble slabs or other facing material are applied to the external surface of steel, reinforced concrete or frame walls.

veneered stock An obsolete term for plywood.

veneered wall A wall having a facing of masonry or other material securely attached to the backing.

veneer plaster A special plaster formulation as a thin coat over veneer base.

veneer tie A wall tie attaching a veneered wall to its backing.

Venetian blind A screen door or window, formed of horizontal slats supported on vertical strips of webbing. It is capable of being collapsed into a small space when raised, and the slats are movable to admit or exclude light.

Venetian blind collector A flat plate solar collector invented by John Peck and Carl Hodges of the University of Arizona. A venetian blind is painted flat black on one side and placed between two panes of glass. When closed with the black side to the sun, it collects heat which is transferred to air circulated between the glass panes.

Venetian dentil molding   A series of contiguous blocks, beveled oppositely and alternately.

Venetian door   A door with side lights.

Venetian mosaic   A type of terrazzo topping in which large chips are incorporated.

Venetian red   A red iron oxide pigment.

Venetian window   The early British term for the prototype of the Palladian window.

vent   Means of escape or passage. *(see vent pipe)*

vented form   A form so constructed as to retain the solid constituents of concrete and permit the escape of water and air.

ventilating bead   A deep bead used in carpentry work.

ventilating brick   An air brick.

ventilating jack   The hood over the inlet to a ventilating pipe that increases the down-draft.

ventilation   Free circulation of air in a room or building; a process of changing the air in a room by either artificial or natural means; any provision made for removing contaminated air or gases from a room and replacing the foul air by fresh air.

ventilator (vent light)   Any means of ventilating a room.

vent pipe   (1) A small diameter pipe used on concrete construction to permit escape of air in a structure being concreted or grouted. (2) A flue or pipe connecting any interior space in a building with the outer air for purposes of ventilation. (3) Any small pipe extending from any of the various plumbing fixtures in a structure to the vent stack.

vent stack   A vertical pipe connected with all vent pipes carrying off foul air or gases from a building. It extends

through the roof and provides an outlet for gases and contaminated air, and also aids in maintaining a water seal in the trap.

vent system   The entire system of pipes installed to provide a flow of air to or from a drainage system, or to provide a circulation of air within such a system to protect the trap seal from siphonage and back pressure.

vent valve   A normally open valve off a tee in the gas line located between two safety shut off valves.

Venturi   A pressure jet that draws in and mixes air.

Venturi flume   A control flume consisting of a short contraction followed by an expansion to normal width. The difference in surface level of the water gives a measure of flow. *(see Parshall measuring flume)*

Venturi meter (Venturi tube)   A flow meter for closed pipes having a throat followed by an expansion to normal width. The pressure is measured at the throat and upstream where the width is normal. The quantity flowing is related to the pressure difference between these points.

veranda   An open portico, sometimes two-storied, usually roofed which is attached to the exterior of a building. Commonly called a porch.

verdigris   Green basic acetate of copper formed as a protective patina over copper which is exposed to air. It may be any color from brown to black.

verge   (1) The edge of tiling, shingles or slate projecting over the gable of a roof, that on the horizontal portion is called the eaves. (2) In Medieval architecture, the shaft of a column. (3) The unpaved edge of a road which forms a part of the legal highway.

verge board   The board under the verge of a gable which is sometimes molded. The term verge board is often corrupted into bargeboard.

verge fillet   A batten fastened on a gable wall to the ends of the roof battens as a neat finish over which the roofing shingles hang.

vermiculated Stone or other material with designs worked on the surface giving it the appearance of being worm-eaten.

vermiculite A group name for hydrated magnesium-aluminum-iron silicate, a micaceous material that exfoliates when heated, splitting into thin laminae, and with further heating into long wormlike pieces. The exfoliated material is used as fill insulation, in place of sand in gypsum plaster, and as an aggregate in lightweight concrete and acoustical plaster.

vermiculite concrete Concrete in which the aggregate consists of exfoliated vermiculite.

vermillion A brilliant red, slightly orange-colored pigment derived from cinnabar composed of mercuric sulphide. It was first used in China. Now considered too expensive for use except in very small quantities.

Vermont marble A group name for a wide variety of marble quarried in Vermont, many of them white or with a ground of white, although there may be considerable veining and clouding. Some are practically pure white. Vermont produces a very fine variety of verd antique which, though classed as marble, is a rock constituted largely of serpentine.

Vernier A device permitting finer measurement or control than standard markings or adjustments.

vertex *(see crown)*

vertical Pertaining to anything, such as a structural member, which is upright in position, perpendicular to a horizontal member, and exactly plumb.

vertical alignment *(see longitudinal profile)*

vertical angle An angle measured in a vertical plane.

vertical broken joint Ceramic tile installation featuring each vertical row offset for half its length.

vertical circle A metal ring which is graduated in degrees and fractions of a degree showing the angle of slope on the survey telescope.

vertical curve The meeting of different gradients in a road or pipe.

vertical drains Usually columns of sand used to vent water squeezed out of humus by the weight of the fill.

vertical grain The edge grain of quarter-sawn lumber.

vertical line At any point on the earth's surface, the line which follows the direction of gravity at that point.

vertical photograph In aerial surveys, a photograph of the ground taken from the air with the camera pointing vertically down. Mosaics are usually built from these photographs.

vertical plane At a point any plane which contains the vertical line at the point.

vertical sand drain A boring through a clay or silty soil filled with sand or gravel to enable the soil to drain more easily. Sand drains speed the drainage of a clay loaded by an earth dam or other heavy weight if their spacing is measurably less than the thickness of the clay. They do not need to reach a permeable soil below the clay, but it is preferable that they do.

vertical sash A window sash.

vertical shaft mixer A cylindrical or angular mixing compartment having an essentially level floor and containing one or more vertical rotating shafts to which blades or paddles are attached; the mixing compartment may be stationary or rotate about a vertical axis.

vertical shingling Shingles hung on a wall.

vertical slip forms Forms which are jacked vertically and continuously during placing of concrete.

vesica (vesica piscis) A lineal figure formed between two arcs of equal radius, each arc passing through the center from which the other arc is drawn.

vestibule A small entrance room at the outer door of a building; an anteroom which is sometimes used as a waiting room.

viaduct Any elevated roadway, especially a bridge with narrow arches of masonry or reinforced concrete supporting high piers carrying a roadway or railroad tracks over a ravine or gorge. They are sometimes of steel construction consisting of short spans carried on high steel towers. Viaducts are sometimes used as a method for carrying water, the most famous being those built by the early Romans.

vibrated concrete Concrete compacted by vibration during and after placing.

vibrating pile-driver A pile-driver which orginated in the USSR. One type has two electric motors rotating in opposite directions mounted on top of the pile to be driven. In the right soil they are silent and rapid due to the acceleration imparted by the vibrator. The principle of vibration is also used in pipe pushing and in extraction of pipe or piles.

vibrating roller A towed or self-propelled roller with a mechanically vibrated roll.

vibrating screen A screen which is vibrated to separate and move material resting on it.

vibration Energetic agitation of freshly mixed concrete during placement by mechanical oscillating devices at moderately high frequency to assist in its consolidation; (a) external vibration employs a vibrating device attached at strategic positions on the forms and is particularly applicable to manufacture of precast items and for vibration of tunnel-lining forms; (b) internal vibration employs a vibrating element which can be inserted into the concrete at selected locations, and is more generally applicable to in-place construction; (c) surface vibration employs a portable horizontal platform on which a vibration element is mounted.

vibration limit That time at which fresh concrete has hardened sufficiently to prevent its becoming mobile when subjected to vibration.

vibrator An oscillating machine used to agitate fresh concrete so as to eliminate gross voids including entrapped air but not entrained air, and produce intimate contact with form surfaces and embedded materials.

vibrator compactor A large roller usually with the engine mounted on the top powering an offset cam or flywheel that sets up a thumping action on the roller as it is being drawn by another power unit. These rollers are usually used for finish work on a fill or roadbed after the primary compaction has been completed.

vibroflot (vibroflotation) A process for compacting clean sands and gravels.

Vicat apparatus A penetration device used in the testing of hydraulic cements and similar materials.

Vicker's hardness test A test used for testing very thin hard cases by the diamond pyramid or softer materials with a steel ball. Indentations are measured by a low-power microscope.

victaulic coupling Pipe fitting. Rubber gasketed compression fitting.

victaulic pipe A pipe with joints which can be moved measurably after fixing and still remain watertight.

Victorian Designating the architecture characteristic of the reign of Queen Victoria (1840–1901).

video Refers to the electronic signal which is the output of a TV camera.

Vierendeel girder (open-frame girder) A Pratt truss without diagonal members and with rigid joints between the top and bottom chords and the verticals.

viga A beam usually made of a whole log with the bark removed, featured usually in Pueblo-style architecture.

vignette In architecture, a small decorative vinelike ornamentation.

Vinal Haven granite An even-textured, fine-grain, light gray granite from Maine which is used for monumental work.

vinyl The name of a class of resins. Vinyl acetate is commonly used in latex paints. Polyvinyl chloride is used in some solvent-thinned coatings in which high chemical resistance is called for. Many other vinyl derivatives appear in various specialized coatings.

vinyl foam A layer of expanded vinyl that forms a cellular resilient layer which is used as a core and/or backing for cushioned sheet goods.

vinyl-to-vinyl adhesive A special adhesive used for joining one vinyl surface to another.

vinyl trim Extruded vinyl moldings for concealing edges, ends, joints and corners.

vinyl wallpaper A flexible film or a liquid bonded by heat to a paper or fabric backing material.

virola (banak) Wood of tropical America which is pale to deep reddish brown, frequently with a purplish hue; used chiefly for veneer.

virtual slope The hydraulic gradient, showing the loss from friction in pressure per unit length.

viscometer (viscosimeter) An instrument for determining the viscosity of slurries, fresh concrete, liquids, etc.

viscosity The measure of the ability of a liquid or solid to resist flow. A liquid with a high viscosity rating will resist flow more readily than will a liquid with a low viscosity. The Society of Automotive Engineers (S.A.E.) has developed a series of viscosity numbers for indicating the viscosity of lubricating oils.

vise (1) A mechanical device for holding a piece of wood or metal rigid while it is being worked. (2) An early British term for a spiral staircase.

visible horizon *(see sensible horizon)*

vista A view as seen through a long narrow passage such as between rows of houses facing on an avenue; a long-range view from a given point.

vitrail The French term for window glass, especially stained glass.

vitreous Derived from or made of glass.

vitreous enamel Porcelain enamel, a glossy composition fused on metal.

vitrified Surface glazed, such as certain clay products.

vitrified brick Bricks which have been surface glazed by heating in a kiln or by salt or other materials being thrown into the furnace.

vitrified tile In building construction, pipes made of clay baked hard and then glazed so they are impervious to water; used especially for underground drainage.

vitrify To glaze during heat treatment.

Vitrolite Colored glass wall tile for bathrooms, the facings of buildings, etc.

vivo The shaft of a column.

V-joint (1) In woodworking, a tongue-and-groove joint in which one face of the boards is cut in a V instead of a butt joint. (2) In masonry, a slight concave horizontal V formed in a mortar joint by tooling.

void In gypsum board a hollow space in the core caused by entrapment of air during the manufacturing process.

void-cement ratio Volumetric ratio of air plus water to cement.

voids Spaces between grains of sand, gravel or soil that are occupied by air or water or both.

voids ratio The ratio of the volume of voids to the volume of the solids in a sample of aggregate or soil. The voids ratio for clay may have to be defined at a stated pressure since clay contracts with a rise in pressure.

volatile A description of liquids which boil at ordinary temperatures or at temperatures below the boiling point of water (100°C).

volatile liquid One which evaporates readily at atmospheric pressure and room temperatures.

volatile material Material that is subject to release as a gas or vapor.

volatile thinner A liquid that evaporates readily and is used to thin or reduce the consistency of finishes without altering the relative volumes of pigments and nonvolatile vehicle.

volcanic tuff A rock composed of the finer kinds of loose volcanic material that results directly from rock disintegration.

volt (1) A unit of measure for the electromotive force which will cause a current of one ampere to flow through a resistance of one ohm. (2) Analogous to water pressure in a pipe.

voltage   Electrical pressure expressed in volts.

voltage drop   A term used to indicate the voltage loss which occurs when wires are overloaded.

voltage regulator (V.R.) tube   A gas-filled diode used to maintain constant voltage.

voltage source   A source of electric potential, e.g. a battery.

volt ampere   A rating unit obtained by multiplying the maximum rated voltage of an electrical appliance by the maximum rated current.

voltohmmeter   A multi-purpose electrical testing instrument.

volume batching   The measuring of the constituent materials for mortar or concrete by volume.

volume change   An increase or decrease in volume *(see deformation)*

volume method of estimating cost   The method of estimating probable total construction cost by multiplying the adjusted gross building volume by a predetermined cost per unit of volume.

volumetric efficiency   In compressors, the relationship between c.f.m. and piston displacement.

volume yield   The volume of lime putty of a stated consistency obtained from a stated weight of quicklime. Also the volume of concrete of a certain mix as obtained from unit weight of cement.

volute   (1) A spiral casing of a fan or a centrifugal pump shaped to gradually reduce the speed of water or air leaving the impeller and transforming it into pressure without shock. (2) The spiral ornament appearing in both the Ionic and Corinthian orders of architecture. The chief characteristic and most distinguishing feature in the Ionic is the convolute spiral ornament.

volute with easement   The spiral portion of a handrail which sometimes takes the place of a newel post in stair building.

vomitorium   The entrance or exit passage of an amphitheater or theater.

voussoir   In architecture, any of the wedge shaped pieces or stones used in forming an arch. The middle one is called the keystone.

voussoir arch   An arrangement of wedge shaped blocks set to form an arched bridge. This method has been replaced by concrete or steel bridges which are cheaper to build and lighter in weight.

Vulcan   A pile driving hammer. The term is most often applied to any single-acting hammer but is actually a trade name.

Vulcanizate   A term used to denote the product of the vulcanization of a rubber compound without reference to shape or form.

Vulcanization   An irreversible process during which a rubber compound, through a change in its chemical structure, e.g. cross-linking, becomes less plastic and more resistant to swelling by organic liquids, and elastic properties are conferred, improved, or extended over a greater range of temperature. (ASTM D-883).

w   water, watt, weight, wicket, wide, width, work, with

W   west, western

WA   with average

WB   water ballast, waybill, wet bulb

WC   water closet

wd   wood, window

wfl   waffle

wg   wing, wire gauge

wh   watt hour

WHP   water horsepower

whr   watt-hour

whse   warehouse

WI   wrought iron

wm   wattmeter

WM   wire mesh

W/M   weight or measurement

w/o   water-in-oil, without

WP   white phosphorus

wpc   watts per candle

wproof   waterproofing

wsct/wains   wainscoting

wt   weight

WT   watertable

ww   white wash

wwf   welded wire fabric

wwm   welded wire mesh

wadding   Cloth placed over the explosive in a hole.

waffle   *(see dome)*

waffle floor   A concrete slab floor with deep square indentations in the soffit. The indents lighten the slab by removing concrete which adds no strength. It spans in two directions and is suitable for large spans.

waffle footing   A flat, reinforced concrete slab foundation with a grid of projections on its lower surface, giving additional rigidity. It is used when bearing capacity of the soil is poor or not firm enough to support a plain flat slab foundation.

waffle slab   A cast in place concrete floor slab. Concrete is poured over steel pans or domes to form the joists and floor slab in one continuous system. It resembles a waffle when viewed from below.

WAG   *(slang)* Wild ass guess. Estimator's term for a bid put together quickly and without sufficient information.

Wagner fineness   The fineness of materials, such as portland cement, expressed as total surface area in square centimeters per gram, determined by the Wagner turbidimeter apparatus and procedure.

wagon   A full trailer with a dump body.

wagon drill   A wheeled frame holding a pneumatic drill and a mechanism for feeding it into the rock and retracting it.

wagon vault   *(see barrel vault)*

wainscot   (1) The wooden paneling of the lower part of an interior wall up to dado height in a room. (2) The walls of an elevator cab extending from the platform to the underside of the car top.

wainscoting   The materials used in lining the interior of walls; also, the process of applying such materials to walls.

wainscoting cap   A molding at the top of a wainscoting.

waist   The narrow part of an object, especially the smallest thickness of a reinforced-concrete stair slab.

Wakeman buff   A sandstone of fine grain and light buff color showing many faint variations commonly called spider web; quarried at Wakeman, Ohio.

wale   Long horizontal member, usually

double, used to hold studs in position; also called waler or ranger.

waler A horizontal brace to hold timbers in place against the sides of an excavation; timbers used in form construction to which the ties are fastened, or against which the end braces are butted; timbers used for holding forms in line. Sometimes called stringers or rangers.

walking beam (trunnion) **(1)** A rigid member whose ends rest on supports that may move up and down independently and whose center is hinged to the load it carries; also known as walking bar. **(2)** A means of mechanically interlocking the direction relays on an elevator control panel. If one direction relay armature is picked up, the other direction relay armature cannot be picked up because of this mechanical interlock.

walking boss *(slang)* A general superintendent. In Britain, he is called a ganger.

walking dragline (walker) A dragline shovel which drags itself along the ground by means of side-mounted shoes, instead of crawler tracks.

walking edger The edger used on pavement and large slabs. The cement mason moves the edger along while in an upright position.

walk-through On-site inspection of a construction project by the owner, architect, and/or a representative of the contractor.

walk-up Multiple dwelling, usually of not over four stories, without elevator service.

walkway A permanent gangway with handrails to provide safe access along a roof.

wall A vertical structure member which encloses, divides, supports or protects a building or room.

wall anchor In carpentry, a steel strap screwed to the end of every second or third common joist and built into brickwork to insure that the joists give lateral support to the wall.

wall bearing construction A structural system in which the floor and roof systems are carried directly by the masonry walls rather than by a structural framing system.

wallboard An artificially prepared sheet material or board used for covering walls and ceilings as a substitute for wooden boards or plaster.

wall board A box built into brickwork to provide a bearing for a beam or joist.

wall bracket A source of artificial light on a wall.

wall cabinet The upper portion of a cabinet that is wall hung, above the base cabinet.

wall column A steel or reinforced-concrete column at least partly built within a wall.

wall covering A term applied to any material used to cover either interior or exterior wall surfaces.

Waller stone A sandstone similar in color and texture to McDermott sandstone, quarried in Scioto County, Ohio.

wall form A retainer or mold so erected as to give the necessary shape, support and finish to a concrete wall.

wall friction Friction between the back of a retaining wall and the retained soil which will generally improve the stability of the wall.

wall furnace Small heating units for installation in wall recesses near a chimney on the main floor.

wall hanger Cast-iron or bent-steel stirrups built into a wall to carry the ends of wood joists; these generally have taken the place of wall boxes in contemporary buildings.

wall joint A mortar joint paralleling the face of a wall.

wall opening *(OSHA)* An opening at least 30 inches high and 18 inches wide, in any wall or partition, through which persons may fall, such as a yard-arm doorway or chute opening.

wallpaper A special paper, plain or printed, for pasting upon a smooth interior wall surface as decoration.

wall plates Horizontal pieces of lumber placed on top of a concrete, brick or stone wall and under the ends of girders, joists, and other lumber to distribute the weight of the load or pressure of the superstructure, especially the roof.

wall plug A two-pronged connection to complete a circuit from an electrical socket or outlet.

walls The vertical or inclined earth surfaces formed as a result of excavation work. Also called sides or faces.

wall section Cross section drawing of a wall, arranged chiefly to show structure characteristics.

wall space Plain wall surface between windows, doors, and like interruptions.

wall stack Flat duct installed in walls for heating upstairs rooms, sometimes called risers.

wall string The string pieces of a stair frame that fasten against a wall.

wall tie A small metal strip or steel wire used to bind tiers of masonry in cavity-wall construction, or to bind brick veneer to the woodframe in veneer construction.

wall tile A tile of burnt clay (glazed or unglazed), terra cotta, concrete, glass, asbestos-cement or plastic used to put a decorative or smooth face on a wall by sticking the tile onto the wall.

wall unit Preassembly of several panels of any type. Units may or may not include trim and may be one or several stories high.

walnut (1) American black walnut: a hard, dark brown wood used chiefly for furniture and interior trim. It is available for architectural uses in limited supply. (2) California walnut: woods of California which produce veneers of tannish brown with prominent black and white stripes and black spots.

wane Bark, or lack of bark or wood from any cause on the edge or corner of a piece of lumber; also the natural curvature of a log or edge of a board sawed from an unsquared log.

wannigan *(slang)* A shanty, house or shelter on skids, sled runners, or a barge, for traveling with men and equipment over water, snow or dry land.

ward (1) A subdivision of a hospital or jail. (2) A baffle in a lock to prevent the full action of the key in the lock operation.

Ward-Leonard control A method of controlling electric winding or other motors with high peak loads.

warehouse set The partial hydration of cement stored for periods of time and exposed to atmospheric moisture.

warm air heating system A heating system in which furnace-heated air moves to living space through a single register or a series of ducts, circulated by natural convection (gravity system) or by a fan or blower in the duct-work (forced system).

warm white Fluorescent lamp resembling color of filament lamp and which blends well with it.

warp (1) Shape distorted by twisting, especially in too rapidly dried wood. (2) The yarn which runs the length of the carpet; pile yarn in woven types.

warped Twisted out of shape.

warping A deviation of slab or wall surface from its original shape, usually caused by temperature or moisture differentials or both within the slab or wall. *(see curling)*

warping joint A joint with the sole function of permitting warping of pavement slabs when moisture and temperature differentials occur in the pavement, e.g., longitudinal or transverse joints with bonded steel or tie bars passing through them.

warranty *(see guarantee)*

Warren girder A truss of triangular shape consisting of sloping members between horizontal top and bottom members and without verticals.

wash (1) The slight slope of a top surface to shed water. (2) An application of color used in rendering of paint or mortar.

washable A term to indicate that a wall covering can be cleaned with a mild soap and water without damage.

washbasin (washbowl) *(see lavatory)*

washboards (1) Transverse corrugations caused on bituminous road by rubber tired traffic on unstable mixtures, thin surfaces or soft subgrades. (2) A baseboard installed on the lower portion of walls for protective purposes.

wash boring　A test hole from which samples are mixed with water; also, sinking a casing to bedrock by means of a jet of water inside it.

washer　In plumbing, a flat ring made of rubber, plastic or fibrous material which is held by a nut to the underside of a water tap to make it watertight. Also, a ring placed under a bolt or nut to distribute pressure.

wash-out closet (wash-down closet)　Obsolete type of the water closet.

washout valve　In hydraulics, a scouring sluice.

wash-point penetrometer　*(see penetrometer)*

washroom　A toilet room, or sometimes a laundry room.

washstand　A lavatory.

wash water (flush)　Water carried on a truck mixer in a special tank for flushing the interior of the mixer after discharge of the concrete.

waste　(1) Refuse material resulting from a building operation. (2) A drain line in plumbing. (3) An overflow line in piping.

waste-disposal unit (garbage disposal)　A small electrically driven garbage grinder placed under a kitchen sink. The garbage is discharged with water down the drain.

waste pipe　A drain pipe which receives the discharge of any fixture receiving human excreta.

waste pulping　The process of grinding waste material to a pulp in the presence of water.

waster　(1) Facing brick with minor defects which can be used as a backing brick. (2) A mason's chisel, either with a claw cutting edge for removing waste stone or a wide chisel.

waste rock　*(see scalp rock)*

waste table　A water table.

wasteway　The channel required to convey water discharged into it from a spillway, escape or sluice; a spillway.

water absorption　The amount of water ingested into the core and surface papers of gypsum board. Expressed as a percent of water added over dry weight.

water back　A coil or chamber near the firepot of a range or heater for hot water supply or storage.

water bar　A strip of material inserted in a joint between wood and stone of a window sill or door sill, to prevent the passage of water from rain or snow.

water-base paints　*(see latex paints)*

water-bearing ground　Ground below the standing-water level.

water-cement ratio　The ratio of the amount of water, exclusive only of that absorbed by the aggregates, to the amount of cement in a concrete or mortar mixture; preferably stated as a decimal by weight. The lower the water-cement ratio, the stronger the cement. It is usually expressed in terms of gallons of water per sack of cement.

water checked casements　Casements with a sill and meeting stile grooved to cut off any possible capillary path for water.

water closet　A flushable toilet.

water content　*(see moisture content)*

water gain　*(see bleeding)*

water gauge　A U-gauge.

water gels (slurry explosives)　A wide variety of materials used for blasting. They all contain substantial proportions of water and high proportions of ammonium nitrate, some of which is in solution in the water. Two broad classes of water gels are those which are sensitized by a material classified as an explosive, such as TNT or smokeless powder; and those which contain no ingredient classified as an explosive which are sensitized with metals such as aluminum or with other fuels. Water gels may be premixed at an explosives plant or mixed at the site immediately before delivery to the bore hole.

water hammer　A fault in plumbing

whereby the surge of suddenly checked water is not properly cushioned against noise.

water level The water level is a piece of clear plastic hose ¼″ to ½″ in diameter and usually about 50′ in length. It is filled with water, from which all air must be removed.

water loss A measurement of the amount of free water evaporated from gypsum board products during the drying stage in manufacturing process. Usually expressed in pounds per 1000 S.F.

water lowering Lowering of groundwater.

water main A water-supply pipe for public or community use.

water meter A device for recording the amount of water flowing through the piping.

water of capillarity Water above the standing water level; sometimes called held water.

water of hydration Water chemically combined with a substance to form a hydrate that can be expelled (as by heating) without essentially altering the composition of the substance.

water paint A paint containing water or water emulsion as the vehicle.

waterpower The power of water employed to move machinery; a fall of water suitable for such use.

waterproof Made secure against flow or permeability of water, as a foundation wall or a ground floor. As applied to plywood, the term is synonymous with exterior; that is, plywood bonded with water resistant adhesives.

waterproofed cement Cement interground with a water repellent material such as calcium stearate. When set, it is watertight.

waterproofing A procedure to make a material impervious to water or dampness. Any of the materials used to waterproof.

waterproofing compound *(see compound, waterproofing)*

water putty A powder which, when mixed with water, makes an excellent filler for cracks and nail holes in wood. It is not suitable for glazing purposes.

water-reducing agent A material which either increases workability of freshly mixed mortar or concrete without increasing water content, or maintains workability with a reduced amount of water.

water-repellent A liquid designed to penetrate into wood and to impart water repellency to the wood.

water-repellent cement A hydraulic cement having a water-repellent agent added during the process of manufacture, with the intention of resisting the absorption of water by the concrete or mortar. *(see waterproofed cement)*

water resistant core A special core formulation with additives to reduce water absorption. Water resistant gypsum backing board is recommended for use as a base for ceramic tile in bath and other wet areas.

water retention The property of mortar, as determined by test, which prevents the loss of water to masonry units having a high suction rate or initial rate of absorption.

water ring Perforated manifold in the nozzle of dry-mix shotcrete equipment through which water is added to the materials.

water seal The water remaining in a plumbing trap after the line has been flushed.

water seasoning Soaking lumber for a period of fourteen days and then air drying it.

water-service pipe That part of a building main installed by or under the jurisdiction of a water department or company.

watershed The dividing line between two catchment areas from which water flows away in two directions.

water sheen Lustrous surface imparted by the evaporation of the bleed water off the concrete.

water spotting Light colored spots, which may or may not be permanent, on a film of paint; caused by drops of water on the surface.

waterspout A duct, pipe or orifice from which water is spouted or through which it is carried.

waterstop Thin sheets of rubber, plastic or other material inserted in a construction joint to obstruct the seepage of water through the joint.

water supply system (1) The water-service pipe, the water distributing pipes, and the necessary connecting pipes, fittings and control valves of a building. (2) A source or process of supplying water usually including reservoirs, tunnels and pipelines.

water table (1) The surface of underground, gravity-controlled water. (2) A slight projection of the lower masonry or brick wall on the outside of a wall a few feet above the ground as a protection against rain.

water test The pressure test for pipes or drains.

water tower A tower or standpipe serving as a reservoir to deliver water at a required head.

water tupelo gum A wood of the southeastern U.S.A. and the Gulf States with white sapwood and pale, brownish gray heartwood.

water turbine A wheel turned by the force of water.

water vapor Water in a vaporous form especially when below the boiling point and diffused in the atmosphere; not ordinarily considered an air contaminant.

water wagon *(slang)* A truck or tractor-drawn tank for water. Pumps on the units supply pressure to a number of nozzles for spraying over a fill area for compaction, or a haul road to keep the dust under control.

water vapor transmission-(WVT) Water vapor flow normal to two parallel surfaces of a material, through a unit area, under the conditions of a specified test such as ASTM E96.

waterwheel A wheel made to rotate by direct action of water; a wheel for raising water.

waterworks (1) An ornamental fountain or cascade. (2) The system of reservoirs, mains, channels and pumping and purifying equipment by which a water supply is obtained and distributed to the users.

watt The measure of the power of a current of one ampere flowing across a potential difference of one volt, one-thousandth of a kilowatt. The watt is the common unit of electric power. There are approximately 748 to one horsepower; one watt is equivalent to 3.41 Btu per hour; 1,000 watt hours is one kilowatt hour (kwh).

wattle Interwoven twigs, wicker, bamboo or other such withes to form a screen or wall surface.

wave length (1) The wave length of a sound wave is the distance a wave travels in one cycle. It is equal to the speed of sound (1,120 ft. per second) divided by the frequency. (2) (wavelength) Radiation received by a solar collector is all of the short wavelength (less than 1.5 microns) type. As the radiation strikes the collector plate a portion of the energy is re-radiated from the coating in the infrared (long wave) portion of the spectrum.

wave pressure Pressures on breakwaters due to waves which may amount to three tons per square foot in exposed places and only one ton per square foot in sheltered places such as the Great Lakes in North America.

wavy grain An attractive curly grain seen in woods such as birch, sycamore, mahogany, etc.

wayleave The British term for permission to pass over land, sometimes including permission to lay cables, pipes, etc. *(see right-of-way)*

waylite Type of expanded slag used as aggregate in lightweight concrete.

weakened-plane joint *(see groove joint)*

wearing course (top course) A layer of treated or untreated road material, well graded from coarse to fine which rests upon the base course or on the natural foundation.

wearlayer The top portion of the floor covering engineered soil to absorb both traffic and wear. Thickness varies from product to product and for specific installations: residential, light commercial and heavy commercial.

weather (1) The amount, measured along the slope, by which a shingle or tile overlaps the next below it. (2) To undergo the changes in color, texture or efficiency brought aboutby continued exposure to wind, sun, rain, frost, etc.

weather bar *(see weather strip)*

weather boarding Boards lapped over each other to prevent rain, etc., from passing through. Also called siding.

weathered joint A water-shedding slope to the outside of the upper part of a mortar joint.

weather fillet A cement fillet.

weathering *(see weather)*

weatherlife The length of time a roofing material will protect the interior of a building from the elements, rain in particular, when applied to a roof surface.

weather molding A molding built into the bottom of an outside door to throw water of the threshold. A stone drip.

weather-o-meter A machine used to test the weatherlife of materials under controlled accelerated conditions, principally by the use of ultraviolet light.

weatherproof So constructed or protected that exposure to the weather will not interfere with successful operation.

weather shingling Vertical shingling.

weatherstrip A thin strip of metal, felt, wood, etc., used to cover the joint between a door or window sash and the jamb, casing or sill, to keep out the air, dust, rain, etc.

weaving Surface and backing yarns of the carpet are interlaced, or woven together, in one operation. Several types of looms are employed:

Axminster Named for a town in England where it was first used. A fairly complicated weave, used chiefly for multi-colored patterns in cut-pile. A distinguishing feature is a heavily ribbed back which can be rolled lengthwise, but not widthwise.

Wilton Also named for a town in England. Employs a Jacquard pattern-making mechanism, operating on the same principle as player piano rolls, with punched pattern cards determining pile height and color selection.

Velvet The simple loom first used to produce carpet with a single-level plush or velvet texture. May be used for cut or looped pile, or other texture variations.

web (1) The middle plate of a girder or the middle section of an I-beam. (2) The cross wall connecting the face shells of a hollow concrete masonry unit.

web bar *(see web reinforcement)*

web belt A commonly used military-type belt adapted to carry hand tools at the job site.

web member A secondary structural member interposed between the top and bottom chords of a truss.

web reinforcement Reinforcement placed in a concrete member to resist shear and diagonal tension.

webstrap (pull strap) A canvas or leather strap attached to the bottom of the upper door panel for manually closing the doors of an elevator.

wedge A piece of wood or metal tapering to a thin edge used to adjust elevation, tighten formwork, etc. Proper wedging entails a wedging force greater than the load ultimately to be carried by the unit or underpinning that is being wedged. For heavy structures this can be accomplished only by pretesting.

wedge anchorage A device for providing the means of anchoring a tendon by wedging.

wedge cut The method of setting the cut holes in tunnelling or shaft sinking so that they slope towards each other like the faces of a wedge.

wedge theory Coulomb's analysis of the force tending to overturn a retaining wall, based on the weight of the wedge of earth which would slide forward if the wall failed. The theory was developed in 1776.

wedge-wire screen A screen made of

wedge-shaped parallel wires with the side edges on top. This screen rarely clogs and is used for dewatering sands with or without vibration.

wedging plate A steel plate placed on top of an underpinning or under a footing against which wedges are driven to pick up the load of the structure on the underpinning.

weep holes Openings left in retaining walls, aprons, linings, foundations, etc. to permit drainage and reduce pressures.

weft In woven carpet, yarns running crosswise between warp yarns.

weigh batcher A batch plant for concrete in which all of the ingredients except water are measured by weight.

weight Force exerted by a mass under local gravitational acceleration conditions. *(see squeeze)*

weight batching Measuring the constituent materials for mortar or concrete by weight.

weighted average An average obtained after each value has received an appropriate weight. The weight of each value corresponds to its trustworthiness and importance. After multiplying the values by their weights they are added together and divided by the sum of the weights, not by the sum of the values; more reliable than a simple average.

weighting (1) Applying weight to observations to obtain a weighted value. (2) Loading a pneumatic caission with cast iron, water or other heavy material to prevent it from floating and make it sink.

weir (1) A structure across a stream or ditch for diverting or for measuring the flow of water. (2) A low dam or wall built across a stream to raise the upstream water level. Termed fixed-crest weir when uncontrolled. Types of weir include broad-crested weir, sharp-crested weir, drowned weir and submerged weir.

weir head The depth of water measured from the bottom of the notch to the upstream water surface. It does not include the velocity of approach.

Weisbach triangle During shaft plumbing, a set-up at the foot of a vertical shaft from which both of the plumb wires can be sighted. This forms a triangle with an angle at the theodolite of up to half a degree. Accurate observations can be taken in this manner. The Weisbach set-up is used for orienting underground workings.

weld To build up or fasten together. A joint made by bringing surfaces heated to plasticity into close contact.

welded butt splice A reinforcing bar splice made by welding the butted ends.

welded-wire fabric A series of longitudinal and transverse wires arranged substantially at right angles to each other and welded together at all points of intersection.

welded-wire fabric reinforcement Welded-wire fabric in either sheets or rolls, used to reinforce concrete.

weldment A base or frame made of pieces welded together, as contrasted with a one piece casting or a bolted or riveted assembly.

well (1) A slot in the front of a hydraulic dredge hull in which the digging ladder pivots. (2) A wall around a tree trunk that protects it from the fill and retains water. (3) The horizontal distance between the flights of a stair. (4) An underground source of water protected for convenient access.

well-conditioned triangle A triangle which is nearly equilateral. An error in measuring an angle makes the smallest error of distance in such a triangle.

well curbing (pit boards) Horizontal sheeting for retaining the earth in a pit.

well drill A churn drill used for water wells. It usually has a limited depth capacity and a truck or trailer mounting.

well-graded aggregate Aggregate having a particle size distribution which will produce maximum density, e.g., minimum void space.

wellhole (1) An open space such as a shaft or well in a building for a staircase; also, the open space about which a circular stair turns. (2) A large vertical boring used when blasting a heavy burden.

Wellington formula The Engineering News formula for driven piles.

wellpoint Perforated pipe sunk into sand to permit the pumping of ground water and excluding the sand.

wellpoint system A series of pipe installed on end in the ground with a header connected to a pump to drain marshy swampy areas by suction.

Welsh arch A lintel form with a loose wedge in the middle.

Welsh groin (underpitch groin) A groin at the intersection of two cylindrical vaults, one of which is of less height than the other.

welt Seam in flexible metal roofing.

western ocean plant A rope sling woven with a rope net in the middle for lifting heavy armatures and shafts.

western pile *(see button-bottom pile)*

western red cedar A wood from the Pacific Northwest widely used for siding and shingles due to its resistance to decay.

westing In surveying, a coordinate measured westward from an origin; a departure to the westward.

Westphal balance An apparatus for measuring the specific gravity of minerals, liquids, etc.

wet A condition where free water is present in a substance.

wet analysis The mechanical analysis of soil particles smaller than 0.06 mm done by mixing the sample in a measured volume of water and checking its density after various periods with a sensitive hydrometer. The test is slow, even using a centrifuge to give the particles a settlement force of many hundreds of times gravity.

wet areas Interior or exterior tiled areas subject to periodic or constant wetting. Examples: showers; sunken tubs; pools; exterior walls; roofs; exterior paving and interior floors.

wet-bulb temperature The temperature of a thoroughly wet body in motion.

wet dock A dock in which the water is kept at high tide. A lock is usually provided to enable vessels to pass in or out at all levels of the tide.

wet edge The length of time paint can stand on a surface and be brushed back into the next stretch and not lap.

wet galvanizing Coating zinc onto steel by passing it through a bath of molten zinc on which a layer of flux floats. Before dipping, the steel is passed through pickling tanks.

wet grinding A process of grinding set concrete with a power grinder and water.

wet head A fire hydrant with the valve in the head, or top, of the hydrant; it floods when hit.

wet heat Any steam or hot water heating system.

wet mix Concrete with too much water.

wet-mix shotcrete Shotcrete wherein all ingredients, including mixing water, are mixed in the equipment before introduction into the delivery hose; it may be pneumatically conveyed or moved by displacement. *(see pneumatic fed; positive displacement)*

wet on wet Painting with special paints where one coat is put on over another before it has completely dried.

wet process In the manufacture of cement, the process in which the raw materials are ground, blended, mixed and pumped while mixed with water; the wet process is chosen where raw materials are extremely wet and sticky, which would make drying before crushing and grinding difficult. *(see dry process)*

wet rot A term used by woodworkers for the decay of lumber or wood, caused especially by moisture and warmth.

wet sand To smooth a finished joint with a coarse wet sponge, a preferred method to reduce dust created in the dry sanding of gypsum board.

wet screening Screening to remove from fresh concrete all aggregate particles larger than a certain size.

wet sieving *(see wet screening)*

wet storage staining   Corrosion products which develop as a result of moisture and limited access to air when coated steels are in contact with one another.

wettest stable consistency   The condition of maximum water content at which cement grout or mortar will adhere to a vertical surface without sloughing.

wetting agent   A substance capable of lowering the surface tension of liquids, facilitating the wetting of solid surfaces and permitting the penetration of liquids into the capillaries.

wet vent   A soil or waste pipe that also serves as a vent.

wet wall   A wall finished with plaster, stucco or other material mixed with water which sets up when dry.

wet weathers   *(slang)* Waterproof coats and leggings for working in rain.

wet well   The sump of a pumping station.

Weymouth seam-face granite   A Massachusetts stone with color blendings of brown or of golden yellow-green; of fine grain, giving fine and easily split seams.

whacker   *(slang)* A hand tamper.

whaler (waler)   2 × 4's which hold studs that make up forms; a horizontal beam in a bracing structure. Also known as a ranger or a stringer.

wheelabrating   Shot blasting with steel grit thrown from a fast spinning wheel.

wheelbarrow   A container, usually metal, with a single wheel in front and two handholds behind by which it is lifted and pushed forward.

wheel, bull   A driving sprocket for a crawler track.

wheel ditcher   A wheel, equipped with digging buckets, carried and controlled by a tractor unit.

wheel load   That portion of the gross weight of a loaded vehicle transferred to a supporting structure under a given wheel of the vehicle.

wheel scraper   A bowl scraper.

wheel, track   One of a set of small flanged steel wheels resting on a crawler track and supporting a track frame.

wheel window   A circular window; its divisions mainly radiating. Also called a Catharine wheel.

whetstone   A natural or artificial stone used for sharpening the cutting edge of tools.

whip line   A large revolving crane mounted on rollers, skids, wheels or gantry.

whirly   *(slang)* A tower crane, hammerhead crane or an ordinary crane mounted on a large, movable base; used primarily in dam and refinery construction.

whiskering   *(slang)* *(see efflorescence)*

whiskey stick   *(slang)* A level.

whispering gallery   An interior space having the accoustic property of reflecting a sound in one or more particular directions with little loss of volume.

whistle stick   *(slang)* A 2×1" square, ⅛" thick with a v-notch in top side on a rod that swivels and attaches to a Universal stick and is used to tie tye wire around conductors.

white bronze   A bronze made lighter in color by a larger proportion of tin.

white cement   portland cement which has been selected and ground without contamination by iron, or to which white pigment has been added. *(see cement)*

white coat   Denoting a gauged lime-putty trowel finish.

white lead   Hydrated carbonate of lead which is used in the making of paint.

white lime   *(see high-calcium lime)*

whitening in the grain   An unpleasant streaky white appearance sometimes seen in varnished or polished woods with coarse texture.

white oak   An American oak of the eastern part of the United States. It is the hardest of American oaks and is characterized by its heavy, close grain. Used extensively where strength and durability are required.

white, 3500K Lamps labeled white or 3500K are slightly more white than warm white. As the color temperature rating (degrees Kelvin) increases, the lamp becomes cooler.

white wash A creamlike solution of slaked lime in water applied as a paint.

whitewood Wood of the tulip tree, yellow poplar, cottonwood, or basswood trees; fine textured and easily worked.

whiting A chalk pigment used in paint and putty.

Whitney stress diagram The diagram of stress distribution in a reinforced-concrete beam according to the ultimate load theory.

whole-brick wall A wall whose thickness is the length of one brick.

whole-circle bearing In surveying, a bearing which defines direction by horizontal angles measured from true north.

wicket A small door or gate opening in a larger door; a small window or opening having a grate over it.

wicket dam A movable barrier made of wickets, or shutters, revolving about a central axis.

wicking The absorption of water by capillary action onto the core of gypsum board.

wide flange structural shape (W-shape) A hot rolled section having parallel flange surfaces.

wide-heel London A wide short trowel used in bricklaying.

wiggle nail *(slang)* A corrugated metal fastener.

Wilkerson sandstone A medium-grain, hard, light gray, easily worked sandstone; quarried in Pierce Country, Washington.

winch A drum that can be rotated in order to exert a strong pull while winding in a line; a small hoist, usually operated by an electric or a gasoline motor.

  capstan A revolving spool that exerts a pull by friction with one or more loops of fiber rope. Also called a cat-head.

  donkey A two-drum towing winch or yarder.oil field An extremely powerful low speed winch on a crawler tractor.

  power control unit A high speed tractor-mounted winch with one to three drums; used chiefly for operation of bulldozers, scrapers and rooters.

  towing A heavy-duty winch mounted on the rear of a crawler tractor.

wind (1) A turn, a bend. A wall is out of wind when it is a perfectly flat surface. (2) A twisting warp in lumber.

wind column A vertical member supporting a wall system designed to withstand horizontal wind loads.

wind beam A beam inserted into a structure for the sole purpose of resisting wind force.

winders Treads of steps used in a winding staircase, or where stairs are carried around curves or angles. The winders are cut wider at one end than at the other so they can be arranged in a circular form.

wind force (wind load) Wind pressure force on a structure multiplied by the area of the structure at right angles to the pressure; the lateral, vertical or uplift forces due to wind blowing in any direction upon a structure.

wind load A load caused by the wind blowing from any horizontal direction.

winding stairs A spiral staircase.

windless A device for hoisting weights, consisting usually of a horizontal cylinder turned by a lever or crank. A cable, attached to the weight to be lifted, winds around the cylinder as the crank is turned, thus raising the load to whatever position is desired. *(see winch)*

window An opening in a wall for light and ventilation, with all its appurtenances.

  casement Having the sash hinged at jamb and opening out or in.

  double-hung Having two balanced sash, one sliding vertically over the other.

  projected Having the sash hinged or pivoted at top or bottom to project entirely outward or inward.

window bar   A glazing bar.

window box   (1) The space adjoining a window stile to permit the action of the sash weights. (2) A box for plants, usually at the outside of the window sill.

window frame   The part of a window surrounding the casements, in which they hinge or slide.

window head   A term applied to the upper portion of a window frame.

window jack   A portable platform which fits over a window sill projecting outward beyond the sill; used principally by painters.

window jack scaffold   A scaffold, the platform of which is supported by a bracket or jack which projects through a window opening.

windowpane   A unit of sash glass; a pane in a window.

window pipe   A dredge discharge pipe with one or more openings in the bottom.

window seat   A seat built into the recess of a window, or in front of a window.

windowsill   The bottom member or group of members of a window opening.

window stile   An upright of the window frame, guiding the sash.

window stool   The inside front-molded horizontal shelf of a window sill.

window type panel   Transparent glass and frame incorporated in panel curtain wall.

wind plumber   (slang) A plumber who runs air tube for controls.

wind pressure   The pressure, measured in pounds per square foot of wall or roof area, due to wind pressure which increases with wind velocity. On sloping roofs, a suction occurs on the lee side which may be nearly as much as the pressure on the windward side.

wind rose   A diagram showing the relative frequency and the average strength of the winds blowing from different directions in a specified region.

windrow   The spill off the ends of a dozer or grader blade; a ridge of loose earth.

windshield   A transparent screen of glass or plastic in front of the driver and occupants of a vehicle or piece of heavy equipment to protect them from the wind.

wind sock (wind sleeve)   A bright colored cloth tube, shaped like a megaphone, which indicates wind direction and velocity; used primarily on air strips and landing fields to assist pilots.

wind stop   Weather stripping.

wind tee   A lighted wind indicator having the form of a tee in a horizontal or slightly tilted plane; marked by green lights.

wind tunnel   A conical or cylindrical structure through which air is blown at measured speeds to test effect on models of suspension bridges, towers, etc., which may be adversely affected by wind.

wind wash   The tendency of the wind blowing across an exposed glass surface to increase the heat transfer and create a 'chill factor' effect.

wing   (1) In building, a term applied to a section, or addition, extending out from the main part of a structure. (2) The projection on an air drill bit.

wing dam   A wall, curb, dike, row of piles or other barrier projecting streamward from the shore; a spur dike.

wing nut (thumb screw)   A nut with wings which can be turned by hand instead of a wrench.

wing pile   A bearing pile, usually of concrete, widened in the upper portion to form part of a sheet pile wall.

wingwall   A wall that guides a stream into a bridge opening or culvert barrel; an abutment wall.

winter air-conditioning   A term sometimes applied to the use of a forced warm air heating system.

wipe   When one contact point moves or rolls across the face of another contact point.

wiped joint   A soldered junction of lead pipes.

wire   Flexible strand or strands of metal, chiefly used to conduct electricity.

wire brushed   A texture achieved by removing the softest part of the grain from the surface of the hardwood floor.

wire cloth Screen composed of wire or rod woven and crimped into a square or rectangular pattern.

wire, cold drawn Wire made from the rods hot rolled from billets and then cold-drawn through dies. *(see reinforcement, cold-drawn wire)*

wire-cut brick Brick made by an extrusion process in which wire is used to cut the units.

wiredrawing (1) Cold drawing. (2) In hydraulics, the pressure drop in a flowing fluid as it passes through a small opening, e.g. the Venturi meter.

wire gauge A method of defining wire diameter by a number which originally reflected the number of passes through a series of increasingly smaller dies making the wire. The number for large wire is therefore smaller than that for thin wire.

wire glass Sheet glass in which wire mesh is embedded as reinforcement.

wire lath A netting of galvanized wire used as a support for plaster.

wire mesh *(see welded-wire fabric)*

wire rope The flexible members from which an elevator car and counterweight are suspended and by which the elevator hoisting machine raises and lowers the elevator car. A wire rope consists of a core, the strands and the wire. *(see steel wire rope)*

wire scratcher In plastering, a devil float.

wireway Sheet-metal troughs with hinged or removable covers for housing and protecting electrical wire and cables in which conductors are installed.

wire winding Application of high tensile wire, wound under tension by machines, around circular concrete or shotcrete walls, domes, or other tension resisting structural components.

withe (wythe) (1) The course or thickness of brick separating flues; each continuous vertical section, or thickness, of brick masonry. (2) A slender flexible branch or twig used as a band or rope.

wobble coefficient A coefficient used in determining the friction loss occurring in post-tensioning, which is assumed to account for the secondary curvature of the tendons.

wobble friction Friction caused by the unintended variation of the pre-stressing steel sheath or duct from its specified profile.

wobble saw *(slang)* A drunken saw.

wobble-wheel roller A pneumatic-tired roller with wheels which are suspended freely on springs to follow the irregularities of the road surface.

wood The cellulose substance inside the bark of trees, cut into lumber and veneer for many uses in building.

wood block Blocks of wood, with grain vertical, used for paving or industrial flooring.

wood-block flooring Many kinds of wood-block flooring are used, e.g., parquet floor, plywood parquet, wood mosaic, etc. The floors are warm and hard wearing.

wood-block paving Softwood blocks used as a road surface by laying them with the grain vertical on a smooth concrete base in hot tar. The process is now obsolete.

wood brick Wood blocks of brick size inserted in the coursing for nailing purposes.

wood butcher *(slang)* A poor carpenter.

wood fiber Non-staining wood particles used as an aggregate with gypsum plaster.

wood float The wood float is sometimes used in place of the flat trowel for floating mortar. It is good for smoothing small irregularities left on the mortar bed, working the surface of the mortar before troweling on the pure coat, or compacting floor and deck mortar.

wood flour Fine sawdust sometimes used as an extender for glues; also used in explosives, plastic wood, etc.

wood mosaic A floor of wood blocks arranged in squares on strong paper, like Roman mosaic with each block surrounded by an oxychloride cement which sticks to any sub-floor including concrete, metal or tile. It is decorative, hard-wearing and flexible because of its many joints.

wood pavior In Britain, a skilled workman who lays and fits wood blocks onto a concrete road foundation and grouts them with hot bitumen or cement. This type of road construction is now obsolete.

wood roll A round-topped piece of wood fixed to roof boarding to allow flexible metal roofing sheets to be lapped over it.

wood sash jamb block Concrete masonry unit which has an end recess for use in the jamb of an opening.

wood screw An ordinary screw for fastening objects on wood.

wood turning The process of shaping pieces of wood or blocks into various forms and fashions by means of a lathe.

woodwork That portion of a building made of wood, particularly the finish woodwork.

wool fiber The traditional carpet fiber whose use goes back as far as 2000 B.C. There has been a series of improvements in wool, such as permanent moth proofing and recent development of shock-free wool to eliminate static electricity. Wool used in carpet comes from special breeds of sheep which have coarse, springy and hardy fibers.

work (1) The entire scope of the work to be performed at the site of the construction project including labor, materials, equipment, transportation and such other facilities as are necessary to fulfill all obligations under the contract. (2) The product of a force and the distance through which it moves. Distinguished from energy and from power which is a rate of doing work.

workability (1) The property of fresh concrete or mortar which determines the ease with which it can be mixed, placed and finished. (2) In woodworking, to distinguish between dense lumber with a twisted grain and soft light lumber with a straight grain.

work arm The part of a lever between the fulcrum and the working end.

work box Sometimes called a hardware box, tote box, or bolt box, used to carry hardware conveniently.

working chamber The space or compartment under air pressure in which the work is being done.

working cycle A complete set of operations of a piece of construction equipment. In an excavator, for example, it usually includes loading, moving, dumping and returning to the loading point.

working drawing Any drawing showing sufficient detail so that whatever is shown can be built without other drawings or instructions; a detail. (see drawings)

working edge (work edge) The face edge of lumber.

working face (work face) The face side of lumber.

working load Load imposed by men, materials and equipment.

working shaft A shaft sunk to excavate a sewer or tunnel and filled in after the construction is completed.

working side Opposite from the ditch side of right of way.

working stress Maximum permissible design stress using working stress design methods.

working stress design A method of proportioning structures or members for prescribed working loads at stresses well below the ultimate, and assuming linear distribution of flexural stresses.

workmanship The quality of executed work.

work order A written order, signed by the owner or his representative, of a contractual status requiring performance by the contractor without negotiation of any sort.

worm (1) (slang) Thread of a piece of pipe. (2) A gear formed of a cylinder with spiral threads cut in its surface. (3) A shaft on which a spiral groove is cut. Also known as endless screw. (4) (slang) Computer program designed to self destruct from within.

worm conveyor A spiral conveyor system.

worm wheel A modified spur gear with curved teeth that meshes with a worm.

worsted yarn Yarn of long staple carpet fiber and combed to parallel the fiber and remove the extremely short fibers.

woven backing Backing produced by a weaving process using natural fiber, such as jute, cotton, ducking or synthetic yarns.

woven-wire fabric A prefabricated steel reinforcement composed of cold-drawn steel wires mechanically twisted together to form hexagonally shaped openings.

woven-wire reinforcement *(see welded-wire fabric)*

wracking forces Horizontal forces, for instance wind or crane surge, which tend to distort a rectangular shape into a parallelogram.

wreath The curved section of a stair rail, curved in both the vertical and horizontal planes; used to join the side of a newel post to the ascending run of the handrail.

wreathed column A column twisted in a spiral form around its vertical axis.

wreath piece (1) In stair building, the curved section of the handrail string of a curved or winding stair. (2) Any ornamental design intertwined into a circular form.

wreck *(see strip)*

wrecking Dismantling or razing a building or other structure; demolition.

wrecking ball A very large metal ball suspended from a crane boom which is used in demolition of structures or buildings; also called a headache ball.

wrecking bar A steel bar used for prying and pulling nails. One end of the bar is slightly bent with a chisel-shaped tip and the other U-shaped with a claw tip for pulling or prying; also called a pinch bar, a crow bar or a pry bar.

wrecking strip A small piece or panel fitted into a formwork assembly in such a way that it can be easily removed before removal of main panels or forms, making it easier to strip major components later.

wrench An adjustable spanner.

wrenchers The laborers who tighten the bolts on the plate which joins two sections of railroad track.

wringing fit A metal-to-metal fit that usually requires selecting assembly.

wrinkle (1) The prune-like appearance of the paint film due to material applied too heavily; it can appear very fine, like haze, and also very large and prominent. (2) An unglued area caused by failure of veneer to slip into place.

wrist action In a bucket, the ability to change its digging or dumping angle by power.

wrought Hammered into shape, as of ductile metals.

wrought aluminum alloy Light alloy which has been cold-rolled, pressed, forged, drawn or extruded and is, for this reason, not described as cast.

wrought iron A soft pure form of iron easily molded into bars and worked into ornamental shapes; widely used for decorative railings, panels, gates, etc.

wrought timber Lumber which has been planed on one or more surfaces.

wye (Y) (1) In plumbing, a fitting or branch pipe, either of cast or wrought iron, which has one side outlet at any angle except a right angle; usually a 45° angle unless otherwise specified. (2) Coils in a three-phase electrical system connected in such a way as to form the configuration of the letter Y.

wye-delta A method of starting an A.C., 3-phase motor.

Wyoming Valley stone *(see Pennsylvania bluestone)*

wythe A masonry wall, one masonry unit, a minimum of two inches thick.

X   experimental
XH   extra heavy
xr   without rights

xw   without warrants
XXH   double extra heavy

X-brace   A paired set of tension or sway braces.

XCU   Letters which refer to exclusions from coverage for property damage liability arising out of (a) explosion or blasting, (b) collapse of or structural damage to any building or structure, and (c) underground damage caused by and occurring during the use of mechanical equipment.

X-mark   *(see face mark)*

Xonotlite   A crystallized mono-calcium silicate hydrate which can be synthesized at steam pressures of about 200-225 psig or higher.

X-ray diffraction   The diffraction of X-rays by substances having a regular arrangement of atoms; a phenomenon used to identify substances having such structure.

X-ray fluorescence   Characteristic secondary radiation emitted by an element as a result of excitation by X-rays, used to yield chemical analysis of a sample.

xylem   The botanical name for wood.

xylol   An aromatic hydrocarbon which is distilled from coal tar. It is a solvent for synthetic resins and gums.

Xylonite   A thermoplastic material similar to celluloid which is used for making models in photo-elastic analysis.

y yard

Y yttrium; wye; Y-branch

yd yard

y.p. yellow pine

Yale lock The brand name for a common cylinder lock.

Yankee gutter The British term for a wooden gutter made by building up a flexible metal gutter directly on the sheathing of a pitched roof near the eaves. The metal is held in place with an upright board at the edge of the roof.

Yankee screwdriver A quick-action screwdriver with a steep thread incised on the shaft. The thread causes the screw to turn when the handle is pushed home. For wood screws, this tool works better screwing in than out.

yard (1) A unit of linear measure; 36 inches. (2) A piece of ground adjacent to and part of a residence or other building. (3) A common term for cubic yard.

yardage The volume of earth filled or excavated, measured in cubic yards; an area in square yards or a length in lineal yards.

yard lumber Lumber of those grades, sizes and patterns generally intended for ordinary construction and general building purposes.

yarn A continuous strand. The basic raw material for textile use which can be fabricated into a carpet. Tufted, woven and knitted carpets are made from yarn; flocked and needlepunched carpets are made from fiber.

yarn ply The number of strands of single yarns twisted together to form one carpet yarn.

Yazoo clay A strata of highly unstable expansive clay found in parts of central Mississippi from Yazoo City north to Hattiesburg south, and from the Mississippi River west to Scott County east. In some areas the clay may reach depths of 35 feet.

Y-ball & dog-nuts *(slang)* Ball clevis and socket eye; used to connect bells and shoes together on overhead distribution lines.

Y-branch In plumbing, a pipe connection shaped like the capital letter Y; used where a change in direction of the pipe is required. *(see wye)*

year ring One of the clearly visible rings in a cross section of a tree trunk showing the amount of annual growth of the tree. Each ring represents one year of growth; also called a growth ring or annual ring.

yellowing Development of yellow color, or cast, in white or clear coatings, on aging.

yelm (yelven) A double handful of reeds, palm fronds or straw laid on a roof as a thatch.

yeso A gypsum whitewash widely used in Mexico.

yield (1) The permanent deformation which a metal piece takes when it is stressed beyond its elastic limit. A piece which yields is commonly called bent, stretched or buckled. (2) A slight horizontal and slighter vertical movement of a loaded retaining wall. (3) The volume of freshly mixed concrete produced from a known quantity of ingredients, the total weight of ingredients divided by the unit weight of the freshly mixed concrete; also, the number of product units, such as block, produced per bag of cement or per batch of concrete.

yield point That point during increasing stress when the proportion of stress to strain becomes substantially less than it has been at smaller values of stress.

yield strength The stress, less than the maximum attainable stress, at which the ratio of stress to strain has dropped well below its value at low stresses, or at which a material exhibits a specified limiting deviation from the usual proportionality of stress to strain.

yoke (1) A tie or clamping device around column forms or over the top of wall or footing forms to keep them from spreading because of the lateral pressure of concrete; also, part of a structural assembly for slip forming which keeps the forms from spreading and transfers form load to the jacks. (2) A curved drawbar on a scraper or trailer which allows pull to be carried over the wheels. (3) The head of a frame for a double-hung window. (4) In plumbing, a wye. (5) A job-built device surrounding a column form, to hold the pressure exerted by wet concrete. *(see column clamp)*

yoke vent A vertical or 45° relief vent of the continuous waste-and-vent type formed by the extension of an upright wye-branch or 45° wye-branch inlet of the horizontal branch to the stack. It becomes a dual yoke vent when two horizontal branches are thus vented by the same relief vent.

Yorkshire bond *(see monk bond)*

yorky *(slang)* A tile or slate with curved cleavage.

Yosemite An asphalt coated and colored granule surfaced roll roofing. The name has been carried over from the time when green granules came from a quarry near Yosemite National Park.

Young's modulus *(see modulus of elasticity)*

yo-yo *(slang)* Two dozers connected by a length of cable; the uphill dozer anchors the pioneering downhill dozer while it operates.

Y-tong block A lightweight, cellular building material made in block form used in construction in the form of block for single-unit walls or for backup for brick or tile facing.

z zero, zone

ZI zone of interior

Z The standard abbreviation for modulus of section.

zax A slater's edged and pointed tool for cutting slate and punching nail holes.

Z-bar (zee-bar) (1) A Z-shaped bar used as a wall tie. **(2)** A non-adjustable. Z-shaped sill support bracket. **(3)** A metal strip to hold carpet next to vinyl.

zebrawood A wood from West Africa which, quarter-sawn, gives a veneer of light straw-colored background with parallel dark brown stripes; heavy, hard texture somewhat coarse.

zein A protein derived from maize. When dissolved in alcohol, it gives a tough film which has become a replacement for shellac.

zener A semiconductor diode designed for its reverse voltage breakdown point.

zero slump concrete Concrete of stiff or extremely dry consistency showing no measurable slump after removal of the slump cone.

zero term In multiple circuits when all inputs are off, all switches are open.

z-furring channel A 'Z' formed metal channel for mechanically attaching gypsum board and insulation material on masonry walls.

Z-metal Galvanized metal to connect siding stacking going upward.

Z-section A member cold formed from steel sheet in the shape of a block "Z".

zig-zag molding Chevron molding.

zig-zag rule A folding rule made of wood or metal pieces pivoted together at the end but not hinged like the fourfold rule.

Zn azimuth, zinc

zinc A metallic element, in commercial form known as spelter; used for galvanizing sheet steel, for making brass, and as an oxide for a pigment for white paint.

zinc chromes Bright yellow pigments which can contain alkali chromatesbut are mostly zinc chromate combined with some zinc hydroxide.

zinc drier In painting, zinc napthenate is the most important zinc drier and is used to prevent wrinkling in stoving. It is also a preservative for wood, sash cord or rope.

zinc dust A powdered zinc used in priming paints to be used on galvanized iron.

zinc oxide (zinc white; Chinese white) A white pigment used in paint.

zirconia Zirconium oxide, a refractory which can be used at very high temperatures.

zocco (zacco; zoccolo; zocle) Variations of the word socle, the lowest member of a column or pilaster.

zone A space or group of spaces within a building combined for common control of heating and cooling.

zone control Any control system using two or more thermostats.

zoned heating The control of the temperature in a room or a group of rooms independently of other rooms.

zone of saturation The ground below the water-table.

zone switch An assembly of electrical contacts used to indicate to the door controller that the elevator is in the proper zone to permit door operation.

zoning Restriction as to size or character of buildings permitted within specific areas, as established by urban authorities.

zoning permit A permit issued by appropriate governmental agencies authorizing land to be used for a specific purpose.

zoom To focus on an object to reduce or increase the size as in a graphic display on a computer.

zwinger A stronghold adjoining a city; a bailey.

CONSTRUCTION ASSOCIATIONS AND INSTITUTES
AND
CONSTRUCTION RELATED GOVERNMENTAL AGENCIES

Acoustical Door Institute
Acoustical and Insulating Materials Association
Advanced Management Research International
Air Conditioning and Refrigeration Institute
Air Conditioning Contractors of America
Air Cooling Institute
Air Diffusion Council
Air Distribution Institute
Air Moving & Conditioning Association
Aluminum Association
Aluminum Manufacturers' Association
Aluminum Siding Association
American Association of State Highway and Transportation Officials
American Boiler Manufacturers Association
American Concrete Institute
American Concrete Paving Association
American Concrete Pipe Association
American Concrete Pressure Pipe Association
American Congress on Surveying and Mapping
American Consulting Engineers Council
American Custom Home Builders Association
American Federation of Labor-Congress of Industrial Organizations
American Forest Products Industries
American Gas Association
American Hardware Association
American Hardware Manufacturers' Association
American Industrial Hygiene Association
American Institute of Architects
American Institute of Building Design
American Institute of Civil Engineers
American Institute of Constructors
American Institute of Consulting Engineers
American Institute of Electrical Engineers
American Institute of Landscape Architects
American Institute of Plant Engineers
American Institute of Steel Construction
American Institute of Timber Construction
American Iron and Steel Institute
American Land Title Association
American Lumber Standards Committee
American National Standards Institute
American Petroleum Institute
American Pipe Fittings Association
American Plywood Association
American Public Works Association
American Railway Bridge and Building Association
American Road Builders Association
American Society for Testing and Materials
American Society of Architectural Hardware Consultants

American Society of Civil Engineers
American Society of Concrete Constructors
American Society of Heating, Refrigeration and Air Conditioning Engineers
American Society of Interior Designers
American Society of Landscape Architects
American Society of Mechanical Engineers
American Society of Planning Officials
American Society of Plumbing Engineers
American Society of Safety Engineers
American Specifications Institute
American Standard Safety Code
American Standards Association
American Subcontractors Association
American Tile Association
American Water Works Association
American Welding Society
American Wood Preservers Association
Architectural Aluminum Manufacturers Association
Architectural Woodwork Institute
Asbestos-Cement Products Association
Asphalt and Vinyl Asbestos Tile Institute
Asphalt Institute
Associated Air Balance Council
Associated Builders and Contractors
Associated Equipment Distributors
Associated General Contractors of America
Associated Landscape Contractors of America
Associated Painting Contractors
Associated Plastering Contractors
Associated Plumbing Contractors
Association of Plumbing, Heating, and Cooling Contractors
Association of Pool Contractors
Association of Blueprints and Allied Industries
Association of Drilled Shaft Contractors
Atomic Energy Commission

Better Heating-Cooling Council
Bituminous Concrete Producers Association
BRAB Building Research Institute
Brick and Tile Manufacturers Association
Brick Institute of America
Bridge, Tunnel and Turnpike Association
British Standard
British Standard Code of Practice
British Standards Institute
Building Officials Conference of America
Building Research Institute
Building Stone Institute
Building Waterproofers Association
Bureau of Apprenticeship and Training
Bureau of Contract Information
Bureau of Explosives
Bureau of Indian Affairs
Bureau of Labor Statistics
Bureau of Land Management

Bureau of Mines
Bureau of National Affairs
Bureau of Reclamation

Canadian Association of Equipment Distributors
Canadian Construction Association
Canadian Prestressed Concrete Institute
Carpet and Rug Institute
Ceiling and Interior Systems Contractors Association
Ceramic Tile Institute
Chain Link Fence Manufacturers' Institute
Civil Service Commission
Clay Products Association
Clay Sewer Pipe Association
Code of Federal Regulations
Compressed Air and Gas Institute
Concrete Contractors Association
Concrete Joint Institute
Concrete Reinforcing Steel Institute
Construction Industry Joint Conference
Construction Industry Manufacturers Association
Construction Specifications Institute
Construction Surveyors Institute
Construction Writers Association
Consulting Engineers Council of the United States
Cooling Tower Institute
Cork Institute of America

Department of Housing and Urban Development
Department of Transportation
Deutsche Industrie Normal (German Industrial Standard)
Douglas Fir Plywood Institute

Economic Development Administration
Edison Electric Institute
Employment Standards Administration
Energy Research and Development Administration
Engineering and Grading Contractors Association
Equal Employment Opportunity Commission
Expansion Joint Institute

Facing Tile Institute
Federal Aviation Administration
Federal Highway Administration
Federal Housing Administration
Federal Mediation and Conciliation Service
Flat Glass Marketing Association
Forest Products Laboratory

Garage Door Manufacturers Association
General Accounting Office
General Building Contractors Association
General Contractors Association
General Services Administration
Glass Tempering Association

Government Printing Office
Gypsum Association
Gypsum Drywall Contractors International

Hardwood Plywood Manufacturers Association
Heat Exchange Institute
Hoist Manufacturers Association
Home Improvement Dealers Association of America
Home Manufacturers Association
Housing and Urban Development Administration
Hydraulic Institute
Hydronics Institute

Illuminating Engineers Society
Independent Contractors Association
Independent Electrical Contractors Association
Industrial Equipment Manufacturers Council
Institute of Boiler and Radiator Manufacturers
Institute of Civil Engineers
Institute of Electrical & Electronics Engineers, Inc.
Institute of Heating and Air Conditioning Industries
Insulation Contractors Association
International Association of Drilling Contractors
International Association of Wall and Ceiling Contractors
International Conference of Building Officials
International Drywall Contractors Association
International Gypsum Drywall Contractors
International Road Federation
International Safety Academy
International Slurry Seal Association
Interstate Commerce Commission

Joint Committee on Building Codes

Landscape Contractors Association
Lath and Plaster Institute
Licensed Contractors Association
Lightweight Aggregate Producers Association
Lumber and Builders Supply Association

Manufactured Housing Association
Maple Flooring Manufacturers Association
Marble Institute of America
Mason Contractors Association of America
Masonry Institute
Mechanical Contractors Association of America
Metal Building Manufacturers Association
Metal Lath Association
Minority Contractors Association

National Acoustical Contractors Association
National Aeronautics and Space Administration
National American Wholesale Lumber Association
National Asphalt Paving Association
National Association of Air Conditioning Contractors
National Association of Architectural Metal Manufacturers

National Association of Elevator Contractors
National Association of Floor Covering Installers
National Association of Home Builders
National Association of Minority Contractors
National Association of Plumbing Contractors
National Association of Plumbing, Heating and Cooling Contractors
National Association of River and Harbor Contractors
National Association of Sheet Metal and Air Conditioning Contractors
National Association of Women in Construction
National Builders Hardware Association
National Building Materials Distributors Association
National Building Products Association
National Bureau for Lathing and Plastering
National Bureau of Standards
National Clay Pipe Institute
National Concrete Masonry Association
National Constructors Association
National Corrugated Metal Pipe Association
National Crushed Stone Association
National Council of Specialty Contractors
National Door Association
National Electrical Contractors Association
National Electrical Manufacturers Association
National Elevators Manufacturing Industry
National Association of Elevator Safety Authorities
National Environmental Systems Contractors Association
National Fire Protection Association
National Forest Products Association
National Home Builders Association
National Home Improvement Council
National Institute for Occupational Safety and Health
National Insulation Contractors Association
National Insulation Manufacturers Association
National Labor Relations Board
National Landscape Nurserymen's Association
National Lumber and Building Material Dealers Association
National Lumber Manufacturers Association
National Metal Trades Association
National Mineral Wool Insulation Association, Inc.
National Oak Flooring Manufacturers' Association
National Paint, Varnish & Lacquer Association
National Park Service
National Particleboard Association
National Precast Concrete Association
National Ready Mixed Concrete Association
National Remodelers Association
National Roofing Contractors Association
National Safety Council
National Sand and Gravel Association
National Slurry Seal Association
National Society of Professional Engineers
National Swimming Pool Institute
National Terrazzo and Mosaic Association
National Woodwork Manufacturers Association
National Utility Contractors Association

Occupational Safety and Health Administration
Office of Minority Business Enterprise

Paint and Wallpaper Association of America
Paintng and Decorating Contractors of America
Paint Research Institute
Perlite Institute
Pipe Fabrication Institute
Pipe Line Contractors Association
Plastic Pipe Institute
Plumbing and Drainage Institute
Porcelain Enamel Institute
Portland Cement Association
Power and Communication Contractors Association
Prestressed Concrete Institute
Producers Council, Inc.

Refrigeration and Air Conditioning Contractors Association
Resilient Flooring and Carpet Association
Rock Products Association
Roofing Contractors Association
Royal Institute of British Architects
Rubber and Vinyl Flooring Council

Sheet Metal and Air Conditioning Contractors National Association
Small Business Administration
Society of Automotive Engineers
Society of Construction Superintendents
Soil Conservation Service
Southern Building Code Congress
Steam Heating Equipment Manufacturers Association
Steel Deck Institute
Steel Door Institute
Steel Field Erectors Association
Steel Joist Institute
Steel Window Institute
Structural Clay Products Institute
Structural Engineers Association
Stucco Manufacturers Association

Tennessee Valley Authority
Thermal Insulation Manufacturers Association, Inc.
Tile Contractors Association of America
Tile Council of America
Truss Plate Institute

Underground Engineering Contractors Association
Urban Mass Transportation Administration

Vermiculite Institute

Wallpaper Institute
Weatherstrip Research Institute
Western Association of State Highway Officials
Western Forest Industries
Western Wood Products Association
Wire Reinforcement Institute
Wood Flooring Institute
Woven Wire Institute

ABSORPTION COEFFICIENTS
For Frequency of 512 Cycles per Second

Material	Coefficient
Open window	1.00
Audience	0.96
Hair felt covered with burlap	0.74
Perforated cane fiber board 1 3/4 in. thick	0.70
Corkboard 1 in. thick	0.30
Acoustical plaster	0.15 to 0.30
Carpet 0.4 in. thick on concrete	0.21
Unpainted brick wall 18 in. thick	0.08
Linoleum	0.10
Wood sheathing	0.10
Wood floor	0.03 to 0.08
Varnished floor	0.03 to 0.08
Lime plaster on wood lath	0.034
Ceramic tile	0.029
Gypsum plaster on hollow tile	0.020
Audience, per person	4.7 units

AGGREGATES — % OF VOIDS
Weights in Pounds per Cubic Yard of Common Mineral Aggregates with Various Percentages of Voids

Kind of Material	Specific Gravity	Percentage of Voids					
		25%	30%	35%	40%	45%	50%
Trap Rock	2.8	3540	3300	3070	2830	2600	2360
	2.9	3660	3420	3180	2930	2690	2440
	3.0	3790	3540	3290	3030	2780	2530
	3.1	3910	3650	3390	3130	2870	2610
Granite and Limestone	2.6	3280	3060	2850	2630	2410	2190
	2.7	3410	3180	2960	2730	2500	2270
	2.8	3540	3300	3070	2830	2600	2360
Sandstone	2.4	3030	2830	2630	2420	2220	2020
	2.5	3160	2950	2740	2520	2310	2100
	2.6	3280	3060	2850	2630	2410	2190
	2.7	3410	3180	2960	2730	2500	2270
Slag	2.0	2530	2360	2190	2020	1850	1680
	2.1	2650	2470	2300	2120	1950	1770
	2.2	2780	2590	2410	2220	2040	1850
	2.3	2900	2710	2520	2320	2130	1940
	2.4	3030	2830	2630	2420	2220	2020
	2.5	3160	2950	2740	2520	2310	2100
Granulated Slag	1.5	1890	1770	1640	1510	1390	1260
Gravel Sand	2.65	3350	3120	2900	2680	2450	2230

NOTE: Most limestone, gravel and sand will absorb one per cent or more water by weight. Free water in moist sand approximates 2 per cent, moderately wet 4 per cent, and very wet 7 per cent.

ALTITUDE

Altitude — An increase in altitude may cause a decrease in engine performance. This is due to the decrease in the air density which affects the fuel-to-air ratio in the combustion chamber of the engine. Since engine manufacturers rate the altitude performance of their engines differently, altitude duration for a specific engine should be obtained from the manufacturer. The following guide lines will be sufficient for the purpose of estimating haulage performance:

4-Cycle Diesel Engine Naturally Aspirated
No loss in performance from sea level to 1000 feet.

Reduce rimpull values by 3% for every 1000' above 1000'.

2-Cycle Diesel Engine Naturally Aspirated
Reduce rimpull values by 1.5% per 1000' between sea level and 6000'. Above 6000' reduce rimpull values by 3% per 1000 feet.

2 & 4-Cycle Turbo-Charged Diesel Engines
No performance loss up to 5000' above sea level and sometimes higher. See the manufacturer's specification sheet. From 5000' (or the higher number) to 10,000' above sea level, subtract 1% from the rimpull values. Above 10,000', subtract 3% per 1000' from the rimpull values.

Horsepower Ratings at Different Elevations
(For Unsupercharged Engines)

Height Above Sea Level—Ft.	Diesel Engine Percentage of HP at Sea Level*	Gasoline Engine Percentage of HP at Sea Level*
0	100	100
1,000	100	97
1,500	100	94
2,000	98	91
3,000	93	88
4,000	89	85
5,000	85	82
6,000	81	79
7,000	78	76
8,000	74	73
9,000	71	70
10,000	67	67
11,000	64	64
12,000	61	61
13,000	57	58
14,000	55	55
15,000	52	52

*Values are average of Handbooks & Engine Manufacturers.

ASPHALT

WEIGHT AND VOLUME RELATIONS FOR VARIOUS TYPES OF COMPACTED ASPHALT PAVEMENTS (Data from The Asphalt Institute)

Note:

Because of the considerable variations of specific gravity, gradation, and other characteristics of mineral aggregates, weight per unit volume of compacted asphalt pavement varies considerably. Exact weights per unit volume should be determined in the laboratory from samples taken from the pavement or prepared in the laboratory with the same materials as used in the field.

Pounds Per Cubic Foot	Pounds Per Cubic Yard	Pounds Per Square Yard Per 1 Inch Depth
100	2700	75
105	2835	79
110	2970	82
115	3105	86
120	3240	90
125	3375	94
130	3510	97
135	3645	101
140	3780	105
145	3915	109
150	4050	112
155	4185	116
160	4320	120

	Pounds Per Cubic Foot Range	Pounds Per Cubic Yard Range	Pounds Per Square Yard Per 1 Inch Depth Range	Frequently Used for Preliminary Estimate
Macadam—A.I. Type I or Penetration Macadam	110-135	2970-3645	82-101	95
Open Graded—A.I. Type II	115-140	3105-3780	86-105	100
Coarse Graded—A.I. Type III	130-150	3510-4050	97-112	105
Dense Graded—A.I. Type IV	135-155	3645-4185	101-116	110
Fine Graded—A.I. Type V	130-150	3510-4050	97-112	105
Stone Sheet—A.I. Type VI	130-150	3510-4050	97-112	105
Sand Sheet—A.I. Type VII	120-140	3240-3780	90-105	100
Fine Sheet—A.I. Type VIII	120-140	3240-3780	90-105	100
Mixed-in-Place Macadam—A.I. Spec RM 1	110-135	2970-3645	82-101	100
Mixed-in-Place Dense Graded—A.I. Spec. RM 2	110-135	2970-3645	82-101	95
Mixed-in-Place Sand Asphalt—A.I. Spec RM 3	100-125	2700-3375	75-94	85

Weights and Volumes of Asphaltic Materials (approximate)

Type and Grade	Pounds per Gallon	Pounds per Barrels *	Gallons per Ton	Barrels * per Ton
MC-30.....................	7.8	328	256	6.1
RC-, MC-, SC-70	7.9	332	253	6.0
RC-, MC-, SC-250	8.0	337	249	5.9
RC-, MC-, SC-800	8.2	343	245	5.8
RC-, MC-, SC-3000	8.3	349	241	5.7
40-50 Pen. A.C............	8.6	361	233	5.5
60-70 Pen. A.C............	8.5	357	235	5.6
85-100 Pen. A.C............	8.5	357	235	5.6
120-150 Pen. A.C...........	8.5	357	235	5.6
200-300 Pen. A.C...........	8.4	353	238	5.7
Emulsified Asphalts	8.3	349	241•	5.7

* A barrel equals 42 U.S. Gallons.
Notes: 1. Since the specific gravity of asphaltic materials varies, even for the same type and grade, the weight and volume relationships shown above are approximate and should be used only for general estimating purposes. Where more precise data are required, they must be computed on the basis of laboratory tests on the specific product.
   2. The approximate data shown above are for materials at 60°F (15.6C).

Data from The Asphalt Institute

Gallons Asphaltic Materials Required at Various Rates of Application
GALLONS PER MILE

Width, Feet	9	12	15	16	20
Gals. per Sq. Yd.					
.10	530	700	880	940	1170
.15	790	1050	1320	1410	1760
.20	1050	1410	1760	1880	2350
.25	1320	1760	2200	2350	2930
.30	1580	2110	2640	2820	3520
.35	1840	2460	3080	3290	4110
.40	2110	2820	3520	3750	4690
.45	2330	3170	3960	4220	5280
.50	2640	3520	4400	4690	5870
1.25	6600	8800	11000	11730	14670
2.00	10560	14080	17600	18770	23470

CONCRETE

Quantities of Cement, Fine Aggregate and Coarse Aggregate Required for One Cubic Yard of Compact Mortar or Concrete

| MIXTURES | | | | QUANTITIES OF MATERIALS | | | | |
| | | | | Fine Aggregate | | Coarse Aggregate | | |
Cement	F. A. (Sand)	C. A. (Gravel or Stone)	Cement in Sacks	Cu. Ft.	Cu. Yd.	Cu. Ft.	Cu. Yd.
1	1.5	....	15.5	23.2	0.86	....	....
1	2.0	....	12.8	25.6	0.95	....	....
1	2.5	....	11.0	27.5	1.02	....	....
1	3.0	....	9.6	28.8	1.07	....	....
1	1.5	3	7.6	11.4	0.42	22.8	0.85
1	2.0	2	8.3	16.6	0.61	16.6	0.61
1	2.0	3	7.0	14.0	0.52	21.0	0.78
1	2.0	4	6.0	12.0	0.44	24.0	0.89
1	2.5	3.5	5.9	14.7	0.54	20.6	0.76
1	2.5	4	5.6	14.0	0.52	22.4	0.83
1	2.5	5	5.0	12.5	0.46	25.0	0.92
1	3.0	5	4.6	13.8	0.51	23.0	0.85

1 sack cement = 1 cu. ft.; 4 sacks = 1 bbl.

Cubic Yards of Concrete in Slabs of Various Areas and Thicknesses

Area (Square Feet)	THICKNESS OF SLABS (Inches)										
	1.0	1.5	2.0	2.5	3.0	3.5	4.0	4.5	5.0	5.5	6.0
10	.03	.05	.06	.08	.09	.11	.13	.14	.15	.17	.19
20	.06	.09	.12	.16	.19	.22	.25	.28	.31	.34	.37
30	.09	.14	.19	.23	.28	.33	.37	.42	.46	.51	.56
40	.12	.19	.25	.31	.37	.43	.50	.56	.62	.68	.74
50	.15	.23	.31	.39	.46	.54	.62	.70	.77	.85	.93
60	.19	.28	.37	.46	.56	.65	.74	.83	.93	1.02	1.11
70	.22	.32	.43	.54	.65	.76	.87	.97	1.08	1.19	1.30
80	.25	.37	.49	.62	.74	.87	1.00	1.11	1.24	1.36	1.48
90	.28	.42	.56	.70	.84	.97	1.11	1.25	1.39	1.53	1.67
100	.31	.46	.62	.78	.93	1.08	1.24	1.39	1.55	1.70	1.85
200	.62	.93	1.23	1.54	1.85	2.16	2.47	2.78	3.09	3.40	3.70
300	.93	1.39	1.85	2.32	2.78	3.24	3.70	4.17	4.63	5.10	5.56
400	1.23	1.83	2.47	3.10	3.70	4.32	4.94	5.56	6.17	6.79	7.41
500	1.54	2.32	3.09	3.86	4.63	5.40	6.17	7.00	7.72	8.49	9.26
600	1.85	2.78	3.70	4.63	5.56	6.48	7.41	8.33	9.26	10.19	11.11
700	2.16	3.24	4.32	5.40	6.48	7.56	8.64	9.72	10.80	11.88	12.96
800	2.47	3.70	4.94	6.20	7.41	8.64	9.88	11.11	12.35	13.58	14.82
900	2.78	4.17	5.56	6.95	8.33	9.72	11.11	12.50	13.89	15.28	16.67
1000	3.09	4.63	6.17	7.72	9.26	10.80	12.35	13.89	15.43	16.98	18.52

NOTE: This table may also be used to estimate the cubic content of slabs of greater thickness and area than those shown. Examples: To find the cubic content of a slab of 1000 sq. ft. area and 8″ thickness, add the figures given under 6″ and 2″ for 1000 sq. ft. To find the cubic content of a slab 6″ thickness and 1500 sq. ft. area, add the figures given for 1000 and 500 sq. ft. under 6″ thickness.

CONCRETE ESTIMATOR

One Cubic Yard of Concrete Will Place					
Thickness	Sq. Ft.	Thickness	Sq. Ft.	Thickness	Sq. Ft.
1"	324	5"	65	9"	36
1¼"	259	5¼"	62	9¼"	35
1½"	216	5½"	59	9½"	34
1¾"	185	5¾"	56	9¾"	33
2"	162	6"	54	10"	32.5
2¼"	144	6¼"	52	10¼"	31.5
2½"	130	6½"	50	10½"	31
2¾"	118	6¾"	48	10¾"	30
3"	108	7"	46	11"	29.5
3¼"	100	7¼"	45	11¼"	29
3½"	93	7½"	43	11½"	28
3¾"	86	7¾"	42	11¾"	27.5
4"	81	8"	40	12"	27
4¼"	76	8¼"	39	15"	21.5
4½"	72	8½"	38	18"	18
4¾"	68	8¾"	37	24"	13.5

Darex Diary

COMPRESSIVE STRENGTHS FOR VARIOUS
WATER-CEMENT RATIOS
(Mixes Recommended by Joint Committee) *

Maximum Allowable Net Water Content, Gal. per Sack of Cement	Probable Minimum Allowable Compressive Strength at 28 Days Lb. per Sq. In.
5	5000
5½	4500
6	4000
6½	3600
7	3200
7½	2800
8	2500
8½	2000

*Report of Joint Committee: "Recommended Practice and Standard Specifications for Concrete and Reinforced Concrete," American Society of Civil Engineers, American Society for Testing Materials, Portland Cement Association, American Concrete Institute, American Railway Engineering Association, American Institute of Architects

CONVERSION FACTORS

Miscellaneous Conversion Factors

Board feet	x 144 sq. in x 1 in.	= cubic inches
Board feet	x .0833	= cubic feet
Cubic feet	x 6.22905	= gallons, Br. Imp.
Cubic feet	x 2.38095 x 10⁻¹	= tons, Br. shipping
Cubic feet	x .025	= tons, U.S. shipping
Degrees, angular	x .0174533	= radians
Degrees, F. (less 32F) x	.5556	= degrees, Centigrade
Degrees, centigrade x	1.8	= degrees, F. (less 32F)
Gallons, Br. Imp.	x .160538	= cubic feet
Gallons, Br. Imp.	x 4.54596	= liters
Gallons, U.S.	x .13368	= cubic feet
Gallons, U.S.	x 3.78543	= liters
Liters	x .219975	= gallons, Br. Imp.
Miles, statute	x .8684	= miles, nautical
Miles, nautical	x 1.1516	= miles, statute
Radians	x 57.29578	= degrees, angular
Tons, long	x 1.120	= tons, short
Tons, short	x .892857	= tons, long
Tons, Br. shipping	x 42.00	= cubic feet
Tons, Br. shipping	x .952381	= tons, U.S. shipping
Tons, U.S. shipping	x 40.00	= cubic feet
Tons, U.S. shipping	x 1.050	= tons, Br. shipping

Note: Br. Imp. = British Imperial

Conversion of Thermometer Scale

Centigrade — Fahrenheit

$$°C. = 5/9 (°F. -32) \qquad °F. = 9/5 °C. +32$$

°C.	°F.	°C.	°F.	°C.	°F.	°C.	°F.	°C.	°F.
—80	—112.	1	33.8	31	87.8	61	141.8	91	195.8
—70	— 94.	2	35.6	32	89.6	62	143.6	92	197.6
—60	— 76.	3	37.4	33	91.4	63	145.4	93	199.4
—50	— 58.0	4	39.2	34	93.2	64	147.2	94	201.2
—45	— 49.1	5	41.0	35	95.0	65	149.0	95	203.0
—40	— 40.0	6	42.8	36	96.8	66	150.8	96	204.8
—35	— 31.0	7	44.6	37	98.6	67	152.6	97	206.6
—30	— 22.0	8	46.4	38	100.4	68	154.4	98	208.4
—25	— 13.0	9	48.2	39	102.2	69	156.2	99	210.2
—20	— 4.0	10	50.0	40	104.0	70	158.0	100	212.0
—19	— 2.2	11	51.8	41	105.8	71	159.8	105	221.
—18	— .4	12	53.6	42	107.6	72	161.6	110	230.
—17	1.4	13	55.4	43	109.4	73	163.4	115	239.
—16	3.2	14	57.2	44	111.2	74	165.2	120	248.
—15	5.0	15	59.0	45	113.0	75	167.0	130	266.
—14	6.8	16	60.8	46	114.8	76	168.8	140	284.
—13	8.6	17	62.6	47	116.0	77	170.6	150	302.
—12	10.4	18	64.4	48	118.4	78	172.4	160	320.
—11	12.2	19	66.2	49	120.2	79	174.2	170	338.
—10	14.0	20	68.0	50	122.0	80	176.0	180	356.
— 9	15.8	21	69.8	51	123.8	81	177.8	190	374.
— 8	17.6	22	71.6	52	125.6	82	179.6	200	392.
— 7	19.4	23	73.4	53	127.4	83	181.4	250	482.
— 6	21.2	24	75.2	54	129.2	84	183.2	300	572.
— 5	23.0	25	77.0	55	131.0	85	185.0	350	662.
— 4	24.8	26	78.8	56	132.8	86	186.8	400	752.
— 3	26.6	27	80.6	57	134.6	87	188.6	500	932.
— 2	28.4	28	82.4	58	136.4	88	190.4	600	1112.
— 1	30.2	29	84.2	59	138.2	89	192.2	700	1292.
0	32.0	30	86.0	60	140.0	90	194.2	800	1472.
								900	1652.
								1000	1832.

DECIMAL EQUIVALENTS

Decimal Equivalents of Fractions

1/64	.015625	33/64	.515625
1/32	.03125	17/32	.53125
3/64	.046875	35/64	.546875
1/16	**.0625**	9/16	**.5625**
5/64	.078125	37/64	.578125
3/32	.09375	19/32	.59375
7/64	.109375	39/64	.609375
1/8	**.125**	5/8	**.625**
9/64	.140625	41/64	.640625
5/32	.15625	21/32	.65625
11/64	.171875	43/64	.671875
3/16	**.1875**	11/16	**.6875**
13/64	.203125	45/64	.703125
7/32	.21875	23/32	.71875
15/64	.234375	47/64	.734375
1/4	**.25**	3/4	**.75**
17/64	.265625	49/64	.765625
9/32	.28125	25/32	.78125
19/64	.296875	51/64	.796875
5/16	**.3125**	13/16	**.8125**
21/64	.328125	53/64	.828125
11/32	.34375	47/32	.84375
23/64	.359375	55/64	.859375
3/8	**.375**	7/8	**.875**
25/64	.390625	57/64	.890625
13/32	.40625	29/32	.90625
27/64	.421875	59/64	.921875
7/16	**.4375**	15/16	**.9375**
29/64	.453125	61/64	.953125
15/32	.46875	31/32	.96875
31/64	.484375	63/64	.984375
1/2	**.5**		

DIGGING & DUMPING

APPROXIMATE DIPPER AND BUCKET EFFICIENCY FOR VARYING CLASSES OF MATERIAL

Conditions. Digging face of sufficient length to allow dipper or bucket to obtain loads as given. Allowance must be made for smaller loads when digging in shallow bank, especially with large capacity dippers or buckets. Higher dipper and bucket factors than those shown below can ordinarily be used for large strippers, shovels or large draglines.

EASY DIGGING	MEDIUM DIGGING	HARD DIGGING	ROCK
Shovel Dipper Factor 0.85 1.00	Shovel Dipper Factor 0.80 0.90	Shovel Dipper Factor 0.70 0.80	Shovel Dipper Factor 0.40
Dragline Bucket Factor 0.85 1.00	Dragline Bucket Factor 0.80 0.90	Dragline Bucket Factor 0.80 0.90	
Loose, soft, free running materials. Close lying, which will fill dipper or bucket to capacity & frequently provide heaped load.	Harder materials that are not difficult to dig without blasting, but break up with bulkiness causing voids in dipper or bucket.	Materials requiring some breaking up by light blasting or shaking. More bulky & somewhat hard to penetrate, causing voids in dipper or bucket.	Blasted rock, hardpan & other bulky materials, which cause considerable voids in dipper or bucket & are difficult to penetrate
Dry sand or small gravel	Clay – wet or dry	Well broken limestone, sand rock & other blasted rocks	
Moist sand or small gravel	Coarse gravel	Blasted shale	
Loam	Clay gravel, packed	Ore formations (not of rock character - requiring some blasting)	
Loose earth	Packed earth	Heavy wet, sticky clay	
Muck	Anthracite coal	Gravel with large boulders	
Sandy clay		Heavy, wet gumbo	
Loose clay gravel		Cemented gravel	
Bituminous coal			
Cinders or ashes			
Very well blasted material			

DUMPING ANGLES

Angles at which different materials will slide out of tipped body)

Ashes, Dry	33°	Coal, Hard	27°
Ashes, Moist	35°	Coal, Soft	30°
Ashes, Wet	26°	Coke	25°
Asphalt	15°	Concrete	30°
Cinders, Dry	33°	Earth, Loose	35°
Cinders, Moist	31°	Earth, Compact	30°
Cinders, Wet	31°	Garbage	30°
Cinders & Clay	30°	Gravel	40°
Clay	45°	Ore, Dry	30°

Ore, Fresh Mined	37°
Rubble	35°
Sand, Dry	40°
Sand, Moist	27°
Sand & Crushed Stone	30°
Stone, Broken	27°
Stone, Crushed	30°

EARTH MOVING

COEFFICIENT OF TRACTION

Materials	Rubber Tires	Tracks
Concrete	90	45
Clay Loam, Dry	55	90*
Clay Loam, Wet	45	70
Rutted Clay Loam	40	70
Dry Sand	20	30
Wet Sand	40	50
Quarry Pit	65	55
Gravel Road (loose)	35	50
Dry Packed Snow	40	50
Ice	10	10
Firm Earth	60	90*
Loose Earth	45	60

*Assumes full grouser penetration

The ability of rubber-tired vehicles to deliver power may be altered on extremely slippery ground or where extremely steep grades cause weight to be transferred onto or off of the drive axle.

ROLLING RESISTANCES

Ground Surface	Rolling Resistance
Asphalt	1.5%
Concrete	1.5%
Dirt – Smooth, hard, dry, well maintained, free of loose material	2.0%
Dirt – Dry, but not firmly packed, some loose material	3.0%
Dirt – Soft, unplowed, poorly maintained	4.0%
Dirt – Soft, plowed	8.0%
Dirt – Unpacked fills	8.0%
Dirt – Deeply rutted	16.0%
Gravel – Well compacted, dry, free of loose material	2.0%
Gravel – Not firmly compacted, but dry	3.0%
Gravel – Loose	10.0%
Mud – With firm base	4.0%
Mud – With soft, spongy base	16.0%
Sand – Loose	10.0%
Snow – Packed	2.5%
Snow – To 4" depth, loose	4.5%

Common Earthmoving Equipment Formulas

1. Rimpull $= \dfrac{\text{H.P. x E x 375}}{\text{M.P.H.}}$

2. Max. Useable Rimpull = G.V.W. x Weight Distribution x Coeff. of Friction

3. Torque $= \dfrac{\text{H.P. x 5252}}{\text{R.P.M.}}$

4. Approx. Horsepower $= \dfrac{(\text{Bore})^2 \text{ x Stroke x R.P.M. x No. Cylinders}}{14,000}$

5. Grade Ability $= \dfrac{\text{Rimpull} - \text{R.R.}}{20 \text{ x G.V.W.}}$

6. Grade Resistance = 20 x % Grade x G.V.W.

7. Rolling Resistance (In Lbs.) = K x G.V.W.

WHERE:

E = Efficiency (Varies from .65 — .90)

G.V.W. = Gross Vehicle Weight   R.R. = Rolling Resistance

K = Rolling Resistance of Roadways in Lbs. per Gross Ton

METALS

Approximate Weight of Various Metals

To find weight of various metals, multiply contents in cubic inches by the number shown; result will be approximate weight in pounds.

Iron	.27777	Lead	.41015
Steel	.28332	Zinc	.25318
Copper	.32118	Tin	.26562
Brass	.3112	Aluminum	.09375

Approximate Weights Per Lineal Foot in Pounds of Standard Steel Bars

Dia. In.	Rd.	Hex.	Sq.	Dia. In.	Rd.	Hex.	Sq.
1/16	.010	.012	.013	1 1/16	1.90	2.10	2.42
3/32	.023	.026	.030	7/8	2.04	2.25	2.60
1/8	.042	.046	.053	15/16	2.19	2.42	2.79
5/32	.065	.072	.083	15/16	2.35	2.59	2.99
3/16	.094	.104	.120	31/32	2.51	2.76	3.19
7/32	.128	.141	.163	1	2.67	2.95	3.40
1/4	.167	.184	.212	1 1/16	3.01	3.32	3.84
9/32	.211	.233	.269	1 1/8	3.38	3.73	4.30
5/16	.261	.288	.332	1 3/16	3.77	4.15	4.80
11/32	.316	.348	.402	1 1/4	4.17	4.60	5.31
3/8	.376	.414	.478	1 5/16	4.60	5.07	5.86
13/32	.441	.486	.561	1 3/8	5.05	5.57	6.43
7/16	.511	.564	.651	1 7/16	5.52	6.09	7.03
15/32	.587	.647	.747	1 1/2	6.01	6.63	7.65
1/2	.667	.736	.850	1 9/16	7.05	7.78	8.98
17/32	.754	.831	.960	1 5/8	8.18	9.02	10.41
9/16	.845	.932	1.08	1 3/4	9.39	10.36	11.95
19/32	.941	1.03	1.20	2	10.68	11.78	13.60
5/8	1.04	1.15	1.33	2 1/8	12.06	13.30	15.35
21/32	1.15	1.27	1.46	2 1/4	13.52	14.91	17.21
11/16	1.26	1.39	1.61	2 3/8	15.06	16.61	19.18
23/32	1.38	1.52	1.76	2 1/2	16.69	18.40	21.25
3/4	1.50	1.66	1.91	2 3/4	20.20	22.27	25.71
25/32	1.63	1.80	2.08	3	24.03	26.50	30.60
13/16	1.76	1.94	2.24				

Weights of Flat Bars and Plates

To find weight per foot of flat steel, multiply width in inches by figure listed below:

Thickness		Thickness		Thickness	
1/16"	.2125	7/8"	2.975	1 3/4"	5.950
1/8"	.4250	15/16"	3.188	1 13/16"	6.163
3/16"	.6375	1"	3.400	1 7/8"	6.375
1/4"	.8500	1 1/16"	3.613	1 15/16"	6.588
5/16"	1.0600	1 1/8"	3.825	2"	6.800
3/8"	1.2750	1 3/16"	4.038	2 1/8"	7.225
7/16"	1.4880	1 1/4"	4.250	2 1/4"	7.650
1/2"	1.7000	1 5/16"	4.463	2 3/8"	8.075
9/16"	1.9130	1 3/8"	4.675	2 1/2"	8.500
5/8"	2.1250	1 7/16"	4.888	2 5/8"	8.925
11/16"	2.3380	1 1/2"	5.100	2 3/4"	9.350
3/4"	2.5500	1 9/16"	5.313	2 7/8"	9.775
13/16"	2.7630	1 5/8"	5.525	3"	10.200
		1 11/16"	5.738		

Standard Steel Sheet Gauges and Weights

U.S.S. (Revised) or Mfrs. Gauge	Thickness Inches*	Wt. per Sq. Ft. (Lbs.)	U.S.S. (Revised) or Mfrs. Gauge	Thickness Inches*	Wt. per Sq. Ft. (Lbs.)
1	. . . .	11.25	16	.0598	2.500
2	. . .	10.625	17	.0538	2.250
3	.2391	10.000	18	.0478	2.000
4	.2242	9.375	19	.0418	1.750
5	.2092	8.750	20	.0359	1.500
6	.1943	8.125	21	.0329	1.375
7	.1793	7.500	22	.0299	1.250
8	.1644	6.875	23	.0269	1.125
9	.1494	6.250	24	.0239	1.000
10	.1345	5.625	25	.0209	.875
11	.1196	5.000	26	.0179	.750
12	.1046	4.375	27	.0164	.6875
13	.0897	3.750	28	.0149	.625
14	.0747	3.125	29	.0135	.5625
15	.0673	2.812	30	.0120	.500

*(3/16" Thick and Heavier Are Called Plates).

To avoid errors specify decimal part of one inch or mention gauge number and the name of the gauge. Orders for a definite gauge weight or gauge thickness will be subject to standard gauge weight or gauge thickness tolerance, applying equally plus and minus from the ordered gauge weight or gauge thickness.

U.S. Standard Gauge—Iron and steel sheets. Note: U.S. Standard Gauge was established by act of Congress in 1893, in which weights per square foot were indicated by gauge number. The weight, not thickness, is the determining factor when the material is ordered to this gauge.

QUICKY COMPUTATIONS

CIRCLE

Area = square of diameter x 0.7854

Area = square of circumference x 0.07058

Area of circular ring = sum of the diameter of the two circles x difference of the diameter of the two circles and that product x 0.7854

Area of sector = length of arc x 1/2 radius

Area of segment = subtract area of triangle from area of sector of equal angle

Circumference = diameter x 3.1416

Circumference of equal circle = side x 3.547

Circumference of circumscribing circle = side x 4.443

Diameter = circumference x 0.31831

Diameter = square root of area x 1.12838

Diameter of equal circle = side x 1.128

(Doubling the diameter of a circle increases its area four times.)

Radius = circumference x 0.0159155

COLUMN OF WATER

To find pressure in pounds per square inch, multiply height of column in feet x 0.434

To find height of column when pressure in pounds per square inch is known, multiply pressure in pounds by 2.309 (2.309 feet water exerts pressure of one pound per square inch).

CONE

Area of surface = area of base + circumference of base x 1/2 slant height

Contents = area of base x 1/3 altitude

Content of frustum = areas of two ends multiplied together and extract square root. Add to this figure the two areas and multiply times 1/3 altitude

Content of frustum = sum of circumference at both ends x 1/2 slant height plus area of both ends

CUBE

Side of inscribed cube = radius of sphere x 1.1547

CYLINDER

Area of surface = area of both ends plus length x circumference

Cubic contents = area of one end x length

Gallons in cylinder or pipe = cubic contents in inches divided by 231

(Doubling the diameter of cylinder or pipe increases its capacity four times.)

ELLIPSE

Area = product of both diameters x 0.7854

HEATING CAPACITY OF BOILER

Heating surface of tubular boiler = 2/3 of the circumference x length of boiler in inches and add to it the area of all the tubes

HORSEPOWER

Evaporation of 30 pounds of water per hour from a feed water temperature of 100° C into steam at 70 pounds gauge pressure equals a standard horsepower

PARABOLA

Area = base x 2/3 of altitude

PARALLELOGRAM

Area = base x altitude

POLYGON

Area of regular polygon = sum of sides x perpendicular from its center to one of its sides divided by 2

RECTANGLE

Area = length x breadth

SPHERE

Circumference = cube root of solidity x 3.8978
Circumference = square root of surface x 1.772454

Contents = diameter x 0.5236
Contents of segment of sphere = height squared plus three times the square of radius of base x height x 0.5236

Cubic inches in sphere = cube of diameter x 0.5236

Diameter = cube root of solidity x 1.2407

Diameter = square root of surface x 0.56419

Side of inscribed cube of sphere = square root of diameter

Solidity = cube of radius x 4.1888
Solidity = surface x 1/6 diameter
Solidity = cube of circumference x 0.016887
Solidity = cube of diameter x 0.5236

Surface = diameter x circumference

SQUARE

Area = height x breadth or height

Side of an equal square = multiply diameter by 0.8862
Side of inscribed square = multiply diameter by 0.7071 or multiply circumference by 0.2251 or divide circumference by 4.4428
Side of square to equal area of circle — diameter x 0.8862
Side of square to equal area of circle — circumference x 0.2821
Side of square multiplied by 1.4142 equals diameter of its circumscribing circle

TANK CAPACITY

To find capacity in U.S. gallons of rectangular tanks, multiply length by width by depth (all in inches) and divide the result by 231.

To find capacity of round tanks; square the diameter in inches, multiply by the length and then by 0.0034.

TRAPEZIUM

To determine area, divide into two triangles and total their areas.

TRAPEZOID

Area = altitude x 1/2 the sum of parallel sides

TRIANGLE

Area = base x 1/2 perpendicular height

Side of inscribed equilateral triangle = diameter x 0.86

WEDGE

Contents = area of base x 1/2 altitude

QUICKY COMPUTATIONS (Continued)

RAPID APPROXIMATION OF MEASUREMENTS

feet	x	0.00019	=	miles
links	x	0.66	=	feet
feet	x	1.5	=	links
square inches	x	0.007	=	square feet
square feet	x	0.111	=	square yards
acres	x	4,840.	=	square yards
square yards	x	0.002066	=	acres
width in chains	x	8.	=	acres per mile
cubic feet	x	0.04	=	cubic yards
cubic inches	x	0.00058	=	cubic feet
U.S. bushel	x	0.046	=	cubic yards
U.S. bushel	x	1.244	=	cubic feet
U.S. bushel	x	2,150.42	=	cubic inches
cubic feet	x	0.8036	=	U.S. bushels
cubic inches	x	0.000466	=	U.S. bushels
U.S. gallons	x	0.13368	=	cubic feet
U.S. gallons	x	231.	=	cubic inch
cubic feet	x	7.48	=	U.S. gallons
cubic inches	x	0.004329	=	U.S. gallons
cylindrical feet	x	5.878	=	U.S. gallons
cylindrical inches	x	0.0034	=	U.S. gallons
pounds	x	0.009	=	cwt (112 lbs)
pounds	x	0.00045	=	long ton (2,240 lbs)
pounds	x	0.0005	=	short ton (2,000 lbs)

ROOFING MATERIALS

WEIGHTS OF ROOFING MATERIALS
(In Pounds per Square)

Heavy		Medium		Light	
Clay tile	1000-2000	Wood shingles	200-300	Copper	80-130
Slate	500-1000	Asphalt shingles	150-300	Terne plate	60- 75
Built-up roofing	300- 600	Galvanized steel	125-200	Prepared	
Asbestos-cement				roofing	35- 80
shingles	400- 700				

SIEVES

Standard Requirements for Certain Sizes of U.S. Standard Sieves

Sieve Size Designation	Size of Sieve Opening		Permissible Variations in Size of Average Opening (Plus or Minus)	Permissible Variations in Size of Maximum Opening (Plus)	Diameters of Wire (Varies according to Difference in Size of Opening)	
	Millimeters	Inches (Approximate Equivalents)			Millimeters	Inches (Approximate Equivalents)
Opening*						
COARSE SERIES						
3 inch	76.2	3.00	2%	3%	4.8 to 8.1	.190 to .320
2½ inch	63.5	2.50	2%	3%	4.4 to 7.1	.175 to .280
2 inch	50.8	2.00	2%	3%	4.1 to 6.2	.160 to .245
1½ inch	38.1	1.50	2%	3%	3.7 to 5.3	.145 to .210
1¼ inch	31.7	1.25	2%	3%	3.5 to 4.8	.140 to .190
1 inch	25.4	1.00	2%	3%	3.43 to 4.50	.135 to .177
¾ inch	19.1	.750	3%	5%	3.10 to 3.91	.122 to .154
½ inch	12.7	.500	3%	5%	2.39 to 3.10	.094 to .122
⅜ inch	9.52	.375	3%	5%	2.11 to 2.59	.083 to .102
¼ inch	6.35	.250	3%	5%	1.60 to 2.11	.063 to .083
Mesh**						
FINE SERIES						
No. 4	4.76	.187	3%	10%	1.14 to 1.68	.045 to .066
No. 8	2.38	.0937	3%	10%	.74 to 1.10	.0291 to .0433
No. 10	2.00	.0787	3%	10%	.68 to 1.00	.0268 to .0394
No. 16	1.19	.0469	3%	10%	.50 to .70	.0197 to .0276
No. 20	.84	.0331	5%	15%	.38 to .55	.0150 to .0217
No. 30	.59	.0232	5%	25%	.29 to .42	.0114 to .0165
No. 40	.42	.0165	5%	25%	.23 to .33	.0091 to .0130
No. 50	.297	.0117	5%	25%	.170 to .253	.0067 to .0100
No. 80	.177	.0070	6%	40%	.114 to .154	.0045 to .0061
No. 100	.149	.0059	6%	40%	.096 to .125	.0038 to .0040
No. 200	.074	.0029	7%	60%	.045 to .061	.0018 to .0024

*Opening is the space in the clear between the wires.
**Mesh is measured from center to center of wire and means the number of openings in a lineal inch.

Sieve analyses, absorptions and specific gravities of concrete aggregates

	Sand percent passing	Gravel percent passing
1/2 inch	100	99.0
3/8 inch	100	98.7
No. 4	94.7	31.1
No. 8	69.8	6.0
No. 16	47.9	3.0
No. 30	28.0	2.0
No. 50	7.6	1.3
No. 100	.8	.8
No. 200	.3	.5
Absorption, percent by weight	.9	1.1
Bulk specific gravity, saturated surface dry	2.61	2.6

SOIL CLASSIFICATION

In order to describe soils, the Public Roads Administration has investigated various soil types which exhibit characteristic field behavior. On the basis of this study soils have been divided into eight distinct classes. These classifications are sufficiently detailed so that characteristics such as compressibility, elasticity, capillary action, cohesion, shrinkage and moisture content — all extremely vital considerations to a good subgrade — can, when considered with local climatic and usage conditions, give a good index to the adequacy of the soil for a desired purpose. These eight soil classifications are as follows:

A-1 — Well graded material, coarse and fine, excellent binder. Highly stable under wheel loads irrespective of moisture conditions. Functions satisfactorily when surface treated or when used as a base for relatively thin wearing courses.

A-2 — Coarse and fine materials, improper grading or inferior binder. Highly stable when fairly dry. Likely to soften at high water content caused either by rains or high capillary rise from saturated lower strata, when an impervious cover prevents evaporation from top layer, or to become loose and dusty in long continued dry weather.

A-3 — Coarse material only, no binder. Lacks stability under wheel loads, but is unaffected by moisture conditions. Not likely to heave because of frost, nor to shrink or expand in appreciable amounts. Furnishes excellent support for flexible pavement of moderate thickness and for relatively thin rigid pavements.

A-4 — Silt soils, without coarse material, and with no appreciable amount of sticky colloidal clay. Has a tendency to absorb water very readily in quantities sufficient to cause rapid loss of stability even when not manipulated. When dry or damp presents a firm riding surface which rebounds but very little upon the removal of load. Likely to cause cracking in rigid pavements as a result of frost heaving, and failure in flexible pavements because of low supporting value.

A-5 — Similar to Group A-4 but have highly elastic supporting surfaces with appreciable rebound upon removal of load even when dry. Elastic properties interfere with proper compaction of macadams during construction and with retention of good bond afterwards.

A-6 — Clay soils without coarse material. In stiff or soft plastic state absorb additional water only if manipulated. May then change to a liquid state and work up into the interstices of macadams or cause failure due to sliding in high fills. Furnish firm support essential in properly compacting macadams only at stiff consistency. Deformations occur slowly and removal of load causes very little rebound. Shrinkage properties combined with alternate wetting and drying under field conditions are likely to cause cracking in rigid pavements.

A-7 — Similar to Group A-6 but at certain moisture contents deforms quickly under load and rebounds appreciably upon removing of load, as do subgrades of Group A-5. Alternate wetting and drying under field conditions leads to even more detrimental volume changes than in Group A-6 subgrades. May cause concrete pavements to crack before setting and to crack and fault afterwards. May contain lime or associated chemicals productive of flocculation in soils.

A-8 — Very soft peat and muck incapable of supporting a road surface without being previously compacted.

To classify a given soil, a sample is run through a series of tests to determine into which of the above groups it most closely falls. The tests to determine its classification are as follows:

1. SIEVE ANALYSIS TEST — This test determines the percent of total quantities that will pass through seven different size sieves. Certain further checks are made to determine the distribution of material passing through a No. 40 sieve.

2. MOISTURE EQUIVALENT TEST — This test determines the percent of weight difference between a dry sample and a moist sample.

3. LIQUID LIMIT TEST — This test is defined as the percent of moisture at which soil changes from a plastic to a liquid condition. The test is conducted by thoroughly mixing a sample with water, smoothing it out, marking a groove in the sample and then determining the number of controlled shocks necessary to close the groove. By repeated tests it is determined what moisture content will permit the groove to close with twenty-five shocks. This moisture content is the liquid limit.

4. PLASTIC LIMIT TEST — This is defined as the percent of moisture at which the soil changes from a solid to a plastic condition. Test is conducted by moistening a sample and rolling it into a 1/8" diameter thread with the palm of the hand. The moisture content at the time the thread begins to crumble determines the Plastic Limit.

5. PLASTICITY INDEX — The numerical difference between the liquid limit and plastic limit.

6. SHRINKAGE TEST — This test determines the "Shrinkage Limit" and the "Shrinkage Ratio." Test is conducted by putting a sample in a test bowl, drying out, and noting volume change.

$$\text{The Shrinkage Limit (\% moisture content)} = \frac{(\text{Volume of dish} - \text{volume dry soil})}{\text{Weight dry soil}} (100)$$

$$\text{The Shrinkage Ratio} = \frac{\text{Weight of dry soil}}{\text{Volume of dry soil}}$$

7. FIELD MOISTURE CONTENT — Minimum moisture content, expressed as a percentage of the weight of the oven dried soil, at which a drop of water placed on a smoothed surface of the soil will not immediately be absorbed, but will instead spread out over the surface and give it a shiny appearance.

8. SOIL ACIDITY OR ALKALINITY — Determine pH value with colormetric test equipment. One purpose is that a lime content has certain beneficial characteristics.

When the above tests have been made the results are compared by use of charts and the soil classed accordingly. Many soils will be borderline cases as to classification.

Although the soil tests and resulting classification will usually give a good index to the behavior of a soil, it does not fill the need for practical soil classification terminology required by the engineer out on the job. Under field circumstances he may be able to test the soil only by visual examination. One of the common classification methods used by many engineers in the field is grouping soils by texture and structure. The terms are general and the range in any one group may be great.

These groups are as follows:

SANDY SOIL — Loose and granular soil, the individual grains of which can readily be seen or felt and may range from very fine sand to coarse sand.

CLAY SOILS — Clay soil is a fine-textured soil which forms hard lumps or clods when dry.

LOAM — A loam is a soil having a relatively even mixture of sand, silt and clay.

SANDY LOAM — A soil containing much sand but having sufficient silt and clay to render it coherent.

SILT LOAM — When this class of soil is dry and powdered, it is often called "rock flour." It is a soil having a moderate amount of fine sand and clay, over half the particles being of the size called "silt." The dry lumps are easily broken and then feel soft and floury.

CLAY LOAM — A fine-textured soil having a large percentage of clay. When dry, the clods are hard and difficult to break.

GRAVELLY OR STONY SOILS — All the above soils, if mixed with a considerable amount of pebbles, are classed as gravelly sand loams; sand clay loams; sandy clay soils, etc.

SOIL COMPACTION

The primary objective of compacting soil by sheepsfoot rollers, flat wheel rollers, pneumatic tired units, or other means is to obtain a soil of a specific density in order that it will carry specified loads without undue settlement. Much has been written on this subject, but soil types, equipment, operating conditions and moisture content are so variable that it is not practical to attempt to state definitely what work is required and what equipment is needed to get certain definite results from compaction.

The work necessary to get the desired compaction on a specific job should be determined by actual test on the job.

Soil settlement occurs under load for two reasons: (1) Air and water are expelled from the earth due to compression; and (2) The earth is forced out laterally into the surrounding soil.

Compaction operations attempt to do these things artificially by means of various types of rollers or tampers so that settlement after construction work is completed will be held to a minimum. To do this, two principles of action are involved.

1. It is necessary to place the earth in layers sufficiently thin to permit air and water to be expelled efficiently and easily. Some soils, depending upon their permeability, may be put down in thicker layers than others. For example, clay must be placed in thin layers whereas a sandy soil could be rolled in thick layers.

2. The second principle to consider is that the compression of soil particles requires movement of the individual particles in order to fit them together and fill in the voids. Before movement can take place friction must be reduced. Lubrication of the soil particles by means of moisture will help to overcome friction. Too little moisture will not materially reduce friction; too much moisture only means that the excess water must be expelled. There is, then, an optimum or ideal moisture content.

Tests have been developed for determining the adequacy of soil compaction. There is some difference in the exact procedure of tests as used by the Army Engineers and the various States, but the fundamental principles remain the same. The tests generally used are based on procedures established by the American Association of State Highway Officials (AASHO). Three main tests are used to test soil for proper compaction

1. Moisture-content test.
2. Unit weight determination or density test.
3. Compaction, test for optimum-moisture content

The MOISTURE CONTENT TEST (Similar to Public Roads Administration "Moisture Equivalent Test") is used to determine the ratio of the weight of the water contained in a given sample to the dry weight of the sample. The answer is expressed in percent. The test is conducted by weighing a moist sample of earth, drying it in an oven, then noting the loss in weight due to the water evaporation. The weight of water lost divided by the weight of the dry sample and multiplied by 100 equals the per cent of moisture content.

The UNIT WEIGHT determination is a test for determining the weight of a unit volume. The answer is expressed in pounds per cubic foot.

The COMPACTION TEST FOR OPTIMUM MOISTURE CONTENT (Modified AASHO method) is an important test used to determine what quantity of moisture in earth will permit the greatest compaction. If too much water is present more work must be done to expel the excess water. If insufficient water is present the dirt will not compact easily. This test is made by compacting in a standard test machine a quantity of the sample dirt which has been thoroughly mixed with water. After compaction the weight per unit volume of the compacted material is determined. Next, samples of the compacted earth are taken and the moisture content is determined as in the MOISTURE CONTENT TEST discussed above. From this information the moisture content for a unit weight of dirt is now known. This same procedure is repeated on several samples with varying amounts of water added until the addition of more water does not give any weight increase for a given volume. The moisture content which results in the greatest weight per volume is the OPTIMUM MOISTURE CONTENT

Reproduced from "Earth Moving and Construction Data."
Courtesy of Allis-Chalmers Manufacturing Company

STOCKPILES

Capacity of Conical Stockpiles
(Angle of Repose = 37°)

Pile Height, Ft.	Pile Radius, Ft.	Pile Diameter, Ft.	Gross Capacity, Cu. Yds.	Gross Capacity, Tons (100#/Ft.³)
10	13¼	26½	68	92
15	20	40	230	310
20	26½	53	545	735
25	33	66	1,060	1,430
30	39¾	79½	1,840	2,490
35	46½	93	2,920	3,950
40	53	106	4,350	5,880
45	59¾	119½	6,200	8,370
50	66¼	132½	8,500	11,450
55	73	146	11,350	15,160
60	79½	159	14,700	19,800
65	86¼	172½	18,700	25,200
70	92¾	185½	23,400	31,500
75	99½	199	28,700	38,880
80	106	212	34,800	47,000
85	112¾	225½	41,800	56,400
90	119¼	238½	49,600	67,000
95	125½	251	58,300	78,600
100	132½	265	68,000	92,000

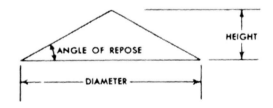

GROSS VOLUME = ⅓ Area Base x Height

GROSS VOLUME, Cu. Yd. = .068 (Height, Ft.)³

GROSS CAPACITY, Tons = 1.35 x Volume, Cu. Yd. (100#/Cu. Ft.)

Live Capacity

Part of Pile that can be removed by conveyor with one feed chute at center of Pile. Approximately ¼ of gross capacity of Pile.

TIMBER

Physical Properties of Timber or Wood

(As determined by tests of seasoned timber, containing 12 per cent or less of moisture) The stresses are given in pounds per square inch.

Name of Wood	Ultimate Resistance to						Modulus of			Ordinary Working Stress			
	Tension	Compression (length)	Compression (cross)	Shearing (length)	Shearing (cross)	Elastic limit	Elasticity	Ultimate bending	Elastic bending	Tension	Compression	Transverse	Weight per cubic foot (pounds)
Ash (American)	17,000	7,200	1,900	1,100	6,820	7,900	1,640,000	10,800	7,900	2,000	1,000	1,200	37
Birch	15,000	8,000			5,600		1,645,000	11,700		2,000	1,000	1,200	33
Cedar (American red)	10,600	6,000	600	400	1,300	5,600	900,000	7,000	5,600	1,300	700	900	24
Chestnut	11,500	5,300			1,500		1,130,000	8,000		1,400	600	900	41
Fir	13,000			1,300			1,500,000						
Gum		7,000	1,400	800	5,800	7,800	1,700,000	9,600	7,600	1,200	900	900	37
Hemlock	8,700	5,700		400	2,760			7,000				750	25
Hickory (American aver.)	19,500	9,500	2,500	1,000	6,200	11,200	2,400,000	17,000	12,000	2,000	1,200	1,800	50
Lignum-vitae	11,800	9,800						11,000		1,500	1,200	1,500	83
Maple	11,000	7,000	1,800	500	6,000	6,400		10,000					49
Oregon pine	13,000	5,700	800	500		6,400	1,600,000	7,800	6,400	1,400	700	1,000	32
Oak (black)	10,000	7,300	1,900	1,100		8,100	1,740,000	10,800	8,100	1,400	900	1,200	45
Oak (white)	13,600	8,500	2,200	1,000	4,400	9,600	2,090,000	13,000	9,600	1,700	1,000	1,500	50
Pine (Southern yellow)	13,000	8,000	1,200	835	5,600	10,000	2,070,000	12,600	9,500	1,600	1,000	1,500	33
Pine (Cuban)	13,000	8,700	1,200	770	5,000	11,000	2,300,000	13,600	10,600				
Pine (loblolly)	13,000	7,400	1,150	800		9,200	2,050,000	11,300	9,400	1,600	900	1,200	33
Pine (white)	10,000	5,400	700	400	2,560	6,400	1,390,000	7,900	6,400	1,200	700	900	24
Poplar	7,000	5,000						6,500		900	600	750	
Spruce (Northern)	11,000	6,000	800	400	3,250		1,400,000	8,000		1,200	700	900	26
Spruce (Southern)	1,200	7,300	1,200	800		8,400	1,640,000	10,000	8,400	1,200	700	900	30
Walnut (black)	10,500	7,500	2,500		4,700	5,700	1,306,000	8,000		1,000	1,000	900	33

Average Safe Concentrated Loads on Wooden Beams—Average Conditions

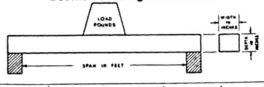

Span	Beam Dimensions		Load (Lbs.)	
	Width	Depth		
4'	6"	6"	2,100	
	8"	8"	4,970	
	8"	10"	7,765	
6'	6"	6"	1,398	
	6"	8"	2,490	
	8"	8"	3,320	
	8"	10"	5,184	
	10"	10"	6,480	
	10"	12"	9,330	
	12"	12"	11,197	
8'	6"	6"	1,050	
	6"	8"	1,866	
	8"	8"	2,488	
	8"	10"	3,888	
	10"	10"	4,860	
	10"	12"	7,000	
	12"	12"	8,400	

Under ideal conditions the load can be increased ¼

Concentrated load = ½ of uniformly distributed load.

WEIGHT OF MATERIALS

Approximate Weight of Materials

MATERIAL	Weight, Lbs. per Cu. Ft.	Weight, Lbs. per Cu. Yd.
Andesite, Solid	173	4,660
Ashes	41	1,110
Basalt, Broken	122	3,300
Solid	188	5,076
Caliche	90	2,430
Cement, Portland	100	2,700
Mortar, Portland, 1:2½	135	3,645
Cinders, Blast Furnace	57	1,539
Coal, Ashes and Clinkers	40	1,080
Clay, Dry Excavated	68	1,847
Wet Excavated	114	3,080
Dry Lumps	67	1,822
Wet Lumps	100	2,700
Compact, Natural Bed	109	2,943
Clay and Gravel, Dry	100	2,700
Wet	114	3,085
Concrete, Asphaltic	140	3,780
Gravel or Conglomerate	150	4,050
Limestone with Portland Cement	148	3,996
Coal, Anthracite, Natural Bed	94	2,546
Broken	69	1,857
Bituminous, Natural Bed	84	2,268
Broken	52	1,413
Cullet	80-100	2,160 to 2,700
Dolomite, Broken	109	2,940
Solid	181	4,887
Earth, Loam, Dry Excavated	78	2,100
Moist Excavated	90	2,430
Wet Excavated	100	2,700
Dense	125	3,375
Soft Loose Mud	108	2,916
Packed	95	2,565

MATERIAL	Weight, Lbs. per Cu. Ft.	Weight, Lbs per Cu. Yd.
Gneiss, Broken	116	3,141
Solid	179	4,833
Granite, Broken or Crushed	103	2,778
Solid	168	4,525
Gravel, Loose, Dry	95	2,565
Pit Run, (Gravelled Sand)	120	3,240
Dry ¼-2"	105	2,835
Wet ½-2"	125	3,375
Gravel, Sand and Clay, Stabilized, Loose	100	2,700
Compacted	150	4,050
Gypsum, Broken	113	3,054
Crushed	100	2,700
Solid	174	4,698
Halite (Rock Salt) Broken	94	2,545
Solid	145	3,915
Hematite, Broken	201	5,430
Solid	306	8,262
Limonite, Broken	154	4,159
Solid	189	6,399
Limestone, Broken or Crushed	97	2,625
Solid	163	4,400
Magnetite, Broken	205	5,528
Solid	315	8,505
Marble, Broken	98	2,650
Solid	160	4,308
Marl, Wet Excavated	140	3,780
Mica, Broken	100	2,700
Solid	180	4,860
Mud, Fluid	108	2,916
Packed	119	3,200
Dry Close	80 to 110	2,160 to 2,970
Peat, Dry	25	675
Moist	50	1,350
Wet	70	1,890
Phosphate Rock, Broken	110	2,970
Pitch	71.7	1,936
Plaster	53	1,431
Porphyry, Broken	103	2,790
Solid	159	4,293
Sandstone, Broken	94	2,550
Solid	145	3,915
Sand, Dry Loose	100	2,700
Slightly Damp	120	3,240
Wet	130	3,500
Wet Packed	130	3,510
Sand and Gravel, Dry	108	2,916
Wet	125	3,375
Shale, Broken	99	2,665
Solid	167	4,500
Slag, Broken	110	2,970
Solid	132	3,668
Slag, Screenings	92	2,495
Slag, Crushed (¼")	74	1,998
Slag, Furnace, Granulated	60	1,620
Slate, Broken	104	2,800
Solid	168	4,535
Stone, Crushed	100	2,700
Taconite	150 to 200	4,050 to 5,400
Talc, Broken	109	2,931
Solid	168	4,535
Tar	71.7	1,936
Trap Rock, Broken	109	2,950
Solid	180	4,870

The above weights may vary in accordance with moisture content, texture, etc.

WEIGHTS & MEASURES – METRIC

Area Measure

1 sq. centimeter = 100 sq. milli-
(cm²)   meters (mm²)

1 sq. meter (m²) = $\begin{cases} 1,000,000 \text{ mm}^2 \\ 10,000 \text{ cm}^2 \end{cases}$

1 are (a)   = 100 m²

1 hectare (ha.) = $\begin{cases} 10,000 \text{ m}^2 \\ 100 \text{ a} \end{cases}$

1 sq. kilometer = $\begin{cases} 1,000,000 \text{ m}^2 \\ 100 \text{ ha} \end{cases}$
(km²)

Linear Measure

1 centimeter (cm.) = 10 milli-
    meters (mm.)

1 decimeter (dm.) = $\begin{cases} 100 \text{ mm.} \\ 10 \text{ cm.} \end{cases}$

1 meter (m.) = $\begin{cases} 1,000 \text{ mm.} \\ 10 \text{ dm.} \end{cases}$

1 dekameter (dkm.) = 10 m.

1 hectometer (hm.) = $\begin{cases} 100 \text{ m.} \\ 10 \text{ dkm.} \end{cases}$

1 kilometer (km.) = $\begin{cases} 1,000 \text{ m.} \\ 10 \text{ hm.} \end{cases}$

Weight

1 centigram (cg.) = 10 milligrams
    (mg.)

1 decigram (dg.) = $\begin{cases} 100 \text{ mg.} \\ 10 \text{ cg.} \end{cases}$

1 gram (g.) = $\begin{cases} 1,000 \text{ mg.} \\ 10 \text{ dg.} \end{cases}$

1 hectogram (hg.) = $\begin{cases} 100 \text{ g.} \\ 10 \text{ dkg.} \end{cases}$

1 dekagram (dkg.) = 10 g.

1 kilogram (kg.) = $\begin{cases} 1,000 \text{ g.} \\ 10 \text{ hg.} \end{cases}$

1 metric ton (t.) = 1,000 kg.

Cubic Measure

1 cubic centimeter (cm³) = 1,000 cubic millimeters (mm³)

1 cubic decimeter (dm³) = $\begin{cases} 1,000,000 \text{ mm}^3 \\ 1,000 \text{ cm}^3 \end{cases}$

1 cubic meter (m³) = $\begin{cases} 1 \text{ stere} \\ 1,000,000,000 \text{ mm}^3 \\ 1,000,000 \text{ cm}^3 \\ 1,000 \text{ dm}^3 \end{cases}$

Volume Measure

1 centiliter (cl.) = 10 milliliters (ml.)

1 deciliter (dl.) = $\begin{cases} 100 \text{ ml.} \\ 10 \text{ cl.} \end{cases}$

1 liter* (l.) = $\begin{cases} 1,000 \text{ ml.} \\ 10 \text{ dl.} \end{cases}$

1 dekaliter (dkl.) = 10 l.

1 hectoliter (hl.) = $\begin{cases} 100 \text{ l.} \\ 10 \text{ dkl.} \end{cases}$

1 kiloliter (kl.) = $\begin{cases} 1,000 \text{ l.} \\ 10 \text{ hl.} \end{cases}$

*The liter is defined as the volume occupied, under standard conditions,
by a quantity of pure water having a mass of 1 kilogram.

Power

1 metric horsepower = $\begin{cases} .986 \text{ U.S. horsepower} \\ 736 \text{ watts} \\ .736 \text{ kilowatts} \end{cases}$ 32,550 ft. lbs. per min.
                                        41.8 BTU per min.

Metric – U.S. Conversion Factors
(Based on National Bureau of Standards)

Length

Centimeters x 0.3937	= inches		Inches x 2.5400	= centimeters
Meters x 3.2808	= feet		Feet x 0.3048	= meters
Meters x 1.0936	= yards		Yards x 0.9144	= meters
Kilometers x 0.6214	= miles*		Miles* x 1.6093	= kilometers
Kilometers x 0.53959	= miles**		Miles** x 1.85325	= kilometers

*Statute miles   **Nautical miles

Area

Sq. cm. x 0.1550	= sq. ins.	Sq. ins. x 6.4516	= sq. cm.
Sq. m. x 10.7639	= sq. ft.	Sq. ft. x 0.0929	= sq. m.
Ares x 1076.39	= sq. ft.	Sq. ft. x 0.00093	= ares
Sq. m. x 1.1960	= sq. yds.	Sq. yds. x 0.8361	= sq. m.
Hectare x 2.4710	= acres	Acre x 0.4047	= hectares
Sq. km. x 0.3861	= sq. miles	Sq. miles x 2.5900	= sq. km.

Volume

Cu. cm. x 0.0610	= cu. ins.	Cu. ins. x 16.3872	= cu. cm.
Cu. m. x 35.3145	= cu. ft.	Cu. ft. x 0.0283	= cu. m.
Cu. m. x 1.3079	= cu. yds.	Cu. yds. x 0.7646	= cu. m.

Capacity

Liters x 61.0250	= cu. in.	Cu. ins. x 0.0164	= liters
Liters x 0.0353	= cu. ft.	Cu. ft. x 28.3162	= liters
Liters x 0.2642	= gals. (U.S.)	Gallons x 3.7853	= liters
Liters x 0.0284	= bushels (U.S.)	Bushels x 35.2383	= liters

Liters x $\begin{cases} 1000.027 & = \text{cu. cm.} \\ 1.0567 & = \text{qt. (liquid) or } 0.9081 = \text{qt. (dry)} \\ 2.2046 & = \text{lb. of pure water at 4C} = 1 \text{ kg} \end{cases}$

Power

Metric horsepower x .98632 = U.S. horsepower
U.S. horsepower x 1.01387 = metric horsepower

Metric – U.S. Conversion Factors (Continued)

Weight

Grams x 15.4324	= grains		Grains	x	0.0648	= g.
Grams x 0.0353	= oz.		Oz.	x	28.3495	= g.
Grams x 0.0022	= lbs.		Lbs.	x	453.592	= g.
Kgs. x 2.2046	= lbs.		Lbs.	x	0.4536	= kg.
Kgs. x 0.0011	= tons (short)		Lbs.		x 0.0004536	= tons*
Kgs. x 0.00098	= tons (long)		Tons (short)		x 907.1848	= kg.
Tons* x 1.1023	= ton (short)		Tons (short)		x 0.9072	= tons*
Tons* x 2204.62	= lbs.		Tons (long)		x 1016.05	= kg.

*metric

Pressure

Kgs. per sq. cm.	x 14.223	= lbs. per sq. in.
Lbs. per sq. in.	x 0.0703	= kgs. per sq. cm.
Kgs. per sq. in.	x 0.2048	= lbs. per sq. ft.
Kgs. per sq. m.	x .204817	= lbs. per sq. ft.
Lbs. per sq. ft.	x 4.8824	= kgs. per sq. m.
Kgs. per sq. m.	x .00009144	= tons (long) per sq. ft.
Tons (long) per sq. ft.	x .0001094	= Kg. per sq. m.
Kgs. per sq. mm.	x .634973	= tons (long) per sq. in.
Tons (long) per sq. in.	x 1.57494	= kg. per sq. mm.
Kgs. per cu. m.	x .062428	= lbs. per cu. ft.
Lbs. per cu. ft.	x 16.0184	= kgs. per cu. m.
Kgs. per m.	x .671972	= lbs. per ft.
Lbs. per ft.	x 1.48816	= kgs. per m.
Kg. m.	x 7.233	= ft. lbs.
Ft. Lbs.	x .13826	= kg. m.
Kgs. per sq. cm.	x 0.9678	= normal atmosphere
Normal atmosphere	x 1.0332	= kgs. per sq. cm.

WEIGHTS & MEASURES – U.S.A.

Linear Measure

1 mile =	{ 8 furlongs 80 chains 320 rods 1760 yards 5280 feet		1 chain =	{ 4 rods 22 yards 66 feet 100 links
1 furlong =	{ 10 chains 220 yards 6.06 rods		1 rod =	{ 5.5 yards 16.5 feet
1 station =	{ 33.3 yards 100 feet		1 yard =	{ 3 feet 36 inches
			1 foot =	12 inches

Gunter's or Surveyor's Chain Measure

1 link = 7.92 inches
1 statute mile = 80 chains

1 chain = { 100 links
4 rods
66 feet
22 yards

Land Measure

1 township =	{ 36 sections 36 sq. miles		1 sq. rod =	{ 272¼ sq. feet 30¼ sq. yards
1 sq. mile =	{ 1 section 640 acres		1 sq. yard =	{ 1,296 sq. inches 9 sq. feet
1 acre =	{ 4,840 sq. yards 43,560 sq. feet 160 sq. rods		1 sq. foot =	144 sq. inches

Cubic Measure

1 cubic yard = 27 cubic feet
1 cord (wood) = 4x4x8 ft. = 128 cu. ft.
1 ton (shipping) = 40 cubic ft.

1 cubic foot = 1728 cubic inches
1 bushel = 2150.42 cu. in.
1 gallon = 231 cu. in.

Weights (Commercial)

1 long ton = 2240 lbs.
1 short ton = 2000 lbs.

1 pound = 16 ounces
1 ounce = 16 drams

Troy Weight (For Gold and Silver)

1 pound = { 12 ounces
5760 grains

1 ounce = { 20 pennyweights
480 grains

1 pennyweight = 24 grains

Liquid Measure

1 pint (pt.)	= $\begin{cases} 4 \text{ gills (gl.)} \\ 28.875 \text{ cu. in.} \end{cases}$	1 hogshead	=63 gallons
1 quart (qt.)	= $\begin{cases} 2 \text{ pints} \\ 57.75 \text{ cu. in.} \end{cases}$	1 barrel	=31½ gallons
1 gallon (gal.)	= $\begin{cases} 4 \text{ quarts} \\ 8 \text{ pints} \\ 32 \text{ gills} \\ 231 \text{ cu. in.} \\ 8\frac{1}{3} \text{ lbs. @ 62° F.} \end{cases}$	1 cu. ft. water	= $\begin{cases} 7.48 \text{ U.S. gals.} \\ 1728 \text{ cu. in.} \\ 62\frac{1}{3} \text{ lbs. @ 62° F.} \end{cases}$

Dry Measure

(When necessary to distinguish the dry pint or quart from the liquid pint or quart, the word "dry" should be used in combination with the name or abbreviation of the dry unit.)

1 quart (qt.)	= $\begin{cases} 2 \text{ pints (pt.)} \\ 67.20 \text{ cu. in.} \end{cases}$	1 bushel (bu.)	= $\begin{cases} 4 \text{ pecks} \\ 32 \text{ quarts} \\ 2150.42 \text{ cu. in.} \end{cases}$
1 peck (pk.)	= $\begin{cases} 8 \text{ quarts} \\ 16 \text{ pints} \\ 537.605 \text{ cu. in.} \end{cases}$		

Mariner's Measure

1 fathom	=	6 feet	1 marine league	=	3 marine miles
1 cable length	=	120 fathoms	1 statute mile	=	$\begin{cases} 7\frac{1}{3} \text{ cable lengths} \\ 5,280 \text{ feet} \end{cases}$
1 nautical mile	=	6,080 feet			

Measures of Power

1 BTU per minute	=	$\begin{cases} .0236 \text{ horsepower} \\ 17.6 \text{ watts} \\ .0176 \text{ kilowatts} \\ 778 \text{ foot lbs. per min.} \end{cases}$
1 ft. lb. per min.	=	$\begin{cases} .0226 \text{ watts} \\ .001285 \text{ BTU per min.} \end{cases}$
1 horsepower	=	$\begin{cases} 746 \text{ watts} \\ .746 \text{ kilowatts} \\ 33,000 \text{ ft. lbs. per min.} \\ 42.4 \text{ BTU per min.} \end{cases}$
1 watt	=	$\begin{cases} .00134 \text{ horsepower} \\ .001 \text{ kilowatts} \\ 44.2 \text{ ft. lbs. per min.} \\ .0568 \text{ BTU per min.} \end{cases}$
1 kilowatt	=	$\begin{cases} 1.341 \text{ horsepower} \\ 1000 \text{ watts} \\ 44,250 \text{ ft. lbs. per min.} \\ 56.8 \text{ BTU per min.} \end{cases}$

Time Measure

The division of time into standard units, as follows:

60 seconds (sec.)	1 minute (min.)
60 minutes	1 hour (hr.)
24 hours	1 day
7 days	1 week (wk.)
30 days	1 month (mo.)
	for computing interest
52 weeks	1 year (yr.)
365 days	1 year
366 days	1 leap year

Circular and Angular Measure

A standard measure expressed in degrees, minutes, and seconds, as follows:

60 seconds (")	1 minute (')
60 minutes	1 degree (°)
90 degrees	1 quadrant
4 quadrant	1 circle or circumference

ARCHITECTURAL

AND ENGINEERING

SYMBOLS

Symbols used by architects and engineers, as on blueprints, are fairly standard. Shown here are commonly used symbols and other markings. It is further suggested that, in reading blueprints, reference be made to the "schedules" used to illustrate the requirements set forth; i.e., a "door schedule" will further explain the size, type and finish of each door shown on the plans, and so forth.

MATERIALS AND DESIGN

Design

Break Line — Long

Break Line — Short

These lines are used when an area cannot or should not be entirely drawn

Center Line

A series of short and long dashes used to designate centers and provide a reference point for dimensioning

Dimension Line

Thin, unbroken lines which designate dimensions

Extension Line

These lines extend, but do not touch, the object lines; they permit dimension lines to be drawn between them

Hidden Line

Short dashes used to show lines that are not visible from the view shown

Leader

The lines are used to connect a note or reference or dimension to the part of the building being illustrated

Object Line

These lines show the main outline of the structure, including exterior walls, interior partitions, porches, patios, driveways, and interior walls. They should be the outstanding lines on the drawing

Section Line

These are heavy lines consisting of a series of one long and two short dashes with arrows at each end pointing away from the area that is cut away for the purpose of sectioning

Materials

Earth

Sand

Concrete

Steel

Brick

Structural Clay Tile

Concrete Block

Cut Stone

Cast Stone

Marble

Slate

Plywood

Wood, Rough

Wood, Finished

Plaster

Ceramic Tile

Insulation Board, Quilt

Insulation, Batts or Fill

Firebrick

Tile, Hollow

Tile, Terra Cotta

Cinders

Structural Steel or Iron

Brick Veneer

Gypsum Board

Flashing, Termite Barrier,
  or Waterproofing

ELECTRICAL

Lighting Outlet

Ceiling Lighting Outlet
  for recessed fixture
  (outline of shape of fixture)

Duplex Convenience Outlet

Duplex Convenience Outlet
  for grounding type plugs

Weatherproof Convenience Outlet

Combination Switch and Convenience Outlet

Range Outlet

Junction Box

Bell-ringing Transformer

Bell

Service Panel

Distribution Panel

Special-purpose outlet with subscript letters
  to indicate use: DW—Dishwasher;
  DF—Drinking Fountain

WH

Single Pole Switch

S

Three Way Switch

S_3

Four Way Switch

S_4

Telephone Outlet

MECHANICAL

Supply Duct Section

Exhaust, Return or Outside Air Duct Section

Supply Outlet: Ceiling Diffuser

Linear Diffuser

Recessed Radiator

Enclosed Radiator

Unit Heater

Louver Opening

Intake Louvers

Convector Radiator

PLUMBING

Water Heater

Cold Water

Hot Wate

Fire Line

Gas-low Pressure

Vent

Ice Watei

Pipe Chase

Floor Drain

Shower Drain

Washing Machine

Water Closet

Urinal

Lavatory

Hose Bib

Hose Rack

STRUCTURAL AND FINISHES

Structural

Stair indicator

UP   DOWN

UP   DOWN

(NOTE: These lines indicate the direction of stairs.)

Doors

Outside

Inside

Double-acting

Windows

Casement

Double-hung

Glass

CPSIA information can be obtained at www.ICGtesting.com
Printed in the USA
LVOW08*0719300514

387840LV00001B/1/P